A Stephen Birnbaum Travel Guide

Birnbaum's
IRELAND
1991

Stephen Birnbaum
Alexandra Mayes Birnbaum
EDITORS

Lois Spritzer
EXECUTIVE EDITOR

Laura L. Brengelman
MANAGING EDITOR

Kristin Moehlmann
Senior Editor

Ann-Rebecca Laschever
Julie Quick
Beth Schlau
Associate Editors

Julie Hassinger Marks
Assistant Editor

HOUGHTON MIFFLIN COMPANY / BOSTON 1990

For Grace and Herbert Mayes, who set the standards and the style

For information about permission to reproduce
selections from this book, write to
Permissions, Houghton Mifflin Company,
2 Park Street, Boston, Massachusetts 02108.

ISBN: 0-395-55728-3
ISSN: 0749-2561 (Stephen Birnbaum Travel Guides)
ISSN: 0896-8691 (Ireland)

Printed in the United States of America

WP 10 9 8 7 6 5 4 3 2 1

Contents

PERSPECTIVES

A cultural and historical survey of Ireland's past and present, its people, politics, and heritage.

THE CITIES

Thorough, qualitative guides to each of the 13 cities most often visited by vacationers and businesspeople. Each section, a comprehensive report of the city's most appealing attractions and amenities, is designed to be used on the spot. Directions and recommendations are immediately accessible because each city guide is presented in consistent form.

DIVERSIONS

A selective guide to more than 20 active and cerebral vacations, including the places to pursue them where the quality of experience is likely to be highest.

For the Experience

For the Body

For the Mind

DIRECTIONS

The most spectacular routes and roads; most arresting natural wonders; and most magnificent castles, manor houses, and gardens — all organized into 12 specific driving tours.

A Word from the Editor

The first night I ever spent in Ireland included several hours at *Bofey Quinn's* pub in the village of Corofin in the west of Ireland. I'd been at the bar there for about 15 minutes, sipping my first ever "jar" of stout from a keg, when a man of the town came up beside me and put his hand on my shoulder. He was dressed in a well-worn tweed jacket, and an equally old tweed cap was on his head.

"Tell me, Boy-o," he began, in a brogue as thick as peat, "where in Ireland is your family from?"

"Poland," I replied, feeling I had scored with a laser-like bon mot.

"Not to worry," he said, not missing a beat, "it's our easternmost county!"

There were lots of lessons to learn from this first encounter on Irish soil. The first, clearly, was not to challenge the wit of the Old Country on its own turf. Second, and perhaps most important, was the depth of hospitality the Irish feel toward visitors, especially those from America.

Hospitality is not a sometime thing in Ireland; it is perhaps the island's single most valuable commodity. Whether in the North or in the Republic, Irish men and women seem to take great delight in making a visitor feel supremely comfortable, and the Irish talent for warmth and welcome has no equal in this wide world.

If you get the idea that Ireland is one of my favorite destinations, you're clearly correct. It's a place to which I return again and again, often inventing excuses to visit with Irish people and to dine out on fine Irish fare.

So it's a very special pleasure to be able to create a guide to Ireland alone, after having been somewhat restricted in our coverage when Ireland was just a part of our old *Great Britain and Ireland* volume. We now have the opportunity to treat a deserving destination in considerably greater detail, and this treatment-in-depth gives us the chance to provide new insights and interests to make an Irish travel experience even more enjoyable.

Such thorough treatment also reflects a new trend among travelers — the frequent return to treasured foreign travel spots. Once upon a time, even the most dedicated travelers would visit distant parts of the world no more than once in a lifetime — usually as part of that fabled old Grand Tour. But greater numbers of would-be sojourners are now availing themselves of the opportunity to visit favored parts of the world over and over again.

So where once it was routine to say that you'd "seen" a particular country after a superficial, once-over-lightly encounter, the more perceptive travelers of today recognize that it's entirely possible to have only skimmed the surface of a specific destination even after having visited that place more than a dozen times. Similarly, repeated visits to a single site permit true exploration of special interests, whether they be sporting, artistic, or intellectual in nature.

For those of us who spent several years working out the special system under which we present information in this series, the luxury of being able to devote nearly as much space as we like to one small island is as close to guidebook heaven as any of us expects to come. But clearly, this is not the first guide to Eire — guides of one sort or another have existed for centuries, so a traveler might logically ask why a new one is suddenly necessary.

Our answer is that the nature of travel to Ireland, and even of the travelers who now routinely make the trip, have changed dramatically. For the past 2,000 years or so, travel to and through the Emerald Isle was an extremely elaborate undertaking, one that required extensive advance planning. Even as recently as the 1950s, a person who had actually been to Ireland could dine out on his or her experiences for years, since such adventures were quite extraordinary and usually the province of the privileged alone.

With the advent of jet air travel in the late 1950s, however, and of increased-capacity, wide-body aircraft during the 1960s, travel to and around this once-distant land became extremely common. In fact, in more than 2 decades of nearly unending inflation, airfare may be the only commodity in the world that has actually gone down in price.

Attitudes, as well as costs, have changed significantly in the last couple of decades. Beginning with the so-called flower children of the 1960s, international travel lost much of its aura of mystery. Whereas their parents might have chosen a superficial sampling of Dublin or Cork, these young people simply picked up and settled in various parts of Europe for an indefinite stay. While living as inexpensively as possible, they adapted to the local lifestyle, and generally immersed themselves in things European.

Thus began an explosion of travel to and in Ireland. And over the years, the development of inexpensive charter flights and packages fueled the new American interest in and appetite for more extensive exploration.

Now, in the 1990s, those same flower children who were in the forefront of the modern travel revolution have undeniably aged. While it may be impolite to point out that they are probably well into their untrustworthy 30s and (some) 40s, their original zeal for travel remains undiminished. For them it's hardly news that the way to get to Killarney is to head toward Cork, make a right, and then wait for the lakes to appear. Such experienced and knowledgeable travelers have decided precisely where they want to go and are more often searching for ideas and insights to expand their already sophisticated travel consciousness.

Obviously, any new guidebook to Ireland must keep pace with and answer the real needs of today's travelers. That's why we've tried to create a guide that's specifically organized, written, and edited for this more demanding modern audience, one for whom qualitative information is infinitely more desirable than mere quantities of unappraised data. We think that this book and the other guides in our series represent a new generation of travel guides, one that is especially responsive to modern needs and interests.

For years, dating back as far as Herr Baedeker, travel guides have tended to be encyclopedic, seemingly much more concerned with demonstrating expertise in geography and history than in any analysis of the sorts of things that more frequently concern a typical modern tourist. But today, when it is hardly necessary to tell a traveler where Dublin is located, it's hard to justify devoting endless pages to historical perspectives. As suggested earlier, it's not impossible that the guidebook reader may have been to Ireland nearly as often as the guidebook editor, so it becomes the responsibility of that editor to provide new perspectives and to suggest new directions in order to make the guide genuinely valuable.

That's exactly what we've tried to do in this series. I think you'll notice a different, more contemporary tone to the text, as well as an organization and focus that are distinctive and more functional. And even a random reading of what follows will demonstrate a substantial departure from the standard guidebook orientation, for we've not only attempted to provide information of a more compelling sort, but we also have tried to present the data in a context that makes it particularly accessible.

Needless to say, it's difficult to decide precisely what to include in a guidebook of this size — and what to omit. Early on, we realized that giving up the encyclopedic approach precluded listing every single route and restaurant, a realization that helped define our overall editorial focus. Similarly, when we discussed the possibility of presenting certain information in other than strict geographic order, we found that the new format enabled us to arrange data in a way that we feel best answers the questions travelers typically ask.

Large numbers of specific questions have provided the editorial skeleton for this book. The volume of mail I regularly receive emphasizes that modern travelers want very precise information, so we've tried to address these needs and have organized our material in the most responsive way possible. Readers who want to know the best restaurants in Cashel or the best golf courses in Portrush will have no trouble whatever finding that data in this guide.

Travel guides are, understandably, reflections of personal taste, and putting one's name on a title page obviously puts one's preferences on the line. But I think I ought to amplify just what "personal" means. I don't believe in the sort of personal guidebook that's a palpable misrepresentation on its face. It is, for example, hardly possible for any single travel writer to visit thousands of restaurants (and nearly as many hotels) in any given year and provide accurate appraisals of each one. And even if it were possible for one human being to survive such an itinerary, it would of necessity have to be done at a dead sprint and the perceptions derived therefrom would probably be less valid than those of any other intelligent individual visiting the same establishments. It is, therefore, impossible (especially in a large, annually revised guidebook *series* such as we offer) to have only one person provide all the data on the entire world.

I also happen to think that such individual orientation is of substantially less value. Visiting a single hotel for just one night or eating one hasty meal in a random restaurant hardly equips anyone to provide appraisals that are of more than passing interest. No amount of doggedly alliterative or oppressively onomatopoeic text can camouflage a technique that is essentially specious on its face. We have, therefore, chosen what I like to describe as the "thee and me" approach to restaurant and hotel evaluation and, to a somewhat more limited degree, to the sites and sights in the other sections of our text. What this really reflects is personal sampling tempered by intelligent counsel from informed local sources; these additional friends-of-the-editor are almost always residents of the city and/or area about which they have been consulted.

The presence of a considerable number of writers, researchers, and local correspondents, and very precise editing and tailoring keep our text fiercely subjective. So what follows is purposely designed to be the gospel according to the Birnbaums, and it represents as much of our own taste and preferences as we can manage. It is probable, therefore, that if you like your cities stylish and your mountainsides uncrowded, prefer small hotels with personality to huge high-rise anonymities, and can't tolerate vegetables or fresh fish that have been relentlessly overcooked, we're likely to have a long and meaningful relationship. Readers with dissimilar tastes may be less enraptured.

I also should point out something about the person to whom this guidebook is directed. Above all, he or she is a "visitor." This means that such elements as restaurants have been specifically picked to provide the visitor with a representative, illuminating, stimulating, and, above all, pleasant experience. Since so many extraneous considerations can affect the reception and service accorded a regular restaurant patron, our choices can in no way be construed as an exhaustive guide to resident dining. We think we've listed all the best places, in various price ranges, but they were chosen with a visitor's perspective in mind.

Other evidence of how we've tried to tailor our text to reflect changing travel habits is in the section we call DIVERSIONS. Where once it was common for travelers to spend a foreign visit nailed to a single spot, the emphasis today is more likely to be directed toward pursuing some athletic enterprise or special interest while seeing the surrounding countryside. So we've selected every activity we could reasonably evaluate and have organized the material in a way that is especially accessible. It is no longer necessary, therefore, to wade through a pound or two of extraneous prose just to find the best salmon stream or the very best crafts shop or the quaintest country inn within a reasonable radius of your destination.

If there is a single thing that best characterizes the revolution in and evolution of current travel habits, it is that most travelers now consider travel a right rather than a privilege. Travel today translates as the enthusiastic desire to sample all of the world's opportunities, to find that elusive quality of experience that is not only enriching but comfortable. For that reason, we've tried to make what follows not only helpful and enlightening but also the sort of welcome companion of which every traveler dreams.

I also should point out that every good travel guide is a living enterprise; that is, no part of this text is carved in stone. In our annual revisions, we refine, expand, and further hone all our material to serve your travel needs even better. To this end, no contribution is of greater value to us than your personal reaction to what we have written, as well as information reflecting your own experiences while using our book. We earnestly and enthusiastically solicit your comments about this guide *and* your opinions and perceptions about places you have recently visited. In this way, we will be able to provide the most current information — including the actual experiences of recent travelers — to make those experiences more readily available to others. Please write to us at 60 E. 42nd St., New York, NY 10165.

We sincerely hope to hear from you.

STEPHEN BIRNBAUM

How to Use This Guide

A great deal of care has gone into the organization of this guide-book, and we believe it represents a real breakthrough in the presentation of travel information. Our aim is to create a new, more modern generation of travel books and to make this guide the most useful and practical travel tool available today.

Our text is divided into five basic sections, in order to best present information in the most useful way on every possible aspect of a vacation in Ireland. This organization itself should alert you to the vast and varied opportunities available, as well as indicating all the specific data necessary to plan a successful visit. You won't find much of the conventional "quaint villages and sublime scenery" type of text in this guide; we've chosen instead to deliver more useful and practical information. Prospective itineraries tend to speak for themselves, and with so many diverse travel opportunities, we feel our main job is to highlight what's where and to provide basic details — how, when, where, how much, and what's best (and what's not) — to assist you in making the most intelligent choices possible.

Here is a brief summary of the five sections of this book and what you can expect to find in each. We believe that you will find both your travel planning and en route enjoyment enhanced by having this book at your side.

GETTING READY TO GO

This mini-encyclopedia of practical travel facts is a sort of know-it-all companion with all the precise information necessary to create a successful trip through Ireland. There are entries on more than 30 separate topics, including how to get where you're going, what preparations to make before leaving, what to expect in the different parts of the country, what the trip is likely to cost, and how to avoid prospective problems. The individual entries are specific, realistic, and, where appropriate, cost-oriented.

We expect you to use this section most in the course of planning your trip, for its ideas and suggestions are intended to simplify this often confusing period. Entries are intentionally concise in an effort to get to the meat of the matter. These entries are augmented by extensive lists of specific sources from which to obtain even more detailed data, plus some suggestions for obtaining travel information on your own.

PERSPECTIVES

Any visit to an unfamiliar destination is enhanced and enriched by understanding the cultural and historical heritage of that area. We have therefore provided just such an introduction to Ireland, its past and present, people, literature, architecture, music and dance, and food and drink, and language.

THE CITIES

Individual reports on the 13 cities most visited by tourists and businesspeople have been created with the assistance of researchers, contributors, professional journalists, and other experts on the spot. Although useful at the planning stage, THE CITIES is really designed to be taken along and used on the spot. Each report offers a short-stay guide within a consistent format: An essay introduces the city as a historic entity and a contemporary place to live and visit; *At-a-Glance* material is actually a site-by-site survey of the most important, interesting (and sometimes most eclectic) sights to see and things to do; *Sources and Resources* is a concise listing of pertinent tourism information, meant to answer a broad range of potentially pressing questions as they arise — from simple things like the address of the local tourist office, how to get around, which sightseeing tours to take, and when special events occur to something more difficult like where to find the best nightspot, to see a show, to play golf, or to get a taxi; and *Best in Town* is our collection of cost-and-quality choices of the best places to eat and sleep on a variety of budgets.

DIVERSIONS

This section is designed to help travelers find the very best locations at which to pursue a wide range of athletic and cerebral activities without having to wade through endless pages of unrelated text. This very selective guide lists the broadest possible range of activities, including all the best places to pursue them.

We start with a list of possibilities that offer various places to stay and eat, and move to those that require some perspiration — sports preferences and other rigorous pursuits — and go on to report on a number of more cerebral and spiritual vacation opportunities. In every case, our suggestion of a particular location — and often our recommendation of a specific resort — is intended to guide you to that special place where the quality of experience is likely to be the highest. Whether you seek crafts shops or fishing boats, luxurious hotels or atmospheric pubs, each entry is the equivalent of a comprehensive checklist of the absolute best in Ireland.

DIRECTIONS

Here are 12 itineraries that range all across the countryside, along the most beautiful routes and roads, past the most spectacular natural wonders, through the most historic cities and countryside. DIRECTIONS is the only section of the book that is organized geographically, and its itineraries cover the touring highlights of both Northern Ireland and the Republic of Ireland in short, independent journeys of 3 to 5 days' duration. Itineraries can be "connected" for longer trips or used individually for short, intensive explorations.

Each entry includes a guide to sightseeing highlights; a qualitative guide to accommodations and food along the road (small inns, castle hotels, hospitable farms, country and off-the-main-road discoveries); and suggestions for activities.

Although each of this book's sections has a distinct format and a special function, they have all been designed to be used together to provide a complete inventory of travel information. To use this book to full advantage, take a few minutes to read the table of contents and random entries in each section to get an idea of how it all fits together.

Pick and choose needed information. Assume, for example, that you have always wanted to take that typically Irish vacation, a driving tour through the southern part of the Republic of Ireland, but you never really knew how to organize it or where to go. Turn first to the *Traveling by Car* section of GETTING READY TO GO, and to the chapters on planning a trip, accommodations, and climate and clothes. These short, informative entries provide plenty of practical information. But where to go? Turn next to DIRECTIONS. Routes and desirable detours are all clearly set forth. Your trip will likely begin or end in Dublin, and for a complete rundown on that remarkable city, you should read the Dublin chapter of THE CITIES. Finally, turn to DIVERSIONS to peruse the chapters on sports, hotels, antiques, and other activities in which you are interested to make sure you don't miss anything along your chosen route.

In other words, the sections of this book are building blocks to help you put together the best possible trip. Use them selectively as tools, sources of ideas, a reference work for accurate facts, and a guide to the best buys, the most exciting sights and sites, the most pleasant accommodations, the tastiest food — *the best travel experiences* that you can have in Ireland.

IRELAND

IRELAND'S NEIGHBORS

SCOTLAND
North Sea
Edinburgh
IRELAND
Irish Sea
Dublin
ATLANTIC OCEAN
ENGLAND
WALES
London
English Channel
Paris
FRANCE

ATLANTIC OCEAN

Miles 60
0
km 100
0

Tory Is.
Dunfanaghy
Falcarragh
Creeslough
Aran I. (Aranmore)
The Rosses
Dungloe
Mts. of Donegal
Ardara
DONEGAL
Glencolumbkille
Donegal
Killybegs
Donegal Bay
Lower L. Erne

Sligo Bay
Sligo
Mullet Pen.
Mts. of Mayo
Ballina
L. Conn
SLIGO
Colloney
Allen
Carrick
Achill I.
Keel
MAYO
Castlebar
Clew Bay
Clare I.
Louisburgh
Westport
Claremorris
ROSCOMMON
Killary Harbour
Delphi Mask
LONG FORD
Renvyle
Leenane
Cong
Roscommon
Letterfrack
Maam
Tuam
L. Ree
Clifden
Corrib
GALWAY
Ballinahinch
Oughterard
Athlone
Roundstone
Carna
Rosmuc
Athenry
Galway
Ballinasloe
Galway Bay
Shannon
Aran Islands
Ballyvaughan
Kinvara
(IRISH
Lisdoonvarna
Gort
Liscannor
Cliffs of Moher
C L A R E
L. Derg
Lahinch
Miltown Malbay
Ennis
TIPPERARY
Kilkee
Thurles
Kilrush
Shannon Airport
Cashel
River Shannon
Limerick
Foynes
Tipperary
Adare
LIMERICK
Dingle Pen.
Castlegregory
Galbally
Cahir
Ballyferriter
Dingle
Anascaul
Tralee
Clonmel
Blasket Is.
Ventry
Killorglin
Mallow
Mitchelstown
WATER-
Dingle Bay
Glenbeigh
Killarney
Fermoy
Cahirciveen
Macgillycuddy's Reeks
L. Leane
C O R K
Youghal
Valentia I.
Iveragh Pen.
KERRY
Ballinskelligs
Sneem
Kenmare
Macroom
Blarney
Cork
Ardmore
Waterville
Lauragh
Caha Mts.
Ballingeary
Midleton
Skellig Rocks
Castletownbere
Adrigole
Glengarriff
Cobh
Ballycotton
Allihies
Bantry
Kinsale
Beara Pen.
Bear Is.
Ballydehob
Skibbereen

(To France)

GETTING READY
TO GO

When and How to Go

What's Where

Ireland, the second largest of the British Isles, lies in the North Atlantic, separated from England by the Irish Sea, from Scotland by the North Channel, and from Wales by St. George's Channel. About one-third the size of the island of Britain, it is 170 miles at its greatest width and 300 miles at its greatest length. Off its western coast are numerous small islands, including the Arans, the Blaskets, Achill, and Clare.

Ireland consists of two political entities: The Republic, also known as Eire, an independent nation of 26 counties, covering 27,000 square miles, takes the lion's share of the island's area; it has a population of 3.5 million. Northern Ireland, a province of the United Kingdom, encompasses six counties — Antrim, Armagh, Down, Fermanagh, Londonderry, and Tyrone — and covers about 5,400 square miles in the northeastern part of the island; its population is 1.5 million.

IRISH REPUBLIC

Prim whitewashed cottages surrounded by verdant pastures and flowering hedgerows — this is the conventional image of Eire. But, in fact, Irish terrain is much more varied — remarkably so for such a small country — and can change abruptly in a matter of just a few miles. In the northwest — counties Donegal, Mayo, and Galway — the landscape is stark and the vegetation brushy. Innumerable stone walls march up steep mountainsides where shaggy cattle graze stubbornly on the rocky land. To the south, the forbidding hills of northern County Clare, which appear to be almost paved with stone, give way to rolling, velvety meadows and powdery strands. The highest mountains in Ireland are in the southwest — on the Dingle, Kerry, and Beara peninsulas. Here, sandstone ridges, such as MacGillicuddy's Reeks and the Caha and Slieve Mish mountains, were shaped by Ice Age glaciers, which also left behind scores of lakes and valleys. The southern coast of Ireland is more gentle — a seascape of quiet coves, saltwater marshes, and little fishing villages — while the southeastern coast is a resort area popular for its sunny weather and sandy beaches. Just south of Dublin is the scenic Glendalough Valley, ringed by mountains, watered by two lakes, and scattered with ancient Christian ruins. The midlands, an area stretching roughly west from Dublin to Limerick, is a low-lying plain with many lakes and bogs. The green fields here are rived with black trenches from which turf has been cut, and the air is sweet with the smell of turf fires.

NORTHERN IRELAND

Most people who have never visited Northern Ireland — or Ulster, as it often is called after the historic province of which it is the largest part — think of it as a drab, gray, and beleaguered country. Although it's true that "the troubles" persist, the scenery is far from drab, and the welcome is as warm as anywhere on the Isle. In the southeast, the majestic Mountains of Mourne really do sweep down to the sea around Kilkeel — it's apparent at once why they are written and sung about. Along the Antrim coast, fierce and perpendicular headlands leap into the ocean, but inland, green and lush pastures are watered by serene loughs (lakes) and hugged by gently heaving hills. Lough Neagh, the largest lake in the United Kingdom, covers 153 square miles in the middle of the country and is bordered by five of the six counties. A major feature of the landscape in the southwest corner of Ulster is the watery, forested county of Fermanagh, which has more than 150 islands in its largest lake, Lough Erne.

When to Go

The decision of exactly when to travel may be imposed by the requirements of a rigid schedule; more likely there will be some choice, and the decision will be made on the basis of precisely what you want to see and do, the activities in which you'd like to participate, or events you'd like to attend, and what suits your mood.

There really isn't a "best" time to visit Ireland. For North Americans as well as Europeans, the period from mid-May to mid-September has long been — and remains — the peak travel period, traditionally the most popular vacation time. As far as weather is concerned, Ireland is at its best then: cooler and more comfortable than many other less temperate destinations on the Continent, where heat waves are inevitable.

It is important to emphasize that Ireland is hardly a single-season destination; more and more travelers who have a choice are enjoying the substantial advantages of off-season travel. Though many of the lesser tourist attractions may close for the winter — around December through *Easter* in rural areas — the major sites stay open and tend to be less crowded, as are the cities. During the off-season, Irish life proceeds at its most natural pace, and a lively social and cultural calendar flourishes. What's more, travel generally is less expensive.

For some, the most convincing argument in favor of off-season travel is the economic one. Simply put, getting there and staying there is less expensive. Airfares drop and hotel rates go down in the late fall, winter, and spring. Relatively inexpensive package tours become available, and the independent traveler can go farther on less, too. Ireland is not like the Caribbean, where high season and low season are precisely defined and rates drop automatically on a particular date. But many Irish hotels reduce rates during the off-season, and savings can be as much as 20% or higher, unless high-season rates continue to prevail because of an important local event — such as the *Spring Show* in Dublin and *St. Patrick's Week* nationwide. Particularly in the larger cities, major trade shows or conferences held at the time of your visit also are sure to affect not only the availability of discounts on accommodations, but the basic availability of a place to stay. Although many smaller guesthouses and bed and breakfast establishments may close during the off-season in response to reduced demand, there still are plenty of alternatives, and cut-rate "mini-break" packages — for stays of more than 1 night, especially over a weekend (when business travelers traditionally go home) — are more common.

It should be noted that what the travel industry refers to as shoulder seasons — the months immediately before and after the peak summer months — often are sought out because they offer reasonably good weather and smaller crowds. But be warned that near high-season prices still can prevail for many popular destinations during these periods.

CLIMATE: The travel plans of most North Americans visiting Ireland traditionally are affected by the availability of vacation time and a desire to visit when the weather is likely to be best — or most appropriate for a particular sport or activity. The most common concerns about off-season travel have to do with questions of temperature and rain. *(Please note that although temperatures in Ireland currently are recorded on both the Fahrenheit and Celsius scales due to the metric conversion in process, for purposes of clarity we use the more familiar Fahrenheit scale.)*

To the extent that it is mild, with no beastly hot summers or bone-chilling winters eliminating chunks of the calendar from consideration, the weather in Ireland cooperates enough to make it a multi-seasonal destination. Warm currents from the Gulf Stream soften extremes of temperature and even provide the surprising touch of palm trees in downtown Dublin.

The climate is hardly perfect, however. For one thing, visitors probably won't come home with a suntan, even in summer. There is a reason for that emerald green countryside and those renowned peaches-and-cream complexions: moisture, meaning frequently overcast skies or even rain. Beautiful mornings often turn into dreary afternoons and vice versa. Because of westerly winds off the Atlantic, there is heavier rainfall in the west than in the east, but because of the island's relatively small size, it has fairly uniform temperatures throughout. Summers are cool and winters are mild. Remember, too, that although winters are not the marrow-freezing scourges of the northern US and Canada, they are damp, and central heating usually is inadequate by American standards. Mid-October through mid-March is admittedly not an ideal time for touring the Irish countryside, though it may be suitable for those with special outdoor interests such as fishing and hunting.

All this doesn't mean that the sun never shines. Days get very long in the summer and there is daylight well into the June night in northernmost areas. In Dublin, average winter temperatures range from 39 to 45F, with January and February the coldest months; average summer temperatures range from 61 to 70F, with July and August the warmest months. April is the driest month, and May and June normally are the sunniest months.

The following chart lists the average low and high temperatures for specific Irish cities at different times of the year to help in planning. (For basic wardrobe information, see *How to Pack,* in this section.)

AVERAGE TEMPERATURES (in °F)

	January	*April*	*July*	*October*
Belfast	36–43	40–54	52–65	45–56
Cashel	35–45	41–54	52–66	45–57
Cork City	36–49	41–56	54–68	45–58
Donegal Town	36–46	40–53	51–65	45–57
Dublin	34–47	40–56	52–68	43–58
Galway City	40–49	43–54	56–68	49–58
Kilkenny Town	35–45	41–54	52–66	45–57
Killarney	41–50	45–56	54–70	49–59
Limerick City	36–47	41–56	54–67	45–58
Londonderry	34–44	38–51	51–65	46–59
Sligo City	35–45	40–53	51–65	44–56
Waterford City	36–46	41–54	53–67	46–58
Wexford Town	36–46	40–53	52–66	46–58

Travelers also can get current readings and 3-day Accu-Weather forecasts through *American Express Travel Related Services'* Worldwide Weather Report number. By dialing 900-WEATHER and punching in either the area code for any city in the US or an access code for any one of 225 major travel destinations around the world, an up-to-date recording will provide current temperature, sky conditions, wind speed and direction, heat index, relative humidity, local time, beach and boating reports or ski conditions (where appropriate), and highway reports. For locations in Ireland, punch in the first three letters of the city. For instance, by entering DUB you will hear the weather report for Dublin — GAL will give you Galway and LIM will give you Limerick. This 24-hour service can be accessed from any Touch-Tone phone in the US and costs 75¢ per minute. The charge will show up on your phone bill. For a free list of the cities covered, send a self-addressed, stamped envelope to *1-900-WEATHER*, 261 Central Ave., Farmingdale, NY 11735.

SPECIAL EVENTS: Many travelers may want to schedule a visit to Ireland to coincide with some special event. The highlight of a sports lover's trip may be attending the Irish championships of his or her game. For a music lover, a concert in a cathedral or Georgian mansion may be a thrilling experience and much more memorable than seeing the same place on an ordinary sightseeing itinerary. For theatergoers, a play by one of Ireland's native playwrights performed by actors with a true Irish brogue may be powerfully evocative. A folklore festival can bring nearly forgotten traditions alive or underscore their continuing significance in modern life.

In Ireland, particularly in the Republic, the calendar of such events is a busy one from spring through fall. In winter, too, in this land of horse lovers, there's racing practically year-round; fishing for one species or another also is possible all year; and winter is the hunting season. Somewhere a bloodstock sale, a rugby match, or a festival of drama, music, or dance is taking place.

The events noted below are the major ones, but they only are a sampling. These events are listed according to the months in which they usually occur. Since there can be variations from year to year, check with the Irish Tourist Board or the Northern Ireland Tourist Board (see *Tourist Information Offices*, in this section) for the exact date of anything you don't want to miss. For more information on major events, see *Feis and Fleadh: The Best Festivals* in DIVERSIONS and *Special Events* in the individual city reports of THE CITIES.

IRISH REPUBLIC

March

   St. Patrick's Week: Celebrations throughout the Republic and Northern Ireland give the patron saint his due. Parades and other festivities in Cork, Dublin, Dundalk, Kilkenny, Killarney, Limerick, Sligo, Waterford, and Wexford.

   World Irish Dancing Championships: Dancers from around the world compete with Ireland's best, chosen in national championships in February. Site changes from year to year.

April

   Dublin Grand Opera: A 2-week spring season at the *Gaiety Theatre*. Dublin, County Dublin.

May

   Cork International Choral and Folk Dance Festival: An international choral competition with folk dancing exhibitions. Cork, County Cork.

   Spring Show and Industries Fair: A weeklong trade and livestock show, with daily horse-jumping competitions — like a huge country fair in the heart of Dublin and one of the city's two biggest annual events. Dublin, County Dublin.

   Pan Celtic Week: Representatives of Scotland, Wales, Cornwall, the Isle of Man, Brittany, and Ireland compete in song, dance, and sports. Killarney, County Kerry.

Fleadh Nua: Pronounced Flah Nuah, this is a festival of traditional music, the second most important one in Ireland. Ennis, County Clare.

Dundalk International Maytime and Amateur Drama Festival: Music, sports, social events, and an international drama festival. Dundalk, County Clare.

Writers' Week: Lectures, workshops, competitions, and camaraderie for writers. Listowel, County Louth.

June

Festival of Music in Great Irish Houses: A week or so of classical concerts held in beautiful 18th-century mansions. Dublin, County Dublin.

July

International Folk Dance Festival: Dancers from Ireland and other countries converge in Cobh, County Cork, for this event.

August

Dublin Horse Show: An outstanding sporting and social event attracting equestrian fans and the smart set from around the Emerald Isle, across the Irish Sea, and from Europe and America. International jumping competitions daily, auctions, band concerts, arts and crafts exhibits, folk dances, dinner dances — it's the gathering of the year. Dublin, County Dublin.

Puck Fair: Actually a 3-day livestock sale and an excuse to keep the Guinness flowing. Men of the village capture a wild billy goat that, once beribboned, watches over the festivities from a pedestal above the square. Killorglin, County Kerry.

Connemara Pony Show: The famous ponies, rounded up from the wild, strut their stuff on the third Thursday of the month. Clifden, County Galway.

Yeats International Summer School: Two weeks of lectures, seminars, and discussions of the poet's work and its background — an entire course with a certificate on completion. Tourists can participate by purchasing single-day admission tickets. Sligo, County Sligo.

Fleadh Cheoil na hÉireann: An all-Ireland *fleadh* and the year's most important gathering of traditional Irish musicians. Some compete and some just play, and for 3 days there is music everywhere. Site changes from year to year.

Rose of Tralee International Festival: One of the country's biggest bashes. A folk festival, dancing and singing, and endless opportunities for merriment occur around the central event: the selection of the Rose of Tralee from a bouquet of fair, young lasses of Irish descent who congregate here from around the globe. Tralee, County Kerry.

September

All-Ireland Hurling Final and *All-Ireland Football Final:* Two rousing finales to a season of Gaelic sports. The hurling final is traditionally held in *Croke Park* on the first Sunday in September, and the Gaelic football final follows 2 Sundays later. Dublin, County Dublin.

Waterford International Festival of Light Opera: Amateur groups from Britain and Ireland vie to give the best performance of a musical or operetta, and for 2 weeks the pubs stay open late. Waterford, County Waterford.

Galway Oyster Festival: The lord mayor opens the first oyster of the season, inaugurating 2 days of feasting on oysters, brown bread, and Guinness stout. Clarinbridge, County Galway.

October

Cork Film Festival: Still an important week on the calendar of international film festivals, though on a smaller scale than before. Cork, County Cork.

Guinness Jazz Festival: A popular event featuring top-notch jazz musicians and vocalists from all over the world. Cork, County Cork.

Dublin Theatre Festival: A fortnight of new plays by Irish playwrights plus imported productions and plenty of opportunity to discuss them. Dublin, County Dublin.

Castlebar International Song Contest: Devoted to popular music, it's one of the most important song contests in Europe. Castlebar, County Mayo.

Wexford Opera Festival: Rarely performed 18th- and 19th-century operas are staged in the small, restored Georgian *Theatre Royal,* and recitals, concerts, exhibitions, and balls go on elsewhere. The 12-day gala has an international reputation. Wexford, County Wexford.

NORTHERN IRELAND

February

Ulster Harp National: The most important steeplechase in Northern Ireland. Downpatrick, County Down.

March

St. Patrick's Week: Concurrent with celebrations in the Republic (see below), there's an important pilgrimage to Slemish Mountain, County Antrim, where the saint tended sheep as a boy, as well as musical and other events in and around Downpatrick, where he is said to have established Ireland's first monastery. Downpatrick, County Down.

April

Festival of Twentieth Century Music: Biennial event featuring both international and local performers and composers. The 1989 event focused on American music; the festival will be held again this year, but as we went to press the theme had not yet been determined. Belfast, County Antrim.

May

Ulster Games: Annual festival of international sporting events held at various sites throughout Northern Ireland. (Note that some of these events may be held as early as March or as late as July.)

June

Northern Ireland Game and Country Fair: Ireland's premier field sports event, covering all aspects of outdoor sports and country life. Bangor, County Down.

July

Orangemen's Day and the Sham Fight: Colorful parades in Belfast and other cities and a sham fight at Scarva in County Down commemorate the Battle of the Boyne.

City of Belfast International Rose Trials: The only open international competition for catalogued roses in the British Isles. Runs through the summer. Belfast, County Antrim.

August

Ancient Order of Hibernians' Processions: Parades, religious services, and sports events commemorate *Lady Day.* Various Ulster cities.

Ould Lammas Fair: A very popular and traditional Irish fair, held annually since the 16th century. Ballycastle, County Londonderry.

November

Belfast Festival at Queen's: Three weeks of classical music, folk music, jazz, opera, ballet, drama, and film at Queen's University. Belfast, County Antrim.

Traveling by Plane

The air space between North America and Europe is the most heavily trafficked in the world. It is served by dozens of airlines, almost all of which sell seats at a variety of prices, under widely different terms. Since you probably will spend more for your airfare than for any other single item in your Irish travel budget, try to take advantage of the low fares offered by either scheduled airlines or charter companies. You should know what kinds of flights are available, the rules and regulations pertaining to air travel, and all the special package options.

SCHEDULED FLIGHTS: *Aer Lingus* flies nonstop from New York to Ireland daily in summer and six times a week in winter. This airline also operates nonstop flights from Boston to Ireland daily during the summer and once or twice a week during the winter, and nonstop flights from Chicago to Ireland twice a week during the summer and weekly during the winter. As we went to press, *Aer Lingus* announced plans to add service from Los Angeles this spring. All *Aer Lingus* flights land first at Shannon International Airport, in the west of Ireland, then fly on to Dublin Airport in the east. *Delta* flies nonstop from Atlanta to Shannon five times weekly in spring and summer and less frequently in winter. *British Airways* flies from the US to Cork, Dublin, and Shannon. Other carriers that go to Britain, but do not fly directly to Ireland, are *Air Canada, American, Continental, Northwest, Pan American, TWA,* and *US Air.* (See "On Arrival" below for details of connecting flights between Britain and Ireland and domestic flights within Ireland.)

Tickets – When traveling on one of the many regularly scheduled flights, a full-fare ticket provides maximum travel flexibility (although at considerable expense), because there are no advance booking requirements: A prospective passenger can buy a ticket for a flight right up to the minute of takeoff — if a seat is available. If your ticket is for a round trip, you can make the return reservation any time you wish, months before you leave, or the day before you return. Assuming the foreign immigration requirements are met, you can stay at your destination for as long as you like. (Tickets generally are good for a year, but can be renewed if not used.) You also can cancel your flight at any time without penalty. However, while it is true that this category of ticket can be purchased at the last minute, it is advisable to reserve well in advance during popular vacation periods and around holiday times.

No matter what kind of ticket you buy, it is wise to reconfirm that you will be using your return reservations. For instance, if you do not call the airline to let them know you will be using the return leg of your reservation, they (or their computer) may assume you are not coming and automatically cancel your seat. For further information, see "Reservations," below.

Fares – Airfares continue to change so rapidly that even experts find it difficult to keep up with them. This ever-changing situation is due to a number of factors, including airline deregulation, volatile labor and fuel costs, and vastly increased competition. Before the Airline Deregulation Act of 1978, US airlines had no choice but to set their rates and routes within the guidelines of the Civil Aeronautics Board (CAB), and they could compete for passengers only by offering better service than their competitors. With the loosening of controls (and the elimination of the CAB), airlines now are engaged in a far more intense competition relating to price and schedule, which has opened the door to a wide range of discount fares and promotional offers. Intensifying the competitive atmosphere has been the creation of several new carriers offering fewer frills and far lower prices. These carriers seem to appear and disappear with dismaying regularity. They have, however, served to drive down fares from time to time and make the older, more entrenched carriers aware that they are in a genuine competition for travelers' dollars. As Europe, too, moves closer to the deregulation of airline fares, the price of intra-European travel is expected to decrease somewhat as well.

Perhaps the most common misconception about fares on scheduled airlines is that the cost of the ticket determines how much service will be provided on the flight. This is true only to a certain extent. A far more realistic rule of thumb is that the less you pay for your ticket, the more restrictions and qualifications are likely to come into play before you board the plane (as well as after you get off). These qualifying aspects relate to the months during which you must travel, how far in advance you must purchase your ticket, the minimum and maximum amount of time you may or must remain abroad, your willingness to make up your mind concerning a return date at the time of booking — and your ability to stick to that decision. It is not uncommon for passengers sitting side by side on the same wide-body jet to have paid fares varying by hundreds of dollars, and all too often the traveler paying more would have been equally willing to accept the terms regulating the far less expensive ticket. The ticket you buy will fall into one of several fare categories currently being offered by scheduled carriers flying between the US and Ireland.

In general, the great variety of fares between the US and Ireland can be reduced to four basic categories, including first class, coach (also called economy or tourist class), and excursion or discount fares. The fourth category, called business class (an intermediate between first class and coach, with many of the amenities of first class and more legroom than coach), has been added by many airlines in recent years. In addition, Advance Purchase Excursion (APEX) and "Eurosaver" fares offer savings under certain conditions.

In a class by itself is the *Concorde,* the supersonic jet developed jointly by France and Great Britain, which cruises at speeds of 1,350 miles an hour (twice the speed of sound) and makes transatlantic crossings in half the time (3½ hours from New York to London) of conventional, subsonic jets. *British Airways* offers *Concorde* service from Miami, Washington, DC, and New York to London. Additionally, *British Airways* has an arrangement with *Enterprise Airlines* for connecting flights between Boston and New York for *Concorde* service. *Air France* also offers *Concorde* service from New York to Paris. Service is "single" class (with champagne and caviar all the way), and the fare is expensive, about 20% more than a first class ticket on a subsonic aircraft. Some discounts have been offered, but time is the real gift of the *Concorde.* As travelers to Ireland actually fly beyond their Irish destination and then have to take a subsonic flight from London to Ireland, this "gift" is more or less valuable as compared to the time of a nonstop flight when taking *Concorde* connections into account.

A first class ticket is your admission to the special section of the aircraft — larger seats, more legroom, sleeperette seating on some wide-body aircraft, better (or more elaborately served) food, free drinks and headsets for movies and music channels, and above all, personal attention. First class fares are about double those of full-fare economy, although both first class passengers and people paying ecomony fares are entitled to reserve seats and are sold tickets on an open reservation system. An additional advantage of a first class ticket is that if you're planning to visit several cities within Ireland or elsewhere in Europe, you may include any number of stops en route to your most distant destination, provided that certain set, but generous, maximum permitted mileage limits are respected. (Travelers to Ireland who wish to fly first class should note that *Aer Lingus* does not offer first class service.)

Not too long ago, there were only two classes of air travel, first class and all the rest, usually called economy or tourist. But because passengers paying full economy fares traveled in the same compartment as passengers flying for considerably less on various promotional or discount fares, the airlines introduced special services to compensate those paying the full price. Thus, business class came into being — one of the most successful of recent airline innovations. At first, business class passengers merely were curtained off from the other economy passengers. Now a separate cabin or cabins — usually toward the front of the plane — is the norm. While standards of comfort and service are not as high as in first class, they represent a considerable improvement over conditions in the rear of the plane, with roomier seats, more leg and shoulder space between passengers, and fewer seats abreast. Free liquor and headphones, a choice of meal entrées, and a separate counter for speedier check-in are other inducements. As in first class, a business class passenger may travel on any scheduled flight he or she wishes, may buy a one-way or round-trip ticket, and have the ticket remain valid for a year. There are no minimum or maximum stay requirements, no advance booking requirements, and no cancellation penalties, and the fare allows the same free stopover privileges as first class. Airlines often have their own names for their business class service — such as Executive Class on *Aer Lingus* or Medallion Class on *Delta.*

The terms of the coach or economy fare may vary slightly from airline to airline, and, in fact, from time to time airlines may be selling more than one type of economy fare. Economy fares sell for substantially less than business fares, the savings effected by limited frills and stopovers. Coach or economy passengers sit more snugly, as many as 10 in a single row on a wide-body jet, behind the first class and business class sections, and receive standard meal service. Alcoholic drinks are not free, nor are the headsets (except on *British Airways,* which does offer these free of charge). If there are two economy fares on the books, one (often called "regular economy") still may include free stopovers. The other, less expensive fare (often called "special economy") may limit stopovers to one or two, with a charge (typically $25) for each one. Like first class passengers, however, passengers paying the full coach fare are subject to none of the restrictions that usually are attached to less expensive discount fares. There are no advance booking requirements, no minimum stay requirements, and no cancellation penalties. Tickets are sold on an open reservation system: They can be bought for a flight up to the minute of takeoff (if seats are available), and if the ticket is round-trip, the return reservation can be made any time you wish — months before you leave or the day before you return. Both first class and coach tickets generally are good for a year, after which they can be renewed if not used, and if you ultimately decide not to fly at all, your money will be refunded. The cost of economy and business class tickets does not vary much in the course of the year between the US and Ireland, though on some transatlantic routes they vary in price from a basic (low-season) price in effect most of the year to a peak (high-season) price during the summer.

Excursions and other discount fares are the airlines' equivalent of a special sale, and usually apply to round-trip bookings. These fares generally differ according to the season and the number of travel days permitted. They are only a bit less flexible than full-fare economy tickets and are, therefore, useful for both business travelers and tourists. Most round-trip excursion tickets include strict minimum and maximum stay requirements and reservations can be changed only within the prescribed time limits. So don't count on extending a ticket beyond the prescribed time of return or staying less time than required. Different airlines may have different regulations concerning the number of stopovers permitted, and sometimes excursion fares are less expensive during midweek. Needless to say, these reduced-rate seats are most limited at busy times such as holidays, when full-fare coach seats sell more quickly than usual. Passengers fortunate enough to get a discount or excursion fare ticket sit with the coach passengers, and, for all intents and purposes, are indistinguishable from them. They receive all the same basic services, even though they have paid anywhere between 30% and 55% less for the trip. Obviously, it's wise to make plans early enough to qualify for this less expensive transportation.

These discount or excursion fares may masquerade under a variety of names, they may vary from city to city (from the East Coast to the West Coast, especially), but they invariably have strings attached. A common requirement is that the ticket be purchased a certain number of days — usually no fewer than 7 or 14 days — in advance of departure, though it may be booked weeks or months in advance (it has to be "ticketed," or paid for, shortly after booking, however). The return reservation usually has to be made at the time of the original ticketing and cannot be changed later than a certain number of days (again, usually 7 or 14 days) before the return flight. If events force a passenger to change the return reservation after the date allowed, the difference between the round-trip excursion rate and the round-trip coach rate probably will have to be paid, though most airlines allow passengers to use their discounted fares by standing by for an empty seat, even if they don't otherwise have standby fares. Another common condition is a minimum and maximum stay requirement; for example, 6 to 14 days or 1 to 6 days, but including at least a Saturday night. Last, cancellation penalties of up to 50% of the full price of the ticket have been assessed — check the specific penalty in effect when you purchase your discount/excursion ticket — so careful planning is imperative.

Of even greater risk — and bearing the lowest price of all the current discount fares — is the ticket where no change at all in departure and/or return flights is permitted, and where the ticket price is totally nonrefundable. If you do buy a nonrefundable ticket, you should be aware of a new policy followed by many airlines, regarding international flights, that may make it easier to change your plans if necessary. For a fee — set by each airline and payable at the airport when checking in — you *may* be able to change the time or date of a return flight on a nonrefundable ticket. However, if the nonrefundable ticket price for the replacement flight is higher than that of the original (as generally is the case when trading in a weekday for a weekend flight), you will have to pay the difference. Any such change must be made a certain number of days in advance — in some cases as little as 2 days — of either the original or the replacement flight, whichever is earlier; restrictions are set by the individual carrier.

In the past, some excursion fares offered for travel to Ireland came unencumbered by advance booking requirements and cancellation penalties, permitted one stopover (but not a free one) in each direction, and had "open jaws," meaning that you could fly to one city and depart from another, arranging and paying for your own transportation between the two. Excursion fares of this type do not, at present, exist on flights between the US and Ireland, but a newer and less expensive type of excursion, the APEX, or Advance Purchase Excursion, does.

As with traditional excursion fares, passengers paying an APEX fare sit with and receive the same basic services as any other coach or economy passenger, even though they may have paid up to 50% less for their seats. In return, they are subject to certain restrictions. In the case of flights to Ireland, the ticket usually is good for a minimum of 7 days abroad and a maximum, currently, of 6 months (depending on the airline and the destination); and, as its name implies, it must be "ticketed" or paid for in its entirety a certain period of time before departure — usually 21 days. The drawback to an APEX fare is that it penalizes travelers who change their minds — and travel plans. The return reservation must be made at the time of the original ticketing, and if for some reason you change your schedule while abroad, you pay a penalty of $100 or 10% of the ticket value, whichever is greater, as long as you travel within the validity period of your ticket. But, if you change your return to a date less than the minimum stay or more than the maximum stay, the difference between the round-trip APEX fare and the full round-trip coach rate will have to be paid. There also is a penalty of $125 or more for canceling or changing a reservation *before* travel begins — check the specific penalty in effect when you purchase your ticket. No stopovers are allowed on an APEX ticket, but it is possible to create an open-jaw effect by buying an APEX on a split-ticket basis; for example, flying to Dublin and returning from London (or some other city). The total price would be half the price of an APEX to Dublin plus half the price of an APEX to London. APEX tickets to Ireland are sold at basic and peak rates (peak season is around May through September) and may include surcharges for weekend flights.

Another type of fare that sometimes is available is the youth fare. At present, most airlines flying to Ireland are using a form of APEX fare as a youth fare for those through age 30. The maximum stay is extended to a year, and the return booking must be left open. Seats can be reserved no more than 3 days before departure, and tickets must be purchased when the reservation is made. The return is booked from Ireland in the same manner, no more than 3 days before flight time. There is no cancellation penalty, but the fare is subject to availability, so it may be difficult to book a return during peak travel periods, and as with the regular APEX fare, it may not even be available for travel to or from Ireland during high season.

Standby fares, at one time the rock-bottom price at which a traveler could fly to Europe, have become elusive. At the time of this writing, most major scheduled airlines did not offer standby fares on direct flights to Ireland. Because airline fares and their conditions constantly change, however, bargain hunters should not hesitate to ask if such a fare exists at the time they plan to travel. Travelers to Ireland also should inquire about the possibility of connecting flights through other European countries (such as Great Britain) that may be offered on a standby basis.

While the definition of standby varies somewhat from airline to airline, it generally means that you make yourself available to buy a ticket for a flight (usually no sooner than the day of departure), then literally stand by on the chance that a seat will be empty. Once aboard, however, a standby passenger has the same meal service and frills (or lack of them) enjoyed by others in the economy class compartment.

Something else to check is the possibility of qualifying for a GIT (group inclusive travel) fare, which requires that a specified dollar amount of ground arrangements be purchased, in advance, along with the ticket. The requirements vary as to the number of travel days and stopovers permitted, and the number of passengers required for a group. The actual fares also vary, but the cost will be spelled out in brochures distributed by the tour operators handling the ground arrangements. In the past, GIT fares were among the least expensive available from the established carriers, but the prevalence of discount fares has caused group fares to all but disappear from some air routes. Travelers reading brochures on group package tours to Ireland will find that, in almost all cases, the applicable airfare given as a sample (to be added to the price of the land package to obtain the total tour price) is an APEX fare, the same discount fare available to the independent traveler.

The major airlines serving Ireland from the US also may offer individual fare excursion rates similar to GIT fares, which are sold in conjunction with ground accommodation packages. Previously called ITX, these fares generally are offered as part of "air/hotel/car/transfer packages," and can reduce the cost of an economy fare by more than a third. The packages are booked for a specific amount of time, with return dates specified; rescheduling and cancellation restrictions and penalties vary from carrier to carrier. When available, these fares are offered to popular destinations throughout Ireland. At the time of this writing, this type of fare was offered to Ireland by *Aer Lingus, British Airways,* and *Delta,* and although their offerings did not represent substantial savings over the standard economy fare, it is worth checking at the time you plan to travel. (For further information on package options, see *Package Tours,* in this section.)

Travelers looking for the least expensive possible airfares should, finally, scan the travel pages of their local newspapers for announcements of special promotional fares. Most airlines traditionally have offered their most attractive special fares to encourage travel during slow seasons and to inaugurate and publicize new routes. Even if none of these factors apply, prospective passengers can be fairly sure that the number of discount seats per flight at the lowest price is strictly limited, or that the fare offering includes a set expiration date — which means it's absolutely necessary to move fast to obtain the lowest possible price. Unfortunately, special fare offers can come and go quickly, and may not be available precisely when you want to travel.

Among other special airline promotional deals for which you should be on the lookout are discount or upgrade coupons, sometimes offered by the major carriers and found in mail order merchandise catalogues. For instance, airlines sometimes issue coupons that typically cost around $25 and are good for a percentage discount or an upgrade on an international airline ticket — including flights to Ireland. The only requirement beyond the fee generally is that a coupon purchaser is required to buy at least one item from the catalogue. There usually are some minimum airfare restrictions before the coupon is redeemable, but in general these are worthwhile offers. Restrictions often include certain blackout days (when the coupon cannot be used at all), usually imposed during peak travel periods. These coupons are particularly valuable to business travelers who tend to buy full-fare tickets, and while the coupons are issued in the buyer's name, they can be used by others who are traveling on the same itinerary.

Given the frequency with which the airfare picture changes, it is more than possible that by the time you are ready to fly, the foregoing discussion may be somewhat out of date. That's why it always is wise to comparison shop, and that requires reading the business and travel sections of your newspaper regularly, and making calls to all the airlines that serve your destination from your most convenient gateway. The potential savings are well worth the effort.

Ask about discount or promotional fares and about any conditions that might restrict booking, payment, cancellation, and changes in plans. Check the prices from other cities. A special rate may be offered in a nearby city but not in yours, and it may be enough of a bargain to warrant your leaving from that city. If you have a flexible schedule, investigate standby fares. But remember that, depending on your departure point, they may not work out to be the rock-bottom price. Ask if there is a difference in price for midweek versus weekend travel, or if there is a further discount for traveling early in the morning or late at night. Also be sure to investigate package deals, which are offered by virtually every airline. These may include a car rental, accommodations, and dining and/or sightseeing features, in addition to the basic airfare, and the combined cost of packaged elements usually is considerably less than the cost of the exact same elements when purchased separately.

If in your research you come across a deal that seems too good to be true, keep in mind that logic may not be a component of deeply discounted airfares — there's not always any sane relationship between miles to be flown and the price to get there. More often than not, the level of competition on a given route dictates the degree of discount, and don't be dissuaded from accepting an offer that sounds irresistible just because it also sounds illogical. Better to buy that inexpensive fare while it's being offered and worry about the sense — or absence thereof — while you're flying to your desired destination.

When you're satisfied that you've found the lowest possible price for which you can conveniently qualify (you may have to call the airline more than once, because different clerks have been known to quote different prices), make your booking. Then, to protect yourself against fare increases, purchase and pay for your ticket as soon as possible after you've received a confirmed reservation. Airlines generally will honor their tickets, even if the operative price at the time of your flight is higher than the price you paid; if fares go up between the time you *reserve* a flight and the time you *pay* for it, you likely will be out of luck. Finally, with excursion or discount fares, it is important to remember that when a reservation clerk says that you must purchase a ticket by a specific date, this is an absolute deadline. Miss it and the airline automatically may cancel your reservation without telling you.

■ **Note:** Another wrinkle on the airfare scene is that if the fares go *down* after you purchase your ticket, you *may* be entitled to a refund of the difference. However, this is possible only in certain situations — availability and advance purchase restrictions pertaining to the lower rate are set by the airline. If you suspect that you may be able to qualify for such a refund, check with your travel agent or the airline (although some airline clerks may not be aware of this policy).

Frequent Flyers – Two of the leading carriers serving Ireland, *British Airways* and *Delta,* now also offer a bonus system to frequent travelers. After the first 10,000 miles, for example, a passenger might be eligible for a first class seat for the coach fare; after another 10,000 miles, he or she might receive a discount on his or her next ticket purchase. The value of the bonuses continues to increase as more miles are logged.

Bonus miles also may be earned by patronizing affiliated car rental companies or hotel chains, or by using one of the credit cards that now offers this reward. In deciding whether to accept such a credit card from one of the issuing organizations that tempt you with frequent flyer mileage bonuses on a specific airline, first determine whether the interest rate charged on the unpaid balance is the same as (or less than) possible alternative credit cards, and whether the annual "membership" fee also is equal or lower. If these charges are slightly higher than those of competing cards, weigh the difference against the potential value in airfare savings. Also ask about any bonus miles awarded just for signing up — 1,000 is common, 5,000 generally the maximum. (For further information on credit cards, see *Credit and Currency,* in this section.)

For the most up-to-date information on frequent flyer bonus options, you may want to send for the monthly newsletter *Frequent.* Issued by Frequent Publications, it provides current information about frequent flyer plans in general, as well as specific data about promotions, awards, and combination deals to help you keep track of the profusion — and confusion — of current and upcoming availabilities. For a year's subscription, send $28 to Frequent Publications, 4715-C Town Center Dr., Colorado Springs, CO 80916 (phone: 800-333-5937).

There also is a monthly magazine called *Frequent Flyer,* but unlike the newsletter mentioned above, its focus is primarily on newsy articles of interest to business travelers and other frequent flyers. Published by Official Airline Guides (PO Box 58543, Boulder, CO 80322-8543; phone: 800-323-3537), *Frequent Flyer* is available for $24 for a 1-year subscription.

Low-Fare Airlines – In today's economic climate, the stimulus for special fares increasingly is the appearance of new airlines along popular routes. These tend to be smaller carriers that offer low fares because of lower overhead, non-union staffs, uncomplicated route networks, and other limitations in their service. On these airlines, all seats on any given flight generally sell for the same price, which is somewhat below the lowest discount fare offered by the larger, more established airlines. It is important to note that tickets offered by the smaller airlines specializing in low-cost travel frequently are not subject to the same restrictions as the lowest-priced ticket offered by the more established carriers. They may not require advance purchase or minimum and maximum stays, may involve no cancellation penalties, may be available one way or round-trip, and may, for all intents and purposes, resemble the competition's high-priced full-fare coach. But never assume this until you know it's so. A disadvantage to many of the low-fare airlines, however, is that when something goes wrong, such as delayed baggage or a flight cancellation due to equipment breakdown, their smaller fleets and fewer flights mean that passengers may have to wait longer for a solution than they would on one of the equipment-rich major carriers.

Virgin Atlantic (phone: 212-242-1330 in New York City; 800-862-8621 elsewhere) flies from Newark to London's Gatwick Airport daily year-round and from Miami to Gatwick four times a week and may be useful to travelers intending to visit both Ireland

and Great Britain. Travelers to Ireland actually will fly beyond their destination, then have to take a second flight from London to Ireland, but still may save money. The airline sells tickets in several fare categories, including business or "upper" class, economy, APEX, and nonrefundable variations on standby called Late Saver fares (which must be purchased not less than 7 days prior to travel) and Late Late Saver fares (which are purchased no later than 1 day prior to travel). At the time of this writing, the Late Saver fare to London was $229 one way during the off-season, rising to $299 one way during the summer. Prices for Late Late Saver fares ranged from $179 for off-season travel to $229 in the summer.

In a class by itself is *Icelandair,* which always has been a scheduled airline but long has been known as a good source of low-cost flights to Europe. *Icelandair* flies from Baltimore/Washington, DC, New York, and Orlando via Reykjavik, Iceland, to Glasgow and London. The airline sells tickets in a variety of categories, from unrestricted economy fares to a sort of standby "3-days-before" fare (which functions just like the youth fares described above but has no age requirement). Travelers should be aware, however, that most *Icelandair* flights stop in Reykjavik for 45 minutes — a minor delay for most, but one that further prolongs the trip for passengers who will wait again in Great Britain to board connecting flights to their ultimate destination in Ireland. As *Icelandair* does not offer connecting flights to Ireland, it may be a better choice for travelers intending to visit Great Britain or the Continent when taking both this delay and the cost of connections into account. For reservations and tickets, contact a travel agent or *Icelandair* (phone: 212-967-8888 in New York City; 800-223-5500 elsewhere in the US).

Intra-European Fares – The cost of the round trip across the Atlantic is not the only expense to be considered. Flights between European cities, when booked in Europe, can be quite expensive. But discounts have been introduced on routes between some European cities (Dublin and London, for instance), and other discounts do exist.

Recent Common Market moves toward airline deregulation are expected to lead gradually to a greater number of budget fares. In the meantime, however, the high cost of European fares can be avoided by careful use of stopover rights on the higher-priced transatlantic tickets — first class, business class, and full-fare economy. If your ticket doesn't allow stopovers, ask about excursion fares and APEX for round trips, and other excursion fares for one-way trips. If the restrictions that govern them allow you to use them (frequently the minimum stay requirement means staying over for at least 1 Saturday night), you may save as much as 35% to 50% off full-fare economy. Note that these fares, which once could be bought only after arrival in Europe, now are sold in the US and can be bought before departure.

It is not easy to inform yourself about stopover possibilities by talking to most airline reservations clerks. More than likely, an inquiry concerning any projected trip will prompt the reply that a particular route is nonstop aboard the carrier in question, thereby precluding stopovers completely, or that the carrier does not fly to all the places you want to visit. It may take additional inquiries, perhaps with the aid of a travel agent, to determine the full range of options regarding stopover privileges. Travelers might be able to squeeze in visits to Paris and London on a first class ticket to Dublin, for instance; and Dublin might be only the first of many free European stopovers possible on a one-way or round-trip ticket to a city in Eastern Europe or points beyond. The airline that flies you on the first leg of your trip across the Atlantic issues the ticket, though you may have to use several different airlines in order to complete your journey. First class tickets are valid for a full year, so there's no rush.

For those traveling in both Great Britain and Northern Ireland, *British Airways* offers a UK Air Pass, which provides substantial savings on flights within these two countries. This pass must be purchased in conjunction with a round-trip transatlantic ticket aboard *British Airways* at least 7 days prior to arrival in Europe. Pass holders can take up to 12 flights on any of *British Airways'* routes within the United Kingdom — including flights between Great Britain and Belfast, Northern Ireland. The price of the pass is based on the number of flights: Flights in or out of London cost $66 each; flights between any other two cities cost $49 each. For information, contact *British Airways* (phone: 800-AIRWAYS).

Taxes and Other Fees – Travelers who have shopped for the best possible flight at the lowest possible price should be warned that a number of extras will be added to that price and collected by the airline or travel agent who issues the ticket. In addition to the $6 International Air Transportation Tax — a departure tax paid by all passengers flying from the US to a foreign destination — there is now a $10 US Federal Inspection Fee levied on all air and cruise passengers who arrive in the US from outside North America (those arriving from Canada, Mexico, the Caribbean, and US territories are exempt). Payable at the time a round-trip or incoming ticket is purchased, it combines a $5 customs inspection fee and a $5 immigration inspection fee, both instituted in 1986 to finance additional inspectors to reduce delays at gateways.

Still another fee is charged by some airlines to cover more stringent security procedures, prompted by recent terrorist incidents. The 8% federal US Transportation Tax, which applies to travel within the US or US territories, already is included in advertised fares and in the prices quoted by reservations clerks. It does not apply to passengers flying between US cities en route to a foreign destination, unless the trip includes a stopover of more than 12 hours at a US point. Someone flying from Los Angeles to New York and stopping in New York for more than 12 hours before boarding a flight to Europe, for instance, would pay the 8% tax on the domestic portion of the trip. Note that all of these taxes *usually* are included in advertised fares and in the prices quoted by airline reservation clerks.

Reservations – For those who don't have the time and patience to investigate personally all possible air departures and connections for a proposed trip, a travel agent can be of inestimable help. A good agent should have all the information on which flights go where and when, and which categories of tickets are available on each. Most have computerized reservation links with the major carriers, so that a seat can be reserved and confirmed in minutes. An increasing number of agents also possess fare-comparison computer programs, so they often are very reliable sources of detailed competitive price data. (For more information, see *How to Use a Travel Agent,* in this section.)

When making reservations through a travel agent, ask the agent to give the airline your home phone number, as well as your daytime business phone number. All too often the agent uses the agency number as the official contact for changes in flight plans. Especially during the winter, weather conditions hundreds or even thousands of miles away can wreak havoc with flight schedules. Aircraft are constantly in use, and a plane delayed in the Orient or on the West Coast can miss its scheduled flight from the East Coast the next morning. The airlines are fairly reliable about getting this sort of information to passengers if they can reach them; diligence does little good at 10 PM if the airline has only the agency's or an office number.

Reconfirmation is strongly recommended for all international flights (though generally it is not required on domestic flights). Some (though increasingly fewer) reservations to and from international destinations are automatically canceled after a required reconfirmation period (typically 72 hours) has passed — even if you have a confirmed, fully paid ticket in hand. It always is a good idea to call ahead to make sure that the airline did not slip up in entering your original reservation, or in registering any changes you may have made since, and that it has your seat reservation and/or special meal request in the computer. Although policies vary from carrier to carrier, some recommend that you reconfirm your return flight 48 to 72 hours in advance. If you look at the back of your ticket, you'll see the airline's reconfirmation policy stated explicitly. If in doubt — call.

Every travel agent or airline ticket office should give each passenger a reminder to reconfirm flights, but this seldom happens, so the responsibility rests with the traveler. Don't be lulled into a false sense of security by the "OK" on your ticket next to the number and time of the return flight. That only means that a reservation has been entered; a reconfirmation still may be necessary.

If you plan not to take a flight on which you hold a confirmed reservation, by all means inform the airline. Because the problem of no-shows is a constant expense for airlines, they are allowed to overbook flights, a practice that often contributes to the threat of denied boarding for a certain number of passengers (see "Getting Bumped," below). Let the airline know you're not coming and you'll spare everyone some inconvenience and confusion. Bear in mind that only certain kinds of tickets allow the luxury of last-minute changes in flight plans: Those sold on an open reservation system (first class and full-fare coach) do, while excursions and other discount fares often are restricted in some way. Even first class and coach passengers should remember that if they do not show up for a flight that is the first of several connecting ones, the airline very likely will cancel all of their ongoing reservations unless informed not to do so.

Seating – For most types of tickets, airline seats usually are assigned on a first-come, first-served basis at check-in, although some airlines make it possible to reserve a seat at the time of ticket purchase. Always check in early for your flight, even with advance seat assignments. A good rule of thumb for international flights is to arrive at the airport *at least* 2 hours before the scheduled departure to give yourself plenty of time in case there are long lines.

Most airlines furnish seating charts, which make choosing a seat much easier, but there are a few basics to consider. You must decide whether you prefer a window, aisle, or middle seat. On flights where smoking is permitted, you also should specify if you prefer the smoking or nonsmoking section.

The amount of legroom provided (as well as chest room, especially when the seat in front of you is in a reclining position) is determined by pitch, a measure of the distance between the back of the seat in front of you and the front of the back of your seat. The amount of pitch is a matter of airline policy, not the type of plane you fly. First class and business class seats have the greatest pitch, a fact that figures prominently in airline advertising. In economy class or coach, the standard pitch ranges from 33 to as little as 31 inches — downright cramped.

The number of seats abreast, another factor determining comfort, depends on a combination of airline policy and airplane dimensions. First class and business class have the fewest seats per row. Economy generally has 9 seats per row on a DC-10 or an L-1011, making either one slightly more comfortable than a 747, on which there normally are 10 seats per row. Charter flights on DC-10s and L-1011s, however, often have 10 seats per row and can be noticeably more cramped than 747 charters, on which the seating normally remains at 10 per row.

Airline representatives claim that most aircraft are more stable toward the front and midsections, while seats farthest from the engines are quietest. Passengers who have long legs and are traveling on a wide-body aircraft might request a seat directly behind a door or emergency exit, since these seats often have greater than average pitch, or a seat in the first row of a given section, since these seats have extra legroom. It often is impossible, however, to see the movie from these seats, which are directly behind the plane's exits. Be aware that the first row of the economy section (called a "bulkhead" seat) on a conventional aircraft (not a widebody) does *not* offer extra legroom, since the fixed partition will not permit passengers to slide their feet under it, and that watching a movie from this first-row seat can be difficult and uncomfortable. A window seat protects you from aisle traffic and clumsy serving carts, and also allows you a view, while an aisle seat enables you to get up and stretch your legs without disturbing your fellow travelers. Middle seats are the least desirable, and seats in the last row are the worst of all, since they seldom recline fully. If you wish to avoid children on your flight or if you find that you are sitting in an especially noisy section, you usually are free to move to any unoccupied seat — if there is one.

If you are overweight, you may face the prospect of a long flight with special trepidation. Center seats in the alignments of wide-body 747s, L-1011s, and DC-10s are about 1½ inches wider than those on either side, so larger travelers tend to be more comfortable there.

Despite all these rules of thumb, finding out which specific rows are near emergency exits or at the front of a wide-body cabin can be difficult because seating arrangements on two otherwise identical planes vary from airline to airline. There is, however, a quarterly publication called the *Airline Seating Guide* that publishes seating charts for most major US airlines and many foreign carriers as well. Your travel agent should have a copy, or you can buy the US edition for $39.95 per year and the overseas edition for $44.95. Order from Carlson Publishing Co., Box 888, Los Alamitos, CA 90720 (phone: 213-493-4877).

Simply reserving an airline seat in advance, however, actually may guarantee very little. Most airlines require that passengers arrive at the departure gate at least 45 minutes (sometimes more) ahead of time to hold a seat reservation. *Aer Lingus,* for instance, may cancel seat assignments and may not honor reservations of passengers not "checked in" 30 minutes before the scheduled departure time for all international and Irish domestic flights. As this is one airline's policy only, it pays to read the fine print on the back of your ticket carefully and plan ahead.

A far better strategy is to visit an airline ticket office (or one of a select group of travel agents) to secure an actual boarding pass for your specific flight. Once this has been issued, airline computers show you as checked in, and you effectively own the seat you have selected (although some carriers may not honor boarding passes of passengers arriving at the gate less than 10 minutes before departure). This also is good — but not foolproof — insurance against getting bumped from an overbooked flight and is, therefore, an especially valuable tactic at peak travel times.

Smoking – One decision regarding choosing a seat has been taken out of the hands of many travelers who smoke. Effective February 25, 1990, the US government imposed a ban that prohibits smoking on all flights scheduled for 6 hours or less within the US and its territories. The new regulation applies to both domestic and international carriers serving these routes.

In the case of flights to Ireland, these rules do not apply to nonstop flights going directly from the US to Europe, or those with a continuous flight time of over 6 hours between stops in the US or its territories. Smoking is not permitted on segments of international flights where the flight time between US landings is under 6 hours — for instance, flights that include a stopover (even with no change of plane) or connecting flights. To further complicate the situation, several individual carriers are banning smoking altogether on certain routes. (As we went to press, this ban had not yet extended to carriers flying between the US and Ireland.)

On those flights that do permit smoking, the US Department of Transportation has determined that nonsmoking sections must be enlarged to accommodate all passengers who wish to sit in one. The airline does not, however, have to shift seating to accommodate nonsmokers who arrive late for a flight or travelers flying standby, and in general not all airlines can guarantee a seat in the nonsmoking section on international flights. Cigar and pipe smoking are prohibited on all flights, even in the smoking sections.

For a wallet-size guide, which notes in detail the rights of nonsmokers according to these regulations, send a self-addressed, stamped envelope to ASH (Action on Smoking and Health), Airline Card, 2013 H St. NW, Washington, DC 20006 (phone: 202-659-4310).

Flying with Children – On longer flights, the bulkhead seats usually are reserved for families traveling with small children. As a general rule, an infant under 2 years of age (and not occupying a seat) flies to Europe at 10% of whatever fare the accompanying adult is paying. A second infant without a second adult pays the fare applicable to children ages 2 through 11. In most cases this amounts to 50% of an adult economy fare and two-thirds of an adult APEX fare.

Although airlines will, on request, supply bassinets for infants, most carriers encourage parents to bring their own safety seat on board, which then is strapped into the airline seat with a regular seat belt. This is much safer — and certainly more comfortable — than holding the child in your lap. If you do not purchase a seat for your baby, you have the option of bringing the infant restraint along on the off-chance that there might be an empty seat next to yours — in which case many airlines will let you have that seat free for your baby and infant seat. However, if there is no empty seat available, the infant seat no doubt will have to be checked as baggage (and most likely you will have to pay an additional charge), since it generally does not fit under the seat or in the overhead racks.

The safest bet is to pay for a seat — this usually will be the same as fares applicable to children ages 2 through 11. You might have to do some number-juggling to determine the cheapest fare for the infant. Excursion fares, which usually are the least expensive, often do not have children's rates, whereas the higher-priced fares usually are the ones that offer discounts for children.

Be forewarned: Some safety seats designed primarily for use in cars do not fit properly into plane seats. Although nearly all seats manufactured since 1985 carry labels indicating whether they meet federal standards for use aboard planes, actual seat sizes may vary from carrier to carrier. At the time of this writing, the FAA was in the process of reviewing and revising airline policies with regard to infant travel and safety devices — it was still to be determined if children should be *required* to sit in safety seats and whether the airlines will have to provide them.

When checking in, and using either a bassinet or infant seat, request a bulkhead or other seat that has enough room in front to use it. On some planes, bassinets hook into a bulkhead wall; on others it is placed on the floor in front of you. Even if you do use a bassinet, babies must be held during takeoff and landing.

The entire subject of flying with children — including a discussion of car seats — is covered in a special supplementary issue of a newsletter called *Family Travel Times,* published by *Travel With Your Children (TWYCH).* An annual subscription (10 issues) is $35, and the "Airline Guide" supplement is available separately for $10, or it will be included free with a subscription. Contact *TWYCH* at 80 Eighth Ave., New York, NY 10011 (phone: 212-206-0688). (For more information on flying with children, see *Hints for Traveling with Children,* in this section.)

Meals – If you have specific diet requirements, be sure to let the airline know well before departure time. The available meals include vegetarian, seafood, kosher, Muslim, Hindu, high-protein, low-calorie, low-cholesterol, low-fat, low-sodium, diabetic, bland, and children's menus. There is no extra charge for this option. It usually is necessary to request special meals when you make your reservations — check-in time is too late. It's also wise to reconfirm that your request for a special meal has made its way into the airline's computer — the time to do this is 24 hours before departure. (Note that special meals generally are not available on intra-European flights on small local carriers. If this poses a problem, try to eat before you board, or bring food with you.)

Baggage – Travelers from the US face two different kinds of rules. When you fly in on a US airline or on a major international carrier, US baggage regulations will be in effect. Though airline baggage allowances vary slightly, in general all passengers are allowed to carry on board, without charge, one piece of luggage that will fit easily under a seat of the plane or in an overhead bin and whose combined dimensions (length, width, and depth) do not exceed 45 inches. (If you prefer not to carry it with you, most airlines will allow you to check this bag in the hold.) A reasonable amount of reading material, camera equipment, and a handbag also are allowed. In addition, all passengers are allowed to check two bags in the cargo hold: one usually not to exceed 62 inches when length, width, and depth are combined, the other not to exceed 55 inches in combined dimensions. Generally no single bag may weigh more than 70 pounds. Note, however, that this weight restriction may vary on some European airlines, ranging from as much as 88 pounds permitted for first class passengers to as little as 50 pounds for economy class — so check with the specific carrier in advance.

On European local or trunk carriers, in general, baggage allowances follow the same guidelines as major carriers. However, especially on regional and local airlines, luggage may be subject to the old weight determination, under which each economy or discount passenger is allowed only a total of 44 pounds of luggage without additional charge. First class or business passengers are allowed a total of 66 pounds. (If you are flying from the US to Europe and connecting to a domestic flight, you generally will be allowed the same amount of baggage as on the international flight. If you break your trip and then take a domestic flight, the local carrier's weight restrictions will apply.)

Charges for additional, oversize, or overweight bags usually are made at a flat rate; the actual dollar amount varying from carrier to carrier. If you plan to travel with a bike, skis, golf clubs, or other sports gear, be sure to check with the airline beforehand. Most have procedures for handling such baggage, but you probably will have to pay for transport regardless of how much other baggage you have checked.

Airline policies regarding baggage allowances for children vary and usually are based on the percentage of full adult fare paid. Children paying 50% or more of an adult fare on most US carriers are entitled to the same baggage allowance as a full-fare passenger, whereas infants traveling at 10% of an adult fare are entitled to only one piece of baggage, the combined dimensions of which may not exceed 45 inches — 39 inches on *TWA*. Particularly for international carriers, it's wise to check ahead. Often there is no luggage allowance for a child traveling on an adult's lap or in a bassinet.

To reduce the chances of your luggage going astray, remove all airline tags from previous trips, label each bag inside and out — with your business address rather than your home address on the outside, to prevent thieves from knowing whose house might be unguarded. Lock everything and double-check the tag that the airline attaches to make sure that it is coded correctly for your destination: BEL for Belfast, DUB for Dublin, or SNN for Shannon Airport, for instance.

If your bags are not in the baggage claim area after your flight, or if they're damaged, report the problem to airline personnel immediately. Keep in mind that policies regarding the specific time limit in which you have to make your claim vary from carrier to carrier. Fill out a report form on your lost or damaged luggage and keep a copy of it and your original baggage claim check. If you must surrender the check to claim a damaged bag, get a receipt for it to prove that you did, indeed, check your baggage on the flight. If luggage is missing, be sure to give the airline your destination and/or a telephone number where you can be reached. Also take the name and number of the person in charge of recovering lost luggage.

Most airlines have emergency funds for passengers stranded away from home without their luggage, but if it turns out your bags are truly lost and not simply delayed, do not then and there sign any paper indicating you'll accept an offered settlement. Since the airline is responsible for the value of your bags within certain statutory limits ($1,250 per passenger for lost baggage on a domestic flight; $9.07 per pound or $20 per kilo for checked baggage and up to $400 per passenger for unchecked baggage on an international flight), you should take some time to assess the extent of your loss (see *Insurance,* in this section). It's a good idea to keep records indicating the value of the contents of your luggage. A wise alternative is to take a Polaroid picture of the most valuable of your packed items just after putting them in your suitcase.

Considering the increased incidence of damage to baggage, it's now more than ever a good idea to keep the sales slips that confirm how much you paid for your bags. These are invaluable in establishing the value of damaged baggage and eliminate any arguments. A better way to protect your precious baggage from the luggage-eating conveyers is to try to carry your gear on board wherever possible.

Be aware that airport security increasingly is an issue all over Europe, and the Irish take it very seriously. Heavily armed police patrol the airports and unattended luggage of any description may be confiscated and quickly destroyed. Passengers checking in at a European airport may undergo at least two separate inspections of their tickets and passports by courteous but serious airline personnel — who ask passengers if their baggage has been out of their possession between packing and the airport or if they have been given gifts or other items to transport — before checked items are accepted.

Airline Clubs – US carriers often have clubs for travelers who pay for membership. These are not clubs solely for first class passengers, although a first class ticket *may* entitle a passenger to lounge privileges. Membership (which, by law, now requires a fee) entitles the traveler to use the private lounges at airports along their route, to refreshments served in those lounges, and to check-cashing privileges at most of their counters. Extras include special telephone numbers for individual reservations, embossed luggage tags, and a membership card for identification. One airline that flies to Ireland and offers membership in such a club is *Delta* — the *Crown Room Club,* single yearly membership $150, spouse an additional $50, 3-year memberships also available for $360. However, such companies do not have club facilities in all airports; other airlines also offer a variety of special services in many airports.

Getting Bumped – A special air travel problem is the possibility that an airline will accept more reservations (and sell more tickets) than there are seats on a given flight. This is entirely legal and is done to make up for "no-shows," passengers who don't show up for a flight for which they have made reservations and bought tickets. If the airline has oversold the flight and everyone does show up, there simply aren't enough seats. When this happens, the airline is subject to stringent rules designed to protect travelers.

In such cases, the airline first seeks ticketholders willing to give up their seats voluntarily in return for a negotiable sum of money, or some other inducement such as an offer of upgraded seating on the next flight or a voucher for a free trip at some other time. If there are not enough volunteers, the airline may bump passengers against their wishes.

Anyone inconvenienced in this way, however, is entitled to an explanation of the criteria used to determine who does and does not get on the flight, as well as compensation if the resulting delay exceeds certain limits. If the airline can put the bumped passengers on an alternate flight that is *scheduled to arrive* at their original destination within 1 hour of their originally scheduled arrival time, no compensation is owed. If the delay is more than an hour — but less than 2 hours on a domestic US flight or less than 4 hours on an international flight — they must be paid denied-boarding compensation equivalent to the one-way fare to their destination (but not more than $200). If the delay is more than 2 hours after the original arrival time on a domestic flight or more than 4 hours on an international flight, the compensation must be doubled (not more than $400). The airline also may offer bumped travelers a voucher for a free flight instead of the denied-boarding compensation. The passenger can choose either the money or the voucher, the dollar value of which may be no less than the monetary compensation to which the passenger would be entitled. The voucher is not a substitute for the bumped passenger's original ticket; the airline continues to honor that as well.

Keep in mind that the above regulations and policies are for flights leaving the US only, and do *not* apply to charters or inbound flights originating abroad, even on US carriers.

In Ireland, each airline is free to determine what compensation it will pay to passengers who are bumped because of overbooking. However, they are required to spell out their policies on the airline ticket. Some foreign carrier's policies are similar to the US policy. Passengers involuntarily bumped may be paid twice the price of a one-way ticket (up to $400) if they reach their destination 4 or more hours late, or may be offered other negotiable compensation — such as a voucher for a free flight — to make up for the inconvenience. However, don't assume every carrier will be as generous.

To protect yourself as best you can against getting bumped, arrive at the airport early, allowing plenty of time to check in and get to the gate. If the flight is oversold, ask immediately for the written statement explaining the airline's policy on denied-boarding compensation and its boarding priorities. If the airline refuses to give you this information, or if you feel they have not handled the situation properly, file a complaint with both the airline and the appropriate government agency (see "Consumer Protection," below).

Delays and Cancellations – The above compensation rules also do not apply if the flight is canceled or delayed, or if a smaller aircraft is substituted because of mechanical problems. Each airline has its own policy for assisting passengers whose flights are delayed or canceled or who must wait for another flight because their original one was overbooked. Most airline personnel will make new travel arrangements if necessary. If the delay is longer than 4 hours, the airline may pay for a phone call or telegram, a meal, and, in some cases, a hotel room and transportation to it.

■ **Caution:** If you are bumped or miss a flight, be sure to ask the airline to notify other airlines on which you have reservations or connecting flights. When your name is taken off the passenger list of your initial flight, the computer usually cancels all of your reservations automatically, unless *you* take steps to preserve them.

CHARTER FLIGHTS: By booking a block of seats on a specially arranged flight, charter operators offer travelers air transportation, often coupled with a hotel room, meals, and other travel services, for a substantial reduction over the full coach or economy fare.

Charters once were the best bargains around, but this is no longer necessarily the case. As a result, charter flights have been discontinued in many areas, but they still can be a good buy to some popular travel destinations, including Ireland. Charters are especially attractive to people living in smaller cities or out-of-the-way places, because they frequently take off from nearby airports, saving travelers the inconvenience and expense of getting to a major gateway to begin their Irish trip.

Where demand persists, charter operators will continue to rent planes or seats from scheduled airlines (or from special charter airlines) and offer flights to the public directly through advertisements or travel agents. You buy the ticket from the operator or the agent, not from the airline owning the plane. With the advent of APEX and various promotional fares on the major airlines and the appearance of low-fare airlines, however, charter flights lost some of their budget-conscious clientele and suffered some lean years, especially on highly competitive routes with a choice of other bargains. At the same time, many of the larger companies running charter programs began to offer both charter flights and discounted scheduled flights (see below). Nevertheless, among the current offerings, charter flights to European cities are common, a sign that they still represent a good value.

Charter travel once required that an individual be a member of a club or other "affinity" group whose main purpose was not travel. But since the approval of "public charters" years ago, operators have had some of the flexibility of scheduled airlines, making charters more competitive. Public charters are open to anyone, whether part of a group or not, and have no advance booking requirements or minimum stay requirements. Operators can offer air-only charters, selling transportation alone, or they can offer charter packages — the flight plus a combination of land arrangements such as accommodations, meals, tours, or car rental.

Though charters almost always are round-trip, and it is unlikely that you would be sold a one-way seat on a round-trip flight, on rare occasions one-way tickets on charters are offered. Although it may be possible to book a one-way charter in the US, giving you more flexibility in scheduling your return, note that US regulations pertaining to charters may be more permissive than the charter laws of other countries. For example, if you want to book a one-way foreign charter back to the US, you may find advance booking rules in force.

From the consumer's standpoint, charters differ from scheduled airlines in two main respects: You generally need to book and pay in advance, and you can't change the itinerary or the departure and return dates once you've booked the flight. In practice, however, these restrictions don't always apply. Today, although most charters still require advance reservations, some permit last-minute bookings (when there are unsold seats available), and some even offer seats on a standby basis.

The savings provided by charters vary, depending on their point of departure in the US and the countries to which they are headed (some governments do not allow charters to land at all; others allow them to undercut scheduled fares by a wide margin). As a rule, a charter to any given destination can cost anywhere from $50 to $200 less than an economy fare on a major carrier, with East Coast charters realizing a greater saving than those from the West Coast.

Some things to keep in mind about the charter game include the following:

1. It cannot be repeated often enough that if you are forced to cancel your trip, you can lose much (and possibly all) of your money unless you have cancellation insurance, which is a *must* (see *Insurance,* in this section). Frequently, if the cancellation made sufficiently far in advance (often 6 weeks or more), you may forfeit only a $25 or $50 penalty. If you cancel only 2 or 3 weeks before the flight, there may be no refund at all unless you or the operator can provide a substitute passenger.
2. Charter flights may be canceled by the operator up to 10 days before departure for any reason, usually underbooking. Your money is returned in this event, but there may be too little time to make new arrangements.
3. Most charters have little of the flexibility of regularly scheduled flights regarding refunds and the changing of flight dates; if you book a return flight, you must be on it or lose your money.
4. Charter operators are permitted to assess a surcharge, if fuel or other costs warrant it, of up to 10% of the airfare up to 10 days before departure.
5. Because of the economics of charter flights, your plane almost always will be full, so you will be crowded, though not necessarily uncomfortable. (There is, however, a new movement among charter airlines to provide flight accommodations that are comfort-oriented, so this situation may change in the near future.)

Bookings – If you do take a charter, read the contract's fine print carefully and pay particular attention to the following:

1. Instructions concerning the payment of the deposit and its balance and to whom the check is to be made payable. Ordinarily, checks are made out to an escrow account, which means the charter company can't spend your money until your flight has safely returned. This provides some protection for you. To ensure the safe handling of your money, make out your check to the escrow account, the

number of which must appear by law in the brochure, though all too often it is on the back in fine print. Write the details of the charter, including the destination and dates, on the face of the check; on the back, print "For Deposit Only." Your travel agent may prefer that you make out your check to the agency, saying that it will then pay the tour operator the fee minus commission. It is perfectly legal to write the check as we suggest, however, and if your agent objects too vociferously (he or she should trust the tour operator to send the proper commission), consider taking your business elsewhere. If you don't make your check out to the escrow account, you lose the protection of that escrow should the trip be canceled. Furthermore, recent bankruptcies in the travel industry have served to point out that even the protection of escrow may not be enough to safeguard a traveler's investment. More and more, insurance is becoming a necessity. The charter company should be bonded (usually by an insurance company), and if you want to file a claim against it, the claim should be sent to the bonding agent. The contract will set a time limit within which a claim must be filed.

2. Specific stipulations and penalties for cancellations. Most charters allow you to cancel up to 45 days in advance without major penalty, but some cancellation dates are 50 to 60 days before departure.

3. Stipulations regarding cancellation and major changes made by the charterer. US rules say that charter flights may not be canceled within 10 days of departure except when circumstances — such as natural disasters or political upheavals — make it physically impossible to fly. Charterers may make "major changes," however, such as in the date or place of departure or return, but you are entitled to cancel and receive a full refund if you don't accept these changes. A price increase of more than 10% at any time up to 10 days before departure is considered a major change; no price increase at all is allowed during the last 10 days immediately before departure.

DISCOUNTS ON SCHEDULED FLIGHTS: The APEX fare is an example of a promotional fare offered on regularly scheduled transatlantic flights by most major airlines. Promotional fares often are called discount fares because they cost less than what used to be the standard airline fare — full-fare economy. Nevertheless, they cost the traveler the same whether they are bought through a travel agent or directly from the airline. Tickets that cost less if bought from some outlet other than the airline do exist, however. While it is likely that the vast majority of travelers flying to Europe in the near future will be doing so on a promotional fare or charter rather than on a "discount" air ticket of this sort, it still is a good idea for cost-conscious consumers to be aware of the latest developments in the budget airfare scene. Note that the following discussion makes clearcut distinctions among the types of discounts available based on how they reach the consumer; in actual practice, the distinctions are not nearly so precise. One organization may operate part of its business in one fashion and the remainder in another; a second organization may operate all of its business in the same fashion, but outsiders — and sometimes the organization itself — would have difficulty classifying it.

Courier Travel – There was a time when traveling as a courier was a sort of underground way to save money and visit otherwise unaffordable destinations, but more and more the once exotic idea of traveling as a courier is becoming a very "establishment" exercise. Courier means no more than a traveler who accompanies freight of one sort or another, and typically that freight replaces what otherwise would be the traveler's checked baggage. Be prepared, therefore, to carry all your own personal travel gear in a bag that fits under the seat in front of you. In addition, the so-called courier usually pays only a portion of the total airfare — the freight company pays the remainder — and the courier also may be assessed a small registration fee.

There are over 4 dozen courier companies operating actively around the globe, and there are at least two travel newsletters that have sprung up for the purpose of publishing courier opportunities. One of these, called *Travel Secrets* (PO Box 2325, New York, NY 10108), lists more than 20 US and Canadian courier companies. The other, *Travel Unlimited* (PO Box 1058, Allston, MA 02135), lists 30 to 40 courier companies and agents worldwide. A particularly useful reference is *A Simple Guide to Courier Travel* by Jesse L. Riddle, published by the Carriage Group (PO Box 2394, Lake Oswego, OR 97035; phone: 800-344-9375), it's available for $14.95, including postage and handling.

And for those traveling to Ireland, *Excaliber International Courier Inc.* often sends couriers to London — an easy connecting flight away from Ireland. For information, contact *Excaliber*'s representative, *Way to Go Travel* (3317 Barham Blvd., Hollywood, CA 90068; phone: 213-851-2572). In addition, courier companies are listed in the yellow pages and, in general, are best used by folks with *very* flexible travel schedules.

Net Fare Sources – The newest notion for reducing the costs of travel services comes from travel agents who offer individual travelers "net" fares. Defined simply, a net fare is the bare minimum amount at which an airline or tour operator will carry a prospective traveler. It doesn't include the amount that normally would be paid to the travel agent as a commission. Traditionally, such commissions amount to about 10% on domestic fares and from 8% to 20% on international tickets — not counting significant additions to these commission levels that are payable retroactively when agents sell more than a specific volume of tickets or trips for a single supplier. At press time, at least one travel agency in the US was offering travelers the opportunity to purchase tickets and/or tours for a net price. Instead of making their income from individual commissions, this agency assesses a fixed fee that may or may not provide a bargain for travelers; it requires a little arithmetic to determine whether to use the services of a net travel agent or those of one who accepts conventional commissions. One of the potential drawbacks of buying from agencies selling travel services at net fares is that some airlines refuse to do business with them, thus possibly limiting your flight options.

Travel Avenue (formerly *McTravel Travel Service*) is a formula fee-based agency that rebates its ordinary agency commission to the customer. For domestic flights, an agent will find the lowest retail fare, then rebate from 8% to 11% (depending on the airline selected) of that price minus an $8 ticket-writing charge. The rebate percentage for international flights varies from 8% to 25% (again depending on the airline), and the ticket-writing fee is $20. The ticket-writing charge is imposed per ticket; if the ticket includes more than eight separate flights, an additional $8 or $20 fee is charged.

Travel Avenue will rebate on all tickets including Max Savers, Super Savers, and senior citizen passes; if the customer is using a free flight coupon, there is an additional $5 coupon processing fee. Available 7 days a week, reservations should be made far enough in advance to allow the tickets to be sent by first class mail, since extra charges accrue for special handling. It's possible to economize further by making your own airline reservation, then asking *Travel Avenue* only to write/issue your ticket. For travelers who live outside the Chicago area, business may be transacted by phone, and purchases may be charged to a credit card.

And for travelers seeking discounts on other travel services, *Travel Avenue* offers a similar net cost service, through which travelers can collect rebates on the cost of hotel accommodations and car rentals if the booking is made through *Travel Avenue*. Upon return home, you simply send *Travel Avenue* a copy of your receipt and they will send you a check for 5% of the total bill — returning part of their agency commission to the consumer. For further information, contact *Travel Avenue* at 641 W. Lake St., Suite 201, Chicago, IL 60606-1012 (phone: 312-876-1116 in Illinois; 800-333-3335 elsewhere in the US).

Consolidators and Bucket Shops – Other vendors of travel services can afford to sell tickets to their customers at an even greater discount because the airline has sold the tickets to them at a substantial discount, a practice in which many airlines indulge, albeit discreetly, preferring that the general public not know they are undercutting their own "list" prices. Airlines anticipating a slow period on a particular route sometimes sell off a certain portion of their capacity to a wholesaler or consolidator at a deep discount. The wholesaler sometimes is a charter operator who resells the seats to the public as though they were charter seats, which is why prospective travelers perusing the brochures of charter operators with large programs frequently see a number of flights designated as "scheduled service." As often as not, however, the consolidator, in turn, sells the seats to a travel agency specializing in discounting. Airlines also can sell seats directly to such an agency, which thus acts as its own consolidator. The airline offers the seats either at a net wholesale price, but without the volume-purchase requirement that would be difficult for a retail travel agency to fulfill, or at the standard price, but with a commission override large enough (as high as 50%) to allow both a profit and a price reduction to the public.

Travel agencies specializing in discounting sometimes are called "bucket shops," a term fraught with connotations of unreliability in this country. But in today's highly competitive travel marketplace, more and more conventional travel agencies are selling consolidator-supplied tickets, and the old bucket shops' image is becoming more respectable. Agencies that specialize in discounted tickets exist in most large cities, and usually can be found by studying the smaller ads in the travel sections of the Sunday newspapers. They deal mostly in transatlantic and other international tickets.

Before buying a discounted ticket, whether from a bucket shop or a conventional, full-service travel agency, keep the following considerations in mind: To be in a position to judge the amount of money you'll be saving, first find out the "list" prices of tickets to your destination. Then, do some comparison shopping among agencies, always bearing in mind that the lowest-priced ticket may not provide the most convenient or most comfortable flight. Also bear in mind that a ticket that may not differ much in price from one available directly from the airline may, however, allow the circumvention of such things as the advance purchase requirement. If your plans are less than final, be sure to find out about any other restrictions such as penalties for canceling a flight or changing a reservation. Most discount tickets are non-endorsable, meaning they can only be used on the airline that issued them, and they usually are marked "nonrefundable" to prevent their being cashed for a list price refund. (A refund of the price paid for the ticket often is possible, but it must be obtained from the outlet from which it was purchased rather than from the airline.)

A great many bucket shops are small businesses operating on a thin margin, so it's a good idea to check the local Better Business Bureau for any complaints registered against the one with which you're dealing — before parting with any money. If you still do not feel reassured, consider buying discounted tickets only through a conventional travel agency, which can be expected to have found its own reliable source of consolidator tickets — some of the largest consolidators, in fact, sell only to travel agencies.

A few bucket shops require payment in cash or by certified check or money order, but if credit cards are accepted, use that option, which allows a purchaser to refuse to pay charges for services they haven't received. Note, however, if buying from a charter operator selling seats for both scheduled and charter flights, that the scheduled seats are not protected by the regulations — including the use of escrow accounts — governing the charter seats. Well-established charter operators, nevertheless, may extend the same protections to their scheduled flights, and when this is the case consumers should be sure that the payment option selected directs their money into the escrow account.

Among the consolidators offering discount fares to Ireland are *Maharaja/Consumer Wholesale* (393 Fifth Ave., 2nd Floor, New York, NY 10016; phone: 212-391-0122 in

New York; 800-223-6862 elsewhere in the US) and *Travac Tours and Charters* (989 Sixth Ave., New York, NY 10018; phone: 212-563-3303).

■**Note:** Although rebating and discounting are becoming increasingly common, there is some legal ambiguity concerning them. Strictly speaking, it is legal to discount domestic tickets but not international tickets. On the other hand, the law that prohibits discounting, the Federal Aviation Act of 1958, consistently is ignored these days, in part because consumers benefit from the practice and in part because many illegal arrangements are indistinguishable from legal ones. Since the line separating the two is so fine that even the authorities can't always tell the difference, it is unlikely that most consumers would be able to do so, and in fact it is not illegal to *buy* a discounted ticket. If the issue of legality bothers you, ask the agency whether any ticket you're about to buy would be permissable under the above-mentioned act.

Other Discount Travel Sources – An excellent source of information on economical travel opportunities is the *Consumer Reports Travel Letter,* published monthly by Consumers Union. It keeps abreast of the scene on a wide variety of fronts, including package tours, rental cars, insurance, and more, but it is especially helpful for its comprehensive coverage of airfares, offering guidance on all the options from scheduled flights on major or low-fare airlines to charters and discount sources. For a year's subscription send $37 to *Consumer Reports Travel Letter* (PO Box 2886, Boulder, CO 80322; phone: 800-525-0643). Another source is *Travel Smart,* a monthly newsletter offering information on a wide variety of trips with additional discount travel services available to subscribers. For a year's subscription, send $37 to Communications House (40 Beechdale Rd., Dobbs Ferry, NY 10522; phone: 914-693-8300 in New York; 800-327-3633 elsewhere in the US).

Still another way to take advantage of bargain airfares is open to those who have a flexible schedule. A number of organizations, usually set up as last-minute travel clubs and functioning on a membership basis, routinely keep in touch with travel suppliers to help them dispose of unsold inventory at discounts of between 15% and 60%. A great deal of the inventory consists of complete tour packages and cruises, but some clubs offer air-only charter seats and, occasionally, seats on scheduled flights. Members pay an annual fee and get a toll-free hot line number to call for information on imminent trips. In some cases, they also receive periodic mailings with information on bargain travel opportunities for which there is more advance notice. Despite the suggestive names of the clubs providing these services, last-minute travel does not necessarily mean that you cannot make plans until literally the last minute. Trips can be announced as little as a few days or as much as 2 months before departure, but the average is from 1 to 4 weeks' notice. It does mean that your choice at any given time is limited to what is offered and if your heart is set on a particular destination, you might not find what you want, no matter how attractive the bargains. Among such organizations offering discounted travel opportunities to Ireland are the following:

Discount Club of America, 61-33 Woodhaven Blvd., Rego Park, NY 11374 (phone: 800-321-9587 or 718-335-9612). Annual fee: $39 per family.

Discount Travel International, Ives Building, 114 Forrest Ave., Suite 205, Narberth, PA 19072 (phone: 800-334-9294). Annual fee: $45 per household.

Encore Short Notice, 4501 Forbes Blvd., Lanham, MD 20706 (phone: 301-459-8020 or 800-638-0930 for customer service). Annual fee: $48 per family.

Last-Minute Travel Club, 132 Brookline Ave., Boston, MA 02215 (phone: 800-LAST-MIN or 617-267-9800). As of this year, no fee.

Moment's Notice, 425 Madison Ave., New York, NY 10017 (phone: 212-486-0503). Annual fee: $45 per family.

Traveler's Advantage, 3033 S. Parker Rd., Suite 1000, Aurora, CO 80014 (phone: 800-548-1116). Annual fee: $49 per family.

Vacations to Go, 2411 Fountain View, Suite 201, Houston, TX 77057; phone: 800-338-4962). Annual fee: $19.95 per family.

Worldwide Discount Travel Club, 1674 Meridian Ave., Miami Beach, FL 33139 (phone: 305-534-2082). Annual fee: $40 per person; $50 per family.

Generic Air Travel – Organizations that apply the same flexible-schedule idea to air travel only and sell tickets at literally the last minute also exist. The service they provide sometimes is known as "generic" air travel, and it operates somewhat like an ordinary airline standby service, except that the organizations running it offer seats on not one but several scheduled and charter airlines.

One pioneer of generic flights is *Airhitch* (2901 Broadway, Suite 100, New York, NY 10025; phone: 212-864-2000), which arranges flights to Europe from various US cities at very low prices. Prospective travelers register by paying a fee (applicable toward the fare) and stipulate a range of acceptable departure dates and their desired destination, along with alternate choices. The week before the date range begins, they are notified of at least two flights that will be available during the time period, agree on one, and remit the balance of the fare to the company. If they do not accept any of the suggested flights, they lose their deposit; if, through no fault of their own, they do not ultimately get on any agreed-on flight, all of their money is refunded. Return flights are arranged the same way. *Airhitch* cautions that, given the number of variables attached to the flights, they are suitable only for travelers willing to accept approximate destinations, although the time period will be the one specified and, for a majority of travelers, the place of arrival, too. At the time of this writing, fares to Ireland ranged from $160 or less one way from the East Coast, $269 or less from the West Coast, and $229 or less from other points in the US. Another of the company's programs, Target, offers greater certainty regarding destinations.

BARTERED TRAVEL SOURCES: Suppose a company buys advertising space for a hotel in a newspaper. As payment, the hotel gives the publishing company a number of hotel rooms in lieu of cash. This is barter, a commmon means of exchange among hotels, airlines, car rental companies, cruise lines, tour operators, restaurants, and other travel service companies. When a bartering company finds itself with excess hotel rooms (or empty airline seats or cruise ship cabin space, and so on) and offers them to the public, considerable savings can be enjoyed.

Bartered-travel clubs often offer discounts of up to 50% to members, who pay an annual fee (approximately $50 at press time) which entitles them to select the flights, cruises, or hotels that the company obtained by barter. Members usually present a voucher, club credit card, or scrip (a dollar-denomination voucher negotiable only for the bartered product) to the hotel, which in turn subtracts the dollar amount from the bartering company's account.

Selling bartered travel is a perfectly legitimate means of retailing. One advantage to club members is that they don't have to wait until the last minute to obtain room or flight reservations. However, hotel rooms and airline seats usually are offered to members on a space-available basis. Ticket vouchers are good only for a particular hotel and cannot be used elsewhere. The same applies to car rentals, cruises, package tours, and restaurants. Among the companies specializing in bartered travel, one that frequently offers members travel services to and in Ireland is *The Travel Guild* (18210 Redmond Way, Redmond, WA 98052; phone: 206-885-1213). The annual membership fee for this club is $48.

CONSUMER PROTECTION: Consumers who feel that they have not been dealt with fairly by an airline should make their complaints known. Begin with the customer service representative at the airport where the problem occurs. If he or she cannot resolve your complaint to your satisfaction, write to the airline's consumer office. In a businesslike, typed letter, explain what reservations you held, what happened, the names of the employees involved, and what you expect the airline to do to remedy the situation. Send copies (never the originals) of the tickets, receipts, and other documents that back your claims. Ideally, all correspondence should be sent via certified mail, return receipt requested. This provides proof that your complaint was received.

If you still receive no satisfaction and your complaint is against a US carrier contact the US Department of Transportation. Passengers with consumer complaints — lost baggage, compensation for getting bumped, smoking and nonsmoking rules, deceptive practices by an airline, charter regulations — should contact the Consumer Affairs Division, Room 10405, US Department of Transportation (400 Seventh St. SW, Washington, DC 20590; phone: 202-366-2220). DOT personnel stress, however, that consumers initially should direct their complaints to the airline that provoked them.

Travelers with an unresolved complaint involving an Irish airline also can contact the US Department of Transportation. DOT personnel will do what they can to help resolve all such complaints, although their influence may be limited.

A more effective direction for your complaint may be the Irish Department of Tourism. Consumers with complaints against Irish airlines or other travel-related services can write to this agency outlining the specifics in as much detail as possible. They will try to resolve the complaint or, if it is out of their jurisdiction, will refer the matter to the proper authorities, and will notify you in writing as to the result of their inquires and/or any action taken. Address your complaint to the attention of James Larkin, Irish Tourist Board, Baggot Street Bridge, Dublin 2 (phone: 1-765871).

The deregulation of US airlines has meant that a traveler must find out for himself or herself what he or she is entitled to receive. The Department of Transportation's informative consumer booklet *Fly Rights* is a good place to start. To receive a copy, send $1 to the Superintendent of Documents, US Government Printing Office (Washington, DC 20402-9325; phone: 202-783-3238). Specify its stock number, 050-000-000513-5, and allow 3 to 4 weeks for delivery.

To avoid more serious problems, *always* choose charter flights and tour packages with care. When you consider a charter, ask your travel agent who runs it and carefully check out the company. The Better Business Bureau in the company's home city can report on how many complaints, if any, have been lodged against it in the past. As emphasized above, protect yourself with trip cancellation and interruption insurance, which can help safeguard your investment if you or a traveling companion is unable to make the trip and must cancel too late to receive a full refund from the company providing your travel services. (This is advisable whether you're buying a charter flight alone or a tour package for which the airfare is provided by charter or scheduled flight.) Some travel insurance policies have an additional feature, covering the possibility of default or bankruptcy on the part of the tour operator or airline, charter or scheduled.

Should this type of coverage not be available to you (state insurance regulations vary, there is a wide difference in price, and so on), your best bet is to pay for airline tickets and tour packages with a credit card. The federal Fair Credit Billing Act permits purchasers to refuse payment for credit card charges where services have not been delivered, so the onus of dealing with the receiver for a bankrupt airline falls on the credit card company. Do not rely on another airline to honor the ticket you're holding, since the days when virtually all major carriers subscribed to a default protection program that bound them to do so are long gone. Some airlines may voluntarily step forward to accommodate the stranded passengers of a fellow carrier, but this now is an entirely altruistic act.

ON ARRIVAL: The major city nearest to Shannon International Airport in the west of Ireland is Limerick, 15 miles away. The government-owned *CIE (Córas Iompair Eireann, National Transport Company)* buses depart Shannon for the Limerick Railway Station every 20 minutes, 24 hours a day. The bus ride is about 45 minutes, and the fare is about IR£3 (at press time, approximately $4.65). A taxi costs around IR£21 (about $32.50). From Limerick there are an average of six trains a day to Dublin, a 2½-hour trip to the east. *CIE* buses connect Dublin Airport, 6 miles north of the city, with Dublin's Central Bus Station (Busaras) on Store St. every 30 minutes up to midnight; the fare is IR£3.50 (about $5.40). The taxi fare to a similar city-center location will be about IR£13 (about $20).

Other alternatives include connecting flights. *Aer Lingus* provides domestic service between Shannon and Dublin, and Dublin and Cork. *Aer Arann* flies between Galway and the Aran Islands in Galway Bay. Air service between Dublin and London is provided by *Aer Lingus,* by *British Airways,* and by Ireland's *Ryanair;* the same and other airlines also connect other Irish and British cities. There are no flights between Belfast, Northern Ireland, and Dublin or Shannon; *British Airways* and *British Midland* both have daily flights between London and Belfast. (An express bus service connects with most flights arriving at Belfast Airport. Travel time to Great Victoria Street Station in the center of the city is 40 minutes and the fare is £2.50, or approximately $4.50.)

Traveling by Ship

There was a time when traveling by ship was extraordinarily expensive, time consuming, utterly elegant, and utilized almost exclusively for getting from one point to another. Times have changed in many ways for ship travel; after a period when the very idea of seaborne transportation was almost completely sunk by the coming of swift, inexpensive jets, cruising has floated to very near the top of leisure travel options.

Alas, the days when steamships reigned as the primary means of transatlantic transportation are gone, when Italy, France, Sweden, Germany, Norway, the Netherlands, and England — and the US — had fleets of passenger liners that offered week-plus trips across the North Atlantic. Only one ship (*Cunard*'s *Queen Elizabeth 2*) continues to offer this kind of service between the US and Europe with any degree of regularity; others make the trip at most a few times a year. At the same time, the possibility of booking passage to Europe on a cargo ship is becoming less practical. Fewer and fewer travelers, therefore, set foot on Irish soil with sea legs developed during an ocean voyage.

Although fewer travelers to Europe are choosing sea travel as the means of transport to their original specific destination, more and more people are cruising around Europe. No longer primarily pure transportation, ocean cruising currently is riding a wave of popularity as a leisure activity in its own right, and the host of new ships (and dozens of rebuilt old ones) testifies dramatically to the attraction of vacationing on the high seas. And due to the growing popularity of travel along coastal and inland waterways, more and more travelers — particularly repeat travelers — are climbing aboard some kind of waterborne conveyance once they've arrived in Europe and seeing Ireland from the banks of a canal or river, or taking a ferry to one of the Irish islands.

The only thing that's lacking from the cruising scene today is much of that old elegance — ships like *Cunard*'s *Sea Goddess I* and *Sea Goddess II* (which sail to London, England, but not Ireland) — though most modern-day passengers don't seem to notice. Cruise ships seem much more like motels-at-sea than the classic liners of a couple of generations ago, but they are consistently comfortable and passengers often are pampered. Prices are reasonable, and cruises focusing on European ports generally last around 2 weeks. What's more, since the single cruise price covers all the major items in a typical vacation — transportation, accommodations, all meals, entertainment, a full range of social activities, and sports and recreation — a traveler need not fear any unexpected assaults on the family travel budget.

When selecting a cruise, your basic criteria should be where you want to go, the time you have available, how much you want to spend, and the kind of environment that best suits your style and taste (in which case price is an important determinant). Rely on the suggestions of a travel agent — preferably one specializing in cruises (see "A final note on picking a cruise," below) — but be honest with the agent (and with yourself) in describing the type of atmosphere you're seeking. Ask for suggestions from friends who have been on cruises; if you trust their judgment, they should be able to suggest a ship on which you'll feel comfortable.

There are a number of moments in the cruise-planning process when discounts are available from the major cruise lines, so it may be possible to enjoy some diminution of the list price almost anytime you book passage on a cruise ship. For those willing to commit early — say 4 to 6 months before sailing — most of the major cruise lines routinely offer a 10% reduction off posted prices, in addition to the widest selection of cabins from which to choose. For those who decide to sail rather late in the game — say, 4 to 6 weeks before departure — savings often are even greater — an average of 20% — as steamship lines try to fill up their ships. The only negative aspect is that the range of cabin choice tends to be limited, although it is possible that a fare upgrade will be offered to make this limited cabin selection more palatable. In addition, there's the option of buying from a discount travel club or a travel agency that specializes in last-minute bargains; these discounters and other discount travel sources are discussed at the end of *Traveling by Plane,* above.

Most of the time, the inclusion of air transportation in the cruise package costs significantly less than if you were to buy the cruise separately and arrange your own air transportation to the port. If you do decide on one of these economical air/sea packages, be forewarned that it is not unusual for the prearranged flight arrangements to be less than convenient. The problems often arrive with the receipt of your cruise ticket, which also includes the airline ticket for the flight to get you to and from the ship dock. This is normally the first time you see the flights on which you have been booked and can appraise the convenience of the departure and arrival times. The cruise ship lines generally are not very forthcoming about altering flight schedules, and your own travel agent also may have difficulty in rearranging flight times or carriers. That means that the only remaining alternative is to ask the line to forget about making your flight arrangements and to pay for them separately by yourself. This may be more costly, but it's more likely to give you an arrival and departure schedule that will best conform to the sailing and docking times of the ship on which you will be cruising.

Prospective cruise ship passengers will find that the variety of cruises is tremendous, and the quality, while generally high, varies depending on shipboard services, the tone of shipboard life, the cost of the cruise, and operative itineraries. Although there are less expensive ways to see Europe, the romance of a sea voyage remains irresistible for many, so a few points should be considered by such sojourners before they sign on for a seagoing vacation (after all, it's hard to get off in mid-ocean). Herewith, a rundown on what to expect from a cruise, a few suggestions on what to look for and arrange when purchasing passage on one, and some representative prices for different sailings.

CABINS: The most important factor in determining the price of a cruise is the cabin. Cabin prices are set according to size and location. The size can vary considerably on older ships, less so on newer or more recently modernized ones, and may be entirely uniform on the very newest vessels.

Shipboard accommodations have the same pricing pattern as hotels. Suites, which consist of a sitting room–bedroom combination and occasionally a private small deck that could be compared to a patio, cost the most. Prices for other cabins (interchangeably called staterooms) usually are more expensive on the upper passenger decks, less expensive on lower decks; if a cabin has a bathtub instead of a shower, the price probably will be higher. The outside cabins with portholes facing the water cost more than inside cabins without views and generally are preferred — although many experienced cruise passengers eschew more expensive accommodations for they know they will spend very few waking hours in their cabins. As in all forms of travel, accommodations are more expensive for single travelers. If you are traveling on your own but want to share a double cabin to reduce the cost, some ship lines will attempt to find someone of the same sex willing to share quarters (see *Hints for Single Travelers,* in this section).

FACILITIES AND ACTIVITIES: You may not use your cabin very much. Organized shipboard activities are geared to keep you busy. A standard schedule might consist of swimming, sunbathing, and numerous other outdoor recreations. Evenings are devoted to leisurely dining, lounge shows or movies, bingo and other organized games, gambling, dancing, and a midnight buffet. Your cruise fare includes all of these activities — except the cost of drinks.

All cruise ships have at least one major social lounge, a main dining room, several bars, an entertainment room that may double as a discotheque for late dancing, an exercise room, indoor games facilities, at least one pool, and shopping facilities that can range from a single boutique to an arcade. Still others have gambling casinos and/or slot machines, card rooms, libraries, children's recreation centers, indoor pools (as well as one or more on open decks), separate movie theaters, and private meeting rooms. Open deck space should be ample, because this is where most passengers spend their days at sea.

Usually there is a social director and staff to organize and coordinate activities. Evening entertainment is provided by professionals. Movies are mostly first-run and drinks are moderate in price (or should be) because a ship is exempt from local taxes when at sea.

To prepare for possible illnesses, travelers should get a prescription from their doctors for pills, patches, or stomach pacifiers to counteract motion sickness. All ships with more than 12 passengers have a doctor on board, plus facilities for handling sickness or medical emergencies.

Shore Excursions – These side trips almost always are optional and available at extra cost. Before you leave, do a little basic research about the ports you'll be visiting and decide what sights will interest you. If several of the most compelling of these are some distance from the pier where your ship docks, chances are that paying for a shore excursion will be worth the money.

Shore excursions usually can be booked through your travel agent at the same time you make your cruise booking, but this is worthwhile only if you can get complete details on the nature of each excursion being offered. If you can't get these details, better opt to purchase your shore arrangements after you're on board. The fact is that your enthusiasm for an excursion may be higher once you are on board because you will have met other passengers with whom to share the excitement of "shore leave." And depending on your time in port, you may decide to forget about the guided tour and venture out on your own.

Meals – All meals on board almost always are included in the basic price of a cruise, and the food generally is abundant and quite palatable. Evening meals are taken in the main dining room, where tables are assigned according to the passengers' preferences. Tables usually accommodate from 2 to 10; specify your preference when you book your cruise. If there are two sittings, you also can specify which one you want at the time you book or, at latest, when you board the ship. Later sittings usually are more leisurely. Breakfast frequently is available in your cabin, as well as in the main dining room. For lunch, many passengers prefer the buffet offered on deck, usually at or near the pool, but again, the main dining room is available.

DRESS: Most people pack too much for a cruise on the assumption that daytime wear should be chic and every night is a big event. Comfort is a more realistic criterion.

Daytime wear on most ships is decidedly casual. For warm-weather cruises, women can wear a cover-up over a bathing suit through breakfast, swimming, sunbathing, and deck activities, lunch, and early cocktails without any change; for men, shorts (with swim trunks underneath) and a casual shirt will be appropriate on deck or in any public room. (Bare feet and swimsuits usually are inappropriate in the dining room.) For travel in cooler seasons, casual, comfortable clothes, including a variety of layers to adjust for changes in the weather, are appropriate for all daytime activities. Also bring along a comfortable pair of rubber-sole, low-heel shoes or sneakers, as sloping gangways and wet decks can be slippery.

Evening wear for most cruises is dressy-casual. Formal wear probably is not necessary for 1-week cruises, optional on longer ones. There aren't many nights when it's expected. Most ships have a captain's cocktail party the first or second night out and a farewell dinner near the end of the cruise. Women should feel comfortable in hostess gowns, cocktail dresses, or stylish slacks. (To feel completely secure, you may want to pack one very dressy item.) Jackets and ties always are preferred for men in the evening, but a long-sleeve, open-neck shirt with ascot or scarf usually is an acceptable substitute. (For further information on choosing and packing a basic wardrobe, see *How to Pack,* in this section.)

TIPS: Tips are a strictly personal expense, and you *are* expected to tip — in particular your cabin and dining room stewards. The general rule of thumb (or palm) is to expect to pay from 10% to 20% of your total cruise budget for gratuities — the actual amount within this range is based on the length of the cruise and the extent of personalized service provided. Allow $2 to $5 for each cabin and dining room steward (more if you wish), and additional sums for very good service. (*Note:* Tips should be paid by and for each individual in a cabin, whether there are one, two, or more.) Others who may merit tips are the deck steward who sets up your chair at the pool or elsewhere, the wine steward in the dining room, porters who handle your luggage (tip them individually at the time they assist you), and any others who provide personal service. On some ships you can charge your bar tab to your cabin; throw in the tip when you pay it at the end of the cruise. Smart travelers tip twice during the trip: about midway through the cruise and at the end; even wiser travelers tip a bit at the start of the trip to ensure better service throughout.

Although some cruise lines do have a no-tipping policy and you are not penalized by the crew for not tipping, naturally, you aren't penalized for tipping, either. If you can restrain yourself, it is better not to tip on those few ships that discourage it. However, never make the mistake of not tipping on the majority of ships, where it is a common, expected practice. (For further information on calculating gratuities, see *Tipping,* in this section.)

SHIP SANITATION: The US Public Health Service (PHS) currently inspects all passenger vessels calling at US ports, so very precise information is available on which ships meet its requirements and which do not. The further requirement that ships immediately report any illness that occurs on board adds to the available data.

So the problem for a prospective cruise passenger is to determine whether the ship on which he or she plans to sail has met the official sanitary standard. US regulations require the PHS to publish actual grades for the ships inspected (rather than the old pass or fail designation) so it's now easy to determine any cruise ship's sanitary status. Nearly 4,000 travel agents, public health organizations, and doctors receive a copy of each monthly ship sanitation summary, but be aware that not all agents fully understand what this ship inspection program is all about. Again, the best advice is to deal with a travel agent who specializes in cruise ships and cruise bookings, for he or she is most likely to have the latest information on the sanitary conditions of all cruise ships (see "A final note on picking a cruise," below). To receive a copy of the most recent summary or a particular inspection report, contact Chief, Vessel Sanitation Program, Public Health Service, 1015 N. America Way, Room 107, Miami, FL 33132 (phone: 305-536-4307).

TRANSATLANTIC CROSSINGS: For seagoing enthusiasts, *Cunard's Queen Elizabeth 2* is one of the largest and most comfortable vessels afloat, having undergone a complete overhaul and refurbishing, from a replacement of its engines to a redecoration of passenger quarters. Each year, in addition to a full calendar of Caribbean and European cruises, plus a round-the-world cruise, the *QE2* schedules approximately a dozen round-trip transatlantic crossings between June and, usually, December.

Although the *QE2* rarely calls at the shores of the Emerald Isle, it does regularly pull into port nearby and therefore may be of interest to travelers combining a trip to Ireland with one to Great Britain. The ship normally sets its course from New York to Southampton, England (a 5-day trip), and then sails directly back to the US, although on a few of the crossings it proceeds from Southampton to Cherbourg, France, or to other European ports before turning back across the Atlantic. (Similarly, on some crossings, the ship calls at various East Coast US ports in addition to New York, thus giving passengers a choice of where to embark or disembark.) On rare occasions, the *QE2* will call at Cork, giving passengers the option to board in Ireland. However, at the time of this writing there were no imminent plans to repeat this itinerary. For travelers headed directly to Ireland, *British Airways* offers travelers the option of paying a supplement for an intra-European flight from Southampton; contact *British Airways* for details. Another alternative is to disembark at Cherbourg and take one of the *Irish Continental Line* ferries to Rosslare (for details, see "Ferries," below).

Transatlantic crossings, however, do not come at bargain prices. Last year, the one-way, per-person cost of passage from New York to either Southampton or Cherbourg ranged from around $1,400 (for the least expensive, two-per-cabin, transatlantic class accommodations at the end of the season) to $8,925 (for one of the grandest travel experiences imaginable). *Cunard* brings a voyage aboard a luxury liner within reach of the less affluent traveler, however, by offering an air/sea package in conjunction with *British Airways*. The one-way ticket to Europe by sea includes an allowance toward return economy class airfare from London to any of 57 North American cities — a free flight home, in essence, provided certain length-of-stay restrictions are respected. The allowance can be applied to an upgraded air ticket if desired, and, if you want to splurge, you can even fly home on a specially reserved *British Airways'* supersonic *Concorde,* provided you make up the difference between the allowance and the *Concorde* fare (the shortfall at press time was $995).

Cunard also offers various European tour packages applicable to the basic air/sea offer. Among the itineraries offered this year is a 17-day Shamrock tour, which will spend 5 full days in Ireland and the balance of its itinerary in England, Scotland, and Wales.

Cunard now also is offering a particularly economical round-trip air/sea option for travelers with a flexible schedule. Special "standby" fares are available on some transatlantic crossings between the US and London (20 sailings were offered between April and December 1990) and include airfare on *British Airways* to a number of US gateways. The package cost (at press time, $1,195 to $1,950 — depending on dates of travel) includes a berth in a double-occupancy "minimum" room on the *QE2* and a one-way *British Airways* economy class ticket to or from London and Boston, Chicago, Detroit, Miami, New York, Philadelphia, or Washington, DC. For an additional $100 supplement charge, passengers may fly to or from other *British Airways* US gateways including Anchorage, Atlanta, Houston, Los Angeles, Pittsburgh, San Diego, San Francisco, and Seattle. Although this fare is offered strictly on a space-available-basis, confirmations are provided 3 weeks prior to sailing. To qualify for this fare, travelers must submit a written application and a $100 deposit to a travel agent or *Cunard;* full payment is due upon confirmation. For information, check with your travel agent or contact *Cunard,* 555 Fifth Ave., New York, NY 10017 (phone: 800-221-4770 or 800-5-CUNARD).

Another interesting transatlantic crossing possibility for those who have the time is what the industry calls a positioning cruise. This is the sailing of a US- or Caribbean-based vessel from its winter berth to the city in Europe from which it will be offering summer cruise programs. Eastbound positioning cruises take place in the spring; westbound cruises return in the fall. Since ships do not make the return trip until they need to position themselves for the next cruise season, most lines offering positioning cruises have some air/sea arrangement that allows passengers to fly home economically — though the cruises themselves are not an inexpensive way to travel.

Among the ships that have been offering positioning cruises for a number of years are *Cunard*'s *Vistafjord* and ships of the *Royal Viking Line* and *Royal Cruise Line.* Itineraries and ports of call vary from year to year. Typically, the ships sail from Florida or San Juan, Puerto Rico, and cross the Atlantic to any one of a number of European ports where the trip may be broken — Barcelona, Cherbourg, Genoa, Le Havre, Lisbon, Málaga, Piraeus, Southampton, Venice — before proceeding to cruise European waters (for example, the Mediterranean, the Baltic Sea, the Black Sea, the Norwegian fjords). Passengers can elect to stay aboard for the basic transatlantic segment alone or for both the crossing and the subsequent European cruise.

Anyone intent on taking a positioning cruise to or from Ireland, however, will be disappointed to find that the nearest point of disembarkation or embarkation usually is London or Southampton. This year, *Royal Viking Lines* is offering a 10-day cruise, aboard the *Royal Viking Sun,* from London to New York, sailing in August via Horta in the Portuguese Azores. Prices for the cruise range from $2,720 to $5,470. This year, the *Royal Viking Sun* also will be making a 14-day cruise from Copenhagen to London, with other ports of call in the Netherlands, Scandinavia, and the Soviet Union. (Prices range from $4,640 to $15,750.)

Those interested in including a cruise to other European waters before, during, or after their trip to Ireland will find that a number of European cruises depart from British ports — primarily London. During the summer, *Royal Cruise Lines*' *Crown Odyssey* is scheduled to make a 13-day round-trip cruise beginning and ending in London and exploring Copenhagen, Helsinki, Oslo, and Stockholm. Fares range from $3,498 to $9,248. In May, the *Crown Odyssey* will make a 12-day cruise called "Great Capitals of Europe," sailing from Venice and ending in London; fares range from $3,598 to $9,198.

In 1990, for instance, while none of the above ships made an eastbound positioning cruise this far north in the Atlantic, two of them made westbound cruises from London to Montreal. The *Royal Viking Line*'s *Royal Viking Sun* made a 21-day leisure trip, calling at Scotland and various ports in Scandinavia and Canada, as well as at Boston and Nantucket en route. The *Royal Cruise Line*'s *Crown Odyssey* made an 8-day direct trip called the "Great Transatlantic High Society Cruise."

Similarly, only infrequently do positioning cruises or their subsequent European cruises even call at Irish ports. An exception this year is *Royal Viking*'s British Isles cruise aboard the *Royal Viking Sea.* This 13-day cruise sails from Copenhagen to London, and includes stops in the Irish ports of Cork, Dublin, and Waterford, in addition to other stops in Great Britain.

For these and other offerings, book well in advance in order to qualify for substantial "early bird" discounts. For information, ask your travel agent or contact the following cruise lines directly: *Cunard* (555 Fifth Ave., New York, NY 10017; phone: 800-221-4770 or 800-5-CUNARD); *Royal Viking Line* (95 Merrick, Coral Gables, FL 33134; phone: 305-447-9660 in Miami; 800-634-8000 elsewhere in the US); *Royal Cruise Line*

(One Maritime Plaza, Suite 1400, San Francisco, CA 94111; phone: 800-792-2992 or 415-956-7200 in California; 800-227-0925 or 800-227-4534 elsewhere in the US).

FREIGHTERS: An alternative to conventional cruise ships is travel by freighter. These are cargo ships that also take a limited number of passengers (usually about 12) in reasonably comfortable accommodations. The idea of traveling by freighter has long appealed to romantic souls, but there are a number of drawbacks to keep in mind before casting off. Once upon a time, a major advantage of freighter travel was its low cost, but this is no longer the case. Though freighters usually are less expensive than cruise ships, the difference is not as great as it once was, and excursion airfares certainly are even less expensive. Accommodations and recreational facilities vary, but freighters were not designed to amuse passengers, so it is important to appreciate the idea of freighter travel itself. Schedules are erratic, and the traveler must fit his or her timetable to that of the ship. Passengers have found themselves waiting as long as a month for a promised sailing, and because freighters follow their cargo commitments, it is possible that a scheduled port could be omitted at the last minute or a new one added.

Anyone contemplating taking a freighter from a US port across the Atlantic should be aware that at press time there were no freighters regularly sailing from the US to Ireland. Several freighter lines, however, do stop in a port reasonably close to Ireland — such as Felixstowe on Great Britain's southern coast — or one that has a ferry connection to Ireland — such as Le Havre, France (see "Ferries," below, for details). Among these freighter lines are the following:

Container Ships Reederi: Sails approximately every 2 weeks from Long Beach, California, via the Panama Canal to Felixstowe, Le Havre, and Rotterdam, taking 23 or 24 days to make the trip. The ships carry from 6 to 9 passengers, and last year, the one-way, per-person fare ranged from $1,975 to $2,315. For information, contact the line's general agent, *Freighter World Cruises* (address below).

Lykes Lines: Carries up to 8 passengers on 13- or 14-day crossings from New Orleans to Felixstowe and Le Havre, calling at Rotterdam and Bremerhaven en route. Ships leave every 8 to 14 days year-round. A one-way ticket costs $1,000 to $1,600. For information, contact *Lykes Lines,* Lykes Center, 300 Poydras St., New Orleans, LA 70130 (phone: 800-535-1861 or 504-523-6611).

Mediterranean Shipping Co.: Sails from Baltimore, Boston, New York, and Newport News (Virginia) to Felixstowe, Le Havre, Antwerp, Bremen, and Hamburg. The trip takes 18 to 19 days; the ships can carry 12 passengers and they leave weekly year-round. Prices vary based on departure point and destination, but on average the one-way fare runs between $1,400 and $2,100. Contact *Mediterranean Shipping*'s representative, *Sea the Difference,* 96 Morton St., New York, NY 10014 (phone: 800-666-9333 or 212-691-3760).

Polish Ocean Lines: This company's freighters accommodate 6 passengers in 3 double cabins on voyages approximately 8 to 10 days in length from Port Newark, New Jersey, to Rotterdam, Bremerhaven, and Le Havre. Last year, the one-way fare from Newark ranged from $1,010 to $1,105 per person, and passengers also could board in Baltimore, Maryland, or Wilmington, North Carolina, for an additional $150; round-trip fares were simply double the one-way fares. For information, contact *Gdynia America Line,* the general agent for *Polish Ocean Lines,* at 39 Broadway, 14th Floor, New York, NY 10006 (phone: 212-952-1280).

Specialists dealing only (or largely) in freighter travel exist to help prospective passengers arrange trips. They provide information, schedules, and, when you're ready to sail, booking services. Among these agencies are the following:

Freighter World Cruises: A freighter travel agency that acts as general agent for several freighter lines. Publishes the twice-monthly *Freighter Space Advisory,* listing space available on sailings worldwide. A subscription costs $27 a year, $25 of which can be credited toward the cost of a cruise. 180 S. Lake Ave., Suite 335, Pasadena, CA 91101 (phone: 818-449-3106).

Pearl's Travel Tips: Run by Ilse Hoffman, who finds sailings for her customers and sends them off with all kinds of invaluable information and advice. 333 E. 79th St., Penthouse S., New York, NY 10021 (phone: 212-734-6327).

TravLTips Cruise and Freighter Travel Association: A freighter travel agency and club ($15 a year or $25 for 2 years) whose members receive the bimonthly *TravLTips* magazine of cruise and freighter travel. PO Box 188, Flushing, NY 11358 (phone: 718-939-2400 in New York; 800-872-8584 elsewhere in the US).

INLAND WATERWAYS: Cruising the canals and rivers of Europe is becoming more and more popular, probably in reaction to the speed of jet travel and the normal rush to do as much as possible in as little time as possible. A cabin cruiser or converted barge averages only about 5 miles an hour, covering in a week of slow floating the same distance a car would travel in a few hours of determined driving. Passengers see only a small section of countryside, but they see it in depth and with an intimacy simply impossible any other way.

Ireland has waterways ideal for cruising. The river Shannon and its lakes, Lough Ree and Lough Derg, cut north to south through a good part of the country, and the Grand Canal traverses its heart from Shannon Harbour to Dublin. A branch of the canal runs south to meet the River Barrow, navigable on to Waterford. Above the Shannon's source, the scenic lakeland of 50-mile-long Lough Erne in Northern Ireland also is popular with cruisers.

There are two ways to cruise the inland waterways: by renting your own self-drive boat or by booking aboard a hotel-boat. If you choose to skipper your own diesel-powered cruiser, you will be shown how to handle the craft and told whom to call if you break down. But once you cast off, you and your party — the boats sleep from 2 to 10 people — will be on your own. You help lock-keepers operate the few gates on the Shannon, and operate untended locks on the Grand Canal yourself. You do your own cooking or eat at restaurants and pubs along the way. The cost of the rental can vary considerably depending on the size of the boat, the season, and the area. A boat sleeping two comfortably can cost from $600 to $700 per week in spring or fall and jump to $1,100 to $1,800 per week at the height of the summer; an eight-berth boat can range anywhere from $1,000 to $8,000 per week. The average rental, however, sleeping four, works out to about $175 to $200 per person per week during the low season and $300 to $350 per person per week in the high season. Fuel is not included.

The alternative is to cruise on a hotel-boat, available in Ireland only on the Shannon. The boats used are specially built or converted river barges sleeping up to 10 to 12 guests plus crew. It's possible for those who crave privacy to charter the boat and have it all to themselves; if not, passengers join other guests aboard. Cruises usually last from 3 days to a week; accommodations can be simple or quite luxurious, and most meals usually are included. When reading the brochure, note the boat's facilities (most cabins have private washbasins, showers, and toilets, but bathrooms also can be separate and shared), as well as the itinerary and any special features, such as sightseeing excursions, that may be offered. Prices can range from $500 per person per week, double occupancy, to well over $1,750.

The Irish Tourist Board publishes an information sheet, "Cruising the Inland Waterways," with particulars on Irish companies — the majority of which rent self-skippered boats. The travel firms listed below, including the operators of hotel-boat cruises and representatives of self-drive boat suppliers, can provide information or arrange your whole holiday afloat in Ireland.

> *Bargain Boating, Morgantown Travel Service:* Books self-skippered boats. PO Box 757, Morgantown, WV 26507-0757 (phone: 304-292-8471).
>
> *Hoseasons Holidays Ltd.:* Offers self-skippered boats. Sunway House, Lowestoft, Suffolk NR32 3LT England.
>
> *Skipper Travel Services:* Books self-skippered boats and hotel-boat cruises. 210 California Ave., PO Box 60309, Palo Alto, CA 94306 (phone: 415-321-5658).

Other sources of information is associations concerned with the use and maintenance of European inland waterways and canals. For instance, the Irish Republic's Office of Public Works, Waterways Division (51 St. Stephen's Green, Dublin 2, Ireland; phone: 1-613111), which maintains and monitors the country's inland waterways, also can provide detailed information for those interested in sailing these waters.

■ **A final note on picking a cruise.:** A "cruise-only" travel agency can best help you choose a cruise ship and itinerary. Cruise-only agents also are best equipped to tell you about a particular ship's "personality," the kind of person with whom you'll likely be traveling on a particular ship, what dress is acceptable (it varies from ship to ship), and much more. Travel agencies that specialize in booking cruises usually are members of an association called the *National Association of Cruise Only Agencies (NACOA).* For a listing of the agencies in your area (requests are limited to three states), send a self-addressed, stamped envelope to *NACOA,* PO Box 7209, Freeport, NY 11520, or call 516-378-8006.

FERRIES: Numerous ferries link Ireland with Great Britain and the rest of Europe. Nearly all of them carry both passengers and cars — travelers simply drive on and drive off in most cases — and most routes are in service year-round. Some operators may offer reduced rates for round-trip excursions, midweek travel, or off-season travel. Space for cars should be booked as early as possible, especially during the high season, even though most lines schedule more frequent departures during the summer months. Note that long journeys, of 8 to 10 hours or more, tend to be scheduled overnight. Most ferry arrivals and departures are well served by connecting passenger trains or buses.

Ferries between Great Britain and Ireland include the daily, year-round *Sealink* services from Holyhead, Wales, to Dún Laoghaire and the joint *Sealink–B & I Line* services, also daily year-round, from Fishguard, Wales, to Rosslare Harbour. Each trip takes about 3½ hours. *B & I Line* ferries make daily trips from Holyhead to Dublin directly (3½ hours) and from Liverpool to Dublin (8 to 9 hours). *Swansea Cork Car Ferries* service between Swansea, Wales, and Cork operates three to five times weekly, depending on the season (a 10-hour trip). Ferry services to Northern Ireland connect Liverpool with Belfast in 9 hours (*Belfast Car Ferries*) and the Scottish port of Cairnryan with Larne in 2 to 2¼ hours (*P & O European Ferries*). The *Sealink* ferry travels between Stranraer, Scotland, and Larne in 2¼ hours.

Irish Continental Line ferries to Ireland from France leave Le Havre several times weekly year-round for Rosslare Harbour (21 hours) and once weekly in summer for Cork (21½ hours); the same ferry line departs Cherbourg for Rosslare Harbour twice weekly in summer and once weekly the rest of the year (17 to 18 hours). *Brittany Ferries* has departures from Roscoff, France, to Cork once a week year-round (14 to 16 hours).

For *Sealink* schedules and prices, contact *BritRail Travel International* (630 Third Ave., New York, NY 10017; phone: 212-599-5400), or other *BritRail* offices in Los Angeles or Dallas. For information on *B & I Line* services, contact *Lynott Tours* (350 Fifth Ave., Suite 2619, New York, NY 10118; phone: 212-760-0101 or 800-537-7575 in New York State; 800-221-2474 elsewhere), and for information on *Irish Continental*

Line services, contact *CIE Tours International* (122 E. 42nd St., New York, NY 10168; phone: 212-972-5600 in New York City; 800-CIE-TOUR elsewhere). Information on other ferry services can be supplied by the Irish Tourist Board or by the *P & O European Ferries* (Channel House, Channel View Rd., Dover, Kent, CP179TJ England; phone: 44-304-203-388), the representative of several lines serving Irish ports. Another good source of information is the *International Cruise Center* (250 Old Country Rd., Mineola, NY 11501; phone: 800-221-3254 or 516-747-8367), the US representative of several European ferry lines.

Traveling by Train

Perhaps the most economical, and often the most pleasant, way to see a lot of a foreign country in a relatively short time is by rail. It certainly is the quickest way to travel between two cities up to 300 miles apart (beyond that, a flight normally would be quicker, even counting the time it takes to get to and from the airport). But time isn't always the only consideration. Traveling by train is a way to keep moving and to keep seeing at the same time, and with the special discounts available to visitors, it can be an almost irresistible bargain. You only need to get to a station on time; after that, put your watch in your pocket and relax. You may not get to your destination exactly at the appointed hour, but you'll have a marvelous time looking out the window and enjoying the ride.

TRAINS AND FARES: While North Americans have been raised to depend on their cars, Europeans long have been able to depend on public transportation. In the Irish Republic, the government-owned *CIE (Córas Iompair Eireann, National Transport Company)* operates the railroads, as well as the country's intercity buses. Main rail routes radiate from Dublin to Belfast, Northern Ireland, and to Sligo, Westport, Galway, Cork, Limerick, Tralee, Waterford, and Wexford. There also are trains between Dublin and the ferry ports of Dún Laoghaire and Rosslare and between Rosslare and Limerick. Shannon Airport is connected by bus with Limerick, from which several trains run daily to Dublin and Cork.

Dublin has two principal train stations — Connolly and Heuston — and it is important to be sure from which station your train will leave. Distances are not great: The trip from Dublin to Belfast, Northern Ireland, on the nonstop city-to-city express takes 2 hours, and trips from Dublin clear across the heart of the country to Galway or south to Cork take about 3 hours. Because of these distances, there is no need for sleeping cars on Irish trains, but normally there is a restaurant or a buffet car or, at the least, light refreshments available on most main routes.

The two classes of travel in the Irish Republic are called standard (second) and super-standard (first), but most routes have only standard class. Fares are based on standard class service; for super-standard service a supplement of IR£3 (approximately $4.65 at press time) is paid for trips up to 130 miles; for trips of 131 miles or more, the supplement is IR£6 (approximately $9.50). Super-standard supplements include seat reservations, which also can be made in standard class (IR£1 charge; about $1.55) as far as 3 months in advance, although not from North America. Reservations usually are not necessary except for travel on weekends or bank holidays. Round-trip tickets (called "return" tickets in Ireland) generally cost quite a bit less than two one-way (or "single") tickets; the same holds true for "day return" or "day excursion" tickets for those returning the same day. Reduced-rate weekend fares can be bought on Fridays, Saturdays, and Sundays, for returns any day up to the following Tuesday. Reduced-rate 4-day return and 8-day return tickets also are sold.

Trains between Dublin and Belfast are operated in cooperation with *Northern Ire-*

land Railways, whose own routes in the northern six counties are few: Belfast to Londonderry via Ballymena and Coleraine; Belfast to Bangor; and Belfast to Larne. Travel on these is either standard class or first class. As in the Republic, reservations generally are not required; however, in Northern Ireland there is no price break for buying a round-trip ticket instead of two one-way tickets.

Visitors also should be familiar with the *Dublin Area Rapid Transit (DART)* commuter rail system. *DART* runs from central Dublin north around Dublin Bay as far as Howth and south as far as Bray, stopping at Connolly Station and other places in the city and at the ferry port of Dún Laoghaire. The service operates daily from approximately 7 AM (later on Sundays) to just before midnight, with trains every 15 minutes or less, depending on the time of day.

Baggage can be checked through to your destination between any two stations in the Republic, but not between the Republic and Northern Ireland or between Ireland and Great Britain — because of customs inspections. Since you therefore will have to keep your luggage with you, keep it light, especially traveling to Great Britain, because porters are not easy to find at the Irish Sea ferry stations. In addition, each passenger is allowed two large suitcases; there is a charge for luggage over this amount. Note that occasionally registered baggage may not travel on the same train that you do — so if it is not at the station when you arrive, it may be on the next train — but just in case it actually has been lost or stolen, ask a conductor. Baggage can be checked overnight at the Left Luggage office (or baggage room) in most stations. (Due to recent bomb scares, lockers are no longer common in railroad stations.)

PASSES: Rail passes are offered by the national railroad companies of most European countries. They allow unlimited train travel within a set time period, frequently include connecting service via other forms of transportation, and they can save the traveler a considerable amount of money as well as time. The only requirement is validation of the pass by an information clerk on the day of your first rail trip; thereafter, there is no need to stand in line — and lines can be very long during peak travel periods — to buy individual tickets for subsequent trips. Designed primarily for foreign visitors, these passes often must be bought in the US (or some other foreign location) prior to arrival in Europe. Although these passes can be among the best bargains around, be sure to look into the comparable cost of individual train tickets which — depending on the number of days you plan to travel — may work out to be less expensive.

The Eurailpass, the first and best known of all rail passes, is valid for travel through the Irish Republic (but not in Northern Ireland) and 16 other countries — Austria, Belgium, Denmark, Finland, France, Germany, Greece, Holland, Hungary, Italy, Luxembourg, Norway, Portugal, Spain, Sweden, and Switzerland. It entitles holders to 15 or 21 days or 1, 2, or 3 months of unlimited first class travel, plus many extras, including some ferry crossings (such as those between France and Ireland), river trips, lake steamers, and transportation by bus and private railroads, as well as scheduled *Europabus* services, and airport to city center rail connections. Since the Eurailpass is a first class pass, Eurail travelers can ride just about any European train they wish, including *ECs*, *ICs*, and other special express trains, without paying additional supplements. The only extras are the nominal reservation fee and sleeper and couchette costs.

At the time of this writing, the prices for first class Eurailpasses were as follows: a 15-day pass cost $340; a 21-day pass cost $440; a 1-month pass cost $550; a 2-month pass cost $750; and a 3-month pass cost $930. A Eurailpass for children under 12 is half the adult price (children under 4 travel free) but includes the same features, whereas the Eurail Youthpass, for travelers under 26 years of age, is slightly different. The Youthpass is valid for travel in second class only. As we went to press, it was available in a 1-month version for $380 and a 2-month version for $500.

The Eurail Saverpass resembles the basic Eurailpass, except that it provides 15 days of unlimited first class travel for three people traveling together during peak season; two people traveling together qualify if travel takes place entirely between October 1 and March 31. Under these restrictions, each 15-day ticket costs $100 less than the 15-day Eurailpass.

Another option is the Eurail Flexipass, which can be used for first class travel on any 5 days within a 15-day period ($198), 9 days within a 21-day period ($360), or 14 days within a 30-day period ($458). All of these passes must be bought before you go, either from a travel agent or from the US offices of the French, German, Italian, or Swiss railway companies. A Eurail Aid Office in Europe will replace lost passes when proper documentation is provided; a reissuance fee is charged.

Both the 7-day Eurailpass and the 9-day Eurail Flexipass can be combined with 3 to 8 days of car rental through *Hertz*. The program, marketed under the name *Hertz* EurailDrive Escape, starts at $229 per person (based on two people traveling together), and the car rental includes unlimited mileage, basic insurance, and taxes, as well as some drop-off options within most of the countries of rental. Reservations must be made in the US at least 7 days in advance by calling *Hertz* at 800-654-3001.

The Eurailpass is a bargain for those who are combining a visit to Ireland with sightseeing on the Continent, but for those who will be traveling strictly within Ireland, the Irish Republic's own Rambler Ticket is more economical. Rambler Tickets are good for unlimited travel in standard class (travelers pay a supplement for super-standard if and when they want it) and come in four versions: 8 or 15 days by rail or bus alone or 8 or 15 days by both. Note that while many rail passes are valid for *consecutive* days of travel, the 8-day rail-only Rambler Ticket is valid for travel on any 8 *individual* days within a 15-day period, and the 15-day rail-only ticket is valid for any 15 days within a 30-day period. The remaining bus-only or combined tickets follow the usual rule; i.e., they are valid for 8 or 15 consecutive days of travel counted from the first day of use. The rail/bus combination should be considered in Ireland, since Irish trains do not go everywhere, and rail and bus routes are well integrated.

Unlike many rail passes, the Rambler Ticket can be bought either before you leave, from any travel agency or from *CIE Tours International* (address below), or after you arrive, at railway or bus stations in Ireland or from the main *CIE* booking office (59 Upper O'Connell St., Dublin). At press time, prices ranged from $78 and $115 for the 8- and 15-day rail or bus versions to $110 and $156 for the 8- and 15-day rail and bus combination. Children under 16 are entitled to their own Rambler Tickets at half the adult fare (children under 3 travel free in Ireland if accompanied by a paying adult). A discounted Youth/Student Rambler Ticket also is available to travelers ages 14 through 26. It provides 8, 15, or 30 days of rail and bus travel, and, like the standard Rambler ticket, may be bought from *CIE* offices in the US or Ireland. The 8-day Youth/Student ticket is $99; the 15-day costs $136; and the 30-day costs $205.

The Rambler Ticket and the Eurailpass can be used only in the Irish Republic, not in Northern Ireland. Another pass, the Irish Overlander, which cost $164 at the time of this writing, is valid for both the Irish Republic and Northern Ireland. It allows unlimited train and bus travel for 15 consecutive days and can be bought from *CIE Tours International* in the US (address below), from the *CIE* booking office in Dublin (35 Lower Abbey St., Dublin 1, Ireland), or from the *Northern Ireland Railways* office at Belfast Central Station (Central Station, Eastbridge St., Belfast BT1 3PB, Northern Ireland) or the *Ulsterbus Ltd.* office (10 Glengall St., Belfast BT3 9BG, Northern Ireland). *Northern Ireland Railways* also offers the Rail Runabout Ticket, which allows 7 days of unlimited travel by rail and is available from April through October in Northern Ireland only. As with the above tickets, the Rail Runabout pass can be bought from *CIE* offices either in the US or Ireland.

FURTHER INFORMATION: For information on train travel in the Irish Republic, or to buy a Rambler Ticket or the Irish Overlander, contact *CIE Tours International*

(122 E. 42nd St., New York, NY 10168; phone: 212-972-5600 in New York City; 800-CIE-TOUR elsewhere in the US). This office also makes available a free timetable of the main intercity train services in the Irish Republic. For information on train travel in Northern Ireland, contact the Northern Ireland Tourist Board (40 W. 57th St., New York, NY 10019; phone: 212-686-6250).

Negotiating the train system on the Emerald Isle is a fairly simple matter, but if Ireland is only part of a more extensive trip through Europe or even farther afield, you may want to consult further sources before finalizing plans. Both the *Eurail Traveler's Guide* (which contains a railroad map) and the *Eurail Timetable* are free from Eurailpass (Box 10383, Stamford, CT 06904-2383), as well as from the Eurail Distribution Center (Box 300, Succursale R, Montreal, Quebec H2S 3K9 Canada). The *Eurail Guide* ($14.95) by Kathryn Turpin and Marvin Saltzman is available in most travel bookstores; it also can be ordered from Eurail Guide Annuals (27540 Pacific Coast Hwy., Mailbu, CA 90265; add $2 per book for postage and handling). *Europe by Eurail* by George Wright Ferguson is available from Globe Pequot Press (PO Box Q, Chester, CT 06412; phone: 203-526-9571). Both of the latter two guides discuss train travel in general, contain information on countries included in the Eurail network (the Saltzman book also discusses Eastern Europe and the rest of the world), and suggest numerous sightseeing excursions by rail from various base cities.

You also may want to buy the *Thomas Cook European Timetable* ($19.95), a weighty and detailed compendium of European international and national rail services that constitutes the most revered and accurate railway reference in existence. The *Timetable* comes out monthly, but because most European countries switch to summer schedules at the end of May (and back to winter schedules at the end of September), the June edition is the first complete summer schedule (and October the first complete winter schedule). The February through May editions, however, contain increasingly more definitive supplements on upcoming summer schedules, which can be used to plan a trip in advance. The *Thomas Cook European Timetable* is sold by some travel bookstores and by the *Forsyth Travel Library* (PO Box 2975, Shawnee Mission, KS 66201-1375; add $3 for airmail postage; Kansas residents add 5½% sales tax). You also can order it by phone and pay by credit card by calling 800-367-7984 or 913-384-0496.

Finally, although any travel agent can assist you in making arrangements to tour Ireland by rail, you may want to consult a train travel specialist, such as *Accent on Travel* (1030 Curtis St., Suite 201, Menlo Park, CA 94025; phone: 415-326-7330 in California; 800-347-0645 elsewhere in the US).

Traveling by Bus

 Going from place to place by bus may not be the fastest way to get from here to there, but that (and, in some cases, a little less comfort) may be the only drawback to bus travel. A persuasive argument in its favor is its cost: Short of walking, traveling by bus is the least expensive way to cover a long distance. On average, a bus ticket between two cities in the Irish Republic costs about two-thirds of the corresponding train fare. For this amount, it is possible to travel comfortably, if not always speedily, and at the same time enjoy an equally scenic view. Buses also reach outposts remote from the railroad tracks, for those so inclined. While train service in Ireland is more limited than it is in many another European country, a map of the bus routes is not much different from a road map: If the way is paved, it's certain that a bus — some bus — is assigned to travel it. The network of express buses — those traveling long distances with few stops en route — is only slightly less extensive. Because of this, Ireland is particularly well suited to bus travel.

In the Irish Republic, the state-owned *CIE (Córas Iompair Eireann, National Transport Company)* operates the trains, the long-distance or provincial buses, and the city buses of Dublin, Cork, Limerick, Waterford, and Galway. There are reduced rates for midweek and weekend return trips, and a number of bus passes are available. *CIE*'s main booking office (59 Upper O'Connell St., Dublin; phone: 1-734222), and the Central Bus Station, or Busaras (Store St., Dublin; phone: 1-720000), provide timetables, maps, and information on how to get anywhere in the Irish Republic by bus or train, as well as tickets. All long-distance buses leave from the Central Bus Station.

CIE also operates a series of half-day or full-day tours by sightseeing bus from major cities. From Dublin, for instance, there are about two dozen itineraries, including city sightseeing itineraries. Tours also leave from Shannon, Limerick, Tralee, Killarney, Cork, Waterford, Wexford, Galway, Sligo, and other cities. They begin as early as March in some areas and may run through September or October, though many are run only at the height of the summer. Departures are daily or several times weekly, and prices range from approximately IR£7 to IR£21 (at press time about $11 to $32.50). Information is available from *CIE Tours International,* 122 E. 42nd St., New York, NY 10168 (phone: 212-972-5600 in New York City; 1-800-CIE-TOUR elsewhere in the US).

In Northern Ireland, *Ulsterbus* operates all bus service. As with train service in this part of the country, it is somewhat more limited than in the Irish Republic. For information on routes, schedules, and fares, write to *Ulsterbus,* 10 Glengall St., Belfast BT3 9BG, Northern Ireland.

BOOKING: Reservations are not normally necessary on most bus routes, which work to established and published schedules. In rural areas of the country in particular, the bus is the main form of transport for the locals. Tickets usually are bought at bus stations or from a central office, although on rural and city routes they may be bought from the bus driver. (Note that exact change often is required.) Sightseeing tours and special programs, however, often require advance reservations.

SERVICES: Buses are not equipped for food service, and few trips are long enough to necessitate meal stops. If you plan to spend some time traveling around Ireland by bus, it is not a bad idea to bring some food aboard to eat en route, though you're probably better off waiting until you reach a stop in a town or city where you can eat more comfortably at a pub or restaurant. Large tour buses often offer special amenities such as air conditioning, toilets, upholstered and adjustable seats, and reading lamps.

FOR COMFORTABLE TRAVEL: Dress casually in loose-fitting clothes. Be sure you have a sweater or jacket (even in the summer) and, for when you disembark, a raincoat or umbrella is a year-long must. Passengers are allowed to listen to radios or cassette players, but must use earphones. Choose a seat in the front near the driver for the best view, or in the middle between the front and rear wheels for the smoothest ride. Smoking is not allowed, even upstairs in double-decker buses that serve Dublin and Belfast.

BUS PASSES: Several bus passes make buses even more of a bargain in Ireland. Although they do not have to be bought before departure, most passes can be bought in the US, and it's a good idea to investigate them while planning the trip.

Since the same company *(CIE)* runs both buses and trains in the Irish Republic, it is only natural that Irish passes are valid for both bus and train travel. The Rambler Ticket is sold for 8 or 15 days of unlimited travel, and either version is available for rail or bus travel alone or in combination. (Use of city bus service is excluded.) The tickets, valid only in the Irish Republic, can be bought from a travel agent or from *CIE Tours International* in the US (address above), at bus and railway stations in Ireland, and at the *CIE* booking office in Dublin (59 Upper O'Connell St., Dublin). Another combination bus and rail pass, the Emerald Card, is valid for 15 days of unlimited travel in both the Irish Republic and Northern Ireland. It, too, is sold by

CIE Tours International in the US, and also is available from the *CIE* booking office in Dublin, as well as the Belfast offices of *Northern Ireland Railways* (Central Station, Eastbridge St., Belfast BT1 3PB, Northern Ireland) and *Ulsterbus* (10 Glengall St., Belfast BT3 9BG, Northern Ireland).

The Freedom of Northern Ireland ticket is a bus-only pass, valid for 1 or 7 days' travel on all *Ulsterbus* services in Northern Ireland. Buy it at bus stations in Northern Ireland.

Though bus timetables can be picked up overseas, it may be useful to have them on hand to help in planning. The *Expressway Bus Timetable* of *CIE* routes in the Irish Republic is available (in very limited quantities) free from *CIE Tours International*. For information on services in Northern Ireland, write to *Ulsterbus Ltd.* (address above). Specify the region of interest or ask for the complete package of timetables (no charge).

Traveling by Car

 After mastering the trick of keeping to the left side of the road, a visitor will quickly find Ireland ideally suited for driving tours. There are few places in Ireland that cannot be reached by train or bus or a combination of the two, yet many visitors are not in the country long before they wish they had a car. Driving certainly is the most flexible way to explore out-of-the-way regions of the country. Trains often whiz much too fast past too many enticing landscapes, tunnel through or pass between hills and mountains rather than climb up and around them for a better view, and frequently deposit passengers in an unappealing part of town. Buses have greater range, but they still don't permit many spur-of-the-moment stops and starts. In a car you go where you want when you want, and can stop along the way as often as you like for a meal, a photograph, or a particularly appealing view.

Ireland is ideally suited for driving tours. The island is small, so distances between major cities and points of interest usually are reasonable. From Shannon Airport across the country to Dublin, for instance, is an average 4-hour drive, and from Cork up to Donegal is a bit more than 7 hours. Most other trips take less time, barring the occasional traffic jam, which is more likely to be caused by a flock of sheep than a crush of cars. In Ireland, the historical and cultural density is such that the flexibility of a car can be used to maximum advantage. A visitor can cover large amounts of territory or spend the same amount of time motoring from village to village and from nook and cranny to crafts shop. (See DIRECTIONS for our choices of the most interesting driving routes.)

Travelers who wish to cover counties in both the north and south can count on a good system of roads to help them make time. Travelers who wish to explore only one region will find that the secondary and even lesser roads are well surfaced and generally in good condition — with the exception of dirt country roads that might not be quite up to par during wetter periods. Either way, there is plenty of satisfying scenery en route.

But driving isn't an inexpensive way to travel. Gas prices are higher in Ireland than in North America, and car rentals seldom are available at bargain rates. Keep in mind, however, that driving becomes more economical with more passengers. Because the price of getting wheels abroad will be more than an incidental expense, it is important to investigate every alternative before making a final choice. Many travelers find this expense amply justified when they consider that rather than just the means to an end, a well-planned driving route also can be an important part of the adventure.

Before setting out, make certain that everything you need is in order. Read about the places you intend to visit and study relevant maps. If at all possible, discuss your intended trip with someone who already has driven the route to find out about road conditions and available services. If you can't speak to someone personally, try to read about others' experiences. Automobile clubs (see below) and Irish tourist board offices in the US (see *Tourist Information Offices,* in this section, for addresses) can be a good source of travel information, although when requesting brochures and maps be sure to specify the areas you are planning to visit. (Also see "Maps," below.)

DRIVING: A valid driver's license from his or her own state of residence enables a US citizen to drive in either the Irish Republic or Northern Ireland. Liability insurance also is required and is a standard part of any car rental contract. (To be sure of having the appropriate coverage, let the rental staff know in advance about the country borders you plan to cross.) If buying a car and using it while abroad, the driver must carry an International Insurance Certificate, known familarly as a Green Card. Your insurance agent or carrier at home can arrange for a special policy to cover you in Europe and automatically will issue your Green Card.

The Irish drive on the left-hand side of the road and pass (or "overtake," as they say) on the right. For this reason, the steering wheel is on the right-hand side of the car and shifting in a car with manual transmission is done with the left hand. The switch is confusing at first, but it is possible to adjust in enough time to enjoy the trip. It generally pays to practice for a few minutes in the parking lot of the rental agency before heading out on the road. And when in doubt, *slow down.* Even with the reversed steering wheel, your automatic reaction when faced with head-on traffic may be to veer to the right — particularly dangerous on the narrow, winding roads found in the Irish countryside. You also should be aware of a tendency of Irish drivers to drive right down the middle of country roads and shift to the left side only when reaching an oncoming car. This jarring experience is best handled by staying to your own side of the road and leaving enough room on the right for oncoming traffic.

High-beam lights should not be used in cities and towns. Use the horn sparingly — only in emergencies and when approaching blind highland curves. In some towns and cities honking is forbidden; flash your headlights instead. In both countries, seat belts are compulsory for the driver and front seat passenger, and children under 12 must travel in the back seat. Motorcycle drivers are required to wear helmets. And watch out for bicycles and motor scooters — they are everywhere.

Pictorial direction signs are standardized under the International Roadsign System and their meanings are indicated by their shapes — triangular signs mean danger; circular signs give instructions; and rectangular signs are informative. Driving in Irish cities can be a tricky proposition, since many of them do not have street signs at convenient corners, but instead identify their byways with plaques attached to the walls of corner buildings. These often are difficult to spot until you've passed them, and since streets often don't run parallel to one another, taking the next turn can lead you astray. Fortunately, most Irish cities and towns post signs pointing the way to the center of the city, and plotting a course to your destination from there may be far easier.

Unlike most of the rest of Europe, distances are measured in miles in Ireland, and they are registered as such on the speedometer — although on main roads and around city centers in the Irish Republic, mileage signs in kilometers are being added, occasionally giving the distinct impression you're getting farther from a place as you approach it. (Older black-and-white signs give distances in miles; newer green-and-white signs, in kilometers.) In the Irish Republic, the speed limit is 55 mph on the open road and 30 to 40 mph in towns and built-up areas. In Northern Ireland, speed limits are as in Great Britain: 70 mph on motorways (expressways) and dual carriageways (4-lane highways), 60 mph on single carriageways (single-lane highways), and 30 mph in towns or built-up areas — unless other limits are posted. Keep in mind when touring along Ireland's scenic roadways that it is all too easy to inch up over the speed limit.

And use alchohol sparingly prior to getting behind the wheel. Both countries also are zealous in prosecuting those who commit infractions under the influence. Sobriety tests are routinely administered and heavy fines or even jail sentences have been imposed. If you've been drinking, do as the natives do and walk home, take a cab, or make sure that a licensed member in your party sticks strictly to soft drinks. Police also have the power to levy on-the-spot fines for other infractions such as speeding, failure to stop at a red light, and failure to wear seat belts.

Traffic congestion is at its worst on main roads — particularly those radiating from major cities — on the days before or after public holidays. Look for signs pointing out detours or alternate routes to popular holiday destinations. Service stations, information points, and tourist offices may distribute free maps of the alternate routes, which may be the long way around but probably will get you to your destination faster in the end by bypassing the bottlenecks.

■ **Note:** Pay particular attention to parking signs in large cities (particularly in Northern Ireland), especially those indicating "control zones," where an unattended parked car presents a serious security risk. If you park in a restricted zone, unlike in the US (where you chance only getting a ticket or being towed), you may return to find that the trunk and doors have been blown off by overly cautious security forces.

Maps – A very good road map of Ireland is Michelin's *No. 405,* on a scale of 6.30 miles to 1 inch. It covers the whole island, outlines particularly scenic routes in green, and includes inset maps showing the main roads into and out of Dublin and Belfast. Michelin maps are readily available in bookstores and map shops throughout the US and all over Europe, and also can be ordered from Michelin Guides and Maps (PO Box 3305, Spartanburg, SC 29304-3305; phone: 803-599-0850 in South Caroline; 800-423-0485 elsewhere in the US). A new edition of each Michelin map appears every year; if you're not buying directly from the publisher, make sure that the edition you buy is no more than 2 years old by opening one fold and checking the publication date, given just under the black circle with the map number.

The Irish Tourist Board distributes a less detailed, free map of Ireland. It, too, covers the whole island and outlines scenic routes in green; in addition, it includes city center maps for Dublin, Belfast, Cork, Limerick, and other cities. If stocks in the US are exhausted, look for it at tourist information offices in Ireland.

Another set of useful maps are those published by the *Ordnance Survey* division of the Irish government. There are four such maps: *Ireland North, Ireland West, Ireland East, Ireland South.* For a price list of all Ordnance Survey maps, write to Ordnance Survey Office (Phoenix Park, Co. Dublin), or to the Government Bookstore (Chichester St., Belfast 1). These maps also may be available at some bookstores and newsstands in Ireland. Road maps also are sold at gas stations throughout Ireland.

Other maps are published by John Bartholomew & Son Ltd., a Scottish map company whose motoring maps, including maps of Ireland, are stocked in many bookstores and map shops around the US. A catalogue of the full line can be obtained by writing to the company at 12 Duncan St., Edinburgh, Scotland EH9 1TA.

Another good source for these and just about any other map available is *Map Link* (25 E. Mason St., Santa Barbara, CA 93101; phone: 305-965-4402). You may want to order their excellent guide to maps worldwide, *The World Map Directory* ($29.95). If they don't have the map you want in stock (not likely — they carry 50 maps of the Irish Republic and 33 of Northern Ireland), they will order it for you.

The *AA Touring Map of Ireland* ($5.95), published by Britain's main automobile club, is available from the *British Travel Bookshop* (40 W. 57th St., New York, NY 10019; phone: 212-765-0898), or by mail from GHS Inc. (Box 1224, Clifton, NJ 07012; add $2.50 for postage and handling; New Jersey residents add 6% sales tax).

The *American Automobile Association (AAA)* also provides several useful reference sources, including a map of Ireland (with Great Britain), an overall Europe planning map, the 600-page *Travel Guide to Europe* (price varies from branch to branch), and the 64-page *Motoring Europe* ($5.95). All are available through local *AAA* offices (see below). The *AAA* is a source of other travel information, and if you are a member you can take advantage of the services of Irish *AA* offices, with whom the *AAA* has a reciprocal agreement. The *AA* will also provide members with suggested routes between destinations that vary from scenic to the most direct. Another invaluable guide, *Euroad: The Complete Guide to Motoring in Europe,* is available for $8.80, including postage and handling, from VLE Limited, PO Box 547, Tenafly, NJ 07670 (phone: 201-567-5536).

Automobile Clubs and Breakdowns – Most European automobile clubs offer emergency assistance to any breakdown victim, whether a club member or not; however, only members of these clubs or affiliated clubs may have access to certain information services and receive discounted or free towing and repair services.

Members of the *American Automobile Association (AAA)* often are entitled automatically to a number of services from foreign clubs. With over 31 million members in chapters throughout the US and Canada, the *AAA* is the largest automobile club in North America. *AAA* affiliates throughout the US provide a variety of travel services to members, including a travel agency, trip planning, free traveler's checks at some locations, and reimbursement for foreign roadside assistance. They will help plan an itinerary, will send a map with clear routing directions, and will even make hotel reservations; these services apply to traveling in both the US and Ireland. Although *AAA* members receive maps, brochures, and other publications for no charge or at a discount (depending on the publication and branch), non-members also can order from an extensive selection of highway and topographical maps. You can join the *AAA* through local chapters (listed in the telephone book under *AAA*) or contact the national office, 1000 AAA Dr., Heathrow, FL 32746-5063 (phone: 407-444-8544).

The main automobile clubs offering information on and service throughout Ireland are the *Automobile Association (AA;* Farnum House, Basing View, Basingstoke, Hampshire RG21 2EA; phone: 256-20123; or 23 Rock Hill, Black Rock, County Dublin, Ireland; phone: 1-833555)) and the *Royal Automobile Club (RAC;* 49 Pall Mall, London SW1Y 5JG; phone: 71-839-7050). Though it isn't necessary to below to these clubs to qualify for emergency assistance, service is cheaper, and sometimes free, if you are a member. Due to a reciprocal agreement, *Automobile Association of America (AAA)* members are granted an automatic temporary membership in the *AA* in Ireland — giving visitors access to informational and emergency rescue services.

If you break down on the road, the first emergency procedure is to get the car off the road. Some roads have narrower shoulders than you're used to, so make sure you get all the way off, even if you have to hang off the shoulder a bit. The universal signal for help is raising the hood, and tying a white handkerchief or rag to the door handle or radio antenna. Don't leave the car unattended, and don't try any major repairs on the road.

Motor patrols usually drive small cars painted a uniform color. In Northern Ireland, both the *AA* and the *RAC* patrol the major highways and maintain emergency phones (yellow call boxes for the *AA* and blue for the *RAC*) on these routes for stranded travelers to dial for roadside assistance. Bear in mind that on secondary, very rural routes in Northern Ireland these boxes may be few and far between. In the Irish Republic there are no special phones available; however, the *AA* and the *RAC* do patrol major routes in this part of the country.

For emergency assistance, you also can call the nationwide emergency number 999 (similar to dialing 911 in the US). For further information on calling for help, see *Mail, Telephone, and Electricity* and *Medical and Legal Aid and Consular Services,* both in this section.

Aside from these options, a driver in distress will have to contact the nearest service center by pay phone. Car rental companies also make provisions for breakdowns, emergency service, and assistance; ask for a number to call when you pick up the vehicle.

GASOLINE – Called "petrol" in Ireland, gasoline is sold by the British or "imperial" gallon, which is 20% larger than the American gallon. One imperial gallon equals about 1.2 US gallons. In both Northern Ireland and the Republic, three grades are available: 4 star, 3 star, and 2 star in Northern Ireland; top grade, middle grade, and lower grade in the Republic.

Gas prices everywhere rise and fall depending on the world supply of oil, and an American traveling overseas is further affected by the prevailing rate of exchange, so it is difficult to say exactly how much fuel will cost when you travel. As gas prices are considerably higher in Ireland, it is not difficult to predict that it will cost roughly twice as much as you are accustomed to paying in the US. At the time of this writing, gas cost an average of about IR£3.90 or £3.30 (about $6) per imperial gallon, or about IR£3.25 or £2.80 (about $5) per US gallon.

Particularly when traveling in rural areas, fill up whenever you come to a gas station. It may be a long way to the next open station. (Even in more populated areas, it may be difficult to find an open station on Sundays or holidays.) You don't want to get stranded on an isolated stretch — so it is a good idea to bring along an extra few gallons in a steel container. (Plastic containers tend to break when a car is bouncing over rocky roads. This, in turn, creates the danger of fire should the gasoline ignite from a static electricity spark. Plastic containers also may burst at high altitudes.)

Considering the cost of gas in Ireland relative to US prices at the time of this writing, gas economy is of particular concern. The prudent traveler should plan an itinerary and make as many reservations as possible in advance, in order to not waste gas figuring out where to go, stay, or eat. Drive early in the day, when there is less traffic. Then leave your car at the hotel and use local transportation whenever possible after you arrive at your destination.

Although it may be as dangerous to drive at a speed much below the posted limit as it is to drive above it, particularly on Northern Ireland motorways — expressways, where the speed limit is 70 mph — at 55 mph a car gets 25% better mileage than at 70 mph. The number of miles per gallon also is increased by driving smoothly. Accelerate gently, anticipate stops, get into high gear quickly, and maintain a steady speed.

RENTING A CAR: Although there are other options, such as leasing or outright purchase, most people who want to drive in Europe simply rent a car. Travelers to Ireland can reserve a rental car through a travel agent or international rental firm before leaving home, or from a local company once they are in Europe. Another possibility, also arranged before departure, is to rent the car as part of a larger travel package (see "Fly/Drive," below, as well as *Package Tours,* in this section).

Renting is not inexpensive, but it is possible to economize by determining your own needs and then shopping around among car rental companies until you find the best deal. As you comparison shop, keep in mind that rates vary considerably, not only from city to city, but also from location to location within the same city. It might be less expensive to rent a car in the center of a city rather than at the airport. Ask about special rates or promotional deals, such as weekend or weekly rates, bonus coupons for airline tickets, or 24-hour rates that include gas and unlimited mileage.

Rental car companies operating in Europe can be divided into three basic categories: large international companies; national or regional companies; and local companies. *Avis, Budget, Hertz,* and other international firms maintain offices in most major European cities. Because of aggressive local competition, the cost of renting a car can be less expensive once a traveler arrives in Europe, compared to the prices quoted in advance from the US. Local companies usually are less expensive than the international giants.

Given this situation, it's tempting to wait until arriving to scout out the lowest-priced rental from the company located the farthest from the airport high-rent district and offering no pick-up services. But if your arrival coincides with a holiday or a peak travel period, you may be disappointed to find that even the most expensive car in town was spoken for months ago. Whenever possible, it is best to reserve in advance, anywhere from a few days in slack periods to a month or more during the busier seasons.

The best guide to sorting through the options may be to contact the local tourist board, which usually can provide recommendations and a list of reputable firms. The Irish Tourist Board and the Northern Ireland Tourist Board have a supply of the rate brochures of numerous Irish car rental companies, many of which have US representatives through whom arrangements can be made directly. Indeed, the large Irish firm *Murray's Rent a Car* is the Irish link in the Europe-wide *Europcar* chain, which is, in turn, the European link of *National Car Rental.*

Renting from the US – Travel agents can arrange foreign rentals for clients, but it is just as easy to do it yourself by calling the international divisions of the following familiar car rental firms:

Avis: Has 18 locations in the Irish Republic and 3 in Northern Ireland. Call 800-331-1084.

Budget: Has 14 locations in the Irish Republic and 1 in Northern Ireland. Call 800-527-0700.

Dollar Rent-a-Car (known in Europe as *Eurodollar*): Has 14 locations in the Irish Republic and 1 in Northern Ireland. Call 800-421-6878.

Hertz: Has 33 locations in the Irish Republic and 1 in Northern Ireland. Call 800-654-3001.

National (known in Europe as *Europcar*): Has 14 locations in the Irish Republic and 4 in Northern Ireland. Call 800-CAR-EUROPE.

All of these companies publish directories listing their foreign locations, and all quote weekly flat rates based on unlimited mileage with the renter paying for gas. Some also offer time and mileage rates (i.e., a basic per-day or per-week charge, plus a charge for each mile driven), which generally are only to the advantage of those who plan to do very little driving — the basic time and mileage charge for a given period of time is lower than the unlimited mileage charge for a comparable period, but the miles add up more quickly than most people expect.

It also is possible to rent a car before you go by contacting any of a number of smaller or less well known US companies that do not operate worldwide but specialize in European auto travel, including leasing and car purchase in addition to car rental, or actually are tour operators with a well-established European car rental program. These firms, whose names and addresses are listed below, act as agents for a variety of European suppliers, offer unlimited mileage almost exclusively, and frequently manage to undersell their larger competitors by a significant margin.

Comparison shopping always is advisable, however, because the company that has the least expensive rentals in one country may not have the least expensive in another, and even the international giants offer discount plans whose conditions are easy for most travelers to fulfill. For instance, *Budget* and *National* offer discounts of anywhere from 15% to 30% off their usual rates (according to the size of the car and the duration of the rental), provided that the car is reserved a certain number of days before departure (usually 7, but it can be less), is rented for a minimum period (5 days or, more often, a week), and, in most cases, is returned to the same location that supplied it or to another in the same country. Similar discount plans include *Hertz*'s Affordable Europe and *Avis*'s Supervalue Rates Europe.

Note: Avis also offers three helpful free services for customers traveling in Northern Ireland (and in Great Britain and on the Continent): the "Know Before You Go" US hot line (phone: 212-876-AVIS); an "On call service" for customers calling once in Europe; and a Europe Message Center, which will take messages for customer traveling in Europe. The first two services provide travelers with tourist information on Northern Ireland (as well as Belgium, France, Germany, Great Britain, Holland, and Switzerland). Topics may range from questions about driving (distances, gasoline prices, and license requirements) to queries about currency, customs, tipping, and weather. (Callers to the US number then receive a personal letter confirming the information discussed.) For the European service, there is a different toll-free number in each country; the numbers are given to you when you rent from *Avis*. The Europe Message Center operates like any answering service in that it will take phone messages any time day or night for *Avis* customers; in addition, if your rental car comes with a car phone, they will give this number to callers (with your permission). For message pick-up, travelers are provided with toll-free numbers for each of the above-mentioned countries. For both services, in Northern Ireland, call 81-7570131 in London.

There are legitimate bargains in car rentals, if you shop for them. Call all the familiar car rental names whose toll-free numbers are given above (don't forget to ask about their special discount plans), and then call the smaller companies listed below. In the recent past, the latter have tended to offer significantly lower rates, but it always pays to compare. Begin your comparison shopping early, because the best deals may be booked to capacity quickly and may require payment 14 to 21 days or more before picking up the car.

Auto Europe, PO Box 1097, Camden, ME 04843 (phone: 207-236-8235; 800-223-5555 throughout the US; 800-458-9503 in Canada). Offers rentals at 7 locations in the Irish Republic.

Cortell International, 17310 Red Hill Ave., Suite 360, Irvine, CA 92714 (phone: 800-228-2535 or 714-724-1003). Has 13 locations in the Irish Republic.

Europe by Car, One Rockefeller Plaza, New York, NY 10020 (phone: 212-581-3040 in New York State; 800-223-1516 elsewhere in the US), or 9000 Sunset Blvd., Los Angeles, CA 90069 (phone: 800-252-9401 or 213-272-0424). Offers rentals in Cork, Dublin, and at the Shannon Airport (all in the Republic).

Foremost Euro-Car, 5430 Van Nuys Blvd., Suite 306, Van Nuys, CA 91401 (phone: 818-786-1960 or 800-272-3299 in California; 800-423-3111 elsewhere in the US). Has 5 locations in the Irish Republic.

Kemwel Group Inc., 106 Calvert St., Harrison, NY 10528 (phone: 800-678-0678 or 914-835-5555). Has 6 locations in the Irish Republic.

For travelers for whom driving is more than just a means of getting from here to there, *European Car Reservations* (349 W. Commercial St., Suite 2950, East Rochester, NY 14445; phone: 800-535-3303) rents BMWs, Mercedes, and Volvos in Ireland, for a 2-week minimum. Prices are hardly inexpensive, but many feel the pleasure of being behind the wheel of a Mercedes 230E or a Volvo 730E is worth the cost. (For those looking for a tamer experience, however, this company also rents more sedate models.) Pick-up and drop-off locations in Ireland include Cork, Dublin, Dún Laoghaire, Galway Airports, Rosslare, Shannon, Sligo, Waterford, and Wexford–Ferry Terminals (all in the Irish Republic).

One of the ways to keep the cost of car rentals down is to deal with a car rental consolidator, such as *Connex International* (983 Main St., Peekskill, NY 10566; phone: 800-333-3949 or 914-739-0066). *Connex*'s main business is negotiating with virtually all of the major car rental agencies for the lowest possible prices for its customers. For example, at the time of this writing, rates for a subcompact car in some parts of Europe (they rent just about everywhere — including both Northern Ireland and the Republic) were as low as $89 a week with unlimited mileage — comparable deals available from other major car rental companies run substantially higher. (*Connex* also can offer significant numbers of other travel services, varying from hotel accommodations to sightseeing programs.)

Local Rentals – It long has been common wisdom that the least expensive way to rent a car is to make arrangements in Europe. This is less true today than it used to be. Many medium to large European car rental companies have become the overseas suppliers of stateside companies such as those mentioned previously, and often the stateside agency, by dint of sheer volume, has been able to negotiate more favorable rates for its US customers than the European firm offers its own. Still lower rates may be found by searching out small, strictly local rental companies overseas, whether at less than prime addresses in major cities or in more remote areas. But to find them you must be willing to invest a sufficient amount of vacation time comparing prices on the scene. You also must be prepared to return the car to the location that rented it; drop-off possibilities are likely to be limited.

The brochures of some of the smaller car rental companies, available from the Irish Tourist Board, can serve as a useful basis for comparison. Overseas, the "Car Hire" section of the local yellow pages is a good place to begin. (For further information on local rental companies, see the individual city reports in THE CITIES.)

Also bear in mind that the rail-and-drive pass offered by *Hertz*, EurailDrive Escape, is valid in the Irish Republic and all the other countries of the Eurail network. (For further information on rail-and-drive packages, see *Traveling by Train*, in this section.)

Requirements – Whether you decide to rent a car in advance from a large international rental company with Irish branches or wait to rent from a local Irish company, you should know that renting a car is rarely as simple as signing on the dotted line and roaring off into the night. If you are renting for personal use, you must have a valid drivers license, and will have to convince the renting agency that (1) you are personally credit-worthy, and (2) you will bring the car back at the stated time. This will be easy if you have a major credit card; most rental companies accept credit cards in lieu of a cash deposit, as well as for payment of your final bill. If you prefer to pay in cash, leave your credit card imprint as a "deposit," then pay your bill in cash when you return the car.

If you don't have a major credit card, renting a car for personal use becomes more complicated. If you are planning to rent from an international agency with an office near your home, the best thing to do is to call the company several days in advance, and give them your name, home address, and information on your business or employer; the agency then runs its own credit check on you. This can be time consuming, so you should try to have it done before you leave home. If planning to pay for your rental car in cash, it is best to make arrangements in advance — otherwise you must bring along a letter of employment and go to the agency during business hours (don't forget to take the time difference into account) so that your employer can be called for verification.

In addition to paying the rental fee up front, you also will have to leave a hefty deposit when you pick up the car — either a substantial flat fee or a percentage of the total rental cost. (Each company has a different deposit policy; look around for the best deal.) If you return the car on time, the full deposit will be refunded; otherwise additional charges will be deducted and any unused portion of the deposit returned.

If you are planning to rent a car once in Ireland, *Avis, Hertz,* and other US rental companies usually *will* rent to travelers paying in cash and leaving either a credit card imprint or a substantial amount of cash as a deposit. This is not necessarily standard policy, however, as *Budget,* some of the other international chains, and many Irish companies *will not* rent to an individual who doesn't have a valid credit card. In this case, you will have to call around to find a company that accepts cash.

Also keep in mind that although the minimum age to drive a car in both Northern Ireland and the Irish Republic is 17 years, the minimum age to rent a car varies with the company. Many firms have a minimum age requirement of 21 years, some raise that to 23 or 25 years, and for some models of cars it rises to 30 years. The upper age limit at many companies is between 69 and 75; others have no upper age limit or may make drivers above a certain age subject to special conditions.

Costs – Given all the competition, the price charged for a rental car changes continuously, rising and falling according to the level of renter traffic. The rate your friend paid last December may have been higher than the one you'll pay in May, and a super-bargain rate may be withdrawn as soon as the advertiser moves some cars off the lot and onto the road again. Nevertheless, there are some constants governing pricing in the international car rental market.

Finding the most economical car rental will require some telephone shopping on your part. As a *general* rule, expect to hear lower prices quoted by the smaller, strictly local companies than by the well-known international names, with those of the national Irish companies falling somewhere between the two.

If you are driving short distances for only a day or two, the best deal may be a per-day, per-mile rate: You pay a flat fee for each day you keep the car (which can be as low as $25), plus a per-mile charge of 12¢ to 40¢ or more. An increasingly common alternative is to be granted a certain number of free miles each day and then be charged on a per-mile basis over that number. Flat weekly rates also are available, and some flat monthly rates that represent a further saving over the daily rate — however, even these longer-term rentals still will not be inexpensive.

A better alternative for touring the countryside may be a flat per-day rate with unlimited free mileage; this is certainly the most economical rate if you plan to drive over 100 miles a day. Make sure that the low, flat daily rate that catches your eye, however, is indeed a per-day rate: Often the lowest price advertised by a company turns out to be available only with a minimum 3-day rental — fine if you want the car that long, but not the bargain it appears if you really intend to use it no more than 24 hours for in-city driving.

Other factors influencing cost include the type of car you rent. Rentals are based on a tiered price system, with different sizes of cars — standard subcompact, compact, mid-size, large, and luxury — often listed as A (the smallest and least expensive) through F, G, or H, and sometimes even higher. The typical A car available in Ireland is a two-door subcompact or compact, often a hatchback, seating two or three adults (such as a small Ford, Fiat, or Renault), while the typical F, G, or H luxury car is a four-door sedan seating four or five adults (such as a Mercedes or BMW). The larger the car, the more it costs to rent in the first place and the more gas it consumes, but for some people the greater comfort and extra luggage space of a larger car (in which bags can be safely locked out of sight) may make it worth the additional expense, especially on a long trip. Be warned, too, that relatively few European cars have automatic transmissions, and those that do are more likely to be in the F group than the A group. Cars with automatic shift must be requested specifically at the time of booking, and they cost more (anywhere from $5 to $10 a day more than the same model with standard shift) and consume more gas. Similarly, cars with air conditioning are likely to be found in the more expensive categories.

Electing to pay for collision damage waiver (CDW) protection will add considerably to the cost of renting a car. You may be responsible for the *full value* of the vehicle being rented, but you can dispense with the possible obligation by buying the offered waiver at a cost of about $13 a day. Before making any decisions about optional collision damage waivers, check with your own insurance agent and determine whether your personal automobile insurance policy covers rented vehicles; if it does, you proba-bly won't need to pay for the waiver. Be aware, too, that increasing numbers of credit cards automatically provide CDW coverage if the car rental is charged to the appropri-ate credit card. However, the specific terms of such coverage differ sharply among individual credit card companies, so check with the credit card company for information on the nature and amount of coverage provided (also see *Credit and Currency,* in this section). Considering that repair costs for a rental car have become a real headache of late, and car rental companies are getting away with steep fees (up to the full retail price of the car) for damage to their property, if you are not otherwise covered it is wise to pay for the insurance offered by the car rental company rather than risk traveling without any coverage.

Overseas, the amount for which renters may be liable should damage occur has not risen to the heights it has in the US. In addition, some Irish car rental agreements include collision damage coverage. In this case the CDW supplement frees the renter from liability for the *deductible* amount — as opposed to the standard CDW coverage, described above, which releases the driver from liability for the full value of the car. In Ireland, this deductible typically ranges from $1,500 to $2,500 at present, but can be more for some luxury car groups. As with the full liability waiver, the cost of waiving this liability — anywhere from $10 to $25 a day — is far from negligible, however. Drivers who rent cars in the US are often able to decline the CDW because many personal automobile insurance policies (subject to their own deductibles) extend to rental cars; unfortunately, such coverage usually does not extend to cars rented for use outside the US and Canada. Similarly, CDW coverage provided by some credit cards if the rental is charged to the card may be limited to cars rented in the US or Canada.

When inquiring about CDW coverage and costs, you should be aware that a number of the major international car rental companies now automatically are including the cost of this waiver in their quoted prices. This does not mean that they are absorbing this cost and you are receiving free coverage — total rental prices have increased to include the former CDW charge. The disadvantage of this inclusion is that you probably will not have the option to refuse this coverage, and will end up paying the added charge — even if you already are adequately covered by your own insurance policy or through a credit card company.

Additional costs to be added to the price tag include drop-off charges or one-way service fees. The lowest price quoted by any given company may apply only to a car that is returned to the same location from which it was rented. A slightly higher rate may be charged if the car is to be returned to a different city in the same country, and a considerably higher rate may prevail if the rental begins in one country and ends in another.

A further consideration: Don't forget that all car rentals are subject to Value Added Tax (VAT). This tax rarely is included in the rental price that's advertised or quoted, but it always must be paid — whether you pay in advance in the US or pay it when you drop off the car. There is a wide variation in this tax rate from country to country: In Northern Ireland, the VAT rate on car rentals currently is 15%; in the Irish Republic, it's 10%.

One-way rentals bridging two countries used to be exempt from tax, but this is no longer the case. In general, the tax on one-way rentals is determined by the country in which the car has been rented, so if your tour plans include several countries, you should examine your options regarding the pick-up and drop-off points. Even if you intend to visit only one country, you still might consider a nearby country as a pick-up point if it will provide substantial savings. For instance, for a visitor planning to explore Northern Ireland, there's a financial incentive (particularly for long-term rentals) to pick up his or her rental car in the Irish Republic, and then drive across the border (at a 5% cost saving).

Some rental agencies that do not maintain their own fleets use a contractor, whose country of registration determines the rate of taxation. An example is the *Kemwel Group,* whose one-way rentals from all countries except Germany, Italy, and Sweden are taxed at the Danish rate, 22% — rentals in Northern Ireland and the Republic are taxed at the standard rate, 15% and 10%, respectively. *Kemwel*'s special programs offer savings to clients planning on touring throughout Europe (particularly where the tax rate is higher) and allow travel agents to earn commissions on CDW fees and on VATs. The SuperSaver Plus and UniSaver Plus tariffs offer inclusive rentals in 24 countries throughout Europe and the Middle East. These programs offer full insurance coverage (with a $100 deductible) and all European VAT, plus unlimited mileage. Rates start at $79 per week and are available in some 35 cities across Europe, including locations throughout the Irish Republic and Belfast in Northern Ireland. If part of a fly/dirve package (see below) booked through *Kemwel,* rates are as low as $39 per week. Bookings must be reserved and paid for at least 7 days before delivery of the car and the vehicle must be returned to the *Kemwel* station from which it originally was rented. For further information, contact *Kemwel Group Inc.,* 106 Calvert St., Harrison, NY 10528 (phone: 800-678-0678 or 914-835-5555).

Rental cars usually are delivered with a full tank of gas. (This is not always the case, however, so check the gas gauge when picking up the car, and have the amount of gas noted on your rental agreement if the tank is not full.) Remember to fill the tank before you return the car or you will have to pay to refill it, and gasoline at the car rental company's pump is always much more expensive than at a service station. This policy may vary for smaller, regional companies; ask when picking up the vehicle.

Finally, currency fluctuation is another factor to consider. Most brochures quote rental prices in US dollars, but these dollar amounts frequently are only guides; that is, they represent the prevailing rate of exchange at the time the brochure was printed. The rate may be very different when you call to make a reservation and different again when the time comes to pay the bill (when the amount owed may be paid in cash in foreign currency or as a charge to a credit card, which is recalculated at a still later date's rate of exchange). Some companies guarantee rates in US dollars (often for a slight surcharge), but this is an advantage only when the dollar is steadily declining overseas. If the dollar is growing stronger overseas, you may be better off with rates in the local currency.

Before you leave the lot, check to be sure the rental car has a spare tire and jack in the trunk. In addition, particularly for extensive touring, you may want to pick up the following equipment: a first-aid kit; a flashlight with an extra set of batteries; a white towel (useful for signaling for help, as well as for wiping the car windows); jumper cables; flares and/or reflectors; a container of water or coolant for the radiator; and a steel container for extra gasoline.

Fly/Drive – Airlines, charter companies, car rental companies, and tour operators have been offering fly/drive packages for years, and even though the basic components of the package have changed somewhat — return airfare, a car waiting at the airport, and perhaps a night's lodging in the gateway city all for one inclusive price used to be the rule — the idea remains the same. You rent a car *here* for use *there* by booking it along with other arrangements for the trip. These days, the very minimum arrangement possible is the result of a tie-in between a car rental company and an airline, which entitles customers to a rental car for less than the company's usual rates, provided they show proof of having booked a flight on that airline.

Slightly more elaborate fly/drive packages can be found listed under various names (go-as-you-please, self-drive, or, simply, car tours) in the independent vacations sections of tour catalogues. Their most common ingredients are the rental car plus some sort of hotel voucher plan, with the applicable airfare listed separately. You set off on your trip with a block of prepaid accommodations vouchers, a list of hotels that accept them (usually members of a hotel chain or association), and a reservation for the first night's stay, after which the staff of each hotel books the next one for you or you make your own reservations. Naturally, the greater the number of establishments participating in the scheme, the more freedom you have to range at will during the day's driving and still be near a place to stay for the night. The cost of these combination packages generally varies according to the size of the car and the quality of the hotels; there usually is an additional drop-off charge if the car is picked up in one city and dropped off in another. Most packages are offered at several different price levels, ranging from a standard plan covering stays in hotels to a budget plan using accommodations such as small inns, farmhouses, or bed and breakfast establishments. Airlines also have special rental car rates available when you book their flights, often with a flexible hotel voucher program. For information on available packages, check with the airline or your travel agent.

Less flexible car tours provide a rental car, a hotel plan, and a set itinerary that permits no deviation because the hotels all are reserved in advance. The deluxe European car tours packaged by *AutoVenture* (425 Pike St., Suite 502, Seattle, WA 98101, phone: 800-426-7501 or 206-624-6033), which can be bought in either a self-drive or chauffeured version, are of this variety. *Avis* offers less deluxe car tours with its Personally Yours program. You must book at least 2 weeks in advance to receive this planned itinerary service. For information on other packagers of car tours, see *Package Tours,* in this section.

LEASING: Anyone planning to be in Europe for 3 weeks or more should compare the cost of renting a car with the cost of leasing one for the same period. While the money saved by leasing — rather than renting for a 23-day (the minimum) or 30-day period — may not be great, what is saved over the course of a long-term lease — 45, 60, 90 days, or more — amounts to hundreds, even thousands, of dollars. Part of the saving is due to the fact that leased cars are exempt from the stiff taxes applicable to rental cars. In addition, leasing plans provide for collision insurance with no deductible amount, so there is no need to add the daily cost of collision damage waiver protection (an option offered by rental companies — see above). A further advantage of a car lease — actually a financed purchase/repurchase plan — is that you reserve your car by specific make and model rather than by group only and it is delivered to you fresh from the factory.

Unfortunately, leasing as described above is offered only in Belgium and France, and the savings it permits can be realized to the fullest only if the cars are picked up and returned at specified locations in these countries. While leased cars can be delivered to other locations in Belgium and France and to other countries there is a charge for this service, which can be as high as $250, to which must be added an identical return charge. If you don't intend to keep the car very long, the two charges could nullify the amount saved by leasing rather than renting, so you will have to do some arithmetic. (Note that at the time of this writing, pick-up or drop-off locations in Ireland were virtually nonexistent, but travelers to Ireland can pick up a car in France and take one of the car-carrying ferry services across to Ireland.)

It is possible to lease a car in countries other than Belgium and France, but most of the plans offered are best described as long-term rentals at preferential rates. They differ from true leasing in that the renter pays tax and collision damage waiver protection (though it may be included in the quoted price), and the cars usually are late-model used cars rather than brand-new.

One of the major car leasing companies is *Renault,* offering leases of new cars for 23 days to 6 months. The cars are exempt from tax, all insurance is included, and there is no mileage charge. *Renault* offers the following pick-up/drop-off options: free pick-up/drop-off in the following French cities: Bayonne, Bordeaux, Calais, Lyons, Marseille, Nice, Paris, Pau, Perpignan, Rennes, Strasbourg, and Toulouse; charges between $50 and $230 in Amsterdam (Holland), Brussels (Belgium), Frankfurt (Germany), London (Great Britain), and Zurich (Switzerland), and several even more expensive locations elsewhere on the Continent. For further information and reservations, ask your travel agent or contact *Renault USA,* 650 First Ave., New York, NY 10016 (phone: 212-532-1221 in New York State; 800-221-1052 elsewhere in the US).

Peugeot also offers a similar leasing arrangement, called the "Peugeot Vacation Plan." In accordance with the standard type of financed purchase/repurchase leasing plan, travelers buy a new car in France, drive it for anywhere between 22 and 175 days, then sell it back to *Peugeot* for a guaranteed price (the original price minus the actual charge for usage). The tax-free "purchase" includes unlimited mileage, factory warranty, full collision damage waiver coverage (no deductible), and 24-hour towing and roadside assistance. Pick-up and drop-off locations and charges are similar to *Renault*'s. *Peugeot*'s "European Delivery" program is a full-purchase program, including shipment of the car to the US, as discussed below. For further information, contact *Peugeot Motors of America* (1 Peugeot Plaza, Lyndhurst, NJ 07071; phone: 201-935-8400). Some of the car rental firms listed above — *Auto-Europe, Europe by Car, Foremost Euro-Car,* and *Kemwel Group* — also arrange European car leases.

BUYING A CAR: If your plans include both buying a new car of European make and a driving tour of Europe, it's possible to combine the two ventures and save some money on each. By buying the car abroad and using it during your vacation, you pay quite a bit less for it than the US dealer would charge and at the same time avoid the expense of renting a car during your holiday. There are two basic ways to achieve this desired end, but one, factory delivery, is far simpler than the other, direct import.

Factory delivery means that you place an order for a car in the US, then pick it up in Europe, often literally at the factory gate. It also means that your new car is built to American specifications, complying with all US emission and safety standards. Because of this, only cars made by manufacturers who have established a formal program for such sales to American customers can be bought at the factory. At present, the list includes Audi, BMW, Jaguar, Mercedes, Peugeot, Porsche, Saab, Volkswagen, and Volvo, among others (whose manufacturers generally restrict their offerings to those models they ordinarily export to the US). The factory delivery price, in US dollars, usually runs about 5% to 15% below the sticker price of the same model at a US dealership and includes the cost of shipping the car home. All contracts except BMW include US customs duty, but the cost of the incidentals and the insurance necessary for driving the car around Europe, are extra except, again, for BMW's plan.

One of the few disadvantages of factory delivery is that car manufacturers make only a limited number of models available each year, and for certain popular models you may have to get in line early in the season. Another is that you must take your trip when the car is ready, not when you are, although you usually will have 8 to 10 weeks' notice. The actual place of delivery can vary; it is more economical to pick up the car at the factory, but arrangements sometimes — but not always — can be made to have it delivered elsewhere for an extra charge. For example, Jaguars must be ordered through a US dealer and picked up at the factory in Coventry, England, although they also can be dropped off for shipment home in any number of European cities. For information, write to *Jaguar Cars,* 555 MacArthur Blvd., Mahwah, NJ 07430 (phone: 201-818-8500).

Cars for factory delivery usually can be ordered either through one of the manufacturer's authorized dealers in the US or through companies — among them *Europe by Car, Foremost Euro-Car,* and *Kemwel Group* (see above for contact information) — that specialize in such transactions. (Note that *Foremost Euro-Car* serves all of the US for rentals and leasing, but they arrange *sales* only for California residents.) Another company arranging car sales abroad is *Ship Side Tax Free World on Wheels BV,* 600B Lake St., Suite A, Ramsey, NJ 07446 (phone: 201-818-0400).

Occasionally an auto manufacturer offers free or discounted airfare in connection with a European delivery program. This year, Mercedes-Benz has a program including discounted round-trip airfare ($500 for two economy fare seats or one business class seat) from any US gateway served by *Lufthansa, Pan American,* or *TWA,* to Stuttgart (where the buyer picks up the car), plus a 1-night stay at the local *Ramada* or *Hilton* hotel, and 15 days' free comprehensive road insurance. For details, contact *Mercedes-Benz of North America,* 1 Mercedes Dr., Montvale, NJ 07645 (phone: 800-458-8202).

The other way to buy a car abroad, direct import, sometimes is referred to as "gray market" buying. It is perfectly legal, but not totally hassle-free. Direct import means that you buy abroad a car that was meant for use abroad, not one built according to US specifications. It can be new or used and may even include — if made for use in Ireland or Great Britain — a steering wheel on the right side. The main drawback to direct import is that the process of modification to bring the car into compliance with US standards is expensive and time-consuming; it typically costs from $5,000 to $7,000 in parts and labor and takes from 2 to 6 months. In addition, the same shipping, insurance, and miscellaneous expenses (another $2,000 to $5,000, according to estimates) that would be included in the factory delivery price must be added to the purchase price of the car, and the considerable burden of shepherding it on its journey from showroom to home garage usually is borne by the purchaser. Direct-import dealers do exist (they are not the same as your local, factory-authorized foreign car dealer, with whom you are now in competition), but even if you use one, you still need to do a great deal of paperwork yourself.

Once upon a time, the main advantage of the direct-import method — besides the fact that it can be used for makes and models not available on factory delivery programs — was that much more money could be saved importing an expensive car. Given today's exchange rates, however, the method's potential greater gain is harder to realize and must be weighed against its greater difficulties. Still, if direct importing interests you, you can obtain a list of those makes and models approved for conversion in this country, and of the converters licensed to bring them up to US specifications, by contacting to the Environmental Protection Agency, Manufacturers' Operations Division, EN-340-F, Investigations/Imports Section, 401 M St. SW, Washington, DC 20460 (phone: 202-382-2505).

If you have special problems getting your car into the US, you might consider contacting a specialist in vehicle importation, such as Daniel Kokal, a regulatory consultant with *Techlaw,* 14500 Avion Parkway, Suite 300, Chantilly, VA 22021 (phone: 703-818-1000).

Package Tours

If the mere thought of buying a package for travel to and through Ireland conjures up visions of a race through ten cities in as many days in lockstep with a horde of frazzled fellow travelers, remember that packages have come a long way. For one thing, not all packages necessarily are escorted tours, and the one you buy does not have to include any organized touring at all — nor will it necessarily include traveling companions. If it does, however, you'll find that people of all sorts — many just like yourself — are taking advantage of packages today because they are economical and convenient, save you an immense amount of planning time, and exist in such variety that it's virtually impossible not to find one that fits at least the majority of your travel preferences. Given the high cost of travel these days, packages have emerged as a particularly wise buy.

Aside from the cost-saving advantages of package arrangements, Ireland itself is ideally suited to package travel. The reason is that, essentially, Ireland is a multifarious country, a roam-and-do destination distinct from, say, the Caribbean, where most visitors go to a single island for a week or two of vacation and unpack everything until they're ready to return home. To be sure, many visitors to Ireland do seek out a single city or area for a concentrated visit, booking themselves into a hotel, country inn, bed and breakfast establishment, apartment, or house that serves as a base from which they make regional tours and visits. But the bulk of North American travelers want to explore as much of Ireland as possible within the restrictions of time and travel funds available. Hence the popularity — and practicality — of package arrangements.

Hundreds of package programs are on the market today. In the US, numerous packages to Ireland are offered by tour operators or wholesalers, some retail travel agencies, airlines, charter companies, hotels, and even special-interest organizations, and what goes into them depends on who is organizing them. The most common type, assembled by tour wholesalers and sold through travel agents, runs the gamut from deluxe everything to simple tourist class amenities or even bare necessities. Fly/drive and fly/cruise packages usually are the joint planning efforts of airlines and, respectively, car rental companies and cruise line operators. Charter flight programs may range from little more than airfare and a minimum of ground arrangements to full-scale escorted tours or special-interest vacations. There also are hotel packages organized by hotel chains or associations of independent hotels and applicable to stays at any combination of member establishments; resort packages, covering arrangements at a specific hotel; and special-interest tours, which can be once-only programs organized by particular groups through a retail agency or regular offerings packaged by a tour operator. They can feature food, music or theater festivals, a particular sporting activity or event, a commemorative occasion, even nature study or scientific exploration.

In essence, a package is an amalgam of travel services that can be purchased in a single transaction. A package tour to and through Ireland may include any or all of the following: round-trip transatlantic transportation, local transportation (and/or car rentals), accommodations, some or all meals, sightseeing, entertainment, transfers to and from the hotel at each destination, taxes, tips, escort service, and a variety of incidental features that might be offered as options at additional cost. In other words, a package can be any combination of travel elements, from a fully escorted tour offered at an all-inclusive price to a simple fly/drive booking allowing you to move about totally on your own. Its principal advantage is that it saves money: The cost of the combined arrangements invariably is well below the price for all of the same elements if bought separately, and particularly if transportation is provided by charter or discount flight, it could even be less than just a round-trip economy airline ticket on a regularly scheduled flight. A package tour provides more than economy and convenience: It releases the traveler from having to make individual arrangements for each separate element of a trip.

Lower prices are possible through package travel as a result of high-volume purchasing. The tour packager negotiates for services in wholesale quantities — blocks of airline seats or hotel rooms, group meals, busloads of ground transport, and so on — and these are made available at a lower per-person price because of the large quantities purchased for use during a given time period. Most packages, however, are subject to restrictions governing the duration of the trip and require total payment by a given time before departure.

Tour programs generally can be divided into two categories — "escorted" (or locally hosted) and "independent" — depending on arrangements offered. An escorted tour means that a guide will accompany the group from the beginning of the tour through to the return; a locally hosted tour means that the group will be met upon arrival in each city by a different local host. On independent tours, there generally is a choice of hotels, meal plans, and sightseeing trips in each city, as well as a variety of special excursions. The independent plan is for people who do not want a set itinerary but who prefer confirmed reservations. Whether you choose an escorted or independent tour, always bring along complete contact information for your tour operator in case problems arise, although US tour operators often have Irish affiliates who are available to give additional assistance or make other arrangements on the spot.

To determine whether a package — or more specifically, *which* package — fits your travel plans, start by evaluating your interests and needs, deciding how much and what you want to spend, see, and do. Gather whatever package tour information is available for your schedule. Be sure that you take the time to read the brochure *carefully* to determine precisely what is included. Keep in mind that travel brochures are written to entice you into signing up for a package tour. Often the language is deceptive and devious. For example, a brochure may quote the lowest prices for a package tour based on facilities that are unavailable during the off-season, undesirable at any season, or just plain nonexistent. Information such as "breakfast included" (as it often is in packages to Ireland) or "plus tax" (which can add up) should be taken into account. Note, too, that prices quoted in brochures almost always are based on double occupancy: The rate listed is for each of two people sharing a double room, and if you travel alone, the supplement for single accommodations can raise the price considerably (see *Hints for Single Travelers,* in this section).

In this age of rapidly rising airfares, the brochure most often will *not* include the price of an airline ticket in the price of the package, though sample applicable fares from various gateway cities usually will be listed separately as extras to be added to the price of the ground arrangements. Before figuring your actual cost, check the latest fares with the airline, because the samples invariably are out of date by the time you read them. If the brochure gives more than one category of sample fares per gateway city — such as an individual tour-basing fare, a group fare, an excursion or other discount ticket, or, in the case of flights to Ireland, an APEX fare — your travel agent or airline tour desk will be able to tell you which one applies to the package you choose, depending on when you travel, how far in advance you book, and other factors. (An individual tour-basing fare is a fare computed as part of a package that includes land arrangements, thereby entitling a carrier to reduce the air portion almost to the absolute minimum. Though it always represents a saving over full-fare coach or economy, lately the individual tour-basing fare has not been as inexpensive as the excursion and other discount fares that also are available to individuals. The group fare usually is the least expensive fare, and it is the tour operator, not you, who makes up the group.) When the brochure does include round-trip transportation in the package price, don't forget to add the round-trip transportation cost from your home to the departure city to come up with the total cost of the package.

Finally, read the general information regarding terms and conditions and the responsibility clause (usually in fine print at the end of the descriptive literature) to determine the precise elements for which the tour operator is — and is not — liable. Here the tour operator frequently expresses the right to change services or schedules as long as equivalent arrangements are offered. This clause also absolves the operator of responsibility for circumstances beyond human control, such as floods or avalanches, or injury to you or your property. In reading, ask the following questions:

1. Does the tour include airfare or other transportation, sightseeing, meals, transfers, taxes, baggage handling, tips, or any other services? Do you want all these services?
2. If the brochure indicates that "some meals" are included, does this mean a welcoming and farewell dinner, two breakfasts, or every evening meal?
3. What classes of hotels are offered? If you will be traveling alone, what is the single supplement?
4. Does the tour itinerary or price vary according to the season?
5. Are the prices guaranteed; that is, if costs increase between the time you book and the time you depart, can surcharges unilaterally be added?

6. Do you get a full refund if you cancel? If not, be sure to obtain cancellation insurance.

7. Can the operator cancel if too few people join? At what point?

One of the consumer's biggest problems is finding enough information to judge the reliability of a tour packager, since individual travelers seldom have direct contact with the firm putting the package together. Usually, a retail travel agent is interposed between customer and tour operator, and much depends on his or her candor and cooperation. So ask a number of questions about the tour you are considering. For example: Has the agent ever used the package provided by this tour operator? How long has the tour operator been in business? Is the tour operator a member of the *United States Tour Operators Association (USTOA)?* (All members of *USTOA* must be bonded, meet certain basic financial levels of capitalization, and have been under the same management for at least three years. A list of members is available upon request; also offered is a useful brochure, *How to Select a Package Tour.* Contact the *USTOA,* 211 E. 51st St., Suite 12B, New York, NY 10022; phone: 212-944-5727. Also check the Better Business Bureau in the area where the tour operator is based to see if any complaints have been filed against it.) Which and how many companies are involved in the package? If air travel is by charter flight, is there an escrow account in which deposits will be held; if so, what is the name of the bank?

This last question is very important. US law requires that tour operators deposit every charter passenger's deposit and subsequent payment in a proper escrow account. Money paid into such an account cannot legally be used except to pay for the costs of a particular package or as a refund if the trip is canceled. To ensure the safe handling of your money, make your check payable to the escrow account — by law, the name of the depository bank must appear in the operator-participant contract, and usually is found in that mass of minuscule type on the back of the brochure. Write the details of the charter, including the destination and dates, on the face of the check; on the back, print "For Deposit Only." Your travel agent may prefer that you make your check out to the agency, saying that it will then pay the tour operator the fee minus commission. But it is perfectly legal to write your check as we suggest, and if your agent objects too strongly (the agent should have sufficient faith in the tour operator to trust him to send the proper commission), consider taking your business elsewhere. If you don't make your check out to the escrow account, you lose the protection of that escrow should the trip be canceled or the tour operator or travel agent fail. Furthermore, recent bankruptcies in the travel industry have served to point out that even the protection of escrow may not be enough to safeguard your investment. Increasingly, insurance is becoming a necessity (see *Insurance,* in this section), and payment by credit card has become popular since it offers some additional safeguards if the tour operator defaults.

■ **A word of advice:** Purchasers of vacation packages who feel they're not getting their money's worth are more likely to get a refund if they complain in writing to the operator — and bail out of the whole package immediately. Alert the tour operator or resort manager to the fact that you are dissatisfied, that you will be leaving for home as soon as transportation can be arranged, and that you expect a refund. They may have forms to fill out detailing your complaint; otherwise, state your case in a letter. Even if the availability of transportation home detains you, your dated, written complaint should help in procuring a refund from the operator.

SAMPLE PACKAGES TO IRELAND: There are so many packages available to Ireland that it's probably safe to say that just about any arrangement anyone might want is available for as long as it is wanted. The keynote is flexibility.

Nevertheless, those seeking the maximum in structure will find that the classic sightseeing tour by motorcoach, fully escorted and all-inclusive (or nearly), has withstood the test of time and still is well represented among the programs of major tour operators. Typically, these tours begin in a major city and take anywhere from 7 days to 2 weeks if visiting Ireland exclusively, and they may last as long as 3 to 4 weeks if combining Ireland with Great Britain (a common arrangement), covering highlighted attractions en route. At their briefest, the tours may begin in Shannon and trace a rough loop south to Limerick, Killarney, and the Ring of Kerry; continue to Blarney and Cork; then work their way north through Waterford and Wexford to Dublin, the terminus for some tours and the turnaround point for others, which then cut west across the country to the Galway area and to Shannon Airport for departure. With more time to spare, the itineraries generally range farther afield in the northwest part of Ireland, pushing into Connemara and visiting Donegal, but for the most part avoiding Northern Ireland itself — except for the occasional foray to visit the Belleek china factory just inside the border.

Hotel accommodations in these packages usually are characterized as first class or better, with a private bath or shower in all rooms, although more than a few tour packagers offer less expensive alternatives by providing more modest lodgings. Breakfast daily almost always is included, whereas the number of lunches and dinners may vary considerably, and meals include wine (or other alcoholic beverages) only when the tour literature clearly states so. Also included are transfers between airport and hotel, baggage handling, tips to maids and waiters, local transportation, and sightseeing excursions and admission fees, as well as any featured evening entertainment, personal expenses for laundry, incidentals and souvenirs, and tips to the motorcoach driver and to the tour escort, who remains with the group from beginning to end — almost everything, in fact, except round-trip airfare between the US and Ireland (which generally is shown separately).

Among these types of escorted, highly structured programs are those offered by *Travcoa*. The 18-day Grand Ireland tour includes the Aran Islands, Connemara, Donegal, Dublin, and Waterford and the 13-day Classic Ireland package tours Ashford, Connemara, Dublin, Killarney, and Waterford. Combination packages include a Scotland and Ireland tour, and an England, Ireland, and Scotland package. All meals are included. For information, conatact *Travcoa* (PO Box 2630, Newport Beach, CA 92658; phone: 800-992-2004 in California; 800-992-2003 elsewhere in the US). These tours are not for the budget traveler, but almost all the well-known tour operators have similar escorted programs of varying length and often with varying categories of hotels, thus creating less expensive alternatives to their standard packages.

Olson Travel World offers similar all-inclusive packages. This year's offerings include a 16-day Irish and British Discovery tour, which visits Cork, Killarney, Limerick, the Ring of Kerry, Shannon, and a number of destinations in England; the 22-day Shannon tour also includes Scotland and Wales. For information, contact *Olson Travel World*, 100 N. Sepulveda Blvd., Suite 1010, El Segundo, CA 90245 (phone: 213-615-0711 or 800-421-5785 in California; 800-421-2255 elsewhere in the US).

Abercrombie & Kent (1420 Kensington Rd., Oak Brook, IL 60521; phone: 708-954-2944 in Illinois; 800-323-7308 elsewhere in the US) offers all-inclusive package tours that take care of just about everything — right down to a traveling bellhop to handle your baggage. These tours, which are grouped under the heading "Great Britain and Europe Express Tours," include packages to Ireland.

David B. Mitchell & Company (200 Madison Ave., New York, NY 10016; phone: 800-696-1323 or 212-696-1323) also offers two 6-day motorcoach tours of Ireland: The Green Eire East tour visits Dublin, Gorey, Kilkenny, Tipperary, and Waterford; the Green Eire West tour includes County Clare, Clifden, Cong, and Letterfrack.

Globus-Gateway, which in 1990 had 79 first class tours of Europe, offers 2 all-Ireland tours, and many of its multi-country tours include Ireland. This year's offerings include an Introduction to Ireland package, which includes 8 days of discovery in Dublin, Kerry, and Waterford, and a 13-day Emerald Island tour, which visits the Aran Islands, Connemara, Dublin, Galway, Kerry, Killarney, Limerick, and Waterford. *Globus-Gateway* is affiliated with *Cosmos,* a tour operator specializing in low-cost motorcoach tours including a number of different Ireland tours. Both agencies can be contacted at 95-25 Queens Blvd., Rego Park, NY 11374 (phone: 800-221-0090 from the eastern US) or 150 S. Los Robles Ave., Pasadena, CA 91101 (phone: 818-449-2019, or 800-556-5454 from the western US).

Maupintour also offers a broad range of 12- to 21-day tours, including a variety of meal plans. Among their recent itineraries were two 15-day tours: a Best of Ireland package including Dublin, Ennis, Galway, Killarney, and Waterford and an England, Ireland, and Scotland tour that stops in Dublin and Limerick. For information, contact *Maupintour,* PO Box 807, Lawrence, KA 66044 (phone: 913-843-1211 in Kansas or abroad; 800-255-4266 elsewhere in the US).

TWA Getaway Tours (phone: 800-GETAWAY) offers a number of escorted tours throughout Ireland, including an 8-day Beauty of Ireland tour (visiting Cork, Dublin, Galway, and Waterford); a 12-day Emerald Islands tour, which follows the coast; a 17-day England, Ireland, and Scotland tour; and a 14-day Britannia tour, including England, Ireland, and Scotland.

Less restrictive arrangements for travelers who prefer more independence than that found on escorted tours are listed in the semi-escorted and hosted sections of tour catalogues. These may combine some aspects of an escorted tour, such as moving from place to place by motorcoach, with longer stays in one spot, where participants are at liberty but where a host or hostess — that is, a representative of the tour company — is available at a local office or even in the hotel to answer questions and assist in arranging activities and optional excursions.

Another equally common type of package to Ireland is the car tour or fly/drive arrangement, often described in brochures as a self-drive or go-as-you-please tour. These are independent vacations, geared to travelers who want to cover as much ground as they might on an escorted group sightseeing tour but who prefer to do it on their own. The most flexible plans include no more than a map, a rental car, and a block of as many prepaid hotel vouchers as are needed for the length of the stay (the packages typically are 4 or 7 days long, extendable by individual extra days or additional package segments), along with a list of participating hotels at which the vouchers are accepted. In most cases, only the first night's accommodation is reserved; from then on, travelers book their rooms one stop ahead as they drive from place to place, creating their own itinerary as they go. When the hotels are members of a chain or association — which they usually are — the staff of the last hotel can make reservations at the next one for you. In other cases, there may be a choice of reserving all accommodations before departure — usually for a fee. Operators offering these packages usually sell vouchers in more than one price category; travelers may have the option of upgrading accommodations by paying a supplement directly to more expensive establishments.

These packages to Ireland most often are offered in two price categories: a standard version covering overnights at hotels and a budget version covering overnights in simple bed and breakfast establishments — Ireland's "town and country homes" — and farmhouses. *CIE Tours International* (122 E. 42nd St., New York, NY 10168; phone: 212-972-5600 in New York City; 800-CIE-TOUR elsewhere in the US), for example, offers both versions. As with many plans, an upgrade option is offered: Those choosing the town and country home/farmhouse plan may upgrade their accommodations to a hotel when they choose by paying a supplement directly to the hotel. A nice touch is that those choosing the hotel plan may spend the night in a farmhouse or other home and receive a home-cooked dinner at no extra charge.

Other tour operators that offer similar self-drive packages include the following:

Brendan Tours, 15137 Califa St., Van Nuys, CA 91411 (phone: 800-421-8446 or 818-785-9696).

Brian Moore International Tours, 116 Main St., Medway, MA 02053 (phone: 800-982-2299).

Celtic International Tours, 161 Central Ave., Albany, NY 12206 (phone: 800-833-4373 or 518-463-5511).

Lismore Tours, 106 E. 31st St., New York, NY 10016 (phone: 212-685-0100 in New York State; 800-547-6673 elsewhere in the US).

Lynott Tours, 350 Fifth Ave., Suite 2619, New York, NY 10118 (phone: 800-537-7575 in New York, or 800-221 2474 elsewhere in the US).

British Airways Holidays (phone: 800-AIRWAYS), a subsidiary of *British Airways,* offers a variety of fly/drive and fly/rail packages, including a choice of mix-and-match independent holiday options ranging from bed and breakfast establishments to deluxe accommodations. Two particularly attractive packages are the Ireland Go-As-You-Wish package, which includes car rental and hotel accommodations (there is no pre-specified length of stay and travelers design their own itineraries), and the London Plus package, which includes a minimum stay of 3 days in London in combination with 3-day stays in Dublin, airport transfers between cities, accommodations, and a half day or more of touring in each city (extended-stay options also are available). Note that although these packages are bought in conjunction with a transatlantic ticket, this airfare may not be included in the basic package price.

Another type of arrangement is more restrictive in that the tour packager supplies an itinerary that must be followed day by day, with a specific hotel to be reached each night. Often these plans are more deluxe as well. The 9- to 14-day Irish itineraries in the Houses and Castles of Ireland and the Country Houses of Britain & Ireland programs designed by *Abercrombie & Kent International* (1420 Kensington Rd., Oak Brook, IL 60521; phone: 312-954-2944 or 800-323-7308) feature stays in hotels that are converted manor houses, castles, and other stately homes. The 7-day Shamrock Road itinerary packaged by *AutoVenture* (425 Pike St., Suite 502, Seattle, WA 98101, phone: 206-624-6033) is similarly deluxe. In addition, the itineraries of both packagers can be bought in either a self-drive or a chauffeured version. *Celtic International Tours* (address above) also has three chauffeur-driven itineraries, one of which — the 4-day Ireland North route — spends half its time in Northern Ireland; custom-tailored itineraries throughout Great Britain are also available.

David B. Mitchell & Company (200 Madison Ave., New York, NY 10016; phone: 800-696-1323 or 212-696-1323) also offers deluxe chauffeured/guided 10-day tours and covering either western or southwestern Ireland. Car tours with reserved but more economical lodgings are available from *Avis* (phone: 800-331-1084); custom itineraries throughout Ireland also are available. (Also see *Traveling by Car,* above.)

A further possibility for independent travelers is a "stay put" package, such as the popular Irish city packages. They appeal to travelers who want to be on their own and remain in one place for the duration of their vacation, although it is not unusual for travelers to buy more than one package at a time. Basically the city packages — no matter what the city — include round-trip transfer between airport and hotel, a choice of hotel accommodations (usually including breakfast) in several price ranges, plus any number of other features you may not need or want but would lose valuable time arranging if you did. Common package features are 1 or 2 half-day guided tours of the city; a boat cruise; passes for unlimited local travel by bus or train; discount cards for shops, museums, and restaurants; temporary membership in and admission to clubs, discotheques, or other nightspots; and car rental for some or all of your stay. Other features may be anything from a souvenir travel bag to tasting of local brews, dinner, and a show. The packages usually are a week long — although 4-day and 14-day packages are available, most packages can be extended by extra days — and often are hosted; that is, a representative of the tour company may be available at a local office or even in the hotel to answer questions, handle problems, and assist in arranging activities and option excursions.

Dublin alone is of interest to some visitors, and a few tour operators have packaged it that way. Both *American Express*'s travel agency (call 800-YES-AMEX or contact the nearest office of *American Express Travel*) and *CIE Tours International* (address above) have city packages to Dublin with some, but not all, of the above-mentioned features.

Such packages often are offered by the package travel divisions of major airlines. For instance, *Aer Lingus* offers a variety of stay-put packages. The Castle Short Stays package includes stays at three elegant Irish castles in County Clare, County Mayo, and County Clare. The package price includes round-trip airfare on *Aer Lingus*, 3 nights of castle accommodations, car rental, and full breakfast daily. Other similar offerings include Short Stay packages in Dublin and Killarney. For information, call 800-223-6537. Other major airlines also offer a variety of similar packages.

Special-interest tours are a growing part of the travel industry, and a staple among these packages to Ireland is the golf tour. The main allure is the opportunity to play at some of the most celebrated courses in the world: the *Killarney, Ballybunion, Portmarnock,* and *Royal Dublin* courses in the Irish Republic; the *Royal Portrush* and the *Royal County Down* courses in Northern Ireland. A fly/drive arrangement usually is involved, with rental car, hotel accommodations for a week or two, often one dinner per day, and some greens fees included. Some packages provide an entire week at one course or a choice of courses, and some combine a golfing holiday in Ireland with a visit to Scottish courses. *Scottish Golf Holidays* (9403 Kenwood Rd., Cincinnati, OH 45242; phone: 800-284-8884 or 513-984-0414) and *InterGolf* (PO Box 819, Champlain, NY 12919; phone: 800-363-6273; or 4150 St. Catherine St. W., Suite 390, Montreal, Quebec H3Z 2Y5, Canada; phone: 514-933-2772) both have self-drive golf packages and tours by escorted motorcoach, and the latter includes escorted sightseeing itineraries for non-golfers in the group. *Marsans Intercontinental* (19 W. 34 St., New York, NY 10001; phone: 212-239-3880 in New York State; 800-223-6114 elsewhere) offers a tour called The Greatest Golf Tour to Ireland Ever, as well as a tour throughout the United Kingdom; both are for serious golfers only. *Perry Golf* (8302 Dunwoody Pl., Suite 305, Atlanta, GA 30350; phone: 404-394-5400 or 800-344-5257) operates a basic 6-night Classic Ireland self-drive package that can be combined with a selection of 3-night "modular tours" to courses in Scotland, as well as with a tour to courses in Northern Ireland.

Other companies offering golf holidays in Ireland include the following:

Adventure Golf Holiday, 815 North Rd., Westfield, MA 01085 (phone: 800-628-9655 or 413-568-2855). Offers packages playing courses throughout the Irish Republic.

Adventures in Golf, 29 Valencia Dr., Nashua, NH 03062 (phone: 603-882-8367). Offers custom golf holidays throughout Ireland.

Atlantic Golf, 235 Post Rd. W., Westport, CT 06880 (phone: 800-443-8075 or 203-454-0090). Offers golf tours including courses in Ballybunion, Killarney, Waterville, and other areas of the Republic.

Berkeley Golf Tours, 275 Madison Ave., New York, NY 10016 (phone: 212-986-9176). Designs custom golf tours throughout in Ireland.

Bestours, Box 1596, Bonita Springs, FL 33959-1596 (phone: 800-231-2431 or 813-495-1500). Offers golf packages throughout Ireland.

Golfing Holidays, 231 E. Millbrae Ave., Millbrae, CA 94030 (phone: 415-697-0230). Offers custom golf packages to Ireland's southwest and east coasts.

Golfpac Inc., Box 940490, 901 N. Lake Destiny Dr., Suite 192, Maitland, FL

32794-0490 (phone: 800-327-0878 or 407-660-8277). Offers custom golf packages throughout Ireland.

Grasshopper Golf Tours, 403 Hill Ave., Glen Ellyn, IL 60137 (phone: 708-858-1660). Offers custom golf packages for individuals and groups.

Henry Hudson Tours, Box 155, Malden on Hudson, NY 12453 (phone: 800-431-6064 or 914-246-8453). Often offers golf tours to Ireland; as we went to press this year's offerings had not yet been determined.

Ireland Golf Tours, 251 E. 85th St., New York, NY 10028 (phone: 800-346-5388 or 212-772-8220). Offers golf tours of the southwest coast and group packages including golf tournaments.

Isle Inn Tours, 113 S. Washington St., Alexandria, VA 22314 (phone: 800-237-9376 or 703-739-2277). Offers fly/drive golf packages throughout Ireland.

ITC Golf Tours, Box 5144, Long Beach, CA 90805 (phone: 800-257-4981 or 213-595-6905). Designs custom golf tours throughout Ireland.

Owenoak International Inc., 88 Main St., New Canaan, CT 06840 (phone: 800-426-4498 or 203-972-3777). Offers a 7-day golf tour in the southwest, including luxury accommodations in hotels or castles. Add-on tours elsewhere in Ireland also are available.

Value Holidays, 10224 N. Port Washington Rd., Mequon, WI 53092 (phone: 800-558-6850 or 414-241-6373). Offers golf packages on the southwest coast; custom packages throughout Ireland also are available.

Information about many more golf packages can be obtained from a travel agent or the Irish Tourist Board or the Northern Ireland Tourist Board.

Among other sports-oriented packages are those focused on — and guaranteeing entrance in — marathons. *Marathon Tours* (108 Main St., Boston, MA 02129; phone: 617-242-7845), which sends runners off to races around the world, and *Grimes Travel* (250 W. 57th St., New York, NY 10019; phone: 212-307-7797 in New York State; 800-832-7778 elsewhere) both offer week-long stays in Ireland for the Dublin Marathon in October.

Fisherfolk might enjoy the opportunity to fish for Irish trout and salmon on one of the fishing tours offered by *Fishing International* (Hilltop Estate, 4010 Montecito Ave., Santa Rosa CA 95404; phone: 800-950-4242 or 707-542-4242). These week-long packages include accommodations in small country inns, all meals, personal guides, and the opportunity to exchange fish stories about the one that got away with fellow enthusiasts.

Horseback riding holidays are the province of *FITS Equestrian* (2011 Alamo Pintado Rd., Solvang, CA 93463; phone: 805-688-9494), whose choices — not for beginners — include 6 days of riding the Connemara trails (nights are spent in hotels), 8 days polishing skills at the *Greystones Equestrian Centre* at Castle Leslie in County Monaghan, as well as an 8-day package in the vicinity of Lough Derg that stresses both riding and cuisine.

A variety of biking packages and hiking trips through rural Ireland are other possibilities. For information on these and other adventure package tours, see *Camping and Caravanning, Hiking and Biking* below.

Still another possibility — and an increasingly popular one — is an inland waterway trip. Many travelers simply rent their own boat, but if you prefer to let someone else do the driving (as well as the cooking), book aboard a hotel-boat cruise. Other inland cruises are discussed in *Traveling by Ship,* in this section, and *Wonderful Waterways and Coastal Cruises* in DIVERSIONS.

Special-interest packages of a non-sporting nature include Crafts of Ireland, an escorted motorcoach tour offered by *Lynott Tours* (address above). Participants on the 10-day trip see Waterford crystal, Belleek pottery, and Donegal carpets and tweeds being made; take in Aran knitting demonstrations; talk to quilters and lacemakers; visit a design center; and spend a day at a school where they get the chance to learn something new about their own craft. The Heritage Roots Tours offered by *Celtic International Tours* (address above) are for travelers of Irish extraction who wish to know more about their ancestors. Each departure in the series focuses on researching specific family names (usually no more than four), and each is escorted by an expert genealogist who accompanies participants to sites pertinent to their family tree while not neglecting the more usual attractions. Tours for music and opera lovers are the specialty of *Dailey-Thorp, Inc.* (315 W. 57th St., New York, NY 10019; phone: 212-307-1555), which regularly combines a visit to the *Wexford Opera Festival* in October with visits to other, non-Irish events.

Off-season, from November through March, numerous long-weekend packages to Ireland become available, usually departing on a Thursday and returning on a Monday. Among these are *Aer Lingus*'s Pub Tour of Ireland and the Shop Ireland package offered by *Matterhorn Travel Service* (2450 Riva Rd., Annapolis, MD 21401; phone: 301-224-2230 in Maryland; 800-638-9150 elsewhere). The novelty for participants in the latter is a few hours of private shopping in the Shannon duty-free shop early in the weekend (in addition to the usual rushed spree before boarding the flight home) and an evening of private shopping at Dublin's *Brown Thomas* department store, dinner included.

For groups of 15 or more travelers, *Travel Concepts* offers a variety of custom-designed theme-oriented tours (your choice of focus) throughout Europe, including Ireland. For information, contact *Travel Concepts,* 62 Commonwealth Ave., Suite 3, Boston, MA 02116 (phone: 617-266-8450).

Other tours also visit major cities each year to enjoy the cultural attractions. For instance, art enthusiasts will enjoy *Prospect Art Tours*' packages visiting key museums and private galleries and art collections, as well as archaeological sites throughout Ireland. For information, contact *Prospect Art Tours* (454-458 Chiswick High Rd., London W45TT; phone: 800-727-2771 or 800-752-4628 throughout the US; 44-81-995-2151 or 44-81-995-2163 elsewhere worldwide) or their US agent, *The British Connection* (Suite 240, 2490 Black Rock Turnpike, Fairfield, CT 06430; phone: 203-254-7221).

Camping and Caravanning, Hiking and Biking

CAMPING AND CARAVANNING: Ireland welcomes campers, whether they come alone or with a group, with tents, or in recreational vehicles — generally known in Ireland as "caravans" (a term that technically refers to towable campers as opposed to fully motorized vehicles, known as "minibuses" or "minivans"). Camping probably is the best way to enjoy the Irish countryside. And, fortunately, campgrounds in Ireland are plentiful.

Where to Camp – Caravanning is extremely popular with European vacationers, and many parks cater more to the caravanner than to the tent dweller. Some campgrounds have minimal facilities, and others are quite elaborate, with a variety of amenities on the premises. Most sites are open from *Easter* through October, but they fill quickly at the height of the summer season, so it's a good idea to arrive early in the day if a "pitch" has not been reserved in advance. In the most popular areas, if you want to camp during the peak summer season, you should reserve a site as early as possible.

In some communities it is possible to camp free on public grounds. Ask the city police or local tourist information office about regulations. To camp on private property you first must obtain the permission of the landowner or tenant — and assume the responsibility of leaving the land exactly as it was found in return for the hospitality.

Irish campgrounds generally are well marked. Still, it's best to have a map or check the information available in one of the comprehensive guides to camping sites (see below). It's also not always easy to find camping facilities open before June or after September, so a guide that gives this information comes in particularly handy off-season.

Directors of campgrounds often have a great deal of information about their region, and some even will arrange local tours or recommend the best restaurants, shops, beaches, or attractions in the immediate area. Campgrounds also provide the atmosphere and opportunity to meet other travelers and exchange useful information. Too much so, sometimes — the popularity of the European campgrounds causes them to be quite crowded during the summer, and campsites frequently are so close together that any attempt at privacy or getting away from it all is sabotaged. As campgrounds fill quickly throughout the season, and the more isolated sites always go first, it's a good idea to arrive early in the day and reserve your chosen spot — which leaves you free to explore the area for the rest of the day. (At the height of the season, however, if you do not have advance reservations, you may be lucky to get even a less desirable site.)

A number of comprehensive guides to sites are available. The Northern Ireland Tourist Board publishes the free booklet *Northern Ireland: Camping and Caravan Parks,* listing more than 100 sites; it is available from Tourist Information Centres in Northern Ireland and from British Tourist Authority offices in the US (see *Tourist Information Offices,* in this section, for addresses). The Irish Tourist Board publishes the yearly guide *Caravan & Camping Parks,* listing all sites meeting the board's minimum standards, as well as a grading of the facilities, descriptions of the sites, and fees. The booklet is distributed free at Irish Tourist Board offices in North America (see *Tourist Information Offices,* in this section).

The *American Automobile Association (AAA)* offers a number of useful resources, including its 600-page *Travel Guide to Europe* and the 64-page *Motoring Europe,* as well as a variety of useful maps; contact the nearest branch of *AAA* or the national office (see *Traveling by Car,* in this section). In addition, the *Automobile Association of Great Britain (AA)* publishes a comprehensive guide, *Camping and Caravanning in Europe* ($12.95), which lists about 4,000 sites throughout Europe, inspected and rated by the *AA,* and provides other information of interest to campers. It is available from the *AA* (Farnum House, Basingstoke, Hampshire RG21 2EA, England). Another guide is *The Campers Companion to Northern Europe* (Williamson; $13.95), which lists over a dozen sites in Ireland; it is available from travel bookstores.

The French international camping organization *Fédération Internationale de Camping et Caravaning* issues a pass, called a *carnet,* that entitles the bearer to information on and modest discounts at many campgrounds throughout Europe. It is available in the US from the *National Campers and Hikers Association* (4804 Transit Rd., Bldg. 2, Depew, NY 14043; phone: 716-668-6242) for a fee of $23, which includes membership in the association, as well as useful camping information. The *carnet* is not necessary for camping in Ireland, but it does open the gates to the sites operated exclusively for members by another major group, the *Camping and Caravanning Club of Great Britain and Ireland* (11 Lower Grosvenor Pl., London SW1WOEY; phone: 44-71-828-1012). The club publishes a free annual guide to its own and other British and Irish sites and provides information and assistance to members, foreign visitors with the *carnet,* and foreign visitors without a *carnet* who become temporary members. Additionally, almost all tourist offices provide brochures about camping in the area, but you will probably have to request it.

Necessities – For outdoor camping, necessities include a tent with flyscreens (the lighter and easier to carry and assemble the better); a sleeping bag; a foam pad, air mattress, or one of the new combination self-inflatable foam mattresses; a waterproof ground cloth; a rain poncho (which, in a pinch, can double as a ground cloth); a first-aid kit (including sunscreen and insect repellent); sewing and toilet kits (including a roll of toilet paper in a plastic bag); a backpack stove; matches; nested cooking pots and cooking utensils; a canteen; a three-quarter ax (well sharpened and sheath-protected); a jackknife; and a flashlight with an extra set of batteries. If you want a campfire, you may want to pick up some supplies (and wood, charcoal, or peat) en route to the campground (though some campgrounds do sell bundles of firewood) — particularly where there is little wood. Be aware, however, that fires are prohibited in many areas.

If you have room bring (or pick up on arrival) a compact Coleman lantern (with extra mantles, fuel, and a funnel) or battery-powered light (with extra batteries); if not, candles will do. You can make a simple windscreen that also will reflect and amplify candlelight using aluminium foil, which also is useful for campfire cooking. Small Coleman-type lanterns that will take either candle inserts or lamp oil are another alternative; these are more practical than the standard lanterns, as they are designed for backpackers and the glass is protected by a metel sheath for safe transport.

For the backpack stove, consider a Mountain Safety Research (MSR) or similar model, which — unlike most stoves, which run only on white gas (which is hard to find in some parts of Europe) — also works with kerosene or alcohol. No matter what kind of camp stove you choose, however, it still is a good idea to bring along extra fuel. A stove helps out when you're knee-deep in the mud of a rainy day, and in-camp cooking is a great way to help stretch your travel funds.

Also include a canteen and/or plastic containers for water. Unless you are told that the campground where you are staying provides purified water, you should use it only for washing (don't even brush your teeth with it). In such cases, use only bottled, purified, or boiled water for drinking. To purify tap water, either use a water purification kit (available at most camping supply stores) or bring the water to a full, rolling boil over a camp stove. Unless deep in the wilderness, it is inadvisable to use water from streams, rivers, or lakes — even purified.

Keep food simple. Unless backpacking deep in the wilds — there is wilderness in Ireland, but you can't get *too* many days away from civilization — you probably will be close enough to a store to stock up on perishables. Staples such as sugar, coffee, powdered milk, rice, and other grains, and a basic assortment of spices, can be carried along. Dehydrated food has become quite popular among both hikers and campers, but it can be expensive. An economical option for the more enterprising camper is to dry a variety of food at home; camping supply stores and bookstores carry cookbooks covering this simple process. Keep in mind, particularly in wilderness areas, that accessible food will lure scavenging wildlife that may invade tents and vehicles. As a basic safety precaution, it is advisable to hang all foodstuffs from a tree some distance from your sleeping area. Bring along an extra waterproof stuff sack (available in a variety of sizes in camping supply stores) and some rope for this purpose.

Most experienced campers (particularly hikers and bikers; see below) prefer to bring their own tried and true equipment, but camping equipment is available for sale or rent throughout Ireland, and rentals can be booked in advance through any number of outfitters. The *AA* guide and some of the other above-mentioned guides to camping and caravanning contain lists of outfitters, and the national tourist offices in the US can supply information on reliable dealers.

Recreational Vehicles – Known in Ireland as caravans (or minibuses or minivans), recreational vehicles (RVs) will appeal most to the kind of person who prefers the flexibility in accommodations — there are countless campgrounds throughout Ireland and many provide RV hookups — and enjoys camping with a little extra comfort.

An RV undoubtably saves a traveler a great deal of money on accommodations, and if cooking appliances are part of the unit, on food as well. However, it is important to remember that renting an RV is a major expense; also, any kind of RV increases gas consumption considerably.

Although the term "recreational vehicle" is applied to all manner of camping vehicles, whether towed or self-propelled, generally the models available for rent in Ireland are either towable campers (caravans) or motorized RVs. The motorized models usually are minivans or minibuses — vans customized in various ways for camping, often with elevated roofs — and larger, coach-type, fully equipped homes on wheels, requiring electrical hookups at night to run the TV set, air conditioning, and kitchen appliances. Although most motorized models are equipped with standard shift, occasionally automatic shift vehicles may be available for an additional charge. Towed vehicles can be hired overseas but usually are not offered by US or international companies.

If you are planning to caravan all over Europe, make sure that whatever vehicle you choose is equipped to deal with the electrical and gas standards of all countries on your itinerary. There are differences, for instance, between the bottled gas supplied in Ireland and on the Continent. You should have either a sufficient supply of the type the camper requires or equipment that can use more than one type. When towing a camper, note that nothing towed is covered automatically by the liability insurance of the primary vehicle, so the driver's Green Card must carry a specific endorsement for the towed vehicle.

Whether driving a camper or towing, it is essential to have some idea of the terrain you'll be encountering en route, and only experienced drivers should drive large campers, particularly in areas such as the mountains of Connemara where the terrain can be quite steep. In fact, grades sometimes can be too steep for certain vehicles to negotiate, and some roads are off limits to towed caravans. Your best source of information on weather and road conditions is one of the automobile clubs discussed in *Traveling by Car,* in this section, or local tourist board offices in Ireland.

Recreational vehicles can be rented from international and Irish car rental companies in the major cities (see *Traveling by Car,* in this section), although you probably will have to do some calling around to find one. RV rentals also can be arranged from the US through several companies, including the following:

Auto-Europe, PO Box 1097, Camden, ME 04843 (phone: 207-236-8235 in Maine; 800-223-5555 throughout the US; 800-458-9503 in Canada). Offers minibus rentals in Dublin, Galway, Killarney, Shannon, and Sligo.

Avis Rent-A-Car, 6128 E. 38th St., Tulsa, OK 74135 (phone: 800-331-1084, ext. 7719). Offers minibus rentals in Cork, Dublin, Galway, Kerry, Limerick, Mayo, Shannon, Waterford, and Wexford.

Connex International, 983 Main St., Peekskill, NY 10566 (phone: 800-333-3949). Offers minibus rentals throughout the Irish Republic.

Foremost Euro-Car Inc., 5430 Van Nuys Blvd., Suite 306, Van Nuys, CA 91401 (phone: 818-786-1960 or 800-272-3299 in California; 800-423-3111 elsewhere in the US). Offers minibus rentals in Cork, Dublin, Galway, Killarney, Limerick, and Shannon.

Kemwel Group, 106 Calvert St., Harrison, NY 10528 (phone: 800-678-0678 or 914-835-5555). Offers minivan rentals in Cork, Dublin, Dún Laoghaire, Rosslare, and Shannon.

The general policy with the above agencies is to make reservations far enough in advance to receive a voucher required to pick up the vehicle at the designated location in Europe. (Early reservations also are advisable as the supply of RVs is limited and the demand great.)

Among companies offering RV rentals in France (which by special arrangement may be transported to Ireland via ferry — but must be returned to France) are the following:

FCI Location, Zone Industrielle de Saint-Brendan, Quentin 22800, France (phone: 33-96-74-08-36). Rents motorized RVs in France.

Trois Soleils, Maison Trois Soleils, 2 Route de Paris, Ittenheim 67117, France (phone: 33-88-69-17-17 for reservations; 33-30-69-06-60 for the Paris branch). Rents motorized RVs, as well as some basic campers in France; pick-up and drop-off locations include Bordeaux, Montpelier, Paris, and Strasbourg.

For information on how to operate, choose, and use a recreational vehicle, see *Living on Wheels* by Richard A. Wholters (Dutton; currently out of print; check your library or bookstore). You also might want to subscribe to *Trailer Life,* published by *TL Enterprises* (29901 Agoura Rd., Agoura, CA 91301; phone: 800-234-3450 or 818-991-4980). A 1-year subscription costs $12; $9 for members of the Good Sam Club, which provides discounts on a variety of services for RV owners and which also is run by *TL Enterprises.*

Another useful resource is the complimentary package of information on RVs offered by the *Recreational Vehicle Industry Association (RVIA).* It includes a catalogue of RV sources and consumer information; write to the *Recreational Vehicle Industry Association* (Dept. RK, PO Box 2999, Reston, VA 22090; phone: 703-620-6003). The *Recreational Vehicle Rental Association (RVRA),* an RV dealers group, publishes an annual rental directory, *Who's Who in RV Rentals;* send $5 to the *Recreational Vehicle Rental Association* (3251 Old Lee Hwy., Suite 500, Fairfax, VA 22030; phone: 703-591-7130).

Finally, you may want to subscribe to *Trailblazer,* a recreational vehicle and motor-home magazine. A year's subscription costs $24; write to *Trailblazer,* 1000 124th Ave. NE, Bellevue, WA 98005.

Horse-drawn Caravans – A caravan vacation in an entirely different spirit is possible in Ireland, where touring in a horse-drawn wagon is common. The vehicle is barrel-shaped, in Gypsy style, and has bunks for up to 4 people, as well as a gas stove for cooking. No experience in handling the horse is required: The company that rents the caravan teaches harnessing and unharnessing, plus the basics of horse care, before anyone sets out. Not much ground can be covered this way (rentals usually are by the week), but the caravan bases generally are located in very scenic areas that are pleasant to explore in depth. Most companies provide a route to follow, pointing out where to find bathroom facilities and the best spots to stop for the night. Cost of renting the caravan starts at approximately $205 per week, including oats for the horse, but no supplementary charges for any grazing the animal might do after parking for the night. The Irish Tourist Board publishes an information sheet, which includes a list of operators to contact to reserve a horse-drawn caravan, something that should be done well in advance to rent one at the height of the summer.

Organized Camping Trips – A packaged camping tour abroad is a good way to have your cake and eat it, too. The problems of advance planning and day-to-day organizing are left to someone else, yet the purchaser still reaps the savings benefits that shoestring travel affords. Be aware, however, that these packages usually are geared to the young, with ages 18 to 35 as common limits. Transfer from place to place is by bus (as on other sightseeing tours), overnights are in tents, and meal arrangements vary. Often there is a food fund that covers meals in restaurants or in the camp; sometimes there is a chef, and sometimes the cooking is done by the participants themselves.

The *Specialty Travel Index* is a directory for special-interest travel and an invaluable resource. Listings include tour operators specializing in camping, as well as myriad other interests that combine nicely with a camping trip, such as biking, ballooning, diving, horseback riding, canoeing, motorcycling, and river rafting. The index costs $5 per copy, $8 for a year's subscription of two issues. Contact *Specialty Travel Index,* 305 San Anselmo Ave., Suite 217, San Anselmo, CA 94960 (phone: 415-459-4900).

Among its numerous outdoor adventures, *Mountain Travel* (6420 Fairmont Ave.,

El Cerrito, CA 94530; phone: 415-527-8100 in California; 800-227-2384 elsewhere in the US) often offers camping tours in Ireland. In addition, a number of packagers listed under "Hiking" and "Biking" (below) also may offer these pursuits in combination with camping — it pays to call and ask when planning your trip.

HIKING: If you would rather eliminate all the gear and planning and take to the outdoors unencumbered, park the car and go for a day's hike.

Walking is a good way to explore any country, and Ireland is no exception. Trails abound in Ireland, as does specific information on how to find them. Tourist authorities distribute information sheets on walking and mountaineering, and there are numerous other sources for those intent on getting about on their own. By all means, cover as much area as you can by foot; you'll see everything in far more detail than you would from the window of any conveyance. For information on suggested hikes throughout Ireland, see *Great Walks and Mountain Rambles* in DIVERSIONS.

The Irish Tourist Board and the Northern Ireland Tourist Board distribute information sheets on walking and mountaineering, and there are several other sources of information for those intent on getting about on their own steam. The *Federation of Mountaineering Clubs of Ireland* (20 Leopardstown Gardens, Blackrock, County Dublin; phone: 1-881266) can be contacted for information and advice, and will provide a list of general and regional walking and climbing guidebooks that can be ordered through its office or bought at bookstores in Ireland. *Irish Walk Guides,* a series of six regional guidebooks published by Gill and Macmillan, are sold in bookstores throughout Northern Ireland and the Republic. Each contains full details of the best hill walks in the area, maps, and notes on climate, flora and fauna, and mountain safety. *The Open Forest,* a guide to state parks and forests, is available free from the Irish Tourist Board in Ireland, as is *Hill Walking and Rock Climbing.* (See *Tourist Information Offices,* in this section, for tourist board addresses.) Guides for touring major cities also are available in bookstores and at newsstands throughout Europe.

For those who are hiking on their own, without benefit of a guide or group, a map of the trail is a must. Ordnance Survey maps of the Landranger series, on the scale of 1¼ inches to 1 mile (1:50,000), cover the whole of Ireland. To obtain a price list, write to the Ordnance Survey Office (Phoenix Park, County Dublin) — Wicklow Way is an especially popular hiking/walking map for those touring on foot; for Northern Ireland, contact the *Government Bookstore* (Chichester St., Belfast 1; phone: 232-234488). A British company that specializes in maps and other publications for hikers and climbers is the *Robertson MacCarta Shop* (122 King's Cross Rd., London WC1X 9DS, England; phone: 71-278-8278).

To make outings safe and pleasant, find out in advance about the trails you plan to hike and be realistic about your own physical limitations. If hiking in higher altitudes, keep in mind that it is easy to underestimate the challenge of the grade combined with the thinner air. Choose an easy route if you are out of shape. Stick to defined trails unless you are an experienced hiker or know the area well. Whether heading out for a short jaunt or a longer trek, particularly in more remote areas, let someone know where you are going and when you expect to be back. If the hike is impromptu, leave a note in or on your car.

All you need to set out are a pair of sturdy shoes and socks; jeans or long pants to keep branches, nettles, and bugs off your legs; a canteen of water; a hat to protect you from the sun; and, if you like, a picnic lunch. It is a good idea to dress in layers, so that you can add or remove clothing according to the elevation and weather. Make sure, too, to wear clothes with pockets or bring a pack to keep your hands free. Some useful and important pocket- or pack-stuffers include trail mix, a jackknife, waterproof matches, a small first-aid kit, a map, and a compass. You also may want to tuck in a lightweight waterproof poncho (available in camping supply stores) in case of unexpected showers.

■ **A word of warning:** It is particularly important to wear socks, long pants, and long-sleeve shirts when hiking in wooded areas due to the danger of Neuro Borreliosis, which is spread through the bite of the deer tick and other ticks. First diagnosed years ago in Europe, this disease recently has become familiar to Americans as Lyme Borreliosis (also known as "Lyme Tick Disease"). A strong insect repellent designed to repel ticks also may be helpful. The initial symptoms of this disease often are a swelling and/or a rash, generally accompanied by flu-like symptoms — such as fever and aching muscles. Readily curable in the early stages through antibiotics, if left untreated it can lead to serious complications. For information on precautions and treatment, contact the *Lyme Borreliosis Foundation,* PO Box 462, Tolland, CT 06084 (phone: 203-871-2900).

Organized Hiking Trips – Those who prefer to travel as part of an organized group should refer to the January/February issue of *Sierra* magazine for the *Sierra Club*'s annual list of foreign outings. The *Sierra Club* offers a selection of trips each year, usually about 2 weeks in length. Recent itineraries included hiking excursions in Ireland, and other tours in Ireland combined hiking with biking. Some are backpacking trips, moving to a new camp each day; others make day hikes from a base camp. Major distances often are traveled in minibuses, and overnights can be in small hotels, inns, guesthouses, bed and breakfast farmhouses, or campgrounds and simple huts. For information, contact the *Sierra Club,* Outing Department, 730 Polk St., San Francisco, CA 94109 (phone: 415-776-2211).

American Youth Hostels (AYH; address below) also sponsors foreign hiking trips, though fewer than its foreign biking trips. As with the *Sierra Club,* the itineraries offered vary from year to year, usually ranging from around 15 to 52 days. *AYH*'s recent roster has included various trips in Ireland. For information on upcoming offerings, contact the *American Youth Hostels* (address below; see *Hints for Single Travelers,* in this section, for membership information.)

Mountain Travel, a company specializing in adventure trips around the world, offers a variety of trips, from easy walks that can be undertaken by anyone in good health to those that require basic or advanced mountaineering experience. This year, an Irish walking tour and a Kerry Ways tour are offered; both include accommodations in guesthouses, and transportation between regions in minibuses. Note that *Mountain Travel* also designs special itineraries for independent travelers. Contact *Mountain Travel,* 6420 Fairmont Ave., El Cerrito, CA 94530 (phone: 415-527-8100 in California; 800-227-2384 elsewhere in the US).

Other companies that offer hiking tours in Ireland include the following:

British Coastal Trails, 150 Carob Way, Coronado, CA 92118 (phone: 619-437-1211). Offers 12-day inn-to-inn hiking tours in the Irish Republic, which cover County Kerry and County Clare and end in Killarney.

English Wanderer, 13 Wellington Court, Spencers Wood, Reading RG7 1BN, England (phone: 44-734-882515). Offers 7-day walking tours of the Irish Republic's Kerry Way.

Forum Travel International, 91 Gregory, No. 21, Pleasant Hill, CA 94523 (phone: 415-671-2900). Offers 6- and 8-day leisurely walking tours through the Kenmarea Bay area, including accommodations in a cozy waterfront hotel. Other enticing itineraries are offered each year, generally in four grades of difficulty — the most energetic grade covering as many as 20 miles (32 km) a day, and geared to those already accustomed to hard mountain walking.

Progressive Travel, 1932 First Ave., Suite 1100, Seattle, WA 98101 (phone: 800-245-2229). Itineraries include inn-to-inn walking tours starting and ending in Shannon. (Also see "Biking," below.)

Sobek Expeditions, PO Box 1089, Angels Camp, CA 95222 (phone: 209-736-4524). This adventure packager offers 8-day walking tours of Galway.

Wilderness Travel, 801 Allston Way, Berkeley, CA 94710 (phone: 415-548-0420 in California or abroad; 800-247-6700 elsewhere in the US). Offers a wide range of hiking trips throughout Europe, including some to Ireland, similar to those packaged by *Mountain Travel,* above. (Also see "Biking," below.)

An alternative to dealing directly with the above companies is to contact *All Adventure Travel,* a specialist in hiking and biking trips worldwide. This company, which acts as a representative for numerous special tour packagers offering such outdoor adventures, can provide a wealth of detailed information about each packager and programs offered. They also will help you design and arrange all aspects of a personalized itinerary. This company operates much like a travel agency, collecting commissions from the packagers. Therefore, there is no additional charge for these services. For information, contact *All Adventure Travel,* PO Box 4307, Boulder, CO 80306 (phone: 800-537-4025 or 303-939-8885.)

BIKING: For young or energetic travelers, a bicycle offers a marvelous way to see a country, especially where the terrain is conducive to easy cycling, as it is in most parts of Ireland, a popular European destination for tourists on two wheels.

Much of Ireland is rural and, except for the environs of industrialized cities, nearly traffic-free. Secondary roads can be found almost everywhere, threaded neatly through picturesque stretches of countryside. The landscape tends to be flat to rolling in the middle of the island, hilly on the coast, and scenic throughout. Biking does have its drawbacks: Little baggage can be carried, travel is slow, and cyclists are exposed to the elements, which in Ireland means a mild climate with cool evenings — and the ever-present possibility of showers. However, should a cyclist need rest or refuge from the weather, there always is a welcoming pub or comfortable bed and breakfast establishment around the next bend. And besides being a viable way to tour Ireland — and to burn calories to make room for unlimited portions of hearty Irish food — biking is a great way to meet people.

Road Safety – While the car may be the bane of cyclists — although Irish motorists are courteous and well accustomed to cyclists — cyclists who do not follow the rules of the road strike terror into the hearts of drivers. Follow the same rules and regulations as motor vehicle drivers. Note that although bicyclists usually follow the flow of cars, in Ireland they most often ride against the traffic — staying to the right while motorists drive on the left. Stay to the right side of the road. Ride no more than two abreast — single file where traffic is heavy. Keep three bicycle lengths behind the cycle in front of you. Stay alert to sand, gravel, potholes, and wet or oily surfaces, all of which can make you lose control. Wear bright clothes and use lights or wear reflective material at dusk or at night, and, above all — even though Irish cyclists often don't — always wear a helmet.

Choosing, Renting, and Buying a Bike – Although many bicycling enthusiasts choose to take along their own bikes, bicycles are available for rent throughout Ireland. Long and short rentals are widely available; however, particularly in rural areas, it may pay to check ahead. Almost all Irish trains have facilities for bike transport at nominal fees (see below).

As an alternative to renting, you might consider buying a bicycle in Ireland, often for less than you might pay in the US. However, the bicycle may take some getting used to — seats especially need breaking in at first — and if you bring it home, it will be subject to an import duty by US Customs if its price (or the total of all purchases made abroad) exceeds $400. When evaluating this cost, take into account additional charges for shipping. Those planning to buy a bicycle, be it in the US or Ireland, should consider a good-quality, lightweight touring bike that has the all-important low gears for hill climbing and riding against the wind. Particularly if you're riding primarily in hilly or mountainous regions, you may want to look at one of the specially designed mountain bikes. A European bicycle purchased in the US should have proof-of-purchase papers to avoid potential customs problems. Bike shops in Ireland that rent and sell bicycles sometimes also sell used ones — a particularly economical option that may be even less expensive than a long-term rental. One such bicycle shop is *The Bike Store* (58 Lower Gardiner St., Dublin 1; phone: 1-725399).

A bicycle is the correct size for you if you can straddle its center bar with feet flat on the ground and still have an inch or so between your crotch and the bar. (Nowadays, because women's old-fashioned barless bikes are not as strong as men's, most women use men's bicycles.) The seat height is right if your leg is just short of completely extended when you push the pedal to the bottom of its arc.

To be completely comfortable, divide your weight; put about 50% on your saddle and about 25% each on your arms and legs. To stop sliding in your seat and for better support, set your saddle level. A firm saddle is better than a soft springy one for a long ride. Experienced cyclists keep the tires fully inflated (pressure requirements vary widely, but always are imprinted on the side of the tire; stay within 5 pounds of the recommended pressure). Do not use top, or tenth, gear all the way; for most riding the middle gears are best. On long rides remember that until you are very fit, short efforts with rests in between are better than one long haul, and pedal at an even pace.

The happiest biker in a foreign country is the one who arrives best prepared. Bring saddlebags, a handlebar bag, a tool kit that contains a bike wrench, screwdriver, pliers, tire repair kit, cycle oil, and work gloves, a bike repair book, a helmet (a rarity among Irish cyclists), a rain suit, a water bottle, a flashlight with an extra set of batteries, a small first-aid kit, and muscles that have been limbered up in advance.

Even the smallest towns usually have a bike shop, so it's not difficult to replace or add to gear; however, because tires and tubes are sized to metric dimensions in some parts of Ireland, when riding your own bike, bring extras from home. Seasoned bikers swear that the second day of any trip always is the worst, so keep this in mind and be ready to meet the mental and physical challenges ahead.

Airlines going from the US (or elsewhere) to Ireland generally allow bicycles to be checked as baggage and require that the pedals be removed, handlebars be turned sideways, and the bike be in a shipping carton, which some airlines provide, subject to availability — call ahead to make sure. If buying a shipping cartons from a bicycle shop, check the airline's specifications and also ask about storing the carton at the destination airport so you can use it again for the return flight. Although some airlines charge only a nominal fee, if a passenger already has checked two pieces of baggage there may be an additional excess baggage charge of $70 to $80 for the bicycle. As regulations vary from carrier to carrier, be sure to call well in advance of departure to find out your airline's specific regulations. As with other baggage, make sure that the bike is thoroughly labeled with your name, a business address and phone number, and the correct airport destination code.

When the going gets rough, remember that cyclists can avoid the arduous parts of the journey by loading their bicycles on the luggage van of a train. Bicycles generally are transported at approximately 25% of the standard (second class) passenger fare on *Northern Ireland Railways* routes; check with the station the day before departure. On trains in the Irish Republic, the cost of transporting a bicycle is about $23 per trip, regardless of the distance traveled. There's a $25 bicycle supplement fee for those with a Rambler Ticket (a special ticket allowing unlimited travel within a set period of time; see *Traveling by Train,* in this section).

A good book to help you plan a trip is *Bicycle Touring in Europe,* by Karen and Gary Hawkins (Pantheon Books; $8.95); it offers information on buying and equipping a touring bike, useful clothing and supplies, and helpful techniques for the long-distance biker. Another good general book is *Europe by Bike,* by Karen and Terry Whitehall (Mountaineers Books; $10.95). The *International Youth Hostel Handbook, Volume One: Europe and the Mediterranean* ($8.95 plus $2 for postage) is a guide to all the hostels of Europe to which members of *AYH* have access; a map of their locations is included. (For information on joining *American Youth Hostels,* see *Hints for Single Travelers,* in this section.)

Whether traveling independently or with an organized tour, cyclists can prepare for all contingencies with the help of *By Bicycle in Ireland,* by Martin Ryle; currently out of print, it is available in libraries. Other sources of information on biking in Ireland are for the Republic, the *Federation of Irish Cyclists* (Halston St., Dublin 7; phone: 1-727524); for Northern Ireland, the *Ulster Cycling Federation* (Ms. Carmel Ann Hunter, 108 Moneymore Rd., Cookstown, County Tyrone, Northern Ireland; phone: 6487-63214). The Northern Ireland Tourist Board distributes a free leaflet, *Cycling in Northern Ireland,* that suggests two tours and lists 20 rental outlets in various areas. The Irish Tourist Board distributes several free leaflets suggesting routes and rental outlets throughout the Republic. (Mopeds, motorcycles, and scooters cannot be rented in Ireland.)

Detailed maps show the scenic byways as well as the route that goes around the mountain, not up it. Such maps are available from a number of sources, but those of the *Bartholomew Leisure Map* series (on a scale of 1:100,000 — 1 centimeter of map equals 100,000 centimeters or 1 kilometer — or approximately five-eighths of a mile of road) are particularly useful for Ireland. If unavailable in the local map store, these can be ordered from *John Bartholomew & Son Ltd.* (12 Duncan St., Edinburgh EH9 1TA, Scotland) or from their US representative, *Hammond, Inc.* (515 Valley St., Maplewood, NJ 07040; phone: 800-526-4953). Ordnance Survey maps also are quite good (see "Maps" in *Traveling by Car,* in this section).

One of the best sources for detailed topographical maps and just about any other type of map (of just about anywhere in the world) is *Map Link* (25 E. Mason St., Santa Barbara, CA 93101; phone: 805-965-4402). Their comprehensive guide *The World Map Directory* ($29.95) includes a wealth of sources for travelers afoot, and if they don't stock a map of the area in which you are interested (or the type of map best suited to your outdoor exploration), they will order it for you. But it is likely that they'll have something to suit your needs — they stock numerous maps of Ireland, including a wide range of topographical maps. Particularly useful is the *Holiday* series, which is published by the Northern Ireland government and includes a wealth of information particularly useful for outdoor explorers on wheels and afoot.

Biking Tours – A number of organizations offer bike tours in Europe. Linking up with a bike tour is more expensive than traveling alone, but with experienced leaders an organized tour often becomes an educational as well as a very social experience which may lead to long-term friendships.

One of the attractions of a bike tour is that shipment of equipment — the bike — is handled by organizers, and the shipping fee is included in the total tour package. Travelers simply deliver the bike to the airport, already disassembled and boxed; shipping cartons can be obtained from most bicycle shops with little difficulty. Bikers not with a tour must make their own arrangements with the airline, and there are no standard procedures for this (see above). Although some tour organizers will rent bikes, most prefer that participants bring a bike with which they are already familiar. Another attraction of *some* organized tours is the existence of a "sag wagon" to carry extra luggage or fatigued cyclists and their bikes, too, when peddling another mile is impossible.

Most bike tours are scheduled from May to October, last 1 or 2 weeks, are limited to 20 or 25 people, and provide lodging in inns or hotels, though some use hostels or even tents. Tours vary considerably in style and ambience, so request brochures from several operators in order to make the best decision. When contacting groups, be sure to ask about the maximum number of people on the trip, the maximum number of miles to be traveled each day, and the degree of difficulty of the biking; these details should determine which tour you join and can greatly affect your enjoyment of the experience. Planning ahead is essential because trips often fill up 6 months or more in advance.

Among the companies offering biking tours in Ireland are the following:

Backroads Bicycle Touring, 1516 Fifth St., Berkeley, CA 94710-1713 (phone: 415-527-1555 in California; 800-533-2573 elsewhere in the US). Offers superior food and accommodations on its 8-day tours of the Ring of Kerry and Killarney.

Breakaway Vacations, 164 E. 90th St., No. 2Y, New York, NY 10128 (phone: 212-722-4221). Offers 9-day inn-to-inn biking tours between Galway and Shannon.

Butterfield & Robinson, 70 Bond St., Suite 300, Toronto, Canada M5B 1X3; phone: 416-864-1354). Offers a number of first class, sophisticated bike trips. Itineraries in Ireland include a Ring of Kerry tour. Bikes are provided, though you can take your own, and there are many departure dates for each itinerary. This company also offers trips for younger riders (ages 17 or older); biking tours are rated at four levels of difficulty.

Country Cycling Tours, 140 W. 83rd St., New York, NY 10024 (phone: 212-874-5151). Offers 9-day biking tours of the Dingle Peninsula.

Eurobike, PO Box 40, DeKalb, IL 60115 (phone: 815-758-8851). Offers a 14-day hotel-to-hotel biking tour along the southwest coast of Ireland.

Peregrine Adventures, PO Box 3838, Park City, UT 84060 (phone: 801-649-0460). Offers a 15-day biking trip through rural areas in Clare, Kerry, and Limerick counties.

Progressive Travel Ltd., 1932 First Ave., Seattle, WA 98101 (phone: 800-245-2229). Offers 9-day inn-to-inn biking tours of the west coast in the vicinity of Galway and Shannon.

Travent International, PO Box 305, Waterbury Center, VT 05677 (phone: 800-325-3009 or 802-244-5420). Offers 10-day inn-to-inn bicycling tours in the southernmost counties of Ireland.

Hundreds of other organizations sponsoring biking tours have sprung up across the Continent in response to the explosion of interest in this form of travel.

The *American Youth Hostels (AYH)* and its local chapters or councils also sponsor a variety of biking tours in Europe each year. You don't have to be a youngster to take an *AYH* trip; membership is open to all ages. The catalogue includes trips for teens and explains the custom trips offered for adults (groups design their own itineraries). *AYH* tours are for small groups of 9 or 10 participants and tend to be longer than average (up to 5 weeks). Departures are geared to various age groups and levels of skill and frequently feature accommodations in hostels — along with hotels for adult groups and campgrounds for younger groups. The *Metropolitan New York Council of American Youth Hostels* is an affiliate with a particularly broad tour program of its own, and is a good source of camping, hiking, and cycling equipment. For information, contact your local council, the national organization (PO Box 37613, Washington, DC 20013-7613; phone: 202-783-6161), or the *Metropolitan New York Council of American Youth Hostels* (91 Amsterdam Ave., New York, NY 10025; phone: 212-932-2300).

The *International Bicycle Touring Society (IBTS)* is another nonprofit organization that regularly sponsors low-cost bicycle tours overseas led by member volunteers. Participants must be over 21. A sag wagon accompanies the tour group, accommodations are in inns and hotels, and breakfast is included. For information, send $2 plus a self-addressed, stamped envelope to *IBTS* (PO Box 6979, San Diego, CA 92106-0979; phone: 619-266-TOUR). The *Sierra Club* also occasionally includes a bike tour to

Ireland in its European offerings. For news about upcoming free-wheeling events, contact the club's Outing Department (address above).

You also may want to investigate the tours of the Continent offered by the *Cyclists' Touring Club (CTC),* Britain's largest cycling association. In addition to offering organized tours (including Ireland), *CTC* has a number of planned routes available in pamphlet form for bikers on their own and helps members plan their own tours. The club also publishes a yearly handbook, as well as magazines. For information, contact the *CTC* at Cotterell House, 69 Meadrow, Godalming, Surrey GU7 3HS, England (phone: 44-4868-7217).

The *League of American Wheelmen* (6707 Whitestone Rd., Suite 209, Baltimore, MD 21207; phone: 301-944-3399) publishes *Tourfinder,* a list of organizations, non-profit and commercial, that sponsor bicycle tours of the US and abroad; the list is free with membership ($25 individual, $30 family) and can be obtained by non-members for $5. The *League* also can put you in touch with biking groups in your area.

Preparing

Calculating Costs

$ After years of living relatively high on the hog, travel from North America to Europe dropped off precipitously in 1987 in response, among other considerations, to the relative weakness of the US dollar on the Continent. Many Americans who had enjoyed bargain prices while touring through Europe only a couple of years before found that disadvantageous exchange rates really put a crimp in their travel planning.

But even though the halcyon days of dollar domination seem over for the present, discount fares and the availability of charter flights can greatly reduce the cost of a European vacation; package tours can even further reduce the price. What's more, Ireland is one of Europe's least expensive destinations, which is part of the reason it always has been popular with both first-time and seasoned travelers. It also is a place where the competition for American visitors works to inspire surprisingly affordable travel opportunities. Nevertheless, most travelers still have to plan carefully and manage their travel funds prudently.

Although a little more expensive than the least expensive Mediterranean countries, Northern Ireland and the Republic are among the least costly countries in Europe. The Northern Ireland Tourist Board, which promotes travel to Northern Ireland, has been very successfully campaigning to call the attention of potential visitors to the low-cost options available for almost every entry in the traveler's budget. Some publications stress this theme, among them a *Bed & Breakfast in Britain* brochure from the British Tourist Authority, an introduction to a most reasonable and pleasant way to bring down the cost of housing for the tourist in Great Britain and Northern Ireland. In the same spirit, the Irish Tourist Board — the dollar is going even farther in the Republic these days than in the North — distributes a leaflet, *Free Attractions in Ireland,* which describes 80 of these events.

In Ireland, estimating the cost of travel expenses depends on the mode of transportation you choose, the part or parts of the country you plan to visit, how long you will stay there, the level of luxury to which you aspire, and in some cases, what time of the year you plan to travel. In addition to the basics of transportation, hotels, meals, and sightseeing, you have to take into account seasonal price changes that apply on certain air routings and at popular vacation destinations, as well as inflation, price fluctuations, and the vagaries of currency exchange. So, while the guidelines in this book will remain useful, costs for both facilities and services may have changed somewhat in the months since publication.

DETERMINING A BUDGET: A realistic appraisal of your travel expenses is the most crucial bit of planning you will undertake before any trip. It also is, unfortunately, one for which it is most difficult to give precise, practical advice. Travel styles are intensely personal, and personal taste determines cost to a great extent. Will you stay in a hotel every night and eat every meal in a restaurant, or are you planning to camp or picnic amidst Ireland's picturesque and peaceful countryside, thus reducing your daily expenses? Base your calculations on your own travel style, and make estimates of expenses from that. If published figures on the cost of travel always were taken as gospel, many trips would not be taken. But in reality, it's possible to economize. On the other hand, don't be lulled into feeling that it is not necessary to do some arithmetic before you go. No matter how generous your travel budget, without careful planning beforehand — and strict accounting along the way — you will spend more than you anticipated.

When calculating costs, start with the basics, the major expenses being transportation, accommodations, and food. However, don't forget such extras as local transportation, shopping, and such miscellaneous items as laundry and tips. The reasonable cost of these items usually is a positive surprise to your budget; such extras as drinks served with imported liquors and airport departure taxes are definite negatives.

Package programs can reduce the price of a vacation in Ireland, because the group rates obtained by the tour packager usually are lower than the tariffs for someone traveling on a freelance basis; that is, paying for each element — airfare, hotel, meals, car rental — separately. And keep in mind, particularly when calculating the major expenses, that costs vary according to fluctuations in the exchange rate — that is, how much of a given foreign currency the dollar will buy.

Other expenses, such as the cost of local sightseeing tours, will vary from city to city. Official tourist information offices are plentiful in Northern Ireland and the Republic, and most of the better hotels will have someone at the front desk able to provide a rundown on the cost of local tours and full-day excursions in and out of the city. Travel agents also can provide this information. Special discount passes that provide tourists with unlimited travel by the day or the week on regular city transportation are available in most large cities. Tourist authorities, as well as railway offices, can provide information on current discount offerings (for offices in the US, see *Tourist Information Offices* and *Traveling by Train,* both in this section). For instance, The British Tourist Authority publishes an information sheet, *Tourist Tickets and Discount Cards,* that lists many transportation and admission discounts in Great Britain, including Northern Ireland. Entries in the individual city reports in THE CITIES also give helpful information on local transportation options.

For purposes of a rough estimate — if you spend every night in a moderately priced hotel and eat every meal in a moderately priced restaurant, you can expect to spend around $200 to $250 for two people per day. This figure does not include transportation costs, but it does include accommodations (based on two people sharing a room), three meals, some sightseeing, and other modest entertainment costs. The accommodations take into consideration the differences between relatively inexpensive lodgings in rural areas (about $50 to $60 per night for two) and moderate hotels in urban areas (about $75 to $100 per night for two). With the exception of major cities — such as Belfast and Dublin — these averages should be about right for a room for two throughout Ireland. You can find places that are much less expensive, or places at which you spend more for a commensurate increase in quality of service and comfort.

Meals are calculated for inexpensive to moderate restaurants. The entertainment calculated in this daily expense figure includes one sightseeing tour and admission to one museum or historic site and/or one recreation — such as greens fees for a round of golf or rental of a mount for an afternoon ride in the countryside.

As noted in *When to Go,* slightly lower hotel rates can be expected in Europe during the off-season — late fall through early spring. Many hotels offer "mini-break" packages, that is, a discount for a stay of 2 or more nights, usually over a weekend; though these discounts may be in effect any time of the year, they are most common when demand is lowest. In large cities, seasonal price variations may be negligible — with the exception of a dramatic rise in the cost of accommodations and services during holidays. During the shoulder season months in spring and fall, prices generally are somewhat more reasonable even for luxury hotels, although, again, high-season prices may prevail in large cities and popular tourist areas.

You should be able to use these averages to forecast a reasonably accurate picture of your daily travel costs, based on exactly how you want to travel. Savings on the daily allowance can occur while motoring in rural areas; budget-minded families also can take advantage of the wide range of inexpensive accommodations available. Campgrounds are particularly inexpensive and they are located throughout Ireland (see *Camping and Caravanning, Hiking and Biking,* in this section). For information on other economical accommodation alternatives, such as bed and breakfast establishments, renting an apartment, house, or cottage, and home exchanges, see the discussion of accommodations in *On the Road,* in this section.

Picnicking is another excellent way to cut costs, and Ireland abounds with well-groomed parks and idyllic pastoral settings. A stop at a local market can provide a feast of cheeses and meats, hearty brown or soda bread, and maybe a fresh fruit tart or sweet bun for dessert at a surprisingly economical price — especially when compared to the cost of a restaurant lunch.

In planning any travel budget, it also is wise to allow a realistic amount for both entertainment and recreation. Are you planning to spend time sightseeing and visiting local museums? (In both Northern Ireland and the Republic, however, often there is no admission charge for major museums.) Is daily golf or tennis a part of your plan? Will your children be disappointed if they don't take a boat ride on the Shannon? If so, charges for these attractions and recreations must be taken into account. General guidelines on the costs of these and other activities can be found in our DIVERSIONS chapters, as well in the *Sources and Resources* sections of the individual city reports in THE CITIES. Finally, don't forget that if haunting pubs, clubs, and other nightspots is an essential part of your vacation, or you feel that one performance at the *Abbey Theatre* in Dublin may not be enough, allow for the extra cost of nightlife. This one item alone can add a great deal to your daily expenditures, particularly in the large cities and major tourist areas.

If at any point in the planning process it appears impossible to estimate expenses, consider this suggestion: The easiest way to put a ceiling on the price of all these elements is to buy a package tour. A totally planned and escorted one, with almost all transportation, rooms, meals, sightseeing, local travel, tips, and a dinner show or two included and prepaid, provides an exact total of what the trip will cost beforehand, and the only surprise will be the one you spring on yourself by succumbing to some irresistible, expensive souvenir.

The various types of packages available are discussed in *Package Tours,* in this section, but a few points bear repeating here. Not all packages are package *tours.* They often are no more than loosely organized arrangements including transatlantic transportation, a stay at a hotel, transfers between hotel and airport, baggage handling, taxes, and tips, which leave the entire matter of how you spend your time and where you eat your meals — and with whom — up to you. Equally common are the hotel-plus-car packages, which take care of accommodations and local transportation. On such independent or hosted "tours," a tour company representative or affiliated Irish travel agent may be available at a nearby office to answer questions, or a host may be stationed at a desk in the hotel to arrange optional excursions, but you will never have to travel in a group unless you wish to.

More and more, even experienced travelers are being won over by the idea of package travel, not only for the convenience and the planning time saved, but above all for the money that can be saved. Whatever elements you include in your package, the organizer has gotten them for you wholesale — and they are paid for in advance, thus eliminating the dismal prospect of returning to your hotel each night to subtract the day's disbursements from your remaining cash, when you should be enjoying a "jar" of stout in a pub in peace.

The possibility of prepaying certain elements of your trip is an important point to consider even if you intend to be strictly independent, with arrangements entirely of your own making, all bought separately. You may not be able to match the price of the wholesale tour package, but at least you will have introduced an element of predictability into your accounting, thus reducing the risk that some budget-busting expense along the way might put a damper on the rest of your plans.

Those who want to travel independently — but also want to eliminate the element of surprise from their accommodations budget — can take advantage of the hotel voucher schemes that frequently come as part of a fly/drive package. Travelers receive a block of prepaid vouchers and a list of hotels that accept them as total payment for a night's stay, and for those who may want to upgrade their lodgings from time to time, there often is another set of hotels that accepts the same vouchers with payment of a supplement.

With the independent traveler in mind, what follows are some suggestions of how to pin down the cost of a trip beforehand. But there are two more variables that will influence the cost of your holiday whether you buy a package or do it all yourself. One is timing. If you are willing to travel during the less trafficked off-season months, when airfares are lower, you'll find many hotels' rates lower also. Keep in mind those periods between the traditional high and low seasons, generally referred to as the shoulder months (approximately late March to mid-May and late September to mid-November). Although costs are only a little lower than in high season and the weather may not be as predictable, you won't be bucking the crowds that in peak months can force a traveler without a hotel reservation into the most expensive hostelry in town. Don't forget, however, to find out what is going on in any place where you plan to spend a good deal of your vacation. The availability and possible economy gained by off-season travel often are negated if a major conference or other special event is scheduled at the time you plan to visit.

Another factor influencing the cost of your trip is whether you will be traveling alone or as a couple. The prices quoted for package tours almost always are based on double occupancy of hotel rooms, and the surcharge — or single supplement — for a room by yourself can be quite hefty. When shopping for a hotel room, you'll find that there are many more double rooms than singles. Don't expect a discount if you occupy a double room as a single, and don't expect single rooms to cost less than two-thirds the price of doubles.

■ **Note:** The volatility of exchange rates means that between the time you originally make your hotel reservations and the day you arrive, the price in US dollars may vary substantially from the price originally quoted. To avoid paying more than you expected, it's wise to investigate rates that are guaranteed in US dollars. Remember that you also can determine whether it's more economical to pay for services in US dollars before departure or in local currency once in Ireland.

TRANSPORTATION COSTS: In earlier sections of GETTING READY TO GO we have discussed the comparative costs of different modes of transportation and the myriad special rates available through package tours, charter flights, train passes, car rental packages, and other budget deals. See each of the relevant sections for specific information. Transportation is likely to represent the largest item in your travel budget (cummulatively, only food and accommodations are likely to be higher), but the encouraging aspect of this is that you will be able to determine most of these costs before you leave. Most fares will have to be paid in advance, particularly if you take advantage of charter air travel or other special offerings.

Airfare is really the easiest cost to pin down, though the range and variety of flights available may be confusing initially. The possibilities were outlined fully in *Traveling by Plane,* earlier in this section. Essentially, you can choose from various types of tickets on scheduled flights, ranging in expense from the luxury of the *Concorde* and first class fares to APEX and discount tickets and charters.

The most important factors in determining which mode of transportation to choose to tour around Ireland are the amount of traveling you plan to do and the length of time you will be abroad. If you intend to move about a great deal among cities, a pass allowing unlimited train or bus travel is likely to be the most economical approach. The Rambler Ticket is valid for travel in the Irish Republic only; the Eurailpass is valid in the Republic and much of the rest of Europe. For travel in Northern Ireland only there is a Rail Runabout pass, and the Emerald Card is valid for travel throughout all of Ireland. For information on these and other economical rail and bus options, see *Traveling by Train* and *Traveling by Bus,* both in this section.

Although driving provides maximum flexibility, renting a car anywhere in Europe is a substantial expense. Car rentals do vary from city to city, as well as according to season (but don't expect rates to be as low as the deeply discounted bargain rates so often found in the US), the type of car you choose, and whether the car is rented independently or as part of a package deal.

If you want to drive through the countryside, you should look carefully into fly/drive arrangements versus straight rentals, and also compare the rates offered by some of the smaller firms specializing in car travel in Europe with the rates offered by the larger, more familiar car rental companies. (For specific information on car rental availability and rates, see *Sources and Resources,* in the individual THE CITIES chapters.) The latter all have discount plans, provided the car is booked a certain number of days before pick-up and the rental is for a minimum period of time. Look for the flat rate that also offers unlimited mileage — usually the best deal. Also, when estimating driving costs, don't forget that the price of gas in Ireland averages more than twice the price you're accustomed to paying in the US, so be sure to take this substantial expense into account. This cost also provides a significant incentive to rent a car that delivers the highest possible mileage per gallon — or liter — of gas.

FOOD: Meals are a more difficult expense to estimate. If you rent an apartment, house, or cottage, or are camping out, you will be able to prepare some meals yourself. Depending on where you're staying, groceries can be more expensive than they are at home, but they certainly will be less expensive than eating out. Restaurant dining — particularly in the better establishments of major cities and prime tourist areas — is going to hit your purse, wallet, or credit card hardest.

Independent travelers eating all of their meals in restaurants should allow roughly $45 to $70 a day for food. This amount includes breakfast, because increasingly the standard breakfast included in the price of accommodations is continental (tea or coffee and rolls or sweet buns), though there is an extra charge for a full Irish breakfast (tea or coffee, porridge, bacon and eggs, grilled tomatoes, toast, marmalade, and so on). Also included is lunch, and an average dinner. The estimate for dinner is based on a fixed menu (at a fixed price) in a moderate, neither-scrimp-nor-splurge restaurant, which at least can include a tasty and occasionally imaginative food selection, but no cocktails before dinner. This also should cover taxes and gratuities, and perhaps a pitcher of stout or a carafe of wine at dinner — but you won't be splurging. If ordering an à la carte dinner and the pick of the imported wine list in one of the major cities, be prepared for the tab to rise much higher, and if you're addicted to *haute gastronomie* (which, contrary to popular opinion, can be found in Ireland), the sky is the limit.

All of this is no reason to forgo your trip, however — remember, it's *dining* that is going to hit your wallet hard. Those who are up to a steady diet of fast food (fish and chips are a particularly good deal) can get by on a lot less. And there is some relief out in the countryside where the breakfast that comes with the bed in the typical bed and breakfast establishment often is a filling one, apt to hold most folks straight through midday (though even travelers on a severe budget are advised not to skip lunch). Pub lunches in general are becoming more and more imaginative everywhere, and they're among the best food buys encountered. If you stick to picnic lunches of local specialties, alternating with "pub grub" or filling afternoon teas, and finish off the day with a carefully chosen meal in a country inn, you will sacrifice nothing in experience and still hold down costs. Our restaurant selections, chosen to give the best value for money — whether expensive or dirt cheap — are listed in the *Best in Town* sections of THE CITIES and in the *Eating Out* sections of each tour route in DIRECTIONS.

ACCOMMODATIONS: There is a wide range of choice and a substantial difference in degrees of luxury provided among the expensive, moderate, and inexpensive Irish hotels. Although room costs in Ireland cover a broad spectrum, for purposes of making an estimate, expect to pay a little less than you would pay in a major American city for equivalent accommodations. Figure on the high side if you're visiting major tourism centers during high season, and slightly lower rates can be expected off-season.

Most expensive — as high as $300 for a double room — will be the luxury hotels of the most expensive cities — such as Dublin. Rates at international hotels with a full complement of business services also tend toward the top of the scale. Generally, the member hotels of international chains in any given city are priced roughly equally. In the larger cities (such as Dublin and Belfast), this ranges from around $125 and up for a double room, although similar hotels elsewhere range from about $60 to $80. There is a big step down from these international class hotels to those in the moderate category in the same cities, and prices generally will be about $20 to as much as $50 less per night.

There is no sacred edict stating that travelers must put up at deluxe hotels, and in fact you might be missing a good deal of the Irish experience by insisting on international standards and skipping over the terrific small hotels, inns, and guesthouses. Hotels in the first class range usually are available at about one-third less than their deluxe counterparts. Second class hotels offer clean, comfortable accommodations and often are thoroughly charming, and in the even more inexpensive range are hotels that many will find perfectly adequate. In rural areas, there also are family-run hotels and inns.

The true staple of the less expensive lodging scene in Ireland are the bed and breakfast establishments located throughout the country. Known as B&Bs, these can be homey or spartan but almost always are clean, and the prices are low, averaging about $15 to $25 per person per night. About the only places that they are not easy to find are in Belfast or Dublin where, as in other large cities, space is at a premium and few private homes have the spare room to rent to passing strangers. Nevertheless, budget accommodations designed to offer basic (but acceptable) lodgings at especially economical prices — a double room may cost as little as $30 to $40, even in some central cities — do exist, and, recognizing the need, travel agents, tour packagers, airlines, and tourist offices are doing what they can to make their whereabouts known.

There are other options for less expensive accommodations for anyone staying in one place for an extended period of time in Ireland. One is renting an apartment or house, called a "self-catering holiday" or a "holiday let." These are available throughout Ireland and can be arranged through travel agents. The other is a home exchange, in which you and an Irish family exchange houses for an agreed-upon period of time.

LOCAL TAXES AND SERVICE CHARGES: A sales tax or VAT (value added tax) is added to both goods and services in many European countries. In Northern Ireland, the standard rate is 15%, whether on accommodations or on goods purchased in local stores. In the Republic, the tax on accommodations is 10%; on goods, 10% to 23%. In both countries, all advertised prices must include VAT. However, tourists can avoid the VAT on purchases by having the goods sent directly to their home address — if the store is willing to do so. In addition, many stores in the Republic participate in the Cashback "retail export" scheme, whereby shoppers pay the tax, have a VAT relief form validated by a customs clerk as they leave the country, and collect a cash refund at the airport. In Northern Ireland (and in those stores in the Republic not participating in Cashback), shoppers receive similar forms to fill out and mail back to the store for their VAT refunds, which usually are in check form. For a full discussion of VAT refunds, see *Shopping,* in this section.

A service charge, usually of 12% to 15% is almost universal on restaurant and hotel bills in Ireland. Nevertheless, there still are many situations not covered by the service charge — or where an additional gratuity is appropriate. For more on these, see *Tipping,* in this section.

■A note on our hotel/restaurant cost categories: There are a great many moderate and inexpensive hotels and restaurants that we have not included in this book. Our *Checking In* and *Eating Out* listings include only those places we think are best in their price range. We have arranged our listings by general price categories: expensive, moderate, and inexpensive. The introductory paragraph of each listing explains just what those categories mean within the context of local prices.

Planning a Trip

123 Travelers fall into two categories: those who make lists and those who do not. Some people prefer to plot the course of their trip to the finest detail, with contingency plans and alternatives at the ready. For others, the joy of a voyage is its spontaneity; exhaustive planning only lessens the thrill of anticipation and the sense of freedom.

For most travelers, however, any week-plus trip to Ireland can be too expensive for an "I'll take my chances" attitude. Even perennial gypsies and anarchistic wanderers have to take into account the time-consuming logistics of getting around, and, even with minimal baggage, they need to think about packing. Hence, at least some planning is crucial. This is not to suggest that you work out every hour of your itinerary in minute detail before you go, but it's still wise to decide certain basics at the very start: where to go, what to do, and how much to spend. These decisions require a certain amount of consideration. So before rigorously planning specific details, you might want to establish your general travel objectives:

1. How much time will you have for the entire trip, and how much of it are you willing to spend getting where you're going?
2. What interests and/or activities do you want to pursue while on vacation? Do you want to visit one, a few, or several different places?
3. At what time of year do you want to go?
4. What kind of topography or climate do you prefer?
5. Do you want peace and privacy or lots of activity and company?
6. How much money can you afford to spend for the entire vacation?

Obviously, your answers will be determined by your personal tastes and lifestyle. These will dictate the degree of comfort you require; whether you select a tour or opt for total independence; and how much responsibility you want to take for your own arrangements (or whether you want everything arranged for you, with the kinds of services provided in a comprehensive package trip).

With firm answers to these major questions, start reviewing literature on the areas in which you're most interested. Good sources of information are airlines, hotel representatives, and travel agents. Also consult such other sources of general travel information as reliable, annually updated guidebooks and maps. Motor clubs (see *Traveling by Car,* in this section) often can be a good source for brochures and other information on Europe. There also are lots of useful little city guides available at newwstands and bookstores on the spot throughout Ireland.

Government departments and affinity clubs focusing on individual outdoor activities — golf, fishing, hunting, boating, mountain climbing, hiking, biking, nature study, and other such special interests — also may be able to provide information on these sports. For information on wilderness trips, hiking, and biking, see *Camping and Caravanning, Hiking and Biking,* in this section, and for information on these and other activities, see the various sections of DIVERSIONS, as well as the individual city reports in THE CITIES.

In addition, the Irish Tourist Board, the British Tourist Authority, and the Northern Ireland Tourist Board all have locations in the US (see *Tourist Information Offices,* in this section, for addresses). Stop in or write to any of these branches — all are ready resources for brochures, maps, and other information on Irish cities and the country-side. (Note that although the British Tourist Authority does not currently promote tourism to Northern Ireland, many of its publications do include useful information on the country.)

Up-to-date travel information on Ireland is plentiful, and you should be able to accumulate everything you want to know, not only about the places you plan to visit, but also about the relevent tour and package options. And if you're visiting Ireland for the first time, make a special effort to read up on its food, history, and culture. A good place to start is the section in this guide called PERSPECTIVES, but if you're planning an extended stay in a particular city or region, you'll probably want to do even more extensive reading.

You now can make almost all of your own travel arrangements if you have time to follow through with hotels, airlines, tour operators, and so on. But you'll probably save considerable time and energy if you have a travel agent make the reservations and arrangements for you. The agent also should be able to advise you of alternate arrangements of which you may not be aware. Only rarely will a travel agent's services cost a traveler any money, and they may even save you some (see *How to Use a Travel Agent,* in this section). Well before departure (depending on how far in advance you make your reservations), the agent will deliver a packet that includes all your tickets and hotel confirmations and often a day-by-day outline of where you'll be when, along with a detailed list of all your flights.

If it applies to your schedule and destination, pay particular attention to the dates when off-season rates go into effect. In major tourism areas, accommodations costs may be lower during the off-season (and the weather often is perfectly acceptable at this time). Off-season rates frequently are lower for other facilities, too, although don't expect to save much on car rental costs during any season. In general, it is a good idea to beware of holiday weeks, as rates at hotels generally are higher during these periods and rooms are heavily booked. (In addition, service is apt to be under par unless more staff people are employed for the holidays, since the regular bellhops, maids, dining room personnel, and others will be trying to cope with a full house instead of being able to provide personal attention to individual guests.)

Make plans early. During the summer season and other holiday periods, make hotel reservations at least a month in advance in all major cities. If you are flying at these times, and want to benefit from savings offered through discount fares or charter programs, purchase tickets as far ahead as possible. The less flexible your schedule requirements, the earlier you should book. Many hotels require deposits before they will guarantee reservations, and this most often is the case during peak travel periods. (Be sure you have a receipt for any deposit, or better yet, charge the deposit to a credit card.) Religious and national holidays also are times requiring reservations well in advance in Ireland.

Before your departure, find out what the weather will be like at your destination.

Consult *When to Go,* in this section, for information on climatic variations and a chart of average temperatures in various Irish cities. See *How to Pack,* in this section, for details on what clothes to take. And see *When to Go,* also in this section, as well as the individual city reports in THE CITIES for information on special events that may occur during your stay. The city chapters also provide essential information on local transportation and other services and resources.

While arranging a vacation is fun and exciting, don't forget to prepare for your absence from home. Before you leave, attend to these household matters:

1. Arrange for your mail to be forwarded, held by the post office, or picked up daily at your house. Someone should check your door occasionally to pick up any unexpected deliveries. Piles of mail or packages announce to thieves that no one is home.

2. Cancel all deliveries (newspapers, milk, and so on).

3. Arrange for the lawn to be mowed and plants watered at regular intervals.

4. Arrange for the care of pets.

5. Etch your social security number in a prominent place on all appliances (television sets, radios, cameras, kitchen appliances). This considerably reduces their appeal to thieves and facilitates identification.

6. Leave a house key and your itinerary with a relative or friend. Notify the police, the building manager, or a neighbor that you are leaving, and tell them who has your key and itinerary.

7. Empty the refrigerator and lower the thermostat.

8. If you use a computer with a hard disk, back up all your files onto diskettes and store them in a safe place away from the equipment.

9. Immediately before leaving, check that all doors, windows, and garage doors are securely locked.

To discourage thieves further, it is wise to set up several variable timers around the house so that lights and even the television set or a radio go on and off several times in different rooms each night.

Make a list of any valuable items you are carrying with you, including credit card numbers and the serial numbers of your traveler's checks. Put copies in your purse or pocket, and leave other copies at home. Put a label with your name and home address on the inside of your luggage to facilitate identification in case of loss. Put your name and business address — *but never your home address* — on a label on the outside of your luggage.

Review your travel documents. If you are traveling by air, check that your ticket has been filled in correctly. The left side of the ticket should have a list of each stop you will make (even if you are only stopping to change planes), beginning with your departure point. Be sure that the list is correct, and count the number of carbons to see that you have one for each plane you will take. If you have confirmed reservations, be sure that the column marked "status" says "OK" beside each flight. Have in hand vouchers or proof of payment for any reservation for which you've paid in advance; this includes hotels, transfers to and from the airport, sightseeing tours, car rentals, and tickets to special events.

Reconfirmation of reservations is strongly recommended for all international flights. Although policies vary from carrier to carrier, it's still smart to reconfirm your flight 48 to 72 hours before departure, both going and returning. This will not, however, prevent you from getting bumped in case the flight is overbooked. Reconfirmation is particularly recommended for point-to-point flights within Europe.

If you will be driving while in Ireland, bring your driver's license and any other necessary identification, proof of insurance, maps, guidebooks, a flashlight with an extra set of batteries, and sunglasses; a small first-aid kit also is a good idea. If driving about for more than a day, upon arrival you may want to pick up emergency flashers, a container of water or coolant for the radiator, and a steel container for extra gas.

Finally, you always should bear in mind that despite the most careful plans, things do not always occur on schedule. If you maintain a flexible attitude at all times, and shrug as cheerfully as possible in the face of postponements and cancellations, you will enjoy yourself a lot more.

How to Use a Travel Agent

 A reliable travel agent remains your best source of service and information for planning a trip abroad, whether you have a specific itinerary and require an agent only to make reservations, or need extensive help in sorting through the maze of airfares, tour offerings, hotel packages, and the scores of other arrangements that may be involved in a trip to Ireland.

You should know what you want from a travel agent so that you can evaluate what you are getting. It is perfectly reasonable to expect your travel agent to be a thoroughly knowledgeable travel specialist, with information about your destination and, even more crucial, a command of current airfares, ground arrangements, and other wrinkles in the travel scene. Most travel agents work through computer reservations systems (CRS) to assess the availability and rates of flights, hotels, and car rentals, and they can book reservations through the CRS. Despite reports of "computer bias," in which a computer may favor one airline over another, the CRS should provide agents with the entire spectrum of flights available to a given destination and the complete range of fares in considerably less time than it takes to telephone the airlines individually — and at no extra charge to the client.

To make the most intelligent use of a travel agent's time and expertise, you should know something of the economics of the industry. As a client, traditionally you pay nothing for the agent's services; with few exceptions, it's all free, from hotel bookings to advice on package tours. Any money the travel agent makes on the time spent arranging your itinerary — booking hotels or flights, or suggesting activities — comes from commissions paid by the suppliers of these services — the airlines, hotels, and so on. These commissions generally run from 8% to 20% of the total cost of the service, although suppliers often reward agencies that sell their services in volume with an increased commission called an override.

Among the few exceptions to the general rule of free service by a travel agent are the agencies beginning to practice *net pricing*. In essence, such agencies return all of their commissions and overrides to their customers and make their income by charging a flat fee per transaction instead (thus adding a charge after a reduction for the commissions has been made). Sometimes the rebate from the agent arrives later, in the form of a check. For further information, see "Net Fare Sources" in *Traveling by Plane*, in this section.

Net fares and fees are a very recent and not widespread practice, but even a conventional travel agent sometimes may charge a fee for such special services as long-distance telephone or cable costs incurred in making a booking, for reserving a room in a place that does not pay a commission (such as a small, out-of-the-way hotel), or for special attention such as planning a highly personalized itinerary. A fee also may be assessed in instances of deeply discounted airfares. In most instances, however, you'll find that travel agents make their time and experience available to you at no charge, and you do not pay more for an airline ticket, package tour, or other product bought from a travel agent than you would for the same product bought directly from the supplier.

This system implies two things about your relationship with an agent:

1. You will get better service if you arrive at the agent's desk with your basic itinerary already planned. Know roughly where you want to go, what you want to do, and how much you want to spend. Use the agent to make bookings (which pay commissions) and to advise you on facilities, activities, and alternatives within the limits of your itinerary. You get the best service when you are requesting commissionable items. Since there are few commissions on camping or driving/camping package tours, an agent is unlikely to be very enthusiastic about helping to plan one. (If you have this type of trip in mind, see *Camping and Caravanning, Hiking and Biking,* in this section, for other sources of information on campgrounds throughout Ireland.) The more vague your plans, the less direction you can expect from most agents. If you walk into an agency and say, "I have 2 weeks in June; what shall I do?" you most likely will walk out with nothing more than a handful of brochures. So do a little preliminary homework.

2. Be wary. There always is the danger that an incompetent or unethical agent will send you to a place offering the best commissions rather than the best facilities for your enjoyment. The only way to be sure you are getting the best service is to pick a good, reliable travel agent, one who knows where to go for information if he or she is unfamiliar with an area — although most agents are familiar with major destinations throughout Ireland.

You should choose a travel agent with the same care with which you would choose a doctor or lawyer. You will be spending a good deal of money on the basis of the agent's judgment, so you have a right to expect that judgment to be mature, informed, and interested. At the moment, unfortunately, there aren't many standards within the travel agent industry to help you gauge competence, and the quality of individual agents varies enormously.

At present, only nine states have registration, licensing, or other form of travel agent-related legislation on their books. Rhode Island licenses travel agents; Florida, Hawaii, Iowa, and Ohio register them; and California, Illinois, Oregon, and Washington have laws governing the sale of transportation or related services. While state licensing of agents cannot absolutely guarantee competence, it can at least ensure that an agent has met some minimum requirements.

Perhaps the best-prepared agents are those who have completed the CTC Travel Management program offered by the *Institute of Certified Travel Agents* and carry the initials CTC (Certified Travel Counselor) after their names. This indicates a relatively high level of expertise. For a free list of CTCs in your area, send a self-addressed, stamped, #10 envelope to *ICTA,* 148 Linden St., Box 82-56, Wellesley, MA 02181 (phone: 617-237-0280 in Massachusetts; 800-542-4282 elsewhere in the US).

An agent's membership in the *American Society of Travel Agents (ASTA)* can be a useful guideline in making a selection. But keep in mind that *ASTA* is an industry organization, requiring only that its members be licensed in those states where required; be accredited to represent the suppliers whose products they sell, including airline and cruise tickets; and adhere to its Principles of Professional Conduct and Ethics code. *ASTA* does not guarantee the competence, ethics, or financial soundness of its members, but it does offer some recourse if you feel you have been dealt with unfairly. Complaints may be registered with *ASTA* (Consumer Affairs Department, PO Box 23992, Washington, DC 20026-3992; phone: 703-739-2782). First try to resolve the complaint directly with the supplier. For a list of *ASTA* members in your area, send a self-addressed, stamped, #10 envelope to *ASTA,* Public Relations Dept., at the address above.

There also is the *Association of Retail Travel Agents (ARTA),* a smaller but highly respected trade organization similar to *ASTA.* Its member agencies and agents similarly agree to abide by a code of ethics, and complaints about a member can be made to

ARTA's Grievance Committee, 1745 Jeff Davis Hwy., Arlington, VA 22202-3402 (phone: 800-969-6069 or 703-553-7777).

Agencies that are members of the *National Association of Cruise Only Agencies (NACOA)* have demonstrated special knowledge in the selling of cruises. For a list of cruise-only agencies in your area (requests are limited to three states), send a self-addressed, stamped envelope to *NACOA* (PO Box 7209, Freeport, NY 11520) or call 516-378-8006. Agencies that belong to a travel consortium, such as *Travel Trust International* (phone: 800-522-2700 in New York; 800-223-8953 elsewhere in the US), have access to preferred rates, as do the huge networks of *American Express* (phone: 800-YES-AMEX) and *Carlson Travel Network* (formerly *Ask Mr. Foster;* phone: 818-788-4118) travel agencies.

A number of banks own travel agencies, too. These provide the same services as other accredited commercial travel bureaus. Anyone can become a client, not only the bank's customers. You can find out more about these agencies, which belong to the *Association of Bank Travel Bureaus,* by inquiring at your bank or looking in the yellow pages.

Perhaps the best way to find a travel agent is by word of mouth. If the agent (or agency) has done a good job for your friends over a period of time, it probably indicates a certain level of commitment and competence. Always ask not only for the name of the company, but for the name of the specific agent with whom your friends dealt, for it is that individual who will serve you, and quality can vary widely within a single agency. There are some superb travel agents in the business, and they can facilitate vacation or business arrangements.

Once you've made an initial selection, be entirely candid with the agent. Budget considerations rank at the top of the list — there's no sense in wasting the agent's (or your) time pouring over itineraries that you know you can't afford. Similarly, if you like a fair degree of comfort, that fact should not be kept secret from your travel agent, who may assume that you wish to travel on a tight budget even when that's not the case.

Entry Requirements and Documents

Despite increased concern about terrorism, a valid US passport is the only document a US citizen needs to enter the Irish Republic or Northern Ireland, and that same passport also is needed to reenter the US. As a general rule, possession of a US passport entitles the bearer to remain in these countries as a tourist for up to 3 months. Resident aliens of the US should inquire at an Irish consulate — concerning the Republic — or British consulate — about Northern Ireland — to find out what documents they need to enter Ireland (see *Tourist Information Offices,* in this section, for addresses); similarly, US citizens intending to work, study, or reside in Ireland should address themselves to the appropriate consulate — again either a British consulate, or an Irish consulate, or both if you will be in both countries.

Vaccination certificates are required only if the traveler is entering from an area of contagion as defined by the World Health Organization, and as the US is considered an area "free from contagion," an international vaccination certificate is no longer required for entering either the Irish Republic or Northern Ireland for a short period of time. Because smallpox is considered eradicated from the world, only a few countries continue to require visitors to have a smallpox vaccination certificate. You certainly will not need one to travel to Ireland or to return to the US.

VISAS: Visas are required, however, for study, residency, or work, and US citizens should address themselves to the appropriate Irish consulate. Visas of this type are available for stays in Ireland of up to 1 year. Note that although visas for study often are issued, it is next to impossible to get a visa to work in Ireland due to the overwhelming unemployment rate. The ready processing of a visa application also may be based on the duration of the visa you are requesting — visas for studying in Ireland for several months are likely to be processed more quickly than residency visas good for 1 year. Proof of substantial means of independent financial support during the stay also is pertinent to the acceptance of any long-term–stay application.

Issuing tourist visas is a routine service provided by the British and Irish consulates — for Northern Ireland and the Irish Republic, respectively — though it is a good idea to apply well in advance. This is particularly important for travelers who live some distance from the nearest British or Irish consulate and are applying by mail. Two items are necessary to apply for a visa: a valid passport and a completed visa form. (These forms may be obtained by sending a self-addressed, stamped envelope to the nearest consulate with a written request.) There is no charge for the issuance of Irish visas. Application must be made at the British or Irish consulate within your jurisdiction (see *Tourist Information Offices,* in this section, for addresses). Visas often are issued on the spot; however, if there is a backlog, you may have to return to pick it up a few days later. To avoid frustration and wasted time, it is a good idea to call ahead to check during what hours and days visa requests are accepted.

PASSPORTS: While traveling in Ireland, carry your passport with you at all times (for an exception to this rule, see our note "When Checking In," below). If you lose your passport while abroad, report the loss to the nearest US consulate or embassy immediately. You can get a 3-month temporary passport directly from the consulate, but you must fill out a "loss of passport" form and follow the same application procedure — and pay the same fees — as you did for the original (see below). It's likely to speed things up if you have a record of your passport number and the place and date of its issue (a Xerox copy of the first page of your passport is perfect); keep this information separate from your passport — you might want to give it to a traveling companion to hold or put it in the bottom of your suitcase. (For a complete list of US consulates and embassies in Ireland, see *Medical and Legal Aid and Consular Services,* in this section.)

US passports now are valid for 10 years from the date of issue (5 years for those under age 16). The expired passport itself is not renewable, but must be turned in along with your application for a new and valid one (you will get it back, voided, when you receive the new one). Delivery can take as little as 2 weeks or as long as a month, and anyone applying for a passport for the first time should allow at least 4 weeks for delivery — even 6 weeks during the busiest season — from approximately mid-March to mid-September.

Normal passports contain 24 pages, but frequent travelers can request a 48-page passport at no extra cost. Every individual, regardless of age, must have his or her own passport. Family passports no longer are issued.

Passport renewal can be done by mail, but anyone applying for the first time or anyone under 16 renewing a passport must do so in person at one of the following places:

1. The State Department passport agencies in Boston, Chicago, Honolulu, Houston, Los Angeles, Miami, New Orleans, New York City, Philadelphia, San Francisco, Seattle, Stamford, CT, and Washington, DC.
2. A federal or state courthouse.
3. Any of the 1,000 post offices across the country with designated acceptance facilities.

Application blanks are available at all these offices and must be presented with the following:

1. Proof of US citizenship. This can be a previous passport or one in which you were included. If you are applying for your first passport and you were born in the United States, an original or certified birth certificate is the required proof. If you were born abroad, a Certificate of Naturalization, a Certificate of Citizenship, a Report of Birth Abroad of a Citizen of the United States, or a Certification of Birth is necessary.

2. Two 2-by-2-inch, front-view photographs in color or black and white, with a light, plain background, taken within the previous 6 months. These must be taken by a photographer rather than by a machine.

3. A $42 passport fee ($27 for travelers under 16), which includes a $7 execution fee. *Note:* Your best bet is to bring the exact amount in cash (no change is given), or a separate check or money order for each passport.

4. Proof of identity. Again, this can be a previous passport, a Certificate of Naturalization or of Citizenship, a driver's license, or a government ID card with a physical description or a photograph. Failing any of these, you should be accompanied by a blood relative or a friend of at least 2 years' standing who will testify to your identity. Credit cards or social security cards do not suffice as proof of identity — but note that since 1988, US citizens *must* supply their social security numbers.

Passports can be renewed by mail with forms obtained at designated locations only if the expired passport was issued no more than 12 years before the date of application for renewal and if it was not issued before the applicant's 16th birthday. Send the completed form with the expired passport, two photos, and $35 (no execution fee required) to the nearest passport agency office.

As getting a passport — or international visa — through the mail can mean waiting as much as 6 weeks or more, a new mini-industry has cropped up in those cities where there is a US passport office. The yellow pages currently list quite a few organizations willing to wait on line to expedite obtaining a visa or passport renewal; there's even one alternative for those who live nowhere near the cities mentioned above. In the nation's capital there's an organization called the *Washington Passport and Visa Service.* It may be the answer for folks in need of special rapid action, since this organization can get a passport application or renewal turned around in a single day. What's more, their proximity to an embassy or consulate of every foreign country represented in the US helps to speed the processing of visa applications as well. *Washington Passport and Visa's* fee for a 3- to 5-day turnaround is $25; for next-day service the charge is $50; for same-day service they charge $75. For information, application forms, and other prices, call 800-272-7776.

If you need an emergency passport, it also is possible to be issued a passport in a matter of hours by going directly to your nearest passport office (there is no way, however, to avoid waiting in line). Explain the nature of the emergency, usually as serious as a death in the family; a ticket in hand for a flight the following day also will suffice. Should the emergency occur outside of business hours, all is not lost. There's a 24-hour telephone number in Washington, DC (phone: 202-634-3600), that can put you in touch with a State Department duty officer who may be able to expedite your application.

■**When Checking In:** It is not at all unusual for an Irish hotel to ask you to surrender your passport for 24 hours (although this practice is far less common in Ireland than elsewhere in Europe). While we all get a little nervous when we're parted from our passports, the US State Department's passport division advises that it's a perfectly acceptable procedure. The purpose usually is a local requirement to check the validity of the passport and ascertain whether the passport holder is a fugitive or has a police record. Many hotels merely will ask that you enter your passport number on your registration card. If a hotel does take your passport, make sure it's returned to you the next day.

DUTY AND CUSTOMS: As a general rule, the requirements for bringing the major-ity of items *into Ireland* is that they must be in quantities small enough not to imply commercial import.

Among the items you may bring into Ireland duty-free are 2 liters of wine, or 2 liters of alcohol under 38.8 proof, or 1 liter above 38.8 proof; 400 cigarettes; 100 cigars; 50 grams of perfume; a quarter of a liter of cologne; and items designated as gifts and valued at less than IR£34 (approximately $50) per item; for children under 15 the limit is IR£17 (about $25) per item.

If you are bringing along a computer, camera, or other electronic equipment for your own use that you will be taking back to the US, you should register the item with the US Customs Service in order to avoid paying duty both entering and returning from Ireland. (Also see *Customs and Returning to the US,* in this section.) For information on this procedure, as well as for a variety of pamphlets on US customs regulations, contact the local office of the US Customs Service or the central office, PO Box 7407, Washington, DC 20044 (phone: 202-566-8195).

Additional information regarding customs regulations is available from the British Tourist Authority or the Northern Ireland Tourist Board in the case of Northern Ireland, or the Irish Tourist Board for the Republic. See *Tourist Information Offices,* in this section, for addresses of offices in the US.

■ **One rule to follow:** When passing through customs, it is illegal not to declare dutiable items; penalties range from stiff fines and seizure of the goods to prison terms. So don't try to sneak anything through — it just isn't worth it.

Insurance

It is unfortunate that most decisions to buy travel insurance are impulsive and usually are made without any real consideration of the traveler's existing policies. Too often the result is the purchase of needlessly expensive, short-term policies that duplicate existing coverage and reinforce the tendency to buy coverage on a trip-by-trip basis rather than to work out a total and continuing travel insurance package that might well be more effective and economical.

Therefore, the first person with whom you should discuss travel insurance is your own insurance broker, not a travel agent or the clerk behind the airport insurance counter. You may discover that the insurance you already carry — homeowner's poli-cies and/or accident, health, and life insurance — protects you adequately while you travel and that your real needs are in the more mundane areas of excess value insurance for baggage or trip cancellation insurance.

TYPES OF INSURANCE: To make insurance decisions intelligently, however, you first should understand the basic categories of travel insurance and what they cover. Then you can decide what you should have in the broader context of your personal insurance needs, and you can choose the most economical way of getting the desired protection: through riders on existing policies; with one-time short-term policies; through a special program put together for the frequent traveler; through coverage that's part of a travel club's benefits; or with a combination policy sold by insurance companies through brokers, automobile clubs, tour operators, and travel agents.

There are seven basic categories of travel insurance:

1. Baggage and personal effects insurance
2. Personal accident and sickness insurance
3. Trip cancellation and interruption insurance
4. Default and/or bankruptcy insurance
5. Flight insurance (to cover injury or death)

6. Automobile insurance (for driving your own or a rented car)
7. Combination policies

Baggage and Personal Effects Insurance – Ask your agent if baggage and personal effects are included in your current homeowner's policy, or if you will need a special floater to cover you for the duration of a trip. The object is to protect your bags and their contents in case of damage or theft any time during your travels, not just while you're in flight and covered by the airline's policy. Furthermore, only limited protection is provided by the airline. Baggage liability varies from carrier to carrier, but generally speaking, for domestic flights, luggage usually is insured to $1,250 — that's per passenger, not per bag. For most international flights, including domestic portions of international flights, the airline's liability limit is approximately $9.07 per pound or $20 per kilo (which comes to about $360 per 40-pound suitcase) for checked baggage and up to $400 per passenger for unchecked baggage. These limits should be specified on your airline ticket, but to be awarded the specified amount, you'll have to provide an itemized list of lost property, and if you're including new and/or expensive items, be prepared for a request that you back up your claim with sales receipts or other proof of purchase.

If you are carrying goods worth more than the maximum protection offered by the airline, bus, or train company, you should consider excess value insurance. Additional coverage is available from airlines at an average, currently, of $1 per $100 worth of coverage, up to a maximum value of $5,000. This insurance can be purchased at the airline counter when you check in, though you should arrive early enough to fill out the necessary forms and to avoid holding up other passengers. Major credit card companies, including American Express and Diners Club, also provide coverage for lost or delayed baggage. In some cases, you must enroll in advance to qualify. Check your membership brochure or contact the credit card company for details (see phone numbers listed in *Credit and Currency,* in this section). Excess value insurance also is included in certain of the combination travel insurance policies discussed below.

■ **A note of warning:** Be sure to read the fine print of any excess value insurance policy; there often are specific exclusions, such as cash, tickets, furs, gold and silver objects, art, and antiques. And remember that insurance companies ordinarily will pay only the depreciated value of the goods rather than their replacement value. The best way to protect the items you're carrying in your luggage is to take photos of your valuables, and keep a record of the serial numbers of such items as cameras, typewriters, radios, and so on. This will establish that you do, indeed, own the objects. If your luggage disappears or is damaged en route, deal with the situation immediately. If an airline loses your luggage, you will be asked to fill out a Property Irregularity Report before you leave the airport. If your property disappears at other transportation centers, tell the local company, but also report it to the police (since the insurance company will check with the police when processing the claim). When traveling by train, if you are sending excess luggage as registered baggage, remember that some trains may not have provisions for extra cargo; if your baggage does not arrive when you do, it may not be lost, just on the next train!

Personal Accident and Sickness Insurance – This covers you in case of illness during your trip or death in an accident. Most policies insure you for hospital and doctor's expenses, lost income, and so on. In most cases, it is a standard part of existing health insurance policies, though you should check with your broker to be sure that your policy will pay for any medical expenses incurred abroad. If not, take out a separate vacation accident policy or an entire vacation insurance policy that includes health and life coverage.

Trip Cancellation and Interruption Insurance – Although modern public charters have eliminated many of the old advance booking requirements, most charter and

package tour passengers still pay for their travel well before departure. The disappointment of having to miss a vacation because of illness or any other reason pales before
the awful prospect that not all (and sometimes none) of the money paid in advance
might be returned. So cancellation insurance for any package tour is a must. Although
cancellation penalties vary (they are listed in the fine print in every tour brochure, and
before you purchase a package tour you should know exactly what they are), rarely will
a passenger get more than 50% of this money back if forced to cancel within a few
weeks of leaving. Therefore, if you book a package tour or charter flight, you should
have trip cancellation insurance to guarantee full reimbursement or refund should you,
a traveling companion, or a member of your immediate family get sick, forcing you to
cancel your trip or *return home early.* The key here is *not* to buy just enough insurance
to guarantee full reimbursement for the cost of the package or charter in case of
cancellation. The proper amount of coverage should be sufficient to reimburse you for
the cost of having to catch up with a tour after its departure or having to travel home
at the full economy airfare if you have to forgo the return flight of your charter. There
usually is quite a discrepancy between the charter fare and the amount charged to travel
the same distance on a regularly scheduled flight at full economy fare.

Trip cancellation insurance is available from travel agents and tour operators in two
forms: as part of a short-term, all-purpose travel insurance package (sold by the travel
agent); or as specific cancellation insurance designed by the tour operator for a specific
charter tour. Generally, tour operators' policies are less expensive, but also less inclusive. Cancellation insurance also is available directly from insurance companies or their
agents as part of a short-term, all-inclusive travel insurance policy.

Before you decide on a policy, read each one carefully. (Either type can be purchased
from a travel agent when you book the charter or package tour.) Be certain that your
policy includes enough coverage to pay your fare from the farthest destination on your
itinerary should you have to miss the charter flight. Also, be sure to check the fine print
for stipulations concerning "family members" and "pre-existing medical conditions,"
as well as allowance for living expenses if you must delay your return due to bodily
injury or illness.

Default and/or Bankruptcy Insurance – Although trip cancellation insurance
usually protects you if *you* are unable to complete — or begin — your trip, a fairly
recent innovation is coverage in the event of default and/or bankruptcy on the part of
the tour operator, airline, or other travel supplier. In some travel insurance packages,
this contingency is included in the trip cancellation portion of the coverage; in others,
it is a separate feature. Either way, it is becoming increasingly important. Whereas
sophisticated travelers have long known to beware of the possibility of default or
bankruptcy when buying a charter flight or tour package, in recent years more than
a few respected airlines unexpectedly have revealed their shaky financial condition,
sometimes leaving hordes of stranded ticketholders in their wake. Moreover, the value
of escrow protection of a charter passenger's funds lately has been unreliable. While
default/bankruptcy insurance ordinarily will not result in reimbursement in time to pay
for new arrangements, it can ensure that you eventually will get your money back, and
even independent travelers buying no more than an airplane ticket may want to consider it.

Should this type of coverage not be available to you (state insurance regulations vary,
there is a wide variation in price, and so on), the best bet is to pay for airline tickets
and tour packages with a credit card. The federal Fair Credit Billing Act permits
purchasers to refuse payment for credit card charges where services have not been
delivered, so the potential onus of dealing with a receiver for a bankrupt airline falls
on the credit card company. You must, however, make your claim within 60 days of
receiving your bill from the credit card company. What's more, do not assume that
another airline automatically will honor the ticket you're holding if it was written by

a bankrupt airline, since the days when virtually all major carriers subscribed to a default protection program are long gone. Some airlines may voluntarily step forward to accommodate stranded passengers, but this now is an entirely altruistic act.

Flight Insurance – US airlines have carefully established limits of liability for the death or injury of passengers. For international flights, they are printed right on the ticket: a maximum of $75,000 in case of death or injury. Although these limitations once were established by state law for domestic flights, each case currently is decided in court on its own merits — this means potentially unlimited liability. But remember, these limits of liability are not the same thing as insurance policies; every penny that an airline must pay in the case of injury or death may be subject to a legal battle.

This may make you feel that you are not adequately protected, but before you buy last-minute flight insurance from an airport vending machine, consider the purchase in light of your total existing insurance coverage. A careful review of your current policies may reveal that you already are amply covered for accidental death, sometimes up to three times the amount provided for by the flight insurance you're buying in the airport.

Be aware that airport insurance, the kind typically bought at a counter or from a vending machine, is among the most expensive forms of life insurance coverage, and that even within a single airport, rates for approximately the same coverage vary widely. Often policies sold in vending machines are more expensive than those sold over the counter, even when they are with the same national company.

If you buy your plane ticket with an American Express, Carte Blanche, or Diners Club credit card, you automatically are issued life and accident insurance at no extra cost. American Express automatically provides $100,000 in insurance to its Green and Gold cardholders, and $500,000 to Platinum cardholders; Carte Blanche provides $150,000; and Diners Club provides $350,000. Additional coverage can be obtained at extremely reasonable prices, but a cardholder must sign up for it in advance. With American Express, $4 per ticket buys an additional $250,000 worth of flight insurance; $7.50 buys $500,000 worth; and $14 provides an added $1 million worth of coverage. (Rates vary slightly for New York residents.) Both Carte Blanche and Diners Club also offer an additional $250,000 worth of insurance for $4; $500,000 for $6.50. Both also provide $1,250 free insurance — over and above what the airline will pay — for checked baggage that's lost or damaged. American Express provides $500 coverage for checked baggage; $500 for carry-on baggage; and $250 for valuables, such as cameras and jewelry.

Automobile Insurance – Public liability and property damage (third-party) insurance is compulsory in Europe, and whether you drive your own or a rental car you must carry insurance. Car rentals in Ireland usually include public liability, property damage, fire, and theft coverage and, sometimes (depending on the car rental company), collision damage coverage with a deductible. In your car rental contract, you'll see that for about $13 a day, you may buy optional collision damage waiver (CDW) protection. (If partial coverage with a deductible is included in the rental contract, the CDW will cover the deductible in the event of an accident, and will cost from $10 to $25 per day.) If the contract does not include collision damage coverage, you may be liable for as much as the full retail value of the car, and by paying for the CDW you are relieved of all responsibility for any damage to the rental car. Before agreeing to this coverage, however, check your own auto insurance policy with your own broker. It very well may cover your entire liability exposure without any additional cost, or you automatically may be covered by the credit card company to which you are charging the cost of your rental.

You also should know that an increasing number of the major international car rental companies automatically are including the cost of the CDW in their basic rates. Car rental prices have increased to include this coverage, although rental company ad campaigns may promote this as a new, improved rental package "benefit." The disadvantage of this inclusion is that you may not have the option to turn down the CDW — even if you already are adequately covered by your own insurance policy or through a credit card company. For more information on this confusing issue, see *Traveling by Car*, in this section.

Your rental contract (with the appropriate insurance box checked off), as well as proof of your personal insurance policy, if applicable, are required as proof of insurance. If you will be driving your own car in Europe, you must carry an International Insurance Certificate (called a Green Card), available through insurance brokers in the US, or take out a special policy for this purpose at customs as you enter the country.

Combination Policies – Short-term insurance policies, which may include a combination of any or all of the types of insurance discussed above, are available through retail insurance agencies, automobile clubs, and many travel agents. These combination policies are designed to cover you for the duration of a single trip.

Two examples of standard combination policies, providing comprehensive coverage for travelers, are offered by *Wallach & Co.* The first, *HealthCare Global,* is available to men and women up to age 84. The medical insurance, which may be purchased for periods of 10 to 180 days, provides $25,000 medical insurance and $50,000 accidental death benefit. The cost for 10 days is $25; for 76 days and over, it is $1.50 a day. Combination policies may include additional accidental death coverage and baggage and trip cancellation insurance options. For $3 per day (minimum 10 days, maximum 90 days), another program, *HealthCare Abroad,* offers significantly better coverage in terms of dollar limits, although the age limit is 75. Its basic policy includes $100,000 medical insurance and $25,000 accidental death benefit. As in the first policy, trip cancellation and baggage insurance also are available. For further information, write to *Wallach & Co.,* 243 Church St. NW, Suite 100D, Vienna, VA 22180 (phone: 703-281-9500 in Virginia; 800-237-6615 elsewhere in the US).

Other policies of this type include the following:

Access America International: A subsidiary of the Blue Cross/Blue Shield plans of New York and Washington, DC, now available nationwide. Contact *Access America,* 600 Third Ave., PO Box 807, New York, NY 10163 (phone: 800-284-8300 or 212-490-5345).

Carefree: Underwritten by The Hartford. Contact *Carefree Travel Insurance,* Arm Coverage, PO Box 310, Mineola, NY 11501 (phone: 800-645-2424 or 516-294-0220).

NEAR Services: Part of a benefits package offered by a travel service organization. An added feature is coverage for lost or stolen airline tickets. Contact *NEAR Services,* 450 Prairie Ave., Calumet City, IL 60409 (phone: 800-654-6700 or 708-868-6700).

Tele-Trip: Underwritten by the Mutual of Omaha Companies. Contact *Tele-Trip Co.,* PO Box 31685, 3201 Farnam St., Omaha, NE 68131 (phone: 402-345-2400 in Nebraska; 800-228-9792 elsewhere in the US).

Travel Assistance International: Provided by Europ Assistance Worldwide Services, and underwritten by Transamerica Occidental Life Insurance. Contact *Travel Assistance International,* 1333 15th St. NW, Suite 400, Washington, DC 20005 (phone: 202-347-2025 in Washington, DC; 800-821-2828 elsewhere in the US).

Travel Guard International: Underwritten by the Insurance Company of North America, it is available through authorized travel agents, or contact *Travel Guard International,* 1145 Clark St., Stevens Point, WI 54481 (phone: 715-345-0505 in Wisconsin; 800-826-1300 elsewhere in the US).

Travel Insurance PAK: Underwritten by The Travelers. Contact *The Travelers*

Companies, Ticket and Travel Plans, One Tower Sq., Hartford, CT 06183-5040 (phone: 203-277-2319 in Connecticut; 800-243-3174 elsewhere in the US).

WorldCare Travel Assistance Association: This organization offers insurance packages underwritten by Transamerica Premier Insurance Company and Transamerica Occidental Life Insurance. Contact *WorldCare Travel Assistance Association,* 605 Market St., Suite 1300, San Francisco, CA 94105 (phone: 800-666-4993 or 415-541-4991).

How to Pack

No one can provide a completely foolproof list of precisely what to pack, so it's best to let common sense, space, and comfort guide you. Keep one maxim in mind: Less is more. You simply won't need as much clothing as you think, and though there is nothing more frustrating than arriving at your destination without the very item that in its absence becomes crucial, you are far more likely to need a forgotten accessory — or a needle and thread or scissors — than a particular piece of clothing.

As with almost anything relating to travel, a little planning can go a long way. There are specific things to consider before you open the first drawer or fold the first pair of underwear:

1. Where are you going — city, country, or both?
2. How many total days will you be gone?
3. What's the average temperature likely to be during your stay?

The goal is to remain perfectly comfortable, neat, clean, and adequately fashionable wherever you go, but actually to pack as little as possible. The main obstacle to achieving this end is habit: Most of us wake up each morning with an entire wardrobe hanging in our closets, and we assume that our suitcase should offer the same variety and selection. Not so — only our anxiety about being caught short makes us treat a suitcase like a mobile closet. This worry can be eliminated by learning to travel light and by following two firm packing principles:

1. Organize your travel wardrobe around a single color — blue or brown, for example — that allows you to mix, match, and layer clothes. Holding firm to one color scheme will make it easy to eliminate items of clothing that don't harmonize, and by picking clothes for their adaptability and compatibility with your basic color, you will put together the widest selection with the fewest pieces of clothing.
2. Use laundries to renew your wardrobe. Never overpack to ensure a supply of fresh clothing — shirts, blouses, underwear — for each day of a long trip. Businesspeople routinely use hotel laundries to wash and clean clothes. If these are too expensive, in Ireland there are local, self-service laundries, called "launderettes," in most towns of any size.

CLIMATE AND CLOTHES: Exactly what you pack for your trip will be a function of where you are going and when, and the kinds of things you intend to do. A few degrees can make all the difference between being comfortably attired and very real suffering, so your initial step should be to find out what the general weather conditions — temperature, rainfall, seasonal variations — are likely to be in the areas you will visit.

Although Ireland is farther north than most of the US — Dublin, sitting astride latitude 53°20′, is as far north as Goose Bay, Labrador — the climate generally is much milder. The Gulf Stream, which warms the coasts, brings moderate temperatures year-round, with few sub-zero winters or blistering hot summers. Winter temperatures rarely dip below 40F and summer temperatures usually rise no higher than 70F. The stereotype about Irish weather being wet is true: It rains often throughout the year, and even on fairly clear days, the air feels damp. Generally speaking, a typical fall wardrobe in the northern tier of the US will probably have everything that's needed for the trip. For example, it's a good idea to bring along a raincoat whatever time of year you travel to Ireland and lightweight wools are worn even in summer.

More information about the climate in Ireland, along with a chart of average low and high temperatures for specific cities, is given in *When to Go,* in this section; other sources of information are airlines and travel agents.

Keeping temperature and climate in mind, consider the problem of luggage. Plan on one suitcase per person (and in a pinch, remember that it's always easier to carry two small suitcases than to schlepp one that's roughly the size of the *QE2*). Standard 26- to 28-inch suitcases can be made to work for 1 week or 1 month, and unless you are going for no more than a weekend, never cram wardrobes for two people into one suitcase.

The dress code in Ireland is casual, relaxed, and conservative. Jeans are not out of place for sightseeing, and sports clothes generally are appropriate for restaurant dining. Attire more formal than a cocktail dress or evening pants for women and something as formal as black tie for men are necessary only for the most elegant occasions — such as one of the gala events held by the *Royal Dublin Society.* A blazer or sport jacket, trousers, and tie will get a man into the finest restaurant anywhere, and, as the dress code tends to be informal, even the tie is not *de rigueur.* For women, a dress or a suit will do in the same situations. Other diners may be more formally dressed, but you won't be turned away or made to feel self-conscious if you do not mirror them. By the same token, you won't feel you've overdone it if you choose to turn an evening at an elegant restaurant into something special and dress accordingly. If you're planning a number of more formal evenings during your trip, bring two or three changes of clothes. Bear in mind that coordinates also are a good way of providing a number of dressier options without adding to your luggage content.

Women should figure on a maximum of five daytime and three late afternoon–evening changes. Whether you are going to be gone for a week or a month, this number should be enough. For daytime activities, women might pack jeans or light slacks, blouses, one or two swimsuits (depending on where you're going), and a pair of comfortable shoes or sneakers. In warmer weather, include T-shirts and a pair of shorts; skirts and summer dresses are a cool choice for touring. As the weather can be damp and chilly even during the summer, also include a lightweight sweater or jacket. In colder weather, pack corduroy or wool slacks, a longer skirt which can be worn with turtlenecks, blouses, and sweaters, and a pair of boots, which will provide a number of comfortable alternatives. Low-heel pumps are appropriate for both dressier daytime and evening wear. Again, before packing, lay out every piece of clothing you think you might want to take. Select clothing on the basis of what can serve several functions, and accessorize everything beforehand so you know exactly what you will be wearing with what. Eliminate items that don't mix, match, or interchange within your chosen color scheme. If you can't wear it in at least two distinct incarnations, leave it home.

Men also will find that color coordination is crucial. Solid colors coordinate best, and a sport jacket that goes with a pair of pants from a suit and several pairs of slacks provides added options. For travel in warmer weather, lightweight cotton shirts and a coordinating cotton sweater paired with casual slacks or chinos (and the sport jacket on damp, chilly days) will suffice for many occasions; also bring along shorts and one or two bathing suits (again, depending on your destination). Include several shirts that can be used for both daytime and evening wear, and sneakers and/or loafers (include at least one pair of double-duty shoes that go with both casual and dressier attire). For touring in colder weather, bring heavier slacks or corduroys, long-sleeve shirts or turtlenecks, a wool sweater, and a warm jacket or coat. Hanging bags are best for packing suits and jackets.

The winter overcoat worn by the Irish generally is not quite as heavy as the one that would be worn in, say, New York or Chicago — no fur or down linings, usually; an unlined loden coat is a classic — but your warmer one will do fine if you are visiting during the often damp and dank winter. Since the prevailing characteristic of the Irish climate is rain, a raincoat with a zip-out lining — and maybe even a hood — is a versatile choice. The removable lining affords adaptability to temperature changes, and the hood is better suited (and less cumbersome) than an umbrella for fine, misty rain, although a practical alternative is a rain hat that can be rolled up in a pocket or carry-on bag. If you do decide to take an umbrella, a compact telescoping model is best.

If your trip will encompass all parts of Ireland, layering is the key to comfort — particularly when touring in parts of the countryside where mornings and evenings can be chilly even when the days are mild. No matter where you are traveling in Ireland, however, layering is a good way to prepare for atypical temperatures or changes in the weather. For damp or unexpectedly cold days or for outings in the countryside, a recommended basic is a lightweight wool or heavy cotton turtleneck, which can be worn under a shirt and perhaps a third layer, such as a pullover sweater, jacket, or windbreaker. In warmer weather, substitute a T-shirt and lightweight cotton shirts or sweaters for the turtleneck and wool layers. As the weather changes, you can add or remove clothes as required, and layering adapts well to the ruling principle of dressing according to a single color scheme. Individual items in layers can mix and match, be used together or independently.

Among the layers, don't forget to include a warm sweater or jacket, even in summer (tweeds are worn year-round). This will not be needed to take the chill off overly air conditioned rooms (air conditioning is not the rule in Ireland), but even on warmer days it will be welcome for exploring castles, cairns, and abbeys. In fact, you probably will be tempted by the great variety of sweaters available throughout Ireland to acquire more layers than you really need, so buy only the very basics before departure.

If you are planning to be on the move — either in a car, bus, train, or plane, or aboard a boat — consider loose-fitting clothes that do not wrinkle, although the recent trend toward fabrics with a deliberately wrinkled look is a boon to travelers. Despite the tendency of designers to use more 100% natural fabrics, synthetics — particularly the new washable rayon blends — are immensely practical for a trip, and they have improved immeasurably in appearance lately. As a general rule, clothes in pure cotton and linen are the most perishable and hard to keep fresh-looking. Lightweight wools and manmade fabrics — such as jerseys and knits, and drip-dry fabrics that can be rinsed in Woolite or a similar cold-water detergent — travel best (although in very hot weather cotton clothing may be the most comfortable), and prints look fresher longer than solids.

Pack clothes that have a lot of pockets, for traveler's checks, documents, and tickets. Then if your bag gets lost or stolen, you will retain possession of the essentials. Men who prefer to keep their pockets free of coins, papers, and keys might consider a shoulder bag, useful for carrying camera equipment as well as daily necessities.

And finally — since the best touring of Irish ruins, churches, and countryside is done on foot — comfortable walking shoes are a must for both sexes, no matter what the season or the fashion. You will do a lot of walking, up and down stairs, up and down hills, to the end of archaeological sites and back. Even in the evening, when you anticipate walking no farther than to the nearest restaurant, women should avoid spike heels. Cobblestones are ubiquitous, and chunkier heels have a better chance of not getting caught — and ruined.

Your carry-on luggage should contain a survival kit with the basic things you will need in case your luggage gets lost or stolen: a toothbrush, toothpaste, all medications, a sweater, nightclothes, and a change of underwear. With these essential items at hand, you will be prepared for any sudden, unexpected occurrence that separates you from your suitcase. If you have many 1- or 2-night stops scheduled, you can live out of your survival case without having to unpack completely at each hotel.

Other items you might consider packing are a flashlight with extra batteries, small sewing and first-aid kits (including insect repellent), binoculars, and a camera or camcorder (see *Cameras and Equipment,* in this section).

Sundries – If you are traveling during the summer and will be spending a lot of time outdoors, particularly along the coast, pack special items so that you won't spend your entire vacation horizontal in a hotel room (or hospital) because of sunburn. Be sure to take a sun hat (to protect hair as well as skin), sunscreen, and tanning lotion, which is available in graduated degrees of sunblock corresponding to the level of your skin's sensitivity. (The quantity of sunscreen is indicated by number: The higher the number, the greater the protection.) A good moisturizer is necessary to help keep your skin from drying out and peeling. The best advice is to take the sun's rays in small doses — no more than 20 minutes at a stretch — increasing your sunbathing time as your vacation progresses.

PACKING: The basic idea of packing is to get everything into the suitcase and out again with as few wrinkles as possible. Simple, casual clothes — shirts, jeans and slacks, permanent press skirts — can be rolled into neat, tight sausages that keep other packed items in place and leave the clothes themselves amazingly unwrinkled. The rolled clothes can be retrieved, shaken out, and hung up at your destination. However, for items that are too bulky or delicate for even careful rolling, a suitcase can be packed with the heaviest items on the bottom, toward the hinges, so that they will not wrinkle more perishable clothes. Candidates for the bottom layer include shoes (stuff them with small items to save space), a toilet kit, handbags (stuff them to help keep their shape), and an alarm clock. Fill out this layer with things that will not wrinkle or will not matter if they do, such as sweaters, socks, a bathing suit, gloves, and underwear.

If you get this first, heavy layer as smooth as possible with the fill-ins, you will have a shelf for the next layer — the most easily wrinkled items, like slacks, jackets, shirts, dresses, and skirts. These should be buttoned and zipped and laid along the whole length of the suitcase with as little folding as possible. When you do need to make a fold, do it on a crease (as with pants), along a seam in the fabric, or where it will not show (such as shirttails). Alternate each piece of clothing, using one side of the suitcase, then the other, to make the layers as flat as possible. Make the layers even and the total contents of your bag as full and firm as possible to keep things from shifting around during transit. On the top layer put the things you will want at once: nightclothes, an umbrella or raincoat, a sweater.

With men's two-suiter suitcases, follow the same procedure. Then place jackets on hangers, straighten them out, and leave them unbuttoned. If they are too wide for the suitcase, fold them lengthwise down the middle, straighten the shoulders, and fold the sleeves in along the seam.

While packing, it is a good idea to separate each layer of clothes with plastic cleaning bags, which will help preserve pressed clothes while they are in the suitcase. Unpack your bags as soon as you get to your hotel. Nothing so thoroughly destroys freshly cleaned and pressed clothes as sitting for days in a suitcase. Finally, if something is badly wrinkled and can't be professionally pressed before you must wear it, hang it overnight in a bathroom where the bathtub has been filled with very hot water; keep the bathroom door closed so the room becomes something of a steamroom. It really works miracles.

LUGGAGE: If you already own serviceable luggage, do not feel compelled to buy new bags. If, however, you have been looking for an excuse to throw out that old suitcase that saw you through 4 years of college and innumerable weekends, this trip to Ireland can be the perfect occasion.

Luggage falls into three categories — hard, soft-sided, and soft — and each has advantages and disadvantages. Hard suitcases have a rigid frame and sides. They provide the most protection from rough handling, but they also are the heaviest. Wheels and pull straps can rectify this problem, but they should be removed before the luggage is turned over at check-in or they may be wrenched off in transit. In addition, hard bags sometimes will pop open, even when locked, so a strap around the suitcase is advised.

Soft-sided suitcases have a rigid frame that has been covered with leather, fabric, or a synthetic material. The weight of the suitcase is greatly reduced, but many of the coverings (except leather, which also is heavy) are vulnerable to rips and tears from conveyor machinery. Not surprisingly, the materials that wear best generally are found on more expensive luggage.

The third category, seen more and more frequently, is soft luggage. Lacking any rigid structural element, it comes in a wide variety of shapes and sizes and is easy to carry, especially since it often has a shoulder strap. Most carry-on bags are of this type because they can be squeezed under the plane seat. They are even more vulnerable to damage on conveyor equipment than soft-sided bags, and as the weak point on these bags is the zipper, be sure to tie some cord or put several straps around the bag for extra insurance. Also be prepared to find a brand-new set of wrinkles pressed into everything that was carefully ironed before packing.

Whatever type of luggage you choose, remember that it should last for many years. Shop carefully, but be prepared to make a sizable investment.

It always is a good idea to add an empty, flattened airline bag or similarly light carrying case to your suitcase; you'll find it indispensable to carry a few items for a day's outing. Keep in mind, too, that you're likely to do some shopping so save room for those items. If you're planning any extensive shopping, you might consider packing one of those soft, parachute-cloth suitcases that fold into a small envelope when not in use.

For more information on packing and luggage, send your request with a self-addressed, stamped, #10 envelope to *Samsonite Travel Advisory Service* (PO Box 39609, Dept. 80, Denver, CO 80239) for its free booklet *Lightening the Travel Load: Travel Tips & Tricks.*

SOME FINAL PACKING HINTS: Apart from the items you pack as carry-on luggage (see above), always keep all necessary medicines, valuable jewelry, and travel or business documents in your purse, briefcase, or carry-on bag — *not in the luggage you will check.* Tuck a bathing suit into your handbag or briefcase, too; in the event of lost baggage, it's frustrating to be without one. And whether in your overnight bag or checked luggage, cosmetics and any liquids should be packed in plastic bottles or at least wrapped in plastic bags and tied.

Golf clubs may be checked through as luggage (most airlines are accustomed to handling them), but tennis racquets should be carried onto the plane. Some airlines require that bicycles be partially dismantled and packaged (see *Camping and Caravanning, Hiking and Biking,* in this section). Check with the airline before departure to see if there is a specific regulation regarding any special equipment or sporting gear you plan to take.

Hints for Handicapped Travelers

From 35 to 50 million people in the US alone have some sort of disability, and at least half this number are physically handicapped. Like everyone else today, they — and the uncounted disabled millions around the world — are on the move. More than ever before, they are demanding facilities they can use comfortably, and they are being heard. The disabled traveler will find that services for the handicapped have improved considerably over the last few years, both in the US and abroad, and though accessibility is far from universal, it is being brought up to more acceptable standards every day.

PLANNING: Good planning is essential: Collect as much information as you can about your specific disability and facilities for the disabled in the area you're visiting, make your travel arrangements well in advance, and specify to all services involved the exact nature of your condition or restricted mobility, as your trip will be much more comfortable if you know that there are accommodations and facilities to suit your needs. The best way to find out if your intended destination can accommodate a handicapped traveler is to write or phone the local tourist association or hotel and ask specific questions. If you require a corridor of a certain width to maneuver a wheelchair or if you need handles on the bathroom wall for support, ask the hotel manager. A travel agent or the local chapter or national office of the organization that deals with your particular disability — for example, the *American Foundation for the Blind* or the *American Heart Association* — will supply the most up-to-date information on the subject. The following sources offer general information on access:

Access to the World, by Louise Weiss, offers sound tips for the disabled traveler abroad. Published by Facts on File (460 Park Ave. S., New York, NY 10016; phone: 212-683-2244), it costs $16.95. Check with your local bookstore; it also can be ordered by phone with a credit card.

Access Travel: A Guide to the Accessibility of Airport Terminals, published by the Airport Operators Council International, provides information on more than 500 airports worldwide — including the major airports throughout Europe — with ratings according to 70 features, including accessibility to bathrooms, corridor width, and parking spaces. For a free copy, write to the Consumer Information Center, Access America (Dept. 563W, Pueblo, CO 81009), or call 202-293-8500 and ask for "Item 563W — Access Travel." To help travel agents plan trips for the handicapped, this material is reprinted with additional information on tourist boards, city information offices, and tour operators specializing in travel for the handicapped (see "Tours," below) in the *Worldwide Edition* of the *Official Airline Guides Travel Planner,* issued quarterly by Official Airline Guides (2000 Clearwater Dr., Oak Brook, IL 60521; phone: 708-574-6000).

Air Transportation of Handicapped Persons is a booklet published by the US Department of Transportation, and will be sent at no charge upon written request. Ask for "Free Advisory Circular #AC-120-32" from the Distribution Unit, US Dept. of Transportation, Publications Section, M-443-2, Washington, DC 20590.

Handicapped Travel Newsletter is regarded as one of the best sources of information for the disabled traveler. It is edited by wheelchair-bound Vietnam veteran Michael Quigley, who has traveled to 93 countries around the world. Issued every 2 months (plus special issues), a subscription is $10 per year. Write to *Handicapped Travel Newsletter,* PO Box 269, Athens, TX 75751 (phone: 214-677-1260).

Information Center for Individuals with Disabilities (ICID), Fort Point Pl., 1st Floor, 27-43 Wormwood St., Boston, MA 02210 (phone: 617-727-5540/1 or 800-462-5015 in Massachusetts only); both numbers offer voice and TDD (telecommunications device for the deaf) service. *ICID* provides information and referral services on disability-related issues and will help you research your trip. The center publishes fact sheets on vacation planning, tour operators, travel agents, and travel resources.

The Itinerary is a travel magazine for people with disabilities. Published bimonthly, it includes information on accessibility, listings of tours, news of adaptive devices, travel aids, and special services, as well as numerous general travel hints. A subscription is $10 a year; write to *The Itinerary,* PO Box 2012, Bayonne, NJ 07002-2012 (phone: 201-858-3400).

Mobility International/USA (MIUSA), the US branch of *Mobility International,* a nonprofit British organization with affiliates in some 35 countries, offers advice and assistance to disabled travelers — including information on accommodations, access guides, and study tours. Its main office is *Mobility International Headquarters* (228 Borough High St., London, SE1 1JX, England; phone: 44-71-403-5688). Among its affiliates in Europe is the *Irish Wheelchair Association* (Aras Chuchulain, Blackheath Dr., Clontars, Dublin 3, Irish Republic; phone: 353-1-338241). Its publications include a quarterly newsletter and a comprehensive sourcebook, *World of Options for the '90s: A Guide to International Education Exchange, Community Service, and Travel for Persons with Disabilities.* Individual membership is $20 a year; subscription to the newsletter alone is $10 annually. For more information, contact *MIUSA,* PO Box 3551, Eugene, OR 97403 (phone: 503-343-1284; voice and TDD — telecommunications device for the deaf).

National Rehabilitation Information Center, 8455 Colesville Rd., Suite 935, Silver Spring, MD 20910 (phone: 301-588-9284). A general information, resource, research, and referral service.

Paralyzed Veterans of America (PVA) is a national veterans service organization. Its members all are veterans who have suffered spinal cord injuries, but it offers advocacy services and information to all persons with a disability. *PVA* also sponsors *Access to the Skies,* a program that coordinates the efforts of the national and international air travel industry in providing airport and airplane access for the disabled. Members receive several helpful publications, as well as regular notification of conferences on subjects of interest to the disabled traveler. For information, contact *PVA/ATTS Program,* 801 18th St. NW, Washington, DC 20006 (phone: 202-USA-1300).

Royal Association for Disability and Rehabilitation (RADAR), 25 Mortimer St., London W1N 8AB, England (phone: 44-81-637-5400), offers a number of publications for the handicapped, including a comprehensive guide, *Holidays and Travel Abroad for the Disabled,* which provides helpful advice to the disabled traveler abroad. Available by writing to *RADAR,* the price, including airmail postage, is £3; *RADAR* requires payment in pounds sterling, so this should be sent via an international money order (available at the post office and at banks).

Society for the Advancement of Travel for the Handicapped (SATH), 26 Court St., Penthouse, Brooklyn, NY 11242 (phone: 718-858-5483). To keep abreast of developments in travel for the handicapped as they occur, you may want to join *SATH,* a nonprofit organization whose members include travel agents, tour operators, and other travel suppliers, as well as consumers. Membership costs $40 ($25 for students and travelers who are 65 and older) and the fee is tax deductible. *SATH* publishes a quarterly newsletter, an excellent booklet, *Travel Tips for the Handicapped,* and provides information on travel agents or tour operators who have experience (or an interest) in travel for the handicapped. *SATH* also offers a free 48-page guide, *The United States Welcomes Handicapped Visitors,* that covers domestic transportation and accommodations, as well as travel insurance and other useful hints for the handicapped traveler abroad. Send a self-addressed, #10 envelope to *SATH* at the address above, and include $1 for postage.

TravelAbility, by Lois Reamy, is a vast database with information on locating tours for the handicapped, coping with public transport, and finding accommodations, special equipment, and travel agents, and includes a helpful step-by-step planning guide. Although geared mainly to travel in the US, it is full of information useful to handicapped travelers anywhere. Previously published by Macmillan, *TravelAbility* is currently out of print, but may be available at your library. *Travel Information Service* at Moss Rehabilitation Hospital is a service designed to help physically handicapped people plan trips. It cannot make travel arrangements, but it will supply information on travel accessibility for a nominal fee. Contact the *Travel Information Service,* Moss Rehabilitation Hospital, 12th St. and Tabor Rd., Philadelphia, PA 19141 (phone: 215-456-9600).

In the Republic of Ireland, the *National Rehabilitation Board* (25 Clyde Rd., Dublin 4, Ireland; phone: 1-684181 or 1-689618) is the central source of information on facilities for the handicapped, and the *Union of Voluntary Organisations for the Handicapped* (29 Eaton Sq., Monkstown, County Dublin, Ireland; phone: 1-809251) will provide addresses and telephone numbers of local volunteer organizations serving the handicapped. In Northern Ireland, the *Northern Ireland Council for the Handicapped, Northern Ireland Council of Social Service* (2 Annadale Ave., Belfast BT7 3JH, Northern Ireland, UK; phone: 232-491011), is the central source of information for the handicapped, and in conjunction with the Northern Ireland Tourist Board publishes and distributes the free booklet *The Disabled Tourist in Northern Ireland: Things to See, Places to Stay,* which provides useful information on everything from access for wheelchair visitors to overnight accommodations and facilities for the hearing-impaired and for visually handicapped people. The Irish Tourist Board (in the Republic) also publishes an annual *Guide to Hotels and Guesthouses,* indicating handicapped accessibility, but its *Accommodation Guide for Disabled Persons,* available free from its Irish offices, is an access guide and is much more useful.

Regularly revised hotel and restaurant guides using the symbol of access (person in a wheelchair — see the symbol at the beginning of this chapter) to point out accommodations suitable for wheelchair-bound guests include *Egon Ronay's Guide* ($18.95) and the *Michelin Red Guide to Great Britain and Ireland* ($17.95), both of which are available in general and travel bookstores.

The *Canadian Rehabilitation Council for the Disabled* publishes a useful book by Cinnie Noble, *Handi-Travel: A Resource Book for Disabled and Elderly Travelers* ($12.95, $2 for shipping and handling, 50¢ each additional copy). This comprehensive travel guide is full of practical tips for those with disabilities affecting mobility, hearing, or sight. To order this book and for other useful information, contact the *Canadian Rehabilitation Council for the Disabled,* 45 Sheppard Ave. E., Suite 801, Toronto, Ontario M2N 5W9, Canada (phone: 416-250-7490).

A few more basic resources to look for are *Travel for the Disabled,* by Helen Hecker ($9.95), and by the same author, *The Directory of Travel Agencies for the Disabled* ($12.95). *Wheelchair Vagabond,* by John G. Nelson, is another useful guide for travelers confined to a wheelchair (softcover, $9.95; hardcover, $14.95). All three are published by Twin Peaks Press (PO Box 129, Vancouver, WA 98666; to order call 800-637-CALM). Additionally, *The Physically Disabled Traveler's Guide,* by Rod W. Durgin and Norene Lindsay, is helpful and informative. It is available from Resource Directories (3361 Executive Pkwy., Suite 302, Toledo, OH 43606; phone: 419-536-5353) for $9.95, plus $2 for postage and handling.

Also check the library for Mary Meister Walzer's *A Travel Guide for the Disabled: Western Europe* (Van Nostrand Reinhold), which gives access ratings to a fair number of hotels along with information on the accessibility of some sightseeing attractions, restaurants, theaters, stores, and more.

It should be noted that almost all of the material published with disabled travelers in mind deals with the wheelchair-bound traveler, for whom architectural barriers are of prime concern. For travelers with diabetes, a pamphlet entitled *Ticket to Safe Travel* is available for 50¢ from the New York chapter of the *American Diabetes Association* (505 Eighth Ave., 21st Floor, New York, NY 10018; phone: 212-947-9707). For those with heart-related ailments, *Travel for the Patient with Chronic Obstructive Pulmonary Disease* is available for $2 from Dr. Harold Silver (1601 18th St. NW, Washington, DC 20009; phone: 202-667-0134); the *American Heart Association* (7320 Greenville Ave., Dallas, TX 75231; phone: 214-373-6300) also provides a number of useful publications. For blind travelers, a wealth of additional information is available from the *American Foundation for the Blind* (15 W. 16th St., New York, NY 10011; phone: 212-620-2147 in New York State; 800-232-5463 elsewhere in the US).

A problem that will restrict the movement of one category of the handicapped, blind people who are dependent on Seeing Eye dogs, is the very strict enforcement of anti-rabies laws in the British Isles, including both Northern Ireland and the Irish Republic. Any dogs brought into either country must spend 6 months in quarantine — and Seeing Eye dogs are not exempt. Since it is not practical to bring a dog for a short stay, blind people should plan to travel with human companions.

PLANE: Advise the airline that you are handicapped when you book your flight. The Federal Aviation Administration (FAA) has ruled that US airlines must accept disabled and handicapped passengers as long as the airline has advance notice and the passenger represents no potentially insurmountable problem in the event that emergency evacuation becomes necessary. As a matter of course, US airlines were pretty good about helping handicapped passengers even before the ruling, although each airline has somewhat different procedures. European airlines also generally are good about accommodating the disabled traveler, but again, policies vary from carrier to carrier. Ask for specifics when you book your flight.

Disabled passengers always should make reservations well in advance, and should provide the airline with all relevant details of their condition at that time. These details include information on mobility, toilet and special oxygen needs, and requirements for equipment that must be supplied by the airline, such as a wheelchair or portable oxygen. Be sure that the person to whom you speak understands fully the degree of your disability — the more details provided, the more effective the help the airline can give you. On the day before the flight, call back to make sure that all arrangements have been prepared, and arrive early on the day of the flight so that you can board before the rest of the passengers. Carry a medical certificate with you, stating your specific disability or the need to carry particular medicine. (Some airlines require the certificate; you should find out the regulations of the airline you'll be flying well beforehand.)

Because most airports have jetways (corridors connecting the terminal with the door of the plane), a disabled passenger usually can be taken as far as the plane, and sometimes right onto it, in a wheelchair. If not, a narrow boarding chair may be used to take you to your seat. Your own wheelchair, which will be folded and put in the baggage compartment, should be tagged as escort luggage to assure that it's available at planeside upon landing rather than in the baggage claim area. Travel is not quite as simple if your wheelchair is battery-operated: Unless it has non-spillable batteries, it might not be accepted on board, and you will have to check with the airline ahead of time to find out how the batteries and the chair should be packaged for the flight. Usually people in wheelchairs are asked to wait until other passengers have disembarked. If you are making a tight connection, be sure to tell the attendant.

Passengers who use oxygen may not use their personal supply in the cabin, though it may be carried on the plane as cargo when properly packed and labeled. If you will need oxygen during the flight, the airline will supply it to you (there is a charge) provided you have given advance notice — 24 hours to a few days, depending on the carrier.

Useful information on every stage of air travel, from planning to arrival, is provided in the booklet *Incapacitated Passengers Air Travel Guide*. To receive a free copy, write to Senior Manager, Passenger Services, International Air Transport Association, 2000 Peel St., Montreal, Quebec H3A 2R4 Canada (phone: 514-844-6311).

For an access guide to hundreds of airports worldwide, write for *Access Travel: A Guide to the Accessibility of Airport Terminals,* a free publication of the *Airport Operators Council International,* which includes detailed information on airports in Cork and Shannon. The US Department of Transportation's *Air Transportation of Handicapped Persons* explains the general guidelines that govern air carrier policies. It is available free when requested in writing. For information on obtaining both of these publications, see the source list above.

The following airlines serving Ireland (either directly or through connecting flights) have TDD toll-free lines in the US for the hearing-impaired: *American* (phone: 800-582-1573 in Ohio; 800-543-1586 elsewhere in the US); *Continental* (phone: 800-343-9195 from 8 AM to 1 AM, Eastern Standard Time); *Pan American* (phone: 800-722-3323); and *TWA* (phone: 800-252-0622 in California; 800-421-8480 elsewhere in the US).

SHIP: Cunard's *Queen Elizabeth 2* is considered the best-equipped ship for the handicapped — all but the top deck is accessible. The *QE2* crosses the Atlantic regularly from April through December between New York and its home port of Southampton, England, sometimes calling at Cherbourg, France, and other European ports, including Ireland. Handicapped travelers are advised to book reservations at least 90 days in advance to reserve specialized cabins. For further information on the *QE2,* see *Traveling by Ship,* in this section.

GROUND TRANSPORTATION: Perhaps the simplest solution to getting around is to travel with an able-bodied companion who can drive. If you are accustomed to driving your own hand-controlled car and are determined to rent one, you may have to do some extensive research, as it is difficult to find rental cars fitted with hand controls in Europe. If agencies do provide hand-control cars, they are apt to be few and in high demand. The best course is to contact the major car rental agencies listed in *Traveling by Car,* in this section, well before your departure, but be forewarned, you still may be out of luck. Other sources for information on vehicles adapted for the handicapped are the organizations discussed above.

The *American Automobile Association (AAA)* publishes the booklet *The Handicapped Driver's Mobility Guide,* available free to members and for $3 to non-members. Contact your local *AAA* office, or send a self-addressed, stamped, 6-by-9-inch envelope to *AAA* Traffic Safety Department, 1000 AAA Dr., Heathrow, FL 32746-5063.

Another quite expensive option is to hire a chauffeured auto. Other alternatives include taking taxis or using local public transportation; however, your mobility may be limited in rural areas.

BUS AND TRAIN: In addition to networks in metropolitan areas, just about anywhere a paved road leads to a town or village there is likely to be an Irish bus route, although frequency and accessibility for handicapped travelers varies widely. Bus travel in Ireland is not recommended for travelers who are totally wheelchair-bound unless they have someone along who can lift them on and off or they are members of a group tour designed for the handicapped and are using a specially outfitted bus. If you have some mobility, however, you'll find local personnel usually quite happy to help you board and exit.

Handicapped travelers with some mobility can make do on short train trips and the major stations have restroom facilities for the handicapped. Train travel for the wheelchair-bound is becoming more feasible in Ireland. Although Irish trains generally cannot accommodate wheelchairs, depending on the type of train, wheelchair passengers sometimes can travel in the guard's van. Arrangements usually are made through the area manager in advance. For further information, contact *CIE Tours International,* 122 E. 42nd St., New York, NY 10168 (phone: 212-697-3914 in New York City;

800-522-5258 elsewhere in New York State; 800-CIE-TOUR elsewhere in the US).

TOURS: Programs designed for the physically impaired are run by specialists who have researched hotels, restaurants, and sites to be sure they present no insurmountable obstacles. The following travel agencies and tour operators specialize in making group and individual arrangements for travelers with physical or other disabilities. All of them have experience in travel to Europe. Because of the requirements of handicapped travel, however, the same packages may not be offered regularly.

Access: The Foundation for Accessibility by the Disabled, PO Box 356, Malvern, NY 11565 (phone: 516-887-5798). Travelers referral service that acts as an intermediary with tour operators and agents worldwide, and provides information on accessibility at various locations. The firm also offers access to its audio/video travel library.

Accessible Tours/Directions Unlimited, 720 N. Bedford Rd., Bedford Hills, NY 10507 (phone: 914-241-1700 in New York State; 800-533-5343 elsewhere in the US). Arranges group or individual tours for disabled persons traveling in the company of able-bodied friends or family members. Accepts the unaccompanied traveler if completely self-sufficient.

Evergreen Travel Service/Wings on Wheels Tours, 19505L 44th Ave. W., Lynnwood, WA 98036-5658 (phone: 206-776-1184 or 800-435-2288 throughout the US). The oldest company in the world offering worldwide tours and cruises for the disabled (Wings on Wheels) and sight impaired/blind (White Cane Tours). Most programs are first class or deluxe, and include a trained escort. *Evergreen* also offers a service called Evergreen Flying Fingers, for the deaf.

Flying Wheels Travel, 143 W. Bridge St., Box 382, Owatonna, MN 55060 (phone: 507-451-5005 or 800-535-6790 throughout the US). Handles both tours and individual arrangements.

The Guided Tour, 555 Ashbourne Rd., Elkins Park, PA 19117 (phone: 215-782-1370). Arranges tours for people with developmental and learning disabilities and sponsors separate tours for members of the same population who also are physically disabled or who simply need a slower pace.

Sprout, 893 Amsterdam Ave., New York, NY 10025 (phone: 212-222-9575). Arranges travel programs for mildly and moderately disabled teens and adults.

Travel Horizons Unlimited, 11 E. 44th St., New York, NY 10017 (phone: 212-687-5121 in New York; 800-343-5032 elsewhere in the US). Travel agent and registered nurse Mary Ann Hamm designs trips for individual travelers requiring all types of kidney dialysis and handles arrangements for the dialysis.

Whole Person Tours, PO Box 1084, Bayonne, NJ 07002-1084 (phone: 800-462-2237 or 201-858-3400). Handicapped owner Bob Zywicki travels the world with his wheelchair and offers a lineup of escorted tours (many conducted by himself) for the disabled. Send a self-addressed, stamped envelope for a general tour brochure of foreign and domestic programs. *Whole Person Tours* also publishes *The Itinerary,* a bimonthly newsletter for disabled travelers (a 1-year subscription costs $10).

Hints for Single Travelers

 Just about the last trip in human history on which the participants were neatly paired was the voyage of Noah's Ark. Ever since, passenger lists and tour groups have reflected the same kind of asymmetry that occurs in real life, as countless individuals set forth to see the world unaccompanied (or unencumbered, depending on your outlook) by spouse, lover, friend, or relative.

There are some things to be said for traveling alone. There is the pleasure of privacy, though a solitary traveler must be self-reliant, independent, and responsible. Unfortunately, traveling alone also can turn a traveler into a second class citizen.

The truth is that the travel industry is not very fair to people who vacation by themselves. People traveling alone almost invariably end up paying more than individuals traveling in pairs. Most travel bargains, including package tours, accommodations, resort packages, and cruises, are based on *double occupancy* rates. This means that the per-person price is offered on the basis of two people traveling together and sharing a double room (which means they each will spend a good deal more on meals and extras). The single traveler will have to pay a surcharge, called a single supplement, for exactly the same package. In extreme cases, this can add as much as 30% to 55% to the basic per-person rate. As far as the travel industry is concerned, single travel has not yet come into its own.

Don't despair, however. Throughout Ireland, there are scores of smaller hotels and other hostelries where, in addition to a cozier atmosphere, prices still are quite reasonable for the single traveler. There are, after all, countless thousands of individuals who *do* travel alone. Inevitably, their greatest obstacle is the single supplement charge, which prevents them from cashing in on travel bargains available to anyone traveling as part of a pair.

The obvious, most effective alternative is to find a traveling companion. Even special "singles' tours" that promise no supplements usually are based on people sharing double rooms. Perhaps the most recent innovation along these lines is the creation of organizations that "introduce" the single traveler to other single travelers, somewhat like a dating service. If you are interested in finding another single traveler to help share the cost, consider contacting the agencies listed below. Some charge fees, others are free, but the basic service offered by all is the same: to match the unattached person with a compatible travel mate, often as part of the company's own package tours. Among the better established of these agencies are the following:

Classic Singles Network: Offers tours catering to the mature single client — the majority of its members are over 45 years old. For information, contact *Classic Singles Network,* 100 N. Sepulveda Blvd., Suite 1010, El Segundo, CA 90245 (phone: 800-421-5785 in California; 800-421-2255 elsewhere in the US).

Contiki Holidays: Specializes in vacations for 18- to 35-year-olds. Packages to Ireland frequently are offered. For information, contact *Contiki Holidays,* 1432 E. Katella Ave., Anaheim, CA 92805 (phone: 714-937-0611; 800-624-0611 in California; 800-626-0611 elsewhere in the continental US).

Cosmos: This agency, specializing in budget motorcoach tours of Europe — including Ireland — offers a guaranteed-share plan whereby singles who wish to share rooms (and avoid paying the single supplement) are matched by the tour escort with like-minded individuals of the same sex and charged the basic double-occupancy tour price. Contact the firm at any one of its three North American branches: 95-25 Queens Blvd., Rego Park, NY 11374 (phone: 800-221-0090 from the eastern US); 150 S. Los Robles Ave., Pasadena, CA 91101 (phone 818-449-0919; 800-556-5454 from the western US); 1801 Eglinton Ave. W., Suite 104, Toronto, Ontario M6E 2H8, Canada (phone: 416-787-1281).

Grand Circle Travel: Arranges extended vacations, escorted tours, and cruises for retired Americans, including singles. Membership, which is automatic when you book a trip through *Grand Circle,* includes discount certificates on future trips and other extras. Contact *Grand Circle Travel,* 347 Congress St., Boston, MA 02210 (phone: 800-221-2610 or 617-350-7500).

Insight International Tours: Offers a matching service for single travelers. Several tours are geared for travelers in the 18 to 35 age group. Contact *Insight Interna-*

tional Tours, 745 Atlantic Ave., Boston MA 02111 (phone: 800-582-8380 or 617-482-2000).

Jane's International: This service puts potential traveling coompanions in touch with one another. No age limit, no fee. Contact *Jane's International,* 2603 Bath Ave., Brooklyn, NY 11214 (phone: 718-266-2045).

Saga International Holidays: A subsidiary of a British company specializing in older travelers, many of them single, *Saga* offers a broad selection of escorted coach tours, cruises, and apartment-stay holidays, including packages, for people age 60 and over or those 50 to 59 traveling with someone 60 or older. Members of the *Saga Holiday Club* receive the club magazine, which contains a column aimed at helping lone travelers find suitable traveling companions. A 1-year club membership costs $5. Contact *Saga International Holidays,* 120 Boylston St., Boston MA 02116 (phone: 800-343-0273 or 617-451-6808).

Singleworld: Organizes its own packages and also books singles on the cruises and tours of other operators; it arranges shared accommodations if requested, charging a one-time surcharge that is much less than the single supplement would be. *Singleworld* actually is a club joined through travel agents for a yearly fee of $20, paid at the time of booking. About two-thirds of this agency's clientele are under 35, and about half this number are women. *Singleworld* organizes tours and cruises with departures categorized by age group. Contact *Singleworld,* 401 Theodore Fremd Ave., Rye, NY 10580 (phone: 914-967-3334 or 800-223-6490 in the continental US).

Travel Companion Exchange: Every 8 weeks, this group publishes a directory of singles looking for travel companions and provides members with full-page profiles of likely partners. Members fill out a lengthy questionnaire to establish a personal profile and write a small listing, much like an ad in a personal column. This listing is circulated to other members who can request a copy of the complete questionnaire and then go on to make contact to plan a joint vacation. It is wise to join as far ahead of your scheduled vacation as possible so that there's enough time to determine the suitability of prospective traveling companions. Membership fees range from $6 to $11 per month (with a 6-month minimum enrollment), depending on the level of service required. The membership package includes a travel newsletter for singles. A sample issue costs $4. Contact *Travel Companion Exchange,* PO Box 833, Amityville, NY 11701 (phone: 516-454-0880).

A special guidebook for solo travelers, prepared by Eleanor Adams Baxel, offers information on how to avoid paying supplementary charges, how to pick the right travel agent, how to calculate costs, and much more. Entitled *A Guide for Solo Travel Abroad* (Berkshire Traveller Press), it's out of print, so check your local library. A new book for single travelers is *Traveling on Your Own* by Eleanor Berman; available in bookstores, it also can be ordered by sending $12.95, plus $2 postage and handling (per book), to Random House, Customer Service Dept., 400 Hahn Rd., Westminster, MD 21157 (phone: 800-726-0600).

The single traveler who is particularly interested in meeting the Irish may want to look into a unique home-stay program. The United States Servas Committee maintains a list of hosts around the world who are willing to take visitors into their homes as guests for a 2-night stay. Servas will send an application form and a list of some 200 interviewers around the US for you to contact. After the interview, if you are accepted as a Servas traveler, you'll receive a certificate making you eligible to become a member. The membership fee is $45 for an individual, with a $15 deposit to receive the host list, refunded upon its return. For more information, contact the United States Servas Committee, 11 John St., Room 706, New York, NY 10038 (phone: 212-267-0252).

WOMEN AND STUDENTS: Two specific groups of single travelers deserve special mention: women and students. Countless women travel by themselves in Europe, and such an adventure need not be feared. You normally will find people courteous and welcoming, but remember that crime is a worldwide problem. (In fact, most Irish cities generally are regarded as safer than American cities — for everyone, including single women.) Keep a careful eye on your belongings while on the beach, or lounging in a park, or traveling on a bus or train; lock your car and hotel doors; deposit your valuables in the hotel's safe; and never hitchhike.

One lingering inhibition many female travelers still harbor is that of eating alone in public places. The trick here is to relax and enjoy your meal and surroundings; while you may run across the occasional unenlightened waiter, a woman dining alone is no longer uncommon. A book offering lively, helpful advice on female solo travel is *The Traveling Woman,* by Dena Kaye. Though out of print, it may be found in your local library.

Studying Abroad – A large number of single travelers are students. Travel *is* education. Travel broadens a person's knowledge and deepens his or her perception of the world in a way no media or "armchair" experience ever could. In addition, to study a country's language, art, culture, or history on site or in one of its own schools is to enjoy the most productive method of learning.

There are many benefits for students abroad, and the way to begin to discover them is to consult the *Council on International Educational Exchange (CIEE).* This organization, which runs a variety of work, study, and travel programs for students, is the US sponsor of the International Student Identity Card (ISIC). Reductions on trains, airfare, and entry fees to most museums and other exhibitions are only some of the advantages of the card. To apply for it, write to *CIEE* at one of the following addresses: 205 E. 42nd St., New York, NY 10017 (phone: 212-661-1414); 312 Sutter St., San Francisco, CA 94108 (phone: 415-421-3473); and 919 Irving St., San Francisco, CA 94122 (phone: 415-566-6222). Mark the letter "Attn. Student ID." Application requires a $10 fee, a passport-size photograph, and proof that you are a matriculating student (this means either a transcript or a letter or bill from your school registrar with the school's official seal; high school and junior high school students can use their report cards). There is no maximum age limit, but participants must be at least 12 years old. The *ID Discount Guide,* which gives details of the discounts country by country, is free with membership. Another free publication of *CIEE* is the informative, annual, 64-page *Student Travel Catalog,* which covers all aspects of youth-travel abroad for vacation trips, jobs, or study programs, and also includes a list of other helpful publications. You can order the catalogue from Dept. ISS — #15 at the New York address given above.

Another card of value in Europe, and also available through *CIEE,* is the Federation of International Youth Travel Organizations (FIYTO) card. This provides many of the benefits of the ISIC card, and will facilitate entry to certain "youth hotels" throughout Europe, including Ireland. In this case, cardholders need not be students, merely under age 26. To apply, send $10 with a passport-size photo and proof of birth date to *CIEE* at one of the addresses above.

CIEE also sponsors charter flights to Europe that are open to students and non-students of any age. Flights between New York and Paris or London (with budget-priced add-ons available from Boston, Chicago, Denver, El Paso, Los Angeles, Las Vegas, Minneapolis, St. Louis, Salt Lake City, San Diego, San Francisco, Seattle, and several other US cities) arrive and depart daily from Kennedy (JFK) or Newark airports during the high season. Regularly scheduled direct flights also are offered from Boston to Brussels.

Youth fares on transatlantic flights currently are offered by most of the scheduled airlines flying to Europe. Although the situation may change in the future, at press time the youth fare was almost the same as the standard APEX fare, and there may be some substantial drawbacks: a 7- or 14-day minimum stay, no stopovers, notification of availability and payment in full 1 to 3 days before the flight, and the return may be left open only if this is arranged before the trip, and again may be subject to 24-hour notice of availability. This space available restriction means that if you really must be home by a certain date, you are better off opting for a different type of ticket. Discount fares vary from carrier to carrier. To find out about current discounts, contact the individual airlines. Also see *Traveling by Plane,* in this section, for more information on economical flight alternatives.

Students and singles in general should keep in mind that youth hostels exist in many cities throughout Ireland. They always are inexpensive, generally clean and well situated, and they are a sure place to meet other people traveling alone. Hostels are run by the hosteling associations of some 60-plus countries that make up the *International Youth Hostel Federation (IYHF);* membership in one of the national associations affords access to the hostels of the rest. To join the American affiliate, *American Youth Hostels (AYH),* contact the national office (PO Box 37613, Washington, DC 20013-7613; phone: 202-783-6161), or the local *AYH* council nearest you. As we went to press, new membership rules and rates were in effect: Membership in *AYH* currently costs $25 for people between the ages of 18 and 54, $10 for youths under 18, $15 for seniors, $35 for family membership. The *AYH Handbook,* which lists hostels in the US, comes with your *AYH* card (non-members can purchase the handbook for $5 plus $2 postage and handling); the *International Youth Hostel Handbooks,* which list hostels worldwide, must be purchased ($10.95 each, plus $2 for postage).

For hostels in Northern Ireland, contact *Youth Hostel Association of Northern Ireland* (56 Bradbury Pl., Belfast BT7 1RU, Northern Ireland; phone: 232-324733); in the Irish Republic, *Irish Youth Hostel Association (An Oige;* 39 Mountjoy Sq., Dublin 1, Irish Republic; phone: 1-363111). These associations also publish handbooks to hostels in their areas. In addition, the tourist boards of both countries publish information sheets on hostels and on hosteling package holidays.

In the Republic of Ireland, a special Student/Youth Rambler Ticket good for rail and bus travel is available for anyone age 14 through 26. The ticket must be purchased prior to departure for Ireland through a travel agent or from *CIE Tours International* (122 E. 42nd St., New York, NY 10168; phone: 212-697-3914 in New York City; 800-CIE-TOUR elsewhere in the US); a minimum of 1 month's advance notice is required.

Eurail's Youthpass, for travelers (including non-students) under 26, is accepted in the Irish Republic, but it is not really economical unless your itinerary includes several other countries on the Eurail network (which does not include Northern Ireland). However, for extensive travel throughout Europe, the Eurail Youthpass entitles the bearer to either 1 or 2 months of unlimited second class rail travel in 17 countries. In addition, it is honored on many European steamers and ferries (including ferry crossings between Ireland and France on the *Irish Continental Line*) and on railroad connections between the airport and the center of town in various cities. The pass also entitles the bearer to reduced rates on some bus lines in several countries. The Eurail Youthpass can be purchased only by those living outside Europe or North Africa, and it must be purchased before departure. Eurailpasses can be bought from a US travel agent or from the national railway offices of the countries in the Eurail network (see *Traveling by Train,* in this section).

Opportunities for study in Europe range from summer or academic-year courses in the civilization of a country designed specifically for foreigners (including those whose school days are well behind them) to long-term university attendance by those intending to take a degree.

Complete details on more than 1,700 available courses and suggestions on how to apply are contained in two books published by the *Institute of International Education*

(IIE Books, 809 UN Plaza, New York, NY 10017; phone 212-883-8200): *Vacation Study Abroad,* $24.95; and *Academic Year Abroad,* $29.95. A third book, *Teaching Abroad,* costs $21.95. All prices include book rate postage; first class postage is $4 extra. IIE Books also offers a free pamphlet, called *Basic Facts on Study Abroad.*

Work, Study, Travel Abroad: The Whole World Handbook, issued by the *Council on International Educational Exchange (CIEE),* is an informative, chatty guide on study programs, work opportunities, and travel hints. To obtain it, send $10.95 plus postage ($1 for book rate; $2.50 first class) to *CIEE,* 205 E. 42nd St., New York, NY 10017 (phone 212-661-1414).

Those who are interested in a "learning vacation" abroad also may want to read *Travel and Learn,* by Evelyn Kaye. This guide to educational travel lists and describes a number of topics — everything from archaeology to whale watching — and provides information on organizations that offer programs in these areas of interest. The book is available in bookstores for $23.95; or you can send $26 (which includes shipping charges) to Blue Penguin Publications (147 Sylvan Ave., Leonia, NJ 07605; phone: 201-461-6918). *Learning Vacations,* by Gerson G. Eisenberg, also provides extensive information on seminars, workshops, courses, and so on — in a wide variety of subjects. The book is $11.95 in bookstores, or it can be ordered from Peterson's Guides (PO Box 2123, Princeton, NJ 08543-2123; add $4.75 for shipping).

Summer study programs particularly are popular in Ireland, and courses are diverse. To start off your research, send for the comprehensive guide *Irish Summer School Directory,* published by the magazine *Inside Ireland* (Rookwood, Stocking Lane, Ballyboden, Dublin 16, Ireland; phone: 1-931906).

Elderhostel is a network of schools, colleges, and universities that sponsors week-long study programs for people over 60 years of age on campuses throughout Europe. Some of its programs are offered in cooperation with the *Experiment in International Living* (see below) and involve home stays. Contact *Elderhostel* (80 Boylston St., Suite 400, Boston, MA 02116; phone: 617-426-7788 or 617-426-8056). An informational videotape describing *Elderhostel*'s programs is available for $5.

The University of New Hampshire, the original sponsor of *Elderhostel,* has its own program for travelers over 50; contact *Interhostel* (University of New Hampshire, Division of Continuing Education, 6 Garrison Ave., Durham, NH 03824; phone: 603-862-1147 weekdays, 1:30 to 4 PM eastern standard time). For more details about both programs, see *Hints for Older Travelers,* in this section.

If you are interested in a home-stay travel program, in which you learn about Irish culture by living with a family, contact the *Experiment in International Living* (PO Box 676, Brattleboro, VT 05302-0676; phone: 802-257-7751 in Vermont; 800-345-2929 elsewhere in the US), which sponsors home-stay educational travel. The organization aims its programs at high school or college students, but it also can arrange home stays of 1 to 4 weeks for adults in more than 40 countries. It is possible, after participating in the programs, to join supplemental travel/activities programs and tour Europe.

National Association of Secondary School Principals (NASSP, 1904 Association Dr., Reston, VA 22091; phone: 703-860-0200), an association of administrators, teachers, and state education officials, sponsors *School Partnership International,* a program in which secondary schools in the US are linked with partner schools abroad for an annual short-term exchange of students and faculty.

Another organization specializing in travel as an educational experience is the *American Institute for Foreign Study (AIFS).* Students can enroll for the full academic year or for any number of semesters. *AIFS* caters primarily to bona fide high school or college students, but its non-credit international learning and continuing education programs are open to independent travelers of all ages. (Approximately 30% of *AIFS* students are over 25.) Contact *AIFS,* 102 Greenwich Ave., Greenwich, CT 06830 (phone: 800-727-AIFS, 203-869-9090, or 203-863-6087 for summer programs; 203-863-6097 for foreign language programs).

Those interested in campus stays should know about the *U.S. and Worldwide Travel Accommodations Guide,* which lists several hundred colleges and universities in Europe that offer simple, but comfortable, accommodations in their residence halls, primarily during the summer season. The accommodations vary from single and double rooms to full apartments and suites with kitchens, and the rooms can be booked by the day, week, or month. Prices range from $12 to $24 per night, with an average of about $18. An added bonus of this type of arrangement is that visitors usually are free to utilize various campus sport and recreation facilities. For a copy of the guide, which describes services and facilities in detail, send $11.95 to *Campus Travel Service,* PO Box 5007, Laguna Beach, CA 92652 (phone: 714-497-3044).

The British Tourist Authority (see *Tourist Information Offices,* in this section) publishes a booklet, *Britain: Stay on a Farm,* that lists working farms throughout the United Kingdom, including Northern Ireland. The Northern Ireland Tourist Board also provides information on private accommodations in its *Northern Ireland: Where to Stay* guide. The Irish Tourist Board publishes its own useful booklet, *Farm Holidays in Ireland,* which lists country homes and working farms. On many farms, travelers will get a room and a hearty breakfast for as little as $15 to $20 a day.

And there's always camping. Virtually any area of the countryside in Ireland has a place to pitch a tent and enjoy the scenery. There are numerous national parks; many of the campsites have showers, laundry rooms, public phones, eating facilities, and shops. And, with permission, it's often possible to camp on private acres of farmland. (For more information, see *Camping and Caravanning, Hiking and Biking,* in this section.)

WORKING ABROAD: Jobs for foreigners in Ireland are not easy to come by and in general do not pay well enough to cover all the expenses of a trip. They do provide an invaluable learning experience, however, while helping to make a trip more affordable.

Those who are at least 18 years old and enrolled as full-time students in a US college or university can work in the Republic for up to 4 months and in Northern Ireland for up to 6 months at any time of the year. Work permits can be obtained through the *Council on International Educational Exchange* (address above) only by students over 18 who are enrolled and working toward a degree in a US college or university and who have 2 years of college education in a foreign language or its equivalent to their credit. The permit allows them to work for 3 months at any time of year, but the students must find their own jobs.

Hints for Older Travelers

Special package deals and more free time are just two factors that have given Americans over age 65 a chance to see the world at affordable prices. Senior citizens make up an ever-growing segment of the travel population, and the trend among them is to travel more frequently and for longer periods of time. No longer limited by 3-week vacations or the business week, older travelers can take advantage of off-season, off-peak travel which is both less expensive and more pleasant than traveling at prime time in high season. In addition, overseas, as in the US, discounts frequently are available.

PLANNING: When planning a vacation, prepare your itinerary with one eye on your own physical condition and the other on a topographical map. Keep in mind variations in climate, terrain, and altitudes, which may pose some danger for anyone with heart or breathing problems.

An excellent book to read before embarking on any trip, domestic or foreign, is Rosalind Massow's *Travel Easy: The Practical Guide for People Over 50,* available for $6.50 to members of the *American Association of Retired Persons (AARP),* $8.95 for non-members (add $1.75 postage and handling per order, not per book). Order from AARP Books (c/o Scott, Foresman, 1865 Miner St., Des Plaines, IL 60016; phone: 800-238-2300). It discusses a host of subjects, from choosing a destination to getting set for departure, with chapters on transportation options, tours, cruises, avoiding health problems, and handling dental emergencies en route. Another book, *The International Health Guide for Senior Citizens,* covers such topics as trip preparations, food and water precautions, adjusting to weather and climate conditions, finding a doctor, motion sickness, and jet lag. The book also discusses specific health and travel problems, and includes a list of resource organizations that provide medical assistance for travelers; it is available for $4.95 postpaid from Pilot Books (103 Cooper St., Babylon, NY 11702; phone: 516-422-2225). A third book on health for older travelers, Rosalind Massow's excellent *Now It's Your Turn to Travel* (Collier Books), has a chapter on medical problems; it is out of print but may be available in your library. (Also see *Staying Healthy,* in this section.) *Travel Tips for Senior Citizens* (State Department publication 8970), a useful booklet with general advice, also currently is out of print but may be found in libraries.

An ideal book for budget-conscious older travelers is *The Discount Guide for Travelers Over 55* by Caroline and Walter Weintz (Dutton; $7.95). Pilot Books (address above) features *The Senior Citizen's Guide to Budget Travel in Europe,* for $3.95. You also may want to send for *101 Tips for the Mature Traveler,* a free publication available from *Grand Circle Travel,* 347 Congress St., Suite 3A, Boston, MA 02210 (phone: 617-350-7500, 800-221-2610, or 800-831-8880).

If you are traveling in the fall, winter, or spring, bear in mind that you will not always find central heating in public places in Ireland and that even if your hotel has it, it may not warm your room up to the temperature you're accustomed to at home. Bear in mind also that even in summer you will need something warm for the evening in many areas throughout the Continent, and there are areas where rainwear year-round is a good idea, too. However, remember that one secret to happy traveling is to *pack lightly.* (For further hints on what to bring and how to pack it, see *How to Pack,* in this section.)

HEALTH: Health facilities in Ireland generally are excellent, and a number of organizations exist to help travelers avoid or deal with a medical emergency overseas. For further information on these services, see *Medical and Legal Aid and Consular Services,* in this section.

Older travelers should know that Medicare does not make payments outside the US, and — contrary to lingering popular belief — Britain's National Health Service, in operation in Northern Ireland, does not provide free medical care to visitors, except in a few instances. If your medical policy does not protect you while you're traveling, there are comprehensive combination policies specifically designed to fill the gap. For a discussion of travel insurance and a list of companies offering attractive combination plans, see *Insurance,* in this section.

Pre-trip medical and dental checkups are strongly recommended, particularly for older travelers. In addition, be sure to take along any prescription medication you need, enough to last *without a new prescription* for the duration of your trip; pack all medications with a note from your doctor for the benefit of airport or other authorities. It also is wise to bring a few common non-prescription over-the-counter medications with you: Aspirin or a non-aspirin pain reliever and something for stomach upset may come in handy. If you have specific medical problems, bring prescriptions and a "medical file" composed of the following:

1. A summary of medical history and current diagnosis.
2. A list of drugs to which you are allergic.
3. Your most recent electrocardiogram, if you have heart problems.
4. Your doctor's name, address, and telephone number.

■ **A word of caution:** Don't overdo it. Allow time for some relaxation each day to refresh yourself for the next scheduled sightseeing event. Traveling across time zones can be exhausting, and adjusting to major climatic changes can make you feel dizzy and drained. Plan on spending at least 1 full day resting before you start touring. If you're part of a group tour, be sure to check the itinerary thoroughly. Some package deals sound wonderful because they include all the places you've ever dreamed of visiting. In fact, visiting all of them can become so hectic and tiring that you'll be reaching for a pillow instead of a camera.

DISCOUNTS AND PACKAGES: Since guidelines change from place to place, it's a good idea to inquire in advance about discounts for transportation, hotels, concerts, movies, museums, and other activities. The Irish tourist boards can give the most up-to-date information about discounts and programs for older travelers in Ireland (see *Tourist Information Offices,* in this section).

Northern Ireland Railways' Rail Runabout Ticket, bought in Northern Ireland and good for 7 consecutive days of unlimited train travel, is half price to senior citizens. (For more information on transportation discounts, refer to *Traveling by Plane, Traveling by Train,* and *Traveling by Bus,* all in this section.)

Many US hotel and motel chains, airlines, car rental companies, bus lines, and other travel suppliers offer discounts to older travelers. Some of these discounts, however, are extended only to bona fide members of certain senior citizens organizations. Because the same organizations frequently offer package tours to both domestic and international destinations, the benefits of membership are twofold: Those who join can take advantage of discounts as individual travelers and also reap the savings that group travel affords. In addition, because the age requirements for some of these organizations are quite low (or nonexistent), the benefits can begin to accrue early. Among the organizations dedicated to helping you see the world are the following:

American Association of Retired Persons (AARP): The largest and best known of these organizations. Membership is open to anyone 50 or over, whether retired or not. *AARP* offers travel programs, designed exclusively for older travelers, that cover the globe; they include a broad range of escorted tours, hosted tours, and cruises, including tours and resort packages. Dues are $5 per year or $12.50 for 3 years, and include spouse. For membership information, contact *AARP Travel Service,* 100 N. Sepulveda Blvd., Suite 1010, El Segundo, CA 90245 (phone: 800-227-7737 or 213-322-7323).

Mature Outlook: Through its *Travel Alert,* last-minute tours, cruises, and other vacation packages are available to members at special savings. Hotel and car rental discounts and travel accident insurance also are available. Membership is open to anyone 50 years of age or older, costs $9.95 a year, and includes its bimonthly newsletter and magazine, as well as information on package tours. Contact the Customer Service Center, 6001 N. Clark St., Chicago, IL 60660 (phone: 800-336-6330).

National Council of Senior Citizens: Here, too, the emphasis always is on keeping costs low. This group offers a different roster of tours each year, and its travel service also will book individual tours for members. Although most members are over 50, membership is open to anyone, regardless of age, for an annual fee of $12 per person or $16 per couple. Lifetime membership costs $150. For information, contact the *National Council for Senior Citizens,* 925 15th St. NW, Washington, DC 20005 (phone: 202-347-8800).

Certain travel agencies and tour operators specialize in group travel for older travelers, among them the following:

Gadabout Tours: Operated by Lois Anderson, this organization offers escorted tours to a number of destinations, including Ireland. See a travel agent or contact *Gadabout Tours,* 700 E. Tahquitz, Palm Springs, CA 92262 (phone: 619-325-5556 or 800-521-7309 in California; 800-952-5068 elsewhere in the US).

Grand Circle Travel: Caters exclusively to the over-50 traveler and packages a large variety of escorted tours, cruises, and extended vacations. *Grand Circle* also publishes a quarterly magazine (with a column for the single traveler) and a helpful free booklet, *101 Tips for the Mature Traveler Abroad.* Contact *Grand Circle Travel,* 347 Congress St., Suite 3A, Boston, MA 02210 (phone: 800-221-2610 or 617-350-7500).

Insight International Tours: Offers a matching service for single travelers. Several tours are geared for mature travelers. Contact *Insight International Tours,* 745 Atlantic Ave., Boston, MA 02111 (phone: 617-482-2000 or 800-582-8380 throughout the US).

Saga International Holidays: A subsidiary of a British company specializing in the older traveler, *Saga* offers a broad selection of escorted coach tours, cruises, and apartment-stay holidays, including packages, for people age 60 and over or those 50 to 59 traveling with someone 60 or older. Among the recent itineraries offered were three motorcoach tours through the Irish countryside. Members of the *Saga Holiday Club* receive the club magazine, which contains a column aimed at helping lone travelers find suitable traveling companions (see *Hints for Single Travelers,* in this section). A 1-year club membership costs $5. Contact *Saga International Holidays,* 120 Boylston St., Boston MA 02116 (phone: 800-343-0273 or 617-451-6808).

Many travel agencies, particularly the larger ones, are delighted to make presentations to help a group select destinations. A local chamber of commerce should be able to provide the names of such agencies. Once a time and place are determined, an organization member or travel agent can obtain group quotations for transportation, accommodations, meal plans, and sightseeing. Groups of 40 or more usually get the best breaks.

Another choice open to older travelers is a trip that includes an educational element. *Elderhostel* is a network of schools, colleges, and universities that sponsors week-long study programs for people over 60 years of age on campuses throughout Europe, including Ireland. An informational videotape describing *Elderhostel*'s programs is available for $5. Accommodations are in residence halls, and meals are taken in student cafeterias. Travel to the programs usually is by designated scheduled flights, and participants can arrange to extend their stay at the end of the program. Elderhostelers must be at least 60 years old (younger if a spouse or companion qualifies), in good health, and not in need of special diets. For information, contact *Elderhostel,* 80 Boylston St., Suite 400, Boston, MA 02116 (phone: 617-426-7788 or 617-426-8056).

Interhostel, a program sponsored by the Division of Continuing Education of the University of New Hampshire, sends travelers back to school at cooperating institutions in 33 countries on 4 continents. Participants attend lectures on the history, economy, politics, and cultural life of the country they are visiting, go on field trips to pertinent points of interest, and take part in activities meant to introduce them to their foreign contemporaries. Trips are for 2 weeks; accommodations are on campus in university residence halls or off campus in modest hotels (double occupancy). Groups are limited to 35 to 40 participants who are at least 50 years old (or at least 40 if a participating spouse is at least 50), physically active, and not in need of special diets. For further information or to receive the three free seasonal catalogues, contact *Interhostel,* UNH Division of Continuing Education, 6 Garrison Ave., Durham, NH 03824 (phone: 603-862-1147 weekdays, 1:30 to 4 PM eastern standard time).

Hints for Traveling with Children

What better way to be receptive to the experiences you will encounter than to take along the young, wide-eyed members of your family? Their company does not have to be a burden or their presence an excessive expense. The current generation of discounts for children and family package deals can make a trip together quite reasonable.

A family trip will be an investment in your children's future, making Irish geography and history come alive to them and leaving a sure memory that will be among the fondest you will share with them someday. Their insights will be refreshing to you; their impulses may take you to unexpected places with unexpected dividends. The experience will be invaluable to them at any age.

The current generation of discount airfares makes flights to Ireland a good deal less expensive than a decent summer camp. In fact, why not send the children to a summer camp for a few days in the Irish countryside? Gaeltacht vacations are offered during the summer months in Irish-speaking regions where children can learn a bit about the language, folklore, and traditions of the Irish people. Riding holidays and pony trekking, as well as traditional camps, are popular, too. Those who would prefer to keep the family together can rent a cottage or visit a family farm in the countryside. The Irish Tourist Board offices have information on how to make arrangements for any of these vacations.

PLANNING: It is necessary to take some extra time beforehand to prepare children for travel. Here are several hints for making a trip with kids easy and fun:

1. Children, like everyone else, will derive more pleasure from a trip if they know something about the country before they arrive. Begin their education about a month before you leave. Using maps, travel magazines, and books, give children a clear idea of where you are going and how far away it is. Part of the excitement of the journey will be associating the tiny dots on the map with the very real places they soon will visit. You can show them pictures of streets and scenes in which they will stand within a month. Don't shirk history lessons, but don't burden them with dates. Make history light, anecdotal, pertinent, but most of all, fun. If you simply make materials available and keep your destination and your plans a topic of everyday conversation, your children will absorb more than you realize.

2. Children should help to plan the itinerary, and where you go and what you do should reflect some of their ideas. If they already know something about the sites they'll visit, they will have the excitement of recognition when they arrive and the illumination of seeing how something is or is not the way they expected it to be.

3. Although the Irish speak English, you may want to learn a few basics in the native Irish tongue like *dia duit* (good day) and *slán agat* (good-bye). You need no other motive than a perfectly selfish one: Thus armed, your children will delight the Irish (particularly those of a more old-fashioned bent) and help break the ice wherever you go. (See *The Irish Language* in PERSPECTIVES for more Gaelic terms and phrases.)

4. Familiarize your children with punts and pounds (see *Credit and Currency,* in this section). Give them an allowance for the trip and be sure they understand just how far it will or won't go.

5. Give children specific responsibilities: The job of carrying their own flight bags and looking after their personal things, along with some other light chores, will give them a stake in the journey. Tell them how they can be helpful when you are checking in or out of hotels.

6. Give each child a diary or scrapbook to take along. Filling these with impressions, observations, and mementos will pass the time on trains and planes and help to focus their experiences.

No matter what your children's reading level, there are books to stimulate their interest in a trip to Ireland. *Irish Books and Graphics* (580 Broadway, Room 1103, New York, NY 10012; phone: 212-274-1923) specializes in Irish books (both new and out of print), maps, posters, and prints, and carries a selection of Irish folk and fairy stories, legends, and poems for young people. Miroslav Sasek's travel series for children, published by Macmillan and available in bookstores, includes *This Is Ireland.* David Macaulay's *Castle* (Houghton Mifflin; $14.95 hardcover; $6.96 paperback), which uses text and drawings to show how castles were built in the 13th century, is particularly suited to helping children understand the many castles they may see in Ireland; *Cathedral: The Story of Its Construction* (Houghton Mifflin; $14.95 hardcover; $6.95 paperback), by the same author, also is appropriate.

And for parents, *Travel With Your Children (TWYCH)* publishes a newsletter, *Family Travel Times,* that focuses on young travelers and offers helpful hints. Membership is $35 a year. For a sample copy of the newsletter, send $1 to *Travel With Your Children,* 80 Eighth Ave., New York, NY 10011 (phone: 212-206-0688).

Another organization that publishes a newsletter for families, as well as functioning as a "family travel club," is *Let's Take the Kids.* They are involved in various activities relating to family travel, including putting together tours and packages and running a "parent travel network," whereby parents who have been to a particular destination can evaluate it for others, and occasionally organize trips for single-parent families traveling together. Annual family memberships in the club are $35, which includes all club services. For information, contact *Let's Take the Kids* (2560 Barrington Ave., Suite 107, Los Angeles, CA 90064; phone: 800-726-4349 or 213-472-4449).

There's also a fairly new organization called *Just Me and the Kids Travel* (PO Box 249, Watkins Glen, NY 14891; phone: 607-535-2966), which puts together trips to popular family destinations for the single-parent family. A membership fee of $25 per family covers the costs of newsletters and travel updates. Another organization, *Parents without Partners* (8807 Colesville Rd., Silver Spring, MD 20910; phone: 301-588-9354), has had chapters (which operate individually) all over the country for many years, offering information for — and activities of interest to — single parents; contact the national office for information on local chapters.

In addition to books, audio cassettes may make Ireland come alive for children. Irish ballads and folk songs, as well as music written just for children, are a lively introduction to the Irish culture and spirit. And be sure to include some Irish bagpipe music — after listening to the resonant tones, children will be surprised to discover what a *uilleann* actually looks like.

PACKING: Choose your children's clothes much as you would your own. Select a basic color (perhaps different for each child) and coordinate everything with it. Plan their wardrobes with layering in mind — shirts and sweaters that can be taken off and put back on as the temperature varies. Take only drip-dry, wrinkle-resistant items that children can manage themselves and comfortable shoes — sneakers and sandals. Younger children will need more changes, but keep it to a minimum. No one likes to carry added luggage (remember that *you* will have to manage most of it!).

Take as many handy snacks as you can squeeze into the corners of your suitcases — things like dried fruit and nut mixes, hard candies, peanut butter, and crackers

— and moist towelettes for cleaning. Don't worry if your supply of nibbles is quickly depleted. Airports and train and bus stations are well stocked with such items.

Pack a special medical kit including children's aspirin or acetaminophen, an antihistamine or decongestant, Dramamine, and diarrhea medication. Do not feel you must pack a vacation's worth of Pampers. Disposable diapers (called "nappies") are available in chemist's (drugstores) and supermarkets. A selection of baby foods also is available in most supermarkets, but in the event that you may not be able to find the instant formula to which your child is accustomed, bring along a supply in the 8-ounce "ready-to-feed" cans. Disposable nursers are expensive but handy. If you breast-feed your baby, there is no reason you can't enjoy your trip; just be sure you get enough rest and liquids.

Good toys to take for infants are the same sorts of things they like at home — well-made, bright huggables and chewables; for small children, a favorite doll or stuffed animal for comfort, spelling and counting games, and tying, braiding, and lacing activities; for older children, playing cards, travel board games with magnetic pieces, and hand-held electronic games. Softcover books and art materials (crayons, markers, paper, scissors, glue sticks, and stickers) ward off boredom for children of most ages, as do audio-cassette players with headphones. Take along a variety of musical and storytelling cassettes, and maybe even an extra set of headphones so two children can listen. *Advice:* Avoid toys that are noisy, breakable, or spillable, those that require a large play area, and those that have lots of little pieces that can be scattered and lost. When traveling, coordinate activities with attention spans; dole out playthings one at a time so you don't run out of diversions before you get where you're going. Children become restless during long waiting periods, and a game plus a small snack — such as a box of raisins or crackers — will help keep them quiet. It also is a good idea to carry tissues, Band-Aids, a pocket medicine kit (described above), and moistened washcloths.

GETTING THERE AND GETTING AROUND: Begin early to investigate all available discount and charter flights, as well as any package deals and special rates offered by the major airlines. Booking sometimes is required up to 2 months in advance. You may well find that charter plans offer no reductions for children, or not enough to offset the risk of last-minute delays or other inconveniences to which charters are subject. The major scheduled airlines, on the other hand, almost invariably provide hefty discounts for children (for specific information on fares and in-flight accommodations for children, also see *Traveling by Plane,* in this section).

PLANE: When you make your reservations, tell the airline that you are traveling with a child. As a general rule, children under 2 travel free in a plane if they sit on an adult's lap — although on some carriers you will have to pay 10% of the adult fare. But it's much safer — and certainly more comfortable — to purchase an adjacent seat for a baby and bring an infant restraint which is then strapped into the airline seat with a regular seat belt. (The airlines do not provide infant seats, so you will have to bring your own. If you do not purchase a seat for your baby and bring the infant restraint along on the off chance that there may be an empty seat next to yours, you will have to pay to check it as baggage if an additional seat is not available.) There is no special fare for an infant, although discounts for children sometimes are in effect, and you can inquire about this when making a reservation — between the ages of 2 and 12, children generally travel at half or two-thirds of the adult fare.

If using one of these infant restraints, you should try to get bulkhead seats, which will provide extra room to care for your child during the flight. You also should request a bulkhead seat when using a bassinet (some airlines do provide bassinets) — again, this is not as safe as strapping a child in. On some planes, bassinets may hook into a bulkhead wall; on others it is placed on the floor in front of you. Even if you do use a bassinet, babies must be held during takeoff and landing. Request seats on the aisle if you have a toddler or if you think you will need to use the bathroom frequently. (Try to discourage children from being in the aisle when meals are served.)

Carry onto the plane all you will need to care for and occupy your children during the flight — formula, diapers, a sweater, books, favorite stuffed animals, and so on. (Never check as baggage any item essential to a child's well-being, such as prescription medicine.) Dress your baby simply, with a minimum of buttons and snaps, because the only place you may have for changing a diaper is at your seat. The flight attendant can warm a bottle for you.

Just as you would request a vegetarian or kosher meal, you are entitled to ask for a hot dog or hamburger instead of the airline's regular dinner if you give at least 24 hours' notice. Some, but not all, airlines have baby food aboard. While you should bring along toys from home, you also can ask about children's diversions. Some carriers have terrific free packages of games, coloring books, and puzzles.

When the plane takes off and lands, make sure your baby is nursing or has a bottle, pacifier, or thumb in its mouth. This sucking will make the child swallow and help to clear stopped ears. A piece of hard candy will do the same thing for an older child.

Avoid night flights. Since you probably won't sleep nearly as well as your kids, you risk an impossible first day at your destination, groggily taking care of your rested, energetic children. Nap time is, however, a good time to travel, especially for babies, and try to travel during off-hours, when there are apt to be extra seats. If you do have to take a long night flight, keep in mind that when you disembark, you probably will be tired and not really ready for sightseeing. The best thing to do is to head for your hotel, shower, have a snack, and take a nap. If your children are too excited to sleep, give them some toys to play with while you rest.

■ **Note:** Newborn babies, whose lungs may not be able to adjust to the altitude, should not be taken aboard an airplane. And some airlines may refuse to allow a pregnant woman in her 8th or 9th month aboard, for fear that something could go wrong with an in-flight birth. Check with the airline well ahead of departure, and carry a letter from your doctor stating that you are fit to travel — and indicating the estimated date of birth.

SHIP, TRAIN, AND BUS: By ship, children under 12 usually travel at a considerably reduced fare. On Irish trains and buses, children under 3 years of age travel free and those from age 3 through 15 travel at half fare. The Irish Republic's Rambler Ticket, which offers unlimited travel within a set period of time, also is offered as a discounted children's fare. A similar pass, the Eurailpass, also valid in the Irish Republic, is half price for children ages 4 through 12. Buy these passes before leaving the US. *Northern Ireland Railways'* unlimited travel pass, the Rail Runabout, is half price to children under 16; the Freedom of Northern Ireland bus pass also is discounted for children under 16. Both can be purchased in Ireland. For further information see *Traveling by Ship, Traveling by Train,* and *Traveling by Bus,* all in this section.

CAR: Without a doubt, a car is the most flexible means of transportation with kids, since driving allows you complete independence in arranging your schedule and itinerary. Keep the car supplied with dried fruits, crackers, candy bars, bottled water, and facial tissue and/or toilet paper. You even may want to pick up a cooler so that you can picnic along the way.

ACCOMMODATIONS AND MEALS: Often a cot for a child will be placed in a hotel room at little or no extra charge. If you wish to sleep in separate rooms, special rates sometimes are available for families; some places do not charge for children under a certain age. In many of the larger chain hotels, the staffs are more used to noisy or slightly misbehaving children. These hotels also are likely to have swimming pools or gamerooms — both popular with most young travelers. Write the hotel in advance to discuss how old your children are, how long you plan to stay, and to ask for suggestions on sleeping arrangements.

You might want to look into accommodations along the way that will add to the color of your trip. For instance, the many country inns, farmhouses, and cottages throughout the Irish countryside prove a delightful experience for the whole family and provide a view of Irish life different from that gained from staying in a conventional hotel. And don't forget castles, many of which double as hotels. Children will love them. Camping facilities often are situated in beautiful, out-of-the-way spots, and generally are good, well equipped, and less expensive than any hotel. For further information on accommodations options for the whole family, see our discussion in *On the Road* and for information on camping facilities, see *Camping and Caravanning, Hiking and Biking,* both in this section.

For the times you will want to be without the children — for an evening's entertainment or a particularly rigorous stint of sightseeing — it is possible to arrange for a baby-sitter at the hotel desk. Many Irish communities have sitter services; check local listings. Whether the sitter is hired directly or through an agency, ask for and check references.

As far as food goes, don't deny yourself or your children the delights of a new cuisine. Encourage them to try new things and don't forget about picnics. There's nothing lovelier than stopping in your tracks at a beautiful view and eating lunch as you muse on the surroundings. (Note that although milk is pasteurized and water is potable in large cities, it's wise to stick to bottled water for small children and for those with sensitive stomachs.)

THINGS TO REMEMBER: If you are spending your vacation traveling, rather than visiting one spot or engaging in one activity, pace the days with children in mind; break the trip into half-day segments, with running around or "doing" time built in; keep travel time on the road to a maximum of 4 or 5 hours a day. First and foremost, don't forget that a child's attention span is far shorter than an adult's. Children don't have to see every museum or all of any museum to learn something from their trip; watching, playing with, and talking to other children can be equally enlightening experiences. Also, remember the places that children the world over love to visit: zoos, country fairs and amusement parks, beaches, and nature trails. Let your children lead the way sometimes — their perspective is different from yours, and they may lead you to things you never would have noticed on your own.

Staying Healthy

The surest way to return home in good health is to be prepared for medical problems that might occur on vacation. Below we've outlined some things you need to think about before you go.

Obviously, your state of health is crucial to the success of a vacation. There's nothing like an injury or illness, whether serious or relatively minor, to dampen or destroy a holiday. And health problems always seem more debilitating when you are away. However, most problems can be prevented or greatly alleviated with intelligent foresight and attention to precautionary details.

Older travelers or anyone suffering from a chronic medical condition, such as diabetes, high blood pressure, cardiopulmonary disease, asthma, or ear, eye, or sinus trouble, should consult a physician before leaving home. A checkup is advisable. A pre-trip dental checkup is not a bad idea, either.

People with conditions requiring special consideration when traveling should consider seeing, in addition to their regular physician, a specialist in travel medicine. For a referral in a particular community, contact the nearest medical school or ask a local doctor to recommend such a specialist. The *American Society of Tropical Medicine and Hygiene* publishes a directory of more than 70 travel doctors across the country. Send a 9-by-12-inch self-addressed, stamped envelope ($1.05 postage) to Dr. Leonard Marcus, Tufts University, 200 W. Boro Rd., North Grafton, MA 01536.

FIRST AID: Put together a compact, personal medical kit including Band-Aids, first-aid cream, antiseptic, nose drops, insect repellent, aspirin, an extra pair of prescription glasses or contact lenses (and a copy of your prescription for glasses or lenses), sunglasses, over-the-counter remedies for diarrhea, indigestion, and motion sickness, a thermometer, and a supply of those prescription medicines you take regularly. In a corner of your kit, keep a list of all the drugs you have brought and their purpose, as well as duplicate copies of your doctor's prescriptions (or a note from your doctor). These copies could come in handy if you ever are questioned by police or airport authorities about any drugs you are carrying, and also will be necessary to refill any prescriptions in the event of loss. Considering the essential contents of this kit, keep it with you, rather than in your luggage.

WATER SAFETY: Ireland is famous for its rocky beaches. It's important to remember that the sea, especially the wild Atlantic, also can be treacherous. A few precautions are necessary. Beware of the undertow, that current of water running back down the beach after a wave has washed ashore; it can knock you off your feet and into the surf. Even more dangerous is the riptide, a strong current of water running against the tide, which can pull you out toward sea. If this happens, don't panic or try to fight the current, because it only will exhaust you; instead, ride it out while waiting for it to subside, which usually happens not too far from shore, or try swimming away parallel to the beach.

INSECTS AND OTHER PESTS: Mosquitoes, horse flies, and other biting insects can be troublesome. We recommend using some form of repellent against bug bites, especially for campers. Mosquitoes can be a terrific nuisance in some areas; vitamin B-1 or thiamine tablets may alter your body chemistry to help repel them. If you are at all susceptible to mosquito bites, you will be amazed at how quickly the vitamins work — although they do not work for everyone. Discuss this strategy with your doctor before trying it. It still *always* is a good idea to use some form of topical insect repellent. As many of the stronger, effective insect repellents have a pungent odor, you may want to try a relatively new alternative, Skin-So-Soft hand lotion, made by Avon. This orderless skin softener actually has been approved by the FDA as an effective insect repellent. Burning mosquito coils containing pyrethrin or citronella candles is another effective precaution.

If you do get bitten — by mosquitoes or other bugs — the itching can be relieved with baking soda or antihistamine tablets. Should a bite become infected, treat it with a disinfectant or antibiotic cream. *Note:* Antihistamines should not be combined with alcohol or cortisone cream, or taken when driving.

If you are bitten and the area becomes painful or swollen and you develop flu-type symptoms, you may have been bitten by a tick carrying what is known as Lyme Borreliosis disease (or "Lyme Tick Disease") in the US. Many Americans believe that this disease is unique to the US; however, it was first diagnosed in Europe — where it is called Neuro Borreliosis — and has been a problem there for years. Caution should be taken in all wooded areas.

Though rarer than insect bites, bites from poisonous spiders or sea creatures such as jellyfish can be serious. If possible, always try to catch the villain for identification purposes. In most cases, particularly if spasms, numbness, convulsions, or hemorrhaging occurs, consult a doctor at once. The best course of action may be to head directly to the nearest emergency ward or outpatient clinic of a hospital. Cockroaches, termites, and waterbugs thrive in warm climates, but pose no serious health threat.

FOOD AND WATER: Water is clean and potable throughout Ireland. Ask if water is meant for drinking, but if you're at all unsure, bottled water is readily available in stores. In general, it is a good idea to drink bottled water at least at the beginning of the trip. This is not because there is something wrong with the water, as far as the residents are concerned, but new microbes in the digestive tract to which you have not become accustomed may cause mild stomach or intestinal upsets. Particularly in rural areas, the water supply may not be thoroughly purified and local residents either have developed immunities to the natural bacteria or boil it for drinking. You also should avoid drinking water from streams or freshwater pools. In campgrounds, water usually is indicated as drinkable or for washing only — again, if you're not sure, ask.

Milk is pasteurized throughout Ireland, and milk products (cheese, yogurt, ice cream, and so on) are safe to eat, as are fresh produce, meat, poultry, and fish.

Following all these precautions will not guarantee an illness-free trip, but it should minimize the risk. As a final hedge against economic if not physical problems, make sure your health insurance will cover all eventualities while you are away. If not, there are policies designed specifically for travel. Many are worth investigating. As with all insurance, they seem like a waste of money until you need them. For further information, also see *Insurance* and *Medical and Legal Aid and Consular Services,* both in this section.

HELPFUL PUBLICATIONS: Practically every phase of health care — before, during, and after a trip — is covered in *The New Traveler's Health Guide* by Drs. Patrick J. Doyle and James E. Banta. It is available for $4.95, plus $2 postage and handling, from Acropolis Books Ltd., 80 S. Early, Alexandria, VA 22304 (phone: 800-451-7771 or 703-709-0006).

The *Traveling Healthy Newsletter,* which is published six times a year, also is brimming with healthful travel tips. For a subscription, which costs $24, contact Dr. Karl Neumann, 108-48 70th Rd., Forest Hills, NY 11375, (phone: 718-268-7290).

For more information regarding preventive health care for travelers contact the *International Association for Medical Assistance to Travelers* (*IMAT;* 417 Center St., Lewiston, NY 14092; phone: 716-754-4883) or write to the US Government Printing Office (Washington, DC 20402) for the US Public Health Service's booklet *Health Information for International Travel* (HEW Publication CDC-86-8280; enclose a check or money order for $4.75 payable to the Superintendent of Documents).

On the Road

Credit and Currency

 It may seem hard to believe, but one of the greatest (and least understood) costs of travel is money itself. If that sounds simplistic, consider that you can lose as much as 30% of your travel dollars' value simply by changing money at the wrong place or in the wrong form. So the one single objective in relation to the care and retention of travel funds is to make them stretch as far as possible. When you do spend money, it should be on things that expand and enhance your travel experience, with no buying power lost due to carelessness or lack of knowledge. This requires more than merely ferreting out the best airfare or the most charming budget hotel. It means being canny about the management of money itself. Herewith, a primer on making money go as far as possible overseas.

CURRENCY: The basic currency unit in both Northern Ireland and the Republic is the pound — the pound sterling in Northern Ireland and the Irish pound (or punt) in the Republic. Although the Republic of Ireland pound once maintained parity with the British pound sterling, it now is linked to other Common Market currencies. Northern Ireland (British) and Republic of Ireland currencies are no longer interchangeable, and they have different values and exchange rates vis-à-vis the American dollar. Republic of Ireland currency is not accepted in Northern Ireland, and vice versa.

In both countries, however, the pound is divided into 100 units, called *pence*. In Northern Ireland, these are distributed in a 100p (£1) coin, as well as 50p, 20p, 10p, 5p, 2p, and 1p coin denominations. It also is still possible to find shillings, equal to 5p, in circulation, leftovers of the pre-decimal currency system. Paper money is issued in Northern Ireland in £50, £20, £10, and £5 notes. The Bank of England stopped printing £1 notes on December 31, 1984, and any £1 notes remaining in circulation ceased to be legal tender in 1985. In the Republic, pence are distributed in 100p, 50p, 20p, 10p, 5p, 2p, 1p coin denominations; paper money is issued in IR£100, IR£50, IR£20, IR£10, and IR£5. As with British currency, the Irish Republic no longer prints IR£1 notes.

Like all foreign currencies, the value of Irish currency in relation to the US dollar fluctuates daily, affected by a wide variety of phenomena. As we went to press, the exchange rate for Northern Ireland's pound sterling was £1 to $1.80 US (or about 55¢ US to £1); the exchange rate for the Irish Republic's pound was IR£1 to $1.55 US (or about .64¢ US to IR£1).

Although US dollars may be accepted in Ireland (particularly at points of entry), you certainly will lose a percentage of your dollar's buying power if you do not take the time to convert it into pounds and pence. By paying for goods and services in the local currency, you save money by not negotiating invariably unfavorable exchange rates for every small purchase, and avoid difficulty where US currency is not readily — or happily — accepted. *Throughout this book, unless specifically stated otherwise, prices are given in US dollars.*

There are no regulations on the amount of currency that a traveler can bring into or take out of Ireland. US law, however, requires that anyone taking more than $10,000 into or out of the US must report this fact on customs form No. 4790, which is available at all international airports. You must do this *before* leaving the US, and you should include this information on your customs declaration when you return.

FOREIGN EXCHANGE: Because of the frequent volatility of exchange rates, be sure to check the current value of Irish currencies before finalizing any travel budget. And before you actually depart on your trip, be aware of the most advantageous exchange rates offered by various financial institutions — US banks, currency exchange firms (at home and abroad), or Irish banks. Almost invariably, the best exchange rate offered for US dollars will be found in Irish banks.

For the best sense of current trends, follow the rates posted in the financial section of your local newspaper or in such international newspapers as the *International Herald Tribune*. It also is possible to check with your own bank. *Harold Reuter and Company*, a currency exchange service in New York City (200 Park Ave., Suite 332 E., New York, NY 10166; phone: 212-661-0826), also is particularly helpful in determining current trends in exchange rates; or check with *Deak International Ltd.* (for the nearest location, call 800-972-2192 in Illinois; 800-621-0666 elsewhere in the US). *Ruesch International* also offers up-to-date foreign currency information and currency-related services (such as converting Irish pound refund checks into US dollars; see *Shopping*, in this section). *Ruesch* also offers a pocket-size *Foreign Currency Guide* (good for estimating general equivalents while planning) and a helpful brochure, *6 Foreign Exchange Tips for the Traveler*. Contact *Ruesch International* at one of the following addresses: 3 First National Plaza, Suite 2020, Chicago, IL 60602 (phone: 312-332-5900); 1925 Century Park E., Suite 240, Los Angeles, CA 90067 (phone: 213-277-7800); 608 Fifth Ave., "Swiss Center," New York, NY 10020 (phone: 212-977-2700); or 1350 Eye St. NW, 10th Floor and street level, Washington, DC 20005 (phone: 800-424-2923 or 202-408-1200).

In Ireland, you will find the official rate of exchange posted in banks, airports, money exchange houses, and some shops. The difference between the exchange rates offered in banks and in hotels varies from country to country — although generally you will get more local currency for your US dollar at banks than at any other commercial establishment. The convenience of exchanging money in your hotel (sometimes on a 24-hour basis) *may* make up for some of the difference in the exchange rate. Don't try to bargain in banks or hotels — no one will alter the rates for you.

Money exchange houses (called "Bureau de Change" throughout Ireland) are financial institutions that charge a fee for the service of exchanging dollars into local currency. When considering alternatives, be aware that although the rate again varies among these establishments, the rates of exchange offered are bound to be slightly less favorable than the terms offered at nearby banks — again, don't be surprised if you get fewer pounds and pence for your dollar than the rate published in the papers.

That said, however, the following rules of thumb are worth remembering:

Rule number one is as simple as it is inflexible: Never (repeat: *never*) willingly exchange dollars for foreign currency at hotels, restaurants, or retail shops, where you are sure to lose a significant amount of your dollar's buying power. If you do come across a storefront exchange counter offering what appears to be an incredible bargain, there's just too much counterfeit specie in circulation to take the chance (see Rule number three, below).

Rule number two: Estimate your needs carefully; if you overbuy you lose twice — buying and selling back. Every time you exchange money, someone is making a profit, and rest assured it isn't you. Use up foreign notes before leaving, saving just enough for airport departure taxes (which often must be paid in local currency), other last-minute incidentals, and tips.

Rule number three: Don't buy money on the black market. The exchange rate may be better, but it is a common practice to pass off counterfeit bills to unsuspecting foreigners who aren't familiar with the local currency. It's usually a sucker's game, and you almost always are the sucker; it also can land you in jail.

Rule number four: Learn the local currency quickly and keep abreast of daily fluctuations in the exchange rate. These are listed in the English-language *International Herald Tribune* daily for the preceding day, as well as in every major newspaper in Europe. Banks post their daily exchange rates, which might vary by only a few cents — or even tenths of a cent — from a neighboring bank's posted rate. Rates change to some degree every day. For rough calculations, it is quick and safe to use round figures, but for purchases and actual currency exchanges, carry a small pocket calculator that helps you compute the exact rate. Inexpensive calculators specifically designed to quickly convert currency amounts for travelers are widely available.

When changing money, don't be afraid to ask how much commission you're being charged, and the exact amount of the prevailing exchange rate. In fact, in any exchange of money for goods or services, you should work out the rate before making any payment.

TIP PACKS: It's not a bad idea to buy a *small* amount of Irish coins and banknotes before your departure. But note the emphasis on the word "small," because, for the most part, you are better off carrying the bulk of your travel funds abroad in US dollar traveler's checks (see below). Still, the advantages of tip packs are threefold: You become familiar with the currency (really the only way to guard against making mistakes or being cheated during your first few hours in a new country); you are guaranteed some money should you arrive when a bank or exchange counter isn't open or available; and you don't have to depend on hotel desks, porters, or taxi drivers to change your money. A "tip pack" is the only Irish currency you should buy before you leave.

If you do run short upon arrival, dollars often are accepted at points of arrival. In other areas, they either *may* be accepted, or someone may accommodate you by changing a small amount — though invariably at a less than advantageous rate.

TRAVELER'S CHECKS: It's wise to carry traveler's checks on the road instead of (or in addition to) cash, since it's possible to replace traveler's checks if they are stolen or lost; travelers usually can receive partial or full replacement funds the same day if they have their purchase receipt and proper identification. Issued in various denominations and available in both US dollars and Irish punts (or pounds sterling in Northern Ireland), with adequate proof of identification (credit cards, driver's license, passport) traveler's checks are as good as cash in most hotels, restaurants, stores, and banks.

You will be able to cash traveler's checks fairly easily in Ireland, but don't expect to meander into a small village and be able to get instant cash. Also, even in metropolitan areas, don't assume that restaurants, small shops, and other establishments are going to be able to change checks of large denominations. Worldwide, more and more establishments are beginning to restrict the amount of traveler's checks they will accept or cash, so it is wise to purchase at least some of your checks in small denominations — say, $10 and $20 or the current equivalent in punts and pounds. Also, don't expect to change them into US currency except at banks and international airports.

When deciding whether to buy your travel funds in US or foreign denomination traveler's checks, keep in mind that the exchange rates offered by the issuing companies in the US generally are far less favorable than those available from banks both in the US and abroad. Therefore, it usually is better to carry the bulk of your travel funds abroad in US dollar denomination traveler's checks.

Every type of traveler's check is legal tender in banks around the world and each company guarantees full replacement if checks are lost or stolen. After that the similarity ends. Some charge a fee for purchase, others are free; you can buy traveler's checks at almost any bank, and some are available by mail. Most important, each traveler's check issuer differs slightly in its refund policy — the amount refunded immediately, the accessibility of refund locations, the availability of a 24-hour refund service, and the time it will take for you to receive replacement checks. For instance, American Express offers a 3-hour replacement of lost or stolen traveler's checks at any American Express office — other companies may not be as prompt. (Note that American Express's 3-hour policy is based on the traveler's being able to provide the serial numbers of the lost checks — without these numbers, refunds can take up to 3 business days.)

We cannot overemphasize the importance of knowing how to replace lost or stolen checks. All of the traveler's check companies have agents around the world, both in their own name and at associated agencies (usually, but not necessarily, banks), where refunds can be obtained during business hours. Most of them also have 24-hour toll-free telephone lines, and some even will provide emergency funds to tide you over on a Sunday.

Be sure to make a photocopy of the refund instructions that will be given to you by the issuing institution at the time of purchase. To avoid complications should you need to redeem lost checks (and to speed up the replacement process), keep the purchase receipt and an accurate list, by serial number, of the checks that have been spent or cashed. You may want to incorporate this information in an "emergency packet," also including your passport number and date of issue, the numbers of the credit cards you are carrying, and any other bits of information you can't bear to be without. Always keep these records separate from the checks and original records themselves (you may want to give them to a traveling companion to hold).

Although most people understand the desirability of carrying travel funds in the form of traveler's checks as protection against loss or theft, an equally good reason is that US dollar traveler's checks invariably get a better rate of exchange than cash — usually by at least 1% (although the discrepancy has been known to be substantially higher). The reasons are technical, but it is a fact of travel life that should not be ignored.

That 1% won't do you much good, however, if you already have spent it buying your traveler's checks. Several of the major traveler's check companies charge 1% for the privilege of using their checks; others don't, but the issuing institution (e.g., the particular bank at which you purchase them) may itself charge a fee. Thomas Cook checks issued in US currency are free if you make your travel arrangements through its travel agency, for example, and if you purchase traveler's checks at a bank in which you or your company maintains significant accounts (especially commercial accounts of some size), you also might find that the bank will absorb the 1% fee as a courtesy. American Express traveler's checks are available without charge to members of the *Automobile Association of America (AAA)* at some *AAA* offices in the US (the policy varies from state to state).

American Express, Citicorp, Thomas Cook, MasterCard, and Visa all offer traveler's checks, but not at all locations. Call the service numbers listed below to find a participating branch near you. Here is a list of the major companies issuing traveler's checks that are accepted widely in Ireland and the numbers to call in case loss or theft makes replacement necessary:

> *American Express:* To report lost or stolen checks in the US, call 800-221-7282. From Ireland, American Express advises travelers to call 721511 from the Irish Republic; 0-800-521313 from Northern Ireland; or 44-273-571600 (in Brighton, England) from either country. Another (slower) option is to call 801-964-6665 in the US, collect; or contact the nearest American Express office.
>
> *Bank of America:* To report lost or stolen checks in the US, call 800-227-3460. From Ireland and elsewhere worldwide, call 415-624-5400 or 415-622-3800, collect.

Citicorp: To report lost or stolen checks in the US, call 800-645-6556; from Ireland and elsewhere worldwide, call 813-623-1709 or 813-626-4444, collect.

MasterCard: To report lost or stolen checks in the US, call 800-223-9920. In Ireland, call the New York office at 212-974-5696, collect.

Thomas Cook MasterCard: To report lost or stolen checks in the US, call 800-223-7373. In Ireland, call the US office, 609-987-7300, collect, or 44-733-502995 (in England) and they will direct you to the nearest branch of Thomas Cook or *Wagons-Lits,* their European agent.

Visa: To report lost or stolen checks in the continental US, call 800-227-6811; from Ireland, call 415-574-7111, collect. From Ireland, you also can call this London number collect: 44-71-937-8091.

CREDIT CARDS: There are two different kinds of credit cards available to consumers in the US, and travelers must decide which kind best serves their needs — although many travelers elect to carry both types. "Convenience" or "charge" or "travel and entertainment" cards — American Express, Diners Club, and Carte Blanche — are widely accepted. They cost the cardholder a basic annual membership fee ($40 to $65 is typical for these three), but put no strict limit on the amount that may be charged on the card in any month. However, the entire amount charged must be paid in full at the end of each billing period (usually a month), so the cardholder is not actually extended any long-term credit.

"Bank cards" also are rarely issued free these days (with the exception of Sears Discover Card), and certain services they provide (check cashing, for example) can carry an extra charge. But this category comprises *real* credit cards, in the sense that the cardholder has the privilege of paying a small amount (1/36 is typical) of the total outstanding balance in each billing period. For this privilege, the cardholder is charged a high annual interest rate (currently three to four times the going bank passbook savings rate) on the balance owed. Many banks now charge interest from the purchase date, not from the first billing date (as they used to do); consider this when you are calculating the actual cost of a purchase. In addition, a maximum is set on the total amount the cardholder can charge, which represents the limit of credit the card company is willing to extend. The major bank cards are Visa and MasterCard, with Discover growing rapidly.

Unless you have established a firm credit history, getting any credit card will involve a fairly extensive credit check. To pass, you will need a job (at which you have worked for at least a year), a certain salary, and a good credit rating.

Note that some establishments you may encounter during the course of your travels may not honor any credit cards and some may not honor all cards, so there is a practical reason to carry more than one. Also keep in mind that some major US credit cards may be issued under different names in Europe. For example, in Ireland, MasterCard may go under the name Access or Eurocard — wherever these equivalents are accepted, MasterCard may be used. The following is a list of credit cards that enjoy wide domestic and international acceptance:

American Express: Emergency personal check cashing at American Express or representatives' offices (up to $500 in cash for all cardholders; traveler's check limits depend on the type of card: up to $500 for Green cardholders; up to $1,000 for Optima cardholders; up to $4,500 for Gold cardholders; and up to $9,500 for Platinum cardholders); emergency personal check cashing for guests at participating hotels (up to $100), and, for holders of airline tickets, at participating airlines in the US (up to $50). Extended payment plan for cruises, tours, and railway and airline tickets, as well as other prepaid travel arrangements. $100,000 to $500,000 travel accident insurance (depending on type of card) if ticket was charged to card; up to $1 million additional low-cost flight insurance available. Contact *American Express,* PO Box 39, Church St. Station, New York, NY 10008 (phone: 212-477-5700 in New York; 800-528-4800 elsewhere in the US; 801-964-6665 abroad; cardholders may call collect).

Carte Blanche: Extended payment plan for air travel (from $2,000 to $5,000, depending on credit line). $150,000 free travel accident insurance on plane, train, and ship if ticket was charged to card, plus $1,250 checked or carry-on baggage insurance and $25,000 rental car insurance. Medical, legal, and travel assistance available worldwide (phone: 800-356-3448 in the US; 214-680-6480, collect, from abroad). Contact *Carte Blanche,* PO Box 17326, Denver, CO 80217 (phone: 800-525-9135 in the US; 303-790-2433 abroad; cardholders may call collect).

Diners Club: Emergency personal check cashing for guests at participating hotels and motels (up to $250 per stay). Qualified card members are eligible for extended payment plan. $350,000 free travel accident insurance on plane, train, and ship if ticket was charged to your card, plus $1,250 checked and carry-on baggage insurance and $25,000 rental car insurance. Medical, legal, and travel assistance available worldwide (phone: 800-356-3448 in the US; 214-680-6480, collect, from abroad). Contact *Diners Club,* PO Box 17326, Denver, CO 80217 (phone: 800-525-9135 throughout the US for customer service; for lost or stolen cards, call one of the following 24-hour service numbers: 800-525-9341 in the US; 303-790-2433, collect, from abroad).

Discover Card: Created by Sears, Roebuck and Co., it provides the holder with cash advance at more than 500 locations in the US, and offers a revolving credit line for purchases at a wide range of service establishments. Other deposit, lending, and investment services also are available. For information, call 800-858-5588 in the US (if you can't reach this number by dialing directly, call an operator, who will be able to place the call).

MasterCard: Cash advances are available at participating banks worldwide, and a revolving credit line can be set up for purchases at a wide range of service establishments. Interest charges on any unpaid balance and other details are set by issuing bank. Check with your bank for information. *MasterCard* also offers a 24-hour emergency lost card service; call 800-336-8472 in the US; 314-275-6690, collect, from abroad.

Visa: Cash advances are available at participating banks worldwide, and a revolving credit line can be set up for purchases at a wide range of service establishments provided by issuer. Interest charges on any unpaid balance and other details are set by issuing bank. Check with your bank for information. Visa also offers a 24-hour emergency lost card service; call 800-336-8472 in the US; 415-574-7700, collect, from abroad.

In addition to the credit card services discussed above, a number of other benefits and/or details are set by the issuing institutions. For instance, some credit cards now offer the added incentive of "bonus" programs. Each time the card is used, the cardholder may gather either points with a monetary equivalent, which can be applied toward the total cost of selected purchases or travel arrangements, or a credit with a specific travel supplier such as frequent flyer mileage bonuses with an airline. When deciding on whether one of these cards provides the best deal, you should compare the potential value of these and other special programs with the variations in interest rates charged on unpaid balances and annual membership fees.

One of the thorniest problems relating to the use of credit cards abroad concerns the rate of exchange at which a purchase is charged. Be aware that the exchange rate in effect on the date that you make a foreign purchase or pay for a foreign service has nothing at all to do with the rate of exchange at which your purchase is billed to you when you get the invoice (sometimes months later) in the US. The amount American Express (and other convenience cards) charges is ultimately a function of the exchange rate in effect on the day your charge is received at an American Express (or other agency) service center, and there is a 1-year limit on the time a shop or hotel can take to forward its charge slips. The rate at which Visa and other bank cards process an item is a function of the rate at which the hotel's or shop's bank processed it.

The principle at work in this credit card–exchange rate roulette is simple, but very hard to predict. You make a purchase at a particular dollar versus local currency exchange rate. If the dollar gets stronger in the time between purchase and billing, your purchase actually costs you less than you anticipated. If the dollar drops in value during the interim, you pay more than you thought you would. There isn't much you can do about these vagaries except to follow one very broad, very clumsy rule of thumb: If the dollar is doing well at the time of purchase, its value increasing against the local currency, use your credit card on the assumption it still will be doing well when the billing takes place. If the dollar is doing badly, assume it will continue to do badly and pay with traveler's checks or cash. If you get too badly stuck, the best recourse is to complain, loudly. Be aware, too, that most credit card companies charge an unannounced, un-itemized 1% fee for converting foreign currency charges to US dollars.

No matter what you are using — traveler's checks, credit cards, or cash — plan ahead. That way you won't live through the nightmare of arriving in a small Irish town on a Friday afternoon without any local currency. If you do get caught in this situation, you may have to settle for a poor exchange rate at a hotel or a restaurant. In this case, exchange just enough dollars to get you through the weekend.

Also, carry your travel funds carefully. You might consider carrying them (cash and traveler's checks) in more than one place. Never put money in a back pocket or an open purse. Money should be kept in a buttoned front pocket, in a money purse pinned inside your shirt or blouse, or in one of the convenient money belts or leg pouches sold by many travel shops. It may be quaint and old-fashioned, but it's safe.

SENDING MONEY ABROAD: If you have used up your traveler's checks, cashed as many emergency personal checks as your credit card allows, drawn on your cash advance line to the fullest extent, and still need money, have it sent abroad via the *Western Union Telegraph Company*. A friend or relative can go, cash in hand, to any of *Western Union*'s 9,000 offices in the US, where, for a minimum transfer fee of $12 (it rises with the amount of the transaction) plus a $17 to $25 surcharge (which varies depending on transfer location), the funds will be transferred either to *Western Union*'s Irish correspondent bank, the *Bank of Ireland* (2 College Green, Dublin) in the Irish Republic, or to a post office in Belfast, Ballymena, Coleraine, Enniskillen, Londonderry, Newryomagh, or Portadown in Northern Ireland. When the money arrives in Ireland, you will not be notified — you must go to the bank or post office to inquire. Transfers generally take anywhere from 2 to 5 business days, although in particularly remote areas, the wait may be much longer. The funds will be turned over in local currency, based on the rate of exchange in effect on the day of receipt. For a higher fee, the US party to this transaction may use his or her MasterCard or Visa card to send up to $2,000 by phone by dialing *Western Union*'s toll-free number (800-325-4176) anywhere in the US.

American Express offers a similar service in the Irish Republic called "Moneygram," completing money transfers in as little as 15 minutes. The sender — who must be an American Express cardholder — must go to an American Express office in the US and can use cash, a personal check, money order, or an American Express Optima, Gold, or Platinum card for the transfer. Optima cardholders also can arrange for this transfer over the phone. The minimum transfer charge is $25, which rises with the amount of the transaction; the sender can forward funds of up to $10,000 (credit card users are limited to the amount of pre-established credit line). To collect at the other end, the receiver must go to American Express's office in Dublin (160 Grafton St.) and present a passport as proof of identification. For further information on this service, call 800-543-4080.

If you are literally down to your last few pence, the nearest US consulate (see *Medical and Legal Aid and Consular Services,* in this section) will let you call home to set these matters in motion.

Accommodations

 From elegant, centuries-old castle resorts and modern high-rises to thatch-roofed cottages and modest and inexpensive guesthouses, it's easy to be comfortable and well cared for on almost any budget in Ireland. Admittedly, in Ireland there are deluxe establishments providing expensive services to people with money to burn, but more affordable alternatives always have been available, particularly in the countryside.

On the whole, deluxe and first class accommodations in Ireland, especially in the large metropolitan centers (such as Belfast and Dublin), are somewhat more expensive than the same types of accommodations in the US (see *Calculating Costs,* in this section). When the dollar is strong, such top-of-the-line establishments are within the range of a great number of travelers who previously would not have been able to afford them. But lately, the generally unfavorable rate of exchange in Ireland and elsewhere on the Continent has rendered princely accommodations very pricey.

If you're watching your budget, however, you will be pleased to find in Ireland an even larger selection and a greater variety of accommodations within your price range than is the case at home. And even at the lower end of the cost scale, you will not necessarily have to forgo charm. While a fair number of inexpensive establishments are simply no-frills, "generic" places to spend the night, even the sparest room may have the cachet of once having been the nightly retreat of a monk or a nun. And some of the most delightful places to stay are the smaller, less expensive, often family-run small inns, guesthouses, and bed and breakfast establishments.

Once upon a time, such things as the superiority of New World plumbing made many of the numerous, less expensive alternatives unacceptable for North Americans. Today, the gap has closed considerably, and in Ireland the majority of the hostelries catering to the tourist trade are likely to be at least adequate in their basic facilities. When shopping around, also keep in mind that although for all accommodations in Ireland the price quoted must include the minimum value added tax (VAT) — which is 15% in Northern Ireland and 10% in the Republic — an additional service charge — usually 12% to 15% — often is added to hotel and guesthouse bills.

Our accommodations choices are included in the *Best in Town* sections of THE CITIES and in the *Checking In* sections of each tour route in DIRECTIONS. They have been selected for a variety of travel budgets, but the lists are not comprehensive; with some diligent searching, before you leave and en route, you can turn up an equal number of "special places" that are uniquely yours. Also consult the brochures and booklets cited in the descriptions below, most of which are available free from the US offices of the Irish Tourist Board or the Northern Ireland Tourist Board (see *Tourist Information Offices,* in this section, for addresses). Other publications can be purchased from the travel bookstores listed in *Books and Magazines,* also in this section.

Hotels and Guesthouses – Hotels may be large or small, part of a chain or independent, new and of the "international standard" type or well established and traditional. There are built-for-the-purposes premises and converted stately homes and villas, resort hotels offering plenty of opportunities for recreation, and smaller tourist hotels offering virtually none.

One way to help you select the type of hotel that fits your finances and personal needs is to become familar with the official hotel grading system used in Ireland. Most of the rooms for rent in the Irish Republic are listed in an accommodations guide issued yearly by the Irish Tourist Board (or *Bord Fáilte,* as it is known in Ireland). *Be Our Guest* details regularly inspected accommodations registered with the Tourist Board, and maximum prices are quoted. Hotels are graded in five categories (A*, A, B*, B, and C), but behind those letter grades may be found anything from a luxurious, turreted castle redolent of Irish history to a large, modern, and functional high-rise or a simple, family-run hostelry.

Guesthouses, somewhat the equivalent in Ireland of the Continent's pensions, are similarly rated (A, B*, B, and C). Though it sometimes is difficult to distinguish between some of the smaller, family-run hotels and the guesthouses, the latter almost always are family enterprises and tend to be more informal and personal in their hospitality. The official dividing line is the meal service: The hotel dining room is open to non-guests. Guesthouses cater exclusively to their guests, and in some cases will serve breakfast only (generally a full one that is included in the room price), though usually a partial- or full-board plan by the day or the week will be available. Guesthouses, too, can vary in atmosphere from old, reconverted Georgian residences to brand-new, built-for-the-purpose premises. Bathroom facilities vary considerably: In an A hotel, most rooms have private bathrooms; in an A guesthouse, some rooms with private bath may be available; in either hotel or guesthouse where a private bath is lacking, the room will have hot and cold running water. In all accommodations in the Irish Republic, the price quoted must include the 10% Value Added Tax (VAT). A service charge, usually of 10% to 15%, often is added to hotel and guesthouse bills.

Hotels and guesthouses in Northern Ireland are listed in the Northern Ireland Tourist Board's official annual *Where to Stay* guide, available from the Northern Ireland Tourist Board. Establishments are graded according to an official rating system similar to the one followed by the Irish Tourist Board in the Irish Republic, with the same hotel ratings as in the Republic (A*, A, B*, B, and C), but with only two grades (A and B) for guesthouses. Another difference is that not all rooms in the listed accommodations have hot and cold running water. The compulsory value added tax (15% in Northern Ireland) is included in the prices quoted; a service charge of 12% to 15% may be added to bills at some properties.

A great many hotels in Ireland are members of chains or hotel associations. Among the well-known, international names with properties in Ireland, particularly in major cities, are the following:

> *Best Western:* Has approximately 50 properties throughout Ireland. Call 800-528-1234.
>
> *Conrad:* The international division of the US *Hilton* hotel chain, with 1 property in Dublin in the Irish Republic. Call 800-445-8667.
>
> *Minotels Europe:* Has 6 properties in Northern Ireland and 16 properties in the Irish Republic. Call 800-336-4668.
>
> *Trusthouse Forte:* Has 4 properties in the Irish Republic: 2 in Dublin, 1 in Ennis, 1 in Kinsale; and 1 property in Belfast in Northern Ireland. Call 800-225-5843.

In addition, *Jurys,* a highly respected Irish chain, has 4 hotels in the Irish Republic: 1 each in Cork, Dublin, Limerick, and Waterford. Although this chain does not have a US representative, you can call their main office in Dublin (phone: 1-605000).

SPECIAL PLACES: Among the most interesting accommodations in Europe are those truly distinctive and frequently historic facilities whose ambience and style reflect something special of the country they are in. Many of these unique hostelries are included in the individual reports in *Best in Town* sections of the individual reports in THE CITIES and in *Checking In* in DIRECTIONS, as well as in various sections of DIVERSIONS.

Relais & Châteaux – Most members of this association are in France, but the group has grown to include dozens of establishments in many other countries, including 9 establishments in the Irish Republic.

Relais & Châteaux members are of particular interest to travelers who wish lodgings reflecting the ambience, style, and frequently the history of the places they are visiting. Some properties actually are ancient castles (several dating back to the 13th century), which have been converted into hotels. Others — the *relais* — are old inns, manor houses, even converted mills, convents, and monasteries. A few well-known city and resort establishments are included, such as *Dromoland Castle* near Shannon, but most are in quiet country surroundings, and frequently are graced with parks, ponds, and flowering gardens.

Members of the *Relais & Châteaux* group often are expensive, though no more than you would pay for deluxe, authentically elegant accommodations and service anywhere in the world (and many are not all that costly). At the time of this writing, the least expensive double room cost about $150 per night — although prices ranged anywhere up to $500 for the most luxurious establishments. (Prices include service and tax; some include breakfast and dinner, but if meals are not included they can add to the cost considerably, since all *Relais & Châteaux* properties have good — and expensive — restaurants.) Accommodations and service from one *relais* or château to another can range from simple but comfortable to elegantly deluxe, but they all maintain very high standards in order to retain their memberships, as they are appraised annually.

An illustrated catalogue of all the *Relais & Châteaux* properties is published annually and is available for $5 from *Relais & Châteaux* (2200 Lazy Hollow, Suite 152D, Houston, TX 77063) or from *David B. Mitchell & Company* (200 Madison Ave., New York, NY 10016; phone: 800-372-1323 or 212-696-1323). The association also can provide information on member properties. Reservations can be made directly with the establishments, through *David B. Mitchell & Company,* or through a travel agency.

BED AND BREAKFAST ESTABLISHMENTS AND OTHER ACCOMMODATIONS: Bed and breakfast establishments are a staple of the lower-cost lodging scene in Ireland, and are found wherever there are extra rooms to let in a private home and a host or hostess willing to attend to the details of this homespun form of hospitality. In Ireland, they are found just about everywhere, and not only in rural areas.

Bed and breakfast establishments (commonly known as B&Bs) provide exactly what the name implies. Though any hotel or guesthouse does the same, it is unusual for a bed and breakfast establishment to offer the extra services found in the other hostelries, and consequently the bed and breakfast route often is the least expensive way to go.

Beyond these two fundamentals, nothing else is predictable about going the bed and breakfast route. The bed may be in an extra room in a family home, in an apartment with a separate entrance, or in a free-standing cottage elsewhere on the host's property. You may have a patio, garden, and pool at your door or only the bare necessities. The breakfast may be a version of the standard continental breakfast (tea or coffee and rolls or sweet buns); however, particularly in rural areas, it generally will be a full Irish breakfast (a hearty meal, also including porridge, bacon and eggs, and so on). And as often as not breakfast is served along with some helpful tips on what to see and do and a bit of family history to add to the local lore. Occasionally, a kitchenette will be included, in which case you may be furnished with the makings of a breakfast you'll have to prepare for yourself. Despite their name, some B&Bs offer an evening meal as well — by prior arrangement and at extra cost.

Irish bed and breakfast establishments range from humble country homes to elegant manor houses. The homes listed in the Irish Tourist Board's annual *Farm Holidays in Ireland* guide are the equivalent of British bed and breakfast accommodations, which consist of the extra rooms of private homes to which adjustments have been made to meet the tourist board's inspection standards. Rarely will a private bathroom be found, but there is hot and cold running water in nearly all rooms in homes approved by the tourist board and listed in the guide. Costs range from about $15 to $25 per person per night (with establishments offering luxurious surroundings running somewhat higher), breakfast included, and many offer weekly rates for partial board. For the same type of accommodation at similar prices in Northern Ireland, see the "Approved Accommodation" and "Farm & Country Houses" headings in the annual *Where to Stay* guide (see above).

Although some hosts may be contacted directly, others prefer that arrangements be made through a reservations organization. The general procedure for making reservations through bed and breakfast services is that you contact them with your requirements, they help find the right place, and confirm your reservations upon receipt of a deposit. Any further information needed will be provided by either the service or by the owner of the bed and breakfast establishment.

Among the bed and breakfast reservations services handling establishments are the following:

> *Anglo-American Reiseburo (AAR;* Bodelschwinghstrasse 13, Westerkappeln 4535, Germany; phone: 49-54-042570). Handles properties throughout the Irish Republic and a few in Northern Ireland. (Note that they have English-speaking personnel, but you may have to call more than once to reach one.)
>
> *Hometours International* (1170 Broadway, New York, NY 10001; phone: 800-367-4668 or 212-689-0851). All properties represented are categorized according to the quality of accommodations and facilities. As we went to press, this company represented only one Irish property (in Dungannon, in Northern Ireland).

The best rule of thumb is to find out as much as you can before you book to avoid disappointment. A useful source of information on bed and breakfast reservation services and establishments overseas is the *Bed & Breakfast Reservations Services Worldwide, Inc.* (a trade association of B&B reservations services), which provides a listing of its members for $3. To order the most recent edition, contact them at PO Box 39000, Washington, DC 20016 (phone: 800-842-1486).

Finally, you may want to subscribe to *Gracious Stays & Special Places,* a publication focusing on guesthouses and bed and breakfast establishments set in historic and architecturally significant buildings. Published by a nonprofit organization, *Person to Person Travel Productions, Inc.* (2856 Hundred Oaks, Baton Rouge, LA 70808; phone: 504-346-1928), the annual membership fee, which starts at $20, includes four issues of the newsletter.

Other B&B publications can be purchased from the *British Travel Bookshop* (40 W. 57th St., New York, NY 10019; phone: 212-765-0898 or 800-448-3039 for book orders only), which can send you a list of all books in stock and an order form for their purchase; postage and handling charges vary from $2 to $7.50 according to the size of the order.

Farmhouses – In the country, city people rediscover the sounds of songbirds and the smell of grass. Suburbanites get the chance to poke around an area where the nearest neighbor lives miles away. Parents can say to their children, "No, milk does not originate in a cardboard carton," and prove it. Youngsters can meet people who live differently, think differently, and have different values. But even if there were no lessons to be learned, a stay at a farm would be a decidedly pleasant way to pass a couple of weeks, so it's no wonder that there are numerous farms welcoming guests all over Ireland.

Farm families who put up guests on a bed and breakfast basis — for a night or two or by the week, with weekly half-board plans available — are included in the Irish Tourist Board's *Farm Holidays in Ireland* guide. Listings in this publication, as well as in the illustrated *Town and Country,* published by the *Town and Country Homes Association* and distributed through the Irish Tourist Board, and in the Northern Ireland Tourist Board's *Farm & Country Holidays* (also illustrated), carry a brief description of each farm, allowing travelers to pick a traditional one or a modern one, a dairy farm over a sheep farm, one with ponies to ride, or one near a river for fishing. If the peace and quiet and the coziness of the welcome are appealing, a farmhouse can be an ideal base from which to explore a region by car or by foot and an especially good idea for those traveling with children.

Apartments, Homes, and Cottages – Another alternative to hotels for the visitor content to stay in one spot for a week or more is to rent a house or an apartment (usually called a "flat" overseas). Known to Europeans as a "holiday let" or a "self-catering holiday," a vacation in a furnished rental has both the advantages and disadvantages of living "at home" abroad. It certainly is less expensive than staying in a first class hotel for the same period of time (although very luxurious and expensive rentals are available, too). It has the comforts of home, including a kitchen, which means saving on food costs. Furthermore, it gives a sense of the country being visited that a large hotel often cannot. On the other hand, a certain amount of housework is involved because if you don't eat out, you have to cook, and though some rentals (especially the luxury ones) include a cleaning person, most don't. (If the rental doesn't include daily cleaning, arrangements often can be made with a nearby service.)

The Irish Tourist Board publishes *Self Catering,* a region-by-region guide to cottages, castles, houses, bungalows, chalets, and flats for rent that meet the tourist board's minimum standards. Entries include a small photo of each property, along with prices (rentals usually are by the week, from Saturday to Saturday) and the names of the owners to contact to make arrangements. Among the properties listed are some typically Irish ones — traditional cottages, many with a thatch roof, refurbished or specially built with all modern conveniences. Located mostly in small towns on the western and southern seaboards, these picturesque dwellings have a romantic appeal all their own. On the practical side, however, they are fairly inexpensive, can be rented by the week, month, or summer season, and have modern kitchens and baths that make them a sensible choice for families with small children. *Irish Cottage Holiday Homes,* a supplement dedicated to thatch-roofed cottage rentals alone, is contained in the above-mentioned self-catering guide and can be requested with the guide or separately. For information on rentals in Northern Ireland, see the Northern Ireland Tourist Board's information bulletin on self-catering or the "Self-Catering Accommodation" section of *Where to Stay.* Tourist boards in Ireland also may have information on local companies arranging rentals. In addition, many tour operators regularly include a few rental packages among their more conventional offerings; these generally are available through a travel agent.

Certain companies in the US specialize in rentals of apartments, houses, cottages, and other properties. They handle the booking and confirmation paperwork, generally for a fee included in the rental price, and can be expected to provide more information about the properties than that which might ordinarily be gleaned from a listing in an accommodations guide. Those listed below have many properties in Ireland; to have your pick you should begin to make arrangements for a summer rental at least 6 months in advance.

At Home Abroad: Offerings in Ireland include two castles, a fishing lodge, and some elegant country houses in the Irish Republic. Photographs of properties and a newsletter are available for a $50 registration fee. 405 E. 56th St., Apt. 6H, New York, NY 10022 (phone: 212-421-9165).

Castles, Cottages and Flats of Ireland and UK, Ltd.: The specialty is cottages in England's heartland, but also featured are properties in the Irish Republic. Small charge ($5) for receipt of main catalogue, refundable upon booking. Box 261, Westwood, MA 02090 (phone: 617-329-4680).

Country Homes and Castles: The specialty is large properties — castles, manor houses, stately homes — and they can arrange luxurious, customized rental packages throughout Ireland. 4092 North Ivy Rd., Atlanta GA 30342 (phone: 404-231-5837), and 900 Wilshire Blvd., Suite 830, Los Angeles, CA 90017 (phone: 213-629-4861).

Eastone Overseas Accommodations: Handles apartments, cottages, houses, and castles in the Irish Republic. 198 Southampton Drive, Jupiter, FL 33458 (phone: 407-575-6991/2), or 20000 Horizon Way, Suite 110, Mount Laurel, NJ 08054 (phone: 609-722-1010).

Hideaways International: Rents apartments, private homes, and manor houses throughout both Northern Ireland and the Republic. 15 Goldsmith St., PO Box 1270, Littleton, MA 01460 (phone: 800-843-4433 or 508-486-8955).

International Lodging Corp.: Handles a few houses and cottages in the Irish Republic. 89-27 182nd Pl., Hollis, NY 11423 (phone: 718-291-1342).

Rent a Vacation Everywhere (RAVE): Modern condominium apartments outside Dublin, plus cottages throughout the Irish Republic. 328 Main St. E., Suite 526, Rochester, NY 14604 (phone: 716-454-6440).

Villas International (formerly *Interchange*): Offers a good selection of simple cottages and a small assortment of more gracious properties throughout the Irish Republic. 71 W. 23rd St., New York, NY 10010 (phone: 212-929-7585 in New York State; 800-221-2260 elsewhere in the US).

HOME EXCHANGES: Still another alternative for travelers who are content to stay in one place is a home exchange: The Smith family from Chicago moves into the home of the Sweeney family in Dublin, while the Sweeneys enjoy a stay in the Smiths' home. The home exchange is an exceptionally inexpensive way to ensure comfortable, reasonable living quarters with amenities that no hotel possibly could offer; often the trade includes a car. Moreover, it allows you to live in a new community in a way that few tourists ever do: For a little while, at least, you will become something of a resident.

Several companies publish directories of individuals and families willing to trade homes with others for a specific period of time. In some cases, you must be willing to list your own home in the directory; in others, you can subscribe without appearing in it. Most listings are for straight exchanges only, but each of the directories also has a number of listings placed by people interested in either exchanging or renting (for instance, if they own a second home). Other types of arrangements include exchanges of hospitality while owners are in residence, or youth exchanges, where your teenager is put up as a guest in return for your putting up their teenager at a later date. A few house-sitting opportunities also are available. In most cases, arrangements for the actual exchange take place directly between you and the foreign host. There is no guarantee that you will find a listing in the area in which you are interested, but each of the organizations given below includes Irish homes among its hundreds or even thousands of foreign listings.

Home Base Holidays: For $42 a year, subscribers receive four listings, with an option to list in all four. 7 Park Ave., London N13 5PG (phone: 44-81-886-8752).

International Home Exchange Service/Intervac US: The $35 fee includes copies of the three directories published yearly and an option to list your home in one of them; a black-and-white photo may be included with the listing for an additional $8.50. A 10% discount is given to travelers over age 65. Box 190070, San Francisco, CA 94119 (phone: 415-435-3497).

InterService Home Exchange, Inc.: An affiliate of *Intervac International*, this service publishes three directories annually that include more than 7,000 exchanges in more than 300 countries worldwide. For $35, interested home-swappers are listed in and receive a copy of the February, March, and May directories; a black-and-white photo of your home may be included with the listing for an additional $10. Box 387, Glen Echo, MD 20812 (phone: 301-229-7567).

Loan-A-Home: Specializes in long-term (4 months or more — excluding July and August) housing arrangements worldwide for students and professors, business-people, and retirees, although its two annual directories (with supplements) carry a small listing of short-term rentals and/or exchanges. $35 for a copy of one directory and one supplement; $45 for a copy of two directories and two supplements. 2 Park La., Apt. 6E, Mt. Vernon, NY 10552 (phone: 914-664-7640).

Vacation Exchange Club: Some 6,000 listings, about half of which are foreign (mostly in Europe). For $24.70 a year, the subscriber receives two directories — one in late winter and one in the spring — and is listed in one. For $16, subscribers receive both directories but no listing. 12006 111th Ave., Suite 12, Youngtown, AZ 85363 (phone: 602-972-2186).

World Wide Exchange: The $45 annual membership fee includes one free listing (for house, yacht, or motorhome) and three free guides. 1344 Pacific Ave., Suite 103, Santa Cruz, CA 95060 (phone: 408-476-4206).

Worldwide Home Exchange Club: Handles over 1,000 listings a year worldwide. For $20 a year, you will receive two listings yearly, as well as supplements. 45 Hans Place, London SW1X OJZ, England (phone: 44-71-589-6055).

Home Exchange International (HEI), with offices in New York, Los Angeles, London, Paris, and Milan, functions in a different manner in that it publishes and directory and shepherds the exchange process most of the way. Interested parties supply *HEI* with photographs of themselves and their homes, information on the type of home they want and where, and a registration fee of $50. The company then works with its other offices to propose a few possibilities, and only when a match is made do the parties exchange names, addresses, and phone numbers. For this service, *HEI* charges a closing fee, which ranges from $150 to $450 for domestic or international switches from 2 weeks to 3 months in duration, and from $275 to $525 for switches longer than 3 months. Contact *Home Exchange International*, 185 Park Row, PO Box 878, New York, NY 10038-0272 (phone: 212-349-5340), or 22458 Ventura Blvd., Woodland Hills, CA 91364 (phone: 818-992-8990).

HOME STAYS: If the idea of actually staying in a private home as the guest of an Irish family appeals to you, check with the United States Servas Committee, which maintains a list of hosts throughout the world (at present, there are about 80 listings throughout Ireland) willing to throw open their doors to foreigners, entirely free of charge. The aim of this nonprofit cultural program is to promote international understanding and peace, and every effort is made to discourage freeloaders. Servas will send you an application form and the name of the nearest of some 200 interviewers around the US for you to contact. After the interview, if you're approved, you'll receive documentation certifying you as a Servas traveler. There is a membership fee of $45 for an individual and there also is a deposit of $15 to receive the host list, refunded on its return. The list gives the name, address, age, occupation, and other particulars of the hosts, including languages spoken. From then on, it is up to you to write to prospective hosts directly, and Servas makes no guarantee that you will be accommodated. If you are, you'll normally stay 2 nights.

Servas stresses that you should choose only people you really want to meet, and that for this brief period you should be interested mainly in your hosts, not in sightseeing. It also suggests that one way to show your appreciation once you've returned home is to become a host yourself. The minimum age of a Servas traveler is 18 (however, children under 18 may accompany their parents), and though quite a few are young people who've just finished college, there are travelers (and hosts) in all age ranges and occupations. Contact Servas, 11 John St., Room 706, New York, NY 10038 (phone: 212-267-0252).

Another organization arranging home stays is *In the English Manner,* which specializes in stays with British families, but also has a number of Irish families (mainly in the Republic) who open their homes to guests. Prospective hosts have been visited by the company to assure that only those genuinely interested in meeting foreigners and making their stay a memorable experience participate. Hosts, in fact, probably are better screened than guests, who need merely supply the company with family members' names and ages, occupations, special interests, and other pertinent data, such as allergies. The company then selects a few possible hosts and lets the client make the final decision. There is a minimum stay of 3 nights, which can be divided among three different families if desired, but no maximum stay except what is mutually agreeable to both hosts and guests. The entire cost of the stay is paid in advance. Meals that guests decide upon in advance also are prepaid; meals and other extras decided upon during the stay are paid in cash on departure (to avoid embarrassment, the company advises clients beforehand what the hosts charge). The program is not for budget travelers, since the cost ranges from $120 per night for two (for lodgings in small houses) up to $200 per night per couple (for castle accommodations), with an average of $160 to $170 per night. But the homes are not ordinary; they include several country houses and some larger stately homes. Single rates are available, and there are reductions for children. Contact *In the English Manner,* PO Box 936, Alamo, CA 95407 (phone: 415-935-7065 in California; 800-422-0799 elsewhere in the US).

You also might be interested in a publication called *International Meet-the-People Directory,* published by the *International Visitor Information Service.* It lists several agencies in a number of foreign countries (37 worldwide, 18 in Europe) that arrange home visits for Americans, either for dinner or overnight stays. To order a copy, send $4.95 to the *International Visitor Information Service* (733 15th St. NW, Suite 300, Washington, DC 20005; phone: 202-783-6540). For other local organizations and services offering home exchanges, contact the local tourist authority.

RESERVATIONS: To the extent that you are able to settle on a precise itinerary beforehand, it is best to make advance reservations for accommodations in any major Irish city or resort area, even if you are traveling during the off-season. To be sure of finding space in the hotel of your choice, booking several months before arrival is not too soon. Hotel rooms in the provincial cities also should be reserved ahead year-round. Because many of them also are important meeting centers, even off-season travelers may find hotel space scarce and "full" signs everywhere if a large convention is being hosted. Also keep in mind that larger hotels are the ones most frequently pre-booked as 2- and 3-day stopover centers for the thousands of tour groups ranging Ireland and the Continent, and major cities may be busiest during off- or shoulder season months due to the simultaneous presence of business and convention travelers and tourists.

During the peak travel season — approximately May through mid-October — visitors should expect to pay a premium for traveling in Ireland. However, not even a willingness to pay for top accommodations will guarantee a room if you don't have reservations. It is wise to make reservations as far in advance as possible for popular tourist destinations throughout Ireland, as well as for hotel, farm, and other accommodations near major summer destinations along the coasts, where the number of rooms and limited facilities, not the price, is likely to be the qualifying factor. Advance reservations also are advisable during the *Christmas* and *New Year*'s holidays and the period surrounding *St. Patrick's Day*.

The simplest way to make a reservation is to leave it all to a travel agent, who will provide this service at no charge if the hotel or guesthouse in question pays a commission. The accommodations guides published by the Irish Tourist Board and the Northern Ireland Tourist Board use a symbol to show which of the establishments listed pay such a commission — the larger and more expensive ones invariably do, and more and more budget hotels are beginning to follow suit. If the one you selected doesn't, the travel agent may charge a fee to cover costs, or you may have to make the reservation yourself.

Reserving a room yourself is not difficult if you intend to stay mainly in hotels that are members of chains or associations, whether European ones with US representatives or American ones with hotels overseas. Most international hotel chains list their toll-free (800) reservation numbers in the white pages of the telephone directory, and any hotel within a chain can assure reservations for you at sister facilities. Naturally, the more links in the chain, the more likely that an entire stay can be booked with a minimum number of letters or phone calls to one central reservations system. If booking with primarily Irish establishments, either a travel agent or the Irish government tourist offices will be able to tell you who in the US represents the chain or a particular hotel. (The US phone numbers of some of these chains and associations operating in Ireland are given in the discussion of hotels above.)

Hotels that are not represented in the US will have to be contacted directly. All the hotel entries in the *Best in Town* sections of THE CITIES chapters include phone numbers for reservations; phone numbers also are included in the *Checking In* sections of DIRECTIONS. If you choose to write rather than telephone, it's a good idea to enclose at least two International Reply Coupons (sold at post offices and banks) to facilitate a response and to leave *plenty* of time for the answer. Give full details of your requirements and several alternate dates, if possible. You probably will be asked to send a deposit for at least 1 night's lodging, payable by check or credit card; in return, be sure to get written confirmation of your reservation and a receipt for any deposit.

Nevertheless, if the hotel you want to visit has no rooms available on your chosen dates, take heart. The advice to make reservations early always is woven into every travel article; making a *late* reservation may be almost as good advice. It's not at all unusual for hotel rooms, totally unavailable as far as 6 months ahead, to suddenly become available a week to a day before your desired arrival. Cancellations tend to occur closer to, rather than farther from, a designated date. One possible strategy is to make reservations at another hotel so you won't be left high and dry, determine the cancellation penalties, if any, and check back with your first choice closer to your date of arrival. It also is true that hotels that report SRO status to travel agents may remarkably discover a room if you call directly (FAX is even better) close to your proposed arrival date.

There also is reason to believe that hotels increasingly are offering one rate to travelers working through travel agents and less expensive rates to clients who book directly. Even if you do use a travel agent, it sounds like a prudent course to double-check hotel rates if saving money is one of your prime travel concerns.

Reservation Services in Ireland – Some people prefer not to contain their wanderlust by making hotel reservations too far in advance. Although the advice still stands to reserve high-season hotel space (particularly in Belfast and Dublin) well beforehand and although the traveler must keep an eye on the special-events calendar to avoid arriving *anywhere* blissfully unaware that the place is already bursting at the seams — *St. Patrick's Week* throughout the country, for instance — it is possible to travel in Ireland reserving as you go. Naturally, the best method is to call ahead to hotels in the next town on your itinerary before checking out of the one you're in because it allows you to alter your course if you don't turn up any vacancies. (Hotels usually will hold rooms on the strength of a phone call provided you arrive no later than expected.)

Though not all travelers would face the prospect of arriving in a strange city without a reservation with equal sangfroid, there are services that help book empty rooms for those who risk it. In the Irish Republic, tourist information offices located throughout the country and at Shannon and Dublin airports and at the ferry ports of Dún Laoghaire will make a reservation for a small fee to cover costs. In Dublin proper, the office is at 14 Upper O'Connell St. Similarly, in Northern Ireland, tourist information offices in Belfast, at Belfast International Airport, Larne Harbour, and in many other towns provide booking services for a small fee. In both countries, the same offices also can be used by those who prefer to book as they go, since they can be used not only to book a room in a locality once you've arrived there, but also to book a room ahead in another part of the country.

When using these services, it is best to arrive at the office as early in the day as possible; at the latest, be there when they open for the afternoon. You may have to stand in line, and there are no guarantees that you will find what you're looking for when your turn comes, but if you are traveling somewhat off the beaten track you should have few really close calls.

OVERBOOKING: Although the problem is not unique to Ireland, the worldwide travel boom has brought with it some abuses that are pretty much standard operating procedure in any industry facing a demand that frequently outstrips supply. Anticipating a certain percentage of no-shows, hotels routinely overbook rooms. When cancellations don't occur and everybody with a confirmed reservation arrives as promised, it's not impossible to find yourself with a valid reservation for which no room exists.

There's no sure way to avoid all the pitfalls of overbooking, but you can minimize the risks. Always carry evidence of your confirmed reservation. This should be a direct communication from the hotel — to you or your travel agent — and should specify the exact dates and duration of your accommodations and the price. The weakest form of confirmation is the voucher slip a travel agent routinely issues, since it carries no official indication that the hotel itself has verified your reservation.

Even better is the increasing opportunity to guarantee hotel reservations by giving the hotel (or its reservation system) your credit card number and agreeing that the hotel is authorized to charge you for that room no matter what. Although many European hotels have strict rules regarding refunds — which apply to both prepaid (written) and credit card (phoned in) deposits — it still *may* be possible to cancel if you do so before 6 PM of the day of your reservation (before 4 PM in some areas). The best course is to check the establishment's policy when making the reservation, and if it does cancel under this arrangement, make sure you get a cancellation number to protect you from being billed erroneously.

If all these precautions fail and you are left standing at the reservation desk with a reservation the hotel clerk won't honor, you have a last resort: Complain as long and as loudly as necessary to get satisfaction! The person who makes the most noise usually gets the last room in the house. It might as well be you.

What if you can't get reservations in the first place? This is a problem that often confronts businesspeople who can't plan months ahead. The word from savvy travelers is that a bit of currency (perhaps attached discreetly to a business card) often increases your chances with recalcitrant desk clerks. There are less venal ways of improving your odds, however. If you are traveling on business, ask an associate at your destination to make reservations for you.

There is a good reason to do this above and beyond the very real point that a resident has the broadest knowledge of local hotels. Often a hotel will appear sold out on its computer when in fact a few rooms are available. The proliferation of computerized reservations has made it unwise for a hotel to indicate that it suddenly has five rooms available (from cancellations) when there might be 30 or 40 travel agents lined up in the computer waiting for them. That small a number of vacancies is much more likely to be held by the hotel for its own sale, so a local associate is an invaluable conduit to these otherwise inaccessible rooms. Another efficient alternative is communciation with the hotel via a FAX machine, which can prove useful in arranging and confirming reservations.

Time Zones, Business Hours, and Public Holidays

TIME ZONES: The countries of Europe fall into three time zones. Greenwich Mean Time — measured from Greenwich, England, at longitude 0°0′ — is the base from which all other time zones are measured. Areas in zones west of Greenwich have earlier times and are called Greenwich Minus; those to the east have later times and are called Greenwich Plus. For example, New York City — which falls into the Greenwich Minus 5 time zone — is 5 hours earlier than Greenwich, England. Ireland is in the Greenwich Mean Time zone, which means that the time is the same throughout Ireland as it is in Greenwich, and when it is noon in Belfast or Dublin, it is 7 AM in New York and Washington, DC.

Like most western European nations, Ireland moves its clocks an hour ahead in the spring and an hour back in the fall, although in both cases the date of the change tends to be about a week earlier (in spring) and a week later (in fall) than the dates we have adopted in the US. For about 2 weeks a year, then, the time difference between the US and Ireland is 1 hour more or less than usual.

Irish and other European timetables use a 24-hour clock to denote arrival and departure times, which means that hours are expressed sequentially from 1 AM. By this method, 9 AM is recorded as 0900, noon as 1200, 1 PM as 1300, 6 PM as 1800, midnight as 2400, and so on. For example, the departure of a train at 7 AM will be announced as "0700"; one leaving at 7 PM will be noted as "1900."

BUSINESS HOURS: Throughout Ireland, most businesses are open Mondays through Fridays from 9 AM to 5 or 5:30 PM. Shops follow roughly the same schedule, from 9 AM to 5:30 or 6 PM, and they also generally are open on Saturdays. In small towns and villages, they may close for an hour at lunchtime, and on at least one weekday they close at 1 PM. Some stores in Dublin skip the early closing and simply don't open on Mondays. Larger stores in shopping centers stay open until 8 or 9 PM at least 1 day a week (Thursdays in most cases, but sometimes also Fridays).

Banking hours in Northern Ireland are from 10 AM to 3:30 PM, with a break for lunch (12:30 to 1:30 PM). In the Irish Republic, banking hours are from 10:30 AM to 3 PM (or 5 PM in some cities), also with a lunch break (12:30 to 1:30 PM). Most banks in both countries are closed on Saturdays, Sundays, and public holidays, although branches at major airports are open 7 days a week.

Restaurant hours are similar to those in the US. Most restaurants are open all week during the high season and close 1 day each week during the off-season — the day varies from restaurant to restaurant. Hours in general tend also to be a bit later in summer, and they vary from city to city; check local listings in THE CITIES and DIRECTIONS.

PUBLIC HOLIDAYS: In the Republic, the public holidays are *New Year's Day* (January 1); *St. Patrick's Day* (March 17); *Good Friday; Easter Monday; June Holiday* (first Monday in June — June 3 this year); *August Bank Holiday* (first Monday in August — August 5 this year); *October Holiday* (last Monday in October — October 28 this year); *Christmas Day* (December 25); and *St. Stephen's Day* (December 26). In

Northern Ireland, they are *New Year's Day* (January 1); *St. Patrick's Day* (March 17); *Good Friday; Easter Monday; May Day* (first Monday in May — May 6 this year); *Orange Day,* or *Battle of the Boyne Holiday* (July 12); *Summer Bank Holiday* (last Monday in August — August 26 this year); *Christmas Day* (December 25); and *Boxing Day* (December 26).

Mail, Telephone, and Electricity

 MAIL: Before you leave home, fill in a "change of address card" (available at post offices), which is the form you need to get the post office to hold your mail until your return. If you are planning an extended stay abroad, you can have your first class mail forwarded to your vacation address. There generally is no charge for this service. (Note that many post offices will need 2 to 3 weeks' notice to put this change of address into effect.)

There are several places that will receive and hold mail for travelers in Ireland. Mail sent to you at a hotel and clearly marked "Guest Mail, Hold for Arrival" is one safe approach. Irish post offices also will extend this service to you if the mail is addressed to the Irish equivalent of US general delivery — called *Poste Restante* in the Republic of Ireland and General Post Office in Northern Ireland. This probably is the best way for travelers to have mail sent if they do not have a definite address. Have your correspondents print your last name in big block letters on the envelope (lest there be any doubt as to which is your last name), and as there often are several post office locations in major cities, it is important that the address and/or specific name of the office be indicated (not just the name of the city), in addition to the words *Poste Restante* or General Post Office. Be sure to call at the correct office when inquiring about mail. Also, don't forget to take your passport with you when you go to collect it. Most Irish post offices require formal identification before they will release anything; there also may be a small charge for picking up your mail.

If you are an American Express customer (a cardholder, a carrier of American Express traveler's checks, or traveling on an *American Express Travel Service* tour) you can have mail sent to its offices in cities along your route; letters are held free of charge — registered mail and packages are not accepted. You must be able to show an American Express card, traveler's checks, or a voucher proving you are on one of the company's tours to avoid paying for mail privileges. Those who aren't clients must pay a nominal charge each time they inquire if they have received mail, whether or not they actually have a letter. There also is a forwarding fee, for clients and non-clients alike. Mail should be addressed to you, care of American Express, and should be marked "Client Mail Service." Additional information on its mail service and addresses of American Express offices in Ireland are contained in the pamphlet *Services and Offices,* available from any US branch of American Express.

US embassies and consulates abroad do not accept mail for tourists. They will, however, help out in emergencies — if you need to receive important business documents or personal papers, for example. It is best to inform them either by separate letter or cable, or by phone (particularly if you are in the country already), that you will be using their address for this purpose.

Irish post office branches are located in every city, town, and hamlet, as well as in many train stations and airports. All post offices in Northern Ireland are open Mondays through Fridays from 9 AM to 5 PM; major post offices in large cities also are open on Saturdays from 9 AM to noon. In the Republic, they usually are open Mondays through Fridays from 9 AM to 5 PM. The main post office in Dublin also is open on Saturday mornings.

Mail rates change frequently, following the upward trend of everything else; stamps are bought at the post office and at authorized tobacconists, as well as at some other shops and hotels. As in the US, letters can be mailed in green letter boxes found on the street, but it is better to mail them (and certainly packages) directly from post offices.

Be advised that delivery from Ireland can be slow (especially if you send something any distance by surface mail) and erratic (postcards often are given lowest priority, so don't use them for important messages). Send your correspondence via air mail if it's going any distance, and to ensure or further speed delivery of important letters, send them registered mail or express or special delivery.

If your correspondence is important, you may want to send it via one of the special courier services: *Federal Express, DHL,* and other international services are available in Ireland. The cost is considerably higher than sending something via the postal services — but the assurance of its timely arrival is worth it.

If you're mailing to an address within Ireland, another way to ensure or speed delivery is to use the postal code. Postal codes are used throughout Northern Ireland, but in the Republic, they only apply to the Dublin area. Including a postal code in a Dublin address will help to speed your letter to its destination, and since small towns in Northern Ireland may have similar names, the postal code always should be specified — delivery of a letter may depend on it. Put it on the envelope immediately after the name of the town or city and on the same line. If you do not have the correct postal code, call the appropriate tourism authority (see *Tourist Information Offices,* in this section, for telephone numbers) — they should be able to look it up for you. Alternatively, you could call the addressee directly — if you have the telephone number — and although this will be costly, it may be worth it to ensure delivery of your correspondence.

TELEPHONE: If you are planning to be away for more than a month, you may be able to save money by asking the telephone company to temporarily suspend your home telephone service. You also can arrange to have your calls transferred to another number.

The Irish telephone system is not too different from our own. It includes direct dialing, operator-assisted calls, collect calls, reduced rates for certain times of the day and days of the week, and so on. The number of digits varies considerably within the country, and to further confuse matters, a city code may be included in the digits quoted as the "local" number. If you dial a number directly and your call does not go through, either the circuits are busy or you may need to add or delete one or several digits. If you have tried several times and are sure that you have the correct number, have an international operator place the call — however, this will be more expensive than dialing directly. (To reach an international operator in the US, dial "0" for a local operator and ask him or her to connect you.)

It is easy enough to call Ireland from the US: dial 011 (the international access code) + the country code + the city code (if you don't know this, ask the international operator) + the local number. (The country code for Northern Ireland — as for the rest of the United Kingdom — is 44; the country code for the Irish Republic is 353.) For instance, to place a call from anywhere in the US to Dublin, dial 011 + 353 + 1 (the city code for Dublin) + the local number; to place a call to Belfast, dial 011 + 44 + 232 + the local number.

The procedure for making a station-to-station call from Ireland to the US (usually a more expensive proposition) is similar to the procedure described above. To call a number in the US from the Irish Republic, dial 16 (the international access code) + 1 (the US country code) + the US area code + the local number; to call a number in the US from Northern Ireland, dial 010 (the international access code) + 1 (the US country code) + the US area code + the local number. For instance, to call a number in New York City from the Irish Republic, dial 16 + 1 + 212 + the local number; to make the same call from Northern Ireland, dial 010 + 1 + 212 + the local number.

Calls between the Irish Republic and Northern Ireland are dialed like other international calls and follow the same basic procedure. To make a call from the Republic to Northern Ireland, dial 16 (the international access code) + 44 (the country for Northern Ireland) + the city code + the local number. To make a call from Northern Ireland to the Republic, dial 010 (the international access code) + 353 (the country code for the Irish Republic) + the city code + the local number.

For calling between cities either within the Irish Republic or within Northern Ireland dial 0 + the city code + the local number; and for calls within the same city code coverage area, simple dial the local number. If you don't know the city code, check the front of a telephone book or ask an operator. Note that Irish telephone directories and other sources may include the 0 (used for dialing within Ireland) as part of the area code; when dialing from the US, follow the procedure described above, *leaving off the 0.*

To reach a local operator in the Irish Republic, dial 10; when in Northern Ireland, dial 100. To reach an international operator in the Irish Republic, dial 114 (or dial 10 for a local operator who can connect you); in Northern Ireland, dial 100 for a local operator who will connect you to an international operator. For information on calling for help in the event of an emergency, see *Medical and Legal Aid and Consular Services,* in this section.

Making connections in Europe sometimes can be hit or miss — all exchanges are not always in operation on the same day. If the number dialed does not go through, try later or the next day. So be warned: Those who have to make an important call — to make a hotel reservation in another city, for instance — should start to do so a few days ahead.

Pay telephones in Ireland can be found in pubs, restaurants, shopping centers, transportation centers, and, less commonly, in booths on the street. (All too often, however, these are out of order — if you're lucky, a sign will warn you.)

The procedure for calling from an Irish pay phone depends on whether it is an older or newer model. To make a call from one of the older pay phones (generally found in very rural areas), place a coin (the pence denomination will be indicated on the phone) in the slot at the top of the phone. When your party answers — and *not* before — push the button at the top of the phone, causing the coin to drop (otherwise the answering party will not be able to hear you). If your party doesn't answer, hang up and simply lift the unused coin out of the slot. In newer pay phones, coins drop automatically when you put them in as in US phones; if your party doesn't answer, you have to press the return button (sometimes repeatedly) to get your money back.

Although the majority of Irish pay phones still take coins, phones that take credit cards or specially designated phone cards are increasingly common. Instituted to cut down on vandalism, the phone cards free callers from the necessity of carrying around a pocketful of change, and are sold in various pence or pound denominations. The units per card, like message units in US phone parlance, are a combination of time and distance. To use such a card, you insert it into a slot in the phone and dial the number you wish to reach. A display gradually will count down the value that remains on your card. When you run out of units on the card, you can insert another.

In the Irish Republic, pay phones that take phone cards generally are found at post offices, which also is where you can purchase the phone cards. In Northern Ireland (as in Great Britain), these special phones are more common; they may be found next to regular phones in metropolitan areas and at major tourist destinations, and phone cards can be purchased at post offices, as well as at newsagents.

A lot of digits may be involved once a caller starts dialing beyond national borders, but avoiding operator-assisted calls can cut costs considerably and bring rates into a somewhat more reasonable range — except for calls made through hotel switchboards. One of the most unpleasant surprises travelers encounter in many foreign countries is the amount they find tacked on to their hotel bill for telephone calls, because foreign hotels routinely add on astronomical surcharges. (It's not at all uncommon to find 300% or 400% added to the actual telephone charges.) A practice initially begun to cover the expense of installing phone equipment and maintaining multilingual personnel to run it around the clock, it now is firmly entrenched as a profit making operation for many hotels.

Until recently, the only recourse against this unconscionable overcharging was to call collect when phoning from abroad or to use a telephone credit card — available through a simple procedure from any local US phone company. (Note, however, that even if you use a telephone credit card, some hotels still may charge a fee for line usage.) Now *American Telephone and Telegraph (AT&T)* offers *USA Direct,* a service that connects users, via a toll-free number, with an *AT&T* operator in the US, who will then put a call through at the standard international rate. A new feature of this service is that travelers abroad can reach US toll-free (800) numbers by calling a *USA Direct* operator, who will connect them. Charges for all calls made through *USA Direct* appear on the caller's regular US phone bill. (As we went to press, this service was available throughout Western Europe, but it was offered only in Northern Ireland, not in the Republic.) For a brochure and wallet card listing toll-free numbers by country, contact International Information Service, *AT&T Communications,* 635 Grand St., Pittsburgh, PA 15219 (phone: 800-874-4000).

It's wise to ask the surcharge rate *before* calling from a hotel. If the rate is high, it's best to use a telephone credit card, or the direct-dial service described above (if you are in Northern Ireland); make a collect call; or place the call and ask the party to call right back. If none of these choices is possible, make international calls from the local post office or special telephone center to avoid surcharges. Another way to keep down the cost of telephoning from Ireland is to leave a copy of your itinerary and telephone numbers with people in the US so that they can call you instead.

■ **Note:** For quick reference, you might want to get a copy of a helpful pamphlet, *The Phone Booklet,* which lists the nationwide, toll-free (800) numbers of travel information sources and suppliers — such as major airlines, hotel and motel chains, car rental companies, and tourist information offices. Send $2 for postage and handling to *Scott American Corporation,* Box 88, West Redding, CT 06896.

ELECTRICITY: The US runs on 110-volt, 60-cycle alternating current. Both Northern Ireland and the Irish Republic run on 220- or 240-volt, 50-cycle alternating current. (Some large tourist hotels also may offer 110-volt currency for your convenience — but don't count on it.) The large difference between US and European voltage means that without a converter, at 220 volts the motor of a US appliance used overseas would run at twice the speed at which it's meant to operate and would quickly burn out.

Travelers can solve the problem by buying a lightweight converter to transform foreign voltage into the US kind (there are two types of converters, depending on the wattage of the appliance) or by buying dual-voltage appliances that convert from one to the other at the flick of a switch (hair dryers of this sort are common). The difference between the 50-cycle and 60-cycle currents will cause no problem — the American appliance will simply run more slowly — but it still will be necessary to deal with differing socket configurations before plugging in. To be fully prepared, bring along an extension cord (in older or rural establishments the electrical outlet may be farther from the sink than the cord on your razor or hair dryer can reach), and a wall socket adapter kit with a full set of plugs to ensure that you'll be able to plug in anywhere.

One good source for sets of plugs and adapters for use worldwide is the *Franzus Company* (PO Box 142, Beacon Falls, CT 06403; phone: 203-723-6664). *Franzus* also publishes a useful brochure, *Foreign Electricity Is No Deep Dark Secret,* which provides information about converters and adapter plugs for electric appliances to be used abroad but manufactured for use in the US. To obtain a free copy, send a self-addressed, stamped envelope to *Franzus* at the above address; a catalogue of other travel accessories is available on request.

Medical and Legal Aid and Consular Services

MEDICAL AID ABROAD: Nothing ruins a vacation or business trip more effectively than sudden injury or illness. You will discover, in the event of an emergency, that most tourist facilities — transportation companies, hotels, and resorts — are equipped to handle the situation quickly and efficiently. Most towns and cities of any size have a public hospital and even the tiniest of Irish towns has a medical clinic or private physician nearby. All hospitals are prepared for emergency cases, and many hospitals also have walk-in clinics designed to serve people who do not really need emergency service, but who have no place to go for immediate medical attention.

Before you go, be sure to check with your insurance company about the applicability of your policy while you're abroad; many policies do not apply, and others are not accepted in Ireland. Older travelers should know that Medicare does not make payments outside the US, and — contrary to lingering popular belief — Britain's National Health Service, in operation in Northern Ireland, does not provide free medical care to visitors, except in (and only in) a few instances. If your medical policy does not protect you while you're traveling, there are comprehensive combination policies specifically designed to fill the gap. (For a discussion of medical insurance and list of inclusive combination policies, see *Insurance,* in this section.)

The level of medical care available in Ireland is generally excellent, providing the same basic specialties and services that are available in the US. In Northern Ireland, the National Health Service (NHS) provides free medical aid to tourists *only* for treatment in hospital accident and emergency wards and for the diagnosis and treatment of certain communicable diseases. Most visitors (except nationals of Common Market countries or of those with which the United Kingdom has reciprocal agreements) are liable for all other medical charges, including hospitalization resulting from an accident or emergency. In the Irish Republic, where the General Medicine Service provides either free hospital coverage or free total health care for nearly all citizens, tourists (again, except from Common Market countries) must pay for all treatment, even in emergencies.

If a bona fide emergency occurs in Northern Ireland, the fastest way to receive attention may be to take a taxi to the emergency room (or "casualty department") of the nearest hospital. An alternative is to dial 999, the free nationwide emergency number used to summon the police, fire trucks, and ambulances. Since ambulance dispatchers are accustomed to taking calls from doctors only, state immediately that you are a foreign tourist and then the nature of your problem and your location.

In the Republic of Ireland, night emergency service rotates among hospitals, so the best recourse is to call 999, the nationwide emergency number here, too, to find out which one in a given area is on duty. The same number can be dialed for an ambulance, but as in Northern Ireland, a taxi may be a faster way to reach help.

If a doctor is needed for something less than an emergency, there are several ways to find one. If you are staying in a hotel or motel, ask for help in reaching a doctor or other emergency services, or for the house physician, who may visit you in your room or ask you to visit an office. (This service is apt to be expensive, especially if the doctor makes a "house" call to your room.) When you register at a hotel, it's not a bad idea to include your home address and telephone number; this will facilitate the process of notifying friends, relatives, or your own doctor in case of an emergency.

In Northern Ireland, check a local telephone directory for neighborhood NHS physicians. Dialing 999 also will be of help in locating a doctor. Callers will be given the name of a general practitioner, since private doctors, usually specialists, almost always see patients upon referral only. For the seriously ill or injured traveler, however, it is best to see a private doctor. Although it goes beyond the bounds of the NHS system to do so, it's usually possible to find a private doctor without referral from a general practitioner through the US consulate (see address and phone number below) or directly through a hospital, especially if you are in an emergency situation. If you already are at the hospital, you may see the specialist there, or you may make an appointment to be seen at his or her office (or "surgery").

In the Irish Republic, General Medicine Service (GMS) doctors also may treat visitors as private patients. To find one in a non-emergency situation, consult the regional health board (there are eight of them) for a list of GMS general practitioners approved for the area served. The office of the Eastern Health Board, which serves Dublin, is at 1 James's St., Dublin 8 (phone: 757951). Private practice is quite common in Ireland, but even doctors working within the General Medicine Service — not on a prepaid salary as British physicians are — tend to schedule tourists quickly. In addition, though general practitioners deliver primary care here, too, there is no violation of protocol in approaching a specialist directly. Call the appropriate department of a teaching hospital or, in Dublin, the US Embassy (address and phone number below), which also maintains a list of doctors. Remember that if you are hospitalized in the Republic, you will have to pay even in an emergency.

Emergency dental care also is available throughout Ireland (see the front page of the local telephone directory), although travelers are strongly advised to have a dental checkup some weeks before the trip to allow time for any necessary dental work to be done. Again, any US consul also can provide a list of English-speaking dentists in the area the consulate serves.

There should be no problem finding a 24-hour drugstore ("Chemist") in any major Irish city — for one thing, chemists who close are required post in the window the addresses of the nearest all-night drugstores or the evening's on-call pharmacy (night duty may rotate in some areas). A call to the emergency room of the local hospital also may produce this information. In small towns, where none may be open after normal business hours, you may be able to have one open in an emergency situation — such as a diabetic needing insulin — although you may be charged a fee for this off-hour service.

Bring along a copy of any prescription you may have from your doctor in case you should need a refill. In the case of minor complaints, Irish pharmacists may do some prescribing and *may* fill a foreign prescription; however, do not count on this. In most cases, you probably will need a local doctor to rewrite the prescription. Even in an emergency, a traveler will more than likely be given only enough of a drug to last until a local prescription can be obtained. As "brand" names vary in different countries, it's a good idea to ask your doctor for the generic names of any drugs you use so that you can ask for their equivalents should you need a refill. Americans also will notice that some drugs sold only by prescription in the US are sold over the counter in Ireland (and vice versa). Though this can be very handy, be aware that common cold medicines and aspirin that contain codeine or other controlled substances will not be allowed back into the US.

Emergency assistance also is available from the various medical programs designed for travelers who have chronic ailments or whose illness requires them to return home. The *Medic Alert Foundation* sells identification emblems which specify that the wearer has a health condition that may not be readily apparent to a casual observer. A heart condition, diabetes, epilepsy, or severe allergy are the sorts of things that these emblems were developed to communicate — conditions that can result in tragic errors if not recognized when emergency treatment is necessary and when you may be unable to speak for yourself. In addition to the identification emblems, the foundation maintains a computerized central file from which your complete medical history is available 24 hours a day by telephone (the phone number is clearly inscribed on the ID badge). The one-time membership fee, between $25 and $45, is tax deductible, and is based on the type of metal from which the emblem is made — the choices ranging from stainless steel to 10K gold-filled. For information, contact the *Medic Alert Foundation,* Turlock, CA 95381-1009 (phone: 800-ID-ALERT or 209-668-3333).

International SOS Assistance also offers a program to cover medical emergencies while traveling. Members are provided with telephone access — 24 hours a day, 365 days a year — to a worldwide, monitored, multilingual network of medical centers. A phone call brings assistance ranging from a telephone consultation to transportation home by ambulance or aircraft, and in some cases transportation of a family member to wherever you are hospitalized. The service can be purchased for 2 weeks ($25), 2 weeks plus additional days ($25, plus $2.50 for each additional day), 1 month ($50), or a year ($195). For information, contact *International SOS Assistance, Inc.,* PO Box 11568, Philadelphia, PA 19116 (phone: 800-523-8930 or 215-244-1500).

The *International Association of Medical Assistance to Travellers (IAMAT)* provides its members with a directory of affiliated medical centers in over 140 countries (500 cities, including Dublin) to call for a list of participating doctors. Participating physicians agree to adhere to a basic charge of around $30 to see a patient referred by *IAMAT.* A nonprofit organization, *IAMAT* appreciates donations; for $25, you will receive a set of worldwide climate charts detailing weather and sanitary conditions. Delivery of this material can take up to 5 weeks, so plan ahead. Contact *IAMAT,* 417 Center St., Lewiston, NY 14092 (phone: 716-754-4883).

The *International Health Care Service* provides information about health conditions in various foreign countries, as well as a variety of travel-related health services. A pre-travel counseling and immunization package costs $185 for the first family member and $165 for each additional member; a post-travel screening is $75 to $135, plus lab work. Appointments are required for all services. Contact the *International Health Care Service* (New York Hospital–Cornell Medical Center, 440 E. 69th St., New York, NY 10021; phone: 212-472-4284). *The International Health Care Travelers Guide,* a compendium of facts and advice on health care and diseases around the world, can be obtained by sending $4.50 and a self-addressed, stamped envelope to PO Box 210 at the address above.

Those who return home ill with a condition they suspect is travel related and beyond the experience of their regular physician should consider seeing a specialist in travel medicine. For information on locating such a specialist in your area, see *Staying Healthy,* in this section.

For a thorough description of the medical services in Ireland's larger cities, see *Traveling Healthy,* by Sheilah M. Hillman and Robert S. Hillman, MD. Unfortunately out of print, it may be found in the library.

Practically every phase of health care — before, during, and after a trip — is covered in *The New Traveler's Health Guide* by Drs. Patrick J. Doyle and James E. Banta. It is available for $4.95, plus $2.50 postage and handling, from Acropolis Books Ltd., 80 S. Early St., Alexandria, VA 22304 (phone: 800-451-7771 or 703-709-0006).

LEGAL AID AND CONSULAR SERVICES: There is one crucial place to keep in mind when outside the US, namely, the American Services section of the United States consulate. If you are injured or become seriously ill, the consulate will direct you to medical assistance and notify your relatives. If, while abroad, you become involved in a dispute that could lead to legal action, the consulate, once again, is the place to turn.

It usually is far more alarming to be arrested abroad than at home. Not only are you alone among strangers, but the punishment can be worse. Granted, the US Consulate can advise you of your rights and provide a list of lawyers (called "solicitors" in Ireland), but it cannot interfere with the local legal process. Except for minor infractions of the local traffic code, there is no reason for any law-abiding traveler to run afoul of immigration, customs, or any other law enforcement authority.

The best advice is to be honest and law-abiding. If you get a traffic ticket, pay it. If you are approached by drug hawkers, ignore them. The penalties for possession of hashish, marijuana, cocaine, and other narcotics are even more severe abroad than in the US. (If you are picked up for any drug-related offense, do not expect US foreign service officials to be sympathetic. Chances are they will notify a lawyer and your family and that's about all. See "Drugs," below.)

In the case of minor traffic accidents, it often is most expedient to settle the matter before the police get involved. If, however, you are involved in a serious accident, where an injury or fatality results, the first step is to contact the nearest US consulate (addresses below) and ask the consul to locate a lawyer to assist you. If you have a traveling companion, ask him or her to call the consulate (unless either of you has a local contact who can help you quickly). Competent lawyers practice throughout Europe, and it is possible to obtain good legal counsel on short notice.

The US Department of State in Washington, DC, insists that any American citizen who is arrested abroad has the right to contact the US embassy or consulate "immediately," but it may be a while before you are given permission to use a phone. Do not labor under the illusion, however, that in a scrape with foreign officialdom, the consulate can act as an arbitrator or ombudsman on an American citizen's behalf. Nothing could be farther from the truth. Consuls have no power, authorized or otherwise, to subvert, alter, or contravene the legal processes, however unfair, of the foreign country in which they serve. Nor can a consul oil the machinery of a foreign bureaucracy or provide legal advice. The consul's responsibilities do encompass "welfare duties" including providing a list of lawyers and information on local sources of legal aid, informing relatives in the US, and organizing and administrating any defense monies sent from home. If a case is tried unfairly or the punishment seems unusually severe, the consul can make a formal complaint to the authorities. For questions about Americans arrested abroad, how to get money to them, and other useful information, call the *Citizens Emergency Center* of the Office of Special Consular Services in Washington, DC, at 202-647-5225. (For further information about this invaluable hot line, see below.)

Other welfare duties, not involving legal hassles, cover cases of both illness and destitution. If you should get sick, the US consul can provide names of doctors and dentists as well as the names of all local hospitals and clinics; the consul also will contact family members in the US and help arrange special ambulance service for a flight home. In a situation involving "legitimate and proven poverty" — of an American stranded abroad without funds — the consul will contact sources of money (such as family or friends in the US), apply for aid to agencies in foreign countries, and in a last resort — which is *rarely* — arrange for repatriation at government expense, although this is a loan that must be repaid. And in case of natural disasters or civil unrest, consulates around the world handle the evacuation of US citizens if it becomes necessary.

The consulate is not occupied solely with emergencies and is certainly not there to aid in trivial situations, such as canceled reservations or lost baggage, no matter how important these matters may seem to the victimized tourist. The main duties of any consulate are administering statutory services, such as the issuance of passports and visas; providing notarial services; distributing VA, social security, and civil service benefits to resident Americans; taking depositions; handling extradition cases; and reporting to Washington the births, deaths, and marriages of US citizens living within the consulate's domain.

We hope that none of the information in this section will be necessary during your stay in Ireland. If you can avoid legal hassles altogether, you will have a much more pleasant trip. If you become involved in an imbroglio, the local authorities may spare you legal complications if you make clear your tourist status. And if you run into a confrontation that might lead to legal complications developing with a citizen or with local authorities, the best tactic is to apologize and try to leave as gracefully as possible. Do not get into fights with residents, no matter how belligerent or provocative they are in a given situation.

Following are the US embassy and consulate in Ireland. (Note that mailing addresses may be different — so call before sending anything to these offices.)

Irish Republic: US Embassy, 42 Elgin Rd., Ballsbridge, Dublin 4, Ireland (phone: 1-688777).

Northern Ireland: US Consulate, Queens House, 14 Queen St., Belfast BTL 6EQ, Northern Ireland (phone: 232-328239).

You also can obtain a booklet with addresses of most US embassies and consulates around the world by writing the Superintendent of Documents, US Government Printing Office, Washington, DC 20402, and asking for publication #78-77, *Key Offices of Foreign Service Posts.*

As mentioned above, the US State Department operates a *Citizens Emergency Center,* which offers a number of services to American travelers abroad and their families at home. In addition to giving callers up-to-date information on trouble spots, the center will contact authorities abroad in an attempt to locate a traveler or deliver an urgent message. In case of illness, death, arrest, destitution, or repatriation of an American citizen on foreign soil, it will relay information to relatives at home if the consulate is unable to do so. Travel advisory information is available 24 hours a day to people with Touch-Tone phones (phone: 202-647-5225). Callers with rotary phones can get information at this number from 8:15 AM to 10 PM (eastern standard time) on weekdays, 9 AM to 3 PM on Saturdays. For emergency calls, from 8:15 AM to 10 PM weekdays, and 9 AM to 3 PM Saturdays, call 202-647-5225. For emergency calls only, at all other times, call 202-634-3600 and ask for the duty officer.

Drinking and Drugs

 DRINKING: It is more than likely that some of the warmest memories of a trip to Ireland will be moments of conviviality shared over a drink in a neighborhood pub. Visitors will find that liquor, wine, and brandies are distilled to the same proof and often are the same labels as those found at home. However, Irish beers and ales have quite a different flavor from those brewed in the US. Whiskey may be tempered with a little water or ice, and ale comes room temperature or cellar-chilled. Guinness stout, dark and syrupy with a thick creamy head and a pronounced bitterness, is the favorite beer. (For a more thorough discussion of Irish beverages, see *Food and Drink,* PERSPECTIVES, and *Pub Crawling,* DIVERSIONS.)

Pub hours vary in Ireland. Most pubs in Northern Ireland are open from 11 AM to 11 PM Mondays through Saturdays, and on Sundays from noon to 2 PM and from 7:30

to 10 PM. In the Irish Republic, pubs are opened from 10:30 AM to 11:30 PM most of the year (until midnight in summer), and on Sundays from 10:30 AM to 3 PM and 4 to 11 PM. Restaurants with liquor licenses can serve alcoholic beverages only during these hours, although they may be open for food service during other times.

As in the US, national taxes on alcohol affect the prices of liquor in Ireland. As a general rule, mixed drinks (which are less common in Ireland) and some types of liquor are more expensive than at home. (If you like a drop before dinner, a good way to save money is to buy a bottle of your favorite brand at the airport before leaving the US and enjoy it in your hotel before setting forth.) Local beers and ales are reasonably priced, so take this opportunity to savor them at the source.

Visitors to Ireland may bring in 2 liters of wine, or 2 liters of alcohol under 38.8 proof, or 1 liter above 38.8 proof per person. If you are buying any quantity of alcohol (such as a case of locally brewed beer) in Ireland and traveling through other European countries on your route back to the US, you will have to pass through customs and pay duty at each border crossing, so you might want to arrange to have it shipped home. Whether bringing it with you or shipping, you will have to pay US import duties on any quantity over the allowed 1 liter (see *Customs and Returning to the US,* in this section).

■ **Two warnings:** The legal age for drinking is 18. Those under 18 are allowed into pubs but cannot be served alcoholic beverages. When setting off to do some serious pub crawling, leave your car behind and make alternate plans for getting back to the hotel; otherwise choose a "designated driver" in your party who will stick strictly to soft drinks. Aside from the obvious danger in which you place yourself and others on the road, there are strict laws against drunk driving in both Northern Ireland and the Republic, and they are zealously enforced.

DRUGS: Illegal narcotics are as prevalent in Ireland as in the US, but the moderate legal penalties and vague social acceptance that marijuana has gained in the US have no equivalents in either Northern Ireland or the Republic. Due to the international war on drugs, enforcement of drug laws is becoming increasingly strict throughout the world. Local narcotics officers and customs officials are renowned for their absence of understanding and lack of a sense of humor — especially where North Americans are involved.

Opiates and barbiturates, and other increasingly popular drugs — "white powder" substances like heroin and cocaine — are as pervasive a problem throughout Europe as in the US. The main drawback to buying any illegal drug (besides the obvious health hazards) is the inherent risk of getting locked up. Most European countries — including Ireland — have toughened laws regarding illegal drugs and narcotics, and these laws do not distinguish between types of drugs — possession of marijuana, cocaine, heroin, and other narcotics are treated with equal severity. Don't assume that you're safe in carrying even small amounts of controlled substances for "personal use" — particularly for foreigners, the maximum penalties may be imposed for possessing even *traces* of illegal drugs. There is a high conviction rate in these cases, and bail for foreigners is rare.

The best advice we can offer is this: Don't carry, use, buy, or sell illegal drugs. The dangers are clear enough when indulging in your own home; if taking drugs while traveling, you may not only endanger your own life but also put your fellow travelers in jeopardy. And if you get caught, you may end up spending your hard-earned travel funds on bail and attorney's fees — and still wind up in jail. There isn't much that the American consulate can do for drug offenders beyond providing a list of lawyers. Having broken a local law, an offender puts his or her fate in the hands of the local authorities.

Those who carry medicines that contain a controlled drug should be sure to have a current doctor's prescription with them. Ironically, travelers can get into almost as much trouble coming through US customs with over-the-counter drugs picked up abroad that contain substances that are controlled in the US. Cold medicines, pain relievers, and the like often have codeine or codeine derivatives that are illegal, except by prescription, in the US. Throw them out before leaving for home.

■ **Be forewarned:** US narcotics agents warn travelers of the increasingly common ploy of drug dealers asking travelers to transport a "gift" or other package back to the US. Don't be fooled into thinking that the protection of US law applies abroad — accused of illegal drug trafficking, you will be considered guilty until you prove your innocence. In other words, do not, under any circumstances, agree to take anything across the border for a stranger.

Tipping

Throughout both Northern Ireland and the Republic (as in most of the rest of Europe) you will find the custom of including some kind of service charge as part of a hotel or restaurant bill more common than in the US. This can confuse Americans not familiar with the custom. On the one hand, many a traveler, unaware of this policy, has left many a superfluous tip. On the other hand, travelers aware of this policy may make the mistake of assuming that it takes care of everything. It doesn't. While "service included" in theory eliminates any question about how much and whom to tip, in practice there still are occasions when on-the-spot tips are appropriate. Among these are tips to show appreciation for special services, as well as tips meant to say "thank you" for services rendered. So keep a wad of IR£1 or a pocketful of £1 coins (at press time, about $1.55 and $1.80, respectively) ready and hand them out like dollar bills. *(Please note that the gratuities suggested below are given in both Irish pounds or punts — IR£ — for the Irish Republic and British pounds sterling — £ — for Northern Ireland. Where coin denominations are suggested, in order to simplify your calculations these amounts should be appropriate tips in either currency.)*

In Irish restaurants, the service charge may appear in one of two ways: It either already is calculated in the prices listed or will be added to the final bill. For the most part, if you see a notation at the bottom of the menu without a percentage figure, the charge should be included in the prices; if a percentage figure is indicated, the service charge has not yet been added. To further confuse the issue, not every restaurant notes if its policy is to include service and at what point the charge is added. If you are at all unsure, you should feel no embarrassment about asking a waiter.

This service charge generally ranges from 10% to 15%. In the rare instance where it isn't added, a 15% tip — just as in the US — usually is a safe figure, although one should never hesitate to penalize poor service or reward excellent and efficient attention by leaving less or more. If the tip has been added, no further gratuity is expected — though it's a common practice in Ireland to leave a few extra pence or a pound or two (depending on the tab) on the table for the waiter.

Although it's not necessary to tip the maître d' of most restaurants — unless he has been especially helpful in arranging a special party or providing a table (slipping him something in a crowded restaurant *may* get you seated sooner or procure a preferred table) — when tipping is desirable or appropriate, the least amount should be IR£3 or £3. In the finest restaurants, where a multiplicity of servers are present, plan to tip 5% to the captain. The sommelier (wine steward) is entitled to approximately 10% of the price of the bottle.

When eating at a self-service, take-out, or fast-food establishment where you pay at the cash register, generally no tip is necessary. There also is virtually no tipping in pubs — unless you become something of a regular and care to offer the barman an occasional drink. It is not uncommon, however, to leave a few pence for a barmaid, and for those served at a table in a bar or cocktail lounge, a small gratuity — 50p to a pound or two (again depending on the tab) — is usual for the server.

In allocating gratuities at a restaurant, pay particular attention to what has become the standard credit-card charge form, which now includes separate places for indicating gratuities for waiters and/or captains. If these separate boxes do not appear on the charge slip presented, simply ask the waiter or captain how these separate tips should be indicated. Be aware, too, of the increasingly common, devious practice of placing the amount of an entire restaurant bill (in which service already has been included) in the top box of a charge slip, leaving the "tip" and "total" boxes ominously empty. Don't be intimidated: Leave the "tip" box blank and just repeat the total next to "total" before signing.

As in restaurants, visitors usually will find a service charge of 10% to 15% included in their final bill at most Irish hotels. No additional gratuities are required — or expected — beyond this billed service charge. It is unlikely, however, that a service charge will be added to bills in small family-run guesthouses or modest bed and breakfast establishments. In these cases, guests should let their instincts be their guide; no tipping is expected by members of the family who own the establishment, but it is a nice gesture to leave something for others — such as a dining room waiter or a maid — who may have been helpful. A gratuity of 50p to £1 per night is adequate in these cases.

If a hotel does not automatically add a service charge, it is perfectly proper for guests to ask to have an extra 10 to 15% added to their bill, to be distributed among those who served them. This may be an especially convenient solution in a large hotel, where it's difficult to determine just who out of a horde of attendants actually performed particular services.

For those who prefer to distribute tips themselves, a chambermaid generally is tipped at the rate of 50p to £1 per day. Tip the concierge for specific services only, with the amount of such gratuities dependent on the level of service provided — about IR£2 or £2 usually is appropriate. If you leave your shoes outside the room at night for a shine, give the hall porter a pound note when you next see him. If you order from room service, 50p to a pound to the waiter for each delivery is sufficient. For other special services, such as personal deliveries, the tip depends on the service rendered, but in most cases a pound or two is more than sufficient.

Bellhops, doormen, and porters at hotels and transporation centers generally are tipped at the rate of 50p per piece of luggage, along with a small additional amount if a doorman helps with a cab or car. Once upon a time, taxi drivers in Ireland would give you a rather odd look if presented with a tip for a fare, but times have changed, and 10% to 15% of the amount on the meter is now a standard gratuity.

Tipping ushers in a movie house, theater, or concert hall used to be the rule, but is becoming less common — the best policy is to check what other patrons are doing and follow suit. Most of the time the program is not free, and in lieu of a tip it is common practice to purchase a program from the person who seats you. Sightseeing tour guides also should be tipped. If you are traveling in a group, decide together what you want to give the guide and present it from the group at the end of the tour. If you have been individually escorted, the amount should depend on the degree of your satisfaction, but it should not be less than 10% and easily could be as high as 50% of the total tour fee. Museum and monument guides also usually are tipped, and it is a nice touch to tip a caretaker who unlocks a small church or turns on the lights in a chapel for you in some out-of-the-way town.

In barbershops and beauty salons, tips also are expected, but the percentages vary according to the type of establishment. Since the prices usually are quite a bit higher in expensive salons (particularly in metropolitan areas), no more than 10% is common; in less expensive establishments, a 15% or 20% tip is in order. (As a general rule the person who washes your hair should get an additional small tip.) The washroom attendants in these places, or wherever you see one, should get a small tip — they usually set out a little plate with a coin already on it indicating the suggested denomination, which is never less than 10p, much more in a very exclusive establishment. Don't forget service station attendants, for whom about 50p for cleaning the windshield or other attention is not unusual.

Tipping always is a matter of personal preference. In the situations covered above, as well as in any others that arise where you feel a tip is expected or due, feel free to express your pleasure or displeasure. Again, never hesitate to reward excellent and efficient attention and to penalize poor service. Give extra and a word of thanks when someone has gone out of his or her way for you. Either way, the more personal the act of tipping, the more appropriate it seems. And if you didn't like the service — or the attitude — don't tip.

Shopping

 Browsing through the department stores, boutiques, street markets, small shops, and crafts centers of Ireland undoubtedly will be one of the highlights of your trip. Visitors from the US may not be quite as enthusiastic about prices as they might have been a few years ago, as prices throughout Europe have risen dramatically. But there still is plenty of value for the money and enough quality and craftsmanship to make many an item irresistible. To help steer visitors toward the best, several sections of this book are devoted to shopping. In THE CITIES, individual city reports include a listing of specific stores and markets, as well as descriptions of special shopping streets where they exist. And sections in DIVERSIONS describe not only where to find antiques and other collectibles, but also — for those who have yet to experience this stimulating form of acquisition — how to buy them at auctions.

HOW TO SHOP AND WHAT TO BUY: The goods are enticing, but even so, top-quality items are not necessarily less expensive in a fashionable boutique in the capital city of the country from which they came than they are in an equally fashionable US store. To be sure, do some homework before you go and arrive prepared with a list of the things you want — as specific as possible, with brands or labels — and the cost of each in the US. In some cases, you will find it less expensive to buy abroad, but frequently you will find it is not, and knowing the difference is crucial to a successful shopping trip. On arrival, it still is necessary to comparison shop as much as time permits, bearing in mind that articles can be less costly the closer you get to the point of manufacture, and least expensive of all in the factory that makes the item — if it sells to the public. Visitors will get a better price on Donegal tweeds, for instance, at small factories and shops in County Donegal than in Dublin. On the other hand, the wholesale price of Waterford crystal is standard throughout Ireland, so variation in its retail price from shop to shop depends on markup only.

In Ireland, crafts are thriving. Products in traditional and modern styles and combinations of the two are found in crafts centers, workshops, and stores throughout the country. Details are in the *Irish Crafts* information sheet available from Irish Tourist Board offices in the US (see *Tourist Information Offices,* in this section). Typical of the work currently being done are the highly prized white wool sweaters and berets knit on the western seacoast and on the Aran Islands, earthenware pottery in modern but natural shapes, and exceedingly well-executed silver and gold jewelry in contemporary styles. Donegal tweed has been hand-loomed for centuries on the Donegal coast of northwest Ireland, and a jacket made of it will likely be the most durable its wearer has ever owned. Pearly Belleek china, luminous Waterford crystal, and Irish lace or linen endow any table with elegance, and Irish smoked salmon only enhances such a setting. For more detailed information on Irish specialties, and a list by category of the best places to find them, see *Shopping Spree,* DIVERSIONS.

VALUE ADDED TAX: Commonly abbreviated as VAT, this is a tax levied by various European countries and added to the purchase price of most merchandise. The standard VAT rate in Northern Ireland is 15% (children's clothes, books, food, and transportation exempt), while in the Irish Republic it is either 10% or 25%, with the higher rate applying to luxury goods such as watches, jewelry, furs, glass, and cameras (food and transportation exempt).

The tax is intended for residents (and already is included in the price tag), but visitors are required to pay it, too, unless they have purchases shipped directly to an address abroad by the store. If visitors pay the tax and take purchases with them, however, they generally are entitled to a refund under retail export schemes that have been in operation in both countries for several years. In the past, returning travelers have complained of delays in receiving the refunds and of difficulties in converting checks written in foreign currency into dollars, but new services recently have been introduced that greatly streamline the refund procedure.

In the Irish Republic, the refund system is called Cashback. To obtain a refund, visitors must shop in stores participating in the scheme (look for the Cashback sign in over 1,000 shops nationwide, including major department stores). A visitor shows the salesperson his or her passport and asks for a Cashback voucher, which the shopkeeper fills out with details of the purchase. It's up to the visitor to fill in his or her name, address, passport number, and other requested information. When leaving the country, visitors should have all of their Cashback vouchers from all stores stamped by customs (customs officials may ask to see the merchandise, so it's a good idea not to pack it in the bottom of a suitcase).

To receive an on-the-spot refund in cash (US or Canadian dollars, British or Irish pounds), go to the Cashback booth in the Arrivals Hall at Shannon Airport or in the Duty-Free Area at Dublin Airport. To receive a refund by check, which will be in dollars if so specified, or as a credit to a credit card account, mail the stamped vouchers to Cashback headquarters, using the pre-addressed (postpaid also, if mailed in Ireland) envelope supplied. Refund checks are sent out within 21 days of receipt of the vouchers, and refunds by credit card generally appear on the cardholder's statement within 1 month of receipt. Note that refunds by credit card are possible even if the purchases were not paid for by credit card — don't forget to write your card number on the vouchers before mailing them, however. Expect a small administrative charge to be deducted from the refund whichever method is chosen.

Those who happen to do their shopping in a store that is not part of the Cashback scheme should not despair. Visitors still are entitled to a VAT refund under the old retail export scheme, although they may have difficulty collecting it unless the store is willing to do the paperwork. Again, it is necessary to show the salesperson a passport and ask for a VAT relief form, which will be filled out on the premises. At departure, have the form validated at the customs desk and mail it back to the *store* (stores generally supply stamped, self-addressed envelopes for this purpose). Note that stores are under no obligation to perform this service and those that do may require a minimum purchase below which they refuse to process the forms. They also usually will deduct a small charge from the refund for doing so. Cash refunds are not possible — the refund will come in the form of a check (usually in Irish currency) mailed to the purchaser's home address or, if the purchase was made by credit card, as a credit to that account.

In Northern Ireland, the VAT refund scheme most often encountered is the same as the one in use throughout the United Kingdom. Although a new streamlined service — called Tourist Tax Free Shopping (TTFS) — has made its debut and has gained wide acceptance among stores in Great Britain, few stores in Northern Ireland participate in it, so most VAT refunds for purchases made here will come about under the older retail export scheme, which is offered by most department stores and shops catering to tourists, but less frequently by smaller, local shops. This scheme functions much like the older one in effect in the Republic, meaning that no VAT will be charged if purchases are shipped by the shop directly to an address abroad. Those who pay the tax and take packages with them should ask the shop for a VAT relief form, have it stamped by customs, and mail it back to the store, which will send out the refund upon its receipt. Where the newer Tourist Tax Free Shopping is offered — participating stores display a TTFS sign — refunds come from a central source, as they do under the Irish Republic's Cashback system. They are sent out within 5 days of receipt of the vouchers and may come in the form of a dollar check, a foreign currency check, or a credit to a credit card account, as preferred, but on-the-spot cash refunds are not possible. (Remember that United Kingdom customs agents must do the stamping for purchases made in Northern Ireland, not agents at the Dublin or Shannon airports. Ask the shop where to go to take care of the formalities.)

Whether shopping in the Irish Republic or Northern Ireland, before making any major purchase, first determine if you are entitled to and will be able to receive a refund. As the tax can add substantially to the purchase price, if you will not be reimbursed you may want to consider shopping elsewhere.

A VAT refund by dollar check or by credit to a credit card account is relatively hassle-free. If it arrives in the form of a foreign currency check and if the refund is less than a significant amount, charges imposed by US banks for converting foreign currency refund checks — which can run as high as $15 or more — could make the whole exercise hardly worth your while.

Far less costly is sending your foreign currency check (after endorsing it) to *Ruesch International,* which will convert it to a check in US dollars for a $2 fee (deducted from the dollar check). Contact *Ruesch International* at one of the following addresses: 3 First National Plaza, Suite 2020, Chicago, IL 60602 (phone: 312-332-5900); 1925 Century Park E., Suite 240, Los Angeles, CA 90067 (phone: 213-277-7800); 608 Fifth Ave., "Swiss Center," New York, NY 10020 (phone: 212-977-2700); and 1350 Eye St. NW, 10th Floor and street level, Washington, DC 20005 (phone: 800-424-2923 or 202-408-1200).

An additional method of reimbursement is possible if the purchases in Ireland are made by credit card: The store may agree to make two credit card charges, one for the price of the goods, the other for the amount of the tax. Then, when the stamped copy of the form arrives from customs, the store simply tears up the charge slip for the sales tax and the amount never appears on your account.

DUTY-FREE SHOPS: If common sense says that it always is less expensive to buy goods in an airport duty-free shop than to buy them at home or in the streets of a foreign city, travelers should be aware of some basic facts. Duty-free, first of all, does not mean that the goods travelers buy will be free of duty when they return to the US. Rather, it means that the shop has paid no import tax acquiring goods of foreign make because the goods are not to be used in the country where the shop is located. This is why duty-free goods are available only in the restricted, passengers-only area of international airports or are delivered to departing passengers on the plane. In a duty-free store, travelers save money only on goods of foreign make because they are the only items on which import tax would be charged in any other store. There usually is no saving on locally made items, although in countries such as Ireland that impose VAT taxes (see above) that are refundable to foreigners, the prices in airport duty-free shops also are minus this tax, sparing travelers the often cumbersome procedures they otherwise have to follow to obtain a VAT refund.

Beyond this, there is little reason to delay buying locally made mechandise and/or souvenirs until reaching the airport. In fact, because airport duty-free shops usually pay high rents, the locally made goods sold in them may well be more expensive than they would be in a downtown store. The real bargains are foreign goods, but — let the buyer beware — not all foreign goods automatically are less expensive in an airport duty-free shop. You can get a good deal on even small amounts of perfume, costing less than the usually required minimum purchase, tax-free. Other fairly standard bargains include spirits, smoking materials, cameras, clothing, watches, chocolates and other food and luxury items — but first be sure to know what these items cost elsewhere. Terrific savings do exist (they are the reason for such shops, after all), but so do overpriced items that an unwary shopper might find equally tempting.

Duty-free shops are located in most major international airports throughout Europe. Shannon International Airport's duty-free shop was the world's first and remains one of the most renowned. There are savings on foreign goods — Lalique crystal, Swiss watches, French perfumes — though not necessarily on Irish-made goods. Those who haven't been able to scout out their souvenirs at the source, however, will find that, generally, they cost no more at Shannon than at Irish shops in downtown areas and certainly cost less than they would back home. And it may be convenient to buy them here rather than carry them along throughout a trip, provided the traveler is willing to take a chance on finding the desired item in the right size and color and provided he or she arrives at the airport in enough time to shop. Shannon also operates a mail-order service that can be used long after leaving Ireland. It's necessary to pay the import duty on the items ordered, but since the purchases are free of a retail store's markup, buyers usually still will pay less than they would in a stateside specialty shop. Pick up a copy of the free mail-order catalogue at Shannon or request it from Shannon Development (757 Third Ave., New York, NY 10017; phone: 212-371-5550). By studying a copy before going, visitors will be better equipped to compare the quality and prices of the merchandise they'll encounter as they shop overseas.

■ **Buyer Beware:** You may come across shops *not* at airports that call themselves duty-free shops. These require shoppers to show a foreign passport but are subject to the same rules as other stores, including paying import duty on foreign items. What "tax-free" means in the case of these establishments is something of an advertising strategy: They are announcing loud and clear that they do, indeed, offer the VAT refund service — sometimes on the spot (minus a fee for higher overhead). Prices may be no better at these stores and could be even higher due to the addition of this service.

Religion on the Road

Ireland is severely split by the two primary religious affiliations that dominate its two regions: Northern Ireland is predominantly Protestant, and the Irish Republic is Catholic. Every town, right down to the most isolated village, has its own church. In larger, more heavily populated areas, some amount of religious variety is reflected in the churches of other denominations, Jewish synagogues, and an occasional mosque or temple.

The surest source of information on religious services in an unfamiliar country is the desk clerk of the hotel or guesthouse in which you are staying; the local tourist information office, an American consul, or a church of another religious affiliation also may be able to provide this information. If you aren't in an area with services held by your own denomination, you might find it interesting to attend the service of another religion. There are many beautiful churches in Ireland and whether in a large city cathedral or a small parish church, visitors are welcome.

Customs and Returning to the US

 Whether you return to the United States by air or sea, you must declare to the US customs official at the point of entry everything you have bought or acquired while in Europe. The customs check can go smoothly, lasting only a few minutes, or can take hours, depending on the officer's instinct. To speed up the process, keep all your receipts handy and try to pack your purchases together in an accessible part of your suitcase. It might save you from unpacking all your belongings.

DUTY-FREE ARTICLES: In general, the duty-free allowance for US citizens returning from abroad is $400, provided your purchases accompany you and are for personal use. This limit includes items used or worn while abroad, souvenirs for friends, and gifts received during the trip. A flat 10% duty based on the "fair retail value in country of acquisition" is assessed on the next $1,000 worth of merchandise brought in for personal use or gifts. Amounts over $1,400 are dutiable at a variety of rates. The average rate for typical tourist purchases is about 12%, but you can find out rates on specific items by consulting *Tariff Schedules of the United States* in a library or any US Customs Service office.

Families traveling together may make a joint declaration to customs, a procedure that permits one member to exceed his or her duty-free exemption to the extent that another falls short. Families also may pool purchases dutiable under the flat rate. A family of three, for example, would be eligible for up to a total of $3,000 at the 10% flat duty rate (after each member had used up his or her $400 duty-free exemption) rather than three separate $1,000 allowances. This grouping of purchases is extremely useful when considering the duty on a high-tariff item, such as jewelry or a fur coat.

There are certain articles, however, that are duty-free only up to certain limits. Individuals are allowed 1 carton of cigarettes (200), 100 cigars, and 1 liter of liquor or wine if over 21. Alcohol above this allowance is liable for both duty and an Internal Revenue tax. Antiques, if they are 100 or more years old and you have proof from the seller of that fact, are duty-free, as are paintings and drawings if done entirely by hand.

To avoid paying duty twice, register the serial numbers of foreign-made watches and electronic equipment with the nearest US Customs bureau before departure; receipts of insurance policies also should be carried for other foreign-made items. (Also see the note at the end of *Entry Requirements and Documents*, in this section.)

Gold, gold medals, bullion, and up to $10,000 in currency or negotiable instruments may be brought into the US without being declared. Sums over $10,000 must be declared in writing.

Personal exemptions can be used once every 30 days; in order to be eligible, an individual must have been out of the country for more than 48 hours. If any portion of the exemption has been used once within any 30-day period or if your trip is less than 48 hours long, the duty-free allowance is cut to $25.

The allotment for individual "unsolicited" gifts mailed from abroad (no more than one per day per recipient) has been raised to $50 retail value per gift. These gifts do not have to be declared and are not included in your duty-free exemption (see below).

Although you should include a receipt for purchases with each package, the examiner is empowered to impose a duty based on his or her assessment of the value of the goods. The duty owed is collected by the US Postal Service when the package is delivered (also see below). More information on mailing packages home from abroad is contained in the US Customs Service pamphlet *International Mail Imports* (see below for where to write for this and other useful brochures).

CLEARING CUSTOMS: This is a simple procedure. Forms are distributed by airline or ship personnel before arrival. (Note that a $5-per-person service charge — called a user fee — is collected by airlines and cruise lines to help cover the cost of customs checks, but this is included in the ticket price.) If your purchases total no more than the duty-free $400 limit, you need only fill out the identification part of the form and make an oral declaration to the customs inspector. If entering with more than $400 worth of goods, you must submit a written declaration.

Customs agents are businesslike, efficient, and not unkind. During the peak season, clearance can take time, but this generally is because of the strain imposed by a number of jumbo jets simultaneously discharging their passengers, not because of unwarranted zealousness on the part of the customs people.

Efforts to streamline procedures include the Citizens' Bypass Program, which allows Americans whose purchases are under $400 to go to the "green line," where they simply show their passports to the customs inspector. Note, however, that as we went to press, this procedure was in the process of being abandoned at most international airport terminals in the US. In a return to an earlier system, American citizens arriving from overseas have to go through a passport check by the Immigration & Naturalization Service (INS) prior to recovering their baggage and proceeding to customs. (US citizens will not be on the same line as foreign visitors; however, this additional wait does delay clearance on re-entry into the US.) Although all passengers have to go through this obligatory passport inspection, those entering with purchases under $400 may be spared a thorough customs inspection, although inspectors still retain the right to search any luggage they choose, so don't do anything foolish.

It is illegal not to declare dutiable items; not to do so, in fact, constitutes smuggling, and the penalty can be anything from stiff fines and seizure of the goods to prison sentences. It simply isn't worth doing. Nor should you go along with the suggestions of foreign merchants who offer to help you secure a bargain by deceiving customs officials in any way. Such transactions frequently are a setup, using the foreign merchant as an agent of US customs. Another agent of US customs is TECS, the Treasury Enforcement Communications System, a computer that stores all kinds of pertinent information on returning citizens. There is a basic rule to buying goods abroad, and it should never be broken: *If you can't afford the duty on something, don't buy it.* Your list or verbal declaration should include all items purchased abroad, as well as gifts received abroad, purchases made at the behest of others, the value of repairs, and anything brought in for resale in the US.

Do not include in the list items that do not accompany you, i.e., purchases that you have mailed or had shipped home. As mentioned above, these are dutiable in any case, even if for your own use and even if the items that accompany your return from the same trip do not exhaust your $400 duty-free exemption. It is a good idea, if you have accumulated too much while abroad, to mail home any personal effects (made and bought in the US) that you no longer need rather than your foreign purchases. These personal effects pass through customs as "American goods returned" and are not subject to duty.

If you cannot avoid shipping home your foreign purchases, however, the US Customs Service suggests that the package be clearly marked "Not for Sale," and that a copy of the bill of sale be included. The customs examiner usually will accept this as indicative of the article's fair retail value, but if he or she believes it to be falsified or feels the goods have been seriously undervalued, a higher retail value may be assigned.

FORBIDDEN ITEMS: Narcotics, most plants, and many types of food are not allowed into the US. Drugs are totally illegal, with the exception of medication prescribed by a physician. It's a good idea not to travel with too large a quantity of any given prescription drug (however, in the event that a pharmacy is not open when you need it, bring along several extra doses) and to have the prescription on hand in case any question arises either abroad or when reentering the US.

In Northern Ireland, any sculpture that is part of an architectural structure, any authentic archaeological find, or other artifacts may not be exported without the permission of the Northern Ireland Department of the Environment. This agency can be called at 232-661621; another alternative is to call the Customs Department in Belfast at 232-234466. Similarly, any historical documents or paintings over 100 years of age cannot be taken out of the Irish Republic without written permission from the Department of Education, which can be contacted at 1-734700 in Dublin. If you do not obtain prior permission of these regulatory agencies, such items will be confiscated at the border, and you will run the risk of being fined or imprisoned.

Tourists have long been forbidden to bring into the US foreign-made US trademarked articles purchased abroad (if the trademark is recorded with customs) without written permission. It's now possible to enter with one such item in your possession as long as it's for personal use.

Customs implements the rigorous Department of Agriculture regulations concerning the importation of vegetable matter, seeds, bulbs, and the like. Living vegetable matter may not be imported without a permit, and everything must be inspected, permit or not. The exceptions include dried bamboo, beads made of most seeds, mushrooms, truffles, nuts, seeds, seashells, shamrocks, spices, straw articles, canned or processed vegetables, and some plants.

Other processed foods and baked goods usually are okay. Regulations on meat products generally depend on the country of origin and manner of processing. As a rule, commercially canned meat, hermetically sealed and cooked in the can so that it can be stored without refrigeration, is permitted, but not all canned meat fulfills this requirement. Be careful when buying European-made pâté, for instance. Goose liver pâté in itself is acceptable, but the pork fat that often is part of it, either as an ingredient or a rind, is not. Even canned pâtés may not be admitted for this reason. (The imported ones you see in US stores have been prepared and packaged according to US regulations.)

Customs also enforces federal laws that prohibit the entry of articles made from the furs or hides of animals on the endangered species list. Beware of shoes, bags, and belts made of crocodile and certain kinds of lizard, and anything made of tortoiseshell; this also applies to preserved crocodiles, lizards, and turtles sometimes sold in gift shops. And if you're shopping for big-ticket items, beware of fur coats made from the skins of spotted cats. They are sold in Europe, but they will be confiscated upon your return to the US, and there will be no refund. For information about animals on the endangered species list, contact the Department of the Interior, US Fish and Wildlife Service (Office of Management Authority, PO Box 27329, Washington, DC 20038-7329; phone: 202-343-5634), and ask for the free publication *Facts About Federal Wildlife Laws.*

For information about transporting plants or wildlife, write to *Quarantines,* US Department of Agriculture (Federal Bldg., Hyattsville, MD 20782), or get in touch with the Animal and Plant Health Inspection Service office nearest your home (check under the US Department of Agriculture listings in your telephone book).

The US Customs Service publishes a series of free pamphlets with customs information. It includes *Know Before You Go,* a basic discussion of customs requirements pertaining to all travelers; *International Mail Imports; Travelers' Tips on Bringing Food,*

Plant, and Animal Products into the United States; Importing a Car; GSP and the Traveler; Pocket Hints; Currency Reporting; Pets, Wildlife, US Customs; Customs Hints for Visitors (Nonresidents); and *Trademark Information for Travelers.* For the entire series or individual pamphlets, write to the US Customs Service (PO Box 7407, Washington, DC 200440, or contact any of the seven regional offices, in Boston, Chicago, Houston, Los Angeles, Miami, New Orleans, and New York. The Customs Service has a tape-recorded message whereby callers using Touch-Tone phones can get more information on various topics; the number is 202-566-8195. These pamphlets provide great briefing material, but if you still have questions when you're in Ireland, you can contact the customs representative at the US Embassy (42 Elgin Rd., Ballsbridge, Dublin 4, Ireland; phone: 1-688777).

Sources and Resources

Tourist Information Offices

The Irish Tourist Board offices and the Northern Ireland Tourist Authority in North America generally are the best sources of travel information, and most of their many, varied publications are free for the asking. (The British Tourist Authority no longer promotes tourism in Northern Ireland, but still offers a variety of useful publications.) For the best result, request general information on specific provinces or cities in which you are interested, as well as publications relating to your particular areas of interest: accommodations, restaurants, special events, guided tours, and facilities for specific sports. There is no need to send a self-addressed, stamped envelope with your request, unless this requirement is specified. Offices generally are open on weekdays, during normal business hours.

The following is a list of the North American offices of the Irish Tourist Board (for information on the Irish Republic), the Northern Ireland Tourist Board (for information on Northern Ireland), and the British Tourist Authority (for publications on Northern Ireland only):

Irish Tourist Board
757 Third Ave., New York, NY 10017 (phone: 212-418-0800).
160 Bloor St. E., Suite 934, Toronto, M4W 1B9 (phone: 416-929-2777).

Northern Ireland Tourist Board
276 Fifth Ave., Suite 500, New York, NY 10001 (phone: 212-686-6250).

British Tourist Authority
John Hancock Center, Suite 3320, 875 N. Michigan Ave., Chicago, IL 60611 (phone: 312-787-0490).
Cedar Maple Plaza, Suite 210, 2305 Cedar Springs, Dallas, TX 75201-1814 (phone: 214-720-4040).
350 S. Figueroa St., Suite 450, Los Angeles, CA 90071 (phone: 213-628-3525).
40 W. 57th St., New York, NY 10019 (phone: 212-581-4700).
94 Cumberland St., Suite 600, Toronto, Ontario M5R 3N3, Canada (phone: 416-961-8124).

Information on Ireland also may be requested from regional tourism organizations, as well as numerous tourist information centers scattered throughout Northern Ireland and the Irish Republic. City tourist offices are cited (with addresses and phone numbers) in the *Sources and Resouces* section of the relevant chapter in THE CITIES section. These offices generally are open Mondays through Fridays. Some are open in summer only and others year-round. For a complete list of all local information centers, seasonal and otherwise, contact the national tourist offices.

Irish Republic
City of Dublin Region, 14 Upper O'Connell St., Dublin 1 (phone: 1-747733).
Cork/Kerry Region, Tourist House, Grand Parade, Cork (phone: 21-273251).

Donegal/Leitrim/Sligo Region, Aras Reddon, Temple St., Sligo (phone: 71-61201).

Eastern Region (includes Dublin, Kildare, Louth, Meath, and Wicklow counties), St. Michael's Wharf, Dún Laoghaire, County Dublin (phone: 1-806984).

Midland Region (includes Cavan, Laois, Longford, Monaghan, Roscommon, and Westmeath counties), Dublin Rd., Mullingar, County Westmeath (phone: 44-48650).

Mid-Western Region (includes Clare, Limerick, and northern Tipperary counties), The Granary, Michael St., Limerick (phone: 61-317522).

South-Eastern Region (includes Carlow, Kilkenny, southern Tipperary, Waterford, and Wexford counties), 41 The Quay, Waterford (phone: 51-75788).

Western Region (includes Galway and Mayo counties), Aras Fáilte, Victoria Place, Galway (phone: 91-63081).

Northern Ireland

Northern Ireland Tourist Board, River House, 48 High St., Belfast, BT1 2DS (phone: 232-231221).

Irish and British Embassies and Consulates in the US

The Irish Republic maintains a number of consulates in the US; one of their primary functions is to provide visas for certain resident aliens, depending on their country of origin, and for Americans planning to visit for longer than 3 months, or to study, reside, or work in Ireland. Consulates also are empowered to sign official documents and to notarize copies or translations of American documents, which often is necessary for those papers to be considered legal abroad.

Listed below are the Republic of Ireland embassy and its consulates in the US.

Boston: Irish Consulate, 535 Boylston St., Boston, MA 02116 (phone: 617-267-9330).

Chicago: Irish Consulate, 400 N. Michigan Ave., Suite 911, Chicago, IL 606011 (phone: 312-337-1868).

New York: Irish Consulate, 515 Madison Ave., 18th Floor, New York, NY 100022 (phone: 212-319-2555).

San Francisco: Irish Consulate, 655 Montgomery St., San Francisco, CA 94111 (phone: 415-392-4214).

Washington, DC: Irish Embassy, 2234 Massachusetts Ave. NW, Washington, DC 20008 (phone: 202-462-3939).

Listed below are the British embassy and its consulates in the US; these offices handle all consular matters for Northern Ireland.

Anchorage: British Consulate, University of Alaska, Anchorage College of Arts and Sciences, 2311 Providence Dr., Anchorage, AK 99508 (phone: 907-786-4848).

Atlanta: British Consulate-General, Suite 2700, Marquis I Tower, 245 Peachtree Center Ave., Atlanta, GA 30303 (phone: 404-524-5856).

Boston: British Consulate-General, 4740 Prudential Tower, Boston, MA 02199 (phone: 617-437-7160).

Chicago: British Consulate-General, 33 N. Dearborn St., Chicago, IL 60602 (phone: 312-346-1810).

Cleveland: British Consulate, 55 Public Sq., Suite 1650, Cleveland, OH 44113-1963 (phone: 216-621-7674).

Dallas: British Consulate, 813 Stemmons Tower W., 2730 Stemmons Fwy., Dallas, TX 75207 (phone: 214-637-3600).

Houston: British Consulate-General, Suite 2250, Dresser Tower, 601 Jefferson, Houston, TX 77002 (phone: 713-659-6270).

Kansas City (Missouri): British Consulate, c/o Hallmark Cards, 2501 McGee Trafficway, Kansas City, MO 64108 (phone: 816-274-5400).

Los Angeles: British Consulate-General, Suite 312, 3701 Wilshire Blvd., Los Angeles, CA 90010 (phone: 213-385-7381).

Miami: British Consulate, Suite 2110, Brickell Bay Office Tower, 1001 S. Bayshore Dr., Miami, FL 33131 (phone: 305-374-1522).

New Orleans: British Consulate, 321 St. Charles Ave., 10th Floor, New Orleans, LA 70130 (phone: 504-586-8300).

New York: British Consulate-General, 845 Third Ave., New York, NY 10022 (phone: 212-888-2112).

Norfolk: British Consulate, Lafayette Towers, Suite 1D, 4601 Mayflower Rd., Norfolk, VA 23508 (phone: 804-627-1934).

Philadelphia: British Consulate, Mather & Co., 226 Walnut St., Philadelphia, PA 19106 (phone: 215-925-0118).

Portland: British Consulate, 3515 SW Council Crest Dr., Portland, OR 97201 (phone: 503-227-5669).

St. Louis: British Consulate, 625 S. Skinker Blvd., St. Louis, MO 63105 (phone: 314-725-5949).

San Francisco: British Consulate-General, 1 Sansome St., Suite 850, San Francisco, CA 94104 (phone: 415-981-3030).

Seattle: British Consulate, 820 First Interstate Center, 999 Third Ave., Seattle, WA 98104 (phone: 206-622-9255).

Washington, DC: British Embassy, 3100 Massachusetts Ave. NW, Washington, DC 20008 (phone: 202-462-1340).

Theater and Special Event Tickets

The Irish Tourist Board and the Northern Ireland Tourist Board can supply information on the many special events and festivals that take place in the Republic and Northern Ireland, though they cannot in all cases provide the actual program or detailed information on ticket prices. In more than one section of this book you will read about events that spark your interest — everything from music festivals and special theater seasons to sporting championships — along with telephone numbers and addresses to write for descriptive brochures, reservations, or tickets. Since many of these occasions often are fully booked well in advance, think about having your reservation in hand before you go. If you do write, remember that any request from the US should be accompanied by an International Reply Coupon to ensure a response (send two of them for an airmail response). Tickets usually can be paid for by an international money order or by foreign draft. These international coupons, money orders, and drafts are available at US post offices and banks.

For further information, write for the *European Travel Commission*'s extensive list of events scheduled for the entire year for its 24 member countries (including Ireland). For a free copy, send a self-addressed, stamped (45¢), business-size (4 x 9½) envelope, to "European Events," *European Travel Commission,* PO Box 1754, New York, NY 10185.

Sports

 Grand castles, stately homes, ruined monasteries, and ancient tombs convey a sense of the Irish past. But for showing off the present — the Irish people at their most energetic, most passionate best — there's nothing like one of the nation's spectator sporting events.

This is particularly true of hurling and Gaelic football matches, because, although all the major international sports are played in Ireland, these two native games — enjoyed only in Ireland and by small groups of exiles in Britain, the US, and Australia — arouse the fiercest sentiments. Competitions are held at the local level throughout the year, except from December through mid-February, and because every man on every team is known to every spectator, feelings run high. They run even higher as the national championships approach — a quarter of a million or more attend the games to cheer in person, and millions more follow the games through the media.

GAELIC GAMES

The Gaelic Athletic Association (GAA) was founded in 1884, the brainchild of a Clareman from the Burren, Michael Cusack, a fiery nationalist and talented athlete, immortalized in James Joyce's *Ulysses* as the "Citizen": "a broadshouldered deep-chested stronglimbed frankeyed redhaired freely freckled shaggybearded widemouthed largenosed longheaded deepvoiced barekneed brawnyhanded hairylegged ruddyfaced sinewyarmed hero." Cusack's purpose was to revive ancient Irish games and, no less important, to wrest control of athletics from the largely Protestant Anglo-Irish Ascendancy, which opposed sports on Sunday, the common worker's only free day at the time. (The Sabbatarian element in this policy was mingled with class discrimination in an attempt to keep Irish athletics exclusive to the professional classes, who were at liberty for games on Saturdays.)

The fundamental unit in the GAA is the club, based on the smallest organized segment of the Irish population, the parish. With few exceptions, there is one club (usually named in honor of a saint or patriot) per parish. Each club is responsible for organizing hurling and football teams in age groups ranging from juvenile to senior. These teams compete in intracounty competitions that culminate in county finals. County champions go on to provincial matches, and the provincial champions to the all-Ireland final. It is the highest ambition of any player to represent his county here.

From the beginning, the GAA was as much a political as an athletic organization. It is credited in no small way with the awakening of national pride at the turn of the century, and, while nominally keeping its distance from revolutionary politics, provided useful cover for those who were active. Hurling, one of the games it promoted, was so nationalistic in its genesis that before 1916 the British occasionally had it banned. The GAA still is nationalistic at heart, although in 1971 it repealed its controversial rule forbidding members to play or watch "foreign" games such as soccer, rugby football, cricket, and hockey. For instance, it excludes the Unionists of Northern Ireland, who in turn regard it as a subversive organization since it refuses to recognize the border and includes IRA supporters in its membership. It also bars from membership British soldiers and members of the Royal Ulster Constabulary. Many members disagree with the organization's political stance, but so far its rules stand.

That the GAA continues withal to grip the imagination of the ordinary Irishman could be seen upon the death of Christy Ring, a respected player from Cork, the greatest hurler of modern times. Sober scholars often have likened Ring's exploits on the field to the heroic deeds of the legendary Cu Chulainn. When Ring died suddenly in 1979, all Ireland went into mourning: Some 50,000 attended his funeral, and that many more lined the route of the funeral cortege.

GAELIC FOOTBALL: Said to hark back to antique customs relating to the decapitation of defeated antagonists, one of Ireland's thrill-a-minute national sports is the fastest and roughest form of football, despite the fact that it has toned down considerably since the days when every contest was an explosion of territorial rivalry. Currently it is part soccer and, to a somewhat greater extent, part rugby. It is played with a soccer-like ball between two teams of 15 on a layout like the hurling field. The scoring method is similar to that in hurling. The ball can be handled, lifted off the ground with the foot, passed between hand and foot, kicked, fisted, or played with the feet on the ground: There is no such thing as offsides and no clear method for getting the ball away from the player who has it.

It is a most spectacular game, especially when played with an aggressive, no-holds-barred will to win — the prevailing spirit of the sport on the Emerald Isle. Of all the athletic trials in the country, Gaelic football consistently attracts the biggest crowds, and as the summer advances through the provincial semifinals in August, only the stoniest souls remain unmoved by the fever over who will compete on the day of reckoning, the *All-Ireland Football Final,* traditionally held on the last Sunday in September, in Dublin's *Croke Park.* For excitement and sheer color, this is every bit the equal of the hurling championships a few weeks earlier.

HURLING: The other Irish national game is fast and dangerous and unique to the Emerald Isle. The game is played on a field by two teams of 15 players each, and the instrument of aggression is the hurley, or *camán* — a 3-foot-long wooden blade of a stick with a curved tip to catch, run with, then use to hurl a leather-covered ball, or *sliotar,* toward the goalpost. The ball moves faster than the speed of light, the hurley sticks whirl, and opportunities for insult or injury are rife. Also a summer game, the hurling season unfolds with the Gaelic football season and reaches its own conclusion at *Croke Park* in the *All-Ireland Hurling Final* — usually on the first Sunday in September. (The Gaelic football final follows at the end of the month and closes out the sports calendar.) Dublin is at its most colorful on the morning of a final as thousands of followers, brandishing county flags and wearing county colors, mill about waiting for the game to begin. Though there rarely is any trouble, there is no segregation of sides in the stadium, and the atmosphere is definitely charged.

OTHER SPORTS

Sports lovers that they are, the Irish demonstrate considerable enthusiasm for other games as well. Now that the GAA ban on "foreign" games is history, both rugby and soccer have their following.

RUGBY FOOTBALL: One of the ironies of the GAA is that the game on which it based Gaelic football was actually a form of rugby football, the preserve of the upper classes and those whom the nationalists scorned as *shoneen,* Irish for "Little John" — or John Bull. And though such associations are largely forgotten, rugby football, once described as "a ruffian's sport, played by gentlemen," still is largely an activity of the middle and business classes, and the schools of those groups tend to go for rugby to the exclusion of other games. As a result, it is something of a minority competition on both sides of the border. Nonetheless, because there is only one rugby union for the entire Emerald Isle, players in international contests get the opportunity to present for a moment what has been beyond the abilities of politicians to achieve on a more permanent basis — a united Irish front. When 15 men of all faiths and political persuasions, all dressed in green jerseys, face the tricolor for the "Irish National Anthem", it is regarded as a small but significant step toward national unity.

The rugby season begins slowly in early autumn, picks up momentum after *Christmas* (when tryouts for places on the Irish team are held), and climaxes in February with the *Internationals,* which draws crowds of over 50,000 to Lansdowne Road in Dublin. These competitions take place, on a home and away basis, among Ireland, England, Wales, and France, with occasional visits from touring teams from New Zealand and Australia. The team that wins all its matches claims the European championship, while the four home teams compete for a mythical honor known as the Triple Crown.

SOCCER: Also banned by the GAA for many years, soccer was not played by the upper classes but was regarded as the preserve of the British army — despite the fact that many city-reared IRA men played soccer and that longtime Irish president and independence leader Eamon de Valera played wing three-quarter for the province of Munster in his youth. Soccer on the Emerald Isle is organized in two separate unions, one north and one south of the border. There are about 15 semi-professional clubs in each country.

Unfortunately, since the financial rewards for playing soccer are small in Ireland, clubs abroad grab up the best players. Home competitions are consequently less exciting than those in Britain and on the Continent. Still, the makings of a national enthusiasm are there. The Irish watch highlights of First Division matches on cross-Channel television on Saturday nights with notable regularity, and spectators at international games, which take place between September and May both in Northern Ireland and the Republic, fill the stadiums. As players, the Irish have been extremely successful both as members of European clubs and in the tough competition of the English First Division, playing for teams such as Liverpool, Arsenal, Everton, Tottenham Hotspur, and others. In 1990, the Irish national team reached the quarter-final round of the *World Cup,* delighting the entire nation with their fine play (under an English coach), and barely missing a chance to reach the final four.

ROAD BOWLING: Played in a small area of Holland and adjacent Germany, where it is called *klootschien,* this type of bowling on public roads also flourishes throughout the year, particularly after *Christmas,* in certain corners of Ireland — specifically Armagh, Cork, and parts of Waterford and Limerick — despite the fact that, as a potential traffic obstruction, it is illegal. It is an odd game, involving two sides: Each player throws a solid iron ball or bowl weighing 16, 21, or 28 ounces along an ordinary road in an attempt to cover a set distance in fewer throws than his opponent. The challenges lie in keeping the bowl on the road and in negotiating bends, either by lofting the bowl over the corner or by curving or putting a spin on the throw. Skill, strength, agility, and a finely honed knowledge of even the slightest slopes in the neighborhood are the requirements. Enthusiasm runs high, and wagering can be lively, both on the outcome and on individual shots; large sums of money often change hands. For the spectator, the best part is the sheer pleasure of passing a few idle hours following the players along gorgeous miles of country lane. The Bowl-Playing Association (An Bol Cumann) is the organizing body for the sport. The *Cork Evening Echo* has regular coverage.

Books and Magazines

Throughout GETTING READY TO GO, numerous books and brochures have been recommended as good sources of further information on a variety of topics. In many cases these have been publications of the Irish Tourist Board or the Northern Ireland Tourist Board and are available free through their offices both here and abroad. Others may be found in the travel section of any good general bookstore. If you still can't find something, the following bookstores and/or mail-order houses, specializing in information on Ireland (and Great Britain), are a further resource.

British Gifts, PO Box 26558, Los Angeles, CA 90026 (phone: 213-666-7778). Mail order only. Stocks a large selection of maps and books, including *Automobile*

Association of Great Britain (AA) and British Tourist Authority publications, which include information on Northern Ireland.

British Market, 2366 Rice Blvd., Houston, TX 77005 (phone: 800-448-0907 or 713-529-9889). Stocks maps and British Tourist Authority literature, as well as a wide range of guidebooks published in both the United Kingdom and the US, some of which include Northern Ireland. Selected price lists are available. Open 9 AM to 6 PM, Mondays through Saturdays, noon to 5 PM on Sundays.

British Travel Bookshop, 40 W. 57th St., 3rd Floor, New York, NY 10019 (phone: 212-765-0898). Carries a complete line of books and maps on all areas of Great Britain, as well as Northern Ireland, especially the *AA (Automobile Association of Great Britain)* and British Tourist Authority material and other books by major and little-known publishers. Book list available. Open 9 AM to 5 PM Mondays through Fridays.

Irish Books and Graphics, 580 Broadway, Room 1103, New York, NY 10012 (phone: 212-274-1923). Sellls a variety of Irish books (both new and out of print), records, cassettes, posters, prints, and maps. This store, the largest supplier of books in Gaelic outside of Dublin, covers just about every subject pertaining to Ireland — including art, architecture, literature, history, and travel. Open 11 AM to 5 PM weekdays; 1 to 4 PM Saturdays.

Irish Books & Media, 1433 Franklin Ave. E., Minneapolis, MN 55404 (phone: 612-871-3505). It's not a bookstore, but a mail-order house specializing in all kinds of books from Ireland — history, fiction, biographies, as well as travel.

The following stores and/or mail-order houses also specialize in travel, though not in travel to any particular country or continent. They offer books on Ireland along with guides to the rest of the world, and in some cases, even an old Baedeker or two.

Book Passage, 51 Tamal Vista, Corte Madera, CA 94925 (phone: 415-927-0960 in California; 800-321-9785 elsewhere in the US). Travel guides and maps to all areas of the world. A free catalogue is available.

The Complete Traveller, 199 Madison Ave., New York, NY 10016 (phone: 212-685-9007). Travel guides and maps. A catalogue is available for $2.

Forsyth Travel Library, PO Box 2975, Shawnee Mission, KS 66201-1375 (phone: 800-367-7984 or 913-384-0496). Travel guides and maps, old and new, to all parts of the world. Ask for the "Worldwide Travel Books and Maps" catalogue.

Gourmet Guides, 2801 Leavenworth St., San Francisco, CA 94133 (phone: 415-771-3671). Travel guides and maps, along with cookbooks. Mail-order lists available on request, including one about Great Britain and Ireland.

Phileas Fogg's Books and Maps, 87 Stanford Shopping Center, Palo Alto, CA 94304 (phone: 800-533-FOGG or 415-327-1754). Travel guides, maps, and language aids.

Tattered Cover, 2955 East First Ave., Denver, CO 80206 (phone: 800-833-9327 or 303-322-7727). The travel department alone of this enormous bookstore carries over 7,000 books, as well as maps and atlases. No catalogue is offered (the list is too extensive), but a newsletter, issued three times a year, is available on request.

Thomas Brothers Maps & Travel Books, 603 W. Seventh St., Los Angeles, CA 90017 (phone: 213-627-4018). Maps (including road atlases, street guides, and wall maps), guidebooks, and travel accessories.

Traveller's Bookstore, 22 W. 52nd St. (lobby), New York, NY 10019 (phone: 212-664-0995). Travel Guides, maps, literature, and accessories. A catalogue is available for $2.

Travel Suppliers, 16735 Lake Forest La., Yorba Linda, CA 93686 (phone: 714-528-2502). Mail-order suppliers of books, maps, language aids, and travel paraphernalia from money belts and pouches to voltage and currency converters. A catalogue is available.

A subscription to the *International Herald Tribune* also is a good idea for dedicated travelers. This English-language newspaper is written and edited mostly in Paris, and is *the* newspaper read most regularly and avidly by Americans abroad to keep up with world news, US news, sports, the stock market (US and foreign), fluctuations in exchange rates, and an assortment of help-wanted ads, real estate listings, and personals, worldwide in scope. Published 6 days a week (no Sunday paper), it is available the same day at newsstands throughout the US and in major cities throughout Europe, including Ireland. Home delivery also is widely available, and you can have your subscription transferred to an address in Ireland. To subscribe, write or call the Subscription Manager, *International Herald Tribune*, 850 Third Ave., 10th Floor, New York, NY 10022 (phone: 800-882-2884 or 212-752-3890).

The New York Times, Wall Street Journal, USA Today, Los Angeles Times, and other US newspapers also can be bought in many of the larger cities and resort areas, at hotels, airports, and newsstands. Note that some papers may cost more than in the US, and some may be available a day or two after publication.

Although Ireland is not particularly well known for its fine food (in comparison to other European countries), sampling the regional fare is still likely to be one of the highlights of any visit. You will find reading about local edibles worthwhile before you go or after you return. *Gourmet,* a magazine specializing in food, now and then features articles on Irish cooking and touring, although its scope is much broader than Ireland alone. It is available at newsstands throughout the US for $2.50 an issue or for $18 a year from *Gourmet,* PO Box 2886, Boulder, CO 80322-2886 (phone: 800-365-2454).

Before or after your trip, you may want to subscribe to various publications devoted exclusively to Ireland. *Ireland of the Welcomes,* a bimonthly magazine published by the Irish Tourist Board, spotlights various parts of the countryside and contains sketches about contemporary and historical personalities. Contact *Ireland of the Welcomes,* PO Box 84, Limerick, Irish Republic; a subscription costs $14 for 1 year, $22 for 2, or $29 for 3. *Inside Ireland,* published independently by Brenda Weir and Gill Bowler, is a quarterly newsletter that reports on a wide variety of topics — shopping, real estate, the arts, restaurants and pubs, retirement in Ireland, and the like. A subscription ($35 for 1 year) also entitles readers to use the publication's information service, to receive special supplements dealing with genealogy, accommodations, and other subjects, and to discounts on shopping, car rentals, and accommodations. For a sample copy of the newsletter send $1 to *Inside Ireland,* Rookwood, Stocking La., Ballyboden, Dublin 16, Irish Republic.

And for some leisurely reading to put you in the Irish spirit, *O Come Ye Back to Ireland* ($16.95 hardcover; $8.95 paper) and *The Pipes Are Calling* ($17.95), both by Christine Breen and Niall Williams, tell the tale of a young American couple's experiences farming in the west of Ireland. These books are available from the publisher, Soho Press, Inc. (1 Union Sq., New York, NY 10003; phone: 212-243-1527). For information on Irish authors and classics, including some wonderfully engrossing fiction, perfect for curling up with on rainy afternoons, see *Literature* in PERSPECTIVES.

Genealogy Hunts

For those interested in their Irish heritage, it's possible to trace Irish ancestors by mail or to hire a professional genealogist. Stateside, researchers can go to the Church of Latter-day Saints' genealogical library in Salt Lake City, where thousands of reels of microfilmed records are filed. But nothing is quite as satisfying as going to Ireland, flipping through the records, and actually visiting the area where an ancestor lived. There's a good chance that it will be possible to worship in a church where some great-great-great-great-grandfather was married, or walk up to the house where his children were born, or read a will written in his own hand, or photograph his moss-covered gravestone in some peaceful country churchyard. Doing the research in person, on the spot, rather than by mail, is more efficient, since clues can be followed up immediately.

It goes without saying, however, that it isn't possible to even begin to search in Ireland until the groundwork has been laid at home. It is necessary to know not only the name of the emigrant ancestor, but also the dates of his or her birth and emigration. It also is important to have a general idea of the area from which he or she came. The names of his relatives also can be useful. From there, it will be possible to consult parish registers and the archives of various public record offices and genealogical libraries. *Note:* Some Protestant marriages on the island were recorded beginning in 1845, while civil registration of births, deaths, and marriages in general began only in 1864.

It was the great potato famine of 1846–48 that drove 4 million Irish across the Atlantic, but several thousand came before that, and hundreds of thousands have come in the years since then. In general, just where to look for the records of forebears will depend on whether they came from the north or the south.

Especially useful, no matter where in Ireland your ancestors hailed from, is *The Handbook on Irish Genealogy* (1984), published by Heraldic Artists, Ltd. (3 Nassau St., Dublin 2). It contains lists of parish registers for the Roman Catholic, Church of Ireland, and Presbyterian churches, plus useful maps and more. Other Irish genealogical materials are available from the same source and from Historic Families (8 Fleet St., Dublin 2). Another helpful resource is *The Irish Ancestor, An Illustrated Journal;* for information write to Ms. Rosemary ffolliott (yes, ffolliott), The Glebe House, Fethard, County Tipperary.

Another useful resource is the comprehensive *Irish and Scotch-Irish Ancestral Research* by Margaret D. Falley. This two-volume set is available from the Genealogical Publishing Company (1001 N. Calvert St., Baltimore, MD 21202; phone: 301-837-8271) for $60. Other detailed publications available from this company include *Irish Emigration Lists, 1833–1839* ($20) by Brian Mitchell; *The Famine Immigrants* ($45) by Ira A. Glazier and Michael H. Tepper; and *Ulster Sails West* ($6) by William F. Marshal.

Before beginning, also get a copy of the Irish Tourist Board's free information sheet called "Tracing Your Ancestors," which offers an excellent summary of genealogical sources and procedures. For further guidance, you may want to contact the Genealogical Office (2 Kildare St., Dublin 2; phone: 1-614877 or 1-611626), which offers a consultation service for a fee of IR£10 (about $15) and also publishes the *Ancestral Trail in Ireland* (included in the consulation fee).

And for those who are heading to Ireland to trace their heritage, Ruth B. Green, an experienced Irish genealogical sleuth, arranges custom tours and will guide you through your search. Contact her at *Shamrock Travel* (6623 Meadowbrook Dr., Fort Worth, TX 76112; phone: 817-457-1993).

REPUBLIC OF IRELAND

Those who are researching ancestors who lived in the Republic will find Catholic marriage records from 1864 to the present and Protestant marriage records from 1845 at the General Register Office, (8-11 Lombard St. E., Dublin 2). Births, marriages, and deaths that occurred before civil registration began may be recorded in parish registers.

Roman Catholic registers normally are held by the parish priest. Many also are on microfilm in the National Library (address below), but even in these cases permission from the parish priest may be necessary. Most of the *surviving* Church of Ireland registers are held by the local clergy. Unfortunately, more than half of them burned in the fire of 1922, along with most probate records and the census records from 1813 to 1851.

This may make research difficult, but various other records do exist. The *Tithe Applotment Books,* containing the nàmes of people whose holdings were subject to tithe in the 1820s and 1830s, are especially useful. These are found in the National Archive (Four Courts, Dublin 7). This office also holds the census records for 1901 and 1911; original wills proved since 1904 and copies of many earlier wills; copies of some Church of Ireland parish registers; and a wide variety of other records. Deeds, leases, mortgages, settlements, and other records of transactions relating to property, dating from as early as 1708, are recorded at the Registry of Deeds (Henrietta St., Dublin 1).

When all else fails, visit the National Library (Kildare St., Dublin 2), where researchers will find the library's Genealogical Office, as well as all manner of books, manuscripts, directories, family histories, and genealogical and historical journals, and also various deeds, letters, and other papers relating to a number of Irish families. Those whose ancestors were Presbyterian can get help from the Presbyterian Historical Society (Church House, Fisherwick Place, Belfast BT1 6DU).

NORTHERN IRELAND

Those whose ancestors lived in the north of Ireland may find the records they need in either Dublin or Belfast. Records of births, marriages, and deaths from the beginning of civil registration until 1922 are in the General Register Office in Dublin (8-11 Lombard St. E., Dublin 2), while post-1922 records are in Belfast at the General Register Office (Oxford House, 49-55 Chichester St., Belfast BT1 4HL). Although a fire in 1922 destroyed many old wills, some thousands of copies, notes, and extracts, as well as the *Tithe Applotment Books* and many other documents relating to the people of the northern part of Ireland, are preserved at the Public Record Office of Northern Ireland (66 Balmoral Ave., Belfast BT9 6NY). On the other hand, the records of the Registry of Deeds in Dublin and of the Genealogical Office in Dublin also can be useful.

The place to turn for help when the trail turns cold is the *Irish Genealogical Association* (162 Kingsway, Dunmurry, Belfast BT17 9AD). Also of assistance are the *Ulster Historical Foundation* (62 Balmoral Ave., Belfast BT9 6NY; phone: 661621) and Donna Hotaling of *All Ireland Heritage* (2255 Cedar La., Vienna, VA 22180; phone: 703-560-4496). Both of these agents lead heritage tours, and the latter also publishes a quarterly magazine, *All Ireland Heritage;* a subscription costs $24 per year.

Weights and Measures

 When you are traveling in Ireland, you'll find that a number of quantities often will be expressed in unfamiliar terms. In fact, this is true for travel almost everywhere in the world, since the US is one of the last countries to make its way to the metric system. It may happen soon in the US, and, depending on where you're traveling, your trip to Ireland may serve to familiarize you with what will one day be the weights and measures at your grocery store.

The Irish Republic is in the process of converting to the continental European metric system, while across the border in the North, they still use the pre-Common Market British system, which is more familiar to US travelers. There are places in the Republic, however, where both systems currently are in use.

There are some specific things to keep in mind during your trip. Fruits and vegetables at a market generally are recorded in pounds and ounces, but your luggage at the airport and your body weight are more likely to be measured in kilos (kilograms). The latter is particularly pleasing to people of significant size, who instead of weighing 220 pounds hit the scales at a mere 100 kilos. (A kilo equals 2.2 pounds and 1 pound is .45 kilos.) Those still following the British system, however, more often discuss body weight in stones (1 stone equals 14 pounds); again, those who weigh 220 pounds will be pleased with the equivalent of approximately 16 stone.

Body temperature is measured in degrees Centigrade or Celsius, as well as on the more familiar Fahrenheit scale, so that a normal body temperature may be expressed as either 37C or 98.6F, and freezing is either 0 degrees C or 32F. Highway signs are written in several styles: in black and white for miles; in green and white for kilometers; or in miles and kilometers (1 mile equals 1.6 kilometers; 1 kilometer equals .62 mile). Where speed limits are in kilometers per hour, think twice before hitting the gas when you see a speed limit of 100 (which means 62 mph). Gasoline is sold by the British or "imperial" gallon, which is 20% larger than an American gallon.

The tables and conversion factors listed below should give you all the information you will need to understand any transaction, road sign, or map you encounter during your travels.

**CONVERSION TABLES
METRIC TO US MEASUREMENTS**

Multiply:	by:	to convert to:
LENGTH		
millimeters	.04	inches
meters	3.3	feet
meters	1.1	yards
kilometers	.6	miles
CAPACITY		
liters	2.11	pints (liquid)
liters	1.06	quarts (liquid)
liters	.26	gallons (liquid)
WEIGHT		
grams	.04	ounces (avoir.)
kilograms	2.2	pounds (avoir.)

US TO METRIC MEASUREMENTS

LENGTH		
inches	25.	millimeters
feet	.3	meters
yards	.9	meters
miles	1.6	kilometers

CAPACITY		
pints	.47	liters
quarts	.95	liters
gallons	3.8	liters

WEIGHT		
ounces	28.	grams
pounds	.45	kilograms

TEMPERATURE
$$°F = (°C \times 9/5) + 32 \qquad °C = (°F - 32) \times 5/9$$

APPROXIMATE EQUIVALENTS

Metric Unit	Abbreviation	US Equivalent
LENGTH		
meter	m	39.37 inches
kilometer	km	.62 mile
millimeter	mm	.04 inch
CAPACITY		
liter	l	1.057 quarts
WEIGHT		
gram	g	.035 ounce
kilogram	kg	2.2 pounds
metric ton	MT	1.1 ton
ENERGY		
kilowatt	kw	1.34 horsepower

Cameras and Equipment

Vacations are everybody's favorite time for taking pictures and home movies. After all, most of us want to remember the places we visit — and show them off to others. Here are a few suggestions to help you get the best results from your travel photography or videography.

BEFORE THE TRIP

If you're taking your camera or camcorder out after a long period in mothballs — or have just bought a new one — check it thoroughly before you leave to prevent unexpected breakdowns or disappointing pictures.

STILL CAMERAS

1. Shoot at least one test roll, using the kind of film you plan to take along with you. Use all the shutter speeds and f-stops on the camera, and vary the focus to make sure everything is in order. Do this well before your departure so there will be time to have the film developed and to make repairs, if necessary. If you're in a rush, most large cities have shops that can process film in as little as an hour. Repairs, unfortunately, take longer.
2. Clean your camera thoroughly, inside and out. Dust and dirt can jam mechanisms, scratch film, and mar photographs. Remove surface dust from lenses and camera body with a soft camel's hair brush. Next, use at least two layers of crumpled lens tissue and your breath to clean lenses and filters, but as they are easily scratched, don't rub hard and don't use water, saliva, or compressed air. Persistent stains can be removed by using a cotton swab moistened with liquid lens cleaner. Anything that doesn't come off easily needs professional attention; a periodic professional cleaning also is advisable. Once your lenses are clean, protect them from dirt and damage with skylight or ultraviolet filters.
3. Check the lithium batteries for your camera's light meter, and take along extras just in case yours wear out during the trip.

VIDEO CAMCORDERS

1. If you haven't used your camcorder lately, use a "practice" videocassette to reacquaint yourself with the various shooting techniques — such as panning, zooming, and segueing (that is, transitioning without pause) from one scene to another. Practice fully before you leave; don't save it for the plane.
2. Clean and maintain your camcorder lenses with a soft, dry cloth. Don't use solvents such as paint thinner or chemically treated cloths. Once your camcorder lenses are clean, protect them from dirt and damage with inexpensive skylight or ultraviolet filters. If your camcorder's heads need cleaning, a recorded tape will tell you. A "snowy" tape is a sign that a head cleaning is needed. If a head cleaning doesn't improve the picture, the problem may lie elsewhere. In that case, take the camcorder to a professional for a check-up. Check the operation of each component on your camcorder, making sure that each feature performs correctly. If there's an internal problem, don't try to fix it yourself. You could void the manufacturer's warranty or, even worse, cause further damage. Even if all appears well at home, take a head cleaner along on your trip to make sure your videos remain clear and sharp.
3. Check the lithium batteries for your camcorder's light indicators, and take along extras just in case yours wear out during the trip. If you took along all your camcorder accessories, your carrying bag would get heavy and cumbersome, but there are a few "musts." Take extra nickel-cadmium (Ni-Cd) batteries so that you always have one or two power sources ready while another is recharging back at the hotel. You never know when a once-in-a-lifetime opportunity will present itself, and if you just used up your 45-minute allotment of power on a local festival, you'll have none left to shoot anything else. Remember that the more features you use, including reviewing what you've taped in the electronic viewfinder, the more battery power you will consume.

EQUIPMENT TO TAKE ALONG

Keep your gear light and compact. Items that are too heavy or bulky to be carried comfortably on a full-day excursion will likely remain in your hotel room, so leave them home.

1. Invest in a broad camera or camcorder strap if you now have a thin one. It will make carrying the camera much more comfortable.
2. A sturdy canvas or leather camera or camcorder bag, preferably with padded pockets (not an airline bag), will keep your equipment organized and easy to find.
3. For cleaning, bring along a camel's hair brush that retracts into a rubber squeeze bulb. Also take plenty of lens tissue, soft cloths, and plastic bags to protect equipment from dust and moisture.

STILL CAMERAS: Lenses and Other Equipment – Most single-lens-reflex (SLR) cameras come with a 50mm, or "normal," lens — a general-purpose lens that frames subjects within an approximately average angle of view. This is good for street scenes taken at a distance of 25 feet or more, and for full-length portraits shot at 8 to 12 feet.

Any lens from 35mm on down offers wide-angle capabilities, which in effect pull segments of the peripheral scene into the picture, and are especially handy for panoramas and landscapes. A wide-angle lens in the 20–28mm range is perfect for castle gardens. Where the normal perspective of a 50mm lens provides only a partial view of the ruins atop the Rock of Cashel, a 20mm incorporates the haunting remains of the cathedral and its majestic tower in one flowing scene. While a 50mm lens only provides a partial view of the Twelve Bens in Connemara, taken from the proper perspective a 20mm lens frames this magnificent sight, as these peaks rise from the rock-strewn moonscape. The wide-angle lens also is excellent for linking people with their surroundings because of its great depth of field — that is, sharp focus from foreground to background — that can focus pictures between 3½ feet and infinity. And it also can be valuable when there's very little space between you and your subject.

Wide-angle lenses are especially handy for panoramas, for cityscapes, and for large buildings or statuary from which you can't step back. For extreme closeups, a macro lens is best, but a screw-on magnifying lens is an inexpensive alternative. Keep in mind that wide-angle lenses have a tendency to distort when used very close to a subject, or when dealing with vertical lines. Tall trees or a high-rise hotel may seem to converge toward the top of the frame, for example. Once you're aware of these effects, you can use them to creative advantage.

Where a wide-angle lens extends normal perspective, a telephoto lens focuses on a portion of the overview, providing perspective in detail. Telephoto lenses, 125mm to 1,000mm, are good for shooting details from a distance and permit dramatic silhouettes of fishing boats against a setting sun, detailed portraits, floral design, and candids — although when choosing a lens, keep in mind that the weight of the higher ranges may prove difficult to support without a tripod (see below).

In addition to individual telephotos, a number of telephoto zoom lenses have become popular with travel photographers. Zooms offer the most versatility as they incorporate a range of focal lengths. A typical telephoto zoom — ranging from 70mm to 210mm, for example — allows you to frame a picture as you want it by choosing the most appropriate lens setting for the situation. That means carrying one lens with millimeter-to-millimeter variations from 70mm to 210mm. Also try a 35mm to 80mm. In general, beware of inexpensive models which can result in poor photographs.

The drawbacks of a zoom lens are its weight and a potential loss of clarity when compared with individual telephotos. This is less of a problem with the better lenses; and both problems are being eliminated by technological advances.

A 2X Teleconverter is a simple addition to a camera kit. Lightweight and easy to carry, the 2X doubles the focal length of various lenses, converting a 20mm into a 40mm, a 50mm into a 100mm, a 70mm to 210mm zoom into a 140mm to 420mm, and so forth. Though there is again a potential loss of clarity, and in low-lighting situations focusing may be somewhat more difficult due to the extra thickness of lens glass, the 2X is a versatile accessory that's easy to use.

While it may seem excessive, a small, lightweight tripod is a real asset in assuring picture quality. This is particularly true when the heavier telephoto lenses are used, or in situations where the available light is limited and shots will be made at speeds slower than 1/60 of a second. For sharp detail, closeups, night, or limited-light pictures while in Europe, a tripod is a must.

A small battery-powered electronic flash unit, or "strobe," is handy for very dim light or night use, but only if the subject is at a distance of 15 feet or less. Flash units cannot illuminate an entire scene (they're only effective up to about a dozen feet), and many museums and other establishments do not permit flash photography, so take such a unit only if you know you will need — and be able to use — it. (If you do violate these rules and take a picture in such a restricted area your film, and even your camera, may be confiscated.)

Subjects as varied as the interiors of cathedrals, castles, and cairns all become photographable with a flash. It also can provide frontal light for a backlit subject and additional light in a variety of dim situations, as it is often overcast in Ireland. If your camera does not have a hot-shoe, you will need a PC cord to synchronize the flash with your shutter. Be sure to take along extra batteries for the flash.

Film – Travel photographs are normally best in color. Good slide films are Kodachrome 64 and Fujichrome 50, both moderate- to slow-speed films that provide saturated colors and work well in most outdoor light. For very bright conditions, try slower film, like Kodachrome 25. If the weather is cloudy, or you're indoors with only natural light, use a faster film, such as Kodachrome 200 or 400. There are now even faster films on the market for low-light situations. The result may be pictures with whiter, colder tones and a grainier image, but high-speed films open up picture possibilities that slower films cannot.

Films tend to render color in slightly different ways. For instance, while Kodachrome results in "warmer" tones and brings out reds and oranges, Ektachrome, a similar film, is "colder" and produces crisp, clear colors — particularly blues and greens. (It is also worth noting that Ektachrome generally can be processed at more photolabs than Kodachrome.) Fujichrome is noted for its yellows, greens, and whites. You might test films as you test your camera (see above) to determine your preference.

If you prefer film that develops into prints rather than slides, try Kodacolor 100 or 400 for most lighting situations. Vericolor is a professional film that comes in speeds of 160 and 400 and gives excellent results, especially for skin tones, but is particularly sensitive to temperature extremes which may cause color alteration. Bring it along for taking shots of people *if* you're sure you can protect it from extreme heat and cold. A newer all-purpose film with similar properties to Vericolor in terms of quality results is Ektar. It is not as sensitive to temperature changes as Vericolor, and comes in three speeds: 25, 125, and 1000. All lens and filter information applies equally to print and slide films.

If you are concerned about airport security X-rays damaging undeveloped film (X-rays do not affect processed film), store it in one of the lead-lined bags sold in camera shops. This possibility is not as much of a threat as it used to be, however. In the US, incidents of X-ray damage to unprocessed film (exposed or unexposed) are few because low-dosage X-ray equipment is used virtually everywhere. However, when crossing international borders, travelers may find that foreign X-ray equipment delivers higher levels of radiation and damage film.

As a rule of thumb, photo industry sources say that film with speeds up to ASA 400 can go through security machinery in the US five times without any noticeable effect. Nevertheless, if you're traveling without a protective bag, ask to have your photo equipment inspected by hand. (Naturally, this is possible only if you're carrying your film and camera on board with you — a good idea, because it helps to preclude loss or theft or the possibility at some airports that checked baggage will be X-rayed with equipment more powerful than normally used for hand baggage.)

In the US, Federal Aviation Administration regulations require that if you request a hand inspection, you get it, but overseas the response may depend on the humor of the inspector. One type of film that never should be subjected to X-rays is the new, very high-speed ASA 1000 film; there are lead-lined bags made especially for it — and, in the event that you are refused a hand inspection, this is the only way to save your film. Finally, the walk-through metal detector devices at airports do not affect film, though film cartridges may set them off.

How much film should you take? If you are serious about photography, pack at least one roll of film (36 exposures) for each day of your trip. Film is especially expensive abroad, and any extra can be bartered away or brought home and safely stored in your refrigerator. (Processing also is more expensive abroad and not as safe as at home.) Nevertheless, if you don't bring enough, you should have no trouble getting any standard film in most places in Ireland; it's sold everywhere.

VIDEO CAMCORDERS: In general, camcorders are self-contained, automated, point-and-shoot devices, though for the more ambitious film-making traveler, 8mm video or movie cameras allow the operator a greater degree of control over the images recorded and superior image quality. What follows is a brief roundup of tips and suggestions for the beginning home moviemaker, and those travelers who need to brush up on their videotaping technique.

Your camcorder has some type of zoom feature, whether it's 4:1, 6:1, or all the way up to 12:1. For most people, that's enough. Although some models have a fixed lens, others, like 8mm video, provide you the option of adding a telephoto for close-up shooting or a wide-angle lens if you often find yourself not being able to fit all of what you want to shoot into the viewfinder. If you do decide to add a lens, check that the one you buy will fit your camcorder. You may be able to double up on your filters, though. As long as it's the same size, your camera filter should be able to fit on your camcorder lens. (See the discussion of filters below.)

Although the lux ratings of camcorders now are low enough to achieve some impressive videos in low-light situations, for good clarity and color saturation you should have an additional light (10 watts or higher) to brighten indoor shooting. Generally, the lights easily can be attached to the camcorder and come with the necessary accessories such as battery charger, battery pack, and light diffuser. All that can get fairly heavy, however, so you might want to leave your light at home. Most museums and churches prohibit the use of video lights — both for security reasons and because they can be harmful to paintings and stained glass, not to mention annoying to other visitors.

In general, Europe operates on 220 volt 50 Hz electric current (although in some parts of Ireland, 125 volt current also may be used), as opposed to the 110 volt 60 Hz current that is the standard in the United States. To compensate for the difference, you'll need to make sure that the battery charger that comes with your camcorder is compatible with the current in the countries you're touring. Most chargers are compatible, but owner's manuals don't always spell this out. So if it's unclear, be sure to call the company and ask. If the charger is incompatible, you'll have to get a voltage converter. Even if your camcorder's charger is compatible with the current and voltage ratings in other countries, you'll need a plug adaptor kit to cope with the variations in plug configurations found in Europe. Voltage converters and adapter plug kits are available from some of the companies listed in *Books and Magazines* (above), specializing in travel paraphenalia; also see *Mail, Telephone, and Electricity,* in this section, for further information and sources.

You'll also be in for a shock if you try to play back your tape through a European TV set or VCR. Whereas the United States and Canada use the NTSC television standard, most European countries operate on the PAL standard. Still other European countries use the SECAM standard, so the chance of your playing back your video movies through a TV set in another country is unlikely. Because the various systems use a different number of lines-per-frame and frames-per-second, they are incompatible with each other. (For the same reason, if you send a tape of your sister's wedding to your brother in Ireland, he won't be able to view it.) In order to review what you've taped, you'll either have to use the electronic viewfinder on your camcorder or have to take along a small portable NTSC TV to which you could connect your camcorder. For the same incompatibility reasons, however, you won't be able to view European telecasts with your portable. Although there are a few multiple-standard TV sets available, don't count on there being one in your hotel room.

Tapes – It usually is best to buy tapes before leaving home, as they probably will be lots more expensive near major tourist and resort areas. It also will be less confusing, since different countries have their own ways of labeling tape. Although the variations in recording and playback standards won't affect your ability to use the tape, they will affect how quickly you record. Because the tape moves slower in a PAL camcorder than in an NTSC camcorder, you will get less recording time from a European tape than is indicated on the label. So if you buy an E-160 tape designed for a PAL camcorder, you really will have only about 2 hours of recording time (T-120) on your NTSC camcorder.

If you do run out of tape while on your trip, you shouldn't have a hard time finding what you need. Most of the major tape brands — TDK, Sony, Memorex, Maxell, BASF, Fuji, and Scotch — are available throughout the US, but when buying tapes abroad, you're bound to run into some unfamiliar names. Stick to what you know, if possible. When choosing, especially among unfamiliar brands, be sure that it is indeed the correct tape format — 8mm, VHS, Super-VHS, Beta, and so on — for your camcorder.

Also, if an unknown brand is priced substantially below the rest, there's probably a reason. First of all, the image quality may be poor. Secondly, the few dollars you save in buying the least expensive videocassettes will mean nothing a few years from now when the tape is showing signs of wear. You also should be aware of the potential problem of low-quality tapes' damaging the heads of camcorders.

Because you'll want to keep your accessories to a manageable number — especially if you're using a full-size camcorder — you should use the longest-length tape possible for recording your trip. Depending on the tape speed of your equipment, the longest 8mm and VHS tapes generally run for 2 hours and VHS-C cassettes run for 20 minutes. VHS and VHS-C cassettes can record in the extended-play mode for 6-hour and 60-minute recordings, respectively, but extending the recording time reduces the picture quality substantially. It's best to record in the standard-play mode, because you'll get the best picture quality.

With the wide variety of grades and types of videocassettes on the market, it's easy to get confused about what kind of tape to buy for a particular application. Certain camcorders can record in stereo, so for those you'll want a hi-fi videocassette for better sound quality. If you have a Super VHS, Super VHS-C, or Hi Band 8mm camcorder, you'll want to buy the corresponding tapes for those high-end machines to achieve the best possible picture quality. A Super VHS-C videocassette will not improve your regular VHS-C video picture, however. Get a high-grade or professional quality tape for the once-in-a-lifetime videos that you plan to watch a lot. Before loading up on videocassettes for your trip, think about how much time you'll actually spend shooting, and about how many tapes you'll really want to view later. Plan on a tape for every other day of your vacation, or, if you intend to use your camcorder heavily, a tape for each day. Remember that you always can edit a tape, and even reuse it if you decide you don't want to keep it.

Your videocassettes generally are safe from the X-rays in airport detector devices, but the electromagnetic fields generated by those devices could cause dropouts in your tapes, which are recorded by an electromagnetic process. The lead-lined bags that protect against X-rays unfortunately don't protect against an electromagnetic field, so your best bet is to take your tapes along for a hand inspection. Because cassettes have been favorite carriers for terrorist explosives over the years, however, airport officials may insist that you put everything through the X-ray machine. If you don't have a choice, put them through and hope for the best.

FILTERS: For both Camcorders and SLR cameras, filters are important considerations. Take a skylight filter (1A or 1B) for each lens. There's no need to remove it, except to replace it with a different filter. Not only will it provide the filtration needed to combat atmospheric haze and ultraviolet light, but it also will protect the lens surface.

A polarizing filter goes one step beyond the skylight variety, cutting out reflections from non-metallic surfaces (water and glass, for instance) and penetrating haze for extra clarity and rich color saturation. It also will add impact to greens and blues in a landscape. While its effects are dramatic, it can be a difficult filter to use as it cuts back on light (it's a dark filter) and creates deep shadows. It will work well only under certain lighting conditions. In spite of these drawbacks, it remains an excellent filter for certain effects.

Unless you plan to experiment with the increasingly diverse range of specialty filters now available (diffraction, multiple image, and closeup, for instance), skylights and a polarizer are just about all you'll need. Stick to the high- to medium-priced glass filters (Hoya, Tiffen, or Vivitar, for example) to assure picture quality.

SOME FINAL TIPS

Get organized. A small, lightweight canvas camera bag with cushioning and Velcro dividers is perfect for carrying lenses, lens tissue, filters, rolls of film or tapes, and a strobe. It's amazing how compact camera equipment is when packed properly. For better pictures, remember the following pointers:

1. Get close. Move in to get your subject to fill the frame.
2. Vary your angle. Shoot from above or below; look for unusual perspectives.
3. Pay attention to backgrounds. Keep it simple or blur it out.
4. Look for details: not just a whole building, but a decorative element; not an entire street scene, but a single remarkable face.
5. Don't be lazy. Always carry your camera gear with you, loaded and ready for unexpected opportunities.

For Better Videos – Try to plan your movie with an introduction, a development, and a conclusion. Sometimes you can't help but get a video collage, but shoot with an eye — and an ear — toward how it's going to look and sound on a TV set. You're not just capturing a moment, as you do with still photography; you're telling a story.

1. To divide the tapes by country or region, use the camcorder's titling feature, if it has one, or shoot museum signs or some other kind of marker that indicates where you are. Use your fade in/fade out feature to provide smooth transitions.
2. Suppress your impulse to point and shoot and then find another object to shoot. Your viewers will need several seconds to focus on a subject and orient themselves

to what they're seeing. Stay on each subject for at least 5 or 6 seconds — longer if the situation warrants.

3. Try not to shoot directly into strong, bright light as this may damage your camcorder. Your subject also is likely to appear as a silhouette because the camcorder will adjust for the brightest source. Some camcorders, however, do have backlight compensating features.

4. Vary your shooting techniques. Using the various buttons available at your fingertips, zoom in and out and pan from side to side to view your subject. If your subject is stationary, walk around (but hold the camera steady) to get a different angle. Your objective should be to create a smooth flow.

5. Your camcorder won't be welcome everywhere, although as they become more popular, they are increasingly accepted. In any event, before lugging your gear with you, check with the places you plan to visit.

■ **A note about courtesy and caution:** When photographing individuals in Ireland (and anywhere else in the world), ask first. It's common courtesy. Furthermore, some governments have security regulations regarding the use of cameras and will not permit the photographing of certain subjects, such as particular government and military installations. When in doubt, ask.

PERSPECTIVES

History

Imagine that you are standing on a windswept headland, a country of lush green glens behind you, the tumultuous sea at your feet. A beautiful girl approaches you, an orphan, she says, but of noble lineage, who tells you a tale so full of romance and heroism and piety and cruelty and *sturm und drang* that you cannot decide whether to laugh or cry, but still find yourself listening enraptured to her compelling voice.

This is Ireland, and the Irish themselves are inclined to surrender to her charms. For centuries, they have been compounding a political and social mythology out of songs, legends, and history, and the heroes of that mythology — Finn MacCool, Brian Ború, Patrick Sarsfield, Wolfe Tone, Daniel O'Connell, and Charles Parnell — remain the controlling models for modern Ireland's political and social behavior. When Patrick Pearse, a leader of the 1916 Easter Rebellion, invoked the Ulster hero Cu Chulainn while British troops besieged his little band in the Dublin General Post Office, he rallied his men with an image from the nation's antiquity. The revival of the Irish language, a cornerstone of government policy, affirms the continuity of the Irish Republic with its remotest antecedents. It is a nation that requires an understanding of its most distant past to complete an understanding of its present.

THE CELTS

The Celts were a family of Indo-European warrior aristocracies related by language, religion, mastery of horsemanship, and a flammable temperament that kept them always at each other's throats. From their arrival in Ireland between 500 and 50 BC, the Celtic clans warred ceaselessly among themselves for territory, tribute, and cattle. Sensitive and superstitious, they were terrorized by their priests (druids) and master-poets (*filidhe;* pronounced *fee*-lee), whose curses carried weight with the gods and in whose memories reposed the only record of tribal histories, genealogies, and myth. These learned, almost Brahmanic castes maintained their own training academies and provided the only source of social unity among the various tribes.

The family was the fundamental Celtic social unit from which all rights and authority flowed. Tribal alliances were matters of military convenience rather than treaty, and not until the 5th century AD did the Irish establish the semblance of a central power. Even then, the high king, ruling from the Hill of Tara, drew his authority not from law but from the tacit consensus of the legislative assemblies of tribal chieftains and nobles. The O'Neill high kings, whose dynasty endured until the 11th century, invoked a national spirit by convening the first such assembly — though each tribe had previously conducted its own and continued to do so. The O'Neills also raised a standing army (the Fianna), but even after they had subdued the Ulaid of Ulster — last of the Celtic tribes to resist Gaelic dominance — in 851, their control of Ireland remained tenuous.

Gaelic civilization flourished unconsumed by the Roman Empire in what W. B. Yeats would call the Celtic Twilight. Its decentralized social structure evolved without interference, and when, in the 5th century, Christianity was introduced by St. Patrick, the new church adapted itself at once to this structure. Abbeys and monasteries patronized by local chieftains and entirely independent of diocesan authority became the seats of church power; out of touch with Rome, the Irish clung to old doctrines long after they had been abandoned or revised elsewhere in Christendom. Yet the monasteries nourished a lively intellectual life; graduates of the poetic academies, attracted by the ascetic ethos, flocked to the monasteries and abbeys, learned to write, and created the stunningly illuminated manuscripts in which the oral literature of the nation was first recorded. By decree of St. Columba (Columcille), a Gaelic prince, poet, and founder of the first native order, lay poets were officially employed in every royal court after 575. The literary arts thus enjoyed the patronage of both church and state.

When the barbarians inundated Europe in the 5th century, Christian learning crawled to high ground in Ireland. As the deluge subsided, Irish missionaries ventured over the European continent, founding monasteries, restoring literacy, and resuscitating the faith amid the ruins of Hellenic civilization. John Scotus Erigena (which means "Irish-born") and his contemporary Sedulius Scotus taught in the palace schools founded by Charlemagne, and the monasteries of Ireland received students from abroad; but while this lively traffic earned Ireland the epithet Isle of Saints and Scholars, it turned Rome's efforts to reforming the doctrinally wayward church and bringing it under central control.

In 795, Ostmen, the predatory Vikings, commenced their raids along the Irish coast, leveling monasteries and torching whole libraries. These Norse pirates built a string of garrisons along the eastern coast, proclaiming themselves kings and establishing Ireland's first cities and ports. The fractious Gaels were helpless to dislodge these ferocious and well-organized intruders. Late in the 10th century, Brian Ború, an obscure chieftain from Clare, overthrew the Danish King of Limerick and, by three usurpations, dispossessed the O'Neills and declared himself High King of Ireland. For a few short years, Brian united the tribes of Ireland behind his leadership; he routed the Danes from their chief stronghold, Dublin, at the Battle of Clontarf in 1014. Brian, alas, lost his life in the battle, and the Irish relapsed into squabbling over succession to the Tara monarchy.

THE NORMAN INVASION

Though their dominance had been broken, the Norsemen remained in Ireland as sailors and merchants, intermarrying with the Gaels and assimilating the native culture. In 1166 they joined with the chiefs of Leinster to overthrow their king, Dermot MacMurrough, who fled to England where he formed an alliance with some Norman adventurers who he hoped would restore him to his realm. In 1169, these mail-clad buccaneers landed on the Baginburn headland in Waterford and in 2 years had seized Leinster for their leader, Richard Fitz-Gilbert de Clare, known as Strongbow. MacMurrough died soon after. Before these brilliant, methodical soldiers the Irish had no defense. In 1171, Strongbow and the rest of the Normans resentfully acknowledged themselves subjects of Henry II, and the High King Rory O'Connor recognized Henry as his sovereign in return for control over all unconquered areas. Ireland had become the property of the English crown.

The Normans marked their holdings with a line called the Pale, a thin strip of land on the eastern coast. But as Norman and Gael intermarried, the former became, as the saying goes, more "Irish than the Irish themselves." (The Irish referred to the Normans as "old foreigners," while the English called those who had gone native "degenerate English.") By 1261, the Gaels had adopted Norman military techniques, putting an end to their conquests, while the Normans had taken up the Gaelic language and culture, maintaining poets and commissioning manuscripts like native chieftains.

The rapprochement displeased the English. In 1297, to consolidate the colony and muster troops from it for his Scottish wars, Edward I convened an Irish Parliament at Kilkenny, which was hostile to the Gaels and assimilated Normans. By 1366, the Parliament had promulgated statutes to separate the "races," but these were largely ignored by a very mixed population. The Normans had built cities, introduced English common law, and mingled names like Bourke, Butler, and Carey with O'Brien, O'Neill, and O'Donnell. Culturally distinct from England and uncomfortable as colonials, the Normans declared parliamentary independence in 1460.

THE PLANTATION

The Reformation and the Tudor monarchy put an end to the Norman's adventure. In 1541, Henry VIII compelled the Irish Parliament to recall his sovereignty. He then asserted his authority to govern the Irish church, as he had already done in England, and imposed the Plantation policy, under which native Irish and some "degenerate English" landholdings were seized and regranted to loyal English fortune seekers. Resistance to the policy centered in Ulster, where the chieftains Red Hugh O'Donnell and Hugh O'Neill, setting aside old rivalries, formed the Tyrone Confederation and, in the first of Ireland's revolutions, rose against Henry's "new earls" (as those who literally bought titles and rights to the land were called). Promises of Spanish assistance were obtained, and from 1594 to 1603 the Tyrone Confederation rebelled with some success against the English. In 1601, a Spanish fleet sailed into Kinsale on the southern coast, and the English Lord Mountjoy turned to attack them, whereupon O'Donnell and O'Neill swept down from the north to besiege the besiegers. The Spanish pressed for a decisive engagement; O'Neill argued for attrition, but O'Donnell forced the issue. The Battle of Kinsale was fought on *Christmas Eve,* 1601, and the Hispano-Gaelic alliance, insufficiently prepared, went down in defeat. The defeated earls, O'Donnell and O'Neill, were permitted to return to Ulster; but after a few years of suffering English rule, they sailed in self-imposed exile to the Continent in 1607, an event often called the Flight of the Earls.

The Plantation policy went forward apace. In Ulster, barely one-tenth of the land was retained by its native inhabitants; the rest was planted with Presbyterian colonists from Scotland, dissenters in their own country. In 1641, Norman soldiers, unemployed and wandering the countryside, enlisted with the Irish chiefs of Ulster in another uprising. The Irish Parliament, now sitting at Dublin, expelled its Catholic members, who gathered at Kilkenny to proclaim a provisional government.

Presiding over this revolution was Owen Roe O'Neill, nephew of Hugh and a statesman of some sophistication; he envisioned for Ireland a centralized and autonomous native government. After Owen Roe's victory over parliamentary forces at Benburb in 1646, Charles I, facing Cromwell's insurgence at home, offered a treaty that would have reversed the Plantation policy; but the Catholic clergy, holding out for emancipation from the Protestant crown, persuaded Owen Roe to reject it. After deposing the king in 1649, Cromwell turned to the reconquest of Ireland, and in September stormed the town of Drogheda, slaughtering 3,500 inhabitants in reprisal for earlier revolutionary terrorism. Owen Roe's death in November signaled the collapse of the resistance. Limerick and Galway capitulated in 1652, and 30,000 Irish soldiers followed their chiefs into exile in what the Irish remember as the Flight of the Wild Geese.

The Cromwellian Act of Settlement in 1652 extended the Plantation policy; Irish lands were seized and distributed among demobilized English soldiers and the financiers of the reconquest. The Catholic church was outlawed and its properties confiscated. Towns were seeded with English burgesses, and native merchants were relocated to the perimeters. The common people were reduced to virtual slavery as tenants on lands immemorially theirs. By 1655, what remained of the Gaelic nation languished among the stony acres west of the Shannon. By 1688, Protestants, though they constituted a tiny minority of its population, owned 78 percent of all the land in Ireland.

STUART vs. ORANGE

With the ascension of James II, a Catholic, in 1685, England's policies in Ireland were somewhat liberalized. But James was deposed in 1688 and fled to France. In 1689 he moved to Ireland, where he hoped to establish in this Catholic nation a base from which to recover his throne. Catholic France rallied to the Jacobites (as his followers were called) and sent a fleet to Kinsale in 1689. But Protestant Europe as determinedly supported William of Orange, James's Protestant successor. Things came to a head in July, 1690, when a mixed army of Danes, Germans, French Huguenots, and English overwhelmed the Jacobites at the Battle of the Boyne. The Irish army, under Patrick Sarsfield, fell back and retrenched beyond the Shannon. They then sallied forth to meet the Protestants at the Battle of Aughrim, and, when defeated again, Sarsfield gathered the remains of his army behind the walls of Limerick and indomitably withstood two lengthy English sieges before finally obtaining favorable terms of surrender, which London was largely to ignore. Sarsfield and his men, like the earls some 40 years before them, fled in exile to France. (Sarsfield joined the French army and died in battle in 1693, crying: "Oh, that this were for Ireland.")

ROBERT EMMET, WOLFE TONEIRISH PROTESTANT PATRIOTISM

The hope of Irish freedom dashed, England imposed the Penal Laws in 1695, the apartheid statutes by which Catholics were denied nearly all rights at law and were reduced to serfdom. (In the words of one lord chancellor: "The law does not take into account the existence of such a person as an Irish Roman Catholic.") Yet while the Penal Laws ensured the privileges of the Ascendancy (Protestant settlers), they also effectively tied most of the Protestant gentry — but not the Protestant magnates — to the land, while tariffs restricted the economy. Furthermore, although the Dublin Parliament was supposedly autonomous in most areas, in fact it merely rubber-stamped the acts of Westminster. All Catholics and many Protestants chafed under the English yoke. In 1791 the Protestant patriot Wolfe Tone founded the United Irishmen, which — inspired by the French Revolution — attempted to bring together Catholics and Protestants in common cause against the English government. The movement gained strength quickly in Ireland but was suppressed in 1794. Tone fled to Paris to raise an army of liberation, and, in 1798, Ireland's third revolution broke out in Wexford. Tone and a French fleet hurried to its aid, but the ragtag rebels, led by two priests, John Murphy and Michael Murphy, were crushed at Vinegar Hill in Enniscorty (County Wexford) before the fleet could arrive. The French, surrounded at Castlebar (County Mayo), surrendered, and Tone, denied an honorable execution before a firing squad and condemned instead to the gallows, slit his throat. In 1801, the Act of Union abolished the Irish Parliament and absorbed Ireland into a United Kingdom. Revolution erupted for the fourth time in 1803, led this time by Robert Emmet, but it collapsed in confusion on the brink of success, and Emmet, whose stirring speech from the dock embedded itself in the Irish memory, was hanged.

CATHOLIC EMANCIPATION

In 1793, a Catholic Relief Bill had ostensibly restored all Catholic rights except that of holding elective office, an omission that rendered the rest meaningless. In 1823, Daniel O'Connell — the brilliant Kerry lawyer and orator who came to be known as "the Liberator" — organized the Catholic Association which, by tithing its members a penny a month, became an organ of legal defense and agitation and the underground government of the Gaelic nation. O'Connell was a peerless organizer, and when defiant voters in Clare elected him to Westminster in 1828, the orchestrated mass movement behind him so intimidated England that he was seated, accomplishing full Catholic emancipation in a stroke.

In 1830, leading a substantial Irish voting bloc in Parliament, O'Connell embarked on a campaign to repeal the Act of Union. Committed to reform within the constitution, activism within the law, and loyalty to the crown, O'Connell threw his party's support behind the Whigs, counting on them to back the repeal movement if they displaced the Tories. But Prime Minister Melbourne's Whig government, once elected, reneged, supported by a Protestant Ascendancy determined to protect its property and power under the Union by force if necessary. The Irish masses stood ready to take up arms at the first word from O'Connell; the Young Ireland party, led by journalist Charles Gavin Duffy and poet Thomas Davis, urged O'Connell to abandon his pacifist principles and lead them in revolution. O'Connell had no such intention. Instead, in 1842–43, he organized and addressed a series of "monster meetings" — rallies in support of repeal; at the one held at Tara, nearly a million people assembled peacefully to hear him speak in the open air. The meetings were perfectly legal, but the English government — mindful of O'Connell's tremendous influence — sent troops to surround the meeting held at Clontarf and threatened violence if the crowd did not disperse. Though he was within his rights and though the assembly could probably have overwhelmed the soldiers, O'Connell canceled the meeting. The next year, he and Duffy were arrested and convicted of sedition. Though the House of Lords later reversed the verdict, O'Connell emerged from 2 months in prison largely stripped of his influence. He split with Young Ireland in 1846; momentum passed to its leaders, and he died in 1847.

THE IRISH FAMINE

In 1847, the potato, staple of the common people, succumbed to blight for the second time and the Great Famine descended over Ireland. It was a catastrophe beyond description; starvation, dysentery, and cholera decimated the population, and tens of thousands fled to America. Ireland lost about 2 million people between 1845 and 1855, yet Britain stuck to its free-trade philosophy and intervened as little as possible on the theory that private enterprise would eventually sort things out. Relief aid actually decreased as the famine worsened. Yet, throughout this Irish holocaust, food was exported from Ireland to pay rents to absentee landlords in England. Great estates went bankrupt and passed into the hands of profiteers who thought nothing of evicting their destitute and starving tenants.

In 1848, under the leadership of William Smith O'Brien and spurred by the writings of John Mitchel (who had been deported to Australia for publishing the seditious journal *United Irishman*), what remained of Young Ireland staged and bungled an armed insurrection. Its participants followed Mitchel to Australia. For almost a decade, the nationalist movement lay dormant and the Irish language and economy languished through neglect. Industrialization was financed by London only in Ulster, which attached itself commercially to the industrial northwest of England, alienating itself still further from the rest of Ireland, where there were virtually no manufacturers. Circumstances were preparing Ulster for separation.

HOME RULE

After the collapse of the repeal movement, the nationalists regrouped behind the Home Rule proposal, which would have restored at least a measure of autonomy to the Irish nation. After 1875, the leader of the Home Rule party at Westminster was Charles Stewart Parnell, an Irish Protestant and charismatic leader who implemented the policy of "obstruction," or withholding his considerable political support to gain concessions for Ireland. Parnell's tactical brilliance secured the admiration and cooperation of William Gladstone, the Liberal prime minister; despite their efforts, however, the Home Rule Bill was twice defeated in Parliament. Shortly thereafter, Parnell suffered a serious blow to his reputation: Two British civil servants were murdered in Dublin's Phoenix Park, and *The Times* published a forged letter — allegedly from Parnell — condoning the killings. Then, in 1888, a divorce proceeding revealed Parnell's liaison with a colleague's wife; he was condemned by Protestant England and Catholic Ireland, his followers dropped away, and he died in disgrace 3 years later at the age of 45.

Nationalist leadership passed to the Sinn Féin (Ourselves Alone), a party founded in 1905 by Arthur Griffith, who favored an independent Irish Parliament. Despite the resistance of Ulster's Orangemen, a society formed to protect the privileges and liberties of Protestants, and the organization of the paramilitary Ulster Volunteers, a Home Rule Bill was finally enacted in 1914. But the Orange militants had succeeded in amending the bill to give Ulster's six counties, with their Protestant majority, the option of seceding from Ireland and remaining in the Union. The outbreak of World War I fatally delayed implementation of the bill, and Ireland, on the eve of its independence, stood divided against itself.

EASTER RISING

The Easter Rebels of 1916, also known as the Irish Volunteers, looked to England's enemy, the Germans, for aid as Hugh O'Neill had looked to the Spanish and Wolfe Tone to the French. On *Good Friday,* 1916, their emissary to Berlin, Roger Casement, was captured by the British while returning to warn that German support would not be forthcoming. (Casement was convicted before a military court and hanged.) The Volunteers canceled what was to have been a national insurgence, but the Dublin contingent, hopeless of success, rose to martyrdom on *Easter Monday.* The 1,200 Volunteers seized strategic buildings around the city; on the steps of the General Post Office, leader Patrick Pearse read the proclamation of an Irish Republic. British troops, ordered to dislodge the rebels, left central Dublin in ruins. Seventeen rebel leaders — including Pearse, Thomas McDonough, John McBride, Joseph Plunkett, and James Connolly — died before a firing squad. Public outrage at the executions persuaded the British to commute the sentences of William Cosgrave, later president of the Free State, and Eamon de Valera, later president of the provisional government of the Republic.

The martyrs, none of them important figures before death, became national heroes afterward. In the elections of 1919, Sinn Féin scored a landslide victory in parliamentary elections, but the deputies refused to take their seats, convening instead the Dáil Éireann (Assembly of Ireland) under de Valera's presidency and proclaiming the Republic once again. England implemented Home Rule, exempting from it the six counties of Ulster, but the Dáil would accept nothing short of total independence. Ireland burst into violence: The Irish Republican Army (IRA) under Sinn Féin leader Michael Collins waged a bloody guerrilla war with the Black and Tans, England's paramilitary police force to whom countless atrocities were attributed; British police fired on the crowds at a sporting event in Dublin's Croke Park; army barracks came under regular attack. The ordinary functions of government dissolved in subversion. In 1921, Griffith and Collins negotiated a treaty with Britain by which a new state, Saorstát Éireann (Irish Free State) was created as a dominion in the commonwealth and under the crown. The Dáil accepted the treaty, but de Valera rejected it and was repudiated by the Dáil. Griffith became the Free State's first president, and Collins, fearing a civil war, made overtures to de Valera, assuring him privately there would be no oath of allegiance to the crown in a new Irish constitution. But de Valera remained adamant and organized an "underground Republic" with himself as president, Sinn Féin as its party, and the IRA as its militia; it would acknowledge neither the crown nor the partition of Ireland.

IRISH FREE STATE

In 1922, incensed by a Free State constitution that embodied the terms of the treaty, IRA troops occupied the Four Courts, the building in Dublin that houses the superior courts of Ireland. Under enormous pressure from Britain, the Free State moved in troops and gunboats and a few days later commenced a series of raids on Republican headquarters in Dublin hotels. Republicans and Free Staters were at war. Political unity once again escaped the Irish, and the country quaked with assassinations and skirmishes. Griffith died in August and Collins a few days later in an ambush near Cork. In 1923, de Valera declared a cease-fire. He agreed to enter the Dáil in 1927, whereupon Sinn Féin drew away from him to the leftist frontier of Republican intransigence. De Valera founded a new party, Fianna Fáil, whose members he urged to take the oath of allegiance to the crown as he had done — with "mental reservations." Fianna Fáil acquired a majority in 1932 and a new government, headed by de Valera, was formed. A new constitution was promulgated in 1937, declaring the nation the Republic of Eire and abolishing the oath of allegiance to the crown. In 1949, Eire withdrew from the commonwealth; at the same time, Britain, to establish a legal basis for partition, referred the question to the heavily Protestant Ulster Parliament seated at Stormont, which put the issue of union before a popular referendum whose outcome was never in doubt.

PARTITION

Since the late 1920s, the industrialized cities of Northern Ireland — Belfast and Derry — and many of the larger towns have divided into sectarian camps. In the 1960s, a Catholic civil rights movement agitated for Catholic representation at Stormont in proportion to the Catholic population, which brought a violent response from the Protestants, to whom the cause seemed synonymous with reunification with the Republic. The IRA, now an extralegal militia outlawed even in the Republic, came to the defense of the Catholic constituency. Confronted by virtual civil war, which Stormont was powerless to stop since it represented only one side, Britain suspended the Northern Ireland legislature in 1972. Stepping between the warring factions, the British army became a target of IRA hostility along with the paramilitary Ulster Defense Force. But now, bound by the legal precedent of the 1949 referendum, Britain has no way of withdrawing from Ulster without a majority mandate, and Ulster has no way of forming a government to which both sides can consent and thereby impose law and order without British intervention.

Ulster Protestants are proud of their heritage and fearful of losing not only property but some of their rights and liberties as British subjects under the Irish Republican constitution, which embodies the moral doctrines of the Catholic church. Efforts within the Republic to conciliate Northern Ireland by expunging from the constitution certain clauses — such as the one against divorce — offensive to Protestants have proven futile. Further, the Republic's economy is weak and agricultural, plagued by unemployment and inadequate social services, while Northern Ireland is industrial and shares the benefits of the British welfare system. The Republicans, however, have never acknowledged Britain's authority over any portion of Ireland, and regard partition as an act of gerrymandering by an illegitimate power. The intransigence of both sides makes reconciliation seem unlikely, despite recent agreements and attempts at rapprochement between the British and Irish prime ministers.

Literature

 In Ireland, the magic of language has from the earliest times conferred a special and exalted status on those who command it. The poets of ancient Ireland had a reputation for supernatural powers and may have belonged to a caste that practiced sorcery. Even in the modern era, men of letters have been accorded high political honors unheard of in other countries. Douglas Hyde (1860–1949), one of those responsible for the revival of the Irish language and literature through the founding of the Gaelic League in 1893, became president of the Republic in 1938, and the poet and Nobel laureate W. B. Yeats (1865–1939) served as a senator from 1922 to 1928. In addition, the Irish language has imparted to the English speech of the country a haunting music and a distinctive, cantering rhythm.

The *filidhe* (master-poets of the Celts) earned their prestige by subjecting themselves to a rigorous course of training at bardic academies where the curriculum demanded memorization of lengthy sagas and learning composition in complex meters. Many graduates of the academies were attracted by monastic life, and their manuscripts and magnificent calligraphy and illumination made them Europe's preeminent students of literature. Between the 8th and 16th centuries these monks transcribed the oral traditions of which they were the living archives and, by keeping them in circulation, preserved them for posterity.

From various manuscript sources scholars can reconstruct the two great saga cycles, that of the Red Branch warriors of Ulster province and that of Finn MacCool and his Fenian band (the Fianna). The Ulster cycle constitutes a portion of the tribal history of the Uliad, who gave their name to the northernmost of Ireland's four provinces, and seems to have become current during the 1st century BC, though a quantity of older lore had been incorporated in the cycle. The king of the Ulidians in the cycle is Conchobar (pronounced *Con*-a-choor), whose castle stood at Emain Macha near modern Keady, County Armagh. But the protagonist is Cu Chulainn, the Hound of Ulster, offspring of the sun god and hero of the tribe.

The cycle centers around the Tain Bo Cualinge (The Cattle Raid of Cooley), an epic narrative in which the semi-legendary Queen Maeve of Connaught leads an expeditionary force toward Cooley (near Dundalk) to steal Conchobar's prized Brown Bull. Cu Chulainn singlehandedly holds the invading army at bay while the Ulstermen recover from a 9-day illness.

Cu Chulainn adds to the conventional virtues of courage and honor an impulsive disdain for any check to his appetites. He is the arch-individualist, a larger-than-life figure who postpones his first encounter with the Connaughtmen to keep a date with a woman, and who slays in single combat his best friend and his only son despite the promptings of human tenderness. His daring and determination together with a roguish impetuosity established a comic tradition in Irish literature.

Cu Chulainn was specifically a hero of the men of Ulster. But between the commencement of the O'Neill dynasty and the height of the Norse incursions, Irish society was challenged to transcend the old clan loyalties for the sake of military unity. This was achieved politically in the person of Brian Ború and in literature through the Fenian cycle, which was the first truly national, rather than tribal, epic.

Finn MacCool, his son Ossian, his grandson Oscar, and his comrades Diarmaid and Cailte commanded the Fianna, the standing army of professional warriors said to have been mustered to the service of Cormac Mac Art, son of the founder of the Tara monarchy, in the 3rd century AD. The Fenians were, from the outset, national rather than tribal heroes. Unlike the Ulster cycle, composed mostly in prose and incorporating myths in a highly learned manner, the Fenian cycle springs directly from popular folklore and employs a ballad meter to which the music of the common people was easily adapted. It is more immediate and dramatic. Its characteristic form is the monologue or dialogue and its setting is the Christian era into which some Fenian hero has survived to speak, often to St. Patrick, of bygone days of glory. Not originally a product of the bardic academies, the Fenian cycle did not enter the courtly repertoire until the 12th century, by which time it had already displaced the Ulster sagas in popular favor.

In contrast to Cu Chulainn, champion of a civilized nobility, the Fenians choose to live outside the pale of settlements and courts, preferring the woods and wilds. They are hunters rather than soldiers, akin to the gods of nature and place worshiped in the vernacular religion. It is from the Fenian tradition that Irish poetry receives its extraordinary sensitivity to nature:

> Arran of the many stags,
> The sea strikes against its shoulder . . .
> Skittish deer are on her peaks,
> Delicious berries on her manes . . .
> — *The Colloquy of the Old Men,*
>   a Fenian romance from a
>   15th-century manuscript,
>   translated by Myles Dillon

From the stories themselves flow the lyrical richness of Irish poetry, the sweetness and nostalgia of popular folk song, and the whole romantic spirit, dash, and panache of Irish history. The Fenian cycle inaugurates a dramatic and intensely personal literary style, which became the expressive mode of the Irish nation and provided the archetype of the outlaw brotherhood in which the 19th-century revolutionaries cast themselves.

The *filidhe* and its elite tradition were destroyed by the social upheavals caused by the Plantation policy, which replaced Irish landowners with English and later Scottish colonists prepared to offer allegiance to the crown. It was not until the 18th century, however, that it was finally extinguished. As late as 1781, a young schoolteacher from Clondagach, County Clare, named Merriman, who had educated himself in the metrical complexities of bardic composition, published an epic satire in the Irish language called *The Midnight Court,* in which the women of Ireland indict the men for contempt of matrimony and obtain a conviction in the court of the Fairy Queen. The poem is elegant, racy, and dreamlike, but its ribaldry proved too strong for a public taste narrowed by oppressive works that were pious and patriotic. The poem was suppressed, though portions of it can be heard recited from memory in some modern Irish-speaking households. Merriman, last of the *filidhe,* wrote nothing more and died in 1805.

Literature in English has been written in Ireland since the 14th century, but many of the Anglo-Irish literati owe little to the national traditions. Irish was the native tongue, and the native populace, denied and excluded from educational institutions by the Penal Laws, produced a glorious but impermanent body of unwritten poetry.

The chief educational institution in Ireland was Trinity College, Dublin, founded in 1592 as a university for the Protestant gentry. Trinity was the intellectual nursery of an extraordinary series of writers whose work places them more properly in a history of English rather than Irish literature. Yet their remarkable singularity of expression was one that could only have been nurtured in an environment where talk, conversation, and language provided the main indoor entertainment.

Chronologically, the first of these writers was Jonathan Swift (1667–1745), author of *Gulliver's Travels,* who is buried in St. Patrick's Cathedral, Dublin, of which he was dean. Next was William Congreve (1670–1729), author of one of the greatest comedies in the English language, *The Way of the World.* Then came Oliver Goldsmith (1730?–74), the son of a Church of Ireland clergyman, most famous for his play *She Stoops to Conquer* and for his friendship with Dr. Samuel Johnson. Finally there was Oscar Wilde (1854–1900), the flamboyant author of the play *The Importance of Being Earnest* and the novel *The Picture of Dorian Gray.*

Two Dubliners who did not attend Trinity need to be mentioned: One is Richard Brinsley Sheridan (1751–1816), the descendant of a famous Anglo-Irish family, whose masterpieces include *The Rivals* and *The School for Scandal;* the other is George Bernard Shaw (1856–1950), widely considered to be the greatest dramatist in the English language after Shakespeare. Shaw spent his first 20 years living in seedy gentility in Dublin. Even after he left to take up residence (and literary sovereignty) in London he never failed to involve himself in Irish affairs, whether they concerned Parnell's divorce or the Irish revolutionary Sir Roger David Casement's homosexuality. Indeed he is one of the few writers in history who is as famous for his political curmudgeonry as for his great works (*St. Joan; Pygmalion; Heartbreak House*). A statue of him by Prince Paul Troubetzkoy stands outside the *National Gallery of Ireland,* to which he left a substantial part of his fortune.

Occasionally the Protestant Ascendancy did produce a writer who was truly Irish in sympathy. One of these was Thomas Moore (1779–1852). Moore was a friend and the eulogizer of Robert Emmet (executed in 1803), the prototype of the Irishman who is both Protestant and nationalist. Emmet himself deserves a place in Irish literature for his speech from the dock which contains the immortal words "Let no man write my epitaph . . ." Moore was a literary, though not a militant, patriot who wrote in the plaintive style of Irish folk song, often to popular airs. Songs like "The Minstrel Boy" and "The Harp That Once Through Tara's Halls" were ambassadors from romantic Ireland to the English gentry and helped revise their image of the Irish as crude and barbarous.

In 1842, *The Nation* magazine began publishing the poems and translations of James Clarence Mangan and Samuel Ferguson. Their work, infused with the energy and misty grandeur of the Irish language, excited interest in ancient literature, particularly the Fenian cycle. Its vibrant tapestry of hunts and fatal love, journeys to the underworld, battles between mortals and ghosts, sojourns in fairyland, and tone of wistful longing for the lost ardor of youth appealed to the romantic temperament of the times.

But the burgeoning political and literary movement did not achieve the status of a renaissance until the appearance of the work of W. B. Yeats (1865–1939), whose early imitations of folk poetry grafted French symbolism onto Irish folklore. Introduced to the Ulster cycle by his friend and patroness of the Irish Literary Renaissance, Lady (Augusta) Gregory, Yeats became fascinated by the figure of Cu Chulainn and meditated on this image of the kind of reckless and heroic action he admired but shrank from in many poems.

Son of an atheist father, the portraitist J. B. Yeats, grandson of the dandyish Church of Ireland rector at Drumcliffe, County Sligo, brother of the expressionist painter Jack Yeats — William Butler Yeats was an unlikely Irishman. He was a member of various occult societies, an admirer of the English and a defender of the Ascendancy, a member of London literary society, and, in his youth, one of those bohemian aesthetes whose tastes and style were schooled by the lyrical poetry of A. C. Swinburne, the humanist doctrines of Walter Pater, and the heroic fantasies of William Morris. Yet he was also an ardent supporter of Charles Parnell, briefly a member of the Fenian Brotherhood, and a student of Irish folklore. Debarred from religious belief by the skepticism inherited from his father, Yeats invented a personal cosmology in which the clash and union of opposites, represented by the phases of the moon, became the dynamic force in history. ("By opposition, square and trine . . .," he says in the poem "In Memory of Major Robert Gregory.") The great poems of his middle years take their intellectual structure from this esoteric and enchantingly bizarre mythology, which perfectly expressed the contradictions of his own nature. Passionately attached to the peasantry, in whom he saw the wellspring of Ireland's creative energy, Yeats was equally passionately the champion of the Ascendancy, whom he regarded as Ireland's intellectual elite capable of giving coherent shape to the emotions of the masses. In his last years he abandoned his highly personalized mysticism to return with new freedom to the subject matter of his earliest days. Pathologically shy, Yeats was nevertheless proud and a trifle vain of his striking good looks. He became one of Ireland's leading public men and it was, ironically, this status rather than his years of obsession with mysticism and folklore that inspired his greatest poem, "Among School Children," with its famous last line, "How can we know the dancer from the dance?"

Yeats often found himself embroiled in controversy because of the parochialism of the Dublin public, whose tastes were circumscribed by oppression and a conservative church. Yeats's own verse was not the source of his troubles; rather it was his defense of his friends and colleagues — Synge, Joyce, O'Casey. That he was a patriot, albeit an eccentric one, a celebrant of the Easter Rising, and, in his youth, a slightly uncomfortable agitator, did not go unrewarded; in 1922 he was appointed a senator of the Irish Free State. In debate, he spoke magnificently and pugnaciously against censorship and also against the constitutional prohibition of divorce, which he characterized as an insult to the Protestant minority. He helped to found the *Abbey Theatre,* now a national institution, but when angry mobs stormed the stage, infuriated at a reference to women's undergarments in Synge's *Playboy of the Western World,* Yeats stepped before the curtains and sternly reproached them. When they did it 20 years later over the appearance of a prostitute in O'Casey's *The Plough and the Stars,* Yeats confronted the mobs a second time, booming at them: "You have disgraced yourselves again!" Ireland loves drama, and Yeats provided drama in abundance. In return, Ireland grudgingly offered him its adoration for the splendor and valor of his quixotic idealism.

Yeats believed that great poetry must be rooted in place, and "The Lake Isle of Innisfree," "The Fiddler of Dooney," "The Man Who Dreamed of Faeryland," and others of his early poems are set close to Sligo Town. But the most important landmarks in his verse are Knocknarea, atop of which stands the pile of stones known as Queen Maeve's Cairn, and Ben Bulben, the limestone mesa across Sligo Bay. Between these two mountains, spectral horsemen called Dananns were said to ride each night:

> The host is riding from Knocknarea
> And over the grave of Clooth-na-Bare;
> Caoilte tossing his burning hair,
> And Niamh calling *Away, come away* . . .
> ("The Hosting of the Sidhe," ca. 1899)

To these horsemen, Yeats, buried in Drumcliffe churchyard at the foot of Ben Bulben, addressed himself in his epitaph:

> *Cast a cold eye*
> *On life, on death.*
> *Horseman, pass by!*
> ("Under Ben Bulben," 1938)

Yeats's work is among the glories of modern literature (he won the Nobel Prize in 1923), yet he was unstintingly generous and supportive of other writers. He encouraged the younger Anglo-Irish writer John Millington Synge to rediscover his roots by visiting the Aran Islands in Galway Bay. Synge's sojourn on Inishmaan, as well as in other Irish-speaking regions, inspired him to combine the realism of Ibsen with the wild, fantastical speech of the Irish countryside in plays that treated the life of Ireland's impoverished rural proletariat with Chekhovian irony and unsentimental honesty. Synge never romanticized, and his plays have no heroes. Christy Mahon, protago-

"The Hosting of the Sidhe," from *The Collected Poems of W. B. Yeats* (New York: Macmillan, 1956). © The Macmillan Company 1956. Reprinted by permission of Macmillan Inc., Macmillan London Ltd., M. B. Yeats, and Anne Yeats.

nist of *The Playboy of the Western World,* finds himself suddenly a celebrity in a strange village after confessing to the murder of his own father and the object, thanks to his prestige, of the affections of Pegeen Mike, the daughter of a publican. When Christy proves innocent of the crime, Pegeen turns on him in a paroxysm of disappointment because, having shown himself to be more tender than wicked, he lacks the notoriety to elevate her life beyond its drudgery; in the last line of the play, having "lost her only playboy of the western world," she realizes, too late, that she loves him. In *Riders to the Sea,* set in the Aran Islands, an old woman accepts the drowning of her last surviving son with a chilly stoicism that is at once tragic and appalling. Synge's is a vision without comfort, as bleak as Dreiser's and as perversely comic as Chekhov's.

Synge died in 1909 at the age of 38, but not before he had given the *Abbey Theatre* and the playwrights of Ireland a dramatic style, often vulgarized, alas, into "peasant-quality" plays in which quaintness and condescending coyness displace Synge's unsparing realism. Synge invented a dialect in which the idioms and constructions of Irish are rendered directly into English. So exquisite a tool did this dialect become that Synge used it to splendid effect in his translations of Petrarch and Villon. But no other playwright could manage the trick.

Synge's example, and Yeats's solicitous encouragement, bore fruit in the work of the next great *Abbey* playwright, Sean O'Casey (1884–1964). Born in the Dublin slums, O'Casey, a Protestant, was the first figure of the Literary Renaissance to spring directly from the proletariat and to make the urban working class the subject of his attention. O'Casey needed no synthetic dialect; the speech of Dublin came naturally to him. His politics, however, came as a mild shock to his colleagues — most especially Yeats, whom O'Casey remembered with wry affection in his memoirs — for he professed to be a Communist. Equally shocking to the public was his insistence on showing Dublin's raw backside. The presence of a prostitute in *The Plough and the Stars* together with the meeting of revolutionary patriots in the unholy precincts of a pub provoked riots at the play's première. Two years later, embittered at *The Plough*'s reception and furious because Yeats refused to produce his next play, *The Silver Tassie,* O'Casey moved to England, never to return. Nothing he wrote thereafter quite equaled his early works, which also included *Juno and the Paycock* and *The Shadow of a Gunman.*

O'Casey's social passion, his sense of grievance, and his identification with his working class characters left him more vulnerable than Yeats and Synge to sentimentality; yet his affection for the outlaw and the outcast recalls the Fenian tradition and rescues his early plays from bathos. O'Casey's spiritual successor among Irish playwrights was Brendan Behan (1923–64). Housepainter, drunkard, and self-made intellectual, Behan, between 1956 and 1958, disposed of his mammoth talent in three works — *Borstal Boy,* his memoir of life in a British reformatory where he was imprisoned for revolutionary terrorism on English soil; *The Quare Fellow,* a drama of prison life under the pall of an inmate's imminent execution; and his magnum opus, *The Hostage,* after which he subsided into notoriety and drink.

Behan's last words, spoken to the nun at his hospital bedside, were: "God bless you, sister, and may all your sons be bishops." He lived and wrote with Rabelaisian gusto. In 1937, he joined the outlawed Irish Republican Army and gave his youth to the cause, although he grew to distrust the fanaticism he saw in it. *The Hostage* is a kind of tragic farce in which an IRA contingent, commanded by a bizarre Ascendancy enthusiast, seizes a young British soldier and holds him hostage in a Dublin brothel on Nelson Street where the residents include, among the working girls, two outrageous homosexuals, a devout and lascivious spinster, and an innocent housemaid who falls in love with the hostage. The Republicans threaten to kill the prisoner in order to force the reprieve of two of their own facing execution in a Belfast jail. The play is punctuated by songs that lampoon Irish piety, by dances and jokes, and, finally, by the gunfire of a police raid in which the hostage is tragically killed. Characters frequently address the audience, the accompanist remains onstage throughout, and no pretense is made that this is anything but theater; yet it captures the emotions anyway, having dispensed with every theatrical convention except the heart's truth.

James Joyce (1882–1941), the titan of Irish prose, exempted himself from the Literary Renaissance — he referred to Yeats's Celtic Twilight as the "Cultic Toilette" — and at age 22 expatriated himself to the Continent. He took with him a handsome but intellectually unprepossessing shopgirl, Nora Barnacle, who became for him the personification of Dublin, in the environs of which Joyce set everything he ever wrote.

Joyce's insistence on fixing his most obscure works to the real, even trivial, details of the city he remembered amounted to the most creative obsession in modern letters. As a young man, growing up in a middle class home, educated in Catholic prep schools and at Trinity College, Joyce had been attracted to the realism of Ibsen and learned Norwegian to read his plays in the original tongue.

Ulysses, the huge novel that established Joyce's preeminent reputation, follows Leopold Bloom, a Dublin Jew, his wife, Molly, and young Stephen Dedalus, Joyce's surrogate, in their minute-by-minute progress through a single day — June 16, 1904 — in Dublin. Joyce employed a stream-of-consciousness technique to record the random associations of his characters' thoughts. Readers were shocked by the eroticism of these interior monologues, and the book was until quite recently banned in Ireland. Yet Dubliners who managed to obtain copies were fascinated by the many living personalities parading across the pages and by the accuracy with which Joyce had observed and remembered the city, its features, and its speech. What few realized was how brilliantly Joyce had transformed the details of Dublin life — newspaper articles from June 16, 1904, brand-name household goods, idioms of local patois — into symbols of Europe's mythological and psychic heritage represented by *The Odyssey,* the novel's controlling metaphor. Nor do many readers appreciate Joyce's love for his characters until Molly Bloom's long interior soliloquy on the edge of sleep.

On Bloomsday, June 16 of every year, dedicated Joyceans gather in Dublin to retrace the routes followed by *Ulysses*'s characters: from the Martello tower (a Napoleonic-era fortress) where Joyce, like Stephen Dedalus, lived briefly in his student days, through the city, past nearly every point of interest or importance, to Eccles Street, where the Blooms resided. Fans of Joyce's next and last book, *Finnegans Wake,* are rather few. It is probably the most frustrating and impenetrable book ever written, for language itself is the subject. Nearly every one of the book's 237,600 words has several meanings at once. Joyce, master of almost every European language, enlisted them all to create this huge stream-of-consciousness work — the sleeping, dreaming thought flow of the Earwicker family of Dublin, whose matriarch, Ann (known also as Anna Livia Plurabelle), is at once the spirit of the river Liffey and the form of the book.

Joyce's works belong to the Red Branch line — comic, cosmic, larger than life — but Samuel Beckett (1906–89), briefly his secretary in the 1930s and another Dublin expatriate who lived on the Continent, belongs to no tradition, though he shows the influence of Joyce and Synge. A founding member of the avant-garde and Ireland's third Nobel Prize winner (after Yeats and Shaw), Beckett's enigmatic plays and novels seem less overtly Irish than the works of his compatriot, although here and there in *Waiting for Godot* one hears echoes of the Irish music hall, and the astute reader or listener will realize that *Play* is set in Foxrock, a Dublin suburb. Beckett, the quintessential absurdist, displays in works as dauntingly obtuse in starkness as *Finnegans Wake* the characteristic daring and individualism of the Irish.

Ireland has dispensed fine writing to the world — this is no provincial tradition — with astonishing abundance in this century. Among the lesser-known luminaries, some of whom have fallen into the shadows of the gods, are Frank O'Connor, memoirist, essayist, translator, and chronicler nonpareil of literary Ireland; Patrick Kavanagh, Ireland's only beat poet; Louis MacNeice, the Belfast poet; Flann O'Brien (*At Swim-Two-Birds*), surrealist virtuoso; Denis O'Donoghue, the literary critic; playwrights Brian Friel and Hugh Leonard, who have enjoyed notable successes on Broadway; poets Thomas Kinsella John Montague, Derek Mahon, and Seamus Heaney; and, to run on and on, Padraic Colum, J. P. Donleavey (who also writes under the pseudonym Myles na Gopaleen), Denis Johnstone, Iris Murdoch, Brian Moore, Edna O'Brien, Liam O'Flaherty, Sean O'Faolain . . . as though all the vital energies of the nation, pent up through 700 years of oppression, were erupting. The spectacle of the Irish literary explosion is without parallel in history.

Architecture

Ireland is full of picturesque ruins and ancient structures, which are part of its charm for Americans unaccustomed to architecture older than a few centuries. Along every Irish road and river lie Stone Age tombs, ruined abbeys, decayed or restored castles, Palladian-style manor houses, and stately Georgian mansions. And the thatch-roofed and whitewashed or fieldstone cottages in the remoter regions are most appealing for their timeless, homespun simplicity.

The oldest structures, some of which have been dated to 3000 BC, are the megalithic monuments — the tumuli and stone circles at Carrowmore in County Donegal and Carrowkeel in County Sligo; the passage grave complex at Brugh na Boinne in County Meath; and the decorated standing stones and dolmens scattered about the countryside. Whether these monuments were built by an indigenous people or by immigrants is not known, but they are similar to those found in Europe and England (Stonehenge is perhaps the best-known example). It is thought that these structures were prehistoric shrines and that the Celts, who began arriving in Ireland around 500 BC, also endowed the sites with religious or magical significance.

The earliest Celtic structures are the *dúns,* fortresses enclosed by dry-stone walls and often built atop megalithic shrines or ring forts. The walls served both to keep cattle in and to protect the settlement from attack. The most famous and impressive of the fortresses is Dún Aengus on the Aran isle of Inishmore in Galway Bay. Dún Aengus is a semicircle; its open side is a cliff that drops precipitously 266 feet to the roiling Atlantic, giving the impression that the missing half of the circle had collapsed into the ocean in some terrible cataclysm. Other notable ringed fortresses include Tara in County Meath and Grianán of Aileach in County Donegal.

Early Celtic dwellings were built of timber and wattle and have not survived. In treeless areas people lived in stone dwellings; their *clocháns* (beehive huts) were constructed in corbeled fashion, with the stones overlapping each other. The early Christian churches were also built in the beehive style, although some variations were introduced — such as a rectangular shape and a pitched roof. Two examples are Skellig Michael, off the Kerry coast, and the Gallarus Oratory in County Kerry; both are thought to date from the 8th century.

The round tower is another relic of early Christian architecture. Ranging in height from 70 to 120 feet, slightly tapered, and topped by a conical roof, these were bell towers as well as places of refuge from the attacks of Viking invaders. (The doorway was located high above the ground; when besieged, inhabitants withdrew the adjoining ladder for safety.) A fine example of an early Christian round tower is the freestanding 11th-century structure at Glendalough in County Wicklow.

Irish monastic and ecclesiastic architecture further developed with the introduction to Ireland of the Romanesque style during the 12th century. It was embraced with some enthusiasm by native artisans, and ornate stone carvings — human and animal heads, chevrons, interlace, and foliage — decorate the arches, doorways, capitals, and sometimes windows of the churches of this period. The Chapel of Cormac, situated on the Rock of Cashel in County Tipperary, is the earliest Irish Romanesque structure in the country, and Clonfert Cathedral in County Galway is perhaps the most ornate; both have heavily embellished portals.

The invasion of the Normans in 1170 changed the face of Irish architecture forever, for they brought with them from England and Wales the designs and styles, proportions, shapes, and decorative devices prevalent there. Eager to colonize, they began a flurry of cathedral and castle building that lasted from the 12th to the 17th century. The numerous churches constructed during this period tended to be large and Gothic in style, with tall lancet windows and pointed arches; St. Patrick's Cathedral in Dublin is a fine example. The typical Norman fortress had a square stone keep enclosed by curtain walls linking four circular corner towers. King John's Castle in Limerick City, built in 1210, combines all of these features. The towerhouse, a structure favored by both Norman and native Irish, dates from the 15th to the 17th century. Most of them were built, however, just after the Statute of 1429, which offered a £10 subsidy to any person building such a tower within the Pale. The so-called £10 houses were fortified dwellings built of stone, four or five stories high, with narrow slitted windows and steeply pitched roofs. A very simple Norman-built towerhouse is Donore Castle in County Meath.

During the late 17th century, domestic dwellings began to look less like fortresses and more like the classical mansions popular in England. This meant that houses were often built of brick, with hipped roofs and dormer windows, as exemplified by Beaulieu in County Louth. Very soon, however, the Irish and English imagination was captured by Palladianism, a reinterpretation of the design principles evolved by Italian architect Andrea Palladio in the mid-16th century. The arrangement of columns and arches in the façade of Bellamont Forest in County Cavan is a typical Palladian motif.

The 18th century saw the architectural expansion and enhancement of Ireland's urban centers — Belfast, Cork, Dublin, Limerick, and Waterford. During this period Dublin received a heady endowment of new buildings designed in the classical style — incorporating elements from ancient Greek and Roman architecture — such as Trinity College, the Four Courts, the Custom House, and the Parliament buildings (now the Bank of Ireland). Georgian architecture was also popular, and elegant Georgian squares — gracious greens presided over by tall brick townhouses with pillared doorways and distinctive fanlights — appeared not only in Dublin (Fitzwilliam and Merrion Squares), but also in Limerick City (Newtown Pery) and in Belfast (Donegall Square). Neo-classicism remained in vogue during the 19th century, although Irish architects also flirted briefly with various revivals of the Gothic style (St. Finbarre's Cathedral in Cork), Italianate (the Custom House in Belfast), and Edwardian (Belfast City Hall).

The common dwellings of Ireland remained virtually unchanged from earliest Celtic times: They were usually only one room heated by a central fireplace that vented its smoke through a hole in the roof. Stables and byres were built adjacent, although animals sometimes shared the living quarters for warmth. The central hearth style with hipped roof was most common in the eastern counties, while homes in the northwest had a bed alcove and room extensions. In the southwest, gables appeared, rising above the thatching, which replaced stone as the common roofing material. Two-story dwellings did not appear until the late 19th century, when, after the depopulation caused by the famine, efforts were made to eliminate the thatch-roofed cottages altogether and replace them with more modern accommodations.

Today, the art of thatching has been practically lost, though many old vernacular houses are still in use. Departing visitors whose route back to Shannon Airport takes them through Adare, County Limerick, can see an especially pretty row of thatch-roofed houses on their way through town, and chances are they'll also see a thatcher at work, because the roofs are meticulously kept. The traditional style has also been revived somewhat in villages of thatch-roofed cottages — with open fireplaces and flagstone floors, as well as electricity, modern heating, and plumbing — built for the use of vacationers. But more than likely, what the visitor will remember most is the haunting picture of the same simple dwellings scattered forlorn and deserted throughout the Irish countryside, left to decay when their owners left for a better life elsewhere. The history of Ireland is indeed told in its architecture.

Traditional Music and Dance

The harp is the instrument most associated with Ireland from ancient times; it was used for centuries by learned bards who entertained the royal Gaelic courts with recitations of poetry and sagas. After the dissolution of the Gaelic courts ordered by the Cromwellian Act of Settlement in 1652, the bards scattered to the countryside, where they mingled with folk poets, and a general intermarriage of their styles ensued. The classical airs that evolved from such collaboration — "The Coolun," "Roisin Dubh," and "Eileen Aroon" — present a refinement and gravity uncommon in folk music.

The harpists traveled among the houses of the rural gentry, playing traditional songs and creating new ones on commission. The greatest of these harpists was Turlough O'Carolan (1670–1738), whose compositions wed a certain European sophistication (perhaps acquired in Dublin) with a native Irish sensibility: Though his melodies are quite lengthy and complex, they also flirt now and again with the popular gapped scales, never losing touch with the folk spirit. Some have become staples of modern Irish ensembles.

Another instrument always associated with Ireland is the bagpipe. The *uilleann* (pronounced *ill*-en) pipes differ from those played in Scotland in that the bellows is pumped with the elbow, a softer reed is used, the drones are slung across the leg of the seated player, and there are keys that change the drone notes when depressed with the heel of the right hand, enabling the player to produce chords. The *uilleann* has been called the "Irish organ," for it is capable of extremely rich, resonant sound, though with its straps and harnesses it resembles an instrument of torture. The west of Ireland, particularly County Clare, was until recently the home of fine Irish piping; but the recent rise in popularity of Irish music throughout the world has persuaded numbers of young Irish (who might otherwise have belabored guitars) to take up the arduous study of this noble and exacting instrument.

While traditional dance music is played on pipes as well as fiddles, the "big airs" — the slow and majestic classical tunes — are especially moving when played on the expansive pipes. Although the older generation of pipers has passed away, many recordings of such great pipers as Willy Clancy and Leo Rowesome still are available. The McPeakes of Belfast were three generations of harpers, pipers, and singers led by Frank McPeake, reputed to have been the first piper skilled enough to sing to his own accompaniment. Today three of the best younger pipers are Paddy Maloney, of the *Chieftains;* Finbar Furey, of the *Furey Brothers;* and the virtuoso Joe McKenna.

The piper produces the melody — trills, grace notes, and other flourishes

— by moving his fingers to open or close the holes of the chanter, or pipe. Flutes and pennywhistles are played in the same way, without tonguing. The great Sligo fiddler Michael Coleman, who emigrated to America and recorded there in the 1920s, evolved a similar ornamental style for his instrument, one which has since become the standard. The musical embellishments used by fiddlers, pipers, flutists, and pennywhistlers perfectly suit the structure of Irish dance music — the jigs, reels, and hornpipes — in which a sinuous and fluid melody rushes along with scarcely a pause for breath, diving and soaring with dizzying exuberance. The stuttering throb of the *bodhrán* (a hand-held drum beaten with a double-headed stick) gives the music an irresistible rhythmic momentum more like jazz or flamenco than anything in the other Celtic musical traditions.

The music of County Kerry tends to be less hectic and more regularly cadenced than that of the rest of the country. Some scholars believe it represents an older style. Polkas and *schottisches* (a Scottish country dance), not found elsewhere in Ireland, are performed in Kerry, as are longer, more elegant dances. A fine example of the latter, which will seem more classical and less Irish to the average listener and more like the harp music of Carolan, is the work of Eugene O'Donnell, the fiddler.

The Connemara region on Ireland's far western coast, a rocky and forbidding region north of Galway City, is famous for its singers and for its stately, mysterious ballads. The vocal technique resembles that of piping and Sligo fiddling; some of the notes are changed or the tempo slowed, and the melody is delivered with a multitude of embellishments. The effect can be quite fascinating, as if one were listening to dance music in slow motion. The recordings of Joe Heaney of Carna provide excellent examples of the ballad style.

Ensembles of singers or musicians are not traditional in Ireland. Solo playing was the rule until the 1920s when record companies began to demand lively and audible renditions of dance tunes to supply the dance market in America; this prompted musicians to seek accompanists. During the 1950s, Sean O'Riada, a "serious" composer and harpsichordist, hearing the *ceildhe* (pronounced *kay*-lee) dance bands that had begun to form and sounded, as someone wrote, "like a tree full of blackbirds," conceived the idea of arranging Irish music for an orchestra of traditional instruments. He gathered a group of fiddlers, pipers, accordionists, whistlers, flutists, and drummers in Dublin and taught them their parts by ear (few could read music). The delightful result was *Ceolteori Cualain,* the first sophisticated folk music ensemble, for whom O'Riada provided many orchestrations that — though they were enriched with harmonies, counterpoint, even rudimentary fugues — never lost their simplicity and drive.

During the 1960s, the *Clancy Brothers* and *Tommy Makem* found an audience among folk music fans in America and introduced them to a species of Irish music worlds away from "Mother Macree" and the other products of the Hibernian division of Tin Pan Alley. Their repertoire included revolutionary and patriotic songs (as well as that pungent Irish subgenre, the antiwar song), sea chanteys, and children's songs, all of them delivered with robust good humor and taste. Since the disappearance of the harpers in the

19th century, music had rarely been a professional undertaking among the Irish, but the Clancys stimulated a new interest, and before long Ireland was in the midst of a ballad boom. Among the more successful groups were the *Dubliners,* a group of four — later five — men including Ronny Drew, a flamenco guitarist and master of the Dublin street ballad, and Barney McKenna, a wizard who pioneered the application of the Sligo style to the tenor banjo. The *Dubliners* have proved to be a durable institution, though, like most Irish musicians who want to earn a living by their art, they have had to seek audiences in England and on the Continent.

After the death of Sean O'Riada, a party of his alumni formed the *Chieftains* to carry on his style and bring it to a wider audience. They tightened the O'Riada sound and began running tunes together in patchwork medleys, sometimes juxtaposing contrasting sounds for dramatic effect. The *Chieftains* fathered a generation of such ensembles in Ireland and Scotland as well as America, where "Celtic" bands have begun to proliferate. Among the best Irish bands are *Planxty, Sweeny's Men,* the *Bothy Band,* and *De Danann;* they preserve the charm and melodic richness of traditional music but deliver it with the instrumental daring and emotional impact of rock.

Music clubs have lately begun to spring up in various Irish cities so that now musicians — who previously gathered only in a few pubs or at government-sponsored summer music festivals — may perform regularly. Concerts are rare, though, and a tourist must search pretty far in the country to find local pubs where musicians play. For years, music was like conversation to the Irish: They would no sooner pay for a song than for a chat. (For more information on dance as well as music, see "Traditional Irish Music" in *The Performing Arts,* DIVERSIONS.)

Food and Drink

 Ireland's location and climate have combined to produce an agricultural abundance: Its lush grasslands support a thriving livestock industry, resulting in good beef, lamb, and pork; its extensive waters yield a fine harvest of fish and seafood: sole, plaice, mackerel, sea trout, salmon, lobster and crab, prawns and scallops, oysters and mussels; its soil and mild climate nurture barley, wheat, sugar beets, and potatoes — as well as other vegetables, when Irish farmers can be persuaded to grow them.

At its best, Irish food is fresh, nourishing, and prepared simply. There are some regional variations and a few local specialties, but the real geographical division is between the coast and the interior. On the coast, which is heavily visited by travelers, food is on the whole good and its presentation attractive. The flat heart of the country has barely emerged from the dark English provincial ages that dominated food in Ireland for a century and a half. The "commercial hotel" — the haven of the turn-of-the-century English business traveler — established a horrendous food pattern that happily is breaking up. A typical meal here consisted of Windsor soup (a nondescript liquid full of floury lumps) and overdone roast beef, crowded on the plate by watery, overcooked vegetables and bathed in a thicker version of the soup called "gravy." This repast concluded with a heavy pudding doused in a nasty, viscous, yellow liquid miscalled "custard." You will rarely find this meal now in its pristine horror, but elements of "commercial" cooking still survive in the midlands and the wary traveler must forage around a little for better food.

That dire warning noted, we will now discuss *real* Irish food. The timing of meals in Ireland is important. The Irish food day is divided into three main meals and almost as many side events. The weight-conscious visitor will simply have to pick and choose and try to be selective.

A typical Irish breakfast starts with porridge (a flavorsome boiled oatmeal topped with cream) and continues through a main course of bacon and eggs accompanied by grilled tomatoes, toast, and orange marmalade. The eggs may be cooked any style and the bacon is good although not crisp. A black or white pudding (both are kinds of blood pudding) or even kidney or liver may accompany the meal. Tea is recommended over coffee with rare exceptions the Irish do not make coffee well. They make their tea strong and serve it with milk but will serve weak tea with lemon if asked.

A breakfast alternative offered on the coast is plaice, a delicate-tasting flounder-type fish, or fresh mackerel if they are running. Try both for a new and delightful breakfast experience.

Instead of toast a coarse, whole-meal "brown bread" — homebaked, nutty, and delicious — or "soda bread" — plain white, usually made without raisins (unlike the unauthentic version often served in American restaurants) may be served.

The midmorning snack — a cup of tea or coffee with a biscuit (cookie) or sweet bun — is very popular in urban Ireland: Some temples to the practice are the *Bewley's Cafés* in Dublin, Limerick, and other major cities (offering sinfully sweet sticky buns and coffee topped with Jersey cream), *Lydon House* in Galway, and *Thompson's* in Cork. Over such matins, much business is conducted, gossip exchanged, and romances started or continued.

To dine or not to dine is a big question for the traveler. For most Irish people, particularly those in the countryside, luncheon is the main meal, taken about 1 o'clock, and usually consists of soup, meat (beef or chicken), vegetables (peas, cabbage, carrots, and usually potatoes), and dessert (the Irish call them "sweets"), generally puddings or pastries. Here or there, a visitor may encounter carrageen sweets, molded jelly with extract of Irish moss, a species of seaweed, flavored with lemon rind and served with heavy cream or fruit. They are mild and subtle and entirely pleasant. Cheese is often offered as an alternative to dessert. Irish cheese is good and some hotels have a tempting cheese board that includes French and other European varieties. Visitors staying with an Irish family should follow custom — others can do as they like. Most hotels and restaurants feature a formal midday meal, and a saving grace is that although it is fundamentally the same meal as that served in the evening, it costs up to 50% less.

The alternatives to a full hot lunch are luckily multiplying in Ireland. Hotel coffee shops or lounges will serve cold plates of smoked salmon, chicken, salads, or sandwiches. The Irish pub — which hitherto concentrated on one thing, drink — is gradually extending its menu from sandwiches (which are thin and bready by American standards) to include soup, cold plates, salads, and hot meat pies. These meals are indicated by signs that say "pub grub." Another option in some towns are fish-and-chip shops; the fish (usually whiting) is good, the chips (fried potatoes) delicious, and the price low.

Or visitors may prefer to skip lunch and sustain themselves until the main evening meal by having afternoon tea. This fine English institution is, like many other colonial relics, slowly fading from Ireland. Afternoon tea is undeniably a spiritual refreshment; it can rise to ritual, however, when it includes delicate finger sandwiches of ham, chicken, or cucumber; strips of toast with honey; chocolate eclairs; heavy fruitcakes; or wedges of apple tart with cream.

The domestic Irish evening dinner meal is usually called tea or supper — "high tea" to distinguish it verbally from the afternoon version. In winter it might be quite a substantial meal — a mixed grill (sausage, bacon, kidney, a small piece of steak, and a lamb chop), steak and potatoes, or fish in the coastal areas; in summer, it may be something lighter, such as boiled eggs with toast, bread and jam, or a plate of sliced cold chicken or ham. Tea is rounded off with cake, a fruit tart, pudding, or scones.

Among the traditional Irish dishes not to be missed are oxtail soup, Irish stew (simmered layers of onion, potato, and mutton), and fresh salmon — in season — for which the country is justifiably famous. Seafood, surprisingly, has only recently become popular in Ireland, though the coastal waters abound with prawns, lobster, mussels, and oysters. Each October, at the beginning of the oyster harvest, a festival is held in Galway City, during which bushels of bivalves meet their doom in a deluge of porter (a dark beer). Briefly thereafter, oysters become available in the shops. Another delicacy sometimes served in restaurants is the periwinkle, a tiny sea snail that is boiled, picked from the shell with sewing needles or wooden pikes, and eaten. Dipped in melted butter laced with garlic, the winkle need not blush before the escargot. (For more details, as well as specific places to whet your appetite, see *Best Eating,* DIVERSIONS).

At fairs or horse races, little bags of dried seaweed are often sold as though it were candy; this is dulse, and it makes a tasty, salty "chaw" — a fine accompaniment to a glass of stout.

This brings us to the subject of drink. The favored beverage is stout, or porter, a dark, pungent brew served by the "jar," with a head like thick cream and a reputation for being able to support life singlehandedly. Guinness is the largest brewer, though other brands are locally obtainable outside Dublin. Good lager and ale, like stout, are drawn at room temperature; the Irish regard the American custom of taking such beverages icy cold with the wry detachment of the anthropologist. They privately think it is a custom suitable only for savages. A dash of sweetened lime juice in a glass of beer makes a refreshing drink called, unsurprisingly, lager and lime.

Most Irish bartenders do not mix drinks, but will sell small bottles of mixers at an extra charge. The spirits of choice are gin, Scotch, and Irish whiskey. The whiskey distributed for home consumption is far smoother than the youthful export stuff, though of slightly lower proof. It is, like the great malt whiskeys of Scotland, a straight liquor, unblended, and it has a distinctive fruity bouquet and trace of sweetness. In recent years, wines have become a popular potable in Ireland, and although only small quantities of wine are produced in the country, a wide assortment of European vintages, as well as selections from as far away as Chile and Australia, are available. California wines, including non-alcoholic varieties, also have gained acceptance in the Irish marketplace. Don't miss a chance to sample that famous after-dinner treat — Irish coffee, a tantalizing concoction of hot coffee and whiskey topped with a thick layer of gently whipped cream. (For a more complete discussion of beers, ales, and liquors, as well as a selection of the best watering holes in Ireland, see *Pub Crawling,* DIVERSIONS.)

The Irish Language

 The official language of the Republic of Ireland is Irish, although the vast majority of people use English as their everyday language. Irish is a Gaelic tongue, and, as such, is often referred to simply as Gaelic, particularly among visitors. Similar in many ways to Scottish Gaelic, the Irish language is also related, to a lesser degree, to Welsh, Cornish, and Breton.

Irish has been in use for at least 2,000 years, dating as far back as the Celts. From the 6th to 9th centuries, it was the sole vernacular in Ireland. It remained dominant throughout the Middle Ages, although other tongues were introduced by the Vikings and the Anglo-Normans. As Great Britain increased its control of Ireland in the 16th and 17th centuries, however, English became the language of the upper classes and the sole language of the government and public institutions. Although the Irish-speaking population remained strong in rural areas (as many as 4 million people spoke Irish in 1835), the language gradually became associated with poverty and social disadvantage. Its usage was undermined by the famine and the subsequent emigration, which reduced the Gaelic-speaking population to 680,000 by 1891.

Enthusiasm for the Irish vernacular was somewhat revived in 1893 with the founding of the Gaelic League *(Conradh na Gaeilge),* a nationwide group devoted to the preservation of Irish language, literature, culture, music, games, dress, and ideas. Consequently, when southern Ireland became a Republic in 1937, its new constitution declared Irish to be "the national language and the first official language," with English as the second official language.

The new Irish government took steps to safeguard the language and to encourage its everyday use: Irish was made an obligatory subject in the curricular of primary and secondary schools, and a knowledge of the language was required for admission to the civil service, police, and army. Most important, government support in the form of grants and concessions was given to certain regions of Ireland where the Irish language was still the vernacular. Each of these regions, seven in all, was officially designated as a *Gaeltacht,* which simply means "Gaelic-speaking area."

To underscore the nation's commitment to the development and promotion of the Irish-language regions, a separate branch of the government, the Department of the Gaeltacht, was established in 1956. Similarly, *Aer Arann,* the airline of the Gaeltacht, was launched in 1970 to connect major Irish-language outposts, such as the Aran islands, to the mainland. In 1972, a radio service, Raidio na Gaeltachta, was introduced to serve the Gaeltacht, with 3 hours of Irish-language broadcasting each day (the service is now up to 10 hours of broadcasting each day).

In general, the Gaeltachts — or, to be linguistically correct, Gaeltachtaí — of Ireland account for about 70,000 people, or 2% of the current population. (The rest of Ireland is overwhelmingly English-speaking, although about a third of the total population claims some level of competence in conversational Irish.) The Gaeltachtaí are situated in remote areas, primarily along the scenic western seaboard. Specifically, they are as follows:

Donegal Gaeltacht — This region, which has the largest native Irish-speaking population (23,000) of any county in Ireland, covers almost the entire length of the county's western coast, from Fanad Head and Downings in the north to Glencolumbkille and Kilcar in the south. It also includes an all-Irish theater at Gweedore, a broadcasting studio for Raidio na Gaeltachta, and several Irish language colleges.

Mayo Gaeltacht — This Gaeltacht is comprised of three regions: the northwest coast surrounding Erris Head and Benwee Head, the eastern half of Achill Island, and the Tourmakeady area at the southern tip of the county. The population is approximately 13,000.

Galway Gaeltacht — Second to Donegal Gaeltacht in population (20,000), Galway Gaeltacht is the largest county in geographical area. It is concentrated primarily in southern Connemara and the coastal villages west of Galway City, as well as the three Aran Islands. There are several Irish colleges in the region, a broadcasting studio for Raidio na Gaeltachta at Casla, and the national theater of the Irish language, *An Taibhdhearc na Gaillimhe,* in Galway City.

Kerry Gaeltacht — The western half of the Dingle Peninsula and the southwest portion of the Iveragh Peninsula (the Ring of Kerry) combine to make the 8,000-strong Irish-speaking areas of County Kerry. A broadcasting studio of Raidio na Gaeltachta is located at Dingle.

Cork Gaeltacht — With an island and a coastal section, Cork Gaeltacht has a combined population of about 4,000. The inland section is in the mountainous northwest corner of the county, between Ballingeary and Ballyvourney, where the first Irish-language college was founded in 1904. The offshore pocket is located on Cape Clear Island, 7 miles southwest of Baltimore.

Waterford Gaeltacht — This is a small outpost of the Gaelic language surrounding the village of Ring, on the southern coast about 40 miles southwest of Waterford City. There is an Irish college here and a population of about 1,100.

Meath Gaeltacht — The smallest (less than 500 people) of Ireland's Gaeltachtaí is comprised of two inland settlements around Ráthcairn and Gibbstown in rural County Meath, about 35 miles northwest of Dublin.

With the exception of the Meath communities, the Gaeltachtaí are located in very scenic and remote parts of Ireland that are poor and underdeveloped. In general, the residents eke out a living from cottage farming, traditional crafts, fishing, small cooperative industries, and tourism.

Visitors flock to the Gaeltachtaí to see the scenery and hear the lilting flow of the Irish language, a combination which can often present difficulties for strangers. In the most remote areas, road or directional signs are strictly in the native language. Because Irish bears little or no resemblance to English, driving around the Gaeltachtaí can be confusing and frustrating. For example, the Irish equivalent of Clonbur in County Galway is "An Fhairche"; just as Recess is known locally as "Sraith Salach"; or Ventry, County Kerry, as "Ceann Trá." It is wise to come equipped with a map spelling out placenames in both languages (such as the Ordnance Survey Maps or some of those distributed by the Irish Tourist Board).

Similarly, the names of shops and businesses in small towns of the Gaeltachtaí usually are in the Irish language. Fortunately, if confusion arises, the vast majority of the local folk speak English as a second language, and they always are willing to direct or even escort visitors to the correct destination or road. Some Irish words that are useful to know include "Mna" (public ladies room), "Fir" (men's room), "Oifig an Phoist" (post office), and "Oifig Fáilte" (tourist office). An Irish police officer is called a "garda" — or "gardaí" (the plural) — which is an abbreviated form of the Irish words "garda síochána" (guardian of the peace).

The Irish language also plays a large part in the placenames of Ireland. Each town and city is known by its Irish as well as its English name; for example, Dublin is designated as "Baile Átha Cliath" (meaning "town of the ford of the hurdles") on many directional signs or bus/train notices.

"Baile," which simply means "a town or village," is one of the most frequently used words in Irish geography; in modern usage, it has also been anglicized to "Bally." Visitors will encounter hundreds of placenames with this prefix — e.g., Ballybofey, Ballybunion, Ballycastle, Ballycotton, Ballyhaunis, Ballyjamesduff, Ballylickey, Ballymaloe, Ballymurphy, Ballynahinch, Ballyporeen, and so on.

Another interesting feature of the Irish countryside is that the same placename will often have two or more spellings, and each will be considered correct. This is because some spellings are strictly Irish, others are a mixture of Irish and English, and still others have evolved from local usage. This explains, for example, why "Clarinbridge" also appears on maps and signposts as "Clarenbridge," "Mulrany" as "Mallaranny," or "Ballysadare" as "Ballisodare."

Other Irish nouns that often are seen as part of modern Irish placenames include the following:

Ard (meaning height, or high) — as in Ardmore (great height), Ardagh (high field), Ardara (height of the ring fort), Ardnamona (height of the bog), and Ardpatrick (height of St. Patrick).

Dun (meaning fort) — as in Dunboy (yellow fort), Duncannon (Ceanann's fort), Dunloe (fort of the river Loe), and Dún Laoghaire (Laoghaire's fort).

Inis (meaning island) as in Inishbeg (little island), Inishmore (great island), Inishmaan (middle island), Inisheer (eastern island), and Inishfree (island of the heather).

Slieve (meaning mountain) — as in Slieve Callan (Callan's mountain), Slieve League (mountain of the flagstones), Slieve Snaght (mountain of the snow), and Slievenamon (mountain of the women).

Kil (meaning church) — as in Kildare (church of the oak grove), Kilkenny (church of St. Cainneach), Killarney (church of the sloes), Killybegs (little churches), and Kilmore (big church).

The Irish language is also used regularly in governmental titles, such as "Dáil Eireann" (Parliament) and "Taoiseach" (Prime Minister). Semi-state bodies are similarly designated by Irish-language names, such as *"Aer Lingus"* (which means "air fleet"), "Bord Fáilte" ("Board of the Welcomes"), *"CIE"* (initials that stand for *"Córas Iompair Eireann,"* meaning "Ireland's Transport Company"), and so on.

It is possible for visitors to Ireland to be totally unfamiliar with the Irish language and still have a great time. There are, however, two phrases that almost everyone comes to know within hours of arrival: *Céad míle fáilte* (meaning one hundred thousand welcomes; pronounced cade *mee*-le-*fal*-che) and *Sláinte* (the standard toast, meaning "To your health"; pronounced *slawn*-che). Other useful everyday words and expressions include the following:

English	Irish	Pronunciation
Good day!	*Dia duit!*	*jee*-a ditch
reply to "Good day!"	*Dia's Muire duit*	*jee*-ass *mwur*-ra ditch
Good-bye!	*Slán agat!*	slawn u*gut*
How are you?	*Cad é mar atá tú?*	*caj*-ay mar ata too
I'm fine. Thank you.	*Tá go maith go raibh. Maith agat!*	taw gu *mayh*, gura. *mah* ugut
Goodnight!	*Oíche mhaith!*	*ee*-ha wah
Excuse me!	*Gabh mo leithscéal!*	gow mu *lay*skal
yes	*tá*	taw
no	*níl*	neel
What is your name?	*Cad is ainm duit?*	kad iss *an*yim ditch?
My name is (name)	(Name) *atá orm.*	a*taw o*rim.
ladies' room	*mna*	men-*aw* (rhymes with "hurrah")
mens' room	*fir*	fear
tourist office	*oifig fáilte*	*aw*-fig *fal*-che
police	*garda siochana*	*gord*-a shea-*kaw*-na
town	*baile*	*ball*-ya
stop	*stop*	stawp
go	*dul*	dull

For visitors who wish to learn more Gaelic, it is possible to take short courses, which last from 1 week to 1 month. They are conducted primarily during the summer months in Donegal and Galway, the two counties richest in Gaelic language traditions. For additional details, contact *Oideas Gael* (2 Bothair Chairi, Mount Merrion, Dublin 14, Ireland; phone: 1-213566), or the *Summer School Office* (University College Galway, Galway, Co. Galway, Ireland; phone: 91-24411).

The local meaning of many seemingly unfamiliar English words may be unfamiliar to Americans traveling in Ireland. The vocabulary of the Irish English is much like that of British English, though it shows more American influence. The following are some frequently used Irish words and phrases:

bank holiday	any legal holiday
basin	any bowl
bathroom	for baths, not a toilet
beer	Always order a type of beer — lager, bitter, and so on — never just "beer."
bitter	a dark, dry beer
lager	American-style beer
light ale	sweet lager
pale ale	light-colored ale
shandy	beer mixed with a soft drink
stout	a dark, sweetish beer
bespoke	custom-tailored
bill	check
Biro	ballpoint pen
biscuit	cookie or cracker
block (of flats)	apartment house
bonnet (car)	hood
boot (car)	trunk
bowler	usually refers to the hat, not a player
braces	suspenders
brolly or bumbershoot	umbrella
busker	street musician
café (pronounced caff)	cheap restaurant
candy floss	cotton candy
car park	parking lot
caravan	RV, mobile home
Chesterfield	sofa
chips	French fries
Christian name	first name
City, the	Dublin
coach	long-distance bus
cold (drinks)	cool, not iced
corn	any edible grain
cot	baby's crib
cul-de-sac	dead end
dispensary	doctor's office
double cream	very heavy sweet cream
dual carriageway	divided highway
dynamo (car)	generator
flat	apartment
flyover	overpass
fortnight	2 weeks
garden	yard
gear lever	gearshift
grammar school	selective middle school
high tea	tea plus light supper
hire purchase	installment plan
hood (car)	soft top of convertible

hoover	vacuum cleaner
hump	carry something heavy
hump that!	To hell with that!
jelly	gelatin dessert (Jell-O)
joint (meat)	roast
kettle	teakettle
knickers	panties
ladder	run in pantyhose
lavatory	toilet
left luggage office	baggage room
lift	elevator
lip balm	Chapstick
loch	lake
loo	toilet
lorry	truck
mackintosh, mac	raincoat
marrow	zucchini
mince, minced meat	hamburger
mineral	soft drink
mod cons	modern conveniences
napkin	diaper
noggin	drink of beer or ale
nosh	hasty meal, not a snack
overtake	pass while driving
pantomime	song and dance show
petrol	gasoline
pram	baby carriage
public school	private school
queue	to stand in line
quid	pound (currency)
rasher	slice of bacon
reception	front desk
return ticket	round-trip ticket
ring	to telephone
roundabout	traffic circle
rubber	eraser
saloon bar	upper class pub
schooner	ordinary beer mug
serviette	napkin
shepherd's pie	mashed potato pie
shop	small store
sick	nauseous (not ill in general)
silencer (car)	muffler
single ticket	one-way ticket
stalls (theater)	orchestra seats
starters	hors d'oeuvres
stone	measure of weight equal to 14 pounds
store	department store
sweet	dessert
telly	television
tights	pantyhose
tenement	apartment house
trainers	sneakers

trillion	a million million
trunk call	long-distance call
vest	man's undershirt
waistcoat	man's vest
whisky	Scotch or Irish whiskey only
yard	paved area
Z	pronounced "zed"
zebra crossing	pedestrian crosswalk

For further information about the Gaeltacht regions, write to *Udarás na Gaeltachta,* Ardoifig na Forbacha, Gaillimh (Galway), Eire (Republic of Ireland).

THE CITIES

BELFAST

As the capital of Northern Ireland, Belfast has been making international headlines for many years. Since 1969, the city has been receiving more than its share of attention because of sharply increased political, religious, and economic upheaval, as well as terrorist activity. However, because most of the violence is directed toward specific targets, tourists have not been drawn into it, and the citizenry seems to take the security measures in stride and carries on with life almost normally. Visitors are unlikely to see many outward signs of "the troubles." A security check on vehicles approaching Belfast's Aldergrove International Airport is possible, though increasingly rare recently, and cars entering and leaving the city center usually undergo a quick parcel inspection (the trunk is opened), but pedestrians are no longer stopped. Indeed, the city center is best seen on foot, since large areas of Belfast's reinvigorated downtown have been reborn as pedestrian shopping districts (closed to private cars) — with such a profusion of flowers, benches, and trees that the city was recognized in the *1986 Beautiful Britain in Bloom* competition.

For travelers trying to appreciate the origins of "the troubles," a look at Belfast's history proves invaluable. Belfast, or *Béal Feirste* in Irish, means "mouth of the Farset," a stream that flows into the river Lagan. It was the natural harbor and strategic defense position formed by the Lagan and Lough Belfast that prompted various marauders over the centuries — Anglo-Norman, Scottish, and Irish — to establish fortified strongholds or castles here. By the 16th century, the area was controlled by the O'Neills, Earls of nearby Tyrone. After the defeat of the great Irish chieftain Hugh O'Neill at Kinsale in 1601, the lands were confiscated by the English Crown and later granted to Sir Arthur Chichester, Governor of Carrickfergus, by Elizabeth I. He built a new castle and supplanted the native Irish with English and Scottish colonists under the Plantation policy — instituted by Mary Tudor (Bloody Mary) in the mid-16th century, and fully carried out under James I in the early 17th century — in the counties that now make up Northern Ireland. In 1613, Belfast was granted a charter of incorporation and was allowed two (Protestant) representatives to the British Parliament. In the years that followed, the Catholic Irish rose up in revolt several times, with no success; they suffered under harsh penal codes, which usurped their property, outlawed their religion, and denied their civil rights.

Soon after the revocation of the Edict of Nantes in France in 1685, Belfast was washed by a new wave of settlers — this time French Huguenots fleeing religious persecution. They brought with them improved weaving methods, which spurred the town's fledgling linen industry into rapid expansion throughout the 18th century. In addition to linen, the development of rope making, engineering, tobacco, and sea trade infused Belfast's economy, causing the town to double in size every 10 years. During this period Roger Mulholland, a local architect, drew up a plan dividing the town into a grid of streets for construction and development. The grid included Donegall Square and was bordered roughly by Wellington Place and Chichester, Great Victoria, May, and Howard Streets. Along these avenues many elegant Georgian buildings were erected by Belfast's prosperous linen merchants.

In 1791, Wolfe Tone, the son of a Protestant Dublin tradesman who was inspired by the American and French revolutions and influenced by radical Belfast Presbyterians, formed the Society of United Irishmen in Belfast. Espousing social as well as political reforms, the society's goal was "to substitute the common name of Irishmen in place of the denominations of Protestant, Catholic, and Dissenter." As Belfast became a center of dissent against the British, the United Irishmen supported an effort by both Presbyterians and Catholics to rid Ireland of English rule. Uprisings in 1798 proved unsuccessful, including a June 7 attack on Antrim, during which the Irish sang the "Marseillaise." The United Irishmen's leader, Henry Joy McCracken, later was hanged in Belfast. Wolfe Tone's Belfast-born ideas of an Irish republic attractive to all the Irish, together with the uprisings, constituted a watershed for the ideal of a united Ireland. Unfortunately, the concept collapsed into sectarianism soon after.

Economically, Belfast continued to burgeon during the 19th century, aided by the Act of Union (which made Ireland part of Great Britain) and by the growth of its shipbuilding industry. Belfast was fancifully called the Athens of the North for its patronage of the arts, and most of its gracious architecture (designed by Sir Charles Lanyon) dates from this era. Unfortunately, the city's prosperity was not shared by all its citizens; the Irish Catholics were still excluded from representation in London, from decent housing, and sometimes even from employment.

In 1920, after much bloody struggle by the Irish for self-government, Britain enacted the Home Rule Bill, which established two new Parliaments — one each in Dublin and Belfast. In 1921, a treaty was signed that formally created an Irish Free State consisting of 26 mostly southern counties and leaving the six northern counties to choose between union with the new republic or with Britain. The Protestant-dominated Belfast Parliament chose the latter course, and the new entity called Northern Ireland was born.

Because the Republic of Ireland remained neutral in World War II, Northern Ireland became strategically vital to the Allied cause. The first American contingent of GIs arrived in Belfast by ship in January 1942, and by the end of that year, there were 100,000 American troops in the province. Generals Eisenhower and Patton oversaw the troop training in Northern Ireland for the massive *D-Day* venture.

Today, Belfast, second in size only to Dublin, is a sturdy, red brick, industrial city ringed by beautiful bluish-purple hills that shelter ancient castles and echo with Irish folklore. Although the city is bothered by continued high unemployment (as in the Republic), a glance around downtown Belfast reveals few visual remnants of prior urban renewal projects or overt terrorist activity. Its basically prosperous appearance reflects the city's role as commercial and cultural capital of Northern Ireland, but until the smoldering internecine conflicts are finally resolved, there will be shadow as well as sun in Belfast's future.

BELFAST AT-A-GLANCE

 SEEING THE CITY: The best views of Belfast are from the top of Cave Hill, 2 miles north of the city. To the south is the Old City, dominated by the copper-domed City Hall in Donegall Square; to the west is Lough Neagh, the largest lake in Ireland. To the northeast, the counties of Carrickfergus, Holywood, and Bangor can be seen from the hill, and on a clear day the Isle of Man may be visible in the Irish Sea to the southeast.

 SPECIAL PLACES: Many of the streets in the 18th-century Old City have been converted to pedestrian walkways and shopping arcades, and automobiles are prohibited. This poses no problem to the tourist, as central Belfast is a compact area best seen on foot. A 1½-mile walking tour is described in the *Belfast Civic Festival Trail* brochure available at the tourist information center, 48 High St.

CITY CENTER

City Hall – A statue of Queen Victoria stands in front of this imposing pillared and corniced gray stone structure capped by a 173-foot-high copper dome. Completed in 1906, its interior is richly decorated in the elaborate Edwardian style with stained glass and marble. It is one of Ireland's most outstanding buildings. Tours are conducted at 10:30 AM, Wednesdays, and require advance reservations; contact the Information Officer (phone: 320202). Donegall Sq. S.

St. Malachy's Church – This is a fine example of the lavish Gothic Roman Catholic churches built in Ireland during the 19th century. Look especially at its remarkable fan-vaulted ceiling, virtually dripping with intricate plasterwork, similar to that found in Henry VII's Chapel at Westminster Abbey in London. 24 Alfred St. (phone: 321713).

Royal Courts of Justice – An imposing building, finished in 1933, the "four courts" is constructed of Portland stone and was a gift from Britain. Chichester St.

Albert Memorial – Looking a little incongruous among parking lots and office buildings, this 116-foot-tall memorial honoring Prince Albert, Queen Victoria's consort, is often called Belfast's Big Ben since it bears such a striking resemblance to London's famous tower. This clock tower, however, has settled slightly to one side, also earning itself the nickname of Belfast's Leaning Tower. At the river end of High St.

Custom House – This squarish, solid-looking building was designed by the architect Sir Charles Lanyon in the richly corniced, somewhat grand Italianate style that was popular in Ireland in the mid-19th century. Sculptures of Britannia, Neptune, and Mercury decorate the pediment on the seaward side. Custom House Sq.

St. Anne's Cathedral – St. Anne's, Belfast's principal Anglican church, took 86 years to build — from 1899 to 1985 — and therefore combines many architectural styles. It is distinguished by some fine Irish Romanesque carving and sculpture. Lower Donegall St. (phone: 328332).

St. Peter's Cathedral – Completed in 1866, this Roman Catholic church is noted for its soaring twin spires and a circular carving by the doorway depicting angels freeing St. Peter from prison. St. Peter's Sq.

First Presbyterian Church – John Wesley preached here in 1789, 6 years after the church was completed. It has a lovely interior. Rosemary St.

ENVIRONS

Port of Belfast – Poised cranes and cables are stock props looming above this busy port, the largest in Ireland. Shipbuilding remains a primary occupation, and numerous ocean liners have been constructed or repaired here. The noted Harland & Wolff (H&W) shipyard grew from 2 acres in 1858 to 300 in the mid-20th century. Once the world's largest shipyard and long renowned for innovative ship design and sophisticated engine and hull construction, H&W today boasts the world's largest dry dock. On April 2, 1912, the *Titanic* set out from its H&W birthplace to Southampton, England, for her maiden transatlantic voyage. Just 12 days later, the *Titanic* struck an iceberg, and in 3 hours the glamorous, "virtually unsinkable" ocean liner sank. Advance booking is required for shipyard tours; contact the Public Affairs Office (phone: 458456).

Stormont – A mile-long road leads uphill through an estate, with extensive gardens, to the erstwhile Parliament House, once the seat of Northern Ireland's legislature, now a government office building. Two statues on the grounds remind visitors of Ulster's political reality. One, at the juncture of the approach avenues, is of Lord Carson, the Dublin lawyer who kept Belfast British during and after World War I; the other, in the main entrance hall of the Parliament building, is of Lord Craigavon, Northern Ireland's first prime minister, best known for his anti-Republican slogans "Not an inch" and "No surrender." Upper Newtownards Rd., just east of the city.

Belfast Castle – Of recent vintage (1870), this mansion — with its turrets, tower, gables, and ornate carving — is a fine example of the romantic Scottish baronial style imported to this area during the Plantation period. Given to the city in 1934 by a former Mayor of Belfast, the Earl of Shaftsbury, the estate — which recently received a $4 million restoration — is now open to the public. There is also a restaurant here offering a splendid view of the city (see *Eating Out*). Antrim Rd., north of the city on Cave Hill (phone: 776925).

Cave Hill – About 2 miles north of the city, Cave Hill is a lovely afternoon's diversion. Stroll through the Hazelwood Gardens, climb to the craggy hill's summit (1,188 feet) and MacArt's Fort (an ancient earthwork), or visit the Belfast Zoo (see below). Easiest access is from the parking lot of Belfast Castle.

Belfast Zoo – Recently expanded and still undergoing major improvements, it features an African House, sea lion pool, penguin exhibit, and a large free-flight aviary. The zoo, renowned for its excellent climate for breeding and conservation, has a new visitors' center with audiovisual exhibits. For hungry guests, there's a restaurant. Open daily, April through September, 10 AM to 6 PM; October through March, 10 AM to 4:30 PM. Admission charge. Take city bus routes 2, 3, 4, 5, or 6 from Donegall Square W., Antrim Rd. (phone: 776277).

Queen's University – When founded in 1845, the school was associated with colleges in Galway and Cork; it became independent in 1909. Its original red brick, Tudor buildings designed by Sir Charles Lanyon are now only a small fraction of the many buildings that make up the university complex. In November the *Belfast Festival at Queen's*, established more than a quarter-century ago and now a rival to the *Edinburgh Festival* as the largest cultural event in the UK, offers a multitude of events — film, music, and drama. The *Queen's Film Theatre* is also open to the public. University Rd. (phone: 245133).

■**EXTRA SPECIAL:** Between Queen's University and the *Ulster Museum* lie Belfast's 28-acre Botanic Gardens, the showpiece of which is the charming Palm House glass conservatory. A famous Victorian-era Belfast landmark, the Palm House was begun in 1839, predating London's Kew Gardens conservatory. It is one of the earliest examples of a curvilinear cast-iron glasshouse. The colorful floral displays in the cool left wing, tropical right wing, and 37-foot-high center dome are open to the public year-round. The Palm House and Tropical Ravine are open Mondays through Fridays, April through September, from 10 AM to noon and from 1 to 5 PM, on Saturdays and Sundays from 2 to 5 PM; during October and March, they're open Mondays through Fridays from 10 AM to noon and from 2 to 4 PM, on Saturdays and Sundays from 2 to 4 PM. The park is accessible at all times. University Rd. (phone: 324902).

SOURCES AND RESOURCES

 TOURIST INFORMATION: The Northern Ireland Tourist Board, River House (48 High St., Belfast BT1 2DS; phone: 231221), offers information, maps, and leaflets, and sells books, postcards, stamps, posters, and slides of the area. The *Belfast City Council Reference Guide* and other information are available at City Hall (Donegall Sq. S.), and *The Visitor's Guide to Northern Ireland* (Hunter Publishing; $10.95) by Rosemary Evans is available at bookshops. For help in tracing ancestral roots, contact the *Ulster Historical Foundation* (68 Balmoral Ave., Belfast BT9 6NY; phone: 681365).

Local Coverage – The *Belfast Telegraph,* the *Newsletter,* and the *Irish News* are all published daily. The *Belfast Telegraph* gives entertainment listings.

Food – The Northern Ireland Tourist Board publishes a booklet, updated yearly, called *Where to Eat in Northern Ireland* ($2.50) that includes an extensive list of eating places in Belfast and throughout the province.

TELEPHONE: The area code for Belfast and the immediate vicinity is 232. When calling from within Northern Ireland, dial 0232 before the local number.

GETTING AROUND: Walking is the best way to tour Belfast's inner core, or the shopping area, since it is off limits to private cars. Travel outside the city is possible by bus, car, or train.

Airport – Belfast International Airport — with connecting flights on *British Airways* and other airlines to London and several other English cities, to Amsterdam via the *NLM Cityhopper,* and to Paris on *Air France* — is 19 miles northwest of Belfast, off M2 (phone: 8494-22888).

Bus – The airport and points south are served by the Ulster Bus Station (Great Victoria St.). Points north can be reached from the station on Oxford St. For information about schedules and departures, call 320011.

Car Rental – Several car rental agencies are represented at Belfast International Airport, including *Avis* (173 Airport Rd.; phone: 8494-52333); *Godfrey Davis* (181 Airport Rd.; phone: 8494-53444); *Hertz* (phone: 8494-52533); and *McCauslands* (phone: 8494-22022), which also has an office in the city (21/31 Grosvenor Rd.; phone: 327211).

Sightseeing Tours – *Citybus* conducts 3½-hour tours of greater Belfast highlights and Carrickfergus Castle at 1:30 PM, late May through September, Mondays through Fridays. The colorful commentary provided by the drivers — a treat in itself — should not be missed. Highlights include city center landmarks, the Queen's University district, the shipyards, Stormont, and the Belfast Zoo. Departure is from Castle Place, outside the general post office. Tours, including afternoon tea, cost $6. Other *Citybus* offerings include tours of parks and gardens, and historic buildings of North Down (phone: 246485).

Taxi – There are taxi ranks at the main bus and rail terminals and at City Hall. These taxis are the familiar old London-type black cabs and have a yellow disk on the windshield. Other taxis may not have meters, so passengers are advised to ask the fare to their destination before setting off. Don't be surprised if you are asked to share a cab when there is a long waiting line — it will cost you less. Or call *Fast Taxi* (phone: 458011), *Dial-A-Cab* (phone: 797777), *Able Taxi* (phone: 241999), or *Fon A Cab* (phone: 233333).

Train – The Belfast Central Station provides service to all destinations in Northern Ireland as well as in the Republic (phone: 230310); trains to Larne for the car ferry to Stranraer, Scotland, leave from York Road Station (phone: 235282). A special *Rail-Link* bus (phone: 235282) runs frequently between the two stations, Mondays through Saturdays from 7:30 AM to 8:30 PM.

 SPECIAL EVENTS: The *Ulster Harp National,* Northern Ireland's most important steeplechase, is held at *Downpatrick Racecourse* in February. A boisterous parade commemorating the Battle of the Boyne — marches through Belfast every July 12. It is often the occasion for much Protestant politicking and speechmaking. In late summer the city holds its *International Rose Trials* at Sir Thomas and Lady Dixon Park, an event that draws rose aficionados from around the world. The *Belfast Festival* at Queen's University in November is an international arts symposium, with presentations of music, drama, and films (phone: 667687).

 MUSEUMS: Belfast's museums of note include the following:

Arts Council Gallery – Contemporary Irish and international art. Bedford House, 16 Bedford St. (phone: 321402).

Octagon Gallery – This gallery exhibits the best work done by local artists. Orpheus Building, York St. (phone: 246259).

Ulster Folk and Transport Museum – Created in 1958, this 136-acre indoor and outdoor complex depicts Northern Ireland's social history. It consists of a gallery of artifacts that offers an evolutionary explanation of rural Ulster life, complemented by 19 buildings — among them a linen mill, spade mill, church, schools, forge, thatched cottiers' cottage, and different styles of terraces and farmhouses — removed stone by stone from Ulster countryside sites. Each building is furnished circa 1900 and has a guide in attendance. Admission charge. Off Bangor Rd. in Cultra, 7 miles northeast of Belfast. Bangor buses depart from Oxford St. Station every half hour (museum phone: 428428).

Ulster Museum – On the grounds of the Botanic Gardens, the collections include Bronze Age horns and pottery, Celtic personal ornaments, early Christian and medieval antiquities (including facsimiles of the 8th- and 9th-century *Book of Kells* and *Book of Armagh*), Irish art, glass and silver, and a display of life in Ireland covering 9,000 years. The most popular exhibit is the Girona treasure, an amazing hoard of gold and silver coins, jewelry (one gold chain weighs 4 pounds and is more than 8 feet long), and other artifacts recovered from a galleon of the Spanish Armada that was wrecked off the Giant's Causeway in 1588. Noted Belgian underwater archaeologist Robert Stenuit salvaged the treasure in 1968, during some 6,000 hours of diving time. University Rd. (phone: 381251).

 SHOPPING: The highlights of Belfast's shopping scene are china, crystal, linen, woolens, and antiques. In addition to the famous *Marks & Spencer* (see below), well-known chain stores are *Body Shop* (10 Castle La.; phone: 223-0651); *British Homes Stores* (24 Castle Pl.; phone: 224-3068); *Littlwoods*

(5 Ann St.; phone: 224-1537); *Next* (Cleaver House, Donegall Pl.; phone: 223-3195); and *Principles* (Cleaver House, Donegall Pl.; phone: 223-8784).

Handicrafts usually are on display, and some may be for sale at the *Local Enterprise Development Unit* (*LEDU;* 17 Linenhall St., 1 block from City Hall; phone: 242582). *LEDU* also offers *A Guide to Northern Ireland Crafts and Craftsmen,* a free booklet with the names, addresses, and specialties of Irish artisans in the six counties, as well as Belfast.

Bell Gallery – Paintings, mainly by Irish artists from the 19th century to the present. 13 Adelaide Pk. (phone: 662998).

Hall's Linen – Fine linen goods. 23 Queen's Arcade (phone: 320446).

Hoggs – Largest selection of Northern Ireland's Tyrone crystal, which is less expensive than Waterford and of comparable quality. There also is a variety of English china and figurines. Seconds sometimes are available. 10 Donegall Sq. W. (phone: 243899).

Irish Linen Shop – More fine linen goods. 46 Fountain Centre, College St. (phone: 322727).

Johnston's Umbrella Shop – Irish shillelaghs and English walking stick in a variety of woods. 33 Ann St. (phone: 232-0729).

Tom Jones – Ireland's best crystal and England's finest china are sold at this elegantly designed shop. 9 Wellington Pl. (phone: 325932).

John and Charlotte Lambe – 18th- and 19th-century furniture, paintings, and silver. 41 Shore Rd. (phone: 370761).

Samuel Lamont & Sons, Ltd. – Irish linen, still woven in Belfast and in other areas of Northern Ireland, is generally exported, but it's available here in large supply, including sheets. Stranmillis Embankment (phone: 668285).

Marks & Spencer – Northern Ireland's largest department store is known for its lamb's wool and Shetland sweaters. Men's woolen suits are of excellent quality and moderately priced. The store has no fitting rooms and credit cards are not accepted. 48 Donegall Pl. (phone: 235235).

Sheepskin Shop – Trendy sheepskin-lined clothing and high-quality leathers. 20 Wicklow St. (phone: 719585).

Sinclair's Antique Gallery – Fine jewelry and silver. 19 Arthur St. (phone: 322335).

Smyth's Irish Linen – Top-quality linen along with needlework and textile crafts. 14 Callender St. (phone: 322983).

 SPORTS AND FITNESS: Fishing – Despite all the commercial shipping in and out of Belfast, fishing can be very good in Lough Belfast. It is best known for its coalfish, pollack, and whiting, but small skate are sometimes taken at Ballymaconnell Point, near Bangor, and it's worth trying for cod from the rocks around Blackhead Lighthouse. The area is best fished from a small boat with an outboard motor. The required game fishing licenses can be obtained from the Northern Ireland Tourist Board (48 High St.), tackle shops, or local hotels. The nearest fishing boat charters are in Bangor; contact Brian Meharg (25 Holborn Ave., Bangor; phone: 247-455321).

Golf – There are ten 18-hole courses: *Balmoral* (518 Lisburn Rd.; phone: 381514); *Malone* (Drumbeg, Dunmurry; phone: 612758); *Helen's Bay* (phone: 247-852815); *Fortwilliam* (Downview Ave.; phone: 771770); *Clandeboye* (Conlig, Newtownards; phone: 247-270767); *Knock* (Dundonald; phone: Dundonald 3251); *Carnalea* (Station Rd., Bangor; phone: 247-461368); *Belvoir Park* (73/75 Church Rd.; phone: 641159); *Royal Belfast* (Craigavad, Holywood; phone: 428165); and *Bangor* (Bangor; phone: 247-3922).

Sailing – *Bangor Sailing School* offers boats for hire, instruction in cruising, and skippered sails around Lough Belfast. Contact John Irwin, 13 Gray's Hill Rd., Bangor, Co. Down (phone: 247-455967).

Swimming – The centrally located *Maysfield Leisure Centre* (East Bridge St.; phone:

241633) and *Avoneil Leisure Centre* (Avenue Rd.; phone: 451564) have indoor pools.

Tennis – Tennis and squash courts are at the *Maysfield Leisure Centre* (phone: 241633) and the *Avoneil Leisure Centre* (phone: 451564).

THEATER: The *Grand Opera House* (Great Victoria St.), adjacent to the *Europa* hotel, is Belfast's finest theater. Drama, ballet, concerts, and other entertainments are scheduled throughout the year. For recorded information, call 249129; for advance booking, call 241919. The *Lyric Players Theatre* (Ridgeway St.; phone: 381081) features Irish drama, the classics, and new works. The *Arts Theatre* (Botanic Ave.; phone: 324936) offers popular plays and musicals. The *Group Theatre* (Bedford St.; phone: 329685) presents mostly amateur theatricals, some of which are quite good.

MUSIC: The *Ulster Orchestra* gives concerts at *Ulster Hall* (30 Bedford St.; phone: 233240 for tickets). There is traditional Irish music on Mondays at the *Errigle Inn* (Ormeau Rd.; phone: 641410); Fridays at *Sunflower Bar* (60 Corporation St.; phone: 231198); most nights at *Madden's* (74 Smithfield; phone: 244114) and *Rotterdam* (54 Pilot St.; phone: 746021); Fridays and Saturdays at *Duke of York* (11 Commercial St., off Lower Donegall St.; phone: 241062); Tuesdays, the *Front Page* on "newspaper row" (108 Donegall St.; phone: 324924); Fridays, *Kelly's Cellars* (38 Bank St.; phone: 324835); and nightly at the *Linenhall Bar* (9 Clarence St.; phone: 248458). Folk music is performed at the *Sunflower Bar* (Corporation St.) on Fridays and at the *Errigle Inn* (Ormeau Rd.; phone: 641410) on Tuesdays. *Harper's Bar* in the *Europa Hotel* (Great Victoria St.; phone: 327000) has been converted into an English-style country pub, offering live music nightly; jazz is featured on Thursdays and Saturdays (phone: 327000).

NIGHTCLUBS AND NIGHTLIFE: Belfast's nightlife has improved dramatically, although many non-hotel bars still shutter at 11:30 PM. *Harper's Bar* at the *Europa* hotel offers music nightly (see *Music* above).

BEST IN TOWN

CHECKING IN: Belfast, like other Irish cities, offers a range of accommodations, from sleek, modern hotels to charming, old hostelries. Expect to pay $125 and up for a double room in a hotel listed as expensive, between $80 and $125 in one listed as moderate. Staying at a guesthouse can be considerably less expensive — rates range from $45 to $80 in the city for two and include full Irish breakfast. A listing of such lodgings is included in the annually updated booklet *Where to Stay,* available from the Northern Ireland Tourist Board (see *Tourist Information*). All telephone numbers are in the 232 area code unless otherwise indicated.

Culloden – On 12 acres of secluded gardens and woodland overlooking Lough Belfast, this former bishop's palace may be Northern Ireland's most luxurious hotel. Its 92 beautifully appointed rooms are done in silks and velvets, and the elegant dining room and public areas are filled with antiques. The bar is part of what was once the bishop's chapel. 142 Bangor Rd., Holywood, 6 miles from downtown Belfast (phone: 2317-5223). Expensive.

Dunadry Inn – Not far from the airport, about 12 miles from downtown Belfast, this atmospheric inn has had past lives as a linen mill and then a paper mill. The linen was once laid to whiten in the sun on the huge lawn. Beetling machines can be seen in the bar, and old mill cottages provide the lodging space (67 rooms in all). 2 Islandreagh Drive, Dunadry, County Antrim (phone: 8494-32474). Expensive.

Europa – Near the *Opera House* and other such sites, this 200-room, modern, high-rise hotel is the city's most centrally located. Its restaurants and bars are popular meeting places for Belfasters. The new *Bewley's* (of Dublin fame) coffee house serves informal fare, from traditional Ulster breakfasts to post-theater refreshments. *Harper's Bar,* recently expanded and redecorated, is an English-style pub serving coffee, tea, and bar food until midnight; it also offers live music nightly, except Sundays. Upstairs is an à la carte restaurant, which serves daily specialties in an elegant library-like atmosphere. Great Victoria St. (phone: 327000). Expensive.

Old Inn – The thatch-roofed portion of this place was built about 1614, and smugglers were said to have used the inn until the close of the 18th century. Many handsome, old pieces of furniture are scattered throughout, and what the rooms lack in size they make up for in charm. The Old English suite has twin brass four-poster beds, and the Azalea Suite has cupboard beds with drapes. All 32 rooms have private baths. In the back of the inn is a tea garden overlooking Crawfordsburn Glen. Just off the Bangor road, 15 Main St., Crawfordsburn (phone: 247-853255). Moderate.

Wellington Park – In the attractive Queen's University neighborhood, this modern building has 50 rooms and a restaurant. It's a good choice during the *Belfast Festival.* 21 Malone Rd. (phone: 381111). Moderate.

Ash-Rowan Guest House – This comfortable house is on a quiet residential street, 3 blocks from the *Ulster Museum* and Queen's University, and an easy walk to restaurants, theaters, and shops. The 4 rooms have private baths. Breakfasts and dinners are prepared by the owners, who are former proprietors of an award-winning restaurant. 12 Windsor Rd. (phone: 661758). Inexpensive.

EATING OUT: Belfast is experiencing a downtown restaurant boom. At least 2 dozen eateries, serving fare from Mexican to Mongolian, have opened in the past few years. The average cost of a three-course meal for two, including VAT and 10% service (but not beverages), will be $55 or more in a restaurant listed as expensive, $35 to $50 in moderate listings, and under $35 in the inexpensive category. Most Belfast hotels have their own dining rooms. The Northern Ireland Tourist Board publishes a booklet, updated yearly, called *Where to Eat in Northern Ireland* ($2.50) that includes an extensive list of eating places in Belfast and throughout the province. All telephone numbers are in the 232 area code unless otherwise indicated.

Restaurant 44 – Conveniently located next to *Ulster Hall,* it's a good choice for an after-theater dinner. The specialty is fresh seafood, including such dishes as scallops in garlic, brill, lemon sole in ginger sauce, and fried mussels. Open Mondays through Saturdays. Reservations necessary. 44 Bedford St. (phone: 244844). Expensive.

Roscoff – With a bright white modern atmosphere and an imaginative menu, this spot has burst onto the Belfast restaurant scene with outstanding success. Specialties include crispy duck confit, pork medallions, terrine of peaches, and French pastries. Open Mondays through Saturdays. Reservations necessary. Lesley House, Shaftsbury Sq. (phone: 331532). Expensive.

Belfast Castle – Housed in a baronial castle set on the slopes of Cave Hill, overlooking the city and Lough Belfast, this restaurant features nouvelle cuisine prepared with fresh ingredients. A hot and cold buffet, carvery, and à la carte menu are offered in the formal dining room. Casual dining is available in the former dungeon decorated with Victorian street scenes. Open daily. Reservations necessary. Antrim Rd., outside the city on Cave Hill (phone: 776925). Dinner, expensive; lunch, moderate.

La Belle Epoque – Delicious French fare is served in this 2-level dining establishment decorated with antiques in a dark atmosphere. The menu includes game in season, fish, and steaks. An accordionist plays some evenings. Closed Sundays. Reservations necessary. 103 Great Victoria St. (phone: 323244). Moderate.

Strand – A brick row house near Queen's University, this popular spot is divided into intimate small rooms decorated with stained glass windows, detailed woodwork, and creative lighting. The excellent fare includes crabmeat, stuffed courgettes (zucchini), chicken roulade, and salmon. Open daily. Reservations necessary. 12 Stranmillis Rd. (phone: 682266). Moderate.

Nick's Warehouse – Housed in a restored warehouse with pine floors and brick walls, this trendy French bistro-style wine bar serves homemade soups, appetizers, and cakes. A more formal restaurant is upstairs. Open daily. Reservations advised. 35-39 Hill St. (phone: 439690). Upstairs, moderate; bistro, inexpensive.

Chez Delbart – Casual and friendly, this lively spot is popular with locals. Specialties include savory and sweet pancakes, steaks, and baked oysters. Have a drink at the long bar if you must wait for a table. Open daily. No reservations. 10 Bradbury Pl. (phone: 238020). Inexpensive.

Saints and Scholars – Small and cozy, with a conservatory section decorated with plants, this eatery features an eclectic menu: stir-fry vegetables, deep-fried Brie, cassoulet. Open daily. Reservations necessary. 3 University St., in the Queen's University area (phone: 325137). Inexpensive.

SHARING A PINT: Just across from the *Europa* (on Great Victoria St.) are two atmospheric old pubs: the *Crown,* a National Trust property with stained glass windows, polished wooden "snugs," and an upstairs oyster bar in Victorian decor, and *Robinson's,* with a big stone fireplace and mahogany bar. Also try *Drury Lane* (2 Amelia St.), for an after-theater dinner; the *Beaten Docket* (48 Great Victoria St.); and *Morning Star* (17 Pottinger's Entry) for an old pub atmosphere (lunch only). Most pubs offer light lunches, some have pub grub dinners. Pub hours are 11:30 AM to 11:30 PM (last drink served at 11 PM), daily except Sundays. A relaxation in licensing laws in Northern Ireland allows pubs to open on Sundays from 12:30 to 2:30 PM and from 7 to 10 PM. While many are taking advantage of the new Sunday opening rules, some publicans continue to observe the traditional Sabbath and remain closed on Sundays.

CASHEL

The Rock of Cashel, with its spectacular grouping of historic ecclesiastical buildings, is one of Ireland's most striking landmarks and one of its most intriguing sights. Among the Irish, it was never referred to by so simple and unimpressive a name as mere Cashel, which is a curt and unromantic anglicization. Instead, it was known as *Caiseal Mumhan,* "the stronghold of Munster" or "Cashel of the kings." For centuries the seat of the Munster kings, it also became the religious center of Ireland.

The small town of Cashel lies on the direct Dublin–Cork road and laps at the foot of the Rock on the south side. Approached from any direction, the 300-foot rocky outcrop — with its towers and battlements spiking out of the plain against the horizon — always jolts the vision and the imagination. Floodlit at night, it is spectacularly beautiful. The Rock of Cashel is no less than Ireland's Acropolis.

A warrior tribe called the Eoghanachta (who probably originated in the present-day Killarney area) arrived here about the 4th century and, after subjugating the original inhabitants, built their stronghold on the Rock. In time they extended their power over the fertile plains until they loosely ruled all of Munster. For 500 years they retained their warlike ways, at the same time growing in political sophistication, and, as Kings of Cashel and then of Munster, refused to acknowledge the overlordship of even the O'Neill Kings of Tara.

From earliest history, Cashel had ecclesiastical connections. St. Patrick came to the Rock in 450 and converted King Aengus to Christianity. The story goes that when Patrick was baptizing the king, the point of his staff accidentally pierced the king's foot. Thinking that this was an essential part of the ceremony, King Aengus bore the wound unflinchingly. Patrick made Cashel a bishopric, and from that time, many of the rulers wielded the crozier as well as the sword.

During the 10th century, the fortress fell prey to Viking marauders, from whom it was rescued by the famous Brian Ború. Thereafter, the O'Briens — the descendants of Brian — held sway over Cashel and in 1101 made the magnanimous gesture of giving the Rock to the church. The Eoghanachta were at this time still lords of Cashel, although internecine warfare had reduced their status. Whatever they thought about Brian's gesture, they obviously came to terms with it. The last of their kings, Cormac, was responsible for the building of King Cormac's Chapel, the finest gem in the Rock's crown.

The Round Tower probably had been on the Rock since the 10th century. Work on the chapel was begun in 1127. The large cathedral that now dominates the group of buildings was begun in the 13th century, some time after King Henry II of England had, so he thought, established his lordship over Ireland.

But nothing remains as simple as that in Ireland. In the centuries of agitation that followed, Cashel had its share of "the troubles." The cathedral was burned down in 1495 by the tempestuous Earl of Kildare because, he explained to Henry, "I thought the archbishop was inside" — an excuse that apparently so charmed the king that he later appointed the earl lord lieutenant of the kingdom. The cathedral was burned down again in 1647 and all inside, including 3,000 townspeople who had taken refuge there, perished.

After those terrible events, the buildings remained abandoned and derelict, except for a short period when they were partly repaired for Protestant use. They were abandoned completely in 1749, and the cathedral roof stripped. It was said that the Archbishop Agar disliked the Sabbath climb to the top of the Rock. In 1874, the ruins were given to the state to be preserved as a national monument.

Compared with the importance and drama of the Rock, the town of Cashel is subdued and modest. It has a population of only about 2,800 and consists of two thoroughfares, Main and Friar Streets, and a handful of side streets. Some 120,000 visitors come to the Rock in a season, tour buses drawing up by the dozens, but their comings and goings hardly impinge on the life of the town. Far from overcommercializing their great site, the townspeople in some perverse way almost refuse to acknowledge it. Hardly a souvenir of Cashel can be found — not a Rock T-shirt in sight. This casual attitude has both its virtues and its shortcomings: It's nice not to be badgered and hustled with plastic Rocks and kelly green towers, but one could wish for more to enliven the evenings than a few old-fashioned pubs and the regular *Irish Nights* at *Brú Ború* in summer (see *Theater*).

Cashel's real preoccupation, as visitors will discover, is not the Rock and its great past, but horses. Cashel stands at the edge of the Golden Vale, a great sweep of fair and fertile lands bounded by the soft folds of Slievenamon, the Galtees, and the Knockmealdown Mountains. On these fertile acres graze some of Ireland's finest bloodstock. Up to a dozen stud farms or training stables are within 10 miles of the town, including that of the almost legendary Vincent O'Brien. And in this tiny town there are four "turf accountants" — bookies, or betting shops.

CASHEL AT-A-GLANCE

 SEEING THE CITY: To get the best view of the Rock from town, walk up Friar Street past both the Catholic church and the Protestant cathedral, and then look back. From here the Rock seems to sit on the roofs of the houses and shops, creating a strange perspective. Guests at the *Cashel Palace,* originally the bishop's palace, get the best view of all. The gardens lead directly to the gate of the Rock enclosure, and a paved way — the Bishop's Walk — leads up through the gardens. At night the Rock is floodlit, taking on something of the mystery of a fairy castle suspended in air, while far below, a fountain is caught in another spot of light.

To see the town, ascend the Rock, and for the highest vantage point, go up into the tower. The small town is spread below, with its few modest 19th-century streets and handful of older buildings. Turn in the other direction and gaze over the miles and miles of emerald grasslands of the Golden Vale. The reason these fertile lands were so much fought over by opposing armies, native and usurper, is apparent.

SPECIAL PLACES: Rock of Cashel – The Rock comprises, in chronological order, the Round Tower, Cormac's Chapel, the cathedral, and the Hall of the Vicars Choral. Entrance is through the Hall of the Vicars Choral, which has been extensively renovated to create an exhibition area and visitors' center, which includes a new audiovisual program about the Rock and the surrounding area.

Vicars Choral – This complex of buildings is the most recent on the Rock, having been built in the 15th century to house the clergy of the cathedral. To the right of the entrance is a vaulted room in which various stone carvings and other local finds are displayed. Here, too, is the massive Cross of St. Patrick, which stood for 800 years outside on the Rock. For safety, it has been brought indoors, and a replica now stands outside. Tradition holds that the base of this cross was the coronation stone of the Kings of Munster. Upstairs is a restored dining hall with a minstrel gallery and kitchen, furnished to the period with authentic 15th-century furniture.

Cathedral – Outside, beyond the replica of the Cross of St. Patrick, is the doorway to the 13th-century cathedral, the largest of the buildings. It has a nave, chancel, two transepts, a tower at the crossing, and a residential tower at the western end. Though roofless and much ruined, it is worth examining for its interesting and attractive details, such as the fine arches of the center crossing and several tombs. Look out for humorous little carved heads peering from pillar tops and archways.

Round Tower – Leaving the cathedral by the doorway you entered, walk to the right around the building to the Round Tower at the northeastern corner. As usual with such structures, its doorway is high above the ground because it was used as a refuge as well as a bell tower in an attack. The exact date of its construction is not known, but it is probably late 10th century, certainly before the Rock was given to the church in 1101.

King Cormac's Chapel – Continue to the right around the cathedral to the gem of the Rock — Cormac's Chapel. Even from a distance, this early small cathedral has a special glow. That's because it is built of warm-colored sandstone, which shows up golden against the cold gray limestone of the larger building. The chapel, with its graceful arcading and steep stone roof, is regarded as the finest example of Irish Romanesque architecture. Notice its two attractively carved doorways and chancel arch. Remnants of paintings can just be discerned on the chancel walls, indicating that once the whole interior glowed with color. There is a superbly carved stone sarcophagus in which a crozier, now in the *National Museum* in Dublin, was found. The chapel was built in 1127, shortly after the Round Tower was completed. When the larger cathedral was begun more than a century later, it had to be carefully fitted between the two, which explains some of the odd connections and dislocations of line.

Buildings on the Rock are open daily 9 AM to 7:30 PM, May through September; 10 AM to 4:30 PM, October through April. Admission charge. Tours are conducted every hour on the hour, or more frequently as needed. Tom Wood is the supervisor guide (phone: 61437). Advice: Even if the day is warm and sunny, bring a windbreaker — this is a drafty spot!

Hore Abbey – The remains of this attractive abbey stand among the fields to the west of the Rock. It began as a Benedictine structure, but in 1272, when the local archbishop dreamed that the Benedictines were plotting to behead him, he banished them, replacing them with Cistercians from Mellifont Abbey in County Louth. The result, after various alterations, is the usual Cistercian plan (simple and utilitarian), except that here the cloisters lie on the north side. (Cloisters were usually on the south so that monks could read and work warmed by the sun.) As it is not locked or guarded, visitors can stroll around the abbey at any time.

Old Palace – First built in 1730 as the archbishop's "palace" and later the residence of the Protestant dean, the Old Palace is now the *Cashel Palace* hotel (see *Checking In*). It is a beautiful example of the Queen Anne style, with a fine hall, original paneling, and a red pine staircase. The gardens run from the back of the house to the slopes of the Rock, with a pathway known as the Bishop's Walk leading to the gate. On the lawn are two sprawling mulberry trees, said to be even older than the house and to have been planted to celebrate Queen Anne's coronation in 1702.

Cashel Diocesan Library (GPA-Bolton Library) – The library of Archbishop Bolton, who built the Old Palace (above) and who died in 1741, is now housed in the Chapter House of the Protestant cathedral. Its treasures include 12th-century manuscripts, 15th-century printed books (incunabula), rare maps, and fine bindings. There is also an exhibition of books (including a first edition of Chaucer), manuscripts, and church silver. Most of the material relates to theological and historical themes. Although there is a published catalogue, this remarkable collection has not been fully studied; it remains a resource for original research. Open 9:30 AM to 5:30 PM Mondays through Saturdays; 2:30 to 5:30 PM Sundays. Admission charge. John St. (phone: 61232).

St. Dominic's Abbey – Now little more than a shell, this abbey, founded in 1243, was an important Dominican establishment in its day. Note the fine 13th-century window. To look inside the walls, get the key from William Minogue, who lives in the cottage at the foot of the Rock. The abbey is just below the Rock in the middle of Cashel.

■**EXTRA SPECIAL: Holy Cross Abbey** – Founded in 1180, though later much altered, the abbey takes its name from a relic of the True Cross that was enshrined here. It has been a place of pilgrimage for centuries. A decade or two ago, it was a gaunt, if picturesque, ruin reflected in the quiet waters of the River Suir. It has since been reroofed and extensively restored for use as a parish church. The interior is starkly plain and white, a treatment that shows its lines and details to best advantage. Note the wall painting of a hunting scene on the north transept and the unusual pillared feature in the south transept, thought to have been where the fragment of the True Cross was kept. The cloisters are fairly well preserved, and there is a meditation garden by the river. The church proper is open daily year-round. A separate building provides facilities for pilgrims and visitors, including a souvenir shop (where an excellent booklet, *Holy Cross Abbey,* can be purchased), a tourist information center, an audiovisual center, and a museum. Facilities open 10 AM to 1 PM and 2 to 6 PM May through September (sometimes for a longer season, depending on traffic). Nine miles north on the Thurles road, R660 (phone: 504-43241).

SOURCES AND RESOURCES

TOURIST INFORMATION: The tourist board is in the Town Hall (Main St.; phone: 61333). It has information, maps, and leaflets — some free, others at nominal cost — and offers a reservation service, particularly useful for arranging on-the-spot bed and breakfast accommodations at local guesthouses. Open weekdays 9 AM to 1 PM and 2 to 5:30 PM May through September.

Local Coverage – The *Nationalist,* which comes out on Thursdays, covers the Tipperary scene and contains a page focusing on people and events in Cashel. The *Tipperary Star* is another good weekly local newspaper. The tourist board, however, is probably the best source of information on happenings.

TELEPHONE: The area code for Cashel and the immediate vicinity is 62. When calling from within the Republic of Ireland, dial 062 before the local number.

GETTING AROUND: Cashel is a small town, best seen on foot.

Bicycle – The nearest bicycles to rent are available from *J. J. O'Carroll,* James St., Tipperary town (phone: 51229).

Bus and Train – Cashel is not on the railway network, but there is daily bus service to Dublin. There is also bus service to Cork City and to Waterford via Cork. For more information, contact *CIE (Córas Iompair Eireann, National Transport Company)* in Dublin (see "Getting Around" in *Dublin,* THE CITIES) or the tourist board in Cashel.

Car Rental – Rentals are available from *O'Doherty & O'Dwyer Ltd.,* Cord Rd. (phone: 61544).

Taxi – Taxis are unnecessary within the town, but to venture farther afield, there is a choice of three: *John Grogan* (phone: 61132); *Donal Feehan* (phone: 61088); or *Tom Devitt* (phone: 61030).

SPECIAL EVENTS: Cashel is a quiet town and has no celebrations beyond the standard holidays. But the town is horse-mad, and racing events at home and abroad bring the place to life. *Tipperary* racecourse, 18 miles away on N24, has a meet every week in summer, with the most important event taking place in July. For betting action, join the crowd at any of the four turf accountants (bookies) in town, especially on the days of the *Grand National* (April), *Cheltenham Gold Cup* (March), or the *Irish Derby* (late June). Check local listings for exact dates.

MUSEUMS: Apart from the Hall of the Vicars Choral on the Rock, there are two small museums that are worth a visit, time permitting.

Bothán Scóir – At the far end of Friar Street is a well-preserved minimal thatched cottage of the Famine period, now used as a folk museum. Open May through September. Admission charge.

Folk Village – An interesting assemblage of stalls with an odd collection of old domestic and farm implements. Open erratically. Admission charge. Just off Main St., behind Town Hall.

SHOPPING: *Pádraig O Mathúna* – The shop/gallery of the master silversmith and enamelist is tucked inconspicuously into a corner almost behind Town Hall. Pádraig is a superb artist and craftsman, and his works have been featured in exhibitions in many countries. Items include silver and gold bowls, plaques, sculptures, and jewelry. Each piece is unique and makes a perfect gift or keepsake. Open usually 9 AM to 6 PM. Ring the bell outside if the shop is closed. 98 Main St. (phone: 61741).

Rossa Pottery and Shanagarry Tweeds – This small pottery shop and adjoining weaving shed are on the Cork road, N8, a mile south of Cashel. The shed offers handwoven scarves and rugs. Open 9:30 AM to 5:30 PM May through September. At other times, knock at the door; if anyone is there, visitors will be welcomed (phone: 61388).

SPORTS AND FITNESS: Fishing – Very good trout and some salmon fishing are to be enjoyed on the lazy river Suir. The manager at the *Cashel Palace* hotel (phone: 61411) will make arrangements for hotel guests. Others should contact Frank Burke at Town Hall (phone: 61166).

Fitness – The sports complex at Larkspur Park offers opportunities for exercise and action: tennis, badminton, and squash courts; snooker room; and a good 18-hole pitch-and-putt course. Visitors welcome; small charge per facility. Open daily 9:30 AM to about 9:30 PM; adults given priority after 6 PM. The Green (phone: 61626).

Fox Hunting – County Tipperary is great hunting country. To join a fox hunt, contact Garrett Dooley in the village of Newinn, south of Cashel on N8 (phone: 62231), who can make all the arrangements.

THEATER: Folk theater, traditional music, song, and dance is offered every evening at *Brú Ború* (phone: 61122), a cultural center. Curtain every evening at 8 PM; additional performances daily on demand.

MUSIC: Daily performances at *Brú Ború*. (See *Theater.*)

BEST IN TOWN

CHECKING IN: Cashel has one excellent hotel; there are two others in Dundrum, 8 miles away on R505. Otherwise the most reliable accommodations are the comfortable and homely (in the best sense) bed and breakfast houses in and around town. Most are within walking distance of the town center, except perhaps for travelers carrying heavy baggage. The selection here is representative of the best, but several others are equally good. The tourist board will make on-the-spot bookings (phone: 61333). In July or August, it may be wise to make advance arrangements, either through the tourist board or directly with the establishment. Expect to pay over $150 for two for accommodations classed as very expensive, $85 to $150 for expensive, $50 to $85 for those listed as moderate, and less than $50 (sometimes far less) for inexpensive ones. All telephone numbers are in the 62 area code unless otherwise indicated.

Cashel Palace – A "grand" hotel on a modest scale, with 20 bedrooms, one of which has a canopy bed, another a four-poster. It dates from 1730, having been built as a residence for the Bishops of Cashel; the Rock begins at the bottom of the garden, which is appropriately named Bishops Walk. The hotel is comfortably furnished in period style — flocked wallpaper, chandeliers, fine old paintings — while offering all modern conveniences. Upon arrival, guests are greeted with tea and scones, and there's a peat fire in the lobby on cold days. There also are 2 restaurants (see *Eating Out*). At the base of the Rock (phone: 61411). Very expensive to expensive.

Dundrum House – This large, airy, Palladian-style manor house, a classic example of 18th-century Georgian architecture, is now a hotel. Standing on wooded grounds where deer and red squirrels abound, it offers good trout fishing in the Multeen River and horseback riding (instruction available), as well as a good restaurant (see *Eating Out*). Dundrum (phone: 71116). Expensive.

Rectory House – A small, family-run place with a sense of style and tradition. Proprietor Paul Deegan prepares elegant meals (see *Eating Out*). Dundrum (phone: 71266). Moderate.

Knock Saint Lour House – Mrs. O'Brien is widely known for her fine breakfasts; she will prepare evening meals as well if contacted in advance. Her modern 2-story farmhouse also has 8 rooms, 4 with private bath. 2 miles south on the main road, N8 (phone: 61172). Inexpensive.

Maryville – Mary and Pat Duane look after guests solicitously in their comfortable, warm house in the center of town. The 13th-century walls of St. Dominic's Abbey adjoin the garden (phone: 61098). Inexpensive.

Rahard Lodge – Mrs. Foley's modern farmhouse and flowering gardens overlook the Rock. Sheep nibble the surrounding lawn and green fields. Only a few minutes' walk from town (phone: 61052). Inexpensive.

Thornbrook House – Besides a pleasant rural setting, guests at Mrs. Kennedy's modern bungalow also enjoy peat fires, wide gardens, and a view of the Rock. On the outskirts of town (phone: 61480). Inexpensive.

 EATING OUT: Cashel does not have a wide variety of dining places, but a few restaurants serve good food in congenial surroundings. The choice in town is among two expensive restaurants, a moderately priced "buttery," pub grub at midday (try *Davern's,* 20 Main St.), and a few small fast-food efforts. Dundrum, 8 miles away on R505, offers two additional choices. Expensive means $60 to $85 for two for dinner, without wine; moderate, about $35 to $45; and inexpensive, $30 or less. All telephone numbers are in the 62 area code unless otherwise indicated.

Chez Hans – This converted Anglican church, with pointed windows and arched doorway, offers what the proprietor calls "honest French food with an Irish touch," such as lamb marinated in homegrown garden herbs and baked *en croûte*. Open 6 PM for dinner only. Reservations necessary. Next to the Rock (phone: 61177). Expensive.

Four Seasons – The main restaurant at the *Cashel Palace* hotel has a reputation for fine food. Try the Lobster Kathleen, with Irish whiskey, cream, leek, and spring onion sauce, or the sole Palace-style, with salmon mousse and watercress sauce. Usually closed weekends October to April. Reservations necessary. *Cashel Palace* (phone: 61411). Expensive.

Bailey's of Cashel – Set in the basement of a Georgian house, this place specializes in succulent steaks and good wines. Reservations advised. Main St. (phone: 61937). Moderate.

Dundrum House – The dining room in the hotel of the same name offers a change of fare and a taste of life in a typical Georgian manor house. Dining is in the conservatory overlooking the lawns and river. Good hearty fare, mainly grills, roasts, and excellent Dublin Bay prawns. Reservations advised. Dundrum (phone: 71116). Moderate.

Rectory House – This charming old house has a Victorian-style dining room — a wonderful spot for a quiet, cozy, candlelit supper featuring Irish and French cuisine. Call ahead to discuss the menu. Reservations advised. Dundrum (phone: 71266). Moderate.

The Buttery – In the cellar of the fine old *Palace* hotel, with flagstone floors, stone walls, and lots of atmosphere, it is a lively and informal place to meet for food or drinks. It features a *flambé* trolley on Thursday, Friday, and Sunday nights, November to March, and a carving trolley at lunchtime. Very popular with the horsey set. Reservations advised. *Cashel Palace* (phone: 61411). Moderate to inexpensive.

SHARING A PINT: The *Buttery* (in the *Palace* cellar), or *Davern's* (20 Main St.) across the road, are the obvious places for visitors to get a drink and a lunchtime snack. Also popular are *Browns* (Main St.), a pub with lovely horse portraits; *Pat's Place,* a delicatessen (at the top of Main St.); and *Golden Vale,* a dance-hall pub with Irish night every Monday. You might get a few good "tips" farther down the road toward Cork, at a little place with a nice antique air, wood paneling, and brass bars on the window. The name *Meany's* is over the door, but in truth the last of a long line of Meanys sold out 10 years ago to Michael and Carl Cregan, who have deliberately avoided making many changes. The talk is mostly of horses, then of greyhounds, and then, they say, of women, if none are present. Get Carl to put a shamrock on your pint!

CORK CITY

The Irish Republic's second city is a bustling, zesty, highly individual place, quite different from Dublin in appearance and atmosphere. Though it lacks the capital's Georgian uniformity, it makes up for the defect in visual variety, mixing the romance of mock-Gothic outlines with the moderation and proportion of the classical style. Dublin is flat, and Cork is hilly. Dublin has a somber tone; Cork is as variegated, light and dark, as its local stones. And while Dublin, as capital, was burdened with an alien tradition of subservience, Cork cultivated a spirit of defiance that earned it the nickname Rebel Cork. It is a busy, assertive, self-made place where Jack is as good as his master and frequently tells him so.

The making of Cork was the river Lee, which flows not only through but in and around the city as it approaches its great estuary. In its valley it formed a great marsh with islands that became, as in Venice, the foundation of the town and the source of its Gaelic name, *Corcaigh,* meaning "a marshy place." The first settlement was, as might be expected, a little Gaelic monastery founded in the 6th century by an obscure but beloved abbot-bishop named Barra of the Fair Hair, or Finbarre. The monastery, on a hill south of the river where the present St. Finbarre's Cathedral stands, grew in power, and it was probably its reputation for wealth that enticed the Vikings in their longboats up the estuary and through the sinuous marsh. The Vikings first founded a trading post here in the 8th century and within 50 years they had fortified one of the islands to become the right and tight little city of Cork.

In time, the Vikings became subjects of the Gaelic prince of the area, MacCarthy Mor, but they nevertheless maintained a degree of independence in their island city under their own *jarl* (ruler) until the Norman invasion in the 12th century forced them to switch allegiance. In the turbulent centuries that followed, the inhabitants of Cork City acquired a reputation for independent-mindedness even to rebellion. King John (as prince) gave them a charter in 1185, they were back under the MacCarthys by 1195, and they were given a more prestigious charter by the king in 1199 and another new one in 1241. But in 1495 they nearly seized the Crown itself when they received the pretender to the throne, Perkin Warbeck, and escorted him to England to proclaim him King of England and Lord of Ireland.

While Dublin's monuments are castle and parliament house and the homes of the great nobles, Cork within its island walls has shops and warehouses and banks. It was essentially a trading town and still is. In the 18th century, it became the great supply port for the American colonies, sending out beef, bacon, and butter, and during the Napoleonic Wars it was the larder of the British army and navy. Gradually, rows of houses began to rise along the winding creeks between the islands and at last Cork expanded beyond its walls and up the sides of the river valley.

As the merchants made money, they developed an appreciation of civilized amenities. Cork silver and glass became tasteful and elegant. A Cork school of painters developed; the neo-classical subjects of James Barry and Robert Fagan, the townscapes of Nathaniel Grogan, and the historical panoramas of Samuel Forde and Daniel Maclise can be admired in the *Crawford Municipal Art Gallery*. Talk has always been a strong art form in Cork; the accent is singsong and musical, but it conceals a sharp verbal wit used with deadly effect on native and visitor. The 19th-century wordsmiths met in drinking clubs and debating societies and produced a circle of essayists and poets including William Maginn, a Johnsonian schoolmaster and satirist, and Francis Sylvester O'Mahony (Father Prout), a mocking ex-priest, both of whom scored in the literary reviews when they emigrated to London, and a gentle lyric poet, J. J. Callanan, who died young in Lisbon.

The 19th century also produced some distinguished architecture in Cork. First the brothers Pain, James and George Richard, pupils of John Nash, came from London and built bridges, jails, a courthouse, some lovely townhouses with gentle Regency bowfronts, and the delightful Gothic fantasy Blackrock Castle at the end of the Marina Walk. They were succeeded by the Deane family, builders of churches, banks, and Cork's University College. From the Deane firm emerged Benjamin Woodward, a genius of the neo-Gothic whose best work is in Dublin and Oxford.

Cork in the 20th century is chronicled in the short stories of Seán O'Faoláin and Frank O'Connor, both natives. It is still a workaday city; shops, warehouses, and factories are part of its fabric. But it is also a good talking town, a great eating-out town, a sports-mad town. During the War of Independence (1919–21) it was a wellspring of nationalistic fervor, losing two mayors and many public buildings to the cause. Since then, it has withstood the worst assaults of modernization, though its cramped island site has given it some real traffic problems, which the city's 136,000 inhabitants manage to live with in their own spirited way. They are a most competent people whose response to good fortune and bad is a mocking laugh and a musical burst of anecdote.

CORK AT-A-GLANCE

SEEING THE CITY: The north slope of the river valley is dominated by the tower of St. Anne's Church, better known simply as Shandon steeple. Cross the river and climb the tower to an outside balcony. The city is spread below, the flat marsh area with its busy streets surrounded by what Edmund Spenser called "The spreading Lee, that like an island fayre / Encloseth Corke with his divided floode." The Lee here forms a north channel and a south channel, and between them is the compact central island known as the "flat of the city." Patrick Street, or St. Patrick Street, the main artery crossing the island, was itself once an open river channel, as were the Grand Parade and the South Mall. In the 18th century ships could still be seen afloat in these channels, but by 1800 the waterways had been turned into thoroughfares for the traffic on foot, hoof, and wheel that crowded into the city's business district. Quieter, more reflective parts of Cork are the slopes that rise to the south and north of the central island. The Gothic towers of St. Finbarre's Cathedral and the graceful Gothic quadrangles of the university are on the south slope, and churches, convents, and hospitals are to the right and left on the north slope.

SPECIAL PLACES: The "flat of the city" is the hub of activity in Cork, and a walk along Patrick Street (affectionately called Pana by residents) and its subsidiary arteries is as traditional an activity as the European evening promenade. Going east to west, the walk is properly done on the left path for a view of the better-preserved right side of the street with its delicately bowfronted 18th-century houses (the left side had to be replaced when British troops burned the street in 1920). Patrick Street leads to the Grand Parade, which runs straight to the south channel of the river and has some traditional weather-slated bowfronts remaining from the 18th century. At the south channel, the Grand Parade meets the South Mall, now the financial district. Here, a few characteristic merchants' houses remain from the days when the South Mall was still an open waterway. Doors at street or water level opened onto basement storerooms so that boats could be unloaded easily, and high outside steps led up to the merchants' living quarters above their shops. Walking is the best way to see the flat of the city. Numerous bridges span the Lee's still-flowing channels providing access to the north and south banks.

FLAT OF THE CITY

Father Matthew Statue – This memorial to Father Theobald Matthew, the Apostle of Temperance, is the work of the celebrated 19th-century Irish sculptor John Henry Foley, who also created the monument to Daniel O'Connell in Dublin and was one of several artists responsible for the Albert Memorial in London. Father Matthew, a superior of the Capuchin order in Cork, was known not only for his crusade in the cause of temperance but also for his work among the poor, especially during the mid-19th-century famines. The statue is a central point of reference in Cork City. Patrick St. at Patrick Bridge.

Crawford Municipal Art Gallery – Housed in a red brick building put up in the early 18th century as the city's custom house, the gallery contains a select collection of works by painters of the 20th-century Irish School: Orpen, Lavery, and Yeats; a good representation by artists of the earlier Cork School: Barry, Grogan, Forde, and Maclise; and some fine examples of Cork silver and glass. Open 9:30 AM to 5:30 PM weekdays, 9 AM to 1 PM Sundays. Emmet Pl.

Church of Saints Peter and Paul – Opened in 1868, this excellent Gothic Revival church by E. W. Pugin is typical of Cork in its casing of red sandstone and its dressing of white limestone. Off Paul St.

Coal Quay Market – This outdoor flea market is open for business daily except Sundays, not on the quays but on a street running from the Grand Parade to Coal Quay. No longer colorful and not exactly sweet-smelling, it takes place in front of a market building with good classical frontage, now privately owned. Corn Market St.

City Market – Fruit, vegetables, fish, and meat — including local specialties such as drisheen (blood pudding or blood sausage) and tripe — are displayed and sold in a stylish late-18th-century market arcade under a cast-iron and glass roof (also referred to by locals as the "English Market," reflecting its origins). When the market is in full swing, daily except Sundays, the scene is animated and the stallholders are full of Cork esprit and chat. Entrances off Patrick St., Princes St., and Grand Parade.

Court House – The Pain brothers designed this stately building with Corinthian porticoes in 1835. Sir Walter Scott, among others, admired it. Washington St.

South and North Main Streets – When Cork was still enclosed by walls, its main gates were at the South Gate Bridge and the North Gate Bridge. Between the two ran the spine of the medieval city, worth walking today for its atmosphere redolent of food and housewares shops. The much-altered 18th-century Protestant Christ Church (South Main St.) is on the site of a medieval parish church that dated from the Normans and was probably the church in which Edmund Spenser married Elizabeth Boyle, his Irish bride, in the 16th century. Another of Cork's medieval parish churches (there were two) was off North Main Street, near which are also many lanes — such as Portney's Lane — that once housed merchants and craftsmen.

Mercy Hospital – When it was built in the 18th century, this was the Mansion House of the Mayor of Cork. The handsome building with its Italianate front is the work of Daviso de Arcort, the Sardinian architect, best known as Davis Ducart; the good stucco ceiling inside is by Patrick Osborne of Waterford. The building is now a hospital. Open to the public during patient visiting hours. Henry St.

Holy Trinity Church – The church of the Capuchin friars, also known as Father Matthew Memorial Church, dates from the 1830s. Internally, it is a charming Regency Gothic creation by George R. Pain. The lantern spire by Coakley is a graceful later addition enhanced by the riverside setting. Father Matthew Quay.

NORTH BANK

St. Patrick's Bridge – This mid-19th-century connection is a very satisfactory classical construction in white limestone. The view from the bridge — upriver over the city's churches, convents, and other institutions and downriver to the ships — is quintessential Cork. Patrick's Hill, a precipitous street housing fashionable doctors, leads up the north bank from the bridge and it's worth the climb for another view over the city. End of Patrick St.

St. Anne's Church, Shandon – The quaint pepper-box tower of this Protestant church, built from 1722 to 1726, is the symbol of Cork. Shandon steeple rises in square tiers to its cupola and weather vane crowned by a golden fish. As in the old jingle "Red and white is Shandon steeple / Party coloured like the people," it has two red sides and two white sides, a combination that is a signature of many Cork buildings. From the top of the steeple, the source of the color scheme is apparent in the river valley: one slope of red sandstone and an opposite one of silvery white limestone. The Shandon churchyard is the last resting place of Francis S. O'Mahony, a fitting spot because it was he, under the pen name Father Prout, who wrote "The Bells of Shandon," a song that made both bells and church famous. Open 9:30 AM to 6 PM in summer, 10:30 AM to 4:30 PM the rest of the year. Church St.

St. Mary's Dominican Church – Kearns Deane, a member of the prominent family of Cork architects responsible for several of the city's classical buildings, designed this church with the solid portico in 1832. Inside is a tiny carved ivory Madonna of 14th-century Flemish origin. Pope's Quay.

St. Patrick's Church – A flurry of construction in the classical style took place in early-19th-century Cork. One good example is this church by George R. Pain (1836) at the foot of the handsome hillside suburbs of Tivoli and Montenotte. The elegant lantern is modeled on the Temple of the Winds in Athens. Lower Glanmire Rd.

SOUTH BANK

Red Abbey – Nothing is left of the abbey of the canons of St. Augustine except the tower of its church, the solitary relic of the early Cork monasteries and, indeed, of medieval Cork. When the Duke of Marlborough besieged the city in 1690, he put a cannon on the tower and directed his fire at the city walls across the south channel of the Lee. Before leaving the spot, walk around the corner to Dunbar Street for a look at St. Finbarr's South, known also as South Chapel, an unusually early (1766) Catholic church (there are very few 18th-century Catholic churches in Ireland) with an altarpiece added by John Hogan, one of the most important Irish sculptors of the last century. Off Mary St.

Elizabeth Fort – The massive curtain walls are all that remain of a 17th-century fort that once housed the Cork garrison. Today, a modern police station stands incongruously within the walls. Off Barrack St.

St. Finbarre's Cathedral – Though somewhat foreshortened on its confined site — where the city's patron saint chose to put his monastery in the 6th century — this Protestant cathedral is considered a brilliant essay in French Gothic by William Burges, an English architect who also designed Cardiff Castle and the quadrangle of Yale University. It was built between 1867 and 1879 to replace an earlier church, which itself replaced a medieval church damaged in the siege of 1690. (A cannonball found 40 feet above the ground in the tower is a reminder of that siege.) Burges's three spires are most successful and his interior detail is rich and inventive. Bishop St.

University College – The main quadrangle is a gem of 19th-century collegiate architecture (reminiscent of the colleges at Oxford) by Thomas Deane and his partner Benjamin Woodward. Later additions do not quite maintain the initial high standard, but the Honan Chapel, architect James J. McMullen's 1915 revival of 12th-century Irish Romanesque style, has interesting exterior details and is stuffed with treasure: stained glass windows, embroideries, tabernacle enamels, and a joyous mosaic floor. The chapel is open daily, except during school holidays. Western Rd.

ENVIRONS

Fota Island – The ornamental estate that belonged to the Smith-Barry family, once Earls of Barrymore, is now owned by University College Cork. Its centerpiece, Fota House, was built in the 1820s by Sir Richard Morrison, who created some of Ireland's finest neo-classical interiors, and it stands today as a splendid example of Regency architecture. The rooms are fully furnished with Irish pieces from the 18th and 19th centuries and decorated with rich period wallpapers and curtains. Most notable are the Irish landscape paintings, dating from the 1750s to the 1870s and constituting the most comprehensive private collection of its kind. On the grounds of the estate are an arboretum, a bee garden, and a wildlife park — including giraffes, zebras, ostriches, antelopes, and other endangered species — covering 70 acres of parkland, woods, and lagoons. During 1991–92, access to Fota Islands attractions may be curtailed at certain times, due to a $70-million development project (scheduled for completion next year), which includes a new hotel, a conference center, sports club, two 18-hole golf courses, golf and tennis schools, a sailing club, and more than 400 vacation homes, apartments, and lodges within the parkland. Check with the tourist office for the latest opening hours. As we went to press, the hours were as follows: Fota House is open 11 AM to 6 PM Mondays through Saturdays, 2 to 6 PM Sundays, April through September; 2 to 6 PM Sundays and holidays the rest of the year. Fota Wildlife Park is open 10 AM to 6PM Mondays through Saturdays, 11 AM to 6 PM Sundays, April through August; 10 AM to 6 PM Saturdays and 11 AM to 6 PM Sundays, September and October. Admission charge. On the main road to Cobh, about 10 miles southeast of Cork in Carrigtwohill (phone: 21-812555).

Blarney – Blarney Castle and the legendary Blarney Stone are a 10-minute drive from Cork City. The castle, which belonged to the MacCarthys, dates from 1446. Although other parts of it were demolished, the massive square keep, or tower, with a battlemented parapet, survived centuries of sieges by such notorious attackers as Oliver Cromwell and William III. The word 'blarney' originated with Cormac MacDermot MacCarthy, a diplomat who was well known in the court of Elizabeth I for his "fair words and soft speech." Blarney has come to mean the ability to deceive without offending. Set in one of the castle walls is the stone that supposedly confers this gift on those who kiss it (leaning over backwards from the parapet). Also on the grounds is Blarney Castle House, a baronial mansion open to the public, and the Rock Close, a garden of ancient trees and stones, reputedly of druidic origin. The Blarney Castle Estate is open daily year-round except *Christmas Eve* and *Christmas Day.* The house is open 10 AM to 5 PM, daily except Sundays, June through September. Admission charge. 5 miles north of Cork City, via R617.

SOURCES AND RESOURCES

 TOURIST INFORMATION: The Cork-Kerry Tourism Office (Grand Parade; phone: 273251) offers information, guidebooks, maps, and leaflets and sells two helpful booklets, *The Cork Guide* (IR£1.50) and the excellent *Tourist Trail* (IR£1), a walking guide to Cork. For books and pamphlets on the city's history and background, visit *Liam Ruiseal's* bookshop around the corner (4950 Oliver Plunkett St.).

Local Coverage – The *Cork Examiner* is the one they call "de payper." It's the morning daily, full of local color. The *Evening Echo,* essential for entertainment information, comes out every evening, and the *Cork Weekly Examiner,* a potpourri of current happenings, appears every Tuesday.

 TELEPHONE: The area code for Cork and the immediate vicinity is 21. When calling from within the Republic of Ireland, dial 021.

GETTING AROUND: In the "flat of the city," walking is easier and faster than going by bus or car because of congested traffic, restricted parking, and one-way circuits. Car drivers should observe the local disc parking system — it works. Books of 10 disc tickets cost IR£2 at tobacco and newspaper shops, garages, and the tourist board. In addition, Cork has three multistory parking garages along the banks of the river downtown — at Lavitts Quay, Paul Street, and Merchants Quay. All are open Mondays through Saturdays (20p to 40p per hour).

Bus and Train – A good city bus service radiates from the Father Matthew Statue. County buses, long-distance buses, and day tours leave from the bus station (Parnell Pl.), a block east of the statue. *Bus Éireann,* a division of *CIE* (*Córas Iompair Éireann, National Transport Company*), operates summer bus tours of the city as well as excursions to Killarney, Bantry Bay, Limerick, and Tipperary (phone: 503399, ext. 318). Trains leave from Kent Station (Lower Glanmire Rd.) on the north bank of the Lee (phone: 504422).

Car Rental – All major international and national firms are represented, including *Johnson & Perrott* (known as *American International Rent-a-Car* in the US; phone: 800-527-0202), which has offices at Emmet Place (phone: 273295) and Cork Airport (phone: 963133). Consult the local yellow pages for more listings.

River Cruises – From mid-May to mid-August, there are afternoon and evening cruises around Cork Harbour and excursions to Fota Island. Schedules and rates are available from the tourist board or *Marine Transport,* Atlantic Quay, Cobh (phone: 811485).

Taxi – Cab ranks are at the stations and in the middle of Patrick Street, opposite the *Savoy Centre,* and at most hotels (phone: 272424, 277000, 961311, or 502680).

Walking Tours – Half- and full-day tours are organized, for a fee, by *Discover Cork Guided Tours* (Belmont, Douglas Rd.; phone: 293873). The tourist office has itineraries and schedules for other, shorter tours that are offered periodically.

 SPECIAL EVENTS: Cork is a festive town. In early May it hosts the *International Choral and Folk Dance Festival,* with colorful and tuneful choirs and lively dancers competing from all over the world. During July, in even-numbered years, the *Royal Cork Yacht Club* organizes *Cork Week,* featuring a variety of contests, including the *European Offshore Team Championship.* Its well-established *Film Festival* of short and feature-length films takes place in September or October, and in late October the town is hopping and bopping with its annual *Jazz Festival.* For information, contact the tourist board, Grand Parade.

 MUSEUMS: Paintings and sculpture by Irish artists and others are in the *Crawford Municipal Art Gallery* (see *Special Places*) and at the *Triskel Arts Centre* (Tobin St.; phone: 272022/23). The *Cork Public Museum* (Fitzgerald Park) contains interesting displays of Cork history from the earliest times to the present, and the surrounding park has a pleasant riverside walk and sculptures by Seamus Murphy, a well-known Cork stone carver who became a sculptor. The museum is open weekdays and Sunday afternoons; the park is open daily (contact the tourist board for the exact hours, which vary with the season). Off Mardyke Rd., a promenade parallel to Western Rd.

SHOPPING: As to be expected of the Republic's second largest metropolitan area, Cork is an excellent shopping center, offering a variety of goods. Major department stores are on Patrick Street. The *Merchant Quay Shopping Centre* (Patrick St. and Merchant's Quay), Cork's newest shopping complex, offers a mix of large department stores, such as *Marks & Spencer* (phone: 275555), international boutiques, such as *Laura Ashley* (phone: 274070), and unique Irish specialty shops. There is also a food court and covered parking. The *Savoy Centre* (Patrick St.) has a variety of large clothing stores, as well as specialty shops carrying Irish linen and fabric, greeting cards, and gift items. Small shops and boutiques abound on Princes and Oliver Plunkett Streets. Paul's Lane, off Paul Street, is home to many antiques shops including *Mills* (3 Paul's La.; phone: 273528), *Anne McCarthy* (2 Paul's La.; phone: 273755), and *O'Regan's* (4 Paul's La.; phone: 509141).

Blarney Woollen Mills – One of the country's busiest craft emporiums, known for fine knits produced on the premises. Also stocks crystal, china, and other gift items. Open daily. In the village of Blarney, 5 miles north of Cork (phone: 385280).

Cash's of Ireland – Cork's equivalent of Dublin's *Switzer's* sells a general range of linen, woolens, tweeds, glassware, and other goods. 18 Patrick St. (phone: 964411).

Cork Arts Society Gallery – Frequent exhibitions of works for sale by local artists. Closed Sundays and Mondays. 16 Lavitt's Quay (phone: 505749).

Fitzgerald – Established in 1860, this shop features Burberry coats and Bally shoes at considerably less than US prices as well as Irish tweeds and cashmere knitwear. 24 Patrick St. (phone: 270095).

Heritage – A variety of local glassware, plus the chance to see local craftsman Sean Murphy at work. 78 Oliver Plunkett St. (phone: 275914).

House of Donegal – The best source for classic trench coats and custom rainwear, with linings of Donegal tweed or silk, all fashioned on the premises. Tweed suits, coats, jackets, tartans, and capes also are made to order. 6/8 Paul St. (phone: 272447 or 502387).

House of James – Housed in a former tea warehouse and candy factory (original cogs and wheels are in evidence), this modern bi-level shop sells locally made pottery, as well as crafts of more than 50 Irish artisans. 20 Paul St. (phone: 272324).

Irish Home Crafts – A tiny place chockful of Irish crocheting, tweeds, handknits, pottery, art, jewelry, and patchwork. 7 Marlborough St. (phone: 273379).

Mainly Murder – For amateur sleuths, this unique bookstore specializes in whodunits from Ireland, England, and many other English-speaking lands. 2-A Paul St., at the corner of French Church St.

Presents – One of the city's better antiques shops, as well as a fine source of sheepskin rugs and handmade craftwork. 75 Oliver Plunkett St. (phone: 275549).

Queen's Old Castle – A traditional department store elegantly converted to a varied shopping mall that includes cafés for the weary. Grand Parade (phone: 275044).

Waterstone's – A bookshop par excellence, for buying or browsing, with an array of volumes on international topics, as well as shelves stacked ceiling-high with books on Irish history, literature, language, politics, cookery, and crafts. Open daily. 69 Patrick St. (phone: 276522).

 SPORTS AND FITNESS: Bicycling – Raleigh touring bikes and all-terrain vehicles can be rented from *Kilcully Stores,* 30 N. Main St. (phone: 273458).

Golf – Several hospitable golf courses surround the city and welcome visitors. The 18-hole *Cork Golf Club* is at Little Island (phone: 353451), about 6½ miles from the center. Others are the *Douglas Golf Club* (phone: 896297), about 3 miles away; the *Muskerry Golf Club* (phone: 385297), about 8 miles away; and *Monkstown Golf Club* (phone: 841376), at Monkstown, a village on the western shore of Cork Harbour, about 5 miles from Cork City. Call for hours. Greens fees average $15 to $20.

Greyhound Racing – Betting is brisk Mondays, Wednesdays, and Saturday nights at the *Cork Greyhound Stadium* (Western Rd.). Details are available in the *Cork Examiner.*

Hurling and Gaelic Football – Cork's *Páirc Uí Chaoimh* stadium on the Marina Walk east of town is the headquarters of Gaelic hurling and football in the south. Matches — of one or the other game — take place most Sunday afternoons through the summer, and *Rebel Cork* is a power to be reckoned with, especially in hurling.

Riding – Three stables are convenient to the city: *Hitchmough Riding School* (Monkstown; phone: 371267); *Pine Grove Riding Centre* (White's Cross; phone: 303857); and *Skevanish Riding Centre* (Innishannon; phone: 775476). Rates average $10 to $15 per hour.

Rugby and Soccer – Both are played at the *University Grounds* (Mardyke Walk). See the sports pages of the *Cork Examiner* for match times.

Sailing – Cork Harbour is a sailor's paradise and the *Royal Cork Yacht Club* (phone: 831440), with headquarters downriver in Crosshaven, welcomes visitors from other clubs.

Tennis – Visitors are welcome at the *Cork Tennis Village* (Model Farm Rd.; phone: 342727). Considered to be one of Ireland's most advanced tennis centers, it offers indoor and outdoor play, 24 hours per day.

 THEATER: The *Cork Opera House* (Emmet Pl.; phone: 270022) is a modern replacement of a romantically decayed theater that burned down in the 1950s. Drama and musical comedies, opera, and ballet are all staged here. *Everyman Palace* offers new plays, foreign and Irish (MacCurtain St.; phone: 503077). From May through December the *Triskel Arts Centre* (Tobin St., off Main St.; phone: 272022) hosts a wide variety of musical events, poetry readings, plays, films, and the performing arts. Check with the tourist board or the *Evening Echo* for details.

MUSIC: For a relatively small city, Cork is fairly rich in music. There are regular lunch-hour concerts of classical music in summer, evening concerts the rest of the year. Check at the tourist board, or call the *Cork School of Music* (phone: 965583). Irish ballads can be heard nightly at *DeLacy House* (74 Oliver Plunkett St.; phone: 270074), at *An Bodhrán* (42 Oliver Plunkett St.; phone: 274544), and at *An Sraid Baile* (*Grand Parade* hotel, 54 Grand Parade; phone: 274391).

NIGHTCLUBS AND NIGHTLIFE: The disco scene is lively. Recommended are *Sparks* (Tucky St.); *Roxanne's* (*Savoy Centre*); *Zoe's* (Oliver Plunkett St.); *Fitzy's* (*Silver Springs* hotel; weekends only); *Mangan's* (16 Careys La.); *Oscar's* (Coburg St); and *Sir Henry's* (Grand Parade). Check the hotels for cabaret and dancing and see the *Evening Echo* for other entertainment listings.

BEST IN TOWN

CHECKING IN: Cork can be jam-packed during high season, so reservations are recommended. Hotels vary from the sleek, modern edifices on the outskirts of town to the downtown dowagers that have been upgraded with bathrooms and coffee shops. Expect to pay $155 and more for a double room in the very expensive category (with Irish breakfast); $105 to $155 in the expensive range; from $70 to $100 in the moderate category; and $60 or less for a room listed as inexpensive. Visitors arriving without a reservation will not be left out in the cold. The tourist board (Grand Parade) will help find a hotel or a good, inexpensive guesthouse. All telephone numbers are in the 21 area code unless otherwise indicated.

Imperial – The dowager of them all, stately in the middle of the South Mall and close to everything, took shape on the drawing board of 19th-century Cork architect Thomas Deane. The grande dame is not as starchy as she looks; in fact, most of the 101 rooms have been renovated with an Art Deco flair, and each has a private bath. Meals in the very competent French restaurant, *La Duchesse,* are served to the accompaniment of piano music. For those who arrive by car, parking can be a problem. South Mall (phone: 274040). Very expensive.

Longueville House – One of Ireland's leading country-house hotels, this 18th-century Georgian mansion is set on a 500-acre wooded estate 20 miles north of Cork. All 16 rooms have a private bath, and the inn is celebrated for the award-winning *Presidents' Restaurant* (see *Eating Out*) and its vineyard, which produces a unique Irish white wine. Closed January and February. In Longueville Mallow village; take the Limerick Rd. to Mallow, then turn left on Killarney and drive 4 miles (phone: 22-47156). Very expensive.

Arbutus Lodge – The lodge is actually an elegant mansion set amid gardens overlooking the city and the river. There are 20 small but good rooms, each with bath, and the Georgian decor is enhanced by a collection of modern Irish art. The best choice if you want to get close to what some consider the best restaurant in Cork, and perhaps in Ireland (see *Eating Out*). Montenotte (phone: 501237). Expensive.

Fitzpatrick Silver Springs – Set on 42 acres overlooking the river Lee on the northeastern fringe of town, this modern 7-story lodging is owned and managed by the Fitzpatricks, one of Ireland's leading hotelier families. This property is constantly undergoing expansion and renovation. The latest development, due for completion early this year, includes 33 new bedrooms and suites, bringing the total to 140. Other additions are a 9-hole golf course and a hilltop activity center, which offers an indoor Olympic-size pool, saunas, steamroom, Jacuzzi, indoor and outdoor tennis courts, squash courts, gym, and aerobic rooms. The hotel has 2 restaurants, one providing river views, a coffee shop, a lounge, and a glass-enclosed elevator. Plenty of parking is available, a rarity for Cork City hotels. Dublin Rd., Tivoli (phone: 507533). Expensive.

Jurys – On the banks of the river Lee, with views of St. Finbarre's Cathedral, this modern 200-room hotel is only a 5-minute walk from the main shopping district. It features the seafood cuisine of *The Fastnet,* an Old World, pubby bar, and a domed, atrium-style pavilion with an indoor-outdoor heated pool, saunas, squash courts, and a gym. Western Rd. (phone: 966377). Expensive.

Metropole – This dowager also manages to keep up appearances. Behind the Victorian (1892) façade of brick and limestone are 91 rooms, each with color TV set, phone, and private bath. On the north bank close to the railway station and ferryport. Complimentary use of a parking garage is available to guests. MacCurtain St. (phone: 508122). Expensive.

Ballymaloe House – Dating from the 17th century with extensions and a chunky stone keep from the 14th-century Fitzgerald Castle, this ivy-walled, old family home about 20 miles from Cork consists of a 400-acre farm replete with grazing sheep and ponies, 29 rooms with bath, and even a cooking school. Some lodging space is assigned in the upgraded courtyard area, the gatehouse, and the gate lodge. Guests and outsiders alike enjoy first class meals in the *Yeats Room* restaurant (see *Ballymaloe* in *Eating Out*). There also is a swimming pool, tennis courts, and a 9-hole golf course. Shanagarry (phone: 652531). Expensive to moderate.

Blarney Park – Convenient for anyone eager to kiss the legendary Blarney Stone, this modern 70-room establishment has a peaceful country setting. All rooms have private baths, and the restaurant, which features nightly entertainment, faces Blarney Castle. A new leisure center is slated to open early this year. Closed January and February. In Blarney, 5 miles north of Cork (phone: 385281). Moderate.

Innishannon House – Just 15 miles outside Cork, this riverside property sits on 9 acres of gardens and woodlands. Built as a private mansion in 1720, it now has 13 guestrooms (each with private bath), a bowfronted dining room, a lounge-library, and a conservatory. Innishannon (phone: 775121). Moderate.

Lotamore House – A sprawling Georgian residence situated on 4 acres along the river Lee, this house is just a 5-minute drive from downtown Cork. All 20 rooms have private baths, orthopedic beds, TV sets, and telephones, while the public rooms retain an 18th-century aura — from a sweeping staircase, ornate plasterwork, and crystal chandeliers to the 1791 drawing room fireplace. Dublin Rd., Tivoli (phone: 822344). Inexpensive.

EATING OUT: Cork is a good eating-out town, largely because the residents eat out quite a bit. Do not ignore the hotel dining rooms; some offer very good value and one in particular may be the best in Ireland. In addition to the restaurants listed here, the natives frequent good dining places half an hour or so from Cork (see "Kinsale" in *West Cork,* DIRECTIONS). Dinner for two without wine or tips will cost $75 and up in places listed as expensive; $40 to $65 in the moderate ones; under $40 in the inexpensive ones. All telephone numbers are in the 21 area code unless otherwise indicated.

Arbutus Lodge – Having won numerous awards (and one coveted star from Michelin), it maintains its standard for excellent and innovative cooking. The seafood is superb (as are most items). The "tasting" menu, if it is on, samples up to a dozen different dishes. A distinguished wine list delights even the most discriminating customers. Reservations necessary. Major credit cards accepted. Montenotte (phone: 501237). Expensive.

Ballymaloe House – Formally known as the *Yeats Room,* the food served here is simple and fresh; nearly everything is grown on the property. Begin with the watercress soup, smoked mackerel, or homemade Danish pâté; follow with summer turkey braised in butter and fresh herbs, roast beef with three sauces, or French casserole of roast pork with Normandy mustard; and top it all with a board of local cheese, fruit tarts, cake, and coffee with *Ballymaloe* chocolates. Open for lunch and dinner. Reservations necessary. Shanagarry (phone: 652531). Expensive.

Clifford's – French nouvelle cuisine is the mainstay at this small but trendy Art Deco–style eatery housed in the old County Library building, near *Jurys* hotel. Chef-owner Michael Clifford changes the menu daily and cooks all dishes to order. House specialties include medallions of monkfish with a prawn *coulis* sauce, breast of duck with baked chicory, and prime filet of beef with glazed shallots. Desserts, such as hot apple and almond tart or orange and lemon pancakes, are especially tempting. Open for lunch and dinner Reservations necessary. 18 Dyke Parade (phone: 275333). Expensive.

Lovetts – French fare is served in this popular restaurant in the suburbs. Seafood is especially recommended; don't miss the brown bread ice cream. Reservations necessary. Churchyard La., off Well Rd., Douglas (phone: 294909). Expensive.

Presidents' – With a hand-painted ceiling, timber floor, and portraits of the Republic of Ireland's former presidents hanging on the walls, this fine establishment at the *Longueville House* hotel serves French fare prepared with fresh ingredients from the 500-acre estate's garden and farm. Menu items include lamb and a variety of fish. Summer dining can be enjoyed in the adjacent 18th-century conservatory. Lunch and dinner served daily. Reservations advised for dinner. Longueville Mallow, 20 miles from Cork; see *Longueville House* in *Checking In* for directions (phone: 22-47156). Expensive.

Jacques – A self-service eatery by day is transformed into a romantic bistro and wine bar each evening. The imaginative dinner menu ranges from cassoulet of shellfish to *noisettes* of lamb with apricot stuffing, roast quail, or chicken Dijon. Homemade desserts include a heavenly almond meringue filled with chocolate cream and rum. Reservations necessary. 9 Phoenix St. (phone: 502387 or 277387). Moderate.

Oyster Tavern – Open since 1742, this traditional eatery, specializing in seafood and steaks, was for sale as we went to press. We hope the new owners will preserve the restaurant's "Old Cork" charm and maintain its long-standing culinary appeal. Since it is in transition, however, check with the tourist office for its current status. Reservations necessary. Market La., off Patrick St. (phone: 27216). Moderate.

Glassialley's – In Cork parlance, "glassialleys" are marbles, and not surprisingly, they dominate the decor of this charming second-floor bistro, with marble-topped tables and marble-accented accessories. Views of the *Municipal Art Gallery* and the *Cork Opera House* add to the ambience. The menu offers an eclectic blend of seafood, steaks, and burgers, with Mexican, Greek, and Chinese influences. Reservations advised. 5 Emmet Pl. (phone: 272305). Moderate to inexpensive.

Mary Rose – Shoppers find the two branches of this restaurant convenient for coffee and pastries, light lunches, snacks, salads, and dinner. In the *Queen's Old Castle* and *Savoy* shopping centers (phone: 507762). Inexpensive.

 SHARING A PINT: Cork's pub system is unusual for Ireland: as in Britain, it consists of independent houses and those linked, or "tied," to a particular brewery. Some pubs serve only Beamish stout, some only Murphy's (the local brews); the independent ones serve both, and Guinness as well. Up to the mid-1950s it was possible to tell who sold what from the outside. Beamish pubs had a classic black and gold nameplate and were called the *Malt Shovel,* the *Black Swan,* the *Winning Post,* and the *Office* ("I was delayed at the *Office,* dear"). The Murphy pubs had a cream and brown trim and usually sailed under their owners' names. Then some irreverent design genius came along and put them both in nondescript contemporary lettering. Inside, however, they keep their individuality. The *Long Valley* (Winthrop St.) is a traditional pub where you can sample both Beamish and Murphy's stouts. *Le Château* (right in the middle of Patrick St.) is crowded but pleasant. Just beside the *Opera House,* audience and actors meet for good talk and the occasional song at the *Grand Circle* (Drawbridge St.). *Beechers Inn* (Faulkners La.) is convenient to the office of the *Cork Examiner,* so the usual liquids come with the customary quota of newspaper rumors. Across the river on the hill beside the old Elizabeth Fort, the *Gateway* (Barrack St.) is supposed to be the oldest pub in Cork. It dates from the 17th century and it is credible that the Duke of Marlborough drank here; certainly legions of his military followers through the centuries did. Good lunchtime eating and drinking pubs include the *Mutton Lane Inn* (Mutton Lane, off Patrick St.); *Maguire's Pennyfarthing Inn* (Grand Parade); *Shandon Tavern* (Lavitt's Quay); and *Dan Lowrey's Seafood Tavern* (MacCurtain St.). *Henchy's* (40 St. Luke's, in the Cork hills) is a fine place to sip a pint and listen to the distinctive Cork accent.

DONEGAL TOWN

Cuddled in the crook of a sheltered Atlantic inlet, near the nest of mountains called the Blue Stacks, Donegal is a tiny town at repose with the world today. But such was not always the case, for in bygone days the drums of history echoed through its streets. Then the stronghold of the powerful O'Donnell clan, rulers of the northwestern kingdom of Tir Connaill (the country of Conall), now the county of Donegal, it was an arena for great and stirring events. In the glory days of that storied Gaelic era beginning in the 13th century, Donegal Town attained a status rivaling the larger, walled cities that had sprung up around the coast of Ireland, and for several centuries this bastion of the O'Donnells exerted a commanding influence on the course of Irish history. The O'Donnell dynasty became a towering symbol of Gaelic hegemony, not the least evidence of which is the fact that in their conquest of Ireland, the invading English had to vanquish the O'Donnells before they could claim a total victory.

The origins of the town are lost in antiquity — the first settlers may have arrived as far back as 2,000 years ago. In the Irish language, Donegal is *Dún na nGall* (fort of the foreigners). It is possible that the original "foreigners" were invaders from Gaul, the vast empire that dominated the western part of continental Europe before the dawn of Christianity. One theory has the Gauls building the first fort on the banks of the river Eske, where the O'Donnells' castle still stands.

What is known with more certainty is that around the 9th century the Vikings built a fortress on this spot that was destroyed by the High King of Ireland in 1159. No trace of this fort has ever been found, however, despite considerable archaeological exploration, although the remains of a number of earthen forts have been excavated in the hills surrounding Donegal Town.

Toward the end of the 15th century, the O'Donnell chieftains erected a massive Norman-style stone tower on the site of the ancient fort. Part of the tower is still attached to the castle that burgeoned from this foundation over the centuries. An English deputy of Queen Elizabeth I, Henry Sydney, wrote of this castle: "It is the greatest I ever saw in Ireland in an Irishman's hands, and would appear to be in good keeping; one of the fairest situated in good soil and so nigh a portable water as a boat of ten tons could come within 20 yards of it." About the same time, the O'Donnells built a friary for the Franciscan order farther down on the estuary, its tumbled remains still visible today.

The O'Donnells were a major branch of the Cineál Conaill (the tribe of Conall), founded by Conall Gulban. Conall was a son of Niall of the Nine Hostages, one of the last pagan High Kings of Ireland, so named for his custom of taking hostages on his many pillaging expeditions in other lands. One of the captives he carried home after a raid on England and sold into slavery was a young boy who was to become St. Patrick, the patron saint of Ireland. Patrick managed to escape to England but later returned to Christianize the pagan Irish.

For 400 years after the initial Anglo-Norman invasion, the O'Donnells defended their northwest kingdom from both native and foreign foes, displaying spectacular gallantry and military skill. Their fame was not founded solely on their prowess in war, for they were also bountiful patrons of education, religion, and the arts. In the late 16th century, Queen Elizabeth I finally succeeded in destroying the old Gaelic dynasties that had ruled Ireland, and the O'Donnells were forced into exile. (Their descendants are still thriving in Spain and Austria, where one of them married into a royal family.)

To prevent Elizabethan forces from using their castle as a base, the O'Donnells deliberately removed the roof and floors and punched a gaping hole in one of the walls. However, when an English captain, Basil Brooke, took possession of it in 1610, he repaired the old tower and built extensive additions to it, using stone from the Franciscan friary, which had been laid waste by the invaders. Toward the end of the 19th century, the castle was handed over to the state and declared a national monument. It is now undergoing a meticulous restoration to return it to its original splendor.

Like the castle, the friary of Donegal is intimately identified with the heyday of Donegal history. Founded in 1474 by the first Red Hugh O'Donnell and his wife, Nuala, it became an illustrious monastic school, attracting scholars from across Europe. Within its cloisters a monumental chronology of Irish history was inked out in scrupulous detail over a period of 4 years. This was the celebrated *Annals of the Four Masters.* The four masters — Franciscan Brother Michael O'Clery and three lay scholars — sat down in their cells to pen what at first was intended to be a comprehensive history of the saints but somehow turned into a year-by-year narrative of the story of Ireland. It is one of the most brilliant achievements of medieval Irish literature.

With the departure of the O'Donnells at the turn of the 17th century, Donegal's heady hour of history ended, and the town's importance as a seat of power began to diminish. Captain Brooke did not stay long in possession of the great castle but moved on to another part of Ireland. (A descendant, also named Basil Brooke, was Prime Minister of Northern Ireland in modern times.) But even though the castle is deserted and the mighty sailing ships are now no more than ghosts in the harbor, the memory of that glorious past still thrives.

Being small, Donegal Town is a perfect microcosm of Irish life as it is today — and as it used to be. It offers an opportunity not only to experience small-town life in Ireland but also to enjoy a countryside of surpassing beauty. Verging Donegal is a majestic landscape of mountains and valleys, lakes and rivers, and vast expanses of lonely moorland, with the waters of the Atlantic forever lapping at the edge of the town.

DONEGAL AT-A-GLANCE

SEEING THE TOWN: The best way to see Donegal Town is on foot, and it is possible to cover nearly all of it in a few hours. The most commanding vantage point is atop Miller's Hill, behind the Roman Catholic church on Main Street. Another splendid viewing point is the hill behind Drumcliffe Terrace, on the north side of the river estuary. From here, there is not only a panorama of the town but also a magnificent outlook across Donegal Bay.

SPECIAL PLACES: Inevitably, most of the places of interest are connected with Donegal's eventful past. A visitor might embark on a tour of the town with a touch of romantic whimsy by starting at the harbor, where the Vikings stormed ashore during an earlier age.

The Diamond – Instead of the more conventional square, a diamond-shaped market-place is a distinctive architectural feature of towns in the northern parts of Ireland. The Donegal Diamond was laid out by the Elizabethan captain Basil Brooke when he took over the town in 1603. Its original outline has not changed over the centuries, despite much rebuilding of the houses and shops that border it. Dominating the Diamond is a 25-foot-high red granite obelisk erected in 1937 to commemorate the Four Masters who, in the nearby Franciscan friary, penned the monumental *Annals,* covering the history of Ireland from 2242 BC to AD 1616. That masterpiece, completed in 1636, is regarded as the most remarkable collection of national tradition and history in the Western world. The architectural style of the obelisk is Irish Romanesque.

Donegal Castle – This impressive keep stands as a symbol of both the lost Gaelic age and the Elizabethan Plantation. It is a combination of the original tower built by the native O'Donnell clan and the Elizabethan manse added on by Captain Brooke, the invader. It is thought that Brooke used stones from the ruined Franciscan friary farther downriver to extend the castle and turn it into a more comfortable residence. The lower parts of the Norman-style tower house still remain, but the most striking feature of the castle is inside the great hall built by Brooke — a magnificent stone fireplace adorned with the arms of Brooke and of his wife's family, the Leicesters. Now a national monument, the castle is open to the public most days. Castle St.

Church of Ireland – This splendid cut-stone building, with a handsome steeple, has been a place of worship for the local Protestant community for more than 100 years. Before it was built, services were held in a small makeshift church amid the ruins of the old friary. Castle St.

Stone Bridge – Built about 1840, this bridge beside the castle spans the river Eske. It bears a plaque commemorating a remarkable Catholic priest and writer, the Rev. Dr. John Boyce, who went to America during the Irish famine to care for the welfare of Irish emigrants and who wrote a number of novels under the pseudonym Paul Pepper-grass, one of which — *Shandy Maguire* — had considerable success. He died in the United States in 1864. Castle St.

Methodist and Presbyterian Churches – On the west bank of the Eske, these two 100-year-old churches are worth a visit. The Methodist, the first glimpsed on the right after crossing the Stone Bridge, is the focal point of a strong Methodist tradition in Donegal. A few steps beyond is the Presbyterian church. Presbyterianism in County Donegal has a close connection with the American sect: Francis Makemie, a minister from Donegal, established that religion in Maryland and, indeed, is regarded as the virtual founder of the US Presbyterian church.

Memorial Church of the Four Masters – Another architectural monument to the monastic authors of the *Annals,* this Catholic church was built in 1935. It is in the Irish Romanesque style and is constructed of red granite. Main St.

Napoleonic Anchor – On the quayside of the river estuary sits an enormous 15-foot-long, 1½-ton anchor believed to have come from the *Romaine,* a French frigate, which was part of a flotilla dispatched by Napoleon to land in Donegal. The expeditionary force of 3,000 was to join Irish revolutionaries in rebellion against the British in 1798, after another French force had been defeated in County Mayo. The second force was routed by British gunboats, and the *Romaine* and two other French ships hid in Donegal Bay. Tradition has it that the *Romaine* cut her anchor and fled back to France on the approach of another British force. Quay St.

Friary – These historic ruins are on the south side of the Eske estuary, just beyond the quay. Built in 1474 by the first Red Hugh O'Donnell for the Franciscan order, the friary became a renowned seat of learning and monastic scholarship. Within its cloisters, the Four Masters penned their epic *Annals.* During the wars with England, the friary was raided several times and once was heavily damaged by an explosion. When the last of the O'Donnells and another great Irish tribe, the O'Neills, were driven into exile in 1607, marking the demise of the ancient Gaelic order, the Franciscans departed the friary forever.

SOURCES AND RESOURCES

TOURIST INFORMATION: The prime source of information and advice for visitors is the headquarters of the Donegal-Leitrim-Sligo Regional Tourism Organization (Temple St., 40 miles south of Donegal Town on N15, in Sligo; phone: 71-61201). This organization's information office (Quay St., Donegal; phone: 21148) is open May to September. The *Four Masters Bookshop* (on the Diamond; phone: 21526) has a good supply of books about Donegal.

Local Coverage – The *Donegal Democrat,* a weekly, is the principal purveyor of local news, announcements, and advertising. Other local weeklies are the *Derry People & Donegal News* and the *Donegal People's Press.*

TELEPHONE: The area code for Donegal Town and the immediate vicinity is 73. When calling from within the Republic of Ireland, dial 073 before the local number.

GETTING AROUND: In this little town, just about everybody walks. There's no municipal bus service, and people hire taxis only for journeys away from town.

Bicycle – During the summer it's pleasant to hire a bike and cycle around the streets, lanes, and byways. Bicycles can be rented from *D. A. McIntyre,* 14 Castle St. (phone: 21942).

Taxi – *John Joseph Culloo* (320 St. Joseph's Ave.; phone: 21645); *James Johnston* (the Mullins; phone: 21349).

Car Rental – It's wisest to rent a car at the port of arrival — usually Shannon Airport or Dublin — where the major rental companies have offices. The car rental closest to Donegal is in Sligo City, 40 miles south on N15. *John Gilbride & Co.,* Bridge St., Sligo (phone: 71-2091).

SPECIAL EVENTS: Hundreds of card players flock to the town every November to take part in a major bridge congress, one of the most notable events in the calendar of the *Contract Bridge Association* of Ireland. Contact Mrs. Gleeson, *Contract Bridge Association,* 17 Beechpark, Athlone, Co. Westmeath (phone: 90-275-549).

SHOPPING: Donegal is the tweed capital of Ireland, and few visitors leave without buying this traditional fabric in some form.

The Antique Shop – The scrupulous business policy of this quaint establishment guarantees that all antiques on show are genuine. Overflowing with old and vintage objects — vases, furniture, brass, and a plethora of paintings — from bargain priced to terribly expensive. Sean Thomas is the curator. The Diamond (phone: 21144).

Donegal Craft Center – An attractive little shopping village just outside town on the Sligo road, N15, where shoppers will find a complete range of traditional Irish crafts as well as a pleasant tea shop for a "cuppa" and delicious home baking. Sligo Rd. (phone: 22053, 22015, 22225, or 22228).

The Gift Shop – Here is a dazzling array of gifts and souvenirs of top-notch quality, including pottery, crystal, hand-crafted jewelry, paintings, and accessories. The Diamond (phone: 21168).

Magee – The supreme tweed shop in Ireland, it displays endless varieties of the versatile fabric, unfinished or tailored to your requirements. The shop was founded in 1881, and it brings together traditional tweed patterns from the looms of Donegal's cottage weavers. There's always a weaver with a loom on hand to demonstrate the subtleties of tweed fashioning, and guided tours are conducted through its factory nearby on the New Row throughout the day. The shop also has a diversity of other classic clothing, including a particularly good selection of woolens. The Diamond (phone: 21100).

Oven Door – A superior pastry and cake shop, loaded with toothsome take-away confections. Cream-bloated buns, icing-encrusted fruitcakes, and home-baked Irish soda bread won't do much for your figure, but they're nonetheless scrumptious. The Diamond (phone: 21511).

SPORTS AND FITNESS: Boating – For cruises around Donegal Bay, boats can be hired in Killybegs Port, 17 miles west of the town. *Mooney Boats,* St. Catherines Rd., Killybegs (phone: 31152).

Fishing – A license is required to fish for salmon and all other species. March to September is open season for salmon and sea trout on the river Eske, and the biggest catches are made in mid-June. Six miles north of town is Lough Eske, which holds char, a very rare fish in Ireland, along with salmon and trout. For angling information, contact Billy Johnston, *Donegal Anglers' Club* (Quay St.; phone: 21039). Rods and tackle are available at *Charles Doherty's* (Main St.; phone: 21119), where permits can also be obtained.

Golf – The 18-hole course at *Donegal Golf Club* is set amid majestic scenery, overlooking the Atlantic. Six miles south on N15 at Murvagh, Ballintra (phone: 34054).

Squash – Visitors are welcome at *St. John Bosco Centre* (Tirconnaill St.), which has 2 excellent squash courts.

Tennis – There are outdoor hard courts at Ardeskin, beyond the Catholic church off Main St.

Swimming – The town has no pool, but a nice sandy beach is west of the town. The Atlantic waters in these parts, unfortunately, can be numbing unless a rare long, hot summer turns on the heat. The beach is off the Mountcharles road, N56, and is signposted.

262 DONEGAL TOWN / Best in Town

MUSIC: Some local pubs have traditional Irish music sessions. Local newspapers carry ads giving details.

NIGHTCLUBS AND NIGHTLIFE: Like so many small Irish towns, the nightlife of Donegal is largely focused on the revered pint of Guinness porter (stout) or "balls of malt" (glasses of Irish whiskey) sipped discreetly in shuttered pubs after dark. It's illegal after 11:30 PM, but that particular law is more honored in the breach than the observance. Lively disco parties are held until near dawn most nights in the *Central* and *Abbey* hotels, both on the Diamond.

BEST IN TOWN

CHECKING IN: We recommend four very good establishments rated as expensive: over $100 a night for two, including a full Irish breakfast. A great many excellent small guesthouses and bed and breakfast establishments in and around the town are of a very high standard and absolutely great value for the money. These often cost far less than $50; we list one below as inexpensive. Some are *very* inexpensive. The tourist board on Quay St. (phone: 21148) has information on vacancies. All telephone numbers are in the 73 area code unless otherwise indicated.

Abbey – A very well run hostelry with 40 rooms, but a bit pricey considering not all rooms have a bath or shower. Excellent service and fine food. The Diamond (phone: 21014). Expensive.

Ernan Park – In sylvan surroundings on a small island joined to the mainland by a causeway, this 19th-century mansion offers a relaxed Old World atmosphere and rooms with views of the Atlantic, as well as first-rate food (see *Eating Out*). Signposted, 2 miles south of town on N15 (phone: 21065). Expensive.

Great Northern – Set on the edge of the Atlantic with breathtaking views, this 96-room Victorian hostelry has an indoor and outdoor swimming pool and an 18-hole golf course. Bundoran, 17 miles southwest of town (phone: 72-412040). Expensive.

Hyland Central – A first class hotel, with a welcoming, courteous staff to make guests feel at home. Tastefully furnished rooms, some overlooking the river Eske, with television sets, radio, and phone. The food is excellent (see *Eating Out*). The Diamond (phone: 21027). Expensive.

Danby House – About 14 miles south of Donegal, in Ballyshannon, is this charming, 20-acre establishment, set on a bluff overlooking Donegal Bay. Owned by the Britton family, the house, built in 1820, has 5 spacious guestrooms, all uniquely decorated with antiques. The restaurant is very good (see *Eating Out*). Ballyshannon (phone: 72-51138). Inexpensive.

EATING OUT: Options for eating out in Donegal Town are limited; restaurants in the hotels recommended above are the best bets. At restaurants listed in the moderate range, expect to pay $35 to $60 for dinner for two, excluding wine and tips; in inexpensive places, expect to pay $30 or less. All telephone numbers are in the 73 area code unless otherwise indicated.

Danby House – In the 1820 guesthouse of the same name, this excellent dining spot is set on a bluff overlooking Donegal Bay. Specialties include seafood — mussels, prawns, smoked salmon — as well as rack of lamb, potatoes, and fresh vegetables.

Hospitality is first-rate here. Reservations necessary. About 14 miles south of Donegal, in Ballyshannon (phone: 72-51138). Moderate.

Ernan Park – The decor in this handsome dining room is pure 19th-century Georgian, with antique furniture, gilt-framed paintings, heirloom silver, and beautifully draped windows that overlook the water. The cuisine is continental and Irish, with an emphasis on seafood. Reservations advised. St. Ernan's Island (phone: 21065). Moderate.

Hyland Central – The best and widest menu range in town — Donegal mountain lamb to Lough Eske salmon and trout, and lobsters from Killybegs — is to be had at the restaurant of this hotel. Famous for very large portions. Reservations advised. The Diamond (phone: 21027). Moderate.

Errigal Grill – Good, serviceable mainstream eatery — a better-quality fast-food place. Reservations unnecessary. Main St. (phone: 21428). Inexpensive.

Magee Café – Located upstairs in *Magee* tweed shop, this café is excellent for lunches and snacks. No reservations. The Diamond (phone: 21100). Inexpensive.

SHARING A PINT: The downstairs bar in the *Central* hotel has softly lit Tudor decor and a roaring peat fire. In addition to the libations, it serves very fine snacks. For a real old-fashioned pub, it's hard to beat *Pat Gallagher's* (Castle St.), where the conversation in the musical Donegal brogue is as exhilarating as the black porter and whiskey.

DUBLIN

Dublin is a friendly city steeped in a history often troubled, sometimes splendid; a city of wide Georgian streets, elegant squares, magnificent doorways; a city of memorable sunsets that bathe the 18th-century red brick façades until the houses seem to glow with their own fire and the windows seem made of gold; a city of ancient churches and cathedrals thrusting their hallowed spires and towers against the skyline; a city where the English language acquires a unique dimension and where the dark, creamy-headed Guinness stout flows abundantly in companionable pubs. This is a city like no other European capital, set like a jewel in the sweep of Dublin Bay. Behind, to the south, rise the Dublin hills and the Wicklow Mountains. Through the city the river Liffey — James Joyce's Anna Livia Plurabelle — wends its leisurely way to the sea, spanned as it passes through Dublin by 11 bridges.

Once there was only one bridge. Indeed, it was not so much a bridge as a mere ford in the river, and it stood approximately where the Father Matthew Bridge stands today. It was built by the first Celtic inhabitants of what is now Dublin. When they came here, we cannot be sure; what is certain is that, by AD 140, they were well established on this site. The Celts themselves probably referred to the spot by a name that endures to this day — the official Gaelic *Baile Atha Cliath* (town of the ford of the hurdles).

It was not, however, until the coming of the Vikings in the 9th century that Dublin as we now know it began to take shape. The old Celtic settlement had at no time been a place of national importance; its significance was as a ford of the Liffey en route to the ancient royal capital of Tara. In AD 837, 65 Viking longboats sailed into Dublin Harbor and up the mouth of the river Liffey. These early Viking settlers established themselves a little downstream from the old Celtic settlement, on a spot where the Poddle, which now flows underground, entered the Liffey, causing it to form a dark pool, or *dubh linn*. The Vikings referred to their settlement by these two Gaelic words, and the anglicized version became the city's modern English name. Dublin rapidly became the focal point of the Viking invasion of Ireland. Then, as the Vikings began to see that trading was ultimately more profitable than plunder, and as they began to settle and intermarry in their new homeland, Dublin became a major center for their extensive European trade. Not long after their arrival, they were converted to Christianity, and in 1034 they erected a cathedral, which became the nucleus of modern Christ Church. The cathedral stood in the center of Viking Dublin and allows us to place the ancient city accurately.

Just over 3 centuries after the coming of the Vikings, new invaders swept Ireland. In 1169 the first contingent of Normans landed on the beach of Bannow, in County Wexford. Two years later, the powerful Baron Richard Gilbert de Clare, otherwise known as Strongbow, arrived at the gates of

Dublin with 1,000 men. The city was taken by storm; its Viking king and inhabitants were forced to flee. Thereafter Dublin became the center of the English conquest, as it had become the center of the Viking conquest.

Not long afterward, the city was fortified by Dublin Castle, built not far from the old Viking cathedral. The cathedral had been taken over by Strongbow and a new and larger edifice had been erected in its place. The city walls were built along with the castle. (Their remains can be seen at St. Audeon's Arch, below Christ Church.) Thus medieval Dublin began to take shape, a small area surrounded by walls.

In shape and in size Dublin did not alter greatly until the arrival of a new viceroy, or king's representative, in 1662 heralded Dublin's rise to a definitive national importance. Dublin, under James Butler, Duke of Ormonde, became and remained the central arena for Ireland's social, political, and cultural life.

Butler, believing that the stability of a government should be reflected in public works, began municipal improvements almost immediately. The solitary, medieval Dublin Bridge was joined by four new bridges across the river; Phoenix Park (to this day the largest enclosed urban park in the world) was walled and several new streets were built.

Dublin's importance as a city and as a seaport increased enormously in the late 17th century. In the 18th century, however, Dublin truly flourished, as it became one of the most brilliant and sparkling capitals in all of Europe. The strong movement toward parliamentary independence that took place at this time was reflected in the splendid Parliament House (now the Bank of Ireland in College Green), commenced in 1729, the first in a series of great public buildings. Extensive rebuilding was carried out on Dublin Castle and Trinity College. The Wide Streets Commission was set up. It was as if the city were proudly preparing for the unprecedented position of importance it would occupy when, in 1782, parliamentary independence was conceded to Ireland by the British Parliament.

Great buildings followed one another in dizzying succession — Leinster House, the Royal Exchange, the Mansion House, the Four Courts, the Custom House. Irish classical architecture, in all its gravity, beauty, and balance, reached full maturity. It flowered in public buildings and private houses, spacious squares and elegant streets. This was Georgian Dublin (various King Georges sat on the British throne in the period): the Dublin of Henry Grattan, Oliver Goldsmith, Jonathan Swift, Bishop Berkeley and Edmund Burke, David Garrick, and Peg Woffington. Handel himself conducted the world premiere of his "Messiah" in this glittering city, whose center was concentrated in the area between Dublin Castle and the Parliament House.

Architecturally, Dublin reached its zenith in the 18th century. Later, its brilliance would be sculpted in the written word rather than in stone. In the 19th century, with the dismantling of the Parliament, Dublin's political and social life suffered a blow from which it was not to recover easily. By contrast, its literary life began to flower, for two great literary movements were born in Dublin — the Gaelic League and the Irish literary renaissance. Between them, the two movements revived and romanticized the early legends and history of Ireland. The literary renaissance — spearheaded by William Butler Yeats, Lady Augusta Gregory, Douglas Hyde, and John Millington Synge, to name but a few — placed a splendid and indelible mark on 20th-century English literature. (Equally renowned are Irish or Ireland-born writers not directly associated with the Irish literary renaissance, such as Samuel Beckett, who was born in Dublin in 1906 and won the Nobel Prize for literature in 1969; George Bernard Shaw, who wrote in England but was born in Dublin; and the Irish playwright Brendan Behan.) The movement found its greatest expression in the creation of the *Abbey Theatre,* associated forever with the brilliant plays of Sean O'Casey. For many years the Abbey was the most famous theater in the world. The Gaelic League had more popular appeal; with its dream of the restoration of the Gaelic language and the reestablishment of a separate Irish cultural nation, it provided a great deal of the inspiration for the Easter Rebellion of 1916.

This uprising, concentrated in Dublin, sparked the 5-year War of Independence, which culminated in the Anglo-Irish Treaty of 1921 (whereby Ireland gained the status of free state). The signing of the treaty was followed by civil war in 1922–23, during which many buildings that had escaped damage in 1916 suffered badly. Today, happily, all the heirlooms of the 18th century have been restored to their original grandeur.

Dublin today, with a population of 1 million, is far larger than it has been at any other stage of its history. Nevertheless, it still is an eminently walkable city. The crossroads of medieval and 18th-century Dublin remain the center of interest. Within a half-mile radius of the Bank of Ireland on College Green lie the cathedrals, the museums, Dublin Castle, the great Georgian public buildings, the parks, and the shops. All are neatly enclosed by the Royal Canal to the north and the Grand Canal to the south.

Thanks to the *Dublin Millennium* celebrations in 1988, the downtown area of the city now enjoys a number of permanent enhancements, including 10 new sculptures by modern Irish craftspersons. The most notable pieces include a freestanding "liberty bell" in St. Patrick's Cathedral Park, a replica of a Viking ship on Essex Quay, and a double arch on a traffic island in Merrion Row, near St. Stephen's Green. In the heart of the city on O'Connell Street there also now is an elaborate fountain, with 40 spouts, designed to represent the course of the river Liffey. The river itself is represented by a larger-than-life sculpture of a reclining female nude, *Anna Livia.*

A major urban improvement is the rejuvenation of Grafton Street as a pedestrian shopping area, with brick walkways, benches, and plants. The shops along Grafton and nearby also have perked up, with smart new façades and signs.

Besides sightseeing, a visitor should sample Dublin's abundant cultural offerings. This year promises to be especially interesting, since Dublin has been chosen as the Cultural Capital of Europe for 1991 (see *Special Events*). As part of the celebration, the city will host the *GPA Dublin International Piano Competition,* which attracts some of the finest young pianists in the world; the *Dublin Literary Festival,* celebrating the works of James Joyce and other of the city's great writers; and the *Irish Traditional Music Spectacular,* with music and dance and an open-air concert. Also scheduled is the official opening of the *Irish Museum of Modern Art* (at the Royal Hospital Kilmainham); the *Dublin Writers Museum;* and the restored Custom House. For further information on cultural events and celebrations during the year, contact the tourist office.

But the true focal point of Dubliners' social life is the pub, and it is there that a visitor must go to find it. Dublin can be a comfortable, "down home" place to visit, so slow down and enjoy it. It has an endearing earthiness, a quality that inspired James Joyce to refer to his native city in off-color, though affectionate, terms as "strumpet city in the sunset" and "dear, dirty Dublin."

DUBLIN AT-A-GLANCE

SEEING THE CITY: Views of this essentially flat city are best from a number of restaurants in the surrounding hills; particularly nice is *Killakee House* in Rathfarnham (phone: 932645 or 932917). Or see Dublin from afar from the neighboring Wicklow Mountains.

SPECIAL PLACES: Central Dublin is very compact. Since traffic can move slowly, by far the best way to see the city is on foot. Making full use of Dublin's splendid, signposted *Tourist Trail,* the determined sightseer should set off on foot to see and experience as much of Dublin as time allows. Walk the wide Georgian squares and avenues, meander down the cobblestone lanes near the Liffey Quays, stroll through the sylvan paths of St. Stephen's Green or along bustling Grafton Street — Dublin's shoppers' paradise — and stop at *Bewley's* (78-79 Grafton St.) for a cup of coffee or at the *Shelbourne* hotel (27 St. Stephen's Green) for a proper afternoon tea.

SOUTH DOWNTOWN

Merrion Square – This is the loveliest of Dublin's Georgian squares, a study in balance and elegance that evokes the graciousness of a vanished age. Note particularly the variety of fanlights on doorways. At No. 1, the young Oscar Wilde lived with his celebrated parents, the surgeon Sir William Wills Wilde and poetess Speranza; No. 42 was the home of Sir Jonah Barrington, 18th-century barrister and raconteur; at No. 58 lived Daniel O'Connell, the "Liberator" who won Catholic emancipation in 1829; No. 70 was the home of tragic Sheridan Le Fanu, author of sinister tales such as *Uncle Silas* and *Through a Glass Darkly* (after his wife's death in 1858, he shut himself up there, appearing only after nightfall to walk in the shadows of Merrion Square); at No. 82 lived William Butler Yeats, poet and Nobel Prize winner. Today, the only house in the square used as a private dwelling is No. 71, where well-known couturière Sybil Connolly has her home and studio.

Leinster House – When young Lord Kildare, Earl of Leinster, chose to build a mansion here in 1745, all of fashionable Dublin protested, for at that time the north side of the city was the fashionable side. Undaunted, he went ahead with his plan, asserting prophetically, "Where I go, fashion will follow." The house Lord Kildare built is said to resemble the White House, whose architect, James Hoban of Carlow, studied in Dublin after the completion of Leinster House. The building was purchased in the 19th century by the Royal Dublin Society, and in 1921 the Parliament of the new Irish Free State chose the building as its meeting place. Leinster House continues to be the meeting place of the Dáil (House of Representatives) and Seanad (Senate). When the Dáil is in session, visitors may watch from the visitors' gallery. Apply for tickets at the main gate. Kildare St., Merrion Sq. (phone: 789911).

National Museum – When Leinster House belonged to the Royal Dublin Society, it became the nucleus of a complex of cultural buildings — the *National Gallery* (phone: 615133), the National Library, the *Museum of Natural History* (phone: 618811), and the *National Museum.* These all are worth visiting, but the *National Museum* especially should not be missed. Its collection of gold objects dating from the Bronze Age to early Christian times almost is without parallel in Western Europe. No admission charge. Kildare St. (phone: 765521).

Genealogical Office and Heraldic Museum – Formerly in Dublin Castle, this is the domain of Ireland's chief herald, the ideal starting point for an ancestry hunt. 2 Kildare St. (phone: 608670).

St. Stephen's Green – Not far from Merrion Square lies St. Stephen's Green, the loveliest of Dublin's many public parks. Its 22 acres contain gardens, a waterfall, and an ornamental lake. In summer, it's an excellent place to sit and watch working Dublin take its lunch; bands play on the bandstand in July and August.

Mansion House – Dublin preceded London in building a Mansion House for its lord mayor in 1715. In the Round Room, the Declaration of Irish Independence was adopted in 1919, and the Anglo-Irish Treaty of 1921 was signed here. The Round Room usually is open to visitors. Dawson St. (phone: 762852).

Trinity College – Dawson Street descends to meet Trinity College, the oldest university in Ireland, founded by Elizabeth I of England on the site of the 12th-century Monastery of All Hallows. Alumni of the college include Oliver Goldsmith, Edmund Burke, Jonathan Swift, Bishop Berkeley (pronounced *Bark*-lee) — who also lent his name to Berkeley in California — William Congreve, Thomas Moore, Sheridan Le Fanu, Oscar Wilde, and J. P. Donleavy, to name but a few. No trace of the original Elizabethan structure remains; the oldest surviving part of the college dates from 1700. The Long Room, Trinity's famous library, is the longest single-chamber library in existence. It contains a priceless collection of 800,000 volumes and 3,000 ancient manuscripts and papyri. The library's chief treasure is the *Book of Kells,* an 8th-century manuscript transcription of the four gospels described as the "most beautiful book in the world." Closed Saturday afternoons and Sundays. Admission charge April to October. College Green (phone: 772941).

Trinity College also is the home of "The Dublin Experience," a 45-minute multimedia sound and light show that traces the history of Dublin from earliest times to the present. It is shown daily, on the hour, from 10 AM to 5 PM, May through October, in the *Davis Theater.* Admission charge. Entrance on Nassau St. (phone: 772941, ext. 1177).

Parliament House – Facing Trinity College is the monumental Parliament House, now the Bank of Ireland. Built in 1729 and regarded as one of the finest examples of the architecture of its period, this was the first of the great series of 18th-century public buildings in Dublin. As its name implies, it was erected to house the Irish Parliament in the century that saw the birth of Home Rule. College Green (phone: 776801).

Dublin Castle – Dame Street leads westward from College Green toward the older part of the city, where the early Viking and Norman settlers established themselves.

Castles have gone up and down on the site of the present castle. A Celtic *rath* (a medieval earthen fort) was almost certainly followed by a wooden Viking fortress, and this in turn was supplanted by the great stone castle erected by John of England in the 13th century. The castle was for 400 years the center of English rule in Ireland; for much of this time it had as grim a reputation as the Tower of London. Although the present building is essentially 18th century, one of the four towers that flanked the original moated castle survives as the Record Tower. The 15th-century Bedford Tower was the state prison; the Georgian State Apartments, formerly the residence of the English viceroys, were beautifully restored between 1950 and 1963 and now are used for state functions. St. Patrick's Hall in the State Apartments was the scene of the inauguration of Ireland's first president, Douglas Hyde; here, too, President John F. Kennedy was made a freeman of Dublin.

Bedford Tower, the Chapel Royal, and the State Apartments can be visited for an admission charge. Dublin Castle (phone: 777129).

Christ Church Cathedral – Not far from Dublin Castle, the massive shape of Christ Church Cathedral crowns the hill on which the ancient city stood. Founded in 1038 by Viking King Sitric Silkenbeard of Dublin, Christ Church was demolished in the 12th century and rebuilt by the Norman Richard Gilbert de Clare (Strongbow), who is buried within its walls. The cruciform building has been much restored through the centuries, but the beautiful pointed nave and the wonderful stonework remain virtually unchanged. These walls have witnessed many dramatic scenes in the course of Irish history. Christ Church today is the Church of Ireland (Protestant) cathedral for the diocese of Dublin. The vaulted crypt remains one of the largest in Ireland. In front of this cathedral Dubliners traditionally gather to ring in the *New Year.* The cathedral and crypt are open. Christ Church Pl. (phone: 778099).

St. Audeon's Arch and the City Walls – The 13th-century church of St. Audeon is Dublin's oldest parish church. It was founded by early Norman settlers, who gave it the name St. Ouen, or Audeon, after the patron saint of their native Rouen. Close to the church is a flight of steps leading down to St. Audeon's Arch, the sole surviving gateway of the medieval city walls. Open daily. High St. (phone: 679-1855).

St. Patrick's Cathedral – Christ Church stood within the old walled city. John Comyn, one of its 12th-century archbishops, felt that while he remained under municipal jurisdiction he could not achieve the temporal power for which he thirsted. Accordingly, he left the city walls and built a fine palace within a stone's throw of Christ Church. Today St. Patrick's is the national cathedral of the Church of Ireland. By the 19th century both cathedrals were in a state of considerable disrepair. Henry Roe, a distiller, came to the aid of Christ Church, restoring it at his own expense; Sir Benjamin Lee Guinness of the famous brewing family came to the assistance of St. Patrick's — hence the saying in Dublin that "Christ Church was restored with glasses, St. Patrick's with pints!" Crane St. off Thomas.

The early English interior of St. Patrick's is very beautiful; the nave is the longest in Ireland. The cathedral's particular fascination, however, lies in its wealth of monuments, especially the Geraldine Door, the Cork Memorial, and the monument to Dame St. Leger. The greatest interest of all, though, is in the long association with St. Patrick's of Jonathan Swift, author of *Gulliver's Travels* and dean of the cathedral for 32 years. Within these walls he is buried, beside his loving Stella. On a slab near the entrance is carved the epitaph he composed for himself, which Yeats described as the greatest epitaph in literature: "He lies where furious indignation can no longer rend his heart." Open to visitors. St. Patrick's Cathedral (phone: 754817).

Guinness Brewery – Founded in 1759 by Arthur Guinness with a mere £100, Guinness's today is the largest exporting stout brewery in the world. The former Guinness Hop Store, on Crane St. adjacent to the main brewery, was once the storage building for the ingredients for the world-famous dark stout, and the aroma remains. Now it is a public hall showcasing traveling displays, art shows, technological works, and contemporary arts. The visitors' center shows an audiovisual presentation about the making of the famous brew, complete with free samples. Also of note are the *Guinness Museum* and the *Cooper's Museum.* Admission charge for the rotating exhibitions (phone: 756701 or 536700).

Royal Hospital – One of Ireland's oldest public buildings, this 17th-century treasure was restored for IR£20 million and reopened in 1985 on its 300th anniversary. Originally built as a home for aged veterans, it is now Ireland's official *National Centre for Culture and the Arts.* Displays range from *National Museum* pieces to traveling art exhibitions from as far away as China. The restoration of the Grand Hall/dining room has been rated as one of Europe's finest achievements of the century. Also used for public concerts, recitals, and lectures (check the Dublin newspapers). Surrounding the building are 50 acres of grounds, including an 18th-century formal garden, a courtyard, a sculpture park, and Bully's Acre, the resting place of many 11th-century Irish chieftains. Closed Mondays. Admission charge. Kilmainham (phone: 718666 or 719147).

NORTH DOWNTOWN

Four Courts – Almost across the river from Guinness's lies the stately Four Courts of Justice, dating from the apogee of the 18th century. The building was begun by Thomas Cooley and completed by James Gandon, the greatest of all the Georgian architects. Court sittings (Supreme and High) are open to the public. No admission charge. Inns Quay (phone: 725555).

St. Michan's Church – Not far from the Four Courts is St. Michan's, a 17th-century church built on the site of a 10th-century Viking church. The 18th-century organ is said to have been played by Handel when he was in Dublin for the first public performance of "Messiah."

Of more immediate interest, perhaps, is the extraordinary crypt, with its remarkable preservative atmosphere: Bodies have lain here for centuries without decomposing, and you can, if you feel so inclined, shake the hand of an 8-foot-tall Crusader! Open weekdays and Saturday mornings. Admission charge. Church St. (phone: 724154).

Irish Whiskey Corner – With so many pubs on every corner of the city, it's no wonder that Irish Whiskey, like Guinness stout, is big business in Ireland. The story of the legendary liquid, known in Gaelic as *uisce beatha* (the water of life), is illustrated in this former distillery warehouse. One-hour tours include a short introductory audio-visual presentation, followed by a visit to an exhibition area with photography archives, distillery memorabilia, and a whiskey-making demonstration. The tour ends at a pub-style "tasting room," where visitors can sample the various brands being brewed today. Tours are available Mondays through Fridays at 3:30 PM. Admission charge. Bow St. (phone: 725566).

Moore Street – Near the historic General Post Office (2 blocks west of Henry Street) is Moore Street. Here, among the fruit and flower sellers, the true voice of Dublin is audible — lively, warm, voluble, speaking an English that is straight Sean O'Casey.

Municipal Gallery of Modern Art – Beyond the Garden of Remembrance (a memorial to those who died for Irish freedom), on the north side of Parnell Square, is Charlemont House. Lord Charlemont, for whom the house was designed by Sir William Chambers in 1764, was a great patron of the arts; it is fitting that his house became, in recent times, the *Municipal Gallery of Modern Art*. The gallery should not be missed; it has an outstanding collection of Impressionist paintings, and the works of more recent artists such as Picasso, Utrillo, and Bonnard are well represented, to say nothing of such prominent Irish painters as Sir William Orpen, John B. Yeats (the poet's father), and Jack Yeats (the poet's brother). Closed Mondays. Parnell Sq. (phone: 741903).

Abbey Theatre – Alas, the original *Abbey Theatre*, founded by Yeats and Lady Gregory on the site of the old city morgue, is no more. In 1951, at the close of a performance of O'Casey's *Plough and the Stars* — a play that ends with Dublin blazing in the aftermath of rebellion — the theater itself caught fire and was burned to the ground. The new *Abbey*, designed by Michael Scott — who was one of the country's foremost 20th-century architects — opened in 1966 on the site of the original building. The lobby, which can be seen daily except Sundays, contains interesting portraits of those connected with the theater's early successes. Performances nightly except Sundays. Abbey St. (phone: 744505 or 787222).

Custom House – This masterpiece of Georgian architecture adorns the north bank of the Liffey, to the east of O'Connell St. It was the *chef d'oeuvre* of James Gandon and is one of the finest buildings of its kind in Europe. Now occupied by government offices and closed to the public, it should nonetheless be seen at close range: The carved riverheads that form the keystones of the arches and entrances are splendid. Custom House Quay (phone: 742961).

SUBURBS

Phoenix Park – Northwest of the city center, this is the largest enclosed urban park in the world. Within its walls are the residences of the President of the Republic and the US Ambassador. The park covers 1,760 acres, beautifully planted with a great variety of trees. Among the attractions are the lovely People's Gardens, a herd of fallow deer, the horse-race course, and the Zoological Gardens. Dublin Zoo is said to be the most beautiful zoo in Europe; it also has a most impressive collection of animals and holds several records for lion breeding. The park and zoo are open daily. Admission charge for the zoo (phone: 213021 or 771425).

Chester Beatty Library – Founded by an American-born, naturalized British resident in Ireland, this library is considered to be the most valuable and representative private collection of Oriental manuscripts and miniatures in the world. The "copper millionaire with a heart of gold," Chester Beatty willed his marvelous library to the people of Dublin. Open Tuesdays through Saturdays. 20 Shrewsbury Rd., Ballsbridge (phone: 692386).

Malahide Castle – In a north city suburb of Dublin, Malahide Castle (now open to the public), was for 8 centuries the home of the Talbots of Malahide. Magnificently furnished in mostly 18th-century style with part of the very valuable National Portrait Collection on view, it is well worth a visit. Also on display is the Fry Model Railway, one of the largest modern railway exhibits in the world, which includes 300 model trains, trams, and items of Irish railway history dating from 1834. Admission charge. Malahide, Co. Dublin (phone: 452337 or 452655).

Newbridge House and Park – Built in 1740, this country mansion is full of memorabilia of the Cobbe family, including original hand-carved furniture collected through the years, portraits, memoirs, daybooks, a museum of world travels, and an extensive doll collection. Downstairs, visitors can view a kitchen and laundry room from 1760, complete with ancient implements. The wooded grounds (365 acres) have picnic areas and walking trails. Five miles north of Dublin Airport and 12 miles from the city center, Newbridge can be comfortably combined with an excursion to nearby Malahide Castle. Open 10 AM to 5 PM weekdays, 2 to 6 PM Sundays, June through October; 2 to 5 PM Wednesdays and Sundays, November through March. Admission charge. Off the Dublin–Belfast road, N1, at Donabate, Co. Dublin (phone: 436534 or 436535).

■**EXTRA SPECIAL:** The beautiful Boyne Valley is one of Ireland's most storied and evocative sites, and it makes an easy and interesting day trip. Leave Dublin by the Navan road, passing through Dunshaughlin (which takes its name from a church founded by St. Seachnall, a companion of St. Patrick). Six miles south of Navan, signposted to the left, is the Hill of Tara. Although only some grassy mounds and earthworks recall a splendid past, it is impossible to remain unmoved by the site's history: This is Royal Tara, where the High Kings of Ireland were crowned on the Lia Fail (Stone of Destiny) before time began. And it was here, at the tribes' great triennial Feis of Tara, that laws were enacted and revised. Now, as Moore wrote in his immortal song, "No more to chiefs and ladies bright / The harp of Tara swells / The chord alone that breaks at night / Its tale of ruin tells."

Returning to the Navan road, you will pass the striking ruins of 16th-century Athlumney Castle on the east bank of the Boyne, about 1½ miles from Navan.

Continue through Donaghmore, with its remains of a 12th-century church and a round tower. Nearby, below the Boyne Bridge, lies Log na Ri (Hollow of the King), where people once swam their herds of cattle ceremoniously across the river to protect them from the "little people" and from natural disasters.

The village of Slane lies on one of the loveliest stretches of the Boyne. There are some delightful Georgian houses, but the history of this small town goes back far beyond the 18th century. On the hill that overlooks Slane, St. Patrick lit the paschal fire on Holy Saturday, AD 433, and drew upon himself the wrath of the high king's druids. Patrick emerged victorious from the ensuing confrontation, and Christianity began its reign in Ireland. On the slopes of the hill are the remains of an ancient earthen fort and the ruins of a 16th-century church. Apart from archaeological interest, the climb up Slane Hill is well worth the effort — rewarding the energetic with fine views across the tranquil Boyne Valley to Trim and Drogheda. Just outside the town lies the estate of Slane Castle, a 19th-century castellated mansion in which the present occupant, Lord Mountcharles, has opened a fine restaurant (phone: 412-4207).

Downstream from Slane is Brugh na Boinne (the Palace of the Boyne), a vast necropolis more than 4,000 years old. Here, beneath a chain of tumuli, Kings of Ireland were laid to rest in passage graves of remarkable complexity. The tumuli of Dowth, Knowth, and Newgrange in particular are of major interest, both for their extent and the amazing diversity of their sculptured ornamentation. Newgrange is one of the finest passage graves in all of Western Europe, and it has been opened to the public. A permanent archaeological exhibition and guided tours are available. Closed Mondays (phone: 41-24274).

Farther down the Boyne Valley is Drogheda, an ancient town that has witnessed many dramatic scenes in the course of Irish history, most of which involve the contention of Royalists and Puritans for the English throne. Oliver Cromwell burned the city to the ground during a vicious siege in the 1640s, and James II was defeated by William of Orange on July 12, 1690. Reminders of Drogheda's past include the 13th-century St. Laurence's Gate, the only survivors of the original ten gates in this once-walled city; the ruins of 13th-century St. Mary's Abbey; the Norman motte-and-bailey of Millmount and the fine *Millmount Museum;* and St. Peter's Church, where the head of St. Oliver Plunkett, martyred Archbishop of Armagh, is enshrined.

Five miles north of Drogheda is Monasterboice, an ancient monastic settlement noteworthy for one of the most perfect high crosses in Ireland — the intricately carved 10th-century Cross of Muireadach. Southwest of Monasterboice are the impressive ruins of Mellifont Abbey. Dating from 1142, this was the first Cistercian foundation in Ireland and heralded a whole new style of ecclesiastical architecture. Note especially the remains of the gate house and the octagonal lavabo.

Return to Dublin via N1.

SOURCES AND RESOURCES

TOURIST INFORMATION: For information, brochures, and maps before departure, contact the Irish Tourist Board (757 Third Ave., New York, NY 10017; phone: 212-418-0800). For on-the-spot information and assistance, call the Dublin Tourism Office (Dublin Airport; phone: 376387; or 14 O'-Connell St.; phone: 747733). The tourist board personnel offer advice on all aspects of a stay in Ireland and can make theater bookings and hotel reservations anywhere in the country. Two useful guides, *Dining in Ireland* and *The Dublin Guide,* are available at the tourist board and at most bookstores.

Tourist Trail, published by the Dublin Tourist Office and available at its offices, is an excellent walking guide to Dublin. Another invaluable publication is *Dublin: Official Guide.* The best city map is the Ordnance Survey Dublin Map; less detailed but generally adequate maps are also available.

The US Embassy is at 42 Elgin Rd., Ballbridge (phone: 688777).

Local Coverage – *In Dublin,* published fortnightly, covers every conceivable activity in Dublin, including theater, cinema, music, exhibitions, sports, and cabarets. The *Dublin Event Guide,* available at no charge at hotels, shops, and tourist offices, is a good resource for a variety of events in Dublin. Large daily newspapers are the *Irish Times,* the *Irish Independent,* and the *Irish Press;* evening papers are the *Evening Herald* and the *Evening Press.*

 TELEPHONE: The area code for Dublin and immediate vicinity is 1. When calling from within the Republic of Ireland, dial 01 before the local number. Be aware that Dublin phone numbers currently are being changed, and that a new system will continue to evolve until 1994. Numbers previously beginning with the digits 23, 24, 26, 27, 28, 70, and 79, for instance, now all begin with a "6." Other changes will be phased in over the next 3 years.

 GETTING AROUND: Airport – Dublin Airport is north of the city at Collinstown. In normal traffic, a trip from the airport to downtown takes 35 to 40 minutes, with an average taxi fare of $15 to $20. CIE (*Córas Iompair Eireann, National Transport Company*) operates a bus service (see below), timed to meet all flights, between the airport and the central bus station.

Bus and Train – *Bus Eireann* and *Irish Rail,* divisions of *CIE,* operate bus and rail services not only in Dublin but nationwide. Cross-city bus routes are extensive. The fare is collected after the passenger is seated (exact fare is not required). Although Dublin has no subway, a commuter rail system, *Dublin Area Rapid Transit* (*DART*), runs from central Dublin along the bay as far north as Howth and as far south as Bray. It is swift, dependable, and safe at all hours.

For extended stays, purchase a new "Explorer Pass," which provides unlimited use of the *DART* system and of all buses and trains within a 20-mile radius. Cost for 4 consecutive days is about $10.

All information regarding bus and rail travel throughout the republic can be obtained by calling 787777. Official *Bus Eireann* and *Irish Rail* timetables are available at newsstands.

Car Rental – Many international companies, such as *Avis, Budget, Hertz,* and *National,* as well as a variety of local firms, offer excellent self-drive opportunities. *Dan Dooley* (42 Westland Row; phone: 772733; or at the airport; phone: 428355); *Murray's* (Baggot Street Bridge; phone: 681777; or at the airport; phone: 378179); *Johnson & Perrott* (at the airport; phone: 370204; or at 12a South Leinstev St.; phone: 767213); and *Cara Rent-a-Car Ltd.* (151 S. Circular Rd.; phone: 537091) are all reliable.

Taxi – There are taxi stands throughout the city, especially near main hotels, and cabs also can be hailed in the streets. Your first conversation with a Dublin cab driver will assure you that you are in fact in Ireland. Among the companies that operate a 24-hour radio service are *Blue Cabs* (phone: 761111), *Co-op Taxis* (phone: 766666), and *National Radio Cabs* (phone: 772222).

Tours – A good way to get one's bearings in Dublin is to take a guided tour. *Bus Eireann* operates half-day motorcoach tours through the city and the nearby countryside, and full-day tours to more distant points, with prices averaging about $12 (half-day) and about $16 (full-day). All tours leave from the Central Bus Station (Store St.; phone: 787777). On a more limited basis, tours also are offered by *Gray Line* (3 Clanwilliam Terrace; phone: 619666).

Walking tours are conducted by several individuals and small firms. *Old Dublin Walking Tours* offers 2-hour tours around the Liberties area, departing from Christ Church Cathedral, daily during summer and on weekends during the rest of the year. The cost is about $5; for reservations and information, phone: 532407 or 556970. Babette Walsh, a guide registered with the Irish Tourist Board, knows every nook and cranny of the city and offers customized tours, including escorted shopping sprees. She is an irresistible storyteller, and her often salty dialogue more than makes up for her occasionally creative view of Irish history. Ms. Walsh leads from 2 to 20 people on private jaunts for about $35 for a half day or $75 for a full day. Contact Ms. Walsh in advance at the *Cottage* (Balscaddon Rd., Howth, Co. Dublin; phone: 391869). The *Dublin Literary Pub Crawl* leads guests to old haunts of the city's illustrious literary figures, such as Samuel Beckett, James Joyce, Brendan Behan, and Patrick Kavanagh, a journalist/writer who wrote about the area. The tour costs about $7.75 and begins at the *Bailey Pub* (Duke St.) on Tuesdays, Wednesdays, and Thursdays, June through August. To book a tour or to obtain additional information, call 540228.

SPECIAL EVENTS: As the *European City of Culture* for 1991, Dublin will be hosting a wide variety of special events throughout the year, involving the arts, culture, and history; for information on specific programs contact the Irish Tourist Board (757 Third Ave., New York, NY 10017; phone: 212-418-0800). Other outstanding annual events include *St. Patrick's Day,* March 17, with a parade and many other festivities; an *Irish Music Festival* (Feis Cheoil) in May; the *Festival of Music in Great Irish Houses* in June, featuring concerts by international celebrities in Georgian mansions near Dublin; *Bloomsday,* June 16, when James Joyce aficionados gather from around the world to follow the circuitous path through Dublin that Leopold Bloom took from morning until late at night in *Ulysses;* the *Dublin Horse Show,* the principal sporting and social event of the year, held at the *Royal Dublin Society* in late July or early August; the *Dublin Theatre Festival* in September and October, featuring new plays by Irish authors; and the *Dublin Marathon,* the last Monday in October. For details about these and other events, inquire at the tourist board (see *Tourist Information,* above).

MUSEUMS: The *National Museum,* the *Heraldic Museum,* and the Royal Hospital are described in *Special Places.* Dublin also is the home of several smaller museums:

Dublin Civic Museum – Adjacent to the *Powerscourt Town House Centre,* it contains artifacts and memorabilia — from old maps and prints to street signs and wooden water mains — reflecting 1,000 years of Dublin history. Closed Mondays. 58 S. William St. (phone: 771642).

Irish Jewish Museum – Housed in a former synagogue, this museum traces the history of Jews in Ireland over the last 500 years. Documents, photographs, and memorabilia are on display. Open Sundays, Tuesdays, and Thursdays, except during winter (open Sundays only). 3/4 Walsorth Rd., off Victoria St. (phone: 832703 or 534754).

Museum of Childhood – Exhibits include dolls, doll houses, and doll carriages, dating from 1730 to 1940, from all over the world. There also are antique toys and rocking horses. Opening days vary, so call in advance. Admission charge. The Palms, 20 Palmerstown Park, Rathmines (phone: 973223).

National Wax Museum – Life-size wax figures of important Irish historical, political, literary, theatrical, and sports figures are on display, as well as international newsmakers from Pope John Paul II and Michael Jackson. Open daily. Admission charge. Granby Row, off Parnell Sq. (phone: 746416).

 SHOPPING: Neatly balanced on both banks of the Liffey, Dublin has two downtown shopping areas: one around O'Connell and Henry Streets, the other centered in Grafton Street and its environs (stores on the south side are more elegant). *Powerscourt Town House Centre,* just off Grafton Street, has a number of clothing, antiques, and craft shops in a courtyard built around a pretty townhouse. Good buys are the chunky Aran sweaters, Donegal tweed, Waterford and Galway crystal, and Belleek china. *Brown Thomas* and *Switzer's* are the main department stores on Grafton Street; *Arnott's, Roche's,* and *Clery's* are reasonably priced department stores in the O'Connell and Henry streets area. The two newest shopping complexes are the *Royal Hibernian Way* on Dawson Street and *St. Stephen's Green Shopping Centre* (housed behind a re-created Regency façade) on the green. Other recommended shops include the following:

Laura Ashley – Fashion and fabrics for the home, women, and children. 60 Grafton St. (phone: 679-5433).

Best of Irish – A wide range of Irish goods — crystal, china, hand-knit goods, jewelry, linen, and tweeds. Open daily. Next to the *Westbury* hotel, on Harry St., off Grafton St. (phone: 679-1233).

Bewley's Café Ltd. – A Dublin landmark, it's an emporium of coffees and teas of all nations, with a tempting candy selection as well. Sampling is encouraged. There are 5 shops in the Dublin area, but only the one on Grafton Street has waitress service. 78/79 Grafton St. (phone: 776761).

Blarney Woolen Mills – A branch of the Cork-based family enterprise, this huge new shop is known for its very competitive prices. It stocks all the visitor favorites, from tweeds and hand-knits to crystal, china, pottery, and souvenirs. 21/23 Nassau St. (phone: 710068).

Cathach Books – Most comprehensive collection of Irish literature and memorabilia in the country. 10 Duke St. (phone: 718676).

The Cheeseboard – Sells fine wines as well the obvious cheese. *Westbury Mall,* off Grafton St. (phone: 679-1422).

Cleo Ltd. – For more than 50 years, one of Dublin's most fashionable sources for hand-knit and handwoven cloaks, caps, suits, coats, and shawls. 18 Kildare St. (phone: 761421).

Sybil Connolly – Ireland's reigning couturière; her romantic ball gowns of finely pleated Irish linen are indeed special. 71 Merrion Sq. (phone: 767281).

Louis Copeland – The city's best bespoken tailor. 18 Wicklow St. (phone: 777038).

Pat Crowley – Silky, seductive blouses and dresses. 3 Molesworth Pl. (phone: 615580).

Dublin Woollen Mills – Large selection of quality woolens. 41 Ormond Quay (phone: 75014).

Dunns – High-quality salmon at very competitive prices. 6 Upper Baggot St. (phone: 602688).

Eason & Son Ltd. – Jam-packed with tomes and paperbacks, maps, records, and stationery. 40/42 Lower O'Connell St. (phone: 733811).

Figgis Rare Books – A fine collection of rare Irish books, maps, and more. 53 Pembroke Rd. (phone: 609491).

Patrick Flood – Silver and gold jewelry in traditional Irish designs. Unit 14C, 1st floor, *Powerscourt Town House Centre* (phone: 770615).

Fred Hanna – Bookseller to Trinity College. New and used books; excellent books and maps on Ireland. 28/29 Nassau St. (phone: 771255).

Hardy's – For new and antique jewelry and timepieces. 11 Johnson's Court (phone: 715587).

Heraldic Artists – A good source for family crests, flags, scrolls, and genealogy tomes. 3 Nassau St. (phone: 762391).

Hodges Figgis – Another terrific bookstore, this one has an exceptional selection of paperbacks. 57/58 Dawson St. (phone: 774764).

Jimmy Hourihan – Ready-to-wear suits, capes, and coats for women. 28 Dublin Industrial Estate, Finglass Rd. (phone: 300033).

House of Ireland – Top-quality Irish and European goods — from Aynsley, Lladro, Spode, Wedgwood, Waterford, and Hummel crystal and china to hand-knits, kilts, linen, and shillelaghs. 37/38 Nassau St. (phone: 716133) and 6465 Dawson St. (phone: 714543).

House of Names – For more good things genealogical; sweaters can be custom-ordered with a family crest and name. 26 Nassau St. (phone: 839733).

H. Johnston Ltd. – Traditional blackthorn walking sticks. 11 Wicklow St. (phone: 771249).

Kapp and Peterson – Tobacco and hand-carved pipes for men *and* women. 117 Grafton St. (phone: 714652).

Kevin & Howlin Ltd. – Men's ready-to-wear and made-to-measure clothing. The store carries some women's tweeds. 31 Nassau St. (phone: 770257).

Knobs and Knockers – Extensive collection of knockers, handles, and pulls. 19 Nassau St. (phone: 710288).

Lace Lady – Yards of antique and modern lace. as well as Irish linen tablecloths, bedcovers, pillowcases, handkerchiefs, and vintage clothes and accessories. 129 Upper Leeson St. (phone: 604537).

McConnell & Nelson – Located downtown, this popular spot is well known for its "wild" salmon. 38 Grafton St. (phone: 774344).

McCullough Pigott – Three floors of records, tapes, and musical instruments. Suffolk St. (phone: 773138).

Memoirs – Spicy potpourri, antique jewelry, miniature toys, porcelain dolls, hair combs, and lots of Victorian nostalgia make this shop very popular with Dubliners. 21 S. Anne St. (phone: 679-1544).

Mullins of Dublin – Coats of arms emblazoned on parchments, plaques, and even doorknockers. 36 Upper O'Connell St. (phone: 741133).

Fergus O'Farrell – For more than 25 years, this has been a showcase for top-quality Irish crafts — from woodcarvings and brass door knockers to beaten copper art; also handmade candles, stationery, and prints from 19th-century woodcuts. 62 Dawson St. (phone: 770862).

M. Samuels – Large selection of antique jewelry and silverplate place settings. 17 S. Anne St. (phone: 11262).

Sheepskin Shop – Just the spot to stock up on high-quality sheepskin and lambskin suits and coats. The shop also has a varied selection of leather trousers, suits, and jackets. 20 Wicklow St. (phone: 719585).

Sleater's – A charming jewelry shop tucked in an alley between Grafton Street and *Powerscourt Town House Centre.* 9 Johnson's Court (phone: 777532).

The Sweater Shop – Wide selection of cashmere, pure wool, mohair, and angora sweaters, all at reasonable prices. 18 Kildare St. (phone: 761421).

Tower Design Craft Centre – Once a sugar refinery, this renovated 1862 tower houses the workshops of more than 30 innovative craftspeople, with work ranging from heraldic jewelry, Irish oak woodcarvings, and hand-cut crystal to Chez Nous Irish chocolates, stained glass, toys, and fishing tackle. Self-service restaurant. Ideal for a rainy day. Pearse St. (phone: 775655).

Trinity College Library – Large assortment of Irish literature and children's books. Trinity College, College Green (phone: 772941).

US Shirtmakers – Besides shirts with detachable collars and mother-of-pearl buttons and made from English cloth, this shop also sells some Irish linen. 13 South Leinster St. (phone: 763013).

Waltons Musical Instrument Galleries – Bagpipes and Irish harps as well as records. 2/5 N Frederick St. (phone: 747805).

Weir's – Fine selection of gold and silver jewelry, antiques, clocks, and bone china in an elegant setting. 96/99 Grafton St. (phone: 779678).

J. & M. Weldon – Frequented by Dubliners because of its antique diamond rings and rare silver decorative items. 18 S. Anne St. (phone: 72742).

SPORTS AND FITNESS: Bicycling – Irish Raleigh Industries operates *Rent-a-Bike* at a number of city firms (phone: 626-1333). Two downtown shops offering bicycle rentals are *Pedal Power* (65 Mespil Rd.; phone: 687923) and *McDonald's* (38 Wexford St.; phone: 752586). Charges average $5 per day or $20 per week.

Gaelic Games – Football and hurling are two fast, enthralling field sports; important matches are played at *Croke Park.* For details, see the calendar of events in *In Dublin* or call Croke Park (phone: 743111).

Golf – More than 30 golf courses are within easy reach of Dublin; visitors are welcome at all clubs on weekdays, but gaining admission can be more difficult on weekends. Two of the finest courses in the world, *Portmarnock* (phone: 323082) and *Royal Dublin* (phone: 336346), are just north of the city and should not be missed.

Greyhound Racing – An exciting spectator sport, racing can be seen regularly at two tracks, *Shelbourne Park Stadium* and *Harold's Cross Stadium,* each an 8-minute ride from the city center. Details in *In Dublin* or at the tourist board.

Horse Racing – *Phoenix Park* is the site of races in the city, but the course is straight, not circular, which makes for frustrating viewing. You can see the start, the middle, or the end, but you won't see the whole race. Better is the well-known racecourse *Curragh,* about a mile outside the town of Kildare in County Kildare, less than an hour's drive from Dublin. Six miles south of the city, Leopardstown has a modern racecourse.

Horseback Riding – A list of riding establishments close to Dublin is available at the tourist board.

Tennis – Ireland has a first-rate international facility — the *Kilternan Tennis Centre* — about a 15-minute taxi ride from the city center. With 4 indoor and 4 outdoor courts, it is open daily from 7 AM to midnight, year-round. Equipment rental at *Pro Shop Kilternan* (phone: 953729 or 955559). There are a few public courts, generally outdoors, in and around Dublin, where visitors can play for a small fee. The most central is Herbert Park (Ballsbridge; phone: 684364). For more information on public courts, contact the *Dublin Corporation* (Community & Environment Dept., 2 Parnell Sq.; phone: 727777).

THEATER: For complete program listings see the publications listed in *Tourist Information,* above. The main theaters are in the city center; smaller theater troupes perform in the universities, in suburban theaters, and occasionally in pubs and hotels. The main theaters are the *Abbey* and the *Peacock* (both at Lower Abbey St.; phone: 744505 or 787222); the *Gate* (the theater of Michael MacLiammoir and Hilton Edwards on Cavendish Row; phone: 744045); the *Gaiety* (S. King St.; phone: 771717), mostly for revues, musicals, and opera; the *Olympia* (Dame St.; phone: 778962), for everything from revues to straight plays; the *John Player Theatre* (S. Circular Rd; phone: 532707), for contemporary drama; the *Focus* (Pembroke Pl.; phone: 763071), for Russian and Scandinavian works; the grand old *Olympia Theatre* (72 Dame St.; phone: 78962), for concerts, pantomime, and plays; and the *Project Arts Centre* (39 E. Essex St.; phone: 712321), very avant-garde. *Andrews Lane Theatre* (9-17 Andrews La.; phone: 679-5720) is one of Dublin's newest theaters, making its mark with performances of contemporary plays. In addition to the main theater, there is a small studio which serves as a stage for avant-garde productions, including occasional lunchtime shows and performances by all-female acting troupes. The *Point* theater (East Link Bridge; phone: 363633), formerly a depot building, features rock bands to Broadway musicals.

For children, the *Lambert Mews Puppet Theatre* in the suburb of Monkstown will prove irresistible. Clifden La., Monkstown (phone: 800974).

It is always advisable to reserve in advance for theater in Dublin. You can make bookings at theaters; the tourist board; and the information desks of *Switzer's* and *Brown Thomas* stores, Grafton St. Most of the theaters accept telephone reservations and credit cards.

 MUSIC: The *National Concert Hall* (Earlsfort Ter., off St. Stephen's Green; phone: 711888) is the center of Dublin's active musical life and the home of the *RTE* (Radio Telefís Eireann) *Symphony Orchestra. RTE* performances are held regularly, as are a variety of other concerts. For a schedule, phone the concert hall or check local publications. The *Royal Dublin Society* stages classical music concerts at the *Members' Hall* — also known as the *Royal Dublin Society Concert Hall* (Ballsbridge; phone: 680645) — from November to March. In April and September the *Dublin Grand Opera Society* holds its spring and winter seasons at the *Gaiety Theatre.* For big-name rock concerts, such as *U2* performances, the popular new venue is the *Point Theatre,* a renovated depot with state-of-the-art acoustics (at East Link Bridge; phone: 363633). The *Olympia* (see above) also hosts occasional rock gigs. Traditional Irish music is a must. Sessions (*seisiún*) are held at many places around the city by an organization called *Comhaltas Ceoltóirí Éireann* (phone: 800295); ballad sessions are held nightly except Sundays in the *Barn* on the ground floor of the *Abbey* (Howth, 10 miles north of the city on the coast; phone: 322006 or 390307). Many pubs offer music informally — *O'Donoghue's* (Merrion Row) is one of the most famous (and least comfortable). Try also *Toner's* and the *Baggot Inn* (both on Lower Baggot St.); *Kitty O'Shea's* (23/25 Upper Grand Canal St.); or *Foley's* (1 Merrion Row). Many other pubs are listed in *In Dublin.*

 NIGHTCLUBS AND NIGHTLIFE: There is little in the way of large-scale cabaret-cum-dancing in Dublin; swinging Dublin tends to congregate on the discotheque scene. Premises range from the large, lively places where an escort is not necessarily required to small, intimate clubs. Most discotheques have only wine licenses.

Among the more established discotheques on a rapidly changing scene are the large and lively *Annabel's* in the *Burlington* hotel, *Raffles* in the *Sachs, Blinkers* at Leopardstown racecourse, and *Rumours* on O'Connell St. Smaller, more intimate clubs are mainly to be found in the Leeson St. area: *Blonds, Samantha's, Styx,* and *Buck's* are a few. The most famous traditional cabaret in Dublin is the established *Jurys Cabaret,* nightly except Mondays from April through October (phone: 605000). Also good are the *Braemor Rooms* (Churchtown; phone: 981016); *Doyle's Irish Cabaret* (open April through October) at the *Burlington* (phone: 605222); and the *Clontarf Castle* dinner show (phone: 332271).

BEST IN TOWN

CHECKING IN: With the opening of three new first class hotels and the refurbishment of several others, Dublin's hotels have risen significantly in quality, but they still are not at the top of world class standards. Expect to pay more than $200 for a double room in hotels classified as very expensive; $135 to $200 for those classified as expensive; $90 to $135 in those listed as moderate; and less than $90 for an inexpensive room. A room with Irish breakfast for two in a private home in a residential neighborhood will cost $50 or less.

Note: The tourist board offers a list of hotels it has inspected and graded; it also offers a computerized reservation service all over Ireland (see *Tourist Information,* above). All telephone numbers are in the 1 area code unless otherwise indicated.

Berkeley Court – The flagship of the Doyle group and the first Irish member of the Leading Hotels of the World group. Close to the city in the leafy suburb of Ballsbridge, it combines graciousness with modern efficiency. Contemporary and antique furnishings harmonize, and the service is exceptionally warm. There are 210 rooms and 6 suites (all with Jacuzzis), including a new 6-room, $2,000-a-night penthouse suite. There also is an excellent dining room (see *Eating Out*), a conservatory-style coffee shop, a health center with indoor pool and saunas, and a shopping arcade. Lansdowne Rd. (phone: 601711). Very expensive.

Conrad – Dublin's newest international hotel — opened in 1990 by the US Hilton hotel chain — is in the heart of the city, opposite the *National Concert Hall* and across from St. Stephen's Green. It offers 192 bright and airy rooms (including 10 suites), all with bay windows. Each room has an executive desk, 2 or 3 telephones, mini-bar, color TV set, and a large marble bathroom. One floor is reserved for nonsmokers. Other facilities include a fully equipped health club, hair salon, a car rental desk, and a garage. The *Alexandra* is the hotel's most elegant restaurant; *Plurabelle* is an informal brasserie; and *Alfie Byrne's* is a lively pub. Earlsfort Terrace (phone: 765555). Very expensive.

Shelbourne – This venerable establishment, a nice mixture of the dignified and the lively, now is more polished than ever after a $5-million face-lift. Some of the 167 rooms are truly splendid, particularly the front rooms on the second floor. Many are supremely comfortable, if compact. But the sense of history in the creaky-floored hallways, the glittering function rooms, and the varied clientele — from socialites to literati — make this establishment especially appealing. The *Horseshoe Bar* is one of the livelier fixtures of Dublin pub life, while the *Aisling* restaurant, with its 1826 plasterwork and trio of Waterford crystal chandeliers, is a showcase for modern Irish cuisine. 27 St. Stephen's Green (phone: 766471; in the continental US or Canada, 800-223-5672). Very expensive.

Westbury – The fashionable centerpiece of a chic mall of shops and restaurants, this hotel is a member of the Doyle group. The management emphasizes elegance, and the 206 rooms have canopied beds and an abundance of mahogany and brass furnishings. Private suites with Jacuzzis also are available. The most noteworthy of its restaurants is the grand *Russell Room.* Grafton St. (phone: 6791122). Very expensive.

Jurys – In Ballsbridge opposite the American Embassy, this modern complex has a multi-story, skylit lobby area and a dome-shape central atrium. The main hotel offers 290 rooms, each with well-equipped bathroom and 100 extra large rooms and suites are in a newer, separate but connected 8-story wing. Known as the

Towers, this section is a first for Ireland — featuring computer-key-accessible rooms, each with a bay window, mini-bar, 3 telephone lines, work area, satellite TV, marble and tile bathroom, walk-in closet, and either king- or queen-size beds. All the *Towers'* rooms are decorated with designer fabrics and specially styled furnishings, such as rocking recliner chairs. Two floors are designated as nonsmoking. The *Towers* has its own hospitality lounge, separate elevators, and entrance. There also are 2 restaurants, a 23-hour coffee shop, 2 bars, an indoor/outdoor swimming pool, and health center. For entertainment, there is *Jurys Cabaret,* Ireland's longest running variety show. Northumberland Rd. (phone: 605000). Very expensive (towers) to expensive (main hotel).

Bloom's – Centrally located, this intimate spot (a member of the Quality Inn group) has a high commitment to service. Its 86 rooms have color TV sets, air conditioning, trouser-pressers, free mixers and ice, and direct-dial telephones. Every corridor has an ice cabinet and a shoeshine. Fine dining is offered in the *Blazes Boylan Grill Room,* and there are 2 lively bars, *Bogie's* and *Yesterday's.* Anglesea St. (phone: 715622). Expensive.

Burlington – Ireland's largest property, with 500 rooms, was completely refurbished in 1989. Restaurants include an international dining room, the *Sussex,* and the cozy *Diplomat* for beef and seafood. The trendy *Burlington Bar,* with its cheery hanging plants, globe lights, and brass, has a popular lunch buffet. A musical revue is performed at *Doyle's Irish Cabaret* on summer evenings, and there's year-round entertainment in *Annabel's* nightclub. Leeson St. (phone: 605222). Expensive.

Gresham – Once considered one of the grandest of Dublin hotels, it has changed ownership a number of times and recently came to rest in the Ryan Holdings Group. Though you hardly could call it grand these days, this 179-room hostelry once attracted lots of luminaries. Upper O'Connell St. (phone: 746881). Expensive.

Montrose – Similar to but larger than the *Tara Tower,* near the National Radio and Television studios and across the road from the Belfield campus of University College, Dublin. About 10 minutes' drive from the city center, on a well-serviced bus route, its 190 bedrooms are comfortable, and it has a good restaurant. Facilities include a grill, bars, a health center, hairdressing salon, and souvenir shop. Stillorgan Rd. (phone: 693311). Moderate.

Russell Court – Two former Georgian houses have been transformed into this convenient place less than a block from St. Stephen's Green. The decor in the public areas is Art Deco, and the 22 modern bedrooms, all with bath, have light woods and pastel tones. Facilities include a restaurant, lounge, and nightclub. 21-23 Harcourt St. (phone: 784991). Moderate.

Skylon – Midway between downtown and the Dublin Airport, this modern northside hostelry has 100 rooms all done in a colorful Irish motif. The hotel also features a restaurant/grill that stays open until midnight. Upper Drumcondra Rd. (phone: 379121). Moderate.

Tara Tower – Modern, comfortable, very reasonably priced, and just 10 minutes' drive from the city center, on a well-serviced bus route, The 100 bedrooms have radio, television sets, and telephone, and many overlook Dublin Bay. The lobby is small, but the hotel's good restaurant/grill is open until midnight. Merrion Rd. (phone: 694666). Moderate.

Ariel House – A homey guesthouse with 15 rooms and a restaurant with a wine license. One block from the *DART* train station for easy commuting to the city center. Room rates include full breakfast. 52 Lansdowne Rd. (phone: 685512). Moderate to inexpensive.

Georgian House – Newly renovated, this centrally located guesthouse is less than 2 blocks south of St. Stephen's Green. It offers 11 bedrooms with private bath/shower, phone, and TV set, but no elevator. There also is a restaurant and an enclosed parking area. 20 Lr. Baggot St. (phone: 604300 or 618832). Moderate to inexpensive.

Anglesea Townhouse – Near the American Embassy, this Edwardian residence is the home of Helen Kirrane, who spoils her guests with hearty breakfasts of fresh fish, homemade breads and scones, fresh juices, baked fruits, and warm cereals. Heirlooms and family antiques add to the ambience of this jewel of a bed-and-breakfast guesthouse. All 7 rooms have private bath/shower, TV sets, and direct-dial telephones. 63 Anglesea Rd., Ballsbridge (phone: 683877). Inexpensive.

Egan's House – Another comfortable guesthouse, offering 23 rooms, all with private baths. There is also a small restaurant. 7 Iona Park (phone: 303611). Inexpensive.

Iona House – A guesthouse with 14 rooms, 12 with private baths, and a restaurant/coffee shop serving breakfast to late snacks. 5 Iona Park (phone: 306217). Inexpensive.

Mount Herbert – Close to the city center in a quaint neighborhood, this well-run, family-owned Georgian mansion has 88 rooms (77 with private baths), a health facility, and a fairly good restaurant. No bar (wine license only) but a very pleasant atmosphere. 7 Herbert Rd. (phone: 684321). Inexpensive.

EATING OUT: Where food is concerned, Ireland, first and foremost an agricultural country, has outstanding raw materials. But truly distinctive and innovative Irish cuisine really does not exist. Traditional dishes such as Irish stew, Dublin coddle, and bacon and cabbage are served, but this kind of dish is a *rara avis* on the menu of most better restaurants, being looked down upon as too common to prepare for discriminating diners.

Where the serving of its enviable agricultural produce is concerned, Ireland's top restaurants can compare with the best anywhere. Dublin offers a wide range of first class restaurants, a somewhat more restricted range of moderately priced establishments, and a number of fast-service, inexpensive eating places.

Dinner for two, excluding drinks, will cost $100 and up in expensive restaurants; $50 to $95 in moderate places; and under $50 in inexpensive ones. Reservations always are advised, especially at expensive and moderate establishments. Unless noted otherwise, most are closed Sundays and holidays. All telephone numbers are in the 1 area code unless otherwise indicated.

Berkeley Court – One of the best hotel dining rooms, this is elegant and lavishly appointed; its prizewinning chef produces highly satisfactory fare. Open daily. Lansdowne Rd. (phone: 601711). Expensive.

Celtic Mews – In an old Georgian mews with a warm, welcoming atmosphere, this is one of Dublin's original fine dining spots. Entrées range from pheasant and lobster to classic Irish stew. Dinner only. 109A Lower Baggot St. (phone: 760796). Expensive.

Le Coq Hardi – Run by owner/chef John Howard, twice Gold Medal winner in the prestigious Hotelympia/Salon Culinaire contest, this is a gracious Georgian establishment. Its extensive à la carte menu offers many house specialties such as Howard's renowned *caneton à l'orange*. Reservations necessary. Major credit cards accepted. 35 Pembroke Rd., Ballsbridge (phone: 689070). Expensive.

Ernie's – Master seafood chef Ernie Evans earned a far-reaching reputation at the *Towers* hotel on the Ring of Kerry. Still specializing in *fruits de mer,* he now works magic on such dishes as Valencia scallops, garlic prawns, and fresh salmon. Open for lunch and dinner; closed Sundays and Mondays. Mulberry Gardens, Donnybrook (phone: 693300). Expensive.

Grey Door – Open since 1978, this restaurant has achieved an enviable reputation for fine Russian and Finnish cuisine. The wine list is good and the more adventurous imbiber can sample such rarities as Russian champagne. The setting behind this elegant doorway in the heart of Georgian Dublin is intimate, rather like dining in a private home. 23 Upper Pembroke St. (phone: 763286). Expensive.

King Sitric – This superb small dining place, right on the bay, serves perfectly cooked fish and excellent wines in a tastefully restored old house. It also specializes in game birds such as grouse and snipe. The service is very good. East Pier, Howth (phone: 325235). Expensive.

Locks – A French provincial eatery on the banks of the Grand Canal near Portobello Bridge. Only the freshest produce is used for such dishes as wild salmon and breast of pigeon. 1 Windsor Ter., Portobello (phone: 538352 or 543391). Expensive.

Lord Edward – Strictly for seafood lovers (no meat on the menu), it is in a tall Victorian building opposite historic Christ Church Cathedral, in the older part of the city. The seafood is prepared and served in the classic French style. Reservations necessary. 23 Christ Church Pl. (phone: 542420). Expensive.

Old Dublin – This cozy eatery has rose-colored linen and walls and roaring fireplaces. Specialties on the menu include Scandinavian-style fish, which owner Eamonn Walsh learned to love while in Finland. For meat eaters there's filet à la Novgorod — chateaubriand sliced and served on sauerkraut alongside fried kasha, spicy mushrooms, caviar, and sour cream. There also is a good wine list. Open weekdays for lunch and dinner; Saturdays for dinner only; closed holidays. 91 Francis St. (phone: 542028 or 542346). Expensive.

Patrick Guilbaud – A trendy place for nouvelle cuisine that draws an equally stylish crowd. Specialties include breast of duck in cider sauce, veal kidneys and sweetbreads, lamb's tongue and brill, and bacon in curry sauce. 46 James Pl., off Baggot St. (phone: 764192 or 601799). Expensive.

White's on the Green – An elegantly appointed gathering place for media stars, celebrities, and expense-account diners, it has the air of a Georgian garden. Dublin's "in" spot features *cuisine moderne* and the finest service traditions. Menu ranges from veal sweetbreads with fennel and celery to roast wild salmon or *panaché* of lamb with fresh tarragon. 119 St. Stephen's Green (phone: 751975 or 751181). Expensive.

O'Casey's – Just south of St. Stephen's Green, it boasts eye-catching decor — bold colors, striped upholstery, rattan chairs, and beautiful paintings by modern Irish artists. Specialties include warm monkfish salad, beef *en croute* with red wine and morels, and sauté of woodcock with bacon and cabbage. Desserts are varied and artfully presented. 17A Lr. Baggot St. (phone: 762050). Expensive to moderate.

Café Klara – Opposite the lord mayor's Mansion House, this new brasserie features a bright and spacious flower-filled decor, with a glass-domed ceiling, tall pillars, and mirrored walls. The menu offers both light and substantial dishes, from salad and soup to pasta and fresh seafood or meat, all available à la carte from noon to almost midnight, daily. 35 Dawson St. (phone: 778611). Moderate.

Coffers – Around the corner from *Bloom's* hotel, this small, comfortable eatery specializes in steaks — varying from a plain filet to a pork steak cooked in fresh apples and Pernod. It features a special pre-theater dinner daily except Sundays. 6 Cope St. (phone: 715900 or 715740). Moderate.

Gallery 22 – A pleasant, gardenlike atmosphere pervades this dining spot near the *Shelbourne* hotel. The innovative menu includes seafood pancakes, rack of lamb, sea trout, and filet steak with vermouth sauce. Vegetarian dishes also are served. A pre-theater dinner is offered. 22 St. Stephen's Green (phone: 616669). Moderate.

La Grenouille – A French-style bistro next to the *Powerscourt Town House Centre*. Each dish on the limited menu is cooked to order. Choices range from rack of lamb or chicken in bleu cheese sauce to steak and duck, all served with an array of fresh vegetables. Open daily for dinner, a rarity in Dublin. 64 S. William St. (phone: 779157). Moderate.

Osprey's – Around the corner from *Jurys* and the American Embassy, this cozy candlelit restaurant has two small dining rooms, each with a fireplace. Flambé cooking is a specialty here, as are such international dishes as beef Wellington, salmon *en croûte,* chicken Madeira, Weiner schnitzel, and Dover sole. 41/43 Shelbourne Rd. (phone: 608087). Moderate.

Shannons – Dubliners looking for a good place to eat have put this place at the top of their list. It is bright and airy, with many plants, flowers, wide windows, and an open kitchen. The menu features the freshest of Irish seafood, produce, and prime meats; unique combination dishes include breast of chicken layered with salmon and a fan of trout with turbot. Service is first rate. Dinner nightly; lunch only on Sundays. The Grove, Stillorgan (phone: 887963). Moderate.

Rudyards – On 3 floors of a tall, narrow house in Crown Alley, it offers a combination of mildly exotic continental dishes, from spinach-stuffed pancakes to navarin of lamb, pasta, and tomato pie and beef in orange sauce. Reservations unnecessary. 15 Crown Alley, off Dame St. (phone: 710846). Moderate to inexpensive.

Unicorn – Established in 1939, this small Italian bistro is a favorite with Irish politicians and literati. All pasta and sauces are made by owners Renato and Nina Sidoli. Open from 10 AM to 10 PM except Sundays. Merrion Ct., off Merrion Row (phone: 762182 or 688552). Moderate to inexpensive.

Bad Ass Café – One of the brightest, and liveliest spots to hit town in some time. Famed as much for its (loud) rock music and videos as for its great pizza. Steaks are another specialty. 9/11 Crown Alley, behind the Central Bank on Dame St. (phone: 712596). Inexpensive.

Beshoff – Owned by a family long known as purveyors of fresh fish, this is a classy version of the traditional Dublin fish-and-chips shop, with a black-and-white marble decor. The menu features chips (French fries) with salmon, shark, squid, turbot, or prawns, as well as the humble cod. Open daily, noon to midnight. 14 Westmoreland St. (phone: 778781) and 5/6 Upper O'Connell St. (phone: 743223). Inexpensive.

Captain America's – Specializes in "genuine American hamburgers," Tex-Mex, and barbecue dishes, served with American beer and rock music. Open daily. Grafton Ct., 1st Floor, Grafton St. (phone: 715266). Inexpensive.

Casper & Giumbini's Drink and Food Emporium – A lively eatery with some traditional Irish dishes, such as Irish stew (not always easy to come by in local restaurants). There's also an exotic range of cocktails and a selection of international beers. Brunch served Saturdays and Sundays. 6 Wicklow St. (phone: 679-4347). Inexpensive.

SHARING A PINT: Until you have been in a pub, you have not experienced Dublin. Here Dubliners come to pursue two serious occupations: drinking and conversation. Many pubs are ugly and modern, complete with Muzak and plastic, but plenty of traditional pubs remain — noisy, companionable places for the pursuit of friendly ghosts of bygone Dublin in an unhurried atmosphere. Some favorites are the *Horseshoe Bar* in the *Shelbourne* hotel (St. Stephen's Green; phone: 766471), favored by the uppity, horsey set; the *Bailey* (2 Duke St.; phone: 772760), a literary pub that actually displays the door of nearby 7 Eccles St., where Joyce's Molly and Leopold Bloom lived; *O'Donoghue's* (15 Merrion Row, off St. Stephen's Green) for Irish ballads; the *Palace Bar* (Fleet St.), a traditional haunt of journalists and literati; the award-winning *Dubliner* in *Jurys* hotel (Northumberland Rd.; phone: 605000), which offers an airy atmosphere with a fireplace and a section called the "Press Room," serving (lethal) seasonal drinks; *Mulligans* (Poolbeg St.), renowned for the quality of its pint, appreciated equally by the dock workers and students (from nearby Trinity College), who form its main clientele; the *Stag's Head* (Dame Ct.), a great haunt of the legal profession, which serves hearty hot lunches at reasonable prices; *Neary's* (Chatham St.), which offers delicacies like smoked salmon and oysters in season; the *Brazen Head* (20 Lower Bridge St.) and *Davy Byrne's* (21 Duke St.) for plain drinking and gab; *Doheny and Nesbitts* (on Merrion Row), which is always known simply as "Nesbitts" — try the bar, not the modernized upstairs lounge; and last, but very far from least, the utterly delightful *Ryans* (Parkgate St.), with its shining mirrors, courteous barmen, and snugs where guests can drink quietly and enjoy first-rate pub grub.

 WINE BARS: A popular addition to the Dublin scene are wine bars, which generally offer light meals and good wines at moderate prices.

Kilmartin's – Originally owned by a turf accountant (a bookie), this bar retains both its name and its racing decor under new owners. Run by two young women, both Cordon Bleu chefs, Kilmartin's specializes in poached salmon and crispy duck. The house wine is particularly good. 19 Upper Baggot St. (phone: 686674).

Mitchell's – In the cellar (where else!) of *Mitchell's Wine Merchants,* this is where swinging Dubliners lunch. The menu is somewhat limited, but the helpings are large, the cooking quite good, and the desserts mouth-watering. Alas, it's not open in the evenings. Get here before 12:30 PM, or you'll find yourself in for a long wait at lunchtime (which you can while away by sampling some of their splendid wines). 21 Kildare St. (phone: 680367).

Shrimp's – Tiny, but charmingly decorated, it is not the place to air your most intimate thoughts. The food, however, is tempting, and you can choose from a good range of wines. 1 Anne's La. (phone: 713143).

GALWAY CITY

The ancient port city of Galway hangs on to a romantic past that has been seasoned as much by myth as by reality. It isn't the glory of the early Gaelic kingdoms that haunts the local folk memory so much as the swashbuckling days of the Spanish Main. It was then that the prevailing sou'westerlies speeded tall ships toward Galway from the ports of Spain. In the 15th and 16th centuries, the two places were engaged in a rich, bustling commerce, and the image of noble Spanish *hidalgos* swaggering through the cobbled streets of Galway still burns bright in the imagination.

Galway is proud of its medieval Spanish connection, almost to the point of forgetting that the really potent influence in shaping the city was Anglo-Norman. The citizenry sees the hand of Spain everywhere, and indeed some of the old back-street townhouses and courtyards are faintly reminiscent of things *español.* Down near the docks, the celebrated Spanish Arch is an extension of the fortress walls that protected the old city and probably got its name from the Spanish sailors who once frequented the nearby alehouses.

Galway nurtures the fables of a colorful past in other ways. Its most famous legend is that of the mayor who hanged his own son. This archetype of the stern father was one James Lynch Fitzstephen who, in 1493, condemned his son Walter as a murderer. Apparently, Walter had killed a visiting Spaniard for stealing his girlfriend. So popular was Walter throughout Galway that no one could be found to hang him, so the father had to do it himself. A stone memorial window marks the execution spot. Even though gray-bearded historians have debunked this story in modern times, a stone window still stands, and most Galwegians are loyal to the legend.

There's a stronger ring of truth to another much-told tale, that of Christopher Columbus discovering Galway before he ever clapped a weather eye on America. It is believed that he called here and prayed in St. Nicholas's Church en route to the uncharted western seas. The church might be considered an auspicious stopping-off place for any would-be discoverer, because this particular St. Nicholas was the patron saint of sea voyagers.

Whatever the truth of the Columbus story, it is hard to shake the faith of Galway natives in their own notable explorer and saint, Brendan. They and many other Irish people believe that St. Brendan discovered the New World centuries before the Italian upstart. Naturally, Brendan sailed from Galway.

Galway's origins go back long before the 6th-century St. Brendan and Christian times. There were settlements on its river in pagan days. The Irish for Galway is *Gaillimh* (pronounced *Goll*-iv), and legend has it that the name comes from a princess, Gaillimh, who was drowned in the river. Nowadays, the river is called the Corrib, and its surging waters rushing into Galway Bay are the pulsing soul and spirit of the city. In summertime, legions of silver salmon swarm in from the Atlantic feeding grounds in response to the im-memorial spawning call and fight their way upriver to the headwaters where they were born. This natural phenomenon used to be one of the more uplifting sights in Galway, and it still is in a way, though the salmon have been thinned out by pollution and the nets of the factory ships.

It was the Normans, not the Spaniards or anyone else, who developed Galway into a thriving mercantile city. During the 13th century they hopscotched from Britain to Ireland with the help of a pope and a traitorous Irish prince, and when their armies reached Galway, they quickly subdued the native tribes, taking over the city. They built stout walls around it to keep out the wild Irish — and then, in a matter of decades, became more Irish than the Irish themselves. Much later, in the mid-17th century, Cromwell smashed his iron fist on the city and reinforced the chains of conquest.

Galway became known as the City of the Tribes because of the 14 dynastic merchant families that controlled its wealth and fortune for several centuries. Outside the walls, across the river, the relics of the ancient Irish civilization survived in the fishing village called Claddagh, which spreads out from Nimmo's Pier at the estuary of Galway Bay. Its thatch-roofed cottages have been torn down and replaced by drab, utilitarian homes, but it still manages to retain its identity and remain independent of Galway City.

From the middle of the 19th century until quite recently, Galway was a port for passenger liners plying the Atlantic between the United States and Europe. The passage was not always comfortable. During the potato famine of the 1840s, thousands of starving Irish peasants sailed from Galway to the New World aboard vessels whose abysmal conditions won them the chilling name "coffin ships."

Only in recent years has Galway expanded rapidly and become highly industrialized. A recent half-mile-radius extension of the city borders increased the city's population overnight, from 30,000 to 55,000, and a massive urban renewal program in the late 1980s transformed the downtown area. This surge of progress, though, barely affected the leisurely rhythm of life here. The old charm still lingers, especially in the back streets and alleyways. It is there that, in fanciful moments, a visitor can almost hear the thrum of Spanish guitars and the clack of Castilian castanets.

Well, why not?

GALWAY AT-A-GLANCE

 SEEING THE CITY: There are no really great vantage points from which to get an overall view of Galway City. For a bird's-eye reconnaissance, try the top of the *Great Southern* hotel (phone: 64041), which is right in the middle of things in front of the railway station on Eyre Square. From the penthouse, spectators can look across the rooftops of the city. Inquire at the reception desk for access to the rooftop, which is available almost anytime.

 SPECIAL PLACES: Galway is a small town, so just about everything worth seeing can be covered in a single day on foot. A walk through the city streets — making sure not to miss those history-haunted back lanes — is highly recommended.

But Galway weather is infuriatingly temperamental, and rain clouds are never far off. Still, even in the gentle drizzle of the Irish "soft day," it's fun to set off with a mac and cover the whole town without risk of drowning. It's even possible to walk out to Salthill, the seaside resort about 1½ miles from downtown. If the clouds have decamped, Salthill offers one of the best views of sunset on Galway Bay.

Eyre Square – This is the heart of the city and the place visitors usually see first. It once was the Fair Green, where livestock and produce were sold, and is now named after one of the ruling merchant tribes, the Eyres. (Charlotte Brontë got the title of her famous novel when she saw the name Jane Eyre on a gravestone during a visit to Galway.) The original pastoral appearance of the green was destroyed by local authorities in an outrageous act of philistinism during the 1960s, when they poured concrete sidewalks along its edges. The park within the square is named after John F. Kennedy, in memory of his Galway visit. There's a fascinating statue of a quirky gnome of an Irish writer named Pádraic O Conaire at the northern end. A splendid cut-stone doorway, of a type seen in the better homes of long ago, also stands in the park, this one from the home of another tribe, the Brownes.

St. Nicholas's Church – This is the place where Columbus is said to have prayed before sailing off to discover America. Originally built by the Anglo-Normans in 1320, it has been greatly altered through the ensuing centuries: It retains its original chancel and is a repository for some striking medieval stone carvings and relics. The three-gabled west front is unparalleled in Ireland. After the Reformation, the church became the prize in a tug-of-war between Protestants and Catholics and changed hands a number of times before Cromwell's forces finally secured it for the Protestants. It is also pleasant to wander through the country market set up outside the church on Saturday mornings. Market St.

Lynch Memorial Window – Just up the street from the church, this stone window marks the spot where the mayor of the city, James Lynch Fitzstephen, is said to have hanged his son Walter for murder in 1493. It isn't the actual window through which the luckless lad exited to the next world — this one was carved some 200 years later. The hanging story is a good one but almost certainly untrue. Market St.

Lynch's Castle – The ubiquitous Lynch tribe that gave so many mayors to the city originally lived in this 16th-century building, regarded by many as the finest town castle in all Ireland. It has been lovingly restored and preserved and is now a bank. Shop St. at the Four Corners (phone: 67041).

Salmon Weir – The centuries-old salmon fishery is below the Salmon Weir Bridge, opposite the new Catholic cathedral. This is a pleasant place to pass an hour in summer watching the salmon on their way up to the spawning grounds.

Catholic Cathedral – On the site of a former jailhouse opposite the Salmon Weir Bridge, this structure, built in the early 1960s, was inspired by Renaissance and other church architecture of the past. It is a large building but not remarkably lovely. Earl's Island.

Spanish Arch – The best-known landmark in Galway, the arch was built in 1594 as an addition to the Old Town wall, as well as protection for the docked Spanish ships unloading their wines nearby. Attached to the arch is a museum (see *Sources and Resources*) through which a traveler can climb to the top of the arch and look across the Corrib to Claddagh. Beside Wolfe Tone Bridge, where the river enters the sea.

Claddagh – This district was originally a fishing village where the native Irish clung to their old culture in defiance of the usurping Anglo-Normans within the walls. Claddagh people no longer fish, nor speak Irish, but they still proudly maintain a sense of separateness from the city. The famous Claddagh ring — two hands clasping a heart surmounted by a crown — was fashioned by local goldsmiths as the traditional wedding band. Cross the Corrib at Wolfe Tone Bridge to reach Claddagh.

Salthill – Galway's seaside resort is really part of the city, a mere 1½ miles from downtown. Salthill has three sandy beaches on Galway Bay, but invariably the weather is hostile to sunbathing and surfing. When the weather is good, swimming is safe and there's no crowding. The *Leisureland* complex that dominates the seafront has a huge heated indoor swimming pool and *Coney Island*–style amusements for children and adults. Southwest of Galway, reachable on foot or by frequent buses from Eyre Square.

Franciscan Abbey – Built in 1836, the abbey is on the site of a 13th-century friary that was founded by the De Burgos (Burkes), the first Norman Lords of Galway. St. Francis St.

University College – The original building, completed in 1849, was modeled in neo-Gothic style on some of the colleges at Oxford. Built as a nondenominational institution, it was once condemned as godless by the Catholic bishops, who forbade Catholics to attend, but the ban was ignored. A small university, it has a friendly, unstuffy atmosphere; someone is always willing to show visitors around. Main entrance to the campus is off University Rd. (phone: 24411).

■**EXTRA SPECIAL:** Generally, Galway is a quiet place, but it does have its moments. In the fall it lets down its hair and stages the closest approximation of *la dolce vita* that anyone will find in Ireland. This is the *Galway Oyster Festival,* held every year over a very long and vertiginous weekend in September. A most sybaritic occasion, it has many more temptations than the oysters everyone ostensibly comes to eat.

The organized events of the festival are rather expensive and must be booked in advance. It's also advisable to reserve a hotel room, especially at the *Great Southern* (see *Checking In*) — the center of the festival — or at any of the other better hotels in Galway. To attend all the events of the festival, from Friday night to Sunday morning, including a reception and dinner, festival banquet, lunch, oyster tasting, and recuperative Irish coffee "morning after," costs about $300 per sore head. This does not include a hotel room, nor does it include the heavy run on your pocket during a weekend of intensive socializing that involves much buying of booze. Count on an outlay of at least $450 for the weekend. For details, contact Ann Flanagan (20 Oaklands, Salthill, Galway, Irish Republic; phone: 22066).

Another festive occasion is *Galway Race Week,* beginning on the last Monday of July. This is a synonym for 6 days of heavy gambling on the ponies running at *Ballybrit Race Course,* within walking distance of the city center. It also entails heroic drinking round the clock and heavy poker sessions in hotel bedrooms, all earthy and great fun even if you don't like horses or cards.

The *Galway Arts Festival,* held for 10 days in July, has developed into one of the most innovative and exciting occasions in Irish life, attracting hosts of young people from all over Ireland and abroad. It features a brilliant array of Irish and international plays, musical events, and art exhibitions, as well as a week-long carnival and all sorts of fringe happenings. Details can be obtained from the tourist board (phone: 63081) or the *Arts Centre* (Nun's Island; phone: 65886).

Finally, don't leave Galway without visiting the Aran Islands (see *Connemara and the Aran Islands,* DIRECTIONS), and, oh, go ahead and take part in one of those medieval banquets in Dunguaire Castle (see *County Clare,* DIRECTIONS). Information on both is available from the tourist board.

SOURCES AND RESOURCES

TOURIST INFORMATION: For comprehensive information and advice, first go to the tourist board, Aras Fáilte, just south of the western side of Eyre Square. During the summer, another office is open on the Promenade in Salthill (phone for either office: 63081). Pick up all of the free literature and maps, including, the *County Galway Tourist Guide* (about $1) and, when available, the Galway Junior Chamber of Commerce listing of summer events in Galway and Salthill. A small booklet, *Tourist Trail of Old Galway* (free at the Junior Chamber of Commerce), describes a walking tour.

Hardiman's *History of Galway* is the definitive work on the city's past and can be bought at the *Connacht Tribune* newspaper office (Market St.) or at *Kenny's Bookshop* (High St.). For more detailed sources, try the County Library in the Hynes Building (St. Augustine St.).

Local Coverage – Two weeklies, the *Connacht Tribune* and the *Connacht Sentinel,* and two giveaways, the *Galway Advertiser* and the *New Galway Observer,* provide strictly local news.

TELEPHONE: The area code for Galway City and the immediate vicinity is 91. When calling from within the Republic of Ireland, dial 091 before the local number.

GETTING AROUND: If the weather allows, it's easy to walk throughout the city without great stress.

Airport – Regularly scheduled *Aer Lingus* flights connect Galway with Dublin. *Ryanair* has daily flights to and from London throughout the year. For information, call 55569.

Bus – The central departure point for all city buses is the west side of Eyre Square. City bus service stops at 11:30 PM. Buses for points outside the city leave from the railway station behind the *Great Southern* hotel. (The only trains leaving the station are for Dublin and intervening stops.) All buses, trains, and touring coaches are run by *Bus Eireann* and *Iarnrod Eireann,* which share the same phone numbers (62141 and 62131).

Car Rental – It's best to pick up a car at the port of arrival in Ireland, usually Shannon or Dublin, where all the major international and local rental companies operate. Rental companies in Galway include *Avis* (at the Aras Fáilte Tourist Office; phone: 68901); *Hertz* (21 Eyre Sq.; phone: 61837); *Budget-Rent-A-Car* (12 Eyre Sq.; phone: 66376); and *Higgins Garage* (Headford Rd.; phone: 68886).

Taxi – Plenty of cabs are available, and they're not too costly. The central cabstand is on the north side of Eyre Sq. (phone: 7888, 55919, 63333, or 61111).

SPECIAL EVENTS: The *Galway Oyster Festival* (see *Extra Special*) and *Galway Race Week* (see *Sports and Fitness*) are held in September and July, respectively. The *Salthill Festival,* featuring a free concert series, pony jumping, fishing competitions, yacht races, and more, is held in early July in the bayside area of Salthill. The *Irish Show Jumping Championship* is held in late July at Salthill Park. The *Galway Arts Festival* also takes place in July, with classical music, poetry readings, art exhibitions, and theatrical happenings (see *Extra Special*).

MUSEUMS: Galway's only notable museum is the *Galway City Museum.* Though tiny, it houses a range of exhibitions that highlight the city's past. A spiral staircase leads from the museum to the top of the Spanish Arch, which offers a fine view across the Corrib to Claddagh. Open Mondays through Saturdays. At the bottom of Quay St. near the Spanish Arch (phone: 68151).

SHOPPING: Good values are to be found in native knitwear and homespun tweeds, as well as Irish glass, bone china, Connemara marble, and other ornamental ware.

Archway Antiques – Pricey but good old china, jewelry, and furniture. Victoria Pl. (phone: 62041).

Aulde Stock – For good, old pine furniture, and the odd silver spoon. Kirwans La., at the bottom of Quay St. (no phone).

Blue Cloak Boutique – Fashions of the times at moderate cost. 31 Upper Abbeygate St. (phone: 67785).

Bridge Mills – A selection of shops (pottery, art gallery, antiques) in a newly renovated old mill. The original mill wheel still turns. O'Brien's Bridge, Bridge St. (phone: 66231).

Browne Doorway – This tiny gift boutique is crammed with Irish-made pottery, silverware, tapestries, linen, woolens, and the work of local painters. Eyre Sq., beside the *Great Southern* hotel (phone: 65757).

Cobwebs – A quaint, old-fashioned shop specializing in curios and offbeat antiques, including nostalgic toys from Edwardian and Victorian times. 7 Quay La., opposite the Spanish Arch (phone: 64388).

Stephen Faller Ltd. – Claddagh rings are the specialty, plus Waterford crystal. Williamsgate St. (phone: 61226).

Galway Irish Crystal – Glass blowing demonstrations are offered at this shop, which sells seconds only. Merlin Pk. (phone: 57311).

House of James – A wide array of handmade Irish items is sold here, including pottery, handwoven rugs, wooden bowls, knitwear, and silver jewelry. A new eatery on the premises serves natural homemade Irish food, from farmhouse cheese to ice cream. Castle St. (phone: 67776).

Margaret Joyce – The designs of a native daughter in cotton, wool, or silk-blend sweaters. 4 Quay St. (phone: 64133).

Kenny's Bookshop and Art Gallery – Housed in two old Galway buildings, the floors may slope but the selections are terrific: from Yeats to Edna O'Brien. There also are prints and maps and a rogue's gallery of Irish autographs. High St. (phone: 62739 or 61014).

Lydon Boutique – High class, trendy fashions for smart young ladies. It's expensive but good value. Shop St. (phone: 66205).

Madame Charyl – Highly styled skirts, jackets, stoles, and scarves in a variety of nice colors. Augustine St. (phone: 66339).

O'Maille's – Everything here is wholesomely Irish — Aran sweaters, Donegal tweeds, and shapeless hats. Pricey, but good quality. Tweed is sold by the yard. Dominick St. (phone: 62696).

Powells Four Corners – *The* place for a wide selection of Irish music on tape. William St. (phone: 68667 or 62295).

Royal Tara China – Visitors are welcome to watch china decoration, as well as purchase seconds at 30–80% discount or perfect pieces at full price. Tara Hall (phone: 51301).

Anthony Ryan – A fine store for men's and women's fashions. 18 Shop St. (phone: 62733 or 67061).

Sheepskin Shop – Very reasonably priced leather jackets, skirts, and pants for men and women. In Corbettcourt (phone: 61619).

Taafe's – A Galway institution — a shop from way back when. Handknit Aran sweaters are the thing. 19 Shop St. (phone: 64006).

Treasure Chest – Housed in a building painted Wedgwood blue is a broad display of high-quality wares, including Irish crystal, pottery, woolens and tweeds, Irish traditional craftwork, and, most notably, classic crocheted garments. William St. (phone: 63862 or 67237).

 SPORTS AND FITNESS: Boating and Sailing – Rowboats and motorboats can be hired for trips up the river Corrib and into Lough Corrib, the big lake upstream. Contact *Frank Dolan* (13 Riverside, Galway City; phone: 65841). For all types of sailing on Galway Bay, contact the *Galway Bay Sailing Centre* (Rinville, Oranmore; phone: 94527).

Fishing – A license must be bought and a fee paid to fish for salmon at the salmon weir (an enclosure in a waterway for trapping fish), near the Salmon Weir Bridge, which has an international reputation among anglers. For details and booking, call the *Galway Fishery* (phone: 62388). There's brown-trout angling on Lough Corrib, for which no license is required. Boats can be hired. Contact *Des Moran* (*Knockferry Lodge*, Knockferry, Rosscahill; phone: 80122), or the tourist board (phone: 63081). To go sea angling for shark, contact *Elmer Kavanagh* (2 Victoria Pl., Galway City; phone: 64789).

Golf – There's a challenging 18-hole course in Salthill, where visitors are welcome (phone: 22169 or 21827).

Horse Racing – The highlight of Galway's equestrian competitions is *Galway Race Week*, held beginning the last Monday in July at the *Ballybrit Race Course*, just 2 miles outside of town. Flat racing, hurdles, and a steeplechase are among the featured events. For more information, contact the *Galway Race Committee* (phone: 53870).

Swimming – The beaches at Salthill are superb, with good bay bathing when the weather is good. The indoor pool at *Leisureland*, on the seafront in Salthill, is open daily (phone: 21455).

THEATER: The *Druid Theatre* (Chapel La.; phone: 68617) has evolved into one of the most exciting theatrical centers in Ireland. It stages traditional and avant-garde productions at irregular intervals, with both lunchtime and evening performances. There's an Irish-language theater — *An Taibhdhearc* (pronounced An *Thigh*-vark) — which has been producing plays in Irish for more than 50 years. The emphasis during the summer tourist season is on traditional Irish music and dance, interspersed with a short play in Irish so heavily mimed that no knowledge of the language is needed. The theater is on Middle St. (phone: 62024).

MUSIC: Traditional Irish music is heard in many pubs in Galway and Salthill; consult the local papers for details.

NIGHTCLUBS AND NIGHTLIFE: Although there are no true nightclubs in Galway, life does not cease at dusk. Most hotels have drinking places that function until near dawn. Some bars, too, continue serving (illegally) after closing time (11:30 PM in summer, 11 PM in winter, except Sundays when it's an hour earlier), and discreet inquiry will gain information about them. There are a number of late-night discos, mostly for young people (under 40); check local newspapers for details. In summer, most Salthill hotels have cabarets and discos. One of the livelier Salthill discos is *CJ's Night Club* (in the *Monterey* hotel; phone: 24017). *Rumur's Night Club* (Salthill; phone: 21371) is a popular late-night haunt of trendy young people.

BEST IN TOWN

CHECKING IN: The better hotels in Galway have become expensive, though it's still possible to find some good hotels in the moderate price range. A few have adopted the so-called European plan and no longer include breakfast in the room rate. Where breakfast *is* included, it's the ample Irish meal of bacon, eggs, and sausages — usually very good — and guests pay for it whether they eat it or not. In the following listings, a private bath is included unless otherwise specified. Expensive means $50 to $70 a night for a double room, and the moderate category is $35 to $50. All telephone numbers are in the 91 area code unless otherwise indicated.

Anno Santo – For those who prefer the quiet life, here is a classy, 13-room intimate place with a relaxed atmosphere. Specify private bath. Threadneedle Rd., Salthill (phone: 22110). Expensive.

Ardilaun House – Once the stately home of an aristocratic family, the building and grounds still retain a patrician aura. The restaurant is first-rate (see *Eating Out*). It's hidden away among trees and shrubs on Taylor's Hill, the best address in town (phone: 21433). Expensive.

Corrib Great Southern – This younger sister of the big Victorian-era hotel on Eyre Square aspires to similar standards. It's modern and comfortable. Dublin Rd. (phone: 55281). Expensive.

Galway Ryan – Each of the 96 rooms in this modern hotel has a bath and shower, a television set, and a direct-dial phone. There is also a gameroom and playroom for both adults and children. Food is conventional and wholesome, and during the summer, musical entertainment and discos are a nightly feature. Dublin Rd. (phone: 53181). Expensive.

Great Southern – A superior hotel, with 120 of the most comfortable rooms in Galway. Its elegant foyer is the center of social life in the city, and it's an easy place to strike up new friendships. The food in the *Oyster* restaurant is fine (see *Eating Out*). A heated swimming pool and sauna are welcome bonuses. Eyre Sq. (phone: 64041). Expensive.

Salthill – A fine, modern hostelry, it overlooks the famous Salthill promenade, offering views of Galway Bay from many of its 47 rooms. All rooms have private bath, TV set, and tea- and coffee-making facilities. There is a good restaurant, too (see *Eating Out*). The Promenade, Salthill (phone: 22448). Expensive.

Adare House – An outstanding guesthouse if bed and breakfast is all that's required (they don't serve other meals). Comfortable rooms, tastefully decorated. Good value. Father Griffin Pl. (phone: 62638). Moderate.

EATING OUT: Strangers to Galway should not venture into any restaurant without having it *reliably* recommended; there are a few shoddy places best avoided. The city does have some exceptionally good eating places, however, and some of the better ones are in hotels. The native beef and lamb are among the world's best, so it's hard to go wrong with steaks or chops. In season, Galway salmon from the river Corrib is superlative, and during the "r" months, the oysters from the bay are possibly the best on the entire globe. To eat really well, stick to the expensive restaurants, though there are a number of commendable ones in the moderate range. Except for those recommended here, stay away from inexpensive places. Expect to pay $65 and up for dinner for two, with wine, in the expensive category; $50 to $60 in the moderate bracket; and $40 or less in inexpensive. Credit cards are accepted. A service charge is included in all meal bills, but a tip (about 5%) is expected all the same. Note that most of the restaurants listed open briefly for lunch, then close and reopen for a 2- or 3-hour dinner period, usually from 7 PM on. Since several are out of town, it's a good idea to check on their serving hours before venturing forth. All telephone numbers are in the 91 area code unless otherwise indicated.

Ardilaun House – With its decorous wood paneling and glass chandeliers, it retains an authentic 19th-century ambience. The food is conventional but of very high quality, and it's a popular dining place for families. Fresh meats and fish are the specialties. Reservations necessary. Taylor's Hill (phone: 21433). Expensive.

Casey's Westwood – It has a neo-Georgian decor and a menu emphasizing French and Irish cooking, with the freshest ingredients. Reservations necessary. Dangan Upper, Newcastle, at University College (phone: 21442). Expensive.

Drimcong House – A lovely 17th-century mansion serves as the backdrop for one of Ireland's best restaurants. Like the decor, the food is elegant yet unpretentious, the service super efficient yet unobtrusive. Chef-owner Gerry Galvin prepares a 5-course dinner; there are à la carte items also, as well as vegetarian dishes and a children's menu. Specialties include excellent wild game in season, oysters from Galway Bay, spiced beef, and salmon. Gerry's wife, Marie, grows fresh vegetables and herbs. It is a dining experience not to be missed. Open Tuesdays through Saturdays for dinner only, Sundays for lunch; closed from *Christmas* through the end of February. One mile past Moycullen village on N59 (phone: 185115). Expensive.

Knockferry Lodge – Highly original dishes are prepared by owner-chef Des Moran in this delightful old house on the shores of Lough Corrib. All the herbs and vegetables are from the garden outside, and magnificent brown trout are caught in the adjoining lake for this very special place, frequented by the food connoisseurs of Galway City. Open May to mid-October for dinner. Reservations necessary. Knockferry, Rosscahill. Take the N59 to Moycullen and turn left at the signpost for Knockferry (phone: 80122). Expensive.

Moran's Oyster Cottage – This lovely thatch-roofed pub, on the edge of the water, is the most famous place in Ireland for oysters. At other times of the year it offers smoked salmon, mussel soup, and other seafoods. Pub hours. Reservations advised. On the Limerick road, 10 miles out of the city; turn right just before the village of Kilcolgan (phone: 96113). Expensive.

Oyster Restaurant – In the *Great Southern* hotel, this is one of the finest all-round restaurants in the city. Try the lamb from Connemara or the Corrib salmon. The continental dishes are good, too. Reservations necessary. Eyre Sq. (phone: 64041). Expensive.

Park House – A stylish eatery that offers, among other delights, a roast duckling that has won an international gold medal. The chicken breasts stuffed with prawns deserve one, too. First-rate lunches are served at the bar. Reservations advised. Forster St. (phone: 68293). Expensive.

Salthill – The food at this hotel is always good, but especially so on Irish nights, when the menu is planned around such native foodstuffs as lamb, salmon, oysters, and prawns. Reservations advised. The Promenade, Salthill (phone: 22711). Expensive.

La Taverna – Mama mia! The only Italian restaurant in western Ireland, and a good one, too, with a full range of pasta dishes. Try the fine *tagliatelle* Bolognese and lasagna. A worthy Italian wine list complements the food. Reservations advised. 169 Upper Salthill (phone: 23174). Expensive.

Ty-ar-mor – It's worth a few miles' driving to get to this seaside Breton eatery set in a cottage. Nets and lobster pots provide the decor, and true to its origin, seafood and crêpes are the specialties. Reservations advised. Sea Point, Barna (phone: 92223). Expensive.

McDonagh's Fish Shop – Practically every kind of fish caught in the Atlantic off the Galway coast finds its way to this dining spot. Served up here in myriad ways, the food is a fish lover's dream. Reservations advised. Quay St. (phone: 65001). Expensive to moderate.

Bentley – Possibly the best value in town for lunch, it serves extra large helpings. The extensive menu, which changes daily, offers such dishes as chicken curry, chicken Kiev, sole, roast beef, and salad. After dark, the eatery becomes a nightclub for people in their 30s. Reservations unnecessary. Eyre Sq. (phone: 64105). Moderate.

Dragon Court – A very fine Chinese restaurant, specializing in Szechuan-style cooking. The decor reflects an authentic and exotic Oriental influence. Reservations advised. 11 Forester St. (phone: 65588). Moderate.

Oriental House – One of the better Chinese dining spots that have begun proliferating all over Ireland. It offers an opulent menu of Peking, Szechuan, and Cantonese dishes, accompanied by exquisite Chinese teas. Reservations advised. 3 Francis St. (phone: 62352). Moderate.

Rabbitt's – Oysters and other succulent sea dishes are the specialties of the house in this 100-year-old bar/restaurant, brought back to life recently through a major refurbishment. Reservations advised. 23/25 Forster St. (phone: 66490 or 62215). Moderate.

Lydon House – Downstairs is a good, stand-up, fast-food eatery; upstairs is a more formal, sit-down restaurant with an orthodox, tasty menu. Reservations advised. 5 Shop St. (phone: 61131). Moderate to inexpensive.

Olde Galway Seafood – Cozy and informal, this spot serves delicious fresh seafood. Reservations advised. 2 High St. (phone: 61410). Moderate to inexpensive.

Brasserie – Tacos, pizza, and such in a nice setting with an open fireplace. No reservations. 19 Middle St. (phone: 61610). Inexpensive.

Fat Freddy's Pizzeria – For pizza, this new spot has some of the city's best. No reservations. Quay St. (phone: 67279). Inexpensive.

Happy Spud – The place to go for Irish potatoes. No reservations. Abbeygate St. (phone: 62966). Inexpensive.

SHARING A PINT: The bars in the hotels listed above are uniformly good, but don't be afraid to let instinct guide you into unfamiliar pubs. The nicest places are often discovered that way. Some pubs have their own attractions. *McDonagh's Thatched Pub* (Main St.) in the village of Oranmore (6 miles from downtown on the Dublin road), is old-fashioned and very friendly, with plenty of atmosphere and an open fire on cold days. *Moran's Oyster Cottage,* mentioned in *Eating Out* for its famous oysters, is also a wonderful place for a "jar" of rich, thick stout (10 miles from downtown on the Limerick road; turn right just before Kilcolgan village). In town, *Seagan Ua Neachtáin* (at the corner of Quay and Cross Sts.) is the definitive Irish pub–cum–general store of 100 years ago. It's frequented by intellectuals and those with pretensions. There are snugs and a fireplace, and a restaurant upstairs. *Freeney's* (High St.) is another old-style pub where there's plenty of chatting while standing at the bar, and *The Yacht* (St. Francis St.) is modern, clean, and comfortable but with an antique flavor. *Hogan's* (86 Bohermore) is a friendly, atmospheric old pub with a blazing fire, tasty food, and occasional traditional music sessions. Several pubs offer good Irish music, including the *Crane* (Sea Rd.), the *Quays* (Quay St.), *Flanagan's* (William St. West), and *King's Head* (High St.). In nearby Salthill, the *Cottage Bar* (Lower Salthill Rd.) and the next door pub *Flaherty's* also offer traditional Irish music.

KILKENNY TOWN

Ireland's best-preserved medieval town is the minute inland city of Kilkenny, 75 miles southwest of Dublin. Beginning as a tiny Gaelic settlement around the monastery of St. Canice (whence its Irish name, *Cill Chainnigh,* "the cell of Canice"), it came to prominence under the Normans when Strongbow, their leader, seized it in 1170 and built a fortification on the hill over the river Nore. The walled town was peopled with a purposeful community of Norman families, of whom ten — "Archdeakin, Archer, Cowley, Langton, Ley, Knaresborough, Lawless, Raggett, Rothe and Shee," as an old list rhymes them off — distinguished themselves particularly and rose to power. Between the Gothic cathedral at one end and the strong castle at the other, the houses, inns, shops, new friaries, and the merchants' parish church crowded inside the city walls on the high bank of the river.

Its reputation as a stable and industrious market town thus established, Kilkenny went on to achieve some notoriety. In the early 14th century, a formidable Norman woman named Dame Alice Kyteler, daughter of a banker, prosperous survivor of four husbands, and wealthy herself through moneylending (a practice, not incidentally, frowned upon by the church), was accused of witchcraft by Richard le Drede, Bishop of Ossory, the local see. Dame Alice was supported by Arnold le Poer, the seneschal, and many powerful friends; the bishop was supported by the law and by the commission he had from the pope to extirpate heresy. A Kilkenny friar records the confrontation: "On Monday . . . the lady Alice Kyteler was tried, found guilty, condemned as a heretic for divers sorceries, manifold heresies, offering sacrifices to demons. . . ." Though her powerful friends resisted and even imprisoned the bishop, he and the authority of the church won that round. Dame Alice fled to Scotland, her maid Petronilla was burned at the stake in her stead, and le Poer died in prison. The bishop did not get off scot-free, however. He was accused of heresy and had to flee to the papal court in Avignon.

Several decades later, the name Kilkenny became associated with infamy. As elsewhere in Ireland, the Normans had been intermarrying with the Irish and adopting some Irish customs as well. Such fraternization was perceived as a threat by the English king, who by now feared being left with too few trustworthy settlers to rule the island on his behalf. Consequently, a parliament held in Kilkenny in 1366 (the city was important enough to be a regular meeting place, along with Dublin, of the Irish Parliament the Normans had instituted) passed the Statutes of Kilkenny. These forbade the Normans to marry the Irish; prohibited them from adopting the Irish language, customs, or dress; and segregated native Irish everywhere beyond the walls of towns.

At the end of the 14th century and for centuries thereafter, the castle of Kilkenny was occupied by the Butlers, Earls of Ormonde, the most powerful family in medieval Ireland and long in the forefront of Irish history. They lived peaceably with the Gaelic chieftains but at the same time were rich from royal favor. They married into the royal family, hosted royal visits, and acted frequently as the king's deputy in Ireland. Under their protection Kilkenny was spared the worst horrors of Henry VIII's Reformation and the devastating cycle of rebellion and repression that ensued during the reign of Elizabeth I. The Butlers conformed to Protestantism and silently suppressed the city monasteries, which became civic property. John Bale, an English friar appointed the first conforming Bishop of Ossory, smashed statues in the cathedral and wrote fiery sectarian pamphlets, but he is better remembered in Kilkenny for the morality plays he wrote and had performed at the Market Cross, which once stood near the center of High Street.

The city could not totally escape the racial and religious conflict of the times, however. When another revolt — the Ulster Rebellion, which would be brutally crushed by Oliver Cromwell — broke out in 1641, Kilkenny became the seat of the independent Irish Parliament set up by Anglo-Irish and Old Irish Catholics united in their common defense. It met from 1642 to 1648, presided over by Lord Mountgarrett, a member of a minor Catholic branch of the Butlers, while the earl, the king's man, sat on the fence. Though the Confederation went so far as to establish a mint, manufacture weapons, raise an army, and receive ambassadors, it fell apart from within when its Norman and Irish factions began to disagree, and it disbanded in confusion. In 1660, Cromwell arrived to take Kilkenny for the English Parliament.

After the ritual window breaking and statue smashing in St. Canice's Cathedral, Cromwell's rule in Kilkenny was less bloody than elsewhere. Families involved in the Parliament were banished west of the Shannon, "to Hell or Connaught," along with the rest of the propertied Catholics who had opposed the Protector. Those from Kilkenny never went, however; they secretly stayed around the city until the Restoration brought back the king, with a Butler again, now Duke of Ormonde, as his viceroy. The duke managed to orchestrate a return of some of the lands confiscated from Kilkenny's leading citizens, but they and the city never quite recovered from the events of the century and never regained their former influence.

Perhaps because of the long, dark years of decline that followed, much of Kilkenny's early architecture remains intact — the city was simply not prosperous enough to tear things down and rebuild them on a grand scale, nor was there any need to do so. The gloom began to lift with a cultural revival in the 19th century and dispersed completely in recent years, leaving only a lingering air of quaintness to temper the changes of a city now in expansion. The Butlers have been gone from the castle since the 1930s but they characteristically and munificently presented it to the people. Its beautiful gardens and park are intact, the art gallery has a notable collection of portraits, and in 1965, the dukes' fine stables became the government-sponsored *Kilkenny Design Workshops,* a wellspring of modern design talent. Since early 1989, the enterprise has been under the stewardship of townspeople. The Rothes' house has been restored as a museum and library; the Shee almshouse has now been refurbished. Once a year, *Kilkenny Arts Week* causes music to resound through castle and cathedral. The little medieval city that witnessed so much Irish history is still the integral core of a busy, modern, yet still traditional community.

KILKENNY AT-A-GLANCE

 SEEING THE CITY: Kilkenny lies in two neat crescents on either side of a river valley basin and does not afford heights for a sweeping panoramic view. From the terraced rose garden in front of Kilkenny Castle (at the Parade plaza), you can survey the city's limits from the castle behind you to the compact, gray St. Canice's Cathedral in the distance, while the river below gives drama and movement. From here, though, the view is *through* the town, catching its recurrences of church spire and Tholsel clock tower. The reverse view is from the top of the round tower at the cathedral, but it is so high up that the city becomes a gray mass; the climb is not recommended for those with vertigo.

 SPECIAL PLACES: The street that straggles from the castle to the cathedral is Kilkenny's Royal Mile. It starts at the castle gates as the Parade, an oblong plaza with the castle's classical stables and a decorous row of Georgian houses on one side and a tree-lined promenade, the Mayor's Walk, along the garden wall on the other side. It then turns into High Street, Kilkenny's main commercial street, with the medieval just under the surface of its respectable Georgian face. The Tholsel, "the house of taxes," is the midpoint of High Street. Beyond it on the right, a unique Kilkenny feature occurs at intervals — the slips, or arched, stepped alleyways giving access to the street at river level. Dashing down slips and side alleys is very much part of sightseeing and shopping in Kilkenny. After High Street, the thoroughfare widens again as Parliament Street, and the restored Rothe House and the classical courthouse come into view. Then it narrows to medieval size for Irishtown and leads to St. Canice's Steps at the foot of the cathedral.

Kilkenny Castle – Kilkenny's most imposing monument looms grandly through trees over the river at the southeastern end of town. Strongbow, the Norman conqueror, had put up earthen fortifications here, and his successor in the early 13th century, William the Earl Marshall, replaced them with an irregular quadrangle of curtain walls reinforced by a fat round tower at each of the four corners. The Butler family, Norman Earls of Ormonde, bought it in 1391, after which they dominated the city. Though the family in residence remained the same for over 5 centuries, the castle itself underwent many changes. When the earls became dukes in the 17th century, the castle was rebuilt as a French château; it was made Gothic in another major reconstruction in the 19th century. The gardens and park are open to the public in daylight hours and the interior may be visited (guided tours are available). Particularly notable is the 19th-century Gothic Revival picture gallery. Designed by Benjamin Woodward, it has a painted hammer-beam roof by J. Hungerford Pollen and a fine collection of Butler family portraits. The old castle kitchen serves home-cooked snacks, tea, and coffee. Open daily June through September; closed Mondays in winter. Admission charge. The Parade (phone: 21450).

Design Centre – Formerly the government-sponsored *Kilkenny Design Workshops,* this cupola-crowned classical group of buildings, with a semicircular courtyard, once formed the castle's stables. The horses' stalls originally had decorated plaster ceilings, and the grooms occupied plainer and more cramped quarters upstairs. In 1965 the buildings became the home of the *Kilkenny Design Workshops,* where everything from traditional craft products to electronic hardware was designed for Irish manufacturers, and young Irish designers gained initial work experience.

Since 1989, however, the complex has shifted from a single government-funded project to a mix of independent enterprises. A group of Kilkenny citizens now operates the *Design Centre Shop,* while the Crafts Council of Ireland has set up a dozen crafts workshops in the courtyard. Visitors can tour the courtyard and watch the craftspeople ply their trade and then enter the shop to purchase items (see *Shopping*). Open daily. The Parade (phone: 22118).

Shee Almshouse – One of the few surviving Tudor almshouses in Ireland, this was founded in 1582 by Sir Richard Shee "for the accommodation of 12 poor persons." The charity thus begun by one of Kilkenny's leading families endured for 3 centuries. After the adjoining St. Mary's Church became Protestant during the Reformation, a chapel in the almshouse was used for Catholic services. In the present century, the house has served as a storehouse, but it has been refurbished and now holds the city's tourist board. Upstairs is a model of Kilkenny as it was in 1642, when the Confederation Parliament made it the capital of Ireland — a status that lasted just a few years. Rose Inn St. (phone: 21755).

St. Mary's Church – Parts of this church are believed to date from the 13th century. A fine display of Tudor and Stuart grave monuments is housed in the north transept. St. Mary's La.

High Street – Kilkenny's main street has undergone considerable change through the centuries, but a pause here and there still helps to recall its earlier days. Numbers 17, 18, and 19 hide a Tudor house (built in 1582) that belonged to the Archers, one of the town's ten leading families, and their crest is visible above the door. Behind it are the remains of the "Hole in the Wall," a supper house famous enough in the late 18th and early 19th centuries to have merited a verse: "If you ever go to Kilkenny /Ask for the Hole in the Wall / You may there get blind drunk for a penny / And tipsy for nothing at all." Above the shopfronts on the north side of High Street, about 100 yards from the main cross street, is a Tudor gable with the impaled arms of Henry Shee and his wife, Frances. He was a Mayor of Kilkenny in the early 17th century and this was their townhouse.

Tholsel – The Saxon word for "the house of taxes" is another name for Kilkenny's Town Hall. Built in the mid-18th century, it has open arcades that provide a market below and support a fine Georgian council chamber above. High St.

Rothe House – John Rothe built this solid Tudor merchant's house — actually three houses around two courtyards, with room for shop, storage, and living quarters — in 1594. Rothe was a member of one of Kilkenny's important families, and his wife, Rose, was an Archer. After the Rothes lost the house in the 17th century because of their association with the Confederation of Kilkenny, it eventually became a school. Finally, the Kilkenny Archaeological Society bought it, restored it, and opened it in 1966 as a library and historical museum. Open Sunday afternoons year-round; weekdays April through October; Tuesday, Friday, and Saturday afternoons the rest of the year. Tours are held weekdays at 3 PM in the summer. Admission charge. Parliament St. (phone: 22893).

St. Francis Abbey – This one-time Franciscan friary is on the premises of the 18th-century Smithwicks Brewery, desolate among beer casks and empty crates but still worth seeing. It was founded in the 13th century by Richard the Marshall and suppressed, along with the rest of the Irish monasteries, in the 16th century. The seven-light east window and the bell tower with its unusual supporting figures are from the 14th century. Off Parliament St.

Black Abbey – The church of the Dominicans, or Black Friars, is on high-walled Abbey Street just beyond Black Freren Gate, the last remaining gate in the city walls.

Its history is similar to that of the Franciscan abbey; both were founded and suppressed at approximately the same time, though the Black Abbey survives today as an active Dominican priory. Immediately after suppression, however, townspeople built thatch-roofed huts within its walls and it was for a time used as a courthouse before being reclaimed, restored, and opened again for worship. Abbey St.

St. Canice's Cathedral – This building, raised in the 13th century by the first Norman bishop, Hugh de Rous, occupies the site of the early Irish monastery of St. Canice and a later Romanesque church. A plain cruciform structure, it is nevertheless impressive for its size — the second largest medieval cathedral in Ireland — and its simplicity. The Master of Gowran (a mason who also worked on a neighboring church at Gowran) contributed some vigorous stone carving, in the west doorway particularly, but the renowned stained glass of the east window survived the Reformation only to be smashed to bits by Cromwell's troops, who also left the cathedral roofless and did considerable damage to its many monuments. The church's collection of 16th- and 17th-century tomb sculptures, many by the O'Tunneys, a local family of sculptors, is still remarkably rich, and its hammer-beam roof (a product of a later restoration) is notable. Outside, the round tower predates the cathedral, though its roof is not the original one. St. Canice's Library, established 300 years ago, has 3,000 old volumes. Open 9 AM to 1 PM and 2 to 5 PM daily. Admission charge to climb to the top of the round tower. Reached via St. Canice's Steps, which are linked to St. Canice's Pl. by Velvet La.

■**EXTRA SPECIAL:** *Kilkenny Arts Week* takes place at the end of August or the beginning of September. It is basically a music festival, with lunchtime recitals and grand evening concerts in the castle and cathedral, the classical music interspersed with programs of traditional music and folk song. Poetry readings — some well-known writers have read their work here — are another fundamental ingredient, as are art exhibitions and street theater. It is a friendly, participatory event that actually lasts for 9 days, each one ending at the *Arts Week Club,* where the social side of the festival goes on until the wee hours. Information: Kilkenny Tourist Office, Alms House, Rose Inn St., Kilkenny (phone: 21755).

SOURCES AND RESOURCES

TOURIST INFORMATION: In Kilkenny, the tourist board (Shee Alms-house, Rose Inn St.; phone: 21755) has information, maps, and leaflets. The city map is free; the *Kilkenny Guide* costs IR£1. A Kilkenny crafts guide is free.

Local Coverage – The *Kilkenny People* is published on Wednesdays. The three Dublin morning dailies are also available. Local events are posted weekly in the Tholsel arcade on High Street; details on daily happenings are available at the tourist board.

TELEPHONE: The area code for Kilkenny and the immediate vicinity is 56. When calling from within the Republic of Ireland, dial 056.

GETTING AROUND: Kilkenny is a walkable city, and there is no city bus service. From castle to cathedral is just over a mile. The railway station, which is a little farther away, is reachable by taxi.

Bus and Train – *Bus Eireann* and *Irish Rail,* divisions of *CIE (Córas*

Iompair Eireann, National Transport Company), serve McDonagh Station, John St. Upper (phone: 22024).

Car Rental – The nearest rental agencies are *Bolands* (New Ross, Co. Wexford; phone: 51-21403), *South East Budget* (New Ross, Co. Wexford; phone: 51-21550), and *EuroDollar* (Ferrybank, Co. Wexford; phone: 53-23511), but they will pick up and drop off at the Kilkenny Tourist Board, where bookings can be made.

Taxi – Cabs are available from *Delaney's* (phone: 22457), *Glendine* (phone: 63600), *Hickey* (phone: 61191), *Howe* (phone: 65874), *Larkin* (phone: 62622), *Martin* (phone: 22979), and *O'Brien* (phone: 61333).

Walking Tours – Guided historical walking tours leave from the tourist office at 10:30 AM and 12:15, 3, 4:30, and 7 PM daily except Sunday mornings in summer. For more information, contact *Tynan Tours* (Shee Almhouse, Rose Inn St.; phone: 61348), which operates out of the tourist office. The cost is about IR£2.

SPECIAL EVENTS: *Kilkenny Arts Week* is held every year in late August or early September (see *Extra Special*). The *Thomas Moore Weekend,* a festival of poetry and story reading, music, and literary gatherings, is held annually in early October.

MUSEUMS: In addition to the Butler family's distinguished portrait collection, the *Kilkenny Castle Art Gallery* (at the Parade plaza) features occasional traveling exhibitions. The restored *Rothe House* (Parliament St.) contains the Kilkenny Archaeological Society's museum of local history (see *Special Places*).

SHOPPING: Synonymous with fine craftsmanship, Kilkenny has a glassware factory and an assortment of interesting crafts shops. Ireland's national Crafts Council also operates a center here, with a group of artisans at work daily in the former stable courtyard of Kilkenny Castle. (Most shops are closed Thursday afternoons.)

Allen & Sons – Good selection of Waterford glass, which they will pack safely and dispatch to overseas addresses duty-free. 94 High St. (phone: 22258).

Liam Costigan – Modern jewelry by a *Kilkenny Design Workshops* graduate. Colliers La. (phone: 62408).

Design Centre – An Aladdin's cave of modern Irish design in silver, glass, pottery, wood, and textiles, many items designed on the premises. Good bargains in household items. There's also a self-service restaurant. The Parade (phone: 22118).

Rudolf Heltzel – Exquisite modern jewelry by a pioneer *Kilkenny Design Workshops* teacher. 10 Patrick St. (phone: 21497).

Kilkenny Crystal – Established in 1969, this glassware shop stocks a variety of hand-cut crystal items, including footed vases, rose bowls, bells, ring-holders, wine glasses, carafes, and decanters. Visitors are also welcome to tour the factory at Callan, 10 miles south of town. 19 Rose Inn St. (phone: 21090).

Marchioness Boutique – Women's clothing with a wide selection of Irish-made ready-to-wear, tweeds, hand-knits, etc. The Parade (phone: 65921).

Monster House – A solid, traditional department store selling woolens, tweeds, glass, and all the rest. 24 High St. (phone: 22016).

P. T. Murphy – Just the spot to find a Claddagh ring, Tara brooch, or Celtic cross, as well as Irish silver, jewelry, Waterford crystal, and Royal Tara china. 84/85 High St. (phone: 21127).

Yesterdays – This eclectic midtown shop offers a variety of antique and modern collectibles, including locally produced scent and soap, vintage brass, bottles, jewelry, toy animals, and dolls. 30 Patrick St. (phone: 65557).

SPORTS AND FITNESS: Bicycling – Bikes can be rented from *J. J. Wall*, 88 Maudlin St. (phone: 21236).

Fishing – There is good trout fishing in the rivers Nore and Dinan north of Kilkenny. Consult J. J. Carrigan at the *Sport Shop* at 82 High St. (phone: 21517).

Golf – The *Kilkenny Golf Club* accepts guests at its pleasant 18-hole course, about 1 mile from town (phone: 61730 or 22125).

Greyhound Racing – Races are held at *St. James's Park* every Wednesday and Friday evening (phone: 21214).

Hill Walking – Join the group that meets Sunday mornings, and wear sturdy hiking boots. Check local paper for time and venue.

Horseback Riding – The best of the nearby stables are *Thomastown Equitation Centre* (Thomastown; phone: 24112), offering year-round indoor and outdoor riding, plus cross-country and training; and the *Mount Juliet* hotel's *Equestrian Centre,* also in Thomastown (phone: 24522), offering a year-round program of riding, trekking, hunting, and cross-country activities.

Horse Racing – The racecourse at lovely *Gowran Park,* 10 miles from the city, is the site of 8 meetings a year (phone: 26126).

Hurling – Ireland's ancient stick and ball game is played most stylishly in Kilkenny. There is usually a game on Sunday afternoons at *Nowlan Park.*

THEATER: The *Kilkenny New Theatre* group presents *Summer Pub Theatre,* a show of light plays, at the *Club House* hotel (Patrick St.) during the summer and at other times in *St. Kieran's College Theatre* (Ormond St.). Other events occur in association with *Kilkenny Arts Week.*

MUSIC: For traditional Irish music, try the *seisiún* presented by *Comhaltas Ceoiltóirí Eireann* once a week in July and August in Kilkenny Castle. In the summer months, the *Newpark* hotel (Castlecomer Rd.) also stages an Irish Night cabaret, usually on Wednesdays. Traditional music can be enjoyed throughout the year on Tuesdays at *P. V.'s Lounge* in the *Kilford Arms* (John St.). *Kilkenny Arts Week* is the best source of information on classical music events; also check the local newspapers.

NIGHTCLUBS AND NIGHTLIFE: Pubs for the mature and discos for the young are the extent of the nightlife in Kilkenny, as in most Irish towns. Irish cabaret is found at the *Kilkenny* hotel on Saturdays and Sundays; on Saturdays at the *Springhill Court,* which also presents *céilí* dancing on Wednesdays. The *Newpark* hotel has dancing on Sunday and Tuesday nights.

BEST IN TOWN

CHECKING IN: Despite its obvious attractions, Kilkenny has not been much of a hotel town until recently. The tourist circuit of Ireland tends to go clockwise around the coast, ignoring the interior, and only lately have hotels in midland towns roused themselves from a rather dull state of commercial plainness. Expect to pay $200 or more for a double room at a hotel we list as very expensive and $100 to $150 for expensive lodgings; most are in the moderate bracket of $65 to $95 per double room; inexpensive ones cost $60 or less. The tourist board is happy to help tourists who can't find rooms. The alternative may be a town or country home or farmhouse. All telephone numbers are in the 56 area code unless otherwise indicated.

Mount Juliet – The Kilkenny area's newest and most luxurious property is set on 1,466 acres, with formal gardens, lawns, woodlands, and parklands along the river Nore. The 18th-century manor house has 23 rooms and 9 suites, all uniquely decorated with antiques and original paintings. Several suites provide private butler service at an additional charge. There is a wide range of sports facilities, including an equestrian center, salmon and trout fishing, pheasant shooting, and fox hunting. By the middle of this year, an 18-hole golf course is expected to open, and a new clubhouse will offer indoor and outdoor tennis, badminton, squash, and a gymnasium with a sauna and a Jacuzzi. Ireland's oldest cricket club also is here. There are two restaurants (see *Eating Out*), a lounge, bar, and a library. Thomastown, 10 miles southeast of Kilkenny (phone: 24455). Very expensive.

Kilkenny – This is a Regency gem built as his own home by William Robertson, the architect who gave Kilkenny Castle its final Gothic trim. His touch here produced a fanciful structure in which the hotel's public rooms have retained some of their former domestic charm. The 60 bedrooms — ultramodern and spacious — are in a separate block. There's also an indoor swimming pool, sauna, hot tub, gym, and tennis courts. College Rd. (phone: 62000). Expensive to moderate.

Newpark – On the north edge of the city, this Victorian country house has been skillfully combined with modern extensions and converted into a comfortable hotel with 60 rooms (each with private bath and phone) in a peaceful garden setting. Facilities include a first-rate dining room (see *Eating Out*), a noon-to-midnight grill room, and a health center with an indoor pool, saunas, Jacuzzi, fully equipped gym, and tennis courts. Irish musical entertainment and twice-weekly discos are featured. The staff is efficient and enthusiastic. Castlecomer Rd. (phone: 22122). Moderate.

Springhill Court – Modern and of the motel type with a castle-like facade, it provides 44 well-equipped rooms (including telephone) and a restaurant and bar. On the southern edge of the city, it's convenient for travelers with a car. Waterford Rd. (phone: 21122). Moderate.

Club House – Almost 200 years old, this downtown hotel is full of atmosphere, with a cozy bar called the *Foxhounds Lounge,* a Georgian-style dining room, and a fine collection of turn-of-the-century magazine cartoons on the walls. There are 23 rooms, 18 with private bath/shower. Patrick St. (phone: 21994). Moderate to inexpensive.

Lacken House – An old Georgian residence about a half-mile east of Kilkenny, this lovely guesthouse has been renovated and updated by the McSweeney family to include 8 rooms, each with private bath, as well as a first class restaurant in the basement. Open year-round, except for a week at *Christmas.* Dublin Rd. (phone: 61085 or 65611). Inexpensive.

 EATING OUT: In the past few years, Kilkenny and its environs have earned a reputation for fine food. Hotel dining rooms often rival local restaurants. For those traveling by car, some worthwhile places in attractive spots at a distance have been included here. Expect dinner for two (without wine or tips) to cost $80 or more in a restaurant listed as very expensive; $60 to $75, expensive; from $35 to $55 in a restaurant listed as moderate; and under $30 in an inexpensive one. All telephone numbers are in the 56 area code unless otherwise indicated.

Lady McCalmont Room – An aura of grandeur prevails at this lovely country house dining place at the *Mount Juliet* hotel. The setting is enhanced by views of the river Nore, fresh flowers from the gardens, and specially patterned linen, crystal, and silver. The menu offers such dishes as salmon with black currant leaf sauce; breast of chicken with cheese mousse and red pepper butter; wrapped rack of lamb; and stir-fried rabbit with leeks. Seven- and eight-course tasting selections also are available. The extensive wine list includes European vintages, as well as choices from the US, Canada, Australia, and New Zealand. Open nightly. Reservations necessary. Thomastown, 10 miles southeast of Kilkenny (phone: 24455). Very expensive.

Damask – The elegant dining room of the *Newpark* hotel features piano music 6 nights a week. The menu ranges from *coquilles St.-Jacques* to châteaubriand, with some imaginative veal and chicken dishes, too. Open daily. Reservations necessary. Castlecomer Rd. (phone: 22122). Expensive.

Lacken House – Chef Eugene McSweeney, formerly of the *Berkeley Court* in Dublin, is making his bid for haute cuisine immortality with this family operation. Fresh fish that comes daily from Dunmore East is the specialty. Dishes range from baked crab au gratin to *paupiettes* of plaice with salmon stuffing, as well as filet of pork and medallions of beef. Closed Sundays and Mondays. Reservations advised. Dublin Rd. (phone: 65611). Expensive.

Maltings – About 10 miles south of Kilkenny, this family-run restaurant is situated right on the river Nore in the idyllic village of Inistioge. Specialties are Nore salmon, minted lamb, chicken *bonne femme,* and duckling with brandy. Open for dinner Tuesdays through Sundays in summer, Thursdays through Saturdays from mid-September to mid-May. Reservations necessary. Inistioge (phone: 58484). Expensive.

Step House – This fine Georgian house serves delicious French meals, including wood pigeon pâté, avocado mousse with Kilmore crab, and wild duck from the Wexford marshlands (in season). Closed Sundays and Mondays and during February. Reservations advised. Borris (phone: 503-73116). Expensive.

Kyteler's Inn – An inn since 1324, this restored medieval tavern has buffet lunches and full-menu dinners. Featured dishes include *langoustines géantes* and veal cordon bleu as well as local salmon and trout. Open daily year-round; in summer, a medieval banquet often is held on Sunday evenings. Reservations necessary. St. Kieran St. (phone: 21064). Moderate.

Lord Bagenal – It's worth the trip to this charming restaurant only 15 miles from Kilkenny, in a historic town at a crossing of the river Barrow. There is bar food throughout the day and a full restaurant menu in the evening, with a variety of dishes, from veal and mushroom pie to filet of beef *en croûte.* Closed Mondays. Reservations necessary. Leighlinbridge (phone: 503-21668). Moderate.

Old Kitchen – An informal alternative at the *Mount Juliet* hotel, this eatery is situated in the basement of the manor house, where the original kitchens were. Cozy and wood-trimmed, it offers hearty fare such as "soup from the cauldron"; chicken and ham pie; beef, Guinness, and mushroom pie; vegetable and herb lasagna; deep-fried prawns; and steaks, as well as salmon from the river Nore, which passes through the grounds. Open daily, 10:30 AM to 10:30 PM. Reservations necessary. Thomastown, 10 miles southeast of Kilkenny (phone: 24455). Moderate.

Mulhall's – A digression off High Street through a small arcade and into a medieval lane leads to this airy, modern restaurant of wood and stone. Excellent coffee and pastries baked on the premises are on the menu all day; light or regular lunches are offered; and dinner is served on Thursdays through Saturdays (until 8 PM). Reservations necessary. 6 High St. (phone: 21329). Inexpensive.

SHARING A PINT: Smithwick's, a medium-tart ale-type beer, has been the local brew for well over 200 years. Free samples are offered on the guided brewery tour (Parliament St.) at 3 PM daily, May through September. To try it elsewhere, pick a pub. They range from the dark and cozy to the modern, well-lighted plastic. A list of the best includes *Tynan's Bar* (2 Horseleap Slip), a turn-of-the-century pub that has survived with its fittings — brass scales, grocery drawers, beer pumps, gilt mirrors — miraculously intact. Locals and cosmopolitans share its great atmosphere and honest drink. The exterior of the *Marble City Bar* (66 High St.) is a museum piece; the interior is less authentic, but its character has not been overwhelmed by modernization. *Kyteler's Inn* (St. Kieran St.) was once the house of the redoubtable Dame Alice. It now has a friendly nest of bars. The *Club House Bar* (Patrick St.), in the hotel of the same name, is a quiet oasis with sporting prints, cartoons, and cast-iron bar tables. Also good for pub grub is *Edward Langton's* (69 John St.), a lively, social spot favored by the young. Other pubs known for their food and convivial atmosphere are the *Court Arms* (9 Parliament St.); *Jim Holland* (60 St. Kieran St.); and *Caisléan Ui Cuan* (*Castle Inn;* Patrick St., facing Kilkenny Castle).

KILLARNEY

Praised by writers from Tennyson and Thackeray to Boucicault and Behan, Killarney is undoubtedly the best known of Ireland's tourism centers. After the capital of Dublin, it is the most visited tourist destination in all of Ireland. Yet, compared with cities like Cork, Galway, or Limerick, Killarney is relatively small (pop. 9,000) and lacks any unique architecture, major cultural outlets, or immediate access to a major airport or seaport. In terms of historic importance, Killarney cannot be ranked with cities like Cashel, Kells, Kilkenny, Wexford, or Waterford, or even with other small towns. Killarney was not the seat of Irish kings as was Tara, nor does it have great Viking or Norman legacies. Killarney is Killarney, and in many ways it is in a class by itself.

Just off the Atlantic in County Kerry, not far from Ireland's southwest coast, Killarney is essentially a sheltered Camelot-like town, surrounded by 23 square miles of idyllic lakes, mountains, floating islands, castles, waterfalls, and parklands. Unlike Camelot, however, the rains and mists come often to Killarney, but then the natives say that the moisture is what keeps Killarney such a naturally verdant paradise, worthy of its sobriquets "Beauty's Home" and "Heaven's Reflex." The rain also provides Killarney with a mild and moderate climate that varies relatively little in temperature.

The place name of Killarney is believed to have come from the Irish or Gaelic name *Cill Aírne,* meaning "church of the sloe." This is well supported by the fact that there are many sloe (*aírne*) or blackthorn woods in the area.

Visitors come to Killarney not just for the town itself but also for its surroundings. The lakes of Killarney and the mountains that hold them reside in a boulder- and rock-strewn land of unrivaled natural beauty, sculpted by the Ice Age and trimmed with gentle woodlands. Ireland's highest range of mountains, MacGillicuddy's Reeks, are a part of this panoramic tableau. To tell the truth, the scenery surrounding Killarney is by far the most compelling reason to visit; tourism's assault on the city proper has turned it into the most commercial (and occasionally tacky) town in the Republic.

Unlike most areas in Ireland, not a great deal is known about Killarney's early days, although some links to a Bronze Age civilization have been found. Earliest historical accounts go back to various monastic sites founded around the lakes during the 7th century and to the rule of early Irish chieftains called McCarthy, O'Donoghue, and O'Sullivan — surnames that predominate still. It was not until the mid-18th century, however, that Killarney began to make an impact and to draw visitors to its beautiful scenery. Thanks to Lord Kenmare, a local landowner, major roads were built from Killarney Town toward Tralee, Limerick, Cork, Kenmare, and beyond.

The mid-19th century brought the railroad to Killarney and the subsequent building of the *Great Southern* hotel. The Lord Kenmare of that time, following his predecessor's lead, gave Killarney another boost in 1861, when he invited Queen Victoria and members of the royal family to visit his lakeland paradise. The people of Killarney spruced up the town in a big way and prepared suitable accommodations for all who were expected to come to see the queen. Following the queen's visit, Victorians became the most enthusiastic travelers to Killarney. The area's purple glens, silent glades, ruined castles, and fairy-tale isles on misty lakes appealed to the Victorian imagination, and the journals of their travels are breathless with wonderment at what they saw.

Even then there was disdain for the traveler on too tight a schedule. William Makepeace Thackeray, in his *Irish Sketch Book,* had little good to say of the "man coming from his desk in London or Dublin and seeing 'the whole lakes in a day.' " Thackeray admonished visitors to "look at these wonderful things leisurely and thoughtfully; and even then, blessed is he who understands them."

Twentieth-century visitors can take heart. The enthralling scenery around Killarney hasn't changed at all, even if the parking lots of the town's hotels are filled with tour buses and the streets are lined with pony traps and jaunting cars for hire. Commercial, yes, but just as the Victorians would be swaddled in lap robes and stashed in the back of horse-drawn carriages, so can today's jet-age sojourners still approximate the feeling of being tucked in and trotted out of town in the turf-scented morning or rainbowed afternoon.

Basically, Killarney's lakes are three in number. Nearest the town is the Lower Lake (also known as Lough Leane, "lake of learning"). This is the largest lake (5,000 acres), with about 30 islands, including Innisfallen, site of a medieval monastery and an early seat of learning. On the eastern shore of the Lower Lake are two other popular Killarney historic sites, Muckross Abbey and Ross Castle.

The wooded peninsula of Muckross separates the Lower Lake from the Middle Lake (680 acres), sometimes called Muckross Lake. On the eastern shore of this body of water is the manor home and folk museum called *Muckross House,* and close by is the 60-foot natural cascade known as Torc Waterfall.

A narrow strait called the Long Range leads to the slender, finger-like Upper Lake (430 acres), which is almost embedded in mountains. The Upper Lake is the smallest but, in the opinion of many, the most beautiful of the lakes, with MacGillicuddy's Reeks rising to the west. Added to the spectacle of the three main lakes are many other, smaller lakes in the folds of the mountains as well as numerous picturesque cascades and waterfalls.

Plant and animal life is also part of Killarney's landscape. The woodlands thrive with a luxuriant medley of oak, birch, yew, ash, cedar, and juniper. Of the smaller native trees are holly, fern, rhododendron, and arbutus (the strawberry tree), the special botanic glory of the area, recognizable by its small, glossy, dark leaves, white flowers in the spring, and brilliant red berries in autumn and winter. All of this is natural habitat for the unique Killarney red deer, the only deer herd of any kind in the country that is of native stock, other animals ranging from Japanese sika deer to black Kerry cattle, and no less than 114 species of birds.

It is not surprising that Killarney is definitely on the beaten tourist track and takes advantage of it. By Irish standards, the town is fiercely commercialized, with an abundance of souvenir and gift shops and visitor services. The local folk scramble to woo visitors to see the sights by motorcoach, mini-bus, private taxi, boat, bicycle, horseback, and, most of all, by jaunting car, the traditional Killarney mode of transport. This is a one-horse-drawn sidecart on which riders sit facing the scenery while the driver (known as a "jarvey") tries to beguile them with commentary laced with a story or song. Even in the most peaceful Killarney surroundings, expect a photographer to appear in the most unlikely spots along the lakeshore, capture the moment on color film, and then eagerly attempt to sell the prints to travelers by mail order.

A polite "No, thank you" will be heeded by jarveys, tour operators, and photographers, but you might think twice, since all this commercialism is designed to provide a memorable visit to Killarney, and that isn't all bad. Be comforted with the knowledge that the very active Urban District Council in the town sets and monitors the prices of all tours and other tourism activities.

To be sure, the town has its detractors who point out that Killarney is more of a tourist center than a representative Irish city — and none the prettier for this transformation. Its fans will answer that this spot has long been a tourist attraction and that there is no denying the beauty of the surroundings. Quite simply, you just haven't seen all of Ireland until you feast your eyes on Killarney.

KILLARNEY AT-A-GLANCE

 SEEING THE CITY: The entire Killarney vista — from the spire of the cathedral to MacGillicuddy's Reeks and the Iveragh Mountains — can be seen on a clear day in one sweeping panorama from Aghadoe Hill (400 feet high). This lookout is about 2 miles north of the town, just off N22, the main Killarney–Tralee road. Another perspective is from a spot 12 miles south of Killarney on the Kenmare road, N71, from which the broad valley of the three lakes can be seen. This vantage point, known locally as "Ladies View," is said to have been named because of the delight expressed by Queen Victoria's ladies-in-waiting on their visit here more than a century ago.

 SPECIAL PLACES: Although the ancient abbeys, stately buildings, manor homes, and castles of Killarney are well worth seeing, the real attraction of this lakeside paradise is the natural beauty of its surrounding parklands and lakeshore countryside. To appreciate the town at its best, allow enough time to see a blend of indoor and outdoor sights.

IN THE TOWN

Kerry Glass – This is Killarney's own glassware factory, where distinctive colored glass designs in vases, bowls, ashtrays, paperweights, and figurines are produced. Visitors are welcome to watch and photograph the craftsmen firing, blowing, shaping, and coloring the glass. Open 8 AM to 1 PM and 2 to 4 PM Mondays through Fridays, year-round. Next to the Franciscan friary, opposite the *Great Southern* hotel at Fair Hill (phone: 32587).

Kerry Poets Monument – Located at the east end of town in a section known as

Fair Hill, this statue was sculpted by Seamus Murphy to depict a *speir bhean* (beautiful woman) as a personification of Ireland. It was erected in 1940 as a tribute to County Kerry's four best-known poets — Pierce Ferriter, Geoffrey O'Donoghue, Egan O'-Rahilly, and Owen Roe O'Sullivan. East Avenue Rd. at Fair Hill.

Knockreer Estate – Once the home of the Kenmare family, this splendid parkland stretches from Killarney Town to the shores of the Lower Lake. A walk around the grounds includes access to the Knockreer House and the gardens, a mix of ancient trees with flowering cherries, magnolias, camelias, rhododendrons, and azaleas. Open daily in summer; weekends at other times. Entrance on New St.

St. Mary's Cathedral – Built between 1842 and 1855, the Catholic Church of St. Mary of the Assumption, as it is officially named, was designed in the Gothic Revival style by the celebrated 19th-century architect Augustus W. Pugin. This fine limestone structure is cruciform in shape, with a massive square central tower capped by a spire. Open daily. New St.

St. Mary's Church – Today belonging to the Church of Ireland, the present structure was built in 1870 in neo-Gothic style. Of more interest is the fact that a succession of churches can be traced to this spot, worship having been continuous here for at least 7 or 8 centuries. According to one theory, this religious place goes back even further and was once the site of the original *Cill Airne,* the medieval church from which Killarney takes its name. Open Sundays. Main St.

National Museum of Irish Transport – Housed in a huge hall near the heart of town, this is the home of a permanent exhibit of antique and veteran cars. Visitors of all ages are fascinated by displays ranging from the world's rarest car (a one-of-a-kind 1907 Silver Stream, built in Kildare), the car of the century (a 1904 Germain), the world's first bicycle (designed by James Starley in England in 1884), and penny-farthing bicycles and tricycles to vintage carriages and more than 2,000 other transport-related items as well as a reference library. Open daily year-round. Admission charge. East Avenue Rd. (phone: 32639).

ENVIRONS

Muckross House – Built in 1843 by the Herbert family, this splendid Elizabethan-style residence is a showcase of 19th-century architecture, with locally made furniture, needlework, mullioned windows, stepped gables, and 62 chimneys. Today it is also a folk museum with exhibits of County Kerry life, history, cartography, geology, plants, and animals. A cluster of basement workshops re-create the crafts of earlier days, with artisans demonstrating weaving, pottery making, bookbinding, spinning, basket making, and blacksmithing. As delightful outside as it is inside, *Muckross House* is surrounded with mature and manicured gardens and is also the focal point of the Killarney National Park. Open year-round. Admission charge. Kenmare Rd. (phone: 31440).

Killarney National Park – The heart of Killarney's legendary beauty, this 25,000-acre natural expanse encompasses three lakes, various nature trails, valleys, islands, rivers, waterfalls, bogs, mountains, and woods. The grounds include the most extensive area of natural oak woodland remaining in Ireland as well as characteristic plants, such as the arbutus, and a rare herd of native red deer that are said to have been here since the end of the last Ice Age. Other inhabitants include Japanese sika deer and a herd of pedigreed Kerry cattle. Free access is available from several points around Killarney, particularly along the Killarney–Kenmare road. The park is best explored on foot, by bicycle, or in a jaunting car.

Ross Castle – Now a ruin, this 15th-century structure is one of the finest examples of castle-building in County Kerry. The remains include a 16th-century tower surrounded by a *bawn* (rampart) with rounded turrets. As a stronghold of the O'Donoghue chieftains, the building's main claim to fame is as the last castle in Ireland to fall to Cromwell's army, in 1652. Standing on a peninsula jutting into the Lower Lake, about 2 miles from the center of Killarney off the Kenmare road, the castle today is the ideal gateway to the lakes and serves as a rendezvous point for rental boats and boatmen.

Innisfallen Island – A 21-acre island floating in the northern end of the Lower Lake, this was once the site of a flourishing abbey, founded about AD 600 by St. Fallen. The *Annals of Innisfallen,* a chronicle of world and Irish history, written in Gaelic and Latin, was compiled here at intervals from the 10th to the 14th century by a succession of 39 monastic scribes (the manuscript is now housed at the Bodleian Library, Oxford). Although the monastery lasted until the 17th century, all that remain today are the ruins of 11th- and 12th-century structures and a remarkably varied terrain of heights and hollows, headlands and bays, woods and open spaces. It is said that many greats from Irish history have visited the island, from Brian Ború to Daniel O'Connell. Boats and boatmen can be hired at Ross Castle.

Muckross Abbey – Founded in the 1440s by the Franciscan friars, this abbey flourished on the edge of the Lower Lake for more than 300 years, until it was suppressed by the Penal Laws. The present well-preserved remains include a church with a wide belfry tower and beautifully vaulted cloisters, with an arched arcade surrounding a square courtyard whose centerpiece is an imposing and ancient yew tree, said to be as old as the abbey. Through the years, the abbey grounds served as a burial place for local chieftains and, during the 17th and 18th centuries, for the famous Kerry poets. Now a part of the Muckross estate, the abbey is in excellent condition. Three miles from Killarney on the Kenmare road, a favorite route for jaunting car drivers.

Torc Waterfall – A footpath winds its way up beside 60 feet of cascading waters, affording magnificent views of the lake district. This impressive waterfall, in its sylvan setting, is about 4 miles from Killarney. The area is well signposted and has its own car park. Off the main road to Kenmare.

Gap of Dunloe – A winding and rocky gorge of Ice Age origin, it winds between MacGillicuddy's Reeks and the Purple and Tomies mountains, 9 miles southwest of Killarney. The best way to experience the Gap is to take one of the full-day tours, which usually depart each morning by bus or jaunting car from the various hotels. Disembarkation is at *Kate Kearney's Cottage,* a former coaching inn turned snack bar, pub, and souvenir shop at the entrance to the Gap. From here, the energetic can walk the 7 miles through the Gap to the shore of the Upper Lake; those less ambitious can opt to ride the route on horseback or with several other passengers via traditional pony and trap. For the first 4 miles, the scene turns extraordinarily remote and gloomy, with massive rocks on either side and an accompanying narrow stream widening here and there into a sullen lake. One of these — Lough Black, or Serpent Lake — is where St. Patrick is said to have drowned the last snake in Ireland. Emerging from the Gap, the wooded Upper Lake, still 3 miles away, comes into view, and Black Valley stretches off in the distance to the right. A popular stop for a picnic lunch (sometimes included in the price of the day's trip) is *Lord Brandon's Cottage,* near the lakeshore, after which everyone boards open boats for the return trip via the Killarney lakes. From the Upper Lake, the boats turn into the Long Range, which grows progressively swifter until the boatmen "shoot the rapids" at the Old Weir Bridge into a beautiful calm spot called the Meeting of the Waters. Next is the Middle Lake, in the shadow of Torc Mountain, and then under Brickeen Bridge into the Lower Lake. The tour ends at 15th-century Ross Castle, where jaunting cars are lined up to take passengers back to Killarney Town. The total price of this day-long, multi-conveyance excursion (about $35) is set and regulated by the Urban District Council, so be sure to check with the tourist office for the current rate.

Crag Cave – Fifteen miles north of Killarney, this underground wonder is believed to be over 1 million years old, although it has been open officially to visitors only since late 1989. One of Ireland's largest cave systems (it is a total surveyed length of 12,510 feet and a depth of over 60 feet), its passageways are spiked with the largest stalactitites in Europe, and there are many unique rock formations. Special lighting produces a haunting effect, showing off dark caverns and obscure crevices that would otherwise go unnoticed. Guided tours are available, and there are exhibit areas, a craft shop, and a restaurant. Open daily, April through October. Admission charge. Castleisland (phone: 66-41244).

SOURCES AND RESOURCES

TOURIST INFORMATION: The Killarney Tourist Board is in the Town Hall (Main St.; phone: 31633). A large facility, it is divided into two sections, one for processing room reservations, the other for information and the sale of pamphlets, guides, and maps. Summer hours are 9 AM to 8 PM Mondays through Saturdays, 10 AM to 1 PM Sundays. The rest of the year, it is open 9:15 AM to 5:30 PM Mondays through Fridays, 9:15 AM to 1 PM Saturdays. Useful publications include *The Killarney Area Guide* (about 80¢), *Killarney — A Guide* (about $3), *The Kerry Guide* (about $2.30), and *The Cork & Kerry Visitor Guide* (issued free and updated annually).

Local Coverage – County Kerry's weekly newspaper, the *Kerryman,* is published every Thursday and contains current information on Killarney area entertainment, sports, and events. Two other publicatons, the *Kingdom Now and Then* (biweekly) and the *Killarney Advertiser* (issued every Friday), are also full of helpful listings and news.

TELEPHONE: The area code for Killarney and the immediate vicinity is 64. When calling from within the Republic of Ireland, dial 064 before the local number.

GETTING AROUND: There is no local public transport within Killarney because the downtown area is relatively small and can easily be explored on foot. A good way to get oriented is to purchase *The Killarney Tourist Trail* (about 80¢) at the tourist board or at a local shop and then follow the route outlined. The disc parking system is in effect on local streets (about 30¢ per hour); discs can be obtained at hotels, shops, or the tourist office.

Bicycles – Bicycling is a particularly enjoyable way to savor the Killarney sights. Most rental dealers are open daily 9 AM to 9 PM May to September, with shorter hours during the rest of the year. A full day's rental averages $6 to $8. The following shops have large rental fleets: *Laurel's Lane Bike Hire* (Old Market La., off Main St.; phone: 32771); *O'Callaghan Bros.* (College St.; phone: 31175); *O'Neill's Cycles* (6 Plunkett St.; phone: 31970); and *O'Sullivan's* (Pawn Office La., off High St.; phone: 31282).

Car Rental – The following companies maintain car rental operations in Killarney: *Budget* (c/o *International Hotel,* Kenmare Pl.; phone: 34341); *Hertz* (c/o *Three Lakes Hotel,* Kenmare Pl.; phone: 34126); *Killarney Autos* (Park Rd.; phone: 31555); and *Randles Car Hire* (Muckross Rd.; phone: 31237).

Jaunting Cars – A pleasant way to see the Killarney lake district is to give in to the tourism flacks and take a ride in a jaunting car, an open horse-drawn cart. The driver, called a "jarvey," not only provides a tour of the most famous sights but also fills the time with lots of local lore.

Since many of Killarney's most scenic lake and parkland areas are not open to automobile traffic, the jaunting car is undoubtedly one of the best ways to get around, especially for those who don't enjoy walking or biking. In many ways, jaunting cars have become synonymous with Killarney, although the experience may not always be as idyllic as presented because the jarveys can be a bit aggressive in pestering visitors to take a ride. The cars usually are lined up along Main Street and Kenmare Place, near the major hotels in town (the *Great Southern* and the *International*), or at the entrance to major sights (such as Muckross House or Ross Castle). Current rates range from about $12 to $37 for one to four people, depending on the duration and distance of the trip. Rates are set and carefully monitored by the Urban District Council, so there is no need to be suspicious of being overcharged.

Taxi – There are taxi stands on College Square and at the *Great Southern* hotel. Taxis also line up to meet arriving trains and buses at the Killarney railway station. To order a taxi by phone, contact *Deros* (phone: 31251), *O'Connor's* (phone: 31052), *Cronin's* (phone: 31521), or *Killarney and Kerry Tours* (phone: 33880).

Tours – During July and August, *Bus Eireann,* a division of *CIE (Córas Iompair Eireann, National Transport Company*), operates full-day sightseeing bus trips around the Ring of Kerry and the Dingle Peninsula, with regular departures from the Killarney railway station, adjacent to the *Great Southern* hotel (phone: 31067). Half-day tours of the Killarney lake district and full-day excursions to the Gap of Dunloe or the Ring of Kerry are also available from *Cronin's Tours* (College St.; phone: 31521); *Deros Tours* (Main St.; phone: 31251); *Killarney and Kerry Tours* (*Innisfallen Mall,* Main St.; phone: 33880); and *Castlelough Tours* (7 High St.; phone: 31115 or 32880).

Trains and Buses – *Irish Rail* and *Bus Eireann,* divisions of *CIE,* connect Killarney to all major Irish cities and towns, such as Dublin, Limerick, Tralee, and Cork. All trains and buses arrive and depart from the Killarney railway station next to the *Great Southern* hotel at the east end of town. For schedules and fare information, call *CIE* (phone: 31067).

Water Excursions – Sightseeing boat trips on the Killarney lakes are operated by *Killarney and Kerry Tours* (*Innisfallen Mall,* Main St.; phone: 33880); *O'Donoghue Bros.* (3 High St.; phone: 31068); and *Lake Tours* (College St.; phone: 32911). Another way to see the lakes is via an enclosed motorized cruise boat, such as the *Lily of Killarney,* operated by *Killarney Watercoach Cruises* (3 High St.; phone: 31068) or the *Waterbus,* operated by *Destination Killarney* (East Ave. Rd.; phone: 32638). These tours last approximately 1 hour and cost about $6.

 SPECIAL EVENTS: The *Easter Folk Festival,* a feast of Irish music, is held annually in March or April. Killarney's principal festival, *Pan Celtic Week,* which convenes each May, is a gathering of musicians, singers, poets, and dancers from the Celtic communities in Scotland, Wales, Cornwall, Brittany, the Isle of Man, and Ireland. The highlight of the week is a "Celticvision" song contest. Further information and advance programs can be obtained from the Killarney Tourist Board (Town Hall, Main St., Killarney, County Kerry; phone: 31633). The *International Motor Rally of the Lakes,* which tours around the lake district, is held in early December. Check with the tourist board.

 MUSEUMS: Besides those mentioned in *Special Places,* a particularly pleasant place to visit on a rainy day is the *O'Connor Gallery* (Town Hall; phone: 31255). This permanent exhibit contains an impressive selection of Irish landscapes and local scenes.

 SHOPPING: As a town that basks in tourism, Killarney has more than its share of souvenir and gift shops. Because there are so many enterprises catering to tourists, the selection and variety of goods are great, quality is high, and the prices usually are competitive. The range of goods is not particularly native to the area but includes all the visitor favorites — Aran hand-knits, Donegal tweed, cashmere, Waterford crystal, and Belleek china. Some local handicrafts, such as hand-thrown pottery, hand-woven clothing, artworks, and Kerry glass, are also sold at many outlets. Official shopping hours are 9 AM to 6 PM, except Sundays, with an early closing Monday afternoons. In high season, however, many of the busier stores remain open until 10 or 11 PM 7 days a week.

Celtic Shop – This all-purpose store offers a wide selection of knitwear and tweeds as well as traditional Irish dolls, road signs, crystal, china, and pewter. 33 College St. (phone: 31126).

Innisfallen Shopping Mall – An enclosed complex of shops and boutiques selling a range of goods from postcards and Irish music tapes to hand-knits, jewelry, and exotic ice creams. Main St.

Kerry Glass – This outlet store for the Kerry Glass Factory sells mostly "seconds" at bargain prices. College St. (phone: 32587).

Kilkenny Shop – Synonymous with fine design, this is an offshoot of the famous Dublin shop of the same name, now owned by the Blarney Woollen Mills of Cork. Like its sister shops, this one sells a wide variety of Irish-made goods, from tweeds and knitwear to crystal, china, pottery, and souvenir items — all at very competitive prices. Main St. (phone: 31888).

Muckross House Crafts – The unique crafts made at the *Muckross House Folk Museum* are sold here. Choices include wrought-iron work, pottery, baskets, and hand-knits. Kenmare Rd. (phone: 31440).

Quills Woollen Market – For hand-knit sweaters of all colors, sizes, textures, and styles. 1 High St. (phone: 32277).

Serendipity – A haven for antique lace, crochetwork, and knitwear in alpaca, mohair, and cashmere, as well as hand-thrown pottery, studio glass, linen, hand-woven bedspreads, antique prints, paintings, copper, and hand-crafted silver and gold. 15 College St. (phone: 31056).

Viking Crafts – The shelves here are stocked with tweed, china, silver, and lace, as well as fishing flies, shamrock seeds, heraldic crests, rugby shirts, Irish ballad books, local shell crafts, Irish coffee mugs, and leprechauns of various sizes and shapes. 3/5 Kenmare Pl. (phone: 33820).

White Heather Home Crafts – Just the spot to find collectors' character dolls, framed dried Kerry flowers, handmade jewelry, crochetwork, lace, and glassware. 48 New St. and Plunkett St. (phone: 31145).

 SPORTS AND FITNESS: Boating – Rowboats can be hired for trips on the Killarney lakes at Ross Castle; contact *H. Clifton* (phone: 32252).

Fishing – On the river Laune and the river Flesk, anglers can enjoy salmon fishing (using spinning gear of any type) and trout fishing (using flies only). Daily permits are required for both types of fishing, and salmon fishermen must also obtain a state license. All of this documentation can be easily obtained from the Fishery Office (c/o Park Superintendent, Knockreer Estate Office, New St., Killarney; phone: 31246), which also will reserve beats (stretches of water) in advance by mail. The salmon season extends from mid-January to mid-October, trout season from mid-February to early October.

Gaelic Games – The Irish national games of hurling and Gaelic football are played most Sunday afternoons during the summer by local teams at *Fitzgerald Stadium* (Lewis Rd.). Check the *Kerryman* newspaper or call the stadium (phone: 31700) for the latest schedule. Admission charge.

Golf – The *Killarney Golf and Fishing Club* (phone: 31242) welcomes visiting golfers to its twin courses, *Killeen* and *Mahoney's Point,* about 3 miles from town. Among the most scenic in Ireland, both courses are lakeside, 18 holes, par 72. The greens fee, approximately $28, entitles players to try both courses in the same day.

Horse Racing – Since 1936, the *Killarney Racecourse* (Ross Rd.) has been drawing people from all parts of Ireland to its annual May and July meets. Check for details in any national or local newspaper, or call the track (phone: 31125).

Horseback Riding – Horses and ponies are available from the *Killarney Riding Stables* (Ballydowney, Killarney; phone: 31686). The rate is usually about $15 per hour; extended trail riding can also be arranged.

Jogging – The *Killarney National Park* offers four fully developed and signposted nature trails, ideal for jogging or walking.

Tennis – Many Killarney hotels, such as the *Cahernane, Dunloe Castle, Europe, Gleneagle,* and *Great Southern,* have tennis courts for guests.

Swimming – The best swimming is available at some of the Atlantic coastal beaches along the Ring of Kerry, such as Castlecove, Rosebeigh, and Waterville, as well as at Inch Strand on the Dingle Peninsula.

THEATER: Evenings from May to October, the *Great Southern* hotel in Killarney presents a varied program of entertainment. Reservations are recommended (phone: 31262). At the *Arus Padraig Hall* (Lewis Rd.; phone: 33516) the local *Dóchas Drama Group* performs plays during the winter, and a traditional Irish dance show is performed here during the summer. The tourist board has times and schedules.

MUSIC: Irish cabaret music sessions are held throughout the summer at Killarney's leading hotels, including *Dunloe Castle* (phone: 44111), *Europe* (phone: 31900), *Great Southern* (phone: 31262), *Aghadoe Heights* (phone: 31766), *Gleneagle* (phone: 31870), *Ryan's* (phone: 31555), and the *International* (phone: 31816). Ballad and folk music is heard regularly at *The Laurels,* a pub (Main St.; phone: 31149); *Danny Mann Inn* (97 New St.; phone: 31640); and the *Eagle's Whistle Singing Pub* (at the *Gleneagle;* phone: 31870). For a change of pace, try the country-and-western repertoire at *Fiddler's Green Inn* (Cork Rd.; phone: 33388).

NIGHTCLUBS AND NIGHTLIFE: Most of Killarney's nightlife is in its pubs. In addition to Irish music, *Danny Mann Inn* (97 New St.; phone: 31640) operates the *Scoundrels Night Club.* Other discos include *Wings Night Club,* at the *Gleneagle* (Muckross Rd.; phone: 31870) and *Revelles,* at the *East Avenue* hotel (Kenmare Pl.; phone: 32522).

BEST IN TOWN

CHECKING IN: As Ireland's most popular pure resort area, Killarney has hundreds of places to stay — from luxurious Old World hotels and modern motels to simple farmhouses and private homes. During the summer, prices are higher than in most other parts of the country, but off-season rates (October/November through April) can provide substantial savings (of up to 35%). In summer, expect to pay $150 a night or more for a double in hotels designated as very expensive, $100 to $145 in the expensive category; $65 to $95 in a moderate hotel or motel, and under $65 for superior guesthouse lodgings. Modest accommodations in private homes and farmhouses, usually without private bath, run less than $35 a night for a double room with a full Irish breakfast. The Killarney Tourist Board operates a full-time reservation service to assist visitors in finding accommodations. All telephone numbers are in the 64 area code unless otherwise indicated.

Aghadoe Heights – Set on a hillside 2 miles west of town, this modern hostelry enjoys panoramic vistas of Killarney, the lake district, and the surrounding mountain ranges. To match the spectacular views, new British-based owners also have renovated the 60 guestrooms and public areas with new furnishings, brass fittings, and other fine touches. The rooftop restaurant, now called *Fredrick's*, also has been redone with plush decor and new kitchens. Salmon fishing is available on a private stretch of the Laune River, and special arrangments can be made at Killarney's two golf courses. Aghadoe, Off N22 (phone: 31766). Very expensive.

Cahernane – Built in 1877 as the manor home of the Herbert family (the Earls of Pembroke), this gracious country inn offers a bucolic parkland setting, complete with rose gardens, on the shores of Killarney's Lower Lake, less than a mile from town. An Old World atmosphere prevails in all the public rooms, including the *Herbert,* an elegant à la carte restaurant, but the 52 bedrooms offer all the 20th-century comforts, including private baths/showers. Guest facilities include tennis courts, pitch and putt, croquet, and reserved fishing privileges. Closed November through February. Muckross Rd. (phone: 31895, 33936, or 33937). Expensive.

Dunloe Castle – This is not an old Irish fortress, but a modern German-owned château-style hotel near the Gap of Dunloe — and adjacent to the ruins of the original 15th-century Dunloe Castle. All 140 rooms have a private bath. Other amenities include an excellent restaurant, a heated indoor pool, sauna, tennis courts, horseback riding, fishing, croquet, a putting green, a fitness track, tropical gardens, and nightly entertainment. Open April through September. Beaufort, west of Killarney off the Killorglin road (phone: 44111). Expensive.

Europe – For unobstructed views of the Lower Lake, this is the hotel of choice. Hugging the shoreline, surrounded by tropical gardens, and next to Killarney's two golf courses, it is a favorite with European visitors. The 176 rooms vary in size, but all have private bathrooms and most have balconies with spectacular views. The *Panorama* restaurant has an international menu with views befitting its name, while the *Tyrol* offers faster service and simpler fare in a skylit, alpine setting. Facilities for guests include an indoor heated swimming pool, a health center, horseback riding, boating, fishing, tennis, and evening entertainment. Open March through October. Fossa, west of Killarney off the Killorglin road (phone: 31900). Expensive.

Killarney Great Southern – On the eastern edge of the town, set on its own grounds and manicured gardens, this 135-year-old, ivy-covered landmark is the grande dame of Killarney hotels. Most of the 180 bedrooms (all with bath/shower) have been refurbished, and 10 deluxe suites have been added. The public areas have been revitalized with classic sofas and armchairs and plush carpeting, but there is still a roaring fire glowing in the lobby, and the Waterford crystal chandeliers, ornate plasterwork, and high ceilings proudly remain. The main dining room is elegant, with dome and pillars, and is as large as a ballroom; for an excellent meal, try the adjoining *Malton Room,* an intimate à la carte restaurant. There is an indoor heated swimming pool, saunas, tennis courts, and a fashionable boutique. During the summer, evening entertainment is provided by various cabaret groups. Open March to December. Off East Avenue Rd. (phone: 31262). Expensive.

Castlerosse – Set on the beautiful Kenmare estate, overlooking lakes and mountains, near Killarney's golf courses, it has 65 motel-style bedrooms, each with private bath/shower. Closed from the end of October to early March. Killorglin Rd. (phone: 31114). Moderate.

Gleneagle – A favorite resort complex for Irish vacationers who are drawn to its entertainment center, which features Irish show bands and pop stars as well as a lively singing pub. There are 140 modern bedrooms (each with a private bath and many with balconies), a restaurant, a grillroom, and a health center with tennis and squash courts, saunas, sunbeds, table tennis, and indoor/outdoor children's playgrounds. Open year-round. Muckross Rd. (phone: 31870). Moderate.

International – Although situated right in the middle of town, the front rooms of this landmark hotel, a Best Western affiliate, offer sweeping views of the mountains. The interior harks back to the grand old days, with a hand-carved central staircase (there's an elevator for those who prefer) and antiques and memorabilia. Each of the 88 rooms has a modern, private bath. Other facilities include a formal dining room, the *Whaler* seafood restaurant, a coffee shop, sun deck, and lounge bar with Irish entertainment nightly during the summer. The hotel supplies complimentary parking discs. Open March through October. Kenmare Pl. (phone: 31816). Moderate.

Ryan – A member of the dependable Irish chain, this 168-room motel-style facility is located just east of the town on its own grounds. All rooms have private bath/shower; other pluses include tennis courts, pitch and putt, children's amusements, and nightly musical entertainment in the summer. Open March to December. Cork Rd. (phone: 31555). Moderate.

Torc Great Southern – This member of the well-known hotel group is a motel-type facility located east of Killarney, about a 5-minute walk from the town. All 96 bright, modern bedrooms have private baths/showers, and a full-service restaurant and cocktail bar are on the premises. The well-tended grounds include a garden and a tennis court. Open April through September. Cork Rd. (phone: 31611). Moderate.

Kathleen's Country House – A family residence that has been extended to include 10 modern bedrooms with private baths/showers, direct-dial phones, and orthopedic beds. This delightful guest home is on spacious grounds, complete with landscaped gardens and a private car park. Open March through October. Madam's Height, 2 miles north on the Tralee road, N22 (phone: 32810). Inexpensive.

Linden House – On the edge of town in a quiet neighborhood near the cathedral, this popular guesthouse is run by the Knoblauch family, known for their German-Irish hospitality. Facilities include 11 rooms, each with a private bath/shower, a full-service restaurant with wine license, and a private car park. Open mid-January through mid-December. New Rd. (phone: 31379). Inexpensive.

EATING OUT: Killarney's restaurants are concentrated within a few blocks in town. For dinner for two, without wine or tips, expect to pay $75 and up in the expensive category, $35 to $70 for a moderately priced meal, and $30 or less at a place indicated as inexpensive. All telephone numbers are in the 64 area code unless otherwise indicated.

Gaby's – Geert and Marie Maes, a Flemish-Irish couple, carry on the tradition of excellent seafood cooking begun by Gaby, Geert's Flemish mother. The atmosphere is bright and nautical, with light knotty pine, colored tablecloths, and a lobster tank at the entrance where diners choose their own. Other entrées include rainbow trout, scallops mornay, turbot, haddock, and seafood combination platters. Open March through November for lunch and dinner. Reservations necessary. 17 High St. (phone: 32519). Expensive to moderate.

Dingles – The decor of this basement bistro is a blend of oak panels, cathedral choir stalls, arched ceilings, and cozy alcoves. The eclectic menu, prepared by owner/chef Gerry Cunningham, includes chicken curry, chile con carne, beef Stroganoff, and Irish stew as well as some exceptional seafood dishes such as monkfish casserole, giant prawns in garlic, and crab and shrimp au gratin. Open nightly for dinner in summer; closed from the end of December through February. Reservations necessary. 40 New St. (phone: 31079). Moderate.

Foley's – A delightful Georgian place, decked out with flowers and candlelight, it offers seafood specialties — mussel soup, Dingle Bay scallops, and local salmon — as well as steaks. The brown bread scones are home-baked. On weekends a tuxedo-clad pianist plays traditional Irish tunes as well as classical and contemporary music. Open for lunch and dinner year-round. Reservations necessary. 23 High St. (phone: 31217). Moderate.

Strawberry Tree – A shopfront eatery, it has a surprisingly romantic atmosphere, with a decor of subtle pink and gray tones, an open fireplace, and classical music played in the background. The fare includes local produce, with such dishes as a trio of gamebirds with wild mushrooms, wild rabbit pie, pan-fried beef in Guinness sauce, and white crab cakes in shallot and wine sauce. Closed Sundays and during February. Reservations necessary. 24 Plunkett St. (phone: 32688). Moderate.

O'Reilly's – A small, informal spot with an open fireplace in the pub room and a skylit dining area in the rear. House specialties include beef filet with prawns, salmon in pastry, scampi, chicken Kiev, and pork filet. Open daily year-round for bar lunches and dinner. Reservations necessary. 45 New St. (phone: 33699). Moderate to inexpensive.

West End House – Housed in a 19th-century structure, which was built by the Earls of Kenmare and over the years served as a school, presbytery, local army headquarters, and private residence, this cozy eatery specializes in charcoal-grilled steaks, spareribs, and chicken. Other dishes include chicken breast in raspberry sauce, pork medallions in brandy cream sauce, rack of lamb, Flemish-style mussels in a casserole, and a vegetarian plate topped with cheese sauce. Closed Sundays and during February. Reservations advised. Lower New St. (phone: 32271). Moderate to inexpensive.

Súgán – Named for the traditional braided straw chair, this cottage-style restaurant emphasizes Irish farm recipes and natural foods. The menu includes potato soup, farmhouse goat cheeses, Irish stew, Killarney lake trout, Kerry lamb cutlets, Lough Leane salmon, and vegetarian dishes. Open May to October for lunch and dinner. Reservations unnecessary. Michael Collins Pl. (phone: 33104). Inexpensive.

SHARING A PINT: Many of Killarney's pubs are the focus of evening entertainment, particularly in the busy summer season. The most popular place for Irish ballads is the *Laurels* (Main St.). Spontaneous and informal music sessions are often on tap at *Dunloe Lodge* and *Tatler Jack's* (both on Plunkett St.). For a quiet drink and an insight into the Kerry football tradition, try *Buckley's Bar* (2 College St.) — the walls are lined with photos and mementos of this favorite Killarney sport. On long summer evenings, an ideal gathering place is *Birdie's Fun Pub* (off College St.), the town's only bar with an outdoor setting and beer garden atmosphere. Seven miles outside of Killarney, at the entrance to the Gap of Dunloe, it's fun to raise a toast in the rustic setting of *Kate Kearney's Cottage,* a former inn and now a cozy watering hole for all those about to embark on the 7-mile trek through the mountainous Gap.

LIMERICK CITY

The fourth-largest city on the Irish Island (pop. 70,000), Belfast included, offers an engaging introduction to the country for those many, many visitors who begin their tour here after the half-hour trip from Shannon Airport. Limerick is a major port, an inevitable product of its enviable position on the river Shannon, and while the city has a reputation for industry, those it is most famous for are all amiably light: traditional Limerick lace, still produced here; wonderfully cured hams and bacon; salmon fishing; and flour milling.

Limerick (in Irish, *Luimneach*) is a city of narrow streets, handsome Georgian houses, and impressive public buildings such as the Custom House and the Town Hall. This gracious architecture hardly reflects Limerick's violent history, however. Invaded by the Danes in the early 10th century, the area suffered many long years of skirmishing, which ended only when the Vikings were finally crushed by the Irish chieftain Brian Ború. He made Limerick the capital of Munster. In the 12th century, the Anglo-Normans conquered the town, and, settling on the island formed by the river Shannon and its tributary, the Abbey, they built stout walls to keep the natives at bay. This area became known as English Town, and the section across the river as Irish Town.

Undeterred by walls, the Irish continued to make sallies into English Town, led by the King of Munster, Donal Mor O'Brien. Upon his death in 1194, however, the Normans consolidated their position, and in 1210 King John ordered a strong castle and fortified bridge built to control the crossing point of the river Shannon. In later years the city walls were extended for added security.

During the 17th century the city was torn between revolts by the Irish, who seized the city, and sieges by the English under King William III and his followers, the Williamites. The Treaty of Limerick, signed in 1691, was to end hostilities and grant political and religious liberty to the Irish Catholics, but repeated violations of the treaty forced thousands into exile. Many of Limerick's most important landmarks — Thomond Bridge, the city walls, and St. Mary's Cathedral — have associations with these turbulent times. This year, the city is celebrating the 300th anniversary of the Treaty of Limerick with a year-long program of events (see *Special Events* below).

As befits a city that is the major western gateway to Ireland, contemporary Limerick has a great deal to offer besides its ancient history and sites. A roster of activities includes fishing, horseback riding, horse racing, golfing, and swimming and boating on the Shannon. The medieval banquets held at the nearby Bunratty and Knappogue castles, as well as the *céilís* at the Folk Park, offer a delightful — if somewhat rowdy — sampling of traditional Irish hospitality. The countryside surrounding Limerick has a quiet beauty, perfect for a peaceful day's rambling: Low hill ranges ruffle the plains, and small towns rise here and there, each with its ruined castle, abbey, or bridge.

Unlike most Irish cities, Limerick does not have important literary connections. It is, however, the home of the limerick, that famous five-line rhyme derived from a round game in which an individual extemporized a nonsense verse, followed by a chorus that included the words "Will you come up to Limerick?" Over the years the term *limerick* became associated with the rhyme scheme *aabba,* devised by the 19th-century nonsense poet Edward Lear. A typical limerick might go like this:

> There was a fair Irish city,
> That lent its good name to a ditty;
>> Though of dubious worth
>> The verse caused great mirth,
> Now the limerick outshines Limerick City.

LIMERICK AT-A-GLANCE

 SEEING THE CITY: The best view of this rather flat city is from the top of King John's Castle; the key to the building is available from Mrs. Maloney, who lives at 5 Castle St., across from the main entrance. As we went to press, however, the castle was closed for excavations of historic ruins, and it was unknown when it would reopen. Another view of the city is from the spire of St. Mary's Cathedral. Contact the caretaker to gain access to the tower.

 SPECIAL PLACES: Limerick is very compact and most of the important sights are located in one area. As traffic is sometimes congested, the city is best seen on foot.

CITY CENTER

Thomond Bridge – The present bridge, dating from 1840, was designed by Irish architect James Pain to replace the 13th-century structure erected by King John to defend the city. The original had a guardhouse and gate at the west end and a drawbridge at the east end near the castle. The Treaty Stone, on which the famous Treaty of Limerick reputedly was signed in 1691, is on the west side of the new bridge.

Medieval Quarter – Newly restored, this area is bordered by Mary and Castle Streets and the Granary on Michael Street. Among other notable buildings, it includes King John's Castle and St. Mary's Cathedral (see below), as well as a number of almshouses. This year the 300th anniversary of the Treaty of Limerick (see *Special Events*) includes a grand opening of this revived area.

King John's Castle – This fortification at the east foot of Thomond Bridge was built in 1210 by King John to guard the city against invaders. It is one of the oldest examples of Norman architecture in Ireland, with rounded gate towers standing sentry over the curtain walls. In the 18th century, military barracks were installed within the walls, and, later, houses were built in the castle yard, some of which remain. As went to press, the castle was closed indefinitely for excavations of what is believed to be a Viking settlement. For more information, contact the tourist office (phone: 317522).

St. Mary's Cathedral – Established in 1172 by Donal Mor O'Brien, the last King of Munster, it has been restored and extended a number of times and combines features from many different centuries. Note especially the unusual (and unique in Ireland) 15th-century choir stalls whose misericords are carved with many medieval emblems, including those of Richard III. The cathedral is open daily, in summer, 9 AM to 1 PM and 2:30 to 5:30 PM; in winter, 9 AM to 1 PM only. Nicholas and Bridge Sts.

Ball's Bridge – The original structure on this location linked the turf of the conquerers — English Town — with that of the natives — Irish Town. The bridge had no battlements, but rather supported a row of houses. These disappeared in 1830 when the present bridge was constructed.

Limerick Walls – Forming a rough diamond shape, the Limerick walls run east and southeast from Ball's Bridge, along Old Clare and Lelia streets to the grounds of St. John's Hospital. There were four main gates: East Watergate, John's Gate, Mungret Gate, and West Watergate. The largest remaining portion of the walls is behind Lelia Street. Traces of the Black Battery (where a small band of defenders successfully resisted the Williamites) are found on the hospital grounds, while a badly deteriorated bit can be seen from Pike's Row in the direction of High Street. There are two other sections — one forming part of the building housing Sinnotts Joinery Works and the other standing in the Charlotte Quay parking lot.

St. John's Cathedral – Originally intended as a parish church, this Gothic Revival cathedral built in the 19th century eventually became the see of the Catholic diocese. It houses two of Ireland's most remarkable ecclesiastical treasures, the magnificently carved miter and crozier made by Cornelius O'Dea, who was one of Limerick's bishops in the 15th century. At 280 feet, St. John's spire is the highest in Ireland; it's more ornate than the rest of the structure. The memorial to Patrick Sarsfield, hero of the 1690–91 sieges, which is located on the cathedral grounds, was rendered by John Lawlor of Dublin in 1881. At Cathedral Place.

St. John's Square – A few steps from the cathedral, this square constructed around 1751 was once lined with fashionable stone houses owned by the local gentry. The square declined slowly over the years until the 20th century, when the houses were used less glamorously as offices, tenements, barracks, and a butcher shop. Eventually they fell into neglect and were abandoned, but the square has recently undergone restoration and the area is being revived.

Newtown Pery – Just 200 years old, this is the "new" part of Limerick — a grid of streets roughly extending between Sarsfield Street on the north and the Crescent on the south. Named after Edward Sexton Pery, a speaker of the Irish House of Commons, under whose patronage the renovation was begun, the development was distinctly Georgian in character, with townhouses constructed of red brick. In the Crescent is a memorial to Daniel O'Connell, "the Liberator" — founder of the movement for Catholic emancipation — rendered by Irish sculptor John Hogan in 1857.

Granary – Originally opened as a Georgian grain store in 1787, this old building was renovated a decade ago and has become the social and commercial hub of Limerick life. Set among the quays near the river Shannon, it includes a tourist office, the city library, shops, restaurants, and taverns. Open daily year-round. Charlotte Quay, Michael St.

ENVIRONS

Bunratty Castle and Folk Park – The original castle on this site was built in the 15th century by the McNamara family but was appropriated around 1500 by Conor

O'Brien, Earl of Thomond. Refurbished in the 1950s, it is now famous for the colorful medieval banquets presented in the great hall every evening (see *Nightclubs and Nightlife*), but the castle also houses an incredible collection of European paintings, furniture, and tapestries dating from the 14th to the 17th century. From the battlements, the view of the surrounding countryside is splendid — as it was for the earl's warriors. Behind the castle is a model village, with cottages, a replica of a 19th-century hotel, school, doctor's office, pub, post office, print shop, workshops, and exhibits demonstrating how people in different regions of Ireland lived and labored years ago. The castle and folk park are both on the main Ennis road. Admission charge.

Quin Abbey – Although the Franciscan friary, dating from 1402, is now roofless and in ruins, the tombs of the founding McNamara clan are still intact. Quin.

Craggaunowen – This project, like Bunratty, was developed to document lifestyles in Ireland long ago. The complex has both a ring fort dating from early Christian times and a *crannóg*, or lake dwelling (stone hut situated on an island), typical of the Bronze Age. The castle on the grounds is a fortress built by the McNamara family in the 14th century. In the intervening years it suffered neglect, but it is now restored and contains many medieval artifacts. Open daily May to October. Quin (phone: 72178).

Ballycasey Craft Courtyard and Design Centre – The crafts workshops here encompass everything from basketry to leatherwork to pottery. Adjacent to the center stands Balleycaseymore House, a Georgian-style building that contains an international art gallery. Both attractions are open daily year-round. Shannon, 10 miles west of Limerick, about 3 miles from Shannon Airport (phone: 362105).

Lough Gur – Around this lake are found a number of ancient ruins, including stone circles, cairns, dolmens, and *crannógs*. Human bones, weapons, and pottery have all been unearthed here and experts estimate earliest habitation of the site to be 2000 BC. A guide to the area ($1.75) and a self-guided walking tour booklet (75¢) can be obtained from the Limerick Tourist Board. Open daily May to September. 12 miles south of Limerick on the Bruff road (phone: 85186).

Hunt Museum – Donated by Celtic historian John Hunt, who also sponsored the Craggaunowen project in Quin (see above), this is a collection of many artifacts found in Ireland dating from the Bronze and Early Iron ages. Open daily 10 AM to 6 PM May through September. University of Limerick, Plassey House, 3 miles east of Limerick, off the Dublin road (phone: 333644).

Flying Boat Museum – An aviation and maritime center at Foynes (a small town southwest of Limerick City on the Shannon estuary), this museum focuses on Ireland's importance in the development of air travel from the US. In the early days of transatlantic flights, from the 1930s to the mid-1940s, Foynes was a principal landing, takeoff, and berthing port in Europe for flying boats and sea planes. The museum houses a variety of memorabilia and equipment including an original terminal; a working version of the Short brothers' *Sunderland Flying Boat;* radio, navigation, and meteorological devices; and film footage from the flying boat era. There is also a tearoom with 1940s-style decor. Open daily, April through October. Admission charge. Foynes (phone: 69-65416).

■ **EXTRA SPECIAL: Knappogue Castle** – Built in 1467 by the McNamara family, this castle was bought in 1966 by an American and restored to its original 15th-century elegance. Surrounded by lush green pastures and grazing cattle, Knappogue presents an imposing front. The interior is no less impressive, with its soaring ceilings and handsome antique furnishings. Ask to see the owners' magnificent private dining room. Open daily May to October. Admission charge. About 12 miles northwest of Limerick, near Quin (phone: 71103 or *Shannon Castle Banquets,* 61788).

SOURCES AND RESOURCES

 TOURIST INFORMATION: For information, brochures, and maps, visit the Shannonside Tourist Board at the Granary (Michael St.; phone: 317522). The staff can answer questions and make hotel reservations anywhere in Ireland. Guides to Limerick, as well as Clare and Tipperary (IR£1 to IR£1.50), are also available.

Local Coverage – The *Limerick Chronicle,* Ireland's oldest newspaper, and the *Limerick Echo* are published weekly. The *Limerick Leader* is published four times a week. The tourist board's annual *Shannon Region Calendar of Events* gives entertainment schedules.

 TELEPHONE: The area code for Limerick and the immediate vicinity is 61. When calling from within the Republic of Ireland, dial 061 before the local number. As we went to press, the telephone number system in the Limerick City area was in a state of transition, and 5-digit numbers were being expanded to meet the Irish Board Telecom's 6-digit format. If you dial a number that has changed since press time, a recording should inform you of the new number; otherwise, check with the local operator or the tourist office.

 GETTING AROUND: Bus – Service between Dublin, Limerick, and Shannon Airport is frequent and convenient. The terminal, Colbert Station, is on Parnell Street. For departure and arrival schedules, call 313333.

Car Rental – All the major Irish and international firms are represented at Shannon Airport. Car rental companies in the Limerick area include *Bunratty Car Hire* (Coonagh Motors, Coonagh Cross, Caherdavin, Limerick; phone: 52781); *Dan Dooley Rent-a-Car* (Knocklong; phone: 62-53103); *Irish Car Rentals* (Ennis Rd., Limerick; phone: 53049); *Cara Rent-a-Car Ltd.* (Ennis Rd.; phone: 55811); and *Treaty Car Rental* (37 William St., Limerick; phone: 46512). The disc parking system is in effect at 20p per hour. Discs can be purchased at shops and at the tourist office.

Sightseeing – Day tours by bus are operated by *Bus Eireann,* a division of *CIE* (*Córas Iompair Eireann, National Transport Company*), from the railway stations at Limerick (phone: 313333) and Ennis (phone: 65-28038) and by *Gray Line Sightseeing,* at the *Limerick Ryan* hotel (Ennis Rd.; phone: 326211).

Taxi – There are cabstands on Thomas Street, Cecil Street, and Bedford Row, and at Colbert Station. Or call for a taxi from *Conway Cabs* (phone: 43947), *Economy Cabs* (phone: 313235), *Limerick Taxi Co-op* (phone: 55533), *Rapid Taxis* (phone: 311211), or *Speedi Cabs* (phone: 318844).

Walking Tours – Walking tours of Old Limerick are conducted from early June to mid-September; they leave at 3:30 PM from the Granary courtyard; the cost is just over $2. Further information is available from the tourist board (phone: 317522).

 SPECIAL EVENTS: The 300th anniversary of the Treaty of Limerick, signed in 1691 — which attempted to guarantee political and religious liberty to Irish Catholics — will be celebrated thoughout the year with a variety of events, including a gala opening of the city's newly restored Medieval Quarter, concerts, recitals, exhibitions, and sports competitions, ranging from a cycling race and triathlon to an American-style football game — New York's Fordham University vs. Worcester's Holy Cross on November 15–17. For a complete schedule of events, contact the Limerick Treaty 300 Committee (15 Shannon St., Limerick, Ireland; phone: 61-311991). The most important annual event in the Limerick area is the annual *Limerick Civic Week* in mid-March, which features a *St. Patrick's Day* parade, a choral competition, a crafts exhibit, an international band competition, and a charity ball hosted by the mayor. Last year the first *Adare Festival,* featuring the *New Jersey Symphony Orchestra,* the *Irish National Symphony Orchestra,* and various soloists, was held during mid-July at the *Adare Manor* hotel in the village of Adare, near Limerick. As we went to press, it was uncertain whether the festival would be held again this year (for more information, call 201-379-6286 in New Jersey, 800-262-7390, or the *Adare Manor* in Ireland, 61-86150). Other notable events include the *Limerick Flower Festival* in August and the *Limerick Summer Festival* in early July, which features the *Limerick Lady Contest,* country and western music, horse racing, water events, and a big fireworks display.

MUSEUMS: The *Limerick City Gallery of Art* (in People's Park, Pery Sq.; phone: 310633) exhibits modern Irish painting; the *Limerick Civic Museum* (1 St. John's Sq.; phone: 47826) documents local history.

SHOPPING: The latest trend in Limerick is the mid-city shopping mall, such as *Arthur's Quay,* a giant 4-story skylit complex, built in Georgian style to meld with the surrounding architecture on Patrick Street. It boasts a variety of big department stores and boutiques, as well as a food court and covered parking. Other large shopping complexes include *Williams Court* (William St.) and *Spaight's* (Henry St.). For shops with traditional Irish crafts, O'Connell Street is still the best bet, although Ellen and Patrick Streets are also worth browsing.

Bunratty Cottage – Northwest of the city, across the street from Bunratty Castle, this shop is a treasure trove of Irish haute couture — from Limerick lace blouses to Donegal tweed capes and hand-crocheted gowns, as well as Celtic designer jewelry, linen, cyrstal, and more. Bunratty (phone: 364321).

Crystallerie – New and distinctively colored glassware is sold at this small workshop/showroom. Visitors can watch artisans as they fire, blow, and cut the glass. The selection of finished items includes goblets, vases, jewelry, and small statues. 9 Ellen St. (phone: 44904).

Good Shepherd Convent – Famous Limerick lace. Clare St. (phone: 45178).

Irish Handcrafts – This spacious midtown shop offers a wide variety of traditional crafts — tweeds, knitwear, crystal, linen, and souvenirs. 26 Patrick St. (phone: 45504).

Leonard's – A good source for Limerick lace, as well as tweeds, cashmeres, and riding wear. 23 O'Connell St. (phone: 45721).

The Stables – Along "Antique Row" on Ellen Street, this is the best of the antiques shops. 11 Ellen St. (phone: 49363).

Todds – Limerick's major department store sells Irish knits, tweeds, and woolens, Waterford crystal, linen, and more. O'Connell St. (phone: 47222).

White and Gold – Fine china, porcelain, and crystal. 34 O'Connell St. (phone: 49977).

Wool Shop – Slightly off the beaten track, this small one-woman shop is a leading source for hand-knit Irish sweaters made with 100% pure new wool. A variety of yarns is for sale, too. Closed Thursdays afternoons and daily from 1 to 2 PM. 3A Lower Cecil St. (no phone).

SPORTS AND FITNESS: Bicycling – Bikes can be rented from *The Bike Shop* (O'Connell Ave.; phone: 315900); *Nestor Brothers Ltd.* (28 O'Connell St.; phone: 44096); or *Emerald Cycles* (1 Patrick St.; phone: 46983).

Boating – In Killaloe, about 12 miles north of Limerick, cabin boats for cruising the river Shannon and neighboring lakes can be rented from *Derg Line Cruisers* (phone: 76364).

Fishing – To fish for salmon in the Shannon or for trout and grilse in the rivers in and near Limerick, you must obtain a permit or a license from the *Shannon Fisheries,* Thomond Weir, Limerick (phone: 55171).

Golf – The *Limerick Golf Club* (at Ballyclough; phone: 44083), the *Shannon Golf Club* (at the airport; phone: 61020), and the *Castletroy Golf Club* (on the Dublin road; phone: 335261) are open to the public; all rent equipment and have a club-house.

Horseback Riding and Hunting – Horses can be hired at *Ashroe Riding School* (Newport, Co. Tipperary; phone: 378271) and *Clarina Riding Centre* (Clarina; phone: 301187). For hunters, the cost of hiring a horse for a day will run about $60, the cap fee about $80. To make arrangements to join a hunt, contact Bryan Murphy, *Foxhunting Centre of Ireland,* c/o *Dunraven Arms Hotel,* Adare (phone: 396209).

Horse Racing – In this part of horse-crazy Ireland, playing the ponies is a most fitting sin. Place your bet at one of Limerick City's many turf accountant (bookie) offices or at the racetrack. Although the two main events, the *Irish Derby* and the *Irish Grand National,* are both held in County Kildare, the excitement runs as high at the smaller races held at *Greenpark,* in the city's southwestern suburbs, and at *Limerick Junction,* about an hour's drive on the Tipperary road. At both courses there will be 10 or 12 colorful turf accountants; lists of runners and the odds being offered are written on blackboards. "Punters" (gamblers) simply walk up to a turf accountant, hand him the money, name their choice of horse, and receive a betting slip with the man's name on it. Winners return their slips to the turf accountant for their payoff — first allowing another race to lapse so that he can make up his cash.

Tennis – Visitors are always welcome at *Limerick Lawn Tennis Club* (Ennis Rd.; phone: 52316), one of Ireland's oldest tennis centers, which has squash courts and a convivial bar as well.

NIGHTCLUBS AND NIGHTLIFE: The *Belltable Arts Centre* (69 O'Connell St.; phone: 319866) has lunchtime and evening performances by local and touring companies, as well as concerts, exhibits, and other year-round cultural events. *Son et Lumière,* a sound-and-light show portraying the history of Limerick, takes place inside 800-year-old St. Mary's Cathedral (near Thomond Bridge) at 9:15 nightly from mid-June to mid-September. For more information, contact the Shannonside Tourist Board (phone: 317522). The *céilí* offered at Bunratty Folk Park is a program of singing, dancing, and storytelling accompanied by an Irish meal. In a similar vein are the banquets held at Bunratty and Knappogue castles — medieval feasts enlivened by traditional music and historical sketches. Both are on or near the main Limerick–Ennis road; for reservations, call *Shannon Castle Banquets* (phone: 61788). Traditional music concerts, followed by *céilí* dancing with audience participation, are held on various nights year-round (check for information on special weekend concerts) at *Cois na hAbhna* (pronounced Cush-na-*how*-na), the Irish Traditional Cultural Centre (Gort Rd., Ennis; phone: 71166). Irish cabaret, a dinner–plus–variety show, is offered by several hotels in the area, as are discos; check with the tourist office for details. Finally, Limerick has many sing-along pubs, and local papers provide information on these.

BEST IN TOWN

CHECKING IN: Because of its proximity to Shannon Airport, the Limerick City hotel scene embraces part of County Clare (in which the airport is located). Hence, many of the hotels listed here are actually west of the city, between the environs of Shannon and downtown Limerick. Expect to pay $200 and up for a double room in a hotel listed as very expensive, between $100 and $150 in the expensive category, and between $50 and $100 for a moderate room. In addition to the large hotels, there are numerous small guesthouses, for which reservations can be made at the tourist board. All telephone numbers are in the 61 area code unless otherwise indicated.

Adare Manor – About 10 miles south of Limerick, this 19th-century Tudor-Gothic mansion is set on the banks of the river Maigue, amid an 840-acre estate. It's the former home of the Earls of Dunraven but was acquired by American owners several years ago; completely restored, it opened as a hotel in 1988. The interior includes barrel-vaulted ceilings, 15th-century Flemish doors, ornate marble fireplaces, the 2-story Long Gallery banquet hall, and an oak-paneled restaurant with views of the river and gardens. There are 64 antiques-furnished bedrooms, each with private bath. Guest activities include salmon and trout fishing, horseback riding, and nature trails. There also is an indoor pool and a fitness center, and an 18-hole golf course designed by Robert Trent Jones, Sr., is under construction, and expected to be ready this year. Adare (phone: 396566). Very expensive.

Dromoland Castle – Unadulterated luxury prevails at this renovated and regal former O'Brien stronghold. Besides 73 large, comfortable bedrooms and suites, it offers 18 holes of golf, horseback riding, tennis, fishing, and pheasant shooting within its spacious grounds. The dining room is formal, as befits a palace, and the food is excellent. Newmarket-on-Fergus (phone: 71144). Very expensive.

Fitzpatrick's Shannon Shamrock – A modern, ranch-style property, owned and managed by two generations of the Fitzpatrick family, who also have major hotels in Dublin and Cork, this hostelry is set back from the main Limerick road amid extensive gardens and grounds, next to Bunratty Castle. Scheduled for completion early this year are 20 additional bedrooms and suites, bringing the total number of rooms to 120. All rooms recently have been refurbished with designer fabrics, many with half-canopy beds, and each room has a remote control TV set. There is a heated pool, a sauna, a lively bar, and a shop. The restaurant serves French and Irish fare. There is ample parking, and a courtesy minibus shuttles guests to and from Shannon Airport. Bunratty (phone: 361177). Expensive.

Jurys – Just over the bridge from the city center, overlooking the river Shannon, this modern hotel offers efficient service and has 100 well-appointed rooms. Its restaurant, the *Copper Room* (see *Eating Out*), is particularly good, and there is also a pub and a coffee shop. Ennis Rd. (phone: 55266). Expensive.

Limerick Inn – This is a modern, comfortable motel with 153 rooms, a continental restaurant that's very good, and service well above average. Amenities include a leisure center with a swimming pool and a gym, plus tennis courts and a putting green. Ennis Rd. (phone: 51544). Expensive.

Clare Inn – With wide-windowed views of the Shannon estuary, this contemporary property is particularly appealing to golf enthusiasts, since it is surrounded by the 18-hole golf course of neighboring *Dromoland Castle.* There also is a new health and fitness center with a heated indoor pool, Jacuzzi, sauna, steamroom, and gym.

The modern rooms offer lovely views of the surrounding County Clare country-side, including the Shannon estuary. Other facilties include a restaurant, a lounge featuring weekend entertainment, and a coffee shop. Newmarket-on-Fergus (phone: 71161). Moderate.

Dunraven Arms – Dating back to the 19th century, this family-run inn is the centerpiece of the picturesque little town of Adare, 10 miles south of Limerick. The 44 guestrooms vary in size and decor, but all have private baths, cable TV, and direct-dial phones. There is also a restaurant, a cozy Old World bar, and lovely gardens. Horseback riding or fox hunting can be easily arranged for guests. Adare (phone: 396209). Moderate.

Limerick Ryan – Part of the dependable Ryan chain, it has 184 rooms and a restaurant. Ennis Rd. (phone: 53922). Moderate.

Two Mile Inn – Named for its location just outside Limerick, this modern hotel (a Best Western affiliate) has a domed atrium, 125 rooms, and a restaurant serving local specialties such as Limerick ham, Burren lamb, and Shannon salmon. Ennis Rd. (phone: 53122). Moderate.

For an extra-special treat, spend the night in a fully staffed, Georgian-style manor house on the grounds of *Dromoland Castle. Thomond House* is the private residence and seat of the Rt. Hon. Lord Inchiquin, Conor Myles John O'Brien, head of the O'Brien clan and the only man in Ireland to hold a British peerage and an Irish chieftaincy. He now welcomes visitors into his home as "private houseguests." There are 5 deluxe bedrooms, each with private bath and views of the 900-acre estate. Lord Inchiquin, in grand fashion, presides over nightly dinners in the candlelit dining room. Rates are approximately $200 per day per person, including breakfast and dinner, available April through October or mid-November. For further information, contact Lord or Lady Inchiquin, Thomond House, Newmarket-on-Fergus (phone: 71304).

EATING OUT: Although it's never been known for its wealth of restaurants, the Limerick-Shannon area has added some distinguished eateries, and you won't be disappointed with a meal at any of the places recommended below. Expect to pay $60 and up for dinner for two (not counting wine) in places listed as expensive, between $30 and $55 in moderate ones, and less than $30 in those listed as inexpensive. All telephone numbers are in the 61 area code unless otherwise indicated.

Copper Room – The best in the downtown area, this rather small but attractive restaurant in *Jurys* hotel offers excellently prepared French fare. Service is efficient and friendly. Open for dinner only; closed Sundays. Ennis Rd. (phone: 55266). Expensive.

MacCloskeys – Encompassing the former mews and wine cellars of Bunratty House, a restored 1804 mansion, this appealing candlelit restaurant is the creation of Gerry and Marie MacCloskey. The cuisine is "French with an Irish flair," with such specialties as Dover sole, rack of lamb, pheasant, and lobster. Open for dinner only; closed Sundays and Mondays. Bunratty Folk Park, Bunratty (phone: 364082). Expensive.

Rose Cottage Mustard Seed – In a historic Old World village setting, this thatch-roofed cottage dining spot is known for its beef Wellington as well as such innovative dishes as scallops and stir-fried vegetables, black grape sorbet, and Baileys and hazelnut ice cream. Open for dinner only; closed Sundays and Mondays and in February. Adare (phone: 396451). Expensive to moderate.

Cronin's – An old house right in the middle of the village of Newmarket-on-Fergus is the setting for this combination restaurant-pub. At any time of day, Irish stew, soup, and snacks are available in the wood-paneled bar lounge, while the adjoining dining room makes an elegant setting to enjoy dinners of filet of beef *en croûte,* *paupiettes* of trout with blue cheese sauce, or prawn tails thermidor. Open daily for lunch and dinner. Main St., Newmarket-on-Fergus (phone: 71157). Moderate.

Restaurant de la Fontaine – Located on the second floor of a downtown storefront building, this charming bistro and wine bar features *cuisine moderne* in the heart of Limerick. The menu includes such dishes as beef flambé, with peppercorns and foie gras; mignons of pork with asparagus; breast of chicken stuffed with smoked salmon and topped with a whiskey and hazelnut cream sauce; and "symphony of the sea," an assortment of fresh seafood presented in watercress and lime sauce. Closed Sundays. 12 Gerald Griffin St. (phone: 44461). Moderate.

Rowan Berry – Part of the Ballycasey craft complex near Shannon Airport, this small eatery is ideal for lunch or a light meal. The offerings include shepherd's pie, homemade scones and pastries, garden vegetable soup, salads, and seafood platters, as well as more predictable fare like pizza, lasagna, and quiche. Closed Sundays. Ballycasey Craft Centre, Shannon (phone: 362105). Inexpensive.

SHARING A PINT: There's always a welcome at *Hogan's* (72 Catherine St.). Known for its cozy snug, chiming antique clock, and small nooks that surround the classic old bar, this pub has been in the same family (named Ryan, not Hogan) for nearly 100 years. A literary atmosphere prevails at the *James Joyce* (4 Ellen St.), where a bust of the author dominates the modern decor, which also includes Joycean photos, sketches, and quotes. *Nancy Blake's* (19 Denmark St.) is a quiet, friendly little pub where local working people drink. The oak-beamed *Vintage Club* (9 Ellen St.) used to be a wine store, so the wines available range from the pedestrian to the extraordinary. The place also serves bar snacks — salads, soup, sandwiches — and attracts a youngish crowd in the late evening, when it can become crowded. The *Olde Tom* (19 Thomas St.) is a family-run place known for its pub meals and fresh salads during the day; in the evenings for impromptu music sessions, dancing, and poetry readings. *Durty Nelly's,* which may be the best-known pub in Ireland, is about 10 miles from Limerick City, right next door to Bunratty Castle. Although often jammed with both tourists and locals, the place is quite attractive and has a restaurant called the *Oyster,* which offers light meals and sandwiches. If you're lucky, you might also catch some music. If *Durty Nelly's* is too crowded, cross the road to *Fibber McGee's,* which features nightly musical entertainment and disco. About 15 miles northeast of Limerick at Birdhill, on the main Dublin road (N7), is a replica of a 19th-century farmer's pub called *Matt the Thresher.* The cottage-like surroundings are replete with open fireplaces, antique furnishings, traditional snugs, and agricultural memorabilia. There's also a full-service restaurant, as well as a wide spectrum of pub grub.

LONDONDERRY

Londonderry — more popularly known by its original name, Derry — is Northern Ireland's second most important city. Although only 75 miles from Belfast, its position in the northwest corner of the country traditionally has rendered it remote from Northern Ireland's other population centers. This condition has been a disadvantage in some ways, but it has served to slow the rate of change and preserve the city's historic character and appearance. A friendly place for strolling, with quiet Georgian corners, Londonderry gives visitors the feeling of a cozy village.

For those who live in the working city, it's the kind of place, says one bartender, where "you can't pretend to be what you're not, because we all know what your grandfather did." It's a cohesive city, even though its very name causes confusion — and rankles Nationalists in both the North and the Republic. Some still consider the prefix *London* — added to Derry in the early 17th century during the controversial Plantation period — an unwelcome intrusion. Today, as discussion and dissension about this matter continue, some have chosen to cope with the issue with some humor by using the name Stroke City, and writing *London/Derry.* Whatever they call their city, its citizens are warm-hearted, good-natured people who have remained so in spite of "the troubles," both recent and historic.

Progress is, however, now beginning to catch up with Londonderry, which is becoming increasingly modernized. With the worst of the bombings in the latest round of internecine battles now more than a decade past, relative relaxation has returned, and it's back to the economic basics, with everybody most interested in keeping the city on its course of commercial invigoration. Firms are encouraged to relocate to the area in an effort to create jobs for a city that has one of the worst unemployment rates in Western Europe. A strong civic pride has surfaced in response to extensive redevelopment in the past 15 years, which has resulted in a city that looks — and feels — attractive, from most angles. Londonderry sports a growing university town atmosphere, as a result of the city's Magee College, now a part of the University of Ulster. The University's College of Tourism, in particular, attracts many students from abroad.

The influx of new people recalls hundreds of thousands who emigrated over several centuries, sailing from Derry's quays, behind the present Guildhall. Most often, it was from economic necessity, and departure was a wrench, as exemplified by the lyrics of the Irish ballad "Danny Boy," sung to the "Londonderry Air," a poignant melody popularized in the 19th century: "'Tis you, 'tis you must go and I must bide." Unfortunately, a lack of jobs still forces many Derry sons and daughters to seek employment on distant shores, but, as one young man expressed it, "Most want to come back. They get withdrawal symptoms very easily." In all, Londonderry's air today is one of cautious optimism. Not only as a doorway to Donegal, but for its own rewards as well, the city deserves a visit.

Derry — derived from the Gaelic word *doire* (oak grove) — was a densely wooded hilltop when St. Columba (Columcille), fleeing a plague in Donegal, arrived in AD 546 to establish his first abbey. During the ensuing centuries, the religious settlement became known as Derry Columcille. The abbey was burned down by piratical Danes in 812 — the first of a succession of invasions Derry was to endure. Neither the Vikings, who marauded in the area for a few hundred years from the 9th century onward, nor the Normans, who crossed the river Bann and headed west in the 12th century, seem to have left much behind except footprints. Nevertheless, the city continued to grow in size and importance, and the magnificent medieval church Templemore was built in about 1164.

Like other Irish cities, Derry came under English control when King Henry II claimed Ireland in the 12th century. The skirmishes that followed did not seriously damage the city until the 1566 rebellion led by Ulster chieftain Shane O'Neill, during which Templemore was destroyed. Queen Elizabeth I sent a small army to fortify Derry, but it failed and withdrew. In 1600, an English army led by Sir Henry Docwra besieged and took possession of the city. Docwra called for the erection of huge earthen bulwarks to protect Derry against further invasions, but in 1608 the Irish chieftain Cahir O'Doherty raided the city, and once again it was ruthlessly sacked. O'Doherty was later killed and his lands confiscated.

With the accession of James I to the English throne in 1603, Derry was made a satellite of the city of London, with the resulting name change to Londonderry. The city fell subject to the policy of Plantation, whereby lands forfeited by vanquished Irish leaders were distributed among English and Scottish colonists. Estates went for a nickel an acre, and the newly created hereditary title of baronet sold for the equivalent of $2,500. The Baron of Belfast, Sir Arthur Chichester, was given the task of selling the city of Londonderry and the district to the Livery Companies (tradesmen associations) of the city of London, at that time the wealthiest corporation on earth. With varying degrees of enthusiasm, the big dozen — clothmakers, tailors, ironmongers, mercers, vintners, salters, drapers, haberdashers, fishmongers, grocers, goldsmiths, and skinners — began to settle the whole area between the river Foyle, the Sperrin Mountains, and the lower river Bann. From 1614 to 1617, the Society of the Governors and Assistants of London of the New Plantation in Ulster within the Realm of Ireland or, more simply, the Irish Society — which still is the ground landlord in Londonderry — built the famous one-mile-long, 18-foot-thick (on average) city walls, made of earth faced with stone. They did an excellent job: Today, the fortifications are the most nearly complete city walls left in Britain. The Plantation of Ulster, of which Derry and its history have formed so significant a part, strained the resources of the city of London and its Livery Companies to the limit. This financial drain played a major role in the catastrophic rift that gradually grew between the commoners and the crown, which in turn helped pave the way toward civil war.

During the 17th century, Londonderry successfully withstood three more sieges, which added to the veracity of her centuries-old epithet "Maiden City," given in recognition of the fact that she has never succumbed to the besieging blandishments of any suitor. In 1641 the Irish rose yet again against the English, and in 1648, during the English Civil War, Derry underwent a 4-month attack by Royalist forces. But it was the third siege that was most memorable.

On December 7, 1688, troops loyal to England's deposed Roman Catholic King James II advanced to the walled city of Londonderry to claim it. (James needed a foothold in Ireland with which to secure his claim to the English crown.) However, their demand for admission to the city at the Ferryquay Gate was met with hesitation by the city fathers who, although not wanting to oppose James openly — he was still their lawful monarch — favored the Protestant William, husband of James's daughter Mary as well as prince of Holland's House of Orange. Deliberation on the issue ended abruptly when a group of 13 apprentice boys took the decision into their own hands, yanking up the drawbridge at Ferryquay and slamming the doors, shutting James out. For a time, James waited by Londonderry's walls, but he eventually wearied of the "obstinate wretches" and retired.

In April 1689, James II resumed in earnest the siege of Londonderry, which was to last an additional 105 days and become, according to 19th-century English historian Thomas Macaulay, "the most memorable siege in the annals of the British Isles." Jacobite troops shelled the city and this time blockaded the river Foyle, throwing a boom across it — at the point where the new Foyle Bridge now spans — to prevent the passage of provision ships. The strategy was to starve the inhabitants into submission. The only person who deserted the city during its difficulties was the governor, Colonel Lundy, who ended his dishonorable term by advising surrender and then escaping from the city by climbing down a pear tree that stood just outside the city walls. (From that year to this, Lundy has been hanged in effigy for his perfidy.) Lundy was succeeded by Reverend George Walker, under whose leadership the city's 30,000 citizens held firm.

Provisions for Londonderry's population soon ran short. Hunger-enfeebled soldiers and civilians seized upon dogs, cats, and rats for food. Contemporary price lists show that a lean mouse cost sixpence; a rat, fattened by human flesh, fetched one shilling and twopence; and a quart of horse's blood brought one shilling and a penny. The inevitable result was disease. More than 7,000 perished, all within sight of a fleet of food-filled ships lying at anchor just beyond the blockade. Nevertheless, when James's troops fired a hollowed cannonball at St. Columb's Cathedral that carried a message with the terms for an armistice, Derry's citizens staunchly replied, "No surrender" — which ever since has been the watchword of the city and of Ulster's Loyal Orange lodges.

Finally, on July 30, 1689, the relief ship *Mountjoy* burst the barrier across the Foyle. In the fighting that followed, "high above the thunder of the Irish guns arose the clamour of the Cathedral bells, and the ramparts blazed with bonfires." That day, the siege was broken, and each year the event is recalled by special celebrations in the city. Not quite a year later, in 1690, on July 1 — which became July 12 when the calendar was changed in the 18th century

— James II finally lost his throne to "King Billy" (William III) at the Battle of the Boyne, fought near Drogheda in the Irish Republic.

From early in the 18th century and continuing into the 19th, Londonderry served as the principal port for the wave of emigrants who left Ulster for New World opportunities across the Atlantic. So many Ulster men and women sailed from Derry Quay to America that they became the second most numerous element in the colonial population (the English being the most numerous at that time). Ulster immigrants played a prominent part in the American Revolution as well as in the settlement of the western frontier. (For more information, see "Ulster–American Folk Park" in *Fermanagh Lakelands,* DIRECTIONS.) Londonderry also served as a major port of embarkation for the mass migrations from all over Ireland as a result of the potato crop failures and famines of the mid- to late-19th century.

In World War II, as the first port across the Atlantic for US and Canadian supply convoys, Derry was tremendously important to the Allies. Many North American troops received early training here for what would eventually be the *D-Day* invasion of Normandy. (The Republic of Ireland declared neutrality during the war, so its ports were closed to the Allies.) In addition to thousands of US Navy personnel in port during the war, at least 5,000 US Army staffers were stationed in Derry, which had a major underground communications center at Magee College. US soldiers were active socially in the community, and the army's Springtown camp remained operative until the mid-1960s.

Derry's more recent history has been less ennobled. After what can be seen as a classic case of gerrymandering in the creation of two new electoral constituencies in Derry in 1966 — which served to exacerbate the conflicts between the Unionists (largely Protestants who wished Northern Ireland would remain part of the United Kingdom) and the Nationalists (mostly Catholics who wanted Ulster to rejoin the Irish Republic) — on October 5, 1968, the first confrontation in the city's current round of "troubles" occurred between civil rights demonstrators and the police. A period of conflict ensued, which, by August 12, 1969, resulted in a state of siege in the Catholic neighborhood of Bogside. Violence was a sadly familiar face on the community during the 1970s. Bombings resulted in the destruction of some buildings and monuments. The remains of some of these — such as Walker's Monument, erected on Royal Bastion of the city walls in 1828 — have been left as memorials to this period and are pointed out by city tour guides. However, visitors to today's Derry generally will find the city cleared of the rubble of the past and its citizens enthusiastically looking ahead.

LONDONDERRY AT-A-GLANCE

SEEING THE CITY: A line in an Irish ballad expresses it thus: "Sure they call it lovely Derry on the banks of the Foyle." And it is a lovely city. Crested by the spires of St. Columb's Cathedral, Londonderry is set on an exposed hill that rises from the Foyle River Valley, ringed by distant hills.

From all sides, green fingers of open land reach in toward the city walls. The best vantage point for views within the city is the roof of O'Doherty Fort Interpretive Centre, which rises well above the city walls. From here, one can see Derry's distinctive, sturdy houses with their brightly colored façades steeply terraced on the hillsides; several steeples that seem to spear clouds from the sky; and the long brick buildings that were linen-shirt factories, a legacy of the mid-19th century. The surrounding walls themselves, however, provide splendid perspectives of sights within the city and over the peaceful landscape well beyond. Other fine views of Derry are available from Brook Park, from along the Waterside district on the opposite banks of the Foyle, and from the Foyle Bridge.

SPECIAL PLACES: The city within the walls, which are roughly rectangular in shape and about a mile in total length, retains its original 17th-century layout, with four main streets radiating from a center square (called the Diamond) to the original gates: Shipquay, Ferryquay (the gate closed against James II by the 13 apprentices in 1688), Butchers, and Bishop. These have all been rebuilt over the centuries, and three newer gates have been added. The main street of the compact city within the walls begins at the Shipquay Gate. As Shipquay Street — arguably the steepest street in Ireland — rises to the Diamond, it exudes a decidedly Georgian flavor, although most of the buildings date from Victorian times. Continuing straight across the Diamond, the road becomes Bishop Street. Along its several blocks before the street reaches Bishop's Gate at the top are many of the city's finest buildings: the Northern Counties Club; the 1830 Deanery, with its fine classical Georgian doorway; The Honourable Irish Society headquarters, inscribed with the date 1764; and the Courthouse. Derry has several good Georgian residential rowhouse terraces, in particular those on Clarendon, Queen, and Bishop Streets.

The Walls – Londonderry's most notable physical feature, the walls, form a terrace walk around the inner city. Each bastion has its own name and story. Coward's Bastion, near O'Doherty's Fort, is so named because it was the safest sector of the city during the siege. On Double Bastion, between Butcher's and Bishop's gates, is Roaring Meg, a brass cannon from 1642 that is a relic of the siege. The cannon, which got its name from the violent bang that heralded its use, overlooks the area from which Jacobite troops attacked the city. As we went to press, the walls were being cleaned and refurbished, and it was uncertain whether visitors would be able to walk on the walls after the project is complete. For current information and for guided tours of the city walls, inquire at the tourist board; see *Tourist Information,* below.

WITHIN THE WALLS

St. Columb's Cathedral – The Church of Ireland Cathedral is the most historic building in Londonderry. Begun in 1628 and finished in 1633, it has undergone much restoration and alteration, although its façade remains basically the simple, austere, well-proportioned Planter's Gothic. The nearby city walls rise higher in this picturesque precinct to protect the cathedral, which fired cannons from its bastions during the 1689 siege. Just inside the door is the hollowed cannonball that was shot into the churchyard with the proposed terms of surrender; elsewhere in the cathedral and in the chapterhouse, other city artifacts are displayed, including locks and keys from the four original gates. A 20-minute video recalls city history and the role of the cathedral in it. Open daily 9 AM to 1 PM and 2 to 5 PM. London St. (phone: 262746).

O'Doherty Fort – Mellowed stones were used to construct this modern castle, which serves as the interpretive center for visitors to the city. The view from the roof is exceptional. Call for details about visiting hours and current exhibitions. Magazine St., inside the walls, opposite the Guildhall (phone: 365151, ext. 205).

Courthouse – Designed by John Bowden, constructed of white sandstone in 1813, the Courthouse is one of Ireland's best examples of Greek Revival architecture. The portico is modeled after the Temple of Erechtheus in Athens. Bishop St.

Bishop's Gate – The most memorable of the city's four original gates, Bishop's was extended upward into a triumphal arch by William III in 1789, on the centenary of the great siege. Sculptured faces on either side of the arch are river gods of the Foyle and the Boyne. At the top of Bishop St., which rises from the Diamond.

WITHOUT THE WALLS

Guildhall – The Guildhall was built in Tudor Gothic style of red sandstone from Antrim in 1890. Its richly decorated façade has mullioned and transomed windows and a four-faced chiming spire clock that is one of the largest in Britain. Striking stained glass windows throughout the building illustrate almost every episode of note in the city's compelling history. The assembly hall, where concerts and other special events are held, has a decorated timber ceiling and one of the finest organs in Europe. Open 9 AM to 4 PM Mondays through Fridays. It's best to call ahead for an appointment for a guided tour. At the foot of Shipquay St. (phone: 365151).

Derry Quay – Celebrated in song and story, often sadly, Derry Quay (the popular name for the Foyle Quay), behind the Guildhall, was the embarkation point for hundreds of thousands of Irish emigrants — including the ancestors of several US presidents — who crossed the Atlantic in the 18th and 19th centuries. A small monument recalls the mass emigrations. Foyle Embankment, behind the Guildhall.

St. Eugene's Cathedral – The Roman Catholic cathedral, with its lofty granite spire, was finished in 1873. Built in Gothic Revival style, it is tall and airy, with exceptional stained glass windows depicting the Crucifixion. In the Catholic district called Bogside; reached from Strand Rd. along Great James St.

Long Tower Church (St. Columba's) – Just outside the city walls to the southwest, this church was built in 1784, and reconstructed in 1908, on the site of the former Templemore (one of the great Irish medieval churches, built in 1164 and destroyed in 1566). The church, which seats 2,000, features attractive hand-carved woodwork, an unusual sloping balcony, and stained glass. The splendid altarpiece of contrasting marbles displays ancient Corinthian column heads that were the gift of Bishop Hervey (see "Downhill" in *Antrim Coast,* DIRECTIONS). The edifice is surrounded by a complex of church schools, and the view from the churchyard across grassy slopes to the city walls is lovely. Long Tower St.

ENVIRONS

Strabane – Americans find Strabane of interest principally because of *Gray's Printing Shop* (see below), which dates from the 18th century and is still in operation. In the room where some 19th-century presses remain, John Dunlap and James Wilson served as apprentices. Dunlap was the first of the two men to emigrate to Philadelphia, where he founded America's first daily newspaper, *The Pennsylvania Packet.* In 1776 he printed the Declaration of Independence from Thomas Jefferson's original manuscript. He was also a captain in General George Washington's bodyguard. By 1807, Wilson too had emigrated to Philadelphia, where he became a judge and a newspaper editor and, eventually, the grandfather of Woodrow Wilson, the 28th President of the United States.

Gray's Printing Shop (49 Main St., Strabane; phone: 504-884094) is open 9 AM to 1 PM and 2 to 5:30 PM year-round, except Thursdays, Sundays, and bank holidays; the 19th-century hand printing presses are on display daily except Thursdays and Sundays, 2 to 5:30 PM April to September. Admission charge. John Dunlap was born at 21 Meetinghouse St., which is marked by a plaque.

Strabane is reached on A5 south from Londonderry, along the river Foyle. Take the pretty, unclassified road eastward to Plumbridge to enter the wild and lovely landscape of the Sperrin Mountains. At Plumbridge, follow B47 for the scenic splendors of the Glenelly Valley. Continue to Draperstown, then swing north and west on B40, B74, and A6 to return to Londonderry.

SOURCES AND RESOURCES

 TOURIST INFORMATION: The Derry Tourist Board (Foyle St.; phone: 267284) is opposite the bus station, near the colorfully painted Craigavon Bridge. Information, maps, and pamphlets on the area are free; the *Derry City Council Official Guide* costs $1.50. Open 9 AM to 1 PM and 2 to 5 PM Mondays to Fridays year-round, and Saturdays June through August. As Londonderry is the doorway to County Donegal in the Republic, the tourist center is also staffed by Bord Fáilte, the Irish tourist board, during peak travel periods (phone: 369501).

Local Coverage – In addition to the daily *Belfast Telegraph,* the *Derry Journal* is published on Tuesdays and Fridays and the *Sentinel* on Wednesdays.

 TELEPHONE: The area code for Londonderry and the immediate vicinity is 504. When calling from within Northern Ireland, dial 0504 before the local number.

GETTING AROUND: Walking is the best way to discover the charms of this friendly city. Within the walls, Londonderry is very compact, although it is steep in spots and flights of stone stairs lead to the tops of the walls.

Airport – Derry is served by Eglinton Airport, 8 miles from the city, which has regular flights to and from Glasgow and Dublin (phone: 810784). Belfast International Airport can be reached by train; disembark at the Antrim stop, 3 miles from the airport.

Bus – There is regular bus service to surrounding towns and to coastal resorts in County Donegal, as well as daily coach and express service to Belfast and Dublin and weekend service to London and Glasgow. For more detailed information, contact *Ulsterbus* (phone: 262261/2/3/4) and the *Londonderry and Lough Swilly Railway Co.* (phone: 262017). Bus station, Foyle St.

Car Rental – Derry has three car rental firms: *Eakin Brothers* (Maydown; phone: 860601), *Hertz* (173 Strand Rd.; phone: 260420), and *Vehicle Services* (Campsie; phone: 810832).

Taxi – There usually are a few taxis waiting at the railway station. In addition, there are several radio taxi services: *Blue Star* (phone: 648888), *Central Taxi* (phone: 61911), *Foyle Car Service and Taxi* (phone: 63905), and *Quick Cabs* (phone: 260515).

Train – *Northern Ireland Rail* operates six trains to and from Belfast Mondays through Saturdays and two trains on Sundays. Waterside Station, Duke St. (phone: 42228).

 SPECIAL EVENTS: Derry has an important cultural heritage. The *Londonderry Feis* (festival), held for a week during February or March, features music, drama, ballet, and speeches. *Feis Dhoire Cholmcille,* with Irish songs, dancing, and instrumental music, is held during *Easter Week* at various venues (such as Guildhall, St. Columb's Hall). Programs may include works by Derry natives Seamus Heaney, the poet, or Brian Friel, the playwright. For more information, contact the tourist board on Foyle St. (phone: 267284).

MUSEUMS: Ballyarnet Field – This is the farm field where Amelia Earhart, the first woman to fly across the Atlantic Ocean solo, brought down her plane on May 21, 1932. The field, which is part of 150 acres of wildlife conservation property, contains a sculptured memorial and a reconstructed cottage where exhibits of photographs and other memorabilia are on display. Call for exhibit information and hours. At Culmore, 1½ miles beyond Foyle Bridge, off Muff Rd., B194 (phone: 53379 or the tourist office).

Foyle Valley Railway Centre – Derry once had four railway lines emanating from it, two standard and two narrow-gauge. This museum houses railroad memorabilia, including steam engines and historic railway displays. Visitors are able to take a short picturesque ride on one of the old trains, departing from Craigavon Bridge. Open Tuesdays through Saturdays from 10 AM to 5 PM and on Sundays from 2 to 6 PM. Admission charge. Foyle Rd. (phone: 265234).

Orchard Gallery – Exhibitions of contemporary and traditional art and craftwork by local, national, and international artists are on display here. The gallery also organizes a schedule of small theater events, films, music, and lectures. Orchard St. (phone: 269675).

SHOPPING: The *Richmond Shopping Complex* (on the Diamond) offers a variety of stores in a single mall. Housed in *Craft Village* (Ship and Quay Sts.) is a collection of shops selling handmade Irish gifts, clothes, and quilts. Most shops in Derry are open 9 AM to 5:30 PM Mondays through Wednesdays, and Saturdays; late night shopping, until 9 PM, is on Thursdays and Fridays.

Arts and Crafts Centre – Supplies — paints, paper, and more — for the artist. Bishop St. (phone: 268402).

Austin's – Derry's main department store, it has a restaurant. The Diamond (phone: 261817).

Bookworm – Traditional Irish literature and recordings. Bishop St. (phone: 261616).

Donegal Shop – A good place to purchase the area's famous tweeds. 8 Shipquay St. (phone: 266928).

Gordon Gallery – The work of established Irish artists. Ferryquay St. (phone: 266261).

Ulster Ceramics – Pottery, kitchenware, tableware, Irish crystal, and table linens — all at factory shop prices. Springtown Industrial Estate, Buncrana Rd. (phone: 265742).

SPORTS AND FITNESS: Boating – Sailboats, rowboats, and power boats are available for hire along the East Bank for 2 miles upstream from Craigavon Bridge. Contact *Prehen Boat Hires* (phone: 43405).

Fishing – The fishing in the river Foyle and its tributaries is legendary. Coarse fishing requires no license; a game rod license for salmon and trout (sea, brown, and rainbow) can be obtained from the *Foyle Fisheries Commission* (8 Victoria Rd.; phone: 42100). Sea fishing is possible from pier or boats. For more information, contact the fisheries commission.

Fitness Centers – The Derry area has several public fitness centers offering swimming pools, squash courts, saunas, weight rooms, and other facilities. For more information, contact the tourist board.

Golf – The 18-hole *City of Derry Golf Club*, which also has a 9-hole practice course, is sprawled scenically along the shores of the river Foyle. Open to the public, the course is in Prehen, 2 miles south of the city on the Strabane road (phone: 42610).

Soccer – *Brandywell Stadium* is home to the *Derry City Football Club*, which has won its way into the premier division of the League of Ireland. On Sundays when the team plays at home, the entire city "goes mad" over the event, which attracts whole families and those of both religious persuasions to what has become a highly popular outlet for civic pride. The stadium is in the Brandywell district. For ticket information, contact the *Derry City Football Club,* Crawford Sq. (phone: 262276).

 THEATER: There is no established theater in Derry, but productions are mounted in St. Columb's Hall auditorium (seating 1,000) or in the complex's *Little Theatre* (seating 100), which serves several thriving amateur theater groups (box office phone: 262880). The *Guildhall* periodically hosts full-scale dramatic productions, including premieres by Derry playwright Brian Friel; for ticket information, contact the Derry City Council Recreation Department (phone: 365151). North of the city center, Magee College of the University of Ulster also stages theater productions (phone: 265621). Visitors also can reserve tickets for most city events at the *Rialto Entertainment Centre,* Market St. (phone: 260516).

 MUSIC: The city has an especially strong musical tradition, and there are still many families in which every member plays an instrument. In his song "The Town I Love So Well," Derryman Phil Coulter, composer and pianist, writes: "There was music there in the Derry air / Like a language that we all could understand. . . ." The *Guildhall* (at the foot of Shipquay St.) is the major city entertainment venue. Its lovely, acoustically superb assembly hall, which seats 700, is the site for performances by the *Ulster Orchestra,* as well as for jazz concerts, organ recitals, cabaret, and other events. Contact Derry City Council Recreation Department (phone: 265151). The *Orchard Gallery* also hosts varied musical events at St. Columb's Hall (Orchard St.; phone: 69675), and the *Everglades* hotel (Prehen Rd.; phone: 46722) offers live piano music nightly from 9 to 11 PM.

BEST IN TOWN

CHECKING IN: Although there are no luxurious hotels to recommend within Londonderry, there are several commendable ones in the immediate vicinity, all with restaurants. The one rated expensive costs $100 or more per night for a double room with a traditional Irish breakfast, those rated as moderate range from $60 to $100, and inexpensive, under $40. Bed and breakfast accommodations in the area range from $30 to $40. The tourist board has information on vacancies. All telephone numbers are in the 504 area code unless otherwise indicated.

Everglades – Set amid landscaped gardens and facing the Foyle, 2 miles south of the city, this modern, 2-story, 58-room property is the best place to stay near Londonderry. It offers 24-hour room service, elegant dining, a bar lounge, piano music (9 PM to midnight Mondays, Wednesdays, Fridays, and Saturdays), and other amenities. Prehen Rd., across the Foyle (phone: 46722 or 44414). Expensive.

Glen House – This cozy place is on the tree-lined main street of a pretty village that was founded by the Grocers' Company during the Plantation era and retains an English appearance. It is a full-service, 16-room hotel with a fine restaurant 9 miles northeast of Londonderry, on the road to Limavady. 9 Main St., Eglinton (phone: 810527). Moderate.

Waterfoot Inn – This new, modern hotel, with 33 rooms (all with private bath, telephone, and a color TV set), is in the Waterside district. There's also a bar and a restaurant (see *Eating Out*). Caw Roundabout, Clooney Rd. (phone: 45500). Moderate.

White Horse Inn – A modern 44-room establishment built around an old pub. Its *Grille Bar* restaurant is a local favorite (see *Eating Out*). For those in search of exercise, there are squash courts. Northeast of Londonderry, on the road to Limavady. 68 Clooney Rd., Campsie (phone: 860606). Moderate.

Clarence House – Within walking distance of the city center, this guesthouse has 7 rooms, none with private bath. 15 Northland Rd. (phone: 265342). Inexpensive.

 EATING OUT: Regional food specialties include Foyle salmon, Donegal lobster, locally cured Londonderry ham and bacon, and Ballarena smoked fish. A three-course meal for two, including service and VAT but not beverages, costs $35 to $50 in the moderate bracket, and $20 to $35 in the inexpensive range. All telephone numbers are in the 504 area code unless otherwise indicated.

L'Azzat – Small and cozy, this spot specializes in Italian, French, and Persian fare. Open nightly for dinner. Reservations advised. Just outside the city walls, 45A Carlisle Rd. (phone: 260033). Moderate.

Bells – An attractive 3-floor restaurant that offers panoramic views of the river Foyle and has a broad menu featuring fresh seafood and rack of lamb. Open daily for dinner; carvery lunch served daily except Saturdays. Also on the premises is *Johnny B's,* an informal wine bar in the cellar that serves inexpensive lunches and dinners. Just past the *City of Derry Golf Club.* Reservations advised. 59 Victoria Rd. (phone: 41078). Moderate.

Grille Bar – This popular hotel restaurant in the *White Horse Inn* features steaks, chicken, and local smoked salmon. Northeast of Londonderry, on the road to Limavady. Reservations unnecessary. 68 Clooney Rd., Campsie (phone: 860606). Moderate.

Brown's – This historic, renovated railway station, with old beams and an all-glass roof, offers European cuisine and vegetarian dishes in an informal bistro or formal restaurant. Open daily except Mondays for lunch and dinner. Reservations unnecessary. At the far side of the Craigavon Bridge. 1 Victoria Rd. (phone: 45180). Inexpensive.

Happy Landing – Brass and mahogany fittings and a large open-hearth fireplace provide a cozy setting for hearty pub-style lunches and dinners. Pepper steak is the house specialty. Reservations necessary for Sunday lunch. Across from *Glen House,* 4 Main St., Eglinton (phone: 810206). Inexpensive.

India House – This local favorite sports modern Indian decor replete with brass and other artifacts, and a menu that includes traditional curry dishes as well as tandoori barbecue. Open daily for dinner. Reservations unnecessary. 51 Carlisle Rd. (phone: 260532). Inexpensive.

Waterfoot Inn – Though unprepossessing outside, this place is highly popular inside with friendly Derry folk, who come here for the good food, good value, and a good time. Set in the Waterside district near the Foyle Bridge, the inn overlooks the river and the city. Open 12:30 to 10:30 PM Mondays through Saturdays. Reservations unnecessary. Caw Roundabout, Clooney Rd. (phone: 45500). Inexpensive.

 SHARING A PINT: Derry offers limited nightlife, but a pub crawl along the pedestrianized Waterloo Street is a popular activity. Many pubs either have scheduled performances or informal sessions of traditional Irish music. *Gweedore Bar* (61 Waterloo St.; phone: 263513) has the best Irish music. Also try *Castle Bar* (11 Castle St.; phone: 263118) or *Dungloe Bar* (Waterloo St.; phone: 260033). For a quiet atmosphere, stop in *Cole's Bar* (Strand Rd.; phone:

265308), with a wood and stained glass decor. The *Metro* (3 Bank Pl.; phone: 267401) offers drinks and pub grub (served daily for lunch) in a relaxed setting. A renowned feature of many of the city's pubs is lively quiz evenings, during which local teams pit their wits against each other. Pubs serve drinks until 11 PM, with a half hour's "drinking up" time. Pubs are now allowed to open on Sundays from 12:30 to 2:30 PM and 7 to 10 PM.

SLIGO CITY

Ireland's greatest poet, W. B. Yeats, spent his childhood summers in Sligo, most of the time staying with his uncle at Rosses Point, a peninsula at the entrance to the harbor. Fortunately for Sligo — and for the county of which it is the principal city — the passion he developed for this rare land inspired verse that immortalized many of the secret places he discovered and explored during his wanderings among the woodlands and on the lake shores and mountains. Yeats, who won the Nobel Prize for literature in 1923, once declared: "The place that really influenced my life was Sligo." His brother, Jack Yeats, who may well be the greatest painter produced by Ireland, also found that Sligo fired his artistic soul and impelled him to enshrine its countless charms on canvas.

Yeats died in France in 1939. When his remains were brought back to Ireland after the war, it was to Sligo that he was carried as the Irish nation mourned. Beneath the noble brow of Ben Bulben, in the churchyard of Drumcliffe, just outside the city, he rests today with the epitaph he wrote. It is the final three lines of "Under Ben Bulben." Carved on a simple piece of limestone, quarried out of the Sligo earth, it reads:

> Cast a cold eye
> On life, on death.
> Horseman, pass by!

Sligo City, set on a verdant, wooded plain, sprawls across the banks of a river that rushes from Lough Gill to the Atlantic Ocean. On all but its ocean side, timeless mountains rise up to form majestic ramparts against the ever-changing western sky. Here, amid these pleasantly watered woodlands and mighty-shouldered mountains, Yeats discovered the poetic soul of Ireland's Celtic past. That past, with its mystical legends and sagas of heroic deeds, haunts the enchanted countryside and crowds the pavements of Sligo City itself. The country dominates the town: While walking the city streets, it's impossible to ignore its brooding presence.

Unlike some other Irish cities, Sligo has no abundance of relics and monuments to chronicle the march of its history, but nearby is a truly astonishing record of its prehistoric past. Just 2 miles south of the city, at Carrowmore, lies a sprawling megalithic burial ground dating from before the Bronze Age. Its primitive rock monuments provide dramatic evidence that there once lived a race of people capable of transporting massive boulders and raising enormous slabs of stone to mark the resting place of their dead. Modern scholars cannot determine whether this race was related to characters in the legends of Finn MacCool and the Fianna — among the most exciting heroes of Celtic mythology — but the locality is rich in ancient folklore, which Yeats transmuted into the lyrical romantic verse of his early poetry. Rising straight up from this prehistoric home of the dead is the noble, flat-topped mountain of Knocknarea (pronounced Knock-na-*ray*), "the hill of the monarchs," surmounted by a rock cairn reputed to be the tomb of Queen Maeve, or Medb, of Connacht, the province in which Sligo is located. According to Celtic myth, Maeve was the powerful queen who sent her warriors into the province of Ulster to capture a prized bull in the celebrated Cattle Raid of Cooley. She is mentioned as Queen Meb in Shakespeare's *Romeo and Juliet,* and, for all the exotic and fanciful legends that surround her, she probably really did exist.

Inishmurray, the only true island off the coast of Sligo, has been occupied from prehistoric to modern times. It was the site of a monastic community that was founded in the 6th century and that flourished until Elizabethan times. St. Columba is said to have retired to Inishmurray after having committed a grievous sin; as part of his penance, he then went to Scotland to found the monastery of Iona.

One of the first mentions of Sligo in old records tells of a raid by Vikings in the 9th century. It is probable that the settlement — on the banks of the river Sligeach, from which it got its name and which is now called the Garavogue — had been established and functioning for many years before it came to the attention of the Norse pirates who were constant visitors to all the coasts of Ireland.

Sligo emerged from the dark veils of early history in the 13th century when an Anglo-Norman named Maurice Fitzgerald arrived and built a castle at the eastern end of what now is called Castle Street. The De Burgo clan, who wielded great power along the western coast, also built a castle in Sligo in 1301. No trace of either fortress can be found today, nor is there evidence of walls having surrounded the medieval city, though primitive forms of earthen defenses are shown on 17th-century maps. The O'Donnells from Donegal destroyed the Fitzgerald Castle in 1270 and again in 1369 after it had been rebuilt.

The most solid relic of Sligo's medieval past is the Dominican abbey, constructed in 1252. The abbey suffered much damage in an accidental fire in 1414, but that was nothing compared with what happened when Cromwell's soldiers, on their rampage of terror across Ireland, arrived in 1641. They not only set fire to the abbey but killed all the friars and then ran amok through the city streets, setting every building ablaze and slaughtering all the inhabitants they could find.

Throughout the 19th century, Sligo was one of the busiest ports in Ireland, with as many as 600 ships using the harbor every year. During the famine in the 1840s, thousands of Irish emigrants bound for North America sailed from Sligo, many risking their lives on the notorious coffin ships, so named because of the appalling conditions on board. Nowadays, Sligo's sea traffic has dwindled to a few small freighters that irregularly call.

From the end of the 17th century to the present, the course of events in Sligo has, for the most part, been remarkably harmonious and trouble-free. Even during the War of Independence, which led to the British departure from the southern part of Ireland in the 1920s, the city managed to avoid much of the violence that convulsed the whole island for several years. Today

Sligo is a prosperous and thriving city with a progressive vision of its future as well as a keen appreciation of the colorful richness of its past.

SLIGO AT-A-GLANCE

SEEING THE CITY: Sligo City lies at the bottom of a bowl formed by spectacular and oddly shaped mountains — some bearing a striking resemblance to the mesas of America's West. The best way to take in an overall view of the city is to head for the hills (preferably on foot or by bike), where there are numerous vantage points from which to see for miles around. From on high, Sligo's setting, with its lakes and woodlands and the great bay opening out into the Atlantic, is unforgettable. For the fastest way into the hills, take N16 for 3 or 4 miles northeast and turn right into any of the three side roads encountered. The reward for this expedition is mountainous country of surpassing loveliness.

SPECIAL PLACES: With a population of 56,000, Sligo is one of Ireland's smallest cities, so there's no great difficulty making a tour of it on foot in 2 to 3 hours. (It's town size, really, having been designated a city only a few years ago.) The compactness of the place makes everything easily accessible. A printed guide and map, plotting out a tourist trail through the city, can be obtained at the Donegal-Leitrim-Sligo Tourist Board, Temple St. (phone: 61201).

CITY CENTER

Dominican Abbey – The ruins of the abbey, built in 1252, consist of choir, nave, and central tower. Much of the original cloisters are still intact, as are several medieval windows, including the beautiful east window. Damage inflicted by Cromwell's Roundheads in 1641 has never been fully repaired, although the Irish government has carried out valuable restoration work in modern times. Abbey St. (ask at No. 6 Abbey St. for a key to the gate).

Town Hall – This imposing edifice, designed in a graceful Italian Renaissance style, was built in 1864 on a hill in Quay Street overlooking the once-busy harbor. It is thought that a Cromwellian fortress may have occupied the site originally. Inside, the Italian palatial theme is maintained with a broad sweeping stone stairway, tall pillars, and a high, arched ceiling. Quay St. (phone: 42141).

Courthouse – A handsome building of Donegal sandstone, this courthouse was built in 1878 to replace an older one, part of which was retained and incorporated into the new structure to maintain historic continuity. A ravaging plague of cholera broke out in Sligo in 1832, during the height of which the old courthouse was turned into a carpenter's shop for the manufacture of coffins. Teeling St. (phone: 42228 or 42429).

St. John's Cathedral (Church of Ireland) – This is the creation of a noted German architect, Richard Cassels, who designed many of Ireland's most distinguished buildings. Much of the original 1730 design has been distorted or wiped away altogether by renovation work carried out some 100 years later, but it is still a building of compelling interest. John Butler Yeats, the poet's father, was wed here in 1863, and the adjoining graveyard contains the remains of the poet's grandfather William Pollexfen, who personally supervised the building of his own tomb. John St. (phone: 426556).

Cathedral of the Immaculate Conception (Roman Catholic) – Another eminent architect, George Goldie of London, designed this fine Norman-style edifice built in 1875. The peal of its bells are to Sligo what the Bow Bells are to London. Temple St. (phone: 61261).

Green Fort – This unusual, square earthen fort dates from the early 17th century. Built on a height above the river Garavogue, it has star-shaped bastions at each corner and commands a sweeping view of the city and countryside northeast of Connaughton Rd.

Yeats Watch Tower – A turret on top of a stone building is where the poet, as a young boy, spent hours every day gazing out over the city and the harbor. The building was owned by his grandfather William Pollexfen, who liked to station himself in the turret with a telescope and watch the comings and goings of the many merchant ships that he owned. Visits can be arranged between 9 AM and 6 PM Mondays through Fridays by calling at the furniture factory that now occupies the building. Corner of Wine and Adelaide Sts.

Riverside Walk – This is a pleasant stroll around the center of town starting at the Douglas Hyde Bridge, which joins Wine Street to Stephen Street, and continuing upstream along the waters of the Garavogue, crossing Thomas Street into Kennedy Parade (named after John F. Kennedy). The walk ends close to the Dominican abbey.

Doorly Park – Continue upstream alongside the Garavogue on Riverside Walk to reach Doorly Park, a spacious and tranquil woodland retreat close to Lough Gill, with splendid views of the surrounding mountains.

ENVIRONS

Drumcliffe – The parish of Drumcliffe, 4 miles north of Sligo on N15, is the most important shrine in Yeats country. The poet is buried here in what is one of the most visited cemeteries in Ireland. The church is on the right, just before the river, and Yeats's grave is just inside the main gate to the left. Yeats's great-grandfather had been rector in this church, set in wildly magnificent scenery at the foot of the mountain called Ben Bulben. The fine Celtic cross in the churchyard dates from the 11th century. Across the road from the church lies the base of an unfinished round tower thought to have been started in the 6th century. Also during that period, St. Columba founded a monastery here to which was attached a house of studies that attracted scholars from many lands in the golden age of Irish Christianity.

Inishmurray – An excursion to this island, 4 miles off the northwest Sligo coast and about 12 miles from Sligo City, is a very worthwhile day trip. Inishmurray, which was inhabited until 1947 (when it still had its own "king"), was the site of a monastic settlement established by St. Molaise in the 6th century. The ruins of the monastery are still there, along with a stone church and the "beehive" cells where the monks lived. All over the island are numerous ancient crosses and tombstones and, reflecting the less ecclesiastical side of life in the past, a collection of the *Clocha Breaca* (pronounced *Kluh*-ha *Brah*-ka), "cursing stones," which were used to invoke curses and misfortune on enemies. The cursing stones were probably used not by the holy men who dwelt on Inishmurray but by the pagans who inhabited the island before their time. Embarkation point for Inishmurray is the tiny and lovely seaport of Mullaghmore. Take N15 north from Sligo to the village of Cliffoney, then turn left at the sign on entering the village. In summer, boats run regularly to and from Inishmurray; contact Bill Mulligan (phone: 66126). Mullaghmore village itself is a charming old port with a famous 200-year-old pub called *Annie's*. It also has a splendid stretch of beach hugging the Atlantic, a very popular gathering place in the hot days of summer.

Carrowmore – This is the location of one of the largest megalithic graveyards in Europe, covering a square mile at the foot of Knocknarea Mountain. There are more than 40 tombs here, some dating from the neolithic or late Stone Age (4500–2300 BC), many undisturbed since they received the dead. An excavation of one of the tombs uncovered the cremated remains of 18 young girls, aged 18 to 22, beside each of whom lay part of the skull of an older male. An arrangement of unopened oyster shells nearby suggests that it might have been a ritual burial. Atop Knocknarea Mountain is a cairn that legend holds is the burial place of Queen Maeve of Connacht, although this story has never been tested by excavation. Carrowmore is 2 miles southwest of Sligo on L132; turn left at Strandhill for the burial ground.

Lissadell House – Set amid rolling wooded hills overlooking the Bay of Drumcliffe, this 19th-century Georgian structure is the childhood home of one of Ireland's greatest woman rebels, Countess Constance Markievicz of the Gore-Booth family. The countess took part in the 1916 insurrection, was imprisoned, and later became the first woman member of Dáil Eireann (the Irish Parliament). Yeats, an intimate friend of the Gore-Booths, often stayed at Lissadell and once reported seeing a ghost at the bottom of the staircase. Members of the Gore-Booth family still live here and always have a welcome for visitors — even the unannounced. To tour the gracious old mansion is to be transported into a past age — every corridor and room scented with nostalgia. To reach Lissadell, travel north on N15, take the first left turn past Drumcliffe, and drive through and beyond Carney for another 6 miles (phone: 63150).

Hazelwood – A lushly wooded area on the northwest shore of Lough Gill, Hazelwood perches on a promontory that juts into the lake and is crisscrossed with shaded paths for walking. There are a number of picnic areas along the water's edge and beneath the trees. Yeats wrote about this area, "I went out to the hazel wood, / Because a fire was in my head. . . ." A stately mansion, Hazelwood House, built in the 18th century, stands unoccupied on the shores of the lake. Take L16 east from Sligo for 3 miles and follow the signposts to the wood.

Rosses Point – With two superb beaches and miles of sand dunes, this peninsula is Sligo's premier seaside resort. Much of Yeats's time in Sligo was spent at Rosses Point in Elsinore Lodge, the residence of his cousins, the Middletons, a wealthy merchant family. Just offshore on a stone pedestal in the sea stands the famous statue of the Metal Man, a 12-foot-high sailor forever pointing to the deepest part of the channel to guide ships into Sligo harbor. In olden days, the area was notorious as a haunt of smugglers. Yeats wrote of people hanging out lanterns at the dead of night near Deadman's Point to guide in smuggling ships carrying contraband cargo from France. L16 northwest from Sligo goes to Rosses Point.

Coney Island – At the entrance to the Sligo harbor, this small island is home to only a handful of people nowadays. It is said that, walking along Green Road, which circumnavigates Coney, one can see all of the rest of County Sligo across the bay. People on the island claim that it gave its name to the more famous Coney Island in New York City. In Irish, Coney Island means "the island of rabbits," and some believe that the captain of the merchant ship *Arethusa,* which regularly sailed between Sligo and New York in the 19th century, observed that the Brooklyn island also was overrun with rabbits and called it Coney, too. The rabbits have since vanished from New York's Coney Island, but they're still hopping about by the thousands among the sand dunes of its Sligo namesake. Boats make the 5-minute trip to Coney Island from the pier at Rosses Point daily in summer; the schedule varies (phone: 77168).

Creevykeel Court Tomb – A magnificent 3,000-year-old court tomb excavated in 1935 by a Harvard archaeologist, it contains several chambers and a gallery, all surrounded by a courtyard. Drive north on N15 to the village of Cliffoney and travel another 1½ miles on the same road to where the tomb is signposted.

Dooney Rock – This is a massive outcrop of rock, smothered in woods and rising dramatically above the southern shore of Lough Gill. A nature walk through the trees leads to the top of the rock and a spectacular view over the island-studded lake. 4 miles east of Sligo on L117.

Strandhill – Because of the shifting sands and strong undertow, swimming is hazardous at Strandhill, a seaside resort famous for the towering Atlantic waves that crash on its long, curved beach. However, some people are willing to take the chance. L132 west from Sligo leads to Strandhill, 12 miles away.

Killaspugbrone – A half-mile north of Strandhill, just past Sligo Airport, is Killaspugbrone, one of Ireland's oldest churches (built in St. Patrick's time). Legend has it that St. Patrick lost a tooth here. Revered for centuries as a relic, the tooth can now be seen in the *National Museum* in Dublin. L132 west from Sligo leads to Strandhill, 12 miles away.

Glencar – One of the loveliest valleys in Ireland, Glencar has massive mountains crowding in on all sides, waterfalls spilling over precipices, and, at the bottom of the glen, a lake so clear that it reflects the tall trees growing in profusion around its banks. A small path leads up the mountain to the principal Glencar waterfall, which plunges 50 feet into a pool at the bottom of a cliff. Small, unpaved roads splendid for hiking run up into the mountains. Glencar Lake and the river that runs through it have fine-size salmon and sea trout in summer. Take N16 from Sligo; 8 miles out, turn left at the "Waterfall" signpost.

Lough Gill – The lake immortalized in one of Yeats's most famous poems, "The Lake Isle of Innisfree" ("I will arise and go now, and go to Innisfree. . . ."), lies just east of Sligo City, linked to it by the river Garavogue. The beauty of Lough Gill compares favorably with that of the fabled lakes of Killarney in County Kerry, and the poetic Innisfree is only one of many wooded islands decorating its waters. Steep rocky cliffs carpeted in greenery rise from the south shore. To the north and west are the peaks of Ben Bulben and the Cuilcagh Mountains. For a land trip around the lake, travel 4 miles south of Sligo on N4, and turn left at the "Lough Gill" signpost onto L117. Make another left at Dromahair onto L112, and 4 miles beyond, turn left again onto L16 back to Sligo. It is also possible to cruise the lake. During the summer, a water bus, the *Queen Maeve,* seating 57 passengers, leaves Riverside daily. The ride includes music and readings of Yeats's poetry. Contact *D. D. Sweeney* (*Larkhill House,* Sligo; phone: 62540). But the best way to enjoy the lake is to rent a rowboat and spend the day exploring its inlets and islands. Contact Peter Henry (*Blue Lagoon Saloon,* Riverside, Sligo; phone: 42530 or 45407).

SOURCES AND RESOURCES

TOURIST INFORMATION: The prime source for all information on Sligo City and the surrounding area is the headquarters of the Donegal-Leitrim-Sligo Regional Tourist Board (Aras Reddin, Temple St.; phone: 61201). A handbook describing a signposted walking tour of the city is for sale. In July and August, conducted walking tours of the city start from Aras Reddin at 11 AM Mondays through Saturdays. Guided tours at other times can be arranged at Aras Reddin. *Keohane's Bookshop* (Castle St.) stocks the most books about Sligo, its lore, and history. For in-depth background on the area, ask for *O'Rorke's History of Sligo* in the County Library (Stephen St.; phone: 42212). Difficult to obtain but highly informative is a little book about Sligo and its famous poet, *The Yeats Country* (Dublin: Dolmen Press, 1977).

Local Coverage – The *Sligo Champion* is the definitive local newspaper, read by everybody. *Sligo Weekender,* a free paper consisting mainly of advertising, can be picked up at most newsstands and hotel reception desks.

TELEPHONE: The area code for Sligo City and the immediate vicinity is 71. When calling from within the Republic of Ireland, dial 071 before the local number.

GETTING AROUND: Walking is the recommended method of seeing the city and that employed by most of its inhabitants. There are, however, other ways to get around.

Airport – There are flights to and from Dublin Airport every day except Sundays. In summer, pleasure and sightseeing trips in small craft are offered. Strandhill, 12 miles west of Sligo on L132 (phone: 68318).

Bicycle – In good weather, biking is a marvelous way to see the city and countryside. Bikes can be hired for any length of time from *Conway Bros.* (Wine St.; phone: 61240) or *W. A. Woods* (Castle St.; phone: 42021).

Bus – Excellent bus service runs to all parts of Sligo. Buses leave regularly from the bus depot at the railway station (Lord Edward St.; phone: 62473). This is also the terminal for provincial bus services, with destinations in all parts of the Republic and Northern Ireland.

Car Rental – It is best to book a car upon arriving in Ireland – either at Shannon Airport or in Dublin. In Sligo, cars can be hired from *John Gilbride & Co.* (Bridge St.; phone: 42091) or *Higgins Garage* (Sligo Airport; phone: 68280).

Taxi – There are no cruising taxis or cabstands in Sligo, but it is possible to call a taxi from *Mark Askey* (phone: 45577), *Martin Furey Ltd.* (phone: 63092), *George Carter* (phone: 42333), or *Jim Fehilly and Sons* (phone: 42596).

Train – The only passenger rail service operating in Sligo is to and from Dublin, with stops along the line. There are three trains each way (morning, early afternoon, and early evening) Mondays through Saturdays, two trains each way (morning and early evening) Sundays. Railway station, Lord Edward St. (phone: 62473).

SPECIAL EVENTS: Considering the Yeatsian influence that permeates Sligo, it's not surprising that the major annual event is the *Yeats International Summer School* and its attendant cultural festival. Started in 1958, the summer school now attracts Yeatsian scholars from all over the world, with Americans predominating. For 2 weeks every August, the hundreds who enroll in the school immerse themselves in a wide range of activities and happenings, from the lighthearted to the heavily studious, all having some connection to the poet. There are visits to all the Yeats shrines, plays and poetry readings, lectures and seminars, and every night the *Festival Club* becomes a stimulating forum for good conversation, intellectual *savoir faire,* and high jinks until dawn. Contact the Secretary, *Yeats Society* (Yeats Memorial Building, Douglas Hyde Bridge; phone: 42693 or 60097). The *Sligo Summer Festival,* usually held the last 2 weeks in August, turns up a lively cocktail of modern and traditional dance; classical, folk, and jazz music; plays; poetry readings; art exhibitions; street busking (performing); and myriad other events. For more information, contact the Sligo Tourist Board (Temple St.; phone: 61201).

MUSEUMS: The *Sligo County Museum* and the *Municipal Art Gallery* share the same buildings attached to the County Library (Stephen St.; phone: 2212). The *County Museum* contains an informative array of objects and artifacts dating from Sligo's richly endowed prehistoric period. The *Municipal Art Gallery* has a fairly comprehensive collection of many of Ireland's major artists including Jack B. Yeats, the poet's brother, and their father, John Yeats, along with oils, watercolors, and drawings by Irish artists such as Paul Henry, Sean Keating, Charles Lamb, and Evie Hone, all with international reputations. In addition, throughout the year various traveling exhibitions by local, national, and international artists are held in the Yeats Memorial Building (phone: 42693), the attractive red brick building at Hyde Bridge, which links Wine and Stephen Streets.

SHOPPING: Sligo is reputed to be the priciest shopping city in Ireland, but visitors from abroad find the tags on Irish-made products still less daunting than those back home.

The Bakery – Scrumptious home-baked pastries and cakes plus hand-dipped chocolates are among the appetizing exotica available here. Thomas St. (phone: 42264).

Cosgrove's – Behind its original 19th-century façade is an old-fashioned food emporium. Perfect for picnic fixings are wild Irish salmon, baked ham, roast lamb, Irish cheeses, salads, and handmade Irish chocolates. 32 Market St. (phone: 42809).

The Curiosity Shoppe – Locally crafted pottery and fine Irish glassware are the specialties of this excellent shop. Thomas St. (phone: 42725).

John Martin & Son – An internationally known tailor shop where traditional hand-sewn methods are still used. Many prominent Americans are listed among its clientele. Wine St. (phone: 62257).

Mullaney Bros. – Large clothing store with a superior line of Irish tweeds and woolens. 9 O'Connell St. (phone: 43278).

My Lady Art Gallery and Bookshop – Dusty old tomes to browse among with a chance of finding something valuable. Also a nice collection of paintings at the rear of the shop. Castle St. (phone: 42723).

Sligo Craft Pottery – Excellent display of very original local ceramics. Great value. Market Yard, at the top of Harmony Hill, which is a continuation of O'Connell St., the main thoroughfare (phone: 62586).

Wehrly Bros. – Beautifully designed gold and silver objects and elegant glassware are found in this high-quality jewelry shop with a vintage Edwardian storefront. There's a hallowed ambience within. 3 O'Connell St. (phone: 42252).

W. A. & A. F. Woods – Vast, old-fashioned store, resembling an American emporium of the 1920s, with just about everything, from nail files to original paintings. Castle St. (phone: 42021).

SPORTS AND FITNESS: Boating and Sailing – The *Sligo Yacht Club* (Rosses Point, at Deadman's Point just beyond the pier; phone: 77168) is the center for sailing and other seafaring activities on the bay. Lessons in sailing are available, and visitors are always welcome. For cruising and rowboating on Lough Gill, see *Special Places.*

Fishing – Lough Gill is a picturesque setting in which to fish for salmon, best during May. In late June and July, sea trout also run up into the lake. The river Garavogue, which runs through Lough Gill and into Sligo City, also has good fishing beats. A license is required to fish for salmon and all other freshwater species. Contact Jim McCarney, Secretary, *The Sligo Anglers,* Annalen, Cornageeha, Sligo (phone: 62385).

Fitness – The *Sligo Sports Centre* has a fully equipped gym for workouts, an indoor track, and squash and badminton courts. At Cleveragh, southeast of the city beside the racecourse. Travel south on Pearse Rd. for a half mile and bear left at the junction (phone: 60539).

Golf – One of Ireland's premier 18-hole golf courses is the *County Sligo Golf Club* (phone: 77134) — popularly known as "Rosses Point" as it is beside the sea on Rosses Point. Every *Easter* it hosts the *West of Ireland Amateur Open Championship.* Visitors are welcome. Take L16 northwest from the city (phone: 77134). A less exacting 9-hole course, ideal for duffers, is at the *Strandhill Golf Club* (12 miles west on L132; phone: 68188).

Horseback Riding – Riding and trekking, at all levels and including instruction if necessary, are available at the *Sligo Equitation Company* in Carrowmore, beside the megalithic graveyard. Carrowmore, 2 miles southwest on L132 (phone: 62758 or 61353).

Swimming – There is an outdoor pool, open daily in summer, on Markievicz Rd. (phone: 43003).

 THEATER: The *Hawk's Well Theatre* (named after an enchanted well from a Yeats poem) is open most of the year both for local productions by the *Sligo Theatre Circle* and for visiting companies. Temple St., in the basement of Aras Reddin, tourist board headquarters (phone: 61526).

 MUSIC: Most musical events, except during the *Sligo Summer Festival* (see *Special Events*), are confined to singing pubs, which bring in various folk and pop groups. Details are carried in the local newspapers. Visits by classical performers are infrequent.

 NIGHTCLUBS AND NIGHTLIFE: Except for the city's discos and after-hours pubs, Sligo packs up early. *Xanadu's* (Teeling, behind the *Grand* hotel), a disco, pulls in mostly a young crowd, "young" in Ireland being anyone under 40. *Papillon* in the *Southern* hotel (Lord Edward St.; phone: 62101) also has the accent on the young side and is one of the trendier rendezvous. Members of the older set will find themselves at home in the *Oasis Nightclub* at the *Blue Lagoon Saloon* (Riverside; phone: 42530), which often fronts the disco beat with big-time acts.

BEST IN TOWN

 CHECKING IN: While there are only a few hotels in and around the city, most are very comfortable and offer good value for the money. Most also include the traditional Irish breakfast in their rate. The expensive category is $55 or more for a double room; moderate, $25 to $50; and inexpensive, $20 to $25. All telephone numbers are in the 71 area code unless otherwise indicated.

Ballincar House – Originally an old country house set in a vast wooded demesne, it is by far the best hotel in the area. Because of the pressing demand for its 20 rooms, it is advisable to book well in advance. It has 6 acres of magnificent gardens as well as views of the Atlantic and, in addition to a telephone, television set, and bath in each room, the property has its own squash complex, tennis court, sauna, and solarium. The restaurant is excellent (see *Eating Out*). Rosses Point Rd. (phone: 45361). Expensive.

Bonne Chere – Located in the heart of town, this establishment offers 19 tastefully decorated rooms — 14 with private bath, cable TV, and telephone. The well-known restaurant serves tasty grilled steaks and seafood. Restaurant reservations necessary. 45 High St. (phone: 42014). Expensive.

Markree Castle – A Gothic gateway leads to this stately 17th-century residence, which has been converted into a luxurious 15-room hostelry. Horseback riding and golf at two 18-hole courses nearby can be arranged. The hotel recently acquired the celebrated *Knockmuldowney* restaurant (see *Eating Out*). Callooney, 7 miles south of Sligo City on the N17 (phone: 67800). Expensive.

Silver Swan – In the city center and perched above the rapids of the river Garavogue, this is a small, homey hostelry with 24 fully equipped rooms. The food served in the *River Room* restaurant is excellent (see *Eating Out*). High Bridge (phone: 43232). Expensive.

Sligo Park – Hidden among trees and surrounded by an expanse of green pastures, this competently run, modern hostelry has 60 comfortable rooms, each with a phone, TV set, bath, and shower. The *Hazelwood Room* serves good chicken and fish dishes and fresh vegetables. Restaurant reservations advised. Pearse Rd. (phone: 60291). Expensive.

Southern – A gracious old hotel, once part of the railway chain of hotels that encircled Ireland, it has been refurbished to a new elegance. The gardens are lovely, and the *Copper Pot* restaurant maintains a consistently high standard (see *Eating Out*). Lord Edward St. (phone: 62101). Expensive.

Yeats Country Ryan – On a mile-long stretch of beach and sand dunes, this hotel rates high on efficiency, service, and comfort, and it also sets a good table. It has tennis courts and is near a the fabled local golf course. Rosses Point; take L16 northwest from Sligo (phone: 77211). Expensive.

 EATING OUT: The better restaurants in and around Sligo are included here. One or two are outstanding in any context. There are several, however, that should not be mentioned in civilized company and are not included here. The expensive category averages around $55 for dinner for two with one bottle of good wine, though if you are lavish with à la carte selections, it's not difficult to spend $70 to $80; the moderate category averages $40, and inexpensive, $25 to $35 (in some cases, a good deal less). All telephone numbers are in the 71 area code unless otherwise indicated.

Ballincar House – Overlooking the hotel's gardens, this much-recommended restaurant specializes in seafood, especially lobster and salmon. Reservations necessary. Rosses Point Rd. (phone: 45361). Expensive.

Knockmuldowney – Originally in Culleenamore, this wonderful dining establishment recently moved to the *Markree Castle* hotel. The food continues to be outstanding; highlights on the menu are fresh game and fish specially supplied to the kitchen. Vegetables and fruit are homegrown. Reservations necessary. Collooney, 7 miles south of Sligo City on the N17 (phone: 67800). Expensive.

Moorings – Old timbers and ships' lanterns give a salty tang of the sea to this inn specializing in seafood served with flair. The lobster is particularly good. Reservations necessary. Rosses Point; take L16 northwest of the city (phone: 77112). Expensive.

Reflections – This intimate little restaurant, with tasteful ambience and superior continental fare, serves delicious entrecôte and lamb kebabs. Reservations necessary. 23 Grattan St. (phone: 43828). Expensive.

Reveries – Irish food of superlative quality is served in this elegant restaurant overlooking Sligo Bay and Knocknarea Mountain. Venison, squab, and veal are given heavenly treatment to produce a memorable eating experience. Reservations necessary. Rosses Point; take L16 northwest of the city (phone: 77371). Expensive.

River Room – Offering panoramic views of the river Garavogue, the *Silver Swan* hotel's dining room offers deliciously prepared deep-fried mushrooms, smoked salmon, and mussels in garlic butter for starters. For the main course there is a wide selection of fresh seafood, including monkfish scampi, prawns, and brill, as well as steak, chicken, and vegetarian dishes. The wine list offers a variety of European vintages. Reservations advised. High Bridge (phone: 43232). Expensive.

Copper Pot – The restaurant in the *Southern* hotel has a soft, intimate atmosphere that complements its versatile range of excellently prepared dishes. Particularly good wine list. Reservations advised. Lord Edward St. (phone: 62101). Moderate.

Kate's Kitchen – Health food, deli fare, and continental fare are served informally on pine tables. Lunch specials daily. Closed Sundays. Reservations unnecessary. 24 Market St. (phone: 43022). Moderate.

Four Lanterns – Good take-away and eat-in, with hamburgers that would rate in the USA, chicken bits, and fish 'n' chips. Great value. Two locations: O'Connell St. and John St. No reservations. No phone. Inexpensive.

 SHARING A PINT: The most famous pub in Sligo is *Hargadon's* (4 O'Connell St.), more than a century old, with ancient mahogany counters, drawers, snugs, and whiskey mirrors. No one should visit Sligo without stopping here. For pubs offering good Irish music, stop in *McLynn's* (Old Market St.) or *Yeat's Tavern* (Drumcliffe).

WATERFORD CITY

Waterford is a gentle city of Georgian doorways and back streets with names like Lady Lane. It stretches for a bit more than half a mile along the southern bank of the river Suir, well up a long inlet from the sea, and during the 17th century its harbor was one of the busiest in the country. Meat, fish, and corn were exported to the Continent, and wine came back. Ships bound for America were provisioned here. Today, one of the principal exports from its still-busy quays is beef, though Waterford crystal is its most famous export.

The old Waterford Glass Factory was founded in 1783, at a time when the city — originally a Viking settlement — was undergoing a burst of development and beginning to outgrow its medieval dimensions. Graceful Georgian homes belonging to the merchant class began to appear along the Mall, and John Roberts, an architect responsible for many of the city's elegant structures, was at work designing the public buildings and churches that are among the city's most prominent landmarks — City Hall and the Catholic and Protestant cathedrals are all his. The latter, which was erected between 1773 and 1779 on the site of a much earlier church, is a stately testimony to Waterford's rich Protestant families, some of whom were carried up the slight incline into Cathedral Square in sedan chairs.

Waterford's most famous landmark, however, is a remnant of Viking times. Sitric the Dane is credited with fortifying the site of the city in the ninth century, and Reginald the Dane, a descendant of Sitric, is believed to have strengthened the fortifications in 1003 by erecting what has since become known as Reginald's Tower. Along with the city walls and two other towers, Reginald's Tower protected the city from invasion first by the Celts and later, when the Norsemen and Celts put aside their differences to join forces against a common enemy, from invasion by the Normans. You can still see part of the old city wall inside the Reginald Lounge, adjacent to the tower.

The Normans finally did take Waterford in 1170, in the person of Richard de Clare, an emissary of Henry II of England. De Clare was better known as Strongbow, for the sureness of his weapons and tactics, and his victory over the city's defenders was both an easy and a far-reaching one. The capture of Waterford was the beginning of the Anglo-Norman domination of Ireland. Strongbow's marriage shortly thereafter to Eva, the daughter of Dermot MacMurrough, the Irish King of Leinster, consolidated the position of the conquering Normans. This fateful event, too, took place in Waterford, reputedly in Reginald's Tower (though the original Viking cathedral, predecessor of Christ Church Cathedral, may have been the actual site).

King John granted the city its first charter in 1205 (his sword and several of the city's subsequent charters are in the Reginald's Tower museum), and for several centuries to come Waterford would be intensely loyal to the English Crown. Henry VII gave it its motto, "Unconquered City," in the 15th century, in gratitude for its successful efforts in fighting off attacks by two pretenders to his throne. But loyalty to the English king in temporal matters did not extend to recognition of the Crown's supremacy in religious matters. The city remained Catholic in the 16th century, and because of this, its charter was eventually withdrawn and its Catholic citizens suffered much in the Cromwellian sieges of the mid-17th century. Their churches were closed and confiscated and many Catholics were sent as slaves to the West Indies.

Several abbeys flourished in Waterford. The ruins of the once extensive 13th-century Dominican friary can be seen. Another large abbey, the Holy Ghost Friary of the Franciscans, or, as it is known locally, the French Church, was built a little later in the same century and is also now in ruins. Both were suppressed by Henry VIII's Dissolution of the Monasteries, the Franciscan friary to become a hospital and then a home to a colony of French Huguenot refugees.

Most visitors come to Waterford to tour the glass factory and concentrate on the gift shops around the quays. But there are revealing detours from the beaten path, such as a walk out to Ballybricken Green, one of the oldest sections. When the Normans controlled Waterford proper, this is where the Irish lived, outside the Patrick Street gate of the city walls. And the side streets and back lanes of this city of 50,000 people are worth discovering for their quaint houses, historic churches, and unexpected finds such as the ancient carvings on the friary wall in Lady Lane. Not much of the great abbeys may remain, but in these narrow passageways, Waterford's medieval atmosphere seems trapped forever like snow in a glass paperweight.

WATERFORD AT-A-GLANCE

SEEING THE CITY: Ignatius Rice Bridge (formerly Redmond Bridge) spans the river Suir at the western end of the city. It can be a quiet spot for viewing the town, which looks not unlike an 18th-century New England coastal village with its large buildings and many church spires. From its hilltop location across the river, the *Jurys* hotel also offers a panoramic view of Waterford.

SPECIAL PLACES: With the exception of the Waterford Glass Factory, about 1½ miles from the center, most of the city's major points of interest are conveniently located in a central area between Ignatius Rice Bridge and Reginald's Tower, either along the quays or just a few blocks from them. The glass factory is best reached by car, taxi, or bus. The rest of the sights can be seen on a walking tour; most of the city's shops, restaurants, pubs, and hotels are in the same vicinity.

Waterford Glass Factory – It is said that 3,000 people a week visit the Waterford Glass Factory to watch Ireland's most famous crystal being mixed, blown, and cut by hand from the raw ingredients of silica sand, potash, and red lead. Not only are the guided tours free, they are also interesting and enjoyable. The original plant opened in 1783 and continued operating until 1851, when English law imposed heavy duties on the exported glass and made the operation unprofitable. With the help of the Irish government, Waterford reopened on a small scale in 1947 and has since outgrown its buildings several times. The company now employs 2,000 people, who cannot keep up with orders for their product, which is exported all over the world (the US is the biggest market). A Waterford chandelier hangs in Independence Hall in Philadelphia and 16 of them are in Westminster Abbey. The factory is closed on weekends and usually is closed during the first 3 weeks of August. Tours are given at 10:15, 11, and 11:45 AM and at 1:45 and 2:30 PM Mondays through Fridays. To check on the times and reserve in advance — reservations necessary year-round — phone 73311; arrangements can also be made through the tourist board. Showrooms are open 9 AM to 5 PM Mondays through Fridays and 9 AM to 12:30 PM on Saturdays. About 1½ miles from the center of Waterford on the Cork road.

St. Saviour's Dominican Church – This handsome church was built in 1874. The solemn interior features Corinthian columns and lovely frescoes over the altar. Corner of Bridge and O'Connell Sts.

Chamber of Commerce – Architect John Roberts designed this aristocratic building in 1795 as a home for the Morris family, which was prominent in the shipping trade. The house was purchased by the Chamber of Commerce in 1815. A large fanlight graces the entrance, and it is worth a look inside to see the beautiful plasterwork and splendid oval staircase. Open weekdays. George's St.

Clock Tower – Nineteenth-century sea captains relied on this landmark along the quays to keep their ships on schedule. It once had troughs of water at its base from which horses could drink, and was thus known as the Fountain Clock. Built in 1861, the original clock was replaced in 1954. The Quay.

Cathedral of the Most Holy Trinity – After the confiscation of their churches in the mid-17th century, the Catholics of Waterford did not receive permission from the city's Protestant-controlled government to build another until 1792. Architect John Roberts designed it for them and it was completed in 1796. The cathedral has a beautifully carved oak pulpit. Barronstrand St.

Lady Lane – This little passage has been described as the best surviving example of a medieval street in Waterford. It is a charming lane with Georgian doorways on one side and two old stone carvings (one dated 1613) visible on the wall of the Franciscan friary on the other side. On Broad St., off Upper Barronstrand St.

Christ Church Cathedral – John Roberts also designed this Protestant church, which was completed in 1779 on the site of an earlier church erected by the Norsemen in 1050. The Norsemen had made Waterford a diocese of its own, and the old church grew in size and property through several centuries until Henry VIII's Dissolution of the Monasteries. Later, Cromwellian troops occupied the original church for a time. The present cathedral incorporates some monuments from the old church and a number of interesting tombs. Cathedral Sq.

French Church – Founded as a Franciscan abbey in 1240, this once included six chambers, a kitchen with four cellars, and stables, in addition to the church whose ruined nave, choir, and Lady Chapel still remain. After it was dissolved by Henry VIII, the friary saw use as a hospital, a burial place for some of Waterford's prominent families, and a parish church for French Huguenot refugees. Architect Roberts is among those buried here. Obtain the key to visit the church from the house across the road; a notice on the door gives the address. Bailey's New St.

Reginald's Tower – This 70-foot stone tower on the quays was built for defense by Reginald the Dane in 1003. It was captured by Strongbow in 1170, and has been used as a mint, a military storehouse, and an air-raid shelter. It now houses a historical museum containing the city's original charters, swords, and municipal muniments. Open 11 AM to 1 PM and 2 to 7 PM Mondays through Fridays, 11 AM to 2 PM Saturdays, April through September; closed in winter. Admission charge. Corner of the Quay and the Mall.

Father Luke Wadding and the Mall – This statue just across the street from

Reginald's Tower commemorates the birth in 1588 of one of Waterford's most distinguished sons. The Franciscan scholar was famous as a linguist and author of the annals of his order, and although he spent most of his life in Rome, he helped his Catholic countrymen both morally and financially in their attempts to establish their own constitution and government. The *Tower* hotel on the left is on the site of the old bowling green. City Hall, completed in 1788 for the merchants of Waterford, now houses a museum (see *Museums*) and the *Theatre Royal* as well as administrative offices. Behind City Hall is the Bishop's Palace, designed in 1741 by Richard Castle, who also designed Powerscourt, Westport House, and the Irish Parliament and the Rotunda Hospital in Dublin. It now is used by the city engineering staff.

■ **EXTRA SPECIAL:** The *Waterford International Festival of Light Opera* has been taking place every September for over 20 years. For 2 weeks, amateur companies from England, Wales, Scotland, Northern Ireland, and the Republic compete to give the best performance of an operetta or musical, and visitors to Waterford have a chance to see and hear again such popular productions as *The Merry Widow, Oliver, South Pacific,* and the like. Fringe events include a ball, band concerts, bridge tournaments, sports competitions, and singing competitions in the pubs, which, as usual during a festival in Ireland, are open late. Tickets are reasonably priced and can be obtained along with specific information on programs and dates from Sean Dower, Secretary of the Waterford Festival, New St., Waterford (phone: 75911 or 75437).

SOURCES AND RESOURCES

TOURIST INFORMATION: The tourist board (41 The Quay; phone: 75788) is open year-round. Hours are usually 9 AM to 6 PM Mondays through Saturdays, May through September; to 5:15 PM weekdays and 1 PM on Saturdays in winter. One of the most helpful pamphlets for sale is the *Waterford Guide* (about $1.55). The tourist board in nearby Tramore (Railway Sq.; phone: 81572), the large seaside resort about 8 miles southwest of Waterford, is open during July and August.

Local Coverage – The *Munster Express,* published Thursdays and Fridays, and the *Waterford News and Star,* published every Thursday, give specific information on entertainment and special events in the city and vicinity.

TELEPHONE: The area code for Waterford and the immediate vicinity is 51. When calling from within the Republic of Ireland, dial 051 before the local number.

GETTING AROUND: Waterford can be a busy turnstile for traffic. Both the Dublin–Cork and Wexford–Tipperary roads pass through the city, but much of the traffic avoids the narrow streets of the old city, traveling instead along the quays and then out along the Mall. Disc parking spaces are plentiful along the quay at (about 30¢ per hour); discs can be purchased at the tourist board and most shops. The city is easily explored on foot, and a change of pace can be provided by an afternoon cruise — with tea en route — on the river Suir. Cruises run April through October; contact the tourist board for details (phone: 75788).

Bus and Train – Local buses board beside the Clock Tower along the Quay, and some buses also leave from Plunkett Station, as do trains for Dublin, Limerick, and Rosslare Harbour (and intervening points); the station is near Ignatius Rice Bridge on the north side of the river Suir (phone: 73401). A taxi into the city center costs about $4, although it is only a short walk.

Car Rental – Among the car rental agencies in Waterford are *Avis* (112 The Quay; phone: 70170); *Hertz* (Waterford Airport; phone: 72891); and *Southeast Budget-Rent-a-Car* (41 The Quay; phone: 21670).

Ferry – Save an hour's driving time to Wexford via N25 by taking the lovely 10-minute car ferry from Passage East, south of Waterford and then picking up L159. Fare per car is about $7.75 round-trip, or about $4.65 one way. No reservations necessary (phone: 82488).

Taxi – Cabs wait at Plunkett Station and along Barronstrand St. Otherwise, a radio cab can be called from *K-Kabs* (phone: 75017). (As a service, the tourist board can call cabs for visitors.) The minimum fare is about $4, with travel outside the city limits costing about 50¢ a mile.

Tours – Bus tours of Waterford and the surrounding area are operated by *Bus Eireann,* a subsidiary of *CIE* (*Córas Iompair Eireann, National Transport Company*), from Plunkett Station June through August (phone: 73401).

SPECIAL EVENTS: The city's *International Festival of Light Opera,* which occurs every September, provides the excuse for a host of fringe events. (For details, see *Extra Special.*)

MUSEUMS: Besides Reginald's Tower (described in *Special Places*), the City Hall contains several items worthy of inspection. During normal business hours, the Council Chamber of this spacious building is open for visitors to view its beautiful glass chandelier, made at the original Waterford factory (a replica of the chandelier hangs in Philadelphia's Independence Hall). There is also a complete dinner service of old Waterford glass, and a flag from the Irish Brigade that fought on the Union side in the American Civil War. The Mall.

SHOPPING: While Waterford is known for its crystal products, the city is also a source for a wide range of Irish-made gifts and souvenirs. You'll find most of the best shops along the Quay and on the long street that begins at Barronstrand. Smaller shops close on Thursdays and some shops stay open late on Friday evenings.

Artwear Galleries – This gem of a shop features paintings and prints plus Irish-made jewelry, linen, and knits. 120 The Quay (phone: 72593).

Book Centre – Large, with a good selection of works by Irish authors. 9 Michael St. (phone: 73823).

The Crystal Gallery – Located at the Waterford crystal factory, this shop sells mouth-blown, hand-cut pieces. Wedgwood china (now owned by Waterford) also is available for purchase. On Cork Road, Kilbarry (phone: 73311).

George's Court Shopping Arcade – An attractive, skylit assemblage of modern boutiques, food shops, and cookery and decor stores encircling a central café. Off George's St.

Hennebry Camera – All the basics and accessories plus kindly proprietors who will try to help when your shutter won't or the flash doesn't. 109 The Quay (phone: 75049).

Joann's – A good place to buy brass, silver, crystal, and china. 30 Michael St. (phone: 73138).

Kelly's – This 2-level department store offers crystal, china, linen, tweeds, silver, copper, coats of arms, and souvenir items from shillelaghs to shamrock seeds. 76 The Quay (phone: 73557).

Joseph Knox – This lovely store behind a Victorian shopfront is a major distributor of Waterford crystal and English bone china, and it's often crowded. If you do more than browse — there are many handsome pieces of porcelain and cut glass on display — you can arrange for your booty to be mailed. 3/4 Barronstrand St. (phone: 75307).

McMahon's – A unique and well-stocked shoe shop, it offers many name brands, including Arianna, Bally, Ecco, and Fogarin. Fashionable sheepskin and leather jackets, coats, and accessories also are available. George's Court, George's St. (phone: 77134).

Midget, Ltd. – Stocked with stacks of appealing hand-crafted baskets, crocks, stoneware, Kilkenny pottery, homespuns, and such. 85 The Quay (phone: 74127).

Penrose – Although its manufacture was revived only in 1978, this locally made glassware dates from 1786 and is well worth a look. Visitors are welcome to watch the craftsmen as they hand-cut the floral motifs into the glass. 32 John St. (phone: 76537).

Quay Antiques – Near Reginald's Tower is a treasure trove of collectibles, posters, brass, and the like. 128 The Quay (phone: 77789).

Shaw & Sons – A homey department store selling a broad range of goods, from Aran sweaters to silver. 53 The Quay (phone: 72977).

Waterford Craft Centre – Prints of old Waterford, etched brass, heraldic crests, and ceramic jewelry are among this shop's wares. 31 Michael St. (phone: 55733).

Woolcraft – Established in 1887, specializing in Aran knit, mohair, Icelandic, and lamb's wool sweaters. Also tapestry jackets, gloves, tams, and scarves. 11 Michael St. (phone: 74082).

SPORTS AND FITNESS: Waterford has a variety of sports facilities both within and just outside the city, and the seaside resort of Tramore has a 50-acre amusement complex and a 3-mile-long beach. In summer, buses to Tramore leave on the half hour from The Quay.

Golf – The 18-hole course of the *Waterford Golf Club* (phone: 76748) is open to the public. It's in a scenic setting about 1½ miles outside the city. Visitors are also welcome at the 18-hole course of the *Tramore Golf Club,* a mile from Tramore (phone: 86170).

Greyhound Racing – The dogs race at *Kilcohan Park* on Tuesdays and Saturdays in June, and daily for a week in August. For specific information, call the *Waterford Greyhound Track* (phone: 74531).

Horseback Riding – Horses can be hired at *Melody's Riding Stables* (Ballmacarberry, near Clonmel, about 15 miles northwest of Waterford; phone: 52-36147); and *Kilotteran Equitation Centre* (Kilotteran, about 3 miles southwest of Waterford; phone: 84158).

Polo – Europe's only residential polo vacation school is at *Whitfield Court,* with 2 polo grounds, wooden horses, an enclosed riding school, video equipment, 20 polo ponies, a heated swimming pool, and a tennis court among its many facilities. One-week sessions are offered from May to August; advance reservations are essential. Major Hugh Dawnay, *Whitfield Court,* Waterford (phone: 84216).

Sailing – Details are available from the *Waterford Sailing Club* in Dunmore East, 9 miles southeast of the city (phone: 83230).

Squash – *Henry Downe's Pub* (10 Thomas St.; phone: 74118) has 2 courts. Other facilities are at the *Celtic Squash Club* (71 Barrack St.; phone: 76541).

Swimming – The *Waterford Glass Swimming Pool* on the Cork road is open to the public. Admission is on the hour for a 45-minute session. Admission charge. Hours vary, so it's probably a good idea to check in advance by calling the pool manager, Waterford Glass Ltd. (phone: 73311, ext. 266). Tramore has a 3-mile beach, with lifeguards on duty in summer. Surfboards and deck chairs can be rented at the beach.

Tennis – *Waterford Tennis Club* (St. John's Hill; phone: 74350) has both grass and hard courts.

THEATER: Special productions take place in summer at the *Theatre Royal* (housed in City Hall, The Mall; phone: 74402). Contemporary plays, films, and concerts are presented year-round at the *Garter Lane Arts Centre and Theatre* (5 O'Connell St.; phone: 55038).

MUSIC: The high point of Waterford's musical season is the 2-week *International Festival of Light Opera* in September. Besides the light opera on the program, there is also a singing pubs competition. (See *Extra Special.*) For traditional and folk music sessions, try *T. & H. Doolan's* pub (32 George's St.); traditional Irish music is offered at any number of pubs, and there is jazz every Sunday at *Reginald's* on the Mall.

NIGHTCLUBS AND NIGHTLIFE: There are often Saturday night dinner dances at the *Granville* hotel (phone: 55111) as well as frequent disco dances at the *Tower* hotel (phone: 75801), the *Jurys* (phone: 32111), and *Xanadu* in the *Bridge* hotel (phone: 77222). *Cheers* (phone: 55089) features an ever-changing agenda of cabaret, dancing, ballad, folk, and disco music Tuesdays through Sundays. Some pubs feature special appearances by singing groups, both popular and traditional. The best way to keep abreast of all evening festivities is to consult the tourist board and the local papers.

BEST IN TOWN

CHECKING IN: Waterford's hotels are convenient to the city center, and they offer the visitor a nice choice between the modern and the old. There are also a number of bed and breakfast houses in the area. The tourist board will help find a vacancy in a house that meets with their approval. Expect to pay over $150 for accommodations listed as very expensive, from $100 to $150 for a double room in an expensive hotel, from $50 to $90 in a moderate one, and under $50 for inexpensive lodgings. All telephone numbers are in the 51 area code unless otherwise indicated.

Waterford Castle – Opened as a hotel in 1988, this luxury property, with a façade of turrets, towers, and battlements, dates back to 1160 and was the home of the FitzGerald family for over 800 years. It is set amid extensive gardens on a 310-acre island in the river Suir about 2 miles south of the city (a short car-ferry ride). The interior is replete with oak-paneled walls, ornate plaster ceilings, historical paintings, and antique furnishings including four-poster or canopy beds in the 20 guestrooms and suites (all with bath). There is a fine restaurant, a fitness center with an indoor pool, and facilities for tennis, horseback riding, salmon and trout fishing, and a variety of water sports; an 18-hole golf course also is in the course of development and expected to be completed this summer. Ballinakill (phone: 78203). Very expensive.

Granville – This Georgian mansion, once the home of Irish patriot Thomas Meagher, is Waterford's classiest hotel in the downtown business area. It exudes an air of graciousness and respectability, with 66 rooms, recently and appealingly redone, and an attractive paneled lounge bar, restaurant (see *Eating Out*), and grill on the premises. The Quay (phone: 55111). Expensive.

Jurys – Set on 38 acres on a hillside along the north banks of the river Suir, this modern 6-story establishment offers panoramic views of Waterford City and the river from each of its 100 rooms. Although the views have always been a major attraction, the hotel itself, formerly the *Ardree,* was rather ordinary until last year, when it was taken over by the Jurys hotel group. A multimillion-dollar refurbishment, scheduled for completion early this year, will transform the property into a first-rate choice, with dark wood furnishings, plush carpets, designer fabrics and linen, and well-lit marble and tile bathrooms. The restaurant, which offers unbeatable vistas (especially at night when the city lights shine) is also being refurbished, and a new chef will prepare Irish dishes with European and Californian influences. The modern leisure center (already in place) has an heated indoor swimming pool, a turbo Jacuzzi, steamroom/Turkish bath, plunge pool, gym, saunas, solariums, hairdressing salons, and 2 tennis courts. The *Waterford Golf Club* is adjacent to the property. There also is ample parking — a rarity among Waterford hotels. Ferrybank (phone: 32111). Expensive.

Tower – Centrally located on the Mall near Reginald's Tower, this 81-room establishment has been tastefully refurbished, with an emphasis on brickwork, mirrors, and flowering plants in the public areas and eclectic furnishings in the bedrooms. Waterford crystal chandeliers hang in the pink-toned dining room, known for such dishes as local river trout. The Mall (phone: 75801). Expensive to moderate.

Bridge – A modern, 49-room hostelry with an Old World atmosphere, particularly in its *Timber Toes* lounge and *Ignatius Rice* restaurant. All rooms have private bath/shower. 1 The Quay (phone: 77222). Moderate.

Dooley's – Formerly a coaching inn, this family-run place has 36 rooms, all with private bath. The restaurant is known for its special-value tourist menus and a nice variety of bar food; a good place to meet the locals. The Quay (phone: 73531). Moderate.

Blenheim House – About 3 miles southeast of Waterford, overlooking the city and the river Suir, this gracious home was built in 1763. The current owners have restored it fully and have furnished it with their own antiques and dazzling collection of Waterford crystal. Each of the 6 guest bedrooms has a private bath. Blenheim Heights, off the Passage East road (phone: 74115). Inexpensive.

EATING OUT: Waterford does not have a large selection of restaurants, but with the inclusion of a few hotel dining rooms, there are enough good ones to keep visitors well fed. For anyone in a hurry or homesick for the US, there is *Chapman's Delicatessen* (61 The Quay). Most pubs serve a lunch of soup and a sandwich or a special of the day costing between $3 and $5. Dinner for two (wine not included) will cost over $60 in an expensive restaurant, between $35 and $55 in a moderate place, and less than $35 in an inexpensive one. All telephone numbers are in the 51 area code unless otherwise indicated.

Galley Cruising Restaurants – Dine while cruising past the sylvan beauties of the rivers Barrow or Nore or down toward the sea (depending on the state of the tide and the inclination of the skipper). The 3-hour dinner trip is fun, and the food — fresh and all home-cooked — is unusually good for the size of the galley. Cruises depart from New Ross, 15 miles northeast of Waterford. Dinner cruises are offered daily in July and August and according to demand in April, May, and September. Two-hour cruises also leave Waterford at 3 PM, and lunch and afternoon cruises depart from New Ross. Reservations essential. New Ross (phone: 21723). Expensive, but the boat trip is included in the price of the meal.

Granville – The cheerfully elegant *Tapestry Room,* handsomest in-town place for lunch or dinner, offers à la carte and table d'hôte choices, reasonably priced chef's specials, and "mini dinners" (three courses with beverage), plus a candlelight dinner dance Saturdays. Open daily. The Quay (phone: 55111). Expensive to moderate.

Jade Palace – On the second floor of a Victorian-style bar managed by the same people, this elegant, award-winning Chinese restaurant specializes in king prawns and duck Cantonese, but it also offers steaks, omelettes, and curry dishes. Dinner daily; lunch Mondays through Fridays. 3 The Mall (phone: 55611). Expensive to moderate.

Dooley's – The restaurant in the hotel of the same name on the quay has earned a reputation for good lunches and dinners at reasonable prices. Open daily. 30 The Quay (phone: 73531). Moderate.

Manners – On the second floor of the trendy *George's Court* shopping arcade, this is a bright and airy restaurant filled with hanging plants. The menus are eclectic, ranging from prime ribs and rainbow trout to seafood paella and weight-watchers' salads. Open daily for lunch and dinner. George's Court and Barronstrand St. (phone: 78704). Moderate.

Manor Court Lodge – Just south of town, en route to the Waterford Glass Factory, this dining place is housed in a 19th-century Gothic-style stone gate lodge, listed on Ireland's National Trust of historic buildings. The decor is rich with stained glass windows and local memorabilia; choir stall seating reflects the Old World atmosphere. The menu features many customary Irish favorites, from stuffed pork steaks and roast stuffed chicken to scampi and filets of plaice, as well as more inventive choices, such as sirloin steaks in brandied peppers, or strips of veal with prawns. Manor Court, Cork Rd. (phone: 78851). Moderate.

Oak Room – Housed in a 300-year-old building that's also home to the popular *Munster Bar*, this small, oak-paneled gem of a restaurant has Waterford crystal chandeliers and an open fireplace make dining on prime ribs and seafood even more enjoyable. During the daytime, the downstairs lounge serves some elegant pub grub, including hot prawns in Pernod and smoked mackerel salad. Closed Sundays for dinner. Factory La., off Bailey's New St. (phone: 74656). Moderate.

Reginald Grill – Newly expanded, this eatery offers several choices. The original grillroom/bar, which is tucked beside Reginald's Tower and contains part of the city's 9th-century walls, is known for its medieval decor, buffet lunches, and creative cocktails. A newer section, in an adjacent house overlooking The Mall, has a more formal atmosphere with fine linen and candlelight dining, plus an imaginative menu that includes baked pink trout *en papilotte,* filet mignon stuffed with stilton, chicken Kiev, and steak Diane. Open daily for lunch and dinner. The Mall (phone: 55087). Moderate to inexpensive.

SHARING A PINT: *Egans* (36/37 Barronstrand St.) is a Tudor-style bar with plenty of room to stretch. It's a convenient place to pause from shopping, enjoy a pint, and listen to the locals discuss the business of the day. *T. & H. Doolan's* (32 George's St.) is a small, old-fashioned gem. The *Reginald Lounge* (on The Mall) usually has a lovely peat fire going, and old armaments hang on a wall that is really a restored section of the original city wall dating from the 12th century. On Sunday afternoons there's often a jazz session by Waterford musicians. Whatever you do, don't leave town without looking in at the *Munster* (on The Mall), a 300-year-old inn revived and added on to by the Fitzgerald family. The entrance to the mellowed though modern lounge, a favorite meeting and greeting spot for young Waterforders, is on The Mall, but walk around to the original Bailey's New St. door to see the men's bar on the right.

WEXFORD TOWN

The main attraction in Wexford Town is the people, whose Irishness is not of the mild, gentle folk strain. Instead, they are keen of mind and quick in discussion, and they often like their wit a bit on the saucy side. Spend a pleasant day browsing among the narrow streets of this hilly town, then head for the nearest bar stool (an easy assignment, as one local claims there are more than 50 pubs in Wexford). A friendly comment or two from a visitor is likely to get a native monologue going, be it a recitation of the local history or a soliloquy on the praiseworthy local weather. An Irish American can expect a lively debate on the political fortunes of the Kennedy family, whose ancestors came from nearby Dunganstown in County Wexford.

The hardy ladies of the country market are easy to engage in conversation as well. They will tell a visitor that from medieval times the market has been the heartbeat of the town and that in the days of the schooners, the ships could dock quite close to unload their goods for sale. They'll also recall that long before the young people started their natural-foods campaign, the wives of Wexford farmers knew the benefits of vegetables grown in chemical-free soil, and they never forsook their homemade breads and jams for commercial substitutes.

This boldness of spirit is not all talk. It has produced such illustrious native sons as John Barry, regarded as the founder of the US Navy, born 10 miles from Wexford at Ballysampson, and Sir Robert J. McClure, discoverer of the Northwest Passage. The boldest and proudest Wexford men of days gone by, however, were those who took part in the Rebellion of 1798. In that year, the United Irishmen were unsuccessful in planning a general uprising against the British, so Father John Murphy, a County Wexford priest, independently led his parishioners, armed with pitchforks, or pikes, in revolt. The rebellion lasted a month before it was suppressed, but it has remained alive in folk memory through Irish ballads such as "The Wearing of the Green" and "The Boys of Wexford."

Wexford has a population of more than 15,300, with another several thousand living in the suburbs. Located where the river Slaney flows into the shallow Wexford Harbour, the town is old and has an impossibly narrow main street, a legacy of its Viking past. It is said that a settlement existed here as early as AD 150, but it was the Vikings who developed it, calling it *Waesfjord,* meaning "harbor of mud flats." Initially, the Vikings used this as a base from which to plunder the countryside and later turned it into a major trading post.

The Anglo-Norman invasion led by Richard de Clare, Earl of Pembroke, known as Strongbow, ousted the Vikings in 1169 and launched a new era of domination. The face of the town also changed. Selskar Abbey rose at its northwestern edge — tradition holds that Henry II came here in 1172 to do *Lenten* penance for the murder of Thomas à Becket, and it was here that

Strongbow's daughter was married — and Wexford soon became a walled town, with five fortified gateways and four castles. The only remains of these defenses are the West Gate, built in the 14th century and used until the end of the 16th century, and a portion of wall nearby.

Norman nobles used one of the town's squares for the bloody sport of bull-baiting and to this day the square is called the Bull Ring. The name stuck, despite the fact that the worst of a much bloodier slaughter, the massacre of Wexford's citizenry by Oliver Cromwell in 1649, occurred in the same place. The townspeople erected no monument to remind them of this deed, but in 1905, when they got around to commemorating the insurgency of 1798, they placed their statue of an Irish pikeman here, in a stroke of independent-mindedness. More of the same spirit lies behind the confusion of Wexford's street names. Many have two names, one dating from the days of British rule, the other from the founding of the Irish Republic in 1922, the latter likely to be the name of a rebel.

The establishment of an industrial estate with German and American firms has brought needed jobs into the area. Lett & Company, which transplants small seed mussels into Wexford Harbour from less nourishing areas, is located in Wexford Town and is the biggest single employer in the Irish fishing industry.

Then there's the tourist industry, which Wexford comes by almost effortlessly, given its location in the sunniest part of Ireland, near the 6-mile beach of Rosslare, which draws Irish holidaymakers unsolicited as honeybees to clover. Tourism is not entirely effortless, however, because the energy that goes into the yearly *Wexford Opera Festival* and all its accompanying fringe events cannot be discounted. At opera time, later in the fall, nearly every family in town has at least one member backstage sewing costumes or painting props, or elsewhere hanging pictures for an exhibition or setting up chairs for a lecture.

That the festival exists at all is the result of another stroke of boldness on the part of Wexford's people. In 1951, a group of residents tired of listening to phonograph records and resolved to hear the real thing, even if they had to produce it themselves. The orchestra was hired, singers were engaged, other professionals were called in, and what eventually was to become an acclaimed event on the international opera calendar was off to a brave beginning.

WEXFORD AT-A-GLANCE

SEEING THE CITY: The best way to see Wexford is on foot. To enjoy the harbor and the sea air, begin at the tourist board on Crescent Quay and walk in a northerly direction. Any street off the quays leads to Main Street, which runs parallel to the harbor and is the central shopping area, but a left turn at the Bank of Ireland onto Common Quay Street (also known as O'Hanlon Walsh Street) brings you to the Bull Ring. This winds around to the right into the Cornmarket and Abbey Street, where *White's* hotel is situated.

SPECIAL PLACES: The town's memorials, churches, and abbey are all within a 5-minute walk of Main Street.

John Barry Memorial – In 1956, the US presented Ireland with this handsome statue of the founder of the US Navy, who was born in County Wexford in 1745. Commodore Barry stands on Crescent Quay where two former American presidents, Dwight D. Eisenhower and John F. Kennedy, laid wreaths on separate occasions. The inscriptions on the monument list a few of Barry's accomplishments during the American Revolution. Walk up the street behind the monument for a lifelike view of the commodore looking out to sea with his mighty cape blowing in the wind. Crescent Quay.

Maritime Museum – A retired lighthouse ship, the *Guillemot* — moored about 15 miles southwest of town at Kilmore Quay — is home to a museum devoted to Wexford's seafaring days. When the ship's flag is flying, the museum is open. Open in summer only, usually from 2 to 8 PM on weekdays and noon to 6 PM on weekends. Admission charge. Kilmore Quay.

Bull Ring – The medieval practice of bull-baiting — killing bulls for sport — once took place in this small, historic square. This is also the place where on October 1, 1649, Oliver Cromwell had 2,000 Irish men, women, and children slaughtered. A statue to a pikeman, done by Oliver Sheppard and erected in 1905, now dominates the square in tribute to the peasants who took part in what came to be known as the Rebellion of 1798. Oscar Wilde's mother lived in the house that is now Diana Donnelly's boutique (legend says that Wilde's mother was born in room No. 10 of the *Old Wexford Coaching Inn*). At the east side of the ring a market is held on Fridays from 9:30 AM to 12:30 PM. Here Wexford women sell their vegetables, baked goods, jams, jellies, honey, and sometimes crafts in buildings dating from 1871.

St. Iberius Church – This Georgian masterpiece (Church of Ireland) was built in 1760 on land occupied by other houses of worship dating from earliest Norse days. The handsome interior and superb acoustics make it a favorite concert hall during the *Wexford Opera Festival*. South of the Bull Ring on Main St.

Wexford Arts Centre – Once the Market House, then Town Hall, this building was restored as a cultural headquarters and special-events site. Its now-elegant second story boasts five Waterford crystal chandeliers. Around the corner from the Bull Ring, Corn Market (phone: 23764).

Twin Churches – The Roman Catholic churches of the Immaculate Conception on Rowe Street and of the Assumption on Bride Street, both designed by Robert Pierce, were inaugurated on the same day in 1858 when Wexford's original nine parishes became two, thanks to the unflagging efforts of Father James Roche, who is buried in the Bride Street church.

Selskar Abbey – It is a pity the town has not done more in restoring and promoting this 12th-century site. The abbey was once quite extensive, although all that can be seen today are a 14th-century battlement tower and church. A long, covered passage runs underground to the far side of town. Tradition says that Henry II did penance here for murdering Thomas à Becket, but historians now think St. Mary's, protected within the town walls, a more likely site for his acts of contrition. Some of the older people in town can remember when the church was still in use. To explore the ruins, visitors must obtain a key from a nearby house (a notice on the gate explains where). Behind the abbey remain the old West Gate, the only one of Wexford's five original gateways still standing, and part of the town walls. Entrance at the intersection of Temperance Row, West Gate, and Slaney St.

Franciscan Friary – Built in the 17th century on the site of an earlier church destroyed during Cromwellian times, this was the parish church for Wexford Town until the twin churches of the Assumption and the Immaculate Conception were completed in 1858. The Franciscan friary was extensively redecorated in the 19th century, when the vaulted ceiling, marble columns, and organ were added. School St.

Irish National Heritage Park – Located about 2 miles north of Wexford Town on the banks of the river Slaney, this new outdoor museum reflects centuries of Ireland's history. Each exhibit is set in an appropriate environment — on the banks of a river estuary, in a woodland, in a marshland, or on a mountain slope. Displays include a *crannog* (an early lake dwelling), ring forts, *souterrains* (underground escape passages), round towers, dolmens, horizontal mills, and a *fulacht fiagh* (an ancient cooking place that used hot stones to heat food). Open daily, except December and January when it is only open on Sundays. Admission charge. Ferrycarrig (phone: 22211 or 47133).

Johnstown Castle – This 19th-century turreted Gothic mansion incorporates an earlier castle and is the former home of the Esmonde, Grogan, and Fitzgerald families. It is now owned by the State Agricultural College, but visitors can tour the beautiful gardens, lakes, and nature trails that surround it. The grounds are open to the public without charge 10 AM to 6 PM daily — take a picnic basket. Exhibits in the *Irish Agricultural Museum* (phone: 53-42888) in the castle's restored farm buildings include harness ware and antique farm machinery as well as a reconstructed farm kitchen and bedroom and a creamery. Open 9 AM to 12:30 PM, 1:30 to 5 PM Mondays through Fridays year-round; also Sundays 2 to 5 PM May through October. Admission charge. Off the Rosslare Harbour road, 2½ miles south of Wexford.

■**EXTRA SPECIAL:** An excellent choice for a day spent outdoors is the Saltee Islands, Ireland's largest and most famous bird sanctuary. During spring and early summer, the Great Saltee (which is 1 mile long) and the Little Saltee are home to more than 3 million gulls, puffins, and other feathered creatures that delight bird watchers. The islands are a 45-minute boat trip off the coast of Kilmore Quay, about 20 miles southwest of Wexford. To arrange a trip, call fisherman Willie Bates (phone: 29644) or Tom O'Brien (phone: 29727). Kilmore Quay itself is a quaint fishing village of thatch-roofed cottages. The lovely, modern *Saltees* hotel (phone: 29601) contains rooms named after different species of birds found on the islands.

SOURCES AND RESOURCES

TOURIST INFORMATION: Wexford's large tourist board on Crescent Quay is open all year, 9 AM to 12:45 PM, 2 to 6 PM Mondays through Saturdays (phone: 23111); winter hours may differ slightly. The board offers extensive information on hotels and sights in the area. In summer the Junior Chamber of Commerce puts out an excellent monthly guide that is available free from the tourist board and from most hotels. It contains names and phone numbers of doctors, dentists, and pharmacists as well as the timetable for buses and trains to Dublin and ferries operating out of Rosslare Harbour. It also has two good maps of the town with a suggested walking tour. The Chamber of Commerce publishes a small brochure with some of the same information in a more condensed form along with a map.

Local Coverage – The *Wexford People,* the town's weekly newspaper, comes out on Thursdays with news and an entertainment listing for the area.

TELEPHONE: The area code for Wexford and the immediate vicinity is 53. When calling from within the Republic of Ireland, dial 053 before the local number.

GETTING AROUND: Plan to park the car and see Wexford on foot. The disc parking system is in effect for all street parking spaces (about 30¢ per hour); discs are sold at the tourist office. Among the dozen or so parking lots, there's a convenient one near the tourist board — a left turn onto Custom House Quay from the bridge, on the right just before the statue of John Barry. (For other lots, see the detailed town map in the Junior Chamber of Commerce guide.) Consider tagging along on an Old Wexford Society walking tour. Its members conduct them throughout the year at hours set to suit visitor demand. Check starting times and places at hotels or the tourist board.

Bicycle – *Hayes Cycle Shop* (108 S. Main St.; phone: 22462) and *The Bike Shop* (9 Selskar St.; phone: 22514) have bikes for rent.

Bus and Train – There is no in-town bus service — it's not necessary. The bus and railway terminals for trips beyond the town are in Redmond Place, near the quays just north of the bridge. *Bus Eireann* and *Irish Rail,* divisions of *CIE* (*Córas Iompair Eireann, National Transport Company*), operate buses and trains between Wexford and Dublin and between Wexford and Rosslare Harbour, 13 miles southeast (not to be confused with Rosslare or Rosslare Strand, the seaside resort between Wexford and Rosslare Harbour). Ferries leave Rosslare Harbour regularly for Wales and for Le Havre and Cherbourg, France. Irish trains and buses are not known for adhering to timetables, so check with *CIE* for delays (phone: 22522 from 6:30 AM to 6 PM). For information on ferries to Wales, call *British Rail* (phone: 33115). For information on ferries to France, call *Irish Ferries* (phone: 33158).

Car Rental – A number of car rental companies operate in Wexford and in nearby Rosslare Harbour, and some have dropping-off stations for their vehicles rented elsewhere. *EuroDollar* (Ferrybank, Wexford; phone: 23511); *Boland's Car Hire* (Rosslare Harbour; phone: 33611); *Murrays Rent a Car* (near the railway station and bus depot at the north end of Wexford; phone: 22122; and at Rosslare Harbour; phone: 32181); and *South East Budget* (Rosslare Harbour; phone: 33318); *Avis* (phone: 81126) and *Hertz* (phone: 33238) also have offices in Rosslare Harbour.

Taxi – Cabs are expensive, but sometimes they're the quickest and most convenient way of reaching a destination in town. To get one, call 22949, 22485, 23196, or 24056.

Tours – *Bus Eireann,* a division of *CIE,* operates afternoon bus tours of nearby scenic areas during July and August from Redmond Pl. (phone: 22522).

SPECIAL EVENTS: Ushering in summer, at nearby Enniscorthy, is the *Wexford Strawberry Festival,* a popular affair held in late June and early July, featuring a week of music and strawberry tasting. The 19th-century *Theatre Royal* (High St.) is the Georgian setting of 12 days of music held in late October and early November. Singers from all over the world present rarely performed operas, usually to sold-out audiences who've waited long and come from afar for the pleasure. The operas, three per festival, can be obscure works of the 17th, 18th, or 19th century or contemporary works, and the performers may be equally unknown, though many are "discovered" here and go on to international careers. Since the theater seats only 446 opera lovers, early booking is necessary — bookings by mail open in June. Contact the *Wexford Opera Festival, Theatre Royal,* Wexford (phone: 22244 or 22144). If you don't get seats, don't despair. Many other events, from concerts, art exhibitions, and lectures to street theater, fashion shows, and fishing contests, take place around the main event, and there is no doubt that this is the liveliest time of year to be in Wexford under any pretext.

SHOPPING: The best method of shopping in Wexford is to walk along Main Street and browse the storefronts. Most stores are open 9 AM to 5:30 PM, slightly later on Fridays and Saturdays; closed Sundays and, in fall and winter, often on Thursdays as well.

Barkers – Established in 1848, this dependable shop offers Waterford crystal, Belleek and Royal Tara china, linen, and other gift items. 36-40 S. Main St. (phone: 23159).

Casket – A small shop with a big stock of Aran knit goods and handmade lace. 43 S. Main St. (phone: 24314).

Martin Doyle – Fine hand-wrought gold and silver jewelery. Lower Rowe St. (phone: 41167).

Faller's Sweater Shop – An enormous emporium of modern Irish-made knitwear, in a rainbow of colors. 4 N. Main St. (phone: 24659).

Hore's – A good place for Irish linen. 31/37 S. Main St. (phone: 22200).

Joyce's China Shop – For more than 40 years this spot has been known for Irish crystal, Belleek china, Wedgwood, Lladro, and other fine European products. 3 N. Main St. (phone: 22212).

Laurence's – A jewelry shop with attractive rings at reasonable prices, as well as crystal, china, and silver. 83 N. Main St. (phone: 24319).

Lowney's Shopping Mall – An enclave of ten little shops under one roof, it offers glassware, ceramics, framed prints, brassware, shell ornaments, and more. 61 S. Main St. (phone: 23140).

Martin's Jewelers – China and crystal, plus traditional Claddagh rings. 14 S. Main St. (phone: 22635).

Wexford Gallery – A showcase for local crafts, this shop sells paintings, pottery, knitwear, crochetwork, hand-cut glass, enamel, and woodwork. Open 7 days. Crescent Quay (phone: 23630).

Wool Shop – For a large choice of Aran sweaters, woven belts, local sheepskin and goatskin rugs. 39/41 S. Main St. (phone: 22247).

SPORTS AND FITNESS: The monthly guide published by the Junior Chamber of Commerce has detailed information on recreational activities. The leisure center in the *Talbot* hotel on the quays is open to non-residents and has a number of facilities including a heated indoor swimming pool, squash courts, and saunas.

Golf – The *Wexford Golf Club* (phone: 42238) has an 18-hole course just one-quarter mile from downtown. The *Rosslare Golf Club* (phone: 32203) has an 18-hole course at Rosslare, 11 miles southeast of Wexford.

Horseback Riding – At *Horetown House* (12 miles west on L160 at Foulksmills; phone: 63633, manor house; 63786, stables), the Young family offers daily rides, all levels of instruction, an indoor ring, and a cross-country course for experienced riders on 17th-century manor grounds. Picnic rides, riding holiday packages, and wonderful home-cooked food are available too. Horses can also be hired at *Laraheen Pony Trekking* (Laraheen House, Gorey; phone: 55-28289) and *Boro Hill Equestrian Centre* (Clonroche, Enniscorthy; phone: 54-44117).

Horse Racing – Flat racing is held five times a year in the small-town atmosphere of Wexford's *Bettyville Racecourse.*

Swimming – Southeast Ireland is known for its comparative abundance of sunshine, which can be enjoyed at a number of beaches around Wexford, including Curracloe, Rosslare, Carne, and Kilmore Quay. Some hotels, such as the *Talbot, Great Southern,* and *Kelly's,* also have indoor swimming pools for guests.

Tennis – Visitors are welcome to use the all-weather courts at *Wexford Harbour Boat Club,* Redmond Rd. (phone: 22039 or 23672).

THEATER: In summer an Irish cabaret is held several nights a week at the *Talbot* hotel (phone: 22566). Special programs take place at the *Wexford Arts Centre* (in the old Market House in the Cornmarket; phone: 23764) and at the *Theatre Royal* (High St.; phone: 22144). The *Riff Raff Theatre* (Larkin's La., off S. Main St.; phone: 22141) offers contemporary plays, plus summertime street and beach entertainment.

MUSIC: Wexford is a lively town at night, with plenty of good singing pubs, cabaret, and ballroom dancing at most of the larger hotels. If you're lucky, *Sonas,* a popular group of five young musicians, will be singing Irish ballads as well as a few humorous, modern tunes. There is Irish music most nights in the *Shelmalier Bar* of *White's* hotel (phone: 22311) and in the *Tavern* of the *Talbot* hotel (phone: 22566). There is jazz on Sundays at the *Talbot.* Look for *seisiún,* an evening — or session — of song and dance sponsored by Comhaltas Ceoltóirí Éireann, a national organization for the promotion of traditional Irish folk music. These very authentic sessions are held in some 30 cities and towns during the summer. In Wexford, they usually take place once a week at *White's* and the *Talbot.* For information on music festivals, see *Special Events.*

NIGHTCLUBS AND NIGHTLIFE: The *Ace of Clubs* disco swings into action on Friday and Saturday nights at *White's* hotel, as does *Speakers Music Bar* next door. *Kelly's Strand* hotel in Rosslare (phone: 32114) also has dancing and entertainment most evenings.

BEST IN TOWN

CHECKING IN: Wexford is a very hospitable town, offering several fine hotels and plenty of bed and breakfast establishments. Most hotels include breakfast in their rates. In summer, an expensive hotel room will cost about $100 and up for a double, a moderate room will run from $65 to $95, and an inexpensive one $60 or less. A single bed and breakfast room will cost about $18, a double about $36. Rates are lower December through March, but about $10 higher per room on bank holidays and during the opera and mussel festivals. All telephone numbers are in the 53 area code unless otherwise indicated.

Ferrycarrig – The top choice in this town is actually out of town, about 2 miles north. Ideally situated, it overlooks the river Slaney estuary, near Ferrycarrig Bridge and opposite the Irish National Heritage Park. Each of the stylishly furnished 40 bedrooms offers a lovely view of the water and surrounding countryside. Facilities include 2 tennis courts and walking trails, as well as a first-rate restaurant (see *Eating Out*). Enniscorthy Rd. (phone: 22999). Expensive.

Talbot – Overlooking Wexford Harbour along the quays, it has 104 rooms, all with bath/shower, and 2 fine restaurants (see *Eating Out*). Its leisure center has a heated indoor pool, gym, squash courts, saunas, and a solarium. The *Tavern* offers live music, from traditional to jazz, and there's a weekly Irish cabaret in summer. Trinity St. (phone: 22566). Expensive.

White's – Originally opened in 1779, it is now also known as the "new" *White's,* with 74 rooms of varying size and quality but all with bath. There are 2 restaurants; *Captain White's* is especially good (see *Eating Out*). The hotel's 2 taverns

— the *Old Wexford* and the *Shelmalier* — are popular for sing-along sessions. George's St. (phone: 22311). Expensive.

Kelly's Strand – A modern 90-room resort hotel on Rosslare Strand, usually booked well in advance, as it is a popular weekend retreat for the Irish, it's known for its good food (see *Eating Out*) and recreation facilities (tennis and squash courts, indoor and outdoor pools, saunas, beach). Closed mid-December to mid-February. Rosslare (phone: 32114). Expensive to moderate.

Great Southern – On a cliff overlooking Rosslare Harbour, it has 100 rooms, all with private bath, plus an indoor heated swimming pool, a tennis court, saunas, and evening entertainment on summer weekends. Open April through October. Rosslare Harbour (phone: 33233). Moderate.

Wexford Lodge – Formerly the *Kincone,* this modern hostelry has 20 rooms, all with bath. There's also a small restaurant. Situated north of town overlooking the Slaney River, adjacent to Wexford Bridge. Dublin Rd. (phone: 23611). Moderate.

Whitford House – Follow the signposts 2 miles south of town to find this modern guesthouse set on its own grounds with countryside views from its wide windows. There are 25 cheery bedrooms, each with private bath, color TV set, and telephone; guests also enjoy a restaurant, lounge bar, reading room, and use of a heated indoor pool and tennis court. New Line Rd. (phone: 43444 or 43845). Moderate to inexpensive.

Killiane Castle – John Mernagh inherited this lovely 230-acre estate, and he and his wife, Kathleen, have converted it into a gracious guesthouse with 8 rooms, all with shared baths. They also rent apartments and hope eventually to restore the 17th-century tower on the grounds. Open April through October. Off Rosslare Harbour Rd., Drinagh (phone: 58885). Inexpensive.

St. Aidan's Mews – A very old place near the Church of the Immaculate Conception, that is now a tidy guesthouse tended by Catherine and Martin Redmond. The 11 rooms share four 4 bathrooms. 25 Lower John's St. (phone: 22691). Inexpensive.

 EATING OUT: Whether a candlelight dinner is desired or a tasty salad in relaxed surroundings, visitors can find a restaurant to suit both appetite and billfold in Wexford. Dinner for two in an expensive restaurant will cost $60 or more; in a moderate one, between $30 and $55; and in an inexpensive one, under $30. All telephone numbers are in the 53 area code unless otherwise indicated.

Captain White's – Comfortable and stylish, this seafood spot with a cozy cocktail bar serves only the freshest fish, done with great skill and respect. Chowder, mussels, scallops, and pink trout with walnut stuffing are commendable; trust the maître d's daily suggestions. There are some meat choices, too. Open daily. In *White's Hotel,* George's St. (phone: 22311). Expensive.

Ferrycarrig – With panoramic views of the river Slaney estuary and the surrounding gardens, this conservatory-style restaurant at the *Ferrycarrig* hotel offers an idyllic setting and good food. The menu, which changes daily, includes such dishes as sautéed Kilmore Quay king scallops in a dill and white wine sauce; breast of duck in a strawberry and vinaigrette sauce; seawater trout and Bannow Bay monkfish baked in fresh herbs; and Wicklow lamb. Save room for the homemade ice cream and pastries. Open year-round. Enniscorthy Rd. (phone: 22999). Expensive.

Kelly's Strand – This elegant hotel dining room offers such tempting dishes as scallops in season and apricot soufflé. Entertainment often rounds out the evening. Open daily; closed mid-December to mid-February. Rosslare (phone: 32114). Expensive.

Guillemot – The main dining room of the *Talbot* hotel, this innovative office has introduced a dual-menu concept to serve both expensive tastes and more moderate budgets. Seafood (especially local lobster, mussels, and pink trout) is a specialty on each menu, and there is an extensive wine list. Open daily. Trinity St. (phone: 22566). Expensive to moderate.

Cellar – Set in the former wine cellar of a 300-year-old Georgian country house, this dining place is known for its carrot and verbena soup, steaks, seafood, and malt health bread. Closed January and February and Sundays and Mondays except June to August. *Horetown House,* Foulksmills, about 20 minutes west of Wexford Town (phone: 63633 or 63706). Moderate.

Farmer's Kitchen – Informal atmosphere, friendly service, good local seafood, and steaks. Bar lunches and restaurant dinners. Open daily. On the Rosslare road (phone: 23295). Moderate.

Granary – Seating is in booths in this quiet, rustic place with a beamed ceiling, wooden pillars, hanging plants, and copper kettles. Its reputation for good food is well established and the menu ranges from veal *à la crème,* chicken flambé, and duck *à l'orange* to lasagna and pork kebabs. Open 7 days for dinner, weekdays only for lunch. Westgate (phone: 23935). Moderate.

Neptune Seafood – This award-winner is set in a fishing village on the river Barrow estuary, about half an hour from Wexford Town. Crab claws, prawns, mussels, and lobster are among the menu's bounty of seafood; other specialties include Hungarian goulash, T-bone steaks, parsnip soup, vegetarian salads, and homemade ice creams. When weather permits, there's outdoor dining on the patio. Closed Mondays November through April. Ballyhack Harbour (phone: 51-89284). Moderate.

Michael's – Pleasant and dimly lit, with aquariums and a nautical motif, its lunch and dinner menus range from steaks to curry to pizza. Open daily. 94 N. Main St. (phone: 22196). Moderate to inexpensive.

Pike Room – The grillroom of the *Talbot* hotel is a good spot for steaks, chops, and seafood, all served in a setting full of historical mementos. Open daily. Trinity St. (phone: 22566). Moderate to inexpensive.

Tim's Tavern – Locals are quick to recommend this casual, folksy spot for lunch and dinner. The steaks are good. Open daily. 51 S. Main St. (phone: 23861). Moderate to inexpensive.

Bohemian Girl – Homemade soup, salads, and appetizing specials make it a particularly good lunch stop. Kay and Seamus McMenamin run this colorful pub named after the opera by William Balfe, who lived in the corner building. N. Main and Monck Sts. (phone: 24419). Inexpensive.

SHARING A PINT: The *Crown Bar* (Monck St.) is one of the oldest pubs in Ireland and has been held by the same family since 1841. Fiona Kelly and her mother, Mrs. Annie Kelly, open for business in the late afternoon and they can help you recall the past when the *Crown* was a stagecoach inn popular with traveling judges and their assistants. You'll see why the *Crown* is also one of Ireland's best-known pubs (it's been seen on television in various European countries) if you sip your drink in the cozy back rooms. They're filled with antique prints, military gear, swords, and other arms — including two guns from the famous Howth gun-running incident of 1914 — that the proprietor's father, the late Aidan Kelly, collected from all over the world. Another stop for a drink and a chat is the *Thomas Moore Tavern* (in the Cornmarket); the poet's mother was born here. *Tim's Tavern* (S. Main St.) has thatching over the bar and good snacks, and *Andy Kinsellas* (also on S. Main St.) is a handsome old place and a quiet refuge from the shopping traffic. The *Westgate Bar* (Ennisworthy Rd.), near the Old City walls, is also worth a visit. If you're looking for an unusual photo setting, Con Macken's "Bar and Undertaker" sign, near Bull Ring, is a classic. Have a drink while enjoying a view of the river Slaney at the *Oak Tavern* (about 2 miles north of town on Enniscorthy Rd. in Ferrycarrig).

DIVERSIONS

For the Experience

Quintessential Ireland

 Ireland's small size tempts visitors to try to see the entire country in a single trip. The distances look short on a map and the miles seem quite modest, but don't be deceived.

Trying to get from Killarney to Galway between lunch and dinner means not only rushing through Counties Limerick and Clare, but also missing the entire point of Ireland. True, even at this speed, it is impossible to miss the rainbow of greens, the rainbows themselves, and the otherwise gorgeous skies and scenery. But the whole point of Ireland is her people — ancient or living, silent or talkative — their histories and connections. Everything in Ireland seems built to human scale. Every nook and cranny has its own name, usually linking it with real or imagined former inhabitants. Scenery, however grand, never intimidates visitors, and otherwise forbidding mountains have names that are musical and wonderfully personal — Ben Lettery, Ben Bulben, and Errigal. Cities and towns are more hospitable to pedestrians than to drivers, and can be walked thoroughly with little strain. Even cosmopolitan Dublin feels cozy for a city of a million souls.

The Irish concept of time is unique and elastic; it often feels imprecise to Americans. In every transaction, there is always time for a chat. Anything after noon can be "evening"; revels of all types start late and go long into the night — making a night of it means the *whole* night. Take your time in Ireland and pretty soon you'll think you have far more of it. Here is just a sampling of the unique experiences that make a visit to Ireland pure magic:

TREADING THE IRISH BOARDS: When the *Abbey*, Dublin's most famous theater, offers productions of plays by early Irish playwrights like Synge, O'Casey, or co-founder W. B. Yeats himself, these classics open the Irish heart and mind to a visitor. The *Abbey* is not the sole keeper of the keys to the kingdom, however. Check local theaters around the country like the *Druid Theatre* and *An Taibdhearc* in Galway, the *Hawk's Well* in Sligo, and the *Guildhall* in Derry for renditions of Irish drama from Wilde and Synge to Brian Friel and Tom Murphy. The level of talent — both professional and amateur — is exemplary, the theaters intimate, and the sound of Irish voices absolutely magical.

SHORTENING THE ROAD: It is not uncommon for Irish vacationers traveling, say, from Dublin to Clifden, a nonstop drive of about 5 hours, to "shorten the road" with a few stops at favorite pubs along the way. They pause as much for spiritual as for liquid refreshment, to take the local conversational temperature as it varies from County Meath to County Roscommon to County Galway. Behind the wheel, all is speed, dash, and more than a little daring. Be assured, however, Irish travelers know how to take their time, pausing to savor a chat more than the scenery. For American visitors, the English language in the mouth of an Irish man, woman, or child sounds like a marvelous new tongue. Few words are rarely used when more will do; color rather than precision is the rule. A pub stop for directions may not clarify the way, but it will illuminate the country.

SHARING A "JAR" AT A COUNTRY PUB: You may park next to a petrol pump, squeeze past bundles of peat and bags of feed and fertilizer, and be distracted by shelves of groceries, but be assured there is a bar in there somewhere. Country pubs are rural Ireland's answer to the mini-mall, invented before the question was even asked, and usually crammed into a space too small to swing a cat. Locals arrive by foot or on bikes, buy milk, bread, and bacon, and have a sociable sip before heading back down their own *boreen* (a tiny, unpaved lane). A wonderfully workable Irish solution to after-hours shopping is the family-owned pub attached to a grocery store. No matter that the shop is dark and long closed, nor that it appears to be a separate entity. A polite inquiry to the barman (and the patience to wait while he attends to the more important business of dispensing pints) will yield the milk or bread or other necessity. If he's very busy, he might just open the door to the shop, tell you to get what you want, and pay at the bar on the way out.

WHEN OYSTERS (AND MORE) "R" IN SEASON: Let there be oysters under the sea — or in this case, Galway Bay — and there will be no question of there being love. Smallish and tasting like a sweet smack of the sea, these exquisitely fresh oysters deserve frequent sampling, and are best washed down with a tall jar of Guinness stout. When September heralds the "r" months once again, the folks in Galway celebrate with an *Oyster Festival:* 2 days of partying that leave visitors feeling they have been celebrating for a month. Happily, another Irish delectable, smoked salmon, is available year-round. Aficionados ask for wild rather than farmed salmon, but when it's well smoked, it is often hard to tell the difference. Enamored visitors have been known to eat smoked salmon scrambled into their breakfast eggs, on slabs of brown bread and butter at lunch, and then again as a "starter" before dinner — all in the same day. Interrupt the seaborne goodies with liberal doses of native cheeses, most of them handmade, all creamy rich and fresh-air infused. Known as farmhouse cheeses, they are made in small batches, usually on the same farm as the goats and cows that produced the raw ingredients. In good restaurants and small grocery stores, look for names like Cashel Blue from County Tipperary, Ireland's answer to Stilton; Lough Caum, a creamy goat cheese from County Clare; or Milleens, a soft cow's milk cheese from County Cork. When in doubt, be sure to try anything made nearby.

GEORGIAN GEM, COUNTY MAYO: A Georgian house, seen in a country setting, emphasizes all the restrained grace of the genre: the solemn, unadorned (but pleasing) geometry of the façade concealing some architectural delight within. At *Newport House,* a hospitable country-house hotel in the little village of Newport, County Mayo, one delight is an elegant lantern — a kind of domed skylight — which admits a lovely light down to the sweeping staircase beneath. During the 1800s, it was as likely to illuminate tweeds and guns and waders as ball gowns. Speaking of waders, the fishing here has an air of the Georgian era as well. Large sections of the Newport River belong exclusively to the manor, a bit of *droit du seigneur* in the late 20th century. Stroll along its rippling banks, casting for salmon or sea trout, and feel that it is yours alone.

A SOFT DAY: It's not exactly raining, but the wipers are on; you don't need an umbrella, but your feet are getting wet. The Irish have many onomatopoeic expressions for precipitation — it may be showering, lashing, belting, or even pissing — but none so apt as "soft." A soft day magically lights up the landscape, for the wet veil over the sun casts a special glow. You may not see the distant mountains standing atop the garden steps of Powerscourt, but the flower borders bloom incandescently and the shadowy ruin of the house comes alive again. Soft days fur the trees and rock walls with mosses, stud the hedgerows with tiny ferns, and transform a country lane into a glade full of magical life. A soft day makes travelers slow down, look about for a rainbow, and understand the genesis of Irish tweed.

TAILORING THE TWEEDS: Irish tweeds perfectly capture the hazy blues and myriad greens, the luminous grays, the dashes of bright fuchsia, and the golden flicker of gorse and lichen on the rocks. Anything made from this sturdy, appealing fabric stands up well however soft the weather, and keeps the wearer dry and cozy (but not burdened). County Donegal is practically a synonym for tweed, and while all manner of tweed items are sold throughout the country, a special cachet lingers over a jacket or skirt purchased on its home ground. Companies like *Magee's* and *John Molloy* still employ home weavers throughout the county, and include the craftsman's name in the garment label. Other counties have their own claims to tweed fame: *Millar's* in Clifden, County Galway, weaves tweed blankets as distinctive as the Connemara landscape; *Avoca Weavers,* whose home is in County Wicklow, captures the soft rainbow colors of Ireland's garden; non-traditional weavers like *Helena Ruuth* in Dublin combine silks and linens in a misty Irish palette. Best get one of each.

SING AN IRISH SONG: Ireland's music, laden with the country's heartbreaking history, ironically inspires the most extraordinarily cheerful evenings. Each part of Ireland has its song, from "The Rose of Alandale" to "The Fields of Athenry"; from "Dublin in the Rare Old Times" to "The Mountains of Mourne" to "The West's Awake." Pubs like the *King's Head* in Galway City, the *Corner Stone* in Lahinch, County Clare, *O'Connor's* in Doolin, County Clare, or *Mannion's* in Clifden, County Galway, post signs announcing "Traditional Music Tonight." Informal playing, however — called a "session" — is common at these and countless other pubs. Impromptu songfests are the Irish version of a digestif at private parties, as well as at country hotels like the *Rock Glen,* near Clifden, County Galway. Every Irish man, woman, and child has a party piece, and everyone participates, entertaining each other with a gusto that feels like television was never invented. Sessions go late into the night, kept afloat with lashings of spirits and pints. Resist the impulse to retire at a sensible hour, be sure to take a turn buying a round of drinks, and don't worry about being in good voice. Participation counts much more than talent, and the hospitable Irish will likely break into "New York, New York" or "I Left My Heart in San Francisco" in reciprocal delight at your contribution.

THE KINGDOM OF CONNEMARA, COUNTY GALWAY: You can drive round it in a day and not see it all in a year. This marvelously diverse western shoulder of County Galway has no official boundaries, but Galway Bay on one side and the Atlantic Ocean on another are generally accepted. There are only rough approximations for the rest.

Just beyond the wooded outskirts of Oughterard, the road bends and rises, the trees disappear, and the looming Maamturk Mountains appear ahead. For travelers from Galway, Connemara begins here with this small taste of astonishing geographical diversity. Farther on, the landscape stretches over bog and lake, one minute wooded and shadowy, the next wild and beautifully stark. The coast is rocky and forbidding, but liberally studded with wide, sandy beaches and hidden, pebbled coves. To make it really your own, ride a Connemara pony along the broad beach at Dog's Bay near Roundstone or on the cliffside fields of Errislannen peninsula. Or see Connemara from one of its high places, like the Sky Road in Clifden, so called because there's more sky than road. For the really energetic, a climb up Diamond Hill in the Connemara National Park will make you feel master of every bog, island, and inlet spread out at your feet.

POETIC PERFECTION, COUNTIES SLIGO AND GALWAY: County Sligo's landscape, draped with song and story, inspired the young W. B. Yeats's poetic imagination. His own legend now clings to those favorite spots, and Glencar Waterfall, the Lake Isle of Inishfree, and the Hazelwood are part of the landscape of great English literature — as lovely as the poems they inspired. Yeats's grave, at the foot of Ben Bulben Mountain, is as dramatic a landmark as he intended and an authentic goose-bump experience — even for non-English majors. Farther south, however, there is another

Yeats landscape, the gentler one surrounding his ancient tower home, Thoor Ballylee in County Galway. Here, where he wrote the mature poems that are the bedrock of his genius, the poet's spirit lingers in the murmur of the little river flowing under the "ancient bridge" by the tower.

ON BLOOM'S TRAIL: Ireland was the country James Joyce loved to hate, but Dublin he simply loved. Never mind that many of the hallowed halls and houses of the hero of *Ulysses* no longer stand; devoted Joyceans follow Leopold Bloom's minutely described footsteps each *Bloomsday,* June 16. For those who never get past page 23, a visit to the Martello Tower overlooking Dublin Bay at Dún Laoghaire, site of stately, plump Buck Mulligan's blasphemous revels, evokes images of the irreverent master.

A WEEK AT THE RACES: The city of Galway is a frenzy during *July Race Week,* for generations a fixture of this horse-mad country. Though crawling with serious fans, this meet has a holiday air and, sure, you need only know the front of a horse from the back to be part of it all. Sit in the stands to get a good view of both the flat and steeplechase racing. Galwegians, however, find the real *craic* (meaning "fun" and pronounced *crack*) in the popular enclosure, where betting, hawking, and all manner of amusements vie with the horses for attention.

THE BURREN, COUNTY CLARE: It means "rocky place" in Irish, and it is an understatement. Hills and fields formed by slabs of limestone in a rainbow of grays conceal a wealth of tiny wildflowers in their crannies. Rivers flow underground, salt spray mists the stony coast, and tiny pastures form astonishingly fertile grassy oases in the rock. The Burren's unique and fragile ecosystem fascinates serious botanists and naturalists, and captivates the rest of us with its haunting, desolate beauty. Ireland's earliest people lived here and left rings of stones which look full of hidden messages. To walk in the ancient silence, broken by the hum and moan of the wind in the rocks, is to feel them trying to speak.

GREAT GOLF, NORTH OR SOUTH: Golf in Ireland is played with something of the spirit of American football, that is, with nearly complete indifference to the weather. At *Royal Portrush,* Portrush, County Antrim, Northern Ireland, it may hail, rain, or blow, but only darkness will surely clear the course. The sight of old Dunluce Castle hovering cliffside in the distance is enough to take anyone's mind off the game, if the wind hasn't blown concentration already. No fear, there's always a warming Bushmill's, Northern Ireland's own whisky from the oldest distiller in the land, to restore the body and soul. Other links we cherish: *Royal County Down,* more often called Newcastle, makes the most of its proximity to the Mountains of Mourne; in the Republic, *Ballybunion*'s *Old Course* ranks among the world's elite.

LAND OF SAINTS: Christianity came to Ireland in the 5th century and took the country by storm. Tempest-tossed relics of this fervent hurricane litter the country; it is impossible to go very far without seeing a roofless church, usually with a companion round tower, both embraced by a crumbling stone wall. Some, like Clonmacnoise on the river Shannon, restored and carefully labeled, are nearly as busy with visitors and faithful as they were in their heyday. Others, like Jerpoint Abbey near Thomastown, County Kilkenny, and Kilmacdaugh near Gort, County Galway, stand wrapped in silence. At small ruins like these, get the key from the caretaker as directed by the sign on the gate, and take a few minutes to find the old, worn small faces carved in the walls. Their simple ancient lines speak of the particular, idiosyncratic kind of faith that still endures in Ireland as nowhere else. Less formal and likely more ancient sacred spots like holy wells and hilltop shrines are known in many country places. A climb up steep, pyramid-shaped Croagh Patrick in County Mayo combines devout pilgrimage with that spirit of jovial outing the Irish bring to their religious observances.

BY THE BOOK: Monks in Ireland's monasteries kept the lamp of learning flickering through Europe's dark ages, by laboring over manuscripts in their dimly lit towers. Another bookish explosion, which began with the Literary Renaissance in the early part of this century and is still going strong, keeps Irish bookshops well stocked with collectible first editions. Almost any Irish bookstore provides a diverting haven on a rainy day. A gem like *Kenny's* on High Street in Galway combines a browser's heaven of old and collectible books and another of prints and maps with an excellent stock of Ireland's contemporary poets and writers. The shop rambles over 5 floors of two back-to-back old Galway houses, and includes a gallery featuring Ireland's best contemporary artists. Each member of the affable Kenny family will happily share his or her expertise or opinion, and while away an afternoon, rainy or otherwise.

Pub Crawling

Ireland has 10,500 pubs in the Republic and another 2,000 in the North — a pub for every 360 people. There are high class bars in expensive luxury hotels, with modern, tiled WCs, and there are age-darkened country pubs with outside toilets (the state of the toilet being a fair indication of the pub's standard). A Roscommon establishment, *James J. Harlow's Funeral Requisites and Furniture Stores,* is at once pub, hardware shop, and gallery of old advertising; Richard MacDonnell's pub in Dingle sells shoes, boots, and leather belts hand-fashioned by the octogenarian proprietor opposite the bar, where he pulls a wonderful pint of Guinness; at *Joe McHugh's Bar* in the lobster-fishing town of Liscannor, County Clare (and at many others like it), it's possible to buy barley sugar, freshly sliced bacon, or a pair of rubber boots along with stout; the *Humbert Inn* in Castlebar, County Mayo, is crammed with musty memorabilia — whips and cudgels from an old English jail, Victorian bottle corkers, and other curiosities. There are sailors' and fishermen's pubs, expatriates' pubs, pubs with gallows and pubs with gardens, pubs with 90-foot bars, country pubs where the dart board is well used and the tables are marked with the rings of a thousand nights of wet-bottomed glasses, city pubs with stained glass and elaborately paneled snugs that have witnessed all manner of clandestine meetings and revolutionary conspiracies in their day. And that's just the beginning. But no matter what its type, the Irish pub — and not the private party — is where weddings, christenings, and funerals invariably end in Ireland, with the Guinness flowing like Niagara Falls and the gossip, discussion, banter, jokes, tales, and information flying fast and furiously, as it can only in Ireland. "A pub is the poor man's university," says a sign in one of them, and talk is at its heart. So don't be afraid to enter into the spirit of things: Upend a pint or two or three, buy a round for your neighbors, accept one from them when your turn comes, and chat with all assembled. If you need advice, it will come in such torrents that you may be hard put to assimilate it all.

The center of pub life, besides the talk, is the distinctive, robust black beer with a creamy white head known as stout. Rich and full-bodied in taste, it was brewed for the first time in Dublin in 1759 and is now consumed in Ireland to the tune of some 2 million pints a day — about half the beer drunk in the country. The singer Burl Ives and the Nobel prize–winning novelist John Steinbeck were devotees of stout, of which three different brands are available: Guinness, which is Dublin's brew, made in Europe's biggest brewery, and two stouts from Cork, Beamish & Crawford and Murphy's. (The Dublin Guinness Brewery has an audiovisual show describing the making of Guinness, after which free samples are handed around — there is no better; phone: 1-756710 or 1-719147.) Each brand has a distinctive flavor, but even the same make varies from one pub to the next, depending on how the pints are pulled. Pulling is considered a high art in Ireland: The method by which the brew is put into the glass is paramount; the stout must be left to rest a minute while the glass is partly filled before being topped off, and the excess foam must be wiped off with a ruler or other straight edge, then topped off again so that the drink can be consumed through the creamy foam. Other factors are equally important, however: the temperature in the cellar where the casks are kept (it must be constant and just so), the distance between cask and tap, and the frequency with which the stout is drawn. It all makes a difference. Certainly, what passes for Guinness stateside would be sent back to the bar straightaway in Ireland.

But stout is not the only drink. There is also Harp, which is brewed in Dundalk, and Smithwick's, the brew for which Ronald Reagan passed up a stout while on a presidential visit to Ballyporeen, County Tipperary, the village of his ancestors. Smithwick's is a bit darker than Harp, but not as dark as stout, and has been made in Kilkenny since 1710 in a brewery on the site of a 12th-century Franciscan monastery whose Romanesque tower still stands.

In addition, reaching deep into Ireland's drinking past is the fiery white distilled spirit known as *poitín* (also known as *poteen* and pronounced put-*cheen*). Many Irish-Americans deeply involved in bootlegging during Prohibition had learned how to distill spirits from making this liquid fire at home in Ireland by boiling together barley, sugar, yeast, and water over a constant flame with the steam running through copper pipe in a barrel of icy water. It was illegal then and continues to be so, though it is still widely manufactured around Connemara and is sold at about half the price of legal liquor. But if it isn't made with scrupulous care — or if it's unscrupulously adulterated with pure alcohol — it can be dangerous, so it's wise to avoid it.

Whiskey is also traditional, the word itself deriving from the Irish *uisge beatha,* meaning "water of life." (Note that it is spelled with an *e,* in contrast to Scotch *whisky.*) Russia's Peter the Great called Irish whiskey "the best of all the wines." The top brands are Jameson, Power, Paddy, and Bushmills — the last made at a distillery dating from 1608, the world's oldest. Located in a pleasant hamlet that gave the liquor its name, this plant is open on weekdays for tours — and samples. (For a reservation, call 2657-31521.) In Ireland, whiskey is seldom drunk with ice, and it used to be that ice was simply unavailable in a bar. A story is told about an American in a rural pub who, requesting his liquor on the rocks, was asked what he meant, and then was told that they had ice in the area only in winter. The American shot is slightly less than the measure (the "half one") in the Republic, slightly more than in Northern Ireland, where drinks cost less in any event, especially beer and stout.

Pub hours vary. In the Republic, they are open Mondays through Saturdays from 11:30 AM to 11 PM in winter, a half hour later in summer; Sunday hours are noon to 10 PM with some closing from 2 to 4 PM. In Northern Ireland, pubs are open Mondays through Saturdays from 11:30 AM to 11 PM. Licensing laws now permit pubs in Northern Ireland to open Sundays from noon to 2 PM and 7 to 10 PM; some publicans, however, choose to remain closed. Pubs in hotels and those with restaurant licenses are open Sundays from about 12:30 to 2:30 or 3 PM and again from 7 to 10 PM; patrons are entitled to drink with a meal then, and visitors who are known or make themselves known may be able to get a drink without a meal. And in both the Republic and Northern Ireland, hotel residents are entitled to drink outside the legal hours, though availability depends on individual circumstances and staffing. Check with the hotel management beforehand about their own policy regarding legal closing time.

Bars are generally quiet in the daytime, since most people don't usually come out to drink until about 9 in the evening. So to meet a few locals and swap some yarns, late evening is the time to start. But while enjoying the convivial drinking scene until the very moment that the publican's "Time, gentlemen, time" sounds serious, remember the saying of the wise old seer: "The first cup for thirst, the second for pleasure, the third for intemperance, and the rest for madness." As for getting over the night before, there's nothing quite like a brisk morning walk in the fresh, unpolluted Irish air, preferably by the sea.

The following is a representative selection of some of the most interesting pubs in Ireland for atmosphere, decor, food, or other unusual features, listed alphabetically by county and town. See "Traditional Irish Music" in *For the Mind* for still other ideas. And be prepared to explore — because there are plenty of others. *Sláinte!*

DERRAGARRA INN, Butlersbridge, County Cavan, Irish Republic: Nobody could miss this pub, probably the best in the midlands and certainly the one with the most character: On the roof stands a life-size replica of a donkey and cart. Inside, turf and log fires in the two large open hearths ward off the chill when the weather demands, which in Ireland is often, and the decor is that of a crammed curio shop, with bric-a-brac from every corner of the world, including a framed signature that Dwight D. Eisenhower presented to owner John Clancy, who worked as a steward on luxury liners for many years and then in some of America's most famous restaurants before purchasing the pub. Since he took over, the place has won 19 awards for its food and its homey decor. Food, all homemade and freshly prepared, is served every day during licensed hours. The steaks are famous throughout the midlands, and none of the meat ever sees a deep freeze, a fact that Clancy relays to visitors in a tone that conveys his horror at the very thought. Details: *Derragarra Inn,* Butlersbridge, County Cavan, Irish Republic (phone: 49-31003).

DURTY NELLY'S, Bunratty, County Clare, Irish Republic: Stationed on the main road within 10 miles of Limerick City and Shannon Airport, this pub is next door to Bunratty Castle, where the buses disgorge great clumps of tourists bound for the medieval banquets (see *Mead and Meat Pies: Historical Banquets*); and so the pub is never without its share of rubberneckers, mostly American. Nonetheless, most of the people in the vast and almost always crowded premises are Irish — and very intent on enjoying themselves in the lounge, where the tourists go; in the local bar, where they do not; or in the piano room, which separates the two, from which the highest volume of music comes. Upstairs is what the management terms the "quiet bar"; and sure enough, it's an oasis of stillness, where the murmuring of the 2 dozen white doves kept by owner Humphrey O'Connor is about the only sound. The *Oyster,* the restaurant on the premises, which has a small stand-up bar, is also pleasant; visitors are permitted to sit at the tables only when ordering a meal. The fare is good, the prices are reasonable, and the restaurant is popular with locals on a night out. Hearty sandwiches and soup are available in the bars. Music and song may erupt at any time; it's welcomed and even encouraged by the enlightened management. Details: *Durty Nelly's,* Bunratty, County Clare, Irish Republic (phone: 61-364861).

FANNY O'DEA'S, Lissycasey, County Clare, Irish Republic: This west Clare pub, about halfway between Ennis and Kilrush, is noteworthy for both its unique history and a unique potable. The notorious Lord Norbury, the "hanging judge" — who once admitted after they had been executed for having sentenced six innocent men to death — was on his way to court in Kilrush, no doubt to create more widows, on a stormy winter's night when his coach broke down. Fortunately for him, he was given bed and board in a nearby cottage, and, grateful for the refuge, the next morning he thanked his hostess, Fanny O'Dea, by granting her a license to sell drink. Today, the specialty is known as an egg flip, which tastes something like *advocaat* (a Dutch eggnog) and is made using an ancient recipe that its custodians will not divulge. Apart from this and other drink, the pub serves only tea, coffee, and sandwiches. The fire on the hearth is said to have been burning nonstop since 1790. Details: *Fanny O'Dea's,* Lissycasey, County Clare, Irish Republic (phone: 65-26304).

HENCHY'S, Cork, County Cork, Irish Republic: Cork City is such a tightly knit community that the rest of the Irish often feel they should show their passports when they enter the environs. This cohesiveness results in large part from the distinctive singsong local accent, whose subtle variations may be heard at the century-old *Henchy's*

— at least by those with an ear fine-tuned to linguistic distinctions. Even those less gifted will still enjoy the spectacle, for all levels of Cork society are represented — even the odd poet, a regular, who is very odd indeed. The pub, a night place if ever there was one, with a fine snug, is owned by Michael Henchy and his mother, Catherine. Details: *Henchy's,* 40 St. Luke's, Cork, County Cork, Irish Republic (phone: 21-501115).

OYSTER TAVERN, Cork, County Cork, Irish Republic: Although this spot was for sale at press time, we hope the new owners will uphold the popular reputation that it has enjoyed for years. While *Henchy's* (address above) is splendid for *drinking* and listening, this not-to-be-missed wonder, tucked away off Patrick St. opposite *Bolger's* (Market La.; phone: 21-274004), is also the place for *eating* and listening. The food, particularly the fish, is superb: The whitebait, when it is on the menu, is delicious and the portion is generous enough to make a main dish in itself. But the real joy is hearing the maître d' sing out, "Your table will be ready in five more minutes, Professor" (or "Doctor," or even, bless the mark, "Surgeon," as the case may be — Cork people are very keen on titles). Details: *Oyster Tavern,* Market La., Cork, County Cork, Irish Republic (phone: 21-272716) or call the tourist board (phone: 21-273251).

SEARSON'S, Midleton, County Cork, Irish Republic: Instead of signing the visitors' book at this Main Street establishment, patrons sign their names on plates, which proprietor Raymond Searson saves, along with others autographed by politicians and celebrities. But that's only one of the points of interest at this pub. Lord Midleton, who was responsible for a good deal that happened in the area, commissioned its design by the English architect A. W. N. Pugin, a proponent of the Gothic Revival who was involved in the design of the British House of Commons and designed a number of cathedrals and churches around Ireland, as well as one other building in Midleton. The pub also serves Midleton very rare whiskey, considered by many to be the best of its kind (so good, according to the proprietor, that you can sip it all night with no ill effect), which is produced here, along with Jameson, Powers, and Hewitts whiskeys, in an exceedingly modern distillery. Also worth sampling is the seafood special, a savory platter of shrimp, fresh prawns, clams, smoked sprats, whelks, periwinkles, whitefish, crab, and roll-mop herring. Details: *Searson's,* Main St., Midleton, County Cork, Irish Republic (phone: 21-631559).

AHERNE'S, Youghal, County Cork, Irish Republic: For complex historical reasons, the Irish are, at best, indifferent to fish, and only very gradually is the prejudice (ludicrous in an island people) being abandoned. In the vanguard of the movement to eradicate it is this North Main Street establishment, owned and managed by John and David Fitzgibbon and their families — perhaps the best and most unpretentious pub restaurant in the south. The bar dispenses delectable smoked mackerel, smoked salmon, oysters, and dressed crab in addition to chicken liver pâté, vegetarian salad, and all kinds of succulent sandwiches; the restaurant offers lobster, scallops, prawns, mussels, black sole, fresh trout, and salmon from the river Blackwater, which enters the sea here, as well as a number of nonpiscine dishes. Youghal (pronounced Yawl) itself is worth the visit anyway: An attractive Victorian seaside resort, it is the spot where, legend has it, Sir Walter Raleigh grew the first potatoes in Europe. The bar food is available all day, but dinner reservations are advised. Details: *Aherne's Pub & Seafood Bar,* 162/163 N. Main St., Youghal, County Cork, Irish Republic (phone: 24-92424).

BAILEY, Dublin, Irish Republic: Once the watering place for generations of Dublin's writers and artists, directly across the street from *Davy Byrne's* (see below), this pub has been preempted by ubiquitous youth, and the clientele is now what can only be described as androgynous. At night, it's jammed with the young and pretty. At other times, there is peace and time enough to admire the handsome iron and marble tables, and many young artists, some writers, and some musicians are still among the crowd. The best way to experience the pub is to come for drinks at noon and, at about 1 PM (having reserved a table), climb the stairs to the restaurant overhead, where the food is good and the service faultless. On the way up or down, don't miss the pub's unique feature — the original door of Leopold Bloom's house at 7 Eccles St., lovingly preserved by the *Bailey's* former owner, artist, and patron John Ryan. Details: *Bailey,* 2 Duke St., Dublin, Irish Republic (phone: 1-773055).

BRAZEN HEAD, Dublin, Irish Republic: Here, legend has it, the winsome Robert Emmet plotted the ragged and abortive little rebellion of 1803. Although only a few hundred yards from the Guinness brewery, this establishment hubristically disdains to serve draft stout. It is a dark and very intimate place, with hallways leading off in all directions, one of them into the little room where the poetry and music sessions are held. The poetry readings have a charmingly inverted nature: One gets the impression that the people are listening to poetry while drinking, rather than the opposite. Outside on the quays and not too far away is the church immortalized by James Joyce in the opening line of *Finnegans Wake:* "riverrun, past Eve and Adam's, from swerve of shore to bend of bay, brings us by a commodious vicus of recirculation back to Howth Castle and environs." While there, pause to watch the seagulls swoop and screech above Anna Livia Plurabella. This 17th-century "hotel," at a site that is said to have been occupied by a tavern since Viking times, is not easily found; better ask a taxi driver. Details: *Brazen Head,* 20 Lower Bridge St., Dublin, Irish Republic (phone: 1-779549).

DAVY BYRNE'S, Dublin, Irish Republic: This, the "moral pub" in which Leopold Bloom had gorgonzola cheese and his glass of burgundy on June 16, 1904, may not bring to mind the place Joyce was visualizing when he wrote of Bloom's visit in *Ulysses.* Despite having undergone much updating, the pub still features murals by Cecil Salkeld (father-in-law of Brendan Behan) that depict famous Irish literary and artistic personalities of the early 20th century, and one of the three bars still bears the name of the novel in which it was immortalized. At the hub of the main shopping and business district of Dublin, it attracts a predictably varied clientele. Food is served all day, the specialties being salads and sandwiches made with fresh or smoked salmon — except on June 16, when gorgonzola and burgundy may take precedence for some. Details: *Davy Byrne's,* 21 Duke St., Dublin, Irish Republic (phone: 1-775217).

DOHENY & NESBITT, Dublin, Irish Republic: Owned and run by Ned Doheny and Tom Nesbitt, this Lower Baggot Street establishment is very small, and late at night, especially on weekends, it's almost impossible to breathe for the heaving mass of trainee architects, students, and tired political pundits taking time off from reporting the proceedings in the Dáil (Parliament) around the corner. So come early, or, better still, sidle in at noontime, when there is breathing space as well as an opportunity to munch on hot beef sandwiches, medium, well done, or (unusual in Ireland) rare. Close to the *National Museum,* National Library, *National Gallery of Art,* and St. Stephen's Green, that wonderful city-center oasis of quietude, ponds, and trees. Details: *Doheny & Nesbitt,* 5 Lower Baggot St., Dublin, Irish Republic (phone: 1-762945).

MULLIGANS, Dublin, Irish Republic: This very old pub, which has been in existence since the 1750s, serves nothing but plain drink. But what it does, it does well, and the Guinness draft offered here is probably the most consistently good, if not the best, in the country. (A constant flow throughout the day is one of the secrets, they say.) The curates — that is to say, the barkeeps — have abandoned their charming aprons, but it is still possible to visualize what it was like to drink here a century ago. Three rooms are in constant use, and since the pub is situated between the harbor, the *Irish Press,* and Trinity College, the patrons include journalists, dock workers, and students. In these frantically egalitarian days, part of the fun of drinking here is guessing whether that long-haired melancholic in the corner is a longshoreman, a music critic, or an aspiring Lionel Trilling. Details: *Mulligan's,* Poolbeg St., Dublin, Irish Republic (phone: 1-775582).

NEARY'S, Dublin, Irish Republic: The back door of this pub opens directly opposite the stage door of the *Gaiety*, the capital's principal variety theater (described in "The Performing Arts" in *For the Mind*), so the noises here are made mostly by actors, musicians, and the sorts of pallid cohorts that these two professions attract. Visiting celebrities from both professions drop in here from time to time, so visitors may find themselves rubbing shoulders with the great. When this happens, the place is full, and there is little comfort; but at lunchtime, it's easy to find consolation in the sandwiches or, in season, fresh oysters. Four beautiful gas lamps stand on the marble counter, the seating is plush and bouncy, and there is usually a young "lounge boy" running his feet off trying to serve everybody at once. Details: *Neary's*, Chatham St., Dublin, Irish Republic (phone: 1-778596).

STAG'S HEAD, Dublin, Irish Republic: Nowadays, this classic, gorgeously turned out right down to its stained glass windows, generally draws a clientele from all strata of society, but at lunchtime on weekdays the observant will note a preponderance of the pinstripe vests, fob watches, and cold noses of members of the legal profession as they dig into their hot-meat-and-two-veg meals. The exact makeup of the crowd is anybody's guess, because the pub is awkward to get to. But the preservationists who yelped with dismay at a recent threat to pull it down are seldom moved to actually visit the place. Details: *Stag's Head*, 1 Dame Ct., Dublin, Irish Republic (phone: 1-779307).

TWELVE PINS, Barna, County Galway, Irish Republic: For those who want to watch the sun go down on Galway Bay, as the Bing Crosby song goes, this pub and restaurant 4 miles from Galway City on the coast road is an ideal vantage point. And since it is on the fringe of Gaelic-speaking Connemara, it is also possible to hear Irish spoken as well. (To guarantee it, it's necessary to penetrate further into the region.) The restaurant is Spanish in style, the wood-paneled pub area more in the Irish tradition. There is also a fish bar where clams on toast, prawns thermidor, king scallops, and other succulents are dispensed. Bar lunches and more elaborate meals are available. To work off any overindulgence, wander down to the nearby harbor to see hookers plying their trade — here, a traditional type of Irish sailing cargo vessel rather than ladies in stiletto heels. Details: *Twelve Pins*, Barna, County Galway, Irish Republic (phone: 91-92368).

SEAGAN UA NEACHTÁIN, TABHARNEOIR, Galway, County Galway, Irish Republic: Ireland's western capital has a number of comfortable and well-run pubs, none as authentic and little changed as this house at the corner of Cross and Quay Streets, which also has a cozy upstairs restaurant. In the old days, the main door of the pub (above which the name of the original owner is still written out in Irish) would not open, and visitors had to go around to the side door on Quay Street and give a knock. They were then quietly ushered into a small room, the pub's one and only, where someone would be singing a lament or playing a tune on the tin whistle. If they made too much noise, they were shushed. The pub is the antithesis of *Durty Nelly's:* Voices are never raised, Irish is often spoken, and potential patrons are carefully screened. Details: *Seagan Ua Neachtáin*, Tabharneoir, 17 Cross St., Galway, County Galway, Irish Republic (phone: 91-66816 or 91-66172).

MORAN'S OF THE WEIR, Kilcolgan, County Galway, Irish Republic: Over 200 years old, this family-run, thatch-roofed pub in the Weir, hard by the tidal river, started serving oysters and crab in a small way back in the 1960s and is now a thriving and much-extended bar and seafood restaurant. For parties of four, five, or eight, its comfortable snugs are perfect for lunch; if the weather is fine, there are tables in the sunshine at the front of the pub. Galway oysters are served with homemade brown bread and butter — which sends most Americans into a swoon — and Guinness. *Moran*'s is an important part of the *Galway Oyster Festival* (see "Feis and Fleadh: The Best Festivals" in *For the Mind*), a jolly gathering much beloved of Ireland's nouveau riche, who descend on the town in force every year in mid-September. Details: *Moran's Oyster Cottage of the Weir*, Kilcolgan, County Galway, Irish Republic (phone: 91-96113).

TOWERS, Glenbeigh, County Kerry, Irish Republic: Hotel bars tend to be much of a muchness, with a few notable exceptions, among them the bar of Dublin's *Shelbourne* and this one, which is really an annex to a justly famous seafood restaurant. The *Towers* is famous for being famous, and dozens of international celebrities have stayed here — understandably, since Glenbeigh is the perfect base for exploring the Ring of Kerry. There is music here every night during July and August, much of it of the inspired amateur variety and some of it even very enjoyable. Details: *Towers,* Glenbeigh, County Kerry, Irish Republic (phone: 66-68212).

EDWARD LANGTON'S, Kilkenny, Irish Republic: Visitors driving from Dublin into this compact, historic city, home of Smithwicks Brewery (off Parliament St.), will encounter this pub about halfway up John Street on the left. It is a superb spot for food and drink as well as for atmosphere. The hanging flower baskets make the façade remarkable even in a city renowned for its shop fronts. The low-ceilinged bar inside, conducive to whispering and gossip, leads out to a conservatory full of light and air from Gothic-style beveled-glass windows, through which remnants of Kilkenny's walls, complete with gun slits, are visible. Owner Eamonn Langton has built a reputation for food of a high standard, including pub grub consisting of five hot dishes daily. Have a drink and admire the slightly gloomy atmosphere, the old prints, the stained glass, the mirrors, and the polished granite tables. Details: *Edward Langton's,* 69 John St., Kilkenny, Irish Republic (phone: 56-65133).

MORRISEY'S, Abbeyleix, County Laois, Irish Republic: This is the sort of pub that a true drinking man would stop into on a cold Monday morning and then not want to leave for a week. With its pot-bellied stove almost as rotund as some of the locals who drink marvelous pints of Guinness here, it looks as if it hasn't changed since the time of our forebears. No meals or snacks are served, as the smell might interfere with the patrons' enjoyment of their drink. An ideal R&R stop en route between Dublin and Cork. Details: *Morrisey's,* Abbeyleix, County Laois, Irish Republic (phone: 502-31233).

STANFORD'S PUB, Dromahair, County Leitrim, Irish Republic: Structurally, this Main Street bar has endured none of the graftings and remodelings of most Irish pubs in the last century. In fact, even the family who owns it is the same: Proprietor Della McGowan is among the fourth generation of Stanfords to run the pub. The ceiling is hung with farm implements, lamps, and mirrors, and behind the bar are a couple of fiddles, a pair of guitars, a melodeon, a mandolin, a tin whistle, and a Jew's-harp — not surprising considering the musical heritage of the area and the melodic inclinations of Tom McGowan. You may be lucky enough to chance upon an impromptu session on some summer evening when "The Blackbird," "Danny Boy," and the locally favored "Isle of Inisfree," made famous by Bing Crosby, ring through the ancient rafters. The actual isle, which the poet Yeats described, can be seen from the shore of Lough Gill, a couple of miles away; Dromahair is on the eastern fringe of the country that the poet roamed in his youth. Pub grub ranges from smoked salmon to Irish stew, and lunches and evening meals are served in the restaurant beside the bar. Details: *Stanford's Pub,* Dromahair, County Leitrim, Irish Republic (phone: 71-64140).

REGINALD, Waterford, Irish Republic: This establishment on the Mall is just behind and adjacent to battle-scarred, 11th-century Reginald's Tower, Waterford's finest historic monument, in whose top-floor banquet hall the Norman conqueror Strongbow sealed his claim to Ireland by marrying Aoife, daughter of Dermot Mac-Murrough, the King of Leinster. The pub incorporates part of the old walls of the tower and the old city, and patrons drink in niches that have been burrowed into the walls. On display in the pub are old weapons, a full suit of armor, and other remembrances of Waterford's history. A lovely peat fire usually burns on the hearth, and on Sunday afternoons Waterford musicians often play some good jazz. Details: *Reginald,* The Mall, Waterford, Irish Republic (phone: 51-55087).

ANTRIM ARMS, Ballycastle, County Antrim, Northern Ireland: One of the oldest hotels in Ireland, built as a coaching inn in 1745, this establishment retains its basic structure and antique appearance, right down to the windows, which are original. Novelist William Makepeace Thackeray's complimentary comments about its comforts in his *Travels Around Ireland* are still entirely relevant. From a whiskey drinker's point of view, however, what stands out are the bar's 100 or so malt whiskeys meant for display as well as for drinking, including the locally distilled Bushmills. Guglielmo Marconi, inventor of wireless telegraphy, stayed here when setting up the first commercial radio link between Ballycastle and Rathlin Island, off the coast. Pub grub and more extensive meals are served year-round. Details: *Antrim Arms,* Castle St., Ballycastle, County Antrim, Northern Ireland (phone: 26-576-2284).

CROWN SALOON, Belfast, County Antrim, Northern Ireland: This venerable, gaslit establishment on Great Victoria Street, opposite the *Europa* hotel and the *Grand Opera House,* has been extensively restored by the National Trust. The windows are stained glass, the floor is mosaic tile, the fireplace is stone, and all around are Victorian fancies — woodcarvings, glass mosaics, plasterwork curlicues, brocades, painted mirrors, and so much more that every nook and cranny seems filled with ornament. As for the snugs — where serious drinkers can hoist their pints in contented privacy — they are in the same good condition as when the place was built back in Victorian days. Details: *Crown Saloon,* 46 Great Victoria St., Belfast, Northern Ireland (phone: 232-249476). Next door, and also notable, is *Robinson's,* which has ornate papered walls, a mahogany bar, polished wooden snugs, and a men's room dubbed "Adam Ant." Details: *Robinson's,* 38 Great Victoria St., Belfast, Northern Ireland (phone: 232-329812).

LONDONDERRY ARMS, Carnlough, County Antrim, Northern Ireland: The horseshoe worn by Ireland's most famous horse, Arkle, when he won one of his three *Cheltenham Gold Cups* in the 1960s, is the proudest possession of Frank O'Neill, whose family has owned the *Londonderry Arms* hotel since 1947. And so it's not surprising that this equine memento occupies the place of honor in its *Oak Panel* bar, along with a painting of the horse and the jockey who rode him to victory, Pat Taaffe. Other adornments include a scattering of driftwood carvings by the local artist John Henshaw and a portrait of Lady Londonderry, who had the hotel built in 1848 and whose grandson, none other than Winston Churchill, inherited it in 1921. Pub grub is served from 12:30 to 2:30 PM, and excellent dinners are served in the hotel dining room in the evenings. Details: *Londonderry Arms,* 20 Harbour Rd., Carnlough, County Antrim, Northern Ireland (phone: 574-85255).

DOBBINS INN, Carrickfergus, County Antrim, Northern Ireland: The bar at this 16th-century former coaching inn is called the *John Paul Jones* because in the bay that the inn overlooks the American naval hero achieved the nascent United States' first naval victory. The decor takes a definitely nautical cue from this circumstance: A ship's wheel is at center stage, prints and pictures of ships hang on the walls, and bands from sailors' hats indicating the ships on which they served — from the aircraft carrier *Ark Royal,* sunk in World War II, to the *Belfast,* now a museum on the Thames in London — are on display. Only Maud, the pub's resident ghost, has nothing to do with the sea. As a young woman, she was having an affair with a soldier from Carrickfergus Castle, whose gaunt outlines can be discerned from the hotel's front door, and was found in a compromising position by her much older husband, who accidentally killed her in the ensuing melee and not at all accidentally laid the blame on the unhappy lover, who was subsequently executed for the deed. While his ghost, Buttoncap, haunts the castle, Maud manifests herself by banging doors and knocking glasses off tables, but never too early in the morning, when people are "curing" themselves — in Ireland even a ghost knows that would be too much of a shock. Pub grub is served weekdays year-round, and the restaurant is open until 9:15 PM. The house specialty is steak John Paul Jones — filet flambéed at the table and served in a creamy sauce flavored with Southern

Comfort, mushrooms, peppers, onions, and garlic. Details: *Dobbins Inn*, 6 High St., Carrickfergus, County Antrim, Northern Ireland (phone: 96-035-1905).

BAYVIEW, Portballintrae, County Antrim, Northern Ireland: This is the only hotel ever to come under naval fire in Ireland, and the *Porthole Bar* displays proof of the attack: a piece of a shell fired by a German U-boat in 1918 at a ship that happened to be facing the hotel. (The shell overshot its target and came through the roof.) The pub grub is of a high standard. The specialty of the house, a steak flambéed with Bushmills and served with a red wine and cream sauce, makes locals who work in the distillery down the road sigh at the waste — but those who eat it feel like Nero after a Roman feast and recommend it as the perfect meal for a hard-drinking man after a rough day. Just down the road is the gaunt clifftop ruin of Dunluce Castle, where cooking of another kind was going on in 1639 when its kitchen crumbled into the sea and took the lives of all who were working there except a handyman who had been mending pots outside. Details: *Bayview*, 2 Bayhead Rd., Portballintrae, County Antrim, Northern Ireland (phone: 26-573-1453 or 26-573-1223).

BLAKE'S OF THE HOLLOW, Enniskillen, County Fermanagh, Northern Ireland: Noted for its handmade lace, its attractive knit sweaters, and its Belleek china, Enniskillen is also home to this handsome old pub, tucked away in a rabbit's warren of streets and alleys not far from St. MacCartan's Cathedral. Lamentably, the stock of rare Old Dublin Potstill Whiskey, an Irishman's collector's item that was once among the alcoholic specialties of the house, has been depleted. But otherwise things are much the same as they were when the premises were last refurbished in 1887 (particularly the long, marble-topped mahogany bar and the pine snugs, attractive enough to warrant praise from Ulster Heritage Societies publications and a government preservation listing). The exterior is still emblazoned with the great stripes of black and red that were originally painted for the benefit of the illiterate among its patrons, the Guinness is well pulled, and the faces of the patrons well creased. As for the mood, it is always subdued, and television intrudes on the drinkers' solitude only during major sporting events. The entrance on Church Street is easiest to find. Details: *Blake's of the Hollow*, 6 Church St., Enniskillen, County Fermanagh, Northern Ireland (phone: 36-522143).

MELLON COUNTRY INN, Omagh, near Newtownstewart, County Tyrone, Northern Ireland: Almost every American touring Northern Ireland visits the Ulster-American Folk Park, which illustrates some of the ties that have been forged down the centuries between Ulster and the US (see *Marvelous Museums*). This modern pub, a mile north of the folk park, provides relaxation, food, and drink for travelers. The menu offers steak sandwiches, surf-and-turf, and the like. A locally bred, hormone-free beef known as Tyrone black — which its producers consider to be Ireland's best — is the house specialty, along with whiskey: There are more than 150 different malt whiskeys in stock, including some from Wales, Japan, and the Isle of Man. Details: *Mellon Country Inn*, 134 Beltany Rd., Omagh, near Newtownstewart, County Tyrone, Northern Ireland (phone: 66-266-1224).

Rural Retreats

To travelers from abroad, one of the most striking features of the Irish countryside is the absence of billboards, the almost total lack of motels, and the abundance of homey inns, guesthouses, and country manors–turned–hotels. The tradition of hospitality goes back centuries, to the year 438, when the law of the land bade all who had the means to do so to entertain visitors, no questions asked. Even then there were guesthouses, where a fire continuously blazed on the hearth and meats were kept hot in vast cauldrons ready for consumption. In the 16th century, the Mayor of Dublin, Patrick Sarsfield, held open house every evening, dispensing libations freely. In today's hostelries, wooden stair treads worn to concavity by the footsteps of travelers through the ages, half-timbered walls, and beamed ceilings impart the same old-time feeling of hospitality.

Some establishments are more noteworthy than others — either because of their decor, the friendliness of their management (more often than not a whole family), their unique setting, or their food. Some even have ghosts, although there does not seem to be a tetchy or morose spirit among them. (An American couple took home a film of the one in *Hilton Park*, which seems a more impressive trophy than even the largest pike.) Here is an assortment of some of the best retreats, in alphabetical order by county, including castle-hotels, inns, and country houses. Some warrant a stop if they're not too far afield; a handful of others, perhaps a shade more wonderful on one or more counts, are worth planning a whole holiday around. (For other ideas, see "Fishing Hotels" in *Gone Fishing*.) Visitors should note that owners are usually a bit casual about when their establishments open and close, muttering things about good tourist seasons and hunting when pressed to name a specific date. So if you are making a special trip — or if there is a specific establishment said to close in October that you want to visit in November — it's a good idea to check in advance before setting your plans in stone.

WORTH A LONG DETOUR

GREGANS CASTLE, near Ballyvaughan, County Clare, Irish Republic: This sprawling country house is eminently comfortable, homey, and atmospheric, with traditional turf fires burning in the handsome fireplaces in the public rooms when the weather is chilly, a marble-floored entrance foyer, gleaming brass ornaments, and antiques scattered throughout. But what really sets the place apart from other hostelries is its location, just an hour from Shannon Airport, in the center of the Burren, an area of enormous interest to serious botanists, amateur plant lovers, and inveterate admirers of magnificent scenery. The whole area is austere, simply mile upon mile of all but bare rock that is by turns pewter-hued, silvery, and brown, riven by slashes of green, where cattle graze. It is an awe-inspiring scene that is miraculously transformed in May and June, when the Burren's unique Alpine plants, their seeds having blown into the area on the same winds that deposited the bits of soil in the rocks' cracks, burst into bloom, like so many jewels in scarlet, white, yellow, and indigo. Most of the comfortable bedrooms have magnificent views over this fabulous land. The restaurant has won awards for its food, and if the selection is not vast, the offerings are good and carefully prepared. As expected at an establishment just 4 miles from the harbor, seafood is a specialty. It also serves a good selection of local Burren cheeses, as well as vegetables fresh from the garden. A golf course is a half hour distant, fishing can be arranged, and the area abounds in antiquities. Botanists who sally forth at odd hours should note that snacks and other viands are also available all day in the *Corkscrew Bar,* named not for the oenophilic instrument but for the adjacent road, a narrow, tortuous lane that clings to the Burren slopes. Open *Easter* through October; 16 rooms, all with baths. Details: *Gregans Castle Hotel,* near Ballyvaughan, County Clare, Irish Republic (phone: 65-77005).

DROMOLAND CASTLE, Newmarket-on-Fergus, County Clare, Irish Republic: This castle sits, gray and graceful, turreted and towered, in the heart of a 450-acre park whose green velvet lawns roll away into dark green woods. Ireland's banner flies from the battlements mirrored in the small lake. And if Dromoland looks like a fantasy come true, it's because it is — for guests who roam its garden, golf on its golf course (a full 18 holes), fish and boat on its lake and streams, ride horseback over neighboring hills, and call it temporary home. It was once the real home of the late Bernard McDonough, a West Virginia gentleman who'd always wanted a castle to call his own and finally realized his impossible dream when he bought this 16th-century seat of the bold O'Briens and restored it as a hotel. A regal job he did, too, and it has since been made even more elegant by the new owners. Inside, antique O'Brien portraits line halls that glow with rich wood paneling, silken fabrics, and sunlight. Through the tall dining room windows, guests can watch deer on the distant morning grass while they try to restrain themselves at the breakfast buffet, laden with fresh fruits, croissants, and fresh-baked pastries; at night its damask walls and polished silver gleam in the chandelier light — a proper setting for the carefully prepared food served therein. Rooms are airy and bright with flowered wallpaper and floral colors. The occasional Irish purist harrumphs and finds it "all a bit too grand." But its many repeat guests wouldn't have it any other way. A member of the Relais & Châteaux group. Open year-round; 73 rooms, each with bath. Details: *Dromoland Castle,* Newmarket-on-Fergus, County Clare, Irish Republic (phone: 61-71144).

SEA VIEW HOUSE, Ballylickey, Bantry, County Cork, Irish Republic: Not the least of this establishment's assets is its location, just 400 yards from a winding inlet of beautiful Bantry Bay in the tiny town of Ballylickey. The house itself, a tall, snowy white structure built in 1890, has been masterfully doubled in size, without altering the lines or charm of the original façade. The 17 guestrooms have been enlarged into suites, all with spacious, modern, private bathrooms. Each room, enhanced by panoramic views of the bay or gardens, has been tastefully refurbished with light oak trim and fixtures, antiques and local period pieces, and designer fabrics. Although there are some ground-level accommodations (one room is equipped for disabled guests), most rooms are on the second or third floors (reached by an elevator). The common areas include newly decorated parlors with open fireplaces and sunlit decks. The gardens recently have been re-landscaped and enlarged. Besides its impressive scenery, the food, prepared by proprietor Kathleen O'Sullivan, is considered the best in Ballylickey. The traditional country-style fare includes fresh seafood, homemade soup and baked goods, local fruits (including peaches and berries), and exotic vegetables from nearby and European markets. All this is served cheerily in a dining room with floor-to-ceiling windows, crocheted placemats, and fresh flowers on the tables. Tea and snacks can be ordered at any time during the day in the new bar lounge. Horseback riding, fishing, boating, and other sports can be arranged. Open April through October. Details: *Sea View House Hotel,* Ballylickey, Bantry, County Cork, Irish Republic (phone: 27-50073).

LONGUEVILLE HOUSE AND PRESIDENTS' RESTAURANT, Mallow, County Cork, Irish Republic: Seen from the outside, this Georgian establishment, built in 1720, is only fractionally smaller than Buckingham Palace. Unlike the royal manse, it stands on a hill surrounded by some 500 acres of grounds scored by the river Blackwater. Inside, there's a lovely formality to the design (notably the noble double staircase) and an abundance of fine interior detail (inlaid mahogany doors, a marble Adam fireplace, Italian plasterwork ceilings). In contrast, the decor is a comforting combination of color and clutter: bowls of flowers, plush chairs, paintings, a Victorian whirligig stand stacked with paperbacks, as well as room-high shelves of rare editions. A gigantic drawing room full of antiques is warmed by a log fire that burns year-round. And the bedrooms will fulfill not a few fantasies — huge and old-fashioned, some with half-canopy beds muffled with curtains that can be used to shut out the Longueville Lady, a friendly shrouded ghost with a riveting history who appears to favored guests strictly without an appointment. Attesting to the fact that these whereabouts have been O'Callaghan soil since the start of Irish time are the massive ruins of Dromineen Castle, a casualty of Cromwell's takeover in the 1640s. A full 300 years later, the land is back in family hands. Now Michael O'Callaghan and his wife, Jane, are the hosts, and their handsome Relais & Châteaux establishment is highly regarded for the food served to its appreciative guests in the magnificent dining room, with portraits of all the Presidents of Ireland presiding (hence its formal name, the *Presidents' Restaurant*). On any given evening, the gooseberry chutney, the cream of tomato and vegetable soups, the chicken, and the pink trout are carefully prepared with sophisticated simplicity and consummate skill by Jane and son William. The sweets — soufflé cake, fresh fruit tarts, homemade ice cream — will dazzle the most demanding palates. Such culinary masterpieces are made possible by the huge kitchen gardens, which support free-range duck, seven kinds of lettuce, almost every sort of berry, and the famous Longueville suckling lambs, which are so young as to be scarcely bigger than hares. The O'Callaghans care a lot, enough to spend their months off "refreshing" — Jane and William at London's Cordon Bleu or with one of France's great chefs, Michael traveling in search of wines for his impressive cellar. (They now boast Ireland's only country inn vineyard, consisting of 3 acres planted with rickensteiner grapes.) Between meals, guests fish for salmon and trout (though tackle is not supplied). It's also possible to ride at nearby stables and play golf in Mallow, 3 miles distant — or just sit and enjoy the sunshine in the palm-lined Victorian conservatory. Outside guests are welcome for dinner only. Open early March to mid-December; 17 bedrooms (including 4 singles), each with bath, at prices that drop with every story up since there is no lift. Details: *Longueville House and Presidents' Restaurant,* Mallow, County Cork, Irish Republic (phone: 22-47156).

BALLYMALOE HOUSE, Shanagarry, Midleton, County Cork, Irish Republic: Beckoning across fields where ponies frolic and grassy lawns where plump sheep graze, this establishment (whose name is pronounced Bally-ma-*loo*) is a lesson in architecture and history enlivened by sumptuous food. Strolling around the premises, one can see the bare skull of rock on which the whole structure is founded and the wall of a castle built in 1500 by the knight of Glin's bastard offshoots. Both the rock and the wall have been incorporated into the building, and one corridor is flanked by the foundations of a 17th-century addition of the Earl of Orrery, who liked everything modern. But the star of the show here is the food, and everyone gathers in the lounge to wait for Myrtle Allen's meals, famed throughout Ireland. The food is simple and gratifying — even at breakfast, which has won a Great Irish Breakfast award — "muesli" cereal, which is grated apple, oatmeal, honey, and a squeeze of lemon; homemade marmalade; and brown bread that is a poem. But then almost everything is, perhaps because, with rare exceptions, everything is grown in the family's 5-acre garden or on its 400-acre farm. Lunch is a cold buffet; the dinner menu is short and straightforward: perhaps crudités with garlic mayonnaise (so perfectly fresh that a cucumber wedge is like ambrosia) or watercress soup to start; then locally smoked mackerel, little pots of hot mussels, or homemade Danish pâté; summer turkey baked in butter and fresh herbs, roast rib of beef with three sauces, or French casserole of roast pork with Normandy mustard sauce; and the board of local cheeses, fruit tarts, cake, and — finally — coffee with *Ballymaloe* chocolates. All of this is an excellent recommendation for the cooking school, which offers a number of sessions of varying lengths throughout the year. Guestrooms are in the main house and in a contemporary modern wing adjoining the gardens and the heated outdoor swimming pool; particularly charming are the Castle Room and the White Room, with their crocheted counterpanes (no ghosts, but it's easy to imagine 15th-century footsteps). Those who are able to waddle after breakfast and lunch can borrow some golf clubs from the management and make their way to the estate's small golf course, work off some calories at tennis or croquet, or wet a line in Ballycotton Bay, 6 miles distant. Open year-round, except for a few days at *Christmas;* 30 bedrooms, each with bath or shower. Details: *Ballymaloe House,* Shanagarry, Midleton, County Cork, Irish Republic (phone: 21-652531).

CASHEL HOUSE, Cashel, County Galway, Irish Republic: This *Cashel* — the other is in County Tipperary — is in Connemara, on the extreme west coast, a magical place of indigo mountains, winding inlets, and violet bog land where wild herds of mouse-colored part-Arab Connemara horses roam the hills and sheep sun themselves on the narrow roads. It is also the home of Dermot and Kay McEvilly's gracious mansion-turned-hotel, a Relais & Châteaux establishment that has welcomed many famous guests, among them General and Mrs. Charles de Gaulle, since it opened its doors in 1968, providing a hideaway where discreet informality is the watchword and the quiet man at the next table could be an American captain of industry, a British prime minister, or a German film star. With the Gulf Stream nearby, exotic plants thrive in the 50-acre gardens, and suites with utmost charm look out onto the brilliant flowers and shrubs. The kitchen emphasizes seafood: Wild mussels, picked from the ocean just 20 yards across the road, make the world's fastest transit from sea to skillet. Dinners are not overly formal, and lunches are packed in picnic baskets or served unfussily in the little bar, with plaice stuffed with smoked salmon mousse a typical offering. Between meals, there's a tiny private beach, glistening white and washed with icy Atlantic water of which those who brave it typically assert: "It's wonderful once you get in." Horseback riding can be arranged, and angling is available on lakes and in rivers and the ocean. Guests can also borrow a small sailing dinghy and rowboat to go out on the quiet waters of the bay not far away. Ask Dermot or Kay about dates for races of Galway Bay hookers — sailing boats rigged like Arab dhows and used to transport cargo. Open March through November; 17 bedrooms and 13 mini-suites. Details: *Cashel House Hotel,* Cashel, County Galway, Irish Republic (phone: 95-31001).

CURRAREVAGH HOUSE, Oughterard, County Galway, Irish Republic: Those who like Victorian fishing lodges built by Anglo-Irish colonels with Indian army links and papered with tiger skins and antler heads will certainly like this place. Visitors can absolutely count on being absolved from the dreary routine of calling home here, for the only connection with the outside world is through a coin-operated phone, at which several pounds of coins are necessary to dial the States. Proprietors Harry and June Hodgson do run a taut ship, meaning that they will unhesitatingly supply the change, if you must. It also means, however, that latecomers to dinner take up their forks at whatever course the general service has reached. The cooking is good in its way — straight from the first Mrs. Beeton, with weekly cyclical overtones ("If it's roast lamb, it must be Wednesday"). There are compensations, however, and the unusual charm of the place is only the first. For anglers there is fishing for salmon, trout, pike, and perch, mainly on Lough Corrib. For fishing widows, there is a pleasant library. And the house, itself surrounded by some 140 acres of woodlands and crowded by overgrown rhododendron and fuchsia, is close to wonderful scenery and ancient ruins. Golf and riding are available locally, and there is even a modern tennis court on the estate. Continental Europeans return year after year, especially the young. Open mid-April to early October (dining room open to non-residents only by prior arrangement); 15 bedrooms, all with baths. Details: *Currarevagh House,* Oughterard, County Galway, Irish Republic (phone: 91-82312 or 91-82313).

PARK, Kenmare, County Kerry, Irish Republic: The late-Victorian premises of this establishment are beautiful, sumptuous, and exquisitely tasteful. Museum pieces are scattered throughout the hotel, beginning in the lobby, where guests register at an antique stockbroker's desk not far from a magnificent Italian water tank standing on dolphins and sea horses, its painted sides twinkling with the bare limbs of gods and goddesses. Some bedrooms are furnished in the plain Georgian style, with cheval mirrors and four-poster beds, while others are massively Victorian, done up with touches of William Morris, or even contemporary. Everywhere, the standard of comfort is superb, and the views over a landscape that defies art, so changing are its moods, are heart-stopping. This alone would make the hotel worth visiting, but the restaurant here (along with the restaurant at the *Arbutus Lodge* in nearby Cork — see *Best Eating*) is a seminal influence on modern Irish cuisine. The food has earned a Michelin star, among other awards. Lobsters and salmon are worth close attention, but game is served in season as well. Breakfast is of the real Irish kind, with the sophisticated addition of scrambled eggs with smoked salmon. The clientele includes the Irish who love luxury and the international set; the owner, Francis Brennan, actually manages to combine family warmth and sophisticated ambience. Open April to January 1; 50 bedrooms (including 6 suites), each with bath. Details: *Park Hotel Kenmare,* Kenmare, County Kerry, Irish Republic (phone: 64-41200).

GREAT SOUTHERN, Parknasilla, County Kerry, Irish Republic: The gardens in this corner of Kerry recall one of the lusher parts of Borneo. A huge plant that looks like a giant, hairy rhubarb, the leaves large enough to shelter an adult, overhang an inlet of the ocean. The odd-shaped fruits of the arbutus — a botanic glory of the area that is better known as the strawberry tree — glow scarlet in fall and winter. Real palm trees grace the gardens, which stretch out toward the bay and include two little islands connected to the mainland by bridge. George Bernard Shaw, who came here twice annually for 15 years, attested that he wrote most of *Saint Joan* here, though how he managed to stay awake long enough to complete the first act is a mystery: The sheer soothing greenness of the place and all the soft air make it the world's greatest cure for insomnia. Although this hotel is state-run, without an especially gracious (or dotty) owner presiding, it does have a very distinguished ghost — the Protestant Bishop of Limerick Charles Graves, grandfather of poet and author Robert Graves, manifests himself occasionally in the west wing. But the place is exceptional for other reasons as well. The property itself is handsome, and the dining room has distinguished itself for its French-accented menu, which offers quenelles of seafood in basil sauce, breast of roast duck sauced with port, and châteaubriand carved at the table, along with the finny preparations to be expected at a seaside location, as well as sweet endings ranging from flambéed puddings to sorbets and homemade ice creams. Moreover, the selection of recreational opportunities is extremely wide: riding, a 9-hole golf course, a heated indoor pool, and more. Two small trawlers can be hired by the day to fish offshore for skate and shark, and freshwater anglers can go after the trout in Long Lake in Tahilla. Prince Rainier of Monaco and his family spent a holiday here, as have the Dutch royal family. Open April through October; 60 bedrooms (including 3 suites) in several grades of comfort and cost, all with bath. Details: *Great Southern Hotel,* Parknasilla, County Kerry, Irish Republic (phone: 64-45122).

MOYGLARE MANOR, near Maynooth, County Kildare, Irish Republic: Tall, gaunt, gray, and highly regarded by architects, this former residence of the Dukes of Leinster and retreat of superannuated duchesses, on attractively landscaped grounds, is more warm and inhabitable than grand, despite its fine plaster ceilings and stately Georgian façade. Peat fires scent the air, creating a real country-house atmosphere, and the rooms of the house, which dates from 1780, are scattered with a handful of fine antiques and interesting pictures. The 17 bedrooms are enchanting, furnished in Victorian style; some are ballroom-size with matching bathrooms, while others have half-tester beds or four-posters. The views leave no doubt as to the primary business of the area: This is horse country. The Curragh (described in "Horsing Around in *For the Body*") is nearby; young horses gambol in the fields of the adjacent stud farm; and fellow guests include breeders, trainers, and foreign buyers. Arrangements can be made for horseback riding at local stables and, in season and for experienced riders, for hunting with the Kildare Foxhounds or the Ward Union. The kitchen here is Franco-Irish-international, and food runs to the hearty rather than haute. On-the-spot, non-equine recreation is provided by a hard tennis court and pitch-and-putt course. All in all, this is a good base for seeing Dublin and its neighborhood. Open year-round, except for a few days at *Christmas;* 12 double bedrooms and a garden suite, all with bath. Details: *Moyglare Manor,* Moyglare, Maynooth, County Kildare, Irish Republic (phone: 12-86351).

MOUNT JULIET, Thomastown, County Kilkenny, Irish Republic: A 2-mile-long driveway provides a scenic introduction to this secluded property; the drive passes neatly fenced green pastures (home of the Ballylinch Stud Farm) dotted with thoroughbreds and strutting pheasants, and lambs grazing beside the banks of the river Nore. The manor house is set high on a hill overlooking the 1,466-acre estate. An elegant Georgian-style structure built in the 1750s, the house is the last of the great homes built by Hamilton Somerset Butler, the eighth Viscount Ikerrin, first Earl of Cork, who named the property "Mount Juliet" after his wife Julianna, or Juliet, as she was known. There are 23 rooms and 9 suites, each with a private bath, direct-dial phones, and a TV set (several suites provide butler service at an extra charge). Offering a view of the river or the gardens, the rooms are individually decorated with antiques or reproduction pieces, four-poster brass beds, armoires, original paintings, fresh flowers, and books. The *Lady Helen McCalmont* restaurant, designed by and named for one of the house's more recent occupants, is a blend of blue Wedgwood wall decorations, fine linen and silver, and a specially commissioned pattern of handcut Tipperary glassware. The menu is equally impressive, with such dishes as trellis of salmon with black currant leaf sauce, steamed breast of free-range chicken with cheese mousse and red pepper butter, breast of squab with onion and sage preserve, rack of lamb wrapped in puff pastry, and stir-fried rabbit with leeks. Seven- and eight-course tasting menus are also available, and there is an extensive wine list. Other public areas include an informal country kitchen–style restaurant and bar and a library. Guests have full run of the estate's formal gardens, woodlands, and parklands, as well as the sporting facilities — an equestrian center and 16 miles of bridle paths, 2 miles of private fishing for salmon and trout on exclusive stretches of the river Nore and its tributary (the King's River), pheasant shooting, and fox hunting with the *Kilkenny Hunt,* which is headquartered on the estate. As we went to press, other facilities were slated to be ready by the middle of this year, including an 18-hole Jack Nicklaus–designed golf course, and golf and fishing academies for on-site instruction. Indoor and outdoor tennis will be available, as well as badminton, squash, and a gymnasium with a sauna and a Jacuzzi. The estate is also the home of Ireland's oldest cricket club. Located just over a mile from Thomastown, County Kilkenny, in the heart of central Ireland; about 10 miles south of Kilkenny; 75 miles southwest of Dublin; and 100 miles southeast of Shannon. Details: *Mount Juliet,* Thomastown, County Kilkenny, Irish Republic (phone: 56-24455).

ADARE MANOR, Adare, County Limerick, Irish Republic: It's not surprising that Adare, one of Ireland's most picturesque communities, is the setting for this truly regal retreat of 840 acres along the river Maigue. The entrance of this walled estate, at the edge of the village, leads to a long and winding driveway of ancient trees and grassy knolls, horse stables and formal gardens, and finally to the huge gray Tudor-Gothic mansion. Built in the early 19th century, this multi-towered and turreted château was the country home of the Earls of Dunraven until a few years ago, when it was acquired by American owners who spent about $10 million to restore, refurbish, and open it as a hotel in 1988. The interior has barrel-vaulted ceilings, 15th-century Flemish doors, more than 50 individually carved fireplaces, and a banquet hall with a 2-story gallery. There are 64 antiques-filled bedrooms, each with a private bath. The restaurant, open to daytime visitors as well as overnight guests, offers a romantic setting with oak-paneled walls, Waterford crystal chandeliers, and floor-to-ceiling windows that frame views of the river and gardens. The menu offers such dishes as lobster in prawn sauce, John Dory sole, grilled local salmon, duck in red wine sauce, and prime ribs of beef carved and served from a rolling silver trolley. A complete resort, the *Manor* offers its guests many daytime activities — from strolling or jogging around the grounds to salmon and trout fishing, horseback riding, fox hunting, and clay pigeon shooting. Also slated to open in the fall of this year is an 18-hole championship golf course designed by Robert Trent Jones, Sr. Details: *Adare Manor,* Adare, County Limerick, Irish Republic (phone: 61-86566).

ASHFORD CASTLE, Cong, County Mayo, Irish Republic: At first glance this establishment looks like the progeny of a marriage between the last of the dinosaurs and the castle inhabited by Snow White's stepmother. The shape is long, low, and gray, with the battlements ridged like the scales down a dragon's back. The river in front is spanned by a stony bridge. Beside it, long Lough Corrib winds down to the sea at Galway. Not really homey, most would think, until they learn that in its present state, give or take a tower, it has been inhabited by several families, most recently by kin of the stout-brewing Guinnesses, in the persons of Lord and Lady Ardilaun. The 18th-century French château section in the middle was home to the Oranmore and Browne families, and the original hefty 13th-century section housed the Norman family known as the De Burgos, who conquered the surrounding land. Many of these illustrious occupants have left their marks. Apart from a fleeting resemblance to the Chartres Cathedral in France (the small dining room being about 45 feet high), the interior is in the comfortable-baronial school of design — just the thing for a comfortable baron who likes a bathroom in which a cocktail party for 30 could be given or who requires a bed the size of a tennis court. A hotel since 1939, unstintingly refurbished in recent years by a consortium of Irish-American owners, the place is luxury incarnate from the thick Oriental-toned carpeting that hushes footsteps in salons and corridors to the Waterford chandeliers that sparkle in gilt mirrors. Fine paintings, sculpture, and uninhabited antique armor are artfully deployed around the public rooms, just to complete the picture. At least one real king has stayed and played here: Edward VII of England, for whom, they say, the billiard room was built. The recreation is of the outdoor kind. Angling for trout, pike, perch, char, rudd, and bream is in adjacent Lough Corrib (and the hotel kitchen, which has always been soundly middle-of-the-road, will prepare the catch). Shooting rights over 25,000 acres — 2,000 of which are a controlled area — provide the chance of bagging pheasant, teal duck, snipe, and woodcock (described in "Stalking and Shooting" in *For the Body*); the lakeside chalet where Lord and Lady Ardilaun spent their wedding night is now in less romantic use as a site for shooters' lunches. Golf and tennis are also part of the picture, and though there is not yet a jousting ground, hunting is an excellent alternative. The sedentary can ramble around the estate in jaunting cars and cruise up the lake in a boat that holds 50. It definitely isn't the place for those who like shops and shopping, although there is one craft shop on the grounds and Cong, the nearest village, is a picturesque spot full of ruined abbeys. Nor is it one of the beacons of the Irish food scene, though the new restaurant seating 32 has begun to win accolades. But despite the scope and the grandeur of it all, the castle is a delightful place, friendly and hospitable. It's easy to understand why King George V of England, who visited here often as Prince of Wales, liked the place so much he could hardly be dislodged. Open year-round; 83 bedrooms and 6 suites, all with bath. A member of the Relais & Châteaux group. Details: *Ashford Castle Hotel*, Cong, County Mayo, Irish Republic (phone: 92-46003).

HILTON PARK, near Clones, County Monaghan, Irish Republic: Johnny and Lucy Madden, whose ancestors moved into the house in 1730, now live here in conditions that are at once shabby and grand. On the one hand is the worn carpet on the stairs; on the other are the giant interconnecting salons, kitchens the size of most houses, and the breast-high four-poster beds equipped with a ladder and covered with slippery, hand-embroidered linen counterpanes. Some bathrooms are the size of parks, but others — among them one with a fine view toward one of the nearby lakes — are minimal, consisting of pitchers and bowls on washstands. The dining room is a gallery of portraits, including clerical and military figures as well as a fellow who looks like a descendant of Count Dracula. Dinners and breakfasts are included, along with snack lunches on request, most of the raw materials for which come from the 550-acre farm and the fine kitchen garden, including unusual vegetables such as sea kale and salsify. The cooking is generally inventive, and Lucy Madden even makes her own cream cheese. One way to enjoy the baronial atmosphere is for four or five couples to take over the entire house for a weekend or a week. Lots do, and keep busy fishing for pike and trout on the two lakes on the property and on others nearby, where they also go swimming and canoeing. Horseback riding and shooting are available by special arrangement nearby, and on the property are tennis courts, a 9-hole golf course, and a lawn for croquet — which is a blood sport here. Open April through September by reservation only and at other times by arrangement (dining room for residents only); 5 double bedrooms, 3 with bath. Details: *Hilton Park,* Scotshouse, Clones, County Monaghan, Irish Republic (phone: 47-56007).

COOPERSHILL, Riverstown, County Sligo, Irish Republic: Think of antlered heads, dogs, antique weapons, portraits of bewigged ancestors and assorted kings, four-poster beds, and a slightly zany atmosphere to get the picture of what it's like here at this 4-story hostelry, a structure in massive cut stone that eerily resembles an Egyptian temple from a production of *Aïda.* A coat of arms above the front door bears the date 1774; the family who built it has occupied it in deteriorating grandeur ever since, with just a single change of name — Cooper to O'Hara. The large bedrooms don't spoil guests with their luxury; "picturesque" is a more accurate description. But there is central heating, supplementing the open fires in the reception rooms, and the food is tasty — breakfasts of porridge, bacon, and black-and-white pudding. Guests, who are French and Japanese as well as Irish, fish for pike on the river Arrow, which runs through the estate, or go after trout with dapped mayflies on nearby lakes. Horseback riding can be arranged. The Rosses Point links of the *County Sligo Golf Club* is a favorite of golfers, and for those who prefer less-physical activity, there is plenty of sightseeing in surrounding Yeats country, which has magical associations for poetry and literature lovers. Open mid-March through October; 5 rooms, each with bath. Details: *Coopershill,* Riverstown, County Sligo, Irish Republic (phone: 71-65108).

WATERFORD CASTLE, The Island, Ballinakill, Waterford, County Waterford, Irish Republic: Of all Ireland's castles, it is the only one that offers a completely secluded setting on a 310-acre island in the river Suir on the southeast Irish coast. Accessible only by a small, chain-link car ferry, the castle has an interesting history. It was built circa 1160 for the FitzGeralds, one of Ireland's most famous ruling families, and remained in their hands for over 800 years. In the 19th century it was the home of Edward FitzGerald, a celebated writer best remembered for his translation of 12th-century Persian poetry, the *Rubaiyat of Omar Khayyam.* Edward FitzGerald's great-grandniece, Princess Caracciolo, was one of the more recent residents before it was purchased by the current owner, Edward Kearns, who has invested millions on masterful restoration and refurbishment. The castle consists of an original Norman keep and two Elizabethan-style wings. It is built entirely of stone with a lead roof, mullioned windows, graceful archways, ancient gargoyles, turrets, towers, and battlements. There are 20 bedrooms and suites of varying sizes, each with antique furnishings and fixtures, four-poster or canopied beds, designer fabrics and linen, hand-carved armoires and vanities, and private bath. The public rooms are replete with spacious sitting areas and huge, stone fireplaces, hand-woven Connemara carpets, oil paintings, oak-paneled walls, and ornate plaster ceilings. Dining by candlelight in the restaurant is appropriately regal — from the Waterford crystal stemware to the Wedgwood place settings and Irish linen. The menu, which changes daily, features locally caught seafood and game and vegetables from the castle gardens. The extensive wine list offers vintages from all over Europe and as far away as Lebanon, Chile, and Australia. Guests enjoy full access to the island's outdoor facilities — tennis, horseback riding, salmon and trout fishing, fox hunting, pheasant and duck shooting, and a variety of water sports. There also is a heated indoor swimming pool with a health and fitness center, and, as we went to press, a new 18-hole championship golf course was slated to open for the 1991 season.

The castle is exclusive, and only overnight guests or visitors with lunch or dinner reservations are given ferry access to the island. Details: *Waterford Castle,* The Island, Ballinakill, Waterford, County Waterford, Irish Republic (phone: 51-78203).

MARLFIELD HOUSE, Gorey, County Wexford, Irish Republic: These days, dowager countesses lead lean lives in picturesque mansions that are much the worse for wear. But it wasn't always that way, as guests will see when visiting this handsome Regency mansion in the southeastern part of the country, the beautifully restored dower house for the Earls of Courtown, where their widows lived after their husbands' demise. This was life on a grand scale, among marble fireplaces and magnificent staircases, surrounded by views of the beautiful grounds seen through tall, elegant windows. As for the Relais & Châteaux hotel that now occupies these premises, there are almost not enough walls in the house to hold the awards that have been heaped on it, the only constant complaint being that the crows in the gardens caw too loudly in the morning. Bedrooms are charmingly furnished with four-poster beds, canopied beds, and other handsome pieces. And the meals are positively sumptuous — as much for their settings as for the food — with breakfasts that include trout as well as porridge and cream, lunches served in the bar, where a mighty log fire blazes continuously and a blue point Siamese gives gracious welcome by allowing himself to be stroked, and dinners laid out in an elegant dining room that looks into a romantic curvilinear Victorian cast-iron conservatory. The fish is so fresh it can be eaten totally plain without the slightest want of flavor. All of the herbs and most vegetables come from the adjacent kitchen garden. The guest list includes most of the monied and influential people in the country and not a few government ministers; they come here for the food, the quiet, and the company. But there's recreation as well: a private tennis court, a golf course a mile away, and long silvery strands at about the same distance. A pack of hounds is within striking distance, and bird watching, shooting, and fishing are all possible. Booking in advance is essential, especially during the tourist season. Open year-round, except for a week or so at *Christmas;* 13 bedrooms and 6 new suites, all with bath. Details: *Marlfield House,* Gorey, County Wexford, Irish Republic (phone: 55-21124).

TINAKILLY HOUSE, Rathnew, County Wicklow, Irish Republic: This enormous gray Victorian mansion stands like a rather surly elephant among the rolling green and purple hills of Wicklow, like hundreds of others that dot the Irish landscape. Inside, however, it gives off a puzzling sense of déjà vu that is not resolved until the realization dawns that the place vaguely resembles one of those grand Cunard liners in which so many films of the 1930s were set — the *Titanic* minus the iceberg leaps to mind (though if this house had been sent to sea, the mahogany doors and massive pine-and-maple shutters could have held their own against any iceberg). Rooms are scattered with needlepoint chairs, marble fireplaces, family silver, and Victorian heirlooms, many of which are nautical in theme. The building was originally put up in the 1870s for Captain Charles Halpin of the Great Eastern, the company that laid the first telegraph cable between Europe and America; as far as possible, the furnishings are of the period. Though there are a few modern bedrooms that are, unfortunately, somewhat lacking in character, many have four-poster or half-tester beds, are very comfortable, and have a strongly masculine character befitting the old salt who built them. As for the food, it has varied over the years as chefs have come and gone; the present incumbent, Johnny Moloney, is highly regarded. However, guests can always count on proprietor Bee Power's superb brown bread. The house is an hour from Dublin along good roads, close to Glendalough and other attractions of County Wicklow, including the famous Mount Usher Gardens (see *Stately Homes and Great Gardens*). There is a tennis court on the grounds, riding can be arranged, and there is access to golf courses. This mansion is very popular with BBC film crews and with actors. Open year-round except in late December and January; 14 bedrooms, each with bath. Details: *Tinakilly House Hotel,* Rathnew, County Wicklow, Irish Republic (phone: 404-69274).

IF YOU'RE NEARBY

BALLYLICKEY MANOR HOUSE, Ballylickey, County Cork, Irish Republic: The former hunting lodge with the Bantry Bay view that was here a few years ago burned in 1983. But the new *Ballylickey* may be even better than the old — more personal and very carefully tailored to the management's ambitions to offer only the best. The main house has been rebuilt according to the plans of the original, but with two wings of suites it provides true seclusion. There are also a number of cottages. Its handsome lawns, gardens, and parkland bordering the Ouvane River and its heated outdoor swimming pool and stables make this Relais & Châteaux establishment a lovely base for tours of Cork and Kerry. Closed November to March; 11 rooms, each with bath. Details: *Ballylickey House,* Bantry Bay, County Cork, Irish Republic (phone: 27-50071).

BANTRY HOUSE AND GARDENS, Bantry, County Cork, Irish Republic: Housed in the east and west wings of this 18th-century brick and stone mansion is an elegant bed and breakfast establishment with 10 rooms (6 with private bath). During a stay, guests can enjoy the fine gardens, as well as many pieces from the Wallace Collection amassed by the second Earl of Bantry during his travels in Europe from 1820 to 1840 (for more information on the collection, see *Stately Home and Great Gardens*). Details: *Bantry House and Gardens,* Bantry, County Cork, Irish Republic (phone: 27-50047).

ASSOLAS COUNTRY HOUSE, Kanturk, County Cork, Irish Republic: This fine 17th-century manor is an idyll inside and out, with its riverside gardens and public spaces and bedrooms full of comfortable chairs and attractive period furnishings. There's a flagstone-floored gameroom inside and a grass tennis court outside — well maintained and ready for use. Open April through October; 10 rooms, all with bath. Details: *Assolas Country House,* Kanturk, County Cork, Irish Republic (phone: 29-50015).

ARD NA GREINE INN, Schull, County Cork, Irish Republic: A farmhouse until the 1970s, this establishment is now a homey country inn full of 18th-century charm, and with its secluded location and extensive gardens it makes a delightful rural retreat. Schull itself is a pretty little fishing port in the shadow of Mount Gabriel, a good departure point for fair-weather trips to the windswept Carbery's Hundred Isles. Open April through October; 7 rooms, each with bath. Details: *Ard Na Greine Inn,* Schull, County Cork, Irish Republic (phone: 28-28181).

RATHMULLAN HOUSE, Rathmullan, County Donegal, Irish Republic: This late-18th-century country house resort (a Relais & Châteaux member) is as snug as can be. Log and turf fires burn in the drawing room and library; the assorted rooms and cottages are stylishly fitted with antiques; and the conservatory-style dining room, with its tented ceiling, makes guests feel that they are dining in a garden. Outside the scenery is magnificent — from the tree-lined shore of Lough Swilly (on whose banks the hostelry sits) to the wildly grand coast and mountains to the west. The gardens are stunning and have won several awards. On its 50 acres of grounds, the hotel also has its own grass tennis court, croquet lawn, and putting green. Open *Easter* to October; 18 rooms, 16 with bath. Details: *Rathmullan House,* Rathmullan, County Donegal, Irish Republic (phone: 74-58188).

KYLEMORE HOUSE, Kylemore, County Galway, Irish Republic: One of the best of a number of superior lodging places in the area. Bordered by 7 wooded acres, it offers country-house elegance as well as good food. It has 6 rooms, 5 with bath. Not to be confused with the *Kylemore Pass* hotel. Open April through October. Details: *Kylemore House Guesthouse,* near Kylemore Abbey, Kylemore, County Galway, Irish Republic (phone: 95-41143).

ROSLEAGUE MANOR, near Letterfrack, Connemara, County Galway, Irish

Republic: Civilized and comfortable, this establishment is in a gracious Georgian manor overlooking a quiet bay edged with woods. With its public rooms decked with antiques and oils and its traditionally furnished bedrooms, it makes a wonderful retreat. Open *Easter* through October; 15 rooms, all with bath. Details: *Rosleague Manor,* Letterfrack, Connemara, County Galway, Irish Republic (phone: 95-41101).

CROCNARAW COUNTRY HOUSE, Moyard, County Galway, Irish Republic: An inviting and homey Georgian house with lovely gardens on 20 acres on the shores of Ballinakill Bay, 6 miles from Clifden. The dining room serves tasty meals that feature fresh seafood, garden vegetables, and dairy products. Open April to October; 6 rooms, 4 with bath. Details: *Crocnaraw Country House,* Moyard, County Galway, Irish Republic (phone: 95-41068).

RENVYLE HOUSE, Renvyle, Connemara, County Galway, Irish Republic: This elegant hotel overlooking the sea was once the country place of Oliver St. John Gogarty, a great Irish wit whom James Joyce immortalized as Buck Mulligan in *Ulysses.* The decor is antique and the atmosphere gracious; the bedrooms have a cottage tone. Fishing is a big deal in these parts. Locals say if you look hard toward the west, you can see Brooklyn. Open late March through December; 40 rooms, each with bath. Details: *Renvyle House Hotel,* Renvyle, Connemara, County Galway, Irish Republic (phone: 95-43511 or 95-43444).

CAHERNANE, Killarney, County Kerry, Irish Republic: A former Victorian home that occupies a peaceful 100-acre estate, with parklands, pastures, lakes, and mountains providing a backdrop. The high-ceilinged, antique-furnished bedrooms in the original mansion are more romantic than those in the modern annex. On-site sports facilities include private river fishing, hard-court tennis, 9-hole miniature golf, and croquet. Open March to October; 52 rooms, each with bath. Details: *Cahernane Hotel,* Muckross Rd., Killarney, County Kerry, Irish Republic (phone: 64-31895, 64-33936, or 64-33937).

NEWPORT HOUSE, Newport, County Mayo, Irish Republic: From its ivy-clad exterior to its graciously furnished interior, this Relais & Châteaux hotel lacks nothing in atmosphere. Many of the bedrooms, which are traditionally furnished, look out onto a pretty courtyard. A highlight of any guest's stay here is dinner, which features wonderful smoked salmon, brown bread, fresh salmon, and berries picked from the gardens in back. There's golf on a 9-hole course, croquet, and all manner of fishing to be enjoyed. Open late March through September; 19 rooms, each with bath. Details: *Newport House Hotel,* Newport, County Mayo, Irish Republic (phone: 98-41222).

CARRIGEEN CASTLE, Cahir, County Tipperary, Irish Republic: This unusual bed and breakfast establishment is not in a castle at all: It used to be a jail — which is not hard to tell from a look at the solid stone walls and turreted top. Guests are accommodated in the cells, cozied up by antiques. Open year-round; 4 rooms, 1 with private bath. Details: *Carrigeen Castle,* Cork Rd., Cahir, County Tipperary, Irish Republic (phone: 52-41370).

CASHEL PALACE, Cashel, County Tipperary, Irish Republic: This former Protestant archbishop's residence, designed by Edward Lovett Pearce around 1730, has fine gardens outside and beautiful paneling, columns, and black marble mantelpieces inside. The luxurious rooms include enormous suites and smaller beamed hideaways; fine period furnishings and attractive fabrics can be found throughout. Open year-round; 20 rooms, all with well-fitted bath. Details: *Cashel Palace Hotel,* Main St., Cashel, County Tipperary, Irish Republic (phone: 62-61411).

DUNDRUM HOUSE, Dundrum, Cashel, County Tipperary, Irish Republic: Built in 1730 on 2,400 acres, this gracious country manor has been extensively renovated and expanded since purchase by its present owners, Austin and Mary Crowe, and the high ceilings, the ornate plasterwork, the carved mantlepieces, and the fine views over the tree-studded grounds make it a delightful place to stay when visiting the Rock of Cashel (see "Ancient Monuments and Ruins" in *For the Mind*). Its dining room offers an opportunity to sample wonderful oak-smoked salmon. Open year-round; 55 rooms, each with bath. Details: *Dundrum House Hotel*, Dundrum, Cashel, County Tipperary, Irish Republic (phone: 62-71116).

HUNTER'S, Rathnew, County Wicklow, Irish Republic: In its fifth generation of ownership by the Gelletlie family, this 200-year-old coaching inn offers a beautiful setting among fine gardens on the banks of the river Vartry. Open year-round; 18 rooms, 10 with bath. Details: *Hunter's*, Newrath Bridge, Rathnew, County Wicklow, Irish Republic (phone: 404-40106).

LONDONDERRY ARMS, Carnlough, County Antrim, Northern Ireland: An old coaching inn built in 1848 by the marquis of Londonderry and inherited by his great-grandson Sir Winston Churchill in 1921, this family-run hostelry is full of unusual pieces of carved furniture, Ulster artists' paintings, early Irish maps, and open fires. It also boasts a fine garden that runs down to the sea. The home-cooked meals feature seasonal local produce. Open year-round; 15 comfortably furnished rooms, each with bath. Details: *Londonderry Arms*, 20 Harbour Rd., Carnlough, County Antrim, BT44 OEU Northern Ireland (phone: 574-885255 or 574-885458).

CULLODEN, Craigavad, Holywood, County Down, Northern Ireland: A splendid Scottish baronial structure on 12 acres of secluded gardens and woodlands, once a bishop's palace, it is possibly the most luxurious hotel in Northern Ireland. Its handsomely decorated guestrooms are full of velvets and silks, and the lovely dining room and public areas are embellished with fine plasterwork ceilings, Louis XV chandeliers, paintings, and other beautiful antiques. The former bishop's chapel is now the bar. Amenities include a pair of squash courts, table tennis, exercise equipment, putting green, tennis, and croquet. Closed *Christmas Day*; 92 rooms, each with bath. Details: *Culloden Hotel*, 142 Bangor Rd., Holywood, County Down, BT18 OEX Northern Ireland (phone: 2317-5223).

A SPECIAL TREAT

One of the greatest pleasures Ireland has to offer is an overnight stay at one of its fine stately homes — those symmetrical Georgian structures that preside graciously over the lush fields here and there throughout the country. Some are available only to groups, but others offer lodging for independent travelers.

To find out more, contact *Elegant Ireland* (15 Harcourt St., Dublin 2; phone: 1-751665) or its agents in the US, *Abercrombie & Kent International* (1420 Kensington Rd., Oak Brook, IL 60521; phone: 800-323-7308 or 312-954-2944).

Best Eating

The Irish know all about potatoes. Traditionally they boil them, bake them, mash them, and mix them with all sorts of other ingredients — with scallions to make a dish called *champ*, with cabbage for *colcannon*, with butter and flour to create *boxty*, and with butter, sugar, brandy, and eggs to make a dessert of puzzling pedigree and hard-to-identify flavors. Potatoes also go into potato cakes, a breakfast dish whose essential accompaniments are bacon and eggs. They are used to make potato scones, light and fluffy at their best and scrumptious when served hot and loaded with butter and Irish honey. The 19th-century suffragette Frances Power Cobbe wrote that housewives before the famine cooked the "delicious tubers . . . in a manner that no English or French Cordon Bleu can approach." Yet despite the ingenuity with which the Irish elaborated on the omnipresent potato then, and have done so since, the nation's cooks have always had a bad reputation. The world at large could see only cabbage and potatoes. Lovers of good food went to Paris when they wanted to eat well but held out little hope for the cuisine of their native land.

All that has changed in the last few years. A whole generation of young Irish chefs, trained on the Continent, at the hotel school in Shannon, and at the cooking school run by Myrtle Allen of *Ballymaloe House* (she's the leading modern interpreter of Irish dishes), have begun discovering other ingredients — and exploiting them with the same invention that the good cooks among their forebears always did with the lowly potato. Soggy sprouts and overcooked plaice, meat roasted to a fare-thee-well, and vegetables that would make the army's steam table offerings look crisp are giving way to sautéed zucchini flowers, grilled lamb marinated in Irish whiskey and carved into juicy pink slices, and the freshest calf's liver served with pan juices flavored with cream, Irish whiskey, and fresh tarragon. The new chefs have a respect for their ingredients that is so intense that they don't just go out and buy the best in the local market. They also work with farmers in the neighborhood to have vegetables planted and grown to their specifications. Or they grow them in their own kitchen gardens and on their own farms. The positive by-products are no longer destroyed through overcooking; and unlike some of the practitioners of the nouvelle cuisine in France, the new Irish chefs tend to be delightfully straightforward and unpretentious about their presentation.

These developments are not lost on the Irish, and a whole group of Irish foodies has evolved; the canniest follow the chef, not the restaurant, and decamp without a moment's hesitation when he or she flounces off to another establishment. The game of musical chefs has become a constant, with chef poaching joining salmon poaching as a national sport.

The following establishments, listed alphabetically by county, are some of the best at press time; consult *Rural Retreats* for other ideas because many of the inns listed there, such as *Ballymaloe House, Longueville House, Newport House, Sea View House, the Park Hotel, Mount Juliet,* and *Waterford Castle,* offer wonderful meals. Almost all except those attached to hotels close on Sundays and public holidays, but it's always a good idea to telephone before detouring to some culinary oasis — to make sure the great chef you heard about is still there as well as to make sure that the restaurant has not suddenly closed for the day to celebrate the marriage of a local dignitary or to go to the races, both of which occasionally happen in rural areas. By the same token, if there's a restaurant you want to visit but expect to be closed, call: The same chefs who will shut up shop earlier in the season if trade is bad occasionally prolong the season if trade is good. In short, always make a phone call before making your plans.

MACCLOSKEYS, Bunratty, County Clare, Irish Republic: A stone's throw up the hill from the fabled Bunratty Castle, the location of this restaurant undoubtedly helped to launch it 10 years ago, but it is the food, impeccably prepared and presented by chef Gerry MacCloskey, that brings customers back time after time. Specialties include veal with sweet and sour sauces, noisettes of lamb with minted béarnaise sauce, black sole on the bone, baked cod with Cajun chili sauce, river Fergus salmon, and West Cork lobster. Desserts are equally tempting — homemade ice cream, strawberry soufflé, chocolate mousse with brandy, baked pear puffs, and grape pudding. The Old World setting is charming, with four cozy candlelit dining areas in the former mews and a 19th-century Georgian wine cellar, with the original white-washed walls, carved archways, and polished slate floors. Fresh flowers or plants adorn every table, along with hand-painted chinaware and fine linens. The chef's wife and partner, Marie MacCloskey, greets every customer individually and offers an aperitif by the fireside, so guests have ample time to explore the menu and savor the ambience. The service is well-coordinated and deft, and chef Gerry often emerges from the kitchen to chat with guests at evening's end. Open for dinner only; closed Sunday and Monday. Details: *MacCloskeys,* Bunratty, County Clare, Irish Republic (phone: 61-364082).

LOVETT'S, Douglas, County Cork, Irish Republic: Proprietor Dermot Lovett, who trained in Ireland, Zurich, and London, has brought a whole menu full of new culinary adventures to a peach-colored, late-19th-century house on an unobtrusive lane beside the sea, a few miles from the heart of Cork. Chief among those adventures are sea urchins, spiny creatures you might consider the hedgehogs of the subterranean world or mines from World War I, depending on your point of view. They are usually eaten raw; when as fresh as they are here and served in clusters on cracked ice with lemon wedges, they are as delicious as the best oyster. Less venturesome diners will relish the smoked eel, the Kenmare Bay oysters, and the brill — a small turbot, but better. High-cholesterol sinners can overdose on fried camembert in fresh tomato sauce, and the most determined of trained eaters can tuck into the 6-course table d'hôte; those with faltering appetites can stick to the equally inventive à la carte menu with no less enjoyment. Presiding over it all is a battery of whiskery Corkonians from Victorian times together with a single alert beauty immortalized in oil on canvas by James Butler Brennan, who tutored William Orpen. The wine list is comprehensive and on occasion is supplemented by an extraordinary yet practically unknown French-made dessert wine, Moulin Touchais from the region of Anjou. A feature that deserves encouragement is the notice on the menu that says there is no service charge and discourages gratuities. Clientele includes local businesspeople and visiting yachtsmen. Open Mondays through Fridays for lunch and dinner, Saturdays for dinner only; closed for a week at *Christmas*. Details: *Lovett's Restaurant,* Douglas, County Cork, Irish Republic (phone: 21-294909).

KINSALE, County Cork, Irish Republic: This brightly painted and beflowered 18th-century town a few miles south of Cork City is like one huge restaurant, with streets instead of stairs; it's the best place for a food lover to be almost any time, but especially during the *Kinsale Gourmet Festival* in early October, when the grub crawling is as furious as the pub crawling. Then, as during the rest of the year, seafood is the specialty, a fact that is not surprising since the town is the hilly backdrop to the picturesque little harbor. Sitting on a dock post with a Guinness in one hand and a fistful of oysters (or periwinkles or crab claws) in the other is one way to go, but everything that ever swam or crept along the ocean floor or gummed itself to a rock on the shoreline also appears on the menus of restaurants like Michael Reise's cozy and romantic *Vintage;* Brian and Anne Cronin's *Blue Haven,* which represented Ireland at *Bloomingdale's* in New York during its Ireland promotion a few years ago; or any of a number of other restaurants and uncounted pubs occupying buildings 2 centuries old or more. At the 11 restaurants of the Kinsale Good Food Circle, the organization that has contributed so greatly to the current culinary state of things, the style ranges from Irish country house to French provincial to nouvelle. Sample the smoked eel, much subtler than smoked salmon, wherever it appears; the brill (a delicate turbot); black sole (Dover sole in America); and, above all, the local native oysters, which will teach those unfortunates who are not already in the know what oysters are all about. Details: *Kinsale Tourist Office,* Kinsale, County Cork, Irish Republic (phone: 21-772234).

ARBUTUS LODGE, Montenotte, County Cork, Irish Republic: One of the great restaurants of Ireland, this one enfolds diners in luxury, cossets them with fine service, and feeds but does not fatten them with the absolute best of food. The Ryan family, who own and run it, have close alliances with the famous Troisgros brothers of France — the two staffs share secrets and inspirations — so the food is classically Franco-Irish, spiced with regional specialties like *drisheen,* a blood pudding native to Cork that is poached in milk. Whether a guest considers this interesting or noxious depends on his or her point of view. Those who are not ethnically inclined can concentrate on the fish, hand-picked from the daily catch of four or five trawlers; the locally smoked salmon; or the game, brought in from the de Vesci estate. Indecisive or gluttonous diners can opt for the eight-course tasting menu for a complete sampling of all the specialties of the house. The hot oysters with herbs from the garden are especially memorable, and the wine list makes connoisseurs gasp. Nearly every important chef in Ireland has done a stint in the kitchen, and *every* important visitor to the southern capital has eaten in the brown and white dining room that shines with damask. In 1802 a master cooper who manufactured butter firkins built the low building on a steep hill known as Montenotte, site of a classy Cork suburb with a plummy accent that earthier Corkonians deride. Guests can munch snacks out on the patio, which offers a spectacular view over the river Lee. Also available are 20 rooms of varying standards, each with bath. Open for lunch and dinner Mondays through Saturdays, with bar food on Sundays; closed a week at *Christmas*. Details: *Arbutus Lodge Hotel,* Middle Glanmire Rd., Montenotte, Cork, Irish Republic (phone: 21-501237).

PARK, Blackrock, County Dublin, Irish Republic: When proprietor Colin O'Daly was at the *Park* hotel in Kenmare, County Kerry, he sent forth a new generation of chefs bearing Olympic torches to rekindle Irish fires that had heretofore been confined to the cooking of bacon and eggs. When he left to start his own restaurant near Dublin in the mid-1980s, he already had a circle of admirers. His establishment's original location, in a storefront building on the main thoroughfare of the Dublin suburb of Blackrock, was cramped and rather unimpressive, compared to the innovative food served inside. Last year, however, O'Daly acquired a new property and created a setting that matches the high standards of his food. Just down the road from the original location, the new spot is housed in an old stone building tucked away from the main street and reached by a landscaped pathway. It is a pleasant and spacious environment, with a blend of natural wood paneling, colorful carpets, and contemporary Irish artworks. The food continues to be superb. Having won competitions and been photographed in many glossy international magazines, O'Daly's plaited sole with sea urchin sauce tastes as good as it looks, as does a glamorous dish of salmon and melon cooked *en papillote* with mango sauce. Among more substantial offerings is chicken breast layered with salmon and served in prawn sauce. Quail eggs are regularly presented as starters, divinely bubbling *en cocotte,* and patrons can count on game in season. It is difficult to get in without a reservation, as it is one of Dublin's chic restaurants, with a regular clientele that includes famous film stars who are very discreetly served. Lunches are more relaxed, but whatever the hour and whoever you are, expect a friendly visit to your table from the very gracious chef-proprietor, who is deeply concerned with how his food is received. Open Tuesdays through Fridays for lunch and dinner, Saturdays for dinner only; closed Tuesdays after public holidays. Details: *Park Restaurant,* The Mews, 40 Main St., Blackrock, County Dublin, Irish Republic (phone: 1-883988).

OLD DUBLIN, Dublin, Irish Republic: Part of an area known as the Liberties, which was inhabited 200 years ago by Huguenot weavers who harbored a deadly animosity toward Roman Catholic butchers, Francis Street is a mixture of inner-city sleaze, strange old crafts, and interesting antiques shops, as well as the home of this restaurant, whose proprietor employs a stout youth to sit outside and watch his patrons' cars. Inside, all is jolly peace and Scandinavian-style fish, which owner Eamonn Walsh learned to love while in Finland. Venalainen smokies — filets of hake, halibut, sea trout, or others hot smoked on the premises and served as an appetizer in a white wine, cream, and dill sauce — are a study in varying tastes and textures. For a main course, try salmon coulibiac. Meanwhile, for meat eaters, there's filet à la Novgorod — a châteaubriand sliced and served Russian-style on sauerkraut alongside fried kasha, spicy mushrooms, caviar, and sour cream. The atmosphere is very clubby, with all the patrons on a first-name basis, and cozy, due in great measure to the rose-colored table linens and walls and the roaring fires. Standouts on the very interesting wine list are the bordeaux, imported directly by the owner and exceptionally priced, especially the St. Emilion Grand Cru 1981. Open Mondays through Fridays for lunch and dinner, Saturdays for dinner only; closed holidays. Details: *Old Dublin Restaurant,* 91 Francis St., Dublin 8, Irish Republic (phone: 1-542028 or 1-542346).

PATRICK GUILBAUD, Dublin, Irish Republic: Secluded in a dim lane off Baggot Street in a mews at the back of a giant bank headquarters, this restaurant is a sort of temple of food, built for the purpose with plaster reproductions of the Parthenon frieze along the walls and greenery hanging from the ceiling. The effect is elegant, if a bit austere, and, as befits a house of worship, the atmosphere is hushed as local devotees dip their reverent beaks into nouvelle concoctions served in bird-size portions (meant for connoisseurs with small appetites rather than for jolly parties). But the pious get viands that are not available elsewhere. Freshwater pike, which chokes up the lakes, is seldom found on Irish tables, but when Guilbaud and his chef Guillaume Lebrun strike it lucky on a fishing expedition in Wicklow, pike is found on the altars here. Woodcock, another rare comestible, is also served here — sometimes in spatchcock fashion, split in halves, beak and all. Pride of the chef's heart is the sea bass, pan-fried in saffron butter and served with herbs and an onion confit, but there are other delightful dishes as well — filets of hare sautéed in walnut oil and served in a fan of paper-thin slices doused with a red-wine-and-juniper sauce. Guilbaud himself, a Breton who worked in England before coming here, is quickly applying the newest fashions in French cookery to his own ideas, though he demonstrates a patriotic attachment to his native land's own produce when it comes to cheese and presents a wicker trolley bearing a superb selection of 30 or so varieties, perfectly presented, after meals. The prosperous clientele, drawn from Ireland's legal eagles and tycoons, is enthusiastic in its appreciation. Open for lunch and dinner Mondays through Fridays; Saturdays for dinner only; closed on public holidays. Details: *Patrick Guilbaud Restaurant,* 46 James Pl., Dublin 2, Irish Republic (phone: 1-764192 or 1-601799).

WHITE'S ON THE GREEN, Dublin, Irish Republic: Among the most fashionable of Dublin's chic dining places, it stands on one side of a pleasant 18th-century garden square whose ponds are full of rare wild duck, a picturesque setting reflected in its decor by floral fabrics, rattan furniture, and Villeroy & Boch china. The food is consistently wonderful. Working with a staff of 11, head chef Jean-Louis Taillebaud, who previously was head chef at *Le Gavroche* in London, works until late at night inventing and perfecting dishes such as his own quenelles of chicken breast with walnut and apple. Equally delicious are the *côte de boeuf* for two, with a sauce made by reducing 40 gallons of stock to 1½ gallons; noisettes of lamb, savory with rosemary and spiced with orange; and *symphonie* of Irish fish, a platter of whatever is freshest steamed with seaweed or grilled and served on a fresh tomato *coulis,* which might come straight from the hand of a Mozart. Owner Peter White is as passionate about his wine as about his food and is justifiably proud of his wine list, which includes costly rarities not found in very many other places. What the two men have created together is a restaurant that has become *the* place to see and be seen for top politicians, businesspeople, and the rich and glamorous of both sexes. At lunchtime, the air turns sulfurous with scandal; it's not surprising that meals that start at 12:30 don't wind down until 6 PM. The tiny bar downstairs serves admirable champagne cocktails. Open Mondays through Fridays for lunch and dinner; Saturdays for dinner only; closed on public holidays. Details: *White's on the Green,* 119 St. Stephen's Green, Dublin 2, Irish Republic (phone: 1-751975 or 1-751181).

DIGBY'S, Dún Laoghaire, County Dublin, Irish Republic: One of the few restaurants in the Dublin environs with a view, this one, a dressy place, looks out over the twinkling lights of Dublin Bay, out of whose waters the chef gets the raw materials for his menus. The magnificent dining room, which is tented in crimson batik, provides the setting for some very creative dishes. Squid in cream sauce — rings of fish stewed in white wine, herbs, and garlic for 4 hours, then thickened with cream — is the consistency of butter, and the proprietor guarantees to replace the dish if the most hardened squid hater is not converted in the first mouthful. Roast mallard comes with orange and walnut stuffing, the pheasant is roasted in a sauce of cider, and the vegetables can be sensational. As the portions are on the large side, diners would be wise to hone their appetites with a walk along the seafront to the nearby Martello tower, where James Joyce set the opening of *Ulysses* and which is now full of exhibits pertaining to the novelist (see "Marvelous Museums" in *For the Mind*). The bar downstairs, which is less grand than the main dining room, is sometimes used for more informal eating. Open weekdays except Tuesdays for lunch and dinner, weekends for dinner only; closed Christmas and Good Friday. Details: *Digby's Restaurant and Wine Bar,* 5 Windsor Ter., Seafront, Dún Laoghaire, County Dublin, Irish Republic (phone: 18-04600 or 18-809147).

O'ROURKE'S, Glenasmole, County Dublin, Irish Republic: Although just 13 miles from Dublin center, the idyllic setting of this restaurant is reminiscent of an earlier era; rushing streams and tiny winding boreens grow ever narrower as one approaches the 200-year-old farmhouse in which the dining room is located. In autumn, tall hedges of rowans laden with berries bend to the ground, grub for the fat thrushes. (These birds gave the place its Irish name, which means "glen of thrushes.") All the herbs, many of the vegetables, and much of the meat come from the surrounding acreage. Lambs baa, ducks quack, chickens cackle, and rabbits hop as the mobile menu literally struts its stuff. And it is all very, very good, from the herbed pâté and kidneys and mushrooms in Madeira served as starters to the chicken with walnut and grape sauce, a sophisticated local favorite. Venison is served in season with a jelly made from whatever rowanberries can be saved from the thrushes, and the cockle soup has to be tasted to be believed. There are always a couple of fish dishes in addition to meat. Lunch is served to the public on Sundays only; weekdays, by prior arrangement, parties of 20 or more can tour the farm, watch the weaving operation from sheep shearing to the finished product, as well as have lunch. Call ahead for directions. Open April through September or during some seasons, through early October, Tuesdays through Saturdays for dinner; Sundays for lunch. Details: *O'Rourke's, Glenasmole Crafts Restaurant,* Bohernabreena, Dublin 24, Irish Republic (phone: 1-513620).

MORAN'S OYSTER COTTAGE, Kilcolgan, County Galway, Irish Republic: The perfect light lunch in a perfect setting, that rare treat, can be found on the road to Shannon from Galway at this establishment, providing one keeps to native oysters, brown bread, and draft stout. (The soup that once glorified the place now, alas, come frequently out of a can, and the smoked salmon is not always of the first quality.) But no one yet has invented instant oysters, the brown bread is mouth-watering as ever, and a pint glass of black stout with its creamy, frothy halo is still a better accompaniment to oysters than any white wine — though some dissenters say it's too heavy; for those, there is always a wine list, which offers some drinkable white burgundy. Those who crave something other than the foregoing should order with care; taste the crab first, ask about the soup's ingredients, and sample it. Then enjoy the food and admire the surroundings: the restaurant itself with its steep thatched roof, its warren of tiny rooms, and the kind of view over the river, lined with ancient castles, that would have had Wordsworth groping for his notebook. Snacks can be eaten inside or out, though the latter is preferable when weather permits. Take the Oranmore road from Galway, turn onto the Limerick road, and watch for a sign on the right near Kilcolgan. Open during pub hours all week; closed on *Good Friday* and *Christmas Day.* Details: *Moran's Oyster Cottage,* Kilcolgan, County Galway, Irish Republic (phone: 91-96113).

DRIMCONG HOUSE, Moycullen, County Galway, Irish Republic: Owner Gerard

Galvin, the moving spirit behind the *Kinsale Gourmet Festival,* has now brought the most inventive food in Ireland to Galway. The fact that the menu changes weekly according to what's best in the garden, the lake, and Galway Bay will not prepare even the most sophisticated diner for what's in store: a dessert sauce flavored with sweet geranium and tasting of rose and lemon simultaneously; baked ham napped in two sauces, one of the wild garlic known as ramson, the other of pink melon; medallions of squab served with pear; hot fish mousse formed into turrets of suave, silky airiness and then moated with tomato and strawberry sauces. The chef also caters to vegetarians and children. Enhancing what can only be described as intense gustatory pleasure is a very attractive setting: a long, low house built in 1680 near a lake that hosts numbers of quacking birds, aromatic turf fires, polished oak tables set with hand-blown Irish glass and creamy Villeroy & Boch china, and the menu itself, seemingly written by the very hand that penned the *Book of Kells.* Drimcong, an 8-mile drive from Galway City, seems half that distance after dinner, due, no doubt, to overwhelming contentment. Open Tuesdays through Saturdays for dinner only, Sundays for lunch; closed from *Christmas* through the end of February. Details: *Drimcong House Restaurant,* Moycullen, County Galway, Irish Republic (phone: 91-85115).

DUNDERRY LODGE, Dunderry, Robinstown, Navan, County Meath, Irish Republic: Dunderry used to have a lot in common with Eton College: Parents put a child's name down at birth and hoped for a place 12 years later. The restaurant here is not quite as difficult to get into, but prospective diners still have to book well in advance to secure a reservation (though it's possible to get lucky with a cancellation). Given that it also is located in practically impenetrable countryside, reached by unmarked roads full of potholes, it seems obvious that something special is in store. This is a place where serious diners can expect to spend several hours over dinner, enjoying the premises — originally a group of cow sheds and an old house, a comfortable hodgepodge architecturally — and eating food that is certainly a strong contender for the Best in Ireland title. The menu is extensive, and the execution is uniformly superb, from the warm salad of duck liver with balsamic vinegar, a rich symphony of delights, to the tiny rose-pink lamb chops scented with rosemary, and the kidneys dijonnaise. The brilliant chef, Catherine Healy, is the wife of the proprietor, Nicholas Healy. Open Tuesdays through Fridays for lunch and dinner; Saturdays for dinner only; closed mid-December through mid-February and *Easter* week. Details: *Dunderry Lodge Restaurant,* Dunderry, Robinstown, Navan, County Meath, Irish Republic (phone: 46-31671).

REVERIES, Rosses Point, County Sligo, Irish Republic: In that raging desert of culinary inactivity known as northwest Ireland, this Yeatsian-named establishment is the single oasis. Run by Damien Brennan and his wife, Dr. Paula Gilvarry (Damian's brother owns the *Park* hotel of Kenmare), it sits quite close to the championship golf course near Sligo City and overlooks spectacular Sligo Bay, with Oyster Island and Coney Island opposite the long window and several houses closely associated with the poet nearby. Chef Paula Gilvarry, a medical doctor with a part-time practice, says that cooking is more creative than doctoring, and it's easy to see why when perusing her menu, which is studded with dishes like mousseline of chicken with leeks, smoked trout with horseradish sauce, venison cutlets with gin and juniper berries, and sporting birds (pheasant, mallard, squab) with kumquat sauce. Natives come from 40 miles around to enjoy the food — and savor it carefully; they know they won't get anything nearly as good without traveling even farther. All the raw materials are obtained locally, except the fish, which comes down from Killybegs in County Donegal. The wine list is rather small, but the menu is gigantic and a frequent award winner. Open Mondays through Saturdays for dinner only (though lunches may be added in the future). Details: *Reveries,* Rosses Point, County Sligo, Irish Republic (phone: 71-77371).

Stately Homes and Great Gardens

Before the mid-17th century, most Irish and Anglo-Irish gentry lived either in battleworthy castles or in long, medieval, thatch-roofed houses. But then a rush of prosperity sparked a building boom, and great houses with gardens appeared all over the country. Many of these homes were torched during the euphemistically named "troubles," the struggle for independence from Britain. Some were spared, by accident or intent. (The kerosene had already been poured in the foyer of Glin Castle when the invalid knight came down and, holding tightly on to his wheelchair, announced that the rebels would have to burn him as well. Stopped in their tracks, they repaired to the local pub, drank until morning, and went on to the next big house.) Of those that remained, some were sold by impoverished owners to religious orders and schools, and some were abandoned entirely. Others remain in the hands of the descendants of their builders, but in conditions of unfortunate decrepitude that are constant reminders to their possessors of the need for conservation and of their perennial lack of the funds necessary to achieve it. Tax rebates, recently legislated for historic houses that open to the public for a period each year, scarcely make a dent in the cost of maintaining such a structure in its original condition. But they do enable the rest of the world to get an idea of the scale on which the wealthy once lived — not as grandly as the wealthy across the Irish Sea, but impressively nonetheless, particularly where the gardens are concerned.

Thanks to an equable climate and an abundance of rain that suit everything but the cactus to perfection, a wide range of trees, shrubs, and plants flourish here. Where the soil is acid, rhododendrons and azaleas have enthusiastically gone native. Giant hedges of fuchsia dominate the roadsides in the western part of the country. Several species of trees have their highest growth rate in the world here. Taking a cue from all this, the brilliant Irish landscape architect William Robinson favored a wild-looking garden where nature appeared to play the dominant role; in his creations and in those of his students and contemporaries, the recesses can be probed only with a machete today.

Many fine castles, stately homes, and gardens are open to the public. St. Stephen's Green in Dublin, full of peaceful walkways, ponds, flower beds, and lush greenery, is only the beginning. The Dublin Corporation Rose Garden in suburban Clontarf is an impressive showcase for thousands of flowers. At the exquisite gardens of Howth Castle, north of Dublin, rhododendrons and azaleas blaze against a spectacular marine backdrop in April, May, and June; there are some 2,000 varieties on just 30 acres. At that same time of year, the gardens of *Muckross House at Muckross* in County Killarney, now a folk museum, are also abloom with rhododendrons and azaleas. Meanwhile, more subtle charms are in evidence at the turn-of-the-century Japanese gardens adjoining the *Irish Horse Museum* on the grounds of the Irish National Stud, where there are bonsai trees, wooden bridges, and the like. (See "Marvelous Museums" in *For the Mind* for more details about the museums.) An intrepid lover of castles might visit medieval Cahir Castle, where parts of the film *Barry Lyndon* were shot; or Russborough, in County Wicklow, a splendid early-18th-century Palladian villa full of fabulous art; or Kilkenny Castle (described in *Kilkenny,* THE CITIES); or Clare's 15th-century Bunratty Castle (see "Marvelous Museums" in *For the Mind*); or exquisite Westport House (see *County Mayo,* DIRECTIONS); and many others. Fairly good listings can be found in the Irish Tourist Board publications *Irish Gardens, Historic Houses, Castles & Gardens,* and *Ireland's Heritage,* and in *The Noble Dwellings of Ireland* by John Fitzmaurice Mills, *In an Irish Garden* by Sybil Connolly and Helen

Dillon, and *The Gardens of Ireland* by Michael George and Patrick Bowe, all of which are available from booksellers.

What follows is a representative and decidedly personal selection of some of the best, listed alphabetically by county. Admission fees are nonexistent to nominal. Be sure to call ahead to check on opening hours.

BELLAMONT FOREST, Cootehill, County Cavan, Irish Republic: Sir Edward Lovett Pearce, architect of Dublin's Bank of Ireland (and the supervising architect for some of the construction on Castletown House, described below), built this most perfect of the British Isles' Palladian villas in 1730 for his uncle by marriage Sir Thomas Coote, and it has changed very little since then. A rosy rectangle of brick crowning a low green hill overlooking water and trees, it is totally symmetrical inside and out, thanks to false doors and windows and concealed doors. There is a massive Doric pedimented portico outside, and the interiors are very handsome, full of beautifully proportioned rooms and fine details. The compartmented ceilings in the saloon and dining room are especially lovely, the former with a central medallion of foliage and garlanded flowers shown off to good advantage by a recent repainting in pastels, the latter coved and embellished with 70 separate hand-molded flowers. Upstairs bedrooms open onto Ireland's earliest lanterned hallway, a corridor illuminated by a windowed cupola with a shallow dome — a "private sky," in the word of one observer, painted blue and white with a hovering eagle in the center. There are no gardens of note, but the surrounding lands, which are state-owned, are worth visiting for the views and the wildlife (herons, red squirrels, waterfowl, deer). Look for the underground tunnel, whose brick cells were once used to incarcerate recalcitrant tenants. Open afternoons year-round and for overnight stays, arranged through *Elegant Ireland* (15 Harcourt St., Dublin 2, Irish Republic; phone: 17-51665), or its agents in the US, *Abercrombie & Kent International* (1420 Kensington Rd., Oak Brook, IL 60521; phone: 312-954-2944 or 800-323-7308).

ANNES GROVE GARDENS, Castletownroche, County Cork, Irish Republic: The beautiful and romantic gardens at Annes Grove, a pretty example of Georgian domestic architecture that has been the home of the Grove Annesley family since 1700, are a Douanier Rousseau jungle. Since the soil is by turns acid and limestone, it supports an enormous mix of plants. The woodland section abounds in the progeny of seed collected in China, Tibet, and Nepal by the great plant hunter Kingdom Ward. Elsewhere, Ward's outstanding deciduous azaleas, rhododendrons, and cherries bloom in spring. June is brightened with the blossoms of many varieties of deutzias from North America and China, including both *Cornus kousa,* their bracts thick and white as waxed paper, and the exquisite little *Cornus alternifolia argentia.* In July, herbaceous borders get star billing along with the astilbes, gunnera, lysichiton, polygonum, sulphur-yellow *Primula florindae,* and superb chalices of *Eucryphia nymansay* that carpet the banks of the river Awbeg, which inspired the Elizabethan poet Edmund Spenser in his *Faerie Queene.* Also at their best in July are the wildflowers that occupy a 4-acre semiwild meadow. August brings the New Zealand hoherias, blissfully happy in the moist, mild climate, while September offers the drama of *Parrottia persica* in its autumn foliage and the pink leaves of cercidophyllums, which are of Japanese origin. The house, which is accessible from the main Fermoy–Mallow–Killarney road, a mile north of Castletownroche, can be shown to groups by prior arrangement, with lunch if desired. Open Mondays through Saturdays and for a few hours on Sundays; closed October through *Easter.* Details: *Annes Grove Gardens,* Castletownroche, County Cork, Irish Republic (phone: 22-26145).

BANTRY HOUSE AND GARDENS, Bantry, County Cork, Irish Republic: In December 1796, amid rumblings that the French were about to invade to help free the nation from English rule, Bantry House owner Richard White helped prepare the defense and was eventually made an earl for his efforts. The title is now extinct, and the present owner, Egerton Shelswell-White, is descended through the female line. However, the brick and stone mansion, built in 1750 as a fairly modest residence and considerably enlarged by baroque grafts in the ensuing years, is very impressive. The second Earl of Bantry traveled in Europe between 1820 and 1840, buying up bits and pieces of the Continent and amassing a collection that came to be known as Ireland's Wallace Collection. Though much has been dispersed over the last 100 years, it is possible to get an idea of its scope from what remains: Russian icons, Pompeiian mosaics, French period furniture, paintings from a Venetian palace, Flemish tapestries, and stained glass from Switzerland, France, Germany, and Flanders. Aubusson tapestries made for Marie Antoinette on her marriage, Gobelin tapestries from another French royal connection, and fireplaces that are believed to have come from Versailles' Petit Trianon embellish one set of grandiose rooms, along with all manner of other objects both curious and rare. The library, among other rooms, is large and beautifully proportioned. As for the blue and gold extravaganza known as the dining room, the word "flamboyant" doesn't do it justice; built-in sideboards on the walls, carved and gilt to the limit, display a wild assortment of ornate bric-a-brac, while extraordinary portraits of King George III, who granted Richard White his peerage, and Queen Charlotte survey the scene from their lofty positions on the walls. The gardens are small but have great charm, their Italianate formality contrasting with the wild beauty of the bay just beyond. Cannon dating from the invasion attempt are ranged along the terrace, along with white-painted nymphs posturing on plinths, up to their classical knees in shrubs. The area is especially pretty in May and June, when wisteria and rhododendrons bloom, and in autumn with the turning of the leaves. Bantry House was one of the first of Ireland's stately homes to be opened to the public after World War II. Its east and west wings have been renovated as a posh bed and breakfast establishment (10 rooms, 6 with bath), giving visitors the opportunity to play at being Earl of Bantry for a night. House and gardens open daily year-round. Details: *Bantry House and Gardens,* Bantry, County Cork, Irish Republic (phone: 27-50047).

GLENVEAGH CASTLE AND GARDENS, Glenveagh, County Donegal, Irish Republic: A battlemented Victorian fantasy of the baronial, on 24,000 wild and remote acres, Glenveagh Castle is filled with exceptional furniture, including many Georgian pieces, some of them fine 18th-century Irish creations and, for its humor, a scattering of Victoriana. But the gardens, created by successive owners and now among the finest in the country, are the real reason to visit here. They are of the utmost beauty — graced with statuary, crisscrossed by secret pathways, full of discrete spaces that are really like outdoor rooms that provide color and interest in every season and that dissolve gradually into the native heather scrub and dwarf oak of the rugged mountains all around. There are terraces, a formal pool, a statue garden, a rose garden, a Gothic orangery, and more. Rhododendrons, some of them 30 feet high, scent the air with almost overpowering fragrance when they bloom in early June. In spite of Glenveagh's position in Ireland's most northerly county, tender exotica such as palms and mimosas prosper, as do all manner of other plants, from the park's thousands of rare shrubs and trees to the less exalted species in the walled kitchen garden — flowers for cutting, fruit bushes, and humble vegetables planted in neat rows to wonderful effect. A great flight of stone steps leads up a mountainside to a grassy terrace overlooking castle and lake; from the steps it is possible to look into the heart of flowering trees, which are like giant bouquets alive with birds. Peregrine falcons and red deer breed on the wild moors (there are some 800 to 900 at any given time), and Lough Veagh, a long tongue of water on the estate, is alive with game fish. The outlying lands were purchased by the government in 1975; the late curator of the *Philadelphia Museum of Art,* Henry McIlhenny, the son of a County Donegal immigrant, purchased the property in 1938 and spent the ensuing decades turning it into the civilized oasis it is today. He gave the gardens and castle to the Irish people in 1981, and the whole complex is now open as a national park, together with the former home of painter Derek Hill at Gartan Lough, where some fine paintings are on exhibit. Since private cars are not permitted in the park, visitors are advised to wear stout shoes or boots and to be prepared for walking if they plan any lengthy inspection. Accessible from the Letterkenny–Gweedore road, about 10 miles from Letterkenny. Grounds open year-round; castle closed late October through late March. (See also *Marvelous Museums.*) Details: *Glenveagh Castle and Gardens,* County Donegal, Irish Republic (phone: 74-37088).

MALAHIDE CASTLE, PARK, AND GARDENS, Malahide, County Dublin, Irish Republic: No other property in Ireland was occupied by a single family as long as this one overlooking the Broadmeadow estuary and the Irish Sea: The Talbot family lived here continuously from 1185, when Richard Talbot founded the estate, until 1973, when the last Lord Talbot died — nearly 8 centuries, with a break of only a few years in Cromwellian times. (The estate had been granted by the Lord Protector himself to one Miles Corbet, who signed Charles I's death warrant and thereby forfeited his own life after the Restoration — much to the relief of the Talbots.) Despite the pedigree, however, this is a smallish, easily managed castle. To the oldest surviving section, a 15th-century tower, many additions have been made. The paneled 16th-century Oak Room, one of the finest in the country, is still very well preserved. Its many individual panels of varying dates, collected from all over the world, are striking in their detail, and the Flemish carved Madonna above the fireplace is a showpiece. Still other rooms show elegant Georgian influence, and the impressive Great Hall remains virtually as it was when built hundreds of years ago, with its blackened woodwork and rafters, minstrels gallery, and mantelpieces. (The castle's small ghost is intermittently seen scampering through the 4-foot door and up the tiny staircase off this room.) Throughout the castle, a number of portraits from the very valuable National Portrait Collection are on display, along with a fine collection of Irish period furniture. Many of these were acquired when death duties forced the family to sell its treasures, so the castle appears more homelike than its slightly gloomy, battle-station exterior would suggest. A very elaborate model railway is also on display.

The 270-acre gardens and park are superb. The last occupant, Lord Milo Talbot de Malahide, was a horticultural enthusiast who specialized in plants of the Southern Hemisphere; he also owned an estate in Tasmania. And between 1948 and his death in 1973, he amassed a collection of some 5,000 species and varieties that flourished in the alkaline soil, the Gulf Stream–warmed climate, the fine breezes, and the low rainfall, including the world's largest collection of olearias, good specimens of euphorbia, eryngium, and ceanothus, and a significant assortment of ozothamnus, which he once used to restock an area in Tasmania after it had been destroyed in bush fires. He also persuaded many extremely tender plants from South America and Africa to prosper in the open here. So the gardens are as exceptional as the castle, which, in addition to the ghost, comes with a closet skeleton: The Talbot family is related by marriage to James Boswell, caches of whose wildly indiscreet papers were found here in outhouses and attics in the 1930s and 1940s. There is also the story of Maud Plunket, whose tomb in the 15th-century Church of St. Sylvester, on the grounds, reads "maid, wife, and widow in one day" — her first husband was killed in battle, along with 14 other Talbots, immediately after the nuptial celebrations. Open year-round during seasonally varying hours. Details: *Malahide Castle,* Malahide, County Dublin, Irish Republic (phone: 1-452655 or 1-450940).

NATIONAL BOTANIC GARDENS, Dublin, Irish Republic: The largest garden of its kind in the world when it opened in 1800, it has since declined in importance. But its 46 acres of flowers, shrubs, and trees in some 20,000 species — fitted between the unfortunately polluted river Tolka on one side and Glasnevin Cemetery on the other — make it one of the most pleasant places to pass a few hours in Dublin, above all during the quiet morning hours. Among the most notable features are a rose bush grown from a cutting of national poet Thomas Moore's original "Last Rose of Summer"; the sadly dilapidated curvilinear mid-19th-century glass conservatories designed by the famous Dublin architect Richard Turner, who also built the Great Palm House at London's Kew Gardens; a specimen of the Killarney fern *Trichomanes speciosum,* virtually exterminated in its native habitat by rapacious Victorian fern hunters; a charming small rose garden reached by a bridge across a millstream; and a number of beds in which plants are arranged by scientific families, making for some groupings (for instance, peonies and anemones) that may surprise some viewers. And there are orchids, oaks, maples, conifers, and more. The gardens, known to Dubliners as the Botanics, are rich in bird life and swarming with red squirrels and rabbits — all of whom are unperturbed by visitors. There are plenty of seats and sheltered places to rest, and a notice board at the entrance lists seasonal attractions. Lovers of English literature will be interested to note that the property previously belonged to *Spectator* founder Joseph Addison, who was secretary to the Earl of Sutherland in Dublin for a short while. Lovers of Victorian cemeteries should wind up their visit with a stop next door, where the headstones are like a roll call of key figures in Irish history, with O'Connell and Parnell at the top of the list. Open daily, year-round. Details: *National Botanic Gardens,* Glasnevin, Dublin, Irish Republic (phone: 1-377596 or 1-374388).

NEWBRIDGE HOUSE, Donabate, County Dublin, Irish Republic: Life upstairs and downstairs is the theme of this Georgian house designed by Edward Lovett Pearce's colleague Richard Castle and built from local stone in about 1740 for Charles Cobbe, Archbishop of Dublin. And though the house has been acquired by the local public authority, Cobbe's descendants still live here, among scores of curiosities from the lives of their forebears: the instruction manual for the harp in the impressive Red Drawing Room, untouched since it was last redecorated in 1830; the chamber pot discreetly concealed under a table in the elegant dining room, for the use of gentlemen after dinner; the hook from a bedroom beam that once supported a swing from which the Cobbe ladies hung while servants laced their corsets; a fine sari holder belonging to an Indian lady who married a Cobbe and was banished to her homeland on her husband's death, her color deemed unacceptable to society of the day. Kitchen, dairy, and laundry room alike are treasure troves of domestic appliances of bygone days, like the Georgian rat trap and the wrought-iron stands for holding oat cakes. An exhibition of estate ledgers from the early 18th century gives touching domestic details; pocket money for the *Donnybrook Fair* appears regularly. Elsewhere are relics of the great Jonathan Swift, who was dean of St. Patrick's in Dublin and a friend of the archbishop. The park surrounding the mansion is pleasant but not noteworthy, except for the remains of ancient and picturesque Landestown Castle. Open year-round; seasonally varying hours and closing days. Details: *Newbridge House,* Donabate, County Dublin, Irish Republic (phone: 1-436534/5).

CASTLETOWN HOUSE, Celbridge, County Kildare, Irish Republic: Under the leadership of the Honorable Desmond Guinness, the Irish Georgian Society did a great deal to nurture the present trend in conservation. This structure, the society's former headquarters, was made an example of what could be achieved through painstaking restoration (and quite an example, since when Guinness borrowed IR£93,000 to wrest it from the developer who bought it after family ownership ended, it was completely empty, the windows broken, and the lead ripped off the roof).

This is Georgian architecture on the most princely scale. The house was built in 1722 for William Conolly, a pubkeeper's son who became an attorney and, after making a fortune dealing in estates forfeited after the Battle of the Boyne in 1690, was elected Speaker of the House of Irish Commons. The structure's architect was the Italian Alessandro Galilei, who had previously designed the façade of Rome's Church of St. John Lateran. Oak, marble, and the finest Irish building materials went into Conolly's grand home — it was even suggested that locks and gates be made of Irish silver. Edward Lovett Pearce, the architect of Bellamont Forest (described above), supervised the execution of the plan with a creative hand as well. The Palladian façade of this building is most impressive, 60 feet tall and flanked on either side by graceful colonnades.

Inside, a good deal of the work was done under the supervision of Lady Louisa, whose husband, Tom, inherited the house on the death of his father, the speaker's widow's nephew. The staircase has airy, elegant, rococo plasterwork by the Francinis, who were renowned in their field at the time; they were very free in their design and even incorporated family portraits in bas relief. The Print Room is a masterwork of panels, garlands, niches, and busts beneath a compartmented ceiling. The Red Drawing Room, with its brocade walls, and the Long Gallery, done in the Pompeiian style and hung with Venetian chandeliers, are equally impressive. The grounds are not the place of grandeur that they once were, but the Folly that the speaker's widow built in 1740, a striking pillar atop a complex of arches, and the Wonderful Barn, a corkscrew-shaped tower affair, invite exploration. Open year-round with varying seasonal admission times. Details: *Castletown House,* Celbridge, County Kildare, Irish Republic (phone: 1-628-8252).

BIRR CASTLE AND GARDENS, Birr, County Offaly, Irish Republic: Originally the Black Castle of the O'Carroll clan, Birr Castle eventually passed into the hands of Laurence Parsons, whose family became the Earls of Rosse and who occupy the house today. The carriage driving championships (described in *Horsing Around*), which the present earl mounts every year in mid-September, are not the only reason to visit the 1,000-acre demesne. The scenery is quite splendid, with fine foliage, a lake fed by the river Camcor, and the Robinsonian 100-acre gardens, where stand specimen trees and shrubs of great rarity: a *Koelreuteria bipinnata,* one of only two in Europe; 35-foot-high boxwood hedges planted in 1782 to frame the formal gardens and now the tallest in the world; and examples of the famous hybrid tree peony named for the present earl's mother, Anne Rosse, in the tiny enclosed garden overlooked by the castle hall. The remains of the Birr Leviathan, a famous telescope developed by the third earl, a distinguished astronomer, and built using local labor in 1845, are also here; its 72-inch reflector made the device the world's largest of its type until 1915. (This distinguished family also included the inventor of the steam turbine, the brother of the fourth earl, who lived here from the mid-19th to early 20th century and continued his father's astronomy experiments.) The castle, the bulk of which dates from the early 1600s, can be toured only by groups who have arranged well in advance; those fortunate enough to fall into this class will see how the premises have been changed and modified since their beginnings. The second earl, an amateur architect, made some colorful changes when he set about repairing the ravages of a fire in the late 18th and early 19th centuries — most notably the colorful courtyard façade, which is pure early Victorian castle, and the Strawberry Hill saloon, a miniature cathedral for domestic comfort named after the architecturally influential English pseudo-Gothic mansion of Horace Walpole. The saloon has the only complete set of Chippendale chairs in private hands, together with a number of family portraits, some Elizabethan. The Great Hall is a fine example of its type, complete with Flemish tapestries and rare furniture; note the cannonballs that lodged in the walls after a siege. The drawing room contains a slightly sinister little wax head of Queen Victoria, modeled from life when she was only eight and thatched with her own hair. The dining room, which seats almost 40, is floridly grand, the walls almost obscured with family portraits. Gardens, telescope, and an annual exhibition mounted by the earl on a theme of family interest are open year-round; specialist groups of 25 to 35 can be entertained at luncheons or champagne receptions in the castle with Lord and Lady Rosse in attendance from April to June or in September and October by special arrangement through *Elegant Ireland* (15 Harcourt St., Dublin 2, Irish Republic; phone: 1-751665). Details: *Birr Castle and Gardens,* Birr, County Offaly, Irish Republic (phone: 509-20056).

MOUNT USHER GARDENS, Ashford, County Wicklow, Irish Republic: The 20 acres of gardens here, crossed by the lovely river Vartry, are a textbook explication of the theories of the famous Irish landscape architect William Robinson, who wrote *The Wild Garden* more than a century ago and liked his bulbs naturalized under trees, his trees growing where they felt happiest, and his plantings lush, wild, and untainted by formality. Now in the hands of an American, Madeleine Jay, who bought the place in 1980, the gardens were planted by Edward Walpole in 1860, beginning with a single acre and then developed by successive generations of his family, who were Dublin's principal linen merchants for several decades. In the woodlands, rare trees vie with each other for the horticulturist's attention. There are no less than 70 species in the eucalyptus group. Gunnera, those giant rhubarb-like plants frequently found in Irish water gardens, grow in vast clumps by the river, and there are fine groups of American and Chinese skunk cabbage. Fern enthusiasts (properly prepared with insect repellent) can creep along a disused millstream to inspect specimens. The property is famous for its eucryphias, most notable among them the original *Eucryphia x nymanensis* Mount Usher, which was first hybridized here from two Chilean species. And since the estate's soil is practically lime-free, rhododendrons and camellias flourish with vigor. The prettiest seasons are midsummer, when there are startling displays of eucryphias and cornuses, and early spring, when carpets of crocuses, snowdrops, wood anemones, sky-blue scillas, and the strange spotted bells of the snake's head fritillary appear. But there is something special to be seen in every month, for the specialist and amateur alike. Accessible via the main Dublin–Wicklow road and open mid-March through October. Details: *Mount Usher Gardens,* Ashford, County Wicklow, Irish Republic (phone: 404-40116).

KILLRUDDERY, Bray, County Wicklow, Irish Republic: Home of the Earls of Meath since 1618, Killruddery as viewed today is largely a creation of the architect Sir Richard Morrison and his son, who designed it around 1820 in Tudor style for the tenth earl. The house is well worth visiting for its impressive drawing room, a study in chilly French grandeur, and the fine if gloomy library, dominated by a portrait of England's Charles II in full fig. There is also a handsome paneled great hall, an impressive staircase, and some ornate plasterwork.

But here it is the gardens that are of prime interest, and they are magic on sunny days when the blue cone of Sugarloaf Mountain shimmers like Mount Fuji in the distance. Perhaps the oldest in Ireland, dating from the mid-17th century, the gardens were planned in accordance with the priority of the day — to provide a place for large numbers of people to stroll and otherwise enjoy themselves. So there is a bowling green, with overlooks from which to watch the action. Hedges of beech delineate pathways encircling a fountain ornamented by dolphin statues and enclose heavily shaded walks where no stray sunbeams could possibly intrude to mar a fair complexion; converging and intersecting hedges of yew and hornbeam, with statues to complete the perspective, offer still other places to walk. The *Sylvan Theatre* has a grass stage and grass banks for seating, with the appropriate deities smiling and scowling from the surrounding thickets. To the rear, behind the fine orangery, a pretty, old-fashioned box parterre with a fountain and ornamental dairy gave the ladies a chance to play at butter making. A unique feature of the garden is a pair of canals, each 550 feet long, that reflect the house and the changing sky and lead the eye toward the cool green of the trees beyond. Accessible by the Greystones road about a mile out of Bray. Open in May, June, and September, and to groups by special arrangement at other times of year. Details: *Killruddery,* Bray, County Wicklow, Irish Republic (phone: 1-863405).

POWERSCOURT ESTATE AND GARDENS, Enniskerry, County Wicklow, Irish Republic: Powerscourt, which was home to several generations of the Wingfield family from the time of James I until 1961, when the house and its contents were sold to the Slazengers, was to have opened to the public for the first time in 1975. But in 1974, a fire caused by a defective chimney ravaged the house, and all of its original furniture, family portraits, rich plasterwork, gilt chandeliers, inlaid floors, and marble mantelpieces went up in smoke. Fortunately, the gardens to which this house was a mere backdrop were unharmed, and they are on a scale so vast that the visitor can only gasp and admire. Steps lead down a set of five terraces that extend for half a mile, flanked by statues, urns, and clipped trees, to a formal lake, the Triton Pool, with a magnificent collection of trees below: a 30-foot aromatic *Drimys winteri,* a cousin of the magnolias; a whole avenue of that curiosity of the Victorians, the monkey puzzle; a eucalyptus over 100 feet tall; and a Sitka spruce that is supposed to be the tallest tree in the country. The statuary is on a heroic scale; the spectacular golden gates for the entrance were bought in Paris in 1867, and there are many others, all glorious. The garden was constructed in so many stages, by so many hands, that no one person can take overall credit, though Richard, the sixth Lord Powerscourt, definitively influenced the shape of the gardens today, lavishing them with costly presents and adornments. In the decade beginning in 1870, he planted some 400,000 trees annually, almost completely afforesting the surrounding mountains. Is all this beautiful? The answer has to be an unqualified yes, although the Irish landscape architect William Robinson must have choked to see it, enamored as he was of the wild in gardens. But nature has not been entirely banished and tamed, for the untouched cone of the Great Sugar Loaf rears itself against the sky, serenely aloof from the clipped formality. And a few miles away is the astonishing Powerscourt Waterfall, 400 feet high and all the more spectacular compared with other cascades because of the reservoir at the top, dug to ensure good water flow before a visit by England's George IV. (John Boorman chose the site to stage the fight between Arthur and Lancelot in his epic 1981 film *Excalibur,* which was filmed almost entirely in Ireland.) This est ate is one of the musts of Irish tourism, though definitely not the place where visitors will pick up ideas for their patches of soil back home. Accessible via the main Dublin–Enniskerry road or the Dublin–Wexford road. Open daily from March 17 through October. Details: *Powerscourt Estate and Gardens,* Enniskerry, County Wicklow, Irish Republic (phone: 1-867676).

Mead and Meat Pies: Historical Banquets

 It would be hard to find a more touristy way to pass an evening than by partaking of one of Ireland's period banquets. Yet, like a good Gothic novel, these entertainments are a painless way to absorb a bit of history, and the chance they provide to slurp down a five-course feast in the best *Tom Jones* fashion — that is, with a knife as the only utensil — can be a lot of fun besides. Knights and ladies in satins and velvets, jesters, minstrels, and maybe a king or queen provide entertainment as participants sup, along with a handful of wenches and colleens to serve and sing.

These usually begin in a foyer where a bit of bread is served with salt "to ward away evil spirits" and everyone's health is toasted with mead — a heady concoction of fermented honey, apples, and spices, "to be drunk for virility and fertility," as the hosts inform their guests by way of explaining the origins of the word *honeymoon,* "one month, or moon, after a wedding" — and then continue, after the mead has taken effect, in a banqueting hall full of long oak trestle tables set with pewter plates, mugs, and the knife with which you're to shovel in your supper. (Most people find this progressively less difficult as the evening wears on — perhaps thanks to the copious quantities of wine and beer that are poured with each remove, as banqueting parlance names the courses.) Serving wenches keep the food coming, and between removes, the singers and jesters and harpists keep people smiling — or at least they try, and actually succeed with some people (and not always the same ones who have swallowed wine and beer enough to put Cu Chulainn himself under the table). You may or may not find the entertainers appealing, depending on your tolerance for the occasionally forgettable. What you find depends on where you go: In the country, the music can be sublime by any lights.

Some banquets operate nightly, and a credit card number is acceptable to secure a reservation. The cost ranges from $40 to $45. Before leaving the US, advance reservations can be made by calling *Brian Moore International Tours* at 800-982-2299 or 508-533-6683. For listings of other feasts, some of them from periods other than the medieval, contact the Irish Tourist Board.

BUNRATTY CASTLE, Bunratty, County Clare, Irish Republic: After climbing the narrow circular stone stairway to the dining hall and quaffing the first goblet of mead, guests can stroll around for a close look at this 15th-century castle's remarkable collection of art and antiques; traditional songs and harp music sustain a pleasantly medieval mood during the banquet. (See also *Marvelous Museums.*) Details: *Shannon Castle Banquets,* Shannon International Airport, County Clare, Irish Republic (phone: 61-361511).

DUNGUAIRE CASTLE, Kinvara, County Galway, Irish Republic: On the site of the King of Connaught's 7th-century castle, is this 500-year-old stone gray castle, which offers a lovely setting overlooking Galway Bay. The menu usually features a taste of the sea (such as fried prawns or fish) as an appetizer, followed by salad or soup, beef, vegetables, pudding, and cheese. The entertainment, a program of music, poetry, and recitations, focuses on light-hearted extracts from literary greats associated with Ireland's west coast, including Synge, Yeats, and Gogarty. Open mid-May through September. Details: *Shannon Castle Banquets,* Shannon International Airport, County Clare, Irish Republic (phone: 61-361511).

KNAPPOGUE CASTLE, Quin, County Clare, Irish Republic: Served in a huge stone dining hall lit by candles and hung with tapestries, the banquet here is very hearty, if not especially medieval: salad, soup, chicken, vegetables, cheese, and fruit. The evening's program features snippets of Irish history and some very fine music performed on the harp and sung by the "ladies of the castle." The castle itself, one of 42 massive structures built by the McNamara tribe that ruled the territory of Clancullen from the 5th to the mid-15th century, deserves a daytime visit in its own right to explore its several elegantly furnished rooms and meander through its verdant and undulating grounds. Its excellent state of preservation is due to the cooperation of its owners, a Houston couple, with the Shannon Free Airport Development Company and the Irish Tourist Board. Details: *Shannon Castle Banquets,* Shannon International Airport, County Clare, Irish Republic (phone: 61-361511).

SHANNON CÉILÍ, Bunratty Folk Park, County Clare, Irish Republic: The music and song at this evening of Irish merriment are purely traditional; there are flutes and fiddles, *bodhráns* and spoons, an accordionist, and singers. The meal is equally traditional: Irish stew, soda bread, apple pie doused with fresh cream, and tea and wine. Open mid-May through September. Details: *Shannon Castle Banquets,* Shannon International Airport, County Clare, Irish Republic (phone: 61-361788).

Antiques and Auctions

Some people are driven to possess a chunk of the past, not content just to admire it in a museum. Those who count themselves as members of this group should be sure to bring their checkbooks when they come to Ireland. The past is everywhere, and the Irish are prepared to part with a bit of it — usually for a price, of course, though a shopper possessed of "a tither o' wit," as they say, can always track down the magic value for the dollar. It might be a little silver photo frame or a pinchbeck muff chain. Or maybe life would not be worth living without that fine piece of Irish Georgian silver. Or that lovely blue and white meat platter with the armorial center — could it be just the thing for Great Aunt Matilda's sister's daughter's wedding present? Or the superb 19th-century dining table inlaid with hundreds of pieces of precious woods, a snip at $5,000 — wouldn't it be perfect in the dining room of your antebellum mansion? Before hesitating and passing that object of desire by, just remember: There's no time like the past — and no time like the present for enjoying it.

Note that any purchase made in the Irish Republic or Northern Ireland that is mailed or shipped by the shop to an address outside the country is free of value added tax (VAT). On purchases that overseas visitors take home in their luggage, the VAT can be refunded; the shop can supply the details on how to go about it. For advice about shipping and customs regulations, and for general information about buying antiques in Ireland, contact the *Irish Antique Dealers Association* (16 Kildare St., Dublin 2; phone: 1-762614), whose members adhere to strict standards of quality and authenticity.

Two publications will also be helpful:

The British Art and Antique Dealers Directory, available from National Magazine House, 72 Broadwick St., London W1V 2BP, England (phone: 14-377144). Details all aspects of the antiques trade and contains a great deal of information about what is available in Ireland, cross-referenced by specialty. Comprehensive, revised annually.

Irish Arts Review Quarterly, Carrick-on-Suir, County Tipperary, Irish Republic (phone: 51-40524). An exceptionally beautiful periodical that keeps collectors up to date on Irish antiques.

A number of distinctly different antiques buying options exist. Though European-style flea markets are little in evidence, there are a number of stalls and secondhand and junk shops in the various arcades and covered markets that spring up here and there in cities and towns. True bargains may be available here — to those willing to sift through the not always interesting and usually rather grubby miscellanea to find them. There are other ways to go as well.

ANTIQUES SHOPS

From Belfast to Killarney there are hundreds of "old curiosity shoppes" in Ireland, whose dealers have made the rounds of the markets and auctions and offer their customers the best of the lots. Over the years, the trade has developed great sophistication, particularly in the fields of furniture, glass and china, table silver, and certain kinds of jewelry.

Few shops specialize in any one thing; they tend to have a little bit of this and that. But whether the quarry be barometers or bond certificates, stamps or steel engravings, there's a shop that stocks some rare, special item. And since ethical standards are high, don't be surprised if a dealer spontaneously divulges defects in an item you've got your eye on; members of the *Irish Antique Dealers Association* (address above) are very good in this way. If a dealer is not forthcoming with caveats about flaws, be sure to question him about what is original, what has been restored or retouched, and what has simply been replaced. By the way, a number of establishments specialize in the restoration of furniture and ceramics. Consult the *Golden Pages,* Ireland's commercial classified phone book, then phone the establishment to try to find out what restoration and subsequent mailing, with insurance, will cost — preferably before buying the piece under consideration. Those who plan to spend any significant sum to acquire an item that has been restored should have the dealer put the qualifications in writing.

And if a whisper lures you to a little shop up a lane in a village about 40 miles away, be sure to phone before leaving home. It might be an early-closing day. Or the quarry may be planning not to open at all, to go to the sale of the late Mr. Murphy's early Cork glass collection.

DUBLIN: In the Republic's capital, the true center of the Irish antiques trade, the many shops are concentrated in several distinct areas.

Baggot, Clare, Duke, Kildare, Molesworth, and South Anne Streets – This area is full of long-established dealers such as the following:

Anthony Antiques: Big stuff in top condition, including French and English furniture, grates, and fenders. Sometimes there are also interesting arms and military antiques. 7/9 Molesworth St. (phone: 1-777222).

Brooks & Co. Antiques: Small items aplenty from books and prints to clocks, lanterns, and curios. 136 Lower Baggot St. (phone: 1-789845).

Byrne's: Unusual jewelry, pectoral crosses, small statues of racehorses in silver. 23 S. Anne St. (phone: 1-718709).

Danker Antiques: Smaller objects, ornaments, and jewelry of good quality, as well as fine 18th-century silver spoons. 10 S. Anne St. (phone: 1-774009).

Ronald McDonnell, Ltd.: Ireland's best-quality stock of furniture and paintings, glass and silver, along with other collectibles, in a beautiful Georgian house. A leader in the trade here and a source of sound advice. 16 Kildare St. (phone: 1-762614).

Molesworth Antiques Gallery, Ltd.: Paintings, engravings, prints. 28 Molesworth St. (phone: 1-614986).

Oriel Gallery: Irish work of the 19th and early 20th centuries, now much sought after. 17 Clare St. (phone: 1-763410).

Rembrandt Antiques: Small things for under $20, plus silver salt spoons and fine china pieces. 24 S. Anne St. (phone: 1-779374).

J. & M. Weldon: A specialist in silver and silver plate, one of the three oldest antiques firms in Dublin. 18 S. Anne St. (phone: 1-772742).

Powerscourt Town House, S. William and Clarendon Sts. – The lovely 18th-century *Powerscourt Town House,* a complex of antiques shops of the same type as those above as well as purveyors of the new and trendy all under one roof, is a wonderful place to spend a rainy hour. Shoppers are under no greater pressure to buy here than they would be in a department store, and they are less likely to encounter the locked door with buzzer that has become a fixture of many establishments that deal in valuables. Shops include *Courtville Antiques, Just Browsing,* the *Silver Shop,* and *Solomon Gallery* — a must for those who love beautiful things.

Irene Fine Art: All kinds of everything, courtesy of Mr. William Kearney, who has been in the business for more than 40 years. 33 Clarendon St. (phone: 1-714932).

Saskia Antiques: Lovely Victorian furniture, rosewood inlaid with mother-of-pearl, George II bedroom furniture, and more. 24 Fitzwilliam Sq. (phone: 1-610440).

Jenny Vander: A cave of wonders, unlike anything else found anywhere, stocked with the odd 1920s dress, paste necklace, Limerick lace christening robe, Worth jacket, traditional knitted white counterpane. 20 Market Arcade, George's St. (phone: 1-770406).

Francis and Patrick Streets – The Liberties, as the district containing these streets has always been known, is among the capital's oldest areas (its name refers to the fact that it did not fall under Dublin's jurisdiction in medieval times), and interesting little antiques shops have always been opening and closing here. In the past few years, though, the antiques scene seems to have taken a firm hold.

Bits and Pieces: Specialists in Art Deco and Art Nouveau light fixtures. 78 Francis St. (phone: 1-541178).

Cooke Antiques and Restoration: Furniture of the 18th and 19th centuries, restoration, and manufacture of reproductions. 79/85 Francis St. (phone: 1-542057).

Gordon Nichol Antiques: Furniture, treen (small woodenware), and decorative pieces. 59/60 Patrick St. (phone: 1-543322).

Gibson O'Neill Antiques: Art Nouveau and Art Deco ceramics and glass. 64/65 Patrick St. (phone: 1-532197).

Timepiece Antiques: Antique clocks and watches. 58 Patrick St. (phone: 1-540774).

The Liffey Quays – Once a great source of underpriced treasures and other fabulous finds, this area still has quite a bit to see, mainly larger items. The shops vary from eccentric little places open every Tuesday when the moon is full, maybe, to really well-stocked emporiums from which collectors could furnish a small mansion. The pieces are similarly mixed in character.

Lawlor Briscoe & Co., Ltd.: Large, well-put-together shop stocked with fine furniture in superb condition. 35 Ormond Quay (phone: 1-732050).

Edward Butler Antiques: Fine pieces in the same atmosphere in which they flourished generations ago, except that an Irish crafts shop now occupies the basement, from a family of former cabinetmakers whose marked furniture is much sought after by collectors. 14 Bachelor's Walk (phone: 1-730296).

Ormond Antiques: Smaller items in brass and porcelain, including some Belleek, plus decorative furniture. 32 Ormond Quay (phone: 1-727257).

BELFAST: With its constant traffic in antiques and curiosities from Scotland and the north of England, this is a great place for the bargain hunter. A few good bets:

Alexander the Grate: One of the most amusing places in Ireland, full of characters and a sure bet for finding That Very Thing. (You'll probably have to charter a cargo boat to get it home, though.) 128 Donegall Pass (phone: 232-232041).

Dara Antiques: Furniture and accessories, with an emphasis on clocks, silver, and porcelain. 35 Donegall Pass (phone: 232-248144).

Great Victoria Carousel: Several antiques shops under one roof. 69A Great Victoria St. (phone: 232-230215)

Trash & Treasure: Frames, plaques, and odd things with holes in the most unexpected places. Finding out what they are could keep the curious occupied for years. 110 Donegall Pass.

HERE AND THERE: Antiques shops are tucked away in nooks and crannies all over the island. A few stops to get you started:

Bunratty, County Clare, Irish Republic – *Mike McGlynn Antiques,* only about 15 minutes from Shannon Airport, deals in very good furniture, porcelain, and works of art, sold from a traditional Irish cottage (phone: 61-364294).

Ennis, County Clare, Irish Republic – *Honan's* is a treasure trove of antique grandfather clocks, candlesticks, stained glass, brass lighting fixtures, and other home furnishings. 14 Abbey St. (phone: 61-28137).

Adare, County Limerick, Irish Republic – *George Stacpoole* has silver, treen, and objects of art, along with a fine collection of really good old prints. Main St. (phone: 61-86409)

Dungannon, County Tyrone, Northern Ireland – *Hurst Antiques* has furniture and old Belleek. Cohannon House, 25 Bovean Rd. (phone: 8687-23253).

AUCTION HOUSES

Auction houses can almost always yield a treasure or two when the circumstances are right. In Ireland, there are generally two kinds of sales: those of objects acquired by the firm from several sources and held on the firm's premises and those held in a private home to dispose of its contents. Not too many visitors turn up at the latter — it's necessary to see the newspaper notice in the first place, find the house (not always the easiest task), and then get there twice, once for the preview and again for the sale. But in a domestic auction there is the opportunity to see objects in their setting — and to see the inside of a fine house before its contents are, sadly, dispersed. Items are often sold in lots on these occasions, so if one bidder ends up with 14 brass doorknobs, he or she may be able to make a deal with the person who got all the ivory bookends.

To find out about upcoming auctions, check the papers and watch for posters. No matter what the auction, be sure to find out about viewing days and times, and go to the preview to examine the wares up close and away from the heat of bidding. Use common sense. Remember that words like "style" or "attributed" are not the same as "fine" or "important." Bearing that in mind and figuring in the taxes and commissions that will be levied, set a spending limit in advance. Then at the sale, stick to that limit. It's best not to try to outbid the dealers, but if you get carried away, well, don't worry, because it's all part of the fun.

DUBLIN: As the focal point for the Irish antiques trade, the auction scene can be lively, and there are salerooms for all purses. Among the best:

> *James Adam & Sons:* Ireland's foremost fine-art auction house. Even the window display is an education. 26 St. Stephen's Green (phone: 1-760261).
>
> *Hamilton, Osborne, King:* Fine furniture, glass, and china dispersal auctions all over Ireland. The firm has a very courteous and helpful staff. Pay a visit to the lovely Georgian building to see what's coming up. 32 Molesworth St. (phone: 1-760251).
>
> *Tormey Brothers:* Weekly auctions of antiques and general household merchandise, including furniture. This is one of several houses of the same ilk, here and elsewhere in the city. Watch for newspaper advertising or consult the Golden Pages of the phone book for a list. 27 Ormond Quay (phone: 1-726781).

BELFAST: There are plenty of auction houses here. For starters, try *Anderson's Auction Rooms,* which has viewings on Tuesdays, sales the next day. 28 Linenhall St. (phone: 232-321401).

RARE-BOOK DEALERS

Browsing among old books, their paper yellowed and brittle and their covers soft leather or beautifully marbled papers, is one of the pleasures of antiques hunting in Ireland, and there are a number of good dealers. However, since many keep their stock at suburban locations or deal out of their own homes, it is generally appropriate to make an appointment.

DUBLIN: There are two establishments worth visiting. *Cathach Books* (10 Duke St.; phone: 1-718676) specializes in Irish books and maps; *Figgis Rare Books* (53 Pembroke Rd.; phone: 1-609491) has a fine collection of a broader range.

CASTLECOMER, County Kilkenny, Irish Republic: The remarkable rare book auctioneer *George Mealy & Sons* (phone: 56-41229) also has rooms here.

BELFAST: Of several sources here, start with *J. A. Gamble* (539 Antrim Rd.; phone: 232-370798). To see his collection of rare books of Irish interest, it's definitely necessary to make an appointment in advance.

ANTIQUES FAIRS

Fairs often bring many dealers — and many wares — together in one place and provide the chance to survey many collections at once. The *Irish Antiques Fair,* held annually in Dublin during July or August, is the premier event. It offers an excellent overview of what's happening on the Irish antiques scene, plus high quality, high prices, and a selection that can't be beat.

Shopping Spree

No matter where the dollar stands relative to the Irish pound, the lure of shopping in Ireland is irresistible. Dublin, a walker's city, can awaken the dormant consumer in even the most monastic visitor. Wonderful covered arcades and centuries-old shops, tucked away on side streets, await the curious. And Belfast, long out of the mainstream, is enjoying a resurgence, especially in the downtown shopping areas. Here, as in all of Northern Ireland, English as well as Irish products are sold (remember that prices are quoted in British pounds sterling).

Quality, durability, and "value for money" are the norm throughout Ireland. A purchase made here will more than likely last for years and never go out of style, partly because it never pretended to be high style to begin with, although this is changing somewhat. Irish fashion designs have made an increasingly noticeable impact over the years. Some clothiers mix natural fabrics and dye them in hues taken from Ireland's lush landscape, while others turn silks and luxurious imported fabrics into stunning evening wear.

Of course, Ireland is a place where it can rain at any moment. When the gentle mist falls, dampening a shopping spree, the true treasure of Irish shopping shines through: The beguiling and chatty shopkeeper can ward off the rainy gloom and prolong any visit, so that it is impossible for anyone to return from Ireland without a bulging carrier full of the hand-knit, the hand-woven, and the hand-thrown.

WHERE TO SHOP

It is possible to find good buys all over Ireland, but knowing where to shop saves steps and ensures satisfaction.

AIRPORT SHOPPING: Shannon's duty-free shopping idea revolutionized airport terminals many years ago. Today, Shannon's emporiums continues to offer Irish and international products, although prices are only variably competitive with other stores in Ireland. Most items are duty-free, but if shipped, the cost of insurance and packaging almost equals the savings. Nevertheless, airport shopping can't be beat for last-minute convenience. Travelers can now pre-shop and have their purchases held until departure. All purchases, at any time, can be packaged and placed on board the aircraft. Payment can be made in any of several currencies, and reimbursements are given for anything lost in transit.

DEPARTMENT STORES: Ireland's department stores offer high-quality goods, attractive prices, and vast selection.

Belfast, Northern Ireland – *Marks & Spencer,* the largest department store in Northern Ireland, is famous for its lamb's wool and shetland sweaters. Men's woolen suits are of excellent quality and moderately priced. (There are no fitting rooms; credit cards are not accepted.) 48 Donegall Pl. (phone: 232-235235).

Other well-known chain stores are *British Home Stores* (24 Castle Pl.; phone: 23-224-3068); *Body Shop* (10 Castle La.; phone: 23-223-0651); *Littlwoods* (5 Ann St.; phone: 23-224-1537); *Next* (Cleaver House, Donegall Pl.; phone: 23-223-3195); and *Principles* (Cleaver House, Donegall Pl.; phone: 23-223-8784).

Cork, Irish Republic – *Cashs of Ireland* is a landmark in this southern city. Among many other items, they stock Waterford crystal, Belleek pottery, and Aran knitwear (18 Patrick St; phone: 21-964411). *Marks & Spencer* is at *Merchant's Quay* (6 Patrick St.; phone: 21-275555).

Dublin, Irish Republic – *Brown Thomas,* Dublin's finest department store, has an excellent selection of Irish linen and English china. The Dawson St. entrance has a riding department that stocks breeches, jodphurs, horse shampoos, riding bits, and caps. 15/20 Grafton St. (phone: 1-679-5666).

Switzer & Company, like *Brown Thomas* across the street, is large, lively, and full of good merchandise, especially Aran Island sweaters. Owned by London's *Harrods,* it's very popular with Dubliners. 92 Grafton St. (phone: 1-776821).

OUTDOOR MARKETS: Never pass a chance to wander through one of Ireland's buzzing, bustling open markets. They're a cross section of local life and a glorious experience for all the senses. The stalls are a riot of form and color — potatoes and tomatoes keep company with spinach and celery — while the calls and clatter of Irish accents delight the ear, and the smells of the flowers and the cheeses and the fish, one aroma blending with the next, assail the nose. Almost every town has such a country market. The capital cities also have permanent flea markets.

Belfast, Northern Ireland – Every Saturday, browsers and collectors can enjoy a flea market of quality goods in the 2-storied *Alexander The Grate* store (128 Donegall Pass; phone: 232-232041), several minutes by car from town center. Also open that day, as well as the rest of the week, are approximately 30 shops and stalls within shops in the vicinity. Most of the furniture, china, and glass is Georgian, Victorian, and Art Deco.

Dublin, Irish Republic – The best weekly markets are located on the south side of the river Liffey, in the heart of "Old Dublin." The *Liberty Market* (Meath St., off Thomas St.) is open from 9 AM to 6 PM on Saturdays, and the *Christ Church Market* (Old Winstanley Factory, High St.) is open from 10 AM to 6 PM on Saturdays and

Sundays. On weekdays, the *Moore Street Market*, an open-air produce market (off Henry St. on the north side), is open from 9 AM to 5 PM.

SPECIAL SHOPPING STREETS AND DISTRICTS: Endowed with character and verve, some streets invite lingering. These areas may be brassy, quaint, or even supremely grand, but they all offer a real spectacle made up partly of the stores, partly of other shoppers. Whether you're buying or just looking, these streets are worth a walk.

Belfast, Northern Ireland – The major stores are in a pedestrian shopping mall that encompasses several streets off Donegall Pass in the center of town. *Queen's Arcade*, although small, has a fine selection of shops. Nearby Howard Street (between Donegall Sq. W. and College Sq. E.) has the newer trendy boutiques.

Cork, Irish Republic – The top shopping thoroughfare for crystal, tweeds, woolens, and general gift items is Patrick Street. Paul Street, home of a mid-city supermarket, also has good book and crafts shops. The "antiques alley" of Cork is Paul's Lane. There are several worthwhile shopping complexes in Cork: The *Merchant's Quay Shopping Centre*, the newest and best of Cork's shopping complexes, offers large department stores and trendy international boutiques, as well as Irish specialty shops, a food court, and covered parking (on Patrick St. at Merchant's Quay). The *Winthrop Arcade* (Winthrop St.) is especially alluring and on the same street, and be sure to visit *Eileen O'Connor's* shop, known for the owner's personalized service.

The *Savoy Centre* (Patrick St.) offers a variety of shops and cafés in the attractive Art Deco setting of a former movie theater. The *Southern Fashion Design Centre*, as well as *W's*, stock all Irish designs. Patrick St.

Queen's Old Castle, a former department store, now houses many shops plus cafés for shoppers' refreshment. Grand Parade.

Dublin, Irish Republic – Shoppers looking for high-quality, typically Irish products should stick to Dawson, S. Anne, and Nassau Streets (Grafton Street has been revitalized and gentrified and is now a pedestrians-only shopping thoroughfare.) For functional woolens, rugged cottons, and everyday wear, shop along Henry Street and nearby *Ilac Center* (about 80 stores in this area).

Powerscourt Town House, the Georgian-style former home of a lord, is an enclosed shopping arcade just a few yards off Grafton on S. William and Clarendon Sts. Three levels crammed with boutiques and pushcarts surround an inner courtyard. The top level has over 20 antiques shops.

The *Royal Hibernian Way*, formerly the site of the *Royal Hibernian* hotel, houses fashionable boutiques, many international. Between Dawson and Kildare Sts.

St. Stephen's Green Shopping Centre offers three skylit levels of shops. At the corner of Grafton and S. King Sts.

BEST BUYS

Ireland is one of the last holdouts against synthetic materials. Some of the products and shops are of a superior quality, which may put them on the road to obsolescence, like the great ocean liners, so let yourself be tempted by classic adornments while they are still available. Ireland is the perfect place for self-indulgence.

BOOKS AND MAPS: Addicted browsers will have to be dragged out of the following haunts:

Dublin, Irish Republic – *Cathach Books* is sheer joy for collectors, since it has the most comprehensive selection of Irish literature and memorabilia in the country. The oldest book here was printed in the 17th century, while hand-drawn maps are from the 16th century. The shop also has first editions of W. B. Yeats and James Joyce. 10 Duke St. (phone: 1-718676).

Eason & Son, Ltd., one of Dublin's finer book stores, is also one of the best places to buy maps. 40/42 Lower O'Connell St. (phone: 1-733811).

Fred Hanna Ltd., a favorite haunt for years, sells both new and used books and maps of Ireland. 27-29 Nassau St. (phone: 1-771255).

The *Trinity College Library Shop* has a large selection of Irish literature and children's books. Trinity College, College Green (phone: 1-772941, ext. 1016).

BRASS: Solid brass articles have religious, artistic, and functional use in Ireland. Door knockers, which adorn Georgian doors in Dublin, are among the most popular items to take home.

Dublin, Irish Republic – *Knobs and Knockers* offers a full range of knockers, handles, and pulls. 19 Nassau St. (phone: 1-710288).*O'Farrell Workshops* has knockers shaped like shamrocks, Claddagh rings, and saints. Most of the religious pieces are designed by the store's owner, who has won many prizes and been commissioned to do larger projects. 62 Dawson St. (phone: 1-770862).

CHINA (CERAMICS, POTTERY): World-famous Irish china — a full range of both decorative and functional items — is produced primarily in factories in Wicklow, Cork, Galway, and Fermanagh. In addition, there are scores of small studio potteries producing varied designs (see local listings). Some of the best outlets are:

Arklow, Irish Republic – *Arklow Pottery* makes heavy, functional ware of modern design. The factory shop is open daily, and several times a month crates are wheeled outside for special sales. Arklow (phone: 402-32401).

Belleek, Northern Ireland – Wafer-thin Belleek parian china is made in the famous Belleek Pottery factory, where tours are given weekdays (in winter months, it is advisable to call ahead for an appointment). The factory shop sells the complete line at retail prices — no seconds. Open Mondays through Saturdays 9 AM to 6 PM. Belleek (phone: 36-565501).

Dublin, Irish Republic – *House of Ireland,* a shop that has one of the largest selections of Irish and English bone china, also sells most of Europe's finest collectibles. 37/38 Nassau St. (phone: 1-716133).

Galway, Irish Republic – *Royal Tara China* welcomes visitors to watch china decoration. Open Mondays through Fridays 10 AM to 5 PM. Advance booking recommended. The factory shops has seconds at 30–80% discount, as well as perfect pieces. Tara Hall (phone: 91-51301).

CRYSTAL AND GLASS: Crystal is manufactured mainly in counties Waterford, Galway, and Cavan in the Irish Republic, and in Tyrone in Northern Ireland.

Belfast, Northern Ireland – *Hoggs* has the largest selection of Northern Ireland's Tyrone crystal, which is less expensive than Waterford and of comparable quality. A variety of English china and figurines are also sold. Mail order possible. Seconds sometimes available. 10 Donegall Sq. W. (phone: 232-243898).*Tom Jones* is an elegantly appointed shop with crystal chandeliers and mahogany shelves displaying Ireland's best crystal and England's finest china. 9 Wellington Pl. (phone: 232-325932).

Dublin, Irish Republic – *House of Ireland,* a full-service store carrying all major brands, has Dublin's largest selection of Waterford. 37-38 Nassau St. (phone: 1-716133).

Dungannon, Northern Ireland – *Tyrone Crystal* rivals Waterford's popularity in recent years. The factory store sells seconds only; first quality can be ordered and shipped. Factory tours are offered. Open Mondays through Fridays 9 AM to 5 PM and Saturdays 10 AM to 4 PM. Oaks Rd. (phone: 86-872-5335).

Galway City, Irish Republic – The factory store of *Galway Irish Crystal* sells seconds only. Tours are not offered at the factory, but glass blowing demonstrations are given in the shop. Open daily 9 AM to 5 PM. Merlin Pk. (phone: 91-57311).

Waterford, Irish Republic – Ireland's most prestigious product, Waterford crystal, is produced here in the world's largest full-lead crystal factory. All pieces are mouth blown, hand cut, and sold at full retail prices. The factory shop — *The Crystal Gallery* — is open year-round; Wedgwood china, now owned by Waterford, is also available. Catalogue sales are possible. One-hour free tours of the factory are conducted Mondays through Fridays 10:15 AM to 2:30 PM. Reservations necessary. Waterford (phone: 51-73311).

Joseph Knox, installed behind a handsome Victorian shopfront in town, is another place to buy Waterford or just to spend a few moments browsing along with the rest of summer's throngs. 3-4 Barronstrand St. (phone: 51-75307).

DESIGNER CLOTHING: Ireland may not share honors with the top fashion centers of the world, but its clothing industry shows signs of lively creativity in a few areas:

Dublin, Irish Republic – Romantic ball gowns made with finely pleated Irish linen are only one of the exceptional productions of Ireland's reigning couturière, Sybil Connelly. Adjacent to the studio is her boutique, which sells ready-to-wear apparel and accessories. Boutique, 71 Merrion Sq. (phone: 1-767281).

Jimmy Hourihan designs ready-to-wear apparel for women: stylish suits, capes, and coats. 28 Dublin Industrial Estate, Finglass Rd. (phone: 1-300033).

Brown Thomas department store has a boutique of top Irish fashion designers: Robert Jacob, Ib Jorgensen, Lainey Keogh, Richard Lewis, Paul Moreland, Michael Mortell, and Mairad Whisker. Many of these clothiers also have their own shops with larger collections (see local listings). 15/20 Grafton St. (phone: 1-679-5666).

FOODSTUFFS AND LIQUOR: Jams and marmalades, blended teas, shortbread, salmon, and other edibles for sale throughout Ireland make wonderful souvenirs — to keep or to give as a gift. Irish whiskeys, which come in a wider selection than ordinarily found in the US, are also appreciated as gifts. Power, Jameson, Paddy, and Tullamore Dew are a few of the better-known brands. Good liqueurs are Bailey's, Emmets, and Irish Mist. Look for special offers in supermarkets and wine shops or purchase them in duty-free shops.

Northern Ireland, in particular, is famous for its bread, which comes in all flavors and shapes. The bakery in the *Marks & Spencer* department store in Belfast has a particularly good selection. Farl, a triangle shape with a rounded edge, is the most popular version of soda bread. Potato bread is also well known in both Northern Ireland and the Republic.

With so many cows in the fields, it's surprising that farmhouse cheeses didn't become popular sooner, but now they are the talk of fine Irish cooks and cheese lovers. The best known types, available in good supermarkets, are Cashel blue (the only Irish blue), cooleeney (camembert type), gubbeen (soft, surface-ripening cheese, both plain and smoked), lavistown (with natural rind, crumbly texture), ring (hard, with a nutty flavor), St. Killian (another camembert type), Burren gold (gouda type), and regatto (sharp, Italian type).

Don't miss the opportunity to pick up a side of Irish salmon, one of the world's great indulgences, before leaving for home. There are three types: "wild," the best and most expensive, comes from the surrounding sea and streams; "farmed" is raised in Irish fish farms; and "imported" (from Canada or California) is only smoked in Ireland. The price of salmon, determined by type and origin, is generally lower in town than at the airports. Be sure it is properly packed for travel. (It's possible to keep vacuum-sealed salmon for up to 2 weeks unrefrigerated.)

Bushmills, Northern Ireland – *Old Bushmills,* the oldest distillery in the world, is open to the public for tours and for samplings of its fine whiskies. There is a souvenir shop on the premises. 2 Distillery Rd. (phone: 26-573-1521).

Dublin, Irish Republic – Behind its beautiful stained glass windows, *Bewley's Café on Grafton* roasts, packs, and brews coffees and teas imported from around the world.

While its confectionery and homemade chocolates are divine, *Bewley's* is more famous for its fresh cream cakes and traditional sticky buns. 78/79 Grafton St. (phone: 1-776761).

The Cheeseboard, in addition to the obvious, sells fine wines. *Westbury Mall,* off Grafton St. (phone: 1-679-1422).

Dunns has excellent quality salmon at very competitive prices. 6 Upper Baggot St. (phone: 1-602688).

McConnell & Nelson is a popular downtown spot well known for its "wild" salmon. 38 Grafton St. (phone: 1-774344).

HANDICRAFTS: Ireland has hand-thrown, hand-woven, hand-spun, and hand-knit products galore. Because it escaped the worst of the Industrial Revolution, many traditional crafts never died out, and the last few years' revival in interest has caused many to flourish as never before. Emigrés from the rest of Europe have brought new ideas and increased sophistication to rural craftsmen, so that workshops and stores throughout the country now stock handmade goods in both traditional and contemporary styles.

Shillelaghs and blackthorn walking sticks are still to be found, and briar pipes are world-famous. There are hand-turned tableware and platters, salt and pepper shakers, and tables and chairs with rustic-looking seats made of twisted hay or straw. Pottery is being produced in studios all over the island in simple sculptured shapes and earthy colors. Metalsmiths produce bowls and bracelets, chains and earrings, pendants and rings, and tea and coffee sets in silver, gold, and copper. Sometimes jewelry is set with semiprecious stones or half-moons of Connemara marble; sometimes the designs are derived from the colorful *Book of Kells.* Other shopping finds are basketwork, stained glass, patchwork quilts, cut stones, St. Bridgit crosses made of straw, decorative items made of turf, candles, handmade carpets, soft toys, and quaint rag dolls. Fine cotton Irish lace, the crafting of which was introduced during the 1840 famine, has died as an industry and is difficult to find except in a few shops or private homes. Every county has its specialty item and its assortment of little shops, some of which keep company with workshops in craft centers (or "craft clusters") where shoppers can watch artisans at work.

Belfast, Northern Ireland – *A Guide to Northern Ireland Crafts and Craftsmen* is available at the Local Enterprise Development Unit (LEDU) Business Center (17-19 Linenhall St.; phone: 232-242582). Some listed crafts are Carrickmacross lace, patchwork, heraldry, glass, and fishing tackle. A collection of crafts from Northern Ireland is on display at the LEDU.

Tucked away in a corner of *Johnston's Umbrella Shop* are Irish shillelaghs and English walking sticks in different woods. 33 Ann St. (phone: 23-232-0729).

Donegal Town, Irish Republic – *Donegal Craft Village* consists of four shops clustered around a courtyard just outside the center of town. Donegal–Sligo Rd. (phone: 73-22053, 73-22015, 73-22225, or 73-22228).

Dublin, Irish Republic – One of the best sources for heraldic plaques, parchments, jewelry, and genealogical research is *Heraldic Artists.* 3 Nassau St. (phone: 1-679-7020).

H. Johnston Ltd., has traditional blackthorn walking sticks. 11 Wicklow St. (phone: 1-771249).

Tower Design Craft Centre, a former sugar refinery, is another good bet. It houses more than 30 innovative craftspeople who produce jewelry, oak woodcavings, crystal, stained glass, Aran sweaters, and more. Visitors are welcome in the individual studios to see craftspeople at work. Pearse St. (phone: 1-775655). There are other crafts centers throughout the country, including ones at Cork and Shannon. For information, contact the *Crafts Council* (phone: 1-679-7368).

Galway City, Irish Republic – *Spiddal Craft Centre* is home to nine craft shops and a gallery. Look for *One of Susan's* shop for exclusive designer knit sweaters, many done in cotton and mohair. She's also famous for intarsia patterns and abstract designs. 12 miles from Galway, on the coast road to Connemara (phone: 91-83149).

HATS: Consistently cool, damp weather has led to a number of distinctive kinds of headgear in Ireland.

Clifden, Irish Republic – *Millars Connemara Tweeds, Ltd.* makes a famous hat known as the Original Irish Country Hat, the Irish Walking Hat, or the Fishing Hat. As they tell it, the only place it may not be worn is to bed. It's made from wool purchased from local farmers and processed in a mill that incorporates part of the town's old railway station, and it's an essential part of every sportsman's wardrobe. Main St. (phone: 95-21038).

HERALDIC CRESTS: Hand-painted heraldic crests immortalizing Irish family names make unique souvenirs.

Dublin, Irish Republic – *Heraldic Artists* is a good place for family crests, flags, scrolls, and genealogy tomes. 3 Nassau St.(phone: 1-679-7020).

JEWELRY: (See also "Silver.") Perhaps the best-known Irish ornament is the Claddagh ring, dating from the 16th century. It is exchanged as a token of friendship, love, and betrothal of marriage. Its design, two hands holding a crown, symbolizes friendship, love, and loyalty. Authentic rings are worked in gold or silver and bear an assay as well as a made-in-Ireland mark. They are sold by fine jewelers throughout the country.

Dublin, Irish Republic – The atmosphere of *Weir's* is one of richness, elegance, and quality. Gold and silver jewelry, antiques, clocks, and bone china selections are the finest. 96/99 Grafton St. (phone: 1-779678).

LACE: Handmade Irish lace is more difficult to find these days — and expensive — as the craft dies out, but it is available. The best outlets are in Limerick and Carrickmacross, where lacemaking is still taught.

Belfast, Northern Ireland – Many women still crochet the Carrickmacross lace in their homes. Contact the LEDU Business Center, 17/19 Linenhall St. (phone: 232-242582), for their addresses.

Dublin, Irish Republic – *The Lace Lady* is owned by Deirdre Ryan, who has scoured Ireland and other countries for yards of lace, antique and modern. She also stocks Irish linen tablecloths, bedcovers, pillowcases, handkerchiefs, and vintage clothes and accessories. 129 Upper Leeson St. (phone: 1-604537).

Limerick, Irish Republic – Handmade Irish lace can be purchased at *Original Designer Lace Ltd.* in the Tait Business Center, Co. Limerick (phone: 61-49477).

LINEN: Authentic Irish linen is expensive. To be sure the linen is made in Ireland, not merely packaged here or bearing an Irish linen design, read the labels carefully.

Belfast, Northern Ireland – The whole area is known for its linen. Consult *A Guide to Northern Ireland Crafts and Craftsmen* (see "Handicrafts") for home addresses or shop at one of the following stores:

Hall's Linen is a tiny shop stocked to the rafters with linens, most made in Northern Ireland. They also carry silver, enamel, brass, and ceramic Celtic jewelry. 23 Queen's Arcade (phone: 232-320446).

Smyth's Irish Linen (also known as Simpson's) is a larger shop selling linen, souvenir items, and yarn. 14 Callender St. (phone: 232-322983).

Ulster Weavers is a leading source for pure Irish linen; visitors can also tour the factory and see the linen being weaved. 47 Linfield Rd. (phone: 232-329494).

Dublin, Irish Republic – *Brown Thomas* department store has a fine selection of pure Irish linen products. 15/20 Grafton St. (phone: 1-679-5666).

MADE-TO-MEASURE (BESPOKE) CLOTHING: Although London is well known for its bespoke shirtmakers and tailors, many Londoners travel to Dublin to have their suits made. Quality here is excellent, the price considerably less.

Cork, Irish Republic – Anthony Boeg, owner of *House of Donegal,* promotes a relaxed attitude toward tailoring. Suits, jackets, and trousers for men and women impeccably fitted in the shop can then be sent by mail. (See also "Woolens.") 6/8 Paul St. (phone: 21-272447).

Dublin, Irish Republic – *Louis Copeland* is Dublin's best bespoke tailor. 18 Wicklow St. (phone: 1-777038).

There's nothing fancy about *US Shirtmakers* except the shirts. They all have mother-of-pearl buttons and are available with detachable collars. Cloth comes from England; some Irish linen available. 13 South Leinster St., 2nd Floor (phone: 1-763013).

Hospital, County Limerick, Irish Republic – *William J. Frazer,* who fits clothing to sit well on horseback, is reputed to be the best hunting attire tailor in the world. He also makes men's and women's suits as fine as any from London's Saville Row. Main St. (phone: 61-83118).

MUSICAL INSTRUMENTS: Traditional Irish musical instruments are made and sold in both Northern Ireland and the Republic.

Northern Ireland – Ulster, in particular, is famous for its craftsmen. *Eamm Maquire* (36 Linden Gardens, Cliftonville Rd.; phone: 23-276-7796) is known for the *bodhrán,* a traditional goatskin drum.

Flutes are the specialty of *Samuel Murray,* 3 Fairyknowe Pk., Whitewell Rd., Newtownabbey, Co. Antrim (phone: 23-277-1406).

For a fiddle, see *Jim McKillop,* 55 Ballymena Rd., Carnlough, County Antrim (phone: 57-485424).

Uilleann pipes are made by *Robbie Hughes,* 100 Ballyduggan Rd., Downpatrick, County Down (phone: 39-64989).

Dublin, Irish Republic –

McCullough Pigott, in the music business for 100 years, offers 3 floors of records, tapes, and musical instruments. Suffolk St. (phone: 1-773138).

Waltons Musical Instrument Galleries stocks Scottish bagpipes, *uilleann* pipes, harps, tin whistles, old violins, and *bodhráns.* Recordings are also available. 2/5 N. Frederick St. (phone: 1-747805).

SHEEPSKINS: The country that manufactures superb woolens (see below) also produces skins.

Belfast, Northern Ireland – *Anderson and McAuley* department store has an ample selection of sheepskin rugs, many dyed soft colors and some with designs. Donegall Pl. (phone: 232-326681).

Dublin, Irish Republic – *Sheepskin Shop* has fashionable sheepskin-lined clothing and fine leathers. 20 Wicklow St. (phone: 1-719585). There is also a branch in Galway at the *Corbettcourt* shopping center, Williamsgate St. (phone: 91-61619).

Shannon and Dublin Airports in the Irish Republic have small sheepskin rugs that are easily rolled and carried on board.

SILVER: Silver ornamentation, which has been made in Ireland for 4,000 years, is available from numerous individual artisans (see local listings) as well as from fine shops:

Dublin, Irish Republic – Many shops on S. Anne Street specialize in antique silver. *J. & M. Weldon* is popular with Dubliners for antique diamond rings and rare silver decorative items. 18 S. Anne St. (phone: 17-72742).

M. Samuels has plenty of antique jewelry and silverplate place settings. 17 S. Anne St. (phone: 17-11262).

WOOLENS: Wool is a way of life in Ireland as well as an attraction for tourists. Superlative tweeds, plaids, and knits are to be found in nearly every shop and department store. Although Irish weavers no longer give the world the kind of homespun, handwoven tweeds that differed from one part of the country to the next (because of regional variations in the wool and dyes), tweed from Donegal on the northwest coast is still one of the country's best buys, as are the items made from it.

Equally renowned are fishermen's sweaters hand-knit from heavily oiled or scoured off-white wool in traditional stitches — tree of life, crooked road, tobacco, carrageen moss, castle, and popcorn-like bobaleen — combined in almost sculptural patterns that sometimes resemble the carvings on Celtic crosses. There's a special meaning to each pattern. Originally, they were made on the Aran Islands, but cottage knitters throughout the west and north now produce them for sale across the nation and around the world. Since no two are quite alike, it's best to shop where the selection is largest — nowadays in Dublin and Galway — and keep looking until you find one you can't resist.

Blarney, Irish Republic – Busloads of shoppers line up outside the mammoth *Blarney Woollen Mills* to buy Aran sweaters, woolens, and every imaginable kind of Irish souvenir (County Cork; phone: 21-385280). A branch (Nassau St., Dublin; phone: 1-710068) carries a complete line of Blarney woolens, but caters more to a town-and-country image.

Cork City, Irish Republic – *House of Donegal* specializes in Irish tweeds and sweaters and raincoats for both men and women. 6/8 Paul St. (phone: 21-272447). See also, "Made-to-Measure (Bespoke) Clothing," above.

County Donegal, Irish Republic – This is the birthplace of Irish tweeds, woven in wonderful herringbones, houndstooth checks, and other patterns. Though synthetic dyes are sometimes substituted, vegetable matter is still the coloring material that yields the distinctively subtle, luscious hues.

Stop by *John Molloy Ltd.* factory store for good buys. A handweaver works on the premises. Killybegs Rd., Ardara (phone: 75-41133).

Magee, in the center of Donegal Town, carries the work of weavers from all over the country. Demonstrations of weaving are usually in progress. The Diamond (phone: 73-21100).

Dripsey, Irish Republic – *Dripsey Woollen Mills, Ltd.* is a true mill shop — not fancy, but well known as exporters of fine tweeds and woolens to international designers. Yarn for Aran-style sweaters is also sold. 14 miles from Cork on the Cork–Killarney Road (phone: 21-334005).

Dublin, Irish Republic – *Cleo Ltd.* offers a wide variety of handwoven and hand-knit sweaters, capes, scarves, and other garments in wool and linen. The quality of the knitting is exceptional, and sweaters in traditional Aran patterns are available in an array of colors reminiscent of an Irish landscape — misty violets and smokey blues, soft greens and intense scarlets. Some take 3 months to make. Woven shawls and travel rugs in muted earth tones are also available. 18 Kildare St. (phone: 1-761421). Also at 2 Shelbourne St., Kenmare, County Kerry (phone: 64-41410).

Dublin Woollen Mills is beside the Ha'Penny Bridge and overflows with quality woolens. 41 Ormond Quay (phone: 17-75014).

Kevin & Howlin Ltd. has been selling Donegal tweed cloth and clothing for 50 years. Their tailors will custom-make a garment in Dublin or send swatches overseas for mail-order customers. There is a limited supply of women's clothing. 31 Nassau St. (phone: 1-770257).

The Sweater Shop has a full range of cashmere, pure wool, mohair, and angora sweaters at reasonable prices. 9 Wicklow St. (phone: 1-713270).

Galway City, Irish Republic – *The Treasure Chest* sells the finest of Irish woolens by designers such as Wolfangel and Jimmy Hourihan. William and Castle Sts. (91-63862 or 91-67237).

Kilmacanogue, Irish Republic – Beside a stream in a lovely village, *Avoca Handweavers* is known for its soft tweeds in muted colors. A full range of mohair products includes throws and sweaters. Kilmacanogue (phone: 1-867482). Other shops that carry the brand are in Avoca (County Wicklow; phone: 402-5105); in Bunratty (County Clare; phone: 61-364029); and at *Connemara Handicrafts* (Letterfrack, County Galway; phone: 95-41058).

For the Body

Great Golf

 True golf devotees contend that some of the finest — and most authentic — golf courses in the world are found in Ireland. This is hardly surprising since the sandy land along its coasts is much the same sort of terrain on which the game was spawned in Scotland. It's hard to believe that less than a century ago golf was virtually unknown anywhere outside Scotland, though the Scots proved great apostles, spreading the word from Perth (where the first recognizable 6-hole course is thought to have been constructed on the city's North Inch), St. Andrews, Prestwick, and Dornoch — icons of a game that has gripped the attention of an entire planet.

At about the time golf leaped the Atlantic in the late 19th century, it also settled into Ireland and grew along the same lines. Consequently, even now, the courses found in Scotland, England, Northern Ireland, and the Irish Republic provide a very different sense of the game than can be acquired anywhere else on earth. Nature was the architect of these courses. As a writer remarked in *The World Atlas of Golf,* "To this day nobody knows who laid [the courses] out . . . there were no fairways, no tees, and no greens, simply agreed starting and finishing points. The game had reached St. Andrews, Carnoustie, Leith, Dornoch, Montrose, North Berwick, and Musselburgh by the beginning of the sixteenth century. Golf thus became established on linksland . . . St. Andrews became — and still is — one long fairway, with nine holes out to a distant point, and nine holes back . . . designs incorporated stone walls, blind shots, hedges, irregularly-shaped mounds and greens in geometric shapes."

But it's more than history that lures generations of modern golfers to the game's breeding grounds. Particularly in Ireland, where there are more golf courses per capita than in any other country in the world — more than 200 courses at last count — there's a friendliness to the sport; it's a community game, not cloistered and clubby. The intensity of the challenge found on these courses remains as vital as ever, and the chance to pit one's skill against the achievements of golf's greatest historic figures is nearly irresistible. Not to play these courses at least once in a lifetime is not to know the real heritage of the game.

A word about particulars: Greens fees average approximately $10 per day, but range up to $45 for some of the top championship courses. The charge usually is per day, not per round. It is wise to book tee times in advance by calling the club secretary. Golf clubs are not generally available to rent, but some clubs do carry a limited number of sets. Caddies, where available, generally must be booked in advance. Caddie carts (usually pullcarts only — there are few motorized carts in Ireland) are available at most clubs for about $1.50 per round. It is best, therefore, to bring only a light "Sunday" bag, as it may be necessary to carry it yourself. Also bring clothing to protect against wind and rain, even on the apparently sunniest days, particularly on coastal courses (Irish golfers rarely pause for weather). That said, we recommend the following courses, listed alphabetically by county:

LAHINCH, Lahinch, County Clare, Irish Republic: Created a century ago by some Irish merchants and a group of Scottish Black Watch regiment members stationed nearby, the extraordinary *Old Course* has been known to inflict players with every conceivable plague, save famine and flood. The *St. Andrews* of Ireland — once famous for its grazing goats (they've died off in recent years) — has one short par 5 that has been toughened a bit by putting something that looks like the Great Wall of China in the middle of the fairway. To add a little extra spice, there's a 145-yard par 3 that's completely blind — a fact that makes for interesting speculation. A second 18-hole course has been added that is less demanding, but of championship standard nonetheless. Our pick for the best fun in the west of Ireland. Details: *Lahinch Golf Club,* Lahinch, County Clare, Irish Republic (phone: 65-81003).

ROYAL DUBLIN, Dollymount, County Dublin, Irish Republic: The "other" Dublin-area golfing magnet, though second to *Portmarnock* (see below), still deserves a place among Europe's best. The winds blow here as well, and the rough grows to a size not normally known in the New World. Founded in 1885, the course is famous for its 4 short holes — the 4th, 6th, 9th, and 12th — all of which call for a keen eye and precision play; the demanding 5th hole, with its narrow valley of a fairway, once prompted the late comedian Danny Kaye to ask his caddy for a rifle. Details: *Royal Dublin Golf Club,* Dollymount, Dublin 3, Irish Republic (phone: 1-336346).

PORTMARNOCK, Portmarnock, County Dublin, Irish Republic: This fabled layout (just outside Dublin) is perhaps the best single course in the Republic. The short flag sticks, which are set on springs to let them swing freely in the breeze, indicate something about the wind hazards here, and the last 5 holes are diabolically difficult. However, the quality of the course, especially the greens, is superb. Be prepared for the strong prevailing northeasterly wind, soaring scores — and a bracing outing. Details: *Portmarnock Golf Club,* Portmarnock, County Dublin, Irish Republic (phone: 1-323082).

BALLYBUNION, Ballybunion, County Kerry, Irish Republic: The original course here is one of the two Irish tracks that Tom Watson plays every year or two just for fun (*Lahinch,* below, is the other), and no less an authority than Herbert Warren Wind calls the *Old Course* one of the ten toughest in the world. Visiting golfers will have no reason to disagree. The course is laid out at the point where the river Shannon estuary meets the Atlantic Ocean. Its 14th, 17th, and 18th holes are all roaring winds, and the out-of-bounds area beside the 1st hole is a graveyard. Welcome to Ireland. A second Robert Trent Jones Sr. 18-holer is also on the club grounds. Details: *Ballybunion Golf Club,* County Kerry, Irish Republic (phone: 68-27146).

DOOKS GOLF CLUB, Glenbeigh, County Kerry, Irish Republic: Between MacGillicuddy's Reeks and Dingle Bay, overlooking the sea, this is one of Ireland's oldest clubs (founded in 1889) and certainly one of its finest. Although short, it has many interesting holes, particularly the 13th, the Saucer, where accuracy is of the essence. It has a fairly new watering system and a renovated clubhouse. *Dooks* is also known for the Natterjack toad (most populous around the 14th to the 17th hole), an endangered species distinctive for the yellow streak down its back and for its three-toed feet, which cause it to walk rather than hop. Details: *Dooks Golf Club,* Dooks, Glenbeigh, County Kerry, Irish Republic (phone: 66-68205).

KILLARNEY GOLF AND FISHING CLUB, Killarney, County Kerry, Irish Republic: The scenery is lovely and dramatic in this fabled spot, and it may take an act of will to keep your head down while playing on one of the two championship courses, though it may not be worth the effort. The sight of the lakes framing the purple mountains is a once-in-a-lifetime experience. The older course presents the more taxing challenge. Details: *Killarney Golf and Fishing Club,* Mahoney's Point, Killarney, County Kerry, Irish Republic (phone: 64-31034).

WATERVILLE GOLF CLUB, Waterville, County Kerry, Irish Republic: A modern resort hotel adjoins this championship course, but don't get the idea that this is an easy resort track; the layout is nearly as rugged as the surrounding countryside. This longest of Irish tracks (7,234 yards from the championship tees) plays between the Atlantic coast and an inland lake that's best known to trout and salmon fishermen. Though long teeing areas allow the course to be shortened to 6,024 yards (society tees), the brave playing from the back are in for a very exhilarating and challenging afternoon. Details: *Waterville Golf Club,* Waterville, County Kerry, Irish Republic (phone: 667-4133 or 667-4102).

COUNTY SLIGO GOLF CLUB, Rosses Point, County Sligo, Irish Republic: More popularly called *Rosses Point,* this western Irish links maintains the conflict between golfer and Atlantic Ocean breezes. How one plays here depends a lot on which way the prevailing hurricane happens to be blowing. *Rosses Point* is not quite as tight a course as the other Irish monsters, and some of its greens are even reachable by mere mortals in regulation figures. Chances are that this is the Irish golf course where spirits (not scores) will soar. Details: *County Sligo Golf Club,* Rosses Point, County Sligo, Irish Republic (phone: 71-77134).

ROYAL PORTRUSH, Portrush, County Antrim, Northern Ireland: Though the "troubles" in Northern Ireland persist, the golf remains above the internecine disputes. Of the two 18-hole layouts here, the *Dunluce* course — the only club in Ireland ever to host the *British Open* — is the championship track. It is named after the striking old castle perched on the white cliffs to its east. The wind off the North Sea is usually intense and constant, and no less an authority than Pete Dye estimated that the course should be ranked eighth best in the world. Details: *Royal Portrush Golf Club,* Dunluce Rd., Portrush, County Antrim BT56 8JQ, Northern Ireland (phone: 265-822311).

ROYAL COUNTY DOWN, Newcastle, County Down, Northern Ireland: This is "where the mountains of Mourne sweep down to the sea." The *British Amateur* championship was played here in 1970, and Gene Sarazen, the noted golf professional, voted it the number one course in the world. So no one should be too surprised to find that some of the hazards can prove rather startling to weak-kneed players. The minutes of the founding club meeting in 1889 reported that "the Secretaries were empowered to employ Tom Morris to lay out the course at a cost not to exceed £4." God alone only knows how Old Tom hacked these holes out of the rough sandhills for that price, but he did make a beauty. Details: *Royal County Down Golf Club,* Newcastle, County Down BT33 0AN, Northern Ireland (phone: 3967-23314).

Tennis

 Although tennis has a long way to go before it becomes the mania in Ireland that it is in the US, there are now thousands of players, and courts are seldom hard to find. While real tennis buffs still wouldn't come here just to play tennis, those who do play should be sure to pack racquet and tennis whites, since a tennis match is a fine, rapid way to get off the standard tourist circuit and into local life. In these circles, playing well is considered important — but playing as if you mean to win at all costs isn't the Irish style. If you pass muster, you may end the match with at least an invitation to the nearest pub.

WHERE TO PLAY

Municipal courts abound in both the Republic and Northern Ireland; tourist literature lists their locations. In addition, many of the more luxurious hotels have their own courts (see listings in THE CITIES and DIRECTIONS). Otherwise, the best sources of information are the following:

> *Dublin Corporation,* Community & Environment Dept., 2 Parnell Sq., Dublin 1, Irish Republic (phone: 1-727777). Can answer questions about playing on public courts around Dublin.
>
> *Irish Lawn Tennis Association,* 22 Upper Fitzwilliam St., Dublin 2, Irish Republic (phone: 1-610117). Can answer questions about playing in both the Republic and Northern Ireland.

For more than just a casual hour a day on the courts, plan your trip around stops at a handful of resorts, such as the following, listed alphabetically by county:

TENNIS VILLAGE CORK, Model Farm Rd., Cork City, County Cork, Irish Republic: Two miles west of downtown, this modern sporting center offers 6 indoor courts and 8 outdoor courts; open year-round, 24 hours per day. The complex also includes a practice area, a tennis boutique, a restaurant, and a bar (phone: 21-342727).

KILTERNAN COUNTRY CLUB, Kilternan, County Dublin, Irish Republic: Set on 2 acres in the sylvan Dublin Mountains, about 15 minutes south of Dublin City, this leisure hotel complex includes an 18-hole golf course, horseback riding, an indoor heated swimming pool, a gym, saunas, and an artificial ski slope. It adjoins a multimillion-dollar national tennis center, whose 8 courts (4 indoor, 4 outdoor) are open from early in the morning until midnight (phone: 1-955559).

PONTOON BRIDGE, Foxford, County Mayo, Irish Republic: Another opportunity to test your skills on grass — there's a single grass court at this modern lakeside hotel (phone: 94-56120 or 94-56151).

KELLY'S STRAND, Rosslare, County Wexford, Irish Republic: Good tennis facilities, with outdoor and indoor courts, at a family-run hotel that's famous for its food (phone: 53-32114).

CULLODEN, Holywood, County Antrim, Northern Ireland: One of Northern Ireland's few first class hotels with tennis facilities, it has one all-weather court. Near Belfast (phone: 23-175223).

SLIEVE DONARD, Newcastle, County Down, Northern Ireland: A fully restored, 19th-century, landmark railway hotel with a recreation center, including 2 all-weather courts set on a lawn facing the Irish Sea and the Mourne Mountains (phone: 3967-23681).

WHERE TO WATCH

The *Irish Open* is the major event of the season. Although it's not now a major tournament, a number of up-and-coming players from the international circuit try to make the scene. The open usually is held during the second week of July, just after *Wimbledon.* To attend, contact the *Fitzwilliam Lawn and Tennis Club* (Appian Way, Dublin 6, Irish Republic; phone: 1-603988). For more information on other Irish tourneys, contact the *Irish Lawn Tennis Association* (above).

Horsing Around

An old Irish saying has it that there are three glories to any gathering — a beautiful wife, a good horse, and a swift hound. In Ireland, the wife and the hound are secondary. It is the horse that provides the excuse to hold the gathering in the first place. (This is, after all, a country that almost unanimously voted a horse as Personality of the Year — the legendary steeplechaser Arkle, the quadruped folk hero who won the *Cheltenham Gold Cup* 3 years running, thereby humiliating, to the immense satisfaction of the Irish, every one of the champion's British counterparts.) Irish horses and their "connections" — trainers, riders, and breeders — are legendary. Hundreds of mares come to Ireland to enjoy the services of celebrated stallions now retired to Irish farms; thanks to a governmental ruling that gives stud fees tax-exempt status, the business is flourishing.

Irish horse gatherings come in all shapes and descriptions, from the snappily elegant *Dublin Horse Show* to the famous *Horse Fair* at Ballinasloe, full of hand-slapping street-corner hard dealing. There are events in which horses are ridden, raced, hunted, bought, sold, jumped, driven, backed, cursed, argued over, and immortalized. And they offer visitors plenty of opportunities to get in on the act.

RACES, SHOWS, MEETS, AND SALES

The Irish are on their favorite turf at these events. There are nearly 300 race days, on the flat and over the jumps, on 2 dozen racecourses each year, all wonderfully entertaining, with the brouhaha of punters placing their bets on named horses and on-course bookies shouting the odds, which are posted on the boards, wiped out, and reposted as wagers are placed. At Dublin's *Phoenix Park Racecourse,* which stages the richest 2-year-old race in the world (the winner of *The Million* gets IR£500,000), there are superb facilities for race-goers and their families. At *Fairyhouse* and *Punchestown,* 14 and 20 miles from Dublin, respectively, there are large enclosures where families picnic on the grass and watch the goings-on. At some festival meetings, all the inhabitants for miles around stop work to go to the races — and a great portion of the rest of the population plan holidays around a favorite meeting.

Since Norman and Elizabethan days, the focal point of Irish racing has been the Curragh, the great plain of Kildare, southwest of Dublin — 6,000 wide-open acres that are home to many of the best stables; at any given time, a few million pounds' worth of bloodstock can be seen trotting over its windswept expanses of short grass. The Curragh is the venue for the five Irish classic races — the *One Thousand Guineas and Two Thousand Guineas* in May, the *Irish Derby* in June, the *Irish Oaks* in July, and the *Irish St. Leger* in October. (Each of these is also referred to by the name of its sponsor, which changes periodically.) Adjacent to the racecourse, whose grandstands brood silently over the plain through most of the year, is the fascinating *Irish National Stud* (Tully, County Kildare, Irish Republic; phone: 45-21251). Each aristocratic stallion has a brass nameplate on his stable door, and the grassy meadows beyond are full of mares and skipping foals — a heart-warming sight to behold. Nearby is the *Irish Horse Museum,* full of objects and information on matters equine, with good coverage of draft horses as well as racing, hunting, show jumping, and steeplechasing; the center of attraction, lovingly admired by all, is the standing skeleton of the steeplechaser Arkle.

Steeplechasing, said to be descended from the Tudor-era wild-goose chase, a pell-mell charge through the fields with no particular end in sight, was born in Ireland in 1752, when two riders in County Cork raced each other from one church to another a few miles away, leaping walls, ditches, hedges, and other impediments en route. Soon it became the height of fashion among Irish horse folk and is still popular today; the greatest steeplechasers on earth are trained here. The thrills are heightened by the ephemeral nature of the sport. For while the victors in a famous flat race, the sort that gets worldwide press attention, can expect to earn their biggest money from post-retirement stud fees, steeplechasers' careers pay the biggest dividends in mere glory: Nearly all jumpers are geldings, who have their moment in the sun — and then are memories.

The best places to watch the Irish and their great horses include *Leopardstown,* a flat course modeled on England's *Sandown,* just south of Dublin, and the following jumping, or national hunt, courses: *Fairyhouse,* the venue for the *Irish Grand National* each *Easter Monday; Punchestown,* steeplechasing's headquarters since 1850, which has a festival meeting in late April or early May; *Galway,* which hosts the *Guinness Hurdle* and the *Galway Plate* on its jumping course in August; *Navan,* County Meath, where there are feature events in January and November; *Gowran,* County Kilkenny, where feature races are run in January, May, and September.

In Northern Ireland, the races at *Downpatrick,* which has a somewhat undulating track, and at *Down Royal,* a good galloping track, enjoy an enthusiastic following. The *Ulster Harp National,* the country's most important steeplechase, is held annually in February.

In addition, there are literally hundreds of well-supported horse shows, or *gymkhanas,* held all over Ireland from February to October — events that last from 1 to 3 days, give neighbors the chance to mingle, visitors the chance to soak up some local color, and participants a crack at qualifying for the *Dublin Horse Show.* Some of the best show jumpers in the country can often be seen at these local events. And nothing warms the heart quite like junior competitions, where pint-size riders on diminutive mounts compete over jumps almost taller than they are. The rivalries are as heated, and the audiences as enthusiastic, as at the *Dublin Horse Show* itself.

Admission to all courses for all kinds of races is about $6 to $8 per adult, a bit more for the bigger races, with an extra charge for the reserved enclosure. There is plenty to eat and drink, and binoculars are for rent at about $5. Don't fail to take in the bumper races — usually the last on the day's card; these events for amateur riders often provide the best sport and the greatest excitement. And since no day at the races is complete without "taking an interest" — that is, putting precious dollars on a nag — those so inclined will want to "study form" in the daily papers — the weekly *Irish Field,* or *Turform Ratings* — which can be purchased at the course for about $3.50. Bets can be placed with the government-run Tote (minimum £1) or with the bookmaker (minimum £5).

Flat races take place from summer through fall, overlapping the commencement of the jumping season, which is in full swing between late December and *Easter,* ending with the late April meeting at *Punchestown.*

The races and equine events listed alphabetically below by town are among the best of their types. For their dates, along with a calendar of all races, contact the *Irish Racing Board,* Leopardstown Race Course, Roxrock, Dublin 18, Irish Republic (phone: 1-892888).

BALLINASLOE HORSE FAIR, Ballinasloe, County Galway, Irish Republic: With Irish horses such valuable exports, traditional sales held at various times in Dublin under the auspices of the Royal Dublin Society and at the renowned *Goffs' Sales Paddocks* at Kill, County Kildare, bring scores of American and European millionaires and Middle Eastern potentates humming in and out in helicopters and wearing costly silks and cashmeres along with their tweeds. The famous October horse and cattle fair in Ballinasloe is different. For this venerable event, the country's largest livestock market and the largest horse fair in Europe in the days of horse-drawn transport, the big, cheerful country town of Ballinasloe leaps out of its usual drowse, sizzles with life, and explodes with the soft, sweet smells of the farmyard. The excitement that characterizes the buying and selling of horses anywhere is crazily mixed up here with the color of a traditional fair in high Irish spirits. Details: *Irish Tourist Board* (see *Tourist Information Offices,* GETTING READY TO GO).

CONNEMARA PONY SHOW, Clifden, County Galway, Irish Republic: These deep-chested, versatile, even-tempered, intelligent native ponies — said to be descended from horses that managed to swim to shore from the wrecks of the Spanish Armada

— have been the focus of increasing attention over the last decade but have been showcased at this professionally run country show held annually on the third Thursday in August for more than 60 years. The animals make fine pets and excellent jumpers, and this fair, at which some 300 of the best are judged, bought, and traded, is a grand one indeed: The breeders are a lively, mixed group — simple farmers and aristocrats alike — and the town goes all out, with Guinness flowing freely. Details: *Connemara Pony Breeders Society,* 73 Dalysfort Rd., Salthill, Galway, County Galway, Irish Republic (phone: 91-22909).

DUBLIN HORSE SHOW, Dublin, Irish Republic: Whereas other cities wilt during the warm days of summer, Dublin is awhirl with activity from late July through early August, as horse lovers from all over Ireland, Great Britain, and the Continent converge on the capital for this equestrian and social event. First held in 1868, it is one of the best shows of its kind in the world and, with its hunt balls and social and diplomatic parties, it is certainly the high point of the year for Dublin society. For *Ladies' Day,* the Thursday of *Horse Show Week,* citizens don their best bib and tucker, and a glittering automobile is presented to the most attractively dressed and suitably groomed lady at the show. The main show jumping events, held on Friday and Saturday, are the *Nations Cup* for the Aga Khan Trophy and the *Grand Prix of Ireland* — the richest jumping competitions in the world. Grandstand tickets for these competitions, as well as for others held during the week, are quite difficult to come by, but standing room is always available. Hotel rooms are scarce as hen's teeth — so hard to find, in fact, that if you haven't booked well in advance, you may end up lodging with a family near the showgrounds. Details: *Royal Dublin Society,* PO Box 121, Ballsbridge, Dublin 4, Irish Republic (phone: 1-680645); for housing details, *Dublin and Eastern Region Tourism Organization,* 13/14 Upper O'Connell St., Dublin 1, Irish Republic (phone: 1-747733).

IRISH GRAND NATIONAL, Fairyhouse, County Meath, Irish Republic: The whole nation knows who is going to win this famous fixture of the jumping season — so the whole nation "takes an interest." Seeing the line of horses taking the first fence on a sunny *Easter Monday* is a sight worth waiting for! Details: *Irish Racing Board* (address above).

GALWAY RACES, near Galway, Irish Republic: These hilarious, exhilarating late July races at Ballybrit, a few miles from city center with a fine view of Galway Bay, are an Irish legend; the whole city practically closes down every afternoon so that the citizenry can make the scene. Racing takes place over a course that is a fair test of stamina for any horse, just as race week's side show of fast-talking hawkers, itinerant musicians, soothsayers, and assorted others of perhaps less than sterling character tries the endurance of visitors and residents. If you make a few dollars while "taking an interest," as most people do (some IR£1 million is put on the line every day), take care that you don't lose it — and more — in a *Galway Race Week* poker game. Details: *Irish Racing Board* (address above).

BUDWEISER IRISH DERBY, Kildare, County Kildare, Irish Republic: Irish racing is world famous, and Irish-bred horses regularly win the Continent's classic competitions; this event, a 1½-miler for 3-year-olds held at the Curragh annually in late June or early July, is Ireland's star race. Among the other classic races that make this track so important are the *Irish One Thousand Guineas* (1 mile for 3-year-old fillies, in May), the *Irish Two Thousand Guineas* (1 mile for 3-year-olds, in May), the *Irish Oaks* (1½ miles for 3-year-old fillies, in July), and the *Irish St. Leger* (1¾ miles for 3-year-olds and up, in October). Details: *Irish Racing Board* (address above).

LAYTOWN STRAND RACES, Laytown, County Meath, Irish Republic: This small resort town at the mouth of the river Nanny, some 30 miles north of Dublin, holds just 1 meet a year, usually in mid-August. It is not the sort of event that draws the top horses or the top jockeys. What makes it exceptional, however, is its venue — the town's long, broad, gently sloping strand. For just this one day a year, the beach is all horse. Stable hands parade the equine competitors around the sandy paddock while trainers and owners look on, bookmakers strike the odds, tipplers drink, and kids beg their parents for candy and souvenirs and then go splashing about at the water's edge. Details: *Irish Racing Board* (address above).

LIMERICK JUNCTION RACECOURSE, Limerick Junction, County Tipperary, Irish Republic: For those who are jaded by big meetings, this small racecourse named after the nearby railway station (and not the distant town) is ideal. In the heart of racing Ireland, 115 miles from Dublin — not far from the home of none other than Vincent O'Brien, one of the world's leading buyers, breeders, and trainers of racehorses — this racecourse hosts events regularly from March through November and draws a crowd that is at least as interesting as the horses. The equine aspect to the features of some of the onlookers is very real: That's what comes of generations of looking after horses. In its own small way, the *Limerick Junction* shows offer everything that is delightful about Irish racing — and Irish character. Details: *Irish Racing Board* (address above).

HEINEKEN HORSE TRIALS, Punchestown, County Kildare, Irish Republic: This annual 3-day competition in late May offers visitors the chance to join Irish equestrians in "full fig" (fully outfitted) from the tips of their hard hats to the toes of their close-fitting boots. Horse lovers, some bringing caravans and mobile homes, come from Bermuda, Canada, Spain, and even New Zealand to enjoy the goings-on: dressage the first day, cross-country steeplechasing the second, show jumping the third. International stars are invariably on hand to show their stuff, but — this being the country of the horse — the hit of the day is just as apt to be the 58-year-old sportsman who gets himself and his half-breed, still together, around the course. Details: *Irish Racing Board* (address above).

TRAMORE RACES, Tramore, County Waterford, Irish Republic: Down in the sunny southeast, by the sea, this mid-August race has a flavor all its own. Nobody takes anything too seriously — except the horses. Those who manage to save something from the bookies can spend it on a piece of crystal from the famous Waterford manufacturer, just down the road. Details: *Irish Racing Board* (address above).

RIDING HOLIDAYS, TREKKING, AND TRAIL RIDING

The Irish flock to horse holidays with exactly the same enthusiasm that Americans flock to dude ranches — except that they are more likely to wear jodhpurs than jeans, swing into saddles without horns as well as with, and do their riding at a stable that doesn't have anything more than a casual arrangement with their lodging place. Top-notch horses, delightful scenery, and the chance to join the natives in one of their favorite pastimes are the main attractions.

Literature describing equestrian holidays often contains bewildering lingo. The term *riding holiday*, for instance, refers to not just any vacation spent on horseback but specifically to one where participants trot, canter, occasionally even take small jumps, and get basic instruction by a full-fledged instructor registered with the Association of Irish Riding Establishments (AIRE), one currently accredited by the British Horse Society (BHSI or BHSAI) or, in smaller establishments, horse folk who instruct as a summer job. The organizations that provide these activities, which are available year-round, may also arrange for their guests to compete in local shows, or *gymkhanas* — great fun — where they can get to know the local horsey set (and in Ireland that's practically everybody). Some riding holiday centers are residential, with accommodations on the premises; others arrange for participants to lodge nearby in small hotels or guesthouses, or even with local families. Rank beginners and advanced equestrians are both welcome. Visitors are advised to check their insurance before going and to look into any limitations on the insurance available through the chosen riding establishment.

Many horsey establishments offer ponies or horses for trekking in nearby mountains or woods. To accommodate novice riders and the less fit, travel is at a walking pace. The great joy, apart from the pleasure of the open air, is the leisurely enjoyment of great sweeps of scenery, of forest-covered hills, and of fields full of bracken or ferns spotted here and there with clumps of purple heather or thistle and foxglove. And all to the gentle rhythm of a walking horse, the squeak of the saddle, the soothing smells of leather and horse sweat mixing with the honeyed scent of golden furze. Children under 14 may find it a bit tedious, but it is the rare experienced day trekker who remains unmotivated to go on to the next level — post trekking or trail riding.

This more ambitious sort of holiday lasts several days and takes riders from one post to the next, 20 to 25 miles a day, in the company of an experienced guide, over rugged hills, through leafy lanes, or across deserted sandy beaches. Picnics, cookouts, and barbecues offer diversion en route, and overnight stops provide for plenty of hot water, huge quantities of food, and good company. Luggage usually is transported separately.

The following, listed alphabetically by county, include some of the best Irish establishments offering riding, trekking, and trail riding. The Irish Tourist Board's *Equestrian Ireland* guide is helpful.

MOUNT PLEASANT PONY TREKKING CENTRE, 13 Bannonstown Rd., Castlewellan, County Down, Northern Ireland: Escorted trekking is available through the 15,000-acre Castlewellan Forest Park and the foothills of the fabled Mournes. Details: *Mount Pleasant Pony Trekking Centre,* 15 Bannanstown Rd., Castlewellan, County Down BT31 9BG, Northern Ireland (phone: 3967-78651).

ASHBROOKE RIDING SCHOOL, Brookeborough, County Fermanagh, Northern Ireland: Instruction for riders of all levels; training includes dressage, show jumping, and cross-country events. Restored housekeeping cottages are available or guests can stay with a family on the Viscount Brookeborough's estate. Details: *Ashbrooke Riding School,* Brookeborough, County Fermanagh, Northern Ireland (phone: 36-553242).

WILLIAM LEAHY, The Connemara Trail, Aille Cross, Loughrea, County Galway, Irish Republic: The particular attractions of this establishment's trail ride along the Connemara Trail, beyond the wonderful landscape that unfolds en route along pretty hill roads and tracks, are the lodgings in places such as Galway's *Great Southern* hotel, where the trip begins and ends, climaxing with a glorious romp down a long and windswept beach. The mounts are hunters or half-breed horses. May through September. Details: *The Connemara Trail,* c/o William Leahy, Aille Cross, Loughrea, County Galway, Irish Republic (phone: 91-41216).

EL RANCHO HORSE HOLIDAYS LTD., Ballyard, Tralee, County Kerry, Irish Republic: This establishment offers, among other things, an adventurous 80-mile, week-long circle trip along out-of-the-way bridle paths through mountain defiles and lovely stretches of sand in the breezy, sea-washed area of rugged hills where the film *Ryan's Daughter* was made. Accommodations en route are in farmhouses and hotels, where the food is both tasty and plentiful. May to October. Details: *El Rancho Horse Holidays Ltd.,* c/o William J. O'Connor, Ballyard, Tralee, County Kerry, Irish Republic (phone: 66-21840).

MOUNT JULIET, Thomastown, County Kilkenny, Irish Republic: Home to the Ballylinch Stud Farm, this expansive 1,466-acre estate is a haven for equestrian enthusiasts. There are 16 miles of profesionally planned bridle paths and qualified instructors for lessons. Equipment and riding gear is also available. Overnight packages include accommodations, breakfast, and dinner at the manor house. Details: *Mount Juliet,* Thomastown, County Kilkenny, Irish Republic (phone: 56-24455).

GREYSTONES EQUESTRIAN CENTRE, Castle Leslie, Glaslough, County

Monaghan, Irish Republic: Riding lessons, with five separate cross-country courses full of prepared fences and all sorts of natural obstacles — rivers, ditches, fallen trees, log piles, stone walls, hedges, drops, and the like; the area was once called "the St. Moritz of equestrianism." Accommodation is provided in a Victorian country house, and meals are typical Irish country fare. Details: *Greystones Equestrian Centre,* Castle Leslie, Glaslough, County Monaghan, Irish Republic (phone: 47-88100).

OLD RECTORY STABLES, Drumcliffe, County Sligo, Irish Republic: Hacking, trekking, residential riding courses, and trail riding are all offered here from March to October, "beneath Ben Bulben's head," in the superb County Sligo landscape that inspired W. B. Yeats to pen some of his finest poetry. Details: *Old Rectory Stables,* Drumcliffe, County Sligo, Irish Republic (phone: 71-63221).

BALLYCORMAC HOUSE, Aglish, near Roscrea, County Tipperary, Irish Republic: Trail rides along the Lough Derg Trail take in a special mix of mountains, rivers, forest, bog, farmland, and lake shore — but few roads and little traffic — and the route jogs and bobs from the tiny 300-year-old *Ballycormac Cottage* guesthouse and the lakeshore Georgian country manor known as the *Gurtnaloughna House* to the family-run *Mountshannon* hotel. Details: *Ballycormac House,* Aglish, County Tipperary, Irish Republic (phone: 67-21129).

EDERGOLE EQUESTRIAN CENTRE, Cookstow, County Tyrone, Northern Ireland: Escorted and unescorted trekking through the Sperrin Mountains, plus British Horse Society–approved instruction at all levels and post trail rides (tours using a succession of farm guesthouses for overnight stays). The riding center also has accommodations. Details: *Edergole Equestrian Centre,* 70 Moneymore Rd., Cookstown, County Tyrone, Northern Ireland BT80 8PY (phone: 6487-62924).

WHITFIELD COURT POLO SCHOOL, Waterford, County Waterford, Irish Republic: It's not surprising that horse-loving Ireland is home to Europe's only residential polo school. Though the game was first played in India over 2,000 years ago and was brought to the West by Her Majesty's Ninth Lancers, the Irish picked it up as if they had been born playing: When the Lancers, most unwisely, challenged the *Meath Hunt* to try out the new sport, they were peremptorily thrashed, and it was one of the Irishmen who exported polo to America. *Whitfield Court* has had beginners and advanced players alike from over 25 countries; some call their polo vacation the most memorable of their lives. Instruction is by Major Hugh Dawnay. Late May through August. (Those who would rather watch than play can catch the polo matches in Dublin's *Phoenix Park* during *Horse Show week* — or observe the practice every Saturday and Sunday afternoon, May through September.) Details: *Whitfield Court Polo School,* Waterford, County Waterford, Irish Republic (phone: 51-84216).

HORETOWN HOUSE, Foulksmills, County Wexford, Irish Republic: Offers week-long packages, including trekking or riding lessons in dressage, show jumping, and cross-country, with lodging in a 17th-century Georgian manor house. More than one guest has gone home applauding and agreeing with the Americans who called *Horetown House* "an authentic Irish country experience, with warm people, a cozy environment, and nourishing fires, food, and talk." Details: *Horetown House,* Foulksmills, County Wexford, Irish Republic (phone: 51-63633).

HORSE-DRAWN CARAVANNING

Meandering along a narrow lane in a horse-drawn wagon, flanked by billowing meadows and fields, with grand vistas stretching off toward a purple-hazed horizon, is one of the most relaxed ways to spend a week — and Ireland is one of the few countries in the world where it's possible to see just why. Agencies in a number of regions rent old-style Gypsy wagons, brightly painted outside and fitted with berths and cooking facilities inside (but without toilets), and the roads of the surrounding countryside are small and traffic-free — perfect for this kind of caravanning. Agents can suggest the most scenic routes; direct their guests to the beaches, overlooks, quaint old pubs, interesting restaurants, and historic sites in the areas through which they'll be passing; and name the best overnight spots, usually about 10 miles apart. The weekly cost for a caravan that will accommodate four is about $300 to $400, depending on the operator and the season. Principal operators include the following:

Dieter Clissmann Horse-Drawn Caravans, Carrigmore Farm, County Wicklow, Irish Republic (phone: 404-8188).

Slattery's Horse-Drawn Caravans, Tralee, 1 Russell St., Tralee, County Kerry (phone: 66-21722).

HUNTING

With just a little effort, riders so inclined could hunt every day of the week in Ireland, in their pick of locations, since riding to hounds — as distinct from shooting, as the Irish call going after game with firearms — is extremely popular here. There are dozens of hunts, including many that welcome guests. The scenery is stupendous, so that a rider may be forgiven for taking a tumble when distracted by the view. And since hunting is very democratic, it provides an opportunity to meet all sorts of people — not only the gentry, but also priests and diplomats, business executives and farmers, secretaries and students. Non-riders often follow the action on foot, by bicycle, or in their cars, standing by to catch a glimpse of the passing hounds and riders as they charge through the fields. From the stirrup cup that almost invariably precedes each meet to the rendezvous afterward in some favored hostelry, the atmosphere is at once efficient, orderly, friendly, and convivial; and the hunter is judged not only on his skill with the horse but also on his ability to hold his own in the best of company.

There's also all sorts of other hunting in Ireland.

FOX HUNTING: Chasing a pack of hounds on horseback, in hot pursuit of the wily fox, is the favorite sport of some of the most fascinating characters in a country full of memorable personalities; fox hunting in Ireland has history, folklore, gossip, and a social flavor all its own. What really counts is your seat on the horse — and whether you keep it!

Hunt secretaries can advise on hiring a mount — usually an Irish-bred horse with fence-taking ability in his blood. Expect to spend just under $150 a day.

County Galway, Irish Republic – Dedicated hunting folk say that if you can hunt in only one place in Ireland, it should be in County Galway, where miles of loose gray limestone walls give gritty character to the landscape and local interest supports no less than three hunts, all of which welcome visitors:

North Galway Hunt, c/o Ms. Helen Howard Taylor, Grassendale Villa, Ballygaddy Rd., Tuam, County Galway, Irish Republic (phone: 93-24843).

County Galway Hunt, c/o Mrs. J. Coveney, Ballingariff, Craughwell, County Galway, Irish Republic (phone: 91-96211). This celebrated hunt is more informally known as the *Galway Blazers.*

East Galway Hunt, c/o Mr. Joe McEvoy, Lawrencetown, County Galway, Irish Republic (phone: 90-585767).

Visiting huntsmen will also find a warm welcome and an understanding and knowledgeable host at the *Great Southern* hotel (Eyre Sq., Galway; phone: 91-64041), described at greater length in "Rural Retreats" in *For the Experience.*

Counties Clare, Cork, and Limerick, Irish Republic – Second to Galway, this is

Ireland's favorite hunt country, notable for great bank ditches of clay and stone that test the mettle of the bravest. A handful of hunts here are of interest because of the variety of terrain and the availability of associated guesthouses and hotels.

County Clare Hunt, c/o Mr. Sean Hurley, Dun Padraig, Tulla Rd., Ennis, County Clare, Irish Republic (phone: 65-21472). The Georgian-style *Ballykilty Manor* hotel in Quin (phone: 65-25627), surrounded by a handsome 50-acre park, and the luxurious *Old Ground* hotel in Ennis (Station Rd.; phone: 65-28127) cater to hunters and organize very enjoyable hunting parties themselves. Until a few years ago, the former was the home of the Blood family, famed for its involvement in the Crown Jewels scandal during the reign of Charles II.

County Limerick Hunt, c/o Mr. Richard Johnson, Ballytigue House, Bruree, County Limerick, Irish Republic (phone: 63-90575).

Duhallow Hunt, c/o Kevin Thompson, Brook Lodge, Mallow, County Cork, Irish Republic (phone: 22-21114). This hunt dates from before 1745.

Other Hunts in the Republic – The *Dunraven Arms* hotel (Adare, County Limerick; phone: 61-396209) specializes in fox hunting arrangements and is affiliated with eight different hunt clubs in Limerick, Clare, Galway, and Tipperary. A tiny guesthouse known as *Ballycormac Cottage* (Aglish, near Roscrea, County Tipperary, Irish Republic; phone: 67-21129) can arrange for visitors to hunt with some of the most famous packs of hounds in the country, including the *Ormond* (the country's oldest), the *Westmeath*, and the *Roscommon Harriers*. The centrally located *Mount Juliet* estate (Thomastown, County Kilkenny; phone: 56-24455), home to the *Kilkenny Hunt*, can arrange for guests to participate in eight additional nearby hunts in Tipperary, Kilinick, Waterford, Wexford, Ormond, Carlow, Kilmoganny, and Bree. Packages include equipment and riding gear (if needed), and accommodations in the manor house.

Northern Ireland – Fox hunting is no less popular here, and there are a number of clubs. The best-known is *East Down Foxhounds*, c/o Miss Diana Kirkpatrick, Church Hill, Newcastle, County Down, Northern Ireland (phone: 39-672-3217).

CUBBING: Most hunts hold cub meets in September, October, and November. Workmanlike affairs whose purpose is to train the hounds, break up litters of young foxes and thin their population, and otherwise get things in order, they are held in early mornings and are open to proficient riders by arrangement with individual hunt secretaries.

HARRIER HUNTING: Less glamorous, with a hare rather than fox as quarry, harrier hunting is done by about 30 Irish hunts. Two near Dublin welcome visitors by appointment:

Bray Harriers, c/o C. J. Warren, 11 Whitethorn Rd., Dublin 14, Irish Republic (phone: 1-694403).

Fingal Harriers, c/o Miss Patricia Murtagh, The Grange, Skerries, County Dublin, Irish Republic (phone: 1-491467).

OTHER FORMS OF MADNESS

Anyone in search of still other ways to enjoy the Irishman's favorite quadruped need not want for opportunities.

HARNESS RACING: This sport is variously known as harness racing, sulky racing, and "Ben Hur with bucket seats." There are tracks at *Portmarnock* in County Dublin and at *Whitehouse* in County Antrim. But nowhere do the locals get into the cut and thrust of sulky racing with the zest of West Cork. The 2-day event at *Leap*, which takes place in a 25-acre field every May, is the biggest of dozens of races all around the country; there are about a thousand spectators and three bookies, and the last few yards of the *Kentucky Derby* won't beat it for heart-stopping tension. Details: *Irish Trotting and Harness Racing Federation,* c/o James Connolly, Maugh House, Dunmanway, County Cork, Irish Republic (phone: 23-45360).

CARRIAGE DRIVING: It would be easy to jump to the conclusion that this is a sport befitting only well-heeled nincompoops, but there's a lot more to it. This can be seen clearly by a visit to the Irish championships, a 2-day all-Ireland event that takes place at the end of August or early September on the splendidly scenic, 1,000-acre demesne of 17th-century Birr Castle, under the auspices of its owner, the Earl of Rosse and his wife, the Countess of Rosse (who is British Princess Margaret's former mother-in-law). The 18-mile-long marathon course along the roads, through the fields, and even in and across streams is ferocious; some riverbanks, for instance, appear to deviate little from the vertical. And the little Shetland ponies that draw the carriages (unprepossessing conveyances that are really more like traps) have to turn into hairy submarines, moving virtually underwater, with only nostrils and ear tips showing, along the bed of the fast-flowing Camcor and Little Brosna rivers. The grounds alone would be worth the trip: The trees are in fine color, and the tall boxwood hedges — the world's tallest, according to *The Guinness Book of World Records* — are as wonderfully fragrant as ever. Details: *Cloonanagh, Silvermines,* c/o Mr. and Mrs. C. H. Powell, Nenagh, County Tipperary, Irish Republic (phone: 67-25256).

Wonderful Waterways and Coastal Cruises

Ireland is a delightfully watery place in the pleasantest possible way. No point is more than 70 miles from the nearest seashore, and the entire country is crisscrossed by rivers and canals and dotted with lakes. As a result, boats play an important role in the lives of many Irish families. Often, they're simply the most convenient way to fish the clear waters, whether fresh or salt. But the calm waters of ancient canals and the challenging seas of the rugged Atlantic seaboard alike also provide access to a whole world of recreation.

The national sailing and boating magazine, *Alfloat* (Shamrock House, Upper Kilmacud Rd., Dundrum, Dublin 14, Irish Republic; phone: 1-988696), provides information on what's going on in every corner of the boating world, at all levels of interest and experience.

SAILING

Sailing has long been a popular Irish sport, thanks to good breezes, excellent waters, a 2,000-mile shoreline, and an almost infinite choice of possible anchorages. For instance, on the most popular cruising coastline, the handsome southwestern seaboard between sheltered Cork Harbour and the impressive Blasket Islands (known informally as "the last parish before America"), it's reckoned that there are 143 different places to tie up, no two alike — and that's just for a quarter of the coastline. Other areas can offer as much variety, and each section of the seas can range from millpond-calm to rough, hard, and roiling; the variety is part of the challenge.

GETTING INFORMATION: The national sailing and boating authority in the Irish Republic is the *Irish Yachting Association* (3 Park Rd., Dún Laoghaire, County Dublin; phone: 1-800239). It provides the first point of contact to the 120 yacht and sailing clubs that play a pivotal role in the country's life afloat. In Northern Ireland, the same function is served by the *Royal Yachting Association* (House of Sport, Upper Malone Rd., Belfast BT9, Northern Ireland; phone: 232-661222). The organizations maintain close ties with each other, as sailing and boating here is essentially an all-Ireland affair, carried on in the friendliest style.

CLUBS: Clubs have played a paramount role in the Irish sailing scene ever since the days of the *Water Club* and its gallant pioneers. And all of them, from the smallest to the grandest, maintain a busy annual program in addition to the active social schedule that has made the Irish après-sailing atmosphere famous among European yachtsmen. Even the *Royal Cork Yacht Club* (Crosshaven, County Cork, Irish Republic; phone: 21-831440), a direct descendant of the old Water Club and the world's senior sailing organization, wears its years lightly and is most hospitable and entertaining.

For visitors, one of the fascinations of sailing in Ireland lies in savoring the different character of the many clubs: on the east coast, the modern *Royal Cork* (address above) and the nearby *Kinsale Yacht Club* (Lower O'Connell St., Kinsale, County Cork; phone: 21-772196), the strikingly contemporary club at Howth, and, in Northern Ireland, the up-to-date harbors at Carrickfergus and Belfast Lough at Bangor in County Down. In Dún Laoghaire, on Dublin Bay, where a huge artificial harbor is home to hundreds of boats, stately yacht clubs with imposing façades line the waterfront with style; elegant reminders of the 19th century though they are, they are welcoming, energetic, and imaginative organizations.

EVENTS: In the early part of the season, during May and June, activity rapidly develops around the main clubs with a hectic program of regional championships, offshore races, and local regattas. Then, during July, the pace quickens with race weeks involving large fleets of cruiser-racers, not only from Ireland but also from abroad. Events of this period include the following:

> *The Round Ireland Race* takes place under the auspices of the *Wicklow Sailing Club* (The Quay, Wicklow, County Wicklow, Irish Republic; phone: 404-67526) and covers 704 nautical miles around the nation's coast. June.
>
> *Cork Week* is staged by the *Royal Cork Yacht Club* (address above) in even years. This includes the *European Offshore Team Championship,* a colorful affair that attracts teams from every continent. July.
>
> *Isora Week* takes place in the Irish Sea in odd-numbered years, alternating between England and Ireland. It's administered by the *Irish Sea Offshore Racing Association* (119 Chelwood Ave., Liverpool L16 2LL, England). July.
>
> *Bangor Offshore Week* is the premier regatta series in Northern Ireland, run by the North's senior club, the *Royal Ulster Yacht Club* (Clifton Rd., Bangor, County Down, Northern Ireland; phone: Bangor 465568). It takes place in July in odd-numbered years.

Later, the emphasis turns from sailing centers near large urban areas to more remote coasts, and the first week of August brings with it a highly entertaining program of rural regattas along the incomparable West Cork seaboard. Dinghy championships are staged at attractive venues such as Sligo, Dunmore East, and Baltimore. And an extensive board-sailing calendar makes a colorful contribution.

At summer's end, though many boats head for home, autumn leagues begin attracting huge fleets to centers such as Cork Harbour, Howth, Lough Belfast, and Strangford Lough. Fall may be the busiest sailing time of all.

SAILING SCHOOLS: More fun than watching is doing it yourself — and, unbeknown to most, Ireland is an excellent place to learn. Week-long sailing courses in dinghies and cruisers, for novices and more advanced sailors alike, are available at dozens of sailing schools and clubs. Administering many of these in the Republic is the *Irish Association for Sail Training* (c/o Confederation House, Kildare St., Dublin 2;

phone: 1-779801). For Northern Ireland, the same service is provided by the *Royal Yachting Association* (*House of Sport*, Upper Malone Rd., Belfast BT9 5LA; phone: 232-661222). Sailing schools such as the following mirror the variety of the clubs:

Baltimore Sailing School, The Pier, Baltimore, County Cork, Irish Republic (phone: 28-20141). Sailing instruction here uses traditional craft and modern dinghies among Carbery's Hundred Isles and around Baltimore, Crookhaven, and Cork.

Bangor Sailing School, 13 Gray's Hill Rd., Bangor, County Down, Northern Ireland (phone: John Irwin, 247-455967). Skippered sails around Lough Belfast, and instruction in cruising. Cruisers, dinghies, canoes, and pedal boats for hire.

Craigavon Water Sports Centre Sailing School, Craigavon Lakes, Portadown, Craigavon, County Armagh, Northern Ireland (phone: 762-342669). Activities here take place on 170-acre Craigavon Lake, not far from several bird sanctuaries and 153-square-mile Lough Neagh, the largest lake in Britain and Ireland.

Dún Laoghaire Sailing School, 115 Lower Georges St., Dún Laoghaire, County Dublin, Irish Republic (phone: 1-806654). This school's extensive course offerings range from 3-hour dinghy instruction to cruises in the Irish Sea and to the Isle of Man.

Fingal Sailing School, Upper Strand Rd., Malahide, County Dublin, Irish Republic (phone: 1-451979). Sailing and windsurfing instruction is available on the safe Broadmeadow Estuary, as well as in Malahide Inlet and along the coast from Howth to Skerries.

Glenans Irish Sailing Center, 28 Merrion Sq., Dublin 2, Irish Republic (phone: 1-611481). Though associated with the famous French sail training group of the same name, this organization has a uniquely Irish character. Bases are located at Baltimore, on Bere Island, and in island-studded Clew Bay on the west coast, and the range of courses for everyone, from absolute beginners through the most experienced offshore sailors, is remarkably comprehensive.

International Sailing Centre, 5 East Beach, Cobh, County Cork, Irish Republic (phone: 21-811237). The ancestors of many Americans bade farewell to the Emerald Isle from Cobh, whose seafaring tradition goes back centuries. Nowadays, *International Sailing Centre* programs visit hidden creeks and wooden coves once frequented by topsail schooners. Sailing, windsurfing, and cruising holidays are available, and lodgings range from simple bunkhouses to comfortable hotels.

Knights Water Sports Centre, Dromineer, Nenagh, County Tipperary, Irish Republic (phone: 67-24295). This family-run sailing school is based on one of Ireland's largest and most attractive lakes, Lough Derg (described in more detail below in the entry on the river Shannon). Fully equipped sailing cruisers can be hired for holidays afloat through an associate company, *Shannon Sailing* (same address and phone as above).

Ulster Cruising School, Carrickfergus Marina, Carrickfergus, County Antrim, Northern Ireland (phone: 9603-68818). This organization offers special pre-flotilla cruise training, offshore sailing in the Irish Sea and the Scottish Hebrides, and other active holidays.

ON YOUR OWN: Crews who wish to make their own way to the many harbors and anchorages around Ireland's coast will find the venerable *Irish Cruising Club*'s two-volume *Sailing Directions* indispensable. The books are available from good nautical booksellers or direct from the club's Honorary Publications Officer (Mrs. Barbara Fox-Mills, The Tansey, Baily, County Dublin, Irish Republic; phone: 1-322823). For information on charters, contact the Irish Tourist Board.

CRUISING THE INLAND WATERWAYS

Complementing the salty waters of Ireland's coast is one of the most fascinating systems of inland waterways in Europe; its fresh, clear, unpolluted waters are one of Ireland's secret attractions. These can be explored gently by charter boats, widely available for hire on the main waterways. From fishing, floating, and feasting while on the water to stops at restaurants and pubs en route, cruising is simple, idyllic, and restorative. It reveals a quieter, more private facet of Ireland's character, and it provides a most unusual way to get to know the people (especially at cruises-in-company, such as the week-long *Shannon Boat Rally* organized by the *Inland Waterways Association of Ireland* every July).

The *Inland Waterways Association of Ireland* (*AWAI*) is responsible for coordinating all inland waterway activities. It is active in the promotion, preservation, and restoration of the canal and river system, and can be contacted in care of its secretary, Stone Cottage, Claremount Rd., Killiney, County Dublin (phone: 1-852258).

THE RIVER SHANNON, Irish Republic: Although the longest river in Ireland, this ancient waterway may seem small by worldwide standards since its navigable sector, which curves westward to the sea from the center of the country, comprises only 140 miles. Nevertheless, the Shannon's quiet majesty as it flows with the tranquillity of a canal between low-lying shores and then swells into vast lakes as temperamental as the ocean itself makes the traditional sobriquet "the lordly Shannon" seem not at all inappropriate. And in actuality, the system is so extensive that overcrowding is well-nigh impossible. For in addition to the riverine portions, it includes three lakes — not only the large Lough Key but also Loughs Ree and Derg, which themselves are practically inland seas. Measuring some 25 miles long and an average 2 to 3 miles across, Derg in particular is a world unto itself, its lovely coastline dotted with delightful miniature ports, each with its own little harbor built to shelter cargo barges in times past and now home to fleets of power and sailing cruisers. Just beyond the banks, soft hills rise green and cool. Nearby there is access to the placid 80-mile-long Grand Canal, a once-bustling commercial link between Dublin and the river Shannon and the even quieter river Barrow. The canal winds between grassy banks speckled with the blossoms of yellow irises, orchids, and daisies in season; sometimes great vistas open up onto the rolling pastureland or wide bogs, sometimes the vegetation closes in like an emerald tunnel. The Barrow, for its part, meanders southward through the southeastern corner of the country, a hidden area of lush farmland, gentle woods, and ancient castles, and ends at the sea near Waterford. Amateur botanists, ornithologists, and peripatetic archaeologists alike should have a field day; there are wildflowers here that do not grow anywhere else in Ireland, as well as herons, swans, curlew, grebes, cormorants, and dozens of other birds.

For particulars, consult the *Inland Waterways Association of Ireland Guide to the Grand Canal and Barrow River* (about $5), the *Shell Guide to the Shannon* (about $20), and other books available in leading bookstores throughout Ireland. Self-skippered charter boats can be rented through several organizations; the Irish Tourist Board can send a complete list. Luxurious hotel-boat cruises, with skipper, meals, and cabins with bath, are also available; for details, contact *Cruise Company, McGregor Travel* (33 Lewis St., Greenwich, CT 06830; phone: 203-622-0203 or 800-825-0826) or *Shannon River Flotels, Ltd* (Killaloe, County Clare, Irish Republic; phone: 61-76364).

LOUGH ERNE, Northern Ireland: Unlike the Shannon and the Barrow, the two huge island-studded lakes that make up the Erne system provide no direct access to the sea, but they are full of character nonetheless — the upper lake a hidden place of winding channels and dense mazes of islands (a few with lakes of their own), the lower lake a majestic place of open water, wide skyscapes, and spectacular scenery. A cruise that takes in the pair is an idyll for anglers, bird watchers, and lovers of wildflowers and churches, castles, caves, ruined monasteries, round towers, and mysterious pagan statues — all of which can be found here, along with dozens of coves and inlets, good hotels, tackle shops, and charter boat operators.

The free booklet *Holidays Afloat and Ashore on the Erne Waterway* will sketch the possibilities. To get a copy, contact the *Erne Charter Boat Association,* Lakeland Visitor Centre, Shore Rd., Enniskillen, County Fermanagh, Northern Ireland (phone: 365-23110).

RIVER BANN, Northern Ireland: In itself, the river Bann would make for a pleasant cruise, with its flourishing bird and plant life, its sedgy shoreline, its uninhabited islets, the thatched shoreside villages where old-fashioned customs maintain their hold just a bit longer than they do elsewhere. But the available cruising grounds multiply, encompassing some 150 square miles, if they include the lake from which the river emerges, Lough Neagh. The largest lake in the British Isles, Neagh supposedly was created when Finn MacCool scooped out a giant-size clod of earth and tossed it into the Irish Sea. According to the same mythology, its depths are the home of Eochu, lord of the underworld, but if that be the case, the sunny beauties of the scenery on a fine day give no hint of it. The wide-open spaces, making up with windswept grandeur what is lost in charming intimacy, are full of the special peace that gentle travel over calm waters can bring.

For more information, contact the Northern Ireland Tourist Board.

Gone Fishing

 Travelers to Ireland can appreciate what outdoor writers really mean when they talk about a "watery kingdom." In this island's 32,000 square miles, there are 9,000 miles of river and over 600,000 acres of lakes (or loughs, as the Irish call the better ones to distinguish them from the English lakes, which they deem inferior), for a total of about an acre of water for every 35 of land. Visitors who cannot find something to dilute their whiskey — and somewhere to wet their line — have only themselves to blame.

Almost all of this water holds fish, and very good fish they are. The limestone bedrock that lies inland from the mostly granite mountains of the Irish coast, which enriches the grass with the bone-building calcium on which the nation's horses thrive, also creates just the right acid balance in the waters that gurgle down from the undulating hills and through the pastures. Under such conditions, the wild brown trout, as well as pike and coarse, are the best in Europe.

It is the sheer number of wild fish, not to mention their fecundity, that sets Ireland apart from the rest of Europe as a prime destination for the freshwater angling enthusiast. The clarity and purity of the waters are also notable: The local fisheries, though not entirely pollution-free, have never been subjected to a great industrial revolution. So the wild fish have survived, to be caught today by anglers in sufficient numbers to make the angling here more than just a bit special.

Irish mountain freshets bear little in the way of food when they make their way to the coastal waters downstream, so the brown trout there do not get fat. But what they lack in size is made up for in heart. The bigger ones, weighing half a pound, create such a fuss at the business end of the tackle when they take the fly and fight so hard for their freedom that the discerning, experienced angler will happily agree with the novice as to the marvels of Irish sport. The salmon and sea trout angler awaits the return of these migratory species to the scenic fresh waters with the eagerness of a child at *Christmas.*

Angling is considered an important tourist activity in the Irish Republic, and the Irish Tourist Board has worked with regional fishery boards to develop the nation's angling to a very high standard, giving attention not only to water management but also to access, parking, bankside facilities such as stiles, footbridges, and platforms, and, on loughs, good moorings, convenient slipways for put-in, and a reasonable supply of rental boats and "ghillies," as guides are generally known here. In addition, the board has given its stamp of approval to a number of salmon, trout, pike, and coarse fishing waters that offer visitors good facilities and reliably good sport. These fisheries are indicated by a special Angling Tourism logo in board literature.

The *Central Fisheries Board* (Mobhi Boreen, Glasnevin, Dublin 9; phone: 1-379206) can provide a vast amount of information about the Irish fishing scene. The Northern Ireland Tourist Board provides comparable services for the six counties in conjunction with the *Department of Agriculture* (Fisheries Division, Stormont, Belfast BT4 3TA; phone: 232-63939), the ultimate authority on the nation's fisheries.

GAME ANGLING

The typical game fisherman has catholic tastes when it comes to the different species. He goes for salmon and brown trout, sea trout and stocked rainbows alike, and he finds them all in Ireland within a remarkably small area. Moreover, since even the heartland of the island is less than 70 miles from the sea, he can salt his game fishing vacation with a day of angling offshore, just for good measure.

BROWN AND SEA TROUT: These fish abound in both rivers and loughs. Sea trout fisheries are all along the coastline, with counties Kerry, Galway, Mayo, Sligo, and Donegal the standouts of those along the Atlantic (and Waterford and Cork providing reasonable sport). The rivers Fane in County Louth, Boyne in County Meath, and Slaney in County Wexford are the most notable of those along the Irish Sea coastline, but there is heavy local club demand.

In Northern Ireland, there is acceptable sea trout fishing near the mouth of the Upper Bann and plenty of brown trout action on the Lower Bann, the Ballinderry, the Moyola, the Maine, and the Blackwater — all rivers that feed 150-square-mile Lough Neagh, the largest lake in Ireland, itself seldom fished with rod and line since most anglers stick to feeder streams. The rivers in the narrow, picturesque valleys known as the Glens of Antrim have good runs of sea trout in July and August. Lough Melvin, in the west, is worth a special visit since it also contains three unique trout species — the sonaghan, the gillaroo, and the ferox — as well as an Ice Age predecessor of trout known as the char.

Throughout the area, Irish sea trout weigh in at a pound on the average — less than those in, say, Scottish waters, but they're tremendous fighters nonetheless. And at about the end of June and into the first week of July, when they start returning to the fresh waters (with the bigger ones leading the way), 3- and 4-pounders are pretty common on fly. For the rest of the season, sea trout offer excellent sport; the fact that they can be taken the day long on Irish rivers and loughs gives the Emerald Isle a special allure. When to go? Never before the final week in June or early July, except perhaps to the Waterville Fishery in County Kerry, which experiences an early run, and never after the close of the season, which is October 12 in most locations.

Brown trout are found almost everywhere. On the better brown trout rivers, the angler will come across enough fish in the ¾-pound range to satisfy, while 2- and 3-pounders are always a possibility to the fly and spinner, and even bigger ones make their presence felt to those fishing the depths with heavy metal or worms. Meanwhile, in loughs, fish of a pound are about average to the fly and spinner, and 2- to 4-pounders are not uncommon. Dapping natural flies brings bigger trout to the surface, especially at mayfly time. A number of fish weighing in at above 10 pounds are taken on the deep troll — but this method is not very popular with the Irish. The season opens on February 15 in many fisheries (though it may be wise to delay visiting until April). Sport is available in one place or another through September.

Stream Trouting – There is a whole world waiting visiting brook, stream, and river angler, much of it to be enjoyed in undisturbed peace. This is because Ireland has a very small population and, particularly on weekdays, the native angler will be at the office.

Fly life on Irish rivers is not widely found until April, except for some large dark olives (adults), which anglers endeavor to simulate with dark olive quill, rough olive, and Greenwells glory patterns. There are also plentiful shrimp, and the March brown and Wickhams fancy are popular artificials. Natural fly becomes more abundant in April, the month of the medium black olive dun, the rough olive, and especially the iron blue dun and jenny spinner. The black duck fly chironimid and a variety of midges and buzzers also appear at this time.

Of the May olives, the iron blue is the most common. It shares the water surface with gray flag, brown flag, and gray Wulff silver sedges, and green drake, gray drake, and spent gnat mayflies in some rivers. Fish feed throughout the day in May, especially on warm evenings.

In June, sedges produce the most exciting sport, with the best fishing in the evening. Spent mayflies, olives, and midges will also be attracting the brown trout's notice.

Conditions are never very good on Irish rivers in July and August. A combination of low water, heavy weed, and occasional sultry weather affects the sport. Olives, sedges, midges, and terrestrials, such as daddy-longlegs, grasshoppers, and white moths, are always evident, but it may take the blue-winged olive and its spent fly (the sherry spinner) to do the trick at dusk. Artificial patterns of the pale watery are also worth trying where there is an August hatch, and some rivers will offer an opportunity for those who can tie a nice brown or red ant pattern.

Weather conditions in September are more favorable, and wet-fly sedge patterns nearly always score.

All legal methods are allowed on most waters, though some, particularly those that are also sea trout rivers, may be confined to fly.

Lough Trouting – All legal methods are allowed on the Republic's loughs, but at certain times some may be limited to fly only. Check with the relevant fishery board. Wet-fly fishing is the norm, but it is different from that practiced in Europe, the US, and many parts of Britain. Anglers fishing on British waters, for instance, must fish deep because of poor water quality, among other reasons, and use all kinds of streamers, dog-hobblers, and weighted nymphs on sinking lines to tease the deep-lying trout.

On Irish loughs, by contrast, floating line and three wet flies, size 10 to 12, are generally used. The fly nearest the rod tip is bobbed along to attract attention and is fished partly dry and partly in the surface film. This is traditional lough wet-fly fishing — and it's a league apart from streamer and lure fishing which, if everyone were honest, would not be termed fly fishing at all.

Fish take at water surface level or in the surface film, which makes for much more excitement. And anglers have a choice of many good and varied drifts and hot spots since, in many loughs, the shallows are not confined to the shore but are scattered here and there, often around the many islands that add such color to Ireland's great bodies of waters.

There are times when, for one reason or another, the fish lie deep. Then, Irish lough anglers may fish a sinking line or a sink-tip, or if conditions are totally against fly angling, they may troll a bait.

Dry-fly anglers also have success on the loughs, though fishing the dry artificial is the exception rather than the rule. A most interesting form of angling known as dapping

— one born among the Irish, extremely popular here, and not used to any great extent elsewhere — often outscores other techniques. Brown trout, sea trout, and salmon all take the dapped insect. And both brown and sea trout that come to the dapped mayfly tend to be larger than those that take wet flies.

Particularly common on the rich limestone loughs or lakes, dapping involves the angler letting his bait drop lightly along the crest of waves while drifting broadside on the breeze and holding the rod tip high so that the bait — live aquatic insects — are carried away from him. A light rod at least 13 feet long is used, with monofilament or blow line and either a large center-pin dapping reel or a spinning reel. At the end of the tackle, a small hook, size 14, is either spliced to the monofilament or eye-tied, and the live insect is attached to the hook. Hooking the fish once it bites demands skill: Since the dapped insect is a natural, the fish must be allowed to take it completely before the angler tries to land it — or the line will not be tight.

Although the lough fishing season opens in February, visitors would be wise to stay home until April. Given mild weather, April can be a great fishing month, especially on Lough Corrib, where duck fly hatches generate great sport. There are generous hatches of other buzzers also, and lake olives become more numerous during April. May and June can be marvelous if conditions are suitable. Good hatches of brighter olives, sedges, buzzers, and the eagerly awaited mayfly provide the best fishing of the year.

Beginning in June, terrestrials find their way onto the water surface, and dapping them — or imitating them with wet- and dry-fly patterns — can provide good creels. Brown trout loughs tend to be a bit less productive during July and early August, except in evenings and early mornings; but fishing can be very lively from the second half of August to the end of the season.

Lough sea trouting offers very special sport from July onward. While a number of sea trout fisheries close on October 1, some stay open through October 12. They are worth a visit, if only because of the scenery (though it would be a very unlucky visiting angler who took home nothing more than memories of pretty landscapes).

Exclusivity again is the name of the game on the Republic's sea trout loughs. The number of boats is limited and, in some cases, the loughs are actually divided into boat beats. For Northern Ireland particulars, contact the *Department of Agriculture* (address above).

Trouting Regulations – In the Republic, state fishing licenses are necessary to fish for both sea trout (a 21-day license, which also covers salmon fishing, costs about $35) and brown trout (a 21-day license costs about $15). Many of the better brown trout rivers and most sea trout rivers are controlled by clubs, and a bag limit may apply. In both instances, visitors are generally welcome, especially on commercially run fisheries, and permission to fish is granted by day or week at about $5 a day on club brown trout streams, slightly more on club sea trout stretches (though on the better sea trout rivers the cost to tourists runs from about $15 to $30 a day — a tremendous value compared with the costs of such exclusivity elsewhere). Many sea trouting streams in the Republic are divided into beats, so the angler has a stretch of possibly a mile or more to himself. Alternatively, the number of rods on the river is strictly measured and controlled.

On many of the best loughs for brown trout, fishing is usually free or available at a nominal charge; loughs under the control of the country's Central or Regional Fisheries boards, for example, can be fished by applying to these organizations for an annual membership in the *Central Fisheries Board* (currently about $15) or by purchasing a day ticket (about $3).

In Northern Ireland, rod licenses are required for brown trout fishing. Many of the waters, including some of the best, are owned and managed by the *Department of Agriculture* (address above), and the permits that are required to fish them (separate from and in addition to rod licenses) are relatively inexpensive — about $10 to $25. The only other cost the angler will incur to fish on a lough is for the hire of a boat — a must — which runs about $25, with an additional $10 charge for one with an outboard engine, or $50 for a package that includes boat, engine, and guide-boatman, the optimal situation. For sea trout fishing, permits are necessary for some waters but not for others. To find out what's required, contact the *Department of Agriculture* (address above); the *Foyle Fisheries Commission* (8 Victoria Rd., Londonderry, County Derry; phone: 504-42100), which controls many waters drained by the Foyle-Mourne-Camowen system, in the northwest of the country; and the *Fisheries Conservancy Board* (1 Mahon Rd., Portadown, County Armagh BT62 3EE; phone: 76-233-4666), which covers the rest of the country.

SALMON: The failure on the part of successive governments in the Republic to introduce a program to ensure a reasonable stock of freshwater fish has taken its toll on wild salmon stocks in the Irish Republic, and spring runs have dwindled to almost nothing. This is sad, since Ireland is responsible for maintaining a considerable percentage of the world's wild Atlantic salmon. Between 1964 and 1975, its contribution to the overall international catch averaged 20% — twice that today. Still, angling for summer salmon and grilse can be good at times, even by international standards. The fish put up a fierce fight, and the cost is a fraction of what anglers would pay in Scotland for the same sport.

Due to the moderating influence of the nearby Gulf Stream, among other factors, the Irish salmon angling season opens as early as the first of January. And since rivers are hardly ever covered with ice here, angling is possible as early as *New Year's Day.* In fact, there usually is some national interest in the season's first salmon from the three rivers that open then — the Liffey (which gives Dublin the distinction of being the only capital where salmon can be caught within the city limits), the Garavogue in Sligo, and the Bundrowes, just 20 miles north of Garavogue, near Bundoran.

Angling opens on a number of other rivers in February and March — most notably the Slaney, Nore, Barrow, the big Munster or Cork Blackwater, Laune, Caragh (Upper and Lower), Waterville system (including the river Inny), Lower Shannon, Corrib, the Bundowragha (part of Connemara's Delphi fishery), and the Owenmore in County Mayo. These are later joined by two other noteworthy Mayo rivers, the Newport and the Moy, which open in April.

Spinning is most popular with Irish anglers on these spring fisheries, where salmon average around 12 pounds and occasionally come in at 15 and 30 pounds. Prawning and worming are also common. Fly fishing with sunken line, with large flies in sizes 2 and 4, and with tube flies will get results whenever conditions are suitable, but the number of early season fly anglers, like the spring salmon, has shown a dramatic decline.

Beginning in late May, certainly by June, the grilse arrive; mature, undersized fish coming inland to spawn for the first time, they dominate the catches for the rest of the season. There is a good supply of summer salmon from as early as April.

Most of the spring fisheries also offer summer angling, but spate fisheries, their waters entirely dependent on flood to provide sufficient water for fish to travel upstream and take freely, account for a considerable portion of the sport. They are unpredictable, but when conditions are right, even the wildest of angling dreams can be realized, and six or seven salmon to a rod is far from unusual; double those numbers are achieved by locals who know how best to tease or coax a take.

The Connemara and Mayo fisheries, where salmon and sea trout generally share, are the big attractions in summer. The *Ballynahinch Castle* hotel fishery (Ballynahinch; phone: 95-31006), the river Erriff, the river Corrib's *Galway Weir Fishery,* and Ballycroy and Burrishoole from July onward are the prime salmon waters that also turn up thousands of sea trout. Add to these the aforementioned spring fisheries and throw in the famed Costelloe, Inver, Gowla, Kylemore, and a few Upper Ballynahinch sea trout gems, where occasional salmon also show, to assemble a truly marvelous selection.

There is also some spring and summer lough salmon angling to be enjoyed — a considerable amount of it on the systems and fisheries mentioned above.

In Northern Ireland, open seasons are April to October 20 for rivers in the Foyle area (from March 1 on loughs), February 1 to September 30 in *Fisheries Conservancy Board* waters such as Lough Melvin (from March 1 for the Erne system), and March through October for the rest, with exceptions here and there.

Regulations and Methods – Required at all times when fishing for salmon in the Republic is a state salmon license (which also covers sea trout and can be purchased in tackle shops or through the fisheries' boards). A 21-day license costs about $35. In addition, though some salmon angling is free (for instance, on the great brown trout loughs such as Melvin, Conn, Corrib, Currane, and Gill, where there are also salmon), other waters are privately held, and permission to fish entails a charge. In general, figure that a day's salmon or sea trout angling will cost about $25 to $35 per rod, occasionally more, including, on the loughs, a guide and boat. On rivers, the ghillie's services cost another $30 for two or more rods.

In Northern Ireland, rod licenses are necessary for salmon, and permits may be necessary in addition. Contact the *Department of Agriculture* (address above) and the Northern Ireland Tourist Board for details.

From March through June and in July and September, the best months for salmon angling, bring a single-handed rod that can cast an 8-to-10 line and 11-pound leader. A double-handed 13-to-15-foot rod can be a godsend on some waters in summer and is always required in spring. The leader to the sunken line for the springers should be at least 15 pounds.

Good spring fly patterns, mostly size 4, include the thunder and lightning, spring blue, Jock Scott, fiery brown, hairy Mary, butcher, black doctor fenian, and the various shrimp. The silver doctor, hairy Mary, blue charm, gray dog, black goldfinch, and shrimp patterns in small sizes, 4 to 9, according to water conditions, score most in summer — nearly always on a floating line. Favorite low-water patterns are the black widow, blue charm, March brown, fiery brown, Lady Caroline, and shrimps in sizes 7 to 10. Dry flies are little used for salmon, but tube flies are popular.

Wading is always necessary in spring, seldom in summer. However, quite a number of fisheries have casting platforms or other improvements that make it nearly possible to fish in shoes. However, short rubber boots, hip waders, or Wellingtons are the norm. And since the better-presented fly often means wading, chest waders are helpful.

COARSE FISHING

All the fish in freshwater rivers and lakes that are not trout or salmon are lumped into the class of coarse fish. These include bream, carp, chub, dace, perch, roach, rudd, eel, and tench. Some pike anglers, especially Europeans, would include this great predator among the list of game fish. In Ireland, however, the pike must put up with being coarse, though it fights with unbridled ferocity.

All of these breed with wild abandon, feed furiously, and grow fatter practically by the minute. Although recently more and more anglers have discovered the joys of Ireland's slow, deep rivers, its half-dozen great lakes, and its thousands of lesser lakes, many waters are still greatly underfished. The fact that these waters also are freer from pollution than those found almost anywhere else in Europe makes for some truly exceptional angling. Not many Irish fish are as heavy as the 42-pound pike caught in the river Barrow or the 38-pounder caught in Lough Corrib a few years back, but most Irishmen believe that plenty of far bigger fish, particularly pike, lurk in the rivers' depths. Some people say that these giants haven't been caught simply because most fishermen aren't equipped to land them.

In the Irish Republic, the river Erne, which runs into Northern Ireland, offers great coarse fishing, with the major centers to be found at lovely Lough Gowna, the source of the Erne, and the area near Belturbet, County Cavan, between the two lakes. At nearby Foley's Bridge and Drumlane Lake, the action is so lively that some locals swear that everyone catches a fish. The river Barrow, flanked by the kind of supremely pastoral countryside that visitors expect when they go to Ireland, has its best fishing at Graiguenamanagh, County Kilkenny, an attractive village in the shadow of Mount Leinster, once a great monastic center. Best of all is the lordly river Shannon, with its three great lakes — lovely 25-mile Lough Derg, 17-mile Lough Ree, and 7-mile Lough Allen. Some of the best centers are at Mohill, County Leitrim, well-organized Carrick-on-Shannon, and Lanesborough, County Longford, in a famous "hot water" stretch, where catches of bream, rudd, and hybrids running into the hundreds of pounds have been made.

Northern Ireland, though still best known for its game fishing, offers some of Europe's finest coarse fishing as well. On the Upper Bann, the section above Lough Neagh is a standout, and individual anglers regularly catch more than 100 pounds of bream and roach in 5-hour matches. The Lower Bann, north of Lough Neagh, also has fine coarse angling, especially for perch. Also superb is Lough Erne, with its two gigantic loughs: The area around Enniskillen, where the world 5-hour match record is regularly broken, still holds the record of 258 pounds, 9½ ounces — which exceeded the previous record by more than 50 pounds. The Fairy Water, a tributary of the Foyle via the Strule, was the first of Northern Ireland's coarse fisheries to come into the public eye, and it still yields roach in immense quantities. Lough Creeve has proved to have a perch growth rate exceeding that of all other Irish waters. And the Quoile, which flows south from its source not far from Ballynahinch, has made a big splash with its rudd production. Pike fishing, another of the province's attractions, is found at its best in both Loughs Erne and in the two Loughs Macnean and Lough Beg, at the mouth of Lough Neagh.

Information and Regulations – In the Republic, a rod license is now required for course fishing (a 21-day license costs about $8), and there is no closed season. For an abundance of detail about these streams and others, get a copy of the Irish Tourist Board's *Coarse Angling* or contact the *Central Fisheries Board* (address above). Bait is available for purchase. Note: Those who wish to bring their own bait should not pack it in soil or vegetable materials, neither of which can be brought into the country.

In Northern Ireland, anglers usually need a rod license and may also need a permit, depending on the waters to be fished. There is no closed season. *Coarse Fishing in Northern Ireland,* published by the Northern Ireland Tourist Board, gives details.

SEA ANGLING

Ireland has hundreds of miles of ragged coastline where anglers reel in anything from half-pound flounders off a sandy bottom to giant mako sharks in deep waters, or wrasse, pollock, and mackerel from the rocks. No license is necessary, and few advance arrangements are required; tackle can usually be hired; and the chefs in most hotels will cook a guest's prize on request. For trips out over the wrecks and sunken reefs where some of the bigger fish lurk, boats and professional skippers are readily available, and a day's outing with a local who can rendezvous with fish on request can be a most rewarding (and reasonably priced) experience. All that's required is a stomach strong enough for a day on the short, choppy seas. Shore fishing for sea bass with a powerful rod and reel requires a little more equipment — namely good oilskins — since these delicious creatures favor "storm beaches," and the best fishing is done when there's a strong onshore wind that will drench an angler to the skin with salt spray.

In the Republic, though sea angling has been organized only for the last quarter century, about 150 clubs sponsor dozens of fishing competitions throughout the year. The big quarry include shark and skate — blue shark, which can weigh in at over 200 pounds and come around the south and west coasts from mid-June to mid-October; porbeagle shark, the Irish record for which was a 365-pound specimen caught off the Mayo coast; the tough-fighting, hard-to-catch mako shark, which visits the south coast in summer; the common skate, a worthy adversary growing to over 200 pounds, which is at its most plentiful around the south and west coasts in deep water from April to early October; and the somewhat smaller white skate, which favors the western seaboard. Flatfish, halibut, conger, monkfish, mackerel, ling, cod, red sea bream, pollock, ray, turbot, plaice, brill, and flounder can be found around the coast. (Note that there is a conservation order on the common skate, and to preserve the species anglers are asked to return to the water any skate caught alive.) Porbeagle shark, in particular, provide the kind of stomach-tightening fight anglers expect to experience only vicariously.

Centers like Youghal, Kinsale, Crosshaven, Baltimore, and Courtmacsherry rank among the best places to fish in the country. In Kinsale, particularly, the angling is well organized, the town is pretty, and there are numerous good lodging places and fine restaurants. Blue shark, skate, and conger are the quarry.

Also good is Fenit, in County Kerry, where monkfish, ray, conger, and skate can be caught right from the ocean pier; boats take anglers out into the even more productive waters of Tralee Bay for larger specimens.

Green Island at the south of Liscannor Bay in Clare is renowned for its rock fishing; porbeagle shark of around 150 pounds have been landed here. Ballyvaughan and Liscannor (birthplace of the inventor of the submarine), farther up the coast, have boats and tackle for hire.

County Mayo has many major sea angling centers. Clew Bay, with its 365 islands in the shadow of Ireland's holy Croagh Patrick, has fast tides that offer splendid shore fishing, while Westport boasts a number of excellent charter boats that go out for the renowned shark and skate fishing, as well as good angling-oriented hostelries, features that attract many Europeans. Lovely Achill Island, once so favored by English anglers that the coastline resounded with their clipped accents, still has superb deep-sea fishing, and past creels have included a number of record-size shark; the main centers are Purteen Harbour and Darby's Point. Belmullet, the peninsula on the northwest coast, is also famous for its deep-sea action and shore fishing, as are Newport and Killala.

In Northern Ireland, the entire coast offers an abundance of rocky points, piers, estuaries, and storm beaches where the action doesn't get nearly the attention it deserves as some of Ireland's best. An Irish record hake was caught in Lough Belfast, and Lough Carlingford in County Antrim has produced a national record tope (66 pounds, 8 ounces). Off Ballintoy, also in County Antrim, is the very unusual fishing for herring on rods with feathered lures, done at dusk and dawn in May and June. Wreck fishing from Portaferry, at the mouth of Strangford Lough, always guarantees good cod, ling, and conger.

Sea Angling Information and Regulations – No licenses or permits are required for sea angling in the waters of the Republic or Northern Ireland.

Sea Angling, published by the Irish Tourist Board, provides details about what can be caught where, with what, when, and from what in the Republic. The *Irish Federation of Sea Anglers* (c/o Mr. Hugh O'Rourke, 67 Windsor Dr., Monkstown, County Dublin; phone: 1-806873) administers local competitions and can provide details. The *Central Fisheries Board* (address above) can also be helpful.

For Northern Ireland, consult the Tourist Board's *Sea Fishing Off Northern Ireland,* a good guide to the possibilities.

FISHING SCHOOLS

Those interested in acquiring or polishing their game fishing techniques have several alternatives in Ireland. A number of salmon and trout ghillies (guides) on the Dempster Fishery and the Blackwater Lodge·Fishery (both on the Munster Blackwater) can instruct in casting and advise on techniques if requested. And in spring, quite a few angling clubs offer courses to members covering the same topics, along with fly tying and entomology. In addition, a number of establishments offer formal angling schools.

BALLYNAHINCH CASTLE, Ballinafad, County Galway, Irish Republic: Casting, fly presentation, and fishing the two-handed rod for salmon are a few of the issues addressed in this week-long school, which convened for the first time in 1987. Practice and instruction are on the Owenmore River, the outlet for the Ballynahinch system. Lodging is available on premises. Details: *Ballynahinch Castle Hotel,* Ballinafad, County Galway, Irish Republic (phone: 95-31006).

ASHFORD CASTLE, Cong, County Mayo, Irish Republic: The internationally known instructors Lee and Joan Wulff head this hotel's program, aimed at improving the casting techniques of American anglers with the single-handed rod, but instructors conversant in Irish methods and techniques are also on hand. Coverage includes stream entomology, water reading, tackle, wading, playing, fly tying, and landing and releasing. Boat angling is done on Lough Corrib, on the edge of the lawns of this fine castle hotel, and stream practice is on the Ballynahinch, Burrishoole, and Delphi salmon and sea trout waters, as well as on the Cong River, a salmon and brown trout stream. Details: *Ashford Castle,* Cong, County Mayo, Irish Republic (phone: 92-46003).

PONTOON BRIDGE, Pontoon, near Foxford, County Mayo, Irish Republic: Held weekly from May to October, courses here cover all areas of casting with fly and spinner for salmon and trout, as well as tuition in float fishing if requested. Students also attend slide-illustrated lectures, receive an introduction to fly tying and entomology, and are instructed in boat and bank angling by Michael Waller, member of the Freshwater Biological Association, and Margaret Cockburn, a fly-tying specialist. The hotel occupies a narrow strip of land between loughs Conn and Cullin, two fine fisheries in the river Moy system, where there is plenty of good brown trout and salmon angling. Details: *Pontoon Bridge Hotel,* Pontoon, near Foxford, County Mayo, Irish Republic (phone: 94-56120 or 94-56151).

MOUNT JULIET FISHING ACADEMY, Thomastown, County Kilkenny, Irish Republic: Slated to open in February or March of this year, this new salmon angling center offers professional instruction to beginning and experienced fishermen alike. Three lakes are maintained and fully stocked for students. In addition, two rivers — the Nore and its tributary, the King's — run through the estate, providing over 2 miles of riverside fishing, including 16 pools that have produced record catches in recent years. Packages include overnight accommodations and meals at the manor house on the estate. Details: *Mount Juliet Fishing Academy,* Thomastown, County Kilkenny, Irish Republic (phone: 56-24522).

FISHING HOTELS

A fishing vacation can be even more pleasant if it includes accommodation in an establishment whose management knows how to meet an angler's needs. One of the beauties of the Irish angling scene is that such hostelries are numerous. They often control rights to stretches of nearby streams; when they don't, they can help make the necessary arrangements. They can also provide fishing maps, information on fishing conditions, and facilities for storing gear or for drying wet clothes overnight. And they may even time meals to suit anglers' habits. Information about town and country houses and guest farms that offer such facilities is available from two sources:

> *Town and Country Homes Association,* Killeaden, Bundoran Rd., Ballyshannon, County Donegal, Irish Republic (phone: 72-51377 or 72-51653).
> *Irish Farm Holidays Association,* Desert House, Clonakilty, County Cork, Irish Republic (phone: 23-33331).

The following hotels and guesthouses with facilities for anglers make a good beginning. Below, we list them alphabetically by county.

DROMOLAND CASTLE, Newmarket-on-Fergus, County Clare, Irish Republic: In a 400-acre park, only 8 miles from Shannon Airport, it offers coarse fishing on a lake and trout and late salmon fishing in a small river. This luxuriously appointed hotel (a member of the Relais & Châteaux group) also makes a good base for fishing Lough Derg when the mayfly is up. Details: *Dromoland Castle,* Newmarket-on-Fergus, County Clare, Irish Republic (phone: 61-71144).

BALLYNAHINCH CASTLE, Ballinafad, County Galway, Irish Republic: For several years the sporting residence of H. H. The Maharajah Jans Sahib of Newanagar, a famous cricketer better known as Rajitsinghi, it is a superb base for the serious salmon, grilse, and sea trout angler. Surrounded by a paradisiacal woods crisscrossed by footpaths, the expertly managed fishery is on the Owenmore River. Its salmon pools are well defined, and the sea trout record is one of Ireland's best. Shooting is also offered. Details: *Ballynahinch Castle Hotel,* Ballinafad, Connemara, County Galway, Irish Republic (phone: 95-31006).

ZETLAND, Cashel Bay, County Galway, Irish Republic: This panoramic hotel established in 1850 overlooking Cashel Bay ranks among the country's most comfortable fishing hotels; the chef is John Prendergast, trained at the Paris Ritz. Certainly, with its traditional turf fires, magnificent views, extensive gardens and lawns, and ambitious kitchen, it does not want for charm. Anglers go for its sea trout fishery, one of the best in the country, on the Gowla fishery's several lakes and rivers. Details: *Zetland Hotel,* Cashel Bay, County Galway, Irish Republic (phone: 95-31111).

ANGLERS REST, Headford, County Galway, Irish Republic: This owner-operated hotel, a few miles from Lough Corrib, boasts a simple, relaxed atmosphere and a long tradition in the care and feeding of anglers. Details: *Anglers Rest Hotel,* Headford, County Galway, Irish Republic (phone: 93-35528).

DOONMORE, Inishbofin Island, County Galway, Irish Republic: A unique site on a beautiful offshore island is only one of the features that has made the Doonmore a favored refuge of deep-sea divers, nature lovers, bird watchers, and artists — not to mention sea anglers, who avail themselves of the hotel's oceangoing boat. Other features include good, unpretentious fare, comfortable accommodations, and friendly management. Details: *Doonmore Hotel,* Inishbofin Island, County Galway, Irish Republic (phone: 95-45804).

KYLEMORE PASS, Kylemore, County Galway, Irish Republic: In addition to a magnificent view from its perch atop one of the Twelve Bens, overlooking Kylemore Lake, guests enjoy the traditional music regularly performed in the hotel bar, the friendly atmosphere, and, above all, the fishing (for sea, river, and lake trout as well as salmon — and for the free brown trout in the hotel's lake). Details: *Kylemore Pass Hotel,* Kylemore, County Galway, Irish Republic (phone: 95-41141).

CORRIB, Oughterard, County Galway, Irish Republic: A popular destination for fishermen because of its proximity to Lough Corrib and the Connemara fisheries — good sources for salmon, sea trout, brook trout, brown trout, and pike. May and

June, the dapping period, are regarded by most local anglers as the best brown trout fishing months. The family-run 26-room hotel is on the western edge of the attractive village; staff can arrange for golf and pony trekking. Details: *Corrib Hotel,* Oughterard, County Galway, Irish Republic (phone: 91-82329 or 91-82204).

CURRAREVAGH HOUSE, Oughterard, County Galway, Irish Republic: This guesthouse, a 19th-century country manor surrounded by woodlands, has long catered to anglers who come to fish for brown trout and grilse when they run in June and July. Details: *Currarevagh House Hotel,* Oughterard, County Galway, Irish Republic (phone: 91-82313).

EGAN'S LAKE, Oughterard, County Galway, Irish Republic: This hotel is in one of the prettiest villages in the west of Ireland, on the shores of 68-square-mile Lough Corrib, the largest free-fishing lake in the British Isles. The mid-May mayfly dapping period produces tremendous creels of salmon and sea trout, the grilse run in mid-June, and pike can be taken year-round, but especially in July. In addition, this family-run hotel — the longest-established in town — can reserve rods on nearby rivers and streams. Details: *Egan's Lake Hotel,* Oughterard, County Galway, Irish Republic (phone: 91-82275).

ROSS LAKE HOUSE, Oughterard, County Galway, Irish Republic: An old Killaguille estate house, this Georgian hotel has taken its name from nearby Ross Lake, which has quite a reputation for pike action; it also adjoins Lough Corrib and the Galway salmon weir fishery. A profusion of amenities, including tennis courts and a sauna, makes it ideal for the angler traveling with a non-fishing spouse. Golf and pony trekking are available locally. Details: *Ross Lake House Hotel,* Rosscahill, Oughterard, County Galway, Irish Republic (phone: 91-80109).

SWEENEY'S OUGHTERARD HOUSE, Oughterard, County Galway, Irish Republic: Owned by the same family since 1913 and occupying a structure dating (in part) from the 18th century, this establishment boasts extensive gardens and a knot of ancient beeches facing the wooded banks of the Owenriff River. There are log and turf fires in the fireplaces, and Irish and classic French cuisine is served in the dining room. Many guests come to angle for free trout, salmon, pike, and perch in Connemara's huge Lough Corrib. Details: *Sweeney's Oughterard House Hotel,* Oughterard, County Galway, Irish Republic (phone: 91-82207).

RENVYLE HOUSE, Renvyle, County Galway, Irish Republic: This hotel-by-the-sea, an excellent choice for the all-around sportsman on holiday with a family, offers trouting on the grounds' Rushduff Lake, as well as shore-fishing, deep-water ocean angling, and, nearby, plenty of action on some fine Connemara sea trout fisheries. Other amenities — on the premises or nearby — include golf, tennis, bowling, horseback riding, snooker, and sauna. Details: *Renvyle House Hotel,* Renvyle, Connemara, County Galway, Irish Republic (phone: 95-43444 or 95-43511).

DUNLOE CASTLE, Gap of Dunloe, County Kerry, Irish Republic: On the grounds of a castle that, along with its historic park and gardens, dates from the 15th century, this luxurious hotel offers elegant decor with splendid period furnishings and amenities such as a heated swimming pool, sauna, tennis courts, and restaurants. To anglers, the prime interest is the river Laune, which flows across the grounds. Salmon season is from mid-January to mid-October, the best periods being from mid-February to the end of July and from mid-August to the close of the season. Trout may be taken from mid-February to mid-October, with the best months from March to July and September and October. Castle is open from April through September. Details: *Dunloe Castle Hotel,* Gap of Dunloe, County Kerry, Irish Republic (phone: 64-44111).

GLENCAR, Glencar, County Kerry, Irish Republic: Salmon, grilse, and brook and brown trout are the sport in the small rocky rivers and rugged mountain lakes in this part of southwestern Ireland. This establishment — which has been one of the country's premier angling hotels for the last century — is a snug, homey place, with plain guest quarters and public rooms ajumble with photos of guests and their catch, antlers, oil paintings in gold frames, and antique furniture from the time of Thomas Sheraton through Queen Victoria, as well as more modern fittings. The best time for salmon fishing is from February to June; for sea trout, from June to September. Details: *Glencar Hotel,* Glencar, County Kerry, Irish Republic (phone: 66-60102).

BUTLER ARMS, Waterville, County Kerry, Irish Republic: Considered one of the country's best fishing hotels almost since it opened more than a century ago, this homey 29-room hotel was a favorite of Charlie Chaplin, who returned annually with his family from the early 1960s into the 1970s. The free salmon and sea trout fishing on Lough Currane — the main attraction — is among Western Europe's best, with optimal periods from the beginning of the season until July. There is sea trout from early May until mid-October, as well as salmon fishing on the Inny, a spate river, when conditions are right. Details: *Butler Arms,* Waterville, County Kerry, Irish Republic (phone: 667-4144).

CURRYHILLS HOUSE, Prosperous, Naas, County Kildare, Irish Republic: A longtime beacon for anglers, this Georgian farmhouse hotel (with a well-regarded restaurant in the Tudor style) is an ideal base from which to head off for some coarse fishing on the Grand Canal, and for 8-to-12-ounce brown trout from local club waters of the river Liffey's middle and upper reaches. Details: *Curryhills House Hotel,* Prosperous, Naas, County Kildare, Irish Republic (phone: 45-68150).

MOUNT JULIET, Thomastown, County Kilkenny, Irish Republic: This 1,466-acre estate boasts two significant rivers, the Nore and its tributary, the King's, with over 2 miles of riverside fishing and 16 pools. The average annual catch of salmon in recent years stands at 257 pounds; the heaviest individual salmon weighed 22 pounds; the average, 9 pounds. Countless trout have been caught, too. Slated to open in February or March of this year, a new fishing academy is also being launched, offering professional instruction at all levels. Packages include equipment and instruction, if needed, and overnight accommodations and meals in the manor house estate. Salmon season runs from June to September; trout, March to September. Details: *Mount Juliet,* Thomastown, County Kilkenny, Irish Republic (phone: 56-24455).

DOWNHILL, Ballina, County Mayo, Irish Republic: Anglers can make arrangements to go for salmon in the pools on the river Moy and for saltwater fish in the ocean, while other family members enjoy a heated pool, squash, sauna, Jacuzzi, and golf on three 18-hole courses. Details: *Downhill Hotel,* Ballina, County Mayo, Irish Republic (phone: 96-21033).

IMPERIAL, Ballina, County Mayo, Irish Republic: Guests at this comfortable family-owned hotel are only a walk away from some of the river Moy's best salmon fishing pools. In addition to salmon and trout fishing on loughs Conn and Cullin, a half hour distant, there is also sea angling in the estuary in the hotel's boat. Accustomed to making anglers feel welcome, the management is friendly and professional. Details: *Imperial Hotel,* Ballina, County Mayo, Irish Republic (phone: 96-22200).

MOUNT FALCON CASTLE, Ballina, County Mayo, Irish Republic: An impressive parkland setting near the river Moy, Ireland's most prolific salmon river, is only one of the features here. For the use of its guests, this elegant establishment also owns and leases four beats on 7½ miles of the river, famous for its massive run of grilse (averaging 5 pounds), from May until mid-August, peaking from early June to mid-July. Spring salmon averaging 10 pounds can be taken in April and May. However, there are runs throughout the season since the loughs Conn and Cullin, of whose system the Moy is a part, provide a good supply of water most of the time. Good creels of wild brown trout are also taken, particularly during the mayfly hatch around the first week of June. Details: *Mount Falcon Castle Hotel,* Ballina, County Mayo, Irish Republic (phone: 96-21172).

ASHFORD CASTLE, Cong, County Mayo, Irish Republic: This ultra-luxurious hotel (a member of the Relais & Châteaux group) has appointed a field sports manager to help make the most of its extensive resources for angling — the Cong River, right on the grounds, which has a good run of grilse in June and July, and Lough Corrib, which laps at the edge of its splendid lawns. Details: *Ashford Castle Hotel,* Cong, County Mayo, Irish Republic (phone: 92-46003).

RYAN'S, Cong, County Mayo, Irish Republic: Anglers have long patronized this family-run hotel in scenic Cong village for the simple but very good food and for its accommodations, which are comfortable, if considerably less luxurious than those at the *Ashford Castle.* Details: *Ryan's Hotel,* Cong, County Mayo, Irish Republic (phone: 92-46004).

HEALY'S, Foxford, County Mayo, Irish Republic: Repeat business is the rule at the Healy family hostelry, a favorite of anglers since it was founded in 1892. The pub conversation alone can make a visit special. Details: *Healy's Hotel,* Pontoon, near Foxford, County Mayo, Irish Republic (phone: 94-56443).

PONTOON BRIDGE, Foxford, County Mayo, Irish Republic: Salmon and trout fishing in Lough Conn (famous for its mayfly, grasshopper, and daddy longlegs dapping periods) and in Lough Cullin, home cooking, peace and quiet, and fantastic scenery are the attractions of this comfortable, modern establishment. Details: *Pontoon Bridge Hotel,* Foxford, County Mayo, Irish Republic (phone: 94-56120 or 94-56151).

NEWPORT HOUSE, Newport, County Mayo, Irish Republic: This handsome country house, the home of the historic O'Donnells, offers good fishing on private waters on the Newport River and Lough Beltra, and sea fishing on the tidal river from the quay facing the estate. A member of the Relais & Châteaux group. Details: *Newport House Hotel,* Newport, County Mayo, Irish Republic (phone: 98-41222).

DUNDRUM HOUSE, Cashel, County Tipperary, Irish Republic: A tributary of the river Suir flows through the grounds of this 18th-century Georgian mansion and offers private brown trout fishing that is exceptionally appealing to dry-fly purists. It also offers horseback riding and a commendable restaurant. Details: *Dundrum House Hotel,* Dundrum, near Cashel, County Tipperary, Irish Republic (phone: 62-71116).

KNOCKLOFTY HOUSE, near Clonmel, County Tipperary, Irish Republic: The former family home of the Earls of Donoughmore, this luxury hotel and time-share complex comprises 105 acres of gardens and pastureland crossed by the river Suir. Features include 1½ miles of bank fishing on the river as well as access to club trout waters nearby. Sea trouting is available on the Blackwater, 24 miles distant, from July onward. Details: *Knocklofty House Hotel,* near Clonmel, County Tipperary, Irish Republic (phone: 52-38222).

SAIL INN, Dromineer, County Tipperary, Irish Republic: A traditional angling hotel on the shores of Lough Derg that was extensively refurbished in 1987, when it came under new management. Many Europeans make it their base when fishing for big pike, for which the lough has a reputation, but it is also a noted producer of big brown trout. Anglers using the dapped mayfly and, in May, spent gnat artificials, enjoy good success, while wet-fly fishing and trolling can be good at other times of year. The nearby Nenagh River has traditionally been an extremely attractive wet- and dry-fly fishery, though this may change if a new drainage scheme currently under consideration goes into effect. Details: *Sail Inn,* Dromineer, County Tipperary, Irish Republic (phone: 67-24114).

BLACKWATER LODGE, Upper Ballyduff, County Waterford, Irish Republic: Owned by an avid Welsh angler, the lodge has been renovated and reorganized to cater to the game angler. It controls 20 of the best beats on the 30-odd miles of high-record salmon waters between Lismore and Mallow on the celebrated Blackwater River; guests usually take a total of 350 to 400 salmon per season — 1988 and 1989 were record years, with an average of 1322 salmon brought in. There is also reasonable fishing for grilse, backend, and sea trout (as well as for wild brown trout, which can range up to 3 pounds, from February 1 to September 30). Details: *Blackwater Lodge Hotel,* Upper Ballyduff, County Waterford, Irish Republic (phone: 58-60235).

OAKVILLE, Enniscorthy, County Wexford, Irish Republic: The owners of this comfortable country home own a private stretch on the river Slaney, a salmon fishery, which they reserve for guests, together with another stretch, which they lease. They will also make reciprocal arrangements with the Cotterell Fishery on the river Nore. Details: *Oakville,* Ballycarney, Bunclody Rd., Enniscorthy, County Wexford, Irish Republic (phone: 54-88626).

BEACH, Portballintrae, County Antrim, Northern Ireland: With fishing on the river Bush, this establishment is now run by the third generation of Maclaines, whose forebears bought it more than 6 decades ago. Details: *Beach Hotel,* Portballintrae, County Antrim BT57 8RT, Northern Ireland (phone: 26-573-1214).

MANVILLE HOUSE, Aughnablaney, County Fermanagh, Northern Ireland: Close by are loughs Melvin and Erne and the river Bundrawes, where the best fishing is from March through May and in August and September. Private instruction is available, and accommodations are in a house about 100 yards from shore, with lovely views from every window. There are 5 rooms — none with private bath. Details: *Manville House,* Aughnablaney, Letter, County Fermanagh BT93 2BB, Northern Ireland (phone: 3656-31668).

CORRALEA LODGE, Belcoo, County Fermanagh, Northern Ireland: Anglers who come for the action in Upper Lough McNean and nearby Lough Erne — many of them German and French — stay in the luxurious guesthouse with 3 rooms or in one of the 6 self-catering chalets. The fishing is mainly for pike, though there are also perch, bream, roach, and trout. Open April through October. Details: *Corralea Lodge,* Belcoo, County Fermanagh BT74 6DX, Northern Ireland (phone: 36586-325).

ELY ISLAND CHALETS, Enniskillen, County Fermanagh, Northern Ireland: When the level of the Lough Erne fell some 80 years ago, a peninsula formed that now connects Ely Island to the mainland. Set on a lovely 277-acre landscaped parkland estate, the 10 log cabins opened here in 1989 are carpeted and finished in pine. Each sleeps 5 to 6, and has a microwave oven, color TV set, private verandah, and jetty. Boats are available for hire. Open year-round. On Lower Lough Erne; 5 miles from Enniskillen. Details: *Ely Island Chalets,* Enniskillen, County Fermanagh BT74, Northern Ireland (phone: 365-89777 or 365-89224).

MAHON'S, Irvinestown, County Fermanagh, Northern Ireland: Fishing on Lough Erne, known for some of the best coarse fishing in Europe, has been a prime drawing card of this antiques-filled, family-owned establishment since it was founded in 1883. There are 19 rooms, 16 with private bath. Open year-round. Details: *Mahon's Hotel,* Irvinestown, County Fermanagh BT74 9XX, Northern Ireland (phone: 3656-21656).

Freewheeling by Two-Wheeler

 The landscapes of Ireland unfold so quickly and with such endless diversity at every bend and turn of the road that traveling through the country quickly by car seems a real shame. The villages full of charming cottages, the rolling hills, the quaint seacoast towns, and the brooding mountains all beg to be explored at bike speed — fast enough to cover a fair amount of terrain, but slow enough to stop to inspect a wildflower or admire a view. It's a real treat to be able to pull over to the side of the road or to pop into a pub with a minimum of fuss or bother. Cycling affords just that. There's something quite special about the rhythm of days spent pedaling on the road — the slow but steady ticking away of the miles, the lure of the unknown just over the next hill, the ready meetings with fellow cyclists on the road or at pubs and hostels, and the special camaraderie that prevails.

Ireland offers not only great scenic variety in a relatively compact area but also an abundance of surfaced, little-trafficked secondary roads. That it also has many facilities for rental and repair and numerous small restaurants, bed and breakfast establishments, guesthouses, and hotels that are no less than delighted to welcome bedraggled pedalers, makes the country a well-nigh perfect candidate for cycling vacations — for beginning tourers and experts alike. Even those who are not particularly experienced and postpone their planning until the last minute can still enjoy a two-wheeling vacation here: Just travel light, start out slowly, don't be too ambitious, and don't give up just because of tender muscles or a little saddle-soreness.

TI Irish Raleigh Limited (Raleigh House, Kylemore Rd., Dublin 10, Irish Republic; phone: 1-6261333) oversees a rental service comprising some 100 dealers throughout the country who provide men's and women's 3-speed, 5-speed, and all-terrain or mountain bikes. (However, bikes hired in Northern Ireland cannot be taken into the Republic and vice versa.) *Rent-A-Bike Ltd.* (58 Lower Gardiner St., Dublin 1, Irish Republic; phone 1-725399) offers Peugeot and Motobecane models from its rental office alongside the bus/rail/air terminal in city center. Rates are about $8 a day or $33 to $38 per week plus an extra $6 for panniers, including insurance; a deposit of at least $45 per cycle is required. Other independent liveries exist in larger towns; count on spending about $5 a day and finding varying levels of quality, comfort, and maintenance.

However, since the amount of pleasure at least partially depends on the bike, cyclists may well want to bring their own. Airlines generally transport bikes as part of a passenger's personal baggage but usually insist that the whole machine be crated. Before leaving home, be sure to check your insurance coverage for personal accident, medical expenses, loss or damage to cycle or luggage, and third-party claims. It is also necessary to bring a basic set of tools and spares. Irish law requires that cycles have two independent brakes and a red rear light and reflector as well as a white light in the front for night riding. Since riding is on the left, it's a good idea to fix the front light onto the right-hand side if it is not already fitted center front. In addition, a good-quality padlock and chain are absolutely essential. (And never leave a bike unattended when loaded with any possessions, even if the bike itself is locked.)

To get out of Dublin without battling traffic is not especially difficult, but cyclists should be aware that it's not possible to put a bike on a city commuter bus or on the handy electric trains of the *DART* (*Dublin Area Rapid Transport*), which runs from Howth to Bray. However, it is possible to go by mainline train on *Irish Rail,* which costs about a fourth of a single passenger fare for the bike in addition to the cost of a regular passenger ticket, usually between $2.50 and $8. Passengers ride in the coach; bikes travel in the guard's van. As for other public transportation, it is sometimes possible to get a bike onto a provincial bus on the *Irish Bus Service* as long as there is room to stow it in the luggage area. Since available storage on any public transportation fills up on peak traveling days, it is best to travel on off-days. Bikes should always be labeled with the cyclist's name and address and station of origin and destination.

BEST CYCLING AREAS

The touring possibilities in Ireland are extensive. Nearly all the roads in both the Republic and Northern Ireland, except for trunk routes between the larger cities, offer cyclists tarred surfaces and light traffic; those in the west and northwest may be somewhat rougher, since local authorities have been cutting back on upkeep in recent years. There are also back roads and unsurfaced mountain tracks — the latter only for the brave and bold.

DUBLIN ENVIRONS, Irish Republic: The wonderful thing about Ireland is that only about 20 miles outside Dublin — or 10 miles from Cork, Derry, Galway, Limerick, or Waterford — the roads are virtually traffic-free. In County Meath, the doorstep of Dublin Airport is the departure point for nearly ideal runs through villages like Ballyboghil and Naul, on to Duleek, and to the remarkable Boyne Valley and the Hill of Tara (whose sites are described in "Ancient Monuments and Ruins" in *For the Mind*). Don't miss the monastic remains at Slane and Navan. South of Dublin, those who like hill climbing can take the road from suburban Rathfarnham to Sally Gap and Devil's Glen and, within a half hour, find themselves out of sight of human habitation in lovely countryside where the lark rising is the only sound to be heard. The small but lovely Wicklow Mountains, which extend from around Dublin in the north to as far south as Arklow and inland for about 25 miles from the sandy shores of the Irish Sea, make for excellent cycling: The wide, long, dune-backed strand at Brittas Bay is one of the best places for a swim here, and Glendalough (described in *Ancient Monuments and Ruins*) is a sightseeing must. Details: *Dublin and Eastern Regional Tourism Office,* 13/14 Upper O'Connell St., Dublin 1, Irish Republic (phone: 1-747733).

MIDWEST, Irish Republic: The 700-foot Cliffs of Moher, which plunge into the foaming sea near the fishing village of Liscannor, the spa town of Lisdoonvarna, the village of Doolin (a home of traditional Irish music), and the Burren — bare and almost lunar in appearance — are some of the notable sites in County Clare, while in more-frequented County Galway, the place to explore is rocky, boggy, lake-studded, and partially Gaelic-speaking Connemara, with the Twelve Bens presiding over flatlands speckled with ruined rock-walled cottages. There are good beaches, seldom busy, and loughs Corrib and Mask (see *Gone Fishing*) are not too distant. Still farther north, small roads meander through pretty quiet villages scattered around the tranquil heather and rhododendron country of less-populated Mayo or hug a coastline as wild and lonesome as anyone tired of city life could ever desire. The routes from Newport and Mulrany by Lough Furnace, over the bridge at Achill Sound to Achill Island, and then around Achill Island are pleasant. Details: *Shannonside Tourism,* The Granary, Michael St., Limerick, Irish Republic (phone: 61-317522); and *Ireland-West Tourism,* Aras Fáilte, Victoria Pl., Galway, Irish Republic (phone: 91-63081).

SOUTHWEST, Irish Republic: Outside busy Cork City, counties Cork, Kerry, and Limerick are quite rural. There are mountains and steep gradients, but gently rolling hills and flat valleys are part of the cycling picture as well. The most dramatic scenery is along the coast, where lovely deep bays are interspersed with cave-pocked cliffs and promontories. Blarney Castle is here, along with the Fota House near Cork City, the fishing town of Youghal, the pretty ports of Kinsale and Cobh on Cork Harbour, the remote district around the Allihies on the coast, Georgian-era Bantry House, Killarney, *Durty Nelly's Inn* (see "Pub Crawling" in *For the Experience*), Ross Castle and the ruined remains of Muckross and Innisfallen Abbey, and the spectacular Gap of Dunloe, which slashes through the countryside between MacGillicuddy's Reeks and the Purple Mountains. The Ring of Kerry and the Dingle Peninsula are particular standouts. Details: *Cork/Kerry Region Tourism Organisation,* PO Box 44, Tourist House, Grand Parade, Cork, Irish Republic (phone: 21-273251).

NORTHWEST, Irish Republic: Head southwest from Sligo and follow an impressive scenic route that passes through Ballina and the Ox Mountains. Loop back east through Bunniconlon and by lovely Lough Tait, and continue northeast to Cloonacool: Pedal through Coolaney Gap, where many a cause was lost, and then by the Bronze Age tombs at Carrowmore, within sight of Knocknarea, a storied spot where the dead were buried after Tuatha De Danaan vanquished the Formorians forevermore after the great battle of Northern Moytura. Second only to Brittany's Carnac in size, this prehistoric graveyard contains the relics of more than 40 graves — mainly standing stones and passages. Then return to Sligo, Yeats country, and picturesque Lough Gill. On another day (or immediately, for strong cyclists), travel east from here to Manorhamilton, an erstwhile strategic center on a high plateau and a very scenic spot surrounded by still other prehistoric sites of note, then through the country of Breffny, where Dervorgilla ran away with Dermot MacMurrough, thereby setting in motion the events that led to the Anglo-Norman conquest and a few centuries of troubles that are not over yet. Then head northwest to breezy Bundoran by the sea, with its fine shore views, and up to the ancient town of Donegal, once the seat of the O'Donnell family. Here is another moment of decision: to head into the wild and very lovely Blue Stack Mountains or to take the relatively easy run north to Ballybofey and Letterkenny, traveling roads by Lough Swilly and Lough Foyle? Let your legs be the judge. Details: *Donegal/Leitrim/ Sligo Region Tourist Information Office,* Temple St., Sligo, Irish Republic (phone: 71-61201).

NORTHERN IRELAND: Northern Ireland's 5,500 square miles encompass some of the most spectacular and varied scenery that one can imagine. Blue mountains and sandy beaches, open moorlands and clear lakes, small towns hidden away in the green places of the countryside, and fishing villages strung out along the rocky shores — and none of this splendor is ever more than an hour from the sea. The only heavy traffic on the excellent network of small, well-signposted roads is the occasional tractor, and the only traffic jams are caused by sheep and cattle changing fields. Perhaps the most rewarding outing for the cyclist is to take the 60-mile coast road from Larne up around the northeast corner of County Antrim to the resort of Portrush. The celebrated Antrim coast road, which passes countless villages, ruined Norman castles, and the nine green Glens of Antrim, is reminiscent of California Highway 1 south of Carmel. Ancient rocks jut out as cliffs in all their brilliant colors — bright red sandstone, white chalk, black basalt, and blue clay. The beckoning hills of Scotland can be seen along part of the route. Stop off at Ballycastle and take a boat across to Rathlin Island, where Robert the Bruce once found sanctuary. If you wish to stay overnight, the *Rathlin Guesthouse* (phone: 2657-63917) has 10 rooms. It is possible to walk or cycle across to the bird sanctuary on the west side and explore the cliffs and caves. Once back on the mainland, pedal on to the strange and remarkable rock formation called the Giant's Causeway, an astonishing complex of basalt columns packed tightly together; the tops of the columns — 38,000 of them — form steppingstones leading from the cliff foot and disappearing into the sea. Details: *Northern Ireland Tourist Board,* River House, 48 High St., Belfast BT1 2DS, Northern Ireland (phone: 232-231221 or 232-246609).

HOW TO PLAN A TOUR

After picking a region to explore, it's a fairly easy matter to sketch out an itinerary. First decide on exactly what to see and do. *Cycling Ireland,* a handy brochure with information on 23 different cycling routes, can be obtained from the Irish Tourist Board. For more ideas, consult local tourist literature as well as articles about touring in bicycling magazines such as the *Cyclists' Touring Club's Route Guide to Cycling in Britain and Ireland* by Christa Gausden and Nicholas Crane (about $5.25; Oxford Illustrated Press, The Gables, Newington, Oxford OX9 8AH, England; phone: Oxford 890026), which lists 370 connecting routes based as far as possible on minor roads and lanes throughout Ireland, suitable for tours lasting anywhere from a single day to several months.

Once a general itinerary has been set, plot out a tour on a large-scale highway map of the country — the sort of map supplied by a national tourist office. Base the daily mileage on what you usually cover on the road at home, but be sure to allot time for dawdling en route — chatting with the locals, stopping to admire the panoramas from picnic spots, walking through ruined abbeys, and the like.

Then, with small-scale topographical maps that show the smallest country lanes and also reveal the contours and elevations of the area to be covered, plot a more detailed route. The best maps to use are ¼- or ½-inch-to-the-mile *Ordnance Survey Maps* or ¼-inch-to-the-mile *Ordnance Survey Holiday Maps* (about $5 each; Ordnance Survey, Phoenix Park, Dublin 8, Irish Republic). The individual county guides produced by the Irish Tourist Board are also useful.

For information about bike rental depots, accommodations, special cycle route sheets, maps, and local information, contact the Irish Tourist Board and the Northern Ireland Tourist Board.

CYCLING HOLIDAYS

For first-time bicycle tourists, for singles, and for gregarious couples and families, a group cycling tour is always a good idea. Many are offered through American or Canadian organizations; for information see *Camping and Caravanning, Hiking and Biking* in GETTING READY TO GO. In Ireland, the possibilities include the following:

Rent-A-Bike Ltd., 58 Lower Gardiner St., Dublin 1, Irish Republic (phone: 1-725399). This organization offers a range of bicycle and youth hostel holidays in the Irish Republic, including cycle hire, accommodations, and maps.

Youth Hostel Association of Northern Ireland, 56 Bradbury Pl., Belfast BT7 1RU, Northern Ireland (phone: 232-324733). The Antrim Coast, the Mourne Mountains, and the Causeway Triangle areas of Northern Ireland are the destinations of cycling and rambling holidays offered by this group.

Stalking and Shooting

Humans have been making sport of their search for game, both large and small, since the time of the pharaohs (who were so enamored of the activity that they looked forward to continuing it in the afterlife) — and the sport's devotees in Ireland are no less enthusiastic. There is immense variety of both game and terrain. Hare, cock pheasant, red grouse, woodcock, snipe, golden plover, gray partridge, pigeon, and flighting mallard, widgeon, teal, and other ducks are all shot, along with red, fallow, and Sika deer. Irish gun dogs, setters and spaniels, are a pleasure, and sportsmen are supportive, offering a variety of schemes to accommodate visitors.

All shooting is done on private land, with strict controls, and it is forbidden to shoot over or into or carry firearms on any lands without the permission of the owner and occupier. Some estates are managed specifically with shooting in mind, and their managers pay careful attention to the development of game stocks, with patrols to guard against poachers and to control pests. The easiest way to plan a shooting holiday on one of these estates is to contact an associated hotel or booking agency.

In addition, a number of organizations offer rough shooting for various bird species, which might include walking up woodcock, snipe, plover, and some pheasant and flighting duck. Pigeon shooting is also available, as are driven pheasant shoots. Bags are mixed and sizes vary, depending on the sportsman's skill, game levels, weather conditions, and terrain, which can be very difficult in some areas.

RULES, REGULATIONS, AND OTHER ESSENTIALS: Season opening and closing dates are published in advance, along with the species that may be shot, and the duration of the season varies from year to year. Geese are often excluded because of concern about their stock levels. (Ireland is an important wintering ground for white-fronted geese.)

Firearms and Firearm Certificates – Any sportsman who wishes to shoot game in the Republic must, for each shotgun he is carrying, have a current Irish firearms certificate, which are available only to visitors who have access to shooting arrangements or who have advance bookings with a recognized shoot. The number of certificates per shoot is controlled. Good for a year from the date of issue, they are available from the Secretary, *Wildlife Service* (OPW, Leeson La., Dublin 2, Irish Republic; phone: 1-615666). The cost, about $25, must be enclosed with the application. Rifles may not be more than 22 inches or 5.6 mm. Up to 500 cartridges may accompany the weapon — but check airline limitations in advance. Shells of any bore can be purchased in the bigger Irish towns; cartridges of less than 12 bore may be difficult to find in smaller villages.

In Northern Ireland, current firearm certificates are also necessary. Write in advance to the Chief Constable, R.U.C., Firearms Branch, Knocknagoney House, Knocknagoney Rd., Belfast BT4 2PP, Northern Ireland (phone: 232-760761).

Hunting Licenses – Sportsmen intending to go for anything but rabbit, pigeon, and pest species in the Republic must carry an Irish hunting license in addition to the appropriate firearms certificate. Applications must be made on special forms (available from the *Forest and Wildlife Service,* Leeson La., Dublin 2, Irish Republic, or from booking agencies) and must include a formal written declaration that the visitor has proper access to shooting in the Irish Republic as the paying or invited guest of a person who controls sporting rights on the land where he will be shooting. Licenses, which expire on July 31 after the date of issue, are free.

Note that applications for both firearms certificate and hunting licenses must be made by post *well in advance* of the trip because certificates and licenses are returned only by mail. Applications in person, upon arrival in the Irish Republic, are not entertained, nor can the necessary documentation be picked up after arrival.

In Northern Ireland, hunting licenses are necessary to go for pheasant, woodcock, grouse, wild duck, pigeon, and snipe in *Department of Agriculture* forests at Fardross in County Tyrone, Drunkeeragh in County Down, and Cam and Iniscarn in County Derry. These are available from the *Forest Service* (Dundonald House, Belfast BT4 3SB, Northern Ireland; phone: 232-650111, ext. 268). For details on walking-up shoots at seven other state forests, contact the Chief Wildlife Officer, *Department of Agriculture,* Forestry Division (Seskinore, County Tyrone, Northern Ireland; phone: 662-841243).

Insurance – Wherever you go and whatever you shoot or stalk, check before leaving home to make sure your insurance is in order. Third-party civil liability is a minimum coverage that you should carry.

BOOKING AGENCIES: These organizations can send the particulars describing several estates, including details on the shooting and fairly complete descriptions of accommodations. Most shoots are organized for groups of four to eight, and it's common for friends to get together to form a shooting party. If a visitor so desires, the agent can try to fit him into someone else's party — though naturally most groups are wary of having an inexperienced sportsman in their midst because of the risk of injury. The organizers will advise a visiting sportsman as to seasonal and bag limits and any local peculiarities and will help him get through the paperwork.

Shooting in the whole of the Emerald Isle is available through two organizations:

Irish Fieldsports Agency, 174 Castlereagh Rd., Belfast BT5 5GX, Northern Ireland (phone: 232-459248).

Luggala Estate, Roundwood, County Wicklow, Irish Republic (phone: 1-818102). Operates largely to the south of the border.

For shooting specifically in the Republic, contact:

Abbey Tours, 50 Garville Ave., Rathgar, Dublin 6, Irish Republic (phone: 1-967314).

Fáilte Travel Ltd., McKee Ave., Finglas, Dublin 11, Irish Republic (phone: 1-344464).

Joe O'Reilly Travel, Blarney, County Cork, Irish Republic (phone: 21-385700).

Des Wallace Travel, 8 Main St., Finglas, Dublin 11, Irish Republic (phone: 1-347888).

Shooting in Northern Ireland is offered by several booking agencies:

Forest Service, Dundonald House, Belfast BT4 3SB, Northern Ireland (phone: 232-650111, ext. 268).

McBride Sports, Haslems La., Lisburn, County Antrim, Northern Ireland (phone: 846-671322).

Sperrin Sports, 112 Seskinore Rd., Omagh, County Tyrone, Northern Ireland (phone: 662-841243)

SHOOTS AND ESTATES: There are a number of shoots and estates in the Republic and Northern Ireland that like to deal directly with visitors — they want to know nearly as much about the sportsman who is planning to shoot with them as he wants to know about them before committing himself to come! A few of these, including private estates and the bigger well-run gun clubs, include the following:

Alpine Club Shoot, Inniscrone, County Sligo, Irish Republic (phone: 096-36252). Snipe and woodcock shoots, plus duck flighting and rough shooting on a 100,000-acre estate attached to the *Alpine* hotel.

Ballywillan Gun Club, 3 Orwell Park, Rathgar, Dublin 6, Irish Republic (phone: 1-975121). Rough shooting, duck, snipe, pigeon, woodcock, and hare on 30,000 acres in County Longford.

Birr Castle Game Syndicate, Croghan, Birr, County Offaly, Irish Republic (phone: 509-20056). Stalking for fallow deer on the estate of the Earl of Rosse, as well as at Newmarket-on-Fergus in County Clare.

Clonalis Shoot, Clonalis, Castlerea, County Roscommon, Irish Republic (phone: 907-20014). Snipe, woodcock, pheasant, hare, and duck rough shooting on the 10,000-acre estate of Mr. Pyers O'Conor–Nash.

Field, Stream & Covert Shoot, c/o R. O'Grady, Corrigeen Anne, Ballinrobe, County Mayo, Irish Republic (phone: 92-41142). Mixed shooting for duck, snipe, hare, plover, and pigeon over 20 square miles.

Luggala Estate, Roundwood, County Wicklow, Irish Republic (phone: 1-818102). Deer stalking, Sika deer stalking, and driven pheasant for parties of ten guns on a number of Irish estates.

Tubbercurry & District Gun Club, c/o Mr. Jerrard Lundy, Rhue, Tubbercurry, County Sligo, Irish Republic (phone: 71-85140). Snipe, woodcock, duck, pigeon, and rabbit walk-up and rough shooting in over 130,000 acres of very exciting terrain.

Ashbrooke Demesne, Brookeborough, County Fermanagh, Northern Ireland (phone: 26553-402). Deer stalking for Japanese Sika deer provided by Viscount Brookeborough.

Baronscourt Estate, Baronscourt, Newtownstewart, County Tyrone, Northern Ireland (phone: 6626-61683). Deer stalking courtesy of the Duke of Abercorn.

Forest Service (address above). Pheasant, woodcock, grouse, duck, pigeon, and snipe at three forests, plus walk-up shooting in seven other forests.

HOTELS FOR SHOOTING HOLIDAYS: A couple of hotels located in good shooting areas also organize shooting holidays for guests, among them:

Ashford Castle, Cong, County Mayo, Irish Republic (phone: 92-46003). Driven pheasant shooting and rough shooting for pheasant, woodcock, snipe, and duck over 2,000 acres, offered by the nation's most luxurious hotel, a sportsman's paradise.

Dromoland Castle, Newmarket-on-Fergus, County Clare, Irish Republic (phone: 61-71144). Rough and driven pheasant shooting and fallow deer stalking over 2,000 acres.

Mount Juliet, Thomastown, County Kilkenny, Irish Republic (phone: 56-24455). Driven shoots for pheasants are offered on this 1,466-acre estate. The pheasant population is at an optimum level of 7,000 birds, and each shoot is confined to a limit of 8 guns, with a bag limit of one brace per gun.

Zetland House, Cashel Bay, County Galway, Irish Republic (phone: 95-31011). Rough shooting of woodcock and snipe over 12,000 acres.

GAME AND COUNTRY FAIRS: These splendid get-togethers for huntin', shootin', fishin', and farmin' folk and all their friends and relations are a must for the traveler of a sporting turn of mind. Exhibits put on by groups ranging from gun and angling shops to specialists in game development and conservation are only the beginning; there are also displays about racing pigeons, ferrets, taxidermy, game keeping, falconry, and bookkeeping, not to mention competitions for gun dogs, archers, riflemen, wildlife photographers, pastry makers, bonnie babies, Wellington boot throwers, tug-of-war teams, and a good deal more. The grandest of the breed include the following:

Dunmanway Annual Agricultural Show, at the *Droumleener Lawn Racecourse,* Dunmanway, County Cork, Irish Republic

This small 1-day fair takes place each July (phone: 23-45419). *Game and Country Fair,* Randalstown, County Antrim, Northern Ireland. Takes place on Shane's Castle estate for 3 days, usually at the end of June or the first week in July; the biggest in the North (phone: 8494-79671). *Limerick Show,* at Greenpark, Limerick City, Irish Republic. A 3-day event held in late August, it includes show-jumping, horticultural exhibits, crafts, and Ireland's largest cattle show (phone: 61-40977 or 61-45519).

Great Walks and Mountain Rambles

 Almost any walker will tell you that it is the footpaths of a country — not its roadways — that show off the landscape to best advantage. A walker is closer to earth than a person driving or even biking, and details that might otherwise be overlooked are more noticeable: incredibly tiny wildflowers blossoming cheerfully in a crack between limestone boulders, for instance, or a fox lurking in the shadows of the woods at dawn. And the scenery moves by at a slow speed, so that hedgerows, fences, and the green velvet pastures can be contemplated at leisure. Churches and barns, old mills and lichen-crusted stone walls, and farms and villages are seldom far out of sight as a walker follows in the footsteps of neolithic man or Bronze Age gold traders or treads tracks first defined by smugglers, cattle drovers, abbots, or coffin carriers, whose ways would often be marked at the tops of passes by the stone piles where they rested their loads. Many paths were literally walked into existence by generations of country folk traveling to work, market, mass, or the pub. And in practice, it is possible to walk more or less freely on all of these paths, provided that what is obviously off limits is respected.

Though some 100-odd forest parks exist throughout Ireland, the walks are mainly short and relatively easy. For longer tramps, it's necessary to head into the wild high

country, mainly along the coast, where tracks are so rare and ill defined that walkers generally cross pathless hills and where map and compass are essential companions. With summits that seldom rise above 3,000 feet, these mountains are no giants, but because the way up begins in valleys that are usually near sea level, the hikes turn out to be a good deal more demanding than one might at first expect. The rewards are abundant, however: The ever-present sea-and-mountain views are awash in incredible blues and intense greens (thanks to the abundant rainfall). And chance encounters en route with fellow ramblers or with shepherds and their collies are a lot of fun.

This is true even when the weather turns rainy, as it may well do even at the height of summer, providing the visitor has come prepared. Stout walking shoes or boots are essential, as is a good rain parka, with leggings. And in addition to the usual walker's gear, a spare sweater is a necessity, even on a day hike — especially in the Irish hills, where conditions can turn arctic within a matter of hours. Hiking and backpacking equipment is best bought in the US, where the selection is greater and prices lower.

Some of the leading walking events, which welcome visitors, include the *Hill Walking Weekend* (in Glencolumbkille, County Donegal; phone: 73-30003), which lasts 3 days in mid-May; the *Kenmare Walking Festival* (in Kenmare, County Kerry; phone: 64-41220), held 3 days in early June; and the *Castlebar International Four Day Walks* (in County Mayo; held in late June; phone: 94-21355).

WHERE TO WALK

Ireland is a rich agricultural nation, and all the low country that is not boggy is checkered with fields separated by hedges and, with the exception of byways and the towpaths of waterways like the Grand Canal, is not particularly good for walking. This situation is not likely to change until the state's scheme to develop waymarked lowland trails to historic castles, forts, and churches around the countryside is more fully developed. For now, the walker and rambler in Ireland will generally choose to go to the hill areas near the coasts, where the scenery ranges from the limestone karst of County Clare's Burren to the bare, rocky quartzite peaks of Connemara, from the dark, vegetation-rich sandstone cliffs of Kerry to the rounded granite domes of Wicklow.

The following are some of the most interesting areas (in alphabetical order by county), together with the names of maps and guidebooks that will be most helpful. Details about the maps and guidelines are given in "Maps and More Information" later in this section.

THE BURREN, County Clare, Irish Republic: The unforgettable karst plateau known as the Burren is mile upon mile of all but bare rock, almost desert-like and making no concession to prettiness; as one Cromwellian lieutenant quipped, it had not enough wood to hang a man, earth to bury him, or water to drown him. But there is magnificence here nonetheless. Distances are short, views across Galway Bay to Connemara and the Aran Islands are magnificent, and in May and June the grikes (cracks) that seam the limestone sprout a stunning and eclectic collection of rare flowering plants unique in Europe — gentians, cranesbill, brilliantly colored saxifrages, rosy Irish orchids — whose seeds arrived on the winds from all over, like the topsoil that nourishes them. Sheltered from the Atlantic winds, their blossoms transform the landscape. The mighty Cliffs of Moher, a few miles to the south, offer a fine cliff-top walk, and the largest cave system in Ireland lies beneath. Most of these underground marvels are dangerous for the inexperienced or improperly equipped, but the Aillwee Cave, which is open to all, conveys the feeling. Discovered and explored by a local shepherd in the 1940s and opened to the public in 1978, it has won the Europea Nostra prize, among other awards, for the completeness with which it blends into the landscape. Refer to ½-inch Map Sheet 14, the Folding Landscapes Map of the Burren, and *Irish Walk Guide: West.*

DONEGAL HILLS, County Donegal, Irish Republic: Here in Ireland's northwest there are plenty of hills to walk and plenty of variety. Close to Donegal Town are the Blue Stack Mountains, granite domes rising from remote boggy valleys, with several attractive walks, most notably that from Lough Eske on the southeast up to crag-bound Lough Belshade and the 2,218-foot summit of Croagh Gorm. At the western extremity of the county, around Glencolumbkille, named for the famous Celtic patron saint of Derry and Donegal, stand 1,972-foot Slieve League and 1,458-foot Slieve Tooey. Though the altitudes are minor, the hills themselves are spectacular, since their cliffs fall directly from summit to sea. Scary tales are told about One Man's Path on the ridge of Slieve League, with a drop of some 1,800 feet into the roiling surf on one side and a near-vertical escarpment on the other; for the inexperienced, it is certainly not a walk for a less than perfectly clear day, nor the place to be when it's windy. But tyros can avoid it by keeping on the inshore side of the ridge for about 100 yards, and the view out over a vast expanse of briny deep and into some five counties makes every skipped heartbeat worthwhile.

In the north of Donegal, the 2,466-foot quartzite cone of Errigal, rising above Dunlewy Lake, is a dominant feature; it is quite easily climbed up the ridge from the road on the east. An isolated summit, it has fine, expansive views across Altan Lough and Muckish to the north coast and southeast over the stark ruin of Dunlewy Church to the huge, gloomy cirque of the Poisoned Glen, so named, legend has it, because plants toxic to cattle once grew there. Nearby is Glenveagh, a national park that is notable for the very fine herd of red deer it shelters and the superb gardens attached to Glenveagh Castle. Refer to ½-inch Map Sheets 1 and 3 and *Irish Walk Guide: North West*.

WICKLOW MOUNTAINS, Counties Dublin and Wicklow, Irish Republic: Stretching southward from Dublin City, these 1,000-odd square miles of granite domes and the deep valleys between them — including Glencree, Glendalough, and Glenmalure — offer some pleasant day hikes. The 1,654-foot summit of Sugar Loaf Mountain, which is easily accessible by bus, stands out as just one example: In the center of an area where the mountains close in on small patches of rolling farmland, it offers fine views out over the sea not far away and, beyond that, on a clear day, all the way to the Welsh mountains. The ascent begins near Rocky Valley, off the main Dublin–Glendalough road; the descent passes through the wooded Glen of the Downs — a steep-banked, 600-foot-deep ravine that the novelist Sir Walter Scott once termed "the most beautiful view" he had ever seen. From Luggala, on the road from Roundwood to Sally Gap, there is a delightful walk down the valley between loughs Tay and Dan, descending through fields on the west of the river, which is crossed via stepping stones, and returning up through the woods on the east. The going is easy, and the views are superb, especially the reflections of the huge Luggala crag in the waters of Lough Tay. Refer to ½-inch Map Sheet 16, the 1:50,000 Wicklow Way Map, *Irish Walk Guide: East*, and *Dublin and the Wicklow Mountains* by members of the *Irish Ramblers Club* (about $2).

CONNEMARA, County Galway, Irish Republic: One of Ireland's most scenic and unspoiled regions, Connemara offers its share of the country's best walking. The quartzite pyramids known as the Twelve Bens, which are the most widely known of the peaks here and look like nothing more than minor hills, provide the quality of experience afforded by real mountains because of their cliffbound ridges and slopes of bare rock and scree. (In fact, the north face of 2,336-foot Bencorr offers some of the country's longest rock climbs.) There are several excellent walks in the Bens, but the going is tough, so allow plenty of time. For instance, the circuit of Glencoaghan, encompassing six fine summits, is only 10 miles long, but it will take a strong walker at least 6 hours. To the east of the Bens is the long chain of the Maumturks, another quartzite range, whose long traverse is one of the greatest walking challenges of Ireland.

The less ambitious walker should not be put off, however; shorter walks like the one up Diamond Mountain near Letterfrack, easily approached through Connemara National Park, will provide vivid insight into the nature of this wonderful wilderness. Refer to ½-inch Map Sheet 10, *Irish Walk Guide: West,* and *The Twelve Bens* by Joss Lynam (about $1).

BEARA PENINSULA, Counties Kerry and Cork, Irish Republic: The Caha Mountains, which form the backbone of the lovely Beara Peninsula and divide Cork from Kerry, are well off the beaten tourist path, and once a bit removed from the popular 1,887-foot Sugarloaf and 2,251-foot Hungry Hill, the highest points in the range, walkers are unlikely to be crowded by fellow enthusiasts. The whole ridge makes a fine 2- or 3-day outing, with overnights at well-placed youth hostels; the less energetic can penetrate easily into the area's distinctive and beautiful cirques. The village of Lauragh is a good point of departure. Refer to ½-inch Map Sheet 24, 1-inch Killarney District Map, and the *Irish Walk Guide: South West.*

IVERAGH AND DINGLE PENINSULA MOUNTAINS, County Kerry, Irish Republic: Ireland's choice offering for walkers and scramblers, this region of relatively unexplored red sandstone country is known first and foremost for the MacGillicuddy Reeks, the high peaks that roof this part of Ireland. The main peak, 3,414-foot Carrantuohill, can provide a good day's workout with fine views as the reward; local guides are available. Strong walkers can tackle the area's finest walk, the ridge line of the reeks, running from the Gap of Dunloe in the east over ten summits to Lough Acoose on the west. But the whole of the Iveragh Peninsula, the largest of Kerry's trio of peninsulas, whose eastern end the reeks occupy, boasts enough equally good walking to keep an intrepid tramper occupied for more than one vacation. The 2,739-foot Purple Mountain is to the east of the Gap of Dunloe and 2,796-foot Mangerton to the south, its summit accessible via the deep lake known as the Devil's Punchbowl, whose waters foam and plummet 60 feet over a series of sandstone crags in one of the country's prettiest waterfalls. Between these two peaks, around Killarney Lakes, is Muckross National Park, where the walks are shorter and easier, but no less beautiful. West of the reeks lies a whole wilderness of mountains — lower (not much exceeding the 2,000-foot mark) but notable for their remote, craggy, lake-filled valleys and bare summits that would be severe but for the warm brown of the stone. (See also "Kerry Way" in "Star Treks," below.)

To the north of Iveragh is the long, narrow, and somewhat grander Dingle Peninsula, with a backbone of interesting summits, such as 2,623-foot Stradbally Mountain and 2,713-foot Caherconree, rising to 3,127-foot Mount Brandon, named for St. Brendan the Navigator, a 5th-century monk who is said to have discovered America when sailing the seas in search of an earthly paradise. The mountain, with its fine conical summit and its long, high wall of crag on the east, dropping almost perpendicularly into a chain of small lakes, has been acclaimed as the finest in Britain and Ireland. The summit, where the remains of the saint's oratory, cell, and well can still be seen, offers superb views to the Blasket Islands in the west. For the less adventurous, there is an easy way up from the west. Refer to ½-inch Map Sheets 20 and 21, 1:50,000 Map Sheet 78, *Irish Walk Guide: South West.*

MAYO MOUNTAINS, County Mayo, Irish Republic: From the north shore of the deep Killary Harbour fjord that separates County Mayo from Galway rises 2,688-foot Mweelrea. The highest mountain in the province of Connacht, it offers a fine walk from Delphi in the east, a remote and beautiful spot on the Aasleagh–Louisburgh road, named by a 19th-century landowner for its resemblance to the Greek original. Farther north, not too distant from the southern shore of Clew Bay, Ireland's holy mountain, 2,510-foot Croagh Patrick, offers yet another good climb. Tens of thousands make the ascent on the last Sunday in July as part of a great national pilgrimage, but even out of season there are plenty of hikers, since its views over island-studded Clew Bay are worth gawking at in any season, a fact that has resulted in a well-worn and relatively easy-to-follow path. Farther north again are the lonely Nephin Beg mountains and, to the west, two fine quartzite summits of Achill Island, 2,204-foot Slievemore and 2,194-foot Croaghaun, the latter standing at the westernmost tip of Achill; there is nothing between its summit and America. Refer to ½-inch Map Sheets 7 and 10 and *Irish Walk Guide: West.*

SOUTHEAST'S SANDSTONE MOUNTAINS, Counties Tipperary and Waterford, Irish Republic: South of Tipperary Town and the rich farmland of the Vale of Aherlow are the Galtee Mountains, a long ridge of peaks that provide pleasant walking, mostly dry-shod, with fine views, especially over the northern edge. To the south is the Mitchelstown Valley, with its well-known caves, and beyond, the Knockmealdown Mountains, another pleasant ridge of rounded summits 20 to 25 miles long. Farther to the east is the Comeragh Plateau, flat and boggy with huge hummocks of peat that would make walking very tiring but for the scenery — the lake-filled coums, steep-sided cirques carved out in the Ice Age, that fringe the plateau, and the dramatic Coumshingaun headwall that rises almost sheer to 2,500 feet. Refer to ½-inch Map Sheets 18 and 22 and *Irish Walk Guide: South East.*

ANTRIM COAST, County Antrim, Northern Ireland: This coast offers a whole range of attractions: the basalt columns of the Giant's Causeway; the high, clean, vertical line of cliffs at Fair Head; the chalk ramparts at Garron Point; the peaceful wooded glens of Glendun and Glenariff; and historic Dunluce Castle, perched on the very edge of the cliffs (so close that the centuries-old story of the kitchen sliding into the sea is almost believable). There is much fenced-off private land here, but all of the sites mentioned here can be reached by public footpath. Refer to 1:50,000 Map Sheet 5 and *Irish Walk Guide: North East.*

MOURNE MOUNTAINS, County Down, Northern Ireland: This granite range in the northeastern section of the island south of Belfast is not very large, but the scenery is especially lovely, with good views, sapphire lakes, and rugged gray rocks. The principal peak of the group, 2,796-foot Slieve Donard, stands out as a particularly good climb, both for its relative ease and its attractiveness, especially when approached from the town of Newcastle. On fine clear days, it's possible to see the Isle of Man, the peaks of the English Lake District, the mountains of Wales, and Scotland's islands. Those with a full day to spare should walk along the ridge to 2,448-foot Slieve Binnian, to see the aptly named Silent Valley and its reservoir, the source of Belfast's water supply, and, beyond it, lonely little Lough Shannagh. Other good hikes include the ascents of 2,394-foot Slieve Bearnagh and of 2,512-foot Slieve Commedagh. The big challenge in the Mournes is to walk the wall that delineates the Belfast Water Supply catchment area, which in fact takes in all the major summits. Refer to the Mourne Country Outdoor Pursuits Map (2½ inches to the mile); J. S. Doran's *Hill Walks in the Mournes,* which describes 21 good hikes (about $1.50 from Mourne Observer Press, Castlewellan Rd., Newcastle, County Down BT33 0JX, Northern Ireland); and *The Irish Walk Guide: North East.* On the spot, the personnel at the various mountaineering club huts can be helpful; for hut locations, inquire locally before heading out, or contact the *Heart of Down Accommodations Association* (Down District Council, Strangford Rd., Downpatrick, County Down, Northern Ireland; phone: 396-614331).

STAR TREKS

The creation of a Round-Ireland Trail, with a number of sections and spur paths, is a plank in the development platform of the Republic's National Sports Council, which has set up a *Long Distance Walking Routes Committee (LDWRC)* to promote development of long-distance footpaths. And while there are still many gaps, a dozen or more paths have now been opened. Each of these walking trails is described in a brochure,

Walking Ireland, available free the Irish Tourist Board in New York (see *Tourist Information Offices,* GETTING READY TO GO). It is possible to take 1-day hikes along any of these (though it may be difficult to get a bus back to the starting point), but the more ambitious can also plan a multi-day walk, with overnights in hostels, bed and breakfast establishments, and guesthouses not far from the trail or, *having asked in advance,* camp on local farms. Note that many of the trails run for considerable distances through state forests, where camping and fires are strictly forbidden.

The most interesting treks are listed below in the order they are encountered along the Round-Ireland Trail. Descriptive leaflets on each of those in the Republic as well as more general information can be obtained from the *LDWRC,* c/o National Sports Council (Hawkins House, 11th Floor, Dublin 2, Irish Republic; phone: 1-714311), or from the Irish Tourist Board. And before hitting the trail, be sure to get the relevant Ordnance Survey Map (see "Maps and More Information," below).

WICKLOW WAY, Marlay Park, County Dublin, to Clonegal, County Carlow, Irish Republic: This 80-mile trek contours the east side of the Wicklow Mountains, then wanders among the smaller hills in the south part of County Dublin, passing through many beautiful valleys, most notably Luggala; Powerscourt, known for its waterfall; and Glendalough, whose monastic ruins are described in *Ancient Monuments and Ruins.* The route then proceeds through lush mature forests over the spurs of the mountains, with fine panoramas of hills and the Irish Sea. The Dublin Way, which crosses the Dublin mountains from east to west and joins the Wicklow Way, offers another diversion. Because both of these run close to Dublin, they are the most frequented of the Irish trails, and good accommodations, including several youth hostels, are within easy reach.

SOUTH LEINSTER WAY, Kildavin, County Carlow, to Carrick-on-Suir, County Tipperary, Irish Republic: Beginning just 4 miles from the end of the Wicklow Way, this 58-mile footpath climbs via forest tracks over the shoulder of Mount Leinster, at the 1,500-foot level, to expose vistas over Wexford to the east and the beautiful river Barrow Valley straight ahead. The trail then descends to the river and follows the riverside towpath for a few miles to Graiguenamanagh, a picturesque market town that is the site of a 13th-century Cistercian abbey. At Graiguenamanagh, it begins climbing again, over the shoulder of Brandon Hill, and thence proceeds over byroads and forest footpaths to the river Nore, at Inistioge, and on to Carrick-on-Suir.

BURREN WAY, Ballinalacken to Ballyvaughan, County Clare, Irish Republic: Covering a distance of 14 miles around the rugged, almost lunar, landscape of County Clare, this is the newest of Ireland's signposted walking trails. The route starts near the Atlantic coast, north of Doolin and slightly west of Lisdoonvarna, and stretches by the valley of Oughtdarra and Ballyryan. It then gently climbs to the uplands of Ballynahown, joining the Green Road through the highlands of the Burren, with its sheets of limestone and shale-covered hills. Next comes the contrasts of the Caher Valley, the Feenagh Valley, and the Rathborney River, ending at Ballyvaughan on the southern slopes of Galway Bay. The path takes in many sights that are indigenous to the Burren: vast stretches of limestone, massive beds of granite, rock pavements, karst land, clints (horizontal slabs), grikes (vertical fissures), caverns and caves, ruined castles, and cliff forts, as well as wildlife, birds, and flora representing a mix of Arctic, Alpine, and Mediterranean species.

EAST MUNSTER WAY, Carrick-on-Suir, County Tipperary, to Lismore, County Cork, Irish Republic: The towpath on the river Suir takes this 36-mile trail as far as Clonmel, where it continues via forest trails and byroads to the end of the Comeragh range and into the pleasant, peaceful Nier Valley. After crossing the Nier, the trail rambles through the woods on the northern side of the Knockmealdown Mountains, affording lovely views of the Galtee Mountains to the northwest, then climbs the aptly named Vee Gap, and finally descends through the woods to the *Lismore Youth Hostel* (phone: 58-54390) in County Waterford.

KERRY WAY, Killarney to Glenbeigh, County Kerry, Irish Republic: This 36-mile stretch of footpath cuts south through the Muckross National Park, past the celebrated lakes of Killarney, to Torc Mountain, an unrivaled viewpoint over the MacGillicuddy Reeks, and then follows the old Kenmare road, now unused, for a few miles before crossing into the remote Black Valley, immediately underneath the reeks. The trail is almost entirely on old Mass paths as it travels westward below the reeks to the rarely visited Bridia Valley and on to Glencar. There it crosses the valley by road and forest path, supplying hikers with good views of Caragh Lake, and then climbs over Windy Gap to descend to Glenbeigh on the Ring of Kerry. Here the adventurous can pick up the trail of the disused railway line that goes almost to Cahirciveen; otherwise, the Round-Ireland Trail has a big gap.

WESTERN WAY, Oughterard, County Galway, to Westport, County Mayo, Irish Republic: From its starting point, an angling center, this 58-mile walk follows the shores of giant Lough Corrib, past one of the few remaining virgin forests in the west of the country, with fine panoramas of the lake's wooded north shore, before plunging into the mountains of Connemara. Ascending only to about 800 feet, the trail does not attain any great altitude, but the feel is definitely alpine as it winds between the bare quartzite peaks of the Maumturks and Twelve Bens before descending to the narrow mountain-fringed Killary Harbour. From Leenane, near the head of this inlet, the trail heads up the Erriff Valley and then through the South Mayo mountains, over the shore of the Sheffry Hills toward Croagh Patrick, Ireland's holy mountain. Beyond the ridge to its east, island-speckled Clew Bay is straight ahead. Then the route turns east and travels along side roads to reach another angling center, Westport.

ULSTER WAY (DONEGAL) Pettigo to Falcarragh, County Donegal, Irish Republic: Connecting to the Ulster Way (described below) at the border town and famous pilgrimage center of Pettigo, this 62-mile trail traverses countryside that is significantly more remote than that of other trails — definitely not for the inexperienced. It begins by skirting holy Lough Derg, where anglers reel in bountiful creels and thousands of pilgrims fast and pray in a cavern on Station Island every summer, then passes beautiful Lough Eske, and steers a careful course over the eastern side of the Blue Stack Mountains. Passing through the Glendowan Mountains, it descends to Glenveagh, crosses by the Poisoned Glen to Dunlewy, and climbs over the shoulder of Errigal before descending past Altan Lough to Falcarragh on the north coast. Accommodations are not plentiful, so take a tent.

SLIEVE BLOOM WAY, Counties Laois and Offaly, Irish Republic: This 32-mile-long route makes a circuit of the Slieve Bloom Mountains, which rise out of the Central Plain between Portlaoise and Tullamore, on the border of County Laois. It can be joined at any one of seven starting points and can be followed in whole or in part through the beautiful wooded valleys and glens of this range, which seems quite grand, despite its rather insignificant height (about 1,700 feet), because of the flat terrain all around. It is also possible to link up with the Kildare Trails, which largely follow the towpaths of the Grand Canal and its branches.

ULSTER WAY, around Northern Ireland: This 500-mile circle of Northern Ireland takes in some of Ireland's finest scenery, including the coast and glens of County Antrim, with the magnificent Atlantic coast cliffs and bays, the Giant's Causeway, the Sperrin Mountains, the Fermanagh Lakeland, the Mourne Mountains, and St. Patrick country, rich in legend and antiquities. From Belfast, the route winds through the quiet wooded valley of the river Lagan. In addition, the trail connects with several in the Republic: the wild and remote 62-mile-long Ulster Way in Donegal (with a junction at Pettigo); the 16-mile-long Cavan Way, short but varied and beautiful (intersecting at Blacklion, County Fermanagh); and the circular Táin Trail, a 19-mile circle through the historic Carlingford Peninsula (with an unwaymarked link to the Ulster Trail at Newry, County Down). Details: *Sports Council of Northern Ireland,* House of Sport, Upper Malone Rd., Belfast BT9 5LA, Northern Ireland (phone: 232-381222).

MAPS AND MORE INFORMATION

When Daniel Boone was asked whether he had ever been lost, he replied, "Nope, but I was a mite confused once for three days." To avoid that fate, and to help plan a trip, it's essential to have the proper maps and guidebooks. The best way to begin planning a trip is to gather general information from the Irish Tourist Board or the Northern Ireland Tourist Board and then consult maps and guidebooks.

MAPS: For general planning, the Ordnance Surveys of Northern Ireland (OSNI) and the Republic jointly publish a set of four holiday maps that cover the whole of Ireland on the scale of 1:250,000 (¼ inch to the mile).

The whole of Northern Ireland is covered by modern maps on the scale of 1:50,000 (1¼ inches to the mile), which give the kind of detail that walkers need; these maps also take in some of the border areas of the Republic. For the Mourne Mountains and Lough Erne, OSNI has also published Leisure Maps, 2½ inches to the mile, a large scale that also shows more specific data on trails and recreational facilities.

The Irish Republic has only two maps on a scale useful to hikers — one for the Wicklow Way and one for the MacGillicuddy Reeks (Sheet 78). For the rest of the Republic, the standard map is ½ inch to the mile, which doesn't show much detail and omits critical information on cliffs, forests, and footpaths.

To get copies of the available maps, contact:

Ordnance Survey Office, Phoenix Park, Dublin, Irish Republic (phone: 1-213171). For the Irish Republic.

Government Sales Office, 10/11 Molesworth St., Dublin 2, Irish Republic (phone: 1-793515). For trails in the Republic.

Ordnance Survey of Northern Ireland, Castleton House, Stranmillis Ct., Belfast BT9 5BJ, Northern Ireland (phone: 232-701444).

Many bookstores also carry stocks of Ordnance Survey maps, at least for their own areas.

GUIDEBOOKS: A reputable guidebook series to consult is *Irish Walk Guides,* published by Gill & Macmillan, which covers the country in six volumes — southwest, west, northwest, northeast, east, and southeast. Each lists about 50 walks, giving a detailed description and an illustrated route map. Most walks are in the hills, but not all of them. The book can be obtained from the guidebook sales officers of the *Federation of Mountaineering Clubs of Ireland:*

Finola O'Donoghue, 20 Leopardstown Gardens, Blackrock, County Dublin, Irish Republic (phone: 1-881266).

Margaret Magennis, 17 Deramore Dr., Belfast BT9 5JR 023, Northern Ireland.

In addition, *Eason & Son* (40/42 Lower O'Connell St., Dublin 1, Irish Republic; phone: 1-723811) carries a selection of guidebooks and maps.

HOSTELS: The tourist boards for the Republic and Northern Ireland can provide information about hotels, guesthouses, bed and breakfast establishments, farmhouses, and other forms of accommodation of interest to travelers. For information about hostels and huts designed specifically to shelter walkers and trampers, consult:

Irish Budget Hostels, Doolin Village, County Clare, Irish Republic (phone: 65-74006).

Irish Youth Hostels Association, 39 Mountjoy Sq., Dublin 1, Irish Republic (phone: 1-363111).

Youth Hostel Association of Northern Ireland, 56 Bradbury Pl., Belfast BT7 1RU, Northern Ireland (phone: 232-324733).

Federation of Mountaineering Clubs of Ireland (addresses of the guidebook sales offices are given above). Though the sales officers don't have the facilities for planning detailed itineraries, they do have information on club-managed huts and will try to answer miscellaneous queries from overseas visitors proposing to walk in Ireland; enclose International Reply Coupons when writing.

GROUP TRIPS

If you don't want to go it alone — or do all the requisite planning — contact the following organizations about group treks:

Association for Adventure Sports (AFAS), c/o Tiglin Adventure Centre, Ashford, County Wicklow, Irish Republic (phone: 404-40169). Mountaineering training courses, walking tours, and adventure holidays in County Wicklow.

Holiday Fellowship, c/o David Hilton, 43 Kincardine Pl., Brankum Hall, Glasgow G74, Scotland. Organizes tours along the Wicklow Way and other trails using good-quality accommodations.

Irish Roamer, 13 Wellington Ct., Spencers Wood, Reading RG7 1BN, England (phone: 734-882515). Has week-long walking tours in the hills and mountains of Ireland, some featuring bicycling and canoeing. Accommodations are in small hotels and inns.

Irish Mountain Holidays, Monafodda, Roscrea, County Tipperary, Irish Republic (phone: 509-31150). Week-long tours, including hotel accommodations and transport by minibus to a half dozen 2,500-foot peaks.

Irish Youth Hostels Association (address above). Summer walking tours based on its network of hostels.

Little Killary Adventure Centre, Salruck, Renvyle, County Galway, Irish Republic (phone: 95-43411). Week-long holidays among the high peaks of Connemara, including Croagh Patrick, the Sheffrys, Mweelrea, the Maumturks, and the Twelve Bens. Overnights are at the center, or 1 or 2 nights are spent under canvas in the hills. All camping equipment and personal belongings are transported to the sites.

Mountain Travel, 6420 Fairmount Ave., El Cerrito, CA 94530 (phone: 800-227-2384 or 415-527-8100). Organizes 2-week tours involving guided walks in the west and south of Ireland, with accommodations in hotels and trips between walks by minibus.

For the Mind

Marvelous Museums

 Ireland's antiquities, impressive by any standards, are mostly concentrated in the *National Museum* in Dublin, which should not be missed under any circumstances. But numerous small museums in the provinces offer local collections and eccentric private collections of varying quality. Ireland also boasts a number of fine open-air facilities that show off the lifestyles of earlier people in vivid detail with restored or reconstructed dwellings and workplaces. Most of these are in settings of great beauty. The selections below, listed alphabetically by county, will provide many days of enlightenment and entertainment. All charge nominal admission, if any, and are open year-round unless otherwise indicated; be sure to call for current hours before making a special trip.

PIGHOUSE COLLECTION, Cornafean, County Cavan, Irish Republic: Housed in Mrs. Phyllis Faris's former piggery and several other outbuildings on her picturesque farm, this collection of folk items is an odd and idiosyncratic hodgepodge of dishes, tools, implements, pictures, bicycles, carriages, parasols, lace, 19th-century costumes, bric-a-brac, and even a few rare treasures. Though a little off the beaten path, it is worth a visit — perhaps as a detour on the way to Killykeen Forest Park — not only for the collection itself but also for the trip through the very pleasant and out-of-the-way countryside. From the midland town of Cavan, take the road west toward Killeshandra, then watch for the signpost. The gallery is about 8 miles from Cavan. Mrs. Faris has no staff, so call ahead to make sure she'll be available. Details: *Pighouse Collection,* Corr House, Cornafean, County Cavan, Irish Republic (phone: 49-37248).

BUNRATTY CASTLE AND FOLK PARK, Bunratty, County Clare, Irish Republic: Associated with the O'Briens, the Lords of Thomond, and now authentically restored and furnished in the style of the period, Bunratty Castle is currently famous for its jovial medieval banquets (see also "Mead and Meat Pies: Historical Banquets" in *For the Experience*). But it is also one of Ireland's finest extant 15th-century castles. Together with the adjoining Folk Park, whose several acres abound with period replicas of Irish rural and town dwellings as they would have appeared at the turn of the century, it provides a glimpse of how the Irish have lived during the last few centuries. Visitors can step into whitewashed or limestone farmhouses, cottages, hovels, and other domiciles from different regions (one of them was moved from a spot that subsequently became a Shannon Airport runway), as well as a typical landowner's *bothán* (hut), a blacksmith's forge, a weaver's shed, and a village street complete with post office, pub, school, doctor's office, hotel, and other shops. Turf fires smolder fragrantly in the hearths, socks hang nearby to dry, an old farm implement leans casually against a wall — so that it all looks as if someone has just left the room. The effect is totally charming. Bunratty House, a substantial late Georgian dwelling of the type once occupied by minor gentry, rounds out Bunratty's fine document of Irish social history. A small, well-illustrated guidebook to the castle, available on the spot, is worth getting. Sometimes closed Mondays in winter. Details: *Bunratty Castle and Folk Park,* Bunratty, County Clare, Irish Republic (phone: 61-361511).

CLARE HERITAGE CENTRE, Corofin, County Clare, Irish Republic: In an attractive small town at the edge of the Burren, a desolately beautiful semidesert of limestone rock that is transformed in May and June by the brilliant blossoms of its rare and unusually varied flowering plants, travelers will find this enterprising project, in the specially converted early-19th-century Church of Saint Catherine. The center's collection, which has won several awards for its creator, Naoise Cleary, includes artifacts and documents from all over the county, attractively displayed alongside texts that are lively and readable as well as informative. It is also now the source of an extraordinarily complete documentation of Clare families over the period from 1800–1860 — an enormous contribution to Irish genealogical and social research. Open daily from 10 AM to 6 PM, May through September. Details: *Clare Heritage Centre,* Corofin, County Clare, Irish Republic (phone: 65-27955 between 9:30 and 11 AM).

CRAGGAUNOWEN PROJECT, near Quin, County Clare, Irish Republic: Craggaunowen Castle, built by the McNamaras around 1550 and furnished with many items of historical and artistic importance from the John Hunt collection, is only the centerpiece of this unique outdoor museum, which comprises a number of other structures that reach deep into the past to convey a sense of life in prehistoric times. On an island in the lake, a dwelling known as a *crannóg* has been reconstructed on the foundations of an original; it is approached by a causeway that may have been used as early as the Bronze Age. There is also a reconstructed ring fort, the farmstead of Ireland's early history, which has an underground passageway for storage and refuge. Patty O'Neill runs a program whose aim is to interest and train young people in the fine traditional art of thatching. Displays also include the *Brendan,* the leather boat in which the writer and amateur sailor Tim Severin crossed the Atlantic a decade or so ago in an attempt to prove that the 5th-century St. Brendan could have discovered America, as legend has it, when sailing the seas in search of paradise. Open April through October. Details: *Craggaunowen Project,* Quin, County Clare, Irish Republic (phone: 61-72178).

GLENVEAGH CASTLE AND GLEBE GALLERY, Glenveagh, County Donegal, Irish Republic: Glenveagh National Park, which sprawls over 25,000 acres of Donegal's wild and remote Derryveagh Mountains, includes in its boundaries the awesome Poisoned Glen; the long tongue of Lough Veagh; and, at the edge of its waters, where salmon leap and red deer come to drink, the grounds of Glenveagh Castle, its towers and battlements constituting one of the more romantic creations of 19th-century Ireland. Successive owners have created gardens of extraordinary beauty — formal, terraced, and graced with statuary, crisscrossed by secret pathways, and dissolving gradually into the native heather scrub and dwarf oak of the surrounding rugged mountains. The government purchased the outlying lands in 1975, Philadelphia's Henry McIlhenny gave the grounds and the castle to the Irish people in 1981, and they are now all open to the public, together with the former home of painter Derek Hill at Gartan Lough, on the edge of the estate.

The castle is filled with rare furniture — mostly Georgian, some Irish, all of it very fine — and a special gallery on the grounds of Hill's studio displays an extensive art collection that includes ceramics by Picasso, lithographs by Kokoschka, paintings and sketches by Annigoni, and wallpapers by William Morris, as well as works by distinguished Irish artists. A number of informed people regard the whole complex as the most wonderful spot in all Ireland. A visitors' center, restaurant, and café are on the premises, and a free minibus takes travelers around the grounds. Closed late September through late May. Details: *Glenveagh National Park and Castle,* Glenveagh, County Donegal, Irish Republic (phone: 74-37088 for the castle and 74-37071 for the gallery).

CHESTER BEATTY LIBRARY, Dublin, Irish Republic: The collection that copper millionaire Chester Beatty bequeathed to the Irish nation in 1968, housed near the

Royal Dublin Society building in plush, embassy-belt Ballsbridge, evokes one superlative after another. The collection of Islamic art and manuscripts, among the finest in the world, includes more than 250 Korans; Persian, Turkish, and Indian painting are also extensively covered. The collection of Chinese jade books is unique. The Chinese snuffbox collection numbers 900 pieces, and that of rhinoceros horn cups includes some 220 items. The collection of Japanese illuminated manuscripts (*nara-e*) ranks with the foremost in Europe, as does the collection of Japanese woodblock prints (*surimono*). The superb group of Western manuscripts includes illuminated books of hours and a volume of gospels from Stavelot Abbey, executed in Flanders in about AD 1000. The important biblical papyri, 11 manuscript volumes of the Bible dating from the early 2nd to the 4th century, are also in the library's possession. Naturally, it is possible to display only a tiny fraction of the library's holdings at a time, but the permanent exhibitions offer a representative sampling, and there are major shows a few times a year. Closed Sundays and Mondays. Details: *Chester Beatty Library,* 20 Shrewsbury Rd., Ballsbridge, Dublin 4, Irish Republic (phone: 1-692386).

MUSEUM OF NATURAL HISTORY, Dublin, Irish Republic: Much loved for its refusal to change an iota over the course of the past century, this museum, originally among the three major Royal Dublin Society collections, was moved over a century ago to a building designed by Thomas Clarendon and constructed on the south side of Leinster Lawn, with an entrance on Merrion Square. The first sight to greet a visitor's eye is that old favorite, the Basking Shark, a huge preserved shark which hangs from the ceiling. Also popular is the display of birds, as well as the three magnificent skeletons of Giant Irish Deer, believed to be about 10,000 years old. On the ground floor, the Irish Room displays Irish fauna and a new exhibition of Irish insects. An impressive collection of big game heads and antlers from India and Africa — bison, panda, giraffe, okapi, rhinos, hippos, elephants, and gorillas — hanging on pillars and walls in the galleries on the upper floor transports museumgoers to late Victorian times. On the next floor are exotic shells, butterflies, and birds — plus skeletons of the extinct dodo, solitaire, and giant bird of Madagascar, with its 11.7-inch egg. A priceless assemblage of glass models of the invertebrates, which dates from the museum's earliest days, is also well worth seeing. Suspended from the roof are the huge skeletons of humpback whales. From the museum's last period of vigorous acquisition — the 1880s to 1914, when deep-sea explorations generated additions to the marine biology and zoology sections — to very recently, there was little activity in the museum; the impressive geological collection has long languished unseen for want of a proper home. In the the geological section there is a small exhibition of Irish rocks and minerals, and the museum has expanded its activities in the field of entomology and marine invertebrates. Closed Mondays. Details: *Museum of Natural History,* Merrion Sq., Dublin 2, Irish Republic (phone: 1-618811).

NATIONAL GALLERY OF IRELAND, Dublin, Irish Republic: Located on the western side of one of Ireland's finest Georgian districts, Merrion Square, within walking distance of the center of town, the *National Gallery* has been called "the best small gallery in Europe." Certainly, considering its chronic shortage of funds, it has a remarkable collection, with some outstanding examples of the works of all major schools, particularly the Italian and Dutch. Under the previous director, James White, and the present director, Homan Potterton, the gallery has shaken off an apparent case of the doldrums, regained much of its style of several decades past, and begun to achieve its potential. Andrea di Bartolo, Fra Angelico, Uccello, Signorelli, Perugino, Titian, Rembrandt, El Greco, and David are all represented; a collection of more than 30 Turner watercolors is shown every January. The Irish School is brilliantly represented by the works of Jack Yeats and earlier painters such as Nathaniel Hone, Walter Osborne, William Orpen, and James Arthur O'Connor. Though staff shortages often cause a number of its rooms to be closed, the gallery is lively and interesting, with an active educational policy, a good research library, a modest bookshop, and an inexpensive restaurant that has become a popular Dublin meeting place. Open daily. Details: *National Gallery of Ireland,* Merrion Sq., Dublin 2, Irish Republic (phone: 1-615133).

NATIONAL MUSEUM, Dublin, Irish Republic: The massive Thomas Deane building on Kildare Street into which the old Royal Dublin Society moved its collection in 1890 and, shortly thereafter, the antiquities from the Royal Irish Academy has lost some of its territory over the years..Its display space is inadequate, and many items are not exhibited to their best advantage. These shortcomings notwithstanding, the museum should not be missed. It has priceless collections of prehistoric gold artifacts, such as solid gold dress fasteners, torques, and lunulae made by the skilled craftsmen of the Bronze and Iron ages. An exhibition area called The Treasury features the museum's important collection of early Christian metalwork, including the *Ardagh Chalice* and the *Cross of Cong.* The Georgian silver, Waterford crystal, and Belleek pottery on display are equally captivating. Visitors should not miss the collection of Irish harps, *uilleann* pipes, and other musical instruments, nor the Derrynaflan chalice, paten, and strainer, found in March 1980 at Killenaule in Tipperary. Finds from the site of Viking Dublin are on display in the museum's exhibition center at nearby Merrion Row. Closed Mondays. Details: *National Museum,* Kildare St., Dublin 2, Irish Republic (phone: 1-618811).

JAMES JOYCE MUSEUM, Sandycove, County Dublin, Irish Republic: Like other Martello towers around the Irish coast, the one that houses this museum was built in 1804 to withstand a threatened Napoleonic invasion, and it would have remained an attractive but fairly anonymous pile of granite had it not been for James Joyce's *Ulysses,* one of the greatest novels in the English language. The novel begins: "Do you pay rent for this tower? — Twelve quid, Buck Mulligan said. — To the Secretary of State for War, Stephen added over his shoulder . . . — Rather bleak in wintertime, I should say. Martello, you call it?" Joyce lived here briefly in 1904 with a medical-student friend named Oliver St. John Gogarty, who paid an annual rent of IR£8 to the War Office for his tenancy, and emerged in print as the "stately plump Buck Mulligan" to Stephen Dedalus, Joyce's alter ego. Sylvia Beach, *Ulysses'* first publisher, opened the tower as a museum in 1962, and it now holds an odd and varied collection of memorabilia: the writer's piano and guitar; his waistcoat, tie, and cane; and letters, manuscripts, photographs, and rare editions. But the chief exhibit is the tower itself, a squat structure looking across Dublin Bay to Howth that is one of the few of its type currently open to the public. On June 16, the day when the events described in *Ulysses* took place, the tower is the beginning for many a Joyce fan's *Bloomsday* tour. Open year-round, but by appointment only from October through April. Details: *James Joyce Museum,* Sandycove, County Dublin, Irish Republic (phone: 1-808571).

MUCKROSS HOUSE AND GARDENS, near Killarney, County Kerry, Irish Republic: The emphasis at this museum, another among the Republic's most forward-looking, is as much on displaying the objects in an interesting way as on preserving them, and a great deal of thought and effort has been put into every exhibit. In addition, potters and weavers can be seen at work, producing the kinds of items displayed in the museum proper. When sated, visitors can go out for a stroll on one of the nature trails that meander across the vast grounds (which, together with the early-19th-century house containing the exhibits, were presented to the nation in 1932 and now comprise the 25,000-acre Killarney National Park). The footpaths alone might warrant a visit here, encircling two of the lakes of Killarney. There is also a superb natural rock garden and an abundance of free-roaming red deer and rare flora. Open daily year-round. Details: *Muckross House Folk Museum,* Kenmare Rd., Muckross, Killarney, County Kerry, Irish Republic (phone: 64-31440).

IRISH HORSE MUSEUM, Tully, County Kildare, Irish Republic: Ireland, which has produced some of the world's greatest thoroughbreds, is still turning them out at the Irish National Stud, on whose grounds this museum is located; a few of these animals — and their progeny — may be seen before and after viewing its collections. Small but interesting, the exhibits trace the history of the horse from the Bronze Age to modern times and cover not only horses involved in racing, hunting, show jumping, and steeplechasing, but also draft horses and others not at the fore of the Irish horse scene. Occupying center stage is the skeleton of the late Arkle (1957–66), one of the nation's greatest and best-loved steeplechasers, who made a place for himself in equine history when he won the *Cheltenham Gold Cup* 3 years in a row — much to the consternation of British trainers and the glee of every Irishman — plus some 27 other victories in only 35 starts. For achievement-oriented visitors, there's an automated quiz and nearby are beautiful Japanese gardens laid out by a turn-of-the-century Japanese landscape architect named Eida. Open daily from *Easter* through October. Details: *National Stud Museum and Japanese Gardens,* Tully, County Kildare, Irish Republic (phone: 45-21251).

MONAGHAN COUNTY MUSEUM, Monaghan, County Monaghan, Irish Republic: One of the Republic's first county museums, this institution — formerly situated in a bleak old courthouse with huge Doric columns that must have put the fear of God into prisoners during the last century — has a stunning and eclectic collection ranging from Neolithic relics to folk items. And it now has a home of its own that provides the showcase they deserve. Stuffed with china dinner sets, lace made in nearby Carrickmacross, and the cotton crochet known as Clones lace, the museum also contains artifacts such as the *Cross of Clogher,* which dates from the early 15th century, as well as a cauldron (ca. 800 BC) found in a bog in 1854, old photographs, and in an open-access exhibition area, a collection of *querns* (hand mills), milk churns, and milestones from the now-unused Ulster Canal. This award-winning museum is one of Ireland's most progressive, and the collections are constantly improving. Closed Sundays September through May. Details: *Monaghan County Museum,* 1/2 Hill St., Monaghan, County Monaghan, Irish Republic (phone: 47-82928 or 47-88109).

COUNTY CASTLE MUSEUM, Enniscorthy, County Wexford, Irish Republic: A medieval air hangs over this town, with its narrow streets winding down to the river Slaney on one side and with Vinegar Hill, where the Irish rebels were defeated in 1798, rising on the other. The museum, housed in a 13th-century Norman castle on which the Elizabethan poet Edmund Spenser once held a lease (one of the few Irish castles not in ruins), contains muskets, pikes, and other relics of the battle, as well as objects from the 1916 Rising (during which this town was the last in the country to surrender). But the museum's contents are not restricted to military impedimenta: A kitchen at the back of the castle and a dairy showcase traditional cooking utensils and tools, including churns used in the old days for making butter and cheese. There are also striking displays of figureheads salvaged from ships wrecked off the coast, a stone covered with *ogham* script, ships' anchors, stone crosses, and chalices dating from the 17th century. A recently added feature is a sports collection, housed in a hitherto unused tower of the castle. And if all this is not enough temptation, the view from the castle roof alone is worth the visit. Open daily, except December and January, when it is only open on Sundays. Details: *County Castle Museum,* Castle Hill, Enniscorthy, County Wexford, Irish Republic (phone: 54-35926).

NATIONAL HERITAGE PARK, Ferrycarrig, County Wexford, Irish Republic: The museum on the sloping banks of the river Slaney estuary is devoted to showing a full range of Irish historic buildings, with structures dating from the time of the earliest settlements to the present — from stone circles and burial sites to early Christian churches, round towers, and the first Viking and Norman communities. It is an elaborate undertaking — and thoroughly splendid. Open daily. Details: *National Heritage Park,* Ferrycarrig, County Wexford, Irish Republic (phone: 53-22211 or 53-41733).

IRISH AGRICULTURAL MUSEUM, Wexford, County Wexford, Irish Republic:
In the restored 19th-century farm buildings of Victorian Gothic Johnstown Castle,
about 3 miles southwest of Wexford Town, this museum provides an excellent picture
of just how much Irish farming has changed in the last 50 years. Its display of old
farming and rural craft items, the country's largest, includes the hand flails, pitchers,
turnip pulpers, butter-making instruments, ploughs, harrows, sowers, mowing machines, harnesses, and carts and traps that were once among every Irish farmer's most
important tools. A complete model of an old kitchen is on exhibit, along with a laundry,
creamery, laborer's bedroom, and stable. There are also displays on coopering, blacksmithing, wheelwrighting, harness making, and traditional Irish country furniture. The
castle's 50-acre gardens — full of meandering pathways, artificial lakes, and interesting
shrubs and flowers — are also a delight, and a tearoom is open at the museum from
June through August. The castle and surrounding farm are used for soil research by
the Agricultural Institute. Open daily, May through October; weekdays only the rest
of the year. Details: *Irish Agricultural Museum,* Johnstown Castle, Wexford, County
Wexford, Irish Republic (phone: 53-42888).

ULSTER MUSEUM, Belfast, County Antrim, Northern Ireland: Housed in a
1920s neo-classical building with a well-designed modern addition that stands right in
the city's delightful Botanic Gardens, the collections are broad-ranging: There's an old,
functioning water wheel (in the Industrial Archaeology section); a group of contemporary paintings and sculpture unrivaled in Ireland (in the Art Galleries); prehistoric
artifacts including the only surviving pair of late Bronze Age trumpets that can still
be played; a display of minerals and gemstones unique in the country (including the
largest group of quartz crystals in Britain and Ireland, an attractive display of fluores-
cent and phosphorescent minerals in a darkened central vault, and a full-size cave); and,
for a touch of glitter, the fabulous collection of jewelry, coins, and other items recovered
from the *Girona,* a galley of the Spanish Armada that went down off the Antrim Coast
in 1588. The Living Sea exhibit abounds with realistic models of marine creatures, and
the Dinosaur Show, a gallery designed with children in mind, features a near-complete
skeleton of *Anatosaurus annecteus* as well as an enormous, now extinct, coelacanth in
the old entrance hall. The museum store sells copies of the gold *No tengo más que darte*
ring, the original of which was worn by a Spanish sailor as he went to his watery grave,
mindful, no doubt, of the sweetheart who gave it to him. Open daily. Details: *Ulster
Museum,* Botanic Gardens, Belfast BT9 5AB, Northern Ireland (phone: 232-381251).

**ULSTER FOLK AND TRANSPORT MUSEUM, Holywood, County Down, North-
ern Ireland:** This is the place for a glimpse of how Ulster folk lived back at the turn
of the century. Brick by brick, stone by stone, terraces of townhouses, as well as
farmhouses, mills, a church, and schools, were moved here, then furnished with the
everyday objects of the appropriate period, and landscaped as they might have been
originally. A farm from mid-Antrim has been reconstructed right down to the stone
walls, hedges, and ditches around the fields. There's also an assortment of galleries filled
with domestic and agricultural artifacts and vehicles used in Irish transport over the
ages — rail, road, air, and sea. In fact, the museum is the home of the finest and most
comprehensive such display in Ireland, with wheelless sledges, elegant horse-drawn
carriages, automobiles (including a De Lorean sports car prototype), and even a verti-
cal-takeoff plane. (Railway rolling stock is kept in Belfast, on Witham Street, off the
Lower Newtownards road.) Throughout the year there are demonstrations of seasonal
crafts. Occasionally soda bread is baked over a traditional turf fire. Open Mondays
through Saturdays from 10 AM to 5 PM. Details: *Ulster Folk and Transport Museum,*
Cultra Manor, Holywood, County Down BT18 0EU, Northern Ireland (phone: 232-
428428).

**ULSTER-AMERICAN FOLK PARK, near Omagh, County Tyrone, Northern Ire-
land:** Born in 1813 in a thatch-roofed cottage near here, Thomas Mellon emigrated to

the New World at the age of 5 and then traveled overland by wagon to western Pennsylvania, where he grew up as the son of struggling small farmers to found the banking empire that bears his name. Now, more than 150 years later, the original Mellon cottage is restored, and it serves as the center of a 26-acre folk park where the Old World and New World stand physically side by side. From 19th-century Ulster, where turf fires burn, blacksmiths work at their forges, craftsmen toil in their thatch-roofed cottages, and hardware stores sell lamp wicks and foot warmers, visitors are transported to a very different American landscape, complete with log cabins, a covered wagon, and a reconstructed Pennsylvania farm complex that has been furnished and equipped exactly like the one in which Mellon spent his boyhood, where demonstrators bake, weave, and churn, and log fires crackle on the hearth. Great attention to detail makes it all feel remarkably real. Closed weekends October to March. Details: *Ulster-American Folk Park,* Camphill, Omagh, County Tyrone, Northern Ireland (phone: 662-3292).

The Performing Arts

The Irish tend to agree with the late theater critic Kenneth Tynan, who once noted "Ireland's sacred duty to send over, every few years, a playwright to save the English theatre from inarticulate glumness." But the attitude cannot be blamed on sour grapes. The contribution of this nation's writers is outstanding and all out of proportion to the island's small population. The names Sheridan, Goldsmith, Wilde, Shaw, Synge, O'Casey, Behan, and Beckett, to name but a few, inevitably crop up whenever great drama is under discussion — and with them, the names of such late great actors and actresses as Barry Fitzgerald and Siobhán McKenna, as well as those of their successors. A special feature of the Irish theater scene is the colorful show of song, dance, and story at Galway's all-Irish *Taibhdhearc na Gaillimhe* (Middle St., Galway; phone: 91-62024).

With all this going on, settling on an evening's entertainment (or an afternoon's, for that matter) can pose some problems. When it comes to theater, one man's meat is another's moan, so before settling on a play, ask a friend or check the daily papers in Dublin, Cork, and Belfast; Galway's *Connacht Tribune;* the fortnightly events guide *In Dublin;* and the monthly *In Belfast.*

Some theaters reliably turn out productions and concerts that are more interesting or wonderful than others, and some are worth a visit in their own right — because they are either particularly beautiful or unusually historic. A few are quite small, so that even the most remote corner affords a fine view of the activities on stage — and the prices are usually relatively low by stateside standards. A few of the best theaters are listed here, alphabetically by county.

ABBEY THEATRE, Dublin, Irish Republic: The fine collection of portraits, including likenesses of W. B. Yeats, Lady Gregory, John Millington Synge, and Sean O'Casey, that graces the foyer of the *Abbey Theatre* — the country's national theater — is a vivid reminder of those heady days when the premieres of O'Casey's *Plough and the Stars* and Synge's *The Playboy of the Western World* were greeted by riot and disorder. Though audiences are less boisterous now and the company is less likely to be arrested (as it was in Philadelphia in 1912, for performing "immoral and indecent" plays), the Abbey still presents the best of contemporary Irish play writing, including productions of works by Brian Friel, Hugh Leonard, and Thomas Murphy, among others, as well as revivals of the classics that made the 85-year-old *Abbey Players* famous. Work of a more experimental nature is presented downstairs, in the Peacock; the opportunity to visit this wonderfully intimate auditorium should not be missed. After the show, slip across the road for a drink in *The Plough,* full of posters of past *Abbey* successes, or in *The Flowing Tide,* with attractive stained glass panels set into the walls — and mingle with the actors who have just taken their bows. Details: *Abbey Theatre,* Lower Abbey St., Dublin 1, Irish Republic (phone: 1-787222).

ANDREWS LANE THEATRE, Dublin, Irish Republic: Tucked in an alley off Dame Street and not far from Trinity College, this is one of Dublin's newest theaters, making its mark with performances of such contemporary plays as *Agnes of God.* In addition to the main theater, there is a small studio which serves as a stage for avant-garde productions, including occasional lunchtime shows and performances by all-female acting troupes. Details: *Andrews Lane Theatre,* 9-17 Andrews La., Dublin 2, Irish Republic (phone: 1-679-5720).

FOCUS THEATRE, Dublin, Irish Republic: Dublin's smallest theater is also one of its most exciting. In 1963, when Deirdre O'Connell returned to Ireland after studying in New York at Lee Strasberg's Actors' Studio, she began to train some Dublin actors in Stanislavskian technique and, by 1967, had formed the nucleus of a company and moved into a converted garage in a lane off Pembroke Street. An evening in this tiny, 72-seat auditorium is never disappointing, whether the play be a classic by Chekhov or the latest offering of a young Irish writer. Besides the resident *Focus Company,* there is a *Studio Company* of young actors-in-training who occasionally present their own improvised and very original adaptations of Irish legends and literature. It is no exaggeration to say that, along with some of the finest actors in Dublin (including O'Connell herself), *Focus* theatergoers glimpse the stars of tomorrow. Details: *Focus Theatre,* 6 Pembroke Pl., Dublin 2, Irish Republic (phone: 1-763071).

GAIETY THEATRE, Dublin, Irish Republic: The *Gaiety* is where many a Dublin child, brought for a special occasion to a pantomime perhaps or a Gilbert and Sullivan musical, gets a first taste of the magic of theater. It was founded in 1871 by Michael Gunn and his brother John (a bust of whom can be seen on the staircase that leads to the circle), and although the original gallery, or "gods," was removed when the theater was renovated in 1955, the theater remains a very fine example of the typical late-Victorian playhouse: It is marvelously opulent, with red carpets, dark pillars, golden draperies, and ornate pink cream plasterwork, and the orchestra pit's brass surround enhances the total effect. In a private box, patrons feel like no less than visiting royalty. The letters patent issued at the theater's founding allows for the production of "any interlude, tragedy, comedy, prelude, opera, burletta, play, farce or pantomime," and today's repertoire remains just that broad. As a result, the list of the famous who have played at the *Gaiety* is formidable, including Lily Langtry, the *D'Oyly Carte Opera Company,* Burgess Meredith, Siobhán McKenna, Paulette Goddard, the *Bolshoi Ballet,* Peter O'Toole — and Dublin's own Jimmy O'Dea, who for nearly 30 years appeared in pantomime and musical and, in the character of Biddy Mulligan, captured the true spirit of the city. Details: *Gaiety Theatre,* South King St., Dublin 2, Irish Republic (phone: 1-771717).

GATE THEATRE, Dublin, County Dublin, Irish Republic: The name of the *Gate Theatre* is synonymous with those of the late Michael MacLiammoir and Hilton Edwards, who organized the company in 1928 to present plays of unusual interest, regardless of nationality or period, at a time when the *Abbey* devoted itself entirely to Irish work. The founders' tradition continues under the direction of Michael Colgan, and theatergoers here are as likely to find a play by Tennessee Williams as one by Brian Friel or a young unknown. The visual emphasis is strong, and the theater has received awards for its stage designs. The auditorium is quite small and, as might be expected from the *Gate*'s reputation for stage design, beautifully decorated, so that it feels less like a modern playhouse than an 18th-century aristocrat's court theater. The young Orson Welles was once employed by the *Gate,* after exaggerating his previous experience, but proved his talents there as, subsequently, elsewhere. James Mason and Geraldine Fitzgerald also began their careers here. Details: *Gate Theatre,* 1 Cavendish Row, Dublin 1, Irish Republic (phone: 1-744045).

OLYMPIA THEATRE, Dublin, Irish Republic: This stage occupies a very special place in the hearts of Dubliners, perhaps because of its connection with music hall, always the most popular form of theater here. Patrons on the 1879 opening night at Dan Lowrey's *Star of Erin* (as the playhouse was then called) enjoyed such wonders as Mademoiselle Miaco, the Boneless Wonder, and Signor Zula, who swung from a high trapeze by his feet, with weights suspended from his teeth. Part of the theater's charm may be gauged from the fact that one of its bars is named not for some famous performer or patron, but for Kathleen Kelly, who served wit and kindness as well as drink from behind its counter for many decades. The only theater in Dublin that still retains its gallery, or "gods," from whose dizzying heights one can see the tops of the performers' heads far below, it is also notable for the Waterford cut-glass chandeliers and the two huge mirrors on either side of the circle in which the spectators can monitor their own reactions while watching the performance. And, though television has meant the end of theatrical variety, the *Olympia* still presents concerts and pantomimes as well as plays, both Irish and foreign, and hosts visiting performers such as mime king Marcel Marceau. After each show, the bars remain open for half an hour and the actors congregate in *Kelly's* bar, attached to the theater, to drink to the memory of days gone by. Details: *Olympia Theatre,* 72 Dame St., Dublin 2, Irish Republic (phone: 17-78962).

THE POINT, Dublin, Irish Republic: Also known as the "Point Depot" because it was formerly a depot building, this new theater–cum–concert hall presents everything from *U2* concerts to Broadway hits, such as *Cats.* Ticket prices are heftier here than at any other performing arts venue in Dublin, and most events are booked well in advance. Details: *The Point,* East Link Bridge, Dublin 1, Irish Republic (phone: 1-363633).

ROYAL DUBLIN SOCIETY CONCERT HALL, Dublin, Irish Republic: While most people think of traditional Irish music when they think of Dublin, it's also true that high-quality classical music can be found here. This is at least in part thanks to the Royal Dublin Society (RDS), which stages recitals from November to March in its 1,206-seat *Members' Hall,* also known as the *RDS Concert Hall.* Although the acoustics are not all that one might desire for small chamber ensembles and soloists, the attractive book-lined walls add a touch of intimacy that is not often encountered in concert halls nowadays, and many distinguished musicians have played here in recent years — among them the *Smetana String Quartet,* Isaac Stern, and Julian Lloyd Webber. Details: *Royal Dublin Society,* Ballsbridge, Dublin 4, Irish Republic (phone: 1-680645.

DRUID LANE THEATRE, Galway, County Galway, Irish Republic: Installed in a former grocery warehouse in the oldest part of the city, near the Spanish Arch, the quays, and the old city walls, the home of the *Druid Theatre Company* is perhaps the most attractive small theater in Ireland, its intimacy enhanced by the way in which the seating surrounds the stage on three sides. The company was founded in 1975 by Garry Hynes, still the artistic director, and in a short time has become renowned for its productions of Irish classics such as Boucicault's *The Colleen Bawn* and Molloy's *Wood of Whispering,* as well as contemporary Irish plays (in particular, those by Tom Murphy) and works from abroad. There's good reason to believe that the lane on which the theater is built is haunted by the ghost of a nun who walks slowly through the street at night. But don't let this get in the way of an evening with this exciting young group. Details: *Druid Lane Theatre,* Druid La. (also known as Chapel La.), Galway, County Galway, Irish Republic (phone: 91-68617).

SIAMSA TÍRE, THE NATIONAL FOLK THEATRE OF IRELAND, Tralee, County Kerry, Irish Republic: In the evenings before television, the country people of Ireland would gather around a turf fire to play music, sing songs, tell stories, and recount the day's activities. Such an occasion was called a *siamsa* (pronounced shee-*am*-sah) and down in The Kingdom, as Kerry is called, *Siamsa Tíre* has taken the spirit of those days of neighborly entertainment and translated it into a stage show that has been received with delight not only abroad but, proof of its faithfulness to tradition, in Ireland itself. The show *Siamsa,* which critic Clive Barnes acclaimed as "absolutely superb," is a whirlwind of song, dance, and music in three acts that re-creates a time when life was simpler, certainly harder, but perhaps more rewarding in its closeness to nature. To watch it in *Siamsa Tíre's* fine new theater in Tralee is to be transported in time to a country kitchen of long ago. The production is not only a re-creation of the past, but also proof of the liveliness of those traditions. June through September. Information: *Siamsa Tíre Theatre,* Godfrey Pl., Tralee, County Kerry, Irish Republic (phone: 66-23055).

GRAND OPERA HOUSE, Belfast, Northern Ireland: When architect Robert McKinstry first went into the deserted building of Belfast's *Grand Opera House and Cirque* in the summer of 1975, he found the house manager's black jacket still hanging on the back of his office door. Crates of bottled beer stood unopened behind the bar where 4 years of dust topped the dour liquids in the half-empty glasses. An upturned chair floated in the orchestra pit. The ashtrays on the backs of the seats in the circle were stuffed with the detritus of chocolate box wrappings and butts of now unfashionable local cigarette brands. In a drawer in the projection room lay a single copy of a pamphlet entitled *How to Emigrate.* But now the *Opera House* has come back to life. The brass rails that once reflected the footlights that illuminated Pavlova and the Divine Sarah (Bernhardt) glisten again, and the turn-of-the-century theater has been restored to its full plush and stucco glory. *Christmas* pantomimes share the bill with drama companies from all over Britain and Ireland, international opera and ballet companies, and major popular entertainers — among them the *National Theatre,* the *Royal Flanders Ballet,* the *Centaur Theatre of Montreal,* the *Berlin Chamber Orchestra,* Carlo Bergonzi, the *Scottish Ballet,* the *Moscow Balalaika Orchestra,* a harp ensemble from Japan, the *Peking Opera,* James Galway, the *Chieftains,* and modern dancers from New York. In July and early August, the house usually is dark. Details: *Grand Opera House,* Great Victoria St., Belfast BT2 7HR, Northern Ireland (phone: 232-249129 for recorded information; 232-241919 for advance booking).

TRADITIONAL IRISH MUSIC

Though there are more concerts, folk festivals, folk clubs, and informal sessions of musicmaking in Ireland than ever before, those magical nights of wild, sweet music and hilarity are still as elusive as the rainbow's end. When the melody rises through the fog of smoke, audiences forget about the uncomfortable chairs, the well-ringed tabletops, the naked walls. The room is transformed. It's all too easy, however, to hit upon the right pub on the wrong night, to settle down beside a stack of musicians only to find that they're more of a mind to chat with each other than to lash out the reels. Before setting out to fill your ears with concertinas and flutes, it's useful to have a pretty good idea about where they might be found.

For information about concerts, folk clubs, and festivals around the country, see the folk column in Friday's *Evening Press.* Also, before leaving Dublin, stop in at the elegant Belgrave Square, Monkstown, headquarters of the *Comhaltas Ceoltóirí Eireann* (phone: 1-800295), where there is entertainment nightly. The *CCE* has traditional music concerts, shows, and informal sessions nightly from May through September and on Friday and Saturday nights year-round; it also sponsors the *All-Ireland Festival,* or *Fleadh Cheoil na hÉireann* (see *Feis and Fleadh: The Best Festivals*), every year on the fourth weekend in August, a *Mardi Gras* of Irish traditional music that attracts up to

100,000 people. In addition, there are more than 30 provincial and county *fleadhanna,* which often produce music of an equivalent standard, but are cozier, more informal, more redolent of regional flavors, and consequently potentially even more interesting. The *CCE* office can provide the particulars, and can tell you where to find traditional music "down the country."

DUBLIN: There is a thorough listing of the traditional goings-on in the fortnightly magazine *In Dublin,* the bi-weekly *Dublin Event Guide* (free at hotels, tourist offices, and shops), and in the ads in the evening newspapers. Some of the best choices in the capital are the famous *O'Donoghue's* (15 Merrion Row); its neighbor, *Foley's* (1 Merrion Row); atmospheric *Kitty O'Shea's* (23/25 Upper Grand Canal St.); the *Abbey Tavern* (in the seaside village of Howth north of the city), heavily beamed and warmed by turf fires; and the creaking old *Brazen Head* (20 Lower Bridge St., at the end of a cobblestone courtyard near the Liffey), said to be the city's oldest pub.

COUNTY CLARE, Irish Republic: Locals deem Clare the home of the very best Irish music. The town of Miltown Malbay hosts the week-long *Scoil Samraidh Willie Clancy,* a traditional music school that draws the county's finest musicians for nonstop music sessions — in the pubs and hotels, on street corners, in tents, and under open skies all day and all night during the first week in July (see *Feis and Fleadh: The Best Festivals*).

In Ennis, often regarded as the center of Irish traditional music, *Kelly's* pub (Carmody St.) has good weekend sessions, while out on the Galway road, the new cultural auditorium, the *Cois na hAbhna,* has programs from Wednesdays through Saturdays in winter for those who want to learn the steps of Irish set dancing. Mondays, Thursdays, and Saturdays in July and August are also lively, with tea and scones and a show served to visitors along with songs and dances and chat. The *Fleadh Nua,* a late-May weekend of music and dancing in Ennis (see *Feis and Fleadh: The Best Festivals*), is definitely worth planning for. Kilmihil, Mullagh, Feakle, and Tulla (home of the *Tulla Céilí Band,* still going strong after 4 decades) are good bets throughout the year. At *Gus O'Connor's,* a homey pub in Doolin, with lobster pots hanging from the ceiling and photos of local musicians on the walls (and a menu of pub grub available in a new restaurant on the premises), Micho Russell can often be found playing his tin whistle in the simple, centuries-old style he learned over 50 years ago. The place itself was established in 1832 and has been owned by the same family for six generations. Other Clare towns that are favorites with traditional musicians are Kilrush (home of *Crotty's*) and Ballyvaughan (home of *The Ballyvaughan Inn* and *Monk's Pub*).

COUNTIES CORK AND KERRY, Irish Republic: The mountainous area of County Kerry known as *Sliabh Luachra,* with its bordering county of north Cork, the land of melodeons, polkas, and slides, is one of the few places in Ireland where people still dance to the music. For as long as anyone can remember, traditional music and dancing have thrived here, and today many an Irish traditional music lover will say that there are more active musicians and dancers per acre here than in any other Irish country district. In tiny Knocknagree, in northwest Cork, the locals — including more than one sprightly octogenarian — have been tripping it out every Friday and Sunday night for a couple of decades at *Dan O'Connell's,* to the accordion music of Johnny O'Leary, widely reckoned to be among the most original masters of the squeezebox in Britain and Ireland; he founded the sessions with the late Denis Murphy, one of the best pupils of that great fiddle master Padraig O'Keeffe. Rathmore is known for its music pubs, as are Newmarket, Kenmare, Scartlaglen, Ballydesmond, and Kanturk, birthplace of the accordionist Jackie Daly, who used to play with the group *De Danann.* Traveling west through Kerry, there's traditional music in various pubs in Tralee and in Irish-speaking Dingle. At the *National Folk Theatre* of Ireland, in Tralee, aficionados can experience the *Siamsa Tíre,* described above. During July and August, similar sessions take place weekly at Finuge, 3 miles from Listowel, and at Carraig, 6 miles from Dingle. *Ceolann,* in the village of Lixnaw, between Tralee and Listowel, hosts periodic concerts and *céilí* dances, including an *oíche cheoil,* or Irish night, the first Friday of the month, giving the visitors a chance to enjoy and join in the musicmaking and dancing.

In neighboring County Cork, best-known spots include the *Folk House,* the *Spaniard,* and the *Shanakee* in Kinsale; *Craigie's* at Castletownbere; and the *Clock House Bar* in Mallow. In Cork City, the best are *An Bodhrán, DeLacy House,* and *An Sraid Baile.*

Killarney is also known for its organized pub music sessions, which can be found at *The Laurels* (Main St.). Spontaneous strains can be heard issuing from the *Dunloe Lodge* (Plunkett St.). In northern Kerry, on the border of County Limerick, the tiny town of Glin is famous for its storybook castle and for the music sessions at *O'Shaughnessy's Pub* on the main square. A *bodhrán* (drum), fiddle, and accordion are a permanent part of the decor here, even when no one is playing them at the regular daytime gatherings. The pub closes at 7 PM.

The Dingle Peninsula is also known for traditional music. Venues include *An Bóthar* at Brandon Creek, Ballydavid; *Tigh Ui Murchu (Murphy's Bar)* at Ballyferriter; *Quinn's Ventry Inn* at Ventry; *Garvey's, O'Flaherty's,* and *Murphy's* of Dingle Town; *Duchas House* at Tralee; and *Kruger's* of Dunquin, named after the Boer War leader Paul Kruger, who is described in a locally famous poem by Brendan Behan.

COUNTY DONEGAL, Irish Republic: Donegal is fiddle country, and it's scarcely possible to pass through it without hearing about the Fiddler King, Johnny Doherty, born in Fintown in 1895 into a family of traveling musicians and tinsmiths. Until his death, this little town drew many musicians and listeners who came to hear him play. Now a noteworthy spot for great bowing (nightly), *Teach Hiudai Bhig* in Bunbeg also has the traditional after-Mass get-together on Sunday mornings. *Teach Leo* in the village of Crolly is also a good bet for music, particularly when the local group *Clannad,* now internationally known, is at home.

The island of Arranmore — only a 50¢ ferry ride from Burtonport — exists in another time and another world, and the sessions go on into the wee hours at Bernadette and Tony Cox's *Plohogue* pub (tucked away at the less frequented top end of the island). Musicians come from the mainland and from Belfast. In August, don't miss the *Festival of International Folk Music* in Letterkenny.

COUNTY GALWAY, Irish Republic: Galway City is known for its swans, the soft speech of its natives, and good Irish music. The *Quays* (Quay St.), *Flanagan's* (William St. West), and the *Crane* (Sea Rd.) offer live music; the latter has established itself as the city's leading traditional music pub over the past few years and offers sessions not only every night but also on Sunday mornings, with some of the finest musicians in the country. Another favorite is the *King's Head* on High St., where traditional music is performed nightly in the back room. In Salthill, within walking distance of the city center, the *Cottage Bar* (Lower Salthill Rd.), around the corner from Devon Park) and the next-door pub, *Flaherty's,* occasionally resound to a few fiddles and banjos (the former on almost any night of the week). Galway is also the gateway to rocky, desertlike, Irish-speaking Connemara, where the musical emphasis is not so much on instruments as on songs, which are sung in the *sean nós* style — solo, heavily ornamented, unaccompanied, and in Irish. Look for music at *An Droighnean Donn* and *Hughes* pubs in the town of An Spideal and at the *Connemara Coast* hotel in Furbo farther into the country. In tiny Cleggan, 10 miles from Clifden, Connemara's capital, there are sessions at the *Pier Bar* on Fridays. Some nights on Inishbofin Island, musicians blast away at *Day's* pub until long after licensing hours — since no *gardai* live on the island, its pubs never have to close. With any luck, visitors can also find good music in East Galway, around Ballinakill, Woodford, and Loughrea, where *Moylan's* has a long-standing Saturday night session.

OTHER MUSICAL SPOTS, Irish Republic: In County Mayo, musicians gather on summer evenings at the *Asgard Tavern* on the Quay in Westport.

The area of south Sligo and north Roscommon is great flute and fiddle country. The local newspapers will note who is playing and where — usually on weekends around Ballymote, Gurteen, and Boyle. Pubs in this area known for their traditional music sessions include *Ellen's* at Maugherow — one of the last of the old Irish thatch-roofed establishments; the *Thatch* at Ballisodare; *Laura's* at Carney; and *McLynn's* (Old Market St.) and the *Yeats Tavern* (Drumcliffe) in Sligo City.

In Limerick, the venue of choice is the the *Vintage Club* (9 Ellen St.); in Wexford, *Tim's Tavern* (S. Main St.); and in Waterford, the *Munster Bar* (on The Mall) and *T. & H. Doolan's* (32 George's St.).

BELFAST: Northern Ireland has a music all its own — a plaintive, almost eerie blend of fiddles and flutes, with long spare notes and little ornamentation — closer to that of the Shetland Islands or Sweden than to Kerry's frolicsome polkas and slides. The music is performed with great verve in many parts, nowhere more so than in Belfast, which has seen a remarkable resurgence of nightlife lately. There are informal traditional Irish music sessions in a number of Docks area pubs such as *Pat's Bar* (109 Princes Dock; phone: 232-744524) and the *Rotterdam* (Pilot St.; phone: 232-746021). Traditional music is played also at the *Errigle Inn* (Ormeau Rd.; phone: 232-641410) on Mondays; most nights at *Madden's* (74 Smithfield; phone: 232-244114); Tuesdays at the *Front Page* (108 Donegall St.; phone: 232-324924); Fridays at *Kelly's Cellars* (38 Bank St.; phone: 232-324835); Saturdays at the *Duke of York* (11 Commercial St., off Lower Donegall St.; phone: 232-241062); and nightly at *Linenhall Bar* (9 Clarence St.; phone: 232-248458).

Belfast's folk club scene is also good. Try the *Sunflower Bar* (Corporation St.) on Friday nights (where a mid-September folk festival convenes annually), or the *Errigle Inn* (Ormeau Rd.) on Tuesdays. For a similar type of musical offering, *Fealty's* (High St. in Bangor, County Down) is particularly lively on Wednesday, Friday, and Saturday nights. *Grace Neill's* (Donaghadee, County Down) is very spontaneous, though Friday and Saturday nights are liveliest; and *Balloo House* (in Killinchy, County Down) is a good bet for a more folky type of music on Tuesdays. *Harper's Bar* in the *Europa* hotel (Great Victoria St.; phone: 232-327000) has live music nightly, except Sundays, including jazz on Thursdays and Saturdays.

OTHER MUSICAL SPOTS, Northern Ireland: In County Antrim, Irish music is played enthusiastically, especially in and around the Glens, and the town of Portglenone is noted for its fine sessions. Also highly recommended is the beautiful thatch-roofed *Crosskeys Inn,* off the main Randalstown–Portglenone road, outside Toomebridge, where on a Saturday night there might be four sessions at once and turf fires warming the old kitchen, one of the loveliest sections of the premises.

In County Fermanagh, *Blake's of the Hollow,* a most handsome spot in Enniskillen, turns musical on Friday and Saturday nights (see "Pub Crawling" in *For the Experience* for details).

Feis and Fleadh: The Best Festivals

 With such a wealth of talent in so many fields, it's hardly surprising that Ireland should be blossoming with festivals. What is surprising is that, without ever depending on having warm and sunny summer weather, they take place virtually year-round and last anywhere from a day or a week to a month or two. Some are oddball events devoted to strawberries or the arcane mysteries of the *uilleann* (elbow) pipes, a type of bagpipes that use the elbow as a bellows to pump air. Others are rooted in the European tradition of street musicians, buskers, and parades. Lisdoonvarna, in Clare, has a matchmaking festival in September, and Belfast an agricultural exhibition in May. There are rallies and angling competitions, horse shows and country fairs, and people stand around in their town's main square listening to bands and ballad singers, meeting neighbors they might not have had a proper chance to speak to since the previous year's event. There is a very good reason for this abundance of festivals: During festival times, the draconian Irish licensing laws ease up a bit, and all bars are allowed to stay open later than usual (though in the cities, late-night drinking — that great source of Irish joy — is confined to a single appointed place). Consequently, the atmosphere is usually jolly, and there is generally a feeling that something is actually happening.

Music festivals are abundant, though it should be said that some kind of music — traditional or popular, jazz or rock — is part of every Irish festival worthy of the name. Cork holds an *International Jazz Festival* annually in late October; Dublin holds a *Festival of Music in Great Irish Houses* every June; and each year, there's usually a major rock music event held outdoors in a natural amphitheater on the sloping banks of the river Boyne at Slane Castle, in County Meath, not far from some of the country's greatest archaeological treasures. In addition, since Ireland is the home of the *Boomtown Rats, U2,* and a host of other international musical heavies, visitors might catch the latest planetary sensation doing a gig at a sports stadium in the provinces or at the *Point* theater and *Royal Dublin Society* in the capital. Rock events, in any case, are held mainly in June and July and can, if the weather is good, be very enjoyable. The same goes for the kind of event known in Ireland as a *fleadh cheoil* (festival of music), which convenes almost every summer weekend somewhere in Ireland. The festivals manage an extraordinary combination of 1960s bonhomie and the long-standing Irish tradition of playing music at fairs. Whether it be the biggest of the breed, the *All-Ireland Festival* (the *Fleadh Cheoil na hEireann*), which generally takes place the fourth weekend in August, or one of the smaller affairs, the experience is fairly unbelievable. Thousands of people, young and old, take over the host town. Guesthouses and hotels don't have a bed to spare, ordinary homes turn into lodging places, and the young put up tents. People drink in the streets, and day and night the music goes on and on. Many of the best interpreters of Irish traditional music and dance show up for performances and competitions alike (so it is not all just drinking and carousing). The size of the throngs who come to listen and take part demonstrates once again how Irish traditional music has grown in importance and popularity over the last decade. For dates, contact the central organizers in Dublin, *Comhaltas Ceoltóirí Eireann,* 32 Belgrave Sq., Monkstown, County Dublin, Irish Republic (phone: 1-800295).

When attending an Irish festival or *fleadh,* it is sensible to buy a program. But buy it as a souvenir, a reminder of the event attended, an aid to identifying some featured celebrity, even a place to take notes. Don't view it as a timetable, even in the loosest sense of the word (timetables are for trains); it is a guide to possibilities. The actual sequence of events will depend on whether the poet caught the bus, whether the loudspeaker has come over from the pier so the archaeologist can start his lecture on the island, whether the *uilleann* piper decided to stay at the *fleadh* on the other side of the county to play an evening of duets with his cousin from Fort Worth. In certain circumstances, the greater part of the attendance may decamp to another town in pursuit of more music or, simply, as they say in Ireland to explain doing practically anything, "for the crack."

The tourist boards of the Irish Republic and Northern Ireland can supply complete listings of events as well as the current dates for the following (listed alphabetically) — some of Ireland's best.

WORTH A LONG DETOUR

DUBLIN THEATRE FESTIVAL, Dublin, Irish Republic: For the last week in September and the first in October, the Irish theater goes mad. Plays open daily — new plays by contemporary Irish authors, high classics by late Irish playwrights, productions by visiting theater companies, late-night revues, and mime shows. Actors get work, directors get work, would-be theater critics get work; theater people are all very happy — and so are visitors. Those who like light comedies will be as gleeful as those who swear by experimental theater. Anyone with stamina and eclectic tastes could spend both weeks watching plays and then rounding off each night in a special festival club where all the casts usually congregate, along with directors and critics. Increasingly, the festival seems to be functioning as a showcase for new works by Irish writers such as Tom Murphy, Hugh Leonard, Stewart Parker, Brian Friel, and J. Graham Reid. Visitors are generally surprised by the quality of the productions. Do remember that seats must be booked in advance — and the better the play, the bigger the queue. Details: *Dublin Theatre Festival,* 47 Nassau St., Dublin 2, Irish Republic (phone: 1-778439).

FESTIVAL OF MUSIC IN GREAT IRISH HOUSES, near Dublin, Irish Republic: At this event, hear Dame Janet Baker sing in stately Killruddery, in County Wicklow, just outside Dublin (described in *Stately Homes and Great Gardens*). Or enjoy a Handel opera in the beautifully restored Royal Hospital, at Kilmainham in Dublin. Or hear the *New Irish Chamber Orchestra* in splendid Castletown House, a mere carriage ride from Dublin for the 18th-century magnate who built it. This festival doesn't just want to sell tickets — it wants to provide music lovers with an opportunity to enjoy the period architecture, the damask curtains, a cool glass of wine in the paved hall during the interval, and the perfumes of the herbaceous border laid down by her ladyship years before. Early June. Details: *Judith Woodworth,* Festival Director, 4 Highfield Grove, Rathgar, Dublin 6, Irish Republic (phone: 1-962021).

FLEADH CHEOIL NA hÉIREANN, varying venues, Irish Republic: The *All-Ireland Festival* is the culmination of the traditional music year in Ireland. Staged in a different town each year, it brings great numbers of Ireland's musicians and singers together for 3 days to compete, to judge, to listen, and above all, to play and sing in concert halls, pubs, car parks, squares, and streets, to audiences numbering in the tens of thousands. Total informality and sheer physical stamina are the order of the day. Visitors are likely to find themselves footing out a handy polka on the macadam surface of some remote main street to fiddle music provided by a local doctor seated on an upturned beer keg. Don't worry — they'll never believe it back home anyway! August. Details: *Comhaltas Ceoltóirí Eireann,* 32 Belgrave Sq., Monkstown, County Dublin, Irish Republic (phone: 18-00295).

FLEADH NUA, Ennis, County Clare, Irish Republic: A little more formal than the clamorous jollifications of the *All-Ireland Festival,* from which it sprang, this late May event showcases Irish musicians, dancers, and singers in a pretty little inland town with some nice Georgian houses and a ruined friary just a few miles down the road from Shannon Airport. Details: Minnie Baker, *Fleadh Nua Office,* Crusheen, County Clare, Irish Republic (phone: 65-27115).

GALWAY INTERNATIONAL OYSTER FESTIVAL, Galway, County Galway, Irish Republic: This western-seaboard city was colonized in the 16th century by Elizabethan Planters, but, in addition, the surrounding bays have always been famous for their oysters and scallops, and in recent years local agencies and fishing cooperatives have actually farmed them. So it's only appropriate that the big annual wingding here, traditionally held during the last weekend in September, just as the bivalves come back into season after a succession of R-less months, is devoted to the succulent creatures. After all the cultural festivals, this is the place to come and relax. The festival begins with the *Irish Oyster-Opening Championship,* followed a couple of days later by the *World Oyster-Opening Championship,* which draws participants from around the globe. Throughout the festival, yacht races, golf competitions, and other festivities take place. To conclude all these activities, head for the pubs of Clarenbridge, where many a tasty bivalve slips down an eager throat on a stream of foaming stout to the accompaniment of terrific Irish brown bread and sweet butter. Or take a boat or plane to the Aran

Islands. Or explore the city: Tudor doorways and coats of arms are still visible on Shop Street. Details: *Aras Fáilte,* Victoria Pl., Galway, Irish Republic (phone: 91-63081).

GUINNESS JAZZ FESTIVAL, Cork, Irish Republic: A magnificent razzle for the those passionate about their upbeats and downbeats, this popular event attracts such international luminaries as Ella Fitzgerald, the *Heath Brothers,* and Cleo Laine, and together with a circle of local swingers, they keep the joints jumping on both banks of Cork's stately river Lee. Don't expect to get too much sleep, and try to book the more important events in advance. October. Details: *Cork Jazz Festival, Metropole Hotel,* MacCurtain St., Cork, Irish Republic (phone: 21-508122).

KILKENNY ARTS WEEK, Kilkenny, County Kilkenny, Irish Republic: Established enough to have acquired a roster of unofficial goings-on known here as a fringe, this event, held at the end of August or the beginning of September, convenes in one of the most pleasant and prosperous of Irish towns, with the added advantage of several very comfortable hotels and a location that makes it feasible to drive down from Dublin (a matter of a couple of hours), have a drink in *The Marble City* or *Tynan's Bar,* catch a lunchtime concert, browse through the arts and crafts exhibitions, see the city's many interesting sights, attend an evening concert in acoustically excellent St. Canice's Cathedral, and then, for those who are not yet worn out, drive back to Dublin. Although many writers — poets Robert Lowell and Ted Hughes among them — have read their work here, music is the main thing, and many of the performers are internationally known. The program offers traditional music and folk songs, along with classical works. Details: *Kilkenny Arts Week,* c/o Kilkenny Tourist Office, Alms House, Rose Inn St., Kilkenny, Irish Republic (phone: 56-21755).

LISTOWEL WRITERS' WEEK, Listowel, County Kerry, Irish Republic: Listowel is the chief town and center of an area distinguished by its writers, among them playwright John B. Keane, who runs a pub here, the short-story writer Brian MacMahon, and the poets Brendan Kennally and Gabriel Fitzmaurice, who are the presiding spirits of this increasingly popular and enjoyable festival usually held during late May or early June. They hold workshops in drama, poetry, and fiction writing for the interested and aspiring, plays are produced by authors new and old, books are launched, and writers give lectures on and readings from their own works and those of others. Yet the atmosphere is anything but academic. Among the musical concerts, art exhibitions, book fairs, and poster showings is the *John Jameson Humorous Essay Open Competition* (first prize: a cut-glass decanter full of Joyce's favorite whiskey). At this event, the main purpose is enjoyment — and people have been known to engage in the pursuit thereof all night. The pubs are friendly, and there's also an official club where a band plays dance music, and the assembled writers, aspiring writers, and other attendant festive spirits — when not drinking — leap about the floor. Details: *Listowel Writers' Week,* c/o The Secretary, PO Box 147, Listowel, County Kerry, Irish Republic (phone: 68-21074).

ROSE OF TRALEE INTERNATIONAL FESTIVAL, Tralee, County Kerry, Irish Republic: Nowadays, nobody takes the competitive element of this beauty-contest-with-a-difference too seriously, but young women still come from all over the world at the end of August or early September to vie for a Waterford crystal trophy and the title Rose of Tralee, first made famous by tenor John McCormack: "She was lovely and fair / Like a Rose of the summer / Yet it was not her beauty alone that won me / O no it was the truth in her eyes ever dawning / That made me love Mary, the Rose of Tralee." But this 6-day event goes beyond McCormack and, as a sort of Irish *Mardi Gras,* provides an extraordinary range of entertainment, from donkey and greyhound races and tugs of war to fireworks, brass band concerts, performances of traditional music, cabarets, and much more. At any given moment, it might be possible to find four or five acts going on in different parts of the town. People roam the streets from early morning until late at night, and the Guinness flows like a flood. There's always

484 DIVERSIONS / Festivals and Fleadh

something happening, and most of it is free. Nearly 100,000 attend. Details: *Festival of Kerry,* 5 Lower Castle St., Tralee, County Kerry, Irish Republic (phone: 66-21322).

ST. PATRICK'S WEEK, countrywide, Irish Republic: Irishmen and Irishwomen by birth, ancestry, or natural conviction descend on the Emerald Isle to celebrate the 17th of March with a week of holiday fun. In Dublin, there are concerts of music and dance in St. Stephen's Green, Gaelic football and hurling matches, an annual dog show hoary with tradition, and the biggest parade the capital can muster — with foreign and local brass bands, silver bands, fife and drum bands, pipe bands, and accordion bands, competitive exhibits on foot and on huge floats, Irish dancers in battalions, Irish and American majorettes, antique cars, and 18th-century ceremonial coaches bearing lord mayors dripping with gold chains and driven by solemn fellows in tricorn hats, not to mention legions of happy visitors, almost every one of them green-hatted and beflagged. It's a great sight, and every child in Dublin exercises his right to attend, festooned with shamrocks and round-eyed with delight. All of Ireland's other villages and towns do as much as they can of the same program — and many have their parades on the Sunday after the big day to give the citizenry the chance to do the whole thing not once but twice. It's March — often wet, cold, and windy. But most of the time visitors don't notice the weather, even if they forget their waterproofs. Details: *Irish Tourist Board* in Dublin (1-747733).

WEXFORD FESTIVAL OPERA, Wexford, County Wexford, Irish Republic: In the latter half of October, when the nights get long and cold, this harbor town comes alive with an event that, from a social point of view alone, is probably one of the most enjoyable in Ireland, filling the town's narrow winding streets with opera lovers from all over the world. The festival's long drawing card is the opera — usually two seldom-performed works by well-known composers and one contemporary opus. Ticket prices are low, even by European standards, and performance quality is very high, as it has been since the festival's inception in 1951. Talented newcomers often use Wexford to launch their careers, and many well-known singers (among them Frederica von Stade) have sung here. Much of the backstage work, the ushering, and ticket selling is done by volunteers, and at least one member each of most local families is directly involved in the festival. As a result of such participation, this otherwise very elite event has become very public and popular. What makes it really special, though, is the setting — a tiny opera house that seats only 446, crouched on a capillary of a side street — plus a general feeling of style and opulence. Among the broad range of events offered are concerts, recitals, and exhibitions and readings at the local arts center. There are also singing competitions in pubs and a window display competition that gets butchers, bakers, grocers, and others in on the act. Rounding out the roster are theater presentations, lectures, walking tours, flower shows and art shows, and other events. To add to the glamour, several of Wexford's public buildings, including a few designed by Pugin, are floodlit for the duration. Details: *Theatre Royal,* High St., Wexford, Irish Republic (phone: 53-22240 or 53-22144).

WILLY CLANCY SUMMER SCHOOL, Miltown Malbay, County Clare, Irish Republic: Following the early death of the great piper Willy Clancy, a delightful man, his friends decided that musicians — particularly pipers — should come together every year in July in his memory to play, teach, and learn the pipes — not hearty warpipes but the cunning, sweetly toned little *uilleann,* traditional and unique to Ireland. It is an instrument that lacks the shrillness of Scottish warpipes and has a wide melodic variation. It's easy to understand the Irish wag's remark about how the Irish exported bagpipes to Scotland — and the Scots haven't yet caught on to the joke. Old and young, American and Irish, novices, experts who can pipe their listeners into a trance, and wildly diverse others jam the pubs, and the music goes on and on. Come official closing time, the doors are locked so that no new merrymakers may enter, but those present remain as long as they can stay awake. Details: *Muiris O'Rochain,* Miltown Malbay, County Clare, Irish Republic (phone: 65-84148).

BELFAST FESTIVAL AT QUEEN'S, Belfast, Northern Ireland: One of the two biggest cultural events in the United Kingdom (the other is the *Edinburgh Festival*), this November event has, since its beginnings in the early 1960s, created excitement on the cultural scene that even "the troubles" have not been able to undermine. Although it covers the entire spectrum of the arts, the emphasis traditionally has been on classical music. But the jazz and film programs are excellent, and folk and popular music are well represented, as is a spectrum of drama, opera, and ballet, with visiting companies from the Republic and the rest of Europe. Superstars like Cleo Laine and Dame Janet Baker, James Galway and Yehudi Menuhin, and Billy Connolly and Michael Palin have performed here. The setting is the Victorian campus of Queen's University; concerts are also presented in the *Grand Opera House,* the *Ulster Hall,* and the *Arts, Lyric,* and *Group* theaters. Details: *Festival House,* 8 Malone Rd., Belfast BT9 5BN, Northern Ireland (phone: 232-667687).

IF YOU'RE NEARBY

AN TÓSTAL, Drumshanbo, County Leitrim, Irish Republic: Over 3 decades ago, when the Irish Tourist Board dreamed of a nationwide festival to launch a new era in the tourist industry, the locals of little Drumshanbo responded with this festival, whose name means "gathering" or "muster," and they've been having it every year ever since. A ballad-singing competition, road races, and an art exhibition are among the goings-on — not especially unusual but a lot of fun. The shindig always kicks off with a parade and the hoisting of the Tóstal flag on Main Street. June. Details: *Mrs. Eva Mooney,* Drumshanbo, County Leitrim, Irish Republic (phone: 78-41013).

CASTLEBAR INTERNATIONAL FOUR DAYS' WALKS, Castlebar, County Mayo, Irish Republic: A friendly get-together for the dedicated tramper, this event also has room for those who enjoy a not overly strenuous stroll in good company in the quiet countryside. June. Details: *Castlebar International Four Days' Walks,* Castlebar, County Mayo, Irish Republic (phone: 94-21355).

CORK INTERNATIONAL CHORAL AND FOLK DANCE FESTIVAL, Cork, County Cork, Irish Republic: This event takes place annually at the beginning of May. Choirs and folk dance teams from all over the world participate, and each year a number of choral works are commissioned from distinguished composers. Details: *Cork International Choral and Folk Dance Festival,* PO Box 68, Cork, County Cork, Irish Republic (phone: 21-213396).

DÚN LAOGHAIRE SUMMER FESTIVAL, Dún Laoghaire, County Dublin, Irish Republic: During the last week in June, this prosperous and well-kept old borough 6 miles from Dublin expresses its essentially Victorian style with art exhibits and musical soirées in the Maritime Institute (High St.), local tours and trips to nearby Dalkey Island, a ball, a regatta, and everything from sea chantey concerts to Punch and Judy shows. Dún Laoghaire's popular harbor is jammed with boats and yachts. Details: *John Murnaghan,* Festival Director, Marine Rd., Dún Laoghaire, County Dublin, Irish Republic (phone: 1-822054).

PAN CELTIC WEEK, Killarney, County Kerry, Irish Republic: Scots, Welsh, Manx, Bretons, Basques, their kin, and their descendants are warmly welcomed back to their home turf with concerts, displays, parades, and plenty of music, song, and dance. May. Details: *Pan Celtic Week,* c/o Killarney Tourist Board, Town Hall, Main St., Killarney, County Kerry, Irish Republic (phone: 64-31633).

STRADBALLY STEAM RALLY, Stradbally, County Laois, Irish Republic: A gathering of steam engines and those who love them, this event associated with the *Irish Steam Museum* (the home of a fine collection of cars, tricycles, fire engines, and other manifestations of the power of steam) swells an otherwise quiet little village with thousands. Owners and attendants are proud, hospitable, and very patient. Two days in early August. Details: *Olive Condell,* Stradbally, County Laois, Irish Republic (phone: 502-252136).

OULD LAMMAS FAIR, Ballycastle, County Antrim, Northern Ireland: A glass or two or three of Bushmills enlivens the conversation at this genuine folk event, the North's most popular traditional fair, and the accents fly thick and fast. For the duration, the otherwise fairly placid little town throbs with activity. Farmers cart in their livestock and stalls sell souvenirs of all imaginable variety, the local specialties being the dried, edible seaweed known as dulse and a sweet known as yellow man. Last Monday and Tuesday in August. Details: Northern Ireland Tourist Board (phone: 232-231221).

SUMMER SCHOOLS

Summer schools, a very particular fixture of the Irish summer season, are not so much over-serious academic gatherings redolent with credits and credentials as they are special-interest festivals that feature, as their entertainment, members of the Irish intelligentsia devoting themselves without restraint to that most venerable of Irish recreations — talk. Some of the best talkers in the country are in attendance, happily moving from one seat of learning to another as the summer advances, so visitors are bound to learn a lot on, and off, the "campus."

MACGILL SUMMER SCHOOL, Glenties, County Donegal, Irish Republic: This school, which convenes on the rugged northwest coast honors the novelist and poet Patrick MacGill, whose first book sold 120,000 copies within 2 weeks of publication and who, like France's Emile Zola, is the voice of the repressed and neglected of his people: the traveling building and agricultural workers of the first half of the century. Accordingly, topics with modern social and political themes are chosen. As at other summer schools, the living creators of modern Irish literature are much in evidence; visitors with literary pretensions might well find room for their latest short stories or epic poems on the elastic program. Details: *Inishkeel Co-op,* c/o Mary Claire O'Donnell, Main St., Glenties, County Donegal, Irish Republic (phone: 75-51103).

MERRIMAN SUMMER SCHOOL, County Clare, Irish Republic: Held during the last week in August in a different Clare town every year, this event is affectionately known as "the lark in Clare air." It fondly recalls its namesake, the 18th-century schoolteacher Brian Merriman, popular for his elegant, racy, and dreamlike satire on ancient bardic epics, "Cúirt an Mheán Oíche" ("The Midnight Court"), in which Ireland's women indict their menfolk for contempt of matrimony in the court of the Fairy Queen, and win. Too strong for public taste of the day, the poem was suppressed for many years. The primary topic of the school varies wildly from one season to the next. Matriculants might find themselves considering the O'Brien family and its 30-foot-long pedigree dating back to 1200 BC, or Ireland's maritime history, or the state of the Irish legal profession. The lecture roll includes politicians, scientists, poets, novelists, and university professors, and all of them are expected to dance the odd reel or jig at the *Merriman Club* each night, to quaff the odd libation, and to entertain the assembled company with the odd song or two. (Thus one learns that there are some very fine singers in Irish academe and on the Front Bench in Government and Opposition.) They are also supposed to get themselves together in the morning — and it's to their credit that they do. Details: *Mary Murphy,* 6 Aravan Court, Bray, County Wicklow, Irish Republic (phone: 1-869305).

PALLADIO ACADEMY, Dublin, Irish Republic: For the artistically inclined, this school offers the best of Ireland's "hands-on" courses, such as a 5-day workshop in decorative painting. The curriculum includes sponging, dragging, rag-rolling, and stippling, as well as marbling and stenciling. Course topics vary from session to session, and the focus is often on conservation and restoration of old buildings, interior landscaping, Art Deco design, Victorian homes, and creative drawing. An offshoot of the London-based academy of the same name, this school offers several summer courses on various dates from May through August. Classes are held at 20 Fitzwilliam Square in the heart of one of Dublin's most fashionable Georgian neighborhoods. Details: *Palladio Academy of Dublin,* c/o Brenda Weir, Director, PO Box 1886, Dublin 16, Irish Republic (phone: 1-931906).

YEATS SUMMER SCHOOL, Sligo, Irish Republic: The poet W. B. Yeats spent a great deal of his childhood in County Sligo, and his feeling for the extraordinarily beautiful scenery that surrounded him there infuses his work, to which this annual August event devotes itself fairly seriously. Professor Elizabeth Butler-Cullingford, one of Ireland's brightest and the current director of the summer school honoring the poet, has theories on Yeats and current Irish political feeling that have drawn fascinating responses from other speakers at the school — people like the internationally known writer and commentator Conor Cruise O'Brien and the writer and critic Denis Donoghue. Performances of Yeats's plays, tours of the countryside, and relaxed evenings in the hospitable pubs of Sligo City soothe the nerves after the stress of such intellectual stimulation. Details: The Secretary, *Yeats Society,* Douglas Hyde Bridge, Sligo, County Sligo, Irish Republic (phone: 71-42693 or 71-60097).

Ancient Monuments and Ruins

A land of 10,000 tales and a 100,000 memories, Ireland is littered with cairns and forts, dolmens and abbeys, standing stones and high crosses, monastic hermitages and feudal castles, with the oldest dating back thousands of years. But though the earliest traces of human life here date from about 6000 BC, it was not until about 3000 BC that humans built on a scale large enough to leave memorials to themselves. Those that survive are tombs of a type known as court cairns — long chambers divided into compartments. The earliest structure that grips the visitor's imagination is the passage grave. Found in groups, each under a huge mound, these typically consist of a long passage leading to a central space onto which other chambers open on three sides, with a floor of large stones, one or more stone basins inside, and, on all the stones, great numbers of incised geometric motifs and even stylized human faces. The group in the Boyne Valley of County Meath, which includes the magnificent Newgrange, is striking.

Equally arresting are Ireland's great standing stones, or dolmens. Outlined against the sky, crowned by an enormous capstone, they were built in about 2000 BC, probably as tombs. Men in pubs call them "beds of Diarmuid and Grainne," referring to the Irish king's daughter who, betrothed to the venerable giant Finn MacCool, eloped with the younger Diarmuid on her wedding night and slept in prehistoric tombs during a furious years-long chase that ended with Diarmuid's death at the snout of an enchanted boar and the wayward lady's marriage. Later, during the Bronze Age, at about the time the Celts arrived here, there were stone circles like the piper's stones of County Wicklow, where, it was believed, the "little people" played the bagpipes for dancers. Hill forts like Tara, the legendary dwelling of the high king of Ireland, came later, in the Iron Age, around 500 BC. A hill fort's outer fortifications enclosed a large area, so the owner was certainly an important figure. Ring forts, of which there are some 3,000 scattered around the country, are smaller, ranging in scale from the Grianán of Aileach in County Donegal to the occasional odd shape in a field.

Christianity came to Ireland in the 5th century, and with it the nation embarked on an era of great building. Monasteries sprang up all over Ireland. Bearing little resemblance to their more modern counterparts, they consisted of simple clusters of stone huts and a sheltering wall, like those on the Dingle Peninsula in County Kerry and at Glendalough in County Wicklow. Round towers, also seen at Glendalough, were put up as refuges from Viking raids. The devout also built crosses which at first were just cross-shaped slabs or slabs incised with a cross motif. Later came the increasingly more ornate high crosses, which had geometric designs and even scenes from the Bible, with a circle around the intersection of the horizontal and vertical arms.

In the 12th century, Irish Romanesque architecture made its debut on the ecclesiastical scene. Examples like the Chapel of Cormac at Cashel, in County Tipperary, and Ballintubber Abbey, in County Mayo, show the distinctive signs: round-headed doorways, fantastic animal and human masks in stone, with intertwining beard and tail, chevrons, and foliage decorating arches, doorways, capitals, and sometimes church windows.

In the 13th century, Franciscans and Dominicans arrived with Gothic ideas in their saddle bags. In cathedral towns like Kilkenny, Kildare, and Limerick, many of the older parish church buildings still in use abound in lancet windows and other distinctive marks of the style. By the 15th century, the Cistercians had risen to the glories of Holy Cross in County Tipperary.

Meanwhile, a more durable class of fortress, the castle, was developing. The Norman invasion sparked the creation of fortresses like Carrickfergus Castle, in County Antrim, and the round keep at Nenagh, in County Tipperary. There was no stopping the masons and their masters of this period. Between 1450 and 1650 every family who was anyone built a castle. Very few of these structures disappeared entirely from the landscape, and some — most notably Bunratty Castle in County Clare — are in splendid shape.

Architecture in PERSPECTIVES gives a somewhat more detailed overview of these trends. For more comprehensive information, consult:

> *National Monuments in the Republic of Ireland* by Peter Harbison (about $8 from Gill and Macmillan Ltd., Goldenbridge, Inchicore, Dublin 8, Irish Republic). This covers monuments in the Republic only.
> *Early Ireland: A Field Guide* by Anthony Weir (Belfast: Blackstaff Press). Currently out of print, this guide covers Northern Ireland as well as the Republic, and is useful enough to warrant a trip to a well-stocked library.

Whether ecclesiastical or secular, each type of building has its saga and its place in Irish history, and with a little imagination, they spring vividly to life when you visit them. Those listed below, in roughly the order in which they were constructed, include some of the most important and most colorful.

NEWGRANGE, Newgrange, County Meath, Irish Republic: Very few relics of the daily life of the people of the Neolithic Age (ca. 3700–2000 BC) survive in Ireland today; it seems as if all the creative energies of the communities of this period were directed toward the construction not of homes for the living but of monumental repositories for the remains of the dead, and the whole valley of the river Boyne, about 30 miles north of Dublin, is scattered with cairns, standing stones, and earthworks both large and small. Of these, Newgrange is the most impressive by far. In fact, this passage grave ranks among the most important of its type in Europe, and scholars have spent centuries studying it. Literature of the ancient Irish links it to a mysterious personage who is sometimes called Oengus an Brógha (Oengus of the palace) and sometimes dubbed Oengus mac an Dagda (Oengus son of the good god); some archaeologists have suggested that Newgrange and similar tombs on the Continent were constructed for the important personages in groups of traders and prospectors who first migrated from Spain or Portugal around 4000 BC. Certainly, they had a civilization far more highly organized than our widespread assumptions about our "primitive" ancestors would credit them — at least if they are to be judged from the sophistication of the building and decorative techniques evidenced here.

HILL OF TARA, near Navan, County Meath, Irish Republic: Little but legend and a handful of earthworks and stones remain of the glories of Tara — but of legend and conjecture there is plenty, and this 512-foot hill about 25 miles from Dublin, commanding a fine view of a vast expanse of lush meadows, is well worth a visit. Already a significant burial place 2 millennia before Christ (as revealed by the excavation of one of the site's most notable monuments, the Mound of the Hostages), it ranked among Ireland's most important political and religious sites for almost 2,000 years. It became the center of priestly rulers even before St. Patrick came to Ireland in the 5th century and long served as a residence for anyone strong enough to make himself at least nominally High King of Ireland. Tara enjoyed one of its most glorious periods in the first centuries after Christ, when the celebrated Cormac the Wise constructed the wooden palaces that are mentioned in some of Ireland's early literature. (It was his daughter who, though betrothed to Finn MacCool, eloped with Diarmuid O'Duibhne and gave rise to the wonderful stories about the lovers' flight from one end of Ireland to the other.) Later, after St. Patrick triumphed in a contest of feats with the druids of High King Laoghaire, whose authority the saint had challenged, the King allowed his subjects to be converted to Christianity (although he himself remained a pagan until his death). Tara's importance declined until its abandonment in 1022. Relics of all of these eras can be seen today. The Mound of the Hostages (Dunha na nGiall), an early passage grave (ca. 1800 BC) with a 17-foot-long corridor, covered by a mound that measures 72 feet in diameter, is at one edge of the large, circular Iron Age ring fort called the Royal Enclosure (Rath na Ríogh), at whose center are two other earthworks — the Royal Seat (Forradh) and Cormac's House (Teach Cormaic), where visitors will see a modern statue of St. Patrick and the 5-foot-long chunk of granite known as the Stone of Destiny (Lia Fail). The latter, according to popular legend, would roar when the king being crowned upon it was acceptable. Just south of the Royal Enclosure is Rath Laoghaire, which is said to be near King Loaghaire's burial place. To the north stand the Rath of the Synods (Rath na Seanad), an erstwhile fortress and burial place; the Banquet Hall (Teach Miodchuarta), where each stratum of society had its own compartment and whose festivities are reported in the 12th-century *Book of Leinster;* the circular Rath Gráinne, named for the fugitive king's daughter; and the odd-shaped Sloping Trenches (Claoin Fhearta), which probably had a ceremonial function of some sort. Also interesting is Adamnán's Stone, a 6-foot-high chunk of sandstone bearing the incised likeness of a human figure — perhaps the horned Celtic Cernunnos or a type of fertility figure known as a *sheila-na-gig* ("sheila of the breasts" — paradoxically a figure that is mostly face and thighs). Details: *Dublin and Eastern Region Tourism Organization* (address above).

GRIANÁN OF AILEACH, Burt, County Donegal, Irish Republic: Ulster cannot boast megalithic monuments of the scope of Leinster's Boyne Valley cemeteries (although several structures do exist with elaborate entranceways that have earned them the name court graves, as well as standing stones and stone circles and dolmens). Here, however, the most characteristic and striking ruins are those of circle-shaped ring forts, which protected farmhouses until AD 1000 (and which are found today by the thousands scattered throughout Ulster's fields). Even more striking are the stone cashels (circular walls enclosing groups of ecclesiastical buildings). The Grianán of Aileach (the sunny place in the territory of Aileach), one of the most important antiquities in the northern part of the country, is among the most noteworthy. Perched atop 800-foot Grianán Mountain, not far from Londonderry, this fortification measures about 77 feet across; the 13-foot-thick walls, restored in the 1870s by the bishop of Derry to their original height of 17 feet, contain galleries and guard chambers and enclose a series of stairway-connected terraces. The views afforded by the topmost of these, out over the blue reaches of loughs Foyle and Swilly, are glorious — fully worthy of the O'Neills, the Kings of Ulster, whose northern branch made this fortification its base from approximately the 5th century AD through the 12th. Already badly battered in 676 during an attack by the southern O'Neills, under Finechta the Festive, the structure was finally destroyed by Murtogh O'Brien, the King of Munster, who, avenging the pillaging of his own residence, instructed each of his men to carry away a single stone of the fort. The exact date of construction is unknown, since no excavations have been made here; in their *Annals of the Kingdom of Ireland,* the Four Masters put its origins back in the Iron Age, while other scholars suggest that it was probably built within a few centuries before or after St. Patrick (who lived in the 5th century AD). The round shape has inspired the church nestling at the foot of the mountain at Burt, one of Ireland's most interesting modern structures. It was built in 1967 after designs by Liam MacCormick and Una Madden. Similar and equally impressive fortifications include Dun Aengus in the Aran Islands and Staigue Fort in County Kerry. Details: *Donegal/ Leitrim/Sligo Region Tourist Information Office,* Temple St., Sligo, County Sligo, Irish Republic (phone: 71-61201).

The earth mound that is the most immediately obvious feature of Newgrange, entirely manmade, using alternate layers of turf and stones, is unusually large — 40 feet high and 300 feet in diameter; estimates put the quantity of stones required for the whole undertaking at 180,000 tons. Now covered with grass, the mound was originally paved with white quartz pebbles so that it glistened brightly enough in the sun to be seen from afar (as indeed it does now, thanks to a careful restoration in the 1960s). Inside, leading into the depth of the hill from the entrance on the southeastern frontage, is a 62-foot-long, yard-wide passage. High enough to let a person walk upright and lined with a series of orthostats, or upright stones, 5 to 8 feet high, it ends at a generally circular burial chamber, whose notable features include its beehive-shaped ceiling paved with overlapping stones (following a method of construction found over and over again at Irish ruins of this period) and, adjoining the main chamber — and giving the tomb's interior a roughly cruciform shape — three recesses containing stone troughs or basins probably once used to contain the ashes of the dead. On the morning of the shortest day of the year, rays of sun shine directly up the passageway to the center of the burial chamber — a design that required some sort of calendar to calculate. The decoration throughout further confirms that sophisticated minds were at work. The ceiling of the north recess, covered with carved spirals, lozenges, triangles, zigzags, diamonds, and other shapes, is particularly noteworthy, as are the gigantic threshold stone, at the entrance to the tomb, and many of the orthostats. The fact that similar motifs appear on many other megalithic stones (and on Mycenean tombs as well) has prompted scholars to theorize that, far from being mere ornament, the designs, probably rooted in the pre-Mycenean civilization of the 3rd millennium BC, are magnificent abstract representations of gods, goddesses, and human beings. A museum and tourist information office at Newgrange can provide details about Newgrange as well as about nearby Dowth and Knowth, the two other major monuments in this area, which is often called Brugh na Boinne (Palace of the Boyne). Note that access to the Newgrange site is available only on the excellent guided tours at the site. Details: *Dublin and Eastern Region Tourism Organization,* 1 Clarinda Park N., Dún Laoghaire, County Dublin, Irish Republic (phone: 1-808571).

GLENDALOUGH, County Wicklow, Irish Republic: Nestled deep in the Wicklow Mountains, about 30 miles south of Dublin, this "valley of the two lakes" is the beautiful setting for one of Ireland's important early Christian monasteries, particularly striking in May when the gorse is in full bloom. Born on the site where St. Kevin settled to renounce human love and live as a hermit during the 6th century, Glendalough, like many other Irish monasteries, was pillaged and sacked many times by the Vikings and assorted other marauders. Famous as a seat of learning, like Clonmacnoise, it was particularly vulnerable and, as at Clonmacnoise, the ruins are extensive: more than half a dozen churches, crosses, grave slabs, a priest's house, a round tower, and old wells. The stone of which most of these are constructed, granite and mica-schist, has chipped and crumbled over the centuries, giving the walls a rough texture and providing a fine medium for the growth of the pale, soft local lichen, so that the buildings at Glendalough have that particularly antique look that many folks imagine all ruins have until they find out otherwise. It's certainly pleasant to spend a day here, poking around among the broken walls, wandering along the pathways between them, and admiring the glass-smooth waters of the upper and lower lakes. Especially noteworthy are the 7th-century cathedral, Ireland's largest pre-Romanesque church; St. Kevin's Church (popularly known as St. Kevin's Kitchen), with its round tower-like belfry rising up above a stone roof; the small, 12th-century Priest's House, perhaps originally a mortuary chapel or even the saint's shrine; the Reefert Church, around whose walls sleep many Leinster kings; and, farther down the valley, accessible via a narrow sylvan path, St. Saviour's Monastery, a 12th-century church probably built by Laurence O'Toole, former abbot of Glendalough, archbishop of Dublin, and Ireland's first canonized saint. There are especially fine walks around the upper lake, which is picturesquely backed by the steep cliffs of 2,296-foot Camaderry and 2,154-foot Lugduff Mountains, ribboned by the rushing Glenealo Stream and a waterfall. Details: *Dublin and Eastern Region Tourism Organization,* 1 Clarinda Park N., Dún Laoghaire, County Dublin, Irish Republic (phone: 1-808571).

CLONMACNOIS, Shannonbridge, County Offaly, Irish Republic: Founded by St. Ciaran in the mid-6th century on a large, serenely beautiful site on a reed-edged curve of the river Shannon between loughs Derg and Ree, Clonmacnois has been plundered and burned by Vikings, desecrated by Danes, harassed by the Normans, and, much later, during the Dissolution, carried away, piece by piece. But until this consummate act of vandalism, it grew strong, flourished, and became the Oxford of medieval Ireland. Fine manuscripts were created here, and some of the country's greatest scholars and intellects came here to live, pray, work, and be buried. What remains are the most extensive monastic ruins in Ireland: eight churches, two round towers, a cathedral, and a castle, as well as three high crosses, parts of two others, and more than 200 6th-through 12th-century gravestones vividly illustrating the many types of graves used in early Ireland. Of all the structures here, the celebrated Flann's High Cross, carved with scenes of the Last Judgment and the Crucifixion, is exceptionally beautiful, and the Nun's Church, whose doorways have capitals crawling with fierce-looking beasts, has the most interesting story: This was where the pathetic Dervorgilla retired in penance after eloping with Dermot MacMurrough, the King of Leinster — thereby setting off the Norman invasion. Rising in lonely tranquillity above the lush green landscape, the ruins possess an air of peace and dignity, as befits a national treasure. Details: *Tourist Information Office,* Dublin Rd., Mullingar, County Westmeath, Irish Republic (phone: 44-48761).

ROCK OF CASHEL, Cashel, County Tipperary, Irish Republic: Even in Ireland's earliest days, before any fortresses or cathedrals or castles were built atop this chunk of carboniferous limestone, the Rock must have looked a bit unreal, rising precipitously — a block of slate gray — above the surrounding rock-studded green plains. Now, capped by the spare and broken remains of structures once frequented by saints, kings, and bishops, the Rock provides a visual experience that is, quite simply, one of Ireland's most stupendous. The longtime capital of the Kings of Munster, the Rock was visited in 450 by St. Patrick, who baptized King Aengus and his brothers. Later, Brian Ború, who defeated the Norsemen in the Battle of Clontarf near Dublin in the 10th century, was crowned king here, and, though it stayed in the hands of his descendants, its political importance declined as its ecclesiastical significance grew; in 1101, it was presented by Brian's grandson, King Muirchertach, to the church, which is responsible for most of the buildings in the tightly grouped complex seen on the Rock today. These are as impressive when viewed at close range as they are from afar. Dominating the group is the cathedral, begun in the 13th century and abandoned in 1749. The central tower offers fine views into the distant mountains and to the Devil's Bit — the mountain pass said to have been created when the Dark Angel took a large bite. (The size of the Rock is said to match the void in the mountain exactly.) A very well-preserved round tower, probably from the 10th century, stands at the corner of the cathedral's north transept; and the massive, rectangular, three-storied archbishop's palace, honeycombed with passageways to explore, adjoins the west end of the cathedral's nave, which was never completed. Nearby is the newly restored 15th-century Hall of the Vicars Choral, used to house laymen who participated in the chanting of the cathedral's services and now home to the 12th-century Cross of St. Patrick, which was recently transferred to this site. Tiny Cormac's Chapel, wedged into a corner between the cathedral's choir and its south transept, is especially interesting. Built in 1127 by Cormac MacCarthy, the Bishop of Cashel and the King of Desmond (in the realm created after a defeat by the King of Connaught divided Munster in half), it is considered by many to be the nation's best example of the Irish Romanesque style, and volumes have been written tracing its origins. Visitors are often most impressed by the elaborate carvings, the ribbed vaulting, twisted capitals, and richly embellished blind arcades; the tympana (the surfaces between the arch and the lintels) surmounting the south door through which visitors enter today, and the far grander north door, through which worshipers gained access to the nave until the construction of the cathedral, are strikingly beautiful. The lions and centaurs seen here are even more exotic than the human heads that peer out from around the chancel. After completing a tour, don't fail to see some of the older structures in Cashel proper (see *Cashel,* THE CITIES). Details: *South Eastern Region Tourist Information Office,* 41 The Quay, Waterford, County Waterford, Irish Republic (phone: 51-75788).

BALLINTUBBER ABBEY, Ballintubber, County Mayo, Irish Republic: The site of this Augustinian community has long been important; tradition tells us that St. Patrick baptized local peasants with water from its well. Later, the monastery became the departure point for pilgrimages to Croagh Patrick. Now it is noteworthy because Mass has been said in its church ever since the community's founding by Cathal Crovdearg O'Conor, the King of Connacht, for the Canons Regular of St. Augustine in 1216 — despite the suppression of the abbey under Henry VIII and the depredations of the Cromwellians in 1653. That there has been no interruption in religious rites for over 760 years makes the church unique in the English-speaking world, and, in addition to its special history, it is also an exceptionally handsome structur e. Thanks to sensitive restoration work begun on the initiative of a former priest, Father Egan, and finished in 1966, a new wooden roof was constructed for the nave and the interior walls whitewashed in the ancient fashion, so that the church looks much as it must have upon its completion. The carving around the three lancet windows in the gable and on the capitals of the chancel exemplifies the best work of a school of talented late-Romanesque carvers who worked in the province of Connacht in the early 13th century after the rest of the country had adopted the Gothic style; and the Augustinians, who were more permissive than other orders, allowed the artists more latitude in their designs — which the results reflect. The wonderfully monstrous snakes twined around each other on the capitals between the triple round-headed window in the front of the church (to see them in those distant gloomy recesses requires field glasses) and the grotesque creatures creeping along the corbels that uphold the chancel's ribbed vaulting are just two examples. Nearby is the well where St. Patrick did his baptizing, as well as the attractive cloisters reconstructed from the ruins of the 15th-century originals with the aid of fragments that came to light in the course of archaeological excavations in the 1960s. Details: *Westport Tourist Information Office,* The Mall, Westport, County Mayo, Irish Republic (phone: 98-25711).

MELLIFONT ABBEY, Drogheda, County Louth, Irish Republic: Near the banks of the narrow river Mattock, 6 miles west of Drogheda, are the meager, but moving and exceedingly graceful, remains of this abbey, Ireland's first of the Cistercian order. There are ruins of rounded chapels in the transepts of a church of continental European design, a fine 2-storied chapter house with a handsomely groined roof in the Norman style, a tall, massive gate house, and other interesting finds, including a crypt under the abbey church, unusual for a structure built in 12th-century Ireland. The whole complex, reputedly commissioned by St. Bernard of Clairvaux and consecrated with great pomp and circumstance in the presence of a papal legate in 1157, initiated a program of reform that quickly took hold and sprouted daughter establishments all over Ireland. At the time of the Dissolution, the abbey was acquired by Edward Moore, and from him it was passed on to the Balfours of Townley Hall, who never lived here. A century ago it was used as a piggery. Details: *Tourist Information Office,* Market Sq., Dundalk, County Louth, Irish Republic (phone: 42-35484).

HOLY CROSS ABBEY, Thurles, County Tipperary, Irish Republic: Ireland certainly has no shortage of ruined abbeys, their gray silhouettes standing stark against the sky. But this one, on the shores of the river Suir, is among the country's most beautiful and best preserved. Founded in 1169 by Donal O'Brien, the King of Thomond, on the site of an earlier Benedictine property, it came into possession of a fragment of the True Cross that Pope Pascal II had given to the founder's father, Donogh O'Brien, the grandson of none other than Brian Ború, in 1110. Because of the presence of this relic the monastery quickly grew, nurtured by gifts brought by the pilgrims who came in multitudes in the 15th and 16th centuries. The glory of the abbey today is its church, which was reroofed with Irish oak and slate and otherwise restored for public worship beginning in 1971. It has magnificent stone carvings, lively Flamboyant traceries, an elaborately groined roof, and handsome windows and arches, along with one of the few wall paintings to be found in any Irish church. (As befits the complex's setting in Tipperary's famous sporting country, the mural depicts a hunting scene.) The chancel, with its ribbed vaulting and fine east window, is considered to be among the best examples of 15th-century architecture in Ireland. Details: *South Eastern Region Tourist Information Office* (address above).

CARRICKFERGUS CASTLE, County Antrim, Northern Ireland: Along with Trim Castle in County Meath, Carrickfergus Castle remains the mightiest symbol of the Norman presence in Ireland after the invasion of 1169. Situated strategically on the shores of Belfast Lough, it is one of Ireland's strongest castles, and its name repeatedly crops up at a number of important junctures in Irish history. Founded in 1180 by John de Courcy, the first Norman Lord of Ulster, it was besieged in 1210 by King John of England, who feared the rising independence of his Norman barons. A century and a considerable amount of construction later, it fell to Robert the Bruce, whose brother Edward had invaded Ireland from Scotland in 1315, but it was returned to the Crown with the defeat of the Bruces a few years later. For nearly 3 centuries, it existed in comparative quiet and increasing decay. Then in 1690, William of Orange landed here during his campaign to defeat the Stuart kings for the possession of Ireland; some 70 years after that, it was taken by a French expeditionary force. In 1778, the American John Paul Jones, captain of the *Ranger,* defeated the HMS *Drake,* which was moored beneath the castle. In the 18th century, the castle was used as a prison for United Irishmen and others. Visitors enter the impressive structure through a gate flanked by two rounded towers and then proceed through the outer ward past a handful of 16th-century storehouses into the middle ward. Adjacent to the middle ward, the inner ward is dominated by the squarish keep — 5 stories, about 90 feet high, 56 feet across, and 58 feet deep. Inside the 8-foot-thick walls is a stairway that climbs from the ground level (where there is an early-20th-century steam engine and an antique wooden dugout canoe) to a group of military exhibits on the floor above and into the great chamber, a spacious room with large windows. Also worth a visit are the walled town's handsome late-18th-century Town Hall and its Church of St. Nicholas, which dates from the 12th and 17th centuries and houses a not-to-be-missed monument to Sir Arthur Chichester, who built the town walls and figured importantly in the establishment of modern Northern Ireland. For details of the medieval fairs and banquets held at the castle during the summer, phone 96-035-1604; for other information, contact the *Northern Ireland Tourist Board* (phone: 232-231221).

DIRECTIONS

Southeast Ireland: Dublin to New Ross

This route traverses only three Irish counties — Dublin, Wicklow, and Wexford — and it stays close to shore most of the time, yet the changing mood and character of the land along the way can be surprising. It may seem impossible, but the splendid isolation of the Wicklow Mountains is a mere half hour's drive from the center of Dublin. Here, great valleys with melodious names such as Glendalough, Clara, and Avoca wind through the hills, and uncrowded roads pass unforgettable sights — a high waterfall, an ancient monastic settlement, a proud estate. Several miles out of Glencree, the boggy terrain, flaked with granite and crusted in late summer with purple heather, seems primitive, still awaiting the arrival of man, whereas the wooded glens met later seem more soothing in their ageless beauty, not quite as lonely.

To the south lies the friendlier, less dramatic landscape of County Wexford, where fertile farmland is served by picturesque villages and the historic town of Wexford itself. The coast is lined with inviting beaches. This sunniest, driest corner of the country is its likeliest spot for sunbathing and beachcombing. There are busy seaside resorts with shooting galleries, amusement rides, and golf courses, but a discerning traveler can also find the secluded and tiny fishing village of Kilmore Quay, its traditional thatch-roofed cottages all freshly painted and still very much occupied.

This area is populated to some extent by urban exiles who have fled the congestion and pace of London and Dublin for the tranquillity of the Wicklow Mountains, weavers and potters with skilled hands musing away in modern bungalows and old cottages, and families cutting and collecting peat throughout the summer along the Military Road through Sally Gap. The people of Wexford congregate in singing pubs and good restaurants, while outside the town, time will seem to recede with the sight of older men in black suits rambling down country lanes, the postman delivering his parcels by bicycle, or women placing statues wrapped in rosary beads at the pilgrim shrines of Lady's Island.

The route heads south through the suburbs of Dublin to the residential and resort town of Dún Laoghaire and keeps to the coast as far as Bray. It then turns inland to the village of Enniskerry and the Powerscourt estate, continues west to Glencree, and turns south again over the Military Road to Laragh, the gateway to the monastic site of Glendalough. The route next passes through the vales of Clara and Avoca and returns to the coast at Arklow, where a succession of smaller and larger beachside resorts and villages leads south and then west to Kilmore Quay, interrupted only by the county town of Wexford on Wexford Harbour. At Kilmore Quay, it is possible to backtrack to Rosslare Harbour (a terminus for ferries to Wales and France) or to proceed to New Ross, from which Kilkenny and Waterford are not very distant.

A double room in a hotel listed as expensive will cost $100 or more; a moderate one, from $50 to $95; and an inexpensive one, less than $40. Dinner for two without wine or tips will come to $80 or more in an expensive restaurant, $50 to $75 in a moderate one, and under $40 in an inexpensive place.

DUBLIN: For a full report on the city, its sights, restaurants, and hotels, see *Dublin*, THE CITIES.

En Route from Dublin – Go south on O'Connell Street and turn left onto Nassau Street, just after Trinity College. Follow the signs to Ballsbridge, passing Merrion Square with its Georgian houses, the American Embassy, and the grounds of the Royal Dublin Society (where the famous horse show is held every summer), and continue until Dublin Bay is visible on the left. This coastal road passes the Booterstown Bird Sanctuary and travels through the small towns of Blackrock and Monkstown and then, 7 miles south of Dublin, into Dún Laoghaire. Craft enthusiasts will enjoy a stop in Blackrock to see the *Dublin Crystal* shop (Carysfort Ave., about a mile off Main St.; phone: 1-887932). This enterprise, begun in 1968, carries on glassmaking traditions that thrived in Dublin from 1764 to 1800. Tours of the factory are available by appointment.

DÚN LAOGHAIRE: As the terminus of the cross-channel ferry route from Holyhead, Wales, this busy residential town, holiday resort, and yachting center is one of the main gateways into Ireland. It has grown considerably as a suburb of Dublin in recent years and has innumerable hotels and restaurants, yet a Victorian charm lies below its modern surface, and a visitor can as easily stay a few days as a few hours. Dún Laoghaire (pronounced *Dun* Leery) was named after a 5th-century Irish king (O'Leary in English) who established a fort, or *dún,* here to protect the lands of the High Kings of Tara from their rivals. In the 16th century, the area figured in the fighting between the English, who had their main port at neighboring Dalkey, and the Irish, who opposed the English from the nearby Wicklow Mountains. (Traces of the ditch marking the Pale, the area under English control, can still be found around Booterstown.) Dún Laoghaire remained primarily a small fishing village until the present harbor was built in 1817, opening the way for mailboat and ferry services with Wales. George IV came to christen the harbor in 1821 (after which the town was renamed Kingston and known thus for the next 99 years), the railway line from Dublin arrived in 1834, and the town rapidly became a fashionable resort for the wealthy — many of the streets with their big Victorian houses are named after English royalty.

If you are just passing through town, head down to the harbor and walk the mile-long east pier, with Howth Head stretching in the distance. In summer, band concerts are sometimes held here, and not too long ago people brought chairs to sit and watch the sunset. On a nice night, many townspeople, children and dogs in tow, still parade the pier to watch the departure of the evening ferry. Nearby People's Park, which has swings and lovely flowers landscaped beneath shady trees, is the place to see next, perhaps after a stop for an ice cream cone at *Teddy's* (The Sea Front, just outside the park). George's Street is the main shopping area, and at the corner of Royal Marine Road is one of the most modern shopping malls in Ireland, with 3 floors of boutiques and gift shops and a tempting delicatessen in the basement. Across the way, St. Michael's Church is worth a visit. Its striking modern design incorporates a 19th-century bell tower from an earlier church destroyed by fire. Farther down Royal

Marine Road are the post office and Town Hall, built in 1878. For fresh salads and picnic or deli fare, the best stop is *Relish* (70 Upper George's St.). Fruit-to-go is the specialty of *P. McGovern & Sons* (65 Upper George's St.).

An enjoyable evening can be spent near Dún Laoghaire at Culturlann na hÉireann, the headquarters of the national organization for the promotion of traditional Irish music, song, and dance known as Comhaltas Ceoltóirí Eireann. The same group that sponsors *seisiún,* sessions of authentic music and dance, throughout the country during the summer has converted a large house into a cultural center, transforming the basement into an Irish kitchen complete with peat fire. Something is happening most evenings from early June to early September: either *seisiún; céilí* (dancing); *fonntrai* (a show spotlighting Irish traditions); or informal sessions of music and talk. There is a nice bar area with tables for socializing. Admission charge. The organization holds off-season programs, too. The building (32 Belgrave Sq., Monkstown; phone: 1-800295) is about 20 minutes on foot from Dún Laoghaire or a short drive by car (it's off the main road, so ask directions to Belgrave Square).

 CHECKING IN: *Fitzpatrick Castle* – Two generations of Fitzpatricks oversee the operation of Dublin's only luxury castle-hotel. Elegantly furnished with antiques and original paintings, it has 100 rooms and suites (many with four-poster beds), a fine dining room (*Truffles*), grillroom, bar, heated indoor pool, saunas, a gym, squash and tennis courts, guest privileges at the nearby *Leopardstown Golf Club,* and 9 acres of grounds with gardens and views of Killiney Bay. Courtesy coach service to the city center and the airport is provided. Killiney Hill Rd., Killiney (phone: 1-851533). Expensive.

Royal Marine – An elegant, older hotel that's set back from the waterfront by a gracious lawn and gardens is a lovely setting for a drink and dinner followed by a romantic stroll down to the harbor. It offers 90 renovated rooms (all with baths). Amenities include saunas, a beauty salon, and a large parking lot that's just behind the shopping mall on George's St. Royal Marine Rd., Dún Laoghaire (phone: 1-801911). Expensive.

Court – Set on 4 acres overlooking Killiney Bay, with a private garden walk to the beach, this converted residence has 34 rooms, all with bath and a view of the bay, and a fine French-Irish restaurant. Downtown Dublin is a 15-minute ride away via the adjacent *DART* (*Dublin Area Rapid Transport*) station. On Killiney Bay (phone: 1-851622). Expensive to moderate.

Scarsdale – This cheery bed and breakfast inn within walking distance of Dún Laoghaire's waterfront is run by Doris Pittman, who lived for several years in Scarsdale, NY. Four of the 5 bedrooms have hot and cold running water; the other, a full private bath. 4 Tivoli Rd., Dún Laoghaire (phone: 1-806258). Inexpensive.

 EATING OUT: *Digby's* – On the seafront, this is an elegant place with a reputation for fine food. The menu usually changes with the seasons to take advantage of whatever is freshest — perhaps wild sea trout, venison, teal, brace of quail, squab, or rack of lamb — and there's also a long list of wines. Open for dinner daily except Tuesdays. 5 Windsor Ter., Dún Laoghaire (phone: 1-804600). Expensive.

Guinea Pig – Former Dalkey town mayor Mervyn Stewart is the chef-owner, and seafood is the specialty, including scallops with crab claws and *symphonie de la mer* — monkfish, salmon, sole, and shellfish simmered in herbs, garlic, butter, and lemon. Open daily for dinner; Sundays — lunch only. 17 Railway Rd., Dalkey (phone: 1-859055). Expensive.

na Mara – A Dublin Bay restaurant in a former train station, known for its good seafood, especially prawns flame-cooked in Pernod, smoked fish pâté, and lobster. 1 Harbour Rd., Dún Laoghaire (phone: 1-806767). Expensive.

Baroque – The atmosphere is Old World, and the menu includes lobster thermidor, rack of lamb, and boneless stuffed duck. Main St., Dalkey (phone: 1-851017). Expensive to moderate.

Salty Dog – Filled with Persian rugs and wall hangings that a roaming salty dog might have brought home from his travels, this pleasant restaurant features dishes such as boneless stuffed duckling, while on Sundays diners can partake of the special Indonesian rice table of 18 different dishes, including deep-fried chicken and spiced lamb. 3A Haddington Ter., Dún Laoghaire (phone: 1-808015). Expensive to moderate.

Pier 3 – Overlooking the water, this new popular spot offers a varied menu, with dishes such as chicken breast stuffed with avocado and smoked bacon; scallops of pork in brandy and pistachio sauce; brace of quail marinated in honey and grape juice, and salmon *en papillotte* with watercress sauce. A different vegetarian dish is also on the menu each night. Open for dinner only, Tuesdays through Saturdays. Marine Parade, Dún Laoghaire (phone: 1-842234). Moderate.

Steers – Steaks — 17-ounce sirloins — are the big attraction at this waterfront restaurant, which also serves seafood. Windsor Ter., Seafront (phone: 1-843498). Moderate.

Wishbone – Right over the *Eagle* pub, this place is popular for steaks, burgers, fresh fish, and crêpes. Open daily for lunch and dinner. 18/20 Glasthule Rd., Sandycove, Dún Laoghaire (phone: 1-808021). Inexpensive.

Dún Laoghaire also has its share of moderate to inexpensive Chinese restaurants. Two current favorites are *Joyous* (69A Upper George's St.; phone: 1-858719) and *Yung* (66B Upper George's St.; phone: 1-803205).

En Route from Dún Laoghaire – The coastal road southeast of town leads to a district known as Sandycove, the site of a Martello tower built as protection against a possible Napoleonic invasion and now a museum dedicated to James Joyce. The author lived in the tower briefly with Oliver St. John Gogarty, and in the opening scene of *Ulysses,* Stephen Dedalus lives there with Buck Mulligan. The museum, which has a small collection of Joyce's letters, books, and other memorabilia, is the starting point of many a Bloomsday tour taken by Joyce fans every June 16, the day in 1904 on which the events of *Ulysses* take place. Visitors can climb to the top of the handsomely restored tower for a great view of the harbor and the Irish Sea as Joyce saw it. The museum is open May through September, by appointment at other times. Admission charge (phone: 1-818571).

A short distance down the coastal road is Bullock Castle, at one time a powerful abbey and inn run by Cistercian monks who exacted tolls from ships entering Bullock Harbour. The castle — now owned by American Carmelite nuns who staff the adjoining nursing home — has been restored, and the tiny prayer cells of the monks and the large dining hall make it an interesting stop. Note the carved head on the corner of the western wall, which dates the castle at about 1160. It is open May through September, by appointment at other times. Bullock Castle is at the northern approach to the small resort village of Dalkey. A major port when Dublin was developing, it was once guarded by no fewer than seven castles, two of which remain on Castle St. (one has been rebuilt as the Town Hall). Continue to follow signs for the coast road, which goes around Sorrento Point and then, via Vico Rd., high over Killiney Hill for a view of Killiney Bay. A local saying, "See Killiney Bay and die," compares the view to that of the Bay of Naples. You can judge for yourself by parking your car and enjoying the beautiful stretch of ocean as far as Bray Head to the south and Dalkey Island to the north — the tiny flecks of black against the blue-gray surface of the water are fishing boats. At the end of Vico Rd., follow the signs to Bray, in County Wicklow; a short

12 miles from Dublin, it's one of Ireland's most popular seaside resorts. Bray has a mile-long beach (a shingly one, compared with those farther south), with a mile-long esplanade running its length to Bray Head. This nearly 800-foot cliff rises sheer from the sea at the end of the esplanade.

After Bray, turn inland and drive the short 3 miles to Enniskerry.

ENNISKERRY: Though this tiny village is very pretty, its main attraction is the 14,000-acre Powerscourt Estate on its southern outskirts (see "Stately Homes and Great Gardens" in *For the Experience,* DIVERSIONS). A fire in 1974 destroyed the interior of the lovely 18th-century mansion, whose substantial skeleton still attests to its grandness, but the wonderful formal terraced gardens with pebble-paved ramps, statuary, and ironwork are still intact in a heady location looking out over the Wicklow hills to Sugar Loaf Mountain. Pleasant Japanese gardens are on the grounds as well as a 400-foot waterfall, the highest in Great Britain and Ireland. The gardens are open March 1 through October; the waterfall area is open year-round. There are also two shops on the estate grounds. Admission charge (phone: 1-867676).

En Route from Enniskerry – Ten miles south of Enniskerry, via the R755, the picturesque mountain village of Roundwood is worth a slight detour before heading on to Glencree. Set 780 feet above sea level, the area usually is referred to as the "highest village in Ireland." Stop for a meal at the rustic old coaching inn (ca. 1750), the *Roundwood Inn* (109 Avondale Rd.; phone: 1-818107 or 1-818125), with stone fireplaces and antique furnishings. Proprietors Jurgen and Aine Schwalm are known for serving fresh seafood, such as Galway Bay oysters, Dublin Bay prawns, or locally caught salmon, plus Irish stew, rack of Wicklow lamb, venison, and international dishes, such as Hungarian goulash. For lunch, try a hearty soup, such as scallop chowder, and sandwiches.

To reach Glencree, head 2 miles back on the R755; next, drive 8 miles west on the R759, then 4 miles north on the R115 until you reach the town. The road climbs into the splendid Wicklow Mountains on a winding course hugged by trees that now and again give way to views of white cottages planted in the midst of brown fields. At Glencree, follow the signs south to Sally Gap over the Military Road, so called because it was built by the British after the Rebellion of 1798 and used to flush out Irish rebels hiding in the glens of the Wicklows. This stretch of the route is a winding one, too, passing peat bogs, glacial lakes, and a landscape somber and unyielding in its flatness till it reaches the crossroads of Sally Gap (1,631 feet) and begins to descend toward Laragh through the valley of Glenmacnass. At the northern end of the glen, where the road joins the course of the river Glenmacnass, is a parking lot. Be sure to stop and walk down to the waterfall, pristine and powerful in its simple beauty as it tumbles over silent slabs of stone into the deep valley below. At the southern end, where the river Glenmacnass meets the Avonmore, is the village of Laragh. Browse for a while in the *Glendalough Craft Centre,* a transformed farmhouse where weavings and jewelry are made on the premises; the wares include sheepskins, woodcarvings, hand-woven clothing, and pottery. Then drive the mile west to the entrance to Glendalough.

GLENDALOUGH: This deep glen, set between two lakes amid the towering wooded slopes and granite hills of the Wicklow Mountains, is at once a place of great natural beauty and immense historical interest. Glendalough means "the valley of the two lakes," and in the 6th century, when St. Kevin came to Wicklow in search of tranquillity, he found it here. But the hermit's sanctity attracted so many disciples that, almost unwittingly, he founded a great monastery that eventually became one of the most renowned centers of learning in Europe. It was sacked by the Vikings in the 9th and

10th centuries, and later (1398) by the English, although some of the buildings remained in use until Henry VIII dissolved the monasteries in the 16th century. Today the ruins of the monastic city are scattered over 1½ miles of a valley that insulates visitors from the present the minute they step through the aged arched gateway at its entrance. It was in the solitude of the Upper Lake at the base of 2,296-foot Camaderry and 2,154-foot Lugduff that St. Kevin first prayed in his stone beehive hut. In the same area, with its gravestones and crosses, is Reefert Church, where the O'Tooles and other local chiefs are buried. Visitors can walk or drive to the upper lake, use the picnic grounds, and (for a small fee) hire a boat that provides some splendid views of the valley and a closer look at St. Kevin's Bed, an excavation in the cliff face about 25 feet above the water level, said to have been used as a retreat by the saint. As it grew, the settlement spread toward the Lower Lake and the entrance, and the ruins in this area include the cathedral, the largest church on the site; St. Kevin's Church, with its sturdy stone ceiling; and the much-photographed Round Tower, over 100 feet high. Built in the 9th century, this was probably a bell tower, lookout point, and place of refuge all in one; the only door is fully 10 feet above the ground. Glendalough's walks and ruins are marked by plaques for easy exploration. After steeping themselves in this ancient beauty made mellow by human habitation, visitors can stop at one of the many tea shops in the vicinity.

 CHECKING IN: *Royal* – Offers 16 renovated bedrooms (all but 3 with private bath), a dining room with views of the river and mountains beyond, and a bar with snacks. Open March through October. Glendalough (phone: 404-5135). Moderate.

En Route from Glendalough – Leaving by the Arklow road, T61, the route once again parallels the course of a river, this time the Avonmore, and passes through the wooded Vale of Clara before reaching the town of Rathdrum, 8 miles south of Laragh. Here it is possible to interrupt the route for an interesting diversion at the nearby *Clara-Lara Fun Park*, an outdoor amusement center featuring rowboats, rides, and a trout farm, where visitors pay $3 for every pound of fish they catch (full barbecue facilities are available on the premises). Admission charge to the park includes fishing pole rental. Open April through October.

About 1½ miles southeast of Rathdrum is Avondale, the lovely birthplace and home of the Irish patriot Charles Stewart Parnell, a member of a Protestant landowning family who became a leader in the fight for Catholic emancipation and land reform in the 19th century. The house was built in 1777 by Parnell's cousin Samuel Hayes, who was interested in forestation and in 1794 wrote the first book on tree planting in Ireland. The 530-acre estate that the Parnell family inherited from Hayes in 1795 belongs to the Forest and Wildlife Service and is used as a forestry school. The guidebook on sale at the estate discusses the wildlife and trees found on the grounds as well as the recommended walks, but for tourists budgeting time, the house, with its lovely furnishings and moldings, is the main interest. Note the poster from the day Parnell addressed the US House of Representatives in 1880 (Parnell's mother was American, the daughter of Admiral Charles Stewart, who fought the British in the War of 1812). The house is open from 2 to 6 PM Fridays through Mondays, May through September; a nature trail on the grounds is open year-round.

From Avondale, return to Rathdrum and pick up the main road, T7, south toward Woodenbridge. The distance between the two towns, approximately 8 miles, is known as the Vale of Avoca, a beauty spot immortalized in verse by Ireland's national poet, Thomas Moore ("There is not in this wide world a valley so sweet / As that vale in whose bosom the bright waters meet"). The Meeting of the Waters, where the rivers Avonmore and Avonbeg join to form the river Avoca, is about 3½ miles south of Rathdrum, and the tree under which Moore is supposed to have sat to contemplate the beauty he saw is marked by a plaque. *The Meetings*, a combination pub, restaurant, nightclub, and crafts shop standing on the site of a cottage where Moore once lived, overlooks this pastoral junction. Visitors can sip an Irish coffee here and listen to the hearty publican, an amateur Moore scholar, discuss the poet's works; he owns an 1889 edition of the poems with the noted tribute to the vale on page 200. If time permits, visit the Motte Stone, signposted near the Meeting of the Waters. The large boulder marks the halfway point between Dublin and Wexford, and from its top the view of the countryside is quite nice. Legend has it that the boulder was the hurling stone of the giant Finn MacCool.

To reach the small, friendly village of Avoca, about 3 miles south of the Meeting of the Waters, turn left at the sign for Avoca on the main road and then left again after the bridge. Here visitors can watch the weaving process at *Avoca Handweavers*. The operation, in a cluster of stone buildings that was once a corn mill, employs about 30 people who prepare, roll, and weave the wool, about 75% of it for export. The remainder, as capes, ponchos, suits, vests, bedspreads, scarves, and so on, can be bought in the mill shop. Besides the weaving mill, Avoca has a short main street that seems like a stage set with its three or four buildings, a couple of them pubs, and several bed and breakfast houses on the main road near the bridge. *Riverview* (phone: 402-5181) is a lovely guesthouse run by May Byrne, a retired schoolteacher and fluent speaker of Irish.

About 2 miles south of Avoca, the rivers Aughrim and Avoca form a second confluence at Woodenbridge, and though no poets have sung its praises, many travelers find it more beautiful than the first. The main road then bears east toward the coast and in 5 miles arrives at Arklow.

ARKLOW: This busy town at the mouth of the river Avoca has long been a fishing and shipping port and a boatbuilding center: *Gipsy Moth IV*, the yacht that took Sir Francis Chichester around the world, was built in an Arklow shipyard. The town is also a popular seaside resort, with beaches to the north and south, and it is the home of *Arklow Pottery*, the largest pottery manufacturer in Ireland. Arklow was founded by the Norsemen, and when they gave way to the Normans, it became the property of the Fitzwalters, ancestors of the Butlers, one of the most powerful families in Irish history. The decisive battle of the Wexford Rebellion of 1798 was fought here; the insurgent leader, Father Michael Murphy (not the same Father Murphy who led the pikemen in Wexford), lost his life in the battle. A statue of him, the 1798 Memorial, commemorates his bravery.

Arklow Pottery, now part of Noritake, a Japanese china company, employs more than 200 people and has been making domestic earthenware since 1934. Though the plant is open to visitors by appointment only (phone: 402-32401), a shop on the premises that sells seconds at discount prices is open daily. Golf, tennis, fishing, and boating are all possible in the Arklow vicinity, but the major attraction outside of town is about 10 miles north, at Brittas Bay. The 3-mile stretch of silver strand and sand dunes can be crowded with picnickers and bathers from Dublin on sunny weekends, but normally there's only a modest crowd.

 CHECKING IN: *Marlfield House* – This 18th-century mansion was once part of the extensive Courtown estate and has been handsomely restored by owners Raymond and Mary Bowe. Some of the furniture belonged to the original estate, and the 13 bedrooms and 6 suites are elegantly decorated. There are beautiful staircases, marble fireplaces, and long windows that look out onto the spacious grounds and award-winning gardens. Vegetables and herbs grown on the premises appear in the dining room, where the dinner menu can include such fare as crab salad, beef Wellington, and chocolate whiskey cake. On the Gorey–Courtown road, Gorey (phone: 55-21572). Expensive.

Tinakilly House – Once the home of Captain Charles Halpin, who laid the first successful cable connecting Europe with America, it is filled with seafaring memorabilia and paintings, family silver, and other precious heirlooms. Now run by the Power family, this house on 7 acres of gardens overlooking the Irish Sea has been completely refurbished. All 14 rooms have private baths, and most have marble fireplaces, needlepoint chairs, wood paneling, and antique Victorian furnishings. The restaurant has 3 dining rooms, and there are tennis courts; a sitting room with a piano; and open fireplaces in all the public rooms. About 2 miles south of Rathnew, right off the main Dublin road (phone: 404-469274). Expensive.

Hunters – This 200-year-old coaching inn is now in the hands of the Gelletlie family's fifth generation. Flowering gardens along the banks of the river Vartry, part of the extensive grounds, also supply the inn's restaurant with fresh vegetables. There are 18 rooms, 10 with bath. Newrath Bridge, Rathnew (phone: 404-40106). Moderate.

 EATING OUT: *Singing Kettle* – Just 200 yards from the beach at Courtown, this lovely candlelight restaurant is run by the McGuinness family. Lunch and dinner daily, June through September; dinner only on weekends the rest of the year. Ardamine, Courtown, about 10 miles south of Arklow (phone: 55-25151). Moderate.

Woodenbridge – Attached to one of Ireland's oldest hotels (ca. 1608), this Tudor restaurant has a warm Old World atmosphere and features local produce and freshwater trout. Open daily for lunch and dinner, morning coffee, and afternoon tea; dancing and entertainment on weekends. Woodenbridge, near Arklow (phone: 40-25146). Moderate.

En Route from Arklow – While the main road south follows the railway line to Wexford, the coastal road, a pleasant, quiet drive of about 40 miles, runs along a succession of sandy beaches in the sunniest and driest part of Ireland. Courtown is a lively resort in summer; besides its 2 miles of beach, it has an 18-hole golf course, typical seaside amusements, and entertainment — Irish nights, *seisiún,* and disco dancing — at a variety of small hotels. In August, the nearby town of Gorey, 3½ miles inland, hosts an arts festival that includes art exhibits, films, theater, and a variety of music from traditional Irish to jazz and rock. The Church of St. Michael and Christ Church are among the things to see at other times of the year. Farther south along the coast, the beaches continue almost uninterrupted to Wexford, including especially good ones at Cahore, Kilmuckridge, Blackwater, and Curracloe, all backed by picturesque villages. South of Curracloe, where the river Slaney runs out to sea, the road crosses the bridge into Wexford.

WEXFORD: Here is a town that combines city sophistication with village warmth. Built on the river Slaney, its narrow streets date from medieval times, so leave your car outside the town proper or in the parking lot on the quays near the tourist board. Wexford was founded by the Vikings, taken by the Normans, suffered terrible destruction at the hands of Oliver Cromwell, and then rose up in the Rebellion of 1798, when a local priest led his parishioners, armed only with pikes, against the English. Wexford has good singing pubs, restaurants, and hotels, but it is best known for its annual *Wexford Opera Festival.* For 12 days every October, rarely performed operas, new and old, are presented in the restored 19th-century *Theatre Royal,* sung by highly regarded, though not yet well known, opera singers from around the world. Wexford's normal population of 15,000 swells by about 6,000 at this time, and the whole town celebrates: There are singing pub competitions, theater presentations, and other festival events. Be sure to have a drink at the intriguing *Crown Bar* (Monck St.) and at the *Thomas Moore Tavern* (in the Cornmarket). The *Bohemian Girl* (at North Main and Monck Sts.) is a good spot for lunch or Irish coffee. For a full report on Wexford, its sights, restaurants, and hotels, see *Wexford* in THE CITIES.

En Route from Wexford – To visit Johnstown Castle, a 19th-century Gothic mansion now owned by the State Agricultural College, proceed south for about 3 miles via an unnumbered country road. The castle grounds have lovely ornamental gardens, walks around artificial lakes, a picnic area, and the *Irish Agricultural Museum,* an interesting exhibition on farming and rural life. Otherwise, start out on the road to Rosslare Harbour, N25. On a fine summer day, this area southeast of Wexford is the stuff of poetry: Clean sea air sweeps over green hedges and down country roads little changed by the 20th century. Turn left onto R740 at Killinick and head for Rosslare, branching left when the main road bears right for Rosslare Harbour. Rosslare, or Rosslare Strand, is a seaside resort in the middle of a wonderful 6-mile beach, which is not its only attraction. There are also public tennis courts, an 18-hole golf course, a playground, fishing and boating, and *Kelly's Strand* hotel (phone: 53-32114), which is a center of activity and a popular year-round retreat for the Irish.

The road south from Rosslare leads to the village of Tagoat and two possibilities. A left turn onto N25 leads to a selection of good hotels and restaurants in Rosslare Harbour, the departure point for ferries to Fishguard, Wales, and Le Havre and Cherbourg, France (but don't follow the road to the end, since it leads directly onto the boats). Driving straight through Tagoat leads to the tiny village of Broadway, which has an enormous tavern and thatch-roofed cottages. Broadway is at the head of Lady's Island Lake, actually a sea inlet, and Lady's Island is in the lake, connected to land by a causeway. The ruins of an Augustinian priory dedicated to the Virgin Mary and a Norman castle with a curiously leaning limestone tower are on the island, which has been the object of pilgrimages for centuries and still is in August and September.

From Lady's Island, the two possibilities are to continue east to Carne Harbour, where there is more beach and a very good seafood restaurant, the *Lobster Pot* (phone: 53-31110), which is open May through August, or to return to Broadway and drive west to Kilmore Quay, one of the most delightful villages in Ireland. Kilmore Quay is a fishing village whose main street is no more than a cozy row of thatch-roofed cottages with a fishermen's cooperative at one end. Visitors with an interest in bird watching can hire a boat to visit the great bird sanctuary of the Saltee Islands, a 45-minute trip off the south coast of County Wexford (call Willie Bates, 29644, or Tom O'Brien, 29727). Watchers should note that about three-quarters of the total Irish bird species have been seen in this county, and most of the birds frequent either Great or Little Saltee, where they rub feathers with many rare migrant birds. Great Saltee (only a mile long) was once inhabited, and caves in its rugged, rocky cliffs were used as hideaways by insurgents after the Rebellion of 1798 was crushed. The small, modern *Saltees* hotel in Kilmore Quay (phone: 53-29601/2) has a restaurant and pleasant accommodations, with rooms named after the various species of birds found on the Saltees.

Less than 20 miles northwest of Kilmore Quay is the town of New Ross, built on a steep hill overlooking the river Barrow. *Galley Cruising Restaurants* (phone: 51-21723) offers 3-hour dinner cruises departing from New Ross at 7 PM daily during the summer and according to demand in April, May, and September. Five miles south of New Ross, on L159, is the John Fitzgerald Kennedy Memorial Park, a splendid 480-acre arboretum commemorating President Kennedy, whose ancestors came from nearby Dunganstown. The park covers the lower slopes of Slieve Coillte, from the top of which, on a nice day, the counties of Wexford and Waterford are visible. Waterford City is 15 miles southwest of New Ross, and Kilkenny Town is 26 miles northwest.

South-Central Ireland

Despite the recent influx of industry and factories, Ireland is still very much a rural, agricultural country, and this route travels through some of the island's best farmland. Tipperary Town is in the midst of the Golden Vale, fertile acreage extending from the valley of the river Suir, east of town, across the border into County Limerick, west of town. The rich pastureland rolls down to Mitchelstown in County Cork, where the vast creamery of the Mitchelstown Cooperative Agricultural Society gathers its bounty, and on to the valley of the river Blackwater, no less known for bounty of another sort. The Blackwater, which cuts across County Cork on its way into the Celtic Sea, is popular with sportsmen, especially fishermen keen on the trout, perch, roach, dace, rudd, and, above all, salmon, in it and its tributaries.

Mountain scenery is not missing: South of Tipperary Town, the Glen of Aherlow is a romantic drive through the mighty Galtee Mountains — motorists might meet a donkey cart or two along the road. Farther south, two other ranges, the Knockmealdowns and the Comeraghs, become a palette of greens in the afternoon light. The route goes around these two, but a detour, a hairpin scenic drive called the Vee, winds through the former. Nor is seascape missing: The route also leads along the Celtic Sea from Cobh, where the great passenger liners once docked, into Youghal, where a version of *Moby Dick* was filmed, past cliffs and miles of beach into quaint Annestown, the seaside resort of Tramore, and, finally, Waterford. The route turns inland after Waterford to enter a landscape where historic castles guarding riverbanks are commonplace, and then it terminates at Cashel, one of Ireland's greatest historical sites. Bad weather actually enhances explorations here. A little fog and mist add a dimension of mystery to the imposing Rock of Cashel, so that you can almost hear the old heroes of Erin clanging their armor among the ruins.

There are areas along this route where few tourists tread and hence they provide a glimpse of Ireland without makeup — raw and beautiful. These quiet stretches are interspersed with the liveliness of good pubs, restaurants, and lodgings that are plentiful from Tipperary back to Cashel. The shingles of artists and craftsmen working at studios and kilns in tiny villages will suggest impromptu breaks in the itinerary from time to time, and the organized tour of the Waterford Glass Factory, where demonstrations of the manufacture of the famous crystal are offered, should not be missed. The route passes through a remote Irish-speaking area, one of the few pockets of Irish not on the west coast, and includes a castle familiar to most visitors from movies. The route blends the pleasure and hospitality of Ireland with the tranquillity and beauty that once made it the land of saints and scholars.

Hotels listed as expensive will charge $100 or more for a double room; those listed as moderate will range from $50 to $95; and inexpensive ones will be

$40 and under — well under in the case of bed and breakfast houses. Dinner for two (without wine) will cost $60 and up in an expensive restaurant; from $35 to $55 in a moderate one; and less than $30 in an inexpensive place.

TIPPERARY: "It's a long way to Tipperary," goes the famous World War I song, but this cozy town in the Golden Vale has developed a personality and prosperity that make the journey worth the distance. Viewed from the footpaths of the hills just outside town, Tip, as it is called by the locals, resembles a quiet New England village bordered by the green back of the Slievenamuck Mountains. But Main Street is a busy place lined with pleasant shops and entertaining pubs. This is prime farmland, and many in the area are employed in the Tipperary Cooperative Creamery at the end of Bridge Street. Fenian leader John O'Leary was born in Tipperary, and the town was famous during the Land League movement of the 1880s, when residents refused to pay property rents to landlord Smith-Barry and established a "New Tipperary" just outside the town borders. The shops and timber houses of Emmet and Dillon Streets are still inhabited, although the plan eventually failed, especially when Smith-Barry discovered he owned the land on which a new butter market had been erected by the rebels and tore it down. *Kiely's Breads* now stands on the site of the butter market, near the town well. Tipperary has had a long history (it grew around a castle built here by King John in the late 12th century), but one that contrived to leave it with few very ancient or notable buildings (it was laid waste during the course of the Desmond Wars in the late 16th century).

It is a friendly place, however, and to sample its hospitality, stop at one of the town's many pubs, such as *Nellie O'Brien's* (Main St.), where guests can sip a pint of beer under a thatch roof, or have a quiet drink at *Tony Lowry's* (46 Main St.), near the Maid of Aran statue at the end of the street.

The Tipperary Tourist Office (3 James St.; phone: 62-51457), open year-round, provides information on the town and surrounding area.

 CHECKING IN: *Dundrum House* – Set on 140 acres, this Georgian house built in 1730 has 55 rooms, each uniquely decorated with antiques and many offering views of the large garden. The dining room, which provides wonderful views of trees and the river, serves fresh seafood; the prawns from Dublin Bay and the scallops in smoked salmon sauce topped with scallop roe are particularly good. On many nights live Irish music is performed in the bar, housed in a former chapel with stained glass windows. A leisure center is scheduled to open later this year, and a golf course will be ready sometime in 1992. Restaurant reservations advised. County Tipperary (phone: 62-71116). Expensive.

Glen – An inviting 24-room hotel on the drive through the Glen of Aherlow, a few miles outside Tipperary. Glen of Aherlow, Tipperary (phone: 62-56146). Moderate.

Royal – Right off Main Street, this older hotel has 16 rooms, each with private bath. Bridge St., Tipperary (phone: 62-51204). Moderate to inexpensive.

Clonmore – Many visitors return to this popular bed and breakfast house run by Mary Quinn in an attractive bungalow. Four rooms with private baths. Open April through October. Cork–Galbally road, Tipperary (phone: 62-51637). Inexpensive.

EATING OUT: *Brown Trout* – Long established and known for its good local fare, ranging from sole on the bone to grilled trout. Light on atmosphere but generous with portions. Bridge St., Tipperary (phone: 62-51912). Moderate to inexpensive.

En Route from Tipperary – Leave by Bridge Street and follow the signs south for the Glen of Aherlow, a valley between the Slievenamuck and the Galtee Mountains that provides a lovely backdrop to a wending, scenic drive. From the car park before the statue of Christ the King, there is a vast view of the valley, which seems untouched by time. Two-story farmhouses are more common than modern bungalows, and donkey carts pulling containers of milk still travel the roads. Follow the signs to Galbally and then on to Mitchelstown, just over the County Cork border.

MITCHELSTOWN: This butter- and cheese-producing town is an interesting mixture of the old and the new. The Catholic Church of the Blessed Virgin Mary with its window-slashed brick interior overlooks Mitchelstown from Convent Hill; it was opened in 1980. In contrast, Kingston College was erected in 1761 by the Earl of Kingston, whose family laid out much of the town. The establishment is a collection of attached stone houses that open onto College Square. Not a college at all, the houses were originally built as almshouses for "decayed gentlefolk" as well as for some of the families who worked for the Kingstons. It is now the home of about 30 retired couples. Each of the Georgian houses has a back garden, and one house is set aside for community affairs, although daily life at the Kingston College once had its unharmonious moments. The houses used to have common entrances, but these gave way long ago to individual doorways so that feuding families would not have to meet. The extensive creamery run by the Mitchelstown Cooperative Agricultural Society can be toured (stop in at the communications office in New Square). The society, which began in 1917 and grew as small cooperatives merged with it, employs about 2,300 people and has 4,500 shareholders, all of whom are farmers. Before leaving Mitchelstown, try the pastries at the *Torten* on Cork Street or stop for a pint at one of the pubs, known for their evocative names — the *Cave, Hunter's Rest,* the *Blackthorn, Foxes' Den.* Mitchelstown Caves, two long, complex caves with large halls and interesting formations that can be visited with a guide, are 6 miles northeast, off the Cahir road.

En Route from Mitchelstown – Drive due south 10 miles to Fermoy, a fairly large, busy town that was once prosperous as a garrison for the British army and is now popular with sport fishermen. The town straddles the river Blackwater, one of the better-known salmon-fishing rivers in Ireland. The Blackwater rises on the Cork-Kerry border and flows 85 miles out to sea at Youghal, and the stretch of the river around Fermoy is the part that is best for salmon. The river is also used for coarse-fishing competitions, and Fermoy has hosted most of the championships. There are numerous sports associations, including five hunt clubs. Castle Hyde House, the beautiful Georgian home of Douglas Hyde, the first President of Ireland, is just outside town; the 6-bedroom house is available for rental (2-week minimum). For details contact *Elegant Ireland* (15 Harcourt St., 2 Dublin; phone: 1-751665). About 3 miles northwest of town, off the Glanworth road and worth a visit, is Labbacallee, or the Hag's Bed, one of the largest wedge-shaped gallery graves in the country. (Gallery graves are those in which the chambers are not distinct from the entrance passages.) It looks like a pile of stones from the roadside, but closer inspection (achieved by climbing over the steps in the stone wall at the side) reveals the massive shape of the two burial chambers covered by three immense capstones. It is guarded by several standing stones and dates from about 1500 BC.

CHECKING IN: *BlackWater Castle* – Located less than 10 miles east of Fermoy, this imposing 12th-century landmark sits high on a rocky peninsula overlooking the Awbeg River in the heart of the Blackwater Valley. Opened as a hotel in 1988, it has been restored and completely renovated, with 10 individually decorated bedrooms, each with antiques and an array of 20th-century amenities, from fully tiled bathrooms to refrigerators, mini-bars, and satellite TV. The public rooms include a well-stocked library, a bar, lounges with open fireplaces, and a restaurant featuring an open kitchen. The grounds offer a putting green, tennis court, croquet lawn, salmon and trout fishing, and acres of gardens and woodlands. It's a remote but surprisingly modern retreat. Fermoy/Mallow Rd. (N72), Castletownroche, County Cork (phone: 22-26333). Expensive.

From Fermoy, head south to Midleton and turn west onto N25, dropping down to T12A at the turnoff for Cobh. The route leads across a strip of water to Great Island (approximately 17 miles by 2 miles) and curves down and around its southern side to where Cobh (pronounced *Cove*) stands facing the greater part of Cork Harbour.

COBH: One of the nicest times of year to enjoy this former port of call for the great transatlantic passenger liners is during the annual *International Folk Dance Festival,* a week of dancing, concerts, fireworks, and parades each July. The blue haze of a summer's evening settles over the harbor and the graceful tower of St. Colman's Cathedral high on the hill above gives the scene a medieval character heightened by the presence of European dancers on the waterfront in traditional costume, singing Irish songs in foreign accents, and waving the flags of their countries. The cathedral, though not medieval (it was built between 1868 and 1915), is Cobh's most striking feature. It tops off the hill of old houses built shoulder to shoulder in ascending height and, from the harbor, looks like a guardian angel hovering over so many members of a family posing for a picture. During the famine years, the harbor at Cobh was the last image of Ireland impressed on the minds of many thousands of Irish emigrants leaving their native soil on ships that all too often were not seaworthy enough to carry them to their destinations. The view then was without the cathedral, but those who survived the coffin ships to do well in the New World sent back money to help build this crowning touch to the town's skyline. Its exterior of Dublin granite is covered with statues and gargoyles, its interior features stained glass windows and a 43-foot-high marble altar alive with carvings, and there are weekly concerts on the 47-bell carillon.

Until the 18th century, Cobh was a small fishing village accessible only by ferry and known simply as the Cove of Cork. In medieval times, it had belonged to an Irish chieftain whose son fought with Brian Ború against the Danes in the Battle of Clontarf (1014). Later, it became the home of Anglo-Irish families such as the Barrys, the Hodnetts, and the Roches, one of whose castles (the 14th-century Belvelly Castle) can be seen near the bridge on the way into town. The British began to develop the fishing village as a strategic naval base during the American Revolution. They erected a military barracks on the site of an ancient monastery across from Cobh on Spike Island (later used as a prison for Irish rebels and now an Irish army coastal defense station) and a naval station west of Spike Island on Haulbowline Island (now the site of a huge steel complex and headquarters of the Irish navy). Many of the town's streets were laid out during the 1800s, as Georgian and Victorian homes for British officers rose along Harbour Row. In 1838, the first transatlantic steamship sailed from Cobh, initiating an era of prominence for the town as an international passenger port, and in 1849 the Cove of Cork became Queenstown, renamed in commemoration of a visit by Queen Victoria. During World War I, both the British and the Americans used Queenstown's port facilities; when a German submarine sank the *Lusitania* off Kinsale in May 1915, it was from here that ships sailed to rescue the survivors. Perpetuating its position as a passenger port, Cunard's *QE 2* calls on Cobh during several of its transatlantic crossings, usually westbound sailings from Southampton, England, to New York.

Today, with its own name, Cobh is a holiday resort focused on its attractive harbor. The *International Sailing Centre* (phone: 21-811237), based near the Town Hall in an old house where equipment lies in colorful disarray, offers courses in sailing. Sea angling can be arranged through the *Cobh Sea Angling Club* (phone: 21-812167). The *Royal Cork Yacht Club* (phone: 21-831440) across the harbor at Crosshaven dates from 1720 and is the oldest in the world. The Lusitania Memorial (Roger Casement Sq.) includes several restored Italianate shops. A local museum is housed in a converted church on High Road. The rest of Great Island can be explored. Victims of the *Lusitania* disaster are buried in the Old Church Cemetery, about a mile north. Nearby at Carrigtwohill is Fota Island, an estate once owned by the Smith-Barry family and now in the care of University College Cork. The family home, built in the 1820s, is a splendid example of Regency architecture. Displayed inside is a private collection of Irish landscape paintings from the 1750s to the 1870s. Open 11 AM to 6 PM Mondays through Saturdays, 2 to 6 PM Sundays, April through September; 2 to 6 PM Sundays and holidays the rest of the year. Also on the grounds are a wildlife center and an arboretum open to the public.

CHECKING IN: *Commodore* – This veteran hotel overlooks the waterfront. It has an Old World atmosphere, modernized facilities (all 36 rooms have private baths), a lovely dining room serving excellent meals, and a heated indoor swimming pool, a squash court, and sauna. Deep-sea fishing trips can be arranged. Cobh (phone: 21-811277). Moderate.

Rinn Ronain – Picturesquely set on the river Lee, this cozy hotel was once the home of J. P. Ronayne, a 19th-century Irish patriot. It has 21 rooms with private baths, and a restaurant with a panoramic view. Open year-round. Rushbrooke, Cobh (phone: 21-812242). Moderate.

En Route from Cobh – The main Cork–Waterford road, N25, leads east to Youghal. But there are several reasons to turn off the road at Castlemartyr and follow the signs to Ballycotton, stopping 3 miles short of the coast at the tiny village of Shanagarry. One is a meal or an overnight stay at Ballymaloe House, a small hotel and family-run restaurant (see *Checking In*) that is one of Ireland's most delightful country properties. Another is a stop at the pottery workshops of Stephen Pearce and his father, Philip. Stephen Pearce, whose brown pottery with frosty white glaze is his trademark, built a studio for himself deep in the Shanagarry woodland a few years ago and has ever since been turning out a distinctive line sold in stores around the world. Philip Pearce, working in a complex of farmhouses known as Shanagarry Pottery, turns out pottery in handsome blacks and whites. Visitors can buy the pottery at a shop in the Ballymaloe House. Before leaving the area, drive down to the cliffs at Ballycotton for a breath of sea air, then return to the main road for the drive east into Youghal.

CHECKING IN/EATING OUT: *Ballymaloe House* – Myrtle and Ivan Allen opened a restaurant in their stone farmhouse in 1964 and a year later began taking overnight guests. Now travelers from all over the world have stayed at this 400-acre rural retreat, an experience something like paying a visit to country cousins. The high ceilings and spacious rooms of the farmhouse, actually part of an old Geraldine castle, have been handsomely renovated, and other buildings, such as the gatehouse and lodge, have been modernized to make a total of 30 rooms, all with private bath or shower. Facilities include a heated swimming pool, tennis courts, a 9-hole golf course, horseback riding, deep-sea fishing (at nearby Ballycotton), and a craft shop well stocked with local wares. Myrtle Allen's award-winning Yeats Room restaurant and her cookbook have spread the hotel's reputation for fine food worldwide. The restaurant is open daily, with a cold buffet on Sundays; reservations advised. Darina Allen, Myrtle's daughter-in-law, also runs a year-round cooking school, with courses lasting from a weekend to an intensive 12-week session. Shanagarry, Midleton (phone: 21-652531). Expensive.

YOUGHAL: Pronounced Yawl, this pleasant resort town on a hill has an old section and a 5-mile beach where the river Blackwater pours into Youghal Bay. The tourist board (South Main St.; phone: 24-92390) in the 18th-century Clock Gate, which once served as a prison where inmates were flogged and often were hung from the windows, offers a Tourist Trail booklet describing a signposted walking tour of the town. The trail leads up and around the Old Town walls, which date from the 15th century and are among the best preserved in Ireland. St. Mary's Collegiate Church, dating from the 13th century, was damaged in 1579 when the town was sacked during the Desmond Rebellion, but it has been restored and is still in use. Nearby Myrtle Grove, an Elizabethan mansion (not open to the public but visible from the church), belonged to Sir Walter Raleigh, who helped put down the rebellion and was granted Irish lands by Elizabeth I for his effort. Raleigh, fresh from Virginia, is supposed to have planted Ireland's first potatoes on the property (and to have smoked the country's first pipe of tobacco here, too), but he probably never lived in the house; he was the Mayor, or Warden, of Youghal for a time in 1588 and 1589. He sold the estate to Sir Richard Boyle, who rose from poverty to great wealth during Elizabeth's reign and became the first Earl of Cork; a monument to him and his family is in St. Mary's. The tourist trail leads past the remains of Tynte's Castle, a tower house built by the English in the 15th century, and past the Benedictine priory, which was Oliver Cromwell's headquarters during his Munster campaign of 1649 and is now partly converted into a tea shop. Stop for a rest here or have a drink in the Moby Dick lounge around the corner from the Clock Gate. The lounge gets its name from the film that was made in Youghal some years back, starring Gregory Peck, and it is appropriately decorated. Other pubs worth a visit are the *Clock Tavern,* the *Yawl Inn, The Nook,* and *Harbour Lights.*

 CHECKING IN: *Devonshire Arms* – A friendly, older hotel convenient to town; all 10 rooms have private bath. Open year-round. Youghal (phone: 24-92827). Moderate.

Hilltop – Just outside town, this modern property has a stone icehouse from the 1800s on its grounds, as well as an outdoor swimming pool and a nightclub. All 50 rooms have private bath. Closed November through March. Youghal (phone: 24-92911). Moderate.

Monatrea House – Surrounded by farmland and overlooking Youghal Bay, this Georgian country house has 14 rooms (8 with bath), a first-rate dining room, an outdoor seawater pool, tennis, sea and river fishing, and horses and ponies for riding. Closed October through April. Ferry Point, Youghal (phone: 24-94301). Moderate.

EATING OUT: *Aherne's* – The best of the local catch is always on the menu here, including lobsters and oysters from the tank as well as succulent crab claws and giant prawns. Lunchtime bar food is plentiful. Open year-round, daily except Mondays. 162/163 N. Main St., Youghal (phone: 24-92424). Expensive to moderate.

Clancy's – Near the old train station by the bay, this restaurant-pub features a railway theme with hot bar lunches during the day and a seafood/steaks menu for dinner. Open year-round except Sundays. Strand Buildings, Youghal (phone: 24-92165). Moderate.

En Route from Youghal – Waterford is 48 miles via the main route, N25, but, time permitting, some of the side roads along the way are worth exploring. Just north of Youghal, the road crosses into County Waterford, and a few miles farther along is a turnoff for Ardmore, a quaint village with impressive cliffs on Ardmore Bay (Ardmore means "the great height") and the site of many a shipwreck. There was an Irish college here whose students included Eamon de Valera and Maud Gonne MacBride. Ardmore is famous for the ruins of a monastery founded by St. Declan in the 7th century, though the buildings that remain are not quite that old. The 12th-century round tower is one of the tallest and best-preserved examples of this type of structure in Ireland. Near it is St. Declan's Church (or Cathedral), Romanesque style, also of the 12th century. St. Declan's Oratory (or Tomb) is a small church traditionally held to be the saint's grave.

Return to the main route and continue north toward Dungarvan, but take the turnoff before Dungarvan and drive down to Ring, near Helvick Head. This is an especially beautiful spot in the evening: Travelers and locals alike can sit on benches in the tall grass along the elevated waterfront and watch the sun set slowly behind the mountains as golden washes of light linger on Dungarvan Bay. Ring is a fishing village in the midst of the Waterford Gaeltacht, one of the few — and scattered — Irish-speaking areas left in Ireland. The Irish college here is half a century old and in summer it is full of students learning the language and studying traditional music and dance. All signs in the area are in Irish, including the stop signs, which read "Stad." Pause for a drink at *Mooney's*, a flagstone bar with a front deck overlooking the water, at the turn in the road leading toward Helvick Head.

Ring is only 5 miles south of Dungarvan, an administrative center for part of County Waterford and a town that comes alive with a market on Thursdays. North of Dungarvan, leave the main route again and take the coastal route, following signs for Stradbally. The road goes inland for a distance and then follows the seacoast through a somewhat isolated region where the wind sweeps over grassy cliffs. Just before Annestown, stop at *Waterford Woodcraft*, a woodworking studio turning out functional and ornamental pieces in native woods including yew, gathered in the nearby Comeragh Mountains. Annestown has a small beach and the distinction of being just about the only village in Ireland without a pub. Its name comes from Anna De La Pore, a Catholic relation of Lord Waterford, who is said to have given Cromwell only buttermilk to drink when he sought accommodation for the night. The coastal route leads next to Tramore, a lively seaside resort whose population nearly doubles in July and August. Tramore has a 3-mile-long beach with lifeguards on duty in summer (surfboards can be rented on the beach), a 50-acre amusement park, 18-hole golf course, horse racing (the most important meeting is in August), and many hotels. The tourist board (Railway Square; phone: 51-81572), open July and August, is well stocked with literature about sports, entertainment, and restaurants in town. From Tramore, it is only 8 miles north on T63 to Waterford.

EATING OUT: *Seanachie* – The name of this thatch-roofed cottage pubrestaurant is Irish for "storyteller." Brother and sister Michael and Laurann Casey, he with an interest in Irish culture, she a graduate of the Cordon Bleu in London, have converted old farm buildings into an intimate dining room and a rustic bar where locals lift a few jars while raising their voices in ballads. The barnyard is now a courtyard for dancing. Open for lunch and dinner; the food is varied. Five miles south of Dungarvan on the main road (phone: 58-46285). Moderate to inexpensive.

WATERFORD: Ireland's fourth-largest city is a busy port on the banks of the river Suir. Reginald's Tower, built by Reginald the Dane in 1003, protected the small Viking settlement from invasion for a time, but in 1170 the Normans captured Waterford anyway, and the centuries of Anglo-Norman domination in Ireland began. The tower, now a museum, is Waterford's most prominent landmark, but the city also has several 18th-century churches and public buildings and the remains of once extensive medieval abbeys. Waterford is best known, however, for the crystal that bears its name, and visitors can watch it being blown and cut on a tour of the *Waterford Glass Factory*, about 1½ miles from the center of town on the Cork road. Tours take place on weekdays, except for the first 3 weeks in August. Reservations are necessary, especially in summer; inquire at the tourist board. Crystal is now sold at the factory as well as in shops in town. For more information on the city's sights, accommodations, restaurants, and entertainment, see *Waterford*, THE CITIES.

En Route from Waterford – The town of Carrick-on-Suir is 17 miles northwest via T13 (N24). Straddling the river, part in County Waterford and part in County Tipperary, the town was another seat of the Butler family of Kilkenny Castle. The Elizabethan manor house built around 1600 by Black Tom Butler, the tenth Earl of Ormonde, is in a style uncommon in Ireland, probably because Black Tom had spent time in England and built it hoping to entice his cousin, Queen Elizabeth I, for a visit. What remains of a 15th-century Butler castle, much damaged by Cromwell, is behind the manor house. Be sure to stop at *Shanahan Willow Crafts* (Chapel St.). John Shanahan learned to make baskets from his father, who learned it from his father, who opened the shop in 1886. The nimble fingers of John and his brother, Michael, have woven some most unusual things — 10-foot goal posts for polo games and passenger baskets for hot air balloons — but their most popular items are shopping baskets and baby cradles, and the prices are quite low for such skillfully crafted, handmade goods. The area's other leading craft enterprise is *Tipperary Crystal*, located about 3 miles west of Carrick-on-Suir at Ballynoran. Staffed by former Waterford Glass craftsmen, this small factory produces fine quality full lead mouth-blown crystal stemware, at prices considerably below the more famous competition. Visitors are welcome at the factory and the adjacent shop. Open daily from May through September and on weekdays during the rest of the year. After Carrick-on-Suir, continue on T13 (N24) to Clonmel, another 13 miles.

CLONMEL: According to legend, ancient settlers were led to this town — "meadow of honey" in Irish — by a swarm of bees. It is the chief town of County Tipperary, an administrative, horse-breeding, and cider-making center. St. Patrick is said to have visited the area, which eventually passed into the hands of the powerful Anglo-Norman Butler family. In 1650, the town fell to Cromwell, but only after a very stiff resistance led by Hugh Dubh O'Neill. Clonmel runs along the river Suir, with wide O'Connell Street as its major thoroughfare. The Main Guard, a 17th-century building at the eastern end of the street, is said to have been designed by Christopher Wren and has been used as a courthouse, prison, and military headquarters. At the other end is West Gate, a 19th-century rebuilding of one of the town's original gates (a portion of the old 14th-century town wall still stands in the graveyard of St. Mary's Church of Ireland on Mary Street). A plaque on one side of West Gate commemorates Laurence Sterne, author of *Tristram Shandy* and a native of Clonmel. Be sure to stop by the 19th-century St. Mary's Catholic Church on O'Connell Street to see the ceiling and the ornate altar with statues; the altar is supposed to have been made for a church in Rome but mysteriously ended up here. The Franciscan friary on Abbey Street has a 13th-century choir wall, a 15th-century tower, and a tiny chapel to St. Francis that is a beauty when the sun shines through the reds and oranges of its modern stained glass windows. Near the entrance is a tomb of the Butler family. (Press the light switch on the wall at the side for a better look at the knight and lady carved on it.) The library on Parnell Street houses a museum of local interest. Also on Parnell Street is *Hearn's* hotel (see *Checking In*), which at one time was the base of operations for the first Irish passenger transport system. In 1815, Charles Bianconi, an Italian-born resident of Clonmel, sent a horse-drawn carriage to Cahir. The number of vehicles and his network grew, and until the coming of the railways, Bianconi cars carried people all over the south of Ireland.

Clonmel has regular horse-racing meetings, weekly greyhound racing, good fishing in the Suir, and pony trekking into the Comeragh Mountains from Ballmacarberry (about 9 miles south of Clonmel). If time permits a detour, there is a magnificently scenic drive through the Knockmealdown Mountains southwest of town. Take the road to Ardfinnan and then on to Clogheen, where a left turn leads to a height of 1,700 feet and the hairpin curve known as the Vee. The descent travels into Lismore, a town on the river Blackwater and the site of Lismore Castle. Built in the 12th century and remodeled in the 19th century, it is not open to the public, though its gardens are. (The castle itself can be rented by the week; for reservations, call 58-54424 at least several months in advance.) The village of Cappoquin is 4 miles east of Lismore, also on the river, and the stretch of valley between the two is especially beautiful. From Cappoquin, return to the route by following the main Dungarvan road, T30, east as far as the turnoff to T27, and then drive the 20 miles north to Clonmel. Slievenamon, the "mountain of the women," rises to a height of 2,368 feet northeast of Clonmel; it is said that the legendary giant Finn MacCool watched while girls raced up to its summit to win him as a husband.

 CHECKING IN: *Clonmel Arms* – Comfortable and nicely furnished, the hotel (a member of the Comfort Inns group) has an elegant dining room and 35 newly decorated guestrooms, most with private bath. Sarsfield St., Clonmel (phone: 52-21233). Expensive to moderate.

Hearn's – The starting point of Charles Bianconi's transport system still has the clock he used to keep the cars on schedule. This pleasant establishment has 25 rooms, more than half of them with bath. Parnell St., Clonmel (phone: 52-21611). Moderate.

 EATING OUT: *La Scala* – Housed in an old limestone building with original rustic log wood and red brick decor, this dining spot serves beef fondue, Stroganoff, chicken in pastry, seafood crêpes, lasagna, and flambé desserts. Market St., Clonmel (phone: 52-24147). Moderate.

En Route from Clonmel – Take N24 west for 10 miles to Cahir. The lands of the Butlers also extended to Cahir (meaning "stone fort," and pronounced *Care*), where the family served as the Earls of Glengall. Richard, the second Earl of Glengall, helped plan much of the town, somewhat to his financial ruin. He commissioned John Nash to design the local Church of Ireland (1817) and also the *Swiss Cottage Fishing Lodge* in Cahir Park. Newly restored in 1989, the cottage was decorated by noted Irish designer Sybil Connolly, and it's now open to the public Tuesdays through Sundays, June through September (admission charge). The town is small but pleasant and it prospers from what seems to be an annual influx of filmmakers to Cahir Castle, one of the largest and most splendid medieval castles in Ireland. Built on a rocky inlet in the river Suir where an ancient ring fort may once have stood, the castle dates mainly from the 15th century. It was thought to be impregnable, but it was captured by Robert Devereux, Earl of Essex and Queen Elizabeth's favorite, in 1599, and by Cromwell in 1650, though each time it returned to the hands of the Butlers. It is now restored and open to the public year-round (admission charge; phone: 52-41011). Cashel is 11 miles north of Cahir via N8.

 CHECKING IN: *Kilcoran Lodge* – A few miles outside Cahir, on the right side of the Mitchelstown road, this former shooting lodge is a charming country hotel on a slope of the Galtee Mountains. The 25 spacious rooms all have private bath. Facilities include a health and leisure center with an indoor pool, steamroom, sauna, and gym. The food served in the airy dining room is good. Cahir (phone: 52-41288). Expensive to moderate.

Carrigeen Castle – For unusual but comfortable accommodations, try the bed and breakfast house run by Peggy Butler on the road to Cork. Built solidly in stone, complete with turrets, it was once a jail. Peggy and her husband have turned the 7 cells into 4 cozy guestrooms decorated with antiques. Only one room has a private bath, but all have hot and cold running water. On the Cork road, Cahir (phone: 52-41370). Inexpensive.

EATING OUT: *Earl of Glengall* – This eatery serves tasty pub lunches, including Irish stew and steak and kidney pie, at very reasonable prices. The Square, Castle St., Cahir (phone: 52-41505). Moderate.

Crock of Gold – The restaurant on the upper level of this little shop serves light meals daily from 9 AM to 9 PM. Castle St., Cahir (phone: 52-41951). Inexpensive.

CASHEL: Dominating the market town that bears its name is the Rock of Cashel, the history of which spans 16 centuries. From the 4th century, the kings of the province of Munster were crowned on this limestone rock rising proudly from the surrounding plain, and they had their palace here. St. Patrick preached Christianity on the site in the 5th century, and Brian Ború was crowned here in the 10th century. In 1101, Brian's grandson King Murtoch O'Brien gave the Rock to the church and a period of great ecclesiastical building began. Today, all of the buildings, even the roofless, retain their grandeur, but tiny Cormac's Chapel is a gem of Irish Romanesque architecture. The Rock is floodlit at night in the summer — an impressive sight — and guided tours are offered. For more information on the town's sights, accommodations, restaurants, and entertainment, see *Cashel,* THE CITIES.

The Dingle Peninsula

The Dingle Peninsula is the northernmost of the mountainous promontories that stick out into the Atlantic from Ireland's southwest coast like toes extended to test the water. It is a jumble of old and varied peaks and cliffs, glacial valleys and lakes, headlands and bays, islands, strands, and great sand dunes stretching 30 miles west from the low-lying country around Tralee through mountains that turn to wild hills and meet the sea in splendid coastlines. The peninsula is blessed with a remoteness that has been an inspiration to poets and religious ascetics alike. It was on Dingle that John Millington Synge wondered why anyone was left in Dublin or London or Paris and whether it wouldn't be better to live "with this magnificent sea and sky, and to breathe this wonderful air, which is like wine in one's teeth."

Dingle's dramatic rendering of nature's bare essentials never ceases to delight visitors. On a clear day it offers stunning views: great panoramic expanses of green stopped by shimmering ribbons of water in the distance, then the farther gray-blue outline of the next peninsula, island, or rocky point, itself backlit by the phosphorescence of fine, silver-edged clouds. On a less clear day when the depth of the scene diminishes, the eye is drawn to the hedgerows by the roadside, made up in spring of white hawthorn or yellow-flowering furze bushes, of languorous drapings of honeysuckle or purplish fuchsia just bursting into bloom. Where they part, they reveal the patchwork of fields beyond and an ample sampling of Ireland's green.

Dingle's topography is mountainous, but not in the alpine way. The landscape rises — from the eastern Slieve Mish Mountains to the western Brandon Mountains — to rounded and treeless peaks, as if some primordial giant had thrown down a heavy carpet to soften the contours and soothe his aching feet. This possibility is not entirely implausible because Dingle is alive with legend and folklore, its remote fastnesses the stamping ground of mythological heroes such as Cu Chulainn, its ports guarded by the larger-than-life Finn MacCool and his warrior army, the Fianna. Visitors may see only innumerable sheep ranging down valleys and over the distant hills, but to locals with longer memories, the land is the home of giants as tall as the tales.

The peninsula is also particularly rich in antiquities, especially prehistoric and early Christian remains, among them *galláns* (standing stones); ogham stones (pillars inscribed with the earliest form of Irish writing); and *clocháns* (circular beehive huts). The latter may be the most suggestive. Grouped in fraternal clusters or alone as solitary cells, monks isolated themselves in these stone huts on Ireland's lonely western fringes in the early days of Irish Christianity. The eremitical offshoot of Irish monasticism was nowhere stronger than in Kerry, and it's not hard for visitors to see why. Perched on the ledge of a wave-pounded rock or on the quieter summit of a deserted hill, the hermit monks could ponder at length both the awesome and the gentle face of God and perhaps, in a radiant flash of sun on sea, witness their own immortality.

Not all beehive huts are ancient, however. Farmers continue to copy the technique for modern animal shelters and sheds, one of many ways Dingle's timeless appearance endures to confound seekers of authenticity. Two decades ago, when scouts were searching for a location to film *Ryan's Daughter,* a story that was supposed to have taken place in 1916, the peninsula was chosen because it looked as though it hadn't progressed much beyond that date, though none of its tiny villages had quite the look of abject poverty required (a model village was built).

Time has also stood still on Dingle in the matter of language. Its western reaches are part of the Gaeltacht, the collective name for the few surviving Irish-speaking areas of Ireland where geography protected what was lost elsewhere under British rule. The native Irish tongue can be heard in villages such as Dunquin and Ballyferriter, whose people use it daily, though they also speak English. During the summer, students come from all over the country to attend the Irish language schools here.

The scenic route around the peninsula is roughly in the shape of a figure eight, with the town of Dingle at the crossing. Roads are narrow and twisting but they're easy to negotiate just the same, and there's no trouble with traffic — though an unsuspecting traveler may round a bend and come upon a traveling bank truck or a collie herding the cattle home. The drive is best on a very bright day and to be avoided, if possible, in mist or continuous rain. The entire peninsula is manageable in a long day trip of approximately 100 miles from Tralee and back, including time for lunch in Dingle Town, through which the route passes twice. Though Tralee, where our route begins, is the usual gateway to Dingle, the peninsula itself offers plenty of bed and breakfast houses and farms plus small hotels and guesthouses and, in Dingle Town, two modern hotels.

A double room in an expensive hotel will cost $100 and up; in a moderate one, from $50 to $99; and in an inexpensive one, $50 or less. A meal for two in an expensive restaurant will cost $60 and up, usually including tip; in a moderate one, from $35 to $55; and in an inexpensive place, $30 or less.

TRALEE: This friendly, busy trading center of 18,000 people is the chief town of County Kerry and one of the most active in southern Ireland. It grew up around the 13th-century Desmond Castle, but because the town was destroyed at the end of the 17th century, its remains — such as the Georgian terraces on Denny Street and in Day Place and St. John's Cathedral Church — are mainly from the 18th and 19th centuries. Its major antiquity is the ruined Rathass Church, about a mile east, dating from the 9th and 10th centuries. Inside is a stone commemorating an 8th-century notable in ogham, the earliest form of Irish writing. Ogham consists of groups of strokes and dots related to a spinal line and it arose, probably on this peninsula, around the beginning of the Christian era.

Tralee has a racecourse and an 18-hole golf course designed by Arnold Palmer, plus salmon and trout fishing in its rivers, excellent deep-sea fishing, a choice of beaches, sailing, skin diving, and horseback riding. Tralee is also the home of *Siamsa tíre* (pronounced *Shee*-am-sah *teer*), the *National Folk Theatre of Ireland,* which brings to life the customs of the Irish countryside through a program of music, singing, dancing, and mime several nights weekly from May through September (phone: 66-23055). Tralee's greatest attraction, however, is the *Rose of Tralee International Festival*, otherwise known as the *Festival of Kerry*, a week of carnival-like pageantry at the end of August or the beginning of September. This is Ireland's biggest bash and its highlight is the crowning of the Rose, the loveliest young woman of Irish descent in the world and the one who best exemplifies the qualities of the original Rose of Tralee, from the song by William Mulchinock, who was born and died here.

CHECKING IN: *Brandon* – One of the largest hotels in County Kerry, this centrally located lodging is standard modern in style but genial in its operation. All 154 rooms have private bath. There's also a dining room, a coffee shop, a pub, a new leisure center with indoor pool, sauna, solarium, steamroom, and gym. Princes St., Tralee (phone: 66-23333). Expensive.

Earl of Desmond – In a grassy setting 2 miles south of Tralee, this modern motor hotel has 50 rooms with private baths and wide picture windows. There are tennis courts and access to a private stretch of the river Laune for fishing. Killarney Rd., Tralee (phone: 66-21299). Expensive to moderate.

Ballygarry House – This country inn with a private garden has an Old World look, complete with open fireplaces, 16 individually decorated bedrooms with private bath, and restaurant serving mostly continental cooking. About 1½ miles from town on the Killarney road, Leebrook, Tralee (phone: 66-21233). Moderate.

EATING OUT: *Chez Jean-Marc* – An elegant second-floor bistro on Tralee's main thoroughfare that serves good French fare — from duck *à la orange* and seafood crêpes to steak *au poivre* and pork ribs. Open nightly for dinner except Sundays. 29 Lower Castle St. (phone: 66-21377). Moderate.

Tankard – This restaurant with sweeping seascape views offers shellfish from Tralee Bay as well as steaks, duck, chicken, and quail. Open for lunch and dinner all year. 6 miles west of Tralee. Fenit (phone: 66-36164). Moderate.

Oyster Tavern – Visit this pub for seafood cooked in a straightforward manner. Favorites include cockle and mussel soup and grilled crab claws. About 3 miles west of Tralee at Spa, site of a popular watering place in the 18th century. Spa (phone: 66-36102). Moderate to inexpensive.

Tommy Doyle's – For lunch or dinner, try its comfortable lounge and bar with an open-hearth fire and delightful staff. Irish ballads in the evenings are a pleasant musical accompaniment. Boherbee, Tralee (phone: 66-23370). Moderate to inexpensive.

Brogue Inn – A big barn of a pub — strewn with agricultural instruments — that's a good place for a light lunch. Rock St., Tralee (phone: 66-22126). Inexpensive.

En Route from Tralee – The road to Dingle (T68) runs along the 19th-century ship canal to Blennerville, which is unusual for its restored windmill and famous among bird watchers for its mudflats in Tralee Bay. Less than a mile farther, where a roadway comes from the left, the 12th-to-13th-century Annagh church is hidden on the right on a site claimed to be the birthplace of Brendan the Navigator, the 6th-century saint, reputed to have discovered America even before the Vikings. (Fenit, across Tralee Bay, is the more likely birthplace.) Continuing out onto the peninsula, along its northern edge, there are wonderfully scenic views. The Slieve Mish Mountains are inland to the left, and to the right a sweep of green tilts gently down to magnificent beaches on the bay, the green scattered with grazing cattle and sheep to the very edge of the pale gold sand.

The remains of the old *Tralee and Dingle* railway are along the route, now on one side, now on the other. Where the road divides just before Camp, going right for Castlegregory and left for Dingle, take the left fork and then turn left again under the broken arch of the old railway line and head straight across the peninsula toward Aughils. The mountain to the left of this road is Caherconree. Near its summit, the curious rock formation with cliffs on three sides and a narrow approach cut off by a substantial wall is a promontory fort dating from the Iron Age (which began in Ireland about 500 BC and lasted until the arrival of St. Patrick in the 5th century AD). It is notable not only because it is inland (most of the other promontory forts on the peninsula are on the coast) but also because it was the home of Cu Roi Mac Daire, a figure from a cycle of legends dealing with Iron Age heroes. Cu Roi was killed by Cu Chulainn, a small, fierce, brave man and a womanizer, after the former had stolen the beautiful Blathnaid, a woman for whom Cu Chulainn had set his cap. There are breathtaking views from the fort, reached via a marked trail that begins some distance farther along the road, and there are equally memorable views — of Dingle Bay and the Iveragh Peninsula — as the road descends to Aughils and Inch. At the sea road at Aughils, turn right. Inch is only 4 miles away.

INCH: This sheltered seaside resort is at the base of the Inch Peninsula. Its name to the contrary, the peninsula provides a 4-mile strip of firm, golden sand that is excellent for bathing. The beach is backed by high dunes that have yielded evidence of mysterious sand hill dwellers who lived here in the Iron Age and perhaps earlier. In the 18th century, this same sandy spit stretching into Dingle Bay was used to wreck ships from the West Indies. A lantern on the head of a moving horse would fool captains into thinking there was another ship ahead, not a sandbar.

ANASCAUL: The inland village of Anascaul, 4 miles west of Inch, is known as the location of the *South Pole Inn.* Now a pub where you can stop for a drink (no food served), this was once the home of Thomas Crean, a member of Robert Falcon Scott's last and fatal expedition to Antarctica (1910–12). A signposted detour north from the town leads, in about 2 miles, to the beautiful Lough Anascaul in a boulder-scattered valley about which there is another Cu Chulainn story. A giant was carrying off a girl, Scál, but Cu Chulainn came to her rescue. From the mountains on either side of the lake, the giants threw great stones at each other. Cu Chulainn was wounded and Scál, thinking him dead, drowned herself in the water.

En Route from Anascaul – Here the road rejoins the main Tralee–Dingle road, T68. Continuing west, it next passes through Lispole. Less than a mile farther, look left for the standing stone, *gallán,* of Ballineetig, about 100 yards from the road. This Bronze Age gravestone is the largest on the peninsula. The roughly pointed tip shows that it was a monument for a man — for women the tips were scooped out.

Still farther, where there is a good view of Dingle Harbour, turn left after the sign for an accident blackspot (a place with a bad record for auto accidents), then make a sharp left at a house. A third of a mile beyond this, in a field on the left, is the little burial place of Ballintaggart, an important site for the study of ogham stones — stones engraved with the Old Irish alphabet. Inside the circular wall are nine stones, rounded, with the base, or spinal, line omitted, an unusual feature. The inscription on one stone commemorates the "three sons of Mailagnos," the next has a long Latin cross, and two others have short Greek crosses, possibly added later as Christianity began to take over from paganism. Before leaving Ballintaggart, take a moment to enjoy the splendid sight of the Skellig Rocks off the coast of the Iveragh Peninsula in the distance. Then return to the main road and drive the remaining 1½ miles into Dingle.

DINGLE: The peninsula's chief town lies at the foot of a steep slope on the north side of the harbor and is bounded on three sides by hills. It was the main port of Kerry in the old Spanish trading days, and in the reign of Queen Elizabeth I it was important enough as an outpost to merit a protective wall. In the 18th century, Dingle became a smuggling center, and during the French Revolution, a local man, Colonel James Rice, was the linchpin of a plot to rescue Marie Antoinette and spirit her to "the highest house on the hill," on Main Street. She refused to go, however, when she learned that her family would not go with her. The house has since been replaced by the Catholic presbytery. Today Dingle's population of 1,400 is dependent on fishing and tourism. Deep-sea fishing facilities are excellent, bathing is good at various beaches in the vicinity, and there is pony trekking into the surrounding hills. Traditional Irish music sessions are often held at the rough-hewn, barnlike *O'Flaherty's Pub* (Bridge St.); order a Guinness, pull up an orange crate, and sit down and listen. Also worth a visit is *Richard MacDonnell's* (Church St.). Known locally as "Dick Mack's," this has to be the only place in Ireland where a customer can buy shoes, boots, and leather belts (hand-fashioned by octogenarian Dick) on one side of the room and enjoy a freshly drawn pint of Guinness on the other. The pub side has two old-fashioned snugs that alone are worth a look.

Dingle is also the gateway to the West Kerry Gaeltacht, the Irish-speaking district, as well as a good base for extended exploration of the archaeological antiquities of this rich area. Begin with the enormous rock called a *bullaun* on Main Street. It has holes in it and was probably used for grinding hard wheat in early Christian times.

 CHECKING IN: Skellig – Under the Quality Inn banner, this contemporary motor hotel sits on the eastern edge of town overlooking Dingle Bay. It offers 50 rooms, all with bath, plus a bay view restaurant, musical entertainment on most summer evenings, and a health complex with a heated indoor pool, an all-weather tennis court, saunas, and tanning beds. Open March through October. Dingle (phone: 66-51144). Expensive.

Benner's – Originally a coaching inn, this 250-year-old hotel in the heart of town has been restored by American owners. Each of the 25 bedrooms has a private bathroom, and the furnishings are a blend of brass, etched glass, and local antiques. Facilities include a restaurant, walled garden, and a pub-type lounge. Open year-round. Main St., Dingle (phone: 66-51638). Moderate.

Doyle's Townhouse – In the heart of town sits this little gem, an outgrowth of the very successful *Doyle's Seafood Bar* next door (see *Eating Out*). The public areas are rich in Victorian and Edwardian antiques, while the 8 rooms of varying sizes all boast telephones, TV sets, adjustable beds, and modern bathrooms of Italian marble. The establishment provides all the comforts of a fine hotel with a homey ambience. Open mid-March through mid-November. John St., Dingle (phone: 66-51174). Moderate.

Alpine House – A modern, centrally heated guesthouse with 14 rooms, each with private bath/shower. At the entrance to Dingle Town, with pleasant views, a lounge, and a dining room. Open March through October. Dingle (phone: 66-51250). Inexpensive.

EATING OUT: Doyle's Seafood Bar – In a small town known for its fine restaurants, this is the leader; its award-winning specialties include crab bisque, éclairs of smoked mackerel pâté, local lobster, and a popular seafood Mornay. Picnickers can buy homemade brown bread and smoked salmon to go. Open for lunch and dinner; closed Sundays and mid-November through mid-March. John St., Dingle (phone: 66-51174). Moderate.

Half-Door – Right next to *Doyle's*, it's not as renowned as its neighbor but is a good alternative. The menu features the best of the local catch, imaginatively prepared in such combinations as sole with banana and chutney, trout in blackberry and vermouth sauce, and salmon in ginger butter. Lobster is featured here, too, as is at least one meat selection. Closed Tuesdays and late November to early March. John St., Dingle (phone: 66-51600). Moderate.

An Cafe Liteartha – Serving simple fare such as salads, casseroles, and sandwiches, this place is best known for its bookshop, with an excellent section on Ireland and the Irish. Closed mid-January to mid-March. Dykegate St., Dingle (phone: 66-51388). Inexpensive.

En Route from Dingle – Head west out of town, and at the junction take the road in the direction of Slea Head. Just beyond a modern cemetery at Milltown is an interesting set of antiquities inside a gate on the right. The site, an ancient burial ground referred to as the "gates of glory," consists of one great *gallán* (standing stone), two others that have fallen, and broken pieces of more stones. The mysterious scribings on top of one of the fallen *galláns* were made by early metalworkers who came to Ireland from Spain some 4,000 years ago. The scooped-out hollows are called cup marks. Many such stones can be found in Kerry, but no one has yet given an adequate interpretation of them.

VENTRY: About 4 miles from Dingle, this little village has a delightful beach. In Irish legend, Ventry Harbour was the scene of a great battle won by the hero Finn MacCool and his warriors, the Fianna, against the forces of the "king of the world," Daire Donn, who crammed the harbor with his ships and was held off for a year and a day before being wiped out to the last man. Keep an eye open for *Quinn's Ventry Inn,* a modern pub with panoramic views and a congenial place to have a drink or a cup of coffee. Beyond the harbor, the road continues to Slea Head on the lower slopes of Mt. Eagle, providing lovely coastal views of Dingle Bay. This cliff-hugging part of the route is particularly scenic and will be familiar to those who saw the film *Ryan's Daughter.* The village of Kirrary in the film was along the coast west of Ventry, but don't look for it: It was built from scratch for the filming and destroyed afterward to preserve the landscape. The area from Ventry to Slea Head is also rich in archaeological remains.

DUNBEG AND FAHAN: Just under 4 miles from Ventry, an Iron Age promontory fort, Dunbeg, can be seen below the road to the left. In addition to the wall that cuts off the triangular promontory, there are four earthen defensive rings, an underground escape passage (*souterrain*) at the entrance, and remains of an inner house. Dunbeg may have been the first bridgehead established by the people who built the ancient town of Fahan, site of the greatest collection of antiquities in all of Ireland. Fahan consists of more than 400 *clocháns* (circular beehive huts constructed without mortar of overlapped or corbeled stones), cave dwellings, standing and inscribed stones and crosses, souterrains, forts, and a church — more than 500 remains in all — strewn along an old road above the main road for about 3 miles. The best way to see this settlement, which was possibly a full-fledged community between the 6th and 10th centuries, as large then as Dingle is now, is to keep to the main road until it passes the small ford at Glenfahan, after which a sign indicates the beehive huts. These are among the most interesting and convenient *clocháns* in the country. The owners of the property expect a small payment from visitors.

SLEA HEAD: The road from Dingle continues to Slea Head at the tip of the peninsula, where the view of the Blasket Islands, the westernmost point in Europe (except for Iceland), is spectacular. In September 1588, four ships of the Spanish Armada were driven by storms through Blasket Sound. Two reached shelter, but a third, the *Santa Maria de la Rosa,* came flying through the sound with its sails in tatters, crashed onto a rock, and sank, as did the fourth, the *San Juan de Ragusa.* (The remains of the *Santa Maria de la Rosa* were found at the bottom of Blasket Sound in the late 1960s.) The beach between Slea Head and the next promontory, Dunmore Head, is Coumeenole strand, attractive but dangerous.

BLASKET ISLANDS: This now-deserted group of seven islands was inhabited from prehistoric times by an Irish-speaking community. The largest island, Great Blasket (4 miles long and ¾ mile wide), was "the next parish to America" until 1953, when the population of barely 100, no longer able to support itself after several disastrous fishing seasons, resettled on the mainland. Blasket islanders were adept at the art of storytelling and produced a number of books. The best-selling *Twenty Years A-growing* by Maurice O'Sullivan; *The Islander,* a masterpiece by Thomas O'Crohan; and *Peig* by Peig Sayers were all written by island natives. Boats to the Blaskets can be hired in Dunquin, north of Slea Head.

En Route from Slea Head – The road leaves the seacoast to cut across Dunmore Head and continues north to Dunquin along a coast where many forms of fossils can be found. At Dunquin Harbour, the colored Silurian rocks in the cliffs are 400 million years old. From Dunquin there are fairly regular sailings in summer to the Blaskets, typically in a boat called a *curragh,* a light, canvas-covered canoe painted with tar. If properly handled, the *curragh* is an extraordinarily seaworthy revival of the ancient boat originally made of skins. After Dunquin, the route passes Clogher Head and turns inland toward the village of Ballyferriter. Watch for Liam Mulcahy's pottery workshop (known in Gaelic as *Potadóireacht na Caolóige;* phone: 66-56229) at Clogher, where travelers can stop and see the potters at work as well as buy some of the simple, colorful pieces they produce.

BALLYFERRITER: Here is a small, mostly Irish-speaking village whose population is increased in summer by students enrolled in Irish language schools. The ruined Castle Sybil, the home of the Anglo-Norman Ferriter family, is about 2 miles northwest of the village just above Ferriter's Cove. The castle was the birthplace of Kerry poet and patriot Piaras Ferriter, an insurgent leader who was hanged by the Cromwellians in 1653. Castle Sybil is said to be named after Sybil Lynch of Galway, who eloped with a Ferriter. When her father sought her out she was hidden in the cave beneath the castle and was drowned by the rising tide.

Smerwick Harbour is about a mile north of Ballyferriter. The *Dún An Oir* — a pleasant hotel popular with families — is named for the small fort of the same name, the "golden" fort that once stood on a promontory in the harbor. In 1580, an expedition of some 600 men financed by the pope — mainly Italians, but also Spanish, Irish, and English — entrenched at the fort to support the cause of the Catholic Irish against the Protestant English in what was the first significant invasion of the British Isles for many centuries. The English (led by Lord Grey and including Edmund Spenser and, possibly, Sir Walter Raleigh) bombarded the fort from land and sea and soon its defenders capitulated. Once disarmed, they were slaughtered, and the massacre of Smerwick rang throughout Europe, a warning to anyone who might again attempt to invade the queen's territory.

En Route from Ballyferriter – Follow the main road east, keeping to the left (avoid the narrow road that bears right up a hill). Turn right over the bridge at a gasoline pump and, almost immediately, right again. The recently excavated eremitical and monastic site of Reask is a short distance farther (about ¾ mile east of Ballyferriter). This gives a good idea of the layout of an early, perhaps 7th- or 8th-century, monastery — the beehive huts, the oblong foundation of a boat-shaped oratory (a small church), the cross pillars (upright stones incised with crosses), and the wall separating the upper, or consecrated, part of the monastery from the rest. Return by the same road, turn right, and follow the signposts for the Gallarus Oratory, about 4 miles northwest of Dingle.

GALLARUS ORATORY: This small, rectangular church in the shape of an upturned boat is the best example of dry-rubble masonry in Ireland and probably the most perfect piece of early Irish architecture extant. Oratories are standard in monastic sites, but everywhere except here and on the remote Skellig Rocks, the unmortared roofs have fallen in from the great weight of their stones. Gallarus, which is still completely watertight, may date from as early as the 8th century, though the mastery of the corbel technique used in its building suggests a later date to some experts — perhaps as late as the 11th or 12th century. Besides a cross pillar, signs of an early monastic settlement around it have yet to be found.

KILMALKEDAR: At the crossroads north of Gallarus, turn sharp left for the remains of Kilmalkedar Church, a fine example of Irish Romanesque architecture. The nave was built in the mid-12th century, the chancel a little later, and it once had a corbeled stone roof, a development of the Gallarus style. Even before the church was built, there was a Christian settlement here, dating from the late 6th and early 7th centuries. Look inside the church for the "alphabet" stone, crudely carved with a Latin cross and the Latin alphabet, used for instruction in an early-7th-century school. There must have been an even earlier, pagan settlement on the site, too. A holed stone inside and another with ogham outside recall Indian yoni stones, through which worshipers would have to pass to achieve regeneration. Reminiscent of these practices, the east window of the medieval church is known as the "eye of the needle," through which the faithful must pass to be saved. A well-carved pre-Christian sundial and a large, crudely cut cross, one of the few in Kerry, are also outside.

Just north of the church is a roadway, and where it forks, the 15th-century St. Brendan's house is on the left. This was probably a presbytery for the church and had nothing to do with St. Brendan. The old Saints' road, which ran through this area bisecting the fork, however, led to the top of Mt. Brandon, named after St. Brendan, who is said to have had his retreat there. After his death, the road was used for pilgrimages to his shrine, a practice that is revived only occasionally.

En Route from Kilmalkedar – Continue on the road beyond town and, at the T-junction, turn right and follow the signposts for Brandon Creek. It was from this spot that St. Brendan is reputed to have set out on his 6th-century voyages searching for the Land of Promise and, the legend goes, discovering America. Two 9th-century manuscripts, one recounting the story of his life and the other the story of his travels, were immensely popular in early medieval Europe and provided inspiration for many voyagers, including Columbus. At least as far as his travels are concerned, however, there may have been some confusion between the name of St. Brendan and that of the hero of an Irish pagan story, *The Voyage of Bran.* Bran and his Kerry companions traveled to magical western islands and, returning from one voyage, put ashore at Brandon Point, northeast of here. By this account, it was Bran, not St. Brendan, who gave his name to the great Mt. Brandon.

From Brandon Creek, turn back toward Dingle. Just 2 miles along, after crossing the Saints' Road again, turn left and drive up as far as possible to the spot from which the 3,127-foot summit of Mt. Brandon, Ireland's second highest peak, is most accessible. It's about a 3½-mile walk to the top, and on a clear day the views are magnificent. After following in the footsteps of the thousands of pilgrims who have made the strenuous trek — or after just enjoying the view of the summit from below — return to Dingle and take the Connor Pass road out of town.

CONNOR PASS: Driving this road demands great care and it should be avoided in bad weather. Leave Dingle by the unclassified road marked Connor (or Conair) Pass, which climbs northeast between the Brandon and the central Dingle groups of mountains. The summit (1,500 feet) provides magnificent views in both directions, south over Dingle Town and Dingle Bay, north to the bays of Brandon and Tralee, the great beaches of north Kerry, and on to the mouth of the Shannon. The road descends between cliffs and valleys and then, below the pass, continues east running parallel to beautiful beaches on Brandon Bay. At Stradbally, take the left fork for Castlegregory.

CASTLEGREGORY: The castle from which this tiny village got its name is now gone. It was built in the 16th century by a local chief, Gregory Hoare, whose daughter-in-law came to grief in 1580 when she poured out all the castle's wine rather than offer it to her country's enemies, Lord Grey and his English troops who were lodging at the castle on their way to attack the fort at Smerwick Harbour. Her husband killed her in a fit of rage, and the next day he himself died suddenly. The village is at the neck of a sandy spit of land that separates the Tralee and Brandon bays. Beyond the limestone tip of the spit are the Maharee Islands, also known as the Seven Hogs. On one of these, Illauntannig, as on nearly every remote outcropping of rock in western Kerry, remains of an early Christian monastic settlement have been found. Arranging a boat to the island can be done only with difficulty, and the ruins are in poor condition. Most visitors are content with a drive out along the spit from Castlegregory or a visit to Lough Gill, west of the village, an attractive lake noted for its waterfowl, including a species of swan that comes all the way from Siberia to winter here.

En Route from Castlegregory – Continue east, and at the town of Camp, take T68 back to Tralee, which is only 20 miles north of Killarney, the gateway to the *Ring of Kerry* route.

County Clare

Clare, in the middle of the west coast of Ireland, is an "island" county: The Atlantic washes its north and west shores; the encircling river Shannon guards it on the east and south. What is left unwashed in the northeastern quadrant is guarded by a chain of hills. In its isolation Clare has retained much of the past — a sturdy political and economic independence, a music livelier and more varied than that of other parts of Ireland, a tenacious grasp of folk traditions, and a speech dotted with the remnants of Irish language forms.

The landscape of Clare is varied, a microcosm of the Irish west coast generally, but with features that give it a distinction of its own. Heading inward from the coast, the terrain changes strikingly, from the wild rocky sea cliffs to the marshy uplands behind them, to the central limestone plain dotted with lakes, to the great brown hills of the east. In the very north is the Burren country, a stony moonscape plateau.

History has left many interesting remains in Clare. Scattered over the northern hills are more than 150 dolmens, or Stone Age tombs, of the farmers who migrated here from France 5,000 years ago. There are nearly 3,000 circular forts in earth and stone, the fortified settlements of their Celtic successors. And more than 200 castles still stand, the earliest ones built by the Normans, the later by the Irish. Traces of the early Catholic church are also found in Clare. Most "churches" are of the eremitical type; a collection of them is on St. Senan's monastic island in the mouth of the Shannon, and they dot the islets and the hillsides up the coast. Such ruins are particularly plentiful in the Burren where the early hermits found the isolation they desired; here the stony desert is dotted with oratories, "saints' beds" or shrines, wells, and stone crosses.

The people of Clare have long been mature and practiced politicians who sum up a situation and pragmatically choose a leader. In the 10th century they picked Brian Ború, head of an obscure clan called the Dalg Cais. They fought for him until he became first King of Munster and then High King of Ireland; they died with him as he defeated the Vikings on the coast of Dublin Bay. At the great upsurge of Irish democracy in the 19th century they voted in Daniel O'Connell as Member of Parliament for Clare, and they supported Charles Stewart Parnell in the Land League Movement. In this century they elected Eamon de Valera Prime Minister and President of an independent Ireland.

Although most Clare folk still pursue a rural lifestyle on small dairy farms, they are gradually adapting to a new world. Many country market towns are beginning to expand with factories, and more people are working in the transport, tourism, and service industries. The international airport at Shannon not only has established a duty-free zone and nurtured an industrial park with many welcome new jobs, but also has made County Clare the major western gateway to Ireland.

Our route begins in Limerick City, which is where most people spend their first night after landing at Shannon. From here, the route travels to Ennis, capital of Clare, then along the river Shannon through numerous little towns out to the lonely peninsula of Loop Head. From this wild Atlantic seascape, the road turns north to the resort towns of Kilkee and Lahinch and on to the great Cliffs of Moher. An eastern leg explores the wonderland of the Burren with its unusual rock formations, caves, flora, and ruins.

Except in the Limerick City area, which has many large new hotels, accommodations in County Clare tend to be small hotels or bed and breakfast houses. Expect to pay $100 and up for a double in those places listed as expensive; from $60 to $95 in the moderate category; and under $60 for inexpensive accommodations. A meal for two, excluding wine, tips, or drinks, will cost about $60 and up in places listed as expensive; $35 to $55 in moderate restaurants; and under $30 in those listed as inexpensive.

LIMERICK CITY: For a detailed report on the city, its hotels, and restaurants, see *Limerick City,* THE CITIES.

En Route from Limerick City – About 12 miles down the main Limerick–Ennis road (N18) is the tiny village of Newmarket-on-Fergus, which owes its name to a track-crazy 18th-century landlord who renamed it after the great center of English horse racing. The long demesne wall beyond the town encloses Dromoland Castle, which is well worth a look. It was once the home of the O'Briens, Earls of Inchiquin, descendants of the High King BrianBorú, and is now the deluxe *Dromoland Castle* hotel (see "Best in Town" in *Limerick City,* THE CITIES).

ENNIS: The county seat of Clare (pop. 8,000), with its narrow, winding main street intersected by even narrower lanes, has a lively medieval charm. Off Francis Street are the ruins of a Franciscan friary founded about 1240 by Donough Mor O'Brien. A monument to Daniel O'Connell, the Liberator, who secured Catholic emancipation and sat in Parliament for Clare, is in O'Connell Square. The modern *Library and Manse Museum* (Harmony Row), which was ingeniously adapted from a disused church, houses mementos of Irish history. Outside of town on the Limerick road are signposts to Clare Abbey, the now undistinguished and abandoned ruins of an Augustinian monastery established in 1189 by Donal Mor O'Brien, King of Munster.

CHECKING IN: *Old Ground* – One of the rooms in this ivy-clad, centrally located 17th-century hotel was once the Town Hall and another was the town jail. It has 61 rooms with bath, some with antiques and others more modern. There is a warming fireplace in the lobby, and the newly refurbished *Poet's Corner* bar is a great spot to meet the locals. O'Connell St., Ennis (phone: 65-28127). Expensive.

West County Inn – Situated just south of town, this is a large, modern Best Western affiliate with 109 rooms, each with private bath. Facilities include a coffee shop, restaurant, nightclub, gymnasium, and sauna. Dinner dances are held every Saturday evening, and Irish cabaret shows are staged on summer evenings. Clare Rd., Ennis (phone: 65-28421). Moderate.

EATING OUT: *Cloister* – Next to Ennis Abbey, this landmark houses both a homey pub and an adjoining fine dining room. The pub is noted for its inexpensive all-day lunch menu including fisherman's pie and hot crab claws;

the restaurant is quite another matter, with such specialties as salmon in champagne sauce, spiced braised duckling, filet of lamb *en croûte,* and Gaelic steak. Save room for chocolate rum mousse, crème de menthe cheesecake, or a melon *frappé.* A pianist or harpist entertains nightly. Abbey St., Ennis (phone: 65-29521). Expensive.

Brogan's – This atmospheric old pub serves steaks, smoked salmon, soup, and sandwiches. There is traditional Irish music on Tuesday and Thursday nights. 24 O'Connell St., Ennis (phone: 65-29859). Moderate.

Lenthall's Inn – Soup, salads, sandwiches, and Irish stew or shepherd's pie are served in the pub lounge during the day. Dinner is served in the upstairs restaurant. The house specialty is steak Considine (named after the proprietor, who created it) — beef cooked with cream and brandy and served flaming. Abbey St., Ennis (phone: 65-22933). Moderate to inexpensive.

En Route from Ennis – L51 travels along the bank of the Shannon estuary all the way to Kilrush. The landscape is gentle and pastoral, offering fine views across "the Shannon spreading like a sea" of the little wooded harbor town of Foynes, of Glin with its Regency castle, and of Tarbert with its lighthouse and electric power station. At Killimer a car ferry crosses every hour on the hour to Tarbert on the Kerry shore.

KILRUSH: The chief market town of southwest Clare, it has a number of small industries, including a factory for processing seaweed. Just outside Kilrush is Cappagh Pier, formerly the terminus for the river steamers that plied the Shannon from Limerick. From here boats go to Scattery Island, the monastic retreat founded in the 6th century by St. Senan. On the island are five early churches dating from the 9th to the 11th century and a 120-foot round tower, the tallest in Ireland.

 EATING OUT: *Malone's Haven Arms Ale House* – Recently restored and refurbished, this Old World pub in the middle of town is a good lunch stop. The menu includes tasty soup, sandwiches, and traditional hot dishes. 10-12 Henry St., Kilrush (phone: 65-51267). Moderate to inexpensive.

En Route from Kilrush – T41 toward Kilkee passes through the rushy, windswept landscape typical of south Clare. About 6 miles out, there's a sign for a holy well; turn left and in 2½ miles the tidily kept holy well dedicated to St. Martin comes into view. Turning back from the well, go straight east, parallel to the estuary.

Doonaha, the first hamlet along the road, was the birthplace of Eugene O'Curry, a pioneer 19th-century Irish scholar and topographer. The road hits the estuary again at Carrigaholt, a picturesque village wrapped around a crescent of beach with a tall O'Brien castle guarding the little harbor. Another 8 miles farther down the spine of the peninsula is the last village, Kilbaha, and 4½ miles beyond that is the lonely lighthouse of Loop Head. From the headland facing south, there are superb views of the mountains of Kerry — MacGillycuddy's Reeks crowned by Carrantuohill, the highest point in Ireland, and Mt. Brandon at the west end of the Dingle Peninsula. To the north are the whale-backed Aran Islands in Galway Bay and the sawtooth peaks of Connemara. Below the lighthouse are some rocks separated from the shore by a deep chasm. Across this, legend has it, the Irish hero Cu Chulainn made a bold leap when pursued by a persistent female.

On the return journey from Loop Head, take the left branch at the village of Kilbaha for a mile to the Moneen church. In a baptistery chapel on the left of the altar is a fascinating relic of the period of anti-Catholic discrimination. What looks like an old-fashioned bathing machine, a little wooden hut with a canvas roof and windows, is in fact the only church allowed in this area in the first half of the 19th century. A bigoted landlord refused to allow a church to be built, so the parish priest — lifting the idea from a horse-drawn carriage in which he had traveled from Kilrush to Ennis — had this structure built. Each Sunday it was drawn onto the beach, where the priest said Mass and his congregation knelt in the open. Known as the Little Ark, the wooden chapel is still an object of veneration, and the story is illustrated in stained glass over the church door.

Just beyond the church is a storm beach of huge rounded boulders; a half-mile farther, a signpost points to the parking lot for the Bridges of Ross. These are curious rock formations carved out by the sea.

Another half mile beyond the village of Cross, make a right turn onto a narrow road, which after 2 miles reaches the coast and the top of Oldtown hill, affording a view of miles of rugged cliffs ahead. The road soon begins to hug the cliff tops, and the next 5 miles into Kilkee are a dramatic unfolding panorama of rock stacks and precipices. Occasionally, remains of castle towers and stone forts are visible in inaccessible places in the rock. The most striking phenomenon is Bishop's Island, a sheer stack of rock that's been cut off from the mainland but retains a beehive oratory and house associated with St. Senan.

KILKEE: This little resort town, with its charming rows of Regency Gothic houses, has been a popular vacation spot for well-to-do people from Limerick since they came by Shannon steamer in the early 19th century. Its powdery, horseshoe-shaped strand is protected from the full force of the Atlantic by two bold headlands and offers safe bathing and boating. Because most of Kilkee's visitors rent houses, there are very few hotels. It's best to stop here for a dip and a drink at the *Central Bar, Richie's, Marrinan's,* the *Hide-Out,* or the *Old Barrell,* pubs with good conversation.

EATING OUT: *Manuel's* – Run by an energetic husband-and-wife team, this eatery is one of the best in town. The menu reflects whatever is in season, and usually includes at least ten different varieties of fresh fish. Open for dinner only; daily in summer; weekends only in April, May, and September. Corbally, Kilkee (phone: 65-56211). Moderate.

En Route from Kilkee – The road to Lahinch runs inland for the next 20 miles, but, time permitting, detour to see the high cliffs of Baltard Bay, guarded by an O'Brien tower, or the White Strand beyond the village of Doonbeg. In the small fishing village of Quilty, the *Leon* pub is named after the Spanish Armada ship that was wrecked off nearby Mutton Island. The distinctive stone walls on the beach here are for drying seaweed, a valued crop.

MILTOWN MALBAY: This village is a strong traditional music center that hosts the Willie Clancy Summer School (named after a beloved local piper) each July. Featured here are the *uilleann* pipes — the Irish type played with a bellows under the elbow. They have a wide melodic variation and none of the shrieking shrillness of their cousins, the Scottish warpipes. On a Sunday or a holiday, and particularly during the school term, almost all the bars in Miltown Malbay have traditional music, as do those in nearby villages such as Mullagh, the Crosses of Annagh, and Quilty. Be warned, however: Traditional music happens spontaneously rather than by schedule, and you have to stalk it.

The nearby resort of Spanish Point commemorates sailors of the Spanish Armada who drowned here in September 1588. Those whom the sea did not claim were butchered by the followers of Loyalist Sir Turlough O'Brien of Liscannor.

LAHINCH: Prettily set on the shores of Liscannor Bay, Lahinch is a cubistic composition of pastel houses perched on a cliff; it has a somewhat exotic Mediterranean look. There's plenty to do: Surfboards can be rented at the beach; bicycles can be hired at the *Lahinch Camping and Caravan Park* (phone: 65-81424); boats are available, both for deep-sea and freshwater fishing; and the celebrated 18-hole championship *Lahinch* seaside golf course is open to guests (phone: 65-81003).

 CHECKING IN: *Aberdeen Arms* – Opened in 1850, this establishment is reputed to be the oldest golf links hotel in Ireland. Now completely refurbished, it offers 55 modern rooms, each with private bath, TV set, telephone, and coffee-maker. Rooms overlook the *Lahinch* golf course or the nearby beach. Public facilities include a restaurant, grillroom, and golf-themed bar, as well as a health center with gym, Jacuzzi, and sauna. Overnight guests are entitled to reduced greens fees on both the old and the new courses at *Lahinch*. Open year-round. Lahinch (phone: 65-81100). Expensive to moderate.

En Route from Lahinch – Take the coast road past the ruined tower house of Dough set among the golf greens on the left; on the right in the sandhills are the "tiger" holes of the golf course. Legend has it that the fairy king Donn of the Sandhills rides his horse here on moonlit nights.

The ruined medieval church of Kilmacrehy is about a mile farther, to the left. Its founder, St. Mac Creiche, fought dragons and cured plagues; he was buried between high and low tides at a spot called "Mac Creiche's bed."

LISCANNOR: An ancient O'Brien tower guards this fishing village and birthplace of John P. Holland, inventor of the submarine and founder of the Electric Boat Company (which became General Dynamics). There is a small museum and library of memorabilia. The road climbs steadily out of Liscannor and at one point comes abreast of a tall urn-crowned column on the left. This is a good stopping point. Below is Liscannor Bay and all the billowy coast toward Miltown Malbay. The column was built to honor local hero Cornelius O'Brien. Beside it is Dabhac Bhrighde, St. Bridget's Well, a vernacular folk shrine still much visited by pilgrims. Its rushing waters, quaint whitewashed courtyard surrounded by scarlet fuchsia, even the *ex voto* offerings of pictures, rosary beads, and a pair of crutches, attest to an abiding religious feeling that dates from pre-Christian times when this was a spring sacred to an ancient Celtic goddess.

 EATING OUT: *Captain's Deck* – On the upper level of an antiques shop overlooking Liscannor Bay, this rustic restaurant is earning a far-reaching reputation for its fresh seafood — from "stowaway's delight" (cod in the rough) to local lobster, salmon steaks, crab claws, and surf and turf. Open daily for lunch (except Sundays) and dinner (except Mondays). Liscannor (phone: 65-81385). Moderate.

CLIFFS OF MOHER: Two miles from St. Bridget's Well, turn right into the parking lot for the Cliffs of Moher, where there is a visitor center with restaurant and craft shop. Follow the path up the hillside to the little tower, built by Cornelius O'Brien, a Clare landlord and patron, who intended it as a teahouse "for the entertainment and refreshment of lady visitors." Now it's just a lookout, but the view from the top is spectacular: north to the Aran Islands and the Connemara mountains and south toward the Cliffs of Moher, a great curtain of sheer cliff face, rippling 5 miles along the coast and hanging over 600 feet above the sea.

En Route from Liscannor – The main road out of Liscannor passes the Cliffs of Moher and offers some marvelous vistas toward the Aran Islands. On Inisheer, the nearest island, are an O'Brien castle and a lighthouse to the left and a village to the right. The inhabitants of Inisheer speak Irish, farm and fish for a living, and retain many of the customs described in the plays and essays of John M. Synge and in the novels of Liam O'Flaherty.

The hills on the right of the road produce a slate flag — called Liscannor or Moher flag — that is used for roofing stables and outhouses and for decorative work in architecture. About 5 miles from the Cliffs of Moher is a detour 2 miles to the left to the village and harbor of Doolin. The village is a single row of thatched fisherman's houses. Beside them is a pub, *Gus O'Connor's,* which is famous for traditional music. Motor launches and *curraghs* cross from Doolin Harbor to Inisheer. In addition, a passenger ferry service links Doolin with the Aran Islands from April through October; the ride takes 30 minutes. For more information, call 65-74189.

EATING OUT: *Bruach na hAille* – This restaurant serves simple but satisfying meals — fresh mackerel, scallops, crab, and other seafood. Open for dinner May through September. Doolin (phone: 65-74120). Moderate.

Ivy Cottage – Also known as "Ilsa's Kitchen," this splendid little ivy-covered stone house is just a few doors down the road from *Gus O'Connor's* music pub. Specializing in wholesome food dishes and locally caught seafood, this health food oasis also doubles as an art gallery. Open for dinner Wednesdays through Sundays May to September. Doolin (phone: 65-74244). Moderate.

Killilagh House – This country house restaurant–cum–crafts gallery serves delicious meals. Open for lunch and dinner April through September. Roadford, Doolin (phone: 65-74183). Moderate.

LISDOONVARNA: Beach hotels and boardinghouses have been part of this spa resort since the 18th century because of its curative sulfur and iron springs. Lisdoonvarna is patronized by area residents in autumn, when, in addition to taking the waters, they play music, dance, and generally enjoy themselves. The *Spa Wells Health Centre* (phone: 65-74023) is open June to October; a sulfur bath costs about $9. Lisdoonvarna also plays host to a folk festival during the second weekend in July, a nonstop music event — folk, rock, traditional, and country. In September, the *Matchmaking Festival of Ireland* is held here. For festival information, contact the local tourist board (phone: 65-74062) during summer or the Limerick City Tourist Board year-round (phone: 61-317522).

En Route from Lisdoonvarna – Two routes go to Ballyvaughan, either the scenic coast road (R477) through Black Head or the Corkscrew Road (N67) through the Burren country.

About a mile out of Lisdoonvarna on the coast road is the 15th-century O'Brien castle, Ballynalacken, a roofless but walled ruin. The castle's parapets offer a great view west across the bay to the Aran Islands and east over the gray hills of the Burren. Continuing north from Ballynalacken, the road runs along a shelf between the sea and overhanging limestone terraces. It's about 10 miles to the lighthouse at Black Head, from which there are fine views across Galway Bay to the mountains of Mayo and Connemara. In another 5 miles the road reaches Ballyvaughan.

The aptly named Corkscrew Road is a narrow, tortuous lane clinging to the Burren hillsides. The vistas are nothing short of breathtaking, with soft mists rising prismlike from the neighboring valleys. The Burren takes its name from the Irish word *boireann,* meaning "rocky." It is literally a rocky desert of silvery gray limestone. General Ludlow, a commander in Cromwell's forces, returned after a reconnaissance to report that the area had "not enough wood to hang a man, earth to bury a man, or water to drown a man!"

The Burren arrived at its present denuded state through the actions of ice, water, air, and frost over scores of centuries. The final effect is unique and not by any means depressing. The color of the rock ranges from a somber pewter to a light silver, and it has been rubbed and carved into marvelous shapes. Long fingers of green reach between the crags to provide relief for the eye and summer grazing for cattle.

Because of the absence of trees or of heavy vegetation the Burren is open to broad untrammeled light, which with all the other weather factors produces the Burren's final glory — its wildflowers. In late spring, the end of May, this desert blooms. The sparse patches of earth and grass on the bare rock face suddenly become bejeweled with as exotic a collection of flora as can be seen anywhere in the world. Clumps of creamy gold mountain avens from the Arctic grow side by side with tall red and white orchids or the scarlet splash of bloody cranesbill from the Mediterranean. Beside these are the intense blue stars of the spring flowering gentian, which also grow in the alps. Small wonder that the monks of nearby Corcomroe named their abbey St. Mary's of the Fertile Rock.

BALLYVAUGHAN: This little coastal village is nestled in one of the green valleys that slope down from the Burren hills. Two miles southeast of the town is Aillwee Cave, the only cave in the Burren open to the public. Its remarkable stalagmites, stalactites, and mysterious bear pits draw more than 100,000 visitors a year. A tea shop, restaurant, craft shop, and the *Burren Gold Cheesemaking* center are all at the entrance to the caves. Open daily year-round (phone: 65-77036).

 CHECKING IN: *Gregans Castle* – Undoubtedly the best place to stay in the region, this family-run inn at the foot of Corkscrew Hill, overlooking the Burren country and Galway Bay, has a charming homey feeling. It is nestled beside the site of a castle ruin dating back to the 17th century — thus its name. Today, it offers modern comforts (16 rooms and suites with private bath) in an Old World atmosphere — antique furnishings, open-turf fireplaces, and a highly acclaimed wine cellar and restaurant serving fresh vegetables from the estate's garden, seafood from the nearby ocean, and a variety of cheeses produced in the Burren. Outside there are colorful flower gardens as well as spectacular views. Open *Easter* through October. Ballyvaughan (phone: 65-77005). Expensive to moderate.

Hyland's – A clean, cheerful, small inn (12 rooms, 9 with baths), run by the seventh and eighth generations of Hylands, with a dining room featuring seafood. Open April to October. Ballyvaughan (phone: 65-77037). Moderate.

EATING OUT: *Manus Walsh's Gallery and Restaurant* – At this jewel of a spot, Manus sells paintings and crafts and his wife, Claire, serves up scrumptious lobster, crab, mackerel, and homemade bread and cakes. Open for dinner April through September. Ballyvaughan (phone: 65-77029). Moderate.

Some atmospheric pubs in town include the *Ballyvaughan Inn,* which offers folk music and talk; *MacNeill O'LocLainn's,* another tiny, traditional pub; and the *Monk's Pub,* at the pier, offering seafood and music.

En Route from Ballyvaughan – About 3 miles from Ballyvaughan, traveling south on R480, is a spectacular tomb, the Poulnabrone Portal dolmen, well worth stopping the car and walking across the field to view. A few miles farther are signposts to the right for Caherconnell, a well-preserved *caher,* or stone ring fort, which protected four Iron Age and early Christian settlements. At the next crossroad stands Leamaneh Castle, a tower house built by the O'Briens in the 15th century, enlarged and fortified in the 17th century, and abandoned in the 18th century in favor of Dromoland Castle. Some features of Leamaneh — a fireplace and gateway — were subsequently moved to the *Dromoland Castle* hotel.

A 4-mile digression west on R476 into the village of Kilfenora is recommended for a look at the remains of its 12th-century cathedral whose chancel has some very good stone carving. In the cemetery are the three Irish high crosses carved with Bible scenes and Celtic and Scandinavian interlace ornamentation. The crosses are typical of Irish art. *The Kilfenora Burren Display Centre* is a worthwhile stop. Here, the unusual and fascinating flora of the Burren is reproduced in wax and silk, with special lighting and models that explain the area's uniqueness. A tearoom and crafts shop are also on the premises. Open daily mid-March through October (phone: 65-88030).

Return to the crossroads and turn south on R476 toward Corofin for a visit to the *Clare Heritage Centre* housed in St. Catherine's Church. This museum portrays the history of western Ireland from 1800 to 1860, a significant period of famine and mass emigration to the US. The collection includes genealogical tracts, local sculptural exhibits, archaeological artifacts, and photographs. Open daily. Admission charge (phone: 65-56112 or 65-27632). From Corofin, it's 13 miles south on R476 to Ennis.

EATING OUT: *Bofey Quinn's* – Situated in the heart of town, this rustic pub-style eatery is ideal for a quick lunch or a casual dinner. Lobsters taken fresh from the seawater tank are prepared in a variety of ways. Other choices include seafood chowder, mussels in wine, *fleurettes* of salmon, "surf and turf," steaks, and duckling. Main St., Corofin (phone: 65-26727). Moderate.

Midway between Corofin and Ennis on Ennistymon Road is Dysert O'Dea Castle, a recently restored local landmark, built by Diarmuid O'Dea between 1470 and 1490. Home of the O'Dea clan until 1961, the castle is now the focus of a newly developed heritage trail that spans a 2-mile radius and includes 25 other historical sites, from Iron Age stone forts and medieval battlefields to a high cross dating to the 12th century. There is also a round tower, built between 900 and 1100, and the foundations of an 8th-century church. The castle houses a museum, archaeology center, exhibits, an audiovisual show, tearoom, and souvenir shop. The castle is open daily, May through September. Admission charge for castle but not for walking trail. For more information, call 65-27722.

An alternative to returning to Ennis is to travel from Ballyvaughan to Galway City by way of Gort and Thoor Ballylee and to connect with the *Connemara and the Aran Islands* tour route.

To take this alternate route, continue east along the coast road, N67, from Ballyvaughan for 9 miles and turn right at the green monument signpost for Corcomroe Abbey. The abbey is reached by a narrow lane (signposted) just beyond the post office. Corcomroe, or St. Mary of the Fertile Rock, was founded in 1196 for the Cistercians by Donal Mor O'Brien, King of Munster. The church is distinguished by some vigorous Irish Romanesque carving on its columns and the important tomb of Conor O'Brien, grandson of the founder.

About 15 miles farther on N67 is Kinvara, where the 15th-century Dunguaire Castle overlooks Galway Bay and offers delightful medieval banquets on summer evenings (phone: 61-61788 or 91-37108).

Take a sharp right along the road signposted for Gort, which is about 11 miles south. About a mile outside Gort, turn left onto N18, the Galway road, and follow signposts into Coole Park. This was the estate of Lady Augusta Gregory, the playwright and founder, with W. B. Yeats, of the *Abbey Theatre* and hostess to such literary lights as Yeats, George Bernard Shaw, John M. Synge, and Sean O'Casey. The house has been demolished, but the garden, with its autograph tree on which Lady Gregory's guests carved their names, survives. Walk by the lake and through the woods so often described by Yeats in his verse.

After Coole Park, continue north on N18 for another mile and turn right at the signpost for Thoor Ballylee; follow the narrow road for a mile or so. Thoor Ballylee, a 16th-century tower house built by the De Burgo family, was Yeats's home from 1917 to 1929 and a frequent symbol in his poetry. Open daily during the summer. Admission charge (phone: 91-31436). Stop in the bookshop for a look and in the tea shop for a cup and a slice of "barm brack" — raisin cake.

From here, it's just 21 miles north on N18 to Galway City, where the *Connemara and the Aran Islands* tour route begins.

County Donegal

Donegal seems forever haunted by its history, harking back to the days when it was a proud and independent enclave ruled by its own kings and chieftains. Spiritually remote from the rest of Ireland, the area retains a strong individuality and a vital awareness of its former glory.

The sense of isolation is emphasized by the towering mountains that hem in much of the county. They are part of the same earth folds that make up the Scottish Highlands, a fact that may help explain the close affinity between Donegal people and the Scots. All this is not to suggest that the Donegal people are not Irish; they are, but they are Irish in their own way.

Donegal people even look different from folks elsewhere in Ireland. They are very easy to spot. Remarkable hair color — sandy to flaming red — cleanly chiseled features, penetrating blue eyes, and lips curled on the brink of whimsicality are some of the giveaway characteristics. Their speech has been set to music in the Ulster mode, more easily understood in the northern capital of Belfast than in the southern one of Dublin. A bit of the skirling lilt of the Scots' brogue sometimes creeps in, too, because so many Donegal people have spent time in Scotland, forced there not only by hard times but by a kinship that goes back many centuries.

Originally, the region was known as Tirconnaill (pronounced Cheer-*kuhn*-il), meaning the Land of Conall, for Conall Gulban, son of an Irish king known as Niall of the Nine Hostages because of his habit of taking prisoners when he raided foreign lands. This piratical king endowed his favorite son, Conall, with the wild territory of Donegal, and it was Conall who in the 5th century founded the kingdom of Tir Connaill, which remained a monarchy until 1071.

The later name, Donegal, comes from the Irish *Dún na nGall,* "fort of the foreigners." It is believed to refer to the Vikings who constantly raided the Irish coast during the 9th and 10th centuries. They may have established the fort that existed where Donegal Town now stands on the river Eske. There's also convincing evidence that this northwestern region of Ireland was settled long before the Norsemen came. The migrant races of the ancient world made successive incursions into Ireland, and traces of some of them, including crude Stone Age weapons and tools, have been found in Donegal.

The most glorious era in Donegal's history began with the emergence of the O'Donnell dynasty around 1200. The mighty O'Donnells held sway over the region for 4 centuries, wielding power not only in Donegal but throughout Ireland. At a time when the old Gaelic chiefs were feuding among themselves, the O'Donnells maintained their independence by virtue of their superior martial skills and with considerable help from the "gallowglasses," mercenary soldiers from the Scottish Isles.

In 1587, one of the clan, young Red Hugh O'Donnell (the second), was kidnapped by an agent of Queen Elizabeth I and held hostage in Dublin Castle in an attempt to extort loyalty to the queen from his father. When Red Hugh escaped after 5 years, he became the hero of Gaelic Ireland. He and another great chieftain, Hugh O'Neill of Tyrone, combined with a Spanish invading force in a final effort to defeat the armies of Elizabeth. Instead, they were themselves crushed at the disastrous Battle of Kinsale on *Christmas Day* 1601. This was the final death rattle of the old Irish chiefs. O'Donnell fled to Spain where he died, apparently from poisoning. His brother and successor, Rory O'Donnell, along with O'Neill, sailed in exile from the Donegal port of Rathmullan in 1607, an event known as the Flight of the Earls. With their departure, all hope of a revival of Gaelic dominance was squashed forever.

These stirring historical events are a vital part of the folk memory of Donegal and have helped shape the character and personality of its people. The O'Donnells may be gone, but their splendid empire of mountain and glen and wild coast is in the good keeping of their descendants. Most of these people live off the land or the sea, and some still make a living weaving the Donegal tweeds that find their way to the fashion salons of the rest of the world. In some parts of the county, Irish is still spoken just as it was in the time of the first Red Hugh.

Our tour, which starts at the most natural departure point, Donegal Town, covers about 200 miles and can be driven comfortably in 4 days. It heads northeast in a huge, straggling circle, girdling the entire county and returning to Donegal Town at the end. The greater part of the tour is along the sea, following a coastline that has some of the most dramatic scenery in Ireland. It also takes in Donegal's magnificent mountains and valleys and lonesome bogs. The roads are not great and in some stretches would unnerve a stunt driver, so ease off the gas pedal.

In the hotels along this route, expect to pay $75 to $130 for a double room in the expensive category; $50 to $70 in a moderate establishment; and about $45 for those listed as inexpensive. Dinner for two with wine in an expensive restaurant will cost $50 and up; in a moderate one, $30 to $40; and in an inexpensive place, under $30.

DONEGAL TOWN: For a complete report on the town, its sights, hotels, and restaurants, see *Donegal Town,* THE CITIES.

En Route from Donegal Town – From Donegal Town, take N15 northeast. Seven miles out is the Barnesmore Gap, a passage through the Blue Stack Mountains joining south and north Donegal. In olden days, the gap was a lucrative hunting ground for highwaymen and assorted brigands who preyed on travelers making their way through the mountains. The road passes through the twin towns of Ballybofey and Stranorlar, which are linked by a bridge over the river Finn, in which there's excellent salmon and trout fishing. At Stranorlar, turn north onto N56 and continue for 10 miles to a signposted T-junction. Turn east onto N13 and head for Manorcunningham, 4 miles away. This is the entrance to the Inishowen Peninsula.

 CHECKING IN: *Jackson's* – Perched on the banks of the river Finn, this comfortable, homey hotel has become famous for its underground nightclub, *Pharaohs,* which will double as a nuclear bomb shelter just in case someone, somewhere, presses the wrong button. Ballybofey (phone: 74-31021). Moderate.

Kee's – A fine, homey hostelry with simple but high-quality fare. Main St., Stranorlar (phone: 74-31018). Moderate.

EATING OUT: *Biddy's O'Barnes* – An unusual and quaint pub at the entrance to the Barnesmore Gap. Unfortunately, refurbishment has stripped away much of its original charm, but it's still a pleasant place to relax with good food and drink. Home-baked brown bread continues to be the specialty of the house, and hearty fresh soup from the kitchen tureen is a joy. Barnesmore Gap, 7 miles north of Donegal Town on N15 (phone: 73-21402). Moderate.

INISHOWEN PENINSULA

This wild, rugged territory juts defiantly into the Atlantic and is almost totally surrounded by the ocean. At one time, it must have been considered an island, because the name Inish Owen means "island of Owen." Owen refers to Cinel Owen (another son of Niall of the Nine Hostages), who ruled the territory during the 5th century. In the generations that followed Cinel, the peninsula was stained by the blood of battle between a succession of tribal chieftains. Inishowen is lavishly beautiful, with towering mountains running up its central spine and vast, open lowlands where heather and bracken grow wild in the bogs. The early Christian church must have been a potent influence on the peninsula, because ecclesiastical ruins and monuments are everywhere. But less reverent forces were also at large in the territory. Much of Inishowen's turbulent spirit can perhaps be blamed on its long-standing boast that the best *poitin* (the original Irish whiskey, now illegal) was distilled here.

En Route from Manorcunningham – About 5 miles north of Manorcunningham, off N13, lie the ruins of Balleeghan Friary, under a mound of ivy beside Lough Swilly. This friary was another monastery built by the O'Donnells for the Franciscans in the 15th century.

Pick up N13 and continue through Newtowncunningham. About 5 miles past this village, the heights of Mount Grianán will come into view on the right. Eight hundred feet up on top of this hill stands one of the most spectacular of Ireland's ancient monuments — the Grianán of Aileach. To reach the site, turn right (south) at the church in Speenoge. It is possible to drive to within a few yards of this imposing fortress, which is thought to have been a temple of the sun during pagan times. The name may be translated as "the sunny place in the land of Aileach" or "the stone house of the sun." The original earthen building could have been erected by druids. Legend also suggests that the fortress was once a sanctuary for the women of the territory when their men were away on war expeditions; hence another of its names, "the weeping place for women." In Christian times, it became the seat of the powerful O'Neill clan, who built the great stone fort on top of the earthen works. The fortress was attacked on numerous occasions, and the Munster king Murtogh O'Brien devastated it early in the 12th century. During the 1870s, Dr. Walter Bernard, the Bishop of Derry, supervised a meticulous restoration of the fort, reinvesting it with much of its original splendor.

Return to N13 and turn right (east). At Bridgend, which is on the border of Northern Ireland, turn left (northwest) for Burnfoot and then right (east) for the village of Muff. From here, head northeast on R238, along the shores of Lough Foyle, to Moville.

MOVILLE: The port of Moville was established during the 18th century by Samuel Montgomery, an ancestor of Viscount Montgomery of El Alamein, the greatest of the British World War II generals and a friendly rival of Dwight Eisenhower. Moville was once a point of departure for steamships bound for America. The town square, shaded by trees, is one of the most attractive in Ireland, and a beautiful seafront promenade leads beyond the town to a long walk that follows the coast beneath tall cliffs and stately mountains. About a mile north of the town is the famous Cooley Cross, a tall stone sculpture dating from the 4th century. What looks like a footprint can be discerned on the rock on which the cross stands; the truly devout believe it came from the foot of St. Patrick.

CHECKING IN/EATING OUT: *Redcastle* – A splendid 17th-century mansion on 22 acres of woodland on the edge of the Atlantic. The original character of the house has been preciously preserved, though a full panoply of modern comforts has been gently worked in. There is a 9-hole golf course, and the hotel specializes in outdoor holidays featuring game-fishing and horseback riding. The hotel's restaurant has won a number of prestigious awards. Three miles south of Moville on R238 (phone: 77-82073). Moderate.

McNamara's – Small and very friendly, this family-run hotel has 15 rooms, most with bath. There's a snug little bar with a log fire, and the restaurant excites the palate with a daily supply of fresh lobster, turbot, crab, and mackerel brought up from the harbor. Main St., Moville (phone: 77-82010). Inexpensive.

GREENCASTLE: Four miles out along the coast road, R241, at a point where the Lough Foyle channel narrows and the opposite shore in Northern Ireland is only a mile away, is one of the Irish Republic's major fishing ports, Greencastle, with its long ribbon of sand along the ocean beyond the harbor. The town's name comes from a nearby castle, the remains of which lie above the town. It was built in 1305 by the Norman Earl Richard de Burgo (Burke) as a gesture of defiance against the two ruling clans of Inishowen, the O'Donnells and the O'Dohertys. Eventually the castle fell into the hands of the O'Donnells, but it was captured from them by Elizabethan Planters. From here, backtrack to Moville.

En Route from Moville – About 7 miles north of Moville on the Culdaff road, R238, is the village of Leckemy, where evidence supports the allegation that sauna baths originated in Ireland. At the foot of Crocknamerragh Hill is a beehive-shaped stone sweathouse, measuring not quite 8 feet high. Such sweathouses are believed to have been used during pagan times to exorcise demons. Later, they were used as treatment for all types of ailments and infirmities. The houses were heated by peat fires. Two or three naked people squeezed into the tiny space and were sealed inside for several hours to sweat. Immediately afterward, in the kind of ritual still followed in Finland today, they plunged into a river or submerged themselves in a tub of ice water.

Drive through Culdaff, and a short distance north is the lovely village of Malin, close to the northernmost tip of Ireland. Malin is a picture postcard hamlet founded by English Planters in the 17th century. Houses of that period surround its central diamond, on which grow sycamore and cherry trees. Spectacular sand dunes rise above the golden strip of beach below the village. It's worth abandoning the car for a while in Malin to walk in the nearby Knockmany Bens (peaks). One of the most exciting hikes in all of Ireland is along the narrow side road that goes from Malin into the heart of the hills, a heather-clad range of low mountains that command magnificent panoramic views across the Atlantic to the Mull of Kintyre in Scotland.

A reasonably good link road, L79, goes all the way to Malin Head, at the very brink of the island of Ireland, for another breathtaking ocean vista. Down below, at the foot of the cliff, the sea races furiously through a channel between needle-pointed rocks in the place known as Hell's Hole, over which clouds of spray hang perpetually like white smoke. To the east, massive cathedral cliffs rear out of the ocean and run for 12 miles down to Glengad Head.

From Malin village, take L79 south toward Carndonagh, and just outside that town bear right (northwest) onto R238 toward Ballyliffin. A graveyard on the left has a large stone cross at the gate. This is St. Patrick's Cross, probably the oldest standing cross in Ireland, dating from the 7th century.

Ballyliffin is a popular resort with a pristine beach running for 2 miles and sand dunes full of rich deposits of calcified and crumbled sea shells, thousands of years old. Three miles south on R238 is Clonmany and the ruins of a church that was built on top of a monastery established by St. Columba (also known as St. Columcille). Downstream on the river Clonmany, at Glenview, is a 40-foot waterfall, at the bottom of which lies a deep pool where brown trout reside. From Clonmany, take the ring road (an unnumbered route that runs in a semicircle northwest through Straid, Kindrohid, Dunaff, and Claggan) through the Mamore Gap for some of the most majestic scenery on the entire peninsula. The road climbs high into the mountains above the sea and then cuts through the gap, a desolate glen of stunning beauty hemmed in by lofty peaks.

From the gap it's a steep downhill run all the way to Buncrana, which has two castles worth visiting and a fine sandy beach. Buncrana is usually crowded with vacationers in summer, when there's an active nightlife with numerous discos and singing pubs open until dawn. Unfortunately, the town has been overrun by tacky gaming arcades, despite the efforts of many citizens to have them closed.

From Buncrana, rejoin R238, which runs south through Fahan to Burnfoot and Bridgend, from which it is possible to double back on N13 to Manorcunningham and from there travel west toward Letterkenny.

 CHECKING IN: *White Strand* – Warm personal attention is a conspicuous feature of this family-owned modern motel. Rooms are comfortable and well equipped, and the food is of high quality. Railway Rd., Buncrana (phone: 77-61059). Moderate.

***Strand* –** Each of 12 rooms in this excellent family-run property has been given an individual touch, along with all the modern facilities, including a television set, radio, and phone. Everything served in the restaurant is fresh or home-produced, and there's a marvelous variety of fish dishes. An added attraction is the beautiful garden at the rear of the hotel. Ballyliffin (phone: 77-76107). Inexpensive.

 EATING OUT: *St. John's* – Housed in a restored Georgian house overlooking Lough Swilly, this elegant restaurant has won a number of well-deserved awards for its cooking: An abundant supply of fresh fish is prepared with great skill, and Donegal lamb is another highlight. Fahan (phone: 77-60289). Moderate.

NORTHWEST DONEGAL

LETTERKENNY: With a population of more than 5,000, Letterkenny, on the banks of the river Swilly, is the county's largest town, and its ecclesiastical center. It derives its name from the Gaelic *Leitir Ceannain* (hillside of the O'Cannons, a clan that inhabited the area before Norman times). Although the town itself is not remarkable, it is a good base from which to enjoy day trips to the northwest coastal areas.

 CHECKING IN/EATING OUT: *Gallagher's* – A small, old-fashioned, and very comfortable place to stay, right in the center of town. The food is fresh and good, and it's served in gargantuan portions. Main St., Letterkenny (phone: 74-22570). Expensive.

***Mount Errigal* –** This modern hostelry has 82 comfortable rooms with private bath and cable TV, and a restaurant serving traditional Irish fare. On the outskirts of Letterkenny on the R245 at Ballyraine (phone: 74-22700). Expensive.

En Route from Letterkenny – At this point it is possible to diverge from the grand tour of County Donegal and become completely immersed in the solitude and splendor of Glenveagh National Park, only 13 miles to the northwest on N56. The route goes first to Kilmacrenan, a hamlet of great charm and particular appeal to anglers because the fast-flowing river Leannan is possibly the best trout water in Donegal and an exciting challenge to the fly caster. The ruins of a 16th-century Franciscan friary, built by one of the O'Donnells, can be found in a churchyard north of the village. Just 1½ miles to the east is Doon Rock, a coronation stone used for many centuries to inaugurate successive O'Donnell chieftains. To reach Glenveagh, travel 3 miles farther along N56, turn left (west) at Termon onto L77, then right (north) at the junction of L82. The entrance to the park is 2 miles beyond on the left.

GLENVEAGH NATIONAL PARK: Glenveagh is very, very precious — a wild domain of nature, almost untouched from the day it was fashioned, with herds of red deer grazing on the uplands, peregrine falcons circling above the lake, and a sequestered glen where civilization and its turmoils are kept at bay and great silences prevail. The privacy of this place was founded in a tragic happening: John George Adair, the man who took over Glenveagh in the 19th century, drove 200 families from their homes on the estate so he could have it all to himself. It was he who built the overembellished Gothic castle above the lake. During the 1930s, Glenveagh came into the possession of a more humane landlord, Henry McIlhenny, a man of limitless wealth gained from the manufacture of gas meters in Philadelphia, where his grandfather, a Donegal man, had emigrated. McIlhenny spent his summers in the castle, living in the resplendent style of a Renaissance prince but winning the affection of the local populace through his generosity. He was a bright light in the international society of the 1930s and 1940s, and many celebrities stayed in the castle as his guests, including Greta Garbo, Cecil Beaton, and Yehudi Menuhin. They slept in sumptuous bedrooms warmed by peat fires and dined in royal style on continental cuisine prepared by European chefs. Upon his death, McIlhenny left the 25,000-acre estate and its castle to the Irish nation, though his widow continued to live in the castle for 36 years. The gardens on the castle grounds are superb, but the real enchantment of Glenveagh is in the wild splendor of its mountainous landscape, where it is possible to walk for miles without seeing a house and to luxuriate in an all-encompassing solitude. It is one of the last real wild places left in Ireland.

En Route from Glenveagh National Park – Before returning to Letterkenny, it's worth traveling 7 miles south on L82 to Gartan, the birthplace of St. Columba. Donegal's remarkable saint evangelized parts of Scotland, where he established a renowned monastery on the island of Iona. His life wasn't entirely one of prayer, however, and in his early years his fiery temper sometimes landed him in trouble. On one notable occasion, he mustered an army to do battle with none less than the High King of Ireland — and defeated him. He died on Iona in 597 at the age of 76. Double back to N56 at the entrance to Glenveagh, and drive south toward Letterkenny. Just outside the town, turn left (east) onto R245, then bear north for Rathmelton and on to Rathmullan.

RATHMULLAN: In all of Ireland there is scarcely a lovelier seaside village than Rathmullan — certainly there is no other tiny spot so richly awash in history. It was here in 1587 that the young Red Hugh O'Donnell (the second) was kidnapped at the behest of Queen Elizabeth I; the youngster was lured aboard a British ship anchored off Rathmullan, chained in the hold, and taken to Dublin, where he was held for 5 years before he escaped and made his way back to Tirconnaill to rally his warriors against Elizabeth.

It was also the scene of one of the most tragic events in Irish history: the Flight of the Earls, when the great chieftains O'Donnell and O'Neill, attended by a retinue of followers, boarded a ship to sail in exile to Europe in 1607. They were the last of the Gaelic chiefs, and their departure cleared the way for the final phase of the English conquest of Ireland.

History was again swept up on Rathmullan's shores in 1798, when the French fleet, planning to invade Ireland and aid a native rebellion against the British, came to grief in Lough Swilly. Aboard one of the captured French ships was the leading insurrectionist, Wolfe Tone, a revered Irish patriot. Tone died, possibly by his own hand, while in prison awaiting execution.

The bay of Lough Swilly, on which Rathmullan is located, is one of the deepest sea anchorages in Europe. Although men-of-war no longer sail into the long, deep harbor, hundreds of yachts, speedboats, and motor launches knife through the sheltered waters in summer. There's great fishing offshore, and fishermen from many lands gather in Rathmullan for the sea angling festival every June.

 CHECKING IN: *Fort Royal* – A delightful country house, with its own beach on Lough Swilly, it has riding stables, tennis courts, and fine food. About one-half mile from Rathmullan on the Portsalon road, immediately beyond the gates of *Rathmullan House:* There's a sign indicating the narrow road that leads to it (phone: 74-58100). Expensive.

Rathmullan House – This magnificent, rambling old mansion, hidden among the trees near the shores of Lough Swilly, is one of the loveliest hotels in Ireland, with very good food. About one-half mile from Rathmullan on the Portsalon road; watch for the sign on the gates at the right (phone: 74-58188). Expensive.

 EATING OUT: *Water's Edge* – Perched on the brink of Lough Swilly, this superb restaurant makes the most of the fish readily at hand. Boned duckling in an exotic sauce is another specialty. Ballyboe, on L77, on the approach to Rathmullan from Rathmelton (phone: 74-58182). Moderate.

En Route from Rathmullan – Visitors can walk for miles unhindered along the sandy shore of Lough Swilly or drive north toward Fanad Head, taking the Knockalla coast road. Follow the signposts (the road is unnumbered) to Portsalon, 8 miles away. It's a precipitous and thrilling drive, for the road first climbs a coastal cliff towering above the Atlantic and then dips suddenly and sweeps downward to Ballymastocker Bay, a crescent of golden sands. As a spectacle, it's a heart stopper. North of Portsalon, the road turns really mean, but it's worth chancing the final 3 miles to Fanad Head just to take in the view from the top of the cliffs here. Then turn south and drive to the village of Tamney, continuing down along the eastern fringe of beautiful Mulroy Bay to Kerrykeel and from there to Milford, at the southern tip of Mulroy Bay.

 EATING OUT: *Village Restaurant* – A small but marvelous little dining place, owned by a chef who has won awards for his special way with seafood. Kerrykeel (phone: 74-50062). Moderate.

SHARING A PINT: *Moore's Inn* – Good drinks and snacks can be had at this flavorsome 19th-century pub where the welcome is warm. Main St., Milford (phone: 74-53123). Inexpensive.

CARRIGART/ROSGUILL: Head north along the western edge of Mulroy Bay on R245 toward Carrigart, 10 miles away. A narrow, elongated inlet with trees edging its shore, the bay is a lovely sight, evoking the Scandinavian fjords. Three miles from Carrigart, the road winds by Cratlagh Wood, where in 1878 one of the most hated landlords in Ireland, the third Earl of Leitrim, was murdered, along with two of his servants. At Carrigart, turn west, and then just on the edge of town, turn right (north) at the signpost for Rosapenna onto R248. This leads onto the Rosguill Peninsula, one of the many Gaeltacht pockets of Donegal, where Irish is still a living language, spoken mostly by the old people. At the headland of Rosguill, another spectacular seascape unfolds along the circular Atlantic Drive. The drive goes through an ecologically devastated "desert," where not a blade of grass grows, and around lovely Dooagh Bay. Leaving the Rosguill headland on the way back to Carrigart, turn right (southwest) onto the road to Creeslough.

CHECKING IN/EATING OUT: *Rosapenna Golf* – The great attraction at this 40-room hotel is the 18-hole golf course, but no less gratifying is the splendid fare served in its restaurant. There are also 2 tennis courts and a restaurant. Right turn at the signpost on the edge of Carrigart, 1 mile onto the Rosguill headland (phone: 74-55301). Expensive.

Carrigart – Noted for its conviviality and warm informality, this hotel also serves good food. Top of Main St., Carrigart (phone: 74-55114). Moderate.

DOE CASTLE/CREESLOUGH: About 6 miles southwest of Carrigart, at the village of Cashel, turn right (north) at the signpost for Doe Castle; it's 1 mile down the side road. Perched on the edge of the sea, the castle is one of the finest fortresses left in Ireland; to explore it, ask for the key in the second house up from the entrance. In the early 16th century, Doe Castle was the stronghold of the MacSweeneys, a clan of "gallowglasses" from Scotland who came to Donegal to fight for the O'Donnell chieftains and gained a foothold in the county themselves. Before he was kidnapped, young Red Hugh O'Donnell lived here briefly under the fosterage of the MacSweeneys. Survivors of the Spanish Armada who swam from their wrecked ships to the Donegal coast found a haven in this castle. The road from Doe Castle runs into Creeslough, a pretty town overlooking the coast. Creeslough is a convenient base for expeditions to Muckish Mountain. Muckish must be climbed because it's there, and the panorama of the north of Ireland from its 2,000-foot peak is a magnificent sight.

EATING OUT: *Corncutters' Rest* – One of the few pub-cum-fast-food eateries in Donegal that can be relied on for cleanliness and efficiency. Snacks downstairs during the day and an à la carte menu upstairs in the evening. Main St., Creeslough (phone: 74-38067). Moderate to inexpensive.

En Route from Creeslough – About 3 miles north, on N56 toward Port-na-Blagh and Dunfanaghy, the texture of the landscape changes suddenly and dramatically, the stark, rugged barrenness giving way to a soft, green-wooded peninsula that juts into Sheep Haven Bay. This is the Ards Forest Park, which is open year-round. It is a relaxing, shaded haven from the outside world amid ancient trees that stand sentinel above the bay. Paths wander through woods and clearings perfect for picnicking, and at the edge of the forest, white strands run down to the sea, where, on those rare days when the sun brings the water up to a bearable temperature, the hardy can swim.

Port-na-Blagh and Dunfanaghy are delightfully unspoiled seaside resorts surrounded by beaches. However, sad to say, it must be noted that although the whole jagged coast of Donegal is a treasure trove of beaches, they are hardly ever used because the rainy and windy weather discourages all but the most valiant of spirit. Just beyond Dunfanaghy, swing right and follow the signpost to Horn Head for another drive around the cliffs above the Atlantic. A strong heart and a steady hand on the steering wheel are prerequisites for Horn Head because at the very top, at the brink of the ocean, a look down those cliffs offers a glimpse of eternity. The massive cathedral cliffs also provide a nesting haven for thousands of seabirds in midsummer, a phenomenon attracting bird watchers from many countries.

Back on N56 again, head southwest to Falcarragh, 7 miles away, which is part of the Gortahork Gaeltacht. Falcarragh has much Gaelic flavor because Irish is still widely spoken, and many students come here every summer to study the native tongue. It is also another point from which to climb Muckish Mountain (see "Doe Castle/Creeslough" earlier in this section). Turn left (south) at the village crossroads and travel the side road 6 miles to the mountain.

CHECKING IN/EATING OUT: *Carrig Rua* – This former coaching inn retains its Old World flavor, and owners Valerie and Cyril Robinson provide an attentive personal touch. The food is splendid. Dunfanaghy (phone: 74-36208). Expensive.

Arnold's – Homey and hospitable, this family-run hostelry is known for indulging its guests. There are 34 rooms, including 2 family units. The excellent restaurant features vegetables from the garden and fresh fish. Dunfanaghy (phone: 74-36208). Moderate.

Port-na-Blagh – The dining room at this large, modern hotel, perched on a cliff overlooking Sheep Haven Bay, has particularly good fish selections. On the left along the road into Port-na-Blagh from Creeslough (phone: 74-36129). Moderate.

TORY ISLAND: Just 9 miles off the coast in the Falcarragh area bobs Tory Island, about which there are many legends. One dating from antiquity tells of an ancient race of giants known as the Formorians inhabiting the island. Their chief was the feared Balor of the Evil Eye, who was said to have supernatural powers and the remains of whose castle still stand on the cliffs at the eastern side of the island. More civilized influences prevailed after the arrival of Christianity, and there are some ruins where Donegal's most famous saint, Columba, once presided over a settlement of monks.

Today there are only about 250 Tory islanders left, and their lifestyle is much the same as that of their ancestors. They speak an Irish with undertones of Scots Gaelic because of the age-old connection between Tory and Scotland. The islanders live in small, thatched cottages and cultivate the meager soil on their tiny holdings, raising oats and potatoes in those parts of the island protected from the fierce Atlantic storms. No trees grow on the island, but some wildflowers manage to bloom in the stony soil. The men still go to sea on fishing expeditions in frail *curraghs* — the tarred-canvas-covered boats used in Ireland for centuries.

Some rather fascinating compensations relieve this hard and bitter life. There are no rats whatsoever on Tory Island. The reason for this — according to the islanders — is that St. Columba banished rats from Tory and blessed the soil so they daren't return. Even better — and perhaps more pertinent today — the islanders don't have to pay any taxes.

While on the island, try to scale the two tors (steep hills) from which Tory gets its name; the view is splendid. On top of one there's a holy stone on which, it is said, if you stand and turn around to the right three times you'll be granted any wish that you make.

There are a number of ports from which it is possible to sail to Tory, and Falcarragh is as convenient as any; contact *James Ferry* (phone: 74-35177). To avoid being marooned on the island, make sure that no bad weather is in the offing on the day of departure. Wild Atlantic storms are frequent, and Tory is often cut off from the mainland for 2 or 3 weeks at a time. But the people are extraordinarily kind and hospitable, so that even an enforced stay can be a pleasant experience.

En Route from Tory Island – Returning to the mainland, get back on N56 in Falcarragh and head southwest to Gortahork. At this point take the signposted road that runs northwest to Meenaclady along the northern coast toward the promontory known as Bloody Foreland. There are magnificent seascapes all along this stretch. Bloody Foreland is at the extreme northwestern tip of the Gaeltacht region known as Gweedore; it got its name from the blood-red color of the rocks as they are struck by the setting sun. Painters and photographers come to Bloody Foreland in summer hoping to catch one of these remarkable sunsets. The road swings around the headland and then turns south through the seaside resorts of Derrybeg and Bunbeg. The latter is a particularly attractive village, tucked away beneath tall cliffs, and has one outstanding curiosity: the smallest harbor in the world. It also has a beautiful and very safe sandy beach surrounded by sand dunes and crags that invite exploration.

Turn left (west) in Bunbeg and follow the signpost to Gweedore village, returning to N56, the main route. From Gweedore, it's 2 miles east to Dunlewy, which is just south of Errigal Mountain.

CHECKING IN/EATING OUT: *Gweedore* – Perched vertiginously on the brink of a cliff way above a golden beach, this smart, ultramodern hostelry offers all the creature comforts, including good food. A signpost on Bunbeg's main street points the way (phone: 75-31177). Moderate.

McFadden's – A venerable and classy family-run hotel, where friendliness and personal attention are the winning points. The food can be recommended, too. Main St., Gortahork (phone: 74-35267). Moderate.

ERRIGAL MOUNTAIN/DUNLEWY: People unskilled in mountain climbing should not attempt Errigal unless they are accompanied by a local guide. From the summit of this 2,466-foot mountain it is possible to see as far away as the Scottish Highlands. While in Dunlewy, take the opportunity to walk south of the village into an exotic valley called the Poisoned Glen. Poisonous weeds known as spurge grow prolifically in the glen and have contaminated a lake, making its waters unsafe to drink. There are no birds in the valley, so when the weather turns hot in summer all sorts of creeping and flying insects infest the place, making it feel uncomfortably like a rain forest — but without the trees!

Return to the main road, N56, and head southwest to the Rosses.

THE ROSSES

The area called "the Rosses" (meaning promontories or headlands, of which there are countless hereabouts) has large, lonely stretches of uninhabited bogland. Its very bleakness has an appeal of its own, and it draws many tourists every summer.

About 3 miles south of Gweedore is the village of Crolly, famous for its Crolly dolls, which are exported all over the world. Visit the doll factory to buy a doll at cut rates. Walk south of Crolly on the Dungloe road, but be prepared for a deafening crash as you pass by a giant glacial boulder. This is the Big Stone of the Leaping Fox, and legend says it will come tumbling down when an honest person passes it — so you've been warned. Instead of taking the main road from Crolly directly to Dungloe, the real heart of the Rosses, turn right (west) at the signposted road to Annagary, which circles the coast through Kincasslagh to Burtonport.

BURTONPORT/ARRANMORE ISLAND: Turn right at the signpost for Burtonport, one of the busiest fishing ports in Ireland, landing more salmon and lobster than anywhere else in the country. At the height of the fishing season, it's fun to watch the activity on the pier as the trawlers come in from the Atlantic to unload their catches. Also from Burtonport, are boats to the island of Arranmore, 3 miles offshore (frequent departures from 10:30 AM; phone: 75-21532) and a ferry that can carry a small number of automobiles. Those who want to relax and do a bit of fishing can catch rainbow trout in Lough Shure; contact Philip Boyle (phone: 75-21508). Those who prefer more strenuous activity can try the 4-mile walk to Rinrawros Point, a lovely spot dominated by a lighthouse.

En Route from Burtonport – Take the signposted road from Burtonport south to Dungloe, considered the capital of the Rosses. Although the town itself is unremarkable, there is some very good trout fishing in the lakes and rivers nearby.

CHECKING IN/EATING OUT: *Ostan Na Rosann* – A good, modern hotel, with an indoor pool and a dining room serving wholesome food in enormous portions. Just outside Dungloe on the road to Burtonport (phone: 75-21088). Moderate.

Viking House – Although there are 8 guestrooms here, the restaurant is the magnet; the accent is on seafood fresh from the Atlantic, just outside the door. It is very popular in summer, so book in advance, preferably the day before. About 7 miles from Crolly on the coast road; watch for the prominent sign on the left of the road after the village of Kincasslagh (phone: 75-43103). Restaurant, moderate; guest-rooms, inexpensive.

SOUTHWEST DONEGAL

En Route from Dungloe – Take N56 south to Maas, 13 miles away, and turn right (west) to reach the pretty villages of Narin and Portnoo, both high above Gweebarra Bay. There is real solitude here because this area has not yet been overrun by tourists, and a number of secluded beaches and coves can be found along the coast. When the tide is out, it is possible to walk across the sands from Narin to the island of Iniskeel to see the ruins of a 6th-century church.

Travel around the circular road from Portnoo, through Rosbeg, to the junction of R261, and then turn right (south) for Ardara, a village that just might be the loveliest in all of Donegal. Ardara is tucked away in a deep valley where the river Owentocker races over rocks and boulders into Loughros More Bay. It is an area renowned for the weaving of Donegal tweed, and many shops in the village offer real bargains in tweed goods. For the more adventurous, signposts point the way to the Maghera sea caves, where moonshiners used to ply their illicit art. Exploring these caves is an exciting experience, but first check the tide schedules to avoid any danger. Be sure to visit the Church of the Holy Family, which contains a very fine work in stained glass by the artist Evie Hone.

Two miles south of Ardara on N56, turn right (west) at the signpost for Glencolumb-kille. At Crobane, 3 miles farther, take the right fork, which runs through the Glengesh Pass, a thrilling drive as the road climbs 900 feet into the clouds and then plunges dizzily to the valley below. The landscape flattens as the road reaches Glencolumbkille.

 CHECKING IN/EATING OUT: *Lake House* – An old-fashioned hostelry offering friendly personal attention and wholesome home-cooked food. Port-noo (phone: 75-45123). Inexpensive.

Nesbitt Arms – A traditional inn where the comfort of guests is always in mind. Great food and a good buy. Main St., Ardara (phone: 75-41103). Inexpensive.

GLENCOLUMBKILLE: This is the lost valley where Columba, the patron saint of Donegal, lived in retreat from the world. He built a monastic prayer house here in the 6th century; even today relics and reminders of his presence are scattered around the glen. The whole place has a timelessness about it; the outside world scarcely intrudes.

On *St. Columba's Feast Day,* June 9, hundreds of people make a 3-mile pilgrimage through the glen, stopping to pray at ancient stone crosses along the way. At one of those crosses, beside the Protestant church, the pilgrims kiss the stone and then peer through an opening in the top in the belief that if they are without sin they may be given a glimpse of the next world.

But not only are Christian memorabilia and artifacts to be found in Glencolumbkille. There's also much evidence of an earlier presence. Nearly 50 monuments traceable to pre-Christian times are scattered throughout the glen, including underground passages and burial places.

Some years back, to provide employment and halt emigration from the glen, the local people formed a cooperative to develop home crafts and industries and to attract more tourists. The results have been some of the most encouraging success stories of rural Ireland. One such enterprise was the building of a village of traditional thatch-roofed cottages. Visitors can rent the cottages at rates that run from inexpensive in low season to moderate during high season. Information about this community can be obtained by contacting the Glencolumbkille Cooperative Society (Glencolumbkille, County

Donegal; phone: 73-30015). To see what life was really like beneath the thatched roofs of Irish cottages in other eras, visit the folk village nearby, where the past has been reconstructed in fine detail.

CHECKING IN: *Glencolumbkille* – The only hotel in the valley offers a reasonable degree of comfort and has an exceptionally friendly staff and good food (phone: 73-30003). Moderate.

En Route from Glencolumbkille – To complete the tour circuit back to Donegal Town, take R263 from Glencolumbkille through Carrick, Kilcar, and Killybegs. Killybegs is Ireland's most important fishing port, and the sight of its fishing fleet coming home in the evening, with thousands of sea gulls shrieking above it, is a great spectacle. Just north of Killybegs, rejoin N56. From here it's a 17-mile run into Donegal Town.

West Cork

Although often overlooked in favor of Kerry, its more famous neighbor, West Cork is a very special part of Ireland. Here the landscape is a palette of infinitely changing colors, and the terrain varies from the soft shoulders of the inland Shehy Mountains to the sandy coves along the southern coast. The area around Bantry Bay — kissed by the warm, gentle Gulf Stream current — abounds with lush palm trees and other subtropical foliage. Pointing to several soaring 80-foot eucalyptus trees, one Corkman boasted: "The trees in this part of Ireland grow as tall as those in Disney cartoons!"

But scenic beauty is by no means Cork's sole attraction. Its fine bathing strands, climbable peaks, excellent fishing waters, and busy marinas make the area a paradise for sports enthusiasts. In addition, there are many lively, cheerful villages where pub regulars have formed singing groups; small mountain towns where the lilt of the ancient Irish tongue is still heard; remote, lovely places where time has stood still. Even on the road, visitors will feel warmly welcomed. Everybody waves: The child on a bicycle beams, the farmer in the field looks up to lift an arm in salute, and conversations at cottage gates pause as heads turn and a company of hands are raised in greeting.

Our route, which begins and ends in Cork City, traces a leisurely circuit around West Cork. First stops are the towns of Macroom and Irish-speaking Ballingeary, and next is the historic, lovely lake of Gougane Barra. The route continues west to balmy Bantry Bay, with an excursion around the Beara Peninsula (which must include a bit of County Kerry), then south and east to the picturesque villages of Skibbereen, Clonakilty, and Kinsale. The entire route is about 200 miles and can be covered easily in 2 to 3 days.

Except perhaps in high season, it's fairly safe to ramble along without hotel reservations, although many places are open only from May to October. A wide selection of accommodations is available, from bed and breakfast accommodations in a simple bungalow to an elegant room with a fine meal in a former mansion. Expect to pay around $100 and up per night for a double room in places listed as expensive, from $50 to $95 in moderate establishments, and less than $50 in inexpensive places. A meal for two (excluding wine, tips, and drinks) will cost $75 and up in a restaurant listed as expensive, between $35 and $70 in moderate ones, and under $30 in the inexpensive category.

CORK: For a detailed report on the city, its sights, hotels, and restaurants, see *Cork City*, THE CITIES.

En Route from Cork – R618 winds along the north bank of the river Lee and passes through the charming village of Dripsey, with its woolen mills, and then through Coachford to Macroom.

MACROOM: At the center of town stands Macroom Castle, granted to Admiral William Penn by Oliver Cromwell in 1654. (Penn, once Governor of Kinsale, was the father of William Penn, founder of Pennsylvania; the younger Penn also spent several years in Ireland handling the family estates.) Over the years, the castle endured much strife and was burned for the final time during the Irish civil war in the early 1920s. The ruins have been declared a monument and are partly restored. There's a 9-hole golf course nearby on a steep slope overlooking the river Sullane.

Macroom owes its existence to its location near the confluence of three rivers — the Lee, Laney, and Sullane — where people have gathered to barter and swap food and produce for centuries. It's still a thriving market town, with an annual agricultural show in summer. Posters for this show advertise competitions for "horses, cakes, sheep, and honey" — a compelling collage of images and flavors.

En Route from Macroom – Go back 1 mile on the Cork road and turn south onto R584 for Inchigeelagh. Past Inchigeelagh, the road hugs the north bank of the long and lovely Lough Allua. But the minor road along the south bank is even more beautiful, so that's the one we recommend.

BALLINGEARY: This village is in the heart of the Gaeltacht — an Irish-speaking district — in West Cork, and every summer young people flock here from all over the country to study in school-sponsored Irish language programs. Villagers, however, greet visitors in perfect and often mellifluous English. *Quill's Woolen Market* (phone: 26-47008), a very good craft and knitwear shop, run by the Quill family, produces and sells handsome garments made from the skins of sheep and goats. Just two doors from this shop is the birthplace of Cardinal Manning, the former Archbishop of Los Angeles.

Make a right turn 3¾ miles beyond Ballingeary, at the sign for Gougane Barra. The fork in the road is marked by a large crucifixion tableau and a memorial to local poet Máire Bhuí Ní Laoghaire.

GOUGANE BARRA: The mountain-encircled lake of Gougane Barra, source of the river Lee, is where St. Finbarre, the founder of Cork, had his hermitage in the 6th century. Joined to the lakeshore by a causeway is an island with a modern Irish Romanesque chapel. The isolation and serenity of the place make it immediately apparent why this valley was chosen for monastic contemplation. The surrounding area is a beautiful forest park with picnic areas and hiking trails. Fishing is free, but don't expect a great catch; as one local put it, "Saint Finbarre let everybody fish free, and that was about a thousand years ago, so I don't expect there's much left to catch."

Return to R584 and continue southwest as the road descends via Keimaneigh Pass and the Ouvane Valley to Ballylickey and Bantry.

 CHECKING IN/EATING OUT: *Gougane Barra* – A family-run hotel that offers 25 rooms, each with a private bath, and a dining room with a lovely view of the lake and hills. It's an ideal base for hiking the spectacularly beautiful 400-acre forest park along the Lee. If given notice, the owner will loan his boat. Open April to October. Gougane Barra (phone: Ballingeary 26-47069). Moderate.

BANTRY: Home of the spectacular, mostly Georgian Bantry House, once the seat of the Earls of Bantry, the mansion is furnished with antiques, tapestries, and paintings chosen by the second Earl of Bantry during his travels in Europe in the early 19th century. Surrounded by elegant terraces and gardens, it overlooks beautiful Bantry Bay. Open daily 9 AM to 6 PM. Admission charge.

Bantry is the perfect base for those interested in water sports; there's a fine beach and facilities for skin diving and water skiing. Check at the tourist board (New St.; phone: 27-50229). It is also a good base for excursions into the Beara Peninsula.

CHECKING IN: *Ballylickey Manor House* – This lovely Georgian mansion was gutted by fire in 1983, but its cottages and a couple of suites in the main house reopened the following year. There are 11 rooms, each with bath. The gardens and grounds were unharmed and remain as beautiful as ever. Amenities include an outdoor swimming pool and poolside restaurant. Open April through October. Ballylickey (phone: 27-50071). Expensive.

***Sea View House* –** Aptly named, this lovely white manor house is perched in a sylvan setting overlooking Bantry Bay. In recent years, enthusiastic proprietor Kathleen O'Sullivan has expanded the house without sacrificing its original charm. There are 17 spacious rooms, each with a modern, private bath, antique furnishings, and panoramic views of the bay or gardens. The public rooms are filled with family heirlooms, include an award-winning restaurant and a new oak-trimmed lounge with an adjacent sun deck. Open April through October. Ballylickey (phone: 27-51555). Expensive to moderate.

***Westlodge* –** Here is a modern 104-room hotel, surrounded by mountains on one side and Bantry Bay on the other. There's a restaurant/grillroom, tavern, an indoor pool, a sauna, an all-weather tennis court, squash courts, and a jogging trail. About 1 mile outside Bantry on N71, the coastal road (phone: 27-50360). Moderate.

***Shangri-La* –** A modern, private residence with hotel-type comforts, it offers 6 rooms, 5 with private bath, a restaurant with wine license, and a car park. It overlooks Bantry Bay, just outside the village. Open year-round. Bantry (phone: 27-50244). Inexpensive.

EATING OUT: *Blair's Cove* – On a country lane southwest of Bantry, overlookng Dunmanus Bay, this restaurant is in a renovated stone barn with a 250-year-old Georgian courtyard. Specialties include seafood, beef, and lamb grilled in an oak fireplace, a buffet of appetizers, and a grand piano that doubles as a dessert trolley. Open daily for dinner and for lunch on Sundays, *Easter* to mid-October; Fridays, Saturdays, and Sundays only, from mid-October to December and from March to *Easter*. Durrus–Barley Cove Rd., Bantry (phone: 27-61127). Expensive.

En Route from Bantry – For a scenic, if curvy, drive into the village of Glengarriff from Bantry or Ballylickey, take the main road, N71, which for the next 10 miles hugs the edge of the bay. Just beyond the mainland, there are views of Whiddy Island, a onetime outpost for offshore oil exploration.

GLENGARRIFF: The name means "rough glen," a description that is only partially true of this lovely village snuggled into a deeply wooded glen at the southeastern corner of the Beara Peninsula. There is nothing rough about it, and sheltered as it is from any harsh winds by mountains on three sides, the village has a justly famous reputation for mild weather and luxuriant vegetation. Arbutus, eucalyptus, fuchsia, rhododendron, and blue-eyed grass are among the plants and trees that flourish in the glen, and on Garinish Island in Glengarriff Harbour, the growth is subtropical. Until the early part of this century, the island was bare, but its owners began to transform it with an extraordinary richness of flowers and foliage laid out in beautiful, Italian-style formal gardens. At the highest point of the island is a Martello tower, the first of many built around Britain and Ireland against the expected Napoleonic invasion of 1804–5. The island, a gift to Ireland in 1939, is now open to the public (admission charge for the gardens). Boats leave Glengarriff 9:30 AM to 6 PM Mondays through Saturdays, 1 to 6 PM Sundays, March through October. There is excellent sea and river fishing in and around the village, and bathing is good along the nearby coves, one of which, Poulgorm ("blue pool") is an extremely picturesque spot just a 2-minute walk from the post office.

Glengarriff also has tennis courts, a golf course, and unlimited terrain for riding and walking.

 CHECKING IN: *Eccles* – Overlooking Glengarriff Harbour, this traditional, but updated and expanded, hotel offers 60 rooms, each with bath. There's also a restaurant, a lounge, and lovely gardens. Open year-round. Glengarriff (phone: 27-63003). Moderate.

En Route from Glengarriff – Route R572 twists west into poor and rocky country along the south coast of the Beara Peninsula, a thinly populated, very underdeveloped region that is also very beautiful and the least frequented of the three great southwestern peninsulas. The full circuit can fill at least a day, but it can be shortened by cutting across the center of the peninsula on the spectacular Healy Pass road. Upon reaching Adrigole village, 12 miles from Glengarriff, take the signposted road, R574, to the right for the Healy Pass.

HEALY PASS: Work on this road began as a relief project during the famine years of the mid-19th century but stopped shortly thereafter. It was resumed in 1928 at the direction of Tim Healy, the first Governor-General of the Irish Free State (a native of Bantry), and was finished 3 years later. The road climbs to a height of 1,084 feet as it crosses the Caha Mountains (and the border between County Cork and County Kerry) to provide rewarding views over Mizen Head and Sheep's Head to the south and Derreen, Kilmakilloge Harbour, the Kenmare River, and the mountains of the Iveragh Peninsula to the north. In early summer, the soft ground beside the pass will be spattered with the blooms of the *Pinguicula grandiflora,* the large-flowered butterwort. The road descends to Lauragh on the northern coast of the peninsula, but those who wish to explore the isolated region farther west can turn back, admiring the splendid sight of Bantry Bay along the way to Adrigole.

En Route from Adrigole – Proceed west on R572. The route to Castletownbere is dominated by the lean, well-named Hungry Hill (a reminder of the famine of 1845 and, at 2,251 feet, the highest point on the peninsula), while Bere Island, with its two Martello towers, emerges to the left in Bantry Bay. The island was named for Beara, a Spanish princess married to Eogan, a partly legendary, partly historical figure who landed here during an invasion of Ireland. Eventually, the whole peninsula was named for the princess. Despite the spare countryside, holly and sally trees flourish, and fuchsia is rampant; in early summer, great drifts of white lilies make a stunning show.

CASTLETOWNBERE: No more than a string of houses along both sides of the street, this village grew up at the beginning of the 19th century when the copper mines at Allihies, west of town, were opened. Its sheltered natural harbor continued to earn it a living as the site of a British naval base until 1938, and it is now becoming one of Ireland's main fishing centers, with tourism increasing. Look at the seven dormer windows, like elegant ships' portholes, over the three houses facing the pier — they are a feature of this area. The ruins of the 15th-century Dunboy Castle, the stronghold of the branch of the O'Sullivans who were lords of this peninsula (the main branch occupied most of the Iveragh Peninsula), are about 2 miles west of town.

 CHECKING IN/EATING OUT: *Craigie's Cametringane House* – Opened in 1985, this family-run inn is nestled in an idyllic setting on Bantry Bay, just outside the village. A good place to relax and enjoy some tennis, sailing, windsurfing, and fishing, it has 13 rooms (10 with private bath), a seafood restaurant, and a convivial pub. Open all year. Castletownbere (phone: 27-70379). Moderate to inexpensive.

En Route from Castletownbere – Continue west on R572 for about 6 miles. When the road divides, with a sign pointing each way to Allihies, take the road to the right, R575. Along the way are good views of the two Skellig Rocks and of Scariff and Deenish islands at the end of the river Kenmare. The road passes the abandoned Allihies copper mines, first worked by Iberian miners some 4,000 years ago and re-opened during the Napoleonic wars by the Puxley family, who made a great fortune. The Puxleys employed no fewer than 1,200 people before the operation succumbed to competition in 1886. When Daphne du Maurier wrote her book about the mines, *Hungry Hill,* she used Puxley family papers as part of her research, though she named the book for a mountain some miles away.

After skirting the little village of Allihies, now a shadow of its former self, follow the signs to Eyeries, then on to Ardgroom and to Lauragh, at the head of Kilmakillage Harbour and the border of County Kerry. On a good day, this stretch of the route provides some of the most striking scenery in all of West Cork and Kerry. It is, however, narrow and twisting most of the way.

LAURAGH: The Healy Pass road across the peninsula joins the scenic sea road, R571, at Lauragh, County Kerry. Close to the village is the estate of Derreen House, whose beautiful subtropical gardens are open to visitors daily, 11 AM to 6 PM, from early April through September. The gardens — much less formal than those of Garinish Island or Muckross House — are remarkable for their rhododendron, camellias, tree ferns, bamboo, and eucalyptus.

En Route from Lauragh – From Lauragh, R571 passes the Cloonie lakes and Lough Inchiquin — well stocked with salmon and sea and brown trout — as it continues east along the coast to Kenmare, County Kerry (see *Ring of Kerry,* DIRECTIONS). From Kenmare, it is 17 miles back to Glengarriff and 29 miles to Bantry via N71.

Head south from Kenmare on N71, which provides fine views of the river Kenmare, adrift with swans, and of the surrounding mountains. The road follows the valley of the river Sheen for several miles, then crosses the river Baureeragh and begins to climb through a series of tunnels, the longest one passing under the border between County Cork and County Kerry. Beyond the main tunnel, far to the right, is Barley Lake, a striking glacial corrie filled with water, with an improbable road snaking up to it. The tortuous Caha Mountains are on the right, and the great stretch of Bantry Bay is visible below, with the tip of Whiddy Island barely discernible. The road then descends through a valley into Glengarriff. Return to Bantry via N71.

En Route from Bantry – Just beyond Bantry, N71 leaves the sea, and the landscape becomes a great patchwork of farm fields, with colors changing every mile. This region has enjoyed an increased affluence in the past decade, and the prosperity is reflected in freshly painted farmhouses and neatly kept yards. In West Cork, as elsewhere in Ireland, cattle are the mainstay of the economy. (The human population of the entire Republic is just over 3.5 million; the livestock population often reaches three times that number.) On the road, it is often necessary to stop your car to give way to lumbering herds, although the Cork farmer may not be leading his cattle on foot, but instead nudging them along with his Mercedes-Benz. One local wit remarked, "Americans can grumble all they like about oil sheiks, but here in Ireland we have milk sheiks!"

From Ballydehob, you can drive directly to Skibbereen or try a scenic side trip westward down the peninsula. First on the detour is Schull, a little village popular with fishermen and sailors; a deep-sea angling competition is held here in July and a regatta in August. Follow the road to Goleen, where the fine strand offers prime sunbathing, then press on to Crookhaven, a pretty harbor town with some small beaches. A few miles farther are the dramatic cliffs of Mizen Head, the southernmost point in Ireland.

Rather than backtrack, return to Schull and Ballydehob via the northern route across the peninsula, which passes Mt. Gabriel (1,339 feet) and the well-preserved castle of Dunmanus, one of the many 15th- and 16th-century strongholds that dot this part of the country.

 CHECKING IN: *Ard Na Greine* – On its own secluded grounds just a mile outside the village and harbor of Schull, this 18th-century farmhouse became a country inn during the 1970s. It's a delightful retreat, with 7 rooms (each with private bath), a seafood restaurant, a pub, and extensive gardens. Open April through October. Schull (phone: 28-28181). Expensive to moderate.

Barley Cove Beach – On a cliff overlooking the Atlantic, this complex includes 70 rooms and chalets (all with private bath), a heated indoor pool, a tennis court, fishing, and a 9-hole golf course. Barley Cove, near Goleen (phone: 28-35234). Expensive to moderate.

SKIBBEREEN: This town offers some first-rate fishing in the nearby Shepperton, Ballinlough, Lissard, and Ballyalla lakes (tackle and boats may be rented). It's also a convenient jumping-off point for exploring the shores and islands of the quaintly named Roaring Water Bay. Eight miles to the southwest, the little town of Baltimore has been one of Ireland's more popular ports of call for hundreds of years because of its sheltered harbor. There are fishing and boating here, and a ferry goes over to the Irish-speaking Cape Clear Island, which boasts megalithic stones, an ancient church, a bird observatory, and a youth hostel. There's also a ferry to Sherkin Island, with its ruins of a Franciscan friary and an *Outdoor Pursuits Centre,* which offers hiking, skin diving, riding, and boating.

En Route from Skibbereen – The drive along the coast road to Kinsale is very pretty and relaxing. Each small town has a particular attraction: Castletownshend's ruined castle and prehistoric stone fort are worth a look; Glandore offers good fishing; Rosscarbery is the site of a monastery established by St. Fachtna in the 6th century; Clonakilty, close to many fine beaches, is also the home of the *West Cork Regional Museum;* and the Franciscan abbey in Timoleague dates from the 14th century.

 CHECKING IN/EATING OUT: *Ardnavaha House* – About 5 miles north of Clonakilty, with 40 acres of woods, meadows, and gardens, this renovated Georgian manor house has a modern extension with 36 rooms, each with a private bath and balcony or terrace. It also has a restaurant, a heated outdoor pool, a sauna, a tennis court, and riding stables with arena. Open year-round. Ballinascarthy (phone: 23-49135). Expensive to moderate.

KINSALE: Clinging to a hill overlooking the Bandon River estuary, Kinsale is an appealing little town (population 2,000) whose tall, whitewashed houses huddle together along narrow, twisting lanes. A morning's stroll along the signposted walking tour takes visitors through the town's most charming streets and past St. Multose Church, an impressive stone structure dating from the 13th century; the Museum/Courthouse on Market Square; Desmond Castle, a 16th-century tower house on Cork St. (also known as the French Prison because Frenchmen were imprisoned there during the Napoleonic wars); and the Carmelite friary, dating from 1314, with its nearby ruins of a Holy Well.

On the outskirts of Kinsale are two magnificent old fortresses: James Fort, a perfect example of a 17th-century star design, was built in 1601; and Charles Fort, begun around 1677 but with many more recent additions, is also laid out on the star plan and was in use as a major harbor fortification until 1922.

The wide, sheltered harbor at Kinsale is one of the most scenic in Ireland, and since the building of a modern marina in 1979 it has become a favorite port with British and

European yachtsmen. Deep-sea fishing, off the Old Head of Kinsale, can be arranged — try the *Kinsale Marine Services Angling Centre* (Lower O'Connell St.; phone: 21-772611), or the *Trident Hotel Angling Centre* (*World's End;* phone: 21-772301) — and the swimming and sunning are very fine on the neighboring strands at Sandy Cove and James Fort. Another attraction is the town's growing reputation as the culinary capital of Ireland. For the town's size, it offers an extraordinary range of top class restaurants whose proprietors sponsor a *Gourmet Festival* every October. In recent years, Kinsale has also won recognition for its gardens (third place in the *European Entente Florale*) and for its overall appearance (top prizewinner in Ireland's *Tidy Town* competition).

Kinsale also provides an important footnote in Irish history, for it was here in 1601 that the Irish forces, led by the chieftains Hugh O'Neill and Hugh O'Donnell, suffered their final defeat at the hands of Queen Elizabeth I's army under Lord Mountjoy. In the annals of world history, this little village was also the focus of attention in May 1915, when the *Lusitania* was torpedoed and sunk off the Old Head of Kinsale with a loss of more than 1,500 lives.

CHECKING IN: *Acton's* – This member of the Trusthouse Forte hotel chain has a terrific location facing the harbor, extensive rose gardens, a seafood restaurant, a nautical tavern, and a leisure complex with swimming pool, saunas, sunbeds, and gymnasium. There are 55 rooms, each with private bath. The Waterfront, Kinsale (phone: 21-772135). Expensive.

***Blue Haven* –** In the middle of the village, this small, cozy hotel has 10 rooms (7 with private bath), some overlooking the main street and others facing the gardens in the rear. Each room is individually named and decorated with furnishings and paintings by local artisans. Extra touches include fresh flowers, coffee- and tea-makers, and mini-refrigerators. For fine dining, visit the hotel's acclaimed restaurant (see *Eating Out*). There is a homey breakfast room, a wood-paneled bar with an open fireplace, and a sunlit conservatory. Open year-round. Pearse St., Kinsale (phone: 21-772209). Expensive to moderate.

***Perryville House* –** Set in a Regency building, this small hotel at the edge of town offers 10 rooms with bath, a pleasant restaurant and bar, and views of the harbor. Open April through October. Long Quay, Kinsale (phone: 21-772731). Moderate.

***Trident* –** A modern concrete and glass structure of 40 bedrooms (each with private bath), this property is short on atmosphere but ideally situated right on the harbor, with a Kinsale version of a Fisherman's Wharf restaurant and a fishing and scuba diving center on the premises. Closed January and February. World's End, Kinsale (phone: 21-772301). Moderate.

EATING OUT: *Blue Haven* – In a town known for its fine restaurants, this is one of the best. Overlooking a garden of flowers and herbs, its decor is bright and airy, with Art Deco furnishings, ceiling fans, and a skylit, domed ceiling. Owners Brian and Anne Cronin have won many accolades over the years for such specialties as prawn tails with salmon mousse, lobster flambé, spring lamb in puff pastry, veal cordon bleu, duck baked in brandy, fish casseroles, and heaping platters of local catch of the day. The adjacent pub is known for its innovative light lunch items, from seafood quiche to salad and pasta. Pearse St., Kinsale (phone: 21-772209). Expensive to moderate.

***Cottage Loft* –** Originally on the edge of town and now in the heart of the action, this award-winning restaurant has all the warmth of an Irish hearth. Featuring a range of dishes from seafood kebab and sole on the bone to Peking pork and duck in black cherry sauce. 6 Main St., Kinsale (phone: 21-772803). Expensive to moderate.

***Man Friday* –** Beautifully situated in its own garden, this dining spot, another award winner, has a rustic decor and a menu ranging from prawns Napoleon and Polynesian chicken to shellfish *nouvelle*. Dinner only. Scilly, Kinsale (phone: 21-772260). Expensive to moderate.

Vintage – A small, vine-covered restaurant with beamed ceilings stands on a winding street near the harbor. The cooking is imaginative, with particular emphasis on local produce. Choices include *noisettes* of lamb, free-range duckling, medallions of monkfish, and Wiener schnitzel. Dinner only. Closed Sundays and January and February. Main St., Kinsale (phone: 21-772502). Expensive to moderate.

Bernard's – The emphasis is on new Irish cuisine, served in a modern bistro setting, with entrées ranging from wild rabbit in cider and chicken stuffed with oysters to a medley of salmon and sole or Kinsale bouillabaisse. Main St. at Emmet Pl., Kinsale (phone: 21-772233). Moderate.

Max's Wine Bar – Tiny but busy, this bistro serves simple meals — salad, soup, oysters, and good lasagna. Open for lunch and dinner, March through September. Main St., Kinsale (phone: 21-772443). Inexpensive.

SHARING A PINT: Kinsale is also well known for its assortment of lively public houses. Try the *Greyhound* or the *Anchor* for pub grub or the *Dock* (Castle Park) for memorable views of Kinsale's inner harbor. Pubs known for their music and entertainment include the *Spaniard* (Scilly), *Shanakee,* and *Folk House* (Guardwell). Other pubs as intriguing as their names are the *White House* (Pearce St.), *Hole in the Wall, Silver Salmon, Cuckoo's Nest,* and *Lord Kingsale.*

En Route from Kinsale – From Kinsale, it's just 18 miles back to Cork City. Any of several routes will do; R600, the most direct, passes by Cork Airport.

The Ring of Kerry

Artists and writers have for centuries celebrated the beauty of the kingdom of Kerry, where the majesty of Ireland's highest mountains contrasts starkly with romantic glens, and the splendor of the rugged coastline gives way to glorious lakes and luxurious forests. It is a landscape of great variety, with the sea and the ever-changing patterns in the sky as much a part of the vistas as the primordial shapes of solid ground or the seasonal come-and-go of blossoming bushes, trees, and green ground cover. A good portion of this southwestern county is made up of three peninsulas that constitute Kerry at its picturesque best: Dingle, Iveragh, and Beara, the latter shared largely with County Cork (see *West Cork,* DIRECTIONS).

The best known of these mountainous projections into the Atlantic is the middlemost one, the Iveragh Peninsula, circled by a much promoted scenic route known as the Ring of Kerry. Browse through a brochure of bus tours of the Emerald Isle, and a day trip around the Ring will rarely be missing. Nor will a stop in Killarney, both the gateway to the Iveragh Peninsula and the focal point of this district of mountains, lakes, and valleys that would put it on the map even if the Ring happened to be nowhere handy.

An air of remoteness still clings to Iveragh, in tiny fishing villages where Irish is still widely spoken and in ancient stones left behind by forgotten peoples. Ascetic monks who withdrew as far as they could from the world built their retreat on Skellig Michael, today a deserted site attracting only the extremely inquisitive. George Bernard Shaw remarked, "No experience that the conventional tourist travel can bring you will stick in your memory so strangely; for Skellig Michael is not after the fashion of this world."

The complete circuit of the peninsula — which extends nearly 40 miles southwest of Killarney and has an average breadth of 15 miles — is an approximately 110-mile round trip that will take most of one day to see in a leisurely way. It is possible to do it counterclockwise as described here (from Killarney to Killorglin and around) or clockwise (from Killarney to Kenmare and around), but the former route is suggested because some of the scenery is seen to best advantage in that direction. (Tour buses take the same route, so as to be on the inside of the sharp curves in the often narrow road.) Do not attempt this scenic run if there is a sea mist, because visibility will be very poor, or during heavy and continuous rain — though the latter seldom lasts more than half a day. If in doubt, get a weather report by calling the Valencia Meteorological Station (phone: 667-2176).

If plans include a night's stay or two on the Ring, estimate that a double room in lodgings classified as very expensive will cost $150 to $250; in the expensive category, $100 to $140 or more; in the moderate category, $60 to $99; and under $60 for an inexpensive room. Dinner for two without wine will be $80 and up in an expensive restaurant, $45 to $75 in a moderate one, and $40 or less in an inexpensive place.

KILLARNEY: For a complete report on the city, its sights, hotels, and restaurants, see *Killarney,* THE CITIES.

En Route from Killarney – To begin the counterclockwise route, take R562 north-west to Killorglin. The jagged mountains to the left are MacGillicuddy's Reeks, reduced to stumps by 200 million years of ruthless erosion but crowned nonetheless by the highest peak in Ireland, Carrantuohill (3,414 feet). Eight miles from Killarney, make a left turn at the signpost for Ballymalis Castle, on the banks of the river Laune. This is one of a line of castles originally built by the Anglo-Normans when they overran the area in the early 13th century. The present castle — partly restored — is a typical 16th-century tower house of 4 stories: the ground floor for storage, the second for defense, the third for sleeping, and the top, a single, splendid living room. Return to R562 and continue the remaining 5 miles into Killorglin.

KILLORGLIN: The presence of another Anglo-Norman castle, now almost totally ruined, gave rise to this small town on the river Laune. Killorglin is famous for its *Puck Fair,* actually a 3-day horse, sheep, and cattle sale, accompanied by unrestricted merrymaking. Held every year from August 10 to 12, it is the area's greatest festival and draws people from all over County Kerry. On the first day, called *Gathering Day,* men of the town go into the mountains and capture the "puck," or wild male goat, who is then decorated with ribbons and enthroned on a platform above the town square, from which he presides over the festivities until *Scattering Day,* the end of the fair. In the meantime, shops are open day and night. The *Puck Fair* has been going on for a long time, but its origins are uncertain. It may date from the worship of the Celtic god Lúg, or it may be an upstart from the 17th century, when a herd of wild goats stampeded through the town ahead of approaching Cromwellian soldiers and thereby saved many lives.

 EATING OUT: *Nick's* – Located in an old stone house in the center of town, this award-winning spot offers hearty pub soup, sandwiches, and light meals by day and full dinner fare at night. Specialties range from game and vegetarian dishes, to local seafoods including fresh lobster. The decor is cozy with alcoves and an open fireplace. Lower Bridge St., Killorglin (phone: 66-61219). Moderate.

En Route from Killorglin – Continue southwest on N70 for 9 miles to Glenbeigh. Along the way, the road passes Lough Caragh on the left. Surrounded by magnificent scenery, it is definitely worth a detour. (There is one viewing point at the parking place up the rough road and another at the end of the path leading to the top of the hill.)

 CHECKING IN: *Ard na Sidhe* – Elegant, quiet, and beautifully secluded in the forest at Lough Caragh. Once a private home, it now has 20 rooms, each with private bath. To find *Ard na Sidhe* (Irish for "hill of the fairies"), look for the signs on N70 between Killorglin and Glenbeigh. Open May through September. Killorglin (phone: 66-69105). Expensive to moderate.

GLENBEIGH: This tiny holiday and fishing resort is situated at the foot of Seefin Mountain (1,621 feet), not far from where the river Behy flows out into Dingle Bay. One of Ireland's oldest golf courses, *Dooks,* overlooks the bay (to play, call the secretary at 66-68205). The Glenbeigh Horseshoe, a semicircle of hills from Seefin to Drung Hill, is known to nature lovers as one of the county's most scenic mountain walks. At the end of the village are the gaunt — and burnt — ruins of Glenbeigh Towers, or "Wynne's Folly," built by the local landlord, Lord Headley Wynne, during the 1870s. Wynne sued his English architect (who kept the actress Ellen Terry as his mistress during the construction) for cost overruns and faulty construction.

A right turn onto an unclassified road beyond Glenbeigh leads, in 1½ miles, to

Rossbeigh Strand, a long spit of land reaching into Dingle Bay to nearly meet its counterpart, Inch Strand, coming across the water from the Dingle Peninsula. The 2 miles of sand beach are backed by dunes, and at the end of the spit is a 19th-century stone tower built to guide ships into Castlemaine Harbour. During the 18th century, many transatlantic ships, driven by terrifying southwest storms, met their end at Rossbeigh, sometimes helped, it is said, by shipwreckers greedy for their cargo.

Also remembered in the area are much more remote incidents connected with the Fenian cycle of Irish legends. Ossian, the son of Finn MacCool (the leader of the Fianna, a sort of standing army of the Iron Age), had met the beautiful, golden-haired Niamh, who persuaded him to return with her to her own kingdom. Together the pair mounted the girl's white horse and galloped out along the Rossbeigh spit into the western ocean to the paradisiacal Land of Youth. Ossian came back 300 years later, but once off the horse he immediately turned into a very old man. Another legend is that of Diarmuid and Grainne, daughter of the King of Ireland, who was betrothed to Finn, whom she found too old. Instead, she forced Diarmuid, a handsome young Kerryman, to elope with her. With a gang of murderous desperadoes (hired by Finn) in hot pursuit, they fled — first to a cave at Glenbeigh. The chase lasted 7 years, and eventually Diarmuid was killed by a magic boar and Grainne did marry Finn. In popular speech, many Irish prehistoric tombs are still called "beds of Diarmuid and Grainne."

CHECKING IN/EATING OUT: *Towers* – A hotel and restaurant that specializes in seafood at night and hearty pub lunches during the day. Lodgings consist of 22 refurbished rooms, each with bath. A new wing with 12 rooms, offering views of the countryside and water, is expected to open in late spring. Closed November to March. Glenbeigh (phone: 66-68212). Moderate.

En Route from Glenbeigh – The main road to Cahirciveen, 17 miles away, encompasses some of the most memorable scenery along the Ring of Kerry. The road rises to Mountain Stage, so called because it was once a station for stagecoaches and it hugs the side of Drung Hill (2,104 feet), providing wonderful views of Dingle Bay and the mountains of the Dingle Peninsula beyond. A cairn near the top of Drung Hill is reputed to be the grave of St. Finian, a major leader of the great religious movement of the 6th and 7th centuries. The road continues high over the sea to Kells, a small resort on Kells Bay, where it descends to a broad valley running on to Cahirciveen. A mile before the town, just beyond the sharp turn left indicated by a series of striking yellow arrows, are the ruins of Carhan House. Daniel O'Connell, the national leader known as the Liberator, who achieved emancipation for Irish Catholics, was born here in 1775.

CAHIRCIVEEN: Set on the river Valencia at the head of Valencia Harbour, Cahirciveen grew up in the early 19th century. Its most notable building is the O'Connell Memorial Church on Main Street, which was intended to honor the centenary of Daniel O'Connell's birth in 1775, but construction was not begun until 1888 when the cornerstone, sent by Pope Leo XIII from the catacombs in Rome, was laid. Across the bridge, about 2½ miles northwest of town, are the remains of Ballycarbery Castle, the magnificent 15th-century castle of MacCarthy Mor, guarded by the old Gaelic O'Connell family. Cromwell's forces destroyed the castle in 1652 and drove the O'Connells to County Clare, though they later returned to the area (a junior member eventually moved to Derrynane). The ruins of an ancient stone fort, Cahergal, are nearby, and another, Leacanabuaile, is a few hundred yards away. The latter, dating from the 9th or 10th century, is one of very few stone forts to have been excavated. Inside, the remains of three stone beehive houses, once occupied by a very poor farming community, were found, along with a square house apparently added later. Note the *souterrain,* originally an escape hatch, a place of refuge, and also a place for storage.

Valencia Harbour was well known in the 18th century as a smuggling port and hiding place for privateers. British naval vessels often anchored here too, but the smugglers earned their tolerance with judicious gifts of brandy. Valencia Island is in the harbor, joined to the mainland by a bridge at Portmagee (there's a good view of the harbor from the bridge).

VALENCIA ISLAND: The inhabitants of this tiny island (7 miles long and 2 to 3 miles wide) live by fishing, farming, and some tourism — the sea fishing is especially good and so are the views from its steep cliffs. The island is one of the most westerly points in Europe, and the first transatlantic telegraph cable, which came to Valencia in 1866, remained in use for 100 years. Knightstown, at Valencia's eastern end, consists of one main street, a lovely harbor and waterfront, and is a popular holiday resort renowned for its deep-sea fishing. The old Western Union cable office is also in Knightstown.

En Route from Cahirciveen – The Ring of Kerry route, N70, turns inland across the tip of the Iveragh Peninsula to Waterville, 11 miles away. Three detours along the way are possible: to Valencia Island (where there's good deep-sea fishing), to the offshore monastic site of Skellig Michael, and to the tiny village of Ballinskelligs on Ballinskelligs Bay. The turnoff for Portmagee and the bridge to Valencia Island is 4 miles southwest of Cahirciveen onto R565, and the turnoff for Ballinskelligs is 2 miles beyond that onto R566. Skellig Michael, one of the Skellig Rocks, can be reached by boat from Portmagee or Valencia Island, but only when the weather permits.

SKELLIG ROCKS: These two small islands, actually pyramids of rock, are 7 and 8½ miles off the coast of Bolus Head. Little Skellig (445 feet high), the smaller of the two and all but inaccessible even by boat, is a bird sanctuary with thousands of seabirds, especially gannets, nesting on its precipitous stone peaks. Bird life — puffins, razorbills, kittiwakes, gannets, and more — is also abundant on Great Skellig (714 feet), or Skellig Michael, but this island is better known for the remains of the simple monastic settlement that existed here for 6 centuries. Founded, according to tradition, by St. Fionan and occupied by hermit monks between the 6th and the 12th century, the monastery has survived in almost perfect condition, probably because of the absence of frost in this mild westerly climate. The ruins, on a rock shelf 550 feet above the sea, consist of six beehive huts, intact and of advanced construction; two oratories evolving into the boat-shaped style that would be used at Gallarus on the Dingle Peninsula; a ruined medieval church; crosses and graves; even tiny patches of imported earth behind retaining walls, where the monks may have attempted to grow something to vary their diet of seaweed, birds, and fish. Three steep stone stairways, corresponding to the three separate landing places whose use once varied according to weather conditions, lead to the settlement. Boats for Skellig Michael leave only if the weather is suitable — a calm day, when the wind is not coming from the east. The trip takes 1½ hours from Portmagee, the point of departure closest to the island (the trip can also be made from Knightstown on Valencia Island and from Bunavalla, below Coomakista, farther along the Ring of Kerry). Allow at least 3 hours for exploration in addition to the 3 hours' travel time. The climb to the monastery by the most common route consists of more than 600 steps, but the site, which must have been terrifying in fierce Atlantic storms, is extraordinarily evocative and beautiful — well worth the effort. For information about a boat trip, contact *Des Lavelle* (phone: 667-6124).

BALLINSKELLIGS: The blessing of a 4-mile beach along the western shore of Ballinskelligs Bay has made this tiny, partly Irish-speaking village a seaside resort. It is part of the Kerry Gaeltacht, and in the summer an Irish language school for children is conducted here. The ruins of a 16th-century MacCarthy castle are west of town, not far from the remains of an Augustinian monastery that was probably founded in the 12th or 13th century by monks returning from the monastic settlement of Skellig Michael. The ruins date from the 15th century and have been much eroded by the sea.

En Route from Ballinskelligs – Follow the signposts back to N70 and Waterville; the right turn onto the main route 6 miles northeast of Ballinskelligs is just above the bridge over the river Inny, 2 miles north of Waterville.

WATERVILLE: This small, unspoiled village lies on a strip of land between the Atlantic Ocean and beautiful Lough Currane, on the eastern shore of Ballinskelligs Bay. Mountains rise from the east and south of the lake, which contains several islands. In addition to Lough Currane, there are many smaller lakes in the vicinity. With all this water, it is hardly surprising that Waterville is a famous angling center. Fishing for salmon, sea trout, and brown trout is free on Lough Currane and some of the smaller lakes and by permit (available from any of the hotels) on still other lakes and the river Inny. No aquatic pursuit is ignored: Boating and bathing are available on the fine sandy beach on the bay shore. Resolute landlubbers can play golf on Waterville's exhilarating championship seaside course; for details contact the *Club Med* (see *Checking In*).

Many early Christian remains — stone forts, religious settlements, beehive huts, and old roadways — are scattered around Lough Currane, and the ruins of a 12th-century Romanesque church can be found on a small island in the lake, Church Island (reachable by boat, which can be hired in Waterville). Waterville and Ballinskelligs Bay figure in many legends. According to one, Noah's son and granddaughter landed here after having been excluded from the Ark. According to another, the alignment of four stones on the skyline to the left of the road 1 mile south of town is the burial place of Scéné, wife of one of the eight leaders of the Milesians in the last, and greatest, of the legendary invasions of Ireland.

 CHECKING IN: *Butler Arms* – A well-known fishing hotel in town, this rambling, crenelated white house has been run by the same family for three generations and was a favorite haunt of Charlie Chaplin. Its restaurant, specializing in shellfish, is quite good. The 29 rooms, all with bath, are open April through October. Waterville (phone: 667-4144). Expensive.

Club Med – Formerly the *Waterville Lake* hotel, this establishment, recently acquired by Club Med, is situated on the outer reaches of the Ring of Kerry, bordered on one side by the Atlantic and on the other by Lough Currane. As we went to press, renovations and expansion were under way on the 50-room property. Existing facilities (which will be enhanced) include a restaurant, an 18-hole championship golf course (the first in Ireland to offer electric carts), a heated indoor swimming pool, a thermal spa pool, a sauna, and a solarium. Waterville (phone: 667-4133). Expensive.

 EATING OUT: *Huntsman* – Furnished with dark oak priory tables and chairs, wrought-iron fixtures, and colorful hanging plants, this restaurant, owned by its chef, provides lovely waterside views with its seafood delights. Open daily for lunch, dinner, and light snacks from noon to 10 PM; closed November through March. Waterville (phone: 667-4124). Expensive to moderate.

Smuggler's – The chef-owner of this renovated farmhouse, with nautical decor and panoramic views, offers seafood specialties such as lobster Newburg, as well as meat and poultry dishes, for lunch and dinner. Selections from an extensive bar menu are also available. Open daily, noon to 11:30 PM for meals. There also are 10 rooms for overnight guests. Cliff Rd., Waterville (phone: 667-4330). Restaurant, expensive to moderate; guestrooms, inexpensive.

En Route from Waterville – Traveling south on N70, the road winds up to a height of 700 feet at the pass of Coomakista, affording superb views of the sharply rising (to 1,600 feet) inland mountains on one side and the lonely Skellig Rocks beyond the mouth of the bay on the other side, out in the open Atlantic. The road then descends in the direction of Derrynane Bay, separated from Ballinskelligs Bay by a point of land called Hog's Head and from the river Kenmare by another point called Lamb's Head. (Even though the river Kenmare is an arm of the sea extending inland as far as Kenmare and is in places as much as 5 or 6 miles wide, only occasionally is it called Kenmare Bay.) Before the village of Caherdaniel, a signposted road to the right leads to *Derrynane House,* ancestral home of the O'Connell family, with a magnificent beach to the front and a more sheltered beach at the side. The O'Connells were a shrewd Irish family who lived by smuggling, importing embargoed goods, and exporting young Catholic Irishmen so they could obtain European educations and jobs denied them at home. Daniel O'Connell, the first Irish Catholic member of Britain's Parliament, inherited the Derrynane property from an uncle and lived here during his political life, often holding consultations on the lawn with troubled constituents, who gathered from miles around to speak to him. The house has now been restored and is open daily year-round as a museum (admission charge), with O'Connell's personal possessions and furniture on display. It is part of Derrynane National Historic Park, which also includes a nature trail through lovely scenery.

Next along the route, near the shore of Derrynane Bay, is Caherdaniel, which takes its name from a stone fort or *caher,* possibly of the 6th century, a short distance outside the village. Near it are the ruins of a much older fort and what seems to be an ancient road system used some 4,000 years ago to link copper mines in the mountains above with the harbor at Derrynane. The route continues along the coast toward the small resort of Castlecove. Just before the village, a signpost points the way to the left for Staigue Fort, 2½ miles off the main road, beautifully positioned at the top of a valley that stretches to the sea.

STAIGUE FORT: Nothing is known of the history of this circular stone fort, which could date as far back as 1000 BC. Though such forts are plentiful in the area, Staigue is one of the largest and most sophisticated, a masterly example of dry-stone construction (no mortar is used). It is also one of the best preserved of all ancient Irish structures. Little has been lost of the wall, which is up to 18 feet high on the north and west sides and 13 feet thick at the base and is scaled by sets of steps up to a long-gone rampart. The area enclosed is 90 feet in diameter but contains no signs of houses, as at Leacanabuaile, leading to speculation that the fort — which has yet to be excavated — may have been occupied by nobility. During the Iron Age, the poor lived in stone houses; royalty and aristocracy rated perishable wooden ones. Admire the quality of the fort's stonework, the sloping back of the walls, the massive lintels, and especially the architectural flourish of the steps inside. On the way back to Castlecove, look for a stone bridge with two spans on the left — apparently in a field going nowhere — part of an old road system. Close by is an exposed rock with copperworkers' scribings.

En Route from Staigue Fort – About half a mile beyond Castlecove village, an unnumbered road branches off the main road to White Strand, a particularly pleasant beach with beautiful views and good bathing. The main road then bends inland to Sneem, 13 miles from Caherdaniel, climbing through a low pass where there is a fine panorama of the Sneem valley, with its great backdrop of mountains stretching as far as MacGillicuddy's Reeks, just dimly to be seen, beside Killarney. The glacial basins, or corries, in the mountains on the left were scooped out during the Ice Age, and antiquities of the Bronze and Iron ages — old fields, roads, settlements, standing and scribed stones — are scattered around them.

SNEEM: With its pink, green, bright red, robin's-egg blue, and even checkered houses freshly painted each year, this is a very colorful and pretty village at the head of the river Sneem estuary. The town is divided in two by the river and has two village greens. Just before the narrow bridge between them, note the tiny Protestant church on the left, with its curiously Elizabethan air, a piece of 18th-century antiquarianism. Because Sneem is in fishing country (trout and salmon abound in the river and nearby mountain lakes), the church's weathervane sports a salmon. Stop just after the bridge to look at the river tumbling over the rocks below, usually quite gently, but spectacularly after a heavy rain. Just beyond is the very attractive 19th-century Italianate Catholic church on the right. The *Blue Bull* — a pleasant country pub and restaurant — is a good stopping place, if only for a quick drink.

 EATING OUT: *Blue Bull* – A charming pub with three different rooms, each decorated with fascinating old prints of County Kerry scenes, and, appropriately, a straw blue bull's head as its centerpiece. In summer, a back room becomes a seafood restaurant, and there's music on most weekends throughout the year. Sneem (phone: 64-45231). Restaurant, moderate; pub, inexpensive.

En Route from Sneem – The Ring of Kerry route turns southeast toward the shore of the river Kenmare. A mile down the road, a detour signposted "Oyster Bed" (so called because oysters thrive here) leads down to a pier where the weary can savor the calm of a garden spot before returning to the main road and driving the remaining mile to Parknasilla. Known for its lush trees, shrubs, and beautiful seascape, Parknasilla owes its subtropical vegetation to its position in a sheltered curve of coastline backed by the 895-foot Knockanamadane Hill. The *Great Southern* hotel (see *Checking In/Eating Out*), on the grounds of the onetime summer home of Charles Graves, Protestant Bishop of Limerick and grandfather of the poet Robert Graves, was a favorite holiday place of George Bernard Shaw. From Parknasilla, N70 runs east toward the upper end of the river Kenmare at Kenmare. Beyond Blackwater Bridge, in a forest on the right, is Dromore Castle, the seat of an old Gaelic family, the O'Mahonys, and the subject of a haunting lullaby. Also on the right, on a rock 2 miles out of Kenmare, are the ruins of Dunkerron Castle, a stronghold of the O'Sullivan family, branches of which occupied both sides of the river Kenmare from the early 13th century, until they were driven out by the Cromwellians in the 17th century.

 CHECKING IN/EATING OUT: *Great Southern* – George Bernard Shaw stayed here at least twice a year for almost 15 years; more recently, Juliana, former Queen of the Netherlands, has been a guest. This luxury hotel (not to be confused with Killarney's *Great Southern*), built in 1896 on the verdant grounds of a former private estate, is carefully and splendidly done in Victorian style, while amenities are up to the minute. There are 60 rooms, each with private bath, a private 9-hole golf course for guests, a heated indoor swimming pool, and fishing or boating on the bay. The food is very good. Closed November through March. Parknasilla (phone: 64-45122). Very expensive to expensive.

KENMARE: This attractive town sits in a limestone niche, surrounded by old red sandstone, at the point where the river Roughty runs into the head of the sea inlet known as the river Kenmare. The location makes it an ideal base for touring either the Iveragh Peninsula to the north or the Beara Peninsula to the south. Kenmare is a planned landlord's town, laid out according to the instructions of the first Marquess of Lansdowne in 1775. A number of houses are built of the local limestone, and there is a fine Roman Catholic church with striking roof timbers. Next to it is the Convent of the Poor Clares, founded in 1861 and well known because of its lacemaking school; the famous point lace and other types produced here are on display daily. The town's oldest monument, the Druid's Circle, is beautifully set on the banks of the river Finnihy on the outskirts of the town and dates from the time of the Beaker folk, copper miners who arrived from Spain 4,000 years ago. This is a circle of 15 stones with a large boulder in the center, an example of a form frequent in and mainly confined to this peninsula. Such circles were places of worship but may also have had secular, ceremonial use as well as astronomical significance — and there is some evidence that human sacrifice was practiced in them.

Kenmare shares the mild climate common to the south coast, and the subtropical foliage evident at Parknasilla is to be seen here, too. There is bathing in the sheltered coves west of the town, extensive salmon and trout fishing, and opportunity for deep-sea fishing.

CHECKING IN: *Park* – Widely acclaimed as one of the country's finest hotels, it is on its own palm tree–lined grounds on Kenmare Bay, just at the edge of the village. Guests are greeted like royalty as they sit down to register at an antique stockbroker's desk in the lobby. There are 50 rooms, each with private bath, including 6 master suites with four-poster beds, hand-carved armoires, and other elegant furnishings. The award-winning restaurant, with romantic bay views on long summer days and candlelight in winter, specializes in seafood, especially salmon and shellfish. Amenities include tennis, croquet, 11 acres of gardens, and an adjacent 9-hole golf course. Open April through January 1. Kenmare (phone: 64-41200). Very expensive.

Kenmare Bay – Located on the outskirts of town, this hotel has 100 airy, modern rooms, a pleasant bar, and a good restaurant. Traditional music and dancing are offered in the lounge on most summer evenings. Closed November through February. Sneem Rd., Kenmare (phone: 64-41300). Moderate.

Hawthorn House – A modern 2-story village home with attractive gardens, this superior bed and breakfast establishment is operated by the Browne family. Each of the 8 bedrooms has a private bath, and an individual name and decor reflecting a different aspect of County Kerry. Open year-round. Shelbourne St. (phone: 64-41035). Inexpensive.

EATING OUT: *Lime Tree* – An old (1821) stone schoolhouse is the setting for one of Kenmare's most highly acclaimed restaurants, next to the grounds of the *Park* hotel. Diners have a choice of the cozy downstairs area, with its warming fireplace, or the skylit gallery overhead. On both levels, paintings by modern Irish artists line the walls. The menu ranges from poached monkfish, trout *almondine,* or fish mousse to rack of lamb with spicy plum sauce. Open April through October. Shelbourne St. (phone: 64-41225). Expensive to moderate.

Star – A modern, bungalow-style restaurant on the edge of town, it serves steaks and seafood as well as a variety of daily specials, such as pan-fried Dover sole, lobster Newburg, and baked filet of lamb. Open daily except Tuesdays for lunch and dinner, April through October. Sneem Rd., Kenmare (phone: 64-41099). Moderate.

Purple Heather Bistro – Seafood is the specialty of the house, with snacks and meals served in the comfortable bar. Open noon to 6:30 PM except Sundays. Henry St., Kenmare (phone: 64-41016). Moderate to inexpensive.

En Route from Kenmare – Upon reaching Kenmare, travelers will have covered 90 miles of the Ring of Kerry route, excluding detours. From here, the most direct road back to Killarney, a distance of 21 miles, is N71 north, which winds over the mountains through Moll's Gap and via Ladies View, a lookout point with a panorama of the wonderful lakes of Killarney that is supposed to have gotten its name because it particularly pleased Queen Victoria's ladies-in-waiting. As alternatives, it's possible to turn south to Glengarriff or west to Coornagillagh and Lauragh for a tour of the Beara Peninsula (see *West Cork,* DIRECTIONS).

Connemara and the Aran Islands

There's scarcely any other part of Ireland where it is possible to be so intimately in touch with the Irish past as in Connemara, that ancient Gaelic kingdom of bogland and mountains that stretches across west Galway to the rocky rim of the wild Atlantic. It is a domain much removed from the modern world, a haunted, mystical land, where some kind of time warp seems to have halted the passage of time.

Most Connemara people still speak the ancient Erse language. Now called Irish, it is the mother tongue that is nearly extinct in other parts of Ireland. Connemara is home to Ireland's biggest Gaeltacht — a region where Irish is the everyday language. But the reality nowadays is that most of the population here, particularly the young, are bilingual, fluent in both Irish and English; with English emerging as the international medium of communication, the preservation of the Irish tongue is increasingly threatened. The mother tongue does live, however, and any visitor going into Connemara who has taken the trouble to learn a few Irish phrases will win an appreciative, warm welcome and won't go short of a drink.

It isn't merely the language that causes the echoes of bygone days to ring plangently through the glens and mountains of Connemara. This rugged and tempestuous land is a rich repository of many facets of the Celtic past. The brooding presence of Ireland's ancient culture and tradition is everywhere, as are vestiges of a way of life that was common to all European peasant societies many centuries ago.

Since those great mountains were sculpted against the western Irish sky and those glens were chiseled deep into the earth, the Connemara landscape has hardly changed, and humankind has barely fixed its stamp on it. It is a stark and unyielding place that has shaped its people into strong, independent individuals with a stoic and earthy eye to the rest of the world.

The land was always begrudging, requiring a fierce will to make it yield even a beggarly subsistence. But the Connemara peasants farmed every arable crevice of flinty earth. In the old days, they lived off potatoes, and when the horrendous potato blight fell upon Ireland during the 1840s, they suffered more than most others during the famine that followed. Thousands died in their thatch-roofed hovels or out in the stony fields and wild bogs, and thousands more fled westward to the shores of "Amerikay." Since then, the region has been sparsely populated, the drain of young people continuing through emigration until today, when industrialization has finally slowed the once inevitable flight from this barren land.

The sea is the other mighty element with which Connemara people continuously wrestle, and their battles have inspired such writers as John Millington Synge and Liam O'Flaherty to powerful prose and poetry. Until recent times, Connemara fishermen rode the Atlantic breakers in fragile *curraghs* to farm the sea. (The *curragh* is a boat of undefinable vintage that originally was made from hides but now is sheathed in tarred canvas.) It is still possible to see *curraghs,* powered by sinew and oar, off the Connemara coast today. They look like black scimitar blades knifing through the waves, seemingly frail and vulnerable but in fact ingeniously crafted to ride out the angriest of storms. They are still widely used by the Aran Islanders.

If at all possible, a visit to Connemara should include a side trip to the Aran Islands. Stripped bare of trees by the Atlantic winds, these three rocky outcrops sit west of the mainland, facing the open mouth of Galway Bay, their isolation helping to preserve ancient traditions: Much of the primeval peasant lifestyle remains intact on the islands — including the clothes worn by the old people. The biggest island, Inishmore, which attracts the preponderance of visitors, is developing some cynical commercial instincts, but the other two, Inishmaan and Inisheer, still almost totally maintain the ambience of an earlier age.

The rapidly developing technologies of the 20th century are only now taking root in Connemara. There are at last factories providing jobs for the young people so that they no longer are inevitably forced onto emigrant ships. The fishing industry is gradually progressing beyond the *curragh* age. These developments, whether welcome or not, have brought a measure of affluence to the land. The old thatch-roofed cottages, with their lime-washed stone walls, are coming down to be replaced by rather alien-looking "mod-con" (that is, "modern convenience") bungalows.

But in Connemara the elemental link between humans, the earth, and the sea is still a force. The old ways survive, and people often face nature with tools that are not much further advanced than those used at the dawn of civilization. Somehow humans seem inconsequential out there on the Connemara landscape, with its great gnarled mountains rearing into the sky, lone and level bogs blending into desolate horizons, rivers racing toward the freedom of the sea, and valleys secluded from the outside world.

Our route starts in Galway City and heads northwest into Connemara territory. The road coils in a serpentine circle through valleys and mountains, at times verging the Atlantic and going through most of the untamed and rugged areas of unsurpassed beauty that have made Connemara famous. The route circles back along the edge of Galway Bay to return to Galway City and then shoves off for the Aran Islands.

An opening word of utmost caution: The roads here are, for the most part, narrow, winding, and roughly surfaced, and Irish drivers often display an unnervingly cavalier attitude at the wheel. So drive slowly, keep very much to the *left,* and at all times be prepared to encounter horse carts, flocks of sheep, or herds of cattle around that next bend.

A double room in a hotel listed as expensive will cost $80 to $100 and up per night; a room listed as moderate will cost $50 to $70. Dinner for two (with wine) in the moderate category will run $30 to $40; a dinner listed as expensive will cost $50 or more.

GALWAY CITY: For a complete report on the city, its sights, restaurants, and hotels, see *Galway City,* THE CITIES.

En Route from Galway City – Take N59 to the village of Oughterard (pronounced *Ook*-ther-ard), 17 miles away. This road runs almost parallel to Lough Corrib, a marvelous fishing lake that is on the right all the way to Oughterard. Most of the side roads to the right lead to the lakeshore, and it is easy enough to hire rowboats or power boats for pleasure trips or for fishing (see "Sources and Resources," *Galway City,* THE CITIES).

OUGHTERARD: At Oughterard, stop off to visit the 16th-century Aughnanure Castle, which is 2 miles southeast of the town (a signpost points the way). It was the redoubt of the ferocious O'Flaherty tribe, who exhibited a sense of hospitality similar to that of the Borgias, once dispatching a dinner guest through a flagstone trap door into the river beneath the banquet hall. The castle has been restored.

But angling is the life and soul of Oughterard. Wander into any of the pubs or hotels and the conversation inevitably concerns the great terminological inexactitudes of fishing lore. Angling tourists from all over Europe come here to pursue the trout and salmon of Lough Corrib, and the fish landed sometimes have been known to be even more immense than the ones that got away. Stop by *Keogh's* emporium (Bridge St., the main street; phone: 91-82212), buy or rent a rod and creel, and get onto the lake for great thrills.

One period of the year, about mid-May, is known as the "carnival of the trout." At this time, great clouds of newly hatched mayflies hover over the lake, and the trout go mad for them. Anglers capture masses of the mayflies, impale them on hooks, and "dap" them on the surface of the water with the aid of a special fishing line; the trout all but come out with their hands up.

 CHECKING IN: *Cloonabinnia House* – Built in the style of a large Swiss chalet, this hotel overlooking Lough Corrib is immensely popular with anglers from all over Europe. It has 14 comfortable rooms and excellent food. Eight miles from Galway City on N59, signposted right turn (phone: 91-85555). Expensive.

Connemara Gateway – A classy, modern motel with 62 comfortable rooms, an outdoor swimming pool, attractive gardens, and a commendable restaurant featuring some homemade specialties. The staff is extremely friendly. On the main road from Galway City, just before entering Oughterard (phone: 91-82328). Expensive.

Corrib – On the main street of Oughterard, this small, delightfully old-fashioned hostelry is famous for its salmon and trout dishes. Bridge St., Oughterard (phone: 91-82329 or 91-82204). Expensive.

Currarevagh House – An aristocratic home on Lough Corrib has been converted into a peaceful and relaxing guesthouse. Open April to October. Reservations necessary. Second right turn on entering Oughterard, signposted for the 4 miles to the lakeside. Oughterard (phone: 91-82312, or 91-82313). Expensive.

EATING OUT: *Drimcong House* – An elegant old country house serves as the backdrop for one of Ireland's best restaurants. Like the decor, the food is elegant yet unpretentious, and the service super-efficient yet unobtrusive. Specialties include excellent wild game, spiced beef, salmon, and oysters. It is a dining experience not to be missed. One mile north of Moycullen village on N59 (phone: 91-85115). Expensive.

Boat Inn – Fresh fish from the nearby Lough Corrib and the Atlantic are the outstanding features of an excellent menu in this friendly tavern. The Square, Oughterard (phone: 91-82196). Moderate.

En Route from Oughterard – Still traveling northwest on N59, you are beginning to move into Connemara, but in this particular area the Irish language is rarely heard. The Gaeltacht areas are much farther. The land beyond Oughterard is desolate and bare, though in a valley to the left are a number of small lakes. Ten miles out, at Maam Cross, turn right onto L100, a very precarious road that must be negotiated carefully — *very* carefully — on the way into the lonely valley of Maam.

When Orson Welles passed this way at the age of 17 — long before becoming the enfant terrible of American radio, stage, and screen — he came riding on a donkey, probably the very best way to travel here. Motorists should stop often and get out and sit on a rock or a stone bridge, just to immerse themselves in the atmosphere or maybe talk to a passing farmer. There is also much to see *above* the land itself. Look upward, if only because generations of artists have come from many lands to do just that in Connemara. Unless there is heavy sea mist or fog or impenetrable overcast, the sky above Connemara is a living mural of constantly changing cloud patterns, with an astonishing interplay of light, color, and shadow, never for a moment the same and always a source of impassioned inspiration and agonizing frustration for painters.

Five miles beyond, at Maam Bridge, turn left to head toward the village of Leenane, 9 miles away. This is the heart of the Maam valley, with the craggy Maumturk Mountains that dominate the Joyce Country (see below) on the left and the hills of south Mayo to the right. There are two diversions worth pursuing here: From Maam Bridge, take a road south into the Joyce Country to the hill of Maumeen, where legend says St. Patrick slept and where a sacred well named after him is still a place of pilgrimage. It is just 10 miles away amid magnificent mountain country. Alternately, 5 miles along the road to Leenane, turn right at the signpost for Lough Nafooey, which lies 5 miles away in a sequestered valley of bogland grandeur. Outside the pages of a book, there is nothing closer to Shangri-La than Nafooey.

 CHECKING IN/EATING OUT: *Peacocks* – A sort of Celtic bazaar at Maam Cross, this establishment offers valuable services to tourists: a big bar for booze and fast grub; a more sedate sit-down restaurant with good fare; a shop with the whole bag of stereotypical Emerald Isle souvenirs — tweeds, wools, pottery; a small supermarket; a car accessories shop; and a filling station. It is even possible to stay overnight. Maam Cross (phone: 91-82306). Moderate.

JOYCE COUNTRY: The Joyce Country, which covers much of the Maam valley and the Leenane area, was named after the clan that ruled this wild territory from the 13th to the 19th century. Originally, the Joyces were of princely Welsh and English stock, remarkable for their tall, striking stature. Tom Joyce, the progenitor of the Irish sept, who came from Wales to Ireland and settled in Connemara during the reign of Edward I, is said to have been 7 feet tall; many of his male descendants were also towering specimens. The clan eventually dispersed from the Joyce Country and resettled all over Ireland and, indeed, the world. The most revered Joyce in modern Ireland was the great writer James Joyce. He must have been conscious of his roots, because during a visit to Galway City with his Galway-born wife, he took time off to make a pilgrimage of his own into the Joyce Country. He also inherited the characteristic Joycean stature, standing well over 6 feet tall.

LEENANE: This lovely village reposes at the bottom of a bowl of mountains, one of whose peaks is called the Devil's Mother. Leenane also lies close to Killary Harbour, the only true Scandinavian-style fjord to be found in Ireland. This long arm of water reaches deeply between giant mountains for 10 miles, and roads lining each side of the inlet provide dramatic panoramas of land and sea. For a view of the Aasleagh Falls on the Erriff River, and maybe to fish for salmon too, walk 3 miles up the road north from Leenane into Mayo.

En Route from Leenane – Head west on the road to Clifden, N59, which runs for a few miles along the shore of Killary Harbour. As the road bends inland, in about 10 miles, Kylemore Abbey, a modern Gothic building, appears across a lake to the right. Built by a doctor in the 19th century as an adoring and lasting monument to his wife, Kylemore is now a prestigious school for girls, run by Benedictines. The nuns show visitors around the abbey library, church, and pottery. They also serve the daintiest teas.

 CHECKING IN/EATING OUT: *Kylemore House* – Not to be confused with the *Kylemore Pass* hotel, this is a truly superior guesthouse, one of a number in the area. It's worth a visit just to see the precious antique furniture and paintings that adorn it. It offers great luxury, 6 rooms (5 with bath), 7 acres of woods, 3 private fishing lakes with salmon and trout, and a table par excellence. A real find. Open April through October. Reservations necessary. Three miles east of Kylemore Abbey on N59, the main Leenane–Clifden road (phone: 95-41143). Moderate.

RENVYLE: About 1 mile west of Kylemore is a signpost on the right for Renvyle, 6 miles away. This road veers north of the main route to the precarious verge of the Atlantic, where the rocky headland juts defiantly out into the water. Locals say that if you look directly west and squint hard while standing there, you'll see the next parish — Brooklyn! Out on the promontory is yet another ruined castle of those terrible O'Flahertys. All around this area are some very lovely, safe beaches. On the way into Renvyle, the route passes through a village called Tully Cross, where there are modern versions of the traditional thatch-roofed Irish cottages that have been fitted with comforts and conveniences unknown to the peasantry of yore. These cottages can be rented at moderate rates, though reservations made well in advance are essential. For information, call Aras Fáilte (phone: 91-63081).

 CHECKING IN: *Renvyle House* – At this elegant hostelry perched above the sea, the decor is of another age, and an air of graciousness prevails. It once was the country residence of the great Irish wit Oliver St. John Gogarty, the prototype of Buck Mulligan in Joyce's *Ulysses.* Closed January, February, and most of March. Signposted on the right, 1½ miles north of Tully Cross, Renvyle (phone: 95-43511 or 95-43444). Expensive.

LETTERFRACK: About 8 miles from Renvyle back through Tully Cross is Letterfrack Village, on the main road from Leenane to Clifden. Letterfrack is a crossroads village of great charm. Visit any of the pubs in the evening to hear some of the best genuine Irish music played on fiddle and tin whistle. The village also lies in the shadow of the towering range of mountains called the Twelve Bens. The Irish government has taken over 3,800 acres of this wild mountainous terrain and turned it into a national park. It shouldn't be missed. The entrance is only about 100 yards south of the main street of Letterfrack. There are wide-open spaces in which to pitch camp, and Diamond Mountain — reaching heavenward in the middle of the park — just begs to be climbed. Here it is also possible to get a close look at the famous Connemara ponies. Indeed, these sturdy and tough little horses, renowned for their endurance, jumping powers, and amiability, can be found roaming all over Connemara. Some people believe that they are descended from Spanish horses that swam to the safety of the Connemara coast from ships wrecked in the Spanish Armada and interbred with local strains. Others say they have Egyptian bloodlines. Whatever the true story, the Connemara pony is now a breed of international celebrity, and there are Connemara pony societies all over the world, including the US.

 CHECKING IN/EATING OUT: *Crocnaraw Country House* – This early-19th-century Georgian country residence, set in 20 acres of gardens and woods on the shores of the Atlantic, is known for its cosseting of guests, free trout fishing, and marvelous home cooking. Open May through October. Moyard on N59, 3 miles west of Letterfrack (phone: 95-41068). Expensive.

Rosleague Manor – Run by members of the famous Foyle family, renowned hoteliers, this gracious pink Georgian manor overlooks a quiet bay and serves very good food. The dining room, decorated with antiques, silver, and crystal chandeliers, offers fine views of the Ballinakill Bay and Diamond Hill. Chef Paddy Foyle prepares a sumptuous six-course meal; the smoked trout and salmon are stars. Open *Easter* through October. Two miles west of Letterfrack on N59 (phone: 95-41101). Moderate.

CLEGGAN/INISHBOFIN: For an interesting (and perhaps lengthy) island excursion, at the village of Streamstown make a sharp right turn onto the unnumbered road to Cleggan. This is the embarkation point for Inishbofin Island, which in recent times has become a haunt of poets, philosophers, and artists from many lands. The mail boat that leaves Cleggan every day at noon — the temperamental Atlantic permitting — will carry passengers to the island. If a really bad storm brews up, though, it is not unknown to be marooned on the island for days (or even weeks), but in view of the hospitality and friendliness of the islanders, there are worse fates. The ruins of a 7th-century monastery are on the island, which was once in the possession of the menacing O'Flahertys. The daring sea queen of the western waters Grainne Ui Mhaille (pronounced *Grawn*-ya Ee *Whal*-ya and translated as Grace O'Malley) also found shelter for her warships here during her rebellion against the sovereignty of Queen Elizabeth I. The iron gauntlet of Cromwell fell on the island in 1652. The barracks where his Roundheads were billeted stands at the harbor entrance.

 CHECKING IN: Day's – Overlooking the harbor on Inishbofin Island, this hotel has a friendly staff, an informal ambience, and cozy, warm rooms. First-rate homemade soup, island lamb, crab, and lobster are served in the restaurant. Musical evenings are held during summer. Inishbofin Island (phone: 95-45827). Inexpensive.

 EATING OUT: Harbour Seafood – At this waterfront eatery with a salty maritime flavor, the skilled cooks do their very best to make sure that the day's catch arrives at the table in its most tempting forms. Cleggan Village (phone: 95-44605). Moderate.

CLIFDEN: Return to the main road, N59, and drive 4 miles southwest to Clifden. This town is cradled in a glen at the head of an Atlantic inlet into which a river rushes. Though it has a population of little more than 1,000, Clifden is called the capital of Connemara, a label that might be challenged by people in southern Connemara, where scarcely anything but Irish is spoken. Clifden is an English-speaking town, a legacy of the days when it was a favorite seaside summer resort of the British gentry. Many army officers from Dublin Castle (the former seat of British rule in Ireland) built or bought estates and manors in and around Clifden, and some of those once splendid residences are now among the better hotels. The town is the site of *Millars Connamera Tweeds* (phone: 95-21038), makers of the traditional Irish country hat; local wool for the hats and other garments is processed in a mill that incorporates part of the old railway station .

Almost forgotten now is the fact that the first wireless messages from Europe to America were sent from Clifden. The inventor of the radio, Marconi, set up a station in Derrygimlagh Bog, 4 miles south of the town. Marconi himself spent much time in Clifden. The buildings that housed the transatlantic wireless station were destroyed during the Irish civil war of the early 1920s, but some of the transmitting masts are still standing. The same bog has claim to another historical distinction: It was on its peaty surface in 1919 that the aviators John William Alcock and Arthur Whitten

Brown landed their biplane, having flown from Newfoundland to complete the first nonstop transatlantic flight. A pile of stones marks the spot today, and nearby is a more imposing limestone monument commemorating the event. These sites are well marked; travel about 4 miles out on the Ballyconneely road to reach them.

Anyone visiting Clifden must ascend the dizzying heights of Sky Road, well named because those toiling up its steep slope feel they may well reach the sky. Signposted from the town's central square, the road is narrow and heart-stoppingly sheer, requiring skilled gear shifting. The precipitous ascent affords a fabulous view of Clifden Bay and the savage rocky west coast as well as the small islands nestled like humpback whales in the Atlantic beyond. At the highest point, there's a walled-in car park where travelers can rest to take in the view at leisure and maybe enjoy a picnic.

CHECKING IN: *Abbeyglen Castle* – The name "castle" was added after architectural tinkering placed castellated turrets on what was a charming old mansion needing no such cosmetics, but it's still a great place to stay, tucked away in a beautiful setting of gardens, waterfalls, and streams, with the monumental Twelve Bens forming a breathtaking backdrop. Sumptuous suites overlook the Atlantic, and the dining room, with its decidedly French accent, has won several prestigious awards. Sky Rd., Clifden (phone: 95-21070). Expensive.

Rock Glen Manor House – A converted 19th-century shooting lodge set amid sylvan glades and stony mountains on the edge of the Atlantic, this beautiful and restful retreat lavishes warm personal attention on its guests. Features include a spacious drawing room stuffed with antiques, an old-fashioned billiards and snooker room, a small intimate bar, and a fine restaurant, hosted most evenings by owner John Roche and his wife, Evangeline. John does all the cooking, specializing in shellfish, wild salmon and trout, and Connemara mountain lamb. There is also a fine selection of Irish cheeses, including County Clare goat cheese, Irish cheddar, and Cashel Blue. One mile south of Clifden on L102, the Ballyconneely road (phone: 95-21035 or 95-21393). Expensive.

Alcock and Brown – Named after the two flyers who made the first nonstop transatlantic flight from Newfoundland to Clifden, this is a well-run modern hotel set right in the center of town. All the necessary creature comforts are provided, including a commendable dining table graced mostly by fresh fish and mountain lamb. Market Sq., Clifden (phone: 95-21086). Moderate.

Barry's – An exceptionally friendly house where management and staff go out of their way to ensure the comfort of their guests, it has pleasant rooms and a good restaurant. Main St., Clifden (phone: 95-21287). Moderate.

Clifden Bay – The original hostelry founded by the Foyle family. A place of warm informality, with music sessions on many evenings, lovely rooms, and fine food. Main St., Clifden (phone: 95-21167). Moderate.

EATING OUT: *Doris's* – A harpist playing by candlelight evokes the past in this unusual and superb eating place, which is housed in a cut-stone building with gnarled wooden beams. The menu includes unique items such as salmon-flavored ice cream. Dinner only. Market St., Clifden (phone: 95-21427). Expensive.

High Moors – Exceptionally fine dinners — with local lamb, fish, and home-grown vegetables — are served in this quaint old house with magnificent views across Clifden Bay. Dooneen, Clifden, signposted three-quarters of a mile outside town on L102, the Ballyconneely road (phone: 95-21342). Moderate.

O'Grady's Seafood – All creatures great and small, shelled and unshelled, from the surrounding Atlantic, find their way onto the tables of this quintessential fish house, among the best in Ireland. Market St., Clifden (phone: 95-21450). Moderate.

Shades – An intimate, softly lighted restaurant that prides itself on an original presentation of a wide variety of seafoods. The prime beef and Connemara lamb are also extremely good. The Square, Clifden (phone: 95-21215). Moderate.

Atlantic Fishery – A cornucopia of fresh fish is served up here at bargain prices throughout the summer. Main St., Clifden (phone: 95-21346). Inexpensive.

En Route from Clifden – Head roughly southeast on the "low road," L102, which hugs the jagged northern coast of the bay almost the whole way and leads quickly into the Gaeltacht area. Although most of the signposts are in Irish here, a traveler is not likely to get lost for any length of time, and most people can speak English well enough to direct a tourist back on the track. Besides, it's a very nice place in which to get lost.

ROUNDSTONE: This is one of the loveliest sea villages in Connemara, and in summer it is crowded with tourists from across the globe. Its Irish name is *Cloch nah Ron,* meaning "rock of the seals," and in the evening the whiskered heads of seals can be seen bobbing in the bay. Two granite piers, built in the 19th century, jut into the bay to protect the fishing boats. Rising almost directly behind the main street is Errisbeg Mountain, which is easy to ascend and from whose summit almost all of the west coast is visible. The two finest beaches in Connemara are off the main road, less than 2 miles west of the village. Stop by husband and wife Malachy and Anne Kearns's factory, *Roundstone Musical Instruments* (phone: 95-35808), where traditional Irish musical instruments are made. *Bodhráns* (Irish drums) are the specialty, but the factory also produces tin whistles, flutes, and harps. Factory and shop hours are 8 AM to 7 PM daily, April through September, and 9 AM to 5 PM weekdays during winter.

CHECKING IN: *Roundstone House* – Maureen Vaughan and her family run this small, friendly hotel, which has spectacular views of Roundstone Bay and the Twelve Bens mountain range. The food, with a distinctively maritime accent, is delicious. Main St., Roundstone (phone: 95-35864). Moderate.

EATING OUT: *Beola* – Lobster is king in this splendid restaurant, which also offers a feast of other viands fresh from the sea outside. The homemade soup is a commendable specialty. Main St., Roundstone (phone: 95-35871). Expensive to moderate.

BALLYNAHINCH: Continue on the coast road, L102, from Roundstone for 10 miles to Ballynahinch, which is signposted and where the splendid Castle of Ballynahinch stands amid woodlands behind turreted gates. In a way, this is the true capital of ancient Connemara, because here resided the powerful, albeit eccentric, Martin family who were simply granted just about all of Connemara by the English king during the 18th century. (One of the Martins had a very nimble intuition: He pledged the right allegiance to the right royal house at the right time.) The dispossessed O'Flahertys (those wild ones again) hated the Martins and put to the sword any who crossed their path, though the Martins themselves were quite competent swordsmen. One of them, Dick Martin, won notoriety as a duelist but redeemed his reckless reputation by founding the Society for the Prevention of Cruelty to Animals, thus earning the name Humanity Dick. The castle, now a hotel (see *Checking In/Eating Out*), has a magnificent setting among mountains, lakes, and woods. The Ballynahinch Fishery is world famous for salmon angling.

Leaving Ballynahinch, double back on the road to reach the signpost for Cashel, then continue southeast along the coast once more. Lush with vegetation and shrubbery, Cashel provides a warm contrast to the stonier, starker face of the Connemara landscape. The view seaward is breathtaking.

CHECKING IN/EATING OUT: *Ballynahinch Castle* – Ancestral home of the Martin dynasty and now a hotel that echoes with history, it offers truly striking scenery and some of the best salmon fishing anywhere. Much frequented by

American visitors. Open June 1 to October 12. Ballynahinch (phone: 95-31006). Expensive.

Cashel House – Often cited as one of Ireland's best hotels, offering sheltered gardens, monastic quiet, and delicious food. Among its distinguished guests was Charles de Gaulle. It's advisable to book well in advance. About 14 miles from Roundstone on the coast road to Galway City. Cashel (phone: 95-31001). Expensive.

Zetland – Set on lushly wooded grounds, this hotel is infused with a warm, hospitable feeling. It has its own fishing facilities (for salmon and sea trout) and a fine dining room. About 14 miles from Roundstone on the coast road to Galway City. Cashel Bay (phone: 95-31111). Expensive.

CARNA: About 10 miles south of Cashel on L102, this sea village is in the heart of the Irish-speaking district. If plans allow, come during July, when there are a number of festivals of a maritime flavor. The old sailing boats called "hookers" and "pucauns" along with the *curraghs* gather off Carna for regattas and races. Carna is also a marvelous place to hear traditional Irish music. Visitors are welcome to join the informal sessions in the pubs or to go to an Irish dance known as a *céilí* (pronounced *kay*-lee). It's also worth taking a trip out to MacDara's Island, the resting place of St. MacDara, protector of fishermen, who still dip their oars in salute as they sail past the island.

From Carna continue along the meandering L102 through Kilkieran to Gortmore and turn right at the signpost to Rosmuc.

 EATING OUT: *Ostan Charna* – A restaurant that is comfortable, pleasant, and quite affordable. The food is nothing fancy, but it's fresh and wholesome, with particularly good lamb and fish. Carna village (phone: 95-32255). Moderate.

ROSMUC: This isolated area is a place venerated in modern Irish history. It was in a cottage here that the mystic poet and philosopher Padraig Pearse, who led the 1916 rising against the British in Dublin, sought seclusion to contemplate Ireland's Celtic past and to dream of revolution and a free nation. Many leading political figures of those times joined him in the cottage to ponder Ireland's destiny. After the rising, Pearse and the other leaders were shot, but their action led to independence for the southern part of Ireland within 5 years. The cottage is a national monument open to the public.

Returning to Gortmore, turn right on L102 and travel to Screeb, 3 miles away, then turn right onto L100 and continue on to Costelloe. From here detour southwest, following the signpost to Carraroe.

CARRAROE: Set amid furze-clad hills and stony fields, this village is a place where the lingering charm of the past is at its strongest. Irish is the lingua franca, and the old traditional ways of cultivating the land are still used on the small farms. Children from all over Ireland come here in summer to gain fluency in the Irish language. A number of pristine beaches are tucked away in niches along the rugged shoreline, including a small coral strand less than 2 miles from the village.

Return to Costelloe and head south on L100. Just before the village of Inverin, the road straightens out and runs directly east to Galway City, 16 miles away, and for the entire run Galway Bay is on the right.

 CHECKING IN: *Ostan Cheathru Rua* – The name (pronounced *Oh*-shtawn Kah-roo Roo-ah) means Hotel Carraroe. The only hostelry that can be recommended unreservedly in this locality, it is comfortable, contemporary, and offers good food. Very often there are enjoyable sessions of Irish music. Open mid-May to mid-September. A highly visible signpost on the village's main street points the way. Carraroe (phone: 91-95116). Expensive.

EATING OUT: *An Ciseog* – A rarity in the area: serving meals alfresco on the sandy beach when the weather permits. It's a popular rendezvous for beach-partying groups in summer. Carraroe Village (phone: 91-95092). Moderate.

Boluisce – Lobster and prawn are the shellfish of choice at this restaurant specializing in seafood. In the village of Spiddal, on L100, the coast road from Carraroe to Galway City (phone: 91-83286). Moderate.

ARAN ISLANDS

Cast adrift from the outermost rim of Europe, the Aran Islands stand guard at the entrance to Galway Bay — stony, immortal bastions of a past that goes back before the primal dawn of civilization. Hewn out of solid limestone and stripped bare of trees by the Atlantic gales, the three islands — collectively known simply as Aran — seem like geographical relics of the Stone Age, abandoned in the Atlantic. Man has taken possession of them, but over the centuries they have only grudgingly yielded to his works and have changed very little since they first emerged from the ocean thousands of years ago. The islands — Inishmore ("the big island"), Inishmaan ("the middle island"), and Inisheer ("the eastern island") — occupy a fascinating place in the lore of the east Atlantic. They have been linked in folk memory with Atlantis, the lost continent, which in the Irish version of the story is known as *Hy Brasil,* the Isle of the Blest.

Whatever ancient mythologies surround Aran, it is certain that the islands were inhabited in prehistoric times, perhaps as far back as 3,000 years before Christianity. The pagan Fir Bolg ("men of the Belgae"), an early Celtic people from Europe, are believed to have been the earliest settlers on the islands. The cyclopean stone *duns* (pronounced *doons*), or forts, for which the islands are famous, may well have been built by the Fir Bolgs, though archaeologists have been unable to fix a definite date on the structures. Some authorities contend that the mightiest of the forts — Dun Aengus on Inishmore — was named for a Fir Bolg deity, Aonghus, god of youth and love. Others suggest it was named in early Christian times after Aenghus, the King of the province of Munster, who was a patron of St. Enda, the monk who evangelized the islands. The son of a 5th-century druid chieftain, Enda (*Naomh Eanna*) had been a young, warlike prince until he was converted to the faith by his own sister, a devout nun. After traveling to Rome (he established a monastery in Italy), Enda landed with a small band of followers on Aran and, using the sword as much as reasoned persuasion in pursuit of his mission, converted the islanders to the new religion.

Enda founded monasteries and built chapels all over the islands, establishing them as a center of monasticism and a fountainhead of religious teaching. Pilgrims from many lands made their way to Aran during the golden age of the early Irish church, which conducted its affairs quite independently of Rome. For more than a thousand years, Aran flourished as one of the great holy places of the west, exerting an influence on the Christian world far out of proportion to its geographic size. Its renown as a sanctuary of cloistered piety and learning equaled that of Scotland's holy island Iona, and indeed the pioneering Scottish evangelist St. Columba (see *County Donegal,* DIRECTIONS) studied under Enda in Aran. It was said that the islands produced as many saints as there are stars in the universe. One ancient scribe wrote: "There are more saints buried in Aran than are known to any but God alone."

Aran's position as a major monastic settlement began to wane during the 14th century, when it first came to the serious attention of the English, who sent a fleet of 50 ships to plunder the islands in 1334. It had been pillaged by the Vikings during the 11th century, but it still managed to hold on to its insular autonomy up to the time when Queen Elizabeth I mounted the throne of England.

Between the 11th and 16th centuries, the powerful O'Brien clan held sway over Aran. For their own benefit, the O'Briens exploited the strategic importance of the islands, located at the entrance to Galway Bay and commanding a vantage point over the busy shipping lanes to prosperous Galway City. They forced the wealthy burghers of Galway to pay a tribute of 3,000 gallons of wine a year to protect the shipping routes from pirates and other predators.

But Queen Elizabeth took possession of the islands in 1587 and handed them over to her countryman John Rawson, who erected Arkyne Castle on Inishmore and garrisoned it with a body of English soldiers. Deprived of their independence, the proud islanders, who to this day speak Irish as a living language, conceived a fierce hatred of Elizabeth and bestowed on her the unflattering name "Betty of the Pigs." Aran was never again in native hands until Ireland gained her independence in the 1920s.

Meanwhile, it was invaded twice more: A small army of Cromwellian Roundheads occupied the islands in 1651 at the end of a year-long siege. The Roundheads took command of Arkyne Castle and built up its fortifications but eventually became absorbed into the island population; a scattering of their descendants are in Aran today. Later, during the Protestant-Catholic struggle of the late 17th century, the islands fell to the forces of the Protestant King William, but those soldiers departed within a few years, and Aran remained Catholic and Irish-speaking.

After these events, the islands were largely forgotten until the middle of the 19th century, when anthropologists, archaeologists, and other researchers of Ireland's past began visiting Aran and letting the outside world know of this strange prehistoric relic in the ocean. They discovered that a way of life that had long since disappeared from almost every other part of Europe was still flourishing in Aran, unchanged over the centuries. The great Irish playwright John Millington Synge was captivated by Aran, and his writings about it helped publicize the islands throughout the world. He spent his summers on Inishmaan in the early part of this century, building a stone "chair" on the edge of the cliffs, where he sat day after day gazing out into the Atlantic. In 1933, the American filmmaker Robert Flaherty made a celebrated documentary — *Man of Aran* — about the hard life on the islands, vividly depicting the rigors of wresting a subsistence from the stone-layered soil and the seas around.

Aran is accessible by plane or boat from Galway City or by fast launch from the nearest point on the County Galway mainland, Rossaveal Harbour in Connemara. Sea trips from Galway City harbor are run by *CIE* (*Córas Iompair Eireann, National Transport Company*) daily in summer and twice a week at other times of the year; for details and reservations, contact *CIE* (Railway Station, Eyre Sq., Galway City; phone: 91-62141). The boats from Rossaveal (20 miles west of Galway on the coast road, L100) operate daily only during summer; for information, contact the Aras Fáilte (off Eyre Sq., Galway City; phone: 91-63081, 91-65201, or 91-65202). Passage on the Dun Aengus boat from Rossaveal can be booked directly by calling 91-72273. Regular daily flights on *Aer Arann* (about $70 round-trip) are from Carnmore Airport, 5 miles north of Galway City off the Monivea road (phone: 91-55437).

Though possible, it's not very satisfying to tour all three islands in a single day. The most enjoyable way to explore Aran is to spend a few days on each island or find a base on one island and make forays to the others. The three islands, only a few minutes' travel from each other, are linked by regular boat service. It is possible to skip from one island to the other in an Aer Arann plane, but under most circumstances that would scarcely be necessary. Available for purchase in any of the island shops or in Aras Fáilte, Galway, is a superb detailed map of the islands called *Oileain Arann* ("the islands of Aran"), which pinpoints not only the numerous historic sites and monuments but nearly all the homes, with the names of the families occupying them. Everything worth seeing is marked on the map — an indispensable item for any visit.

It's best to start a tour of Aran on the biggest island, Inishmore. All boats from the mainland berth at the principal port, Kilronan, where bicycles can be hired. This is perhaps the best way to sightsee in Inishmore, although the extremely steep hills can knock the breath out of those less fit. A more leisurely way of getting around, and certainly less strenuous, is by pony-drawn sidecar, or trap (which looks like a large dog cart). These can be hired, with driver, for $15 and up, depending on length of use or distance traveled. It is possible to walk without too much stress: This island is about 10 miles long and little more than 2 miles wide at any point (but the hills are very steep).

On Inishmore, there are three great ring forts, the most impressive of which is Dun Aengus, prized as one of the most spectacular of megalithic monuments in all of Europe. It towers above the southwest cliffs of the island, some 6 miles west of Kilronan. About 4 miles east of Dun Aengus on the same coast is Dun Cuchathair, the Black Fort. Although much of it has fallen into the sea, it remains an awesome sight. At the western end of the island, south of the village of Eoghanacht, about 8 miles from Kilronan, is another massive fortress called Dun Eoghnachta, estimated to be 3,000 or more years old. At Killeany, beside the airstrip and about 1½ miles southeast of Kilronan, is the most sacred reliquary in Aran — the ruins of the church built by St. Enda, where the saint is reputed to be buried. Beside Killeany pier are the ruins of Arkyne Castle, which was garrisoned by successive waves of invading soldiers from Elizabeth's time onward.

Take the boat from Kilronan first to Inishmaan and then to Inisheer. Inishmaan is the most primitive-looking of the islands, rising sharply out of the ocean and blanketed in great gray slabs of limestone. Dry-stone walls, some of which were built many centuries ago, encircle the barren fields and form a jagged pattern of crisscrossed rocks right across the island. Here the hills are steepest of all and exhausting to negotiate on foot in the full heat of summer — and it is on foot that one has to travel, as bicycles or horse-drawn vehicles are hard to procure on Inishmaan. Still, it is a small island, no more than 4 by 2 miles, which means there isn't too much territory to cover. The only major road bisects the island, going from the landing pier on the east coast to the west coast. It's both a tortuous and torturous route but, blessedly, passes close to most of the sites worth seeing on the island. A mile inland, to the left of the road, is Dun Conchuir (Connor Fort). Rivaling Dun Aengus in breathtaking splendor, it alone is worth a visit to Inishmaan. The thatch-roofed cottage on the other side of the road, just before the fort, is where the playwright Synge stayed during the many summers he spent in Aran.

A little farther is the island's museum, a traditional cottage inside which the furniture and fittings of a centuries-old peasant society are preserved intact, reflecting a lifestyle that has not changed much on the island with the passing of time. Continue on the same road for another ½ mile to reach the site of Synge's stone chair on the high cliffs overlooking Gregory's Sound. While sitting here, Synge was inspired to write *Riders to the Sea,* among the greatest one-act plays ever penned.

Inisheer, a 5-minute boat ride from Inishmaan, is the tiniest of the Aran Islands, only about 2 miles by 2 miles and with fewer than 500 inhabitants. Bicycles can be hired at the pier, though some parts of Inisheer are not accessible on wheels, so walking is recommended. There's one formidable hill on the northeast side of the island; otherwise the terrain is flat, though very rocky in parts. This is the best island for swimming (by an odd quirk of nature, the ocean waters around Aran are always a few degrees warmer than those at the mainland beaches). The sheer cliffs on the eastern side of the island, close to where a wrecked steamer, stranded on the rocks some years back, lies incongruously rusting away, provide a dramatic location from which to drop a fishing line into the broiling waters far below for deliciously edible mackerel or rock salmon.

Inisheer does not boast the great forts found on the other two islands. The antiquities are practically all connected with the early church. Right beside the pier is an ancient circular graveyard from which bronze urns have been unearthed. A mile to the southeast is the island's most venerated holy place — the Church of St. Kevin, now almost completely buried in sand, even though it was in use as recently as 100 years ago. The remains of another early church — named after St. Gobnait, who is said to have been the only woman allowed into the monasteries of Aran — can be found about ¼ mile south of the landing pier. Atop the high hill on the northeast side of Inisheer, the ruins of the O'Brien castle tower proudly above everything else on the island. Immediately south of the castle is an ancient cemetery called the Grave of the Seven Daughters, about which little is known.

Apart from explorations into the Celtic past, there are many other intriguing things to see and do on Aran. Shops at Kilronan harbor stock traditional Aran knitwear (also sold in many fine stores on the mainland), and tiny pubs, some of them roofed in thatch, are often scenes of merriment and song. There are fishermen willing to take passengers out for a ride in a *curragh,* a thrilling experience. The sheer cliffs rearing out of the ocean will test the nerve of anyone with a mountaineering spirit. Most precious of all, for many visitors, is the elemental timelessness of the place and the peaceful silence that envelops the islands, tempered only by the eternal sea sounds that soothe the mind and soul.

Most accommodations on the islands are provided in private homes and are generally of a high standard. Arrangements can be made for bed and breakfast or for partial board (includes dinner in the evening) or full board (includes both lunch and dinner). The map *Oileain Arann,* previously mentioned, has a fairly complete list of all the homes offering accommodation. Bed and breakfast accommodations for two average $25 to $30 a night; partial board, $40 to $45; and full board, about $55 to $60. A list of homes approved by Bord Fáilte, the Irish Tourist Board, is available at the Galway City office (Aras Fáilte, off Eyre Sq.; phone: 91-63081, 91-65201, or 91-65202). Dinner for two at a restaurant listed as moderate will cost about $30 to $40, excluding wine and tip.

CHECKING IN: *Inisheer* – The only true hotel on Aran and quite a good one, although it has only 10 rooms. The food is commendable, traditional, and with no frills. A few hundred yards south of the landing pier, Inisheer (phone: 99-75020). Inexpensive.

Johnston Hernon's Kilmurvey House – A comfortable 8-bedroom guesthouse, close to Dun Aengus. There's nothing pretentious on the menu, but the food is wholesome and usually includes excellent fresh fish. Kilmurvey village, about 6 miles west of Kilronan, Inishmore (phone: 99-61218). Inexpensive.

EATING OUT: *An tSean Cheibh* – As might be expected, fish, in endless varieties, is the strong point of the house, although native lamb and beef dishes, conjured up with French flair or in traditional home-cooked style, are top rate. The restaurant (whose name is pronounced *Un Chan Cave,* meaning "the old pier") is in the style of an Aran cottage, with lime-painted stone walls and an outdoor terrace overlooking the sea for alfresco dining. By far the best restaurant on the islands, it is open from morning until late at night from May to September. A 3-minute walk from the landing pier, Kilronan, Inishmore (phone: 99-61228). Moderate.

An tSéanDun Aonghusa – An atmospheric restaurant that serves very good food, with fish predominant, in pleasant, old-fashioned surroundings, including timbered stone walls and an enormous open fireplace. Beside the landing pier, overlooking Galway Bay, Kilronan, Inishmore (phone: 99-61104). Moderate.

County Mayo

Above brooding Connemara, the Mweelrea and Partry mountains and the Sheeffrey Hills of southern County Mayo give way to a gentler landscape that wraps around beautiful, island-studded Clew Bay. Croagh Patrick, the stately mountain where St. Patrick is said to have prayed and fasted for 40 days for the salvation of the Irish people, is the dominant feature of the bay's southern shore, while Achill Island, Ireland's largest offshore island, guards the northwestern reaches of the bay. Inland, a series of lakes, most notably Lough Mask, which feeds into Lough Corrib near Mayo's border with County Galway, offer anglers excellent trout fishing. The more northerly regions of the county offer dramatic mountain and cliff scenery. Mayo's natural amenities and leisure facilities present traditional Ireland at its best, and many names associated with local heritage are famed in song and story.

The coastline, which presents a succession of sandy beaches, rugged headlands, and dramatic cliffs, is steeped in the legends of Grace O'Malley (Grainne Ui Mhaille), the 16th-century warrior sea queen who made herself ruler of the district that surrounds Clew Bay and its islands after the death of her father. While some doubt the veracity of her legendary exploits, stories about her have been handed down in the spoken tradition of the islanders and in the historical novel *Queen of Men* by William O'Brien. One of the most interesting tales concerns a marriage contract she made with her second husband, MacWilliam Oughter. They agreed that either party could dissolve the union after 1 year merely by saying, "I dismiss you!" Grace O'Malley took advantage of the escape clause at the end of the year, but not before she had garrisoned all of Oughter's coastal castles with her own followers, strengthing her position as ruler of the area.

And while the authenticity of Irish history reaches back no farther than the 7th century, the plain of Southern Moytura near Cong is said to have been the scene of the first battle between two mythical tribes that ruled this area 3,000 years ago — the Fir Bolg, a race of small dark men, and the fair Tuatha De Denaan, said to be a race of magicians. Though the Denaan were victorious here, they were later overcome in the Celtic conquest. Legend says the defeated Denaan changed themselves into fairies and ever since have inhabited the hills, forts, and caves of Ireland. Beneath the rocks of Cong lie more than 40 dark, unearthly looking caves, and not a few locals will attest that many of the "little people" went to live there.

There is more historical certainty about the role that Mayo men played in the agitations of the Land League, formed to help tenant farmers resist tyrannical, rent-racking landlords. Michael Davitt, one of the founders of the league, was born at Straid, near Castlebar, and Captain Charles Boycott, one of the league's targets, lived at Lough Mask House, on the shores of the southern Mayo lake.

The northern part of the county also has resounded to a few epics of history, notably in 1798, when the French Revolution swept up on its shores. A force of more than 1,000 French soldiers sailed into Killala Bay and stormed ashore to join in the insurrection that had been stirred up by the patriots, called the United Irishmen, in different parts of Ireland. What followed was a mixture of comic opera and bitter tragedy, all well reconstructed in a novel by the American writer Thomas Flanagan called *The Year of the French*. The French were joined by a ragtag band of Irish peasants who knew nothing about warfare and, initially, enjoyed a heady victory in Castlebar, where they established the Republic of Connacht in the province where Mayo is located. Eventually, they went down to inglorious defeat at the hands of the English, who then took a terrible revenge on the native inhabitants, slaughtering them and burning their homes, while at the same time granting clemency to the French invaders.

Earlier, during the reign of Queen Elizabeth I, there had been another invasion of the northwest Mayo coast when a number of ships of the Spanish Armada, fleeing from the wrath of Sir Francis Drake, put in at Blacksod Bay. The Spanish officers tried to goad the natives into rebellion but, getting no response, were forced to sail toward Scotland and were wrecked in a storm.

Our County Mayo route originates in Galway City, from which it is a pleasant 20-mile drive into southern Mayo and the historic village of Cong. The route then skirts the western edges of Lough Mask, beneath the Partry Mountains, heading north to Castlebar. From this busy town in the heart of the limestone plain country, it turns north to the great salmon and fishing territory that encompasses the scenic lakes and rivers around Foxford, Pontoon, and Ballina. The route then follows the Atlantic cliffs to the bleak boglands of Erris and Belmullet and the wonderful seascapes beyond this wilderness. From there, the tour heads east and inland to Crossmolina, then south again and west to Newport and Achill Island. After an excursion to the island, it continues around Clew Bay, traveling through Westport and Louisburgh, then dips south into Joyce Country (described in the *Connemara and the Aran Islands* route) before returning to Cong or Galway. The route, a meandering 150 miles, can be covered comfortably in 3 to 4 days.

Expect to pay $80 to $150 for a double room at a hotel rated as expensive, from $50 to $80 at one rated as moderate, and $35 or less for one rated as inexpensive. Dinner for two at an expensive establishment will cost a minimum of $65; at a moderate one, two can dine well for $30 to $50.

GALWAY CITY: For a complete report on the city, its sites, hotels, and restaurants, see *Galway City,* THE CITIES.

En Route from Galway City – Take N84 north around the eastern shore of Lough Corrib, passing through Cloonboo and Headford. The well-preserved ruins of 14th-century Ross Abbey are nearby. At Headford, pick up R334 northwest through Bunnafollistran and Cross. At Cross, bear west onto R346 to Cong.

CONG: This tiny village, on an isthmus between Lough Mask and Lough Corrib, is best known for the ruins of the 12th-century Cong Abbey and the luxury hotel *Ashford Castle* (see *Checking In*). It may also be familiar to Americans as the setting for much of that quintessential Irish-American movie *The Quiet Man,* which was filmed in these precincts. Another claim to fame: former President Reagan once stayed here.

Cong Abbey, founded for Irish Augustinians by Turlough O'Connor, King of Ireland, is considered one of the finest examples of early architecture in Ireland. The ruins preserve several doorways and windows of a type transitional between Romanesque and Gothic and are best seen from the cloisters garth. Behind the west end of the abbey garth is a small stone house constructed so that the river Cong flows through a gully beneath the floor. The structure is known as the Monks' Fishing House because monks from the abbey supposedly fished through a trapdoor in its floor.

The ruins of the abbey are beside one of the entrance gates to the lovely grounds of Ashford Castle, which commands some of the finest acreage along Lough Corrib. The oldest part of the castle was built in the 18th century, but the castellated towers and a bridge on the river's edge were added later by Sir Benjamin Guinness. There are some 25 miles of landscaped walks through the demesne (grounds) of the castle, which was converted into a hotel in 1939. Parts of the grounds are open to the public.

Besides the abbey, there are several interesting historical artifacts and monuments connected with Cong and its environs. The celebrated *Cross of Cong* (now in the *National Museum* in Dublin) was discovered in a chest in the village early in the 19th century. Made of oak plated with copper and decorated with beautiful gold filigree work of Celtic pattern, it is a masterpiece of religious art. The little ruined church and the ancient Stone of Lunga, on the low wooded island of Inchagoill in Lough Corrib, belong to the age of St. Patrick. The stone is a 2½-foot-high obelisk that bears ancient Roman characters thought to be the oldest Christian inscription in Europe outside the Catacombs.

The stream connecting Lough Mask and Lough Corrib runs underground at Cong and is accessible from a number of caves that honeycomb the plateau of cavernous limestone between the lakes. The most accessible cave is the Pigeon Hole, reached by turning right onto New Saw Mill, a mile west of the village. At the first cottage on the right, an iron gate opens to a field; a short way from the gate, 61 stone steps lead down to the underground chamber.

Another underground curiosity is the Dry Canal, which was built as a relief scheme during the Great Famine of 1846 with the idea of connecting Lough Corrib and Lough Mask to extend navigation. When it was completed, however, it was discovered that despite the cut-stone banks and locks, the canal was incapable of holding water because of the porous limestone bed.

About half a mile from the village on all three approach roads to Cong, a visitor may notice small mounds of wooden crosses, called *crusheens.* For centuries, it has been the practice of funeral corteges to stop at these spots to say a prayer and add another cross to the pile.

About 4 miles north of Cong, on a minor road along the shores of Lough Mask, are the ruins of a castle that belonged to Captain Charles Boycott. The name of Boycott, a retired British army officer who was unpopular with his tenants, came to stand for ostracism and isolation because workers refused to help him during the harvest season during the Land League agitation during the 1880s.

Cong is a center for hunting and fishing. Lough Mask is noted for large trout and pike; Lough Corrib — Ireland's second-largest lake — is renowned for brown trout, pike, and salmon. The season for salmon and trout fishing in the lakes runs from February 15 to September 30, and on the rivers from March 1 to September 30. No fishing license is required. Horses can be hired locally, and a secluded sandy cove for bathers can be reached from an approach road off the Cong–Clonbur road, 1 mile west of the village.

CHECKING IN/EATING OUT: *Ashford Castle* – One of the finest castle hotels in Europe, its public rooms have paneled ceilings and impressive wood carvings and stonework, set off by period furniture, Waterford chandeliers, and military memorabilia. Each of the 83 rooms and 6 suites has a view of the lake or the hotel's formal gardens and wide lawns, and there is a 9-hole golf course on the grounds. The dining room, which is walled in mirrors and looks out over the lake, serves elaborate French cuisine. Although the restaurant is open to non–hotel guests, reservations must be made well in advance. On 98A just east of Cong (phone: 92-46003). Expensive.

En Route from Cong – The route north to Castlebar follows an unnumbered minor road along the western bank of Lough Mask, beside the Partry Mountains, passing through Tourmakeady, a small Irish-speaking village. At the village of Partry, take N84 about 3½ miles north, where a road on the right leads to the largely restored Ballintubber Abbey, which has been in almost uninterrupted use as a place of worship since it was founded by Augustinians in 1216. The abbey consists of a cruciform church with nave transepts and choir. Three blocked windows of Norman design with double dog-tooth molding are over the altar. The monastic buildings are at the end of the south transept. In a chapel to the south of the choir is an elaborate altar tomb with a row of figures on the pediment. Return to N84 and continue north to Castlebar.

CASTLEBAR: The administrative capital of County Mayo, Castlebar is a thriving commercial center that began as a settlement where a castle was built by the de Barra family. It became famous during the 1798 rebellion because a joint Irish-French force defeated the British army here in a battle known as the Races of Castlebar. The remains of John Moore, President of the Republic of Connaught, which was proclaimed after the battle, are buried in the town's pleasant, tree-lined mall. The Castlebar Tourist Board (phone: 94-21207) is open only during summer.

CHECKING IN: *Breaffy House* – An elegant Georgian mansion with modern additions, it's set on 60 acres of wooded parkland. There are 43 pleasantly appointed rooms and evening entertainment during the summer months. Two miles from Castlebar on the Castlebar–Claremorris road, N60 (phone: 94-22033). Expensive.

EATING OUT: *Castle Bistro* – Seafood is one specialty at this attractive restaurant and bar reminiscent of a French bistro. Food is also served in the bar area all day. Castle St., Castlebar (phone: 94-22809). Moderate.

***Davitt* –** Excellent steaks and other straightforward fare are served in this well-run open-kitchen eatery. There's a fireplace in the bar. Rush St., Castlebar (phone: 94-22233). Moderate.

En Route from Castlebar – In the pretty village of Turlough, 3 miles northeast of Castlebar on N5, is a well-preserved round tower beside the ruins of a 17th-century church. Head northeast from Turlough on N5 and turn north onto N58 at Bellavary village to reach Foxford and Pontoon.

FOXFORD: The river Moy flows through Foxford on its way into the Atlantic at Killala Bay. The Moy is a regal river for salmon fishing and, in its heyday around the turn of the century, constantly recorded the biggest annual catches of any salmon water in Ireland or Britain. Overfishing (not here, but in the Atlantic areas to which the Moy salmon migrate and feed before attempting to return to home waters), pollution, and poaching, among other hazards, have reduced the stocks in the Moy, but it still attracts anglers from many parts of the world and can still yield fine catches. The little town of Foxford (or nearby Pontoon; see next entry) is an ideal base from which to fish the mighty Moy. Local anglers will be happy to suggest the best methods and lures to catch the big ones. For information, contact Peter Tolan, Church Rd., Foxford (phone: 94-56157).

Foxford is also renowned for the woolen mills established by an order of nuns alongside the Moy in 1892. Visitors are welcome to tour the venerable buildings and purchase, at reduced prices, any of the superb range of woolen products. A bronze bust in the town honors one of its most illustrious sons, Admiral William Brown, the man who founded the Argentine navy.

PONTOON: Take the left fork just outside Foxford and travel along L22 to Pontoon on Lough Conn. The name of the town comes from the bridge that was built to span the narrow stretch of water that links Conn with the smaller Lough Cullin. Both lakes are superb salmon waters, and Pontoon, situated in the midst of forests and majestic mountains fringing the lake shores, is an idyllic setting for anglers.

 CHECKING IN/EATING OUT: *Pontoon Bridge* – Perched on the edge of Lough Conn, this is a favorite haunt of anglers because it provides boats and tackle, along with ghillies (angling guides), for fishing trips. Some of the bedrooms have striking views of the lake. The dining room has an excellent reputation. Pontoon (phone: 94-56120 or 94-56151). Expensive.

Healy's – A small but exceptionally good hotel that's been run by the same family since 1892, it is set amid lush woodland at the foot of a mountain, between loughs Conn and Cullin. Warm personal attention is given to all visitors, and a high standard of cooking is consistently maintained, with a welcome emphasis on traditional Irish fare. Salmon from the lakes is king, but the wild fowl is also worth a try. Pontoon (phone: 94-56443). Moderate.

BALLINA: The drive north to Ballina on L134 offers some of the loveliest lake scenery in Ireland. Ballina is Mayo's largest town and one of its most attractive. Designed and founded by a local landlord in the mid-18th century, the town straddles the Moy at a point where the river broadens before entering the estuary leading to Killala Bay. It's famous for its salmon fishing and in particular for the Ridge Pool, just above the Ham Bridge. In summer, the Ridge teems with salmon, resting there before battling their way upriver to the spawning grounds. It is not unknown for an angler to hook 20 salmon or more during a day on the Ridge, which is probably the most prolific fishing pool in Ireland. The best time is May to September. For salmon fishing, contact the Fishery Manager (*Moy Fishery Company,* Ballina; phone: 96-21332). There is also a good run of sea trout in the Moy from July to September. The locals take boats onto the estuary and use strips of mackerel as bait to catch these delectable fish in huge numbers. For sea trout fishing and boats, contact Judd Ruane (*Riverboat Inn,* The Quay, Ballina; phone: 96-22183).

 CHECKING IN: *Belleek Castle* – Clever refurbishment has given the interior of this 19th-century mansion an Elizabethan atmosphere. Timbers from shipwrecks have been used to create the *Spanish Armada Bar,* which has a cavernous stone fireplace. The basement dungeons house a museum with an impressive collection of old European armor and weapons. There are four-poster beds and medieval-style furniture in many of the bedrooms. The famous river Moy flows through the wooded grounds, which have secluded forest walks and a private golf course. The food is imaginative, adventurous, and very good. Castle Rd., Ballina (phone: 96-22061 or 96-21878). Expensive.

Downhill – Catering to the health-conscious, this long-established luxury hotel on the banks of the river Bunree has a heated indoor swimming pool, squash courts, sauna, sunbed, Jacuzzi, and a studio gym with instructor. For those of a more hedonistic bent, there's the late-night *Frogs Piano Bar and Disco.* The hotel food is quite good. Bunree, Ballina (phone: 96-21033). Expensive.

Mount Falcon Castle Guest House – Tucked away on 100 acres of forested parkland, this authentic period country residence of cut stone preserves the ambience of a past age: Log fires heat the rooms. Produce from the castle gardens and farm is served in the hotel dining room, celebrated for its home cooking. The Aldridge family, who own the castle, also hold the rights to one of the best fishing stretches on the Moy, which meanders through the grounds. For a small fee, guests can book a day's angling. Mount Falcon, on N57 south of Ballina (phone: 96-21172). Expensive.

EATING OUT: *Imperial* – A century-old hotel in the middle of town, its 35 rooms have been refurbished to handsome, modern standards, while retaining much of the original charm. The cuisine is of a high order, with superb, fresh salmon in season. Pearse St., Ballina (phone: 96-22200). Expensive.

Swiss Barn – The Swiss chef-owner of this continental restaurant dispenses superlative dishes, among the most noteworthy of which are fondue bourguignon, lobster thermidor, and steak tartare. For dessert, there are homemade ices. Open for dinner only. Reservations essential. Foxford Rd. (N57), Ballina (phone: 96-21117). Moderate.

ARDNAREE: Just east of Ballina on L133, on the east bank of the river Moy, is the village of Ardnaree ("the hill of the execution" in Irish), where four brothers were hanged for the murder of a bishop in the 7th century. Because the murderers were princes of the blood, they were given a royal burial despite their foul deed, and a dolmen (megalithic tomb) marks the place where they are interred at Knockleagh, close to the railway station in the southwestern part of the town. Ardnaree was the scene of another hanging during the French invasion of 1798, when a scout for the French forces, Patrick Walsh, was captured by the British and executed on the spot. Ballina fell to the French and their Irish rebel allies, whose forces were billeted in the town for a number of days before marching to Castlebar, where they routed the English garrison. Also in Ardnaree are the ruins of a 14th-century Augustinian abbey and the 19th-century Catholic cathedral of St. Muredach, which has some beautiful stained glass windows.

En Route from Ballina – R314 runs north from Ballina for 7 miles along the western edge of Killala Bay to the village of Killala and then turns northwest along the Atlantic cliffs almost to Belmullet and the Mullet Peninsula before it joins R313. However, travelers who wish to omit this part of the drive can proceed directly west from Ballina on N59 to Crossmolina and, from there, south to Newport and Achill Island (see "Crossmolina" and "En Route from Crossmolina" below).

KILLALA: A sleepy, lovely seaport, Killala was at one time the most important ecclesiastical center in Mayo, the seat of an influential bishopric. The Church of Ireland (Protestant) still maintains a cathedral that was built during the 17th century above the ruins of the original Catholic cathedral. According to legend, none other than St. Patrick himself established the first church here. Moreover, there is also a local belief that it was from Killala that the young Patrick made his escape from Ireland, where he had been taken and put into slavery as a boy, only to return years later to Christianize the country.

Standing above the harbor is one of the best preserved round towers in Ireland, built by monks as a refuge against pillagers. At Carricknass, just west of the village, are the interesting ruins of a medieval castle built by the Burke clan, who were one of the most powerful Anglo-Norman families to settle in Ireland during the 12th century.

Killala's most memorable moment in history came on an August morning in 1798 when three French men-of-war sailed into the bay and hove to off Kilcummin strand, just north of the village. A force of 1,067 French soldiers, tough products of the revolution that had recently swept their own land, were rowed ashore in relays of longboats to take part in Ireland's revolution against England, engineered by the radical United Irishmen. The French were commanded by the swashbuckling General Humbert, a confrere of Napoleon, and they had been led to believe that a well-armed and sternly disciplined band of Irish rebels were ready to join them when they came ashore. Instead, they found ill-clad and ill-fed Irish peasants, who had no knowledge whatever of war and who could speak only Gaelic, flocking to their revolutionary flag. This motley army met little resistance at the start, and both Killala and Ballina were taken in a matter of hours. They then marched to Castlebar to achieve a famous victory over the British garrison there, routing the English so ignominiously that the episode went down in history as the Races of Castlebar. However, their march across Ireland came to a sorry end when they encountered superior English forces at Ballinamuck, in County Longford, and were speedily defeated. The French were chivalrously treated as prisoners of war; the Irish were summarily executed, their supporters and families in Mayo also slaughtered.

Resume the tour north on L133, which, after passing through the village of Ballycastle, swings west, high above the sea in the direction of Belmullet.

BALLYCASTLE: Ballycastle is a charming, old-fashioned village that still has one or two thatch-roofed cottages on the main street. (Thatch-roofed cottages elsewhere in the area are available for rent; contact the Galway Tourist Board; phone: 91-63081.) Linger here awhile and walk along the side road that leads to Downpatrick Head, a sheer cliff promontory that has legendary connections with St. Patrick. Using great caution, walk to the edge of the precipice and peer down at Dun Briste ("the broken fort"), a huge rocky chunk of land that seems to have been severed from the mainland and cast adrift in the Atlantic. According to folklore, Dun Briste was the home of a pagan god, Crom Cruach, and St. Patrick cut it off from the mainland with a blow of his staff, thus isolating paganism from Ireland forever. The pleasant river Ballinglen, flowing through Ballycastle, holds a plentiful supply of lively brook trout and can be fished free of charge. Outside the village, there's a beautiful crescent of sandy beach, washed by Atlantic breakers and ideal for swimming when the weather is hot.

EATING OUT: *Doonfeeny House* – Perched on wooded cliffs above the Atlantic, this is a superb restaurant whose talented owner-chef specializes in fresh fish and game in season. It's a small, hushed, candlelit place, with a respectable wine cellar to complement the excellent viands. Dinner only. Ballycastle, 2 miles northwest on R314, signposted (phone: 96-43092). Moderate.

En Route from Ballycastle – Heading west to Belmullet Town, R314 passes through some of the most deserted countryside in all of Ireland, with miles and miles of furze-covered bogland stretching to the south. On the northern side, sheer cliffs plunge vertiginously down to the wild Atlantic, and small remote beaches beckon from among the rocks.

BELMULLET: This quaint old town, with a rather fetching down-at-the-heels appearance, is the gateway to the Mullet Peninsula, a large, desolate tract of land that juts out into the Atlantic. It's possible to tour the peninsula on its one good road in an hour or so. The most interesting part is at the southern tip, where a splendid lighthouse rises from the rocky shore at Blacksod. The area is steeped in history and legend. At Cross Point, near a lake 5 miles southwest of Belmullet, are the remains of an abbey that is thought to be connected with St. Brendan the Navigator, the adventurous sea voyager and holy man whom the Irish believe discovered the New World many centuries before any visit by Columbus. Two miles out in the ocean from Cross Point is the island of Inishglora, where in Celtic mythology the children of Lir, who had been changed into swans by their evil stepmother, dwelt for hundreds of years, waiting for the sound of a church bell to return them to human form.

The Mullet forms the western shore of Blacksod Bay, regarded as one of the finest natural deep-water harbors in Europe, though it is little used nowadays. At the bottom of the bay, the largest of the galleons that sailed with the Spanish Armada — *La Rata* — has been lying since 1588, when it went down in a storm while trying to make its way back to Spain after being routed by Queen Elizabeth's naval forces. *La Rata* and a smaller ship, the *Nuestra Señora de Begona,* sought sanctuary in Blacksod, anchoring offshore and sending emissaries into the Mullet in a bid to stir up a local rebellion against the British. *La Rata* sank as it was leaving the bay, but the *Nuestra Señora de Begona* made it safely home to Spain.

On the peninsula, 8 miles south of Belmullet, the derelict remains of the whaling station that once flourished in Elly Harbour are still visible. Until the close of the 19th century, the Elly station was one of the busiest in Europe, and the bay was often crowded with tall-masted whalers waiting to unload their catches. Small fishing boats still sail out of Elly and, in sharp contrast to the whaling tradition, a doll factory now occupies one of the warehouses where the whales were once processed.

En Route from Belmullet – Travel east on R313 to Bangor Erris and from there take N59 farther east (not south) to the village of Crossmolina. This route passes through the tiny hamlet of Bellacorick, the location of one of Ireland's most intriguing "believe it or not" oddities. The coping stones on the north side of the bridge that crosses the river Oweninny give out musical notes when vigorously rubbed or hit hard with a rock, a phenomenon that no one has been able to explain satisfactorily.

 CHECKING IN/EATING OUT: *Ostan Synge* – *Ostan* is Irish for "hotel" or "inn," and this establishment is named after the celebrated Irish playwright John Millington Synge, who spent much time in the west of Ireland absorbing color and lore for his writings. His most famous play, *The Playboy of the Western World,* is set in the Belmullet area. The hotel is modern and comfortable, featuring rooms with balconies overlooking Blacksod Bay. For anyone who wants to escape the fast-track bustle of city life, the isolated location is a near-perfect answer, and the food usually is good — lamb from the nearby hills and salmon from the surrounding sea. Geesala, 5 miles southwest of Bangor Erris; take the signposted side road (phone: 97-86801). Moderate.

CROSSMOLINA: Continue east on N59 to Crossmolina, another premier angling center with plenty of large brown trout in the river Deel, which flows through the village. Bordering Crossmolina are the northern shores of Lough Conn, and it is easy to hire a boat to go out onto the lake; contact Daniel Hiney (Mullinmore St., Crossmolina; phone: 96-31202). On the lake shore, southeast of town, are the remains of Errew Abbey, built for the Augustinians in the 15th century, and near the point where the Deel enters the lake are the remains of 16th-century Deel Castle.

 CHECKING IN/EATING OUT: *Enniscoe House* – Guests at this 7-room Georgian house, on the shore of Lough Conn, can take advantage of fishing, boating, or shooting facilities, or simply enjoy the restful atmosphere. The house is furnished with fine antiques and paintings. Meals are ample. Closed October to *Easter.* Castlehill, 2 miles south of Crossmolina on the R315 (phone: 96-31112). Expensive.

En Route from Crossmolina – From Crossmolina, head south on L140 for 5 miles and take the right fork onto L137. At the L136 T-junction, turn left and travel south to Beltra. Here, turn right onto the continuation of L137, which runs into Newport, another good angling village. From Newport, drive northwest on N59 as far as Mulrany, the entrance to Corraun Peninsula, and pick up R319, which bridges Achill Sound to Achill Island.

 CHECKING IN/EATING OUT: *Mulrany Bay* – Ideally situated overlooking the bay, this hotel offers 43 rooms, 36 with bath, plus tennis courts, a swimming pool, and, for children, a playroom and playground. The food is adequate. Mulrany (phone: 98-36222). Expensive.

Newport House – A 21-room, white Georgian house with Regency decor, this is situated bayside. The French chef prepares superb food, with fresh ingredients from the hotel's own gardens, farm, and fishery. The smoked salmon is particularly good, as are the oysters and lobsters, which come fresh from nearby Clew Bay, and the Irish lamb and pork. Newport (phone: 98-41222). Expensive.

ACHILL ISLAND: The largest of Ireland's offshore islands, Achill is a popular holiday center, though it's little known to foreign visitors. It is dominated by three mountains, and its coast is marked by dramatic cliffs as well as several charming resort villages with long, broad, sandy beaches. The town of Achill Sound, just across the bridge from the mainland, is the island's principal shopping center. It also has facilities for bathing, boating, and fishing. Beyond Achill Sound, the Atlantic Highway bears right off L141, the island's main road, and passes a keep of the O'Malleys. This road traverses the windswept tracts of peat bog that cover much of the island and supply fuel to the islanders. Black-faced sheep dot the rolling bogs and occasionally block the winding road. Dooega, a small village at the mouth of a valley on the west side of Minaun Mountain, is a convenient place from which to climb the mountain or the Minaun Cliffs, rising to 800 feet.

Just before reaching Keel, the island's main resort town, the route passes the spectacular Cathedral Rocks, water-carved cliffs that resemble a Gothic cathedral jutting up from the ocean. Keel, on a curving bay sheltered by Slievemore Mountain on the north and Croghun Mountain on the west, is a center for surfing and diving. In addition to its 3-mile-long sandy beach, it has a 9-hole golf course and tennis courts.

Two miles beyond Keel are the whitewashed cottages of Dooagh, on a bay famous for salmon netting. Keem Bay, which has a narrow, fine-sand beach sheltered by the steeply rising Moyteoge Head, is 3 miles farther west. Basking sharks occasionally frequent Achill waters in spring and are trapped in nets at Keem Bay and then killed with lances by island crews working from small canvas-covered *curraghs*. A steep road leads from Keem Bay to the summit of Croaghaun Mountain, with a 4-mile line of superb cliffs reaching as high as 2,000 feet above the ocean.

Heading back through Keem Bay, a road to the left leads north across the island to Dugort, a north shore village from which boatmen take visitors to the Seal Caves that extend far into the cliffs under Slievemore Mountain, a mass of quartzite rock and mica that rises to 2,204 feet.

In addition to sea angling, there is fishing for trout in Achill's lakes and the river Dooega, and in recent years the island has become a popular locale for mountain climbing, windsurfing, canoeing, orienteering, and scuba diving. (For diving information, contact John P. O'Malley at the post office in Keel; phone: 98-43125). There are numerous small hotels and guesthouses on the island that are open to visitors in summer. Among the restaurants are *Calvey's* (phone: 98-43158) and the *Boley House* (phone: 98-43147), both featuring very reasonably priced seafood. May and June are the best months to visit, but the Achill Tourist Board is open in July and August (phone: 98-45384).

En Route from Achill Island – N59 follows the curve of Clew Bay south from Mulrany to Westport, 8 miles below Newport.

WESTPORT: This charming seigneurial town, in a hollow on the arm of Clew Bay, was planned for the Marquess of Sligo by James Wyatt, a famous British architect of the Georgian period. Its main street, known as the Mall, runs along both sides of the gentle river Carrowbeg, which is crossed by several picturesque stone bridges and sheltered by a colonnade of lime trees. Westport is an important center for sea angling and was the site of a meeting at which the Irish Land League was formed in 1879. The town also provided the setting for a number of novels by George A. Birmingham, the pen name of James Owen Hannay, who was rector of the Church of Ireland here from 1893 to 1913. A mile and a half west of the town center, on a lovely estate overlooking Clew Bay and the Atlantic Ocean, is *Westport House,* a fine Georgian mansion that was the home of the Marquess of Sligo. The house is open to the public from April 1 through October 5 (phone: 98-25141 or 98-25430). Designed by the German architect Richard Cassels in 1730 and altered 50 years later by Wyatt, it houses fine collections of old English and Irish silver, paintings by Sir Joshua Reynolds and James O'Connor (perhaps the best of Irish landscape painters), Waterford crystal, and fine old furniture. The attractive marble staircase was built by Italian artisans brought here specifically for that purpose. The basement area contains a warren of shops, an amusement arcade, and a tea shop. Outside, horse caravans (no longer in use) are on display. *Westport House Country Estates* (phone: 98-25430) rents holiday homes and has a campground.

Just outside the gates to the grounds of Westport House is Westport Quay, where boats can be rented for boating and fishing on Clew Bay. On Collanmore Island in the bay, there is a sail-training center for beginners and intermediates. For information, contact *Glenans Irish Sailing Centres* (28 Marion Sq., Dublin 2; phone: 1-767775 or 1-611481). Good swimming can be found at nearby Bertra Beach. The *Westport Golf Club* (3 miles from town; phone: 98-25113) has an 18-hole, par 73 championship course across the bay from Croagh Patrick. One of its most interesting holes is the 15th (par 5), which requires a carry from the tee across Clew Bay.

Each June, a 4-day international sea angling festival and the 3-day *Westport Horse Show,* one of Ireland's most important, are held here. Ballad sessions are held in some hotels and pubs in summer. The Westport Tourist Information Office is on The Mall (phone: 98-25711).

CHECKING IN: *Olde Railway* – An old-fashioned, friendly hostelry on a tree-shaded street overlooking the river in which the rooms are comfortable, and the food is very good. The Mall, Westport (phone: 98-25166). Expensive.

Westport – The highest standards in the town are maintained at this modern, 49-room hotel. The staff is exceedingly friendly, and the food is first-rate. Westport, across the bridge at the bottom of James St., entering Newport Rd.; take the first left turn (phone: 98-25122). Expensive.

Westport Ryan's – Set on wooded grounds beside the lake, it offers 56 modest rooms. Westport, on the road from town to The Quay (phone: 98-25811). Expensive.

EATING OUT: *Ardmore House* – Specializing in fresh seafood, this small, intimate, candlelit restaurant overlooks Clew Bay. Owner-chef Pat Hoban prepares excellent continental and Irish dishes, while his wife Noreen supervises the dining room. Reservations advised in summer. Rosbeg, Westport, 1 mile from the town center (phone: 98-25994). Expensive.

Asgard – Owner-chef Michael Cadden specializes in seafood. The dining room, supervised by his wife, Mary, is candlelit and intimate. A lunch menu is available in the pub. The Quay (phone: 98-25319). Moderate.

Quay Cottage – Clams, lobster, mussels, and other shelled denizens of the deep are served all day in this quaint seaside inn. The Quay, Westport (phone: 98-26412). Moderate.

Railway – A family-run hostelry with Old World character and a popular pub where visitors can enjoy excellent seafood crêpes or just order a Guinness and mix with the locals. The Mall (phone: 98-25166). Moderate.

En Route from Westport – The graceful Croagh Patrick, Ireland's holy mountain, 5 miles west of town off R335, is one of the most impressive landmarks in the west of Ireland. Its 2,510-foot summit offers an inspiring view of the island-dotted bay, making the 2-hour climb worth the effort. St. Patrick is said to have spent 40 days and 40 nights in prayer and fasting atop the mountain in 441, and each year Catholics make pilgrimages to the mountain on the last Sunday in July. The route up the mountain begins near Murrisk Abbey, which was built in the 14th century for the Augustinians and has a notable east window.

Eight miles farther west is Louisburgh, a pleasant fishing village at the mouth of the river Bunowen. There are several good sandy beaches nearby at Old Head, Carramore, Berta, Carrowniskey, and Thallabawn. In addition to several small hotels and guesthouses, there are 10 self-catering cottages available through *Rent an Irish Cottage Ltd.;* for details, contact the tourist board (Eyre Sq., Galway; phone: 91-63081). A minor road west from Louisburgh leads to Roonah Quay, where boats are available for trips to Clare Island.

CLARE ISLAND: Steeped in the legends of the 16th-century sea queen Grace O'Malley, Clare Island guards the entrance to Clew Bay and offers visitors a sense of peace and remoteness. Grace O'Malley's massive square castle, on the east coast of the island above the harbor, was converted into a coast guard station more than 150 years ago and is not particularly interesting. Tradition says that the ferocious Grace was interred in Clare Abbey, a small 15th-century church about a mile and a half southwest of the harbor, but even if this is untrue, the abbey is worth seeing for its frescoes. There is only one small hotel on the island — Chris O'Grady's 13-room *Bayview* (phone: 98-26307) — but day-trippers can take advantage of several good beaches for bathing or picnics. A colorful regatta is held at Clare Island every July.

En Route from Clare Island – Back on the mainland, the route south from Louisburgh, R335, crosses a desolate moor and climbs past the village of Cregganbaum before descending to the Delphi valley, which has a series of lakes and is flanked by the Sheeffrey Hills (2,504 feet) on the left. A sharp turn south leads to the northern shore of Killary Harbour and to the handsome waterfall where the river Erriff comes down from the mountain. At Leenane, a sparse fishing village at a bend in the Killary, the road to the right, R336, leads through Joyce Country (see the *Connemara and the Aran Islands* route), along the northern banks of Lough Corrib, and back to Cong. Alternatively, follow R336 to Maam, then pick up N59 south to Galway City.

Antrim Coast

In many ways reminiscent of the California coast as seen from Highway 1, the 70-mile stretch of northeastern coastline between Larne and Portrush offers some of the most exceptional coastal scenery in Europe, with spectacular views of the sea and sky at every twist and turn. And along the eastern edge of the Antrim Coast, as far north as Ballycastle, drivers will be tempted to turn inland and explore the Glens of Antrim, a series of nine lovely valleys formed 20,000 years ago by retreating glaciers. Of great interest to scientists, the coastline is a veritable textbook illustration of the geological history of the earth, with its rock layers of red sandstone, white chalk, black basalt, and blue clay jutting out from beneath ancient lava flows.

Antrim has been inhabited for at least 5,000 years and probably for a great deal longer than that. In Glenballyeamon, near Cushendall, stone "ax factories" dating from the Neolithic period have been discovered, and it is known that some of the tools made here of the local stone, diorite, were "exported" to countries outside Ireland. A Harvard University archaeological expedition has uncovered several layers of flint tools in a cliff face at Cushendun; the archaeologists think these may be the key to the Irish Stone Age. So many ancient artifacts have been found near the ruins of Olderfleet Castle in Larne that fragments from Ireland's Stone Age are termed "Larnian." And Danish archaeologists believe that this area is a prime example of the development of post–Ice Age society.

Although not part of the Roman Empire, Antrim was visited by the Romans, and trade developed with Britain. Upon the decline of the empire and the weakening of its defense, Irish kings launched raiding parties to steal booty and capture slaves. One of the most famous of these slaves, Patrick, son of a Roman centurion, who was later to become Ireland's patron saint, spent 7 years as a shepherd on Slemish Mountain (1,437 feet) in County Antrim before he escaped to Gaul. The region resounds with anecdotes about the saint's activities.

Many Irish missionaries who set out to convert Europe to Christianity hailed from the north of Ireland, most notably St. Columbanus and St. Gall, who went to Germany, Switzerland, and Italy, and St. Columba, who went to Scotland. Because of the proximity of Ireland and Scotland, there has always been much traffic between the two countries. Besides Christianity, Ireland gave Scotland its Gaelic language (which replaced Pictish from the 5th century on), shared the game of hurling (called shinny or shinty in Scotland), and even sent over the famous bagpipes (there's a joke hereabouts that the Irish exported the bagpipes to Scotland and the Scots haven't seen the joke yet).

The town of Carrickfergus is named in honor of Fergus, a Gael who was monarch of the ancient kingdom of Dalriada. Two Scotsmen, Robert the

Bruce and his brother Edward, who had freed their country from English rule, attempted to do the same for Ireland, but succeeded only briefly — Edward was declared King of Ireland in 1316, but his death 2 years later threw Ireland back into its feud with the English crown. The wars continued until the end of the 16th century, culminating in the conquest of the north by the soldiers of Queen Elizabeth I. To tighten English control, a new policy — the "plantation of Ireland" — was devised. This plan for introducing Scottish and English Protestant settlers into the area was quite effective. A few Plantation manor houses still exist today and can be seen along this route in Ballygally, on Rathlin Island, and other places.

Whatever their roots, the people in the Antrim area are exceptionally friendly. In the countryside, visitors will be bidden the time of day and perhaps engaged in a conversation, for as the Irish are fond of saying, "When God made time, he made plenty of it."

The first stop on our Antrim Coast route is Carrickfergus on the east coast, 9 miles northeast of Belfast. From Carrickfergus, the route hugs the northeastern shore of Ireland. The road from Larne to Cushendall (25 miles), mostly at the foot of cliffs, was a great engineering feat when it was constructed in the 1830s. Its magnificent east coast curves around the base of steep headlands between which the beautiful nine glens of Antrim open to the sea. Almost every bay along the coast is a link in a chain of picturesque fishing ports and attractive holiday resorts. Torr Head, the northeasternmost point of the mainland, is only 12 miles from Scotland. Farther west along the coast is the Giant's Causeway, a curious basalt rock formation that is Ireland's most celebrated natural wonder, and a UNESCO World Heritage Site. Portrush forms the western boundary of the Antrim Coast and County Antrim. The tour ends at the ancient walled city of Londonderry.

Generally, hotels in Northern Ireland are not first class by international standards, but they are always clean and congenial. Most hotels have a dining room, where the food served is fresh and hearty, and occasionally haute cuisine. Hotels listed here as expensive will charge $80 and up for a double room with bath and full breakfast; those listed as moderate will run $60 to $80, and those listed as inexpensive will cost $60 or under. Guesthouses will generally cost $30 to $40. An expensive meal for two, including VAT but no beverages, usually costs $50 or more; from $35 to $50 for moderate; and less than $35 for inexpensive.

En Route from Belfast – For a full report on the city's sites, hotels, and restaurants, see *Belfast,* THE CITIES. Take M5 from Belfast to Newtownabbey; then pick up A2 to Carrickfergus, a total distance of about 9 miles.

CARRICKFERGUS: Said to be one of the oldest towns in Northern Ireland, Carrickfergus was the north's main port and principal town until Belfast began to expand in the 17th century. Its proud history is personified by the grand castle built on a spit of basalt rock and standing watch over the harbor. Northern Ireland's largest and best-preserved Norman castle, Carrickfergus, has been carefully restored. Note especially the 14th-century portcullis and the machinery that operates it. Sections of the castle were begun by John de Courcy, Earl of Ulster, in about 1180 and construction was completed by his successor, Hugh de Lacy, by about 1205, although renovations were made as late as the 17th century to accommodate newly developed artillery. The stronghold's central feature is the rectangular keep. About 90 feet high and 60 feet square, it has 5 stories linked by a spiral stone staircase that winds up to the roof and ramparts. From here sentries could survey the sea for hostile ships, and troops could defend the fortress.

Carrickfergus has seen many aggressors: King John in 1210 attempted to subordinate the Earl of Ulster; Robert the Bruce of Scotland and his brother Edward took the castle in 1315 (in an unsuccessful attempt to drive the English from Ireland); and the French in 1710 under General Thurst merely wanted to steal food and money. For 7 centuries, the castle was continuously garrisoned; then, in 1928, it became a museum. Visitors can inspect the banqueting hall, view the old castle well, and sneak down into the impressive dungeon. The castle also houses the *Regimental Museum*, which features armor, artillery, cavalry uniforms, and displays on the history of the Inniskilling Dragoons, Irish Hussars, and North Irish Horse. Open 10 AM to 6 PM daily (2 to 6 PM Sundays), April through September; daily 10 AM to 4 PM (Sundays, 2 to 4 PM) the rest of the year. Admission charge (phone: 9603-51273).

St. Nicholas Church, first built in 1185, retains some of the original 12th-century arcades and other features added in the 14th century, but most of the present structure dates from the 17th and 18th centuries. The 16th-century Flemish John-the-Baptist window in the nave is possibly the oldest stained glass in Ulster. The pretty churchyard is entered through a reconstruction of a distinctive, early-19th-century archway and bell tower.

Sections of Carrickfergus's town wall remain, particularly the North Gate, which is the strongest due to restoration work in 1911. The four walls of the old County Antrim Courthouse on High Street, which date from 1613, are now the exterior walls of the Town Hall. Also on High Street are some attractive 18th-century houses.

One mile east of town is Boneybefore, where the grandparents of Andrew Jackson (seventh President of the United States) lived. A monument marks the site of their home, while a reconstruction of their late-18th-century thatch-roofed, dirt-floor cottage, which contains period furnishings and exhibits, stands nearby. Open daily 10 AM to 1 PM, 2 to 5 PM, June through September; 10 AM to 1 PM and 2 to 4 PM, October through May. Small admission charge. (phone: 9603-64972).

LARNE: Continue north on A2 to Larne. Second only to Belfast in its importance as a port in Northern Ireland, Larne is the closest point in Ireland to Britain, and the ferry trip to Stranaer, Scotland, takes just a bit over two hours. Huge freight ships as well as smaller pleasure craft rock in the harbor. A 95-foot tower is Larne's landmark. Modeled after the traditional Irish round tower, it was built to honor James Claine, a member of Parliament who so loved the harbor's view that he was buried upright so he "would never lose sight of it."

ISLAND MAGEE: Only a short ferry ride from Larne, Island Magee is actually a peninsula attached to the mainland just north of Carrickfergus. Most of its acreage is given over to farming, but there are plenty of spots for exploring and picnicking. The 250-foot basalt cliffs on the eastern coast of the island, called the Gobbins, are inhabited by flocks of singing sea birds. (Be careful on the cliffside walkways; they can be dangerous.) At Portmuck, north of the Gobbins, are the ruins of a castle believed to have been the home of a Scottish family, the Magees, from whom the snip of land takes its name. On the island's northern tip, near Brown's Bay, is the 9-hole course at the *Larne Golf Club* (phone: 9603-72043).

En Route from Larne – The road to Ballygally, A2, passes Ballygally Head, a cluster of irregular rock pillars formed by lava that bubbled to the surface in the Cenezoic era.

Overlooking Ballygally Bay is Ballygally Castle, a Plantation manor house built in 1625 by a Scottish landowner, James Shaw, and turned into a hotel in 1948.

At Glenarm, the first of Antrim's nine glens, and oldest of the glen villages, turn left on B97 for a scenic diversion that temporarily takes visitors inland from the sea. Behind the village is Glenarm Castle, residence of the 13th Earl of Antrim. (The first earl to live there was Sorley Boy MacDonnell, an active Irish foe of Queen Elizabeth I.) The ancient estate is divided in two by the Glenarm River. On the east side is Glenarm Forest, a lovely public park, and on the west side is Glenarm Castle, completed in 1636. The castle, visible from several points on the road, has been greatly altered over the years and now strikingly resembles the Tower of London. The castle is not open to the public.

After passing the castle, follow B97 south and then west, turning onto A42, passing through The Sheddings. To the south is a solitary extinct volcano, Slemish Mountain (1,437 feet). Legend holds it was on the slopes of Slemish that a young slave, Patrick, served his master Miluic as a swine herder. Years later Patrick became a priest, and in his *Confessio* described himself as but "a beardless boy" of 16 when Irish pirates carried him away (ca. 389) from his family, who were Romans, probably living in what today is Wales. On Slemish Mountain, Patrick supposedly received divine visions urging him to ready himself for a life of Christian missionary activity; after 7 years of hardship and loneliness he escaped from Ireland to Gaul to fulfill that vision. For centuries since, Slemish has been a popular site for pilgrimages on *St. Patrick's Day*.

At Broughshane, head 2½ miles northeast to the dramatically situated ruins of Skerry Hill Old Church, built on the supposed site of the of the *rath* (ring fort) of Miluic, Patrick's master. Just outside the church is a "footmark" in rock, which legend holds to be that of the Angel Victor, made as he ascended to heaven after one of his earthly visits to Patrick. Next, retrace your way on the A42 through Glencloy, a valley crosscut by streams and splashed by waterfalls, back to Carnlough on the coast.

Carnlough, an old limestone quarrying town embraced by a sandy bay, is a popular summer vacation spot. In season, the picturesque limestone harbor is abob with pleasure boats full of expectant anglers. In the center of town is a bridge over the main street that was built by the Marquess of Londonderry in 1854 to carry the small railway that transported limestone from the quarries in the hills above the harbor. Other limestone landmarks in the town include a square clock tower, the former Town Hall, and the harbormaster's office.

En Route from Carnlough – North from Carnlough is Garron Point, with a lookout point that provides visitors the opportunity to savor the hillsides of one of the most scenic of Antrim's glens, Glenariff. At the foot of Glenariff is Red Bay, which takes its name from the sloping, red sandstone cliffs. The cliffs are punctured at two points by tunnels through which the road passes.

At the end of the bay's straggling shorefront village of Waterfoot, turn left on A43 for a 5-mile drive up the side of Glenariff to the Glenariff Forest Park. The park has a café, a shop, toilets, a ranger office, and picnic tables. Wonderful views can be had walking; signposted routes range from half a mile to 4 miles (phone: 26637-232). Return to the coast.

 CHECKING IN/EATING OUT: *Ballygally Castle* – A 17th-century manor house with a 20th-century addition, this hotel has lovely views of Ballygally Bay and 30 modern bedrooms, some with sea views in the old manor house tower. The sleek dining room, enclosed by picture windows facing the sea, is a good choice for coffee, tea, or dinner. The fresh fish is especially well prepared. 274 Coast Rd., Ballygally (phone: 574-83212). Expensive.

Drum-Na-Greagh – This clifftop hotel offers 16 comfortable rooms, each with private bath and either a sea or glen vista. Fish is a specialty at the two restaurants on the premises. Three miles north of Ballygally on Coast Rd. in Glenarm (phone: 574-84651). Expensive.

Londonderry Arms – Filled with carved furniture and sporting an open fire, Carnlough's ivy-covered hotel retains its cozy Georgian coaching-inn air. Built in 1848 by the Marchioness of Londonderry, it was passed down to one of her descendants, Sir Winston Churchill, in 1921. Since 1947, the 14-room hotel has been owned by the O'Neill family, who enjoy a reputation for dispensing good food and who also operate *Hessie's,* a bistro featuring seafood and a wine bar, down the street overlooking the harbor. Afternoon tea is served in the hotel. There is an Irish crafts shop on the premises. 20 Harbour Rd., Carnlough (phone: 574-885255, 574-885458, or 574-885459). Moderate.

CUSHENDALL/CUSHENDUN: The next stop on A2 is Cushendall, a bustling town whose streets are lined with stately Georgian and Regency houses. In the village center is a structure called Curfew Tower, a sort of jail built by Frances Turnley in 1809. Cushendall is a holiday center, offering swimming, boating, and fishing.

A few miles west of Cushendall, on an unnumbered country road, are signs for Ossian's Grave, a court cairn or burial mound made of stones. The Ossian in question was a poet warrior in the 3rd century AD and supposedly the son of that mythological Irish hero Finn MacCool. Be warned that it's not an easy climb up the lower slopes of Tievebulliagh Hill to the grave. Return to A2, and on to Cushendun.

Cushendun is regarded by some as one of the most attractive Irish villages. Threaded by the river Glendun, Cushendun occupies a lovely sandy crescent of shore washed by the bay and anchored by sandstone cliffs at either end. The Cornish-style cottages on the north side of the river were designed by Clough William Ellis, an imaginative and innovative architect whose most famous work is at Portmeirion in Wales. Cushendun's whitewashed stone cottages and the surrounding countryside are now maintained by the National Trust, which operates an information center, gift shop, and tea shop in the village. This area has been much painted by artists, and in summer they are often busy at work. Despite traffic, the village is delightfully tranquil. Boats are available for hire, and the many caves in the sandstone cliffs are open for exploration. One of these is 20 miles deep and leads to Cave House, once the vacation home of the poet John Masefield and now owned by the Catholic church. The famous Irish chieftain Shane O'Neill (Shane the Proud), an opponent of Queen Elizabeth I and a leader of an Ulster revolt against England, was decapitated by the MacDonnells in Cushendun in 1567.

En Route from Cushendun – For a pleasant side trip, take A2 slightly east, then north, over the Glendun Viaduct, an 82-foot-high bridge that crosses the river Glendun and offers an impressive panorama of the area. Across the bridge, the road continues to Loughareema, called locally the "vanishing lake": When there is a downpour, the lake can rise and fall dramatically because of the permeable chalk bed underneath. Near Loughareema is Balleypatrick Forest with a 4½-mile scenic drive. It's also a good spot for picnicking, pony trekking, or just walking.

Returning to Cushendun, take the Torr road along the coast to Fair Head and then continue on A2 to Ballycastle.

 CHECKING IN: Villa – Up a steep lane is this 19th-century hilltop guesthouse with 3 rooms (2 with private bath) and a truly spectacular view of sheep grazing on startlingly green fields, the sea far below. Morning coffee, afternoon tea, and strawberries and cream are served in the garden in season. Open April through October. 185 Torr Rd., Cushendun (phone: 26674-252). Inexpensive.

FAIR HEAD: A short detour off the Torr Road leads to the summit of this impressive 636-foot-high cliff. Fair Head rises from huge sandstone blocks and towers over Murlough Bay. The terrain across the mouth of the bay and opposite the head is gentler, with lush green vegetation carpeting the slope right down to the sandy beach. This area was much loved by Roger Casement, the Irish patriot and international philanthropist, and a monument to him stands here. The descent to Murlough Bay is steep, although the road is in good condition. Be sure to sound your horn on blind curves. Return to the Torr road, drive west to Ballyvoy, and rejoin A2 to Ballycastle.

BALLYCASTLE: At the mouth of the river Glenshesk and overlooked by the 1,696-foot-high Knocklayd Hill, Ballycastle is actually two towns linked by Quay Road, a pretty avenue lined with trees and Georgian and Victorian homes. Lower Town is a seaside resort with facilities for swimming, tennis, boating, golf, and fishing. Upper Town, the older of the two, has restaurants, shops, and many fine houses. The center of Upper Town is called the Diamond, where, centuries ago, the castle of the Scottish MacDonnell family, for whom the town was named, once stood. Today, in its place, is the Greek-style Holy Trinity Church, built in 1756, as well as a memorial to George O'Connor, one of the town's patrons. The Diamond is also the scene of the annual *Ould Lammas Fair,* a kind of flea market where all sorts of new and used articles are sold, including the local specialties of dulse (edible seaweed) and yellow man (toffee). First chartered in 1606, *Ould Lammas* is the oldest of Ireland's traditional fairs. It's held the last Monday and Tuesday in August. Along the side streets leading from the Diamond are a few shops, such as *D. Donnelly & Co.* (14 Ann St.; phone: 2657-62395), which feature paintings by local artists.

On the outskirts of town is the Franciscan Bonamargy Friary, founded by the MacQuillan family in 1500. Damaged by fire in 1589, it was refurbished and occupied until 1642, after which it gradually fell into decay; in 1931 the friary underwent final restoration. Note the family tomb of the Earls of Antrim (MacDonnell).

The town has mythological as well as religious associations, for it was in the nearby Sea of Moyle that the tragic Children of Lir, who were changed into swans by their jealous stepmother, had to spend 300 of their 900 years' transmutation.

RATHLIN ISLAND: A visit to Rathlin Island can be a delightful interlude in a driving journey, for cars must be left behind and the island explored on foot. The 6-mile crossing from Ballycastle takes 50 minutes by motorboat and should be undertaken only in good weather, as the Rathlin Sound can be treacherous when rough. (Long ago the sound was called the Cauldron of Brecain because it was in these stormy waters that Brecain — grandson of the legendary King of Ireland, Niall of the Nine Hostages — perished with his fleet.)

The approach to the harbor in Church Bay provides a good view of Rathlin's steep, 200-foot-high white limestone cliffs that surround almost all of the island. Fishing is the main occupation on the island; lobster, conger eel, and many varieties of fish are found in Church Bay. To go fishing, talk to one of the local fishermen about arranging an outing.

With a population of only about 100 — down from 1,000 a century and a half ago — people are a minority here. The island is really owned and occupied by the thousands of sea birds that nest on Rathlin's crags and cliffs. The best vantage point for bird watching is West Lighthouse, on the western end of the island. And Kebble, nearby, is a breeding ground for the island's puffin, guillemot, and razorbill population.

Although tiny, Rathlin has seen much history. The island's most famous landmark is Bruce's Cave, on the eastern end, to which Robert the Bruce retreated in 1306 with 3,000 of his men, after his defeat to the English at Perth, Scotland. A favorite Irish legend holds that while sitting in the cave in the spring of 1307, brooding over his military loss, Bruce spied a spider, subsequently referred to by Winston Churchill as "the most celebrated in history." While Bruce watched, the spider repeatedly tried to ascend to the cave's roof by a gossamer strand. Seven times Bruce saw the spider attempt to hook its web from one rock to another before finally succeeding. Inspired by the spider's persistence, Bruce returned to Scotland to fight again, and eventually gained the Scottish throne at the Battle of Bannockburn.

At Knockans are the ruins of an Irish sweathouse, a primitive version of the sauna, for which steam was produced by pouring water on heated stones. (Remember Tomas Larkin purging his soul — and sweating off a drunk — in the Leon Uris novel *Trinity?*) In the center of the island, Brockley is the site of a Stone Age ax factory, and, slightly north, Doonmore once was the site of an ancient hill fort. Near the harbor is an 18th-century manor house built by Viscount Gage.

 CHECKING IN: *Rathlin Guest House* – Down on the harbor a few minutes' walk from Tony McCuaig's pub is a small guesthouse with a reputation for hearty breakfasts. It has 5 rooms, none with private bath. Snacks, soup, and sandwiches are available; dinner is by arrangement. The Quay, Rathlin (phone: 2657-63917). Inexpensive.

En Route from Rathlin Island – The coastal road (B15), west of Ballycastle and leading to Giant's Causeway, provides about a dozen miles of some of the Antrim's most charming sites. Kinbane Castle, one of the least known but most picturesque ruin sites, is poised on a white chalk pinnacle surrounded by the sea. The ruins here are what remains of a 16th-century castle built by Colla MacDonnell, the brother of Sorley Boy (see "Dunluce Castle"). From the parking lot, there is a steep path, with a handrail, that can be slippery. The area offers a fine view across to Rathlin Island.

At the turn-off for Carrick-a-Rede (rock in the road) Island, proceed to the parking lot and then follow the National Trust footpath to the coast. There, a swaying 63-foot wooden plank bridge with a wire handrail provides the only access for salmon fishermen and tourists to cross over a narrow 80-foot deep chasm from the mainland to Carrick-a-Rede Island. On the island, salmon fishermen lower and hoist their boats from the rocky peak with a derrick. The bridge, re-erected early each May and dismantled in mid-September, swings in the winds, even in summer, but the superb coastal scenery is worth the perils of crossing.

Slightly farther along the coast, follow a snaking S-curve road down to Ballintoy Harbor, a photographer's dream, with the sea set between white piers, plus a white beach beneath a sheer black volcanic cliff, and an archipelago of small jagged islands. There is a picnic site in the area, and a café is open in season. A pretty white church at a bend in the road down to the harbor was used as a refuge by Protestants during the 1641 rebellion.

Just past Ballintoy Harbor is White Park Bay, a lovely mile-long crescent of white sand with a backdrop of dunes and cliffs, which is one of Ireland's most beautiful beaches. Leading from the beach are footpaths to Ballintoy Harbor and the Giant's Causeway. At the western end of White Park Bay is Portbraddon, a hamlet of a half dozen houses tucked into a cleft in the cliffs. It's the home of Ireland's smallest church, measuring 12 feet by 6½ feet.

GIANT'S CAUSEWAY: After visiting White Park Bay take B146 off A2 to the Giant's Causeway. Traveling by stagecoach from London in the 18th century, Dr. Samuel Johnson wrote that the Giant's Causeway is "worth seeing but not worth going to see." Today, the Causeway remains worth seeing, and thanks to good roads, and the other memorable sights along the Antrim Coast that have been mentioned here, today's travelers have reason to disagree with the second part of Johnson's statement. The Giant's Causeway, in the care of the National Trust, was included on UNESCO's official World Heritage list of sites in 1987. It was at the end of the 17th century that the peculiar beauty of the Causeway — with its roughly 40,000 basaltic "stepping stones" (largely six-sided) which fit together so exactly that the natural volcanic wonder looks like the work of human hands — first attracted written attention. However, stories surrounding Northern Ireland's most famous sight are far more ancient. One tale has it that the giant, Finn MacCool, champion of Ireland, was much aggrieved at the insolent boasting of a certain Caledonian giant, who claimed he could beat all who came before him in Scotland. He told Finn that if it wasn't for getting himself wet in the sea, he would swim over to Ireland and give MacCool a thrashing. Finally, Finn could stand it no more and applied to the King of Ulster, who gave him leave to construct a stone causeway to Scotland. (Similar rock formations are found off the Scottish Isle of Staffa, at Fingal's Cave, named in honor of Finn.) When the causeway was completed, the Scot giant walked over the water to Ireland to fight Finn. By this time, however, Finn had become somewhat frightened at the thought of confrontation with the Caledonian. In a hastily hatched ploy, his wife helped him don baby clothes, and when the Scot giant arrived for battle, she pointed to Finn saying, "This is the baby; you should see his father." That was enough for the Caledonian giant, who fled back to Scotland, destroying the causeway behind him.

The more prosaic explanation for the causeway's existence is that it was formed by the quick-cooling lava that burst to the earth's surface in the Cenozoic era about 70 million years ago. Altogether there are about 40,000 basalt columns packed together in a shape so regular they seem constructed by craftsmen rather than by nature. Some sections of the lava were naturally molded into unique designs that have been given nicknames such as Lady's Fan, Lord Antrim's Parlour, the Giant's Horseshoe, and the Giant's Coffin. Another, called the Giant's Organ, is an astonishing 60-yard series of pillars of incredible regularity. Providing a backdrop to the causeway are large basalt pillars called the Chimney Tops; in 1588, the retreating Armada aimed an attack on these columns, thinking they were part of Dunluce Castle. Past these stacks is Port Na Spania Bay, where one of the Spanish galleons, the *Girona,* was shipwrecked. In recent years, the wreckage of the sunken ship was explored, and the items that were recovered are on display at *Ulster Museum* in Belfast. The collection consists of Renaissance jewelry, including a cross of the knight of Malta belonging to Captain Fabricio Spinola, some tableware, and artillery.

The *Giant's Causeway Interpretation Centre* houses entertaining and educational exhibits, from a size 25 shoe marked "Finn MacCool's boot?" to detailed geological explanations of the area. Also on view are displays on local flora and fauna, the fishing industry, and details about the interesting history of tourism to the Causeway. Mark Twain visited here in the 19th century during an era when local guides were spinning a "blatant brand of blarney" about the origins of the Causeway. An excellent 24-minute multimedia presentation on all aspects of the Giants's Causeway is shown in the center's 56-seat theater. Open year-round; 10 AM to 7 PM during July and August; closes as early as 4 PM the rest of the year, depending on the season. The center has a restaurant and National Trust shop, both open from *St. Patrick's Day* through October (phone: 2657-31855).

The adventurous can hire a boat and a boatman to wander through the nearby caves of the Causeway; one called the Runkerry is 700 feet long.

En Route from the Giant's Causeway – Bushmills, a pleasant hamlet 2 miles southwest on A2, is the home of the well-known Old Bushmills Distillery Co. Ltd., the oldest licensed distillery in the world, established by Thomas Phillips in 1608 and still in operation. Visitors to the distillery have included Peter the Great of Russia, who declared (in 1697), "Of all the beverages the Irish is the best." Today's visitors are welcome Mondays through Thursdays, 9 AM to noon and 1:30 to 3:30 PM; also open Friday mornings. The tour, which takes about an hour, includes each stage of the triple distillation whiskey-making and bottling process, ending at the reception center where visitors can sample the product and browse in the gift shop. Since the company is small, appointments are suggested during the summer and essential on inclement days (phone: 2657-31521).

 CHECKING IN/EATING OUT: *Bayview* – A small, comfortable hotel facing a harbor, it offers 16 rooms, each with private bath, pool room, restaurant, and 24-hour guest pantry. Guests can chase away any chill in front of the inviting lobby fireplace. About a mile from Bushmills in the fishing village of Portballintrae (phone: 2657-31453 or 2657-31223). Moderate.

Bushmill's Inn – A recently refurbished 200-year-old coaching inn, it has 11 rooms, all with private bath and country-style decor. The common rooms have pine wood, peat fires, and Ulster charm. For French provincial fare and a carvery, dine at the hotel's formal restaurant. There's also a less formal brasserie. Lunch and dinner are served daily (last order at 9 PM). Main St., Bushmills (phone: 2657-32339). Moderate.

DUNLUCE CASTLE: Two miles west on A2, is Dunluce Castle, built by Richard de Burgh, Earl of Ulster, in about 1300. Awesomely placed on a basalt rock jutting from the sea, the structure is reached by a wooden walkway (which replaced the former drawbridge) and has five towers linked by a curtain wall. Since its builders thought — with some justification — that the fortress was impregnable, the castle doesn't have a keep. A cave passage through the rock beneath the castle, though, served as a secret exit and entryway. Dunluce was held for centuries by the de Mandevilles (also called the MacQuillans). In 1584, the Irish MacDonnells captured Dunluce from its English occupants when one of their countrymen employed in the castle hauled men up the cliff in a basket by night. In about 1595, with proceeds from the sale of treasure salvaged from the Spanish Armada galleon *Girona,* which had been wrecked nearby in 1588, the MacDonnells reconstructed Dunluce Castle, adding a magnificent banqueting hall. Preparing for a splendid repast in the hall, the kitchen was a hive of activity one stormy night in 1639 when, without warning, the entire kitchen tumbled into the sea 100 feet below. Of the staff, only a tinker mending pans in a window embrasure is thought to have survived. From that night, the Countess of Antrim refused to live at Dunluce. Over the centuries Dunluce gradually fell into decay, and today is the one of some of Ireland's most romantic ruins. Open Mondays through Saturdays from 10 AM to 7 PM and on Sundays, 2 to 7 PM, April through September; also open Tuesdays through Saturdays from 10 AM to 4 PM and on Sundays from 2 to 4 PM (closed 1 to 3:30 PM), October through March (no phone).

Continue on A2 for 7½ miles to Portrush. This resort town has long sandy beaches and facilities for tennis, boating, and fishing. It is most famous, however, for the outstanding links courses at *Royal Portrush Golf Club,* the only Irish club to have hosted the *British Open* (in 1951). *Royal Portrush*'s two 18-hole courses and one 9-hole course are located on 480 acres of wildflower-covered dunes, which are among the natural hazards that rule out the need for many bunkers. The scenic *Dunluce* course is the championship 18. Guests are welcome; weekdays are best, except Wednesday afternoons (phone: 265-822311).

For the first time, this route veers inland from Portrush to Coleraine via A29.

EATING OUT: *Ramore* – A chic harborside restaurant offering sophisticated food and service. Reservations required. Open Tuesdays through Saturdays for dinner only, 7 to 10 PM. An adjacent wine bar is open Mondays through Saturdays from noon to 2 PM and 5:30 to 9 PM and on Sundays, 7 to 10 PM. Portrush (phone: 265-824313). Moderate.

COLERAINE: A 17th-century Plantation town at the head of the river Bann estuary, Coleraine was established by the London Company on land granted by James I in 1613.

Since then Coleraine has become a bustling industrial center engaged in the distilling of whiskey and in the linen trade; it is a good regional shopping center. Some say that Coleraine's roots stretch far beyond the 17th century to prehistoric times, and, indeed, nearby archaeological excavations have indicated that there were settlements here as early as about 7000 BC. A mile south of Coleraine, on the east bank of the Bann, is Mountsandel, the ruin of a fort once held by an early King of Ulster and later by the de Courcys. This is also where the Mesolithic artifacts thought to be the earliest traces of civilization in Ireland were discovered.

Whatever Coleraine's ancient origins, most of its architecture is of relatively recent vintage because many earlier structures were either washed away, burned out, pillaged, or replaced. The newest additions are the modern concrete and brick buildings of the University of Ulster, a few miles north off Portrush Road.

From Coleraine, take the coast road, A2, to Downhill.

 CHECKING IN/EATING OUT: *Macduff's* – About 6 miles south of Coleraine, this charming Georgian establishment serves continental dinners featuring local country produce, fresh salmon, and game in season. Open from 7 to 9:30 PM Tuesdays through Saturdays. Reservations necessary. All 6 Georgian period bedrooms have private bath. 112 Killeague Rd., Blackhill (phone: 265-868433). Hotel, expensive; restaurant, moderate.

DOWNHILL: Most historians consider Downhill the private domain of the colorful — and eccentric — Bishop Frederick Augustus Hervey, fourth Earl of Bristol, who in 1779 began his reign in Derry, the second wealthiest of Ireland's church districts. He was a man of extremes: He lived extravagantly, collected art avidly, and traveled extensively. He always took a large group of attendants on his journeys, and hotel owners were so eager for his business that they sometimes named their establishments in his honor — hence, the many Bristol Hotels throughout Europe. Hervey's ostentatious lifestyle even included running horse races for the pleasure of his clergymen at Magilligan Strand, the 6-mile-long beach (Ireland's longest) below the castle. Hervey, however, was not all frivolity. His more serious accomplishments include putting into practice the Catholic Relief Act of 1791, leading a private army on horseback to the Volunteer Convention in Dublin, and supporting demands and rallies for an Irish Parliament.

No fewer than four different architects were employed in designing the bishop's splendid estate. The castle's interior was destroyed by fire in 1851 and refurbished in 1876, but the restoration bore little resemblance to the original. Parts of the estate still standing are the Bishop's Gate, an arched portal with Doric columns; the Lion Gate, a sandstone structure carved with the two animals that are on the Bristol coat of arms; and the Mussenden Temple, a circular structure with Corinthian columns built in 1783 by Michael Shanahan and modeled after the Italian temples of Vesta. Established as a memorial to Hervey's cousin — some say mistress — the temple was also used as the bishop's library. To reach the windswept temple, perched on a cliff above the sea, visitors can walk up a garden path at the Bishop's Gate, over a stile, across fields where sheep graze, and past the ruins of the former bishop's castle. Allow at least 45 minutes for the trip there and back, and wear sturdy shoes. Maintained by the National trust, the temple is open from 2 to 6 PM daily in July and August, and on weekends and holidays only, April through June and in September (phone: 265-848281). At Magilligan Point (the west end of the 6-mile Magilligan Strand) stands a Martello tower, one of the many early-19th-century fortresses built in response to Napoleonic invasions. From Magilligan Point it's 1 mile across the mouth of Lough Foyle to County Donegal.

En Route from Downhill – Take the steep-climbing Bishop's Road (yet another creation of Frederick Hervey) to Limavady. Along the scenic 9-mile road, stop at

Gortmore, a picnic site and lookout point offering a wonderful, far-reaching view of the mountains of Donegal, the Foyle estuary, and the Magilligan Plain, a flat triangle of sand dunes and farmlands. Farther along Bishop's Road the scenery varies from treeless, high moorland to deep forests. The road ends at B201; turn right to Limavady.

LIMAVADY: This old Georgian town set in the valley of the river Roe is perhaps best known as the place where Jane Ross heard and transcribed in 1851 the traditional Irish tune "Londonderry Air" (widely recognized as the music set to the lyrics of "Danny Boy") as it was played by a wandering fiddler named MacCormick. (The original composer is believed to have been Rory O'Caghan, a blind 16th-century harpist.)

When visiting Limavady's parish church, note its finely crafted woodwork and tapestried kneelers. Each of the latter has a different design; all were rendered by local women.

Limavady actually means "dog's leap" and refers to the legendary dog who leaped over a wide crevice to deliver an important message to the chieftain of north Derry Rory Dall O'Caghan. The parish church contains a carving of the "dog of Limavady," and a spot in Roe Valley Country Park is designated Dog's Leap in commemoration. Also in the park are picnic and camp sites, walking trails, and a memorial called O'Caghan's Rock, which marks the site where O'Caghan's castle once stood.

In 1896 some valuable Celtic gold objects were found in Broighter, the marsh area near Limavady. Although it is thought that these items — a miniature boat and pieces of jewelry — date from early Christian times, no one has ever determined to whom they belonged or whether they were hidden or lost. They are now on display at the *National Museum* in Dublin.

En Route from Limavady – Two and a half miles west of Limavady, on A2 to Londonderry, the route passes through Ballykelly Forest. Sometimes called Walworth Wood, it was planted in the 17th century to honor Sir William Walworth, head of the London Fishmongers' Company in the late 14th century. Walworth House, also part of the grounds, is now in ruins except for a few of its towers.

Continue along A2 to Londonderry.

LONDONDERRY: Most often bypassed by travelers en route to Donegal or Belfast, this hardworking city (also called Derry) astride the river Foyle deserves a visit as well. It's quite compact, and the major sites can be easily covered in a day's walk. Most of the special places are on the west side of the river within and just outside the old walls. For a complete report on the city, its sights, restaurants, and hotels, see *Londonderry,* THE CITIES.

County Down and the Mountains of Mourne

With a distinctive mixture of mountains, sea, and green-growing fields, long the subject of songs and stories, County Down's magic tapestry weaves itself over the southeast corner of Northern Ireland. The Down town of Newcastle, for example, is rhapsodized in the popular melody "Where the Mountains of Mourne Sweep Down to the Sea," while Irish courting customs are evoked in the ballad "Star of the County Down." More serious reflections on the landscape can be found in the novels and theological essays of C. S. Lewis, a native of north Down, and observations of the skyscape in the writings of such well-traveled authors as H. V. Morton, who described it as the most dramatic in Europe.

The 19th-century novels of the three Brontë sisters — Charlotte, Emily, and Anne — whose father was a native son, are perhaps the best-known literary works inspired by County Down. Patrick Brontë passed on to his daughters in Yorkshire the self-sufficient pride of his rural Down forebears as well as his own inclinations for writing. Episodes, characters, and landscapes in *Wuthering Heights, Jane Eyre,* and all the Brontë books owe something to Patrick's memories and stories of his youth in County Down. The Brontë Homeland Route, included in this driving tour, gives travelers a sense of the powerful impact the ancestral soil and soul had on these writers' works.

With the inclusion of the city of Armagh, our driving tour also encompasses aspects of Ireland that led it to become known as the "land of saints and scholars." St. Patrick's roots are deeper in Ulster than anywhere else on the island, and nowhere as deep as in Armagh and Downpatrick. This area was inhabited, however, well before Patrick's 5th-century Christian missionary work. The earliest settlements in County Down date from the Mesolithic period (about 7000 BC). Later, in the neolithic period (4000–2000 BC), inhabitants practiced rudimentary farming; then, around 700 BC, the Celts arrived from central Europe with their iron weapons. The principal northern stronghold for the Celts, a society of warriors ruled by high kings, was Emain Macha, just outside Armagh. Surviving nearly until the time of St. Patrick, their settlements were *raths,* or ring forts, circular earthen fortifications, usually on hilltops, inside of which the community or individual existed in relative safety.

Monks in the early centuries of the Christian era were the chroniclers of Down history, especially of the warfare among Irish chieftains. The remains of the monasteries and fortified homesteads of the period survive in great numbers (some 1,300 are said to exist in County Down alone). From the 9th to the 11th century, Viking raids on the exposed Down coast were numerous and merciless. During the 12th century, the Anglo-Normans invaded and conquered the area, often building their castles on the remains of hill forts. The Norman era was followed by Elizabethan attempts to rule through the policy of Plantation, so the 17th century saw the settlement of Northern Ireland, including Down, by tens of thousands of immigrant English and Scots. The Scots, more numerous and mostly Presbyterian, were fine farmers. Getting the best agricultural land, while the native Irish got mostly hill country, they set about building houses, towns, and roads. Their industry gave Northern Ireland much of the character it retains today. During the 19th century, the Industrial Revolution began to take hold in north Down, although the country was still significantly agricultural. Shipbuilding and linen manufacturing created far more prosperity for the north than for the south of Ireland.

Dominating the region are the almost impenetrable Mourne Mountains: No road reaches their center — often called the Wilderness — so they naturally beckon the walker. Within the space of 25 miles, 15 summits rise above 2,000 feet. Slieve Donard (a mountain named for one of St. Patrick's disciples, a hermit who spent his life on its slopes), near Newcastle, has the highest peak, at nearly 2,800 feet. Roads ringing these Inner Mournes provide the motorist with a constantly changing panorama. C. S. Lewis wrote of the Mourne vista: "Imagine the mountains . . . Sometimes they are blue, sometimes violet; but quite often they look transparent — as if huge sheets of gauze had been cut into mountainous shapes and hung up there."

The Mournes are "young" mountains — contemporary with the Alps — but much worn down by glaciers. Five varieties of granite — from gray to pink — were created during volcanic action about 75 million years ago. Over the centuries, Mourne granite provided the ballast for many ships. As the stonecutting industry developed, the granite was used to pave the streets of English cities. Light gray granite boulders strewn throughout the rich Down soil has always made plowing difficult. For generations, the boulders have been dug up by farmers and built into miles of dry-stone walls that mark the boundaries of some 15,000 small fields in the Mourne region. Smaller stones left in the fields provide the good natural drainage necessary for potatoes — an important product in all of Down, but with the highest yield in the Annalong-Kilkeel area.

Agriculture still is the main industry in southeast Northern Ireland, but there is considerable forestry and sea fishing as well. Because of the lack of good land routes through the Mournes, the sea often compensates as the major means of commercial transportation. While timber and "taties" (potatoes) are shipped out from the seaside towns and villages of County Down and the Ards Peninsula, fish are hauled in to local harbors. The cultivation limit is about 700 feet in the Mournes, since the growing season above that altitude is too short to be economical. With soil crops financially unfeasible, much of the higher Mourne land is given over to sheep grazing. In addition to the grass and scrub growth on which the sheep feed, mountain vegetation includes bristly brilliant yellow gorse (whin), several hues of heather, bog cotton, purple moon grass, fuchsia, and reddish bracken.

While this touring area is a delight for those whose intellects run to antiquities and antiques, even citified souls will respond to the natural environment. Sea, sun, soil, shadow, sheep, and the stillness of mountains combine here to produce a rare effect in modern life: a soothing tranquillity. And after an invigorating session of historical sightseeing, from ring forts to round towers, there's always a warming pot of tea, or a pint, at the end of the trail.

Our driving route begins and ends in Belfast, starting in a southwesterly counterclockwise direction to the coast — with a detour to Armagh — and looping around the main mass of the Mournes (except for scenic inland incursions) northeast to St. Patrick country around Downpatrick. It returns by way of the Ards Peninsula, sampling the best of both its coastlines. The approximate distance from west to east (Armagh to Portaferry) is 55 miles; north to south (Belfast to Rostrevor), 45 miles.

An expensive hotel in the area will charge $95 to $130 for a double room with private bath and breakfast. Moderate accommodations will cost $60 to $90, and inexpensive, less than $60. Staying at a guest or farmhouse can be considerably less expensive. A three-course meal for two, including service and VAT (but not beverages), will cost an average of $55 or more in an expensive restaurant, $35 to $50 in a moderate one, and $25 to $35 in places listed as inexpensive.

BELFAST: For a complete report on the city, its sights, hotels, and restaurants, see *Belfast,* THE CITIES.

En Route from Belfast – Take M1 southwest from Belfast. After the Lisburn bypass, pick up A1 south for Hillsborough. Follow the signs off A1 into Hillsborough. The total distance from Belfast is 12 miles.

HILLSBOROUGH: This architecturally elegant town is a fashionable suburb of Belfast and the capital of Northern Ireland's antiques trade. It was little more than forest and moorland when Moyses Hill, a native of Devon, England, arrived in Ireland in 1573. He served as an officer in the army of the Earl of Essex, sent by Elizabeth I to subdue the rebellious O'Neills. When the wars were over, Hill remained, holding important offices under the Crown, yet identifying himself with the Irish by marrying Alice, sister of Sorley Boy MacDonnell (see entry for "Dunluce Castle," *Antrim Coast,* DIRECTIONS). Over generations, the Hill family became numbered among the wealthiest landowners in Ireland. This town was named after them when Charles II chartered it as a borough in 1662.

The Hillsborough Parish Church (Church of Ireland, Episcopal), a beautifully situated town landmark, was enlarged from an earlier edifice at enormous expense to Wills Hill, Earl of Hillsborough and first Marquis of Downshire, who completed the improvements in 1773. The church remains one of the finest examples of Gothic Revival architecture in Ireland, essentially unaltered by later renovation. It is but one example of the efforts made by generations of the Hill family to make Hillsborough a tasteful showplace. From the church's sturdy tower, which houses a peal of 10 bells, rises a graceful 120-foot spire. The 1772 organ by John Snetzler, the most famous organ builder of the 18th century, and the 1795 small organ by George Pike England frequently are used for concerts. The State Chair is used by Northern Ireland's secretary of state, who resides in Hillsborough Castle, or by members of the royal family when they visit. Facing each other by the entrance gates, across the gracious tree-lined mall that leads to the church, are the sexton's house and the parish room, which were the girls' and boys' schools, respectively, when built in 1773.

On rising ground next to the church is Hillsborough Fort, built in 1630. It has been much altered since then, but the well-preserved stone structure retains many of the original architectural details. After the Restoration, Charles II made it a royal fort and named Arthur Hill the hereditary constable. The title carried with it the responsibility, as well as the expense, of maintaining a private garrison of 20 armed men, whom Hill dressed in uniforms of white, black, and scarlet. Called the Castlemen, the garrison was employed well into the 20th century. King Billy (England's William III) spent 4 nights in Hillsborough Fort in 1690 on his way to victory at the Battle of the Boyne. The fort is open year-round (closed Mondays). A lake behind the fort has a footpath around it.

At the top of steep Main Street, handsomely lined with Georgian buildings, is Hillsborough Castle on the Square, completed in 1797. Formerly known as Government House, the castle was the official residence of the governor of Northern Ireland from 1925 until the termination of the office in 1973. Today, in addition to housing the official representative of the queen, it accommodates visiting members of the royal family and foreign diplomats. The ornamental ironwork entrance gates, built by the brothers Thornberry in 1745, are the finest example of their kind surviving in Northern Ireland. The Georgian Market House on the Square is preserved as a Historic Monument.

CHECKING IN: *White Gables* – This medium-size full-service hotel, the only one in Hillsborough, is on the outskirts of town. It has 25 double rooms with private baths, landscaped gardens, good facilities for children, and opportunities for fishing. There's also a fine restaurant (see *Eating Out*). 23 Dromore Rd., Hillsborough (phone: 846-682755). Expensive.

EATING OUT: *Hillside Bar* – The bar menu offers a salad bar and homemade pâté and soups, while the à la carte menu features spareribs, salmon mayonnaise, and beef *chasseur.* Open noon to 2:30 PM and 7 to 9:30 PM, Mondays through Thursdays; 12:30 to 2 PM on Sundays. 21 Main St., Hillsborough (phone: 846-682765). Moderate.

White Gables – A well-appointed restaurant in the hotel of the same name, it features French fare prepared with fresh, locally grown vegetables and game in season. All desserts and pastries are baked on the premises. Open daily 12:30 to 2:15 PM for lunch and 5:30 to 9:15 PM (8 PM on Sundays) for dinner. 23 Dromore Rd., Hillsborough (phone: 846-682755). Moderate.

Marquis of Downshire – Dine on specialties such as grills, scampi, and salads in a comfortable pub atmosphere. Open Mondays through Saturdays, noon to 2:30 PM and 8 to 10 PM. Pub grub served from 11:30 AM to 11 PM. 48 Lisburn St., Hillsborough (phone: 846-682095). Inexpensive.

Plough Inn – For those who seek local character, this is the place for drinks and tasty pub grub. Open Mondays through Saturdays from 11:15 AM to 11 PM and on Sundays from 12:15 to 10 PM. On the Square, opposite Hillsborough Castle (phone: 846-682985). Inexpensive.

BANBRIDGE: Return to A1 and continue southwest to Banbridge, a pleasant market and industrial town on the upper river Bann. The town's main thoroughfare (Bridge and Newry St.) is split into three sections, with dignified shop-lined terraces on each side and an underpass through the center of the steep street. The Banbridge "cut" was made in 1834, when the town was an important stop on the Belfast–Dublin stagecoach route, out of consideration for the horses pulling uphill. In the center of the road, near where a bridge crosses the Bann, is the Crozier Monument (1862), featuring four polar bears in stone. It stands in remembrance of Captain Francis Crozier, born in a house opposite, who went with Admiral Peary to the Arctic and died on the tragic expedition to Greenland.

ARMAGH: Take A50 northwest from Banbridge to Gilford; from there, pick up A51 to Armagh, a total of less than 20 miles. Armagh, with a population of about 15,000, is the ecclesiastical capital of Ireland. It has two cathedrals — one Church of Ireland (Anglican), the other Roman Catholic — both named for St. Patrick, who founded his principal church here in AD 445.

The story of the city of Armagh starts much farther back, however, since it has a claim to being Ireland's oldest recorded settlement. Ptolemy, the 2nd-century geographer who produced a map of the known world based on earlier maps and reports from travelers and seamen of the period, included among several regions and rivers mentioned in Ireland a specific place identified as Isamnion, which most scholars consider a form of *emain* (meaning "palace") *Macha* (a war queen in Ulster who lived about 300 BC). Two miles west of present-day Armagh, the 18-acre site — nearly circular and situated on a drumlin surrounded by farmland — was the principal settlement in Ireland in the time of Christ. It is well identified by historical markers and open for the public to roam at will. Excavation at Emain Macha, now more popularly known as Navan Fort, has revealed traces of occupation from the Late Stone Age (about 2000 BC). The most important structure on the site dates back to a settlement by the Celts in the Late Bronze Age (about 700 BC). It was a circular, thatch-roofed building, nearly 45 yards in diameter, with a center oak post (which allowed for highly accurate tree-ring dating by Queen's University, Belfast). Presumably, this building served as a ceremonial, spiritual, and political center of Ulster, since the construction of the ramparts and ditches of Emain Macha indicate that it was not used for defense.

Emain Macha was the setting for the Ulster cycle, the ancient record of the legendary deeds of Cu Chulainn and the Red Branch Knights. The cycle has been compared by many scholars to Homer's epics. The greatest King of Emain Macha, Conchobor mac Nessa, died in AD 33. The Ulster cycle tells how he had been seriously wounded by the Connaught champion, who had hurled a ball (made from the calcified brain of the King of Leinster) that lodged deep in Conchobor's head. The king's physicians stitched up the wound, leaving the ball inside, and advised the king to rest. However, upon hearing of the death of Christ, King Conchobor became so enraged that the ball burst out of his head, and he died. Since the king had died in reaction to the death of Christ, he was regarded as the first Irish martyr and the first pagan in Ireland to have reached heaven.

The death of Conchobor marked the passing of the old pagan order in Ulster legend. Many historians believe that Emain Macha fell in AD 332, when the last of the traditional Ulster kings, Fergus Fogha, was killed in battle with the three *collas* from the south, who afterward burned Emain. But some believe that Emain did not fall until about 450. This theory would support another popular belief, that St. Patrick came here, drawn to the political center of Ulster to preach Christianity. In either case, as a former slave in Ulster, Patrick would have known that the power was based at Emain Macha and that this was the place he had to convert if his mission was to succeed — two good reasons to explain why Patrick came to the area of Armagh. The past glory and political importance of pagan Emain Macha would have provided a symbolism and authority acceptable to early Irish Christians and, along with its early association with the Christian movement, would have fostered the rise of Armagh as the Christian capital of Ireland.

Although at first denied the hilltop site he wanted for his principal church in Armagh, Patrick eventually acquired the land from the chieftain Duire. Once his headquarters in Armagh was established, Patrick founded over 700 other Christian communities throughout Ireland. Patrick's era was the beginning of Ireland's reputation as the "land of saints and scholars." Around Patrick's church in Armagh there grew a school of monastic learning that became famous throughout Europe during the Dark Ages, until the Danes destroyed it during the 9th and 10th centuries. Some 1,200 scholars were based in Armagh in 807, when *The Book of Armagh* — the first section of which is the *Life of Patrick* — was hand-produced here. The ornamented portions are contemporary with and equal in importance to the famous *Book of Kells.* Both books are in the library of Trinity College in Dublin.

Patrick called Armagh "my sweet hill," and there's still an air of quiet dignity and refinement in this most venerated of Irish cities. On the hill where Patrick's stone church once stood is now the Church of Ireland cathedral, with its squat, square Norman tower. The exterior of the Anglican cathedral is essentially 12th century, although it has been rebuilt at least 17 times — most recently in 1912 — and reveals a strong Victorian influence inside and out. Grimacing gargoyles feature prominently in a frieze of carved heads around the exterior. In the adjoining chapter house is a collection of pagan statues. The sexton on the premises assists visitors Mondays through Fridays; ring the bell at 3 Vicar Hill for access on weekends. A marker in the west wall of the lovely cathedral close indicates the grave of BrianBorú, first king of all Ireland, who drove out the Norse invaders in 1014. Treasures in the cathedral library (open afternoons, Mondays through Saturdays) include a copy of *Gulliver's Travels* annotated by Swift. Streets surrounding the cathedral follow the rings of the Celtic *rath* (hill fort) which originally stood on the site that Patrick selected for his church.

Facing the Church of Ireland cathedral from an opposing hilltop is the twin-spired Catholic cathedral, begun in 1840. It is flanked by two larger-than-life archbishops in marble who benignly survey the town from the same superior perspective that visitors on the cathedral steps do. The interior is a striking contrast to that of the Church of Ireland cathedral, this one being almost Byzantine in its use of mosaics, carvings, and colors. On the pale blue ceiling and walls are represented every Irish saint and a multitude of angels.

Armagh has many graceful Georgian Regency buildings, the legacy of native son Francis Johnston, the distinguished 18th-century architect who also left his mark on Georgian Dublin. Encouraged by Archbishop Robinson and other wealthy patrons, Johnston and his contemporaries created The Mall (attractive buildings surrounding a rectangular town green on which cricket is played on the weekends), as well as the notable courthouse, market house, observatory, Royal School, Bank of Ireland building, and Charlemont Place. All were built in the warm-colored local yellow limestone that makes the city glow even on the dullest day. The doorsteps and pavement on The Mall glow pink, from polished red limestone (called Armagh marble). Most streets retain a historic character, especially in the area of the Shambles, which features antiques shops and a Friday livestock market.

Armagh County Museum is one of the finest small museums in the country. Exhibits include prehistoric implements and artifacts, Irish lace and linen, carved Black Bog oak jewelry, displays and documents on Viking raids, natural history, and paintings by George Russell (on The Mall; phone: 861-523070). Open daily, except Sundays, 10 AM to 1 PM and 2 to 5 PM. No admission charge. The Sovereign's House (also on The Mall) contains the *Royal Irish Fusiliers Regimental Museum.* Hours variable (best to call in advance). No admission charge (phone: 861-522911). The *Astronomy Center* (on College Hill) comprises a public observatory, a planetarium, and a hall of astronomy. Open daily, except Sundays, 2 to 4:45 PM. No admission charge. There are planetarium shows on Saturdays at 2 and 3 PM and daily, except Sundays, in July and August; advanced booking advised. Admission charge (phone: 861-523689).

Because of its surrounding fertile farmland, Armagh is often called "the garden of Ireland." In May and June, signposts guide motorists on scenic routes through beautifully blooming orchards. Outside the city, a traveler may be lucky enough to come across a game of road bowls or "bullets" — played only in the Irish counties of Armagh and Cork — in which an iron ball is thrown along a winding road, the object being to cover a set course of several miles in the fewest shots. Competitions are held in July and August.

CHECKING IN: *Charlemont Arms* – The only hotel in the center of Armagh, it's situated between the two hilltop cathedrals and convenient to most of the other major sites. The hotel has 18 rooms, 11 with private bath, and a restaurant. 63 Upper English St., Armagh (phone: 861-522028). Inexpensive.

EATING OUT: *Swallows* – Also near the cathedrals, this restaurant offers a broad menu; its specialties are porterhouse steaks and bacon-stuffed courgettes (zucchini). Open 12:30 to 2:30 PM and 6 to 10 PM Mondays through Saturdays (closed Mondays for dinner); noon to 2 PM and 6 to 9 PM, Sundays. 17 Lower English St., Armagh (phone: 861-524956). Moderate.

Archway – Homemade soup, sandwiches, and pastries are served in a cozy tearoom atmosphere. Morning coffee, lunch, and tea are available from 10 AM to 5 PM Tuesdays through Saturdays; closed July. On The Mall, 5 Hartford Pl., 100 yards from the *Armagh County Museum,* Armagh (phone: 861-522532). Inexpensive.

En Route from Armagh – Backtrack east on A51 to Tandragee. Turn south on A27 and, after a couple of miles, east into Scarva, a hamlet on the now unused Newry Canal. Scarva is noted for its annual "sham fight" — a colorful pageant on July 13 in which the Battle of the Boyne (1690) is reenacted in full dress. Pipe, brass, and silver bands from many of Northern Ireland's Orange Lodges parade and perform. Follow B10 from Scarva to Banbridge and watch for signposts for the Brontë Homeland Route.

BRONTË HOMELAND ROUTE: This signposted driving route extends over 10 square miles between Banbridge and Rathfriland to the southeast. Numerous Brontë relatives — grandparents, father, aunts, and uncles — of the famous novelists Charlotte, Emily, and Anne lived in this area. The scenic, serene, and remote river valley setting of the Brontë homeland sprawls over gently rolling hills, with the Mountains of Mourne rising romantically in the distance. The future father of the famous novelist sisters was the firstborn (on *St. Patrick's Day* in 1777) in the first home of Hugh and Alice Brunty, in Emdale. The house was a thatch-roofed, 2-room stone cottage, the foundations and walls of which are preserved and marked by a plaque. The eldest of ten children, Patrick Brunty was born of a poor but happy mixed — Catholic and Protestant — marriage. Patrick's father was an imaginative storyteller and entertained the local people as he tended a corn kiln. Literacy was not the rule in rural Ireland in those days, but Patrick taught himself to read from the few books his almost illiterate parents chanced to own. Although he was apprenticed to a blacksmith and then a linen weaver, he was also encouraged to educate himself, and local clergymen instructed him and loaned him books. By the time he was 16, Patrick was teaching in the Presbyterian school at Glascar. He also started writing the *Cottage Poems* (published in 1811). Unfortunately, when it became known that Patrick had kissed one of his senior pupils, the school was closed. However, in 1798, at age 21, he obtained another teaching job, this one at the parish school of Drumballyroney, and also served as tutor to the children of the rector of Drumballyroney parish church, the Reverend Thomas Tighe, a good friend of the great preacher John Wesley. Visitors are welcome at the hilltop parish church and school, beside which are picnic tables with fine views. In the church's lovely little green rolling cemetery, where six of Patrick's brothers and sisters are buried, is a relatively recent Brontë stone with "The Lord Is My Shepherd" engraved on it. Tighe coached Patrick, lent him a little money, and sponsored him at St. John's College, Cambridge University, which Patrick entered in 1802. Whether by confusion in university records or by choice — perhaps influenced by the fact that the King of Naples had made Admiral Nelson the Duke of Brontë in 1800 — from this period onward Patrick was known by this grander version of his original Brunty name. Patrick took his degree in 1806, was ordained, and held curacies in Essex and Shropshire before going to Yorkshire in 1809. In 1812 he married Maria Branwell. Six children were born of the marriage, the last, Anne, in 1820, the year Patrick was appointed to the incumbency at Haworth, Yorkshire. Sadly, his wife died the following year, but from that time on, Haworth remained the family home.

Although Patrick returned to Ulster only once — and preached a sermon at Drumballyroney church — he never forgot his roots. He filled his daughters with tales of his youth in County Down. Episodes in all the Brontë novels owe something to the father's memories of the hills near Rathfriland. The character of Heathcliff in Emily's *Wuthering Heights* is said to be her wild great-uncle Welsh, who, like Heathcliff, was an adopted child. (Welsh once traveled to London to threaten his niece's critics with a stick.) To his brother Hugh back in Emdale, Patrick sent an early copy of *Jane Eyre* with the message: "This is the first work published by my daughter Charlotte, under the fictitious name of C. Bell, which is the usual way at first by authors." Hugh showed the novel to the local minister, who pronounced it "the grandest novel that has been published in my time," and further claimed, "It bears the Brunty stamp on every sentence and idea." Patrick's brothers and sisters were said to recognize many of their father's old stories of Ulster in *Jane Eyre*. Patrick outlived all his children and died at the age of 84.

Following the signposts along the Brontë Homeland Route in the small rural lanes may sometimes seem to lead in circles, but there is hardly prettier, more welcoming countryside in which to get slightly lost. If exploration doesn't detect the main sites — the Brontë cottages at Emdale and Drumballyroney (1 mile south of Ballyroney, which is on B7, 3 miles northeast of Rathfriland) — ask directions from any of the friendly farmers along the roadside. Return to B7 and follow it southwest into Rathfriland.

RATHFRILAND: This hilltop Plantation-era market town has marvelous views of the Mourne Mountain range and a flavorful country Irish atmosphere. Steep streets lead to a pleasing square with an old market house in the middle. People from the surrounding countryside crowd the square on Wednesdays for the general market and on Tuesdays for livestock sales. *Graham's,* near the square, is a favorite local stop for homemade ice cream.

En Route from Rathfriland – Take B25 south from Rathfriland to Hilltown, named for the Hill family of Hillsborough renown, who founded it in 1766. A pretty parish church built in 1776 and a Georgian market house sit on the tree-lined main square. The village holds a market on the second Tuesday of every month and a sizable sale of hill sheep each autumn. For its small size (population about 600), Hilltown is particularly well endowed with pubs, a legacy from the 18th century, when it was the main distribution point for spirits being smuggled via the Brandy Pad path from Kilkeel on the coast over the mountains.

From Hilltown, scenic roads reach out in all directions. Follow B8 in the direction of Newcastle (to the left); then take B27 (toward Kilkeel) for 4 miles to Spelga Dam in the midst of the Mournes. Retrace the route back to Hilltown. For a particularly fine ride, take B8 southwest from the center of Hilltown toward Mayobridge. At the "Yellow Road" signpost on the left, follow the very rural, unnumbered Yellow Road past heathered hillsides and up a steep landscape that soon looks down on a world of irregularly shaped fields outlined by stone fences and flecked with sheep. Depending on the weather — which can change completely in the twinkle of an Ulsterman's eye — massive clouds may be sweeping over the Mourne foothills, with sudden shafts of sunlight illuminating farms in the distance, or brilliant sunlight may reveal a tapestry of farm fields in at least twenty shades of green. The only sounds in the wild moorland at the peaks will be the wind and, perhaps, a waterfall. Although there is seldom another car on this road, it's well to be warned of the possibility of one appearing over a blind rise, or of a shepherd and his border collie moving a flock along the road from one field to another. Head over the hills in a generally southern direction, toward the sea and Rostrevor.

ROSTREVOR: Nestled in the lee of the mountains facing Carlingford Lough, a tidal inlet, this is the most sheltered spot in Northern Ireland, with palms, mimosa, and Chilean flame trees thriving in the open. The village square of this pretty resort features ancient trees. A turn into Bridge Street reveals a lovely stone bridge over the little river Kilbroney. Flowing down the Fairy Glen Valley, the river affords a fine walk on sylvan paths past small waterfalls. A signpost in the village identifies Forest Drive, which climbs up to a car park with an information office. From there, proceed on foot for about a half-mile to gain a panoramic view of Lough Carlingford and the mountains. A more strenuous extension of the path continues to Cloghmore (meaning "big stone"), a peculiar boulder moved by a glacier which, according to myth, is supposed to have been thrown at an enemy by Finn MacCool, the Irish giant said to have built the Giant's Causeway. Across Lough Carlingford are the Carlingford Mountains, locally called the Cooley Mountains, because Finn MacCool is supposed to be buried there. At the western edge of Rostrevor, near a tiny quay, is a granite obelisk in memory of Major General Robert Ross, who in 1814 captured Washington, DC, and burned the White House, after he and his officers ate President Madison's dinner and drank his best wine.

 EATING OUT: *Cloughmor Inn* – An enjoyable, casual eatery, featuring hamburgers and meat or savory pies. Open daily 11:30 AM to 11:30 PM; inquire about Sundays. 2 Bridge St., Rostrevor (phone: 6937-38007). Inexpensive.

If you have time, upon reaching the A2, the main coastal road, turn right and head northeast on a short drive to the *Narrow Water Castle Gallery* (Warrenpoint; phone: 6937-53940), housed in the vaulted ceiling cellars of the handsome 1840 Tudor revival–style home of the Hall family, residents of the town since the 17th century. The gallery, open Tuesdays through Saturdays from 2 to 6 PM, has rotating exhibits of Irish and international artists. The castle is signposted to the right off the A2, opposite the picturesque waterside ruins of the Old Narrow Water Castle, which dates from 1560. Return to Rostrevor on the A2.

En Route from Rostrevor – Take A2 southeast from Rostrevor in the direction of Kilkeel. At the river Cassy Water, a signpost offers "Welcome to the Kingdom of the Mournes." This area extends to St. Patrick's Stream, south of Newcastle, inland to the tops of the mountains. Tradition holds that in Celtic times the region was ruled by a cowherd king, Boirche, from the summit of Slieve Binnian, which overlooks the whole area.

Just past the walled wooded estate of Mourne Park, seat of the Earls of Kilmorey, turn left onto Ballymageogh Road for an exceptionally lovely ride through country where hedges and lichen-stenciled, gorse-draped stone walls separate grazing sheep from cultivated fields. The road leads upward to a splendid semicircular view of brilliantly green domesticated fields that rise to become heathered moorlands that, still higher, become the barren peaks of the Mournes. Follow the road downhill and turn right through the hamlet of Attical, the last place in the Mournes where the Irish language was spoken. A short distance beyond the hamlet, turn right onto B27, which heads into Kilkeel, 4 miles away.

KILKEEL: Kilkeel is the main fishing port on the south Down coast, sometimes called "the capital of the kingdom of Mourne." A bustling, cheerful commercial center of some 3,000 inhabitants, the town has a harbor constructed in 1866; the principal catch includes herring, prawns, skate, sprats, and haddock. Quayside auctions are interesting to watch.

CHECKING IN: *Heath Hall* – A simple bed and breakfast establishment, this stone farmhouse with spacious gardens and views of the mountains and the sea has 2 double rooms (no private baths). Open May through September. On B27 1½ miles north of Kilkeel. 160 Moyadd Rd., Kilkeel (phone: 6937-62612). Inexpensive.

En route from Kilkeel – Retrace the route inland on B27 to a right turn marked Silent Valley (Head Rd.). Silent Valley serves as a reservoir for the Belfast area, supplying 30 million imperial gallons of water a day. Built between 1923 and 1932, it is half a mile wide and 2½ miles long and can hold 3 billion gallons. Silent Valley, which comprises beautiful parkland as well as the dam, is the only place from which the inner Mournes can be reached by car. The catchment area is encircled by the Mourne Wall, a massive dry-stone wall 6 feet high and 22 miles long, ascending and descending the 15 peaks surrounding the inner Mournes.

Head Road itself runs through the foothills of the Mournes, parallel to the sea, which is visible in the distance below. On a clear day it is possible to see the mountainous peaks of the Isle of Man. The green fields of the small tidy farms on either side of the road are a maze of gray granite dry-stone walls — termed "ditches" locally. There is a constantly changing play of sun and shadow over the landscape that begs to be photographed. Follow Head Road to the end and turn right. When you reach the main road, turn right again into Annalong.

ANNALONG: Northeast of Kilkeel on A2, Annalong is a small, picturesque harborside village. It's best to park at the Annalong Cornmill and Marine Park, where there are public toilets, a café/gift shop, an exhibit on mills, and an herb garden. Guided tours of a fully restored, water-powered corn mill from the early 1800s are available 2 to 6 PM daily June through September (phone: 3967-68736). Use the free, self-guiding *Annalong Marine Park Trail* brochure for a more complete exploration by foot, and be sure to take the short path over the river Annalong, which powers the mill, to Annalong harbor.

During the early 1900s, Annalong was one of the area's chief ports, busy with fishing fleets and trading schooners exporting Mourne granite and Down potatoes. Only a small fleet of skiffs, used to catch herring and mackerel, now remains. The kippering store at the harbor still uses smoldering oak shavings to preserve the herring for export. Near the Annalong corn mill are several granite mills where the stone is cut and polished.

CHECKING IN: *Glassdrumman Lodge* – This converted farmhouse offers unrivaled views of the Mourne Mountains and the Irish Sea. Situated on a 30-acre working farm, it has 8 tasteful rooms, each with bath. Guests can collect their own eggs for a hearty farm breakfast. 85 Mill Rd., Annalong (phone: 3967-68585 or 3967-68451). Expensive.

EATING OUT: *Glassdrumman House* – A complex of new and restored buildings that includes two good restaurants: The *Kitchen Garden,* open 11 AM to 9:30 PM daily, serves everything from morning coffee or afternoon tea to three-course meals (moderate). The elegant *Memories,* which features French cuisine, faces a walled garden and is open year-round 7 to 9:30 PM for dinner Wednesdays through Saturdays and from 12:30 PM for lunch Sundays. It is also open for lunch Mondays through Fridays in July and August (reservations advised; expensive). Several shops in the complex provide the makings of a perfect picnic — bread and pastries from the bakery; meats, salads, cheeses, and homemade pickles and preserves from the deli. Signposted on A2, Annalong. For more information and for restaurant reservations, call 3967-68585.

Fisherman – On the ground floor of a comfortable, multi-windowed house, this restaurant features fresh local prawns, lobster, salmon, clams, and turbot. Try the pâté and stuffed mushrooms. Open for dinner only, 5 to 9:30 PM Tuesdays through Fridays, 5 to 10:30 PM Saturdays, and 5 to 8:30 PM Sundays July and August; Thursdays through Sundays September through June. Reservations advised. 43 Kilkeel Rd., signposted on A2, Annalong. (phone: 3967-68733). Inexpensive.

Harbour Inn – In a sturdy stone building at the quaint harbor, this spot serves fresh fish, steaks, shepherd's pie, and good desserts. Food served Mondays through Thursdays from 11:30 AM to 3 PM and to 6 PM on Fridays and Saturdays. No reservations. 6 Harbour Dr., Annalong (phone: 3967-68678). Inexpensive.

NEWCASTLE: Head north on A2, with the Irish Sea on the right and the Mourne Mountains on the left. Newcastle is an attractively situated seaside resort that stretches in a broad crescent along a 5-mile sandy shore on the Irish Sea. The beauty of the town's setting inspired Irish songwriter Percy French to compose "Where the Mountains of Mourne Sweep Down to the Sea," made world-famous by the classical tenor John McCormick. (A fountain in the seafront promenade gardens commemorates the composer.) The Mournes' highest summit, the barren peak of Slieve Donard (2,796 feet), less than 2 miles away, dominates Newcastle with its mysterious and distinctive hazy blue and purple hues.

Nature and bygone gentry have endowed Newcastle with beautiful scenery and fine forests, which provide a venue for walks, pony trekking, and rock climbing. There are a café and exhibition center at Tollymore Forest Park in the Clanbressel barn, built about 1730. Nearby, the Barbican Gate — a Gothic folly — leads to a long avenue of Himalayan cedars. The Mourne Countryside Centre, on the Central Promenade at Newcastle, informs visitors about anything to do with Mourne country, from geology to flora and fauna to the best routes into — and out of — the mountains by foot or car. In addition to information, the center has photographic displays and three-dimensional maps of the region. Open daily 9 AM to 5 PM (to 8 PM in July and August). June through September; mornings only and by request October through May (phone: 3967-22222).

Tropicana, a recreational facility in the Newcastle Center on the Central Promenade, has a heated outdoor seawater pool and sheltered sunbathing patio (phone: 39-672-2222). Other recreational features of the town include a putting green, bowling green, tennis courts, and boating lake. Insinuating itself nearly into the center of Newcastle is the magnificent *Royal County Down Golf Club,* which Gene Sarazen, the noted golf professional, voted the number one course in the world. The links, which run parallel to the Irish Sea, offer rolling dune holes in valleys of heather and gorse. The splendid 9th hole, where one must drive blindly "on the spire" of the nearby *Slieve Donard* hotel, is acknowledged as one of the world's most spectacularly beautiful. Contact the Secretary, *Royal County Down Golf Club,* Newcastle (phone: 3967-23314).

 CHECKING IN: *Burrendale* – Offering the most modern comforts in the area, here is both a hotel and a country club, all surrounded by trees and gardens. There are 50 bedrooms (4 executive suites), each with private bath. It also boasts a health club and spa, which includes a heated swimming pool, saunas, solarium, Turkish steam rooms, Jacuzzis, exercise room, massage parlor, beauty salon, and refreshment bar. The restaurant features fresh local produce and seafood. The *Cottage Bar,* with its interior thatch roof and open fire, is a cozy retreat for pub lunches, high tea (supper), and drinks. Just outside town at 51 Castlewellan Rd., Newcastle (phone: 3967-22599). Expensive.

Slieve Donard – A favorite with the Northern Irish, this attractive, atmospheric, turn-of-the-century hotel, built to be convenient to the former railway station nearby, occupies a wonderful site on the Irish Sea, with views of Slieve Donard and other Mournes sweeping down to the shore. Extensively renovated, it has a health club, heated indoor swimming pool, lobby bar lounge and restaurant (see *Eating Out*), as well as 2 tennis courts and 6 acres of grounds that back up to the

Royal County Down Golf Club. Just steps from the front door are several miles of sandy beaches stretching in both directions. All 120 rooms have private facilities; request a front one, preferably a room with bay windows that take in both the sea and the Mournes. Newcastle (phone: 3967-23681). Expensive.

 EATING OUT: *Enniskeen* – The dining room at this 12-room country-house hotel, set at the foot of the Mourne Mountains, offers wonderful views. A full table d'hôte lunch is served for about $10.50, and for dinner an à la carte menu offers sweetbreads, fresh vegetables (some straight from the hotel's gardens), locally caught salmon, chicken, and vegetarian dishes. Homemade pies, pizzas, and the like are served at the bar. Reservations advised for window views at dinner. 98 Bryansford Rd. (phone: 3967-22392). Moderate.

***Percy Frengh Grill Bar* –** At the *Slieve Donard* hotel, overlooking the beach, this Tudor-style eatery offers pub fare between 12 and 2:30 PM and an à la carte menu in the evening. Dinner specialties include vegetarian dishes, lamb, steaks, roast duckling, chicken in white wine sauce, jumbo shrimp scampi, and salmon steaks. Open daily. Reservations advised for dinner on weekends. Newcastle (phone: 3967-23681). Moderate to Inexpensive.

***Strand* –** A 50-year-old establishment overlooking the sea, its specialties include pancakes, sandwiches, home-baked goods, and ice cream. Open daily in summer 10 AM to 11 PM; limited hours during winter. There's a bakery on the second floor over the restaurant. 53 Central Promenade, Newcastle (phone: 3967-23472). Inexpensive.

CASTLEWELLAN: Take A50 inland 4 miles to Castlewellan, a picturesque market town nestled between the High Mournes and the Slieve Croob hills of central Down. Spires from the Church of Ireland and the Roman Catholic church rise at the eastern and western ends of the wide main street, which passes through two squares shaded by chestnut trees. Market day is Monday.

Signposted immediately north of town is Castlewellan Forest Park, 1,500 acres that once were a nobleman's estate. The park surrounds Lake Castlewellan, more than one-half–mile long, where boats can be hired in season. The Scottish baronial-style castle overlooking the lake was built in 1856 to replace an earlier mansion of the Earls of Annesley, who once owned most of the Mournes. The farmstead was built around 1720 and includes courtyards, a barn, and a belfry in superb Queen Anne style. An inexpensive café — the *Grange Coffee House,* open daily 10:30 AM to 6:30 PM *Easter* through September and weekends in winter — offers quiche, salads, and pizza (phone: 3967-71290). Perhaps the finest feature of the park is the National Arboretum, one of the best in the British Isles. Begun in 1790, it contains trees and plants from around the world. Some of the outstanding plantings are Scots pine, beech, Irish yew, and a variety of cypress called Castlewellan Gold. A guidebook is available at the information office.

For an overland adventure to the Legananny Dolmen, considered one of Ireland's finest neolithic tombs (ca. 2000 BC), pick up A50 outside Castlewellan Forest Park and head west toward Banbridge. In about 3 miles, a sign for Legananny Dolmen indicates a right turn; from here, the antiquity is 5½ miles away, over well-paved but very rural roads. Though it may not always seem so, the route is accurately signposted. The monument finally is visible off Dolmen Road, up a dirt lane to the right past a small farm. Beyond this unusually tall, tripod dolmen, standing at an altitude of 850 feet on Cratlieve Mountain, is a magnificent view over the Mournes. Bring stout shoes for hiking in this beautiful, virgin setting. Retrace the route to Newcastle.

En Route from Newcastle – Heading northeast of Newcastle on A2 toward Dundrum, look for a sign on the right for the Murlough Nature Reserve. The National

Trust has provided paths, notice boards, and an information center so that visitors can learn about the birds, flowers, and geology of this rich land of dunes and heaths. The boardwalk-type path from the car park to the beach is about one-half mile.

Next, follow signs for Dundrum Castle. The remains of this Norman stronghold, built about 1177 by John de Courcy, rest strikingly on a 200-foot hill that offers splendid views of the mountains and the sea. The castle was taken by King John in 1210 and was bombarded by Cromwell's troops in 1652. Grounds are open at all times; keep is open April through September from 10 AM to 7 PM, Tuesdays through Saturdays, and 2 to 7 PM, Sundays; October through March, 10 AM to 4 PM on Saturdays, and 2 to 4 PM, Sundays (no phone).

From Dundrum, take the A24 north through Clough to Seaforde where the Tropical Butterfly House of the Seaforde Nursery is located. Over 30 species of free-flyings tropical butterflies are here, as well as tropical insects and reptiles from four continents. Open April through September, Mondays through Saturdays from 10 AM to 5 PM and on Sundays from 2 to 6 PM (phone: 39687-225). Next, continue on A2 to Clough, and turn right (east) on A25 for Downpatrick.

 EATING OUT: *Woodlands* – This dining place offers such specialties as Strangford scallops, game in season, and hazelnut and apricot meringue. Open Thursdays through Saturdays 7:30 to 9:30 PM. Reservations advised. At Clough, head north on A24 to Ballynahinch. 29 Spa Rd., Ballynahinch (phone: 238-562650). Moderate.

DOWNPATRICK: The administrative center for the rural, largely agricultural Down District of Southeast Northern Ireland, Downpatrick obtained its name from close association with St. Patrick and from a local landmark, the great fort, or *dún*, of the Red Branch knight known as Celtair, which is thought to have been located on what is now Cathedral Hill. Although the area was vulnerable to Viking raids for 300 years or more, Downpatrick grew in importance as a religious center. In 1176, Henry II granted the counties of Down and Antrim to John de Courcy, a Cheshire knight. De Courcy established a stronghold in Downpatrick and then secured his territory by dividing it into administrative units controlled by minor overlords. Attempting to further impose their ways on the local population, the Normans replaced existing churches and clergy with their own orders of monks in elaborate religious houses. To placate the Irish, de Courcy enshrined the local relics of St. Patrick, St. Brigid, and St. Columba. The picturesque ruins of the Abbey of Inch (see below) still stand outside the town on the banks of the river Quoile, but there are records of the existence of 6 other religious establishments in Downpatrick from that era, although no traces of these remain.

During the Middle Ages, Downpatrick suffered at the hands of the Scots and English, who burned and plundered many of its buildings, but by the early 18th century stability and prosperity had returned. This was especially due to the influence of the Southwells, a Bristol family who acquired the Manor of Downpatrick through marriage in 1703. Much of the development of the town can be attributed to the work of the Southwell family, who erected a quay on the river Quoile and encouraged markets and fairs and the building of hotels and houses. Three old streets with distinguished architecture — much of it Georgian — are English, Scotch, and Irish streets, which meet at the center of Downpatrick. The layout and naming of these streets typifies the Elizabethan system of dividing settlements into racial quarters. Buildings of note include the Southwell charity schools and almshouses (1733) on English Street, as well as the imposing courthouse and county hall, the judges' residence, and *Denvir's* hotel (15 English St.; phone: 396-612012), part of which dates from 1642. The assembly rooms dominate the town center at the junction of English, Scotch, and Irish Streets, with a fanciful high clock tower and arcade.

Down Cathedral (Cathedral Church of the Holy Trinity) stands at the top of English

Street, on the great *dún,* or royal residence, of the mighty Celtair, one of the 12 chiefs of Ulster, who may have predated St. Patrick by 400 or more years. The story of the church on this site is one of repeated destruction and reconstruction. We know that by the 6th century there was a great church here, but from the late 8th until the early 12th century, the town and the religious buildings on its hill were regularly pillaged by the Danes. In those days the river Quoile almost surrounded the site of the cathedral, affording the raiders easy access by ship. The site was occupied by monks of the order of St. Augustine until the 1172 Anglo-Norman invasion headed by John de Courcy, when the Augustinians were replaced by Benedictine monks from Chester. In 1245, the church was destroyed by an earthquake. In 1316, it was burned by Edward Bruce, the brother of Robert the Bruce of Scotland. In 1538, it was destroyed yet again, this time by the English. From 1538 the cathedral lay in ruins. In 1744, a writer of a history of County Down recorded, "The Cathedral is yet venerable in its ruins." The Rev. John Wesley, founder of Methodism, first visited Downpatrick in 1778 and wrote in his diary, "At the head of English Street stands the Abbey on a hill. It is a noble ruin, the largest building I have seen in the Kingdom." The cathedral languished in ruin for more than 250 years, and then restoration, arranged through an Act of Parliament, began in 1790. In the course of the restoration, the features of the ancient structures were retained as much as possible, and the restored building was erected on the walls and arches of the abbey choir — probably built during the 14th century after the destruction of de Courcy's original building by Edward Bruce. The cathedral was reopened for service in 1818, and has since undergone extensive repairs, the most recent round of which was completed in 1987.

Approaching from English Street, visitors first see the east door of the cathedral; in front of it stands a badly weathered 10th-century High Cross. From the west door are distant views of the Mournes. In the cemetery to the side is a great Mourne granite slab marked "Patric" that was placed here in 1900 as a reminder that the saint is traditionally believed to be buried close to the cathedral. (It is also thought that St. Brigid and St. Columba were later buried with St. Patrick.) The most striking interior features are the capitals, which include carved vine leaves, oak leaves with acorns, animals, birds, clusters of berries, and human heads. Some are genuine 14th- and 15th-century work, while others are the work of 18th-century restorers. The choir screen with stalls underneath is the only remaining screen of its kind in Ireland. Down Cathedral possesses one of the two largest, most complete and original 18th-century organs remaining in Ireland (the other is in Hillsborough).

Just down English Street from the cathedral is the St. Patrick Heritage Centre, in the gatehouses of the 18th-century former gaol (jail). The center tells the story of Ireland's patron saint through large-scale illustrations and other displays, emphasizing the strong links between southeast Ulster and Patrick and early Irish Christianity. The old Down County Gaol, built between 1789 and 1796, serves as headquarters for the new *Down Museum,* which presents exhibits on the area's natural history and archaeological past. Open 11 AM to 5 PM Tuesdays to Fridays, 2 to 5 PM Saturdays, except during July and August — open 11 AM to 5 PM Mondays through Fridays; 11 AM to 5 PM Saturdays and Sundays. English St. (phone: 396-615218).

EATING OUT: *Rea's* – An atmospheric bar-restaurant with dark wood paneling and working fireplaces, where everything from soup to sauce is homemade from fresh produce. Specialties are the beef sandwich, barbecued chicken, and fresh seafood, including mussels, squid, brill, and prawns. Open for lunch Mondays through Saturdays noon to 11:30 AM to 3 PM; for dinner Thursdays through Saturdays 6:30 to 9:30 PM. 78 Market St., Downpatrick (phone: 396-612017). Moderate.

INCH ABBEY: Take A7 toward Belfast for about half a mile, then turn left at the signpost for Inch Abbey. Set in a lovely rural area on an island in the river Quoile, the extensive ruins are the remains of a Cistercian abbey founded in the 1180s by John de Courcy, who built it in atonement for having destroyed in war another abbey south of Downpatrick. The abbey was built on the foundations of an ancient church that was devastated by a Viking raid in AD 1001. Although within sight of Downpatrick Cathedral across the river, the island site ensured a degree of seclusion and today preserves something of the peace and independence sought by the Cistercians away from the distractions of everyday life. Inch was for centuries a center of English influence; Irishmen were not allowed to enter the community. The abbey was burned in 1404, perhaps the occasion for reducing the size of the church, and monastic life there ended in 1542. Nineteenth-century illustrations show the ruin ivy-covered and buried deep in fallen rubble. In 1910, the ruins were placed in the care of the state, and in 1980 a larger area — embracing most of the medieval precinct — was annexed. Within the precinct is the site of a 5th-century Celtic monastery, possibly connected to St. Patrick. Inch Abbey, accessible by a short walk from the car park, is open from April through September on Tuesdays through Saturdays from 10 AM to 7 PM and on Sundays from 2 to 7 PM; October through March on Saturdays from 10 AM to 4 PM and on Sundays from 2 to 4 PM (closed 1 to 1:30 PM both days).

SAUL: From Downpatrick, head northeast on A25, following the sign for Strangford. After about a mile, turn right for Saul and Saul Brae. Look for the gray granite church with a distinguishing replica of a Celtic round tower. The church was erected in 1932 to commemorate the 1,500th anniversary of Patrick's return to Ireland; it is open to the public daily.

Patrick received religious training in France, where he was consecrated as a bishop by Germanus of the See of Auxerre and directed to return to Ireland to Christianize the heathen. Landing at Wicklow, Patrick intended to go first to Ulster, site of his early years as a slave on Slemish Mountain in Antrim. As he made his way up the east coast of Ireland by ship, strong currents forced him instead into Lough Strangford, where he landed at the mouth of the river Slaney. Coming ashore to rest, Patrick and his company were met by a good-natured heathen named Dichu. When Dichu saw Patrick, he "became gentle, and believed." Patrick baptized his first convert, and, in return, Dichu gave Patrick a barn for his first church in Ireland. The area has since been known as Saul, a form of the Irish word for barn, *sabhal.* It is often claimed to be the country's holiest site. Patrick always loved Saul, and it was here he came to rest from his travels. It is said that when Patrick neared death, the angel Victor told him that Saul was the appointed place for him to die, and, indeed, it was here that Patrick received his last Eucharist from a bishop named Tassach. Many towns and monasteries vied for the honor of burying Patrick. According to tradition, an angel advised that a pair of untamed oxen be harnessed to a cart bearing Patrick's body; the oxen should "proceed wherever they wish, and where they shall rest let a church be founded there in honor of his body." The oxen supposedly stopped at Cathedral Hill in Downpatrick.

During his lifetime, Patrick founded Saul Abbey, placing it in the care of St. Duminius. For more than 300 years, the abbey existed unmolested. Eventually, however, because of its easy accessibility from Lough Strangford, it came to the attention of the Danes, who raided and burned it. It was rebuilt by the Bishop of Down as an Augustinian priory but was again destroyed by Edward Bruce in 1316. After this, the site was neglected for centuries. In 1788, a new church — a simple whitewashed building — was erected. In 1932, the Church of Ireland replaced that building with the present one, a replica of an ancient Celtic church. It is the parish church for a small number of neighboring families; services are held each Sunday at noon. Special services are held on the *Festival of St. Patrick,* March 17, when many modern pilgrims make their way to Saul. In the graveyard is one remaining wall of the original Saul Abbey and two small corbeled cells, one of which was used as a tomb. The other may have been an anchorite cell, where life was spent in prayer and meditation. Decorative stones from the abbey can be viewed at the back of the present church.

On the commanding slope of nearby Slieve Patrick is a 33-foot granite statue of Patrick, also erected in 1932; its base is decorated with bronze panels depicting scenes from the saint's life. Leading up the mountain to an open-air altar are 12 small altars commemorating the significant moments in Christ's life.

En Route from Saul – Return to A25 and drive 4 miles toward Strangford. On the western outskirts of town, turn left for Castle Ward, a popular National Trust home on 800 acres overlooking Lough Strangford. The stately three-story residence of Bath stone was built between 1762 and 1768 for Bernard Ward, the first Lord Bangor, and his wife, Lady Anne. Owing to the differing and uncompromising architectural tastes of Lord and Lady Bangor — he preferred classical, she the then-fashionable Neo-Gothic — Castle Ward has a southwest façade that is Palladian, while the northeast is Gothic. The same dichotomy of style is maintained throughout the interior. Lady Bangor's eccentric boudoir is one of the most peculiar rooms in Ireland, featuring ornate plasterwork, paneling, and painted doors. Not surprisingly, the couple later separated. The house is surrounded by beautiful gardens with walks. Also on the grounds are a *Victorian Laundry Museum,* an 18th-century summer house, a crafts workshop, and the *Castlewood Tea Rooms,* serving lunch, scones, cakes; open during viewing hours. The grounds are open free from dawn to dusk year-round. The house is open 1 to 6 PM daily, except Thursdays, May through August; and 2 to 6 PM on weekends in April, September, and October (phone: 396-86204). Admission charge; parking costs are additional.

STRANGFORD: Strangford is a pretty village clustered on the shore of a double cove on the western shore of Strangford Lough narrows, through which St. Patrick sailed in 432 before landing in Saul. Some 400 million tons of water pass through the narrows during each daily tidal change. The powerful current so impressed raiding Vikings in the 10th century that they named the lough "strong fjord," the name it retains today. There is a walkable path along the Strangford shore that passes Strangford Castle (a tower house from the 16th century) and the defensive tower of Old Court (residence of Baroness de Ros, Premier Baroness of Great Britain, a title created in 1264).

En Route from Strangford – Strangford village is one of the terminals for the Strangford Lough car ferry that sails to Portaferry, on the opposite shore, eliminating what would otherwise be a 50-mile detour around the lough. The ferry carries 24 cars and runs year-round from each port every half hour or so from 7:30 AM to 10:45 PM (phone: 39686-637). The one-way fare is about 90¢ for car and driver. The lough, a large inlet of the Irish Sea, is 18 miles long and an average of 3½ miles wide. It is noted for multitudes of birds and marine creatures — nearly 700 species have been recorded.

PORTAFERRY: On the picturesque narrows opposite Strangford, Portaferry seems pleasantly removed from modern life. The long waterfront has Scottish-style cottages and some Georgian and early Victorian houses. The town, which has several interesting churches, rises steeply up a hill. The *Northern Ireland Aquarium* contains 70 species of fish housed in the lough; displays include models of the seabed. Open 10 AM to 8 PM Tuesdays through Saturdays, 1 to 8 PM Sundays, April through August; 10:30 AM to 5 PM Tuesdays through Saturdays, 1 to 5 PM Sundays, September through March. Admission charge. Rope Walk (phone: 2477-28062).

 CHECKING IN/EATING OUT: *Portaferry* – Nearly opposite the car ferry slip, well within the sound of sea gulls on the lough, this place has 5 double rooms, each with private bath, and two restaurants: A cozy neighborhood-style bar/lounge facing the water serves pub grub lunches; a more formal restaurant specializes in seafood — stuffed mussels, fried oyster, and turbot. Reservations advised. On the Strand, Portaferry (phone: 2477-28231). Moderate.

En Route from Portaferry – Head northeast on A2, up the North Down Ards Peninsula, to Cloghy and a 2-mile sweep of beach and dunes on the open Irish Sea. Continue to Portavogie, a classically pretty harbor with a colorful fishing fleet. In Portavogie, boats are built, sailed, and discussed night and day. The largest local catches are prawns and herring; on most evenings there is a fish auction on the quay. The inhabitants are markedly Scottish in speech and traditions. Continue north to Ballywalter, then turn west onto B5 to Greyabbey on the lough side of the peninsula, which has a noticeably different feeling from the sea side.

GREYABBEY: This graceful village is most noted for its well-preserved ruins of a Cistercian abbey, founded in 1193 by Affreca, daughter of the King of the Isle of Man and wife of John de Courcy, the Norman conqueror of Ulster. The abbey, which has lovely grounds, was used as a parish church until 1778. An effigy tomb in the north wall of the choir may be that of Affreca. For more information contact the tourism section of the Ards Burough Council (2 Church St., Newtownards, County Down, Northern Ireland ET2 34AP; phone: 247-812215). The village has several antiques shops.

En Route from Greyabbey – About 3 miles north on A20 is an abrupt right turn, marked with a signpost, into the National Trust site of Mount Stewart House and Gardens. The house was the birthplace of Lord Castlereagh, foreign secretary of England during the Napoleonic Wars. The house is overshadowed by its gardens, which are among the finest in the British Isles. Laid out during World War I by Edith Lady Londonderry, the gardens offer unrivaled collections of plantings and vistas: topiary in the Shamrock Garden; a Temple of the Winds; an 18th-century folly that is a copy of an Athenian temple; and unusual locally carved animal statuary — dodos, dinosaurs, griffins, satyrs, crocodiles, duck-billed platypuses. A detailed guide is available at the entrance. The house is open 1 to 6 PM (gardens noon to 6 PM) daily, except Tuesdays, June through August; open weekends and holidays, April, May, September, and October. Admission charge (phone: 24774-387).

NEWTOWNARDS: Continue northwest on A20 to Newtownards, a flourishing commercial center, with Ulster's finest Georgian town hall and an old Market Cross. Just southwest is steep Scrabo Hill, made conspicuous for miles by its 135-foot-high tower (122 steps to the top), built in 1857 as a memorial to the third marquis of Londonderry, one of Wellington's generals. The tower is now a countryside center with information and visual displays. There are exceptional views of north Down from both hill and tower. The tower is open free of charge noon to 5:30 PM daily (except Mondays), June through September; at other times by arrangement (phone: 247-811491).

En Route from Newtownards – The most direct route to the center of Belfast is A20 west. Alternatively, drive north on A21 to the seaside suburban town of Bangor, then west and south on A2, passing Cultra and the *Ulster Folk and Transport Museum* (see "Museums" in *Belfast,* THE CITIES).

Fermanagh Lakelands

Fermanagh is famous for its lakes — one-third of the county is water — and for its mountain-and-moor loveliness. The largest lake, the 50-mile waterway of Upper and Lower Lough Erne — separated by the island town of Enniskillen, ancient seat of the Irish Maguire chieftains — refreshes the whole region. Hills and mountains punctuate the scenery, and vantages like Lough Navar Viewpoint provide monumental perspectives. Sir John Davies, attorney general to Queen Elizabeth I, wrote in 1609 that Fermanagh is "so pleasant and fruitful, that if I should make a full description thereof it would be taken as a poetical fiction."

In addition to the lake scenery, there are many other sights to occupy the traveler: Plantation period castles, splendid stately houses, traditional craft factories, and pagan and early Christian monuments, to mention a few. But overall, life proceeds at a relaxed pace in this quiet corner of Ulster. There's a feeling of "Summertime, and the livin' is easy. / Fish are jumpin'...." And indeed they are, for Enniskillen is one of the angling capitals of Europe. Even those who don't actively participate can sample the catch in local restaurants. Fermanagh's lakes are also for cruising — cabin cruisers can be hired from any one of seven companies (most of which have a 1-week minimum) — for canoeing, sailing, water skiing, and swimming, or for painting, photographing, or simply contemplating.

During early Christian times, the islands in Lough Erne were populous ports of call. People then traveled with more ease on water than on land, and the Erne was a great highway from the sea to deep inland. Churches and monasteries, built in Fermanagh since the 6th century, were especially concentrated on the islands and shores of Lough Erne. These were not only retreats for religious contemplation, selected for their privacy and safety, but way stations for travelers along the inland waterway. Later, during medieval times, parish churches occupied many of these island and lough shore sites, and some continued the tradition of hospitality. The Erne was important as a route of pilgrimage northwest to St. Patrick's Purgatory. (This was the spot where St. Patrick had a vision of purgatory; just over the border into Donegal near Lough Derg, it has been a pilgrimage site for centuries.) At that time Fermanagh's population was three times the 50,000 it is today, and many of the 154 Lough Erne islands that now are uninhabited supported substantial numbers of residents. Then, as today, the islands and shore revealed grass-covered vestiges of prehistoric and pre-Christian peoples.

Throughout the late 16th century, Queen Elizabeth's attempt to subjugate the Irish — ostensibly because of her fear that Spain would attack England through Ireland — was challenged by the leaders of the Gaelic aristocracy. Nowhere were her generals more fiercely opposed than in west Ulster by the O'Neills, O'Donnells, and Maguires. Her successor, King James, used the

Flight of the Earls (the escape of the defeated Irish chieftains) in 1607 as an excuse to confiscate land, and he granted it in large parcels to English and Scottish "Planters," on the condition that they build settlements and provide strongholds loyal to himself. The Planters, mainly English and Lowland Scottish opportunists, finding themselves among a hostile native population, built defenses. These reflected the varied origins of their builders, from the troubled Scottish borders where castles were still in use to the more peaceful parts of southern England where the spread of Renaissance ideas fostered neoclassical designs. The Plantation castles and houses of Ulster are a unique blend of these different architectural styles. About ten sturdy stone castles were added to Fermanagh's existing fortresses during the Plantation era. Now they are mostly in ruins, but their remains are among the principal attractions for visitors to west Ulster.

The history of the post-Plantation 18th and 19th centuries is one of large-scale emigration to the New World, as illustrated by the stimulating displays at the Ulster–American Folk Park outside Omagh in County Tyrone (the northernmost portion of our driving tour). Today, although Fermanagh's antiquities and Plantation castles (which are in remarkable condition considering their turbulent history) attract many visitors, the area's main appeal is still its scenery: The lakes and islands offer the same peace and serenity to 20th-century travelers that they did to 7th-century monastics.

Our driving tour, which begins west of Belfast and ends south of Londonderry, is primarily in County Fermanagh, with some sites farther north in County Tyrone. From Dungannon in the east to Belleek in the west, the drive is about 70 miles; from Enniskillen in the south to Omagh in the north, it's about 30 miles, although the mileage in this vicinity is difficult to calculate since the route circles and loops several times as we cover a concentration of sites around Lough Erne. The area can be sampled in depth, including side trips and walks, in 4 to 5 leisurely days.

In hotels listed as expensive, a double room with private bath and full breakfast costs $100 and up; in those listed as moderate, $55 to $100; and in inexpensive places, $50 or less. A three-course meal for two, including 10% service and VAT (but not beverages), costs $50 or slightly more in the expensive category, $35 to $50 is considered moderate, or under $35, inexpensive.

En Route from Belfast – Leave Belfast on M1 west, following the sign for Lisburn; or from Belfast International Airport, take A26 south and pick up M1 west at the attractive village of Moira. At Exit 12 (about a 30-minute drive from Belfast), change to B196, which loops north through Maghery and then back south to M1.

Residents of Mahgery claim that emigrants from their town, a former fishing village on Lough Neagh, named New York's Coney Island after the wooded islet at the mouth of the river Blackwater. (Residents of Sligo City in the Republic of Ireland also claim this distinction for their island in Sligo Bay.) Today, a greater contrast between places would be hard to imagine. The Irish Coney Island, now owned by the National Trust, has no inhabitants except birds, especially waterfowl. A monument near the ruins of an ancient circular church declares that St. Patrick often "resorted to this island" for prayers and meditation in the 5th century. During the rule of Elizabeth I, Coney Island

was a penal settlement; the execution mound can still be traced in the dense under-
growth. The island, reachable by boat from Mahgery, is open at all times.

Lough Neagh is Ulster's inland sea, the biggest lake in the British Isles (20 miles long
and 11½ miles at its widest), nearly as large as Switzerland's Lake Geneva. Local lore
accounts for its origin: The Irish giant Finn MacCool, in a rage during a fight with rival
giants, tore up a vast fistful of earth and hurled it toward England. The piece of Irish
sod thrown by Finn fell short of England, landing in the Irish Sea, and became known
as the Isle of Man. The hole left in Ulster soil became Lough Neagh. This tale is
dubiously supported by the remarkable similarity in shape and size of Lough Neagh
and the Isle of Man. A more scientific explanation is that Lough Neagh is a "glacial
puddle" that formed following the melting at the end of the last ice age.

Continue on B196 past the Peatlands Park (also called the Birches), which has more
than 900 acres of peat faces (surfaces in a peat bog from which bricks of turf are cut),
tracts of rhododendron, a small lake, characteristic bogland ecology, a visitors' center,
and a narrow gauge railway (phone: 762-851102). One mile south of the park, follow
signs to rejoin M1 west to Dungannon. At Exit 15, the end of the motorway, take A29
north for about 2 miles into the town center.

DUNGANNON: The mound above Market Square in Dungannon — now surmounted by two towers from a castle built in 1790 — was for centuries the site of the
castle and seat of the O'Neill Kings of Ulster and the Earls of Tyrone. Once the most
powerful of the four ancient Irish kingdoms, Ulster adopted as its emblem the O'Neill
Red Hand. The story of the Red Hand survives from a distant era, when rivals from
an unknown land sailed to Ireland for the purpose of conquering it. Nearing the Ulster
coast, the shipboard warriors agreed that whoever touched Irish soil first would be lord
over it. One daring chief, whose landing boat was lagging behind the others, cut off his
left hand and threw it onto the shore, thus claiming he had touched land first. From
this man descended the O'Neills, the royal race of Ulster. The last of the great O'Neills
was Hugh, Earl of Tyrone, who alternately warred with and submitted to Elizabeth I
until his escape to France in 1607 in the notorious Flight of the Earls.

Dungannon's noteworthy Tyrone Crystal Ltd. — producers of mouth-blown, hand-
cut, full-lead crystal — was opened in 1970, just 2 miles from and 200 years after the
founding of one of the first crystal glasshouses in Ireland, at Drumreagh, under famed
glassmaker Benjamin Edwards. Today, despite its relatively recent origins, Tyrone
Crystal, which is owned by a local cooperative and employs 150 people, has become
well established among the world's foremost crystal manufacturers. Vistors may observe the cut-crystal production process, from melting, blowing, and cooling to cutting,
washing, polishing, and packing. From the beginning to the end of the process, some
30 people handle each piece.

To get to the factory from Dungannon town center, take the turn for Cookstown;
at the roundabout soon afterward, exit at about "5 o'clock" onto the Coalisland road.
The factory is less than 2 miles beyond on the right-hand side of the road. Free tours
are available year-round, Mondays through Thursdays from 9:30 AM to noon and from
1:30 to 3 PM; on Fridays, 9:30 AM to noon. The factory is closed 2 weeks during
mid-July. Advanced booking is requested. The shop sells "imperfects" at about one-
third less than the prevailing retail prices in Northern Ireland, which are in turn about
50% less than prices in the US. Shop hours are 9 AM to 5 PM, Mondays through
Fridays; 10 AM to 1 PM and 2 to 4 PM on Saturdays; closed *Easter* weekend and July
12 and 13. Oaks Rd., Dungannon (phone: 8687-25335).

 CHECKING IN: *Grange Lodge* – This Georgian country house on 20 tree-
shaded acres offers 3 double rooms (1 with private bath), a good restaurant
(reservations necessary), a tennis court, table tennis, and darts. From M1 Exit

15, take A29 south for 1 mile and turn left at the sign for the Grange Meeting House. 7 Grange Rd., Dungannon (phone: 8687-84212 or 8687-22458). Restaurant, expensive; hotel, moderate.

 EATING OUT: *Castle Grill* – Light meals and snacks are available at this little place conveniently located in the town center. Open 9 AM to 5:30 PM Mondays through Saturdays. Reservations unnecessary. 33 Market Sq., Dungannon (phone: 8687-22681). Inexpensive.

Dunowen Inn – Set lunches, pub grub, and à la carte dinners. Open noon to 10:30 PM Mondays through Saturdays. Reservations unnecessary. Market Sq., Dungannon (phone: 8687-22030). Inexpensive.

En Route from Dungannon – Leave Dungannon on A29 south and pick up A4 west for Enniskillen. At Ballygawley, about 15 miles from Dungannon, a signposted left turn leads to President Ulysses S. Grant's ancestral home, 4 miles east in the hamlet of Dergina. The Simpson family farm buildings have been restored and furnished with period pieces. In addition to a gift shop and a visitors' center, which offers a video on Irish immigration to North America and tells President Grant's family story (the president's maternal great-grandfather was born in the small thatch-roofed farmhouse), the site includes interesting exhibits of rural Irish life. The 10-acre farm is still worked by 19th-century methods; the livestock are purebred Irish goats, "mountainy" cattle, and poultry. Open 10:30 AM to 6:30 PM Mondays through Saturdays and 2 to 6 PM Sundays, May through September; 10:30 AM to 4:30 PM Mondays through Fridays, October through April; call for information in other months. Admission charge. Dergina (phone: 662-527133).

Ballygawley is one of several villages along or just off A4 located in the 18-mile-long Clogher Valley, along the river Blackwater. This gentle green region is rich in antiquities. Just northwest of Augher, off B83, is Knockmany Forest, the site of prehistoric ruins. On the summit of a steep wooded hill (650 feet) is the Late Stone Age Knockmany chambered cairn, Northern Ireland's best-known example of a passage grave, with excellent examples of rock-carved art. Elaborate designs include concentric circles and zigzag and "snake" patterns. Queen Aine of the 6th-century kingdom of Oriel is supposedly buried at Knockmany.

The next village down the road, Clogher, also occupies an ancient site. The diocese of Clogher — the oldest bishopric in Ireland — is believed to have been established by St. Patrick himself; its first bishop was his disciple St. MacCartan. The small classical-style Church of Ireland cathedral (1744) is named for MacCartan (as is another cathedral in Enniskillen; see below). From the square tower, there is a good view of the Clogher Valley. Ask at the rectory for access.

It is just 5 miles from Clogher to Fivemiletown, so named for being located 5 miles from each of its neighboring villages. (An Irish mile, now only an unused historical oddity, was longer than an English or American statute mile; it measured 6,720 feet rather than 5,280. All signposts today show statute miles, although an occasional old road post shows Irish mileage.) The *Fivemiletown Display Centre,* in the library on Main St., has changing displays of old photographs of the Clogher Valley, farm and kitchen utensils, craftsmen's tools, and antique bottles; it occasionally hosts exhibitions of lacemaking, a local cottage industry.

CHECKING IN/EATING OUT: *Blessingbourne* – Owned by the same family for 300 years, this is a striking Victorian Gothic country home with original fittings and furnishings set on a 500-acre estate. There are only 3 rooms — none with private bath, one with a four-poster bed. The baronial dining room overlooks the lake. Other facilities include tennis courts, fishing, and a library. Reservations essential. Turn right off the A4 at Fivemiletown; continue for about one-quarter mile, and turn right onto the estate at the gate lodge entrance (phone: 3655-21221). Expensive.

Just west of Fivemiletown, the route passes from County Tyrone to County Fermanagh, the most western of the 6 counties of Northern Ireland. Follow A4 the rest of the way to Enniskillen (a total of 46 miles from Dungannon).

ENNISKILLEN: Fermanagh's county seat is also by far its largest town, with 13,000 inhabitants. (The next-largest towns are Lisnaskea and Irvinestown.) It sits on an island in the river Erne, which connects the Lower and Upper Lough Erne, a 50-mile natural waterway. Enniskillen, whose origins predate recorded history, was a midlake link of great strategic significance, situated on the main highway between the ancient Irish kingdoms of Ulster and Connaught. It was the medieval seat of the Maguires, chieftains of Fermanagh, who policed the loughs with a private navy of 1,500 boats, stationed principally at Hare Island and at the clan's waterside castle at Enniskillen.

Enniskillen was at the center of Irish resistance to Tudor domination, and so its history in the 16th century was one of siege, capture, burning, and battering — between the Maguires and the rival O'Neill clan and the English. During the closing stages of the war between Elizabeth I and Hugh O'Neill, the Maguire's Enniskillen Castle was severely damaged, partly by the Maguires themselves, to prevent the English from using it against them. When Planter Captain William Cole arrived as constable of the royal fort of Enniskillen, soon after the Flight of the Earls in 1607, he found only a crumbling wall enclosing the burned-out shell of a tower house. Cole succeeded in creating a working fort out of the ruins of the Maguire castle, adding the Watergate, which is still a picturesque Enniskillen landmark. He probably intended this as an architectural enhancement for an otherwise functional fortress, since there is no sign that it ever served as a gateway. When William Cole (by then a knight) died in 1658, he left his family rich in lands in Enniskillen and beyond. There were Coles living in the castle until the 18th century when, as the Earls of Enniskillen, they moved to Florence Court (see below). After that, Enniskillen Castle gradually deteriorated, such that on a visit in 1762, Methodist preacher John Wesley noted that there was *no* castle. Attempted French invasions in the west of Ulster stimulated rebuilding late in the 18th century. A brand-new barracks was built in 1790, and in 1796 funds were allocated to refurbish the site as the Castle Barracks.

From the 17th century, the town of Enniskillen became distinct from its castle, its fame coming mainly from the Royal Inniskilling Fusiliers and the Inniskilling Dragoons, regiments that were first raised in the area and whose battles included the Boyne, Waterloo, and the Somme. It is possible that an 18th-century marching air of the Inniskillings, who served in America in 1814 as part of the British forces in the War of 1812, was adopted as the tune for "The Star Spangled Banner." A few documents that pass as evidence for this case can be viewed in the *Regimental Museum* (phone: 365-323142) which, with the *Fermanagh County Museum,* is housed in the 3-story remains of the medieval Maguire castle keep; these consist of ground-level chambers, probably originally used for defense and storage, and rebuilt upper stories.

The *Fermanagh County Museum* evokes the history of Fermanagh from the Middle Stone Age to the end of the early Christian period through archaeological finds, realistic dioramas, and large-scale models and displays, among which are fiberglass copies of the famed White Island figures (see below). An excellent 20-minute audiovisual program includes presentations on the Maguire chieftains, the Elizabethan wars, and the Plantation period. Open year-round, 10 AM to 1 PM and 2 to 5 PM Mondays through Fridays; 2 to 5 PM Saturdays, May to September; 2 to 5 PM Sundays, July and August.

No admission. Maguire Castle Keep, Castle Barracks, Enniskillen (phone: 365-325050).

The *Regimental Museum* contains the brilliant uniforms, arms, colors, regimental plate, Napoleonic battle trophies, metals, engravings, and photographs that trace the history of the famous Fusiliers. A prized possession on display is the bugle that sounded the charge at the bloody Battle of the Somme (1916). Open year-round, 9:30 AM to 12:30 PM and 2 to 4:30 PM Mondays through Fridays; weekends by arrangement. Admission charge. Maguire Castle Keep, Castle Barracks, Enniskillen (phone: 365-323142).

Enniskillen's considerable historical and architectural interest is exemplified by its winding main street, which carries six different names between the bridges at either end. This street is also a major shopping center in Fermanagh, with a lively Thursday market and numerous specialty stores, including outlets for cottage industries, arts, crafts, and antiques. Aran sweaters, Irish lace, handmade jewelry, and local pottery are good buys. The following are some of the best stores: *The Wool Centre* (3 Diamond St.; phone: 365-322672) specializes in traditional patterned Aran knitwear, with Fermanagh's largest stock of woolens. *L. W. N. Hall, Booksellers* (10 High St.; phone: 365-324341) sells maps and guides. *Armstrong & Kingston's* (8 High St.; phone: 365-322113) is the place for men's quality tweeds, knitwear, and outerwear. *Fermanagh Cottage Industries* (14 East Bridge St.; phone: 365-322260) offers handmade lace, other crocheted items, and hand-embroidered table and bed linens. *Ann McNulty* (Fermanagh Enterprise Centre, Down St.; phone: 365-323117) creates decorative stoneware and hand-thrown pots.

North of the main street, between Water and Market streets (where the street market was held in the past), is a warren of alleys, including Corn and Butter markets (alleys where these products were sold), that retain some of the architectural atmosphere of Old Enniskillen. Remnants of gray stone arches add character.

Two churches dominate the town. On Church Street, Enniskillen's large, rather plain Gothic-style St. MacCartan's Cathedral (1842) incorporates a font, north porch, and tower from a 17th-century church. One of the ten bells of the tower's carillon was cast from cannon captured at the Battle of the Boyne. The fine interior galleries house old colors of the Enniskillen regiments, and there is a pulpit preserved from the 1688–89 Siege of Derry. (Another church named for St. MacCartan is in Clogher; see above.) Almost opposite the Cathedral is St. Michael's Catholic Church, completed in 1875 in the French Gothic style. The exterior view of the rear section, on sloping ground, emphasizes its massive proportions. A third church, the Convent Chapel (Belmore St.), built in 1904 in the Byzantine style, features 15 windows by Michael Healy, Lady Glenavy, and Sarah Purser, noted Irish stained glass artists of the Dublin School.

Because it is on an island, Enniskillen offers varied views of the Erne; the best are from Watergate, the Broadmeadow — at which the Lakeland Forum, a public recreational facility, or leisure center, offers a swimming pool, squash, aquatic sports, and many other recreational facilities — and from the Round O landing stage (departure point for cruises).

The Lakeland Visitor Centre, on Shore Rd., by the town center car park, provides comprehensive area tourist information, accommodation booking services, displays and printed information on major sites, and crafts sales. The center is open Mondays through Fridays 9 AM to 5 PM (late in the summer), Saturdays and Sundays 9 AM to 6 PM, June to September; also open on Saturdays from *Easter* to June, 10 AM to 5 PM. Center may be closed from 1 to 2 PM for lunchtime; closed weekends the rest of the year (phone: 365-323110). In summer, the visitors' center can also help to arrange walking tours of Enniskillen.

Overlooking the town from the east is Fort Hill Park, with such charming features as a Victorian bandstand topped by an elaborate clock. At the top of the hill is Cole

Column, a monument surmounted by a statue of General Sir Galbraith Lowry Cole, who was a descendant of William Cole, founder of Plantation Enniskillen. The later Cole fought in the Peninsula Wars and became governor of the Cape Colony in South Africa. The column can be climbed — 108 steps — for a panoramic view of Fermanagh's lakes and mountains. Open late May to mid-September, Mondays through Fridays 4 to 6 PM; Saturdays and Sundays 2 to 6 PM; other times by appointment. Admission charge. Fort Hill, reached from Belmore St. in town (phone: 365-325050).

Portora Royal School, established by decree of James I in 1608, is to the west of town on a hill above the river Erne. The ruins of the 1619 Portora Castle, partially blown up in 1859 by experimenting chemistry students, are on the grounds. Colonnades and wings added to the main building in 1837 give the school an imposing appearance worthy of its history. Old boys of Portora include Oscar Wilde and Samuel Beckett. Derrygonnelly Rd., Enniskillen (phone: 365-322658).

Castle Coole, on the Dublin Road, a National Trust property considered to be the finest neo-classical house in Ireland, recently reopened after the most extensive renovation ever undertaken by the National Trust in the UK. Castle Coole's restrained white splendor startles the eye, as was the intention of its builder, the first Earl of Belmore, who was said to be jealous of his brother-in-law's creation, Florence Court, on the other side of Upper Lough Erne (see below). It took 9 years (beginning in 1789) and vast sums of money to realize the earl's fantasy. All of the Portland stone for the house was transported from England by sea and then by bullock and cart from Ballyshannon. Today, Castle Coole is still a showpiece, with its fine plasterwork friezes, Cuban mahogany doors, and Scagliola columns. Many of the handsome Regency pieces — thought to have been made by the same craftsman who outfitted Buckingham Palace — were designed for the exact locations they occupy today. The lake is a breeding colony for greylag geese, and the Enniskillen golf course runs through the grounds. The visitors' center at the car park has a gift shop and exhibits on the restoration. House open 2 to 6 PM daily in June through August; weekends and holidays only in April, May, and September. Admission charge. Grounds are open daily from dawn to dusk, no admission charge. The entrance to Castle Coole is opposite the *Ardhowen Theatre,* on the Dublin Road, a half-mile southeast of Enniskillen (phone: 365-322690).

The *Ardhowen Theatre Centre,* a focal point for the arts in Fermanagh, is beautifully set on a hill overlooking Upper Lough Erne and its wooded shoreline. The center includes a 300-seat theater, a lovely outdoor terrace, a marina, picnic facilities, and a restaurant that is a popular coffee and lunch spot. The restaurant is open 10:30 AM to 4:30 PM. The box office is open daily, except Sundays, 10 AM to 4:30 PM and 6 to 8 PM on performance evenings. Dublin Road, Enniskillen (phone: 365-325440).

 CHECKING IN: *Killyhevlin* – A well-appointed hotel on Upper Lough Erne, it has 22 rooms (each with private bath), some with lake views, and 14 self-catering 2-bedroom lakeside chalets. The welcoming, many-windowed lounge overlooks the lake; the *Oak Bar,* with its fireplace, conversation couch corners, and piano, exudes a pleasant spirit that sometimes is expressed in song. The restaurant and lounge offer a broad menu (see below). Signposted on A4 just before the *Ardhowen Theatre,* about one-half mile outside Enniskillen. Dublin Road, Enniskillen (phone: 365-323481). Expensive.

EATING OUT: *Coral* – The dining room/restaurant in the *Killyhaven* hotel offers an extensive à la carte dinner menu and friendly service. A luncheon buffet, with salad bar, is served in the lounge, which offers scenic views of Lough Erne. Carvery luncheon (roasts, cut to order) is a specialty on Sundays. Snacks are always available at the adjoining bar (with fireplace). Open daily for lunch, served 12:30 to 2:30 PM, and dinner, with last orders taken at 9:15 PM (8 PM on Sundays). Reservations advised. Signposted on A4 just before the *Ardhowen*

Theatre, about one-half mile east of Enniskillen. Dublin Road, Enniskillen (phone: 365-323481). Moderate.

Franco's Pizzeria – This eatery offers pasta, pizza, and kebabs in a cozy, fireside atmosphere — with a tree growing up the middle. Open Sundays through Thursdays from noon to 11 PM; Fridays and Saturdays noon to 11:30 PM. Reservations unnecessary. Queen Elizabeth Rd., just off High St., Enniskillen (phone: 365-324424). Moderate.

Blake's of the Hollow – A fine late-Victorian pub that is a favorite with locals. Serves sandwiches and pub grub. Open Mondays through Saturdays 11:30 AM to 11 PM. 6 Church St. (phone: 365-322143). Inexpensive.

En Route from Enniskillen – Before following the route straight to Monea Castle and the village of Belleek, consider a detour to any one, or all three, of the following sites: Devenish Island, Florence Court House and Forest Park, and Marble Arch Caves.

DEVENISH ISLAND: The most extensive remains of early and medieval Christian settlements in Northern Ireland are 2 miles north of Enniskillen, on a 70-acre island in Lower Lough Erne. The monastery on Devenish was founded by St. Molaise in the 6th century and remained functional as late as the 16th century. The most conspicuous landmark is an 82-foot, 12th-century round tower, the best preserved in Ireland, with a richly decorated cornice incorporating four carved heads. (Round towers were used to safeguard valuables from Vikings and local raiders.) The Teampull Mor (Great Church), nearest the ferry jetty, dates from about 1225 in its first phase. It has a fine roll-molded south window characteristic of the transition from Romanesque to Gothic architecture. The south chapel was added later as a mausoleum for the Maguires, whose coat of arms is still visible. Other sites on the island include the house of St. Molaise, which faces the round tower; St. Mary's Abbey, the largest and most recent (1449) of the ecclesiastical buildings on the island; the high cross in the cemetery south of the abbey; and a small museum that contains artifacts from the island. The best view is downslope from the east end of St. Mary's Abbey.

A 2-hour narrated cruise of Lough Erne stops at Devenish Island. The boat, which has a covered deck and a snack bar, sails from Round O jetty at Brook Park on the west bank of the river Erne. Departure times: in May and June, Sundays at 3 PM; in July and August, daily at 11 AM and 3 PM, with additional departures on Thursdays, Saturdays, and Sundays at 7 PM; September, Tuesdays, Thursdays, Saturdays, and Sundays at 3 PM. Fare is about $3.50. Contact *Erne Tours Ltd.* (phone: 365-322882).

Visitors who want more than a short stopover on Devenish, but no guided tour, can take the ferry from Trory Point jetty, about 3 miles north of Enniskillen, signposted off B82 toward Kesh. The ferry operates daily except Mondays from mid-April through September, 10 AM to 7 PM; Sundays 2 to 7 PM. Fare less than $2. Contact *Devenish Island Ferry* (phone: 365-322711, ext. 230).

FLORENCE COURT FOREST PARK: About 8 miles southwest of Enniskillen is Florence Court. One of Ulster's most important historic houses, it commands extensive parklands on the northeast shoulder of Cuilcagh Mountain. Head west on A4 (the Sligo Road) for 3 miles, turn south onto A32, and follow the signposts to Florence Court Forest Park.

The park includes woodlands (of 200-year-old oaks), moorland, and farmland. A walled garden near the car park, originally planted in the 1870s, has been restored; look for the famous 220-year-old Florence Court Yew, the parent of all Irish yews world-wide. Walks from the car park are marked for difficulty and duration. Park open daily from 10 AM to dusk.

Florence Court House, a National Trust property since the 1950s, is a fascinating example of Irish Georgian (mid-18th-century) architecture. It is also one of the most beautifully situated houses in Northern Ireland, with mountain peaks visible in three directions. Sir John Cole, mayor of Enniskillen, decided about 1710 that the cold, comfortless Enniskillen Castle was not a worthy home for his adored wife, Florence, and built this country estate for her. Among its excellent decorative arts, Florence Court is best known for its intricate and charming plasterwork, the handiwork of the Dublin romantic stuccadore Robert West, who unified a mélange of interior architectural styles by placing flamboyant plaster cherubs, birds, flowers, and foliage everywhere. The plasterwork is best exemplified by the dining room ceiling — it is original, unlike some of the others, which had to be restored following a serious fire in 1955 — thought to be the finest in Ireland. Four puffing cherubs, representing the four winds, stand out in white against a blue background. The Venetian Room, with its gorgeous white-on-gray plaster ceiling of various birds and flowers, is just one example of how carefully the house was restored after the fire. From this delightful room a visitor can look out to the "ha-ha," a dry moat that kept cattle off the main lawn but allowed them to graze close enough to the house to be picturesque. In Lady Florence's bedroom is an elaborately embroidered Irish linen bedspread and equally detailed pillowcases. Tours of the house are self-guided (reading materials provided), which allows lingering appreciation. In addition to a "pleasure ground" of plants and shrubs cultivated for the connoisseur, there is an icehouse and eel bridge. The National Trust recently acquired additional working parts of the estate, including the forge, weighbridge, sawmill, carpenter's shop, and others, many of which are open to the public during the ongoing restoration. There is a gift shop and a café (see *Eating Out*). Open daily, except Tuesdays, from 2 to 6 PM, June through August; weekends and holidays only from 2 to 6 PM in April, May, and September. No admission charge. Swanlinbar Rd. (phone: 36582-249).

CHECKING IN: *Tullyhona House* – On a working sheep-and-cattle farm, this guesthouse offers 7 rooms (4 with private bath), plus a sunroom and lounge with a TV set. Open year-round. About 1½ miles from Marble Arch Caves, on Marble Arch Rd., Florence Court (phone: 36582-452). Inexpensive.

EATING OUT: *Florence Court* – Housed on the ground floor of one of the Florence Court pavilions, the café serves such luncheon staples as quiche, stew, and meatloaf, with wheat bread. Open 1 to 6 PM when the house is open (see above). At Florence Court House, Swanlinbar Rd. (phone: 36582-249). Inexpensive.

MARBLE ARCH CAVES: When rejoining Swanlinbar Road outside Florence Court Forest Park, turn left (west), then left again (south) onto Marlbank Scenic Loop, a semicircular drive that crosses the Cuilcagh plateau, the finest caving area in Ireland, and ends near Marble Arch Caves.

The Marble Arch Caves are the best known in the subterranean labyrinth of Cuilcagh. The 1½-hour tour of Marble Arch begins with a cruise across an underground lake, ending at the "junction," the spot where, in 1895, the earliest documented exploration and survey of the caves was begun by Edouard Martel, an eminent French speleologist — probably on the invitation of the third Earl of Enniskillen, a famous geologist in his own right. The caves developed in Darty limestone, a sedimentary rock 600 feet thick that was deposited about 330 million years ago. The huge cave system has been formed by three acidic underground streams that, over time, have etched away millions of tons of limestone. This has created an entire underworld of lakes, rivers, waterfalls, passageways, and reflecting pools that mirror the growths on the roofs of lofty chambers. The entire Marble Arch system is a superb natural laboratory; the Showcave at its center is special for its size and for the variety of its formations. Only recently opened to the public, the caves now offer an experience of exploration formerly available only to serious spelunkers. A path about two-thirds of a mile long winds past an array of fascinating formations: stalactites, mineral veils, and curtains draped along fissures and fractures, rimstone pools, and cascades of cream-colored calcite coating the walls with a Belleek-like sheen. The sound of water is constant — dripping, flowing, and falling. Excellent commentary is provided. The caves are displayed as naturally as possible: White light is the predominant illumination, although some colored lights are also used. Wear shoes appropriate for wet surfaces, and bring a sweater and waterproof jacket. The Marble Arch Cave site has refreshment facilities and a shop. Open daily *Easter* through October from 11 AM; closing times vary at the duty officer's discretion. It is advisable to check in advance to ensure date and time of choice. Admission charge. Marlbank Scenic Loop, Florence Court, Enniskillen (phone: 36582-8855).

Return to A32 toward Enniskillen. Turn right (east) toward Arney and Bellanaleck and, if desired, follow signposts for the *Sheelin* restaurant on A509. Or return to Enniskillen via A509.

EATING OUT: *Sheelin* – A 200-year-old, thatch-roofed, whitewashed cottage that serves superb home-cooked food, often before a turf fire. Open year-round for morning coffee, lunch, high tea (fresh scones, snacks, soup, bread, and salads), and dinner. Dinner selections include Chinese marinated steaks, lamb with orange and cream, and caramelized peaches. Dinner reservations essential. There is also a crafts shop on the premises, with hand-crocheted woolen caps, scarves, shawls, ties, traditional hand-knit and tweed clothing, and soft toys. Rt. A509, Bellanaleck (phone: 36582-232). Lunch, inexpensive; dinner, expensive.

En Route from Enniskillen – From Enniskillen head northwest on A46, then turn left onto B81 and travel west for about 3 miles. Turn right at signs for Monea Castle.

Monea is one of Northern Ireland's finest examples of a Plantation castle as well as one of the largest and best preserved. Believed to be the site of a 15th-century Maguire stronghold and headquarters of that clan before Enniskillen became its capital, Monea's present ruins date from a 1618 castle built for Malcolm Hamilton, rector of Devenish, who later became archbishop of Cashel. The castle rises on a rocky bluff, surrounded on three sides by swampy ground. Just to the south is a small lake with a *crannog*, an artificial island built for defense (the water was the barrier, instead of stone or earthen banks), suggesting prehistoric settlement of the site. Monea Castle is built of limestone with sandstone dressings. It has two 3-story towers with Scottish-style corbeling and crow-stepped gables. Part of the defensive *bawn* (ramparts) remains. Even in its relatively decayed state, Monea's strength and Scottish architectural ancestry are apparent. The castle was captured by the Maguires in 1641 but was quickly retaken by the Planters. In 1688, it was held by Gustavus Hamilton, Governor of Enniskillen. Abandoned after an 18th-century fire, Monea reverted to state care in 1954. It is open at all times; no admission charge.

Return to B81 and turn right (north) for Derrygonnelly, a small village with a pleasant green and a Plantation period church ruin. Follow signs for Glennasheevar Rd. for another 4½ miles west to the Lough Navar Forest Scenic Drive. Continue on this drive for 7 miles through a wilderness of conifer forests, where it is possible to stop at any number of places along the way to enjoy self-guiding nature trails and footpaths. At the far end of the semicircular scenic drive is a car park, beyond which is the Lough Navar Viewpoint, an overlook affording one of the grandest views in Ireland. From here, it is possible to see the steep sandstone Cliffs of Magho and nearly the whole of Lower Lough Erne and its islands. On a clear day, the mountains of several counties are visible, as well as the Atlantic shore of Donegal Bay to the west. The colors of lake, mountain, and sky are most impressive at sundown. For more information, call the head forester: 36564-256.

Complete the scenic drive, then turn right onto the main (unnumbered) road. After driving about 4 miles through moorland and bog, turn right onto B52 and follow signs to Belleek.

BELLEEK: A border village whose western outskirts lie in County Donegal, Belleek is known far and wide for its lustrous parian ware, a fine, white, decorative porcelain. The pottery was established in 1857 by John Bloomfield, owner of Caldwell Castle on Lower Lough Erne. On the grounds of his estate, Bloomfield found a superior quality of feldspar, an important ingredient of porcelain. His curiosity about the feldspar was initially aroused by the distinctive brilliance of the whitewash of his tenants' cottages. Originally the pottery produced earthenware, but by 1863 the formula for parian ware had been perfected by William Bromley, who came from Stoke-on-Trent to work at Belleek. Bromley achieved the renowned eggshell thinness of some of the pieces by refining the casting process. By 1869, prestigious orders, such as a tea service for the German royal family as a gift from Queen Victoria, were being received for parian ware. Since then Belleek has been best known for finely decorated china, although earthenware was produced until 1947. Today, the delicate, translucent ivory tint and painstakingly detailed decoration for which the factory is known are perhaps most apparent in the open-trellis basketware pieces embellished with flowers. Belleek china appears in many museums and private collections worldwide. In some families, the tradition of collecting Belleek began when emigrants left Ireland for the New World. The original *Statue of Liberty Museum* displayed Belleek as the typically cherished possession of an Irish immigrant. The designs of many of the 200 pieces in production today, such as the popular shamrock basketweave, were introduced during the 19th century. Some of the designs were taken from the ornamental letters in the *Book of Kells.* More than 8,000 individuals — including many Americans — belong to the Belleek Collectors' Society, for whom limited editions are created.

The factory (which employs 140 people from both sides of the border) is on the right, just across the bridge at the entrance to Belleek. Tours begin with the raw materials: china clay, feldspar, ground flint glass, frit, and water. These are ground and mixed into a thick, creamy substance called "slip." After the slip is sieved, visitors can see it poured into plaster of Paris molds, which absorb the water. When dry, the shaped pieces begin their artistic journey through many stages of decoration and firings. A piece that emerges less than perfect from any stage is destroyed — the Belleek factory allows no "seconds."

The factory welcomes visitors Mondays through Fridays year-round (except *Easter,* the first two weeks of August, and several local holidays), from 9:30 AM to 12:15 PM and 2:15 to 4:15 PM (3:15 PM on Fridays). There is a small charge for tours, which last 25 minutes and depart about every half hour. The factory has a new visitors center, with a museum of unique pieces and a shop that has the world's most complete stock of Belleek. Prices are the same as in local shops, approximately 50% less than in the US. The shop is open 9 AM to 6 PM Mondays through Fridays, 10 AM to 6 PM on Saturdays, and 2 to 6 PM on Sundays, March through September; 9 AM to 5 PM Mondays through Fridays, October through February. The Belleek pottery tearooms are open 9:30 AM to 6 PM, Mondays through Saturdays, and 2 to 6 PM on Sundays. On A47 by the river Erne, Belleek (phone: 36565-501).

 EATING OUT: *Cleary's Corner Bar* – Overlooking the river Erne, this spot serves pub grub Mondays through Saturdays from noon to 10 PM. Near the Belleek factory; 5 Main St. (phone: 36565-403). Inexpensive.

En Route from Belleek – Take A47 east of Belleek, on the northern side of Lower Lough Erne. Once across the bridge to the west end of 5-mile-long Boa Island, watch for signs on the right indicating the old cemetery of Caldragh, site of two of the oldest and strangest stone figures in Ireland, perhaps dating from the 1st century. The so-called Janus statues have a face on each side. (Janus was a Roman god with two faces; he could see the past and the future.) A hollow in the top of the Janus figure may have been used to hold drink or blood offerings to the gods. It is necessary to walk over rough ground to reach the stones.

A47 joins A35 north of Kesh. Bear south into Kesh on A35, and then bear right onto B82, which leads to Castle Archdale Forest and Marina. Ferries to White Island operate from the end of April to early September, 10 AM to 7 PM Tuesdays through Saturdays, 2 to 7 PM Sundays, and other times on request (no service Mondays). Ferry charge about $2. Castle Archdale Marina (phone: 3656-21588).

Also at Castle Archdale are the *Drumhoney Stables,* which offer guided pony treks by Lough Erne, old-time horse-drawn cart rides, and a café (phone: 3656-21892).

WHITE ISLAND: White Island was the site of an early monastery, although its patron saint remains unknown. The 74-acre island attracts archaeologists, historians, and travelers from around the world to its 8 inscrutable statues, found at various times over a period of several decades, the last in 1958. They are now placed side by side on a wall of the ruined 12th-century church in which they were discovered. The figures are impressive in scale, in their powerful modeling, and in the individuality of their faces. Each is distinct, but they share similarities: All stare fixedly forward; all have very small hands and feet; and all wear a tunic with a bottom hem. Why the figures were concealed, which are pagan and which Christian, and what they represent have been the subjects of much discussion. The church itself, a ruin since 1600, was restored in 1928. Its fine south door is the only intact Romanesque door surviving in Northern Ireland.

En Route from White Island – Once back on the mainland, take B72 for 2 miles northeast, then connect with A35 southeast to Irvinestown. From Irvinestown, drive 20 miles northeast on A32 through Dromore to Omagh.

 CHECKING IN/EATING OUT: *Mahon's* – A family-run hotel for three generations, it has 19 rooms, most with private bath. The cozy bar is noted for its cocktails, and there's also entertainment. The restaurant is open daily for lunch and snacks from 12:30 to 2:30 PM, for dinner from 6 to 9 PM. Hotel moderate; restaurant inexpensive. Enniskillen Rd., Irvinestown (phone: 3656-21656).

For an overnight stay at a hostelry that is well worth a detour, once back on the mainland from White Island, continue south from Castle Archdale on B82 toward Enniskillen. At Trory, make a sharp left turn northeast onto A32, then a right (east) onto B46 toward Ballinamallard and Errington. About 1 mile beyond the Fish Farm out of Ballinamallard, turn left into a residential driveway marked "Jamestown."

 CHECKING IN/EATING OUT: *Jamestown Country House* – People go out of their way to stay at this unusually gracious and historic bed and breakfast establishment. The house, which dates from 1760, has a projecting central bay and a handsome stableyard. Grounds include a tennis court and a croquet lawn. Guests are sometimes escorted on fishing or shooting expeditions on the estate by owner Arthur Stuart. In the evening, a gathering in front of the drawing room fire is followed by a gracious dinner featuring local produce and game in season. Picnic lunches are available on request. There are 3 double rooms (2 with private bath). Reservations advised. Magheracross, Ballinamallard (phone: 36581-209). Moderate.

To resume the route, follow B46 northeast through Kilskeery, Trillick, and Ballyard to Dromore. There, pick up A32 to Omagh.

OMAGH: The capital and principal market town of County Tyrone, Omagh occupies open fertile country where the Carnowen and Drumragh rivers meet to form the Strule. All three rivers are good for fishing; the Strule is also noted for its mussel pearls. Omagh is a pleasant town with lovely river views, but it has little architectural distinction, since it was completely destroyed by fire in 1743. It does have some Georgian-style and late-19th-century houses, and the main thoroughfare, High St., has a classical-style courthouse at its height. Its most notable building is the Catholic cathedral, the Church of the Sacred Heart, designed by William Hague, which has Gothic-style steeples of unequal height, particularly lovely when viewed approaching the town. During the warmer months, Omagh hosts various festivals, agricultural and livestock exhibitions, and show jumping and gun dog trials. Souvenirs of the area include locally made linen, crochet lace, and turfcraft — plaques and statues of Irish mythological figures molded from compressed peat from the nearby Black Bog.

CHECKING IN/EATING OUT: *Royal Arms* – Centrally located on the main thoroughfare, this hostelry has 16 double rooms and 5 singles, all with private bath. Its restaurant offers morning coffee, afternoon tea, and a full lunch and dinner menu. Open daily; last dinner orders taken at 9:30 PM (8:30 PM Sundays). 51 High St., Omagh (phone: 662-3262). Hotel moderate; restaurant inexpensive.

ULSTER–AMERICAN FOLK PARK: Three miles north of Omagh on A5 toward Newtownstewart, the Ulster–American Folk Park commemorates Ulster emigration to America, relating the history of the hundreds of thousands of nameless settlers, as well as that of the more famous figures in American government and commerce. The folk park opened in July 1976 to coincide with the bicentennial of American independence, in which immigrants from Ulster played so prominent a part (five signed the Declaration of Independence, a sixth was secretary to the Congress that adopted it, and a seventh printed it).

There were two waves of emigration to America. Those in the first, during the 18th and early 19th centuries, are most often referred to as the Scotch-Irish (so called because many of their ancestors had come from Scotland to Ulster several generations earlier during the Plantation period of the 17th century). Many of the Scotch-Irish settled in America on farms or were pioneers on the ever-expanding frontier. The folk park is constructed around the thatch-roofed farmhouse birthplace of Judge Thomas Mellon, a first-wave emigrant who left with his family in 1818 at the age of 5. His enormously successful scions helped found and fund the folk park, which re-creates the lifestyle of Ulster people, both in Ireland before departure and in America after the crossing, with original and reconstructed buildings of the kind lived and worked in on both sides of the Atlantic, as well as with exhibition galleries, large-scale models, shops, demonstrations, and an excellent introductory 15-minute audiovisual program.

The second wave of Irish emigrants to America reached its peak in the mid-19th century. These people, who came from all over Ireland, were victims of the Great Famine. They settled in America's fast-growing cities or helped build canals or railroads. Known in America as the Irish-Americans, they are represented at the park by the boyhood home of John Hughes, who was born only 20 miles away from the park site and who rose to eminence by becoming Archbishop of New York and builder of St. Patrick's Cathedral on Fifth Avenue.

It is difficult to overstate the influence Ulster had on the developing American nation. One-quarter of US presidents have had Ulster roots, and three were the nation's only first-generation presidents. From Daniel Boone, Davy Crockett, and Sam Houston to Cyrus McCormick, Andrew McNally, Horace Greeley, and Stephen Foster to astronauts John Glenn, James Irwin, and Neil Armstrong, the folk park points to the strong links forged over centuries between Ulster and the US.

The park comprises 26 acres. An exhibit features a reconstructed early-19th-century emigrant ship — with realistic sounds, smells, sensations, and other details of difficult Atlantic crossings — and an authentically re-created Ulster dockside departure port with costumed interpretive guides. Visitors should allow at least 2 hours to see the outdoor exhibits (including the Mellon cottage, meeting house, schoolhouse, weaver's cottage, Hughes house, Aghalane house, blacksmith forge, log cabins, bars, and Conestoga wagon, as well as a replica of the larger house the Mellons built in America) and additional time for the film and numerous indoor exhibits. The visitor center has a café and a crafts/gift shop. Open *Easter* through early September, Mondays through Saturdays 11 AM to 6:30 PM, Sundays and holidays 11:30 AM to 7 PM; late September to *Easter,* Mondays through Fridays 10:30 AM to 5 PM (except holidays). Last admission 1½ hours before closing. Admission charge. Camphill, on the Newtonstewart road, A5 (phone: 662-3292).

En Route from Ulster–American Folk Park – Return to A5 and continue 30 miles north to Londonderry, passing through Strabane (see "Environs" in *Londonderry,* THE CITIES). Alternatively, take A5 south to Ballygawley, then A4 east to its junction with M1; drive east approximately 75 miles to Belfast.

Index